Introducing Pearson One

Each title in the Pearson One series is part of a collaborative global editorial development process that aligns the talent and expertise of Pearson authors, editors, and production people from all over the world. Titles in the Pearson One series will offer students increased understanding of the global business environment through content and cases, with both local and global relevance.

The First in the Pearson One Series

Marketing Management: An Asian Perspective, 5th Edition is an adaptation of **Marketing Management, 13th Edition**, an international best seller by Philip Kotler and Kevin Keller in the US. It has been translated into 26 different languages and also adapted into other English language editions for Canada, Europe, Africa, the Middle East, South Asia, Australia as well as China. The current edition was simultaneously developed and produced to launch around the world through an innovative publishing model that brought our authors and editors together in a truly global endeavor.

Readers of the Asian edition will benefit from these local perspectives and expertiese through our international case studies, authored by our partners worldwide. These cases will be identified by a marginal note in each chapter linked to relevant content and available through links on our Companion Website.

FIFTH EDITION

MARKETING MANAGEMENT

AN ASIAN PERSPECTIVE

PHILIP KOTLER
KEVIN LANE KELLER
SWEE HOON ANG
SIEW MENG LEONG
CHIN TIONG TAN

Prentice Hall

Singapore London New York Toronto Sydney Tokyo Madrid
Mexico City Munich Paris Capetown Hong Kong Montreal

Published in 2009 by
Prentice Hall
Pearson Education South Asia Pte Ltd
23/25 First Lok Yang Road, Jurong
Singapore 629733

Pearson Education offices in Asia: *Bangkok, Beijing, Hong Kong, Jakarta, Kuala Lumpur, Manila, New Delhi, Seoul, Singapore, Taipei, Tokyo*

Authorized adaptation from the United States edition, entitled MARKETING MANAGEMENT, 13th Edition, ISBN: 0136009980 by KOTLER, PHILIP; KELLER, KEVIN, published by Pearson Education, Inc, publishing as Prentice Hall, Copyright © 2009.

Printed in Singapore

4 3 2
12 11 10 09

ISBN 13 978-981-06-7993-4
ISBN 10 981-06-7993-9

While every effort has been made to trace the copyright holders of reproductions, we have been unsuccessful in some instances. To these, we offer our sincere apologies and hope that they will take our liberty in good faith. We would appreciate any information that would enable us to acknowledge the copyright holders in future editions of this book.

Prentice Hall
is an imprint of

www.pearsoned-asia.com

About the Authors

Philip Kotler is the S. C. Johnson & Son Distinguished Professor of International Marketing at the Kellogg Graduate School of Management, Northwestern University. He received his M.A. from the University of Chicago and his Ph.D. from the Massachusetts Institute of Technology. He is the author of over 20 books, including *Principles of Marketing, Marketing: An Introduction,* and *Strategic Marketing for Nonprofit Organizations.* He has contributed over 100 articles to leading journals, including *Harvard Business Review, Sloan Management Review, Management Science, Journal of Marketing Research,* and *California Management Review.* He is the only three-time winner of the Alpha Kappa Psi award for the best annual article published in the *Journal of Marketing.* Professor Kotler has also received the Paul D. Converse Award, Distinguished Marketing Educator Award, and Charles Coolidge Parlin Award. He has served as chair of the College of Marketing of The Institute of Management Sciences, a director of the American Marketing Association, and a trustee of the Marketing Science Institute. He has consulted for such major companies as AT&T, Bank of America, Ford, General Electric, and IBM.

Kevin Lane Keller is the E. B. Osborn Professor of Marketing at the Tuck School of Business, Dartmouth College. He has degrees from Cornell, Carnegie-Mellon, and Duke universities. Previously, he was on the marketing faculty of the Graduate School of Business, Stanford University, the University of California at Berkeley, and the University of North Carolina at Chapel Hill. He was also Visiting Professor at Duke University and the Australian Graduate School of Management. His widely-cited research on branding has been published in the *Journal of Marketing, Journal of Marketing Research,* and *Journal of Consumer Research.* He has also served on the editorial boards of these journals and has received numerous research awards from his over 50 publications. He is author of *Strategic Brand Management.* He is also an academic trustee for the Marketing Science Institute. Professor Keller has consulted for such leading businesses as Accenture, American Express, Bank of America, Disney, Intel, Levi Strauss, Kodak, Shell, and Unilever.

Swee Hoon Ang is an Associate Professor at the NUS Business School, National University of Singapore. She received her Ph.D. from the University of British Columbia. She was a Visiting Professor at the University of California at Berkeley, Helsinki School of Economics and Business Administration, and the China-Europe International Business School. She is a co-author of *Principles of Marketing: An Asian Perspective.* In addition, she has written numerous articles for journals and conferences, including *Journal of Advertising, Marketing Letters, Long Range Planning, Journal of Business Ethics,* and *Journal of Cross-Cultural Psychology.* Her research and teaching interests are in advertising and cross-cultural consumer behavior. She has consulted for such companies as Citibank, Johnson & Johnson Medical, and Singapore Pools.

Siew Meng Leong is a Professor at the NUS Business School, National University of Singapore. He received his MBA and Ph.D. from the University of Wisconsin, Madison. He was a Visiting Professor at the University of California at Berkeley. He is a co-author of *Marketing in the New Asia* and *Strategic Marketing Cases for 21st Century Asia.* He has published in *Journal of Consumer Research, Journal of Marketing, Journal of Marketing Research,* and other international journals and conference proceedings. His publications focus on consumer behavior, sales management, and marketing research. Professor Leong is an advisory board member of Behavioral Marketing Abstracts, and an editorial board member of *International Journal of Research in Marketing, Academy of Marketing Science Review,* and *Journal of Marketing Communications.* He was an advisory council member of the Association for Consumer Research and now serves on the Academic Standards Council of u21 Pedagogica. He has consulted for such clients as Citibank, DuPont, Philips, and Singapore Pools.

Chin Tiong Tan is a Professor and Deputy President at the Singapore Management University. He received his Ph.D. from Pennsylvania State University. He has taught at the Helsinki School of Economics and Business Administration and the University of Witwatersrand, and was a Visiting Scholar at the Stanford Business School. He is the co-author of *The Chinese Tao of Business, New Asian Emperors: The business Strategies of the Overseas Chinese* and several other books in marketing. He has published in *Journal of Consumer Research, Journal of International Business Studies, Journal of Business and Industrial Marketing, International Marketing Review, European Journal of Marketing,* and other international journals and conference proceedings. Professor Tan sits on the boards of several companies and committees of government agencies. He was academic advisor to the Singapore Airlines' Management Development Center, and has consulted for companies like Acer Computer, Altron Group, Inchcape, and Singapore Telecom. He was the President of the Marketing Institute of Singapore.

Brief Contents

About this Book **xxix**
Preface **xxxiii**

PART 1 Understanding Marketing Management 2
Chapter 1 Defining Marketing for the 21st Century 3
Chapter 2 Developing Marketing Strategies and Plans 33

PART 2 Capturing Marketing Insights 72
Chapter 3 Gathering Information and Scanning the Environment 73
Chapter 4 Conducting Marketing Research and Forecasting Demand 99

PART 3 Connecting with Customers 130
Chapter 5 Creating Customer Value, Satisfaction, and Loyalty 131
Chapter 6 Analyzing Consumer Markets 159
Chapter 7 Analyzing Business Markets 195
Chapter 8 Identifying Market Segments and Targets 225

PART 4 Building Strong Brands 258
Chapter 9 Creating Brand Equity 259
Chapter 10 Crafting the Brand Positioning 299
Chapter 11 Dealing with Competition 327

PART 5 Shaping the Market Offerings 358
Chapter 12 Setting Product Strategy 359
Chapter 13 Designing and Managing Services 389
Chapter 14 Developing Pricing Strategies and Programs 421

PART 6 Delivering Value 458
Chapter 15 Designing and Managing Marketing Channels and Value Networks 459
Chapter 16 Managing Retailing, Wholesaling, and Logistics 495

PART 7 Communicating Value 526
Chapter 17 Designing and Managing Integrated Marketing Communications 527
Chapter 18 Managing Mass Communications: Advertising, Sales Promotions, Events and Public Relations 559
Chapter 19 Managing Personal Communications: Direct Marketing and Personal Selling 599

PART 8 Creating Successful Long-Term Growth 640
Chapter 20 Introducing New Market Offerings 641
Chapter 21 Tapping into Global Markets 677
Chapter 22 Managing a Holistic Marketing Organization 715

Appendix **A1**
Endnotes **E1**
Glossary **G1**
Image Credits **C1**
Name Index **I1**
Company, Brand, and Organization Index **I2**
Subject Index **I5**

Contents

About this Book xxix
Preface xxxiii

PART 1 Understanding Marketing Management 2

Chapter 1 **Defining Marketing for the 21st Century 3**

The Importance of Marketing 4
The Scope of Marketing 5
What is Marketing? 5
What is Marketed? 5
MARKETING MEMO The Rewards of Branding Asian Countries 8
Who Markets? 8
Marketing in Practice 11
Core Marketing Concepts 13
Needs, Wants, and Demands 13
Target Markets, Positioning, and Segmentation 13
Offerings and Brands 14
Value and Satisfaction 14
Marketing Channels 14
Supply Chain 15
Competition 15
Marketing Environment 15
The New Marketing Realities 15
Major Societal Forces 15
New Company Capabilities 17
Company Orientations Toward the Marketplace 18
The Production Concept 18
The Product Concept 19
The Selling Concept 19
The Marketing Concept 19
The Holistic Marketing Concept 20
Relationship Marketing 20
MARKETING MEMO Marketing Right and Wrong 20
BREAKTHROUGH MARKETING Nike 22
Integrated Marketing 23
Internal Marketing 24
Performance Marketing 25
Financial Accountability 25
Social Responsibility Marketing 26
Marketing Management Tasks 28
MARKETING MEMO Marketers' Frequently Asked Questions 28

Developing Marketing Strategies and Plans 29
Capturing Marketing Insights and Performance 29
Connecting With Customers 29
Building Strong Brands 29
Shaping the Market Offerings 29
Delivering Value 30
Communicating Value 30
Creating Long-term Growth 30
Summary 31
Application 31

Chapter 2 Developing Marketing Strategies and Plans 33

Marketing and Customer Value 34
The Value Delivery Process 34
The Value Chain 35
Core Competencies 37
A Holistic Marketing Orientation and Customer Value 39
The Central Role of Strategic Planning 41
MARKETING INSIGHT Views on Marketing from Chief Executive Officers 42
BREAKTHROUGH MARKETING Intel 43

Corporate and Division Strategic Planning 44
Defining the Corporate Mission 44
Establishing Strategic Business Units (SBUs) 46
Assigning Resources to Each SBU 47
Assessing Growth Opportunities 47
Organization and Organizational Culture 50
Marketing Innovation 54
MARKETING INSIGHT Creating Innovative Marketing 55

Business Unit Strategic Planning 55
The Business Mission 56
SWOT Analysis 56
MARKETING MEMO Checklist for Performing Strengths/Weaknesses Analysis 58
Goal Formulation 58
Strategic Formulation 59
MARKETING INSIGHT Same Bed, Different Dreams 61
Program Formulation and Implementation 62
MARKETING INSIGHT Marketing's Contribution to Shareholder Value 63
Feedback and Control 63

Product Planning: The Nature and Contents of a Marketing Plan 64

MARKETING MEMO Marketing Plan Criteria 64

Contents of the Marketing Plan 65

Sample Marketing Plan: Pegasus Sports International 66

Summary 71

Application 71

PART 2 Capturing Marketing Insights 72

Chapter 3 **Gathering Information and Scanning the Environment 73**

Components of a Modern Marketing Information System 74

Internal Records and Marketing Intelligence 75

The Order-to-Payment Cycle 75

Sales Information Systems 75

Databases, Data Warehousing, and Data Mining 76

The Marketing Intelligence System 76

MARKETING MEMO Clicking on the Competition 78

Analyzing the Macroenvironment 78

Needs and Trends 78

MARKETING INSIGHT Megatrends Shaping the Asian Consumer Landscape 79

Identifying the Major Forces 79

The Demographic Environment 79

BREAKTHROUGH MARKETING Google 80

Worldwide Population Growth 81

Population Age Mix 83

Ethnic and Other Markets 83

MARKETING INSIGHT Friends for Life 84

Educational Groups 85

Household Patterns 85

Geographical Shifts in Population 86

Other Major Macroenvironments 86

Economic Environment 86

Social-cultural Environment 87

Natural Environment 90

MARKETING INSIGHT Green Marketing 91

Technological Environment 92

Political-Legal Environment 93

Summary 97

Application 97

Chapter 4 Conducting Marketing Research and Forecasting Demand 99

The Marketing Research System 100

The Marketing Research Process 101

Step 1: Define the Problem, the Decision Alternatives, and the Research Objectives 102

Step 2: Develop the Research Plan 102

MARKETING INSIGHT Conducting Informative Focus Groups 104

MARKETING MEMO Questionnaire Do's and Don'ts 105

MARKETING INSIGHT Getting into Consumers' Heads With Qualitative Research 108

MARKETING INSIGHT Understanding Brain Science 109

Step 3: Collect the Information 111

MARKETING MEMO Pros and Cons of Online Research 112

MARKETING INSIGHT Global Online Market Research Challenges 113

Step 4: Analyze the Information 114

Step 5: Present the Findings 114

Step 6: Make the Decision 114

Overcoming the Barriers to the Use of Marketing Research 115

Marketing Research in Asia 116

Measuring Marketing Productivity 117

Marketing Metrics 117

Marketing-Mix Modeling 118

Marketing Dashboards 118

MARKETING INSIGHT Marketing Dashboards to Improve Effectiveness and Efficiency 119

Vocabulary for Demand Measurement 122

Estimating Current Demand 124

Estimating Future Demand 126

Summary 129

Application 129

PART 3 Connecting with Customers 130

Chapter 5 Creating Customer Value, Satisfaction, and Loyalty 131

Building Customer Value, Satisfaction, and Loyalty 132

Customer Perceived Value 133

Total Customer Satisfaction 136

Monitoring Satisfaction 137

Product and Service Quality 139

Maximizing Customer Lifetime Value 140
Customer Profitability 140
Measuring Customer Lifetime Value 142
MARKETING MEMO Calculating Customer Lifetime Value 143
Cultivating Customer Relationships 144
Customer Relationship Management (CRM) 144
MARKETING INSIGHT Company Response to Customer Empowerment 145
Attracting and Retaining Customers 146
Building Loyalty 148
MARKETING MEMO Creating Customer Evangelists 149
Win-Backs 152
Customer Databases and Database Marketing 152
Customer Databases 152
Data Warehouses and Data Mining 153
BREAKTHROUGH MARKETING Tesco 154
The Downside of Database Marketing and CRM 155
Summary 157
Application 157

Chapter 6 **Analyzing Consumer Markets 159**
What Influences Consumer Behavior? 160
Cultural Factors 160
Social Factors 162
MARKETING INSIGHT China's Young Consumers 164
Personal Factors 165
MARKETING INSIGHT Face-Saving and the Chinese Consumer 166
BREAKTHROUGH MARKETING Ikea 170
Key Psychological Processes 171
Motivation: Freud, Maslow, Herzberg 171
Perception 174
Learning 176
Memory 177
The Buying Decision Process: The Five-Stage Model 179
Problem Recognition 180
Information Search 180
Evaluation of Alternatives 182
Purchase Decisions 184
Postpurchase Behavior 186
Other Theories of Consumer Decision Making 188
Level of Consumer Involvement 188

Decision Heuristics and Biases 189
Mental Accounting 189
MARKETING INSIGHT How Consumers Really Make Decisions 190
MARKETING MEMO Decision Traps 191
Profiling the Customer Buying Decision Process 191
Summary 193
Application 193

Chapter 7 Analyzing Business Markets 195
What is Organizational Buying? 196
The Business Market Versus the Consumer Market 196
MARKETING INSIGHT Big Sales to Small Business 197
Buying Situations 198
Systems Buying and Selling 199
Participants in the Business Buying Process 200
The Buying Center 200
Buying Center Influences 201
Buying Center Targeting 201
The Purchasing/Procurement Process 203
Purchasing Orientations 203
Types of Purchasing Processes 203
Purchasing Organization and Administration 204
Stages in the Buying Process 204
Problem Recognition 205
General Need Description and Product Specification 205
Supplier Search 206
E-Procurement 206
MARKETING INSIGHT The Business-To-Business (B2B) Cyberbuying Bazaar 207
MARKETING INSIGHT The Asian B2B Environment 208
Proposal Solicitation 209
Supplier Selection 209
MARKETING MEMO Developing Compelling Customer Value Propositions 210
Order-Routine Specification 211
Performance Review 212
Managing Business-to-Business Customer Relationships 212
The Benefits of Vertical Coordination 212
BREAKTHROUGH MARKETING General Electric 213
MARKETING INSIGHT Rules of Social and Business Etiquette 214

MARKETING INSIGHT Establishing Corporate Trust and Credibility 215
Business Relationships: Risks and Opportunism 217
Relationship Marketing in the Keiretsu and Chaebol 218
Institutional and Government Markets 219
MARKETING INSIGHT Government Procurement in Korea 220
Summary 222
Application 222

Chapter 8 **Identifying Market Segments and Targets 225**
Levels of Market Segmentation 226
Segment Marketing 226
Niche Marketing 228
MARKETING INSIGHT Chasing the Long Tail 230
Local Marketing 231
BREAKTHROUGH MARKETING HSBC 232
Individual Marketing 233
Bases for Segmenting Consumer Markets 233
Geographic Segmentation 233
Demographic Segmentation 235
MARKETING INSIGHT Trading Up (and Down): The New Consumer 239
MARKETING INSIGHT Marketing to Generation Y 240
Psychographic Segmentation 241
Behavioral Segmentation 243
Bases for Segmenting Business Markets 248
Marketing Targeting 250
Effective Segmentation Criteria 250
Evaluating and Selecting the Market Segments 251
Selective Specialization 251
Product Specialization 252
Market Specialization 252
Full Market Coverage 252
Additional Considerations 253
Summary 256
Application 256

PART 4 Building Strong Brands 258

Chapter 9 **Creating Brand Equity 259**
What is Brand Equity? 260
The Role of Brands 260

BREAKTHROUGH MARKETING Procter & Gamble 262

The Scope of Branding 263
Defining Brand Equity 263
Brand Equity as a Bridge 265

MARKETING MEMO A Checklist for Developing Global Asian Brands 267

Brand Equity Models 267

Building Brand Equity 270

Choosing Brand Elements 271
Designing Holistic Marketing Activities 277

MARKETING INSIGHT Applying Permission Marketing 277

Leveraging Secondary Association 280

Measuring Brand Equity 281

MARKETING INSIGHT The Brand Value Chain 282

Brand Valuation 283

Managing Brand Equity 283

Brand Reinforcement 283

MARKETING INSIGHT What is a Brand Worth? 284

Brand Revitalization 285

Devising a Branding Strategy 287

Branding Decision 288
Brand Extensions 289
Brand Portfolios 292

Customer Equity 294

MARKETING INSIGHT 21st Century Branding 294

Summary 296
Application 296

Chapter 10 **Crafting the Brand Positioning 299**

Developing and Communicating a Positioning Strategy 300

Competitive Frame of Reference 301
Points-of-Parity and Points-of-Difference 301

BREAKTHROUGH MARKETING Shanda Interactive Entertainment 302

Establishing Category Membership 304
Choosing POPs and PODs 305
Creating POPs and PODs 306

MARKETING MEMO Writing a Positioning Statement 307

Differentiation Strategies 308

MARKETING MEMO How to Derive Fresh Consumer Insights to Differentiate Products and Services 308

Product Life-Cycle Marketing Strategies 310

Product Life Cycles 310
Style, Fashion, and Fad Life Cycles 311
Marketing Strategies: Introduction Stage and the Pioneer Advantage 312
Marketing Strategies: Growth Stage 314
Marketing Strategies: Maturity Stage 315

MARKETING INSIGHT Competitive Category Dynamics 316

Marketing Strategies: Decline Stage 319
Evidence on the Product Life-Cycle Concept 321
Critique of the Product Life-Cycle Concept 322

MARKETING MEMO How to Build a Breakaway Brand 322

Market Evolution 322

Summary 325
Application 325

Chapter 11 Dealing with Competition 327

Competitive Forces 328
Identifying Competitors 329
Analyzing Competitors 330

Strategies 330

MARKETING INSIGHT High Growth Through Value Innovation 331

Objectives 332
Strengths and Weaknesses 333

MARKETING MEMO Benchmarking to Improve Competitive Performance 334

Selecting Competitors 334
Selecting Customers 334

Competitive Strategies for Market Leaders 335

BREAKTHROUGH MARKETING Accenture 336

MARKETING INSIGHT When Your Competitor Delivers More for Less 337

Expanding the Total Market 338
Defending Market Share 339

MARKETING INSIGHT *Sun Tzu Bing Fa:* Modern Strategy Insights from Ancient China 340

Expanding Market Share 345

Other Competitive Strategies 346

Market-Challenger Strategies 346

MARKETING MEMO Making Smaller Better 349
Market-Follower Strategies 350
MARKETING INSIGHT Counteracting Counterfeiting 351
Market-Nicher Strategies 352
MARKETING MEMO Niche Specialist Roles 353
MARKETING MEMO Strategies for Entering Markets Held by Incumbent Firms 353
Balancing Customer and Competitor Orientations 354
Competitor-Centered Companies 354
Customer-Centered Companies 354
Summary 356
Application 356

PART 5 Shaping the Market Offerings 358

Chapter 12 **Setting Product Strategy 359**
Product Characteristics and Classifications 360
Product Levels: The Customer Value Hierarchy 360
MARKETING INSIGHT Metamarkets and Metamediaries 361
Product Classifications 362
Differentiation 364
Product Differentiation 364
BREAKTHROUGH MARKETING Toyota 367
Design 369
Services Differentiation 369
MARKETING INSIGHT Design as a Powerful Marketing Tool 370
Product and Brand Relationships 372
The Product Hierarchy 372
Product Systems and Mixes 372
Product-Line Analysis 373
Product-Line Length 375
MARKET INSIGHT When Less is More 376
Product-Mix Pricing 379
Co-Branding and Ingredient Branding 381
Packaging, Labeling, Warranties and Guarantees 383
MARKETING MEMO Making Ingredient Branding Work 384
Packaging 384
Labeling 385
Warranties and Guarantees 386
Summary 387
Application 387

Chapter 13 **Designing and Managing Services 389**

The Nature of Services 390
Service Industries are Everywhere 390
Categories of Service Mix 391
Distinctive Characteristics of Services 392

Marketing Strategies for Service Firms 396

A Shifting Customer Relationship 396

MARKETING MEMO Recommendations for Improving Service Quality 397

MARKETING INSIGHT The Japanese Philosophy of Service 397

BREAKTHROUGH MARKETING Southwest Airlines 399

Holistic Marketing for Services 401

Managing Service Quality 404

Customer Expectations 404

MARKETING INSIGHT The Role of Expectations on Service Quality Perceptions 406

MARKETING MEMO Assessing E-Service Quality 407

Best Practices of Service-Quality Management 407

MARKETING MEMO The Seven Deadly Sins of Service Management 409

MARKETING INSIGHT Developing Customer Interface Systems 410

Managing Service Brands 412

Differentiating Services 413
Developing Brand Strategies for Services 414

Managing Product Support Services 416

Identifying and Satisfying Customer Needs 416
Postsale Service Strategy 417

Summary 418

Application 418

Chapter 14 **Developing Pricing Strategies and Programs 421**

Understanding Pricing 422

A Changing Pricing Environment 422
How Companies Price 423

MARKETING INSIGHT Giving it all Away 424

Consumer Psychology and Pricing 425

Setting the Price 430

Step 1: Selecting the Pricing Objective 430
Step 2: Determining Demand 432
Step 3: Estimating Costs 435

Step 4: Analyzing Competitors' Costs, Prices, and Offers 438
Step 5: Selecting a Pricing Method 439
BREAKTHROUGH MARKETING Ebay 443
Step 6: Selecting the Final Price 445
MARKETING INSIGHT Stealth Price Increases 446

Adapting the Price 447
Geographical Pricing (Cash, Countertrade, Barter) 447
MARKETING MEMO Guidelines for Countertraders 448
Price Discounts and Allowances 449
Promotional Pricing 450
Differentiated Pricing 450

Initiating and Responding to Price Changes 451
Initiating Price Cuts 451
Initiating Price Increases 452
Responding to Competitors' Price Changes 453
MARKETING MEMO How to Fight Low-Cost Rivals 454

Summary 456
Application 456

PART 6 Delivering Value 458

Chapter 15 **Designing and Managing Marketing Channels and Value Networks 459**

Marketing Channels and Value Networks 460
The Importance of Channels 460
Channel Development 461
Hybrid Channels 461
Understanding Customer Needs 462
Value Networks 462

The Role of Marketing Channels 463
Channel Functions and Flows 464
Channel Levels 465
Service Sector Channels 467

Channel-Design Decisions 467
Analyzing Customers' Desired Service Output Levels 467
Establishing Objectives and Constraints 467
Identifying Major Channel Alternatives 470
Evaluating the Major Alternatives 473

Channel-Management Decisions 474
Selecting Channel Members 474
Training and Motivating Channel Members 475
Evaluating Channel Members 476
Modifying Channel Design and Arrangements 477

MARKETING MEMO Designing a Customer-Driven Distribution System 478

Channel Integration and Systems 478
Vertical Marketing Systems 478

MARKETING INSIGHT The Importance of Channel Stewards 479

Horizontal Marketing Systems 481
Multichannel Marketing Systems 481

MARKETING MEMO Multichannel Shopping Checklist 482

Conflict, Cooperation, and Competition 483
Types of Conflict and Competition 483
Causes of Channel Conflict 484
Managing Channel Conflict 484
Dilution and Cannibalization 484
Legal and Ethical Issues in Channel Relations 485

E-Commerce Marketing Practices 486
Pure-Click Companies 487

BREAKTHROUGH MARKETING Amazon.com 488

Brick-and-Click Companies 490
M-Commerce 490

MARKETING INSIGHT E-Tailing Lessons for the Asia Pacific 491

Summary 493
Application 493

Chapter 16 Managing Retailing, Wholesaling, and Logistics 495

Retailing 496
Types of Retailers 496

MARKETING INSIGHT Enhancing Online Shopping in Asia 499

MARKETING INSIGHT Franchise Fever in Asia 500

The New Retail Environment 501
Marketing Decisions 503

MARKETING INSIGHT Making Labels Smarter 507

MARKETING MEMO Helping Stores to Sell 509

Private Labels 512
Role of Private Labels 512

BREAKTHROUGH MARKETING Wal-Mart 513

MARKETING INSIGHT *Feng Shui* and its Application to Retailing and Marketing in the Far East 514

The Private Label Threat 515

MARKETING MEMO How to Compete Against Store Brands 516

Wholesaling 516

Trends in Wholesaling 517

Market Logistics 518

MARKETING INSIGHT Toyota's Supplier Relationships 518

Integrated Logistics Systems 519

Market-Logistics Objectives 520

Market-Logistics Decisions 521

Organizational Lessons 524

Summary 525

Application 525

PART 7 Communicating Value 526

Chapter 17 **Designing and Managing Integrated Marketing Communications 527**

The Role of Marketing Communications 528

Marketing Communications and Brand Equity 528

The Communication Process Models 532

Developing Effective Communications 534

Identify the Target Audience 534

Design the Communications 535

MARKETING INSIGHT Celebrity Endorsements as a Strategy 538

MARKETING INSIGHT Collectivism, Consensus Appeals, and Credibility 539

MARKETING INSIGHT Comparative Advertising in Asia 540

Select the Communications Channels 542

Establish the Total Marketing Communications Budget 544

Deciding on the Marketing Communications Mix 546

BREAKTHROUGH MARKETING Intel 547

MARKETING INSIGHT Marketing Communications and the Urban Chinese Consumer 548

Characteristics of the Marketing Communications Mix 549

Factors in Setting the Marketing Communications Mix 550

Measuring Communications Results 551

Managing the Integrated Marketing Communications Process 552

Coordinating Media 553

MARKETING MEMO How Integrated is Your IMC Program? 554

Summary 556

Application 556

Chapter 18 **Managing Mass Communications: Advertising, Sales Promotions, Events, and Public Relations 559**

Developing and Managing an Advertising Programmme 560

Setting the Objectives 560
Deciding on the Advertising Budget 562
Developing the Advertising Campaign 563
MARKETING INSIGHT Advertising Guidelines for Modern Asia 565
MARKETING MEMO Print Ad Evaluation Criteria 567

Deciding on Media and Measuring Effectiveness 568

Deciding on Reach, Frequency, and Impact 568
Choosing Among Major Media Types 569
Alternative Advertising Options 570
Evaluating Alternative Media 574
Selecting Specific Vehicles 574
MARKETING INSIGHT Playing Games with Brands 575
Deciding on Media Timing and Allocation 576
Evaluating Advertising Effectiveness 577
Sales Promotion 580
Objectives 580
Advertising versus Promotion 581
Major Decisions 582

Events and Experiences 587

Events Objectives 587
Major Decisions 588
Creating Experiences 590
MARKETING INSIGHT Experiential Marketing 590

Public Relations 591

MARKETING INSIGHT Managing a Brand Crisis 592
Marketing Public Relations 593
Major Decisions in Marketing PR 593
BREAKTHROUGH MARKETING Virgin Group 594

Summary 597
Application 597

Chapter 19 **Managing Personal Communications: Direct Marketing and Personal Selling 599**

Direct Marketing 600

The Benefits of Direct Marketing 600
Direct Mail 602
MARKETING MEMO When Your Customer is a Committee 603

Catalog Marketing 604
Telemarketing 605
Public and Ethical Issues in Direct Marketing 606
Interactive Marketing 606
Advantages and Disadvantages of Interactive Marketing 606
BREAKTHROUGH MARKETING Yahoo! 608
Placing Ads and Promotion Online 609
Word of Mouth 614
Buzz and Viral Marketing 614
Opinion Leaders 615
Blogs 616
Measuring the Effects of Word of Mouth 616
MARKETING MEMO How to Start a Buzz Fire 616
Designing the Sales Force 618
Sales Force Objectives and Strategy 619
Sales-Force Structure 620
MARKETING INSIGHT Major Account Management 622
Sales-Force Size 622
Sales-Force Compensation 623
Managing the Sales Force 623
Recruiting and Selecting Representatives 624
Training and Supervising Sales Representatives 624
Sales Rep Productivity 626
Motivating Sales Representatives 627
Evaluating Sales Representatives 628
Principles of Personal Selling 630
The Seven Steps 631
Negotiation 632
Relationship Marketing 634
MARKETING INSIGHT Culture and Relationship Marketing 636
Summary 638
Application 638

PART 8 Creating Successful Long-Term Growth 640

Chapter 20 **Introducing New Market Offerings 641**
New-Product Options 642
Make or Buy 642
Types of New Products 642
Challenges in New-Product Development 643
The Innovation Imperative 643
New-Product Success 643
New-Product Failure 645

Organizational Arrangements 647

MARKETING INSIGHT The Effects of National Culture on New-Product Development 647

Budgeting for New-Product Development 648

Organizing New-Product Development 649

Managing the Development Process: Ideas 651

Idea Generation 651

MARKETING MEMO Ten Ways to Great New-Product Ideas 651

MARKETING INSIGHT P&G's New Connect-and-Develop Approach to Innovation 652

MARKETING MEMO Seven Ways to Draw New Ideas from Your Customers 653

MARKETING INSIGHT Developing Successful High-Tech Products 654

MARKETING INSIGHT New-Idea Generation In Japanese Companies 655

Idea Screening 656

Managing the Development Process: Concept to Strategy 658

Concept Development and Testing 658

Marketing Strategy 661

Business Analysis 662

Managing the Development Process: Development to Commercialization 663

Product Development 664

Market Testing 665

Commercialization 668

BREAKTHROUGH MARKETING Apple iPod 670

The Consumer-Adoption Process 671

Stages in the Adoption Process 671

Factors Influencing the Adoption Process 671

Summary 675

Application 675

Chapter 21 Tapping into Global Markets 677

Competing on a Global Basis 678

BREAKTHROUGH MARKETING Samsung 678

Deciding Whether to Go Abroad 680

Deciding Which Markets to Enter 681

How Many Markets to Enter 681

Developed versus Developing Markets 682

MARKETING INSIGHT Spotlight on Key Developing Asian Markets 683
Regional Free Trade Zones 684
MARKETING INSIGHT Emerging Market Companies 685
Evaluating Potential Markets 686
MARKETING INSIGHT China Post-WTO 688
Deciding How to Enter the Market 689
Indirect and Direct Export 689
Using a Global Web Strategy 690
Licensing 691
Joint Ventures 692
MARKETING INSIGHT *Guanxi* and its Application to Marketing in Greater China 693
Direct Investment 694
MARKETING MEMO Guidelines for Managing Joint Ventures in Asia 695
Deciding on the Marketing Program 696
MARKETING INSIGHT Global Standardization or Adaptation? 696
MARKETING MEMO The Ten Commandments of Global Branding 698
MARKETING INSIGHT Establishing Global Service Brands 699
Product 699
Communications 701
Price 704
MARKETING INSIGHT Unauthorized Sales — Dealing with the Gray Market and Counterfeit Products 706
Distribution Channels 707
Country-of-Origin Effects 709
Building Country Image 709
Consumer Perceptions of Country-of-Origin 710
Deciding on the Marketing Organization 711
Export Department 711
International Division 711
Global Organization 711
Summary 712
Application 712

Chapter 22 Managing a Holistic Marketing Organization 715

Trends in Marketing Practices 716
Internal Marketing 716

MARKETING MEMO Characteristics of Customer-Driven Company Departments 717

Organizing the Marketing Department 718
Relations with Other Departments 722
Building a Creative Marketing Organization 722

MARKETING INSIGHT The Marketing CEO 723

MARKETING INSIGHT Fueling Strategic Innovation 724

Socially Responsible Marketing 724

BREAKTHROUGH MARKETING Starbucks 726

Corporate Social Responsibility 727
Socially Responsible Business Models 729

MARKETING INSIGHT Confucius and Marketing in East Asia 729

Cause-Related Marketing 730

MARKETING INSIGHT New Views on Corporate Social Responsibility 731

Social Marketing 733

MARKETING MEMO Making a Difference 734

Marketing Implementation 735
Evaluation and Control 736

Annual-plan Control 736
Profitability Control 740
Efficiency Control 744
Strategic Control 744

The Future of Marketing 748

MARKETING MEMO Major Marketing Weaknesses 749

Summary 750
Application 750

Appendix A1
Endnotes E1
Glossary G1
Image Credits C1
Name Index I1
Company, Brand, and Organization Index I2
Subject Index I5

Each title in the Pearson One series is part of a collaborative global editorial development process that harnesses the talent and expertise of Pearson authors, editors, and production people from all over the world. And we combine content from many cultures, giving students greater insight into what they have in common with the world, and at the same time, we offer material that is locally relevant.

Our History

Pearson imprints have a rich heritage of academic, business, and professional books. For more than 100 years, we have provided educational tools to more than 100 million people across the globe. Our diverse network of brands encompasses a comprehensive range of solutions in testing, assessment, and enterprise software; the very best in online consumer and professional learning; and textbooks written by the most notable authors for higher education around the world. We help teachers teach and students learn across the globe.

The First in the Pearson One Series

Readers of the Asian edition will benefit from these local perspectives and expertise through our international case studies, authored by our partners worldwide. These cases will be identified by a marginal note in each chapter linked to relevant content and available through links on our Companion Website.

MARKETING MANAGEMENT

AN ASIAN PERSPECTIVE

Now into its fifth edition, this book continues to showcase the excellent content that Kotler has created with examples and case studies that are easily recognised. This enables students to relate to and grasp marketing concepts better.

IN THIS EDITION, YOU WILL FIND THAT WE HAVE:

1 Global brand names to provide a balanced look at Marketing Management

2 An in-depth look at emerging markets and trends

3 A greater focus on technology and marketing

Global cases to provide a balanced look at Marketing Management

The cases and examples in *Marketing Management : An Asian Perspective* (Fifth Edition) have been carefully selected to provide your students with a comprehensive understanding of marketing in today's world.

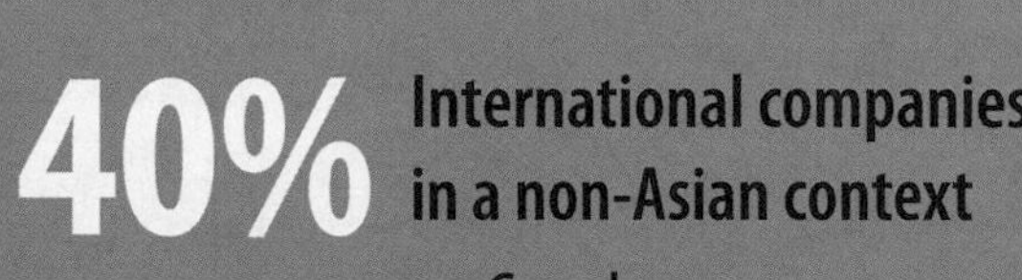

40% **International companies in a non-Asian context**

- Google
- Burger King's "Subservient Chicken"
- Apple and the iPod
- Coach

20% **Asian companies in an Asian context / non-Asian context**

- Li & Fung
- Hindustan Unilever
- Shanda Interactive Entertainment

40% **International companies in an Asian context**

- Disney in Hong Kong
- IKEA in Asia
- Gillette in Japan
- Cisco in China

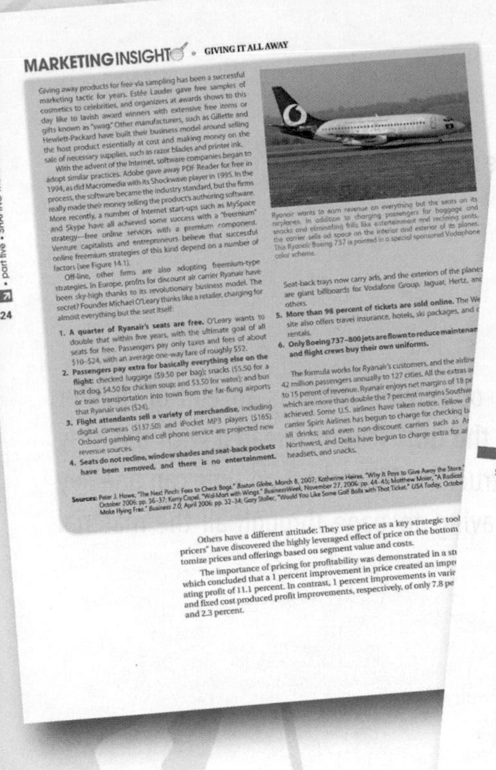

Cases on emerging markets and trends

Students are kept up-to-date and informed of emerging markets and trends around the world.

- Marketing to metrosexual men in India
- The "freemium" business model in the airline industry
- Counteracting counterfeiting

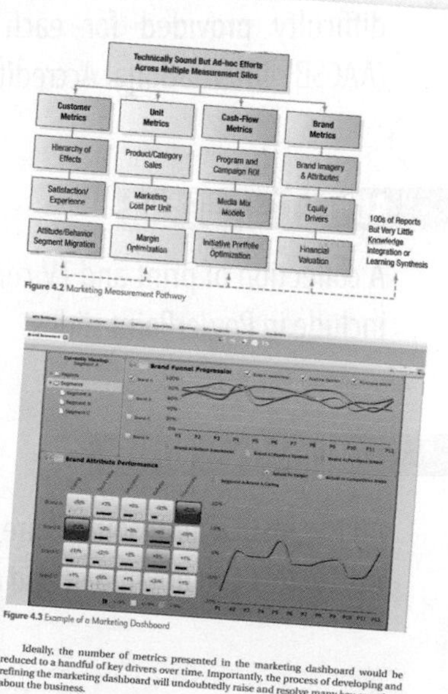

More focus on technology

A focus on heightened e-marketing activities helps students to understand the ever-increasing integration of technology into marketing in today's connected world.

- Buzz and viral marketing
- Use of technology in marketing research
- Customer empowerment with interactive marketing

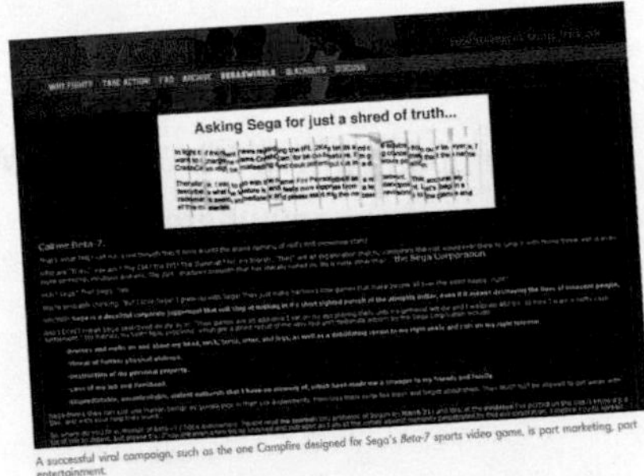

Instructor Resources

We have designed and developed a comprehensive range of resources that are unique to this Asian edition to help instructors prepare for their course effectively.

INSTRUCTOR'S MANUAL

The instructor's manual includes chapter/summary overviews, key teaching objectives, answers to end-of-chapter materials, exercises, projects, and detailed lecture outlines. The "Professors on the GO!" feature, created with the busy professor in mind, is also included. It brings key material upfront, where an instructor who is short on time can find key points and assignments that can be incorporated into the lecture without having to page through all the material provided for each chapter.

POWERPOINT SLIDES

Teaching slides are available for easy customization and sharing.

TEST ITEM FILE

The Test Item File contains more than 3,000 multiple-choice, true-false, short answer, and essay questions with level of difficulty provided for each question. It supports the Association to Advance Collegiate Schools of Business (AACSB) International Accreditation.

ADVERTISING BANK

A collection of print and TV commercials is available upon request in a CD for instructors to showcase during lessons or to include in PowerPoint slides.

COMPANION WEBSITE

All the instructor resources are available at the Kotler Companion Web site at http://www.pearsoned-asia.com/kotler. Instructors can download and access these files at anytime, from anywhere.

Preface

What Is Marketing Management All About?

Welcome to the fifth edition of *Marketing Management: An Asian Perspective.* Since our fourth edition was published in 2006, we have witnessed economic boom and turbulence, and escalating oil prices. This new edition highlights some of these recent environmental factors impacting on marketing, making it the leading marketing text because its content and organization consistently reflect changes in marketing theory and practice.

Asian businesses must acknowledge and respond to the new elements in today's marketplace. The Internet has multiplied the number of ways consumers buy and companies sell and how companies conduct their businesses. With increased liberalization and deregulation of regional markets, Asian businesses face competitors from a growing number of countries. They must exploit the explosion of communication channels to reach their more media-savvy customers. Margins have thinned considerably, and power is shifting to Asian consumers, who are telling companies what product features they want, what communications they will tolerate, what incentives they expect, and what prices they will pay. While the U.S. is reeling from the sub-prime crisis and the increased oil price is affecting the cost of businesses worldwide, attention continues to be diverted to Asia as its consumers experience, in some cases, new-found purchasing power.

In response, forward-thinking Asian companies are shifting gears from managing product portfolios to managing customer portfolios. They are compiling databases on individual customers to better understand them and to construct individualized offerings and messages. They are doing less product and service standardization and more niching and customization. They are improving their methods of measuring customer profitability and customer lifetime value. They are measuring the return on their marketing investment and its impact on shareholder value.

As companies change, so does their marketing organization. Marketing is no longer a company department charged with a limited number of tasks—it is a company-wide undertaking. It drives the company's vision, mission, and strategic planning. Marketing includes decisions like who the company wants as its customers; which of their needs to satisfy; what products and services to offer; what prices to set; what communications to send and receive; what channels of distribution to use; and what partnerships to develop. Marketing succeeds only when all departments work together to achieve goals: when engineering designs the right products, finance furnishes the required funds, purchasing buys high-quality materials, production makes high-quality products on time, and accounting measures the profitability of different customers, products, and areas.

To address all these different shifts, good marketers are practicing holistic marketing. *Holistic marketing* is the development, design, and implementation of marketing programs, processes, and activities that recognize the breadth and interdependencies of today's marketing environment. Four key dimensions of holistic marketing are:

1. **Internal marketing**—ensuring everyone in the organization embraces appropriate marketing principles, especially senior management.
2. **Integrated marketing**—ensuring that multiple means of creating, delivering, and communicating value are employed and combined in the best way.
3. **Relationship marketing**—having rich, multifaceted relationships with customers, channel members, and other marketing partners.
4. **Performance marketing**—understanding returns to the business from marketing activities and programs, as well as addressing broader concerns and their legal, ethical, social, and environmental effects.

These four dimensions are woven throughout the book and at times spelled out explicitly. The text specifically addresses the following tasks that constitute modern marketing management in the 21st century:

1. Developing marketing strategies and plans
2. Capturing marketing insights and performance

3. Connecting with customers
4. Building strong brands
5. Shaping the market offerings
6. Delivering and communicating value
7. Creating successful long-term growth

What Makes *Marketing Management* the Marketing Leader?

Marketing is of interest to everyone, whether they are marketing goods, services, properties, persons, places, events, information, ideas, or organizations. As it has maintained its respected position among students, educators, and businesspeople, *Marketing Management: An Asian Perspective* has kept up-to-date and remains contemporary. Students (and instructors) feel that the book is talking directly to them in terms of both content and delivery.

Marketing Management: An Asian Perspective owes its marketplace success to its ability to maximize three dimensions that characterize the best marketing texts—depth, breadth, and relevance—as measured by the following criteria:

- **Depth.** Does the book have solid academic grounding? Does it contain important theoretical concepts, models, and frameworks? Does it provide conceptual guidance to solve practical problems?
- **Breadth.** Does the book cover all the right topics? Does it provide the proper amount of emphasis on those topics?
- **Relevance.** Does the book engage the reader? Is it interesting to read? Does it have lots of compelling examples?

This fifth edition builds on the fundamental strengths of past editions that collectively distinguish it from all other marketing management texts:

- **Managerial Orientation.** The book focuses on the major decisions that marketing managers and top management face in their efforts to harmonize the organization's objectives, capabilities, and resources with marketplace needs and opportunities.
- **Analytical Approach.** *Marketing Management: An Asian Perspective* presents conceptual tools and frameworks for analyzing recurring problems in marketing management. Cases and examples illustrate effective marketing principles, strategies, and practices.
- **Multidisciplinary Perspective.** The book draws on the rich findings of various scientific disciplines—economics, behavioral science, management theory, and mathematics—for fundamental concepts and tools directly applicable to marketing challenges.
- **Universal Applications.** The book applies strategic thinking to the complete spectrum of marketing: products, services, persons, places, information, ideas and causes; consumer and business markets; profit and nonprofit organizations; domestic and foreign companies; small and large firms; manufacturing and intermediary businesses; and low and high-tech industries.
- **Asian Insights.** This book provides insights with an Asian flavor, drawing from regional thinkers and business leaders (from Confucius and Sun Tzu to Jong-Yong Yun and Carlos Ghosn, among others), institutions (*chaebol*, *keiretsu*, and so on), Asian trends and events (China's WTO entry, Beijing Olympic Games, demographic changes, etc.), and practices which impact Asian marketing (*guanxi*, *mianzi*, *feng shui*, counterfeiting, etc.)
- **Comprehensive and Balanced Coverage.** *Marketing Management: An Asian Perspective* covers all the topics an informed marketing manager needs to understand to execute strategic, tactical, and administrative marketing.

Other features include new concepts, examples, guidelines, and developments as detailed below.

Revision Strategy for the *Fifth Edition*

As marketing techniques and organization have changed, so has this text. The fifth edition is designed not only to preserve the strengths of previous editions, but also to introduce new material and organization to further enhance learning. We retained the key theme of holistic marketing, and the recognition that "everything matters" with marketing and that a broad, integrated perspective is often necessary. This theme is not developed so deeply, however, that it would restrict or inhibit an instructor's flexibility and teaching approach. To provide flexibility in the classroom, we also retained the new modular structure and eight parts corresponding to the eight key marketing management tasks. The fifth edition was changed to include the following:

- All chapters have brief commentary and new introductory vignettes that set the stage for the chapter material to follow. By covering topical brands or companies, the vignettes serve as great discussion starters.
- Breakthrough Marketing boxes replace the Marketing Spotlight boxes from the fourth edition. Each chapter has one box appearing in an appropriate spot to highlight innovative, insightful marketing accomplishments by leading organizations that businesses, including those in Asia, can learn from.
- Approximately four Marketing Insight and Marketing Memo boxes are included in each chapter; at least half, on average, are new. **Marketing Insight** boxes delve into important marketing topics such as "*Guanxi* and Its Applications to Marketing in Greater China," often highlighting current research findings. **Marketing Memo** boxes offer practical advice and direction in dealing with various decisions at all stages of the marketing management process. Topics covered include "Guidelines for Managing Joint Ventures in Asia" and "A Checklist for Developing Global Asian Brands."
- About ten in-text boxes are included in each chapter. These in-text boxes provide vivid illustrations of chapter concepts using actual companies and situations. The boxes cover a variety of products, services, and markets, and many have accompanying illustrations in the form of ads or product shots. These in-text boxes not only cover examples in Asia, but also those in the world that Asian businesses can learn from.
- Chapters are updated throughout, especially in terms of academic references.
- At the end of each chapter, the *Marketing Applications* section has two practical exercises to challenge students: *Marketing Debate* suggests opposing points of view on an important marketing topic from the chapter and asks students to take a side. *Marketing Discussion* identifies provocative marketing issues and allows for a personal point of view.

Chapter-by-Chapter Changes

Once again, this edition has been both streamlined and expanded to bring essentials and classic examples into sharper focus, while covering new concepts and ideas in depth. Following is an overview of some of the new or expanded material in each chapter:

Chapter 1

- Role of Chief Marketing Officer (CMO)
- What makes a great marketer
- Internal marketing and effective marketing departments

Chapter 2

- Market sensing and becoming more market-driven
- Assigning resources to SBUs
- Corporate culture and innovative marketing

Chapter 3

- Database marketing
- Important new marketplace trends
- Generations and cohorts
- Green marketing

Chapter 4

- Ethnographic research
- Brain science
- Marketing dashboards
- Marketing-mix modeling

Chapter 5

- Measuring customer satisfaction
- Methods to calculate customer lifetime value
- The new customer empowerment

Chapter 6

- New consumer trends
- Consumer decision-making

Chapter 7

- Customer references
- Lead generation
- Customer value proposition

Chapter 8

- Niche marketing and the "long tail"
- Consumers trading up and down
- Brand funnel

Chapter 9

- Brand equity models
- Internal branding
- Brand valuation
- Customer equity

Chapter 10

- Creating new markets and categories
- Building a breakaway brand

Chapter 11

- Value innovation ("blue ocean thinking")
- Selecting customers
- Competing with value-based rivals

Chapter 12

- Product returns
- Product and product line simplification

Chapter 13

- Customer empowerment
- Coproduction
- Customer interface systems
- Service strategies for product companies

Chapter 14

- The changing pricing environment
- "Freemium" pricing strategies
- Price optimization
- Strategies to fight low-cost rivals

Chapter 15

- Channel stewardship
- E-marketing
- M-marketing

Chapter 16

- The new retail environment
- "Fast forward" retailers
- RFIDs
- Private-label competition

Chapter 17

- The changing marketing communication environment
- Interactive marketing
- Word-of-mouth marketing

Chapter 18

- New developments in place advertising
- New developments in marketing events and experiences

Chapter 19

- Consumer-generated ads
- Types of interactive marketing
- Word of mouth, buzz and viral marketing, blogs, and podcasts

Chapter 20

- Innovation imperative
- "Connect and develop" innovation approaches
- Generating ideas from customers
- Designing brainstorming sessions

Chapter 21

- Emerging markets
- Regionalization
- Gray markets and counterfeit products

Chapter 22

- New developments in social responsibility
- Cause marketing guidelines
- Marketing metrics
- Marketing creativity and discipline

The Teaching and Learning Package

Marketing Management: An Asian Perspective is an entire package of materials available to students and instructors. This edition includes a number of ancillaries designed to make the marketing management course an exciting, dynamic, interactive experience.

INSTRUCTOR'S MANUAL

The Instructor's Manual includes chapter/summary overviews, key teaching objectives, answers to end-of-chapter materials, exercises, projects, and detailed lecture outlines. Also included is the feature, "Professors on the Go!" which was created with the busy professor in mind. It brings key material upfront, where an instructor who is short on time can find key points and assignments that can be incorporated into the lecture, without having to page through all the material provided for each chapter.

TEST ITEM FILE

The Test Item File contains more than 3,000 multiple-choice, true-false, short-answer, and essay questions, with page reference and difficulty level provided for each question. *Please note that an entire section is dedicated to application questions.* These real-life situations take students beyond basic chapter concepts and vocabulary and ask them to apply marketing skills.

The Test Item File supports Association to Advance Collegiate Schools of Business (AACSB) International Accreditation. Each chapter of the Test Item File was prepared with the AACSB curricula standards in mind. Where appropriate, the answer line of each question* indicates a category within which the question falls. This AACSB reference helps instructors identify those test questions that support that organization's learning goals.

*Please note that not all the questions will offer an AACSB reference.

POWERPOINT SLIDES

Teaching slides are available for easy customization and sharing. Instructors who prefer to customize PowerPoints can also make use of the ad bank, a collection of print and TV commercials.

ADVERTISING BANK

A collection of print and TV commercials is available in a CD for you to showcase during lessons or to include your PowerPoint slides.

COMPANION WEB SITE

Available at www.pearsoned-asia.com/kotler. This is where instructors can access our complete array of teaching materials. Simply go to the Instructor's Resource page for this text and click on the Instructor link to download the Instructor's Manual, Test Item File, and PowerPoint slides. NOTE: Prentice Hall manually checks every password request and verifies each individual's instructor status before issuing a password.

Acknowledgments

The fifth edition of Marketing Management: An Asian Perspective bears the imprint of many people. Our colleagues at the Kellogg Graduate School at Northwestern University, Dartmouth College, the National University of Singapore, and the Singapore Management University continue to have an impact on our thinking. We also want to thank our respective academic leaders, Deans Dipak Jain at Kellogg, Paul Danos at Tuck, and Christopher Earley at NUS for their continuous support of our research and writing efforts.

The talented staff at Pearson Education deserve praise for their role in shaping this book. We thank Geoffrey da Silva at Temasek Polytechnic for his work on the instructor's manual, Test Item File, and PowerPoint slides. Our overriding debt continues to be to our families who provided the time, support, and inspiration to prepare this edition.

We are grateful to the following individuals and companies for providing us permission to use some of the materials for this book:

Banyan Tree Hotels and Resorts
Billabong – Peter Thew, Sharmin Lee
Books Kinokuniya Singapore
Cerebos (Singapore) Pte Ltd
Cisco
Essilor – Sim Peng Tak
Eu Yan Sang (Singapore) Pte Ltd
HSBC
ICICI Prudential Life Insurance Company Ltd
Japan Sangaria Beverage Co., Ltd
Lenovo Group Ltd
Li & Fung Group
Professor Ivan Png, National University of Singapore
Mr Lawrence Ang Swee Leng
Shiseido Company Ltd
Singapore Zoo – Fanny Lai, Frederic Eng
Sony Corporation
Tesco plc
Unilever Singapore Pte Ltd – Dove
Warner Music

Philip Kotler
Kevin Lane Keller
Swee Hoon Ang
Siew Meng Leong
Chin Tiong Tan

Understanding Marketing Management

Downtown Shanghai, an example of the many faces of marketing today.

1 Defining Marketing for the 21st Century

Marketing is everywhere. Formally or informally, people and organizations engage in a vast number of activities called marketing. Good marketing has become an increasingly vital ingredient for business success. And marketing profoundly affects our day-to-day lives. It is embedded in everything we do—from the clothes we wear, to the Web sites we click on, to the ads we see.

Two teenage girls walk into their local Starbucks in Shanghai. One goes to the crowded counter and waits to hand a coupon to the barista for two free green tea frappucinos. The other sits at a table and opens her Lenovo ThinkPad notebook computer. Within a few seconds, she connects to the Internet, courtesy of Starbucks' deal with China Mobile to provide its customers with wireless access to hotspots on the China Mobile network. Once on the Net, the girl uses Baidu—the Chinese search engine—to search for information about the latest online game release from China's Shanda Interactive. In addition to links to various reviews, news sites, and fan pages, Baidu's search results feature a link to a chat room where hundreds of other gamers are discussing the game. The girl enters the chat room to ask whether people who have played the game recommend it. The response is overwhelmingly positive, so she clicks on a sponsored link from the results page, which generates a sliver of paid-search revenue for Baidu and takes her to Shanda's official site, where she sets up an account.

Now her friend has returned with green tea frappucinos in hand. She is eager to show off her parents' gift to her for doing well in her exams—a pink Samsung L600 mobile phone created for women after months of market research and consumer tests. She thinks this is so cool, especially for the long subway rides home from school. The two girls are admiring the slender phone when it receives a text message announcing the availability of Shanda's latest game for mobile download. The girls turn to the laptop, so they can gauge the online buzz for the mobile version of the game.

In this chapter, we will address the following questions:

1. Why is marketing important?
2. What is the scope of marketing?
3. What are some fundamental marketing concepts?
4. How has marketing management changed?
5. What are the tasks necessary for successful marketing management?

Good marketing is no accident, but a result of careful planning and execution. Marketing practices are continually being refined and reformed in virtually all industries to increase the chances of success. But marketing excellence is rare and difficult to achieve. Marketing is both an "art" and a "science"—there is constant tension between the formulated side of marketing and the creative side. It is easier to learn the formulated side, which will occupy most of our attention in this book; but we will also describe how creativity and passion operate in many companies. This book will help to improve your understanding of marketing and your ability to make the right marketing decisions. In this chapter, we lay the foundation for our study by reviewing important marketing concepts, tools, frameworks, and issues.

The Importance of Marketing

Financial success often depends on marketing ability. Finance, operations, accounting, and other business functions will not really matter if there is no sufficient demand for products and services. There must be a top line for there to be a bottom line. Organizations of all kinds—from consumer goods makers to health care insurers and from nonprofit organizations to industrial product manufacturers—trumpet their latest marketing achievements in press releases and on their Web sites.

Marketing is tricky, however, and it has been the Achilles' heel of many formerly prosperous companies. Large, well-known businesses such as Sony, Levi's, and Kodak have confronted newly empowered customers and new competitors, and have had to rethink their business models. Even market leaders such as Microsoft, Wal-Mart, Intel, and Nike recognize that they cannot afford to relax. Jack Welch, GE's brilliant former CEO, repeatedly warned his company: "Change or die."

Xerox—Xerox has had to become more than just a copier company. The blue-chip icon with the name that became a verb sports the broadest array of imaging products in the world and dominates the market for high-end printing systems. It's making a huge product-line transition as it moves away from the old-line "light lens" technology to digital systems. Xerox is preparing for a world that is no longer black and white, and in which most pages are printed in color. In addition to revamping its machines, Xerox is beefing up sales by providing annuity-like products and services that are ordered again and again: document management, ink, and toners. Having been slow at one time to respond to the emergence of Canon and the small copier market, Xerox is doing everything it can to stay ahead of the game.[1]

Making the right decisions is not always easy. Marketing managers must decide what features to design into a new product, what prices to offer customers, where to sell products, and how much to spend on advertising or sales. They must also make more detailed decisions such as the exact wording or color for new packaging. The companies at greatest risk are those that fail to carefully monitor their customers and competitors and to continuously improve their value offerings. They take a short-term, sales-driven view of their business and ultimately, they fail to satisfy their stockholders, their employees, their suppliers, and their channel partners. Skillful marketing is a never-ending pursuit.

The Scope of Marketing

To prepare to become a marketer, you need to understand what marketing is, how it works, what is marketed, and who does the marketing.

What is Marketing?

Marketing deals with identifying and meeting human and social needs. One of the shortest definitions of marketing is "meeting needs profitably." When eBay recognized that people were unable to locate some of the items they desired most and created an online auction clearing-house or when IKEA noticed that people wanted good furniture at a substantially lower price and created knock-down furniture, they demonstrated their marketing savvy and turned a private or social need into a profitable business opportunity.

The American Marketing Association offers the following formal definition: *Marketing is an organizational function and a set of processes for creating, communicating, and delivering value to customers and for managing customer relationships in ways that benefit the organization and its stakeholders.*[2] Coping with exchange processes calls for a considerable amount of work and skill. Marketing management takes place when at least one party to a potential exchange thinks about the means of achieving desired responses from other parties. We see **marketing management** as the art and science of *choosing target markets and getting, keeping, and growing customers through creating, delivering, and communicating superior customer value.*

We can distinguish between a social and a managerial definition of marketing. A social definition shows the role marketing plays in society. A social definition that serves our purpose is: *Marketing is a societal process by which individuals and groups obtain what they need and want through creating, offering, and freely exchanging products and services of value with others.* For a managerial definition, marketing has often been described as "the art of selling products," but people are surprised when they hear that the most important part of marketing is not selling! Selling is only the tip of the marketing iceberg. Peter Drucker, a leading management theorist, puts it this way:

> *There will always, one can assume, be need for some selling. But the aim of marketing is to make selling superfluous.The aim of marketing is to know and understand the customer so well that the product or service fits him and sells itself. Ideally, marketing should result in a customer who is ready to buy. All that should be needed then is to make the product or service available.*[3]

When Apple designed its iPhone, when Sony designed its PlayStation, and when Toyota introduced its Lexus automobile, they were swamped with orders because they had designed the "right" product based on careful marketing homework.

What is Marketed?

Marketing people are involved in marketing 10 types of entities: goods, services, experiences, events, persons, places, properties, organizations, information, and ideas.

GOODS

Physical goods constitute the bulk of most countries' production and marketing effort. Each year, companies worldwide market billions of fresh, canned, bagged, and frozen food products and millions of cars, refrigerators, television sets, machines, and various other mainstays of a modern and global economy. Not only do companies market their goods, but thanks in part to the Internet, even individuals can effectively market goods.

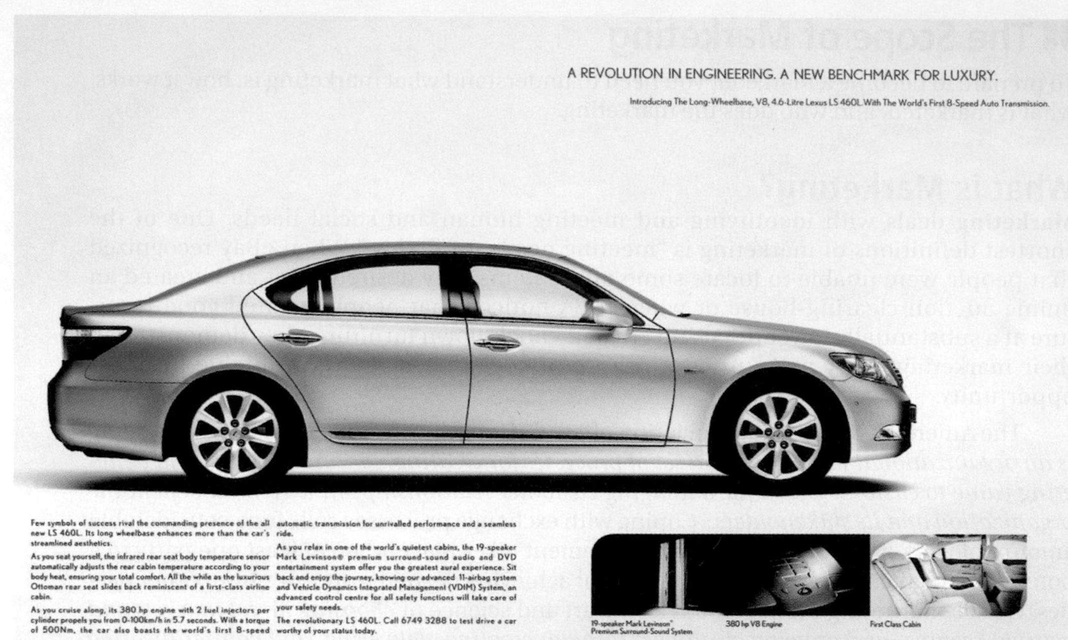

With its latest flagship model, Lexus has switched to emphasizing the performance and comfort offered to its customers.

SERVICES

As economies advance, a growing proportion of their activities is focused on the production of services. Developed economies usually have a 70–30 services-to-goods mix. Services include the work of airlines, hotels, car rental firms, barbers and beauticians, maintenance and repair people, as well as professionals working within or for companies, such as accountants, bankers, lawyers, engineers, doctors, software programmers, and management consultants. Many market offerings consist of a variable mix of goods and services. At a fast-food restaurant, for example, the customer consumes both a product and a service.

EVENTS

Marketers promote time-based events, such as major trade shows, artistic performances, and company anniversaries. Global sporting events such as the Olympics or World Cup are promoted aggressively to both companies and fans. There is a whole profession of meeting planners who work out the details of an event and make sure it comes off perfectly.

EXPERIENCES

By orchestrating several services and goods, a firm can create, stage, and market experiences. Tokyo Disneyland and DisneySea represent experiential marketing: customers visit a fairy kingdom, a pirate ship, or a haunted house. So does the Hard Rock Café, where customers can enjoy a meal or see a band in a live concert. There is also a market for customized experiences, such as spending a week on eco-tourism in remote natural habitats in Asia, or learning about recycling at the Singapore Zoo.

PERSONS

Celebrity marketing is a major business. Today, every major film star has an agent, a personal manager, and ties to a public relations agency. Artists, musicians, CEOs, physicians, high-profile lawyers and financiers, and other professionals are also getting help from celebrity marketers.[4] Some people have done a masterful job of marketing themselves—think of Korean singing sensation Rain, and film stars Jackie Chan and Zhang Ziyi. Management consultant Tom Peters, being a master at self-branding, has advised each person to become a "brand."

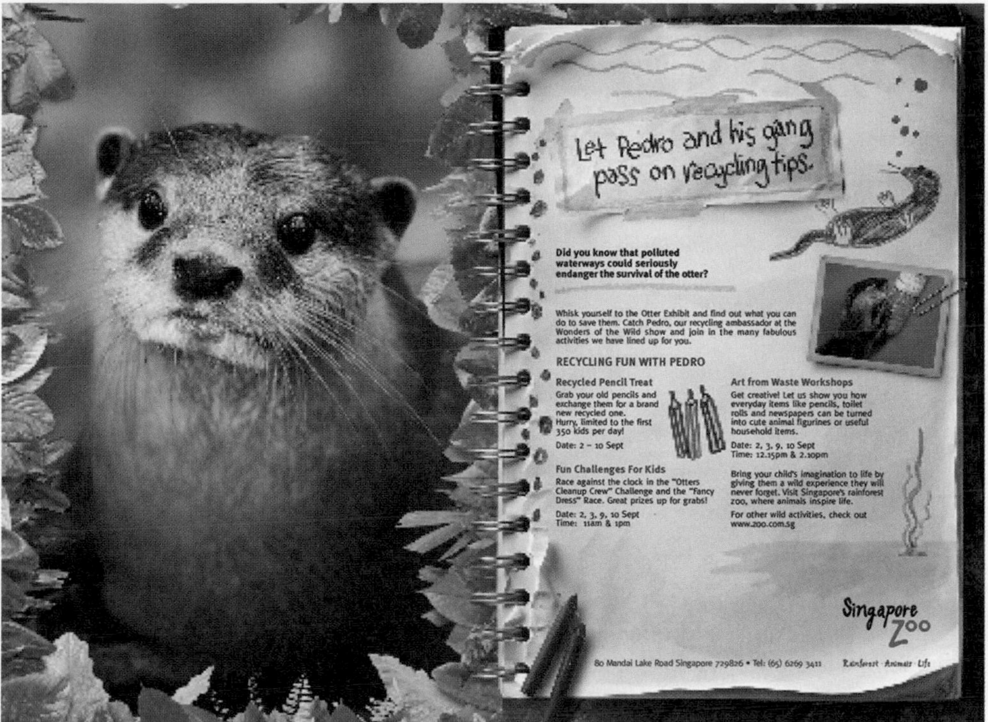

The Singapore Zoo offers varied experiences. During a school break, it organized recycling activities for children to experience what it takes to save the rainforest.

PLACES

Cities, states, regions, and whole nations compete actively to attract tourists, factories, company headquarters, and new residents.[5] Place marketers include national tourism agencies, economic development specialists, real estate agents, commercial banks, local business associations, and advertising and public relations agencies. For example, Asian countries have been marketed by their respective tourism promotion boards to woo regional and international visitors. Some campaign taglines used include: "Malaysia—Truly Asia," "Amazing Thailand," "Hong Kong: Live It. Love It!," "Uniquely Singapore," Macau's "A Heritage of Two Cultures," and Taiwan's "Touch Your Heart" (see "Marketing Memo: The Rewards of Branding Asian Countries").

Outdoor ad from Tourism Thailand promoting the amazing wonders that Thailand offers.

PROPERTIES

Properties are intangible rights of ownership of either real property (real estate) or financial property (stocks and bonds). Properties are bought and sold, and this requires marketing. Real estate agents work for property owners or sellers or buy residential or commercial real estate. Investment companies and banks are involved in marketing securities to both institutional and individual investors.

ORGANIZATIONS

Organizations actively work to build a strong, favorable, and unique image in the minds of their target public. Companies spend money on corporate identity ads. This is certainly the case with Philips "Sense and Simplicity" campaign.

MARKETING MEMO • THE REWARDS OF BRANDING ASIAN COUNTRIES

Regional brand management consultant Paul Temporal argues that just like companies, Asian countries must promote themselves as brands to achieve important national objectives. These include:

1. Increasing currency stability
2. Restoring international credibility and investor confidence
3. Reversing international ratings downgrades
4. Increasing international political influence
5. Increasing exports of branded goods and services
6. Increasing inbound tourism and investment
7. Stimulating stronger international partnerships
8. Enhancing nation-building (confidence, pride, harmony, ambition, resolve)
9. Reversing negative perceptions of environmental and human rights issues
10. Diffusing allegations of corruption and cronyism
11. Increasing access to global markets
12. Improving the ability to succeed against regional and global business competitors, and to defend home markets.

Source: Paul Temporal, "Why Asian Countries Need Branding." *Asia-Inc,* December 2001, pp. 46-47.

Royal Philips—Philips researchers asked 1,650 consumers and 180 customers in dozens of in-depth and quantitative interviews and focus groups what was most important to them in using technology. Respondents from the U.K., the U.S., France, Germany, the Netherlands, Hong Kong, China, and Brazil agreed on one thing: they wanted the benefits of technology without the hassle. With its "Sense and Simplicity" advertising campaign and focus, Philips believes, "our brand now reflects our belief that simplicity can be a goal of technology. It just makes sense." The campaign consists of print, online, and television advertising directed by five experts from the worlds of health care, lifestyle, and technology whose role is to provide "additional outside perspectives on the journey to simplicity."[6]

INFORMATION

Information is essentially what schools and universities produce and distribute at a price to parents, students, and communities. Magazines such as *Her World* and *PC World* supply information about the fashion world and computers respectively. The production, packaging, and distribution of information is one of our society's major industries.[7] Even companies that sell physical products attempt to add value through the use of information. For example, the CEO of Siemens Medical Systems, Tom McCausland, says, "[our product] is not necessarily an X-ray or an MRI, but information. Our business is really health-care information technology, and our end product is really an electronic patient record: information on lab tests, pathology, and drugs as well as voice dictation."[8]

IDEAS

Every market offering includes a basic idea. Charles Revson of Revlon observed: "In the factory, we make cosmetics; in the store we sell hope." Products and services are platforms for delivering some idea or benefit. Social marketers are busy promoting such ideas as "Say No to Drugs," "Exercise Daily," and "Eat Healthy Food." In Asia, governments often engage in social marketing. The Singaporean government is noted for its social marketing, including encouraging graduate women to get married and have more children.

Who Markets?

MARKETERS AND PROSPECTS

A **marketer** is someone seeking a response (attention, a purchase, a vote, a donation) from another party, called the **prospect.** If two parties are seeking to sell something to each other, we call them both marketers.

Marketers are skilled in stimulating demand for a company's products, but this is too limited a view of the tasks they perform. Just as production and logistics professionals are responsible for supply management, marketers are responsible for demand management. Marketing managers seek to influence the level, timing, and composition of demand to meet the organization's objectives. Eight demand states are possible:

1. ***Negative demand***— Consumers dislike the product and may even pay a price to avoid it.
2. ***Non-existent demand***— Consumers may be unaware or uninterested in the product.
3. ***Latent demand***— Consumers may share a strong need that cannot be satisfied by an existing product.
4. ***Declining demand***— Consumers begin to buy the product less frequently or not at all.
5. ***Irregular demand***— Consumer purchases vary on a seasonal, monthly, weekly, daily, or even hourly basis.
6. ***Full demand*** — Consumers are adequately buying all products put into the marketplace.
7. ***Overfull demand*** — More consumers would like to buy the product than can be satisfied.
8. ***Unwholesome demand***— Consumers may be attracted to products that have undesirable social consequences.

In each case, marketers must identify the underlying cause(s) of the demand state and then determine a plan for action to shift the demand to a more desired state.

MARKETS

Traditionally, a "market" was a physical place where buyers and sellers gathered to buy and sell goods. Economists describe a market as a collection of buyers and sellers who transact over a particular product or product class (e.g., the housing market or grain market). Modern economies abound in such markets.

Five basic markets and their connecting flows are shown in Figure 1.1. Manufacturers go to resource markets (raw material markets, labor markets, money markets), buy resources and turn them into goods and services, and then sell finished products to intermediaries, who sell them to consumers. Consumers sell their labor and receive money with which they pay for goods and services. The government collects tax revenues to buy goods from resource, manufacturer, and intermediary markets and uses these goods and services to provide public services. Each nation's economy and the global economy consist of complex interacting sets of markets linked through exchange processes.

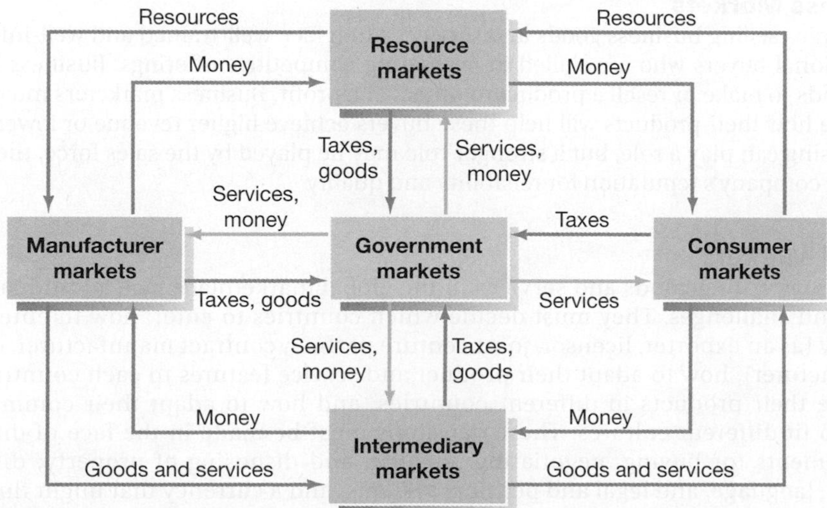

Figure 1.1 Structure of Flows in a Modern Exchange Economy

Marketers often use the term *market* to cover various groupings of customers. They view the sellers as constituting the industry and the buyers as constituting the market. They talk about need markets (the slimming-seeking market), product markets (the shoe market), demographic markets (the youth market), and geographic markets (the China market); or they extend the concept to cover other markets, such as voter markets, labor markets, and donor markets.

Figure 1.2 shows the relationship between the industry and the market. Sellers and buyers are connected by four flows. The sellers send goods and services and communications (ads, direct mail) to the market; in return they receive money and information (attitudes, sales data). The inner loop shows an exchange of money for goods and services; the outer loop shows an exchange of information.

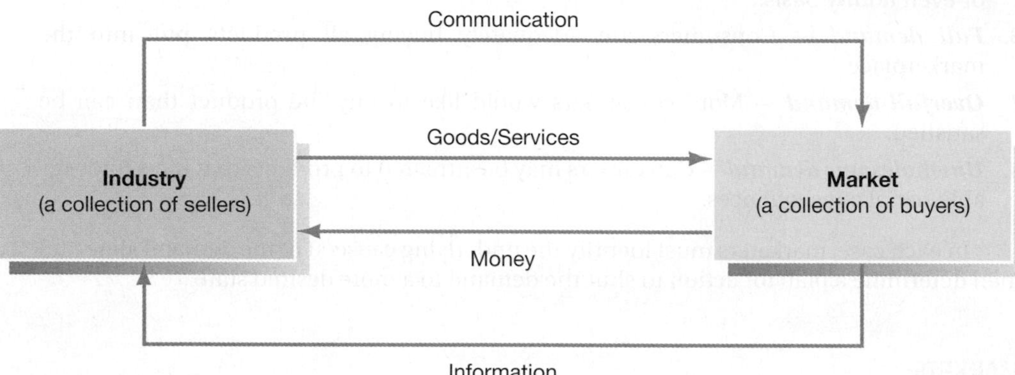

Figure 1.2 A Simple Marketing System

KEY CUSTOMER MARKETS

Consider the following key customer markets: consumer, business, global, and non-profit.

Consumer Markets

Companies selling mass consumer goods and services such as soft drinks, cosmetics, air travel, and athletic shoes and equipment spend a great deal of time trying to establish a superior brand image. Much of a brand's strength depends on developing a superior product and packaging, ensuring its availability, and backing it with engaging communications and reliable service.

Business Markets

Companies selling business goods and services often face well-trained and well-informed professional buyers who are skilled in evaluating competitive offerings. Business buyers buy goods to make or resell a product to others at a profit. Business marketers must demonstrate how their products will help these buyers achieve higher revenue or lower costs. Advertising can play a role, but a stronger role may be played by the sales force, the price, and the company's reputation for reliability and quality.

Global Markets

Companies selling goods and services in the global marketplace face additional decisions and challenges. They must decide which countries to enter; how to enter each country (as an exporter, licensor, joint venture partner, contract manufacturer, or solo manufacturer); how to adapt their product and service features to each country; how to price their products in different countries; and how to adapt their communications to fit different cultures. These decisions must be made in the face of different requirements for buying, negotiating, owning, and disposing of property; different culture, language, and legal and political systems; and a currency that might fluctuate in value.

McDonald's—With China's informal out-of-home eating industry estimated to be worth over $135 billion, McDonald's is pouncing on this opportunity by opening over 1,000 outlets. It is relying on a combination of the traditional and the new to capture a large slice of the market. It has a $2 million innovation center in Hong Kong dedicated to coming up with suitable products. Alongside the Big Mac and fries, Chinese diners can choose from green pea pies, rice burgers, and a mint-flavored soda called Blue Haven. It also offers a chicken-and-mushroom pie in the shape of a pinwheel because according to Chinese folklore, the pinwheel is supposed to bestow good luck. When the company opened its first drive-through outlet in Guangzhou, it realized that this concept is foreign to the Chinese. Customers would drive up, collect their food, and then park their cars before entering the restaurant to eat their meal. Yet, with the anticipated boom in the Chinese auto market, McDonald's will be opening more car-friendly outlets. It has an agreement with Sinopec, the state-owned oil company, to give it first refusal on locating its outlets at any of Sinopec's 30,000 fuel stations across China.[9]

With an over $135 billion out-of-home dining industry, McDonald's is entering China in a big way with innovative food items for the Chinese tastebuds. These include rice burgers and a chicken-and-mushroom pie in the shape of a pinwheel, a lucky symbol for the Chinese.

Non-profit and Governmental Markets

Companies selling their goods to non-profit organizations such as churches, universities, charitable organizations, or government agencies need to price carefully because these organizations have limited purchasing power. Lower prices affect the features and the quality that the seller can build into the offering. Much government purchasing calls for bids, with the lowest bid being favored in the absence of extenuating factors.

MARKETPLACES, MARKETSPACES, AND METAMARKETS

The marketplace is physical, as when you shop in a store; marketspace is digital, as when you shop on the Internet.[10]

Sawhney proposed the concept of a *metamarket* to describe a cluster of complementary products and services that are closely related in the minds of consumers but are spread across a diverse set of industries. The automobile metamarket consists of automobile manufacturers, new and used car dealers, financing companies, insurance companies, mechanics, spare parts dealers, service shops, auto magazines, classified auto ads in newspapers, and auto sites on the Internet. In purchasing a car, a buyer will get involved in many parts of this metamarket, and this has created an opportunity for metamediaries to assist buyers to move seamlessly through these groups, although they are disconnected in physical space. Metamediaries can also serve other metamarkets such as the home ownership market, the parenting and baby care market, and the wedding market.[11]

Marketing in Practice

How is marketing done? Increasingly, marketing is *not* done only by the marketing department. Marketing needs to affect every aspect of the customer experience, meaning that marketers must properly manage all possible touch points—store layouts, package designs, product functions, employee training, and shipping and logistics methods. Marketing must also be heavily involved in key general management activities, such as product innovation and new-business development.

To create a strong marketing organization, marketers must think like executives in other departments, and executives in other departments must think more like marketers.[12] CMO (Chief Marketing Officer) and later CEO (Chief Executive Officer) of WalMart.com, Carter Cast, noted that what surprised him most when he became CMO was "that I would interact so much with functions outside of marketing. I didn't realize it is a holistic assignment. Then I realized I really had to understand things like product supply, cost break-evens, and accounting."[13]

Companies generally establish a marketing department to be responsible for creating and delivering customer value, but as the late David Packard of Hewlett-Packard observed, "Marketing is far too important to leave to the marketing department." Companies now know that every employee has an impact on the customer and must see the customer as the source of the company's prosperity. So they're beginning to emphasize interdepartmental teamwork to manage key processes. They're also placing more emphasis on the smooth management of core business processes, such as new-product realization, customer acquisition and retention, and order fulfillment.

In practice, marketing follows a logical process. The marketing *planning* process consists of analyzing marketing opportunities, selecting target markets, designing marketing strategies, developing marketing programs, and managing the marketing effort. In highly competitive marketplaces, however, marketing planning is more fluid and is continually refreshed. Companies must always be moving forward with marketing programs, innovating products and services, staying in touch with customer needs, and seeking new advantages rather than relying on past strengths.

The changing new marketing environment is putting considerable demands on marketing executives. Marketers must have diverse quantitative and qualitative skills, an entrepreneurial attitude, and a keen understanding of how marketing can create value within their organization.[14] They must work in harmony with the sales function.

There are five key functions for a CMO in leading marketing within the organization: (1) Strengthening the brands; (2) Measuring marketing effectiveness; (3) Driving new product development based on customer needs; (4) Gathering meaningful customer insights; (5) Utilizing new marketing technology.

Quelch and McGovern note that there is tremendous variability in the responsibilities and job descriptions for CMOs.[15] They offer eight ways to improve CMO success (see Figure 1.3).

1. Make the mission and responsibilities clear. Be certain that the case for having a CMO is strong and the mission is well understood by leaders in the organization, particularly the CEO, the board, and line management. Without a clear need (real or perceived), the role will be rejected by the organization.

2. Fit the role to the marketing culture and structure. Avoid having a CMO in a marketing-led company that has many individual brands rather than a single corporate umbrella—unless the person appointed to the position is a well-connected insider.

3. Choose a CMO who is compatible with the CEO. Beware of the CEO who wants to hire a CMO but doesn't want to relinquish any marketing control. Find a CEO who recognizes his or her responsibility to be the cheerleader for marketing and the brand, but realizes the need to be guided and coached by a marketing specialist.

4. Remember that showpeople don't succeed. The CMO should work hard to ensure the CEO is successful at being the principal cheerleader for the brand.

5. Match the personality with the CMO type. Be certain that the chief marketer has the right skills and personality for whichever of the three CMO models he or she might fill (VP of Marketing Services, Classic CMO, or "Super" CMO). There is little tolerance for on-the-job training.

6. Make line managers marketing heroes. By stretching their marketing budgets, CMOs can improve a division's marketing productivity and help business unit leaders increase their top-line revenues.

7. Infiltrate the line organization. Have the CMO support the placement of marketing professionals from the corporate marketing department into divisional marketing roles. Provide input from the CMO into the annual reviews of line marketers.

8. Require right-brain and left-brain skills. The most successful CMO will have strong creative and technical marketing expertise, be politically savvy, and have the interpersonal skills to be a great leader and manager.

Figure 1.3 Improving CMO Success

Source: Gail McGovern and John A. Quelch, "The Fall and Rise of the CMO." *Strategy&Business*, Winter 2004. Reprinted by permission.

Core Marketing Concepts

To understand the marketing function, we need to understand the following core set of concepts.

Needs, Wants, and Demands

Needs are the basic human requirements. People need food, air, water, clothing, and shelter to survive. People also have strong needs for recreation, education, and entertainment. These needs become *wants* when they are directed to specific objects that might satisfy the need. A Japanese needs food but may want *tempura, soba,* and *ocha.* A Thai needs food but may want a coconut drink and rice with green curry, followed by glutinous rice with mango for dessert. Wants are shaped by one's society. *Demands* are wants for specific products backed by an ability to pay. Many people want a Mercedes; only a few are willing and able to buy one. Companies must measure not only how many people want their product but also how many would actually be willing and able to buy it.

These distinctions shed light on the frequent criticism that "marketers create needs" or "marketers get people to buy things they don't want." Marketers do not create needs: needs preexist marketers. Marketers, along with other societal factors, influence wants. Marketers might promote the idea that a Mercedes would satisfy a person's need for social status. They do not, however, create the need for social status.

Understanding customer needs and wants is not always simple. Some customers have needs of which they are not fully conscious, or they cannot articulate these needs, or they use words that require some interpretation. What does it mean when the customer asks for a "powerful" fan, an "anti-bacterial" hand soap, an "attractive" bathing suit, or a "restful" hotel? Consider the customer who says he wants an "inexpensive car." The marketer must probe further. We can distinguish among five types of needs: (1) *Stated needs* (the customer wants an inexpensive car); (2) *Real needs* (the customer wants a car whose operating cost, not its initial price, is low); (3) *Unstated needs* (the customer expects good service from the dealer); (4) *Delight needs* (the customer would like the dealer to include an onboard navigation system); (5) *Secret needs* (the customer wants to be seen by friends as a savvy consumer).

Responding only to the stated need may shortchange the customer. Many consumers do not know what they want in a product. Consumers did not know much about mobile phones when they were first introduced. Nokia fought to shape consumer perceptions of them. Simply giving customers what they want is not enough any more—to gain an edge, companies must help customers learn what they want.

Positioning: "The First SUV with Anti-Rollover Technology." A Volvo ad focuses on the company's central benefit—safety.

Target Markets, Positioning, and Segmentation

A marketer can rarely satisfy everyone in a market. Not everyone likes the same *dim sum,* hotel room, restaurant, automobile, college, or movie. Thus marketers start by dividing the market into segments. They identify and profile distinct groups of buyers who might prefer or require varying product and services mixes by examining demographic, psychographic, and behavioral differences among buyers. The marketer then decides which segments present the greatest opportunity—which are its *target markets.* For each chosen target market, the firm develops a *market offering.* The offering is *positioned* in the minds of the target buyers as delivering some central benefit(s). For example, Volvo develops its cars for buyers to whom automobile safety is a major concern. Volvo, therefore, positions its car as the safest a customer can buy. Companies do best when they choose their target market(s) carefully and prepare tailored marketing programs.

Offerings and Brands

Companies address needs by putting forth a value proposition, a set of benefits they offer to customers to satisfy their needs. The intangible value proposition is made physical by an *offering*, which can be a combination of products, services, information, and experiences.

A *brand* is an offering from a known source. A brand name such as McDonald's carries many associations in the minds of people: hamburgers, fun, children, fast food, convenience, and golden arches. These associations make up the brand image. All companies strive to build brand strength—that is, a strong, favorable, and unique brand image.

Samsung—Samsung commissioned a study on consumer's perceptions of various brands. It found that while it was perceived as fashionable yet not flashy, Nokia was seen as a curious and classic brand with innovative and easy-to-use products. Sony was viewed as visionary and mature with quality and functional products. Panasonic was seen as a popular and older brand offering stable and reliable products, while Motorola was boring but well-known.[16]

Value and Satisfaction

The offering will be successful if it delivers value and satisfaction to the target buyer. The buyer chooses between different offerings on the basis of which is perceived to deliver the most value. *Value* reflects the perceived tangible and intangible benefits and costs to customers. Value can be seen as primarily a combination of quality, service, and price (QSP), called the "customer value triad." Value increases with quality and service, and decreases with price, although other factors can play an important role.

Value is a central marketing concept. Marketing can be seen as the identification, creation, communication, delivery, and monitoring of customer value. *Satisfaction* reflects a person's comparative judgments resulting from a product's perceived performance (or outcome) in relation to his or her expectations. If the performance falls short of expectations, the customer is dissatisfied and disappointed. If the performance matches the expectations, the customer is satisfied. If the performance exceeds expectations, the customer is highly satisfied or delighted.

Marketing Channels

To reach a target market, the marketer uses three kinds of marketing channels. *Communication channels* deliver and receive messages from target buyers and include newspapers, magazines, radio, television, mail, telephone, billboards, posters, fliers, CDs, audiotapes, and the Internet. Beyond these, communications are conveyed by facial expressions and clothing, the look of retail stores, and many other media. Marketers are increasingly adding dialogue channels (email and toll-free numbers) to counterbalance the more normal monologue channels (such as ads).

The marketer uses *distribution channels* to display, sell, or deliver the physical product or service(s) to the buyer or user. They include distributors, wholesalers, retailers, and agents.

Coca-Cola—Coca-Cola in Japan popularized the idea of canning coffee and making it available through vending machines. While Americans can enjoy a hot cup of coffee in most places, Japanese traditionally drink *ocha* or green tea. However, Coca-Cola found that the Japanese enjoy coffee but just can't get it readily. Hence, in a country where vending machines are a common form of retailing, Coca-Cola's Georgia brand canned coffee can be bought from many of the thousands of vending machines to suit Japanese lifestyle needs.

The marketer also uses *service channels* to carry out transactions with potential buyers. Service channels include warehouses, transportation companies, banks, and insurance companies that facilitate transactions. Marketers clearly face a design problem in choosing the best mix of communication, distribution, and service channels for their offerings.

Supply Chain

The supply chain is a longer channel stretching from raw materials to components to final products that are carried to final buyers. The supply chain for women's purses starts with hides, and moves through tanning operations, cutting operations, manufacturing, and the marketing channels bringing products to customers. The supply chain represents a value delivery system. Each company captures only a certain percentage of the total value generated by the supply chain. When a company acquires competitors or moves upstream or downstream, its aim is to capture a higher percentage of supply chain value.

Competition

Competition includes all the actual and potential rival offerings and substitutes that a buyer might consider. Suppose Toyota is planning to buy steel for its cars. There are several possible levels of competitors. The car manufacturer can buy steel from Nippon Steel or other integrated steel mills in Japan or abroad (e.g., from China or Korea); or buy steel from a mini-mill at a cost savings; or buy aluminum for certain parts of the car to lighten the car's weight; or buy engineered plastics for bumpers instead of steel. Clearly, Nippon Steel would be thinking too narrowly of competition if it thought only of other integrated steel companies. In fact, Nippon Steel is more likely to be hurt in the long run by substitute products than by its immediate steel company rivals. It must also consider whether to make substitute materials or stick only to those applications where steel offers superior performance.

Marketing Environment

Competition represents only one force in the environment in which the marketer operates. The marketing environment consists of the task environment and the broad environment.

The *task environment* includes the immediate actors involved in producing, distributing, and promoting the offering. The main actors are the company, suppliers, distributors, dealers, and the target customers. Included in the supplier group are material suppliers and service suppliers such as marketing research agencies, advertising agencies, banking and insurance companies, transportation companies, and telecommunications companies. Included with distributors and dealers are agents, brokers, manufacturer representatives, and others who facilitate finding and selling to customers.

The *broad environment* consists of six components: demographic environment, economic environment, physical environment, technological environment, political–legal environment, and social–cultural environment. These environments contain forces that can have a major impact on the actors in the task environment. Market actors must pay close attention to the trends and developments in these environments and make timely adjustments to their marketing strategies.

The New Marketing Realities

We can say with some confidence that "the marketplace isn't what it used to be." Marketers must attend and respond to a number of significant developments.

Major Societal Forces

Today the marketplace is radically different as a result of major, sometimes interlinking societal forces that have created new behaviors, new opportunities, and new challenges:

- ***Network information*** — The digital revolution has created an Information Age. The Industrial Age was characterized by mass production and mass consumption, stores stuffed with inventory, ads everywhere, and rampant discounting. The Information Age promises to lead to more accurate levels of production, more targeted communications, and more relevant pricing. Moreover, much of today's business is carried over electronic networks: intranets, extranets, and the Internet.

i-mode—i-mode in Japan capitalized on the craze in accessing the Internet over mobile phones. Consumers can send emails, make reservations for dinner, view a concert, or access Web sites for leisure or information as they commute or wait for friends. It is regarded as a personal concierge. Given the long commuting time between home and office or school in Japan, i-mode has become an indispensable service.

- ***Globalization*** — Technological advances in transportation, shipping, and communication have made it easier for companies to market in other countries and easier for consumers to buy products and services from marketers in other countries.
- ***Deregulation*** — Many countries have deregulated industries to create greater competition and growth opportunities. Companies in the telecommunication, domestic air travel, and electrical utilities industries may face foreign competition and may enter other local markets.
- ***Privatization*** — Many countries such as China have converted state-owned enterprises to private ownership and management to increase their efficiency.
- ***Heightened competition*** — Brand manufacturers are facing intense competition from domestic and foreign brands, which is resulting in rising promotion costs and shrinking profit margins. They are being further buffeted by powerful retailers who command limited shelf space and are putting out their own store brands in competition with national brands. Many strong brands are extending into related product categories, creating megabrands with much presence and reputation.

- ***Industry convergence*** — Industry boundaries are blurring at an incredible rate as companies are recognizing that new opportunities lie at the intersection of two or more industries. Pharmaceutical companies, at one time essentially chemical companies, are now adding biogenetic research capacities to formulate new drugs, new cosmetics (cosmoneuticals), and new foods (nutriceuticals). Shiseido, the Japanese cosmetics firm, markets a portfolio of dermatology drugs. The computing and consumer electronics industries have converged as Dell, Gateway, and Hewlett-Packard released a stream of entertainment devices—from MP3 players to plasma TVs and camcorders. The shift to digital technology, in which devices needed to play entertainment content are more and more like PCs, is fueling this massive convergence.[17]
- ***Retail transformation*** — Small retailers are succumbing to the growing power of giant retailers and "category killers." Store-based retailers are facing growing competition from catalog houses; direct-mail firms; newspaper, magazine, and TV direct-to-customer ads; home shopping TV; and e-commerce on the Internet. In response, entrepreneurial retailers are building entertainment into stores with coffee bars, lectures, demonstrations, and performances. They are marketing an "experience" rather than a product assortment.
- ***Disintermediation*** — The amazing success of early online dot-coms such as Amazon, Yahoo!, eBay, E*Trade, and dozens of others who created *disintermediation* in the delivery of products and services struck terror in the hearts of many established manufacturers and retailers. In response to disintermediation, many traditional companies engaged in *reintermediation* and became "brick-and-click," adding online services to their existing offerings. Many brick-and-click competitors became stronger contenders than the pure-click firms, since they had a larger pool of resources to work with and well-established brand names.

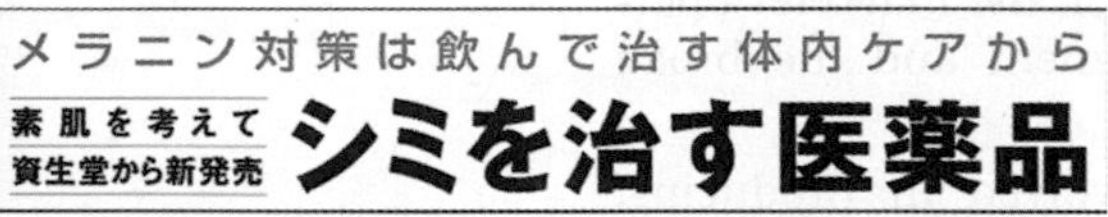

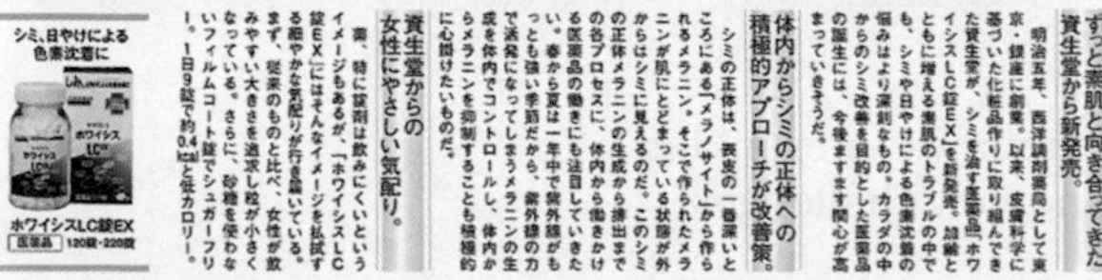

Cosmoneuticals: An ad for dermatology drugs marketed by Shiseido, the Japanese cosmetics firm. The WH/SIS product line targets spots and freckles, and includes cleanser, lotion, emulsion, day/night whitening beauty essence, and medication to be taken orally. It is sold only in Japan, mainly in drugstores. This is an example of industry convergence.

The societal forces that spawned this Information Age have resulted in many new consumer and company capabilities. The digital revolution has placed a whole new set of capabilities in the hands of consumers and businesses. Consider what consumers have today that they didn't have yesterday:

- ***A substantial increase in buying power*** — Buyers today are only a click away from comparing competitor prices and product attributes on the Internet. They can even name the price they want to pay for a hotel room, airline ticket, or mortgage, and see if there are any willing suppliers. Business buyers can run a reverse auction where sellers compete to capture the buyer's business. Buyers can join with others to aggregate their purchases to achieve deeper volume discounts.
- ***A greater variety of available goods and services*** — Today, a person can order almost anything over the Internet. Amazon.com advertises itself as the world's largest bookstore, with over three million books in its catalog; no physical bookstore can match this. Further, buyers can order these goods from anywhere in the world, which helps people living in countries with very limited local offerings to achieve great savings. It also means that buyers in countries with high prices can reduce their costs by ordering in countries with lower prices.
- ***A great amount of information about practically anything*** — People can read almost any newspaper in any language from anywhere in the world. They can access online encyclopedias, dictionaries, medical information, movie ratings, consumer reports, and countless other information sources.
- ***A greater ease in interacting and placing and receiving orders*** — Today's buyers can place orders from home, office, or mobile phone 24 hours a day, seven days a week, and the orders will be delivered to their home or office quickly.
- ***An ability to compare notes on products and services*** — Today's customers can enter a chat room centered on some area of common interest and exchange information and opinions.
- ***An amplified voice to influence peer and public opinion*** — The Internet fuels personal connections and user-generated content through social media such as MySpace and single-use social networks such as Wikipedia (encyclopedia articles), and YouTube (video).[18]

KFC, Converse, William Wrigley Jr.—Although Chinese citizens are still prohibited from criticizing the government online, they have thousands of online forums for airing grievances about poor customer service, misleading ad campaigns, shoddy products, safety standards, and more. Chinese consumers are vocal and active, and when enough of them voice a complaint, companies listen. When a Chinese TV spot for Yum! Brand Inc.'s KFC Corp. depicted a hardworking student who didn't pass his exams and two carefree children who enjoyed KFC fried chicken and did, KFC received so many complaints for suggesting hard work doesn't pay that it changed the ad to show all three children doing well. Smart companies are enlisting their opinionated Internet consumers to give input before a product is launched. Converse and Wm. Wrigley Jr. conducted a joint promotion encouraging Chinese consumers to come up with their own cool designs for Converse sneakers that featured Wrigley's Juicy Fruit logo.[19]

New Company Capabilities

New forces also have combined to generate a new set of capabilities for today's companies:

- **Marketers can use the Internet as a powerful information and sales channel**, augmenting their geographical reach to inform customers and promote their businesses and products worldwide. By establishing one or more Web sites, they can list their products and services, history, its business philosophy, job opportunities, and other information of interest to visitors.
- **Researchers can collect fuller and richer information** about markets, customers, prospects, and competitors. They can also conduct fresh marketing research using the

Internet to arrange for focus groups, send out questionnaires, and gather primary data in several other ways.

- **Managers can facilitate and speed internal communication among their employees** by using the Internet as a private intranet. Employees can query one another, seek advice, and download or upload needed information from and to the company's main computer.
- **Companies can also facilitate and speed external communication among customers** by creating online and off-line "buzz" through brand advocates and user communities.
- **Target marketing and two-way communication are easier** thanks to the proliferation of special-interest magazines, TV channels, and Internet newsgroups. Extranets linking suppliers and distributors let firms send and receive information, place orders, and make payments more efficiently. The company can also interact with each customer individually to *personalize* messages, services, and the relationship.
- **Marketers can send ads, coupons, samples, and information to customers** who have requested them or have given the company permission to send them. They can now assemble information about individual customers' purchases, preferences, demographics, and profitability. British supermarket giant Tesco uses its Clubcard data to personalize offers according to individual customer attributes.[20]
- **Companies can reach consumers on the move** with mobile marketing. Using GPS technology, for instance, Americans can download company logos so they can spot brands such as Dunkin' Donuts or Baskin-Robbins when they're on the road.[21] Firms can also advertise on video iPods and reach consumers on their mobile phones through mobile marketing.[22]
- **Firms can produce individually differentiated goods,** whether they're ordered in person, on the phone, or online, thanks to advances in factory customization, computers, the Internet, and database marketing software. For a price, customers can buy M&M candies with their names on them. BMW's technology allows buyers to design their own models from among 350 variations, with 500 options, 90 exterior colors, and 170 trims. The company claims that 80 percent of the cars bought by individuals in Europe and up to 30 percent bought in the United States are built to order.
- **Managers can improve purchasing, recruiting, training, and internal and external communications.** Aerospace and defense contractor Boeing has joined large, high-profile companies Walt Disney, General Motors, and McDonald's in embracing corporate blogging to communicate with the public, customers, and employees. External blogs allow dialogues with a marketing vice president and a glimpse into the flight testing of new aircraft models; internal blogs allow conversations on hot topics and anonymous feedback.[23]
- **Corporate buyers can achieve substantial savings** by using the Internet to compare sellers' prices and to purchase materials at auction or by posting their own terms. Companies can improve logistics and operations to reap substantial cost savings, at the same time improving accuracy and service quality.
- **Firms can also recruit new employees online,** and many are also preparing Internet training products for download to employees, dealers, and agents.

Company Orientations Toward the Marketplace

Given these new marketing realities, what philosophy should guide a company's marketing efforts? Increasingly, marketers operate consistently with a holistic marketing concept. Let's review the evolution of earlier marketing ideas.

The Production Concept

The production concept is one of the oldest concepts in business. It holds that consumers will prefer products that are widely available and inexpensive. Managers of production-oriented businesses concentrate on achieving high production efficiency, low costs, and mass distribution. This orientation makes sense in developing countries such as China where the largest PC manufacturer, Lenovo, and domestic appliances giant, Haier, take advantage of the country's huge inexpensive labor pool to dominate the market. It is also used when a company wants to expand the market.[24]

The Product Concept

The product concept holds that consumers will favor those products that offer the most quality, performance, or innovative features. Managers in these organizations focus on making superior products and improving them over time. However, these managers are sometimes caught up in a love affair with their products. They might commit the "better mousetrap" fallacy, believing that a better mousetrap will lead people to beat a path to their door. A new or improved product will not necessarily be successful unless the product is priced, distributed, advertised, and sold properly.

The Selling Concept

The selling concept holds that consumers and businesses, if left alone, will ordinarily not buy enough of the organization's products. The organization must, therefore, undertake an aggressive selling and promotion effort. The selling concept is epitomized in the thinking of Sergio Zyman, Coca-Cola's former vice president of marketing: the purpose of marketing is to sell more stuff to more people more often for more money in order to make more profit.[25]

The selling concept is practiced most aggressively with unsought goods, goods that buyers normally do not think of buying, such as insurance, encyclopedias, and funeral plots. Most firms practice the selling concept when they have overcapacity. Their aim is to sell what they make rather than make what the market wants. However, marketing based on hard selling carries high risks. It assumes that customers who are coaxed into buying a product will like it; and that if they do not, they will not return it or bad-mouth it or complain to consumer organizations, or might even buy it again.

The Marketing Concept

The marketing concept emerged in the mid-1950s.[26] Instead of a product-centered, "make-and-sell" philosophy, business shifted to a customer-centered, "sense-and-respond" philosophy. The job is not to find the right customers for your products, but the right products for your customers. The marketing concept holds that the key to achieving organizational goals consists of the company being more effective than competitors in creating, delivering, and communicating superior customer value to its chosen target markets.

Levitt drew a perceptive contrast between the selling and marketing concepts:

> *Selling focuses on the needs of the seller; marketing on the needs of the buyer. Selling is preoccupied with the seller's need to convert his product into cash; marketing with the idea of satisfying the needs of the customer by means of the product and the whole cluster of things associated with creating, delivering, and finally consuming it.*[27]

Several scholars have found that companies who embrace the marketing concept achieve superior performance.[28] This was first demonstrated by companies practicing a *reactive market orientation*—understanding and meeting customers' expressed needs. Some critics say this means companies develop only low-level innovations. Narver and his colleagues argue that high-level innovation is possible if the focus is on customers' latent needs. He calls this a *proactive marketing orientation*.[29] Companies such as 3M, Hewlett-Packard, and Motorola have made a practice of researching or imagining latent needs through a "probe-and-learn" process. Companies that practice both a reactive and proactive marketing orientation are implementing a *total market orientation* and are likely to be the most successful.

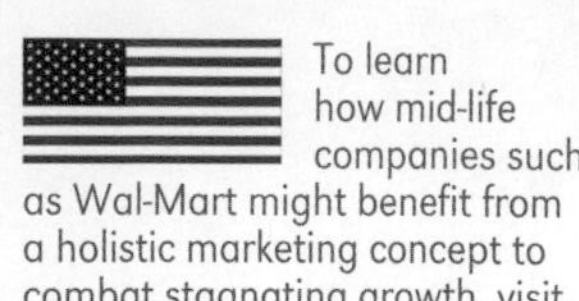
To learn how mid-life companies such as Wal-Mart might benefit from a holistic marketing concept to combat stagnating growth, visit wps.prenhall.com/bp_kotler_mm_13/.

The Holistic Marketing Concept

Without question, the trends and forces defining the 21st century are leading business firms to a new set of beliefs and practices. Today's best marketers recognize the need to have a more complete, cohesive approach that goes beyond traditional applications of the marketing concept. "Marketing Memo: Marketing Right and Wrong" suggests where companies go wrong—and how they can get it right—in their marketing.

The **holistic marketing** concept is based on the development, design, and implementation of marketing programs, processes, and activities that recognize their breadth and interdependencies. Holistic marketing recognizes that "everything matters" with marketing and that a broad, integrated perspective is often necessary.

Holistic marketing is thus an approach to marketing that attempts to recognize and reconcile the scope and complexities of marketing activities. Figure 1.4 provides a schematic overview of the four broad themes characterizing holistic marketing: relationship marketing, integrated marketing, internal marketing, and performance marketing. We will examine these major themes throughout the book.

Successful companies will be those that can keep their marketing changing with the changes in their marketplace—and marketspace. "Breakthrough Marketing: Nike" describes how that company has successfully changed—and thrived—through the years.

Relationship Marketing

Increasingly, a key goal of marketing is to develop deep, enduring relationships with people and organizations that could directly or indirectly affect the success of the firm's marketing activities. **Relationship marketing** aims to build mutually satisfying long-term relationships with key constituents to earn and retain their business.[30]

MARKETING MEMO • MARKETING RIGHT AND WRONG

The Ten Deadly Sins of Marketing

1. The company is not sufficiently market-focused and customer-driven.
2. The company does not fully understand its target customers.
3. The company needs to better define and monitor its competitors.
4. The company has not properly managed its relationships with its stakeholders.
5. The company is not good at finding new opportunities.
6. The company's marketing plans and planning process are deficient.
7. The company's product and service policies need tightening.
8. The company's brand-building and communications skills are weak.
9. The company is not well-organized to carry on effective and efficient marketing.
10. The company has not made maximum use of technology.

The Ten Commandments of Marketing

1. The company segments the market, chooses the best segments, and develops a strong position in each chosen segment.
2. The company maps its customers' needs, perceptions, preferences, and behavior and motivates its stakeholders to obsess about serving and satisfying the customers.
3. The company knows its major competitors and their strengths and weaknesses.
4. The company builds partners out of its stakeholders and generously rewards them.
5. The company develops systems for identifying opportunities, ranking them, and choosing the best ones.
6. The company manages a marketing planning system that leads to insightful long-term and short-term plans.
7. The company exercises strong control over its product and service mix.
8. The company builds strong brands by using the most cost-effective communication and promotion tools.
9. The company builds marketing leadership and a team spirit among its various departments.
10. The company constantly adds technology that gives it a competitive advantage in the marketplace.

Source: Adapted from Philip Kotler, *Ten Deadly Marketing Sins*, (Hoboken, NJ: John Wiley, 2004).

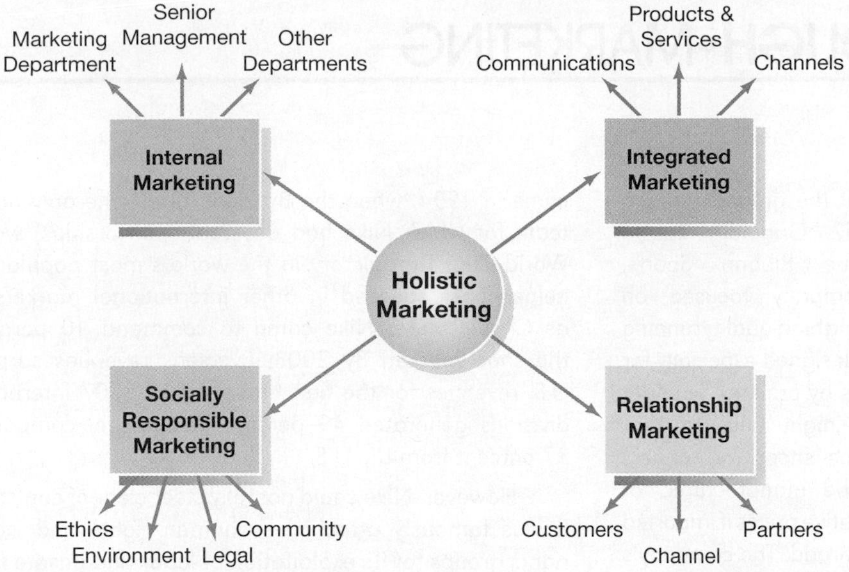

Figure 1.4 Holistic Marketing Dimensions

Four key constituents for relationship marketing are customers, employees, marketing partners (channels, suppliers, distributors, dealers, and agencies), and members of the financial community (shareholders, investors, analysts). Marketers must respect the need to create prosperity among all these constituents and develop policies and strategies to balance the returns to all key stakeholders. To develop strong relationships with these constituents requires an understanding of their capabilities and resources, as well as their needs, goals, and desires.

The ultimate outcome of relationship marketing is a unique company asset called a marketing network. A **marketing network** consists of the company and its supporting stakeholders—customers, employees, suppliers, distributors, retailers, ad agencies, university scientists, and others—with whom it has built mutually profitable business relationships. The operating principle is simple: build an effective network of relationships with key stakeholders, and profits will follow.[31]

Relationships and networks take on added importance in Asian marketing. In East Asia, the cultivation of personal relationships and the use of *guanxi* (personal connections) in business are still evident. In countries like China, which have a long history of being exploited by other nations, personal relations are useful in developing trust among business partners. To conduct business successfully in Asia, hiring a consultant or an intermediary to foster *guanxi* may be fruitful, and selecting a joint-venture partner who has valuable connections with the local government may also prove beneficial.

A growing number of today's companies are also shaping separate offers, services, and messages to *individual customers,* based on information about past transactions, demographics, psychographics, and media and distribution preferences. By focusing on their most profitable customers, products, and channels, these firms hope to achieve profitable growth, capturing a larger share of each customer's expenditures by building high customer loyalty. They estimate individual customer lifetime value and design their market offerings and prices to make a profit over the customer's lifetime.

Another goal of relationship marketing is to place more emphasis on customer retention. Attracting a new customer may cost five times as much as doing a good enough job to retain an existing one. A bank aims to increase its share of the customer's wallet; a supermarket aims to capture a larger share of the customer's "stomach." Companies build customer share by offering a larger variety of goods to existing customers. They train their employees in cross-selling and up-selling.

BREAKTHROUGH • MARKETING

NIKE

Nike is widely acknowledged as one of the most skilled advertisers around.

Nike hit the ground running in 1962. Originally known as Blue Ribbon Sports, the company focused on providing high-quality running shoes designed especially for athletes by athletes. Founder Philip Knight believed that high-tech shoes for runners could be manufactured at competitive prices if imported from abroad. The company's commitment to designing innovative footwear for serious athletes helped it build a cult following among U.S. consumers.

Nike believed in a "pyramid of influence" where product and brand choices were influenced by the preferences and behavior of a small percentage of top athletes. Therefore, from the start, Nike's marketing campaigns featured winning athletes as spokespeople. Nike's first spokesperson, runner Steve Prefontaine, had an irreverent attitude that matched the company's spirit.

In 1985, Nike signed up then-rookie guard Michael Jordan as a spokesperson. Jordan was still an up-and-comer, but he personified superior performance. Nike's bet paid off: the Air Jordan line of basketball shoes flew off the shelves, with revenues of over $100 million in the first year alone.

In 1988, Nike aired the first ads in its $20 million "Just Do It" ad campaign. The campaign, which ultimately featured 12 TV spots in all, subtly challenged a generation of athletic enthusiasts to chase their goals; it was a natural manifestation of Nike's attitude of self-empowerment through sports.

As Nike began expanding overseas to Europe, however, it found that its U.S.-style ads were seen there as too aggressive. Nike realized it had to "authenticate" its brand in Europe the way it had in the U.S. That meant building credibility and relevance in European sports, especially soccer (known outside the U.S. as football). Nike became actively involved as a sponsor of youth leagues, local clubs, and national teams.

Authenticity also required that consumers see athletes using the product, especially athletes who win. The big break came in 1994, when the Brazilian team (the only national team for which Nike had any real sponsorships) won the World Cup. That victory in the world's most popular sport helped Nike succeed in other international markets such as China, where Nike came to command 10 percent of the shoe market. By 2003, overseas revenues surpassed U.S. revenues for the first time, and by 2007 international divisions generated 49 percent of revenue, compared to 37 percent from the U.S.

However, Nike could not fully steer clear of controversy. It was famously attacked by human rights and workers' rights groups for its exploitation of labor and unsafe factory conditions in Asia. Nike responded by implementing major changes in corporate labor policy. In 2004, a Nike ad featuring basketball star LeBron James was banned in China. Chinese regulators were offended that an American sports icon could defeat a dragon, a symbol of Chinese culture, and a martial arts master, a symbol of national pride. Nike quickly withdrew the ad and apologized.

Another 2004 ad resonated better among Chinese mainlanders. When hurdler Liu Xiang became China's first Olympic gold medalist, Nike launched a television commercial showing Liu destroying the field and superimposing a series of provocative, if not nationalistic, questions. "Asians lack muscle?" asked one. "Asians lack the will to win?" Then, Liu raised his arms above the trademark Swoosh on his shoulder: "Stereotypes are made to be broken." The commercial was an instant success.

In addition to expanding overseas, Nike moved into new athletic footwear, apparel, and equipment product categories. These included the Nike Golf brand of footwear, apparel, and equipment, which were all endorsed by megastar Tiger Woods. In 2005, Nike introduced an urban-themed collection of retro footwear and apparel bearing the name of the original company, Blue Ribbon Sports. Blue Ribbon Sports designs—which included jeans, belts, sweaters, and woven shirts—were sold at high-end retailers.

Today, Nike dominates the athletic footwear market. Swooshes abound on everything from wristwatches to golf clubs to swimming caps. As a result of its expansion across geographic markets and product categories, Nike is the top athletic apparel and footwear manufacturer in the world, with corporate fiscal 2007 revenues of over $16.3 billion.

Sources: Justin Ewers and Tim Smart, "A Designer Swooshes In." *U.S. News & World Report*, January 26, 2004, p. 12; "Corporate Media Executive of the Year." *Delaney Report*, January 12, 2004, p. 1; "10 Top Nontraditional Campaigns." *Advertising Age*. December 22, 2003, p. 24; Chris, Zook, and James Allen, "Growth Outside the Core." *Harvard Business Review*, December 2003, 8, p. 66; "Nike Hones Rebel Reputation with Controversial Asian Ads." *Columbia Daily Tribune*, December 8, 2004; "How Nike Figured Out China." *Time*, October 25, 2004; <www.nike.com>.

> **ExxonMobil, Shell, Caltex, and SPC**—In Singapore, petrol companies are increasingly relying on their rewards programs to hold on to their customers. ExxonMobil has an upgraded Smiles reward program that gives a more favorable earn rate and a higher discount for petrol purchases. It also introduced a Gold Tier scheme which gives 30 percent bonus points to customers who spend at least S$250 a month. Shell's Escape program changed its awards based on number of liters pumped instead of amount spent. With increasing petrol prices, the point issuance based on liters insulates customers against pump price changes. Caltex's Thanks! Program rewards high-value customers with a Platinum Pack that includes fuel discount vouchers, free beverages, and bonus Thanks! Points. SPC's program saves the customer the trouble of keeping track of the points and deciding what to redeem them for. The company's computer system stores the points earned in a given month and gives upfront discounts over and above other discounts the following month.

Marketing must skillfully conduct not only customer relationship management (CRM), but partner relationship management (PRM) as well. Companies are deepening their partnering arrangements with key suppliers and distributors, thinking of these intermediaries not as customers but as partners in delivering value to final customers so everybody benefits.

Integrated Marketing

The marketer's task is to devise marketing activities and assemble fully integrated marketing programs to create, communicate, and deliver value for consumers. Marketing activities come in all forms. McCarthy classified these tools into four broad groups that he called *the four Ps* of marketing: product, price, place, and promotion.[32]

The particular marketing variables under each P are shown in Figure 1.5. Marketing-mix decisions must be made for influencing the trade channels as well as the final consumers. Figure 1.6 shows the company preparing an offering mix of products, services, and prices, and utilizing a communications mix of advertising, sales promotion, events and experiences, public relations, direct marketing, and personal selling to reach the trade channels and the target customers.

The firm can change its price, sales force size, and advertising expenditures in the short run. It can develop new products and modify its distribution channels only in the long run. Thus the firm typically makes fewer period-to-period marketing-mix changes in the short run than the number of marketing-mix decision variables might suggest.

The four Ps represent the sellers' view of the marketing tools available for influencing buyers. From a buyer's point of view, each marketing tool is designed to deliver a

Figure 1.5 The Four P Components of the Marketing Mix

Communications mix

Offering mix

Company | Products Services Prices

Advertising

Sales promotion

Events and experiences

Public relations

Direct marketing

Personal selling

Distribution channels

Target customers

Figure 1.6 Influencing Marketing-Mix Strategy

customer benefit. A complementary breakdown of marketing activities has been proposed that centers on customers. Its four dimensions (SIVA) and the corresponding customer questions are: (1) **S**olution: How can I solve my problem? (2) **I**nformation: Where can I learn more about it? (3) **V**alue: What is my total sacrifice to get this solution? (4) **A**ccess: Where can I find it?

Winning companies will be those that can meet customer needs economically and conveniently and with effective communication.

Two key themes of integrated marketing are that (1) many different marketing activities are employed to communicate and deliver value, and (2) all marketing activities are coordinated to maximize their joint effects. In other words, the design and implementation of any one marketing activity is done with all other activities in mind. Businesses must integrate their systems for demand management, resource management, and network management.

For example, an integrated communications strategy involves choosing communication options that reinforce and complement each other. A marketer might selectively employ television, radio, and print advertising, public relations and events, and PR and Web site communications so that each contributes on its own as well as improves the effectiveness of others. Integrated channel strategy involves ensuring that direct (e.g., online sales) and indirect channels (e.g., retail sales) work together to maximize sales and brand equity.

Companies such as Kinokuniya are using Web sites as part of their integrated communications strategy to maximize sales and brand equity.

Internal Marketing

Holistic marketing incorporates *internal marketing*, ensuring that everyone in the organization embraces appropriate marketing principles, especially senior management. Internal marketing is the task of hiring, training, and motivating able employees who want to serve customers well. Smart marketers recognize that marketing activities within the company can be as important as—if not even more so—than marketing activities directed outside the company. It makes no sense to promise excellent service before the company's staff is ready to provide it.

Internal marketing must take place on two levels. At one level, the various marketing functions—sales force, advertising, customer service, product management, marketing research—must work together. Too often, the sales force thinks product managers set prices or sale quotas "too high"; or the advertising director and a brand manager cannot agree on an advertising campaign. All these marketing functions must be coordinated from the customer's point of view. The following example highlights the coordination problem:

The marketing vice president of a major Asian airline wants to increase the airline's traffic share. His strategy is to build up customer satisfaction through providing better food, cleaner cabins, better-trained cabin crews, and lower fares; yet he has no authority in these matters. The catering department chooses food that keeps food costs down; the maintenance department uses cleaning services that keep down cleaning costs; the human resources department hires people without regard to whether they are naturally friendly; the finance department sets the fares. Because these departments generally take a cost or production point of view, the vice president of marketing is stymied in creating an integrated marketing mix.

At the second level, marketing must be embraced by the other departments; they must also "think customer." Marketing is not a department so much as a company orientation. Marketing thinking must be pervasive throughout the company (see Table 1.1).

Internal marketing thus requires vertical alignment with senior management and horizontal alignment with other departments, so everyone understands, appreciates, and supports the marketing effort. A study conducted by Booz Allen Hamilton asked 2,000 executives to describe the marketing structure within their organizations and to detail the tasks they consider integral to their missions. The researchers identified six types of marketing organizations (see Figure 1.7 for a breakdown and descriptions). In the most successful type, Growth Champions, marketing heavily influenced all aspects of the organization. Growth Champions were 20 percent more likely to deliver revenue growth and profitability than the other types of marketing organizations.

Growth Champions (8.8%) emphasize growth-support functions, leading such general-management activities as product innovation and new-business development.

Marketing Masters (38.4%) oversee company-wide marketing efforts and the customer-focused side of new product and service launches, although are typically not involved with strategic decisions.

Senior Counselors (16.9%) specialize in marketing strategy, advising the CEO and individual businesses, and may drive major communication programs, although not typically new product development.

Best Practices Advisors (8.9%) work with individual business units to improve their marketing effectiveness but are less likely to be linked with above-average growth than both the Growth Champions and the Marketing Masters.

Brand Builders (12.2%) support brands by providing marketing services like communications strategy, creative output, and campaign execution, but exhibit little strategic leadership.

Service Providers (14.7%) coordinate marketing communications, but often work in firms with lower revenue growth and profitability.

Figure 1.7 Types of Marketing Organizations

Performance Marketing

Holistic marketing incorporates *performance marketing* and understanding the returns to the business from marketing activities and programs, as well as addressing broader concerns and their legal, ethical, social, and environmental effects. Top management is going beyond sales revenue to examine the marketing scorecard and interpret what is happening to market share, customer loss rate, customer satisfaction, product quality, and other measures.

Financial Accountability

Marketers are thus being increasingly asked to justify their investments to senior management in financial and profitability terms, as well as in terms of building the brand and growing the customer base.[33] As a consequence, they're employing a broader variety of financial measures to assess the direct and indirect value their marketing efforts create. They're also recognizing that much of their firms' market value comes from intangible assets, particularly their brands, customer base, employees, distributor and supplier relations, and intellectual capital.

Table 1.1 Assessing which Company Departments are Customer-Minded

R&D
- They spend time meeting customers and listening to their problems.
- They welcome the involvement of marketing, manufacturing, and other departments to each new project.
- They benchmark competitors' products and seek "best of class" solutions.
- They solicit customer reactions and suggestions as the project progresses.
- They continuously improve and refine the product on the basis of market feedback.

Purchasing
- They proactively search for the best suppliers.
- They build long-term relationships with fewer but more reliable, high-quality suppliers.
- They don't compromise quality for price savings.

Manufacturing
- They invite customers to visit and tour their plants.
- They visit customer plants.
- They willingly work overtime to meet promised delivery schedules.
- They continuously search for ways to produce goods faster and/or at lower cost.
- They continuously improve product quality, aiming for zero defects.
- They meet customer requirements for "customization" where possible.

Marketing
- They study customer needs and wants in well-defined market segments.
- They allocate marketing effort in relation to the long-run profit potential of the targeted segments.
- They develop winning offers for each target segment.
- They measure company image and customer satisfaction on a continuous basis.
- They continuously gather and evaluate ideas for new products, product improvements, and services.
- They urge all company departments and employees to be customer-centered.

Sales
- They have specialized knowledge of the customer's industry.
- They strive to give the customer "the best solution."
- They make only promises that they can keep.
- They feedback customers' needs and ideas to those in charge of product development.
- They serve the same customers for a long period of time.

Logistics
- They set a high standard for service delivery time and meet this standard consistently.
- They operate a knowledgeable and friendly customer service department that can answer questions, handle complaints, and resolve problems in a satisfactory and timely manner.

Accounting
- They prepare periodic "profitability" reports by product, market segment, geographic areas (regions, sales territories), order sizes, channels, and individual customers.
- They prepare invoices tailored to customer needs and answer customer queries courteously and quickly.

Finance
- They understand and support marketing expenditures (e.g., image advertising) that produce long-term customer preference and loyalty.
- They tailor the financial package to the customer's financial requirements.
- They make quick decisions on customer creditworthiness.

Public Relations
- They send out favorable news about the company and "damage control" unfavorable news.
- They act as an internal customer and public advocate for better company policies and practices.

Source: Philip Kotler, *Kotler on Marketing*, (New York, NY: The Free Press, 1999), pp. 21–22.

Social Responsibility Marketing

The effects of marketing clearly extend beyond the company and the customer to society as a whole. Marketers must carefully consider their role in broader terms, and the ethical, environmental, legal, and social context of their activities.[34] Increasingly, consumers demand such behavior, as Starbucks Chairman Howard Schultz has observed:

> *"We see a fundamental change in the way consumers buy their products and services ... Consumers now commonly engage in a cultural audit of providers. People want to know your value and ethics demonstrated by how you treat employees, the community in which you operate. The implication for marketers is to strike the balance between profitability and social consciousness and sensitivity. ... It is not a program or a quarterly promotion, but rather a way of life. You have to integrate this level of social responsibility into your operation."*[35]

This realization calls for a new term that enlarges the marketing concept. We propose calling it the "societal marketing concept." The *societal marketing concept* holds that the organization's task is to determine the needs, wants, and interests of target markets and to deliver the desired satisfactions more effectively and efficiently than competitors in a way that preserves or enhances the consumer's and society's long-term well-being. Sustainability has become a major corporate concern in the face of challenging environmental forces. Firms such as Hewlett-Packard have introduced recyclable computers and printers and reduced greenhouse emissions; McDonald's strives for a "socially responsible supply system" encompassing everything from healthy fisheries to redesigned packaging.[36]

The societal marketing concept calls upon marketers to build social and ethical considerations into their marketing practices. They must balance and juggle the often conflicting criteria of company profits, consumer want satisfaction, and public interest. Table 1.2 displays some different types of corporate social initiatives, illustrated by McDonald's.[37]

Companies see cause-related marketing as an opportunity to enhance their corporate reputation, raise brand awareness, increase customer loyalty, build sales, and increase press coverage. They believe that customers will increasingly look for signs of good corporate citizenship that go beyond supplying rational and emotional benefits.

Table 1.2 Corporate Social Initiatives by McDonald's in Asia

Type	Description	Example
Corporate social marketing	Supporting behavior change campaigns	McDonald's sponsorship of Clean Community Days in China through which it encourages participation in tree planting and recycling programs.
Cause marketing	Promoting social issues through efforts such as sponsorships, licensing agreements, and advertising	McDonald's use of funds raised during World Children's Day to sponsor dictionaries for needy children in China. In Japan, McDonald's sponsors an annual All-Japan Rubber Baseball Tournament. Rubber baseball is an original Japanese product, created to provide a safe way for children to play baseball.
Cause-related marketing	Donating a percentage of revenues to a specific cause based on the revenue occurring during the announced period of support	During the relief efforts for the 2004 Asian tsunami, McDonald's India saw employees donating a day's pay, while McDonald's Singapore committed a portion of sales from popular menu items, and employees from McDonald's Hong Kong volunteered for UNICEF.
Corporate philanthropy	Making gifts of money, goods or time to help non-profit organizations, groups, or individuals	McDonald's Singapore donated part of the proceeds made on World Children's Day to support children with HIV/AIDS.
Corporate community involvement	Providing in-kind or volunteer services in the community	In Mumbai, McDonald's was involved in restoring a designated "heritage structure" in a historically and commercially important part of the city.
Socially responsible business practices	Adapting and conducting business practices that protect the environment, and human and animal rights	McDonald's Japan leads in energy efficiency programs. It has tracked its energy use for the past 14 years and has developed metrics to monitor carbon dioxide emissions. To date, it has reduced its gas emissions by 14.6 percent or 23 metric tons per restaurant.

Source: Philip Kotler and Nancy Lee. *Corporate Social Responsibility: Doing the Most Good for Your Company and Your Cause*, (Hoboken, NJ: John Wiley , December 2004); <www.mcdonalds.com/corp/values.html>.

Bata Indonesia—Bata Indonesia is different from other shoe manufacturers. While some sports apparel manufacturers have been labeled negatively for exploiting cheap Asian sweatshop labor, Bata Indonesia's factory compound looks better as a park than Jakarta's few parks do. Wide, tree-lined avenues lead to clean, spacious work sheds. There is also a grassy pitch for soccer matches, and a clean, well-stocked medical clinic situated near the main gate. While stories of other factories that force and lock their workers out of the factory grounds during lunchtime are rampant, Bata Indonesia provides two canteens for its staff. This display of social welfare is the reason that it was chosen by Bienestar, a U.S.-based clothing manufacturer, to make its No Sweat sneakers. While a pair of Nike sneakers cost $2, No Sweat's cost $4.50 a pair. The extra cost for workers' benefits, ranging from free health care and a monthly rice allowance, to a pay package that is about 30 percent above the minimum wage in Indonesia, is detailed on every No Sweat shoe box.[38]

Marketing Management Tasks

These core concepts and others provide the input for a set of tasks that make up successful marketing management. We'll use the following hypothetical situation to illustrate these tasks in the context of the plan of the book. ("Marketing Memo: Marketers' Frequently Asked Questions" is a good checklist for the questions marketing managers ask, all of which we examine in this book.)

Emperor, Inc. operates in several industries, including chemicals, cameras, and film. The company is organized into Strategic Business Units (SBUs). Corporate management is considering what to do with its Oriental camera division. At present, Oriental produces a range of 35 mm and digital cameras. The market for cameras is intensely competitive. Although Emperor has a sizable market share and is producing much revenue for the company, the 35 mm market itself is growing very slowly and its market share is slipping. In the faster-growing digital camera segment, Emperor is facing strong competition and has been slow to gain sales. Emperor's corporate management wants Oriental's marketing group to produce a strong turnaround plan for the division. Marketing management has to come up with a convincing marketing plan, sell corporate management on the plan, and then implement and control it.

MARKETING MEMO • MARKETERS' FREQUENTLY ASKED QUESTIONS

1. How can we spot and choose the right market segment(s)?
2. How can we differentiate our offerings?
3. How should we respond to customers who buy on price?
4. How can we compete against lower-cost, lower-price competitors?
5. How far can we go in customizing our offering for each customer?
6. How can we grow our business?
7. How can we build stronger brands?
8. How can we reduce the cost of customer acquisition?
9. How can we keep our customers loyal for longer?
10. How can we tell which customers are more important?
11. How can we measure the payback from advertising, sales promotion, and public relations?
12. How can we improve sales force productivity?
13. How can we establish multiple channels and yet manage channel conflict?
14. How can we get the other company departments to be more customer-oriented?

Developing Marketing Strategies and Plans

The first task facing Oriental is to identify its potential long-run opportunities given its market experience and core competencies (see Chapter 2). Oriental can design its cameras with better features. It can also consider making a line of video cameras, or it can use its core competency in optics to design a line of binoculars and telescopes. Whichever direction it chooses, it must develop concrete marketing plans that specify the marketing strategy and tactics going forward.

Capturing Marketing Insights and Performance

Oriental needs a reliable marketing information system to closely monitor their marketing environment. Its microenvironment consists of all the players who affect the company's ability to produce and sell cameras—suppliers, marketing intermediaries, customers, and competitors. Its macroenvironment consists of demographic, economic, physical, technological, political–legal, and social–cultural forces that affect sales and profits (see Chapter 3).

Oriental also needs a dependable marketing research system. To transform marketing strategy into marketing programs, marketing managers must measure market potential, forecast demand, and make basic decisions on marketing expenditures, marketing activities, and marketing allocation.[39] To make these allocations, marketing managers may use sales-response functions that show how sales and profits would be affected by the amount of money spent in each application (see Chapter 4).

Connecting With Customers

Oriental must consider how to best create value for its chosen target markets and develop strong, profitable, long-term relationships with customers (see Chapter 5). To do so, Oriental needs to understand consumer markets (see Chapter 6). Who buys cameras, and why do they buy? What are they looking for in the way of features and prices? Where do they shop? Oriental also sells cameras to business markets, including large corporations, professional firms, retailers, and government agencies (see Chapter 7), where purchasing agents or buying committees make the decisions. Oriental needs to gain a full understanding of how organizational buyers buy. It needs a sales force that is well-trained in presenting product benefits.

Oriental will not want to market to all possible customers. It must divide the market into major market segments, evaluate each segment, and target those market segments that the company can best serve (see Chapter 8).

Building Strong Brands

Oriental must understand the strengths and weaknesses of the Emperor brand with customers (see Chapter 9). Is its 35 mm film heritage a detriment in the digital camera market? Suppose Oriental decides to focus on the consumer market and develop a positioning strategy (see Chapter 10). Should Oriental position its cameras as the "Mercedes" brand, offering superior cameras at a premium price with excellent service and strong advertising? Should it build a simple, low-priced camera aimed at more price-conscious consumers? Or something in between? Oriental must also pay close attention to competitors (see Chapter 11), anticipating its competitors' moves and knowing how to react quickly and decisively. It may want to initiate some surprise moves, in which case it needs to anticipate how its competitors will respond.

Shaping the Market Offerings

At the heart of the marketing program is the product—the firm's tangible offering to the market, which includes the product quality, design, features, and packaging (see Chapter 12). To gain a competitive advantage, Oriental may provide various services, such as leasing, delivery, repair, and training (see Chapter 13).

A critical marketing decision relates to pricing (see Chapter 14). Oriental must decide on wholesale and retail prices, discounts, allowances, and credit terms. Its price should be commensurate with the offer's perceived value; otherwise, buyers will turn to competitors' products.

Delivering Value

Oriental must also determine how to properly deliver the value embodied by these products and services to the target market. Channel activities include the various activities the company undertakes to make the product accessible and available to target customers (see Chapter 15). Oriental must identify, recruit, and link various marketing facilitators to supply its products and services efficiently to the target market. It must understand the various types of retailers, wholesalers, and physical-distribution firms and how they make their decisions (see Chapter 16).

Communicating Value

Oriental must also adequately communicate the value embodied by their products and services to the target market. It will need an integrated marketing communication program that maximizes the individual and collective contribution of all communication activities (see Chapter 17). Oriental needs to set up mass communication programs consisting of advertising, sales promotion, events, and public relations (see Chapter 18). It also needs to set up more personal communications in the form of direct and interactive marketing and must also hire, train, and motivate salespeople (see Chapter 19).

Creating Long-term Growth

Based on its product positioning, Oriental must initiate new-product development, testing, and launching (see Chapter 20). The strategy also will have to take into account changing global opportunities and challenges (see Chapter 21).

Finally, Oriental must build a marketing organization that is capable of implementing the marketing plan (see Chapter 22). Because of surprises and disappointments that can occur as marketing plans are implemented, Oriental will need feedback and control to understand the efficiency and effectiveness of its marketing activities and how it can improve them.[40]

Summary

1. From a managerial point of view, marketing is the process of planning and executing the conception, pricing, promotion, and distribution of ideas, goods, and services to create exchanges that satisfy individual and organizational goals. Marketing management is the art and science of choosing target markets and getting, keeping, and growing customers through creating, delivering, and communicating superior customer value.
2. Marketers are skilled at managing demand: they seek to influence the level, timing, and composition of demand. Marketers are involved in marketing many types of entities: goods, services, events, experiences, persons, places, properties, organizations, information, and ideas. They also operate in four different marketplaces: consumer, business, global, and nonprofit.
3. Marketing is not done only by the marketing department. Marketing needs to affect every aspect of the customer experience. To create a strong marketing organization, marketers must think like executives in other departments, and executives in other departments must think more like marketers.
4. Today's marketplace is fundamentally different as a result of major societal forces that have resulted in many new consumer and company capabilities. These forces have created new opportunities and challenges, and marketing management has changed significantly in recent years as companies seek new ways to achieve marketing excellence.
5. There are five competing concepts under which organizations can choose to conduct their business: the production concept, the product concept, the selling concept, the marketing concept, and the holistic marketing concept. The first three are of limited use today.
6. The holistic marketing concept is based on the development, design, and implementation of marketing programs, processes, and activities that recognizes their breadth and interdependencies. Holistic marketing recognizes that "everything matters" with marketing and that a broad, integrated perspective is often necessary. Four components of holistic marketing are relationship marketing, integrated marketing, internal marketing, and socially responsible marketing.
7. The set of set of tasks necessary for successful marketing management include developing marketing strategies and plans, connecting with customers, building strong brands, shaping the market offerings, delivering and communicating value, capturing marketing insights and performance, and creating successful long-term growth.

Application

Marketing Debate—Does Marketing Create or Satisfy Needs?

Marketing has often been defined in terms of satisfying customers' needs and wants. Critics, however, maintain that marketing does much more than that and creates needs and wants that did not exist before. According to these critics, marketers encourage consumers to spend more money than they should on goods and services they really do not need.

Take a position: *Marketing shapes consumer needs and wants* versus *Marketing merely reflects the needs and wants of consumers.*

Marketing Discussion

Consider the broad shifts in marketing. Are there any themes that emerge in these shifts? Can they be related to the major societal forces? Which force has contributed to which shift?

PART 1

A Zara store in Singapore.

Developing Marketing Strategies and Plans 2

A key ingredient of the marketing management process is insightful, creative marketing strategies and plans that guide marketing activities. Developing the right marketing strategy over time requires a blend of discipline and flexibility. Firms must stick to a strategy but must also find new ways to constantly improve it.[1] Marketing strategy also requires a clear understanding of how marketing works.[2]

Walk into a trendy boutique and you might see high-fashion T-shirts selling for $250. Step into a Zara clothing store and you can see a version of the same style for $25. Started as a small lingerie company based in Spanish town La Coruna, Zara has grown to become one of the biggest and most successful clothing retailers. It introduces 11,000 new garments at breakneck speed in a typical year, with many lines available for only a few weeks before they are replaced. Zara's secret lies in its total control of every part of the business from design to production to distribution. By controlling the entire process from factory to shopfloor, Zara can react quickly to changing fashion trends and customer tastes, providing a "newness" that has captivated the world by storm. While its rivals start planning their lines on average nine months before they hit the shelves, Zara takes just two to three weeks. This lead-time advantage also lets Zara operate with lower inventory levels and permits frequent line changes, giving customers a sense of exclusivity.

Zara is also not afraid to withdraw items from shelves and write off items that are not selling. Its designers get a daily report on what has and has not been sold. The information is used to decide which product lines and colors are kept or altered and whether new lines are created. Customers also have direct input into what the shops sell, as feedback is sent back to the designers too. Zara calls this the "democratization of fashion."

Another trend-bucking aspect of Zara's business model is its approach to advertising. Fashion retailers spend, on average, 3.5 percent of revenue on advertising. Zara spends just 0.3 percent. It thinks advertising is a pointless distraction and that its shop windows are all the advertising it needs.

Zara has expanded globally with its first Asian store in Hong Kong. In Asia, Zara now has stores at prime locations in Indonesia, Japan, Malaysia and Singapore, and plans to enter China, Taiwan, the Philippines, and Thailand. Globally, Zara intends to double its number of stores to 4,000, with more than 100 stores in Asia. Franchised outlets, which currently account for only 10 percent of stores, are expected to fuel this growth.

In this chapter, we will address the following questions:

1. How does marketing affect customer value?
2. How is strategic planning carried out at different levels of the organization?
3. What does a marketing plan include?

This chapter begins by examining some of the strategic marketing implications involved in creating customer value. It then provides several perspectives on planning and describes how to draw up a formal marketing plan.

Marketing and Customer Value

Marketing is about satisfying consumers' needs and wants. The task of any business is to deliver customer value at a profit. In a hypercompetitive economy with increasingly rational buyers faced with abundant choices, a company can win only by fine-tuning the value delivery process and choosing, providing, and communicating superior value.

The Value Delivery Process

The traditional view of marketing is that the firm makes something and then sells it. As shown in Figure 2.1(a), marketing takes place in the second half of the process. The company knows what to make and the market will buy enough units to produce profits. Companies that subscribe to this view have the best chance of succeeding in economies marked by shortage of goods where consumers are not fussy about quality, features, or style—for example, with basic staple goods in developing markets.

(a) Traditional Physical Process Sequence

Make the product
Sell the product
Design product
Procure
Make
Price
Sell
Advertise/ promote
Distribute
Service

(b) Value Creation and Delivery Sequence

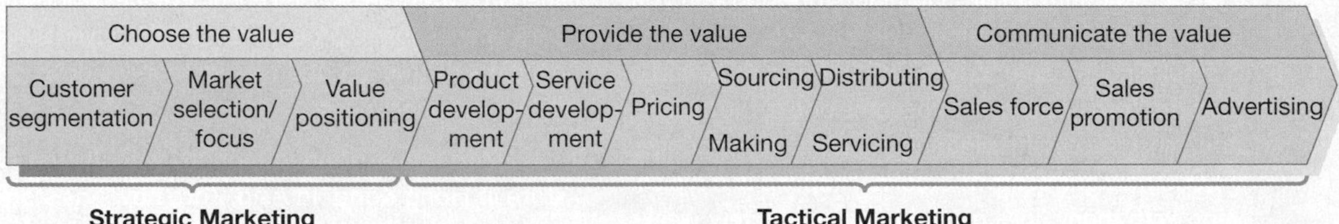

Figure 2.1 The Value Delivery Process

The traditional view of the business process, however, will not work in economies where people face abundant choices. There, the "mass market" is actually splintering into numerous micromarkets, each with its own wants, perceptions, preferences, and buying criteria. The smart competitor must design and deliver offerings for well-defined target markets. This belief is at the core of the new view of business processes, which places marketing at the beginning of planning. Instead of emphasizing making and selling, these companies see themselves as part of a value delivery process.

Figure 2.1(b) illustrates the value creation and delivery sequence. The process consists of three parts. The first phase, *choosing the value*, represents the "homework" marketing staff must do before any product exists. The marketing staff must segment the market, select the appropriate market target, and develop the offering's value positioning. The formula "segmentation, targeting, positioning (STP)" is the essence of strategic marketing. Once the business unit has chosen the value, the second phase is *providing the value*. Marketing must determine specific product features, prices, and distribution. The task in the third phase is *communicating the value* by utilizing the sales force, sales promotion, advertising, and other communication tools to announce and promote the product. Each of these value phases has cost implications.

As Figure 2.1(b) shows, the value delivery process begins before there is a product and continues while it is being developed and after it becomes available. The Japanese have further refined this view with the following concepts:

- ***Zero customer feedback time*** — Customer feedback should be collected continuously after purchase to learn how to improve the product and its marketing.
- ***Zero product-improvement time*** — The company should evaluate all improvement ideas and introduce the most valued and feasible improvements as soon as possible.
- ***Zero purchasing time*** — The company should receive the required parts and supplies continuously through just-in-time arrangements with suppliers. By lowering its inventories, the company can reduce its costs.
- ***Zero setup time*** — The company should be able to manufacture any of its products as soon as they are ordered, without facing high setup time or costs.
- ***Zero defects*** — The products should be of high quality and free of flaws.

SCOCO—Japanese women are responsible for 70 to 80 percent of the nation's consumer spending. They are staying single longer, earning more, and shopping at *conbini*, as the popular stores are known, rather than in supermarkets. Even after they marry, Japanese women tend to control the family purse strings. Thus COCO, which runs more than 900 convenience stores in Japan, decided to be the first chain that targets women specifically. It added "S" (for "she") to its logo. The "S" also stands for "slender, smart, and stylish." SCOCO is staffed entirely by women, who developed the original concept and saw it through the planning stages. The store's restroom is called a "powder room" where a customer can touch up her make-up, change her stockings and clothes, brush her teeth, and remove oil from her skin. Part of the floor is raised to create a clean space for her to kick off her shoes and change her stockings and clothes. SCOCO's inexpensive *bento* or take-out lunches are smaller than usual to fit the average Japanese woman's appetite. The cosmetics offered are in tune to current trends and seasonal influences. In winter, lipsticks sold prevent chapped lips; in summer, hairclips are sold to pin the hair up. There are no male magazines, sports newspapers, and canned coffee, items bought mainly by men. SCOCO has a nook called Eat in Café, where women can sit down and chat.[3]

Kumar has put forth a "3 Vs" approach to marketing: (1) define the *value segment* or customers (and his/her needs); (2) define the *value proposition*; and (3) define the *value network* that will deliver the promised service.[4] Webster views marketing in terms of: (1) *value defining processes* (e.g., market research and company self-analysis); (2) *value developing processes* (e.g., new product development, sourcing strategy, and vendor selection); and (3) *value delivering processes* (e.g., advertising and managing distribution).[5]

The Value Chain

Michael Porter has proposed the **value chain** as a tool for identifying ways to create more customer value (see Figure 2.2).[6] According to this model, every firm is a synthesis of activities performed to design, produce, market, deliver, and support its product. The value chain identifies nine strategically relevant activities—five primary activities and four support activities—that create value and cost in a specific business.

The *primary activities* cover the sequence of bringing materials into the business (inbound logistics), converting them into final products (operations), shipping out final products (outbound logistics), marketing them (marketing and sales), and servicing them (service). The *support activities*—procurement, technology development, human resource management, and firm infrastructure—are handled in certain specialized departments, as well as elsewhere. Several departments, for example, may do procurement and hiring. The firm's infrastructure covers the costs of general management, planning, finance, accounting, legal, and government affairs.

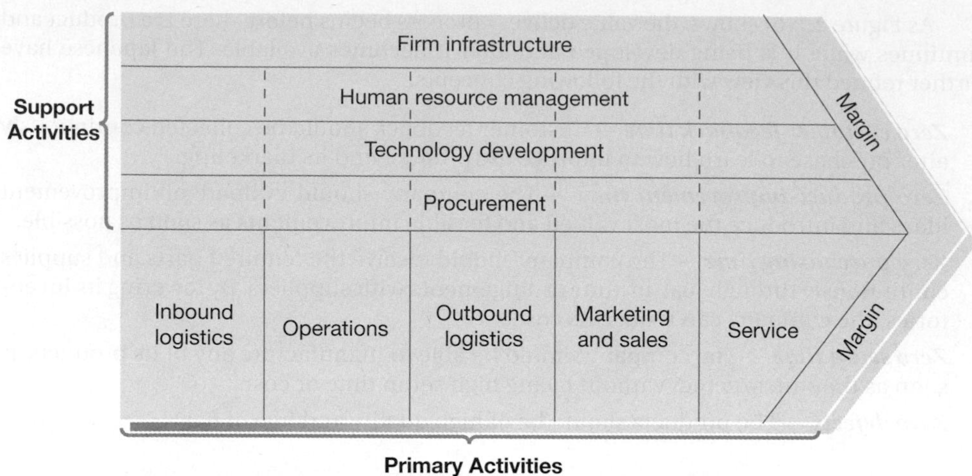

Figure 2.2 The Generic Value Chain

The firm's task is to examine its costs and performance in each value-creating activity and look for ways to improve it. The firm should estimate its competitors' costs and performances as *benchmarks* against which to compare its own costs and performance. It should go further and study the "best of class" practices of the world's best companies.[7]

Cisco Systems Inc.—Although Cisco Systems continues to grow, it is not growing at the breakneck speed of the 1990s, so its supply base needs have changed. The company has reduced its number of suppliers and aligned itself more closely with the remaining suppliers for each of its product-based teams—from Application Specific Integrated Circuits (ASIC) to microprocessors and broadband chips. Steve Darendinger, vice president of supply chain management for Cisco, says, "With ASIC we have gone from more than 20 suppliers to 3 suppliers," and "the three have a greater level of ASIC leverage ..." Involving suppliers in new-product development lets Cisco tap into its partners' expertise in improving time to volume, cutting costs, and improving supplier quality.[8]

The firm's success depends not only on how well each department performs its work, but also on how well the various departmental activities are coordinated to conduct *core business processes*.[9] These core business processes include:

- ***The market sensing process*** — All the activities involved in gathering market intelligence, disseminating it within the organization, and acting on the information.
- ***The new offering realization process*** — All the activities involved in researching, developing, and launching new high-quality offerings quickly and within budget.
- ***The customer acquisition process*** — All the activities involved in defining target markets and prospecting for new customers.
- ***The customer relationship management process*** — All the activities involved in building deeper understanding, relationships, and offerings to individual customers.
- ***The fulfillment management process*** — All the activities involved in receiving and approving orders, shipping the goods on time, and collecting payment.

Strong companies develop superior capabilities in managing and linking their core business processes. They are also re-engineering the workflows and building cross-functional teams responsible for each process.[10] At Xerox, a Customer Operations Group links sales, shipping, installation, service, and billing so that these activities flow smoothly into one another. Winning companies are those that excel at managing core business processes through cross-functional teams. For instance, Motorola has re-organized its employees into cross-functional teams. Cross-functional teams are also found in non-profit and government organizations.

To be successful, a firm also needs to look for competitive advantages beyond its own operations, into the value chains of suppliers, distributors, and customers. Many companies today have partnered with specific suppliers and distributors to create a superior **value delivery network** also called a **supply chain.**[11]

Core Competencies

Traditionally, companies owned and controlled most of the resources that entered their businesses, but this situation is changing. Many companies today outsource less critical resources if they can be obtained at better quality or lower cost. Frequently, outsourced resources include cleaning services, landscaping, and auto fleet management. Indian companies are known for operating call centers for many multinational companies worldwide.

The key, then, is to own and nurture the resources and competencies that make up the essence of the business. Nike, for example, does not manufacture its own shoes, because certain Asian manufacturers are more competent in this task; Nike nurtures its superiority in shoe design and shoe merchandising, its two core competencies. We can say that a **core competency** has three characteristics: (1) it is a source of competitive advantage in that it makes a significant contribution to perceived customer benefits; (2) it has applications in a wide variety of markets; and (3) it is difficult for competitors to imitate.[12]

Competitive advantage also accrues to companies that possess distinctive capabilities. Whereas core competencies tend to refer to areas of special technical and production expertise, *distinctive capabilities* tend to describe excellence in broader business processes. George Day sees market-driven organizations as excelling in three distinctive capabilities: market sensing, customer linking, and channel bonding.[13] In terms of market sensing, he believes that tremendous opportunities and threats often begin as "weak signals" from the "periphery" of a business.[14] He offers a systematic process for developing peripheral vision, and practical tools and strategies for building "vigilant organizations" attuned to changes in the environment, by asking questions in three categories (see Table 2.1).

Table 2.1 Becoming a Vigilant Organization

Learning from the past
- What have been our past blind spots?
- What instructive analogies do other industries offer?
- Who in the industry is skilled at picking up weak signals and acting on them?

Evaluating the present
- What important signals are we rationalizing away?
- What are our mavericks, outliers, complainers, and defectors telling us?
- What are our peripheral customers and competitors really thinking?

Envisioning the future
- What future surprises could really hurt or help us?
- What emerging technologies could change the game?
- Is there an unthinkable scenario that might disrupt our business?

Source: George S. Day and Paul J. H. Schoemaker, *Peripheral Vision: Detecting the Weak Signals That Will Make or Break Your Company*, (Boston, MA: Harvard Business School Press, 2006).

Competitive advantage ultimately derives from how well the company has fitted its core competencies and distinctive capabilities into tightly interlocking "activity systems." Competitors find it hard to imitate companies such as Singapore Airlines, Dell, or IKEA because they are unable to copy their activity systems. Business realignment may be necessary to maximize core competencies. It involves three steps: (1) (re)defining the business concept (the "big idea"); (2) (re)shaping the business scope (the lines of business); and

(3) (re)positioning the company's brand identity (how customers should see the company). Consider what Kodak is doing to re-align its business:

Kodak—With the advent of the digital era and consumers' new capacity to store, share, and print photos using their PCs, Kodak faces more competition than ever, both in-store and online. In 2004, after being bumped from the Dow Jones Industrial Average, where it had held a spot for more than 70 years, the company started the painful process of transformation. It started off by expanding its line of digital cameras, printers, and other equipment, and also set out to increase market share in the lucrative medical imaging business. Making shifts is not without challenges, however. The company announced in the summer of 2006 that it would outsource the making of its digital cameras. Kodak eliminated almost 30,000 jobs between 2004 and 2007 and it spent money acquiring a string of companies for its graphics communications unit. Not only must Kodak convince consumers to buy its digital cameras and home printers, but it also must become known as the most convenient and affordable way to process digital images. So far, the company faces steep competition from Sony, Canon, and Hewlett-Packard.[15]

However, many multinationals find it difficult to replicate their core competencies in China. Williamson and Zeng found that multinationals have clear advantages over local companies in China in two areas—industry-specific technology and managerial competence.[16] However, such core competencies are handicapped by several characteristics in the Chinese business landscape.

- ***Poor infrastructural support*** — China's poor infrastructural support means scarce market research and compromised supply chains. Toshiba, for instance, spent more than five years establishing a local supplier for a component that it needed for laptop computer production.
- ***Inflexibility*** — The lack of flexibility means higher costs when integrating local operations.
- ***Fragmented market*** — A fragmented Chinese market suggests that multinationals cannot reap economies of scale. Otis Elevator, for example, discovered that it needed to maintain production facilities in several regions in China to respond to the buying preferences of local authorities.
- ***Less developed market*** — Many markets in China are still in an early stage of development. Over one billion of China's consumers can only afford products that serve their basic needs.

In contrast, Chinese competitors have three competitive advantages over MNCs:

- ***Better understanding*** — Chinese companies have a better understanding of what will work in the local environment. For example, detergent producer Nice had a TV commercial showing a young girl helping her just-laid-off mother with the family's laundry. The ad resonated well with the community because it reflected *dongshi*, the critical period when a child understands his or her responsibilities to the family.
- ***Leaner and more flexible*** — Chinese companies tend to be leaner and more flexible with lower costs. Many successful Chinese companies are run by highly entrepreneurial people.
- ***Opportunity to catch up*** — The open global markets allow Chinese companies to buy much of technology and expertise that they need to catch up. In the PC market, the latest tools and technologies developed in Silicon Valley arrive in China within months. This allows Dongguan, a small city in Guangdong province that has the world's highest concentration of component manufacturers, to provide Chinese PC makers with a ready supply of world-class technology.

McKinsey found that many successful Asian companies adopt at least one of three strategies to harness their core competence:[17]

- ***Expand quickly to capture global market opportunities*** — Being the best company in a domestic market no longer guarantees survival since global players have the ability to attack incumbents in their home markets and erode their profits. Half of the top 10 value creators, on average, earned more than half of their revenues outside their home markets, often by leveraging Asia's low-cost labor or mastering its complicated and inefficient supply chains. Example: Hong Kong-based Johnson Electric, manufacturer of micro motors, derives more than 70 percent of its revenue from Europe, Japan, and the U.S. It benefited from the relatively low cost of skilled labor to capture global market share.
- ***Become atomizers*** — These companies receive more than 80 percent of their revenues from a single main industry sector. Unlike the typical Asian conglomerate, these focused companies have resisted the temptation of empire-building. For example, Taiwan Semiconductor Manufacturing Company is a specialized circuit foundry. Its founder, Morris Chang, has enshrined in its corporate charter a single-minded preoccupation with the semiconductor foundry business, thus preventing the company from attempting to move into the production of its own branded products and from competing against its customers.
- ***Become asset-light by using intangibles*** — Physical assets are becoming less relevant in the global battle for supremacy. The more profitable Asian companies focus on intangibles such as fostering human capital, exploiting network effects, and creating synergies based on reputation. For example, Hong Kong's Li & Fung, which manages supply chains for international companies, does not own any production facilities. Instead, it specializes in offering its customers a one-stop service ranging from the development of products through sourcing raw materials and managing production to consolidation of shipping.

A Holistic Marketing Orientation and Customer Value

A holistic marketing orientation can also provide insight into the process of capturing customer value. One conception of holistic marketing views it as "integrating the value exploration, value creation, and value delivery activities with the purpose of building

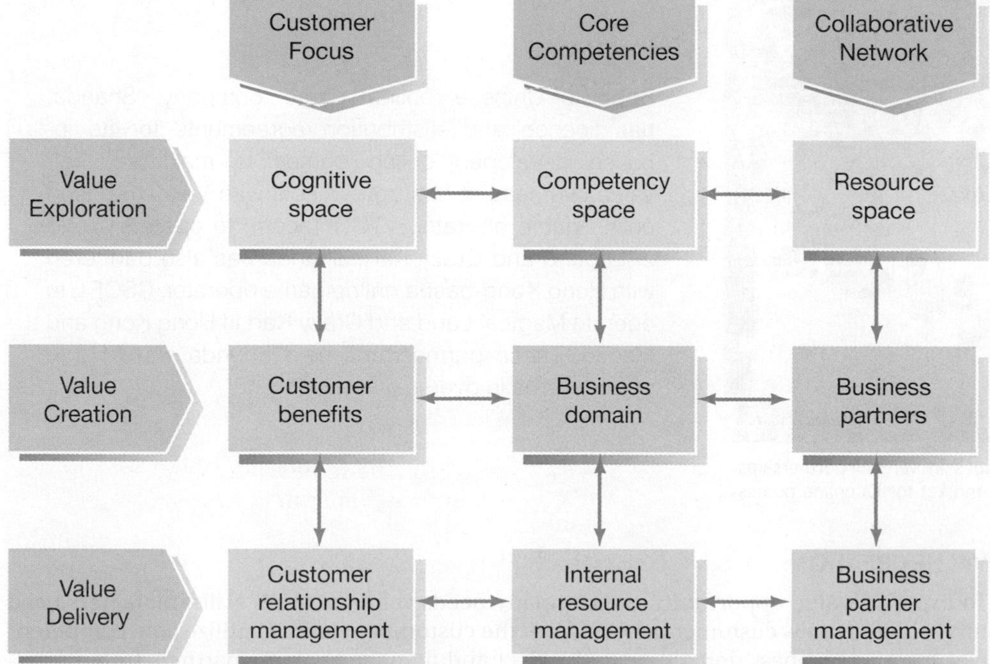

Figure 2.3 A Holistic Marketing Framework

Source: P. Kotler, D.C. Jain, and S. Maesinee, "Formulating a Market Strategy." In *Marketing Moves* (Part 1), Fig 1-1, (Boston: Harvard Business School Press, 2002), p. 29.

long-term, mutually satisfying relationships and co-prosperity among key stakeholders."[18] According to this view, holistic marketers succeed by managing a superior value chain that delivers a high level of product quality, service, and speed. Holistic marketers achieve profitable growth by expanding customer share, building customer loyalty, and capturing customer lifetime value. Figure 2.3, a holistic marketing framework, shows how the interaction between relevant actors (customers, company, and collaborators) and value-based activities (value exploration, value creation, and value delivery), helps to create, maintain, and renew customer value.

The holistic marketing framework is designed to address three key management questions:

1. ***Value exploration*** — How can a company identify new value opportunities?
2. ***Value creation*** — How can a company efficiently create more promising new value offerings?
3. ***Value delivery*** — How can a company use its capabilities and infrastructure to deliver the new value offerings more efficiently?

VALUE EXPLORATION

Because value flows within and across markets that are themselves dynamic and competitive, companies need a well-defined strategy for value exploration. Developing such a strategy requires an understanding of the relationships and interactions among three spaces: (1) the customer's cognitive space; (2) the company's competence space; and (3) the collaborator's resource space. The customer's *cognitive space* reflects existing and latent needs and includes dimensions such as the need for participation, stability, freedom, and change.[19] The company's *competency space* can be described in terms of breadth—a broad versus focused scope of business; and depth—physical versus knowledge-based capabilities. The collaborator's *resource space* involves horizontal partnerships, where companies choose partners based on their ability to exploit related market opportunities, and vertical partnerships, where companies choose partners based on their ability to serve their value creation. Here's an example of vertical partnerships.

Shanda enhances value when it engages in vertical partnerships with foreign distributors to expand the market for its online games overseas.

Shanda—Chinese online game company, Shanda, has licence and distribution agreements for its in-house developed online games to maximize their value overseas. It has agreements with Vietnam-based online game operator, VTC Intecom, to operate World of Legend and Crazy Kart. Shanda has also partnered with Hong Kong-based online game operator, CSOFT, to operate Magical Land and Crazy Kart in Hong Kong and Macau. These partnerships help Shanda seize future opportunities in overseas markets.[20]

VALUE CREATION

To exploit a value opportunity, the company needs value-creation skills. Marketers need to: (1) identify new customer benefits from the customer's view; (2) utilize core competencies from its business domain; and (3) select and manage business partners from its collaborative networks. To craft new customer benefits, marketers must understand what the customer thinks about, wants, does, and worries about. Marketers must also observe who customers admire, who they interact with, and who influence them.

Hindustan Unilever—In India, many cosmetic brands such as Avon, L'Oréal, Ponds, and Garnier are selling skin-lightening products. Darker-skinned women want to have fairer skin to look prettier. The competition is stiff. While Hindustan Unilever's Fair & Lovely used to focus on the whitening quality of its products, it now focuses on a slightly different benefit. In a sign of the times, the ads show lighter skin conferring a different advantage: helping a woman land a job normally held by men, like that of an announcer at cricket matches.[21]

Hindustan Unilever's Fair & Lovely established a foundation that empowers women to do better economically.

VALUE DELIVERY

Delivering value often means substantial investment in infrastructure and capabilities. The company must become proficient at customer relationship management, internal resource management, and business partnership management. *Customer relationship management* allows the company to discover who its customers are, how they behave, and what they need or want. It also enables the company to respond appropriately, coherently, and quickly to different customer opportunities. To respond effectively, the company requires *internal resource management* to integrate major business processes (e.g., order processing, general ledger, payroll, and production) within a single family of software modules. Finally, *business partnership management* allows the company to handle complex relationships with its trading partners to source, process, and deliver products. Below is an example of how Coca-Cola in Japan uses its internal resource management to understand and serve its customers better.

Coca-Cola—In Japan, Coke is known for its "intelligent" distribution networks. It uses vending machines that can compute data such as unit sales, sellouts, when a customer is short-changed, and when mechanical failures occur. This information is uploaded to the handheld terminal of a salesperson. The salesperson can then analyze out-of-stock rates, replenishment rates, etc., as well as identify underperforming machines. The system also allows Coke to understand which products sell better and quickly adjust the product mix in a machine to avoid out-of-stock situations and respond to market trends faster. This system saw sales increase 10 percent overall, and other associated costs decrease 46 percent. Additionally, the number of vending machines that could be managed per salesperson increased by as much as 42 percent. By the end of 2008, Coke will have equipped all its vending machines in Japan to accept payment through Felica, contactless credit cards on mobile phones developed by cellular industry leader NTT DoCoMo and electronics giant Sony. The system will make it possible to buy any soft drink, coffee, tea, or fruit drink in Coca-Cola machines by holding up a mobile phone to the machine, with the cost of the refreshment going on a monthly phone bill. Coke benefits from electronic payment which is less expensive in maintenance costs than bills or coins.[22]

The Central Role of Strategic Planning

Successful marketing thus requires having capabilities such as understanding customer value, creating customer value, delivering customer value, capturing customer value, and sustaining customer value. "Marketing Insight: Views on Marketing from Chief Executive Officers" addresses some important senior management priorities in improving marketing. Only a handful of companies stand out as master marketers: Procter & Gamble, Nike, Disney, Wal-Mart, and McDonald's in the U.S.; Toyota, Sony, Canon, and Samsung in Asia;

MARKETING INSIGHT • VIEWS ON MARKETING FROM CHIEF EXECUTIVE OFFICERS

Marketing faces a number of challenges in the 21st century. Based on an extensive research study, McKinsey identified three main challenges as reflected by differences in opinion between chief executive officers (CEOs) and their most senior marketing executives or chief marketing officers (CMOs).

- ***Doing more with less*** — CEOs need and expect all areas of their organizations to be more efficient; CMOs indicate that they anticipate that their budgets will grow.
- ***Driving new business development*** — CEOs want marketing to play a more active role in driving new business development— not just new products but also new markets, channels, and lines of business; CMOs cited new-product development as their primary concern.
- ***Becoming a full business partner*** — CEOs look for marketing to become a more central business partner that helps to drive profits; CMOs are unsure that their groups have the skills to do so.

McKinsey suggests that bridging these gaps will require changes in spending, organization skills, and culture for many marketers. To accommodate the pressure to simultaneously grow revenues while also reducing marketing costs as a percentage of sales, they offer three recommendations:

1. Link spending priorities to profit potential, for example, as measured by size and anticipated growth rate of current customers—not historical performance;
2. Focus spending on brand drivers (features and benefits truly important to customers), not antes (features and benefits that a brand needs to stay in the game); and
3. Deepen insights on how customers get product information and make buying decisions.

Based on research on companies that successfully develop big ideas, McKinsey identifies three characteristics that help to position marketers as business development leaders:

1. Force the widest view when defining their business, assets, and competencies;
2. Combine multiple perspectives, for example, using attitudinal and need profiles as well as behavior-based segments, to identify market opportunities or sweet spots; and
3. Focus idea generation through a combination of marketing insight and business analysis—but identify profitable unmet needs before they brainstorm creative solutions.

Finally, McKinsey offers two recommendations to overcome CEOs' concerns about the role and performance of marketing.

1. Marketers must test and develop programs more quickly as they enhance planning processes and research approaches; and
2. Marketers must more effectively evaluate the performance and profit impact of investments in the expanding marketing arena (e.g., CRM technology, sponsorships, Internet marketing, and word of mouth).

Source: David Court, Tom French, and Gary Singer, "How the CEO Sees Marketing." *Advertising Age*, March 3, 2003, p. 28.

and IKEA, Club Med, Bang & Olufsen, Electrolux, Nokia, and Lego in Europe. "Breakthrough Marketing: Intel" describes how that company created customer value and built a brand in a category for which most people thought branding impossible.

These companies focus on the customer and are organized to respond effectively to changing customer needs. They have well-staffed marketing departments, and their other departments also accept the concept that the customer is king. To ensure that they select and execute the right activities, marketers must give priority to strategic planning in three key areas: (1) managing a company's businesses as an investment portfolio; (2) assessing each business's strength by considering the market's growth rate and the company's position and fit in that market; and (3) establishing a strategy. For each business, the company must develop a game plan for achieving its long-run objectives.

Most large companies consist of four organizational levels: the corporate level, the division level, the business unit level, and the product level. Corporate headquarters is responsible for designing a corporate strategic plan to guide the whole enterprise; it makes decisions on the amount of resources to allocate to each division, as well as on which businesses to start or eliminate. Each division establishes a plan covering the allocation of funds to each business unit within the division. Each business unit develops a strategic plan to carry that business unit into a profitable future. Finally, each product level (product line, brand) within a business unit develops a marketing plan for achieving its objectives in its product market.

The **marketing plan** is the central instrument for directing and coordinating the marketing effort. The marketing plan operates at two levels: strategic and tactical. The **strategic marketing plan** lays out the target markets and the value proposition that will be offered,

BREAKTHROUGH • MARKETING

INTEL

A lighter-than-you-ever-imagined notebook? Everything is possible with me inside.
INTEL® CENTRINO® DUO PROCESSOR TECHNOLOGY.
It's what drives your notebook's performance, wireless connectivity, and amazing battery life. It's the difference between a good computer and a great one.
GREAT COMPUTING STARTS WITH INTEL INSIDE.
intel
Centrino
Duo

Ads like this were part of Intel's strategy for building a brand in a product area where no brand name had ever existed before—microprocessors.

Intel makes the microprocessors that are found in 80 percent of the world's personal computers. In the early days, Intel microprocessors were known simply by their engineering numbers, such as "80386" or "80486." Intel positioned its chips as the most advanced. The trouble was, as Intel soon learned, numbers can't be trademarked. Competitors came out with their own "486" chips, and Intel had no way to distinguish itself from the competition. Worse, Intel's products were hidden from consumers, buried deep inside PCs. With a hidden, untrademarked product, Intel had a hard time convincing consumers to pay more for its high-performance products.

Intel's response was a marketing campaign that created history. The company chose a trademarkable name—Pentium—and launched the "Intel Inside" marketing campaign to build awareness of the brand and get its name outside the PC and into the minds of consumers.

Intel used an innovative cooperative scheme to extend the reach of the campaign: it would help computer makers who used Intel processors to advertise their PCs if the makers also included the Intel logo in their ads. Intel also gave computer manufacturers a rebate on Intel processors if they agreed to place an "Intel Inside" sticker on the outside of their PCs and laptops.

Intel continues its integrated ingredient campaigns to this day. For example, when launching its Centrino mobile microprocessor platform, Intel began with TV ads that aired in the U.S. and 11 other countries. These ads include the animated logo and now familiar five-note brand signature melody. Print, online, and outdoor advertising followed shortly thereafter. Intel created eight-page inserts for major newspapers that urged the wired world to not only "unwire," but also "Untangle. Unburden. Uncompromise. Unstress."

Intel even held a "One Unwired Day" event that took place in major cities such as New York, Chicago, San Francisco, and Seattle. In addition to allowing free trial Wi-Fi access, the company held festivals in each city that included live music, product demonstrations, and prize giveaways.

The "Unwired" campaign was another Intel success in marketing. The $300 million total media effort for the Centrino mobile platform, which also included cooperative advertising with manufacturers, helped generate $2 billion in revenue for Intel during the first nine months of the campaign.

Going forward, Intel launched a new brand identity in 2006, supported by a $2 billion global marketing campaign. The company introduced a new logo with a different font and updated visual look and also created a new slogan: "Leap Ahead." In addition to the new logo and slogan, Intel developed a new microprocessor platform called Viiv (rhymes with "five") aimed at home entertainment enthusiasts. These moves were designed to create the impression of Intel as a "warm and fuzzy consumer company," with products that went beyond the PC. Intel remained one of the most valuable brands in the world, its $31 billion brand valuation earning it seventh place in the 2007 Interbrand/*BusinessWeek* ranking of the Best Global Brands.

Sources: Don Clark, "Intel to Overhaul Marketing in Bid to Go Beyond PCs." *Wall Street Journal*, December 30, 2005; Cliff Edwards, "Intel Everywhere?" *BusinessWeek*, March 8, 2004, pp. 56–62; Scott Van Camp, "ReadMe.1st," *BrandWeek*, February 23, 2004, p. 17; David Kirkpatrick, "At Intel, Speed Isn't Everything." *Fortune*, February 9, 2004. p. 34; "How to Become a Superbrand." *Marketing*, January 8, 2004, p. 15; Roger Slavens, "Pam Pollace, VP-Director, Corporate Marketing Group, Intel Corp. " *B to B*, December 8, 2003, p. 19; Kenneth Hein, "Study: New Brand Names Not Making Their Mark." *BrandWeek*, December 8, 2003, p. 12; Heather Clancy, "Intel Thinking Outside the Box." *Computer Reseller News*, November 24, 2003, p. 14; Cynthia L. Webb, "A Chip Off the Old Recovery?" *Washingtonpost.com*, October 15, 2003; "Intel Launches Second Phase of Centrino Ads." *Technology Advertising & Branding Report*, October 6, 2003.

based on an analysis of the best market opportunities. The **tactical marketing plan** specifies the marketing tactics, including product features, promotion, merchandising, pricing, sales channels, and service.

Today, teams develop the marketing plan with inputs and sign-offs from every important function. These plans are then implemented at the appropriate levels of the organization. Results are monitored, and necessary corrective action taken. The complete planning, implementation, and control cycle is shown in Figure 2.4. We next consider planning at each of these four levels of the organization.

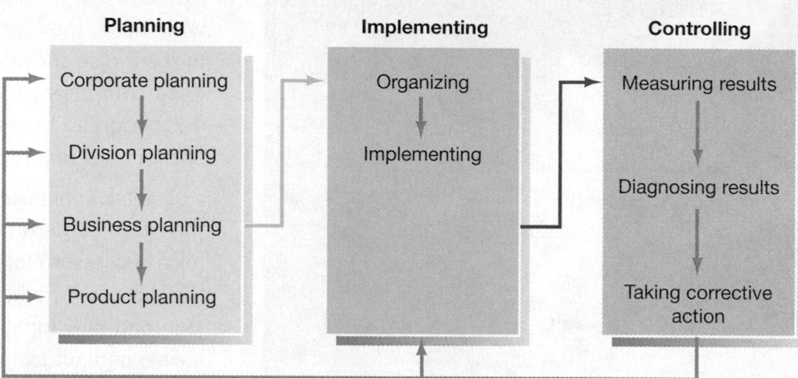

Figure 2.4 The Strategic Planning, Implementation, and Control Processes

Corporate and Division Strategic Planning

Some corporations give their business units a lot of freedom to set their own sales and profit goals and strategies. Others set goals for their business units but let them develop their own strategies. Still others set the goals and participate in developing individual business unit strategies.[23]

All corporate headquarters undertake four planning activities: (1) defining the corporate mission; (2) establishing strategic business units (SBUs); (3) assigning resources to each SBU; and (4) assessing growth opportunities.

Defining the Corporate Mission

An organization exists to accomplish something: to make cars, lend money, provide lodging, and so on. Its specific mission or purpose is usually clear when the business starts. Over time the mission may change to take advantage of new opportunities or respond to new market conditions. Amazon.com changed its mission from being the world's largest online bookstore to aspiring to become the world's largest online store. eBay changed its mission from running online auctions for collectors to running online auctions covering all kinds of goods.

To define its mission, a company should address Peter Drucker's classic questions:[24] What is our business? Who is the customer? What is of value to the customer? What will our business be? What should our business be? These simple-sounding questions are among the most difficult a company will ever have to answer. Successful companies continuously raise these questions and answer them thoughtfully and thoroughly. [25]

Organizations develop **mission statements** to share with managers, employees, and (in many cases) customers. A clear, thoughtful mission statement provides employees with a shared sense of purpose, direction, and opportunity.

Mission statements are at their best when they reflect a vision, an almost "impossible dream" that provides a direction for the company for the next 10 to 20 years. Sony's former president, Akio Morita, wanted everyone to have access to "personal portable sound," so his company created the Walkman and portable CD player. Table 2.2 gives examples of the mission statements of three Asian businesses.

Table 2.2 Sample Mission Statements

Samsung (Korea)
"We will devote our people and technology to create superior products and services, thereby contributing to a better global society."
Cathay Pacific (Hong Kong)
"Our vision is to make Cathay Pacific the most admired airline in the world by ensuring that safety comes first, providing service straight from the heart, encouraging product leadership, delivering superior financial returns, and providing rewarding career opportunities."
Kasikornbank (Thailand)
"Kasikornbank aims to be a strong Thai financial institution that provides a variety of financial services of world-class quality by harmoniously combining technology and human resources so as to achieve good and balanced benefits to customers, shareholders, employees, and the country."

Good mission statements have three major characteristics. First, they focus on a limited number of goals. The statement, "We want to produce the highest-quality products, offer the most service, achieve the widest distribution, and sell at the lowest prices" claims too much. Second, mission statements stress the company's major policies and values. They narrow the range of individual discretion so that employees act consistently on important issues. Third, they define the major competitive spheres within which the company will operate:

- ***Industry*** — The range of industries in which a company will operate. Some companies will operate in only one industry; some only in a set of related industries; some only in industrial goods, consumer goods, or services; and some in any industry. For example, Siam Cement prefers to operate in the industrial market, whereas Jollibee concentrates on the consumer market, and Matsushita operates in both industrial and consumer markets. Until recent corporate restructuring, many Asian conglomerates such as the state-owned enterprises of China, the government-linked corporations of Singapore, and the *chaebol* of Korea would get into almost any industry where they thought they could make money.
- ***Products and applications*** — The range of products and applications a company will supply. Sony, Panasonic, and Samsung sell electronics from home entertainment devices like television and DVD players to mobile phones; while Sharp concentrates only on household items like washing machines and entertainment products, not mobile phones.
- ***Competence*** — The range of technological and other core competencies that a company will master and leverage. Japan's NEC has built its core competencies in computing, communications, and components to support production of laptop computers, television receivers, and handheld telephones.
- ***Market segment*** — The type of market or customers a company will serve. For example, Porsche markets only expensive cars.
- ***Vertical*** — The number of channel levels from raw material to final product and distribution in which a company will participate. At one extreme are companies with a large vertical scope. Japanese production *keiretsu*, for instance, comprise large auto-makers such as Toyota and their suppliers. At the other extreme are "hollow corporations" or "pure marketing companies" consisting of a person with a phone, fax, computer, and desk who contracts out for every service, including design, manufacture, marketing, and physical distribution.[26]
- ***Geographical*** — The range of regions, countries, or country groups in which a company will operate. At one extreme are companies that operate in a specific city or state. At the other are multinationals such as Procter & Gamble and Sony, which operate in many countries.

The fourth characteristic of mission statements is that they take a long-term view. They should be enduring; management should change the mission only when it ceases to be relevant. Finally, a good mission statement is as short, memorable, and meaningful as possible. Marketing consultant Guy Kawasaki even advocates developing short three- to four-word corporate mantras rather than mission statements, like "peace of mind" for

FedEx. Compare the rather vague missions statements on the left with Google's mission statement and philosophy below:

To build total brand value by innovating to deliver customer value and customer leadership faster, better, and more completely than our competition. We build brands and make the world a little happier by bringing our best to you.	**1.** Never settle for the best. **2.** It's best to do one thing really, really well. **3.** Fast is better than slow. **4.** Democracy on the Web works. **5.** You don't need to be at your desk to need an answer. **6.** You can make money without doing evil. **7.** There is always more information out there. **8.** The need for information crosses all borders. **9.** You can be serious without a suit. **10.** Great just isn't good enough.

Source: *The Economist: Business Miscellany* (London: Profile Books Ltd, 2005), pp. 32–33.

Establishing Strategic Business Units (SBUs)

Companies often define their businesses in terms of products: They are in the "auto business" or the "clothing business." But Levitt argues that market definitions of a business are superior to product definitions.[27] A business must be viewed as a customer-satisfying process, not a goods-producing process. Products are transient; basic needs and customer groups endure forever. Transportation is a need: the bicycle, the automobile, the railroad, the airline, and the truck are products that meet that need.

Levitt encouraged companies to redefine their businesses in terms of needs, not products. IBM redefined itself from a hardware and software manufacturer to a "builder of networks." Table 2.3 gives several examples of companies that have moved from a product to a market definition of their business. It highlights the difference between a target market definition and a strategic market definition.

Table 2.3 Product-Oriented versus Market-Oriented Definitions of a Business

Company	Product Definition	Market Definition
Canon	We make copying equipment.	We help improve office productivity.
Petronas	We sell gasoline.	We supply energy.
Sony Pictures	We make movies.	We market entertainment.
Encyclopaedia Britannica	We sell encyclopedias.	We distribute information.
Toshiba	We make air-conditioners.	We provide climate control in the home.

A *target market definition* tends to focus on selling a product or service. Pepsi could define its target market as everyone who drinks a cola beverage and competitors would therefore be other cola companies. A *strategic market definition* could be everyone who might drink something to quench his or her thirst. Suddenly, Pepsi's competition would then include non-cola soft drinks, bottled water, fruit juices, tea, and coffee. To better compete, Pepsi might decide to sell additional beverages whose growth rate appears to be promising.

A business can be defined in terms of three dimensions: customer groups, customer needs, and technology.[28] Consider a small company that defines its business as designing incandescent lighting systems for television studios. Its customer group is television studios; the customer need is lighting; and the technology is incandescent lighting. The company might want to expand. It could make lighting for other customer groups, such as homes, factories, and offices; or it could supply other services needed by television studios, such as heating, ventilation, or air-conditioning. It could design other lighting technologies for television studios, such as infrared or ultraviolet lighting.

Large companies normally manage quite different businesses, each requiring its own strategy. General Electric classified its businesses into **strategic business units (SBUs)**. An SBU has three characteristics:

1. It is a single business or collection of related businesses that can be planned separately from the rest of the company.
2. It has its own set of competitors.
3. It has a manager who is responsible for strategic planning and profit performance and who controls most of the factors affecting profit.

The purpose of identifying the company's strategic business units is to develop separate strategies and assign appropriate funding. Senior management knows that its portfolio of businesses usually includes a number of "yesterday's has-beens" as well as "tomorrow's breadwinners." Yet it cannot rely on impressions; it needs analytical tools to classify its businesses by profit potential.[29]

Assigning Resources to Each SBU

Once it has defined SBUs, management must decide how to allocate corporate resources to each. The 1970s saw several portfolio-planning models introduced to provide an analytical means for making investment decisions. The GE/McKinsey Matrix classifies each SBU according to the extent of its competitive advantage and the attractiveness of its industry. Management would want to grow, "harvest" or draw cash from, or hold on to the business. Another model, the BCG's Growth-Share Matrix, uses relative market share and annual rate of market growth as criteria to make investment decisions.

Portfolio-planning models like these have fallen out of favor as oversimplified and subjective. More recent methods firms use to make internal investment decisions are based on shareholder value analysis, and whether the market value of a company is greater with an SBU or without it (whether it is sold or spun off). These value calculations assess the potential of a business based on potential growth opportunities from global expansion, repositioning or retargeting, and strategic outsourcing.

Assessing Growth Opportunities

Assessing growth opportunities involves planning new businesses, downsizing, or terminating older businesses. The company's plans for existing businesses allow it to project total sales and profits. If there is a gap between future desired sales and projected sales, corporate management will have to develop or acquire new businesses to fill it.

Figure 2.5 illustrates this strategic-planning gap for a major manufacturer of blank compact discs called Musicale (name disguised). The lowest curve projects the expected sales over the next five years from the current business portfolio. The highest curve describes desired sales over the same period. Evidently, the company wants to grow much faster than its current businesses will permit. How can it fill the strategic-planning gap?

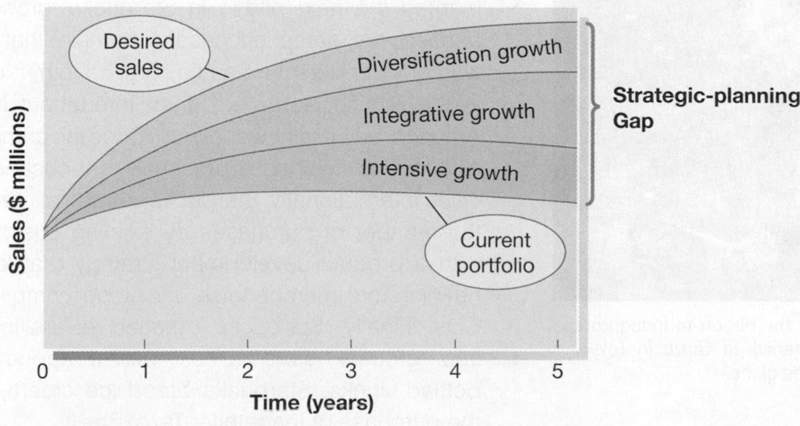

Figure 2.5 The Strategic-Planning Gap

The first option is to identify opportunities to achieve further growth within current businesses (intensive opportunities). The second is to identify opportunities to build or acquire businesses that are related to current businesses (integrative opportunities). The third is to identify opportunities to add attractive businesses that are unrelated to current businesses (diversification opportunities).

INTENSIVE GROWTH

Corporate management's first course of action should be a review of opportunities for improving existing businesses. Ansoff proposed a useful framework for detecting new intensive growth opportunities called a "product-market expansion grid" (see Figure 2.6).[30]

	Current Products	New Products
Current Markets	1. Market-penetration strategy	3. Product-development strategy
New Markets	2. Market-development strategy	(Diversification strategy)

Figure 2.6 Three Intensive Growth Strategies: Ansoff's Product-Market Expansion Grid

Source: Adapted and reprinted by permission, *Harvard Business Review*. From "Strategies for Diversification," by Igor Ansoff, September-October 1957. Copyright © 1957 by the President and Fellows of Harvard College. All rights reserved.

The company first considers whether it could gain more market share with its current products in their current markets (market-penetration strategy). Next it considers whether it can find or develop new markets for its current products (market-development strategy). Then it considers whether it can develop new products of potential interest to its current markets (product-development strategy). Later it will also review opportunities to develop new products for new markets (diversification strategy).

Starbucks—Starbucks is a company that has achieved growth in many different ways. When Howard Schultz joined the company in 1982, he recognized an unfilled niche for cafés serving gourmet coffee directly to customers. This became Starbucks' market-penetration strategy, and helped the company attain a loyal customer base in Seattle. The market-development strategy marked the next phase in Starbucks' growth: it applied the same successful formula that had worked wonders in Seattle, first to other cities in the Pacific Northwest, then throughout North America, and finally, worldwide. Once the company established itself as a presence in thousands of cities internationally, Starbucks sought to increase the number of purchases by existing customers with a product-development strategy that led to new in-store merchandise, including compilation CDs. Finally, Starbucks pursued diversification into grocery store aisles with Frappuccino® bottled drinks, Starbucks brand ice cream, and the purchase of tea retailer Tazo® Tea.[31]

Howard Schultz of Starbucks waves after cutting the ribbon to inaugurate Starbucks' first store opening outside North America, in Ginza in Tokyo, August 1996. Today Starbucks has stores across the globe.

How might Musicale use these three major intensive growth strategies to increase its sales? Musicale could try to encourage its current customers to buy more. This could work if its customers could be shown the benefits of using more compact discs for recording music or for data storage. Musicale could try to attract competitors' customers. This could work if Musicale noticed major weaknesses in competitors' products or marketing programs. Finally, Musicale could try to convince non-users of compact discs to start using them. This could work if there are still enough people who are not able to or do not know how to burn a compact disc.

How can Musicale use a market-development strategy? First, it might try to identify potential user groups in the current sales areas. If Musicale has been selling compact discs only to consumer markets, it might go after office and factory markets. Second, Musicale might seek additional distribution channels in its present locations. If it has been selling its discs only through stereo equipment dealers, it might add mass-merchandising channels. Third, the company might consider selling in new locations in its home country or abroad. If Musicale is sold only in Asia, it could consider entering the U.S. market.

Management should also consider new-product possibilities. Musicale could develop new features, such as additional data storage capabilities or greater durability. It could offer the CD at two or more quality levels, or it could research an alternative technology such as digital audiotape.

By examining these intensive growth strategies, management may discover several ways to grow. Still, that growth may not be enough. In that case, management must also look for integrative growth opportunities.

INTEGRATIVE GROWTH

A business can increase sales and profits through backward, forward, or horizontal integration within its industry.

Media companies have long reaped the benefits of integrative growth. Here's how one business writer explains the potential that NBC could reap from its merger with Vivendi Universal Entertainment to become NBC Universal. Although it's a far-fetched example, it gets across the possibilities inherent in this growth strategy.[32]

NBC Universal—[When] the hit movie *Seabiscuit* (produced by Universal Pictures) comes to television, it would air on Bravo (owned by NBC) or USA Network (owned by Universal), followed by the inevitable bid to make the movie into a TV series (by Universal Television Group), with the pilot being picked up by NBC, which passes on the show, but it's then revived in the "Brilliant But Canceled" series on cable channel Trio (owned by Universal) where its cult status leads to a Spanish version shown on Telemundo (owned by NBC) and the creation of a popular amusement-park attraction at Universal Studios.

How might Musicale achieve integrative growth? The company might acquire one or more of its suppliers (such as plastic material producers) to gain more control or generate more profit (backward integration). It might acquire some wholesalers or retailers, especially if they are highly profitable (forward integration). Finally, Musicale might acquire one or more competitors (horizontal integration). However, these new sources may still not deliver the desired sales volume. In that case, the company must consider diversification.

DIVERSIFICATION GROWTH

Diversification growth makes sense when good opportunities can be found outside the present businesses. A good opportunity is one in which the industry is highly attractive and the company has the right mix of business strengths to be successful. For example, from its origins as an animated film producer, Walt Disney Company has moved into licensing characters for merchandised goods, entering the broadcast industry with its own Disney

To understand how Group Danone has used internalization to focus its growth strategy in the food products sector, visit www.pearsoned.co.uk/marketingmanagementeurope.

Channel as well as ABC and ESPN acquisitions, operating a cruise line, and developing theme parks and vacation and resort properties.

Several types of diversification are possible. First, the company could seek new products that have technological or marketing synergies with existing product lines, even though the new products themselves may appeal to a different group of customers (concentric strategy). It might start a laser disc manufacturing operation because it knows how to manufacture compact discs. Second, the company might search for new products that could appeal to current customers even though the new products are technologically unrelated to its current product line (horizontal strategy). Musicale might produce compact disc cases, even though producing them requires a different manufacturing process. Finally, the company might seek new businesses that have no relationship to its current technology, products, or markets (conglomerate strategy). Musicale might want to consider such new businesses as making application software or personal organizers.

DOWNSIZING AND DIVESTING OLDER BUSINESSES

Companies must not only develop new businesses, they must also carefully prune, harvest, or divest tired old businesses to release needed resources and reduce costs. Weak businesses require a disproportionate amount of managerial attention. Managers should focus on growth opportunities, not fritter away energy and resources trying to salvage hemorrhaging businesses.

Organization and Organizational Culture

Strategic planning is done within the context of the organization. A company's **organization** consists of its structures, policies, and corporate culture, all of which can become dysfunctional in a rapidly changing business environment. Whereas structures and policies can be changed (with difficulty), the company's culture is very hard to change. Yet changing a corporate culture is often the key to successfully implementing a new strategy.

Corporate culture is an elusive concept, which some define as "the shared experiences, stories, beliefs, and norms that characterize an organization." Yet, walk into any company and the first thing that strikes you is the corporate culture—the way people are dressed, how they talk to one another, and the way they greet customers.

Sometimes corporate culture develops organically and is transmitted directly from the CEO's personality and habits to the company employees. Such is the case with Microsoft, which began as an entrepreneurial upstart. Even as it grew to a $51-billion company in 2007, Microsoft did not lose the hard-driving culture established by founder Bill Gates. In fact, most feel that Microsoft's ultra-competitive culture is the biggest key to its success and to its much-criticized dominance in the computing industry.[33]

Corporate culture varies markedly among Asian companies. Overseas Chinese businesses are characterized by fast, autocratic, experience-based, and action-oriented decision making. These businesses seem to invest and risk their capital without much analysis. In reality, the overseas Chinese collect and analyze data tirelessly to make rapid decisions. Many leverage their core competencies in hoarding information and erecting barriers to outsiders' acquisition of such information. However, their corporate culture may change as a new generation of Western-trained managers assumes leadership of their parents' businesses.

The Asian financial crisis in the late 1990s also impacted cultural change. Victor Fung, of Hong Kong's Li & Fung, notes that during the boom years, "you could run a large empire with very few people making few decisions. Now you need a large number of small decisions." Consequently, overseas Chinese tycoons can no longer rely on their extended families to run their businesses, but have to recruit outside professionals. The Internet is also transforming the corporate culture of overseas Chinese businesses. First, it enhances market efficiency by making information abundant, instantaneous, and accessible. This reduces the advantage secured via proprietary marketing information from the network of personal relationships built by overseas Chinese businesses.

Second, the Internet enables the rapid rise of new companies by lowering barriers to entry. Third, Internet businesses rely more on equity funding by venture capitalists as well as stock options as compensation to employees—groups which demand greater transparency.[34]

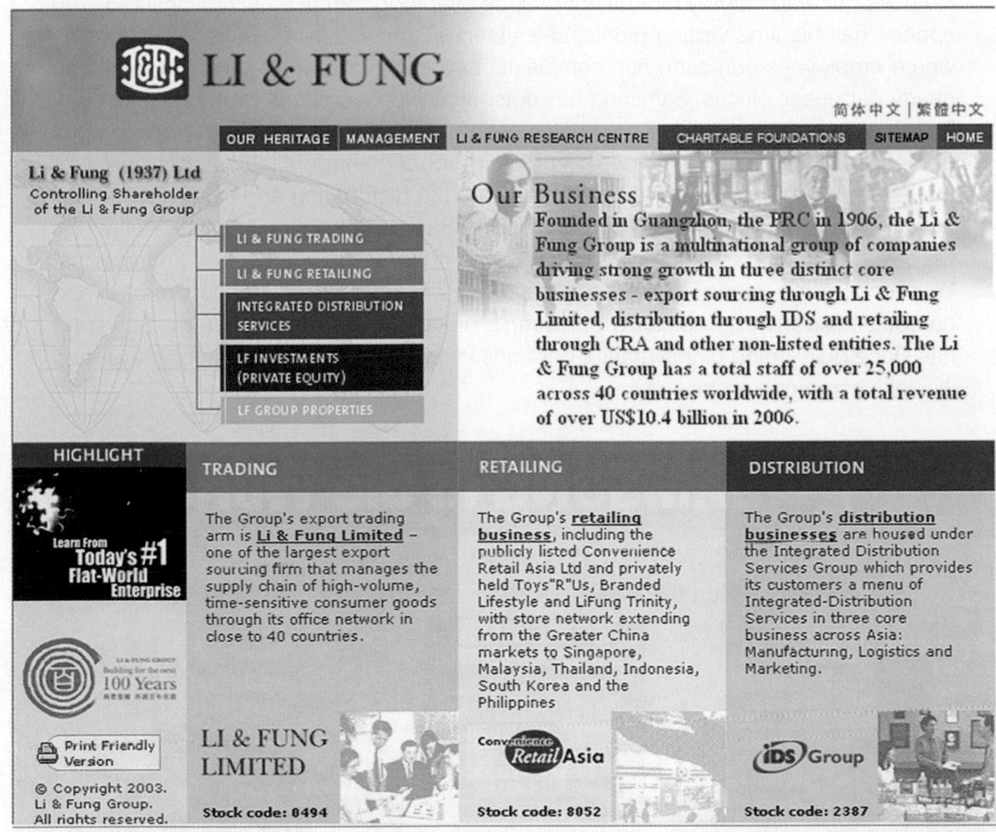

The Internet is transforming the corporate culture of overseas Chinese businesses by enhancing efficiency, lowering barriers to entry, and providing more transparency.

Corporate culture may also be transformed when state-owned enterprises are privatized as is occurring in many parts of Asia. Some private-sector Asian businesses have also undergone remarkable changes in corporate culture in response to the changing marketing environment, as illustrated by Samsung Electronics.[35]

Samsung Electronics—In 1997, Jong-Yong Yun was appointed CEO of Samsung Electronics. Earnings had weakened due to a long decline in memory chip prices, Samsung's main source of profit. Yun reinvented Samsung through a four-step process which he calls "the cycle of change." First, "chaos making" involved shaking up the old structure. Yun slashed debt by selling $1.9 billion in assets and exiting 16 marginal businesses like dishwashers, pagers, and juice mixers. Defying such Korean business traditions as lifetime employment and seniority as the means to advance, he cut a third of the payroll and replaced about half of the senior managers. Second, Yun shook the complacency out of his managers who emphasized market share over profits, using the slogan: "First survival, then growth." Third, Yun instilled new values. He appointed three foreigners to Samsung's corporate board to tap their expertise and signal acceptance of international financial practices and standards. Yun also hired over 50 young Koreans with American MBAs in marketing and assigned

(Continued ...)

(*Continued ...*)

them to every division as catalysts for making the company more attuned to global customers. He meets regularly with them and other high-flyers to obtain feedback and to encourage them. Yun also abolished Samsung's top-down power hierarchy. He does not read lengthy reports nor preside over long formal meetings. Instead, Yun spends half his time visiting plants, sales offices, and retailers. He has a PC hotline where employees can send him complaints and suggestions directly. Yun insists on nearly paperless offices. Samsung has outsourced its secretarial work and mailroom. Fourth, Yun restored order by implementing a quick, simple, and autonomous managerial approach. He handed 17 global product managers total responsibility for the entire value chain, from R&D and production to distribution and sales. Inventories have thus been reduced by 75 percent, saving Samsung billions. Innovative offerings were also launched in high-growth businesses such as mobile phones and laptops. Yun encouraged inter-divisional cooperation by mixing wireless, semiconductor, and computer expertise to actualize Samsung's digital-convergence strategy. Samsung has since built strong global market positions in memory chips, thin-film displays, and wireless communications.

Samsung has undergone remarkable changes in corporate culture in response to the changing marketing environment. Today, it is ranked in the top 20 brands by Interbrand.

What happens when companies with clashing cultures enter a joint venture or merger? In a study by Coopers & Lybrand of 100 companies with failed or troubled mergers, 85 percent of executives polled said that differences in management style and practices were the major problem.[36] Conflict was certainly the case when Germany's Daimler merged with Chrysler in 1998. Daimler preferred to operate a classic bureaucracy, while Chrysler traditionally gave decision making ability to managers lower in the ranks. Such fundamental differences contributed to early departures by executives, a stock price slide, management restructuring, and considerable losses at Chrysler.[37] Nonetheless, there exist cases of successful cultural integration, as illustrated by Renault's acquisition of Nissan, and the appointment of Carlos Ghosn to head its management.[38]

Nissan—When Carlos Ghosn joined Nissan in 1999, the company had not been doing well for seven years and losing market share for 27 years. Problems included too much focus on chasing competitors and too little on customers, excessive hierarchy, and a lack of urgency. In July 1999, Ghosn created nine cross-functional teams to probe Nissan's key functional areas like manufacturing, purchasing, and engineering to formulate a turnaround strategy. In October 1999, Ghosn launched his Nissan Revival Plan amidst much skepticism. The plan trimmed 21,000 jobs at Nissan plants worldwide. Ghosn also shut down five domestic factories, successfully demanded a 20 percent savings from car-parts suppliers, and reduced the number of *keiretsu* companies tied by cross-shareholdings to Nissan. Breaking traditions, he lured a senior designer from a rival company, introduced stock options to key staff, based promotions on performance rather than seniority, and substituted consensus gathering with quick decision making. Ghosn eliminated advisors and coordinators who had no defined responsibilities and gave all his executives direct operational authority. By 2002, Nissan reported record profits. Remarkably, Ghosn transformed Nissan's corporate culture without destroying its morale. As a Nissan board member notes, Ghosn "is able to restructure people's mind-sets." By allowing designers greater freedom, Nissan developed such new models as the Murano SUV, the Altima sedan, and the Cube micro-van. This helped Nissan create "segment-defining" models and a stronger brand identity. Ghosn hopes that consumers will purchase Nissan not only because it is a rational buy of reliable quality and low price, but also because of more emotional aspects like design and status. Ghosn's success has made him a celebrity CEO, an image he is leveraging to sell cars: "You buy cars from somebody you like." Combined, Nissan and Renault are now the world's fourth largest auto-maker and enjoy the highest margins between them. In an industry first, Ghosn became CEO at both global auto companies in 2005.

What organizational factors drive high-performing Asian businesses? Deshpandé and Farley profiled high-performing firms in six Asian countries. Their sample included 500 of the largest firms (including state-owned businesses) in major Asian industrial cities selected from stock market and local business directory listings.[39] The results showed that the four organizational factors which affected business performance in Western industrialized nations—market orientation, innovativeness, corporate culture, and organizational climate—were also operative in diverse Asian settings. The most successful Asian companies also looked very similar regardless of their country's political and economic system.

However, Deshpandé and Farley found that there was no homogeneous Asian model of business performance. Instead, there were many country-specific findings. Chinese and Indian companies seem to be positioned especially well to be globally competitive as they tended to have more entrepreneurial cultures. This indicates that the next set of global challengers will come from China and India.

In contrast, Japanese firms have non-entrepreneurial cultures, reflecting the value placed on consensus in Japanese society. This may hinder their cultivation of growth markets in future, both at home and abroad. Thailand's firms similarly demonstrate an above-average consensual corporate culture, stemming from the country's strong Buddhist tradition. India and Vietnam appear to be grappling in different ways with the legacy of central economic planning, with India's private sector showing signs of entrepreneurialism, while Vietnamese firms are more bureaucratic. Perhaps given its unique history of melding Asian and European cultures, Hong Kong was the only country where firms did not demonstrate a single clear profile of corporate culture.

Although Deshpandé and Farley uncovered much variation among firms in the six Asian countries, its major thesis should be of universal interest to marketing managers: competitive and entrepreneurial firms perform better, and more consensual and bureaucratic firms perform worse than their national peers. Similarly, more market-oriented firms which place customer interest first, and innovative businesses which help create new customers, perform better regardless of where they are based. Despite a fast-changing and increasingly globalized world, these features remain constant.

Marketing Innovation

Innovation in marketing is critical. The traditional view is that senior management hammers out the strategy and hands it down. Hamel offers the contrasting view that imaginative ideas on strategy exist in many places within a company.[40] Senior management should identify and encourage fresh ideas from three groups that tend to be underrepresented in strategy making: employees with youthful perspectives; employees who are far removed from company headquarters; and employees who are new to the industry. Each group is capable of challenging company orthodoxy and stimulating new ideas.

Nokia—Finnish giant Nokia remains the frontrunner in the mobile phone industry with annual sales of $80.5 billion across 130 countries and a global market share of 38 percent, by installing a culture of innovation at all levels, and using small, nimble, creative units to let new ideas bubble up through the ranks. Innovations are as likely to come from a junior application designer as from a seasoned engineer. One example of how the company creates its culture can be seen in the company cafeteria where employees view a slide show as they eat. It's not just any slide show, but one of pictures taken with camera phones by some of Nokia's 1,500 employees—part of an internal corporate competition that rewards staff creativity. Nokia even has a watchword for its culture of continuous innovation: "renewal."[41]

Jump Associates, an innovative strategy firm, offers five key strategies for managing change in an organization:[42]

1. **Avoid the innovation title.** Pick a name for the innovation team that won't alienate co-workers.
2. **Use the buddy system.** Find a like-minded collaborator within the organization.
3. **Set the metrics in advance.** Establish different sets of funding, testing, and performance criteria for incremental, experimental, and potentially disruptive innovations.
4. **Aim for quick hits first.** Start with easily implemented ideas that will work to demonstrate that things can get done, before quickly switching to bigger initiatives.
5. **Get data to back up your gut.** Use testing to get feedback and improve an idea.

"Marketing Insight: Creating Innovative Marketing" describes how some leading companies approach innovation.

Strategy must be developed by identifying and selecting among different views of the future. The Royal Dutch/Shell Group pioneered scenario analysis. A **scenario analysis** consists of developing plausible representations of a firm's possible future that make different assumptions about forces driving the market and include different uncertainties. Managers think through each scenario with the question: "What will we do if it happens?" They adopt one scenario as the most probable and watch for signposts that might confirm or disconfirm that scenario.[43]

MARKETING INSIGHT • CREATING INNOVATIVE MARKETING

When IBM surveyed top CEOs and government leaders about their agenda priorities, their answers about innovation were revealing. Business-model innovation and coming up with unique ways of doing things scored high. IBM's own drive for business-model innovation led to much collaboration, both within IBM itself and externally with companies, governments, and educational institutions. CEO Samuel Palmisano noted how the breakthrough Cell processor, based on the company's Power architecture, would not have happened without collaboration with Sony and Nintendo, as well as competitors Toshiba and Microsoft.

Procter & Gamble similarly has made it a goal for 50 percent of the new company's products to come from outside P&G's labs—from inventors, scientists, and suppliers whose new-product ideas can be developed in-house.

Collins' research emphasizes the importance of systematic, broad-based innovation: "Always looking for the one big breakthrough, the one big idea, is contrary to what we found: To build a truly great company, it's decision upon decision, action upon action, day upon day, month upon month.... It's cumulative momentum and no one decision defines a great company." He cites the success of Walt Disney with theme parks and Wal-Mart with retailing as examples of companies who were successful after having executed a big idea brilliantly over such a long period of time.

Sawhney and his colleagues outline 12 dimensions of business innovation that make up the "innovation radar" and suggest that business innovation is about increasing customer *value*, not just creating new *things*; business innovation comes in many flavors and can take place on any dimension of a business system; and business innovation is systematic and requires careful consideration of all aspects of a business.

Prahalad believes much innovation in industries from financial and telecom services to health care and automobiles can come from developments in emerging markets such as India. Forced to do more with less, Indian companies and foreign competitors are finding new ways to maximize minimal resources and offer quality products and services at low prices. Consider Bangalore's Narayana Hrudayalaya hospital, which charges a flat fee of $1,500 for heart bypass surgery that would cost 50 times that much in the U.S. The low cost is a result of the hospital's low labor and operating expenses and an assembly-line view of care that has specialists focus just on their own area. The approach works—the hospital's mortality rates are half those of U.S. hospitals. Narayana also operates on hundreds of infants for free and profitably insures 2.5 million poor Indians against serious illness for 11 cents a month.

Finally, to find breakthrough ideas, some companies find ways to immerse a range of employees in solving marketing problems. Samsung's Value Innovation Program (VIP) isolates product development teams of engineers, designers, and planners with a timetable and end date in the company's center just south of Seoul, Korea, while 50 specialists help guide their activities. To help make tough trade-offs, team members draw "value curves" that rank attributes such as a product's sound or picture quality on a scale from 1 to 5. To develop a new car, BMW similarly mobilizes specialists in engineering, design, production, marketing, purchasing, and finance at its Research and Innovation Center or Project House.

Sources: Steve Hamm, "Innovation: The View From the Top." *BusinessWeek*, April 3, 2006, pp. 52–53; Jena McGregor, "The World's Most Innovative Companies." *BusinessWeek*, April 24, 2006, pp. 63–74; Rich Karlgard, "Digital Rules." *Forbes*, March 13, 2006, pp. 31; Jennifer Rooney and Jim Collins, "Being Great Is Not Just a Matter of Big Ideas." *Point*, June 20, 2006; Moon Ihlwan, "Camp Samsung." *BusinessWeek*, July 3, 2006, pp. 46–47; Mohanbir Sawhney, Robert C. Wolcott and Inigo Arroniz, "The 12 Different Ways for Companies to Innovate." *MIT Sloan Management Review*, Spring 2006, pp. 75–85; Pete Engardio, "Business Prophet: How C.K. Prahalad Is Changing the Way CEO's Think." *BusinessWeek*, January 23, 2006, pp. 68–73.

Business Unit Strategic Planning

The business unit strategic-planning process consists of the steps shown in Figure 2.7. We examine each step in the sections that follow.

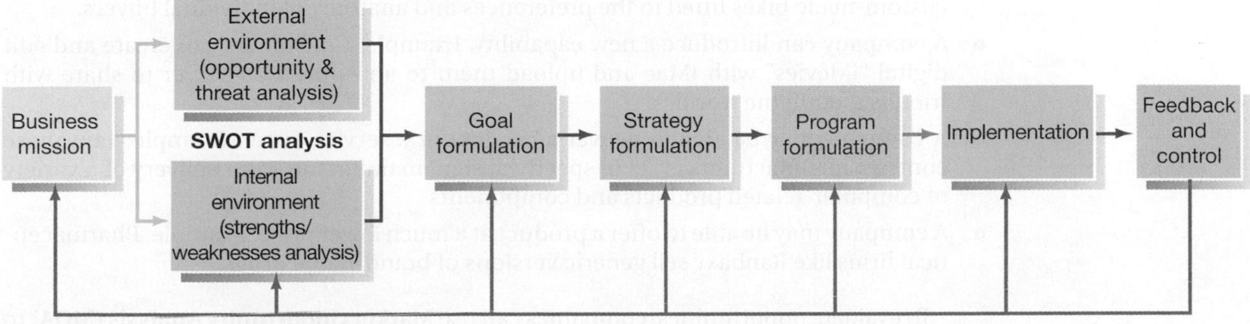

Figure 2.7 The Business Unit Strategic-Planning Process

The Business Mission

Each business unit needs to define its specific mission within the broader company mission. Thus a television studio-lighting-equipment company might define its mission as, "The company aims to target major television studios and become their vendor of choice for lighting technologies that represent the most advanced and reliable studio lighting arrangements." Notice that this mission does not attempt to win business from smaller television studios, win business by being lowest in price, or venture into non-lighting products.

SWOT Analysis

The overall evaluation of a company's strengths, weaknesses, opportunities, and threats is called SWOT analysis. It involves monitoring the external and internal marketing environment.

EXTERNAL ENVIRONMENT (OPPORTUNITY AND THREAT) ANALYSIS

A business unit has to monitor key *macroenvironment forces* (demographic-economic, natural, technological, political-legal, and social-cultural) and significant *microenvironment actors* (customers, competitors, suppliers, distributors, and dealers) that affect its ability to earn profits. The business unit should set up a marketing intelligence system to track trends and important developments and any related opportunities and threats.

Good marketing is the art of finding, developing, and profiting from opportunities.[44] A **marketing opportunity** is an area of buyer need and interest in which there is a high probability that a company can profitably satisfy that need. There are three main sources of market opportunities.[45] The first is to supply something that is in short supply. This requires little marketing talent, as the need is fairly obvious. The second is to supply an existing product or service in a new or superior way. There are several ways to uncover possible product or service improvements: by asking consumers for their suggestions (*problem detection method*); by asking consumers to imagine an ideal version of the product or service (*ideal method*); and by asking consumers to chart their steps in acquiring, using, and disposing of a product (*consumption chain method*). The third source often leads to a totally new product or service.

Opportunities can take many forms, and marketers have to be good at spotting them. Consider the following:

- A company may benefit from converging industry trends and introduce hybrid products or services that are new to the market. Example: Major mobile phone manufacturers have released phones with MP3 players and Global Positioning System.
- A company may make a buying process more convenient or efficient. Example: Consumers can now use the Internet to find more books than ever and search for the lowest price with a few clicks.
- A company can meet the need for more information and advice. Example: Zuji.com facilitates finding travel information by providing several flight and hotel alternatives.
- A company can customize a product or service that was formerly offered only in a standard form. Example: National Bicycle's Panasonic Order System manufactures custom-made bikes fitted to the preferences and anatomy of individual buyers.
- A company can introduce a new capability. Example: Consumers can create and edit digital "iMovies" with iMac and upload them to an Apple Web server to share with friends around the world.
- A company may be able to deliver a product or a service faster. Example: Taiwanese contract manufacturers excel in speedy design, manufacture, and delivery of a variety of computer-related products and components.
- A company may be able to offer a product at a much lower price. Example: Pharmaceutical firms like Ranbaxy sell generic versions of brand-name drugs.

To evaluate opportunities, companies can use **Market Opportunity Analysis (MOA)** to determine the attractiveness and probability of success:

1. Can the benefits involved in the opportunity be articulated convincingly to a defined target market(s)?
2. Can the target market(s) be located and reached with cost-effective media and trade channels?
3. Does the company possess or have access to the critical capabilities and resources needed to deliver customer benefits?
4. Can the company deliver the benefits better than any actual or potential competitors?
5. Will the financial rate of return meet or exceed the company's required threshold for investment?

In the opportunity matrix in Figure 2.8(a), the best marketing opportunities facing the TV-lighting-equipment company are listed in the upper-left cell (Number 1). The opportunities in the lower-right cell (Number 4) are too minor to consider. The opportunities in the upper-right cell (Number 2) and lower-left cell (Number 3) should be monitored for any improvement in attractiveness and success probability.

An **environmental threat** is a challenge posed by an unfavorable trend or development that would lead, in the absence of defensive marketing action, to lower sales or profit. Threats should be classified according to seriousness and probability of occurrence. Figure 2.8(b) illustrates the threat matrix facing the TV-lighting-equipment company. The threats in the upper-left cell are major, because they can seriously hurt the company and they have a high probability of occurrence. To deal with them, the company needs contingency plans that spell out changes it can make before or during the threat. The threats in the lower-right cell are very minor and can be ignored. The threats in the upper-right and lower-left cells need to be monitored carefully in the event that they grow more serious.

INTERNAL ENVIRONMENT (STRENGTHS/WEAKNESSES) ANALYSIS

It is one thing to find attractive opportunities and another to be able to take advantage of them. Each business needs to evaluate its internal strengths and weaknesses. It can do so by using a form like the one shown in "Marketing Memo: Checklist for Performing Strengths/Weaknesses Analysis."

(a) Opportunity Matrix

Attractiveness \ Success Probability	High	Low
High	1	2
Low	3	4

1. Company develops more powerful lighting system
2. Company develops device to measure energy efficiency of any lighting system
3. Company develops device to measure illumination level
4. Company develops software program to teach lighting fundamentals to TV studio personnel

(b) Threat Matrix

Seriousness \ Probability of Occurrence	High	Low
High	1	2
Low	3	4

1. Competitor develops superior lighting system
2. Major prolonged economic depression
3. Higher costs
4. Legislation to reduce number of TV studio licenses

Figure 2.8 Opportunity and Threat Matrices

MARKETING MEMO • CHECKLIST FOR PERFORMING STRENGTHS/WEAKNESSES ANALYSIS

	Performance					Importance		
	Major Strength	Minor Strength	Neutral	Minor Weakness	Major Weakness	Hi	Med	Low
Marketing								
1. Company reputation								
2. Market share								
3. Customer satisfaction								
4. Customer retention								
5. Product quality								
6. Service quality								
7. Pricing effectiveness								
8. Distribution effectiveness								
9. Promotion effectiveness								
10. Sales force effectiveness								
11. Innovation effectiveness								
12. Geographical coverage								
Finance								
13. Cost or availability of capital								
14. Cash flow								
15. Financial stability								
Manufacturing								
16. Facilities								
17. Economies of scale								
18. Capacity								
19. Able, dedicated workforce								
20. Ability to produce on time								
21. Technical manufacturing skill								
Organization								
22. Visionary, capable leadership								
23. Dedicated employees								
24. Entrepreneurial orientation								
25. Flexible or responsive								

Clearly, the business does not have to correct all its weaknesses, nor should it gloat about all its strengths. The big question is whether the business should limit itself to those opportunities where it possesses the required strengths or whether it should consider opportunities that mean it might have to acquire or develop certain strengths.

Sometimes a business does poorly not because its people lack the required strengths, but because they do not work together as a team. In one major electronics company, the engineers look down on the salespeople as "engineers who couldn't make it," and the salespeople look down on the service people as "salespeople who couldn't make it." It is therefore critical to assess interdepartmental working relationships as part of the internal environmental audit.

Goal Formulation

Once the company has performed a SWOT analysis, it can proceed to develop specific goals for the planning period. This stage of the process is called **goal formulation**. Managers use the term *goals* to describe objectives that are specific with respect to magnitude and time.

Most business units pursue a mix of objectives including profitability, sales growth, market share improvement, risk containment, innovation, and reputation. The business unit sets these objectives and then manages by objectives (MBO). For an MBO system to work, the unit's objectives must meet four criteria:

1. **They must be arranged hierarchically, from the most to the least important.** For example, the business unit's key objective for the period may be to increase the rate of return on investment. Managers can increase profit level by increasing revenue and reducing expenses. Revenue can be increased by increasing market share and prices.
2. **Objectives should be stated quantitatively whenever possible.** The objective "increase the return on investment (ROI)" is better stated as the goal "increase ROI to 15 percent within two years."
3. **Goals should be realistic.** They should arise from an analysis of the business unit's opportunities and strengths, not from wishful thinking.
4. **Objectives must be consistent.** It is not possible to maximize sales and profits simultaneously.

Other important trade-offs include short-term profit versus long-term growth, deep penetration of existing markets versus developing new markets, profit goals versus non-profit goals, and high growth versus low risk. Each choice in this set of trade-offs calls for a different marketing strategy.

Many believe that adopting the goal of strong market share growth may mean having to forego strong short-term profits. This longer term view of the market was held by Japanese businesses, which have traditionally placed less emphasis on meeting quarterly profit targets. Yet some believe that most businesses can be a growth business and can grow profitably, citing success stories such as Citibank and GE Capital.[46]

Strategic Formulation

Goals indicate what a business unit wants to achieve; **strategy** is a game plan for getting there. Every business must design a strategy for achieving its goals, consisting of a *marketing strategy,* and a compatible *technology strategy* and *sourcing strategy.*

PORTER'S GENERIC STRATEGIES

Michael Porter has proposed three generic strategies that provide a good starting point for strategic thinking: overall cost leadership, differentiation, and focus.[47]

- ***Overall cost leadership*** — The business works hard to achieve the lowest production and distribution costs so that it can price lower than its competitors and win a large market share. Firms pursuing this strategy must be good at engineering, purchasing, manufacturing, and physical distribution. They need less skill in marketing. The problem with this strategy is that other firms will usually compete with still lower costs and hurt the firm that rested its whole future on cost.
- ***Differentiation*** — The business concentrates on achieving superior performance in an important customer benefit area valued by a large part of the market. The firm cultivates those strengths that will contribute to the intended differentiation. Thus the firm seeking quality leadership, for example, must make products with the best components, put them together expertly, inspect them carefully, and effectively communicate their quality.
- ***Focus*** — The business focuses on one or more narrow market segments. The firm gets to know these segments intimately and pursues either cost leadership or differentiation within the target segment.

The online air travel industry provides a good example of these three strategies: Travelocity is pursuing a differentiation strategy by offering the most comprehensive range of services to the traveler; Lowestfare is pursuing a lowest-cost strategy; and Last Minute is pursuing a niche strategy in focusing on travelers who have the flexibility to travel on very short notice.

According to Porter, firms pursuing the same strategy directed to the same target market constitute a **strategic group**. The firm that carries out that strategy best will make the most profits. Firms that do not pursue a clear strategy and try to be good on all strategic dimensions do the worst.

Porter drew a distinction between operational effectiveness and strategy.[48] Competitors can quickly copy the operationally effective company using benchmarking and other tools, thus diminishing the advantage of operational effectiveness. Porter defines strategy as "the creation of a unique and valuable position involving a different set of activities." A company can claim that it has a strategy when it "performs different activities from rivals or performs similar activities in different ways."

STRATEGIC ALLIANCES

Even giant companies—P&G, IBM, Sony—often cannot achieve leadership either nationally or globally, without forming alliances with domestic or multinational companies that complement or leverage their capabilities and resources.

Just doing business in another country may require the firm to license its product, form a joint venture with a local firm, or buy from local suppliers to meet "domestic content" requirements. As a result, many firms are rapidly developing global strategic networks, and victory is going to those who build the better global network. Star Alliance, for example, brings together 20 airlines including Lufthansa, United Airlines, Air Canada, ANA, Austrian Airlines, Air China, Singapore Airlines, SAS, Thai Airways, Air New Zealand, Asiana Airlines, and Spanair into a huge global partnership that allows travelers to make nearly seamless connections to about 700 destinations.

Many strategic alliances take the form of marketing alliances. These fall into four major categories.

1. ***Product or service alliances*** — One company licenses another to produce its product, or two companies jointly market their complementary products or a new product. For instance, Sanrio licenses companies to have its Hello Kitty moniker on various products.
2. ***Promotional alliances*** — One company agrees to carry a promotion for another company's product or service. Visa, for example, has a lucky draw with Hong Kong Disneyland for its cardholders.
3. ***Logistics alliances*** — One company offers logistical services for another company's product. For example, Hong Kong's Li & Fung manages Avon's supply chain.
4. ***Pricing collaborations*** — One or more companies join in a special pricing collaboration. Hotel and rental car companies often offer mutual price discounts.

A celebration of a Star Alliance inaugural. Star Alliance brings together 20 airlines that cover most of the globe.

Companies need to give creative thought to finding partners that might complement their strengths and offset their weaknesses. Well-managed alliances allow companies to obtain a greater sales impact at less cost. In contrast, poorly managed alliances often end in failure (see "Marketing Insight: Same Bed, Different Dreams"). To keep their strategic alliances thriving, corporations have begun to develop organizational structures to support them and have come to view the ability to form and manage partnerships as core skills (called **Partner Relationship Management, PRM**).[49] For example, biotech and pharmaceutical companies like ImClone Systems and Bristol-Meyers Squibb are partnering to leverage each other's respective strengths in research and marketing.

MARKETING INSIGHT • SAME BED, DIFFERENT DREAMS

Despite the many good reasons for pursuing alliances, a high percentage end in failure. A study by McKinsey & Company revealed that roughly one-third of 49 alliances failed to live up to the partners' expectations. Yet such painful lessons are teaching companies how to craft a winning alliance. Three keys seem to be:

1. ***Strategic fit*** — Before even considering an alliance, companies need to assess their own core competencies. Then they need to find a partner that will complement them in business lines, geographic positions, or competencies. A good example is the link between Microsoft and HSBC which enables the latter's customers to manage their personal accounts on their home PCs using Microsoft Money. The agreement combines Microsoft's expertise in computer software and interface design with HSBC's experience in running Hexagon, an online banking system for commercial clients in more than 40 countries.
2. ***A focus on the long term*** — Rather than joining forces to save a few dollars, strategic partners should focus more on gains that can be harvested for years to come. Corning, the glass and ceramics maker, is renowned for making partnerships. It has derived half of its products from joint ventures and even defines itself as a "network of organizations." That network includes German and Korean electronics giants Siemens and Samsung, and Mexico's glassmaker, Vitro.
3. ***Flexibility*** — Alliances can last only if they are flexible. Traditionally, high-tech Japanese firms often created alliances among fellow *keiretsu* members, such as the Mitsubishi or Mitsui group of firms. However, future successful firms may be networked corporations with multiple alliances outside their *keiretsu* or even with their competitors. Sony and Sanyo have joined forces to produce panel display technology. Sony contributes advanced polysilicon display technology, while Sanyo develops special manufacturing techniques.

In the Asian context, Vanhonacker analyzed the failures of several equity joint ventures (EJVs) in China. He gave two broad sets of reasons for the failure of these alliances: China's tradition of a planned economic system, and the conflicting perceptions and expectations between Chinese and foreign businesses.

First, China's planned economy left a rather rigid and hierarchical structure. All Chinese companies belong to and operate under a mix of local, provincial, and central government authority, each with its own agenda, all competing for resources and regulatory protection. An EJV trying to do business outside its authorized territory can easily run into trouble. For example, China's fixed-line telephone network is owned and operated by the Ministry of Posts and Telecommunications (MPT). Shanghai Bell, Alcatel's EJV with a MPT-related company, thus has an advantage selling to the local operating companies and commands a high market share.

However, NEC, Siemens, and AT&T have partners under different ministries with no such regulatory authority and enjoy no such benefits. China's fragmented industrial system also confined Chinese businesses to a narrow line of products or to operate in a narrow niche. Thus very few Chinese companies have a national presence and those that do, have been cherry-picked by early MNC entrants. New entrants to China would thus find it difficult to locate a qualified local partner.

Second, there is the problem of market access. Some Chinese partners are unable to find buyers for the EJV's output. For example, Matsushita wanted to capitalize on its EJV partner Hualu Electronics' extensive domestic network. Hualu was to buy 80 percent of the EJV's VCR components for installation in VCRs to be sold in China. However, Hualu was unable to absorb the output from the EJV's 45 production lines.

Third, the *guanxi* of some Chinese companies has been found to be limited, or may take the foreign partner in directions that are difficult to control, or not be strategically useful, or not be cost effective. For example, Danish company Novo Nordisk, while negotiating with two potential pharmaceutical partners, realized that it could get approvals to do business as well as to access the Beijing government without their assistance. It decided to establish a wholly-owned biotechnology company in Tianjin.

Fourth, some Chinese companies may lack the experience to keep up with the rapid changes in the Chinese market. They tend to view sales and marketing with an order-taking approach. Free-market competition is alien to many Chinese. Chinese partners have proven hard to motivate once the EJV has attained a comfortable position. Krohne's EJV in Shanghai achieved a 60 percent market share for flow meters in China and a significant profit within five years of its establishment. The result delighted the Chinese partner who took it as a signal to relax. Krohne, in contrast, saw that its success invited competition and urged its Chinese partner to increase its investments. Unable to agree on the EJV's direction, Krohne and its partner went into legal negotiations.

Fifth, there is the issue of technology transfer. This is perhaps the grayest area of doing business in China. How much should

(continued ...)

MARKETING INSIGHT • SAME BED, DIFFERENT DREAMS

(continued...)

foreign companies share with local partners? Chinese companies desire as much information as possible, while foreign investors are reluctant to provide advanced, proprietary technology given China's patchy enforcement of intellectual property rights.

Sixth, Chinese partners seek profits on a shorter time horizon than foreign businesses. Some fear that China's experiment with capitalism may not last, given the large swings in recent government policy. In contrast, foreign companies entering China are sometimes willing to sustain losses for growth and to re-invest their profits for expansion. For example, an EJV between Saint Gobain and a Shanghai tool manufacturer lost money soon after it began. The Chinese lost complete interest in the project to the extent that morale problems led to a rare worker strike. After long negotiations and additional investments, Saint Gobain bought out its Chinese partner.

Sources: Sherman Stratford, "Are Strategic Alliances Working?" *Fortune,* September 21, 1992, pp. 77–78; Peter Gloster, "Tie-up Brings Easier Online Banking," *Asian Business,* April 1996, p. 63; Ray Tsuchiyama, "Networking for the 21st Century," *Asian Business,* May 1996, p. 38; Wilfried Vanhonacker, "Entering China: An Unconventional Approach," *Harvard Business Review*, March–April 1997, pp. 130–141.

Program Formulation and Implementation

Even a great marketing strategy can be sabotaged by poor implementation. If the unit has decided to attain technological leadership, it must plan programs to strengthen its R&D department, gather technological intelligence, develop leading-edge products, train the technical sales force, and develop ads to communicate its technological leadership.

Once the marketing programs are formulated, the marketing people must estimate their costs. Questions arise: Is participating in a particular trade show worth it? Will a specific sales contest pay for itself? Will hiring another salesperson contribute to the bottom line? Activity-based cost (ABC) accounting should be applied to each marketing program to determine whether it is likely to produce sufficient results to justify the cost.[50]

In implementing strategy, companies also must not lose sight of their multiple stakeholders and their needs. Traditionally, most businesses focused on stockholders. Today's businesses are increasingly recognizing that unless they nurture other stakeholders—customers, employees, suppliers, distributors—the business may never earn sufficient profits for the stockholders. A company can aim to deliver satisfaction levels above the minimum for different stakeholders. For example, it might aim to delight its customers, perform well for its employees, and deliver a threshold level of satisfaction to its suppliers. In setting these levels, a company must be careful not to violate the various stakeholder groups' sense of fairness about the relative treatment they are receiving.[51]

A dynamic relationship connects the stakeholder groups. A smart company creates a high level of employee satisfaction, which leads to higher effort, which leads to higher-quality products and services, which creates higher customer satisfaction, which leads to more repeat business, which leads to higher growth and profits, which leads to high stockholder satisfaction, which leads to more investment, and so on. This is the virtuous circle that spells profits and growth. "Marketing Insight: Marketing's Contribution to Shareholder Value" highlights the increasing importance of the proper bottom-line view to marketing expenditures.

According to McKinsey & Company, strategy is only one of seven elements in successful business practice.[52] The first three elements—strategy, structure, and systems—are considered the "hardware" of success. The next four—style, skills, staff, and shared values—are the "software."

The first "soft" element, *style,* means that company employees share a common way of thinking and behaving. Giordano's employees smile at the customer, and Lenovo employees are professional in their customer dealings. The second, *skills,* means that the employees have the skills needed to carry out the company's strategy. The third, *staffing,* means that the company has hired able people, trained them well, and assigned them to the right jobs. The fourth, *shared values,* means that the employees share the same guiding values. When these elements are present, companies are usually more successful at strategy implementation.[53]

Another study of management practices found that superior performance over time depended on flawless execution, a company culture based on aiming high, a structure that is flexible and responsive, and a strategy that is clear and focused.[54]

MARKETING INSIGHT • MARKETING'S CONTRIBUTION TO SHAREHOLDER VALUE

Companies normally focus on profit maximization rather than on shareholder value maximization. Doyle, in his *Value-Based Marketing*, charges that profit maximization leads to short-term planning and under-investment in marketing. It leads to a focus on building sales, market share, and current profits. It leads to cost cutting and shedding assets to produce quick improvements in earnings, and erodes a company's long-term competitiveness by neglecting to invest in new market opportunities.

Companies normally measure their profit performance using ROI (return on investment, calculated by dividing profits by investment). This has two problems:

1. **Profits are arbitrarily measured and subject to manipulation.** Cash flow is more important. As someone observed: "Profits are a matter of opinion; cash is a fact."
2. **Investment ignores the real value of the firm.** More of a company's value resides in its intangible marketing assets—brands, market knowledge, customer relationships, and partner relationships—than in its balance sheet. These assets are the drivers of long-term profits.

Doyle argues that marketing will not mature as a profession until it can demonstrate the impact of marketing on shareholder value, the market value of a company minus its debt. The market value is the share price times the number of shares outstanding. The share price reflects what investors estimate is the present value of the future lifetime earnings of a company. When management is choosing a marketing strategy, Doyle wants it to apply shareholder value analysis (SVA) to see which alternative course of action will maximize shareholder value.

If Doyle's arguments are accepted, marketing will finally get the attention it deserves in the boardroom. Instead of seeing marketing as a specific function concerned only with increasing sales or market share, senior management will see it as an integral part of the whole management process. It will judge marketing by how much it contributes to shareholder value

Source: Peter Doyle, *Value-Based Marketing: Marketing Strategies for Corporate Growth and Shareholder Value*, (Chichester, England: John Wiley, 2000).

Feedback and Control

As it implements its strategy, the firm needs to track the results and monitor new developments especially as the marketplace changes. Haier is a good example.

Haier—Founded in 1984 from its predecessor, Qingdao Refrigerator, Haier first marketed refrigerators from a German company called Liberherr. It made the headlines when its inferior-quality products were smashed just before they went off the production line—an inauspicious beginning for a company whose vision is "Committing Yourself to the Motherland by Pursuing Excellence." Yet, over the next 16 years, Haier's sales rose by 11,600 times while its product offering grew from a single refrigerator model to nearly 70 products in almost 11,000 designs. Haier is now China's leading maker of washing machines and ranks second in refrigerator sales worldwide. Its products are sold in over 160 countries and over 38,000 outlets. However, after largely having the Chinese market to itself for a decade, Haier now faces competition from domestic upstarts and such foreign entrants as Samsung, Siemens, and Electrolux. A price war in 2001 lowered appliance prices and pressured Haier's margins. Haier has responded by partnering with Sanyo and Taiwan's Sampo in production and distribution alliances. It also makes digital TVs with LG Electronics. Finally, it is diversifying its business in areas such as finance, computers, and mobile phones.[55]

A Haier ad in Charles de Gaulle International Airport, Paris.

A company's strategic fit with the environment will inevitably erode because the market environment changes faster than the company's 7 Ss. Thus a company might remain efficient while it loses effectiveness. Drucker pointed out that it is more important to "do the right thing" (effectiveness) than "to do things right" (efficiency). The most successful companies excel at both.

Once an organization fails to respond to a changed environment, it becomes increasingly hard to recapture its lost position. Consider what happened to Lotus Development Corporation, whose Lotus 1-2-3 software was once the world's leading software program. Its market share in desktop software has now slipped so low that analysts do not even bother to track it.

Organizations are set up as efficient machines, and it is difficult to change one part without adjusting everything else. Yet organizations can be changed through strong leadership, preferably in advance of a crisis. The key to organizational health is the willingness to examine the changing environment and to adopt new goals and behaviors.

Product Planning: The Nature and Contents of a Marketing Plan

Working within the plans set by the levels above them, product managers come up with a marketing plan for individual products, lines, brands, channels, or customer groups. Each product level (product line, brand) must develop a marketing plan for achieving its goals. A **marketing plan** is a written document that summarizes what the marketer has learned about the marketplace and indicates how the firm plans to reach its marketing objectives.[56] It contains tactical guidelines for the marketing programs and financial allocations over the planning period.[57] It is one of the most important outputs of the marketing process.

Marketing plans are becoming more customer- and competitor-oriented and better reasoned and more realistic than in the past. The plans draw more inputs from all the functions and are team-developed. Marketing executives increasingly see themselves as professional managers first, and specialists second. Planning is becoming a continuous process to respond to rapidly changing market conditions.

Most marketing plans cover one year. The plans vary in length from under five to over 50 pages. Some companies take their plans very seriously, whereas others see them only as a rough guide to action. Eisenhower once observed: "In preparing for battle I have always found that plans are useless but planning is indispensable." The most frequently cited shortcomings of current marketing plans, according to marketing executives, are lack of realism, insufficient competitive analysis, and a short-run focus (see "Marketing Memo: Marketing Plan Criteria" for some guideline questions to ask in developing marketing plans).

What, then, does a marketing plan look like? What does it contain?

MARKETING MEMO • MARKETING PLAN CRITERIA

Here are some questions to ask when evaluating a marketing plan.

1. ***Is the plan simple?*** Is it easy to understand and act on? Does it communicate its content easily and practically?
2. ***Is the plan specific?*** Are its objectives concrete and measurable? Does it include specific actions and activities, each with specific dates of completion, specific persons responsible, and specific budgets?
3. ***Is the plan realistic?*** Are the sales goals, expense budgets, and milestone dates realistic? Has a frank and honest self-critique been conducted to raise possible concerns and objections?
4. ***Is the plan complete?*** Does it include all the necessary elements?

Source: Tim Berry and Doug Wilson, *On Target: The Book on Marketing Plans*, (Eugene, OR: Palo Alto Software., 2000).

Contents of the Marketing Plan

- ***Executive summary and table of contents*** — The marketing plan should open with a brief summary of the main goals and recommendations. The executive summary permits senior management to grasp the plan's major thrust. A table of contents that outlines the rest of the plan and all the supporting rationale and operational detail should follow the executive summary.
- ***Situation analysis*** — This section presents relevant background data on sales, costs, the market, competitors, and the various forces in the macroenvironment. How is the market defined, how big is it, and how fast is it growing? What are the relevant trends affecting the market? What is the product offering and what are the critical issues facing the company? Pertinent historical information can be included to provide context. All this information is used to carry out on a SWOT (strengths, weaknesses, opportunities, and threats) analysis.
- ***Marketing strategy*** — Here the product manager defines the mission, and marketing and financial objectives. The manager also defines those groups and needs which the market offerings are intended to satisfy. The manager then establishes the product line's competitive positioning, which will inform the "game plan" to accomplish the plan's objectives. All this is done with inputs from other organizational areas, such as purchasing, manufacturing, sales, finance, and human resources, to ensure that the company can provide proper support for effective implementation. The marketing strategy should be specific about the branding strategy and customer strategy that will be employed.
- ***Financial projections*** — Financial projections include a sales forecast, an expense forecast, and a break-even analysis. On the revenue side, the projections show the forecasted sales volume by month and product category. On the expense side, the projections show the expected costs of marketing, broken down into finer categories. The break-even analysis shows how many units must be sold monthly to offset the monthly fixed costs and average per-unit variable costs.
- ***Implementation controls*** — The last section of the marketing plan outlines the controls for monitoring and adjusting implementation of the plan. Typically, the goals and budget are spelled out for each month or quarter so management can review each period's results and take corrective action as needed. A number of different internal and external measures must be taken to assess progress and suggest possible modifications. Some organizations include contingency plans outlining the steps management would take in response to specific environmental developments, such as price wars or strikes.

Sample Marketing Plan: Pegasus Sports International*

1.0 Executive Summary

Pegasus Sports International is a start-up aftermarket inline skating accessory manufacturer. In addition to the aftermarket products, Pegasus is developing SkateTours, a service that takes clients out, in conjunction with a local skate shop, and provides them with an afternoon of skating using inline skates and some of Pegasus' other accessories such as SkateSails. The aftermarket skate accessory market has been largely ignored. Although there are several major manufacturers of the skates themselves, the accessory market has not been addressed. This provides Pegasus with an excellent opportunity for market growth. Skating is a booming sport. Currently most skating is recreational. There are, however, a growing number of skating competitions, including team competitions such as skate hockey as well as individual competitions such as speed skate racing. Pegasus will work to grow these markets as well as develop the skate transportation market, a more utilitarian use of skating. Several of Pegasus' currently developed products have patents pending, and market research indicates that there is great demand for these products. Pegasus will achieve fast, significant market penetration through a solid business model, long-range planning, and a strong management team that is able to execute on this exciting opportunity. The three principals on the management team have over 30 years of combined personal and industry experience. This extensive experience provides Pegasus with the empirical information as well as the passion to provide the skating market with much-needed aftermarket products. Pegasus will sell its products initially through its Web site. This "Dell" direct-to-the-consumer approach will allow Pegasus to achieve higher margins and maintain a close relationship with the customers, which is essential for producing products that have a true market demand. By the end of the year, Pegasus will have also developed relationships with different skate shops and will begin to sell some of its products through retailers.

Table 1.0 Sales Forecast

Sales Forecast			
Sales	**2008**	**2009**	**2010**
Recreational	$455,740	$598,877	$687,765
Competitive	$72,918	$95,820	$110,042
Total Sales	$528,658	$694,697	$797,807
Direct Cost of Sales	**2008**	**2009**	**2010**
Recreational	$82,033	$107,798	$123,798
Competitive	$13,125	$17,248	$19,808
Subtotal Cost of Sales	$95,158	$125,046	$143,606

2.0 Situation Analysis

Pegasus is entering its first year of operation. Its products have been well-received, and marketing will be key to the development of brand and product awareness as well as the growth of the customer base. Pegasus offers several different aftermarket skating accessories, serving the growing inline skating industry.

2.1 Market Summary

Pegasus possesses good information about the market and knows a great deal about the common attributes of the most prized customer. This information will be leveraged to better understand who is served, what their specific needs are, and how Pegasus can better communicate with them.

Target Markets

- Recreational
- Fitness
- Speed
- Hockey
- Extreme

Table 2.1 Target Market Forecast

Target Market Forecast							
Potential Customer	**Growth**	**2008**	**2009**	**2010**	**2011**	**2012**	**CAGR**
Recreational	10%	19,142,500	21,056,750	23,162,425	25,478,668	28,026,535	10.00%
Fitness	15%	6,820,000	7,843,000	9,019,450	10,372,368	11,928,223	15.00%
Speed	10%	387,500	426,250	468,875	515,763	567,339	10.00%
Hockey	6%	2,480,800	2,628,800	2,768,528	2,953,720	3,130,943	6.00%
Extreme	4%	2,170,000	2,256,800	2,347,072	2,440,955	2,538,593	4.00%
Total	10.48%	31,000,000	34,211,600	37,784,350	41,761,474	46,191,633	10.48%

*Modification of a sample plan provided by and copyright Palo Alto Software, Inc. <www.mplans.com/spv/3407/index.cfm?affiliate=mplans> Find more complete sample plans at www.mplans.com.

2.1.1 Market Demographics

The profile for the typical Pegasus customer consists of the following geographic, demographic, and behavior factors:

GEOGRAPHICS

- Pegasus has no set geographic target area. By leveraging the expansive reach of the Internet and multiple delivery services, Pegasus can serve both domestic and international customers.
- The total targeted population is 31,000,000 users.

DEMOGRAPHICS

- Male and female users, with an almost equal ratio between the two.
- Ages 13–46, with 48 percent clustering around the ages 23–34. The recreational users tend to cover the widest age range, including young users through active adults. The fitness users tend to be ages 20–40. The speed users tend to be in their late 20s and early 30s. The hockey players are generally in their teens through their early 20s. The extreme segment is of similar age to the hockey players.
- Of the users who are over 20, 65 percent have an undergraduate degree or substantial undergraduate coursework.
- The adult users have a median personal income of $47,000.

BEHAVIOR FACTORS

- Users enjoy fitness activities not as a means for a healthy life, but as an intrinsically enjoyable activity in itself.
- Users spend money on gear, typically sports equipment.
- Users have active lifestyles that include some sort of recreation at least two to three times a week.

2.1.2 Market Needs

Pegasus is providing the skating community with a wide range of accessories for all variations of skating. Pegasus seeks to fulfill the following benefits that are important to its customers:

- ***Quality craftsmanship.*** The customers work hard for their money and do not enjoy spending it on disposable products that only work for a year or two.
- ***Well-thought-out designs.*** The skating market has not been addressed by well-thought-out products that serve skaters' needs. Pegasus' industry experience and personal dedication to the sport will provide it with the needed information to produce insightfully designed products.
- ***Customer Service.*** Exemplary service is required to build a sustainable business that has a loyal customer base.

2.1.3 Market Trends

Pegasus will distinguish itself by marketing products not previously available to skaters. The emphasis in the past has been to sell skates and very few replacement parts. The number of skaters is not restricted to any one single country, continent, or age group, so there is a world market. Pegasus has products for virtually every group of skaters. The fastest-growing segment of this sport is the fitness skater. Therefore, the marketing is being directed to service this group. BladeBoots will enable users to enter establishments without having to remove their skates. BladeBoots will be aimed at the recreational skater, the largest segment. SkateAids, on the other hand, are great for everyone.

The sport of skating will also grow through SkateSailing. This sport is primarily for the medium-to-advanced skater, and its growth potential is tremendous. The sails which Pegasus has manufactured have been sold in Europe, following a pattern similar to windsurfing.

Another trend is group skating. More and more groups are getting together on skating excursions in cities all over the world. The market trends are showing continued growth in all directions of skating.

2.1.4 Market Growth

With the price of skates going down due to competition by so many skate companies, the market has had steady growth throughout the world, with 22.5 million units sold in 2000 to over 31 million in 2003. The growth statistics for 2004 were estimated to be over 35 million units. More people are discovering—and in many cases rediscovering—the health benefits and fun of skating.

2.2 SWOT Analysis

The following SWOT analysis captures the key strengths and weaknesses within the company, and describes the opportunities and threats facing Pegasus.

2.2.1 Strengths

- In-depth industry experience and insight.
- Creative, yet practical product designers.
- The use of a highly-efficient, flexible business model utilizing direct customer sales and distribution.

2.2.2 Weaknesses

- The reliance on outside capital necessary to grow the business.
- A lack of retailers who can work face-to-face with the customer to generate brand and product awareness.
- The difficulty of developing brand awareness as a start-up company.

2.2.3 Opportunities

- Participation within a growing industry.
- Decreased product costs through economy of scale.

- The ability to leverage other industry participants' marketing efforts to help grow the general market.

2.2.4 Threats

- Future/potential competition from an already established market participant.
- A slump in the economy that could have a negative effect on people's spending of discretionary income on fitness/recreational products.
- The release of a study that calls into question the safety of skating or the inability to prevent major skating-induced traumas.

2.3 Competition

Pegasus Sports International is forming its own market. Although there are a few companies that do make sails and foils that a few skaters are using, Pegasus is the only brand truly designed for and by skaters. The few competitors' sails on the market are not designed for skating, but for windsurfing or for skateboards. In the case of foils, storage and carrying are not practical. There are different indirect competitors who are manufacturers of the actual skates. After many years in the market, these companies have yet to become direct competitors by manufacturing accessories for the skates that they make.

2.4 Product Offering

Pegasus Sports International now offers several products:

- The first product that has been developed is BladeBoots, a cover for the wheels and frame of inline skates, which allows skaters to enter places that normally would not allow them in with skates on. BladeBoots come with a small pouch and belt which converts to a well-designed skate carrier.
- The second product is SkateSails. These sails are specifically designed for use while skating. Feedback that Pegasus has received from skaters indicates skatesailing could become a very popular sport. Trademarking this product is currently in progress.
- The third product, SkateAid, will be in production by December. Other ideas for products are under development, but will not be disclosed until Pegasus can protect them through pending patent applications.

2.5 Keys to Success

The keys to success are designing and producing products that meet market demand. In addition, Pegasus must ensure total customer satisfaction. If these keys to success are achieved, Pegasus will become a profitable, sustainable company.

2.6 Critical Issues

As a start-up business, Pegasus is still in the early stages. The critical issues are for Pegasus to:

- Establish itself as the premier skating accessory company.
- Pursue controlled growth that dictates that payroll expenses will never exceed the revenue base. This will help protect against recessions.
- Constantly monitor customer satisfaction, ensuring that the growth strategy will never compromise service and satisfaction levels.

3.0 Marketing Strategy

The key to the marketing strategy is focusing on the speed, health and fitness, and recreational skaters. Pegasus can cover about 80 percent of the skating market because it produces products geared toward each segment. Pegasus is able to address all of the different segments within the market because, although each segment is distinct in terms of its users and equipment, Pegasus' products are useful to all of the different segments.

3.1 Mission

Pegasus Sports International's mission is to provide the customer with the finest skating accessories available. "We exist to attract and maintain customers. With a strict adherence to this maxim, success will be ensured. Our services and products will exceed the expectations of the customers."

3.2 Marketing Objectives

- Maintain positive, strong growth each quarter (notwithstanding seasonal sales patterns).
- Achieve a steady increase in market penetration.
- Decrease customer acquisition costs by 1.5 percent per quarter.

3.3 Financial Objectives

- Increase the profit margin by 1 percent per quarter through efficiency and economy-of-scale gains.
- Maintain a significant research and development budget (as a percentage relative to sales) to spur future product developments.
- A double- to triple-digit growth rate for the first three years.

3.4 Target Markets

With a world skating market of over 31 million and steadily growing (statistics released by the Sporting Goods Manufacturers Association), the niche has been created. Pegasus' aim is to expand this market by promoting SkateSailing. The Sporting Goods Manufacturers Association survey indicates that skating now has more participation than football, softball, skiing, and snowboarding combined. The breakdown of participation of skating is as follows: 1+ percent speed (growing), 8 percent hockey (declining),

7 percent extreme/aggressive (declining), 22 percent fitness (nearly seven million—the fastest growing), and 61 percent recreational (first-timers). Our products are targeting the fitness and recreational groups, because they are the fastest growing. These groups are gearing themselves toward health and fitness, and combined, they can easily grow to 85 percent (or 26 million) of the market in the next five years.

3.5 Positioning

Pegasus will position itself as the premier aftermarket skating accessory company. This positioning will be achieved by leveraging Pegasus' competitive edge: industry experience and passion. Pegasus is a skating company formed by skaters for skaters. Pegasus management is able to use its vast experience and personal passion for the sport to develop innovative, useful accessories for a broad range of skaters.

3.6 Strategies

The single objective is to position Pegasus as the premier skating accessory manufacturer, serving the domestic and international markets. The marketing strategy will seek to first create customer awareness concerning the offered products and services and then develop the customer base. The message that Pegasus will seek to communicate is that it offers the best-designed, most useful skating accessories. This message will be communicated through a variety of methods. The first will be the Pegasus Web site. The Web site will provide a rich source of product information and offer consumers the opportunity to purchase. A lot of time and money will be invested in the site to provide the customer with the perception of total professionalism and utility for Pegasus' products and services.

The second marketing method will be advertisements placed in numerous industry magazines. The skating industry is supported by several different glossy magazines designed to promote the industry as a whole. In addition, a number of smaller periodicals serve the smaller market segments within the skating industry. The last method of communication is the use of printed sales literature. The two previously mentioned marketing methods will create demand for the sales literature, which will be sent out to customers. The cost of the sales literature will be fairly minimal, because it will use the already-compiled information from the Web site.

3.7 Marketing Mix

Pegasus' marketing mix comprises the following approaches to pricing, distribution, advertising and promotion, and customer service.

- ***Pricing*** — This will be based on a per-product retail price.
- ***Distribution*** — Initially, Pegasus will use a direct-to-consumer distribution model. Over time, Pegasus will use retailers as well.
- ***Advertising and Promotion*** — Several different methods will be used for the advertising effort.
- ***Customer Service*** — Pegasus will strive to achieve benchmarked levels of customer care.

3.8 Marketing Research

Pegasus tested its products not only with its principals, who are accomplished skaters, but also with the many other dedicated and "newbie" users. The extensive product testing by a wide variety of users provided Pegasus with valuable product feedback and has led to several design improvements.

4.0 Financials

This section will offer the financial overview of Pegasus related to marketing activities. Pegasus will address break-even analysis, sales forecasts, expense forecast, and indicate how these activities link to the marketing strategy.

4.1 Break-even Analysis

The break-even analysis indicates that $7,760 will be required in monthly sales revenue to reach the break-even point.

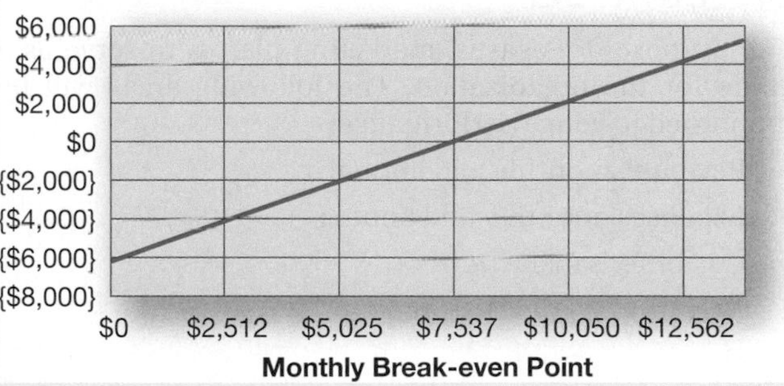

Break-even Analysis
Break-even point is where line intersects with 0

Table 4.1 Break-even Analysis

Break-even Analysis	
Monthly Units Break-even	62
Monthly Sales Break-even	$7,760
Assumptions	
Average Per-Unit Revenue	$125.62
Average Per-Unit Variable Cost	$22.61
Estimated Monthly Fixed Cost	$6,363

4.2 Sales Forecast

Pegasus feels that the sales forecast figures are conservative. It will steadily increase sales as the advertising budget allows. Although the target market forecast (Table 2.1) listed all of the potential customers divided into separate groups, the sales forecast groups customers into two categories: Recreational and Competitive. Reducing the number of categories allows the reader to quickly discern information, making the chart more functional.

4.3 Expense Forecast

The expense forecast will be used as a tool to keep the department on target and provide indicators when corrections/modifications are needed for the proper implementation of the marketing plan.

Table 4.2 Marketing Expense Budget

Marketing Expenses Budget	2008	2009	2010
Web site	$25,000	$8,000	$10,000
Advertisements	$8,050	$15,000	$20,000
Printed Material	$1,725	$2,000	$3,000
Total Sales and Marketing —Expenses	$34,775	$25,000	$33,000
Percent of Sales	6.58%	3.60%	4.14%
Contribution Margin	$398,725	$544,652	$621,202
Contribution Margin/Sales	75.4%	78.40%	77.86%

5.0 Controls

The purpose of Pegasus' marketing plan is to serve as a guide for the organization. The following areas will be monitored to gauge performance:

- Revenue: monthly and annual
- Expenses: monthly and annual
- Customer satisfaction
- New product development

5.1 Implementation

The following milestones identify the key marketing programs. It is important to accomplish each one on time and on budget.

5.2 Marketing Organization

Helen Li will be responsible for the marketing activities.

5.3 Contingency Planning

Difficulties and Risks

- Problems generating visibility, a function of being an Internet-based start-up organization.
- An entry into the market by an already established market competitor.

Worst Case Risks

- Determining that the business cannot support itself on an ongoing basis.
- Having to liquidate equipment or intellectual capital to cover liabilities.

Table 5.1 Milestones

Milestones			Plan		
Milestone	**Start Date**	**End Date**	**Budget**	**Manager**	**Department**
Marketing plan completion	1/1/08	2/1/08	$0	Helen	Marketing
Web site completion	1/1/08	3/15/08	$20,400	outside firm	Marketing
Advertising campaign #1	1/1/08	6/30/08	$3,500	Helen	Marketing
Advertising campaign #2	3/1/08	12/30/08	$4,550	Helen	Marketing
Development of the retail channel	1/1/08	11/30/08	$0	Helen	Marketing
Total			$28,450		

Summary

1. The value delivery process involves choosing (or identifying), providing (or delivering), and communicating superior value. The value chain is a tool for identifying key activities that create value and costs in a specific business.
2. Strong companies develop superior capabilities in managing core business processes such as new-product realization, inventory management, and customer acquisition and retention. Managing these core processes effectively means creating a marketing network in which the company works closely with all parties in the production and distribution chain, from suppliers of raw materials to retail distributors. Companies no longer compete—marketing networks do.
3. According to one view, holistic marketing maximizes value exploration by understanding the relationships between the customer's cognitive space, the company's competence space, and the collaborator's resource space; maximizes value creation by identifying new customer benefits from the customer's cognitive space, utilizing core competencies from its business domain, and selecting and managing business partners from its collaborative networks; and maximizes value delivery by becoming proficient at customer relationship management, internal resource management, and business partnership management.
4. Market-oriented strategic planning is the managerial process of developing and maintaining a viable fit between the organization's objectives, skills, and resources and its changing market opportunities. The aim of strategic planning is to shape the company's businesses and products so that they yield target profits and growth. Strategic planning takes place at four levels: corporate, division, business unit, and product.
5. The corporate strategy establishes the framework within which the divisions and business units prepare their strategic plans. Setting a corporate strategy entails four activities: defining the corporate mission, establishing strategic business units (SBUs), assigning resources to each SBU based on its market attractiveness and business strength, and planning new businesses and downsizing older businesses.
6. Strategic planning for individual businesses entails the following activities: defining the business mission, analyzing external opportunities and threats, analyzing internal strengths and weaknesses, formulating goals, formulating strategy, formulating supporting programs, implementing the programs, and gathering feedback and exercising control.
7. Each product level within a business unit must develop a marketing plan for achieving its goals. The marketing plan is one of the most important outputs of the marketing process.

Application

Marketing Debate—What Good is a Mission Statement?

Virtually all firms have mission statements to help guide and inspire employees as well as signal what is important to the firm to those outside the firm. Mission statements are often the product of much deliberation and discussion. At the same time, some critics claim that mission statements sometimes lack "teeth" and specificity. Moreover, critics also maintain that in many cases, mission statements do not vary much from firm to firm and make the same empty promises.

Take a position: *Mission statements are critical to a successful marketing organization* Versus *Mission statements rarely provide useful marketing value.*

Marketing Discussion

Consider Porter's value chain and the holistic marketing orientation model. What implications do they have for marketing planning? How would you structure a marketing plan to incorporate some of their concepts?

PART 2

Capturing Marketing Insights

fake hurts real. imitations are poorly made, giving you no protection.

Adidas' campaign against counterfeits in the Philippines.

3

Gathering Information and Scanning the Environment

Developing and implementing marketing plans involves a number of decisions. Making those decisions is both an art and science. To provide insights into and inspiration for marketing decision making, companies must possess comprehensive and current information on both macro trends as well as micro effects particular to their business. Holistic marketers recognize that the marketing environment is constantly presenting new opportunities and threats, and they understand the importance of continuously monitoring and adapting to that environment.

Adidas shoes, Louis Vuitton bags, Callaway golf clubs, Intel computer chips. Pick any product from any well-known brand, and chances are that there is a counterfeit version of it in Asia. The World Customs Organization estimates that counterfeiting accounts for 5 to 7 percent of global merchandise trade, the equivalent of as much as $512 billion in lost sales annually. In 2006, EU customs officers seized 253 million fake products at the external borders of the bloc, up from 85 million in 2002. DaimlerChrysler figures that phony Daimler parts have grabbed 30 percent of the market in China, Korea, and Taiwan.

While knockoffs were traditionally of luxury products, they have now extended to consumer products such as Gillette Mach 3 razors and Head & Shoulders shampoo, both Procter & Gamble products. At Unilever, knockoffs of its shampoos, soaps, and teas are growing by 30 percent annually. Reasons for this boom include the Internet which makes it easier to find customers, and the development of cheap, high-quality printing equipment that allows criminals to mass-produce packaging. The latest victim of counterfeiters is the iPhone. In Taiwan, "aifungs" (the Chinese pronunciation for iPhones) were sold six months before the iPhone went on sale in the U.S. The counterfeiter designed the fakes from pictures posted on the Internet before Apple's Chief Executive, Steve Jobs, unveiled the iPhone.

China accounts for nearly two-thirds of these counterfeit goods. Many fakes are getting so good that in some instances, it takes a forensic scientist to distinguish them from the real thing. While the counterfeiters are piling up profits, the MNCs are spending more on stopping them. LVMH Möet Hennessy Louis Vuitton spent more than $16 million annually on investigations, busts, and legal fees.[1]

In this chapter, we will address the following questions:

1. What are the components of a modern marketing information system?
2. What are useful internal records?
3. What is involved in a marketing intelligence system?
4. What are the key methods for tracking and identifying opportunities in the macroenvironment?
5. What are some important macroenvironment developments?

In this chapter, we consider how firms can develop processes to track trends. We also identify a number of important macroenvironment trends. Chapter 4 reviews how marketers can conduct more customized research that addresses specific marketing problems or issues.

Components of a Modern Marketing Information System

Although every manager in an organization needs to observe the outside environment, marketers have two advantages. First, they have disciplined methods for collecting information, including **marketing information systems (MIS)** that furnish the management with rich detail about buyer wants, preferences, and behavior. Second, they spend more time interacting with customers and observing competition.

Motorola—Motorola dispatches teams of market researchers to far-flung locations in China. From this, they discover that even consumers in rural China are becoming more discerning. "In the lower-tier cities, the young people look at value, but they're also very individualistic," says Motorola China boss Michael Tatelman. Thus its designers are devoting more resources to the lower end of the market. For example, Motorola's least expensive phones allow users to download MP3 songs and customize their ringtones. While Motorola does not design phones specifically for China, it is now better at getting the right handsets to each location—bigger supply of cheaper phones in rural areas, and snazzier ones in cities. "The demographic differences have always been there, but we've become more sophisticated in our ability to identify them," Tatelman says.[2]

However, many business firms are not sophisticated about gathering information. Many do not have a marketing research department. Others have a department that limits its work to routine forecasting, sales analysis, and occasional surveys. Many managers complain about not knowing where critical information is located in the company; getting too much information that they cannot use and too little that they really need; getting important information too late; and doubting the information's accuracy. Companies with superior information enjoy a competitive advantage. The company can choose its markets better, develop better offerings, and execute better marketing planning.

Every firm must organize and distribute a continuous flow of information to its marketing managers. Companies study their managers' information needs and design a MIS to meet these needs. An MIS consists of people, equipment, and procedures to gather, sort, analyze, evaluate, and distribute needed, timely, and accurate information to marketing decision makers. A marketing information system is developed from internal company records, marketing intelligence activities, and marketing research. The first two topics are discussed here; the latter topic is reviewed in the next chapter.

The company's MIS should be a cross between what the managers think they need and what they really need, and what is economically feasible. An internal MIS committee can interview a cross-section of marketing managers to discover their information needs. Table 3.1 displays some useful questions.

Table 3.1 Information Needs Probes

1. What decisions do you regularly make?
2. What information do you need to make these decisions?
3. What information do you regularly get?
4. What special studies do you periodically request?
5. What information would you want that you are not getting now?
6. What information would you want daily? Weekly? Monthly? Yearly?
7. What magazines and trade reports would you like to see on a regular basis?
8. What topics would you like to be kept informed of?
9. What data analysis programs would you want?
10. What are the four most helpful improvements that could be made in the present marketing information system?

Internal Records and Marketing Intelligence

Marketing managers rely on internal reports on orders, sales, prices, costs, inventory levels, receivables, payables, and so on. By analyzing this information, they can spot important opportunities and problems.

The Order-to-Payment Cycle

The heart of the internal records system is the order-to-payment cycle. Sales representatives, dealers, and customers send orders to the firm. The sales department prepares invoices and transmits copies to various departments. Out-of-stock items are back-ordered. Shipped items are accompanied by shipping and billing documents that are sent to various departments.

Today's companies need to perform these steps quickly and accurately. Customers favor firms that can promise timely delivery. Customers and sales representatives fax or email their orders. Computerized warehouses quickly fill these orders. The billing department sends out invoices as quickly as possible. More companies are using the Internet and extranets to improve the speed, accuracy, and efficiency of the order-to-payment cycle.

Sales Information Systems

Marketing managers need timely and accurate reports on current sales. Consider 7-Eleven in Japan:

> **7-Eleven**—At the heart of a Japanese 7-Eleven store is an NEC personal computer that not only feeds data about the customer and his purchase, but also helps the store manager track how fast each product is selling. He knows what type of food products to restock between 7 p.m. and 9 p.m. to attract young salaried men. He also knows which areas of his store are contributing the most to sales and profits. Sometimes, a message from 7-Eleven's headquarters is flashed on the screen, telling him of a new drink that is a hit in other stores and may possibly be a hot seller at his store as well.

The 7-Eleven chain in Japan customizes its merchandise using a sophisticated sales information system.

Companies must carefully interpret the sales data so as not to get the wrong signals. Michael Dell gave this illustration: "If you have three yellow Mustangs sitting on a dealer's lot and a customer wants a red one, the salesman may be really good at figuring out how to sell the yellow Mustang. So the yellow Mustang gets sold, and a signal gets sent back to the factory that, hey, people want yellow Mustangs."

Databases, Data Warehousing, and Data Mining

Today, companies organize their information in databases—customer databases, product databases, salesperson databases—and then combine data from the different databases. For example, the customer database will contain every customer's name, address, past transactions, and even demographics and psychographics (activities, interests, and opinions) in some instances. Instead of a company sending a mass "carpet bombing" mailing of a new offer to every customer in its database, it will rank different customers according to purchase recency, frequency, and monetary value (RFM) and send the offer only to the highest scoring customers. Besides saving on mailing expenses, this will often achieve a double-digit response rate.

Coca-Cola—Coca-Cola wanted to maximize the impact of its carbonated soft drink in Japan. It was already very successful with its canned coffee, Georgia. Once, it ran a sweepstakes from a database of 9.5 million Georgia drinkers. From this database, Coca-Cola learnt how young Japanese responded to soft drinks.

Companies warehouse these data and make them easily accessible to decision makers. Further, by hiring analysts skilled in sophisticated statistical methods, they can "mine" the data and garner fresh insights into neglected customer segments, recent customer trends, and other useful information. The customer information can be cross-tabbed with product and salesperson information to yield even deeper insights. To manage all the different databases efficiently and effectively, some firms use business integration software.

Ben & Jerry's—At its headquarters, each pint of Ben & Jerry's ice cream is stamped after manufacture and its tracking number put in an Oracle database. Using Business Objects software, the sales team can see which flavors are generating the most sales. The marketing department can check whether online orders require added philanthropic donations. The finance people can record sales and close their books more quickly. Consumer affairs can match up the pints with the roughly 225 calls and emails the company receives weekly to ensure that there are no systematic problems with any particular ingredient.[3]

The Marketing Intelligence System

The internal records system supplies *results* data, but the marketing intelligence system supplies *happenings* data. A **marketing intelligence system** is a set of procedures and sources managers use to obtain everyday information about developments in the marketing environment. Marketing managers collect marketing intelligence by reading books, newspapers, and trade publications; talking to customers, suppliers, and distributors; monitoring social media on the Internet via online discussion groups, emailing lists and blogs; and meeting other company managers.

A company can take several steps to improve the quality of its marketing intelligence.

- **Train and motivate the sales force to spot and report new developments.** Sales representatives are positioned to pick up information missed by other means, yet they often fail to pass on that information. The company must "sell" its sales force on their importance as intelligence gatherers. Sales representatives should know the types of information to be sent to the various managers. Reliance on the sales force for information is particularly important in rural marketing. Hindustan Unilever faces a situation where India's 600 million rural population is split among 560,000 villages. Only 45 percent of rural Indians can be reached by motorable roads. The company uses its salespeople to visit these villages regularly and find out what products these villagers want.

- **Motivate distributors, retailers, and other intermediaries to pass along important intelligence.** Many companies hire specialists to gather marketing intelligence. Service providers often send mystery shoppers to their stores to assess how employees treat customers. Mystery shoppers for McDonald's discovered that only 46 percent of its U.S. restaurants met internal speed-of-service standards, forcing the company to rethink processes and training.[4] Retailers also use mystery shoppers. They find that stores that consistently score high on service have the best sales. Typical questions their mystery shoppers report on are: (1) How long before a sales associate greeted you? (2) Did the sales associate act as if he or she wanted your business? and (3) Was the sales associate knowledgeable about products in stock?[5]
- **Network externally.** It can purchase competitors' products; attend open houses and trade shows; read competitors' published reports; attend stockholders' meetings; talk to employees, dealers, distributors, suppliers, and freight agents; collect competitors' ads; and look up news stories about competitors.

  Companies can still gain useful information in the field. On a fact-finding trip to Asia for a U.S. textile company, Fuld & Co., a Cambridge consulting firm that specializes in competitive intelligence, snapped a photo of a goat munching grass on a field. This wasn't just any goat, but proof that the rival company's much-heralded new Indonesian plant wasn't where it was rumored to be. Armed with that information, the textile company was able to change its defensive strategy.[6]

  Competitive intelligence gathering must be legal and ethical. Procter & Gamble reportedly paid a multimillion-dollar settlement to Unilever when some external operatives hired as part of a P&G corporate intelligence program to learn about Unilever's hair care products were found to have engaged in such unethical behavior as "dumpster diving."[7]
- **Set up a customer advisory panel.** Members might include representative customers or the company's largest customers or its most outspoken or sophisticated customers. Many business schools have advisory panels made up of alumni and recruiters who provide valuable feedback on the curriculum.
- **Take advantage of government data resources.** Population census and trade data are valuable sources for a first cut about the market.
- **Purchase information from outside suppliers.** Well-known data suppliers include A.C. Nielsen and Taylor Nelson Sofrés. These research firms gather consumer-panel data at a much lower cost than the company can on its own.
- **Use online customer feedback systems to collect competitive intelligence.** Online customer review boards, discussion forums, chat rooms, and blogs can distribute one customer's evaluation of a product or supplier to a large number of other potential buyers and, of course, to marketers seeking information on the competition. Chat rooms allow users to share experiences and impressions, but their unstructured nature makes it difficult for marketers to find relevant messages. Thus some companies have adopted structured systems, such as customer discussion boards or customer reviews (see "Marketing Memo: Clicking on the Competition" for a summary of the major categories of structured online feedback systems).[8]

Some companies circulate marketing intelligence. The staff scans the Internet and major publications, extracts relevant news, and disseminates a news bulletin to marketing managers. They collect and file relevant information and assist managers in evaluating new information.

MARKETING MEMO • CLICKING ON THE COMPETITION

There are four main ways marketers can find relevant online information on competitors' product strengths and weaknesses, and summary comments and overall performance rating of a product, service or supplier.

- ***Independent customer goods and service review forums*** — In the U.S., these forums include Web sites such as Epinions, RateItAll, ConsumerREVIEW.com, and BizRate. Consumer feedback can come from members who provide ratings and feedback to assist other shoppers, and survey results on service quality collected from customers. These sites have the advantage of being independent from the goods and service providers, which may reduce bias.
- ***Distributor or sales agent feedback sites*** — These sites offer both positive and negative product or service reviews, but the stores or distributors have built the sites themselves. Amazon, for instance, offers an interactive feedback opportunity through which buyers, readers, editors, and others may review all products listed in the site, especially books.
- ***Combo-sites offering customer reviews and expert opinions*** — This type of site is concentrated in financial services and high-tech products that require professional knowledge. ZDNet, an online advisor on technology products, offers customer comments and evaluations based on ease of use, features and stability, along with expert reviews. ZDNet summarizes the number of positive and negative evaluations and total download numbers within a certain period (commonly a week or a month) for each software program. The advantage of this type of review site is that a product supplier can compare opinions from the experts with those from consumers.
- ***Customer complaint sites*** — These forums are designed mainly for dissatisfied customers. Reviewers at most opinion sites tend to offer positive comments due to financial incentives and potential lawsuits for slanderous or libelous negative comments. In contrast, some Web sites offer a complaining forum with a moderator. For instance, PlanetFeedback and Complaints.com allow customers to voice unfavorable experiences with specific companies.
- ***Public blogs*** — Tens of millions of blogs exist online and their numbers continue to grow. Consultancy firms analyze blogs and social networks to provide firms with insights into consumer sentiment: drug firms want to know what questions are on patients' minds when they hear about problems with a medication; car companies are looking for better ways to spot defects and work out what to do about them.

Sources: "The Blogs in the Corporate Machine," *Economist*, February 11, 2006, pp. 55–56; and adapted from Robin T. Peterson and Zhilin Yang, "Web Product Reviews Help Strategy," *Marketing News*, April 7, 2004, p. 18.

Analyzing the Macroenvironment

Successful companies recognize and respond profitably to unmet needs and trends.

Needs and Trends

Enterprising individuals and companies manage to create new solutions to unmet needs. FedEx was created to meet the need for next-day mail delivery. Dockers were created to meet the needs of baby-boomers who were unable to wear jeans, but wanted a physically and psychologically comfortable pair of pants at that point of time. Amazon.com was created to offer more choice and information for books and other products.

We can draw distinctions among fads, trends, and megatrends. A **fad** is "unpredictable, short-lived, and without social, economic, and political significance." A company can cash in on a fad such as Tamagotchi or Beanie Babies, but this is more a matter of luck and good timing than anything else.[9]

A **trend** is a direction or sequence of events that has some momentum and durability. Trends are more predictable and durable than fads. A trend reveals the shape of the future and provides many opportunities. For example, the percentage of Asian women wanting fairer skin has risen steadily over the years. Marketers of cosmetics cater to this trend with appropriate products and communications. Christian Dior has a Dior Snow, Origins a Light Snow, and L'Oréal a White Perfect.

Megatrends have been described as "large social, economic, political, and technological changes [that] are slow to form, and once in place, they influence us for some time—between 7 and 10 years, or longer."[10] "Marketing Insight: Megatrends Shaping the Asian Consumer Landscape" lists the forces in play.

MARKETING INSIGHT • MEGATRENDS SHAPING THE ASIAN CONSUMER LANDSCAPE

1. From nation-states to networks as seen in Japan, giving way to overseas Chinese networks.
2. From export-led to consumer-driven economies, with the expanding Asian middle class reaching half a billion consumers.
3. From Western influence to the Asian way. Asia will modernize free of Western welfare statism.
4. From government-driven to market-driven economies, as government controls give way to reliance on the market.
5. From villages to supercities, as agricultural societies move into the Information Age.
6. From labor-intensive to high-technology industries.
7. From male dominance to the emergence of female economic power, as Asian women join the workforce.
8. From West to East, as Asia becomes the center of the world.

Source: John Naisbitt, *Megatrends Asia*, (London, UK: Nicholas Brealey Publishing, 1995).

Trends and megatrends merit close attention. A new product or marketing program is likely to be more successful if it is in line with strong trends rather than opposed to them, but detecting a new market opportunity does not guarantee success, even if it is technically feasible. For example, some companies now sell portable "electronic books," but there may not be enough people interested in reading a book on a computer screen or willing to pay the required price. This is why market research is necessary to determine an opportunity's profit potential.

Identifying the Major Forces

Companies and their suppliers, marketing intermediaries, customers, competitors, and public all operate in a macroenvironment of forces and trends that shape opportunities and pose threats. These forces represent "non-controllables," to which the company must monitor and respond. In the economic arena, companies and consumers are increasingly affected by global forces.

The beginning of the new century brought a series of new challenges: the steep decline of the stock market, which affected savings, investment, and retirement funds; corporate scandals; and the rise of terrorism. These dramatic events were accompanied by the continuation of other, already-existing longer-term trends that have profoundly influenced the global landscape. In 2005, more transistors were produced (and at a lower cost) than grains of rice; the U.S. blog-reading audience is already 20 percent of the size of the newspaper-reading population; and insatiable world oil consumption is expected to rise.[11]

Within the rapidly changing global picture, the firm must monitor six major forces: demographic, economic, social-cultural, natural, technological, and political-legal. We will describe these forces separately, but marketers must pay attention to their interactions, because these will lead to new opportunities and threats. For example, explosive population growth (demographic) leads to more resource depletion and pollution (natural), which leads consumers to call for more laws (political-legal), which stimulate new technological solutions and products (technological), which, if they are affordable (economic), may actually change attitudes and behavior (social-cultural). "Breakthrough Marketing: Google" describes how that company has successfully capitalized on the new marketing environment.

The Demographic Environment

Demographic trends are highly reliable for the short and intermediate run. There is little excuse for a company being suddenly surprised by demographic developments. The Singer Company should have known that its sewing machine business would be hurt in urban areas by smaller families and more working wives, although it is less affected in emerging economies.

The main demographic force that marketers monitor is *population*, because people make up markets. Marketers are keenly interested in the size and growth rate of population in cities, regions, and nations; age distribution and ethnic mix; educational levels; household patterns; and regional characteristics and movements.

BREAKTHROUGH • MARKETING

GOOGLE

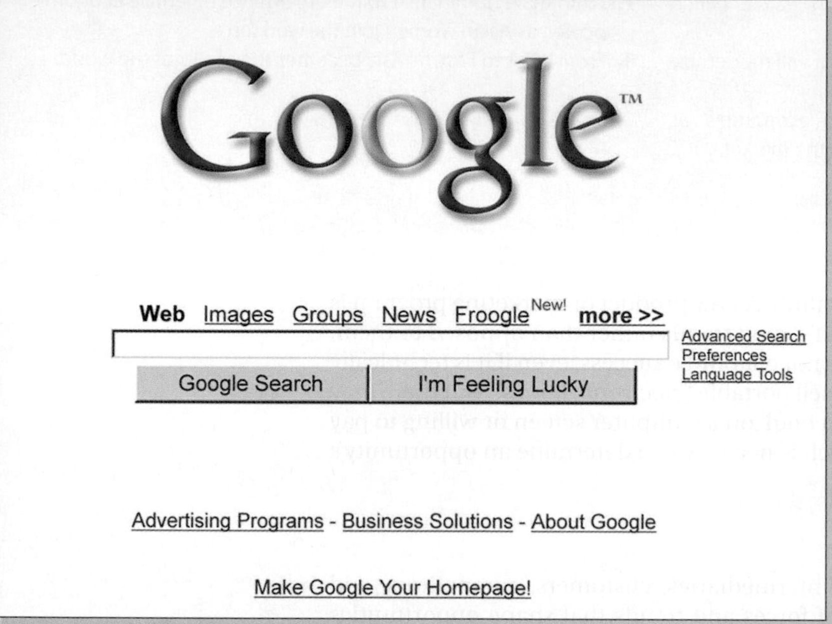

Google has become a business leader in the new marketing environment.

Founded in 1998 by two Stanford University PhD students, search engine Google's name is a play on the word *googol*—the number represented by a 1 followed by 100 zeroes—a reference to the massive quantity of data available online, which the company helps users make sense of. Google's stated corporate mission is "to organize the world's information and make it universally accessible and useful."

The company has become the market leader for search engines through its business focus and constant innovation. As Google grew into a primary destination for Web users searching for information online, it attracted a host of online advertisers. These advertisers drove Google's revenue by buying what are called "search ads," little text-based boxes shown alongside search results that advertisers pay for only when users click on them. Google's search ad program, called AdWords, sells space on its search pages to ads linked with specific keywords. Google auctions off the keyword ads, with the prime key words and prime page locations going to the highest bidder. The advertisers pay only if Internet users click on their ads.

In addition to offering prime online "real estate" for advertisers, Google adds value to advertisers by providing them with a variety of means to better target their ads to users and better understand the effectiveness of their marketing. Google Analytics, which Google provides free to advertisers, provides advertisers with a custom report, or dashboard, detailing how Internet users found the site, what ads they saw and/or clicked on, how they behaved while at the site, and how much traffic was generated. Google client Discount Tire was able to identify where visitors to the site encountered problems that led them to abandon a purchase midstream. After modifying its site and updating its keyword search campaign, Discount Tire measured a 14 percent increase in sales within a week.

With its ability to deploy data that enable up-to-the-minute improvements of a Web marketing program, Google supported a style of marketing where the advertising resources and budget could be constantly monitored and optimized. Google called this approach "marketing asset management," implying that advertising should be managed like assets in a portfolio, with management marshalling certain resources at one time or place online and others at a different time or place, depending on the market conditions. Rather than follow a marketing plan that had been developed months in advance, companies could use the real-time data collected on their campaigns to optimize the campaign's effectiveness by making it more responsive to the market.

Google has augmented its search capabilities with additional services and features for Internet users, including Google Maps, Google Local, Google Finance, Gmail (a Google email service), and Google Video (which was bolstered by the $1.65 billion acquisition of video hosting site YouTube in 2006). These new efforts all offered opportunities for Google to grow by selling the additional targeted advertising space that was created.

Going overseas, Google has to make some adjustments. Previously, Google services in China were poor. The Web site was down 10 percent of the time, and when users were able to reach it, it was slow and sometimes stalled. It resolved this by creating a local presence. Google set up a new site (www.google.cn), but to satisfy authorities in Beijing, Google censored its search services. The new version restricts access to sensitive terms and Web sites.

Sources: <www.google.com>; Catherine P. Taylor, "Google Flex." *Adweek*, March 20, 2006, cover story; Richard Karpinski, "Keywords, Analytics Help Define User Lifetime Value." *Advertising Age*, April 24, 2006, p. S2; Danny Gorog, "Survival Guide," *Herald Sun*, March 29, 2006; Julie Schlosser, "Google." *Fortune*, October 31, 2005, pp. 168–169; Jefferson Graham, "Google's Profit Sails Past Expectations." *USA Today*, October 21, 2005; Andrew McLaughlin, "Google in China." January 27, 2006; <www.googleblog.blogspot.com>; "Google Censors Itself for China." January 25, 2006, <www.news.bbc.co.uk>.

Singer's sewing machines are less popular in urban areas where there are more working women and smaller families. In suburban towns, Singer still see good sales. This Singer store is located in the old part of a Malaysian town.

Worldwide Population Growth

The world population is showing explosive growth: it totaled 6.1 billion in 2000 and will exceed 7.9 billion by the year 2025.[12] Here is an interesting picture:

> *If the world were a village of 1,000 people, it would consist of 520 women and 480 men, 330 children and 60 people over age 65, 10 college graduates, and 335 illiterate adults. The village would contain 52 North Americans, 55 Russians, 84 Latin Americans, 95 East and West Europeans, 124 Africans, and 584 Asians. Communication would be difficult because 165 people would speak Mandarin, 86 English, 83 Hindi/Urdu, 64 Spanish, 58 Russian, and 37 Arabic, and the rest would speak one of over 200 other languages. There would be 329 Christians, 178 Muslims, 132 Hindus, 62 Buddhists, 3 Jews, 167 non-religious, 45 atheists, and 86 others.*[13]

The population explosion has been a source of major concern. Unchecked population growth and consumption could eventually result in insufficient food supply, depletion of key minerals, overcrowding, pollution, and an overall deterioration in the quality of life.

Moreover, population growth is highest in countries and communities that can least afford it. The less developed regions of the world currently account for 76 percent of the world population and are growing at 2 percent per year, whereas the population in the more developed countries is growing at only 0.6 percent per year. In developing countries, the death rate has been falling as a result of modern medicine, but the birth rate has remained fairly stable. Feeding, clothing, and educating children, while also providing a rising standard of living, are nearly impossible in these countries.

Table 3.2 contains the population data of the 12 Asian countries of principal interest in this book, given their greater market potential in the region. Overall, these 12 countries account for nearly three billion consumers, or nearly half the world's population. Five of these countries have population growth rates far above the world's average: Malaysia, Singapore, India, the Philippines, and Indonesia. This, coupled with the large population bases in such nations as India, Indonesia, and Malaysia, appears to offer attractive potential for marketers.

Explosive population growth has major implications for business. A growing population does not mean growing markets unless these markets have sufficient purchasing power.

Table 3.2 Asian Population Statistics

Country	Population (Million)	Population Growth (Percent)
China	1,254	0.9
India	998	1.8
Indonesia	207	1.6
Japan	127	0.1
Vietnam	77	1.3
The Philippines	74	1.7
Thailand	60	0.8
South Korea	47	0.9
Malaysia	23	2.4
Taiwan	22	0.5
Hong Kong	7	1.1
Singapore	4	1.9
Total Asia – 12	**2,900**	**1.3**
The U.S.	278	1.2
European Union	293	0.2
World	5,978	1.4

Source: World Bank, *Little Data Book* (2001).

Nonetheless, companies that carefully analyze their markets can find major opportunities. For example, to curb its skyrocketing population, the Chinese government has passed regulations limiting families to one child. One consequence of these regulations: these children are spoiled and fussed over as never before. Known in China as "Little Emperors," Chinese children are being showered with everything from candy to computers as a result of the "six pocket syndrome." As many as six adults—parents, grandparents, great-grandparents, and aunts and uncles—may be indulging the whims of each child. This trend has encouraged toy companies, such as Japan's Bandai Company, Denmark's Lego Group, and the U.S.'s Hasbro and Mattel to enter the Chinese market aggressively.[14]

Local marketers like BabyCare have also exploited this opportunity.

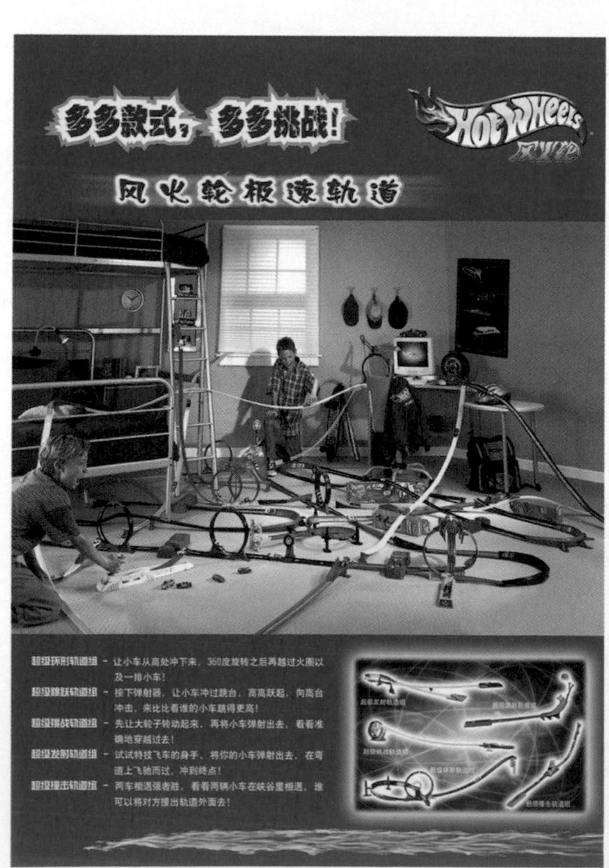

A Mattel ad in Chinese for its Hot Wheels toy. The headline reads: "Hot Wheels performance tracks–great varieties, great challenges!"

BabyCare—This Beijing child-care facility is aimed at helping infants develop their spatial perception and motor skills through play. There are also homework assignments in which mothers are to practice what they have learned with their kids. Consistent with the Chinese proverb that says the first three years are critical to a child's future, BabyCare was formed to exploit China's large market potential for nutritional supplements for expectant mothers and infants. Its facilities educate women on pregnancy and child-rearing, and sell them supplements at the same time. The bulk of its profits come not from classes but from sales of vitamins, baby formula, and educational toys. However, the centers, which offer everything from classes on Lamaze birthing techniques and breast-feeding to how to be a good grandparent, are key to attracting new customers. BabyCare employs 4,500 sales representatives, most of whom are ex-customers.[15]

More importantly, the first batch of Little Emperors has become young adults now and are starting their own families. They never had to worry about money nor did they ever have to share. They grew up on a diet of foreign brands and Western notions of consumption. Additionally, with few local brands to rival Western companies, these young consumers are likely to favor non-Chinese brands.[16]

Population Age Mix

National populations vary in their age mix. At one extreme is Indonesia, a country with a young population and rapid population growth. At the other extreme is Japan, a country with one of the world's oldest populations. Milk, diapers, school supplies, and toys would be important products in Indonesia while Japan's population would consume more adult products.

There is a global trend toward an aging population. According to a survey in *The Economist*, more people will grow old in this century than ever before. It is the start of what the Japanese are calling the Silver Century. The graying of the population is affected by another trend, the widespread fall in fertility rates. In most countries, women are not having enough babies to replace the people who die. While there are currently about 11 working people for every retiree in Asia today, it is estimated that by 2050, the number of workers will fall to four per retiree. There will be a huge problem of having to support a vastly larger population of elderly people. However, future Asian retirees are envisaged to be more affluent, active, cosmopolitan, and youthful than their parents. This implies good prospects for marketers of travel, entertainment, health care, wealth management, and beauty care offerings.

A population can be subdivided into six age groups: preschool, school-age children, teens, young adults aged 25–40, middle-aged adults aged 40–65, and older adults aged 65 and above. Some marketers like to focus on cohorts. **Cohorts** are groups of individuals who are born during the same time period and travel through life together. The "defining moments" they experience as they become adults can stay with them for a lifetime and influence their values, preferences, and buying behaviors. "Marketing Insight: Friends for Life" summarizes one breakdown of cohorts in the U.S. market that can be used for the Asian market.

For marketers, the most populous age groups shape the marketing environment. For example, in Japan, the proportion of over-65-year olds is already 20 percent. By 2020, it will approach 30 percent. This provides a significant business opportunity for elderly facilities, particularly given Japan's becoming less family-oriented. One of the most profitable operators is Message Co.

Message Co.—This Japanese chain facility provides high-quality care, with a focus on individual freedom, at reasonable prices. Its staff is required to treat patients with respect. They must make appointments with their patients, and residents can schedule meals, baths, or recreation whenever they wish. Ultra-efficiency keeps care quality high and costs low. Stopwatch-wielding managers follow workers around and use the data to work out detailed schedules so that no time is wasted. Finally, Message leases, rather than buys, its properties.[17]

Ethnic and Other Markets

Countries also vary in ethnic and racial make-up. At one extreme is Japan, where almost everyone is Japanese; at the other is the U.S., where people come from virtually all nations. Ethnic groups have certain specific wants and buying habits. They prefer certain types of food and clothing. They speak different dialects and languages, which may necessitate the employment of salespeople and telemarketers of different ethnicities and linguistic skills, and use of suitably translated marketing communications materials and appropriate media vehicles.

Yet, marketers must be careful not to overgeneralize about ethnic groups. Within each ethnic group are consumers who are quite different from each other. Asia's ethnic diversity is reflected in Tables 3.3 and 3.4 which display the more than 20 major languages and the

MARKETING INSIGHT • FRIENDS FOR LIFE

Schewe and Meredith have developed a generational cohort segmentation scheme based on the concept that the key defining moments that occur when a person comes of age (roughly ages 17–24) imprints core values that remain largely intact throughout life. They divide the U.S. adult population into seven distinct cohorts, each with its own unique value structure, demographic make-up, and markers.

Depression Cohort

Aged from the mid-80s onwards, this rapidly dwindling group grew up with economic strife and elevated unemployment rates. Financial security—what they most lacked when coming of age—rules their thinking. They are no longer in the workforce, but they have had a clear impact on many of today's management practices.

World War II Cohort

These are people in their early 80s. Sacrifice for the common good was widely accepted among members of the World War II cohort. This cohort was focused on defeating a common enemy during their coming-of-age years, and its members are team-oriented and patriotic.

Postwar Cohort

These individuals experienced a time of remarkable economic growth and social tranquility. They participated in the rise of the middle class, sought a sense of security and stability, and expected prosperous times to continue indefinitely.

Leading-Edge Baby Boomer Cohort

They championed causes such as Greenpeace, civil rights, and women's rights; yet were simultaneously hedonistic and self-indulgent (pot, free love, sensuality).

Trailing-Edge Baby Boomer Cohort

This group witnessed the fall of Vietnam, and experienced the oil embargo and the raging inflation rate. Hence, they are less optimistic about their financial future than the leading-edge boomers.

Generation X Cohort

Many members of this cohort are latch-key children or have parents who divorced. They have delayed marriage and children, and they do not take those commitments lightly. More than other groups, this cohort accepts cultural diversity and puts personal life ahead of work life. Members show a spirit of entrepreneurship unmatched by any other cohort.

N Generation Cohort

The advent of the Internet is a defining event for this cohort, and they will be the engine of growth over the next two decades. Although still a work in progress, their core value structure is different from that of Gen X. They are more idealistic and social-cause oriented, without the cynical, what's-in-it-for-me, free-agent mind-set of many Xers.

Sources: Charles D. Schewe and Geoffrey E. Meredith, "Segmenting Global Markets by Generational Cohort: Determining Motivations by Age." *Journal of Consumer Behavior*, October 4, 2004, pp. 51-63; Geoffrey E. Meredith and Charles D. Schewe, *Managing by Defining Moments: America's 7 Generational Cohorts, Their Workplace Values, and Why Managers Should Care*, (New York: John Wiley, 2002); Geoffrey E. Meredith, Charles D. Schewe, and Janice Karlovich, *Defining Markets Defining Moments*, (New York: John Wiley, 2001).

more than 12 major religions in the 12 Asian countries. Just as significant is the number of major languages and religions in some of the countries, which suggests substantial diversity within their national borders.

Table 3.3 Major Asian Languages

Country	Language(s)
China	Mandarin, Chinese dialects (Cantonese, Shanghainese)
Hong Kong	Chinese dialect (Cantonese), English
India	English, Hindi
Indonesia	Bahasa Indonesia, English, Dutch, local dialects (Javanese)
Japan	Japanese
South Korea	Korean
Malaysia	Bahasa Melayu, English, Chinese dialects, Tamil
The Philippines	Tagalog, English
Singapore	English, Mandarin, Chinese dialects, Bahasa Melayu, Tamil
Taiwan	Mandarin, Taiwanese dialect
Thailand	Thai, English
Vietnam	Vietnamese, English, French, Chinese, Russian

Source: *The CIA World Factbook 2001*, various country statistics.

Table 3.4 Major Asian Religions

Country	Major Religions
China	Taoist, Buddhist, Muslim 2–3%
Hong Kong	Buddhist and Taoist 90%, Christian 8%
India	Hindu 81.3%, Muslim 12%, Christian 2.3%
Indonesia	Muslim 88%, Protestant 5%, Roman Catholic 3%, Hindu 2%, Buddhist 1%, Others 1%
Japan	Mainly Shintoist and Buddhist
South Korea	Christian 27%, Buddhist 23%, Confucianist 0.5%
Malaysia	Muslim 60.4%, Buddhist 19.1%, Christian 9.2%, Hindu 6.3%, Taoist 2.6%, Others 2.4%
The Philippines	Roman Catholic 82.9%, Protestant 5.4%, Muslim 4.6%
Singapore	Buddhist 42.5%, Muslim 14.9%, Christian 14.6%, Taoist 9.5%, Hindu 4%
Taiwan	Buddhist, Confucianist, and Taoist 93%
Thailand	Buddhist 95%, Muslim 3.8%, Christian 0.5%
Vietnam	Buddhist 50%, Catholic and Protestant 30%, Muslim, Caodaist, and Harmonist 20%

Source: PriceWaterCoopers, *From New Delhi to New Zealand*, (October 2002).

Educational Groups

The population in any society falls into five educational groups: illiterates, high school dropouts, high school degree holders, college degree holders, and professional degree holders. In Japan, 99 percent of the population is literate, whereas the rate is much lower in less developed countries and rural communities. In India, for example, 35 percent of children in fifth grade cannot read or write. Some 75 percent of those enrolled drop out by 8th grade, and 85 percent quit by 12th grade. Less than half of those remaining graduate.[18] However, this still translates to some 100,000 Indians heading to the country's 975 private engineering colleges alone each year. As a result, the student loan market in India is burgeoning, given that the typical urban middle-class household earns $800 monthly, while the tuition fees can amount to $9,000 over 4 years.[19] The desire for Asians to upgrade their knowledge and skills spell a high demand for quality books, magazines, and educational programs in the region. Many universities have established offshore campuses in various Asian countries or have partnered local schools to introduce joint degree and executive programs. Online courses such as those offered by Universitas 21 Global, a consortium of leading research-intensive universities, have also been launched.

Household Patterns

The "traditional household" consists of a husband, wife, and children (and sometimes grandparents). In Asia, extended families are common. In the Indian subcontinent, for example, the household may also include dependent brothers and sisters. In some countries, there may be "non-traditional" households which include single live-alones, adult live-togethers of one or both sexes, single-parent families, childless married couples, and empty-nesters. More people are divorcing or separating, choosing not to marry, marrying later, or marrying without the intention to have children. Each group has a distinctive set of needs and buying habits. For example, people in the SSWD group (Single, Separated, Widowed, Divorced) need smaller apartments; inexpensive and smaller appliances, furniture, and furnishings; and smaller-size food packages. Marketers must increasingly consider the special needs of non-traditional households, because they are growing rapidly.

Married couple households have slipped among the more developed Asian economies. Asians are delaying marriage longer than ever, cohabitating in greater numbers, forming more same-sex partnerships, living far longer, and remarrying less after splitting up. But singles can also have significant buying power and spend more on themselves than those who live in larger households.

Geographical Shifts in Population

This is a period of great migratory movements between and within countries. One particularly Asian phenomenon that made impact was in 1997 when Hong Kong, then a British colony, was reverted to China. The migration of Hong Kongers to other countries such as Australia, Britain, Canada, Singapore, and the U.S. brought about increased demand for housing and education, as well as marketing sensitivities to the likes and dislikes of these immigrants.

Migration also occurs under more normal circumstances. For example, the establishment of Special Economic Zones along coastal China led many inlanders moving to such cities as Shenzhen. Meanwhile, neighboring Hong Kongers have also flocked to the city for its better job prospects and lower cost of living. This has led to a narrowing of property prices between the two cities, and the launch of more housing projects in Shenzhen. The entry of China into the World Trade Organization may also see the influx of migrants and the return of those who had left China earlier. Forward-looking companies and entrepreneurs are taking advantage of the growth in immigrant populations and marketing specifically to these new and successful members of the population.

Other Major Macroenvironments

Other macroenvironment forces profoundly affect the fortunes of marketers. Here we review developments in the economic, social-cultural, natural, technological, and political-legal environments.

Economic Environment

The available purchasing power in an economy depends on current income, prices, savings, debt, and credit availability. Marketers must pay careful attention to trends affecting purchasing power because they can have a strong impact on business, especially for companies whose products are geared to high-income and price-sensitive consumers.

INCOME DISTRIBUTION

There are four types of industrial structures: *subsistence economies* like Laos (few opportunities for marketers); *raw-material-exporting economies* like Brunei (oil), with good markets for equipment, tools, supplies, and luxury goods for the rich; *industrializing economies* like China and India, where a new upper class and a growing middle class demand new types of goods; and *industrial economies* like Japan which are rich markets for all sorts of goods.

In a global economy, marketers need to pay attention to the shifting income distribution in countries, particularly countries where affluence levels are rising.

India—With its surfeit of low-cost, high-IQ, English-speaking employees, India is snapping up programming and call-center jobs once held by Americans, in a wave of outsourcing that shows no signs of stopping. While India's ascendance inevitably means lost jobs and anguish for American white-collar workers, it also means a larger market for American and Western goods—and anguish for traditional Indian families. Along with training in American accents and geography, India's legions of call-center employees are absorbing new ideas about family, material possessions, and romance. "I call these kids 'liberalization children'," says Rama Bijapurkar, a Mumbai-based marketing consultant. "This generation has a hunger in the belly for achievement." Liberalization children are questioning conservative traditions such as arranged marriages and no public kissing. They want to watch Hollywood movies, listen to Western music, chat on mobile phones, buy on credit—rather than saving—and eat out in restaurants or cafés. And they are being targeted relentlessly by companies that have waited to see India develop a Western-style consumer class.[20]

Sometimes, growing affluence hides a hidden struggle as the following example shows:

Taiwan's middle class—Consumption of mid-level products in Taiwan is decreasing even though Taiwan's overall economic growth is favorable and unemployment stays around 4 percent. The middle class has cut down on extras such as gym memberships, travel, and movies as wages stagnate and jobs move to China. Sales of cars have decreased.[21]

Marketers often distinguish countries with five different income-distribution patterns: (1) very low incomes, (2) mostly low incomes, (3) very low, very high incomes, (4) low, medium, high incomes, and (5) mostly medium incomes.

Consider the market for Lamborghinis, an automobile costing more than $150,000. The market would be very small in countries with type (1) or (2) income patterns. One of the largest single markets for Lamborghinis turns out to be Indonesia (income pattern (3)—one of the poorer countries in Asia, but one with enough wealthy families to afford expensive cars.

Aside from cross-national income differences, companies must also consider intra-country variations in income. Procter & Gamble has won over consumers in China's hinterlands with a budget detergent called Tide Clean White, while holding onto city consumers with the more expensive Tide Triple Action. General Motors targets the wealthiest Chinese with the Cadillac, middle management with the Buick Excelle, office workers with the Chevrolet Spark, and rural consumers with the Wuling minivan. Similarly, Lenovo not only manufactures PCs costing $2,000 or more that double as home entertainment centers, but also simple machines costing a few hundred dollars for poorer families who want their children to be computer literate. Geely makes the $17,000 Mybo as a family sedan for city drivers, while the $3,700 Haoqing is aimed at recent college graduates buying their first car.[22]

SAVINGS, DEBT, AND CREDIT AVAILABILITY

Consumer expenditures are affected by savings, debt, and credit availability.

The Japanese have a high savings rate, about 13 percent of their income, or nearly three times more than U.S. consumers. Despite such a high savings rate, the 1990s recession ate into Japanese pockets and marketers responded accordingly. Minicars such as the Suzuki Wagon R and utility wagons—which are safe and energy efficient—boomed. Muji, which sells a range of well-made but generic clothing, furniture, and household goods, did well too. The recession also led to an increased preference for eating in. 7-Eleven Japan increased its share of the processed food market as well as branched out into offering such services as easing bill payments, dispensing cash, and parcel delivery.[23] Many retailers established 100-yen (85-cent) stores, including am/pm Japan, Three F, Lawson 100, as well as 24-hour chains like Shop 99 and Hyper Convenience USMart.[24]

Social-cultural Environment

Society shapes the beliefs, values, and norms that largely define these tastes and preferences. People absorb, almost unconsciously, a worldview that defines their relationships to themselves, to others, to organizations, to society, to nature, and to the universe.

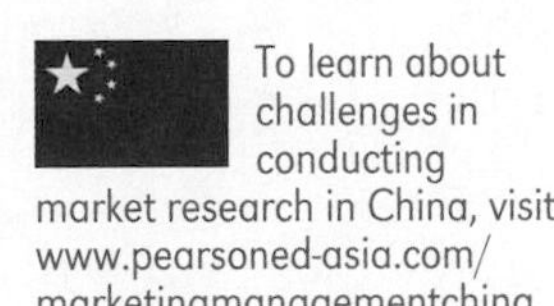

To learn about challenges in conducting market research in China, visit www.pearsoned-asia.com/marketingmanagementchina.

- ***Views of themselves*** — People vary in the relative emphasis they place on self-gratification. Marketers must recognize that there are many different groups with different views of themselves. Grey Global's survey of young Indians and Chinese found they were overwhelmingly positive about the future, believed success was in their hands, and viewed products as status symbols. Over 60 percent viewed themselves as individualists.[25] Similarly, young Japanese also consider themselves to be individualists, with attendant marketing implications:

More and more Japanese teenagers view themselves as individualists these days.

Levi's—Levi's found that Japanese teenagers were cynical of advertising and perceived Levi's jeans as any other pair of jeans. Levi's thus launched its Engineered Jeans with Japanese pop star, Takuya Kimura. This was followed by a physically interactive campaign involving Japanese teenagers expressing their creativity, individuality, and originality—values consistent with Levi's. The world's largest photocopier, big enough to accommodate a human being, was used to this end. Pop stars and Levi's customers were invited to hop onto the copier to create their own completely original poster ad. The campaign became self-generating as each poster was unique. People came in, bought a pair of Levi's, climbed up onto the copier, and expressed their originality. Each printout became an instant point-of-sale poster expressing the customer's and Levi's view of themselves as being original and unique. The campaign was a success as Levi's brand image as an "Individual" rose from 29 to 44 percent over the campaign period.

- ***Views of others*** — People are concerned about the homeless, crime and victims, and other social problems. They would like to live in a more humane society. At the same time, people are seeking out their "own kind" and avoiding strangers. They hunger for serious and long-lasting relationships with a few others. These trends portend a growing market for social-support products and services that promote direct relations between human beings, such as health clubs, cruises, and religious activities. They also suggest a growing market for "social surrogates," things that allow people who are alone to feel that they are not, such as television, home video games, and chat rooms on the Internet.
- ***Views of organizations*** — People vary in their attitudes toward corporations, government agencies, trade unions, and other organizations. Most people are willing to work for these organizations, but there has been an overall decline in organizational loyalty. Company downsizings and corporate accounting scandals have bred cynicism and distrust. Many people today see work not as a source of satisfaction, but as a required chore to earn money to enjoy their non-work hours. This outlook has several marketing implications. Companies need to find new ways to win back consumer and employee confidence. They need to make sure that they are good corporate citizens and that their consumer messages are honest.
- ***Views of society*** — People vary in their attitudes toward their society. Some defend it (preservers), some run it (makers), some take what they can from it (takers), some want to change it (changers), some are looking for something deeper (seekers), and some want to leave it (escapers).[26] Consumption patterns often reflect social attitude. Makers tend to be high achievers who eat, dress, and live well. Changers usually live more frugally, drive smaller cars, and wear simpler clothes. Escapers and seekers are a major market for movies, music, surfing, and camping.

- ***Views of nature*** — People vary in their attitudes toward nature. Some feel subjugated by it, others feel in harmony with it, and still others seek mastery over it. A long-term trend has been humankind's growing mastery of nature through technology. Others are concerned with nature's fragility and finite resources. They recognize that nature can be destroyed by human activities. Among other business opportunities, this has led to eco-tour operators packaging tours to wilderness areas.
- ***Views of the universe*** — People vary in their beliefs about the origin of the universe and their place in it. Asia is multireligious. There are Buddhists, Christians, Hindus, Muslims, and Taoists. However, the extent of religious conviction and practice varies. Those who are not strong in their religious orientation seek self-fulfillment and immediate gratification. At the same time, every trend seems to breed a countertrend, as indicated by a worldwide rise in religious fundamentalism.

Other cultural characteristics of interest to marketers are the persistence of core cultural values and the existence of subcultures.

HIGH PERSISTENCE OF CORE CULTURAL VALUES

The people living in a particular society hold many *core beliefs* and values that tend to persist. Most Asians still believe in hard work, filial piety, getting married, and education. Core beliefs and values are passed on from parents to children and are reinforced by major social institutions—schools, religious organizations, businesses, and governments. *Secondary beliefs* and values are more open to change. Believing in the institution of marriage is a core belief; believing that people should wed early is a secondary belief. Marketers have more chance of changing secondary values than core values. Thus, family-planning marketers could make some headway arguing that people should get married later, rather than that they should not get married at all.

The modern and traditional in Asia: A Coca-Cola vending machine next to a traditional Chinese temple.

EXISTENCE OF SUBCULTURES

Each society contains **subcultures**, groups with shared values emerging from their special life experiences or circumstances. Japan's Harajuku Kids and Korea's Orange Youths represent subcultures who share common beliefs, preferences, and behaviors. To the extent that subcultural groups exhibit different wants and consumption behavior, marketers can choose particular subcultures as target markets.

Marketers sometimes reap unexpected rewards in targeting subcultures. Marketers have always loved teenagers because they are society's trendsetters in fashion, music, entertainment, ideas, and attitudes. Marketers also know that if they attract someone as a teen, there is a good chance they will keep the person as a customer later in life. Another rising submarket is the metrosexuals.

Shah Rukh Khan popularized the metrosexual trend in India. His image has led to several endorsements including this one by Hyundai.

Metrosexuals in India—Personal care companies are targeting Indian men as rising incomes allow them to buy more deodorants and shaving gels. Metrosexuals—urban, heterosexual men who pay close attention to grooming and fashion—were popularized in India by Bollywood actors such as Shah Rukh Khan. The growing attention to male grooming in India mirrors a trend in North America and Europe. While there is still a social stigma against male grooming products, there is a growing trend. A Gillette survey found that urban Indian men spend 20 minutes in front of the mirror each morning compared to women's 18. The fastest growing segment of the male personal care market is toiletries—grooming products other than shaving gels. Products such as Brylcreem Talc and Helen Curtis India's Park Avenue International Soap are garnering sales. Emami, which makes beauty and health-care products, developed its whitening cream for men because surveys showed they were consuming 30 percent of the women's version.[27]

Natural Environment

The deterioration of the natural environment is a major global concern. In many world cities, air and water pollution have reached dangerous levels. There is great concern about "greenhouse gases" in the atmosphere due to the burning of fossil fuels, about the depletion of the ozone layer due to certain chemicals, and about growing shortages of water. However, in many less developed Asian countries, such environmental concern is lacking. Air, water, and noise pollution are common.

Imposing new regulations may hit certain industries very hard. Steel companies and public utilities in some countries like the U.S. have had to invest heavily in pollution-control equipment and more environmentally-friendly fuels. The auto industry has had to introduce expensive emission controls in cars. The soap industry has had to increase its products' biodegradability. The major hope is that companies will adopt practices that will protect the natural environment. Great opportunities await companies and marketers who can create new solutions that promise to reconcile prosperity with environmental protection. Consider how the auto industry has adjusted to environmental concerns.[28]

The Toyota Prius, once scoffed at by auto experts, is enjoying brisk sales as consumers become increasingly concerned with the environment.

Toyota Prius—Some auto experts scoffed when Toyota launched its Prius sedans with hybrid gas-and-electric engines in 2001 and predicted sales of 300,000 cars within five years. But by 2004, the Prius was such a huge hit in the U.S. that it had a six-month waiting list. Toyota's winning formula consists of a powerful electric motor and the ability to quickly switch power sources—resulting in 55 miles per gallon for city and highway driving—with the roominess and power of a family sedan and an eco-friendly design and look, for a little over $20,000. The lesson? Products that consumers see as good for the environment and that are functionally successful can offer enticing options. Toyota is now rolling out hybrids throughout its auto line-up, and U.S. automakers have followed suit. It recently announced that it will introduce plugged-in cars by 2010.

Consumers often appear conflicted about the natural environment. Young people especially are more likely to feel that nothing that they do personally makes a difference. Increasing the number of green products that are bought requires breaking consumers' loyalty habits, overcoming consumer skepticism about the motives behind the introduction of green products and their quality level, and changing consumer attitudes about the role they play in environmental protection (see "Marketing Insight: Green Marketing").

MARKETING INSIGHT • GREEN MARKETING

Although environmental issues have long affected marketing practices, especially in Europe, their relevance has increased recently though they have been muted in Asia. Some "environmentally-friendly" products and marketing programs have appeared to capitalize on consumers' perceived increased sensitivity to environmental issues.

From a branding perspective, however, "green marketing" programs have not been entirely successful. In a study conducted by environmentalists, Toshiba and Acer received low scores of 22 and 39, respectively, for not being environmentally-friendly. In contrast, Asian companies praised for their green marketing include Sony, Samsung, and LG. They have committed to reducing, substituting, and eliminating, wherever possible, the use of substances that are potentially hazardous to the environment.

What obstacles have marketers of green sales pitches encountered over the last decade?

- ***Overexposure and lack of credibility*** — So many companies made environmental claims that the public became skeptical of their validity and consider them as marketing gimmicks.
- ***Consumer behavior*** — Studies have shown that most consumers are not willing to pay a premium or give up the benefits of other alternatives to choose green products. For example, some consumers dislike the performance, appearance, or texture of recycled paper and household products. Others are unwilling to give up the convenience of disposable products such as diapers.
- ***Poor implementation*** — Many firms did a poor job implementing their green marketing programs. Products were poorly designed in terms of environmental worthiness, overpriced, and inappropriately promoted. Some ads failed to make the connection between what the company was doing for the environment and how it affected individual consumers.

However, there are ways to avoid such green marketing myopia. These include:

Consumer Value Positioning

- Design environmental products to perform as well as (or better than) alternatives.
- Promote and deliver the consumer-desired value of environmental products and target relevant consumer market segments (such as market health benefits among health-conscious consumers).
- Broaden mainstream appeal by bundling (or adding) consumer-desired value into environmental products (such as fixed pricing for subscribers of renewable energy).

Calibration of Consumer Knowledge

- Educate consumers with marketing messages that connect environmental product attributes with desired consumer value (e.g., "pesticide-free produce is healthier"; "energy-efficiency saves money"; or "solar power is convenient").
- Frame environmental product attributes as "solutions" for consumer needs (e.g., "rechargeable batteries offer longer performance").
- Create engaging and educational Internet sites about environmental products' desired consumer value (e.g., Tide Coldwater's interactive Web site allows visitors to calculate their likely annual money savings based on their laundry habits, utility source (gas or electricity), and zip code location).

Credibility of Product Claims

- Employ environmental product and consumer benefit claims that are specific, meaningful, unpretentious, and qualified (i.e., compared with comparable alternatives or likely usage scenarios).
- Procure product endorsements or eco-certifications from trustworthy third parties, and educate consumers about the meaning behind those endorsements and eco-certifications.
- Encourage consumer evangelism via consumers' social and Internet communication networks with compelling, interesting, and/or entertaining information about environmental products (e.g., Tide's "Coldwater Challenge" Web site included a map of the United States, so visitors could track and watch their personal influence spread when their friends requested a free sample).

There have been some notable green marketing successes through the years. McDonald's has introduced several well-publicized environmental initiatives such as unbleached paper carry-out bags and replacing polystyrene foam sandwich clamshells with paper wraps and lightweight recycled boxes.

Sources: Jacquelyn A. Ottman, *Green Marketing: Opportunity for Innovation*, 2nd ed., (Chicago: NTC/Contemporary Publishing Company, 1998); Jacquelyn A. Ottman, Edwin R. Stafford, and Cathy L. Hartman, "Avoiding Green Marketing Myopia." *Environment*, June 2006, pp. 22–36; Geoffrey Fowler, "Green Sales Pitch Isn't Moving Many Products." *Wall Street Journal*, March 6, 2002, p. B4; Lynn J. Cook, "Our Electrons are Greener." *Forbes*, June 23, 2003, p. 101; Kevin Lane Keller, *Strategic Brand Management*, 3rd ed., (Upper Saddle River, NJ: Prentice Hall, 2007); Maggie Jackson, "Earth-Friendly Company Changes Come From One 'Green Champion' At A Time," *Boston Globe*, May 9, 2004, p. G1; Sam Varghese. "Green Group Urges Dirty Computer Boycott." <www.smh.com.au>, June 8, 2005.

Technological Environment

One of the most dramatic forces shaping people's lives is technology. Technology has released such wonders as penicillin, open-heart surgery, and the birth control pill. It has released such horrors as the hydrogen bomb, nerve gas, and the submachine gun. It has also released such mixed blessings as the automobile and video games.

Every new technology is a force for "creative destruction." Computers hurt the typewriter industry, xerography hurt the carbon paper business, autos hurt the railroads, and MP3s hurt the music industry. Instead of moving into the new technologies, many old industries fought or ignored them, and their businesses declined. Yet it is the essence of market capitalism to be dynamic and tolerate the creative destructiveness of technology as the price of progress.

Look at Dell, Hewlett-Packard, Apple, and Microsoft. According to some, "smart" mobile phones will eventually eclipse the PC.

Smart phones—"One day, two or three billion people will have mobile phones, and they are all not going to have PCs," says Jeff Hawkins, inventor of the Palm Pilot and chief technology officer for PalmOne. "The mobile phone will become their digital life," Hawkins predicts. After a slow start, mobile phones have become more ubiquitous—there are 1.5 billion in the world today—and smarter. Today's mobile phones are used to send email, browse the Web, take pictures, play video games, and even have Global Positioning Systems in place. Hawkins predicts that within the next few decades, all phones will be mobile phones, capable of receiving voice and Internet signals at broadband speeds, and that mobile phone bills will shrink to a few dollars a month as phone companies pay off their investment in new networks. New smart phones include Palm's pocket-size Treo600, with a tiny keyboard, a built-in digital camera and slots for added memory, and Motorola's MPx, which features a "dual-hinge" design. The handset opens in one direction and appears to be a regular phone, but it also flips open on another axis to look like an email device, with the expanded phone keypad serving as a small QWERTY keypad.[29] The latest iPhone 3G combines three products in one—a phone, a widescreen iPod, and an Internet device.

The economy's growth rate is affected by the number of major new technologies that are discovered. Unfortunately, technological discoveries do not arise evenly through time—the railroad industry created a lot of investment, and then investment petered out until the auto industry emerged. Later, radio created a lot of investment, which then petered out until television appeared. In the time between major innovations, an economy can stagnate. They involve less risk, but they also divert research effort away from major breakthroughs.

New technology also creates major long-run consequences that are not always foreseeable. The contraceptive pill, for example, led to smaller families, more working wives, and larger discretionary incomes—resulting in higher expenditures on vacation travel, durable goods, and luxury items. Here is one technology that gives mothers more quality time:

Yujin Robotics—Korean robot maker, Yujin Robotics, introduced iRobi, a home robot, to alleviate a mother's chores. It can sing, dance, and teach English to young children. And when a mother is out, she can use a wireless link to peek in on things through the robot's video camera eyes and send video messages to her children through an embedded monitor.[30]

The marketer should monitor the following trends in technology: the pace of change, the opportunities for innovation, varying R&D budgets, and increased regulation.

ACCELERATING PACE OF CHANGE

Many of today's common products were not available 40 years ago. Electronic researchers are building smarter chips to make our cars, homes, and offices more responsive to changing conditions. More ideas than ever are in the works, and the time between the appearance of new ideas and their successful implementation is all but disappearing. So is the time between introduction and peak production. Apple quickly ramped up in a little over five years to sell 23.5 million iPods in 2006.

UNLIMITED OPPORTUNITIES FOR INNOVATION

Some of the most exciting work is being done in biotechnology, computers, microelectronics, telecommunications, robotics, and designer materials. Researchers are working on AIDS cures, happiness pills, painkillers, totally safe contraceptives, and non-fattening foods. They are designing robots for firefighting, underwater exploration, and home nursing.

> **Samsung**—In an ambitious endeavor, Samsung has launched a digital home business. In Korea, Samsung has 6,000 networked homes that are outfitted with Internet-enabled ovens, refrigerators, security cameras, and wall-mounted flat panel displays. Samsung is looking to take the idea abroad. Wiring homes in the U.S. will cost from $2,000 to $10,000, making adoption relatively affordable. However, besides overcoming a few technical challenges, Samsung must also contend with consumers who worry about the complexity or even the need for such products. But experts look to the further penetration of broadband access to propel the adoption of the digital home as consumers learn to access digital media and commerce from more devices.[31]

Companies are already harnessing the power of *virtual reality* (VR), the combination of technologies that allows users to experience three-dimensional, computer-generated environments through sound, sight, and touch. Virtual reality has already been applied to gathering consumer reactions to new automobile designs, kitchen layouts, exterior home designs, and other potential offerings.

VARYING R&D BUDGETS

Although the U.S. leads the world in annual R&D expenditures, Japan is fast increasing its R&D expenditures, mostly on non-defense-related research in physics, biophysics, and computer science. Many companies are content to put their money into copying competitors' products and making minor feature and style improvements. Even basic-research companies such as DuPont, Bell Laboratories, and Pfizer are proceeding cautiously, and more research directed toward major breakthroughs is being conducted by consortiums of companies rather than by single companies.

INCREASED REGULATION OF TECHNOLOGICAL CHANGE

As products become more complex, the public needs to be assured of their safety. Consequently, government agencies' powers to investigate and ban potentially unsafe products have been expanded. Safety and health regulations have also increased in the areas of food, automobiles, clothing, electrical appliances, and construction. Marketers must be aware of these regulations when proposing, developing, and launching new products.

Political-Legal Environment

Political and legal environment is composed of laws, government agencies, and pressure groups that influence and limit various organizations and individuals. Sometimes, these laws also create new opportunities for business. For example, a recycling law would give the recycling industry a major boost and spur the creation of new companies making new products from recycled materials. Four major trends deal with the increase in business legislation, the growth of special-interest groups, market reform, and corruption.

INCREASE IN BUSINESS LEGISLATION

Business legislation has four main purposes: (1) to protect companies from unfair competition, (2) to protect consumers from unfair business practices, (3) to protect the interests of society from unbridled business behavior, and (4) to charge businesses with the social costs created by their products or production processes.

A major purpose of business legislation and enforcement is to charge businesses with the social costs created by their products or production processes. A central concern is this: At what point do the costs of regulation exceed the benefits? The laws are not always administered fairly; regulators and enforcers may be lax or overzealous. Although each new law may have a legitimate rationale, it may have the unintended effect of sapping initiative and retarding economic growth.

India's pharmaceutical industry—India passed a patent protection law in 2005 to bring its legislation in line with World Trade Organization norms. This means that Indian companies can no longer ignore the patents of MNC drug companies and produce unlicensed generics. This tougher patent protection law has spurred rapid growth in new drug research. India has more than 50 drug research centers and more are expected to be set up. Besides selling licensed generics, these Indian companies also want to have their own branded, patented drugs.[32]

Legislation affecting businesses has increased steadily over the years. Governments worldwide have been examining and enacting laws covering competitive behavior, product standards, product liability, and commercial transactions. Others have passed strong consumer protection legislation: Thailand requires food processors selling national brands to market lower price brands as well, so that low-income consumers can find economy brands. In India, food companies need special approval to launch brands that duplicate what already exists on the market such as another cola drink or brand of rice. However, marketers can sometimes get around regulations as the following example illustrates:

Dahongying—Tobacco advertising is banned in China. Yet Dahongying, which sells cigarettes, has its name regularly seen on TV, billboards, and in-store displays. This is because Dahongying trumpets the company's other similarly-named businesses in trading and education. It has even built libraries named Dahongying in China's rural schools.[33]

Regulations on counterfeiting are also increasing. Asian exporters are expected to face tougher European Union customs controls. Popular counterfeited brands include Chanel, Christian Dior, Louis Vuitton, Timberland, and Rolex. Beijing's Silk Market, Bangkok's Silom Street market, and Shenzhen's shopping malls are abundant with counterfeit products, although Shanghai's Xiangyang Market has been disbanded. Even clones of fast-food restaurants exist. Although the production and sale of counterfeits is illegal, the rules against purchasing them are vague. While it is technically illegal to buy counterfeits, it is not a crime if a buyer is not aware or claims not to know the items are fake, or is not buying them for trade or business.

Sometimes, legislation is passed to protect home industries. In Asia, such practices are more prevalent where local businesses may be less competitive than multinationals.

KFC—The KFC outlet in Bangalore was closed for alleged overuse of monosodium glutamate and its New Delhi outlet was closed for allegedly containing harmful chemicals and having unhygienic practices. However, rumors abound that the reason for the closures was to protect local food retailers.

Cisco—While Cisco continues its commitment to China, it is concerned over the Chinese government's provision of loans and other support to favored domestic rivals such as Huawei Technologies and Harbor Networks. Further, China's less-than-rigorous intellectual property protection, which puts Cisco's patented products in jeopardy, is another sore point, although Cisco has successfully sued Huawei for intellectual property theft. Instead, Cisco has expanded its operations in India. It believes that the deregulation of India's telecom industry will generate huge demand for broadband networks. Also, unlike China, there appears to be no homegrown rival to Cisco in India.[34]

In Shanghai, a clone of KFC operates, right down to the colors and Colonel Sanders icon.

In Beijing, the clone has even opened an establishment next to KFC.

To counter these protectionistic policies, some foreign companies introduce new local brands. Asia Pacific Breweries has a "made-in-Thailand" Heineken beer as well as a "made-in-Cambodia" Tiger beer. During the Asian economic crisis, many MNCs sought local sourcing not only for cost effectiveness, but also because they wanted to convince local customers that they were "local" companies. For example, Fila Korea emphasized that all its fabric and materials were from domestic sources.

Laws have also been eased to encourage business. China has relaxed its restrictions on foreign ad agencies. Previously, foreign ad agencies had to operate as joint ventures with local partners. That restriction was lifted in 2005 under commitments China made when it joined the World Trade Organization.

Marketers must have a good working knowledge of the major laws protecting competition, consumers, and society. Some companies have legal review procedures to guide their marketing managers, and as more business takes place in cyberspace, marketers must establish new parameters for doing business ethically.

GROWTH OF SPECIAL-INTEREST GROUPS

The number and power of special-interest groups have increased over time. One important force affecting business is the **consumerist movement**—an organized movement of citizens and government to strengthen the rights and powers of buyers in relation to sellers. Consumerists have advocated and, in some countries, won the right to know the true interest cost of a loan, the true cost per standard unit of competing brands (unit pricing), the basic ingredients in a product, the nutritional quality of food, the freshness of products, and the true benefits of a product.

With consumers increasingly willing to swap personal information for customized products from firms—as long as they can be trusted—privacy issues will continue to be a public policy issue.[35] Consumer concerns are that they will be robbed or cheated; that private information will be used against them; that someone will steal their identity; that they will be bombarded with solicitations; and that children will be targeted.[36] Several companies have established consumer affairs departments to help formulate policies and respond to consumer complaints. Companies are careful to answer their emails and to resolve and learn from any customer complaints.

Clearly, new laws and growing numbers of pressure groups have put more restraints on marketers. Marketers have to clear their plans with the company's legal, public relations, public affairs, and consumer affairs departments. For instance, Japan's product liability law empowers consumers to sue ad agencies for creating ads that mislead or project wrong images. Thus agencies like Dentsu are providing more detailed instructions on product use and placing warning labels more prominently.

MARKET REFORM

Governments may also introduce market reforms to be consistent with their nation-building agenda. These reforms take time to bear fruit and businesses need to be patient, particularly in less developed Asian countries. Vietnam's economic reform program, *doi moi*, has been criticized for being too slow with too much bureaucracy, overregulation, and inefficiency. Further, joint ventures fail because many foreign businesses felt that their Vietnamese counterparts do not understand practical business processes. In China, the corporatization of state-owned enterprises has led to burgeoning non-state enterprises (*qiye jituan*) that do not promise lifetime employment and income benefits. As government subsidies are withdrawn and benefits such as free housing removed, the reform saw the property market booming as urban workers began to buy private residential property.

CORRUPTION

Observations have been made that corruption among Asian political officials and businesspeople is rife. Such corruption may hinder economic development as bribes have to be paid to get the smallest of clearances. In one Indonesian incident, there were 96 different levies imposed, accounting for 30 percent of the cost of doing business. From another point of view, it may be worthwhile for foreign businesses to consider greasing the machinery as part of conducting businesses in Asia in return for faster processing of business documents and procedures. In a survey called the Bribe Payers Index, Chinese businesspeople were the most willing to pay bribes, followed by South Koreans and Taiwanese. Asian governments have made efforts to clean up such behavior for long-term economic dividends.

Summary

1. To carry out their analysis, planning, implementation, and control responsibilities, marketing managers need a marketing information system (MIS). The role of the MIS is to assess the managers' information needs, develop the needed information, and distribute that information in a timely manner.
2. An MIS has three components:
   a. an internal records system, which includes information on the order-to-payment cycle and sales reporting systems;
   b. a marketing intelligence system, a set of procedures and sources used by managers to obtain everyday information about pertinent developments in the marketing environment; and
   c. a marketing research system that allows for the systematic design, collection, analysis, and reporting of data and findings relevant to a specific marketing situation.
3. Many opportunities are found by identifying trends (directions or sequences of events that have some momentum and durability) and megatrends (major social, economic, political, and technological changes that have long-lasting influence).
4. Within the rapidly changing global picture, marketers must monitor six major environmental forces: demographic, economic, social–cultural, natural, technological, and political–legal.
5. In the demographic environment, marketers must be aware of worldwide population growth; changing mixes of age, ethnic composition, and educational levels; the rise of non-traditional families; large geographic shifts in population; and the move to micromarketing and away from mass marketing.
6. In the economic arena, marketers need to focus on income distribution and levels of savings, debt, and credit availability.
7. In the social–cultural arena, marketers must understand people's views of themselves, others, organizations, society, nature, and the universe. They must market products that correspond to society's core and secondary values, and address the needs of different subcultures within a society.
8. In the natural environment, marketers need to be aware of raw materials shortages, increased energy costs and pollution levels, and the changing role of governments in environmental protection.
9. In the technological arena, marketers should take account of the accelerating pace of technological change, opportunities for innovation, varying R&D budgets, and the increased governmental regulation brought about by technological change.
10. In the political–legal environment, marketers must work within the many laws regulating business practices, engage with various special-interest groups, exploit opportunities arising from market reform, and deal with corruption.

Application

Marketing Debate—Is Consumer Behavior More a Function of a Person's Age or Generation?

One of the widely debated issues in developing marketing programs that target certain age groups is how much consumers change over time. Some marketers maintain that age differences are critical and that the needs and wants of a 25-year-old in 2008 are not that different from those of a 25-year-old in 1978. Others dispute that contention and argue that cohort and generation effects are critical and that marketing programs must therefore suit the times.

Take a position: *Age differences are fundamentally more important than cohort effects* versus *Cohort effects can dominate age differences.*

Marketing Discussion

What brands and products do you feel successfully "speak to you" and effectively target your age group? Why? Which ones do not? What could they do better?

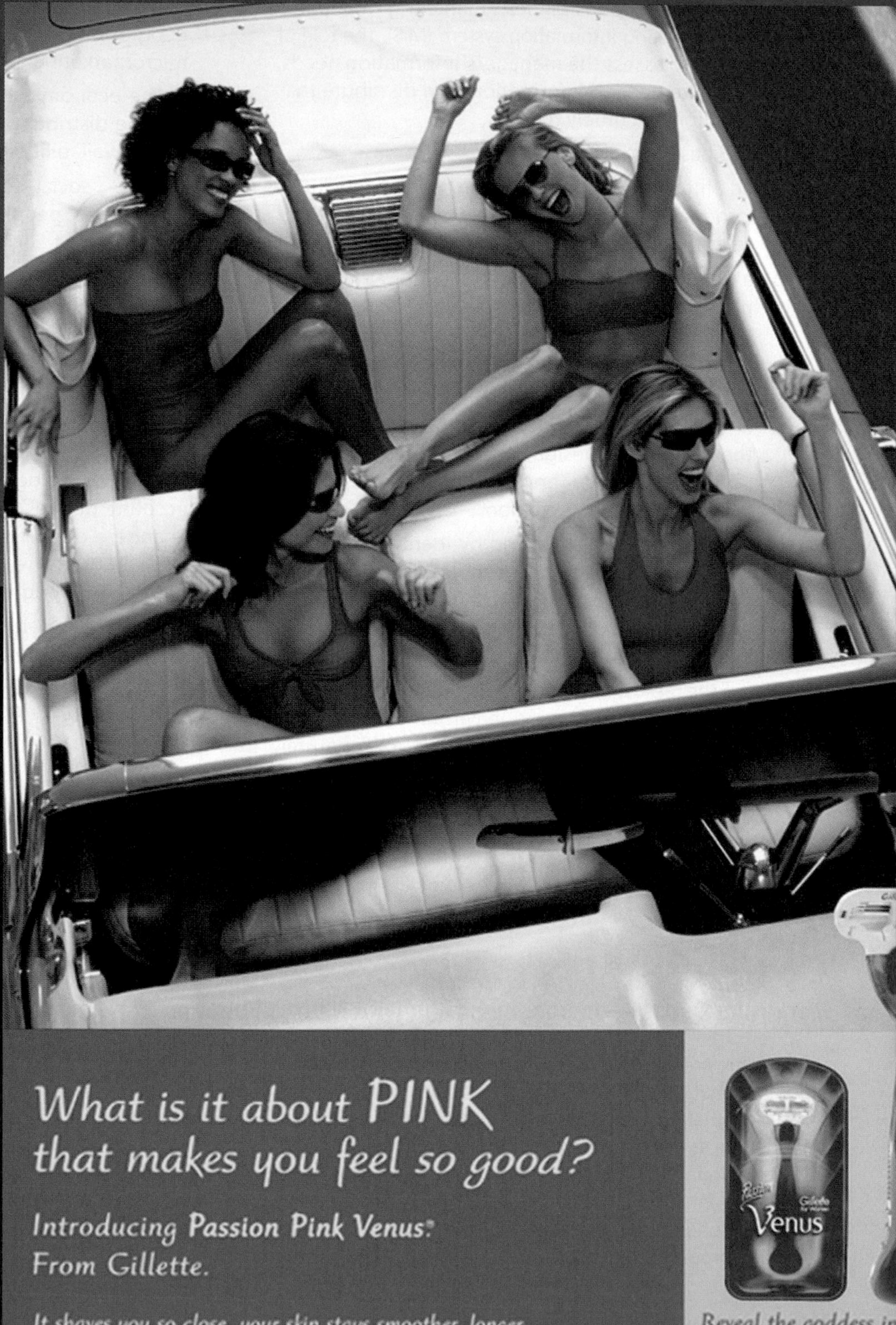

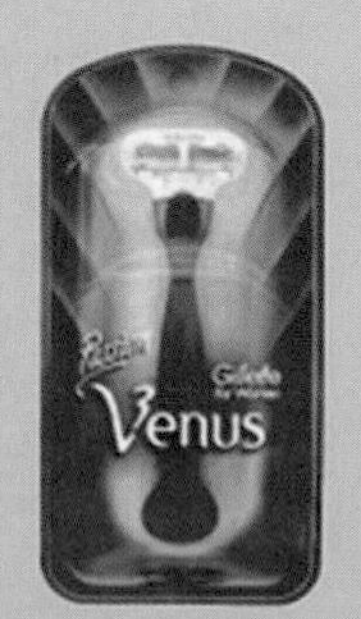

What is it about PINK
that makes you feel so good?
Introducing Passion Pink Venus.
From Gillette.
It shaves you so close, your skin stays smoother, longer.
Venus
Reveal the goddess in

Marketing research led to many of the successful features of Gillette's Venus, the first razor designed for women.

Conducting Marketing Research and Forecasting Demand

4

In addition to monitoring a changing marketing environment, marketers also need to develop specific knowledge about their particular markets. Good marketers want information to help them interpret past performance as well as plan future activities. Marketers need timely, accurate, and actionable information on consumers, competition, and their brands. They need to make the best possible tactical decisions in the short run and strategic decisions in the long run. Discovering consumer insights and understanding the marketing implications can often lead to a successful product launch or spur the growth of a brand.

hat is it about PINK
at makes you feel so good
oducing Passion Pink Venus
n Gillette.

As part of a $300 million budget for the development of its first razor designed solely for women, Gillette conducted extensive consumer research and performed numerous market tests. The razor, called Venus, was a marked departure from previous women's razor designs, which had essentially been colored or repackaged versions of men's razors. After research revealed that women change their grip on a razor about 30 times during each shaving session, Gillette designed the Venus with a wide, sculpted rubberized handle offering superior grip and control, and oval-shaped blade in a storage case that could stick to shower walls. Research also indicated that women were reluctant to leave the shower to replace a dull blade, so the case held spare blade cartridges. The research paid off for Gillette, as the Venus brand accounted for more than $2 billion in revenue in the four years following its 2001 retail launch and held more than 50 percent of the global women's shaving market in 2005. More recently, Gillette successfully leveraged customer insights in creating the six-bladed Fusion.[1]

In this chapter, we will address the following questions:

1. What constitutes good marketing research?
2. What are good metrics for measuring marketing productivity?
3. How can marketers assess their return on investment of marketing expenditures?
4. How can companies more accurately measure and forecast demand?

In this chapter, we review the steps involved in the marketing research process. We also consider how marketers can develop effective metrics for measuring marketing productivity. Finally, we outline how marketers can develop good sales forecasts.

The Marketing Research System

Marketing managers often commission formal marketing studies of specific problems and opportunities. They may request a market survey, a product-preference test, a sales forecast by region, or an advertising evaluation. It is the job of the marketing researcher to produce insight into the customer's attitudes and buying behavior. We define **marketing research** as the systematic design, collection, analysis, and reporting of data and findings relevant to a specific marketing situation facing the company.

A company can obtain marketing research in a number of ways. Most large companies have their own marketing research departments, which often play crucial roles within the organization.[2]

Procter & Gamble—P&G's large market research function is called Consumer and Market Knowledge (CMK). Its goal is to bring consumer insight to decision making at all levels. Dedicated CMK groups work for P&G businesses worldwide, including Global Business Units (GBUs), which focus on long-term brand equity and initiative development, and Market Development Organizations (MDOs), which focus on local market expertise and retail partnerships. There is also a relatively smaller, centralized corporate CMK group which, in partnership with the line businesses, focuses on three kinds of work: (1) proprietary research methods development; (2) expert application of, and cross-business learning from, core research competencies; and (3) shared services and infrastructure. CMK leverages traditional research basics such as brand tracking. CMK also finds, invents, or co-develops leading edge research approaches such as experiential consumer contacts, proprietary modeling methods, and scenario-planning or knowledge synthesis events. CMK professionals connect market insights from all these sources to shape company strategies and decisions. They influence day-to-day operational choices, such as which product formulations are launched, as well as long-term plans, such as which corporate acquisitions best round out the product portfolio.

Companies normally budget marketing research from 1–2 percent of company sales. A large percentage of that is spent on the services of outside firms. Marketing research firms fall into three categories:

1. ***Syndicated-service research firms***— These firms gather consumer and trade information, which they sell for a fee. Example: A.C. Nielsen Media Research.
2. ***Custom marketing research firms***— These firms are hired to carry out specific projects. They design the study and report the findings.
3. ***Specialty-line marketing research firms***— These firms provide specialized research services. The best example is the field-service firm, which sells field interviewing services to other firms.

Sony—Sony uses both in-house and market research firms to ascertain the effectiveness of its various marketing campaigns. In one campaign for its PlayStation, Sony ran 30-second commercials as part of the previews in more than 1,800 theaters and on 8,000 movie screens. Their commissioned ad-tracking study showed that unaided recall in cinema advertising was very effective. Another example of measurement is Sony's Generation Y youth marketing efforts. The online campaign promoted the NetMD, ATRAC CD Walkman, and Cybershot. Sony found that more than 70 percent of the click-throughs were spurred by rich media ads via Eyeblaster versus static banners. Sony has also developed a direct marketing solution which it sells to other companies who want to measure marketing effectiveness. The product, called eBridge™, allows marketers to use video, measure the effectiveness of the campaign, and gain insight into the target audience, all in one package.

Small companies can hire the services of a marketing research firm or conduct research in creative and affordable ways, such as:

1. ***Engaging students or professors to design and carry out projects*** — The Business School at the National University of Singapore has several projects with companies where students engage in case analyses and consultancy. Some of the companies that the business school has worked with include Samsung and Kimberly-Clark.
2. ***Using the Internet***— A company can collect considerable information at very little cost by examining competitors' Web sites, monitoring chat rooms, and accessing published data.
3. ***Checking out rivals***— Many small companies routinely visit their competitors.

Marketing research can be carried out by everyone in the company—and by customers, too.

Hindustan Unilever—This company has added a new concept to its consumer research in India—consumer windows. Besides its traditional market research, it has also established direct customer contact where its managers can log in to a Web site and request for an interface with any type of consumer across India. The request is then processed by the research agency which will organize meetings between the managers and the consumers. Hindustan Unilever claims that after this window was set up, about nine managers will contact consumers in some 20 locations across five consumer groups every day. This tool has helped it find solutions to specific problems. When the sales of one of its top brands Lifebuoy tapered off, the consumer window sessions helped the company realize that consumers preferred a non-carbolic product, and thus repositioned the soap as a family product.[3]

The Marketing Research Process

Effective marketing research involves the six steps shown in Figure 4.1. We will illustrate these steps with the following hypothetical situation:

Japan Airlines (JAL) is looking for new ways to serve its passengers. It is reviewing many new ideas, especially to cater to its first-class passengers on very long flights, many of whom are businesspeople whose high-priced tickets pay most of the freight. Among these ideas are: (1) to supply an Internet connection with limited access to Web pages and email messaging; (2) to offer 24 channels of satellite cable TV; and (3) to offer a 50-CD audio system that lets each passenger create a customized playlist of music and movies to enjoy during the flight. The marketing research manager was assigned to investigate how first-class passengers would rate these services and how much extra they would be willing to pay if a charge was made. He was asked to focus specifically on the Internet connection. One estimate says that airlines might realize revenues of $70 billion over the next decade from in-flight Internet access, if enough first-class passengers would be willing to pay $25 for it. JAL could thus recover its costs in a reasonable time. Making the connection available would cost the airline $90,000 per plane.[4]

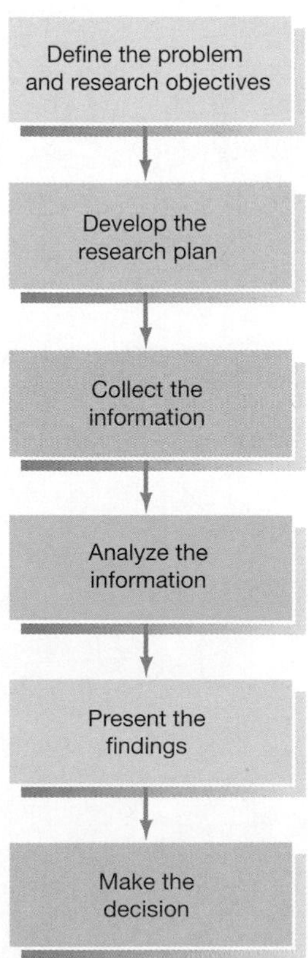

Figure 4.1
The Marketing Research Process

Step 1: Define the Problem, the Decision Alternatives, and the Research Objectives

Marketing managers must be careful not to define the problem too broadly or too narrowly for the marketing researcher. A marketing manager who instructs the marketing researcher to "Find out everything you can about first-class air travelers' needs," will collect a lot of unnecessary information. One who says, "Find out if enough passengers on board a B747 flying direct between Los Angeles and Tokyo would be willing to pay $25 for an Internet connection so that JAL would break even in one year on the cost of offering this service," is taking too narrow a view of the problem. The marketing researcher might even raise this question: "Why does the Internet connection have to be priced at $25 as opposed to $10, $50, or some other price? Why does JAL have to break even on the cost of the service, especially if it attracts new users?"

In discussing the problem, JAL's managers discover another issue. If the new service was successful, how fast could other airlines copy it? Airline marketing research is replete with examples of new services that have been so quickly copied by competitors that no airline has gained a sustainable competitive advantage. How important is it to be first, and how long could the lead be sustained?

The marketing manager and marketing researcher agreed to define the problem as follows: "Will offering an in-flight Internet service create enough incremental preference and profit for JAL to justify its cost against other possible investments JAL might make?" To help in designing the research, management should first spell out the decisions it might face and then work backward. Suppose management spells out these decisions: (1) Should JAL offer an Internet connection? (2) If so, should the service be offered to first class only, or include business class, and possibly economy class? (3) What price(s) should be charged? (4) On what types of planes and lengths of trips should it be offered?

Now management and marketing researchers are ready to set specific research objectives: (1) What types of first-class passengers would respond most to using an in-flight Internet service? (2) How many first-class passengers are likely to use the Internet service at different price levels? (3) How many extra first-class passengers might choose JAL because of this new service? (4) How much long-term goodwill will this service add to JAL's image? (5) How important is Internet service to first-class passengers relative to providing other services such as a power plug or enhanced entertainment?

Not all research projects can be this specific. Some research is exploratory—its goal is to shed light on the real nature of the problem and to suggest possible solutions or new ideas. Some research is descriptive—it seeks to ascertain certain magnitudes, such as how many first-class passengers would purchase an in-flight Internet service at $25. Some research is causal—its purpose is to test a cause-and-effect relationship.

Step 2: Develop the Research Plan

The second stage of marketing research calls for developing the most efficient plan for gathering the needed information. The marketing manager needs to know the cost of the research plan before approving it. Suppose the company made a prior estimate that launching the in-flight Internet service would yield a long-term profit of $50,000. The manager believes that doing the research would lead to an improved pricing and promotional plan and a long-term profit of $90,000. In this case, the manager should be willing to spend up to $40,000 on this research. If the research would cost more than $40,000, it is not worth doing.[5] Designing a research plan calls for decisions on the data sources, research approaches, research instruments, sampling plan, and contact methods.

DATA SOURCES

The researcher can gather secondary data, primary data, or both. *Secondary data* are data that were collected for another purpose and already exist somewhere. *Primary data* are data freshly gathered for a specific purpose or for a specific research project.

Researchers usually start their investigation by examining some of the rich variety of secondary data to see whether the problem can be partly or wholly solved without collecting costly primary data. Secondary data provide a starting point and offer the advantages of low cost and ready availability. When the needed data do not exist or are dated, inaccurate, incomplete, or unreliable, the researcher will have to collect primary data. Most marketing research projects involve some primary-data collection. The normal procedure is to interview some people individually or in groups, to get a sense of how people feel about the topic in question, and then develop a formal research instrument, debug it, and carry it into the field.

RESEARCH APPROACHES

Primary data can be collected in five main ways: through observation, focus groups, surveys, behavioral data, and experiments.

Observational Research

Fresh data can be gathered by observing the relevant actors and settings.[6] Consumers can be unobtrusively observed as they shop or as they consume products. Ogilvy & Mather's Discovery Group creates documentary-style videos by sending researchers into consumers' homes with handheld video cameras. Hours of footage are edited to a 30-minute "highlight reel" which the group uses to analyze consumer behavior. Other researchers equip consumers with pagers and instruct them to write down what they are doing whenever prompted, or hold more informal interview sessions at a café or bar. The JAL researchers might meander around first-class lounges to hear how travelers talk about the different carriers and their features. They can fly on competitors' planes to observe in-flight service.

Ethnographic Research

This is a particular observational research approach that uses concepts and tools from anthropology and other social science disciplines to provide deep understanding of how people live and work.[7] The goal is to immerse the researcher into consumers' lives to uncover unarticulated desires that might not surface in any other form of research.[8] Firms such as IBM, Intel, and Motorola have embraced ethnographic research to design breakthrough products. After observing the popularity of Chinese-character text messaging in Shanghai, Motorola developed the A732 mobile phone, with which users could write messages directly on the keypad using a finger.

Ethnographic research is not limited just to consumer companies in developed markets. GE's ethnographic research into the plastic-fiber industry showed the firm that it was not in a commodity business driven by price as much as it was in an artisanal industry with customers who wanted collaborations at the earliest stages of development. GE completely reoriented the way it interacted with the companies in the plastic-fiber industry as a result. Ethnographic research can be especially useful in developing markets, especially far-flung rural areas, where companies do not know consumers as well.[9]

Focus Group Research

A **focus group** is a gathering of 6 to 10 people who are carefully selected based on certain demographic, psychographic or other considerations and brought together to discuss various topics of interest at length. Participants are normally paid a small sum for attending. A professional research moderator provides questions and probes based on a discussion guide or agenda prepared by the marketing managers responsible to ensure that the right material gets covered.

Moderators attempt to track down potentially useful insights as they try to discern the real motivations of consumers and why they are saying and doing certain things. The sessions are typically recorded in some fashion, and marketing managers often remain behind two-way mirrors in the next room. In the JAL research, the moderator might start with a broad question, such as "How do you feel about first-class air travel?" Questions then move to how people view the different airlines, different existing services, different proposed services, and specifically, Internet service. Although focus group research has been shown to be a useful exploratory step, researchers must avoid generalizing the reported feelings of the focus group participants to the whole market, because the sample size is too small and the sample is not drawn randomly. "Marketing Insight: Conducting Informative Focus Groups" has some practical tips to improve the quality of focus groups.

MARKETING INSIGHT • CONDUCTING INFORMATIVE FOCUS GROUPS

Focus groups allow marketers to observe how and why consumers accept or reject concepts, ideas, or any specific notion. The key to using focus groups successfully is to *listen*. It is critical to eliminate biases as much as possible. Although many useful insights can emerge from thoughtfully run focus groups, there can be questions as to their validity, especially in today's marketing environment.

Some researchers believe that consumers have been so bombarded with ads, they unconsciously (or perhaps cynically) regurgitate what they have already heard as compared to what they think. There is also a concern that participants are just trying to maintain their self-image and public persona or have a need to identify with the other members of the group. Participants may not be willing to admit in public—or may not even recognize—their behavior patterns and motivations. There is also always the "loudmouth" problem—when one highly opinionated person drowns out the rest of the group. It may be expensive to recruit qualified subjects, but getting the right participants is crucial.

Even when multiple groups are involved, it may be difficult to generalize the results to a broader population. Focus group findings often vary from region to region. Some consumers tend to be highly critical and generally do not report that they like much. Too often, managers become comfortable with a particular focus group format and apply it generally and automatically to every circumstance. Asians typically need more time than American marketers typically are willing to give—a focus group in Asia there rarely takes less than two hours and often more than four.

Participants must feel as relaxed as possible and feel a strong obligation to "speak the truth." Physical surroundings can be crucial. Researchers at one agency knew they had a problem when a fight broke out between participants at one of their sessions. As one executive noted, "we wondered why people always seemed grumpy and negative—people were resistant to any idea we showed them." The problem was the room itself: cramped, stifling, forbidding: "It was a cross between a hospital room and a police interrogation room." To fix the problem, the agency gave the room a make-over. Other firms are adapting the look of the room to fit the theme of the topic—like designing the room to look like a playroom when speaking to children.

Although many firms are substituting observational research for focus groups, ethnographic research can be expensive and tricky: researchers must be highly skilled, participants have to be on the level, and mounds of data have to be analyzed. The beauty of focus groups, as one marketing executive noted, is that, "it's still the most cost-effective, quickest, dirtiest way to get information in rapid time on an idea." In analyzing the pros and cons, Americus Reed might have said it best: "A focus group is like a chain saw. If you know what you're doing, it's very useful and effective. If you don't, you could lose a limb."

Sources: Naomi R. Henderson, "Beyond Top of Mind." *Marketing Research*, September 1, 2005; Rebecca Harris, "Do Focus Groups Have a Future?" *Marketing*, June 6, 2005, p. 17; Malcolm Gladwell, *Blink: The Power of Thinking Without Thinking*, (New York: Little Brown, 2005); Linda Tischler, "Every Move You Make." *Fast Company*, April 2004, pp. 73-75; Jeffrey Kasner, "Fistfights and *Feng Shui*." *Boston Globe* July 21, 2001, pp. C1-C2; Alison Stein Wellner, "The New Science of Focus Groups." *American Demographics*, March 2003, pp. 29-33; Dennis Rook, "Out-of-Focus Groups." *Marketing Research*, Summer 2003, 15(2), p. 11.

At Singapore Changi Airport, feedback on the airport service is regularly collected. Passengers now give their feedback through touch-screen terminals.

Survey Research

Companies undertake surveys to learn about people's knowledge, beliefs, preferences, and satisfaction, and to measure these magnitudes in the general population. JAL might prepare its own survey instrument to gather the information it needs, or it might add questions to an omnibus survey that carries the questions of several companies at a much lower cost. It can also put the questions to an ongoing consumer panel run by itself or another company. It may do a mall intercept study by having researchers approach people in a shopping mall and ask them questions.

Behavioral Data Research

Customers leave traces of their purchasing behavior in store scanning data, catalog purchases, and customer databases. Much can be learned by analyzing these data. Customers' actual purchases reflect preferences and often are more reliable than statements they offer to market researchers. People may report preferences for popular brands, and yet the data show them actually buying other brands. For example, grocery shopping data show that high-income people do not necessarily buy the more expensive brands, contrary to what they might state in interviews; and many low-income people buy some expensive brands. Clearly, JAL can learn many useful things about its passengers by analyzing ticket purchase records.

Experimental Research

The most scientifically valid research is experimental research. The purpose of experimental research is to capture cause-and-effect relationships by eliminating competing explanations of the observed findings. To the extent that the design and execution of the experiment eliminate alternative hypotheses that might explain the results, research and marketing managers can have confidence in the conclusions.

Experiments call for selecting matched groups of subjects, subjecting them to different treatments, controlling extraneous variables, and checking whether observed response differences are statistically significant. To the extent that extraneous factors are eliminated or controlled, the observed effects can be related to the variations in the treatments. JAL might introduce in-flight Internet service on one of its regular flights from Los Angeles to Tokyo. It might charge $25 one week and charge only $15 the next week. If the plane carried approximately the same number of first-class passengers each week and the particular weeks made no difference, any significant difference in the number of calls made could be related to the different prices charged. The experimental design could be elaborated by trying other prices and including other air routes.

RESEARCH INSTRUMENTS

Marketing researchers have a choice of three main research instruments in collecting primary data: questionnaires, qualitative measures, and mechanical devices.

Questionnaires

A questionnaire consists of a set of questions presented to respondents. Because of its flexibility, the questionnaire is by far the most common instrument used to collect primary data. Questionnaires need to be carefully developed, tested, and debugged before they are administered on a large scale. In preparing a questionnaire, the researcher carefully chooses the questions and their form, wording, and sequence. The form of the question can influence the response. Marketing researchers distinguish between closed-end and open-end questions. Closed-end questions specify all the possible answers and provide answers that are easier to interpret and tabulate. Open-end questions allow respondents to answer in their own words and often reveal more about how people think. They are especially useful in exploratory research, where the researcher is looking for insight into how people think rather than measuring how many people think a certain way. Table 4.1 provides examples of both types of questions; and see "Marketing Memo: Questionnaire Do's and Don'ts."

MARKETING MEMO • QUESTIONNAIRE DO'S AND DON'TS

1. **Ensure that questions are without bias.** Do not lead the respondent into an answer.
2. **Make the questions as simple as possible.** Questions that include multiple ideas or two questions in one will confuse respondents.
3. **Make the questions specific.** Sometimes it is advisable to add memory cues. For example, it is good practice to be specific with time periods.
4. **Avoid jargon or shorthand.** Avoid trade jargon, acronyms, and initials not in everyday use.
5. **Steer clear of sophisticated or uncommon words.** Only use words in common speech.
6. **Avoid ambiguous words.** Words such as "usually" or "frequently" have no specific meaning.
7. **Avoid questions with a negative in them.** It is better to say "Do you ever . . . ?" than "Do you never . . . ?"
8. **Avoid hypothetical questions.** It is difficult to answer questions about imaginary situations. Answers cannot necessarily be trusted.
9. **Do not use words that could be misheard.** This is especially important when the interview is administered over the telephone. "What is your opinion of sects?" could yield interesting but not necessarily relevant answers.
10. **Desensitize questions by using response bands.** For questions that ask people their age or companies their employee turnover, it is best to offer a range of response bands.
11. **Ensure that fixed responses do not overlap.** Categories used in fixed response questions should be sequential and not overlap.
12. **Allow for "other" in fixed response questions.** Precoded answers should always allow for a response other than those listed.

Source: Adapted from Paul Hague and Peter Jackson, *Market Research: A Guide to Planning, Methodology, and Evaluation,* (London: Kogan Page, 1999). See also Hans Baumgartner and Jan Benedict E.M. Steenkamp, "Response Styles in Marketing Research: A Cross-National Investigation," *Journal of Marketing Research,* May 2001, pp. 143–156.

Table 4.1 Types of Questions

Name	Description	Example
A. Closed-end Questions		
Dichotomous	A question with two possible answers.	In arranging this trip, did you personally phone JAL? Yes No
Multiple choice	A question with three or more answers.	With whom are you traveling on this flight? ❑ No one ❑ Children only ❑ Spouse ❑ Business associates/friends/relatives ❑ Spouse and children ❑ An organized tour group
Likert scale	A statement with which the respondent shows the amount of agreement/disagreement.	Small airlines generally give better service than large ones. Strongly disagree 1__ Disagree 2__ Neither agree nor disagree 3__ Agree 4__ Strongly agree 5__
Semantic differential	A scale connecting two bipolar words. The respondent selects the point that represents his or her opinion.	JAL Large .... Small Experienced .... Inexperienced Modern .... Old-fashioned
Importance scale	A scale that rates the importance of some attribute.	Airline food service to me is Extremely important 1__ Very important 2__ Somewhat important 3__ Not very important 4__ Not at all important 5__
Rating scale	A scale that rates some attribute from "poor" to "excellent."	JAL food service is Excellent 1__ Very Good 2__ Good 3__ Fair 4__ Poor 5__
Intention-to-buy scale	A scale that describes the respondent's intention to buy.	If an in-flight telephone were available on a long flight, I would Definitely buy 1__ Probably buy 2__ Not sure 3__ Probably not buy 4__ Definitely not buy 5__
B. Open-end Questions		
Completely unstructured	A question that respondents can answer in an almost unlimited number of ways.	What is your opinion of JAL?
Word association	Words are presented, one at a time, and respondents mention the first word that comes to mind.	What is the first word that comes to your mind when you hear the following? Airline ______ JAL ______ Travel ______
Sentence	An incomplete sentence is presented and respondents complete the sentence.	When I choose an airline, the most important consideration in my decision is ______
Story completion	An incomplete story is presented, and respondents are asked to complete it.	"I flew JAL a few days ago. I noticed that the exterior and interior of the plane had very bright colors. This aroused in me the following thoughts and feelings. . . ." Now complete the story.
Picture	A picture of two characters is presented, with one making a statement. Respondents are asked to identify with the other and fill in the empty balloon.	 WELL HERE'S THE FOOD.
Thematic Apperception Test (TAT)	A picture is presented and respondents are asked to make up a story about what they think is happening or may happen in the picture.	

Qualitative Measures

Some marketers prefer more qualitative methods for gauging consumer opinion because consumer actions do not always match their answers to survey questions. *Qualitative research techniques* are relatively unstructured measurement approaches that permit a range of possible responses. Qualitative research techniques are a creative means of ascertaining consumer perceptions that may otherwise be difficult to uncover. The range of possible qualitative research techniques is limited only by the creativity of the marketing researcher. Here are seven techniques employed by design firm IDEO for understanding the customer experience:[10]

- ***Shadowing***— Observing people using products, shopping, going to hospitals, taking the train, using their mobile phones.
- ***Behavior mapping***— Photographing people within a space, such as a hospital waiting room, over two or three days.
- ***Consumer journey***— Keeping track of all the interactions a consumer has with a product, service, or space.
- ***Camera journals*** — Asking consumers to keep visual diaries of their activities and impressions relating to a product.
- ***Extreme user interviews*** — Talking to people who really know—or know nothing—about a product or service and evaluating their experience using it.
- ***Storytelling*** — Prompting people to tell personal stories about their consumer experiences.
- ***Unfocused groups*** — Interviewing a diverse group of people. To explore ideas about sandals, IDEO gathered an artist, a bodybuilder, a podiatrist, and a shoe fetishist.

Because of the freedom afforded both researchers in their probes and consumers in their responses, qualitative research can often be a useful first step in exploring consumers' brand and product perceptions. There are also drawbacks to qualitative research. The in-depth insights that emerge have to be tempered by the fact that the samples involved are often very small and may not necessarily generalize to broader populations. Moreover, given the qualitative nature of the data, there may also be questions of interpretation. Different researchers examining the same results from a qualitative research study may draw very different conclusions. "Marketing Insight: Getting into Consumer Heads with Qualitative Research" describes some popular approaches.

Technological Devices

Technological devices are occasionally useful in marketing research. Galvanometers can measure the interest or emotions aroused by exposure to a specific ad or picture. The tachistoscope flashes an ad to a subject with an exposure interval that may range from less than one hundredth of a second to several seconds. After each exposure, the respondent describes everything he recalls. Eye cameras study respondents' eye movements to see where their eyes land first, how long they linger on a given item, and so on.

Technology has now advanced to such a degree that marketers can use devices such as skin sensors, brain wave scanners, and full body scanners to get consumer responses.[11] Some advertising technology companies study the eye movements and brain activity of Web surfers to see which ads grab their attention.[12] "Marketing Insight: Understanding Brain Science" provides a glimpse into some new marketing research frontiers studying the brain.

Technology has replaced the diaries that participants in media surveys used to keep. Audiometers attached to television sets in participating homes now record when the set is on and to which channel it is tuned. Electronic devices can record the number of radio programs a person is exposed to during the day, or, using Global Positioning System (GPS) technology, how many billboards a person may walk by or drive by during a day. Technology is also used to capture consumer reactions to programming content.

MARKETING INSIGHT • GETTING INTO CONSUMERS' HEADS WITH QUALITATIVE RESEARCH

Here are some commonly used qualitative research approaches to get inside consumers' minds and find out what they are thinking or feeling about brands and products:

1. ***Word associations*** — People can be asked what words come to mind when they hear the brand's name. "What does the Casio name mean to you? Tell me what comes to mind when you think of Casio watches." The primary purpose of free association tasks is to identify the range of possible brand associations in consumers' minds. But they may also provide some rough indication of the relative strength, favorability, and uniqueness of brand associations.
2. ***Projective techniques*** — People are presented an incomplete stimulus and asked to complete it or given an ambiguous stimulus that may not make sense in and of itself and are asked to make sense of it. The argument is that people will reveal their true beliefs and feelings. One such approach is "bubble exercises" based on cartoons or photos. Different people are depicted buying or using certain products or services. Empty bubbles, like those found in cartoons, are placed in the scenes to represent the thoughts, words, or actions of one or more of the participants. People are then asked to "fill in the bubble" by indicating what they believed was happening or being said. Another technique is comparison tasks. People are asked to convey their impressions by comparing brands to people, countries, animals, activities, fabrics, occupations, cars, magazines, vegetables, nationalities, or even other brands.
3. ***Visualization*** — People can be asked to create a collage from magazine photos or drawings to depict their perceptions. ZMET is a research technique that starts with a group of participants, who are asked in advance to select a minimum of 12 images from their own sources (e.g., magazines, catalogs, and family photo albums) that represent their thoughts and feelings about the research topic. The participants bring these images to a personal one-on-one interview with a study administrator, who uses advanced interview techniques to explore the images with the participants and reveal hidden meanings. Finally, the participants use a computer program to create a collage with these images that communicates their subconscious thoughts and feelings about the topic. One ZMET study probed what women thought of panty hose. Twenty hose-wearing women were asked to collect pictures that captured their feelings about wearing panty hose. Some of the pictures showed fence posts encased in plastic wrap or steel bands strangling trees, suggesting that panty hose are tight and inconvenient. Another picture showed tall flowers in a vase, suggesting that the product made a woman feel thin, tall, and sexy.
4. ***Brand personification*** — People can be asked to describe what kind of person they think of when the brand is mentioned: "If the brand were to come alive as a person, what would it be like, what would it do, where would it live, what would it wear, who would it talk to if it went to a party (and what would it talk about)?" Thailand's Boon Rawd Brewery conducted a brand personification study and found that Leo, a local beer, was perceived to have a mature personality that values Thai heritage. Singha, another local beer, was perceived as having an international Thai personality—someone who is modern and proud to be a Thai, and yet a citizen of the world with international ambitions. Heineken was viewed as the Master European Brewer, while Chang, a low-cost beer targeted at the rural market, had no clear brand personality.
5. ***Laddering*** — A series of increasingly more specific "why" questions can be used to gain insight into consumer motivation and consumers' deeper, more abstract goals. Ask why someone wants to buy a Nokia mobile phone. "They look well-built" (attribute). "Why is it important that the phone be well-built?" "It suggests that the Nokia phone is reliable" (a functional benefit). "Why is reliability important?" "Because my colleagues or family can be sure to reach me" (an emotional benefit). "Why must you be available to them at all times?" "I can help them if they are in trouble" (brand essence). The brand makes this person feel like a Good Samaritan, ready to help others.

Sources: Allen Adamson, "Why Traditional Brand Positioning Can't Last." *BrandWeek,* November 17, 2003, pp. 38–40; Todd Wasserman, "Sharpening the Focus." *BrandWeek,* November 3, 2003, pp. 28–32; Linda Tischler, "Every Move You Make." *Fast Company,* April 2004, pp. 73–75; Gerald Zaltman, *How Customers Think: Essential Insights Into the Mind of the Market,* (Boston: Harvard Business School Press, 2003).

SAMPLING PLAN

After deciding on the research approach and instruments, the marketing researcher must design a sampling plan. This calls for three decisions:

1. **Sampling unit—Who is to be surveyed?** The marketing researcher must define the target population that will be sampled. In the JAL survey, should the sampling unit be only first-class business travelers, first-class vacation travelers, or both? Should travelers under age 18 be interviewed? Should both husbands and wives be interviewed? Once the sampling unit is determined, a sampling frame must be developed so that everyone in the target population has an equal or known chance of being sampled.
2. **Sample size—How many people should be surveyed?** Large samples give more reliable results than small samples. However, it is not necessary to sample the entire target population or even a substantial portion to achieve reliable results. Samples of less than 1 percent of a population can often provide good reliability, with a credible sampling procedure.

MARKETING INSIGHT • UNDERSTANDING BRAIN SCIENCE

As an alternative to traditional consumer research, some researchers have begun to develop sophisticated techniques from neuroscience that monitor brain activity to better gauge consumer responses to marketing stimuli.

For example, a group of researchers at UCLA used functional Magnetic Resonance Imaging (fMRI) to measure how consumers' brains responded to 2006 Super Bowl advertisements. The research demonstrated how consumers' stated preferences often contradict their inner thoughts and emotions. The fMRI showed that the "I'm going to Disney World" ad featuring members of both teams rehearsing the famous line elicited the highest levels of positive brain activity, followed by a Sierra Mist commercial starring an airport security screener and a traveler. Yet in a consumer poll conducted independently, a Bud Light ad rated highest, despite not generating significant positive reaction in the fMRI tests.

Although it can be more effective in uncovering inner emotions than conventional techniques, neurological research is costly, running as much as $100,000 per project. One major finding to emerge from neurological consumer research is that many purchase decisions are characterized less by the logical weighing of variables than was previously assumed and more "as a largely unconscious habitual process, as distinct from the rational, conscious, information-processing model of economists and traditional marketing textbooks." Even basic decisions, such as the purchase of gasoline, are influenced by brain activity at the sub-rational level.

Neurological research can be used to measure the type of emotional response that consumers exhibit when presented with marketing stimuli. A group of researchers in England used an electroencephalograph (EEG) to monitor cognitive functions related to memory recall and attentiveness for 12 different regions of the brain as subjects were exposed to advertising. Brain wave activity in different regions indicated different emotional responses. For example, heightened activity in the left prefrontal cortex is characteristic of an "approach" response to an ad and indicates an attraction to the stimulus. In contrast, a spike in brain activity in the right prefrontal cortex is indicative of a strong revulsion to the stimulus. In yet another part of the brain, the degree of memory formation activity correlates with purchase intent. Other research has shown that people activate different regions of the brain in assessing the personality traits of people versus brands.

The term *neuromarketing* has been used to describe brain research on the effect of marketing stimuli. By adding neurological techniques to their research arsenal, marketers are trying to move toward a more complete picture of what goes on inside consumers' heads. Given the complexity of the human brain, however, many researchers caution that neurological research should not form the sole basis for marketing decisions. These research activities have not been universally applauded though. Critics think that such a development will only lead to more marketing manipulation by companies.

Sources: Carolyn Yoon, Angela H. Gutchess, Fred Feinberg, and Thad A. Polk, "A Functional Magnetic Resonance Imaging Study of Neural Dissociations between Brand and Person Judgments." *Journal of Consumer Research,* June 2006, 33, pp. 31–40; Daryl Travis, "Tap Buyers' Emotions for Marketing Success." *Marketing News*, February 1, 2006, pp. 21–22; Deborah L. Vence, "Pick Someone's Brain." *Marketing News*, May 1, 2006, pp. 11–13; Louise Witt, "Inside Intent." *American Demographics,* March 2004, pp. 34–39; Samuel M. McClure, Jian Li, Damon Tomlin, Kim S. Cypert, Latané M. Montague, and P. Read Montague, "Neural Correlates of Behavioral Preference for Culturally Familiar Drinks." *Neuron,* October 14, 2004, 44, pp. 379–387; Melanie Wells, "In Search of the Buy Button." *Forbes*, September 1, 2003.

3. **Sampling procedure—How should the respondents be chosen?** To obtain a representative sample, a probability sample of the population should be drawn. Probability sampling allows the calculation of confidence limits for sampling error. Thus one could conclude after the sample is taken that "the interval five to seven trips per year has 95 chances in 100 of containing the true number of trips taken annually by first-class passengers flying between Tokyo and Los Angeles." Three types of probability sampling are described in Table 4.2, Part A. When the cost or time involved in probability sampling is too high, marketing researchers will take non-probability samples. Table 4.2, Part B describes three types. Some marketing researchers feel that nonprobability samples are very useful in many circumstances, even though they do not allow sampling error to be measured.

However, probability sampling is difficult to achieve in some countries like China. This follows from China's large size and the time, cost, and difficulty of accessing respondents in all parts of the country due to lack of communication, transportation, and other infrastructural set-ups. Regional variations in cultural traditions and the economic situation present additional problems, particularly as economic development has been accompanied by increasing diversity across the country. The frequent need to obtain authorization from the relevant authorities when undertaking surveys may also result in gaining cooperation from a research unit affiliated with a particular ministry but difficulty in sampling potential respondents affiliated with other ministerial systems.[13]

Table 4.2 Probability and Non-Probability Samples

A. Probability Sample	
Simple random sample	Every member of the population has an equal chance of selection.
Stratified random sample	The population is divided into mutually exclusive groups (such as age groups), and random samples are drawn from each group.
Cluster (area) sample	The population is divided into mutually exclusive groups (such as city blocks), and the researcher draws a sample of the groups to interview.
B. Non-Probability Sample	
Convenience sample	The researcher selects the most accessible population members.
Judgment sample	The researcher selects population members who are good prospects for accurate information.
Quota sample	The researcher finds and interviews a prescribed number of people in each of several categories.

CONTACT METHODS

Once the sampling plan has been determined, the marketing researcher must decide how the subject should be contacted: mail, telephone, personal, or online interview.

Mail Questionnaire

The *mail questionnaire* is the best way to reach people who would not give personal interviews or whose responses might be biased or distorted by the interviewers. Mail questionnaires require simple and clearly worded questions. Unfortunately, the response rate is usually low or slow.

Telephone Interview

Telephone interviewing is the best method for gathering information quickly; the interviewer is also able to clarify questions if respondents do not understand them. The response rate is typically higher than in the case of mailed questionnaires. The main drawback is that the interviews have to be short and not too personal. Telephone interviewing is getting more difficult because of consumers' growing antipathy toward telemarketers calling them in their homes and interrupting their lives.

Personal Interview

Personal interviewing is the most versatile method. The interviewer can ask more questions and record additional observations about the respondent, such as dress and body language. At the same time, personal interviewing is the most expensive method and requires more administrative planning and supervision than the other three. It is also subject to interviewer bias or distortion. Personal interviewing takes two forms. In *arranged interviews,* respondents are contacted for an appointment, and often a small payment or incentive is offered. *Intercept interviews* involve stopping people at a shopping mall or busy street corner and requesting an interview. Intercept interviews can have the drawback of being non-probability samples, and the interviews must not require too much time.

Online Interview

There is increased use of online methods. There are many ways to use the Internet to do research. A company can include a questionnaire on its Web site and offer an incentive to answer the questionnaire; or it can place a banner on some frequently visited site such as Yahoo!, inviting people to answer some questions and possibly win a prize. The company can sponsor a chat room or bulletin board and introduce questions from time to time, or host a real-time panel or virtual focus group. A company can learn about individuals who visit its site by following how they *clickstream* through the Web site and move to other sites. A company can post different prices, use different headlines, offer different product features on different Web sites or at different times to learn the relative effectiveness of its offerings.

Online product testing, in which companies float trial balloons for new products, is also growing and providing information much faster than traditional marketing research techniques used to develop new products. For instance, marketers for Mattel's Hot Wheels toys rely heavily on the Web to interact with collectors to help develop new products, promotions, and licensed goods. Following one fan survey, marketing executives learned that they could expand licensed offerings to boys aged 11–16 to keep them into the brand franchise, resulting in extended partnerships with Bell Motorcycles and BMX bikes.[14]

Hershey's Food Corp.—Candymaker Hershey was an early innovator in the area of online product testing. In 1999 through 2000, the company moved its new product testing online along with its entire historical product testing. It combined more than 1,200 historical concept tests with about 300 to 400 online test results to create an online "turnkey" system that works both as a reporting tool and as an archival system. The move to online product testing has cut Hershey's new product development process by two-thirds—a strategic advantage in a mature market—and keeps a wealth of institutional data on hand even as research personnel change over the years.[15]

In China, CIC, a company specializing in online research, has found some success:

CIC—CIC is a company that tracks and analyzes online chats on specific products. It developed a software that allows it to track specific strings of conversation. In China, there are some 137 million people online, relatively small compared to the population. However, these affluent urbanites with Internet access are also those who buy cars and Nike shoes. Hence, companies like Nike use CIC's services to find out what customers like and dislike. Automakers also use CIC to find out what the buzz is on their cars and what potential buyers are interested in. Says Sam Fleming, its co-founder, "I can tell you which models had tens of thousands of mentions in the month of August. We can tell clients how much talk there is. Is the talk good or bad? Where is it happening?" CIC first started when it developed proprietary software platform specifically to track conversations in Chinese. "You listen and then, as a brand, you can figure out how to meaningfully participate in this online world where more and more consumers are spending time," added Fleming.[16]

While marketers are right to be infatuated with the possibilities of online research, it is important to remember that the field is still in its infancy and is constantly evolving to meet the needs of companies, advertising agencies, and consumers. "Marketing Memo: Pros and Cons of Online Research" outlines some of the advantages and disadvantages of online research thus far.

Step 3: Collect the Information

The data collection phase of marketing research is generally the most expensive and the most prone to error. In the case of surveys, four major problems arise. Some respondents will not be at home and must be contacted again or replaced. Other respondents will refuse to cooperate. Still others will give biased or dishonest answers. Finally, some interviewers will be biased or dishonest. Getting the right respondents is critical.

Data collection methods are rapidly improving, thanks to computers and telecommunications. Some research firms conduct interviews from a centralized location. Professional interviewers will sit in booths and draw telephone numbers at random. When the phone is answered, the interviewer reads a set of questions from a monitor and types the respondents' answers into a computer. This procedure eliminates editing and coding, reduces errors, saves time, and produces all the required statistics. Other research firms have set up interactive terminals in shopping centers. Persons willing to be interviewed sit at a terminal, read the questions from the monitor, and type in their answers.

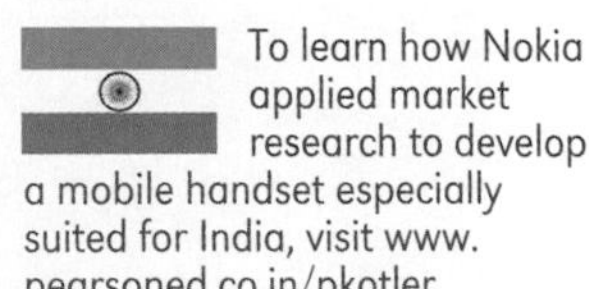

To learn how Nokia applied market research to develop a mobile handset especially suited for India, visit www.pearsoned.co.in/pkotler.

MARKETING MEMO • PROS AND CONS OF ONLINE RESEARCH

Advantages

- **Online research is inexpensive**. The cost of gathering survey information electronically is much less expensive than by traditional means. A typical email survey costs about half of what a conventional survey costs, and return rates can be as high as 50 percent.
- **Online research is faster**. Online surveys are faster to complete since they can automatically direct respondents to applicable questions and be sent electronically to the research supplier once finished. One estimate is that 75 to 80 percent of a survey's targeted response can be generated in 48 hours using online methods, as compared to a telephone survey that can take 70 days to obtain 150 interviews.
- **People tend to be more honest online than they are in personal or telephone interviews.** People may be more open about their opinions when they can respond to a survey privately and not to another person who they feel might be judging them, especially on sensitive topics.
- **Online research is more versatile.** The multimedia applications of online research are especially advantageous. For instance, virtual reality software lets visitors inspect 3-D models of products such as cameras, cars, and medical equipment, and product characteristics can be easily manipulated online. Even at the most basic level, online surveys make answering a questionnaire easier and more fun than paper-and-pencil versions.

Disadvantages

- **Samples can be small and skewed.** Perhaps the largest criticism leveled against online research is that not everyone is online. Research subjects who respond to online surveys are more likely to be tech-savvy middle-class males. A high percentage of households do not have access to the Internet. These people are likely to differ in socioeconomic and education levels from those online. While marketers can be certain that more and more people will go online, it is important for online market researchers to find creative ways to reach certain population segments that are less likely to be online. One option is to combine offline sources with online findings. Providing temporary Internet access at locations such as malls and recreation centers is another strategy. Some research firms use statistical models to fill in the gaps in market research left by offline consumer segments.
- **Online market research is prone to technological problems and inconsistencies.** Because online research is a relatively new method, many market researchers have not gotten survey designs right. A common error is transferring a written survey to the screen. Others overuse technology, concentrating on the bells and whistles and graphics, while ignoring basic survey design guidelines. Problems also arise because browser software varies. The Web designer's final product may be seen very differently depending upon the research subject's screen and operating system.

Sources: Catherine Arnold, "Not Done Net: New Opportunities Still Exist in Online Research." *Marketing News,* April 1, 2004, p. 17; Nima M. Ray, and Sharon W. Tabor, "Contributing Factors: Several Issues Affect e-Research Validity." *Marketing News*, September 15, 2003, p. 50; Louella Miles, "Online, On Tap." *Marketing,* June 16, 2004, pp. 39–40; Joe Dysart, "Cutting Market Research Costs with On-site Surveys." *The Secured Lender,* March/April 2004, pp. 64–67; Suzy Bashford, "The Opinion Formers." *Revolution,* May 2004, pp. 42–46; Bob Lamons, "Eureka! Future of B-to-B Research is Online." *Marketing News,* September 24, 2001, pp. 9–10.

Neopets.com—With more than 22 million members and 27,000 new ones joining everyday, Neopets is one of the most popular children's Web sites. The Web site is free, and it allows users to create, nurture, and care for cyberpets as they earn "neopoints." They raise their neopet in a virtual neighborhood that includes eating at McDonald's, watching Disney movie clips, feeding pets General Mills cereal, or playing Reese's Puffs Mini Golf with them. In this unique form of interactive product placement, advertisers pay to become part of the branded Neopet environment. In return, they get increased exposure to their products or services and data on their target market's consumer behavior. "We live and breathe market research," says Rik Kinney, the company's executive vice president. The primary research mechanism at Neopets is a link to an online survey, prominently displayed on the home page. Members are rewarded with Neopoints for answering questions about their shopping habits, and users complete 6,000–8,000 surveys a day. Interestingly, despite building a profitable business around selling information on its loyal users, Neopets has won kudos from privacy advocates because it only releases data about its user base as a whole or about certain segments, rather than revealing any facts on individual users.[17]

One savvy marketer gets primary data via online surveys from a highly coveted demographic as they play games.

It is important to recognize that not everyone in the sample population will be online (see "Marketing Insight: Global Online Market Research Challenges").

When collecting information, it is also important to protect the personal information of the respondents. However, the level of privacy protection in Asia lags behind Western industrialized countries. In 2005, Japan instituted a law to protect personal information after several leaks of customer data occurred. When Japanese businesses and organizations seek personal information, they are required to explain the purposes for which the data will be used. When they provide personal data to a third party, they must obtain the consent of the individuals involved. They must also disclose the personal data they have on file to the individuals upon request. Several issues give rise to such leaks. One is the level of access employees have to personal data. Many companies fail to sufficiently restrict staff access to ensure protection. The growing trend towards outsourcing and flexible staffing based on the use of temporary workers also poses a data management problem. Further, Japan's traditional corporate culture of *keiretsu* means that customer information is shared widely among different departments and affiliated companies.[18]

MARKETING INSIGHT • GLOBAL ONLINE MARKET RESEARCH CHALLENGES

When chipmaker Intel wanted to know how people in countries around the world use technology, it sent an anthropologist to find out. Dr. Genevieve Bell visited 100 households in 19 cities in seven countries in Asia and the Pacific. She returned with 20 gigabytes of digital photos, 19 field notebooks, and insights about technology, culture, and design that would challenge company assumptions about digital technology.

Clearly, Intel would want to know how technology is used in its international markets. Yet all companies have a stake in knowing how the rest of the world sees and uses what most Westerners take for granted: Internet technology. With online research becoming the fastest growing market research tool, marketers with global ambitions need to know which countries are online and why or why not.

Internet penetration is low in most parts of Asia, Latin America, and Central and Eastern Europe. In Brazil, for example, only 7 percent of the population is online. While most people assume that the low penetration is due to economies that don't support an expensive technological infrastructure, there are other factors involved. There's climate, for one. In Malaysia, power surges caused by monsoons can fry computer motherboards. Government is also a powerful spur or barrier to Internet penetration. While the Chinese economy is zooming ahead, it's unlikely the authoritarian Chinese government will feel comfortable with market researchers gathering information from its citizens via the Internet. Contrast this with South Korea, where the government has made widespread broadband Internet access a priority, and has provided incentives to PC makers to bring cheaper models to market.

Other significant factors that can keep computers, Wi-Fi, and data ports from crossing the threshold are religion and culture. Bell found that values of humility and simplicity are deemed incompatible with Internet technology and make it less welcomed in some Hindu homes in India or Muslim homes in Malaysia and Indonesia. She also noted that while Americans have private space in the home for leisure activities, Japan's tighter quarters afford little privacy. This may explain the huge popularity of text messaging on mobile phones among Japan's young people.

Bell's findings on global responses to technology highlight one of the biggest obstacles to conducting international research, whether online or not: a lack of consistency. Nan Martin, global accounts director for marketing research firm Synovate, says: "In global research, we have to adapt culturally to how, where, and with whom we are doing the research. A simple research study conducted globally becomes much more complicated as a result of the cultural nuances, and it's necessary for us to be sensitive to those nuances in data collection and interpretation." For instance, suppose Internet penetration is equal. In Latin America, where consumers are uncomfortable with the impersonal nature of the Internet, researchers might need to incorporate interactive elements into a survey so participants feel they are talking to a real person. In Asia, focus groups are challenging because of the cultural tendency to conform. Online surveys may bring more honest responses and keep respondents from "losing face."

And what if a researcher collects data face-to-face in Mexico, but by Internet in the U.S.? Nan Martin says, "Not only are the subjects answering the question differently because of cultural difference, but the data is being collected by a different method. That can shake the underpinnings of how research scientists feel about collecting data: that every time you change a variable, you're making interpretation of the results more challenging. It is so challenging, in fact, that some say this is an area where global marketers are best served by hiring an expert—an outside research firm with an expertise in acquiring and analyzing international data."

Sources: Arundhati Parmar, "Stumbling Blocks: Net Research is Not Quite Global." *Marketing News*, March 3, 2003, p. 51; Catherine Arnold, "Global Perspective: Synovate Exec Discusses Future of International Research." *Marketing News*, May 15, 2004, p. 43; Michael Erard, "For Technology, No Small World After All." *New York Times*, May 6, 2004, p. G5 (3), Deborah L. Vence, "Global Consistency: Leave it to the Experts." *Marketing News*, April 28, 2003, p. 37.

Step 4: Analyze the Information

The next-to-last step in the process is to extract findings from the collected data. The researcher tabulates the data and develops frequency distributions. Averages and measures of dispersion are computed for the major variables. The researcher will also apply some advanced statistical techniques and decision models in the hope of discovering additional findings.

Step 5: Present the Findings

As the last step, the researcher presents the findings. The researcher should present findings that are relevant to the major marketing decisions facing management. The main survey findings for the JAL case show that:

1. The chief reasons for using in-flight Internet service are to pass the time surfing, and to send and receive messages from colleagues and family. The charge would be put on passengers' charge accounts and paid by their company.
2. About five first-class passengers out of every 10 during a flight would use the Internet service at \$25; about six would use it at \$15. Thus a charge of \$15 would produce less revenue (\$90 = 6 × \$15) than \$25 (\$125 = 5 × \$25). By charging \$25, JAL would collect \$125 per flight. Assuming that the same flight takes place 365 days a year, JAL would annually collect \$45,625 (= \$125 × 365). Since the investment is \$90,000, it will take approximately two years before JAL breaks even.
3. Offering in-flight service would strengthen the public's image of JAL as an innovative and progressive airline. JAL would gain some new passengers and customer goodwill.

Step 6: Make the Decision

The managers who commissioned the research need to weigh the evidence. If their confidence in the findings is low, they may decide against introducing the in-flight Internet service. If they are predisposed to launching the service, the findings support their inclination. They may even decide to study the issues further and do more research. The decision is theirs, but hopefully the research provided them with insight into the problem (see Table 4.3).[19]

Table 4.3 The Seven Characteristics of Good Marketing Research

1. Scientific method	Effective marketing research uses the principles of the scientific method: careful observation, formulation of hypotheses, prediction, and testing.
2. Research creativity	At its best, marketing research develops innovative ways to solve a problem: a clothing company catering to teenagers gave several young men video cameras, then used the videos for focus groups held in restaurants and other places teens frequent.
3. Multiple methods	Marketing researchers shy away from overreliance on any one method. They also recognize the value of using two or three methods to increase confidence in the results.
4. Interdependence of the type of information sought	Marketing researchers recognize that data are interpreted from underlying models that guide the type of information sought.
5. Value and cost of information	Marketing researchers show concern for estimating the value of information against its cost. Costs are typically easy to determine, but the value of research is harder to quantify. It depends on the reliability and validity of the findings and management's willingness to accept and act on those findings.
6. Healthy skepticism	Marketing researchers show a healthy skepticism toward glib assumptions made by managers about how a market works. They are alert to the problems caused by "marketing myths."
7. Ethical marketing	Marketing research benefits both the sponsoring company and its customers. The misuse of marketing research can harm or annoy consumers, increasing resentment at what consumers regard as an invasion of their privacy or a disguised sales pitch.

A growing number of organizations are using marketing decision support systems to help their marketing managers make better decisions. John Little defines a **marketing decision support system (MDSS)** as a coordinated collection of data, systems, tools, and techniques with supporting software and hardware by which an organization gathers and interprets relevant information from business and environment and turns it into a basis for marketing action.[20]

A classic MDSS example is the CALLPLAN model which helps salespeople determine the number of calls to make per period to each prospect and current client. The model takes into account travel time as well as selling time. When launched, the model was tested at United Airlines with an experimental group that managed to increase its sales over a matched control group by 8 percentage points.[21] Once a year, *Marketing News* lists current marketing and sales software programs that assist in designing marketing research studies, segmenting markets, setting prices and advertising budgets, analyzing media, and planning sales force activity.

Overcoming the Barriers to the Use of Marketing Research

Despite the rapid growth of marketing research, many companies still fail to use it sufficiently or correctly, for several reasons:[22]

- ***A narrow conception of the research*** — Many managers see marketing research as a fact-finding operation. They expect the researcher to design a questionnaire, choose a sample, conduct interviews, and report results, often without a careful definition of the problem or of the decisions facing management. When fact-finding fails to be useful, management's idea of the limited usefulness of marketing research is reinforced.
- ***Uneven caliber of researchers*** — Some managers view marketing research as little more than a clerical activity and treat it as such. Less competent marketing researchers are hired, and their weak training and deficient creativity lead to unimpressive results. The disappointing results reinforce management's prejudice against marketing research. Management continues to pay low salaries to its market researchers, thus perpetuating the basic problem.
- ***Poor framing of the problem*** — In the famous case where Coca-Cola introduced New Coke after much research, the failure of New Coke was largely due to not setting up the research problem correctly from a marketing perspective. The issue was how consumers felt about Coca-Cola as a brand and not necessarily the taste in isolation.
- ***Late and occasionally erroneous findings*** — Managers want results that are accurate and conclusive. They may want the results tomorrow. Yet good marketing research takes time and money. Managers are disappointed when marketing research costs too much or takes too much time.
- ***Personality and presentational differences*** — Differences between the styles of line managers and marketing researchers often get in the way of productive relationships. To a manager who wants concreteness, simplicity, and certainty, a marketing researcher's report may seem abstract, complicated, and tentative. Yet in the more progressive companies, marketing researchers are being included as members of the product management team, and their influence on marketing strategy is growing.

Failure to use marketing research properly has led to numerous gaffes, including this historic one:

Star Wars—In the 1970s, a successful marketing research executive left General Foods for Hollywood to give film studios access to the same research that had spurred General Foods' success. A major studio asked him to research and predict the success or failure of a science fiction film proposal: his views would inform their decision whether to back the film. He concluded the film would fail. First, Watergate had made America less trusting of its institutions and, as a result, Americans in the 1970s prized realism and authenticity over science fiction. Second, the film had the word "war" in its title; he reasoned that America, suffering from its post-Vietnam hangover, would stay away in droves. The film was *Star Wars*. What this researcher delivered was information, not insight. He failed to study the script itself, to see that it was a fundamentally human story—of love, conflict, loss, and redemption—that merely played out against the backdrop of space.[23]

Marketing Research in Asia

The conduct of marketing research in Asia presents its own unique set of challenges.[24] Indeed, much data on Asian markets—particularly less economically developed countries—is non-existent, unreliable, or very costly to collect. Consider the problems with secondary data in the region. Many countries estimate their population by asking local authorities to estimate local population; they will get pure guesses or just extrapolations of past numbers. China relies on birth registration records for population size. However, in rural areas, many families have more than one child and do not register their younger children with the population census. The national income estimate may be based on tax returns but no allowance is made for widespread unreported or underreported income.

There are also few comparable databases available. For instance, in counting the number of travelers leaving their countries, Taiwan, South Korea, Japan, Hong Kong, and the Philippines have varying approaches. In Taiwan, an exit visa with trip destination and duration information is required for each departure. In contrast, only the departure flight number is recorded for each traveler leaving Hong Kong.

Collection of primary data is also saddled with problems. Survey research suffers from a lack of sampling lists, few or unqualified interviewers, poor language translation of questions, respondent refusals to be interviewed, metric equivalence, or less than truthful responses. For example, the Japanese desire not to contradict makes for more "yea-saying" and upward social bias than in a Western culture. Chinese have been observed to use their group as reference for expressed opinions rather than speaking their own mind. Does using a 5- or 7-point scale lead to more responses in the mid-point of the scale in China than in the U.S.? Japanese managers have been found to not adequately understand the scale anchors "agree/disagree" that are commonly used in Likert-type scales. Further, semantic differential scales are difficult to construct in the Chinese language as the language does not readily provide good antonyms. Chinese have a problem answering hypothetical questions as well. Quality control also varies. While the standard of market research in Japan matches the best standards worldwide, this may not be true for all of Asia, especially those countries where market research has developed in the recent past. In a research commissioned by the Hong Kong Tourism Board, several interviewers were charged with fraud after they were found fabricating the data.

Additionally, researchers should bear in mind the connotations Asians associate with certain product features. For example, when asking Asians for their reactions toward price, remember that Asians tend to equate high price with high quality. A warranty on a durable product may be viewed as a signal of quality by an American consumer, but might be viewed as an extrinsic cue of little value to the Chinese consumer. In countries where imports are restricted or highly taxed, like South Korea and the Philippines, "imported" and especially "made-in-U.S.A." are strong product claims, and thus associated with quality. Further, words such as "high quality," "colorful," and "expensive" have varying meanings from country to country.

Researchers must also be aware of the cultural variations in Asian countries. For example, it may be decided that the wife be interviewed. However, in some Muslim countries, men have several wives. Who is to be interviewed?

In many countries, the researcher cannot send a mailed questionnaire because of low population literacy or poor postal service; and telephone interviews are not feasible where telephone ownership or service is poor. This means that researchers must rely primarily on personal interviewing, focus group interviewing, and observational research to arrive at a fair picture of the marketplace. However, over-explanation of the research topic may occur, resulting in inadvertently leading questions. While a lot of insight into the market can be gained from these methods, they cannot be sure of how representative the findings are.

Asian countries also vary in their research capabilities. Hong Kong, Japan, the Philippines, and Singapore have fairly advanced research industries; while those in China and Indonesia are more limited, although improving.

Thus companies going abroad face a problem: they need reliable data because they know little about other countries' cultures, distribution, and economics; yet the data often are poor for making key decisions. Researchers should also be attuned to the high rate of change in the Asian region. Information may thus be outdated very quickly. Marketing research is most useful insofar as it can forecast patterns of behavior. Where rates of change are rapid, the future is more difficult to predict.

Several solutions have been suggested to overcome some of these problems. First, it may be unwise to develop one marketing research study for all of Asia. Rather, a sequence of piloting, adaptation, and rollout may be preferable. External validation among data sources is also advised. For example, travel departure statistics of Japan are known to be accurate and can be used to check the incoming travel figures that South Korea keeps for Japanese visitors. Standardized question structure, back-translation, and logic checks of questions may also be useful research strategies. It has also been recommended that samples be based on future demographic profiles to account for Asia's high rate of change. Finally, as more companies enter Asia, the marketing research capabilities and infrastructure in the region will improve.

Measuring Marketing Productivity

An important task of marketing research is to assess the efficiency and effectiveness of marketing activities. Marketers increasingly are being held accountable for their investments and must be able to justify marketing expenditures to senior management.[25] In a recent Accenture survey, 70 percent of marketing executives stated that they did not have a handle on the return on their marketing investments.[26] Another study revealed that 63 percent of senior management said they were dissatisfied with their marketing performance measurement system and wanted marketing to supply prior and posterior estimates of the impact of marketing programs.[27]

Marketing research can help address this increased need for accountability. Two complementary approaches to measure marketing productivity are: (1) marketing metrics to assess marketing effects, and (2) marketing mix modeling to estimate causal relationships and how marketing activity affects outcomes. A third, marketing dashboards, is a structured way to disseminate the insights gleaned from these two approaches within the organization.

Marketing Metrics

Marketers employ a wide variety of measures to assess marketing effects. **Marketing metrics** is the set of measures that help firms to quantify, compare, and interpret their marketing performance. Marketing metrics can be used by brand managers to design marketing programs and by senior management to decide on financial allocations.

Ambler suggests that if firms think they are already measuring marketing performance adequately, they should ask themselves five questions:[28]

1. Do you routinely research consumer behavior (retention, acquisition, usage, etc.) and why consumers behave that way (awareness, satisfaction, perceived quality, etc.)?
2. Are the results of this research routinely reported to the board in a format integrated with financial marketing metrics?
3. In those reports, are the results compared with the levels previously forecasted in the business plans?
4. Are they also compared with the levels achieved by your key competitor using the same indicators?
5. Is short-term performance adjusted according to the change in your marketing-based asset(s)?

Ambler believes firms must give priority to measuring and reporting marketing performance through marketing metrics. He believes evaluation can be split into two parts: (1) short-term results and (2) changes in brand equity. Short-term results often reflect profit and loss concerns as shown by sales turnover, shareholder value, or some combination of the two. Brand-equity measures include awareness, market share, relative price, number of complaints, distribution and availability, total number of customers, perceived quality, and loyalty/retention. Ambler also recommends developing employee measures and metrics, arguing that "End users are the ultimate customers, but your own staff are your first; you need to measure the health of the internal market." Table 4.4 summarizes a list of popular internal and external metrics from Ambler's survey.

Table 4.4 Sample Marketing Metrics

I. External	II. Internal
Awareness	Awareness of goals
Market share (volume or value)	Commitment to goals
Relative price (market share value/volume)	Active innovation support
Number of complaints (level of dissatisfaction)	Resource adequacy
Consumer satisfaction	Staffing/skill levels
Distribution/availability	Desire to learn
Total number of customers	Willingness to change
Perceived quality/esteem	Freedom to fail
Loyalty/retention	Autonomy
Relative perceived quality	Relative employee satisfaction

Sources: Tim Ambler, "What Does Marketing Success Look Like?" *Marketing Management*, Spring 2001, pp. 13–18.

Marketing-Mix Modeling

Marketing accountability also means that marketers can more precisely estimate the effects of different marketing investments. *Marketing-mix models* analyze data from a variety of sources, such as retailer scanner data, company shipment data, pricing, media and promotion spending data, to understand more precisely the effects of specific marketing activities. To deepen understanding, multivariate analyses are conducted to sort through how each marketing element influences marketing outcomes of interest such as brand sales or market share.[29]

Especially popular with packaged goods marketers such as Procter & Gamble, Clorox, and Colgate, the findings from marketing-mix modeling are used to allocate or re-allocate expenditures. Analyses explore which part of ad budgets are wasted, what optimal spending levels are, and what minimum investment levels should be.[30] Although marketing-mix modeling helps to isolate effects, it is less effective at assessing how different marketing elements work in combination. Reibstein notes three other shortcomings:[31]

- Marketing-mix modeling focuses on incremental growth instead of baseline sales or long-term effects.
- Despite their importance, the integration of metrics such as customer satisfaction, awareness, and brand equity into marketing-mix modeling is limited.
- Marketing-mix modeling generally fails to incorporate metrics related to competitors, the trade, or the sales force (the average business spends far more on the sales force and trade promotion than on advertising or consumer promotion).

Marketing Dashboards

Firms are also employing organizational processes and systems to make sure they maximize the value of all these different metrics. Management can assemble a summary set of relevant internal and external measures in a *marketing dashboard* for synthesis and interpretation. Marketing dashboards are like the instrument panel in a car or plane, visually displaying real-time indicators to ensure proper functioning. They are only as good as the information on which they're based, but sophisticated visualization tools are helping bring data alive to improve understanding and analysis.[32]

Some companies are also appointing marketing controllers to review budget items and expenses. Increasingly, these controllers are using business intelligence software to create digital versions of marketing dashboards that aggregate data from disparate internal and external sources.

As input to the marketing dashboard, companies should include two key market-based scorecards that reflect performance and provide possible early warning signals.

- A **customer-performance scorecard** records how well the company is doing year after year on such customer-based measures as those shown in Table 4.5. Management should set norms for each measure and take action when results get out of bounds.

- A **stakeholder-performance scorecard** tracks the satisfaction of various constituencies who have a critical interest in and impact on the company's performance: employees, suppliers, banks, distributors, retailers, and stockholders. Again, management should take action when one or more groups register increased or above-norm levels of dissatisfaction.[33]

Table 4.5 Sample Customer Performance Scorecard Measures

- Percentage of new customers to average number of customers.
- Percentage of lost customers to average number of customers.
- Percentage of win-back customers to average number of customers.
- Percentage of customers falling into very dissatisfied, dissatisfied, neutral, satisfied, and very satisfied categories.
- Percentage of customers who say they would repurchase the product.
- Percentage of customers who say they would recommend the product to others.
- Percentage of target market customers who have brand awareness or recall.
- Percentage of customers who say that the company's product is the most preferred in its category.
- Percentage of customers who correctly identify the brand's intended positioning and differentiation.
- Average perception of company's product quality relative to chief competitor.
- Average perception of company's service quality relative to chief competitor.

Some executives worry that they will miss the big picture if they focus too much on a set of numbers on a dashboard. Some critics are concerned about privacy and the pressure the technique places on employees. But most experts feel the rewards offset the risks.[34] "Marketing Insight: Marketing Dashboards to Improve Effectiveness and Efficiency" provides practical advice about the development of these marketing tools.

MARKETING INSIGHT • MARKETING DASHBOARDS TO IMPROVE EFFECTIVENESS AND EFFICIENCY

Marketing consultant Pat LaPointe sees marketing dashboards as providing all the up-to-the-minute information necessary to run the business operations for a company—such as sales versus forecast, distribution channel effectiveness, brand equity evolution, and human capital development. According to LaPointe, an effective dashboard will focus thinking, improve internal communications, and reveal where marketing investments are paying off and where they aren't.

LaPointe observes four common measurement "pathways" marketers are pursuing today (see Figure 4.2).

- The **customer metrics pathway** looks at how prospects become customers, from awareness to preference to trial to repeat purchase. Many companies track progression through a "hierarchy of effects" model to follow the evolution of broad market potential to specific revenue opportunities.
- The **unit metrics pathway** reflects what marketers know about sales of product/service units—how much is sold by product line and/or by geography; the marketing cost per unit sold as an efficiency yardstick; and where and how margin is optimized in terms of characteristics of the product line or distribution channel.
- The **cash-flow metrics pathway** focuses on how well marketing expenditures are achieving short-term returns. Program and campaign ROI models measure the immediate impact or net present value of profits expected from a given investment.
- The **brand metrics pathway** tracks the development of the longer-term impact of marketing through brand equity measures that assess both the perceptual health of the brand from customer and prospective customer perspectives as well as the overall financial health of the brand.

LaPointe feels a marketing dashboard can present insights from all the pathways in a graphically related view that helps management see subtle links between them. A well-constructed dashboard can have a series of "tabs" that allow the user to toggle easily between different "families" of metrics organized by customer, product, brand, experience, channels, efficiency, organizational development, or macroenvironmental factors. Each tab presents the three or four most insightful metrics, with data filtered by business unit, geography, or customer segment based upon the users' needs (see Figure 4.3 for example.)

Source: Adapted from Patrick LaPointe, *Marketing by the Dashboard Light–How to Get More Insight, Foresight, and Accountability from Your Marketing Investments*, © 2005, Patrick LaPointe.

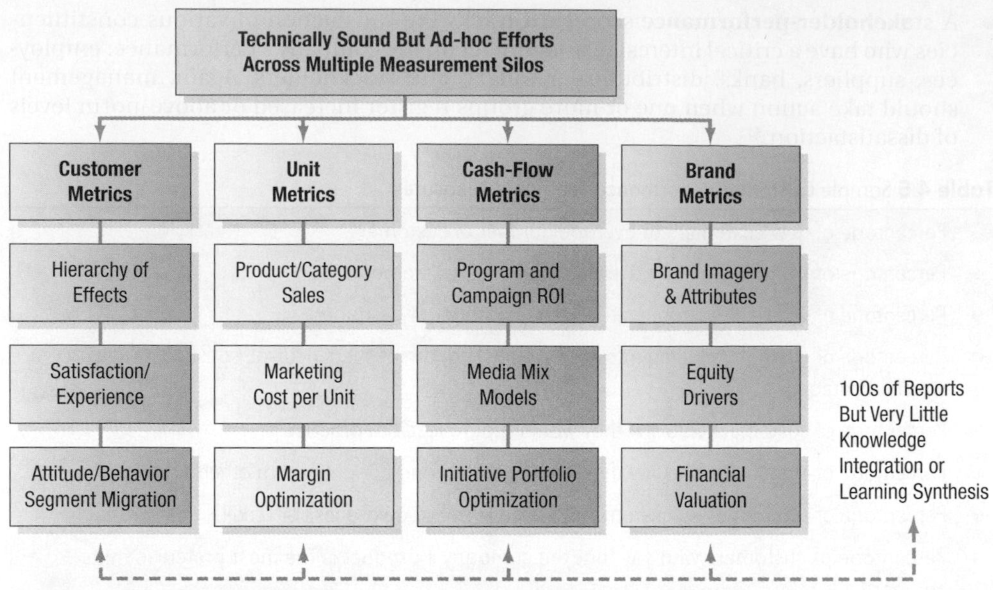

Figure 4.2 Marketing Measurement Pathway

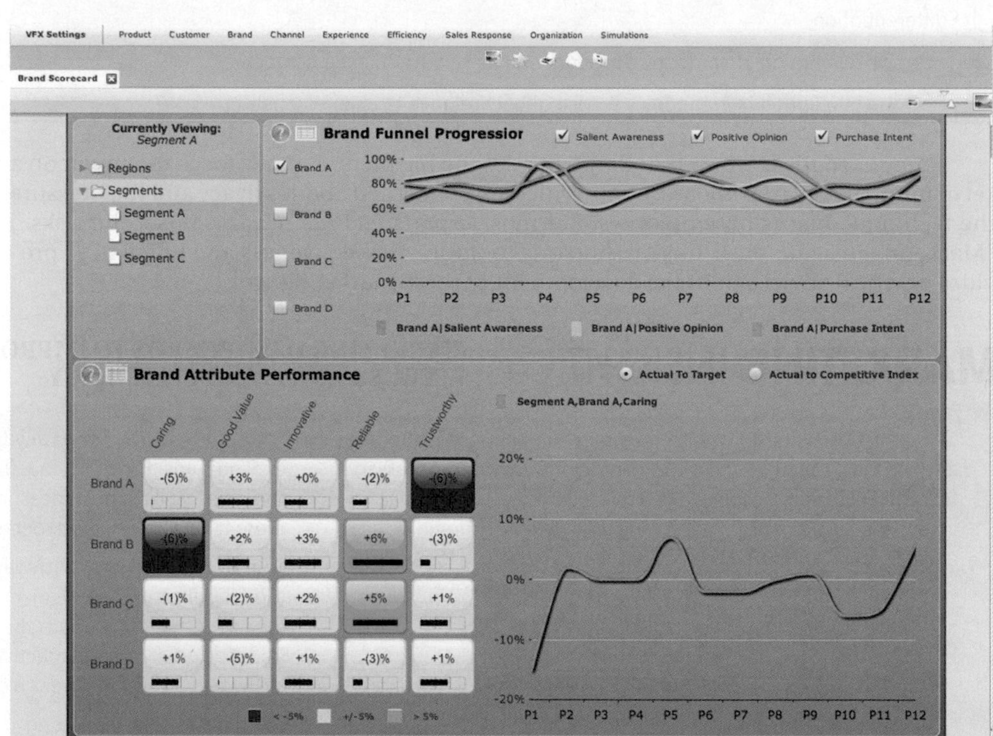

Figure 4.3 Example of a Marketing Dashboard

Source: Adapted from Patrick LaPointe, *Marketing by the Dashboard Light – How to Get More Insight, Foresight, and Accountability from your Marketing Investments.* © 2005, Patrick LaPointe.

Ideally, the number of metrics presented in the marketing dashboard would be reduced to a handful of key drivers over time. Importantly, the process of developing and refining the marketing dashboard will undoubtedly raise and resolve many key questions about the business.

One major reason for undertaking marketing research is to identify market opportunities. Once the research is complete, the company must measure and forecast the size, growth, and profit potential of each market opportunity. Sales forecasts are used by the finance department to raise the needed cash for investment and operations; by the manufacturing department to establish capacity and output levels; by purchasing to acquire the right amount of supplies; and by human resources to hire the needed number of workers. Marketing is responsible for preparing the sales forecasts. If its forecast is far off the mark, the company will be saddled with excess inventory or have inadequate inventory. Sales forecasts are based on estimates of demand. Managers need to define what they mean by market demand. Here is a good example of the importance of defining the market correctly:

Coca-Cola—When Roberto Goizueta became CEO of Coca-Cola, many people thought that Coke's sales were maxed out. However, Goizueta reframed the view of Coke's market share. He said Coca-Cola accounted for less than two ounces of the 64 ounces of fluid that each of the world's 4.4 billion people drank on average daily. "The enemy is coffee, milk, tea, water," he told his people at Coke, ushering in a huge period of growth.

Companies can prepare as many as 90 different types of demand estimates (see Figure 4.4). Demand can be measured for six different product levels, five different space levels, and three different time levels.

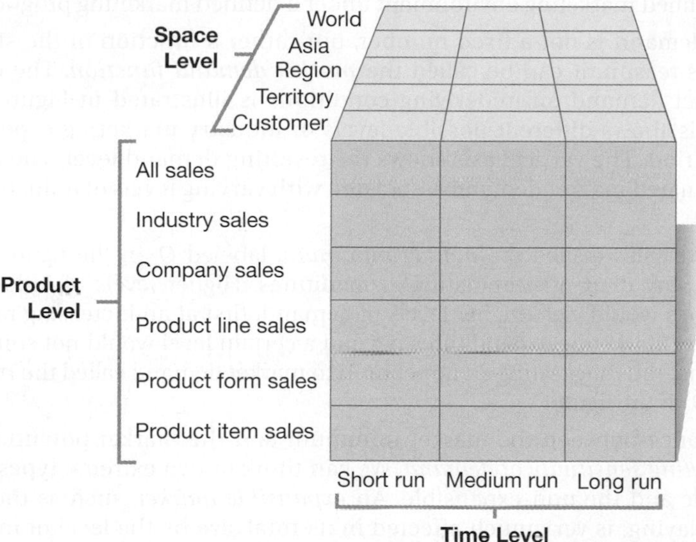

Figure 4.4 Ninety Types of Demand Measurement (6 × 5 × 3)

Each demand measure serves a specific purpose. A company might forecast short-run demand for a particular product for the purpose of ordering raw materials, planning production, and borrowing cash. It might forecast regional demand for its major product line to decide whether to set up regional distribution.

Forecasts also depend on which type of market is being considered. The size of a market hinges on the number of buyers who might exist for a particular market offer. But there are many productive ways to break down the market:

- The **potential market** is the set of consumers who profess a sufficient level of interest in a market offer. However, consumer interest is not enough to define a market. Potential consumers must have enough income and must have access to the product offer.
- The **available market** is the set of consumers who have interest, income, and access to a particular offer. For some market offers, the company or government may restrict sales to certain groups. For example, a particular state might ban motorcycle sales to anyone under 21 years of age. The eligible adults constitute the *qualified available market*—the set of consumers who have interest, income, access, and qualifications for the particular market offer.
- The **target market** is the part of the qualified available market the company decides to pursue. The company might decide to concentrate its marketing and distribution effort on the northern provinces. The company will end up selling to a certain number of buyers in its target market.

- The **penetrated market** is the set of consumers who are buying the company's product.

These definitions are a useful tool for market planning. If the company is not satisfied with its current sales, it can take a number of actions. It can try to attract a larger percentage of buyers from its target market. It can lower the qualifications of potential buyers. It can expand its available market by opening distribution elsewhere or lowering its price; or it can reposition itself in the minds of its customers.

Vocabulary for Demand Measurement

The major concepts in demand measurement are market demand and company demand. Within each, we distinguish among a demand function, a sales forecast, and a potential.

MARKET DEMAND

As we have seen, the marketer's first step in evaluating marketing opportunities is to estimate total market demand. **Market demand** for a product is the total volume that would be bought by a defined customer group in a defined geographical area in a defined time period in a defined marketing environment under a defined marketing program.

Market demand is not a fixed number, but rather a function of the stated conditions. For this reason, it can be called the *market demand function.* The dependence of total market demand on underlying conditions is illustrated in Figure 4.5(a). The horizontal axis shows different possible levels of industry marketing expenditure in a given time period. The vertical axis shows the resulting demand level. The curve represents the estimated market demand associated with varying levels of industry marketing expenditure.

Some base sales (called the *market minimum,* labeled Q_1 in the figure) would take place without any demand-stimulating expenditures. Higher levels of industry marketing expenditures would yield higher levels of demand, first at an increasing rate, then at a decreasing rate. Marketing expenditures beyond a certain level would not stimulate much further demand, thus suggesting an upper limit to market demand called the *market potential* (labeled Q_2 in the figure).

The distance between the market minimum and the market potential shows the overall *marketing sensitivity of demand.* We can think of two extreme types of markets, the expansible and the non-expansible. An *expansible market,* such as the market for racquetball playing, is very much affected in its total size by the level of industry marketing expenditures. In terms of Figure 4.5(a), the distance between Q_1 and Q_2 is relatively large. A *non-expansible market*—for example, the market for opera—is not much affected by the level of marketing expenditures; the distance between Q_1 and Q_2 is relatively small. Organizations selling in a non-expansible market must accept the market's size (the level of *primary demand* for the product class) and direct their efforts to winning a larger **market share** for their product (the level of selective demand for the company's product).

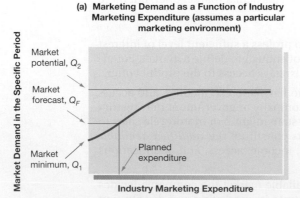

(a) Marketing Demand as a Function of Industry Marketing Expenditure (assumes a particular marketing environment)

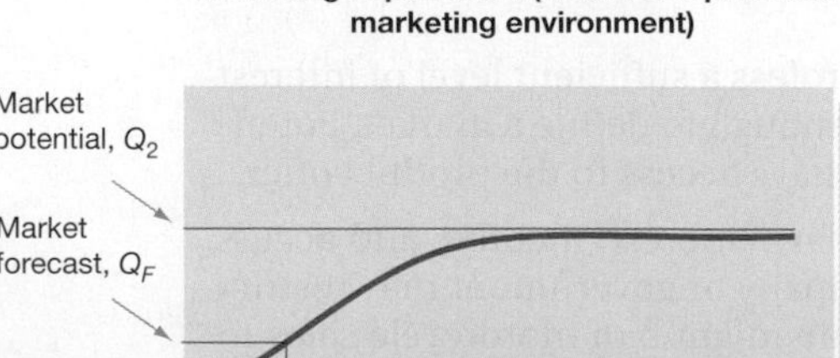

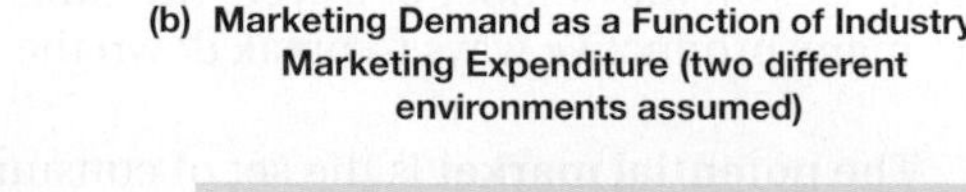

(b) Marketing Demand as a Function of Industry Marketing Expenditure (two different environments assumed)

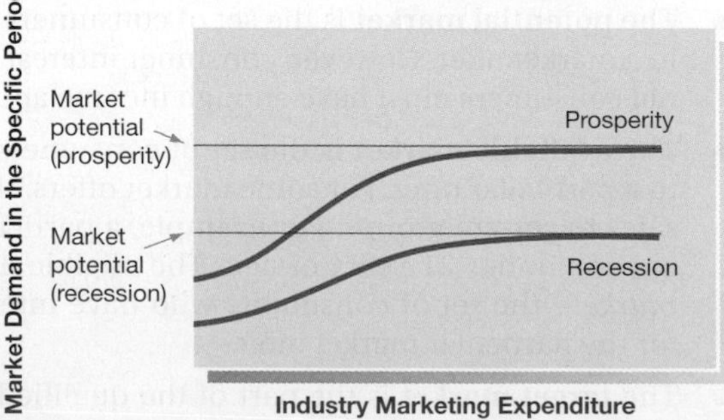

Figure 4.5 Market Demand Functions

It pays to compare the current level of market demand to the potential demand level. The result is called the **market penetration index**. A low market penetration index indicates substantial growth potential for all the firms. A high market penetration index suggests that there will be increased costs in attracting the few remaining prospects. Generally, price competition increases and margins fall when the market penetration index is already high.

A company should also compare its current market share to its potential market share. The result is called the company's **share penetration index**. A low share penetration index indicates that the company can greatly expand its share. The underlying factors holding it back could be many: low brand awareness, low brand availability, benefit deficiencies, too high a price. A firm should calculate the share penetration increases that would occur with investments to remove each deficiency, to see which investments would produce the greatest improvement in share penetration.[35]

It is important to remember that the market demand function is not a picture of market demand over time. Rather, the curve shows alternative current forecasts of market demand associated with alternative possible levels of industry marketing effort in the current period.

MARKET FORECAST

Only one level of industry marketing expenditure will actually occur. The market demand corresponding to this level is called the **market forecast**.

MARKET POTENTIAL

The market forecast shows expected market demand, not maximum market demand. For the latter, we have to visualize the level of market demand resulting from a "very high" level of industry marketing expenditure, where further increases in marketing effort would have little effect in stimulating further demand. **Market potential** is the limit approached by market demand as industry marketing expenditures approach infinity for a given marketing environment.

The phrase "for a given market environment" is crucial. Consider the market potential for automobiles in a period of recession versus a period of prosperity. The market potential is higher during prosperity. The dependence of market potential on the environment is illustrated in Figure 4.5(b). Market analysts distinguish between the position of the market demand function and movement along it. Companies cannot do anything about the position of the market demand function, which is determined by the marketing environment. However, companies influence their particular location on the function when they decide how much to spend on marketing.

Companies interested in market potential have a special interest in the **product penetration percentage**, which is the percentage of ownership or use of a product or service in a population. Companies assume that the lower the product penetration percentage, the higher the market potential, although this assumes that everyone will eventually be in the market for every product.

COMPANY DEMAND

We are now ready to define company demand: **Company demand** is the company's estimated share of market demand at alternative levels of company marketing effort in a given time period. The company's share of market demand depends on how its products, services, prices, communications, and so on are perceived relative to the competitors'. If other things are equal, the company's market share would depend on the size and effectiveness of its market expenditures relative to competitors. Marketing model builders have developed sales-response functions to measure how a company's sales are affected by its marketing expenditure level, marketing mix, and marketing effectiveness.[36]

COMPANY SALES FORECAST

Once marketers have estimated company demand, their next task is to choose a level of marketing effort. The chosen level will produce an expected level of sales. The **company sales forecast** is the expected level of company sales based on a chosen marketing plan and an assumed marketing environment.

The company sales forecast is represented graphically with company sales on the vertical axis and company marketing effort on the horizontal axis, as in Figure 4.5. Too often the sequential relationship between the company forecast and the company marketing plan is confused. One frequently hears that the company should develop its marketing plan on the basis of its sales forecast. This forecast-to-plan sequence is valid if "forecast" means an estimate of national economic activity or if company demand is non-expansible. The sequence is not valid, however, where market demand is expansible or where "forecast" means an estimate of company sales. The company sales forecast does not establish a basis for deciding what to spend on marketing. On the contrary, the sales forecast is the result of an assumed marketing expenditure plan.

Two other concepts are worth mentioning in relation to the company sales forecast. A **sales quota** is the sales goal set for a product line, company division, or sales representative. It is primarily a managerial device for defining and stimulating sales effort. Management sets sales quotas on the basis of the company sales forecast and the psychology of stimulating its achievement. Generally, sales quotas are set slightly higher than estimated sales to stretch the sales force's effort.

A **sales budget** is a conservative estimate of the expected volume of sales and is used primarily for making current purchasing, production, and cash flow decisions. The sales budget is based on the sales forecast and the need to avoid excessive risk. Sales budgets are generally set slightly lower than the sales forecast.

COMPANY SALES POTENTIAL

Company sales potential is the sales limit approached by company demand as company marketing effort increases relative to that of competitors. The absolute limit of company demand is, of course, the market potential. The two would be equal if the company got 100 percent of the market. In most cases, company sales potential is less than the market potential, even when company marketing expenditures increase considerably, relative to competitors. The reason is that each competitor has a core of loyal buyers who are not very responsive to other companies' efforts to woo them.

Estimating Current Demand

We are now ready to examine practical methods for estimating current market demand. Marketing executives want to estimate total market potential, area market potential, and total industry sales and market shares.

TOTAL MARKET POTENTIAL

Total market potential is the maximum amount of sales that might be available to all the firms in an industry during a given period, under a given level of industry marketing effort and environmental conditions. A common way to estimate total market potential is as follows: Estimate the potential number of buyers times the average quantity purchased by a buyer times the price.

If 100 million people buy books each year, and the average book buyer buys three books a year, and the average price of a book is $20, then the total market potential for books is $6 billion (100 million × 3 × $20). The most difficult component to estimate is the number of buyers for the specific product or market. One can always start with the total population in a country, say 261 million people. The next step is to eliminate groups that obviously would not buy the product. Let us assume that illiterate people and children under 12 do not buy books, and they constitute 20 percent of the population.

This means that only 80 percent of the population, or approximately 209 million people, would be in the suspect pool. We might do further research and find that people of low income and low education do not read books, and they constitute over 30 percent of the suspect pool. Eliminating them, we arrive at a prospect pool of approximately 146.3 million book buyers. We would use this number of potential buyers to calculate total market potential.

A variation on this method is the *chain-ratio method.* It involves multiplying a base number by several adjusting percentages. Suppose a brewery is interested in estimating the market potential for a new light beer. An estimate can be made by the following calculation:

Demand for the new light beer = Population × personal discretionary income per capita × average percentage of discretionary income spent on food × average percentage of amount spent on food that is spent on beverages × average percentage of amount spent on beverages that is spent on alcoholic beverages × average percentage of amount spent on alcoholic beverages that is spent on beer × expected percentage of amount spent on beer that will be spent on light beer.

AREA MARKET POTENTIAL

Companies face the problem of selecting the best territories and allocating their marketing budget optimally among these territories. Thus they need to estimate the market potential of different cities, states, and nations. Two major methods of assessing area market potential are available: the market-buildup method, which is used primarily by business marketers, and the multiple-factor index method, which is used primarily by consumer marketers.

Market-Buildup Method

The **market-buildup method** calls for identifying all the potential buyers in each market and estimating their potential purchases. This method produces accurate results if we have a list of all potential buyers and a good estimate of what each will buy. Unfortunately, this information is not always easy to gather.

Consider a machine-tool company that wants to estimate the area market potential for its wood lathe in the Suzhou area. Its first step is to identify all potential buyers of wood lathes in the area. The buyers consist primarily of manufacturing establishments that have to shape or ream wood as part of their operation, so the company could compile a list from a directory of all manufacturing establishments in the Suzhou area. Then it could estimate the number of lathes each industry might purchase based on the number of lathes per thousand employees or per $1 million of sales in that industry.

Multiple-Factor Index Method

Like business marketers, consumer companies also have to estimate area market potentials, but the customers of consumer companies are too numerous to be listed. The method most commonly used in consumer markets is a straightforward index method. For example, a fruit seller might assume that the market potential for fruits is directly related to population size. If the state of Sabah has 1.7 percent of the Malaysia population, the company might assume that Sabah will be a market for 1.7 percent of total fruits sold.

However, a single factor is rarely a complete indicator of sales opportunity. Regional fruit sales are also influenced by per capita income and the number of food stalls per 10,000 people. Thus it makes sense to develop a multiple-factor index, with each factor assigned a specific weight. The numbers are the weights attached to each variable. For example, suppose Sabah has 2.5 percent of Malaysians' disposable personal income, 2 percent of Malaysia retail sales, and 1.7 percent of Malaysia population, and the respective weights are 0.5, 0.3, and 0.2. The buying-power index for Sabah would be 2.19 [0.5(2.5) + 0.3(2) + 0.2(1.7)]. Thus 2.19 percent of the nation's fruit sales might be expected to take place in Sabah.

The weights used in the buying-power index are somewhat arbitrary. Other weights can be assigned if appropriate. Further, a manufacturer would want to adjust the market potential for additional factors, such as competitors' presence in that market, local promotional costs, seasonal factors, and local market idiosyncrasies.

Many companies compute other area indexes as a guide to allocating marketing resources. Suppose the drug company is reviewing six Chinese cities listed in Table 4.6. The first two columns show its percentage of China brand and category sales in these six cities. Column 3 shows the **Brand Development Index (BDI)**, which is the index of brand sales to category sales. For example, Shanghai has a BDI of 114 because the brand is relatively more developed than the category in Shanghai. Chengdu has a BDI of 65, which means that the brand in Chengdu is relatively underdeveloped. Normally, the lower the BDI, the higher the market opportunity, in that there is room to grow the brand. However, other marketers would argue the opposite, that marketing funds should go into the brand's strongest markets—where it might be important to reinforce loyalty or more easily capture additional brand share.[37]

Table 4.6 Calculating Brand Development Index (BDI)

Territory	(a) Percent of China Brand Sales	(b) Percent of China Category Sales	BDI (a ÷ b) × 100
Shanghai	3.09	2.71	114
Chengdu	6.74	10.41	65
Tianjin	3.49	3.85	91
Beijing	.97	.81	120
Shenzhen	1.13	.81	140
Suzhou	3.12	3.00	104

After the company decides on the city-by-city allocation of its budget, it can refine each city allocation down to census tracts if these are available. *Census tracts* are small, locally defined statistical areas in metropolitan locations and some other counties. Data on population size, median family income, and other characteristics for these geographic units have been found to be useful for identifying high-potential retail areas within large cities.

INDUSTRY SALES AND MARKET SHARES

Besides estimating total potential and area potential, a company needs to know the actual industry sales taking place in its market. This means identifying competitors and estimating their sales.

The industry trade association will often collect and publish total industry sales, although it usually does not list individual company sales separately. With this information, each company can evaluate its performance against the whole industry. Suppose a company's sales are increasing by 5 percent a year, and industry sales are increasing by 10 percent. This company is actually losing its relative standing in the industry.

Another way to estimate sales is to buy reports from a marketing research firm that audits total sales and brand sales. A.C. Nielsen Media Research audits retail sales in various product categories and sells this information to interested companies. These audits can give a company valuable information about its total product-category sales as well as brand sales. It can compare its performance to the total industry or any particular competitor to see whether it is gaining or losing share.

Business-goods marketers typically have a harder time estimating industry sales and market shares. Business marketers have no Nielsens to rely on. Distributors typically will not supply information about how much of competitors' products they are selling. Business-goods marketers therefore operate with less knowledge of their market-share results.

Estimating Future Demand

Very few products or services lend themselves to easy forecasting; those that do generally involve a product whose absolute level or trend is fairly constant and where competition is non-existent (public utilities) or stable (pure oligopolies). In most markets, total demand and company demand are not stable. Good forecasting becomes a key factor in company success. The more unstable the demand, the more critical is forecast accuracy, and the more elaborate is forecasting procedure.

Companies commonly use a three-stage procedure to prepare a sales forecast. They prepare a macroeconomic forecast first, followed by an industry forecast, followed by a company sales forecast. The macroeconomic forecast calls for projecting inflation, unemployment, interest rates, consumer spending, business investment, government expenditures, net exports, and other variables. The end result is a forecast of gross national product, which is then used, along with other environmental indicators, to forecast industry sales. The company derives its sales forecast by assuming that it will win a certain market share.

How do firms develop their forecasts? Firms may do it internally or buy forecasts from outside sources such as marketing research firms, which develop a forecast by interviewing customers, distributors, and other knowledgeable parties. Specialized forecasting firms produce long-range forecasts of particular macroenvironmental components, such as population, natural resources, and technology.

All forecasts are built on one of three information bases: what people say, what people do, or what people have done. The first basis—what people say—involves surveying the opinions of buyers or those close to them, such as salespeople or outside experts. It includes three methods: surveys of buyer's intentions, composites of sales force opinions, and expert opinion. Building a forecast on what people do involves another method—putting the product into a test market to measure buyer response. The final basis—what people have done—involves analyzing records of past buying behavior or using time-series analysis or statistical demand analysis.

SURVEY OF BUYERS' INTENTIONS

Forecasting is the art of anticipating what buyers are likely to do under a given set of conditions. Because buyer behavior is so important, buyers should be surveyed. For major consumer durables (for example, major appliances), several research organizations conduct periodic surveys of consumer buying intentions. These organizations ask questions like the following:

Do you intend to buy an automobile within the next six months?

0.00	0.20	0.40	0.60	0.80	1.00
No chance	Slight possibility	Fair possibility	Good possibility	High possibility	Certain

This is called a **purchase probability scale**. The various surveys also inquire into consumers' present and future personal finances and their expectations about the economy. The various bits of information are then combined into a consumer confidence or consumer sentiment measure. Consumer durable-goods producers subscribe to these indexes in the hope of anticipating major shifts in buying intentions so they can adjust production and marketing plans accordingly.

For business buying, research firms can carry out buyer-intention surveys regarding plant, equipment, and materials. Their estimates tend to fall within a 10 percent error band of the actual outcomes. Buyer-intention surveys are particularly useful in estimating demand for industrial products, consumer durables, product purchases where advanced planning is required, and new products. The value of a buyer-intention survey increases to the extent that the cost of reaching buyers is small, the buyers are few, they have clear intentions, they implement their intentions, and they willingly disclose their intentions.

COMPOSITE OF SALES FORCE OPINIONS

When buyer interviewing is impractical, the company may ask its sales representatives to estimate their future sales. Each sales representative estimates how much each current and prospective customer will buy of each of the company's products.

Few companies use sales force estimates without making some adjustments. Sales representatives might be pessimistic or optimistic, or they might go from one extreme to another because of a recent setback or success. Further, they are often unaware of larger economic developments and do not know how their company's marketing plans will influence future sales in their territory. They might deliberately underestimate demand so that the company will set a low sales quota, or they might lack the time to prepare careful estimates or might not consider the effort worthwhile. To encourage better estimating, the company could offer certain aids or incentives. For example, sales reps might receive a record of their past forecasts compared with actual sales and also a description of company assumptions on the business outlook, competitor behavior, and marketing plans.

Involving the sales force in forecasting brings a number of benefits. Sales reps might have better insight into developing trends than any other single group. After participating in the forecasting process, reps might have greater confidence in their sales quotas and more incentive to achieve them. Also, a "grassroots" forecasting procedure provides detailed estimates broken down by product, territory, customer, and sales rep.

EXPERT OPINION

Companies can also obtain forecasts from experts, including dealers, distributors, suppliers, marketing consultants, and trade associations. Large appliance companies periodically survey dealers for their forecasts of short-term demand, as do car companies. Dealer estimates are subject to the same strengths and weaknesses as sales force estimates. Many companies buy economic and industry forecasts from well-known economic-forecasting firms. These specialists are able to prepare better economic forecasts than the company because they have more data available and more forecasting expertise.

Occasionally, companies will invite a group of experts to prepare a forecast. The experts exchange views and produce a group estimate (*group-discussion method*); or the experts supply their estimates individually, and an analyst combines them into a single estimate (*pooling of individual estimates*). Alternatively, the experts supply individual estimates and assumptions that are then reviewed and revised by the company. Further rounds of estimating and refining follow (this is the Delphi method).[38]

PAST-SALES ANALYSIS

Sales forecasts can be developed on the basis of past sales. *Time-series analysis* consists of breaking down past time-series into four components (trend, cycle, seasonal, and erratic) and projecting these components into the future. *Exponential smoothing* consists of projecting the next period's sales by combining an average of past sales and the most recent sales, giving more weight to the latter. *Statistical demand analysis* consists of measuring the impact level of each of a set of causal factors (e.g., income, marketing expenditures, price) on the sales level. Finally, *econometric analysis* consists of building sets of equations that describe a system, and proceeding to fit the parameters statistically.

MARKET-TEST METHOD

When buyers do not plan their purchases carefully or experts are not available or reliable, a direct-market test is desirable. A direct-market test is especially desirable in forecasting new-product sales or established product sales in a new distribution channel or territory. (We discuss market testing in detail in Chapter 20.)

Summary

1. Companies can conduct their own marketing research or hire other companies to do it for them. Good marketing research is characterized by the scientific method, creativity, multiple research methods, accurate model building, cost-benefit analysis, healthy skepticism, and an ethical focus.
2. The marketing research process consists of defining the problem and research objective, developing the research plan, collecting the information, analyzing the information, presenting the findings to management, and making the decision.
3. In conducting research, firms must decide whether to collect their own data or use data that already exist. They must also decide which research approach (observational, focus-group, survey, behavioral data, or experimental) and which research instruments (questionnaire or mechanical instruments) to use. In addition, they must decide on a sampling plan and contact methods.
4. Conducting marketing research in Asia is challenging due to non-existent and unreliable secondary data, non-comparability of databases cross-nationally, poor research infrastructure, cultural differences in consumer response, variations in research capabilities, and high rates of change in the marketplace. Solutions include sequencing the piloting, adapting, and rollout of surveys regionally, external validation of data sources, use of samples based on future demographic profiles, and investment in enhancing research capabilities and infrastructure.
5. Two complementary approaches to measuring marketing productivity are: (1) marketing metrics to assess marketing effects, and (2) marketing-mix modeling to estimate causal relationships and measure how marketing activity affects outcomes. Marketing dashboards are a structured way to disseminate the insights gleaned from these two approaches within the organization.
6. There are two types of demand: market demand and company demand. To estimate current demand, companies attempt to determine total market potential, area market potential, industry sales, and market share. To estimate future demand, companies survey buyers' intentions, solicit their sales force's input, gather expert opinions, or engage in market testing. Mathematical models, advanced statistical techniques, and computerized data collection procedures are essential to all types of demand and sales forecasting.

Application

Marketing Debate—What is the Best Type of Marketing Research?

Many market researchers have their favorite research approaches or techniques, although different researchers often have different preferences. Some researchers maintain that the only way to really learn about consumers or brands is through in-depth, qualitative research. Others contend that the only legitimate and defensible form of marketing research involves quantitative measures.

Take a position: *Marketing research should be quantitative* versus *Marketing research should be qualitative.*

Marketing Discussion

When was the last time you participated in a survey? How helpful do you think was the information you provided? How could the research have been done differently to make it more effective?

Connecting with Customers

Ritz-Carlton's focus on its guests helped it win the prestigious Baldrige Award twice and placed it among the Top 20 on the Brand Keys Customer Loyalty Index.

Creating Customer Value, Satisfaction, and Loyalty

Today, companies face their toughest competition ever. Moving from a product and sales philosophy to a marketing philosophy, however, gives a company a better chance of outperforming competition. And the cornerstone of a well-conceived marketing orientation is strong customer relationships. Marketers must connect with customers, informing, engaging, and maybe even energizing them in the process. John Chambers, CEO of Cisco Systems, put it well: "Make your customer the center of your culture." Customer-centered companies are adept at building customer relationships, not just products; they are skilled in market engineering, not just product engineering.

The Ritz-Carlton hotel chain, owned by Marriott International, is known throughout the world for its singular focus on providing guests with luxurious amenities and exceptional service. This customer-centered approach is expressed by the company's motto: "We are ladies and gentlemen serving ladies and gentlemen." Guests at any of the 62 Ritz-Carlton hotels in 21 countries notice the brand's famed personal touch immediately upon checking in, when they are greeted by name. To ensure guests' total experience at the hotel is of the utmost quality, Ritz-Carlton creates a daily "Service Quality Index" (SQI) at each of its locations, so employees can continually monitor key guest service processes and swiftly address potential problem areas. At the brand's corporate headquarters in Maryland, SQIs for each hotel are displayed in a central command room, allowing instant analysis of how well a single location is performing. Other customer service initiatives include the CLASS (Customer Loyalty Anticipation Satisfaction System) database, which contains preferences and requirements of repeat Ritz-Carlton guests, and a room maintenance system known as CARE (Clean and Repair Everything), which ensures all guestrooms are free of defects every 90 days. These initiatives helped Ritz-Carlton win its second Malcolm Baldrige National Quality Award in 1999, becoming the only service company to win twice. Its dedication to its customers also enables Ritz-Carlton to forge lasting relationships with them, as evidenced by the hotel's Top 20 ranking on the Brand Keys 2006 Customer Loyalty Index. Its Osaka and Singapore hotels won the *Condé Nast Traveler* 2006 Top 100 Best in the World awards, while that in Kuala Lumpur was voted one of the World's Best Business Hotels in 2006 by *Travel and Leisure*.[1]

In this chapter, we will address the following questions:

1. What are customer value, satisfaction, and loyalty, and how can companies deliver them?
2. What is the lifetime value of customers and how can marketers maximize it?
3. How can companies cultivate strong customer relationships?
4. How can companies both attract and retain customers?
5. What is database marketing?

As Ritz-Carlton's experience shows, successful marketers are the ones that fully satisfy their customers. In this chapter, we detail how companies can go about winning customers and beating competitors. The answer lies largely in doing a better job of meeting or exceeding customer expectations.

Building Customer Value, Satisfaction, and Loyalty

Creating loyal customers is at the heart of every business.[2] As marketing experts Don Peppers and Martha Rogers say:

> *The only value your company will ever create is the value that comes from customers—the ones you have now and the ones you will have in the future. Businesses succeed by getting, keeping, and growing customers. Customers are the only reason you build factories, hire employees, schedule meetings, lay fiber-optic lines, or engage in any business activity. Without customers, you don't have a business.*[3]

Managers who believe the customer is the company's only true "profit center" consider the traditional organization chart in Figure 5.1(a)—a pyramid with the president at the top, management in the middle, and frontline people and customers at the bottom—obsolete.

Successful marketing companies invert the chart (see Figure 5.1(b)). At the top are customers; next in importance are frontline people who meet, serve, and satisfy customers; under them are the middle managers, whose job is to support the front-line people so that they can serve customers well; and at the base is top management, whose job is to hire and support good middle managers. We have added customers along the sides of Figure 5.1(b) to indicate that managers at every level must be personally involved in knowing, meeting, and serving customers.

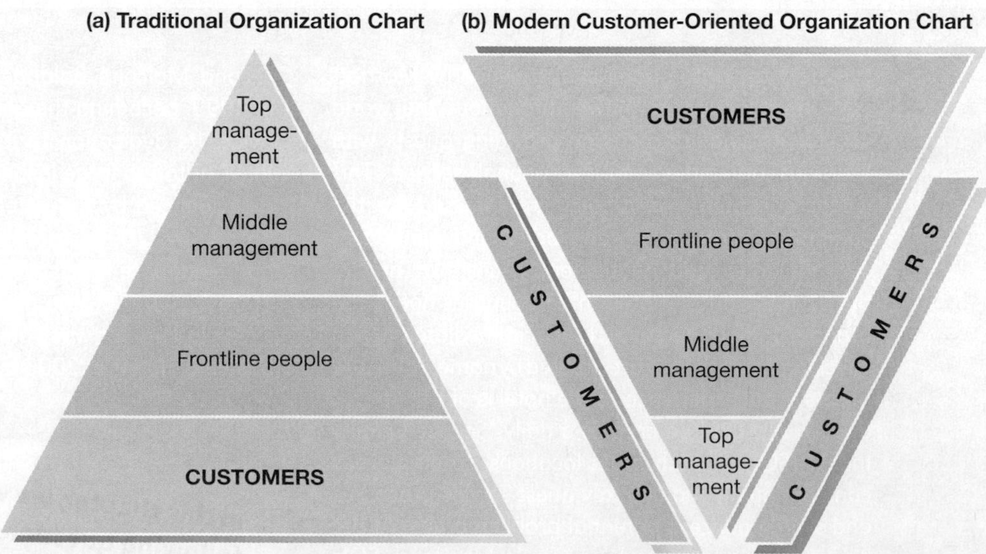

Figure 5.1 Traditional Organization Chart versus Modern Customer-Oriented Organization Chart

Some companies have been founded with the customer-on-top business model and customer advocacy has been their strategy—and competitive advantage—all along. Ralph's, one of Philippines' biggest distributors of wines and spirits, is an example.

Ralph's—Ralph's was set up in 1975 in a small 30-square-meter shop at a time when most Filipinos' concept of a drink was largely limited to beer, gin, and local concoctions. In 30 years, it has grown to a network of 22 branches all over the country. Company founder, Robert Joseph, attributes its growth and staying power to its close relationship with its base of customers. While other companies invested in advertising and other expensive marketing ventures, Ralph's stuck to nurturing an intimate relationship with its core customers. It held free wine-tasting sessions every week to inform customers about the latest wines. It also tracks its biggest customers through data collected from invoices and point-of-sale equipment to ensure quality service. These are on top of the discount and promotional programs that usually go with the launch of a new bottle of wine or spirit. "We always involve the customer because the customer is king. We say that whatever they want, we have it for them," says Joseph. However, he notes that a customer relationship management program can only go so far if it is not tied with good customer service. Hence, Ralph's invests in staff training so that the staff can help customers pick the right kind of wine to suit their taste, budget, and occasion.[4]

Customer Perceived Value

Consumers are more educated and informed than ever, and they have the tools to verify companies' claims and seek out superior alternatives.[5] How then do they ultimately make choices? Customers tend to be value-maximizers, within the bounds of search costs and limited knowledge, mobility, and income. Customers estimate which offer will deliver the most perceived value and act on it (see Figure 5.2). Whether or not the offer lives up to expectation affects customer satisfaction and the probability they will purchase the product again.

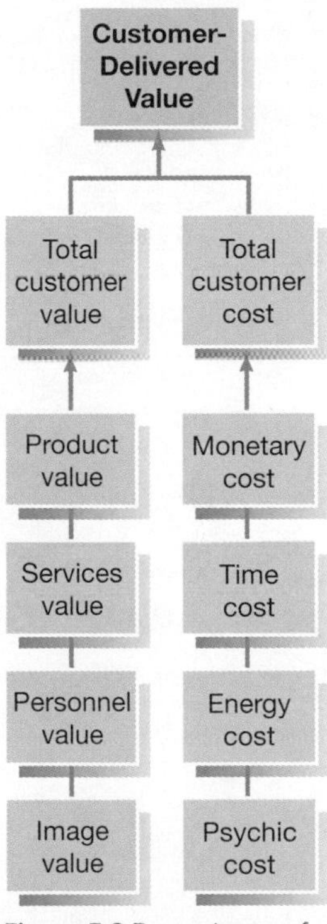

Figure 5.2 Determinants of Customer-Delivered Value

Customer perceived value (CPV) is the difference between the prospective customer's evaluation of all the benefits and all the costs of an offering and the perceived alternatives. *Total customer value* is the perceived monetary value of the bundle of economic, functional, and psychological benefits customers expect from a given market offering. *Total customer cost* is the bundle of costs customers expect to incur in evaluating, obtaining, using, and disposing of the given market offering, including monetary, time, energy, and psychic costs.

Customer perceived value is thus based on the difference between what the customer gets and what he or she gives for different possible choices. The customer gets benefits and assumes costs. The marketer can increase the value of the customer offering by some combination of raising functional or emotional benefits and/or reducing one or more of the various types of costs. The customer who is choosing between two value offerings, V1 and V2, will examine the ratio V1:V2 and favor V1 if the ratio is larger than one, favor V2 if the ratio is smaller than one, and will be indifferent if the ratio equals one.

APPLYING VALUE CONCEPTS

Suppose the buyer for a large construction company wants to buy a tractor from Caterpillar or Komatsu. The competing salespeople carefully describe their respective offers. The buyer wants to use the tractor in residential construction work. He would like the tractor to deliver certain levels of reliability, durability, performance, and resale value. He evaluates the tractors and decides that Caterpillar has a higher product value based on perceptions of those attributes. He also perceives differences in the accompanying services—delivery, training, and maintenance—and decides that Caterpillar provides better service and more knowledgeable and responsive personnel. Finally, he places higher value on Caterpillar's corporate image. He adds up all the values from these four sources—product, services, personnel, and image—and perceives Caterpillar as delivering greater customer value.

Does he buy the Caterpillar tractor? Not necessarily. He also examines his total cost of transacting with Caterpillar versus Komatsu, which consists of more than the money. As Adam Smith observed over two centuries ago, "The real price of anything is the toil and trouble of acquiring it." Total customer cost includes the buyer's time, energy, and psychic costs. The buyer evaluates these elements together with the monetary cost to form a total customer cost. Then the buyer considers whether Caterpillar's total customer cost is too high in relation to the total customer value it delivers. If it is, the buyer might choose the Komatsu tractor. The buyer will choose whichever source he thinks delivers the highest perceived customer value.

Now let us use this decision making theory to help Caterpillar succeed in selling to this buyer. Caterpillar can improve its offer in three ways. First, it can increase total customer value by improving product, services, personnel, and/or image benefits. Second, it can reduce the buyer's non-monetary costs by reducing the time, energy, and psychic costs. Third, it can reduce its product's monetary cost to the buyer.

Suppose Caterpillar concludes that the buyer sees its offer as worth $20,000. Further, suppose Caterpillar's cost of producing the tractor is $14,000. This means that Caterpillar's offer potentially generates $6,000 over the company's cost, so Caterpillar needs to charge a price between $14,000 and $20,000. If it charges less than $14,000, it will not cover its costs; if it charges more than $20,000, it will price itself out of the market.

The price Caterpillar charges will determine how much value will be delivered to the buyer and how much will flow to Caterpillar. For example, if Caterpillar charges $19,000, it is creating $1,000 of customer perceived value and keeping $5,000 for itself. The lower Caterpillar sets its price, the higher is the customer perceived value and, therefore, the higher is the customer's incentive to purchase. To win the sale, Caterpillar must offer more customer perceived value than Komatsu does.[6]

Very often, managers conduct a **customer value analysis** to reveal the company's strengths and weaknesses relative to those of various competitors. The steps in this analysis are:

1. **Identify the major attributes and benefits that customers value.** Customers are asked what attributes, benefits, and performance levels they look for in choosing a product and vendors.
2. **Assess the quantitative importance of the different attributes and benefits.** Customers are asked to rate the importance of the different attributes and benefits. If their ratings diverge too much, the marketer should cluster them into different segments.
3. **Assess the company's and competitors' performances on the different customer values against their rated importance.** Customers describe where they see the company's and competitors' performances on each attribute and benefit.
4. **Examine how customers in a specific segment rate the company's performance against a specific major competitor on an individual attribute or benefit basis.** If the company's offer exceeds the competitor's offer on all important attributes and benefits, the company can charge a higher price (thereby earning higher profits), or it can charge the same price and gain more market share.
5. **Monitor customer values over time.** The company must periodically redo its studies of customer values and competitors' standings as the economy, technology, and features change.

Gillette—When Gillette introduced the five-blade Fusion in Japan, its market share jumped from 21 percent to 33 percent. Prior to that, Gillette had stagnant or single-digit growth. What prompted this success? Gillette began to dissect its shortcomings and understand the Japanese market better. While the Japanese were moving toward preferring ads featuring local celebrities and athletes rather than foreign models, Gillette was slow to pick up on this changing trend. It was also targeting at hyper-masculine Western men which did not go down well with Japanese men. Through its research, Gillette began to understand the market better. Japanese tend to favor electric razors than dry shavers. Japanese men often shower in the evening and shave the next morning. They shave less frequently than men in other parts of the world. Then, for a first, Gillette appointed a local to run its Japanese operations. It also intensified its advertising, customized its merchandise, and negotiated better shelf space and long-term displays at stores. One such effort was an alliance with the Japanese barbers' association to run a shaving bar in the Tokyo financial district. Some barbers even sold Fusion blades and razors in their shops. More recently, Gillette's understanding of its market is evident in its launch of the black and silver version of the Fusion. Following the Japanese trend, Gillette will, for the first time, feature local athletes and celebrities like DJ Chris Peppler and swimmer Kosuke Kitajima. Also, the razor is not called Phantom, as it is in the rest of world, because it does not translate well in Japan. Instead, it is called Air.[7]

CHOICES AND IMPLICATIONS

Some marketers might argue that the process we have described is too rational. Suppose the customer chooses the Komatsu tractor. How can we explain this choice? Here are three possibilities:

1. **The buyer might be under orders to buy at the lowest price.** The Caterpillar salesperson's task is to convince the buyer's manager that buying on price alone will result in lower long-term profits.
2. **The buyer will retire before the company realizes that the Komatsu tractor is more expensive to operate.** The buyer will look good in the short run; he is maximizing personal benefit. The Caterpillar salesperson's task is to convince other people in the customer company that Caterpillar delivers greater customer value.
3. **The buyer enjoys a long-term friendship with the Komatsu salesperson.** In this case, Caterpillar's salesperson needs to show the buyer that the Komatsu tractor will draw complaints from the tractor operators when they discover its high fuel cost and need for frequent repairs.

The point of these examples is clear: buyers operate under various constraints and occasionally make choices that give more weight to their personal benefit than to the company's benefit.

Customer perceived value is a useful framework that applies to many situations and yields rich insights. Here are its implications:

First, the seller must assess the total customer value and total customer cost associated with each competitor's offer to know how his or her offer rates in the buyer's mind.

Second, the seller who is at a customer perceived value disadvantage has two alternatives: to increase total customer value or to decrease total customer cost. The former calls for strengthening or augmenting the offer's product, services, personnel, and image benefits. The latter calls for reducing the buyer's costs by reducing the price, simplifying the ordering and delivery process, or absorbing some buyer risk by offering a warranty.[8]

DELIVERING HIGH CUSTOMER VALUE

Consumers have varying degrees of loyalty to specific brands, stores, and companies. Oliver defines **loyalty** as "a deeply held commitment to re-buy or re-patronize a preferred product or service in the future despite situational influences and marketing efforts having the potential to cause switching behavior."[9]

The **value proposition** consists of the whole cluster of benefits the company promises to deliver; it is more than the core positioning of the offering. For example, Volvo's core positioning has been "safety," but the buyer is promised more than just a safe car; other benefits include a long-lasting car, good service, and a long warranty period. Basically, the value proposition is a statement about the resulting experience customers will gain from the company's market offering and from their relationship with the supplier. The brand must represent a promise about the total experience customers can expect. Whether the promise is kept depends on the company's ability to manage its value-delivery system. The **value-delivery system** includes all the experiences the customer will have on the way to obtaining and using the offering.

Singapore Airlines (SIA)—SIA continues its efforts to provide customers with an excellent pre- and on-board flight experience. Its online services allow customers to select their seats from those available at the time of booking, as well as check-in from 48 hours up to 2 hours before departure. SIA automatically notifies passengers of flight alerts through text and email messages. Passengers can also access up-to-date information on SIA's services via their personal digital assistant (PDA), WAP phone, or i-mode phone. First- and business-class passengers enjoy a myriad of exclusive privileges. They are escorted to a reception lounge to relax while check-in is handled by a Premium Services Officer. A private entrance from the lounge leads them directly to immigration customs and then to the boarding gate. A Book the Cook service is available in advance where passengers can order exclusive meals created by its international panel of chefs. Additionally, such passengers will find porters waiting to unload their baggage when they arrive at the airport.[10]

Total Customer Satisfaction

Whether the buyer is satisfied after purchase depends on the offer's performance in relation to the buyer's expectations. In general, **satisfaction** is a person's feelings of pleasure or disappointment resulting from comparing a product's perceived performance (or outcome) in relation to his or her expectations. If the performance falls short of expectations, the customer is dissatisfied. If the performance matches the expectations, the customer is satisfied. If the performance exceeds expectations, the customer is highly satisfied or delighted.[11]

DaimlerChrysler—DaimlerChrysler's Southeast Asian operations spends $1.3 million annually to raise customer satisfaction across the region. Called the "Mercedes Benz Service Excellence Award," the initiative involves over 100 dealers from Brunei, Indonesia, Malaysia, Singapore, South Korea, and Thailand who compete to determine who best meets the expectations of Mercedes Benz drivers. J.D. Power & Associates, an independent research company, has been appointed to assess dealer performance. This assessment utilizes a biannual customer survey to develop a customer satisfaction index and a twice-yearly mystery shopper's test for repair quality.[12]

Although the customer-centered firm seeks to create high customer satisfaction, that is not its ultimate goal. If the company increases customer satisfaction by lowering its price or increasing its services, the result may be lower profits. The company might be able to increase its profitability by means other than increased satisfaction (e.g., by improving manufacturing processes or investing more in R&D). Also, the company has many stakeholders, including employees, dealers, suppliers, and stockholders. Spending more to increase customer satisfaction might divert funds from increasing the satisfaction of other "partners." Ultimately, the company must operate on the philosophy that it is trying to deliver a high level of customer satisfaction subject to delivering acceptable levels of satisfaction to the other stakeholders, given its total resources.

How do buyers form their expectations? From past buying experience, friends' and associates' advice, and marketers' and competitors' information and promises. If marketers raise expectations too high, the buyer is likely to be disappointed. However, if the company sets expectations too low, it will not attract enough buyers (although it will satisfy those who do buy).[13] Some of today's most successful companies are raising expectations and delivering performances to match. Korean automaker Kia found success in the U.S. by launching low-cost, high-quality cars with enough reliability so that it could offer a 10-year warranty.

A customer's decision to be loyal or to defect is the sum of many small encounters with the company. One consulting firm says that for all these small encounters to add up to customer loyalty, companies need to create a "branded customer experience."

Monitoring Satisfaction

Many companies are systematically measuring customer satisfaction and the factors shaping it. For example, IBM tracks how satisfied customers are with each IBM salesperson they encounter, and makes this a factor in each salesperson's compensation.

A company would be wise to measure customer satisfaction regularly because one key to customer retention is customer satisfaction. A highly satisfied customer generally stays loyal longer, buys more as the company introduces new products and upgrades existing products, talks favorably about the company and its products, pays less attention to competing brands and is less sensitive to price, offers product or service ideas to the company, and costs less to serve than new customers because transactions are routine.

The link between customer satisfaction and customer loyalty, however, is not proportional. Suppose customer satisfaction is rated on a scale from one to five. At a very low level of customer satisfaction (level one), customers are likely to abandon the company and even bad-mouth it. At levels two to four, customers are fairly satisfied but still find it easy to switch when a better offer comes along. At level five, the customer is very likely to repurchase and even spread good word of mouth about the company. High satisfaction or delight creates an emotional bond with the brand or company, not just a rational preference. Xerox's senior management found out that its "completely satisfied" customers were six times more likely to repurchase Xerox products over the following 18 months than its "very satisfied" customers.[14]

When customers rate their satisfaction with an element of the company's performance—say, delivery—the company needs to recognize that customers vary in how they define good delivery. It could mean early delivery, on-time delivery, order completeness, and so on. The company must also realize that two customers can report being "highly satisfied" for different reasons. One may be easily satisfied most of the time and the other might be hard to please but was pleased on this occasion.[15]

MEASUREMENT TECHNIQUES

A number of methods exist to measure customer satisfaction. *Periodic surveys* can track customer satisfaction directly. Respondents can also be asked additional questions to measure repurchase intention and the likelihood or willingness to recommend the company and brand to others.

Companies can monitor the *customer loss rate* and contact customers who have stopped buying or who have switched to another supplier to learn why this happened. Finally, companies can hire *mystery shoppers* to pose as potential buyers and report on strong and weak points experienced in buying the company's and competitors' products. Managers themselves can enter company and competitor sales situations where they are unknown and experience firsthand the treatment they receive, or phone their own company with questions and complaints to see how the calls are handled.

For customer satisfaction surveys, it is important that companies ask the right questions. Reichheld suggests that perhaps only one question really matters: "Would you recommend this product or service to a friend?" He maintains that marketing departments typically focus surveys on the areas they can control, such as brand image, pricing, and product features. According to Reichheld, a customer's willingness to recommend to a friend results from how well the customer is treated by frontline employees, which in turn is determined by all the functional areas that contribute to a customer's experience.[16]

In addition to tracking customer value expectations and satisfaction, companies need to monitor their competitors' performance in these areas. One company was pleased to find that 80 percent of its customers said they were satisfied. Then the CEO found out that its leading competitor had a 90 percent customer satisfaction score. He was further dismayed when he learned that this competitor was aiming for a 95 percent satisfaction score.

INFLUENCE OF CUSTOMER SATISFACTION

For customer-centered companies, customer satisfaction is both a goal and a marketing tool. Companies need to be especially concerned today with their customer satisfaction level because the Internet provides a tool for consumers to spread bad word of mouth—as well as good word of mouth—to the rest of the world. On Web sites like TroubleBenz and LemonMB, angry Mercedes-Benz owners have been airing their complaints on everything from faulty key fobs and leaky sunroofs to balky electronics that leave drivers and their passengers stranded.[17]

CUSTOMER COMPLAINTS

Some companies think they are getting a sense of customer satisfaction by tallying complaints, but studies of customer dissatisfaction show that customers are dissatisfied with their purchases about 25 percent of the time but that only about 5 percent complain. The other 95 percent either feel complaining is not worth the effort, or they do not know how or to whom to complain, and they just stop buying.[18]

Of the customers who register a complaint, between 54 percent and 70 percent will do business with the organization again if their complaint is resolved. The figure goes up to a staggering 95 percent if the customer feels the complaint was resolved *quickly.* Customers who have complained to an organization and had their complaints satisfactorily resolved tell an average of five people about the good treatment they received.[19] The average dissatisfied customer, however, gripes to 11 people. If each of them in turn tells other people, the number of people exposed to bad word of mouth may grow exponentially.

The fact is, no matter how perfectly designed and implemented a marketing program is, mistakes will happen. The best thing a company can do is to make it easy for the customer to complain. Suggestion forms, toll-free numbers, Web sites, and email addresses allow for quick, two-way communication. The 3M Company claims that over two-thirds of its product improvement ideas come from listening to customer complaints.

Given the potential downside of having an unhappy customer, it is critical that marketers deal with the negative experience properly.[20] Beyond that, the following procedures can help to recover customer goodwill:[21]

1. **Set up a 7-day, 24-hour toll-free "hotline" (by phone, fax, or email) to receive and act on customer complaints.**
2. **Contact the complaining customer as quickly as possible.** The slower the company is to respond, the more dissatisfaction may grow and lead to negative word of mouth.
3. **Accept responsibility for the customer's disappointment.** Do not blame the customer.
4. **Use customer-service people who are emphatic.**
5. **Resolve the complaint swiftly and to the customer's satisfaction.** Some complaining customers are not looking for compensation so much as a sign that the company cares.

Product and Service Quality

Satisfaction will also depend on product and service quality. What exactly is quality? Various experts have defined it as "fitness for use," "conformance to requirements," "freedom from variation," and so on.[22] We will use the American Society for Quality Control's definition: **Quality** is the totality of features and characteristics of a product or service that bear on its ability to satisfy stated or implied needs.[23] This is clearly a customer-centered definition. We can say that the seller has delivered quality whenever the seller's product or service meets or exceeds the customers' expectations. A company that satisfies most of its customers' needs most of the time is called a quality company, but it is important to distinguish between *conformance* quality and *performance* quality (or grade). A Lexus provides higher performance quality than a Hyundai: the Lexus rides smoother, goes faster, and lasts longer. Yet both a Lexus and a Hyundai can be said to deliver the same conformance quality if all the units deliver their respective promised quality.

Raja Fashions—Raja Fashions is Hong Kong's biggest made-to-order business and the world's most-wanted tailor. Founded more than 50 years ago when his tailor grandfather moved from Mumbai to Hong Kong, Raja Daswani has produced custom-made suits for the rich and famous with the help of technology. He travels to Europe and the U.S. nine months a year to make these top-of-the-line suits. Instead of setting up a business in Europe, which is costly, Raja and his entourage base themselves in a hotel suite. He takes photos of clients on a digital camera and emails them to his tailors in Hong Kong and China so that they know the exact shape of the clients. He says that the body shape is crucial and a good suit hides imperfections in the posture. Unlike Saville Row and Jermyn Street, Daswani says he does not tell the customer what to wear, but "will make anything you want, any way you want, and we're not proud." His more democratic approach, together with the technology-enhanced tailoring, has helped bring made-to-measure tailoring to a wider audience. So good is he at keeping his customers satisfied, Daswani receives 800 email messages every day for orders over the Net. Moving forward, Raja Fashions is investing in the latest computer technology that will scan a customer's body and recommend the style and fabric that will suit him.[24]

Raja Fashions has expanded to include Raja of London.

According to GE's former Chairman, John F. Welch Jr., "Quality is our best assurance of customer allegiance, our strongest defense against foreign competition, and the only path to sustained growth and earnings."[25] The drive to produce goods that are superior in world markets has led some countries—and groups of countries—to recognize or award prizes to companies that exemplify the best quality practices (e.g., the Deming Prize in Japan, the Malcolm Baldridge National Quality Award in the U.S., and the European Quality Award).

IMPACT OF QUALITY

Product and service quality, customer satisfaction, and company profitability are intimately connected. Higher levels of quality result in higher levels of customer satisfaction, which support higher prices and (often) lower costs. Studies have shown a high correlation between relative product quality and company profitability.[26] Companies that have lowered costs to cut corners have paid the price when the quality of the customer experience suffers.[27]

- When Home Depot decided to expand into the contractor supply business, while also cutting costs and streamlining operations in its U.S. stores, it replaced many full-time workers with part-time employees who soon made up about 40 percent of store staff. The chain's customer satisfaction index dropped to the bottom among major U.S. retailers and its share price slid 24 percent during the biggest home improvement boom in history.
- Although Northwest Airlines stopped offering free magazines, pillows, movies, and even minibags of pretzels on domestic flights, the carrier also raised prices and reduced its flight schedule. As one frequent flier noted, "Northwest acts low cost without *being* low cost." Not surprisingly, Northwest came in last of all top U.S. airlines in both the ACS index and J.D. Power & Associates customer satisfaction poll.

Quality is clearly the key to value creation and customer satisfaction.

TOTAL QUALITY

Total quality is everyone's job, just as marketing is everyone's job. Marketers play several roles in helping their companies define and deliver high-quality goods and services to target customers. First, they bear the major responsibility for correctly identifying the customers' needs and requirements. Second, they must communicate customer expectations properly to product designers. Third, they must make sure that customers' orders are filled correctly and on time. Fourth, they must check that customers have received proper instructions, training, and technical assistance in the use of the product. Fifth, they must stay in touch with customers after the sale to ensure that they are satisfied and remain satisfied. Sixth, they must gather customer ideas for product and service improvements and convey them to the appropriate departments. When marketers do all this, they are making substantial contributions to total quality management and customer satisfaction, as well as to customer and company profitability.

Maximizing Customer Lifetime Value

Ultimately, marketing is the art of attracting and keeping profitable customers. Yet every company loses money on some of its customers. The well-known 20–80 rule says that the top 20 percent of the customers may generate as much as 80 percent of the company's profits. In some cases the profit distribution may be more extreme—the most profitable 20 percent of customers (on a per capita basis) may contribute as much as 150 percent to 300 percent of profitability. The least profitable 10 percent to 20 percent of customers, on the other hand, can actually reduce profits between 50 percent and 200 percent per account, with the middle 60 percent to 70 percent breaking even.[28] Figure 5.3 displays one customer profit distribution. The implication is that a company could improve its profits by "firing" its worst customers.

It is not always the company's largest customers who yield the most profit. The largest customers demand considerable service and receive the deepest discounts. The smallest customers pay full price and receive minimal service, but the costs of transacting with small customers reduce their profitability. The midsize customers receive good service and pay nearly full price and are often the most profitable.

Customer Profitability

What makes a customer profitable? A **profitable customer** is a person, household, or company that over time yields a revenue stream that exceeds by an acceptable amount the company's cost stream of attracting, selling, and servicing that customer. Note that the emphasis is on the lifetime stream of revenue and cost, not on the profit from a particular transaction.[29] Customer profitability can be assessed individually, by market segment, or by channel.

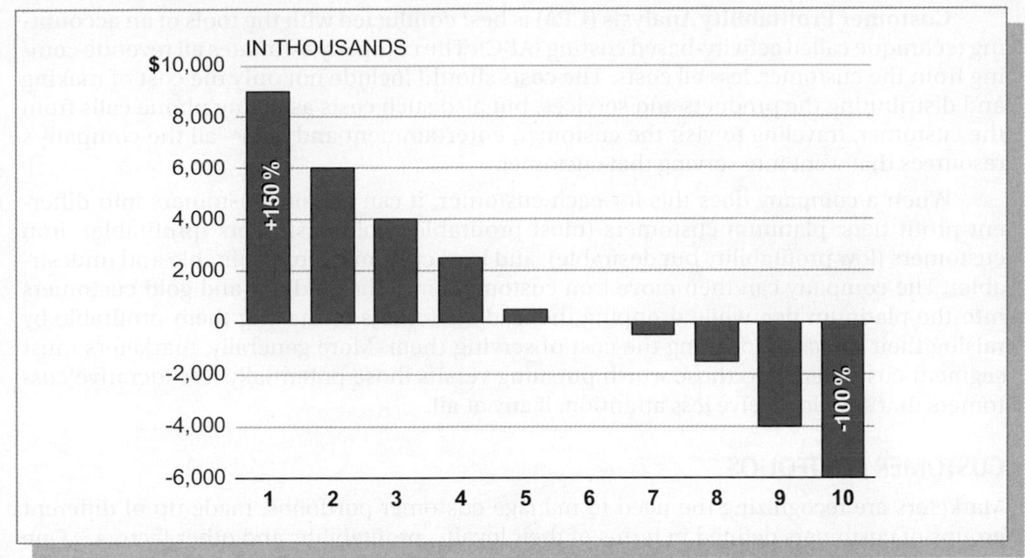

Figure 5.3 The 150–20 Rule: "The 20% Most Profitable Customers Generate as Much as 150% of the Profits of a Company; the 20% Least Profitable Lose 100% of the Profits"

Source: Larry Selden and Yoko S. Selden, "Profitable Customer: The Key to Great Brands." *Point*, July–August 2006, p. 9.

Although many companies measure customer satisfaction, most companies fail to measure individual customer profitability.[30] Banks claim that this is a difficult task because a customer uses different banking services and the transactions are logged in different departments. However, the number of unprofitable customers in their customer base has appalled banks that have succeeded in linking customer transactions. Some banks report losing money on over 45 percent of their retail customers.

CUSTOMER PROFITABILITY ANALYSIS

A useful type of profitability analysis is shown in Figure 5.4.[31] Customers are arrayed along the columns and products along the rows. Each cell contains a symbol for the profitability of selling that product to that customer. Customer 1 is very profitable; he buys three profit-making products (P1, P2, and P4). Customer 2 yields a picture of mixed profitability; he buys one profitable product and one unprofitable product. Customer 3 is a losing customer because he buys one profitable product and two unprofitable products.

What can the company do about Customers 2 and 3? (1) It can raise the price of its less profitable products or eliminate them, or (2) It can try to sell them its profit-making products. Unprofitable customers who defect should not concern the company. In fact, the company should encourage these customers to switch to competitors.

Products	C_1	C_2	C_3	
P_1	+	+	+	Highly profitable product
P_2	+			Profitable product
P_3		−	−	Losing product
P_4	+		−	Mixed-bag product
Customers	High-profit customer	Mixed-bag customer	Losing customer	

Figure 5.4 Customer-Product Profitability Analysis

Customer Profitability Analysis (CPA) is best conducted with the tools of an accounting technique called activity-based costing (ABC). The company estimates all revenue coming from the customer, less all costs. The costs should include not only the cost of making and distributing the products and services, but also such costs as taking phone calls from the customer, traveling to visit the customer, entertainment and gifts—all the company's resources that went into serving that customer.

When a company does this for each customer, it can classify customers into different profit tiers: platinum customers (most profitable), gold customers (profitable), iron customers (low profitability but desirable), and lead customers (unprofitable and undesirable). The company can then move iron customers into the gold tier and gold customers into the platinum tier, while dropping the lead customers or making them profitable by raising their prices or lowering the cost of serving them. More generally, marketers must segment customers into those worth pursuing versus those potentially less lucrative customers that should receive less attention, if any at all.

CUSTOMER PORTFOLIOS

Marketers are recognizing the need to manage customer portfolios, made up of different groups of customers defined in terms of their loyalty, profitability, and other factors.[32] One perspective is that a firm's portfolio consists of a combination of "acquaintances," "friends," and "partners" that are constantly changing.[33] The three types of customers will differ in their product needs, their buying, selling, and servicing activities, and their acquisition costs and competitive advantages.

Another perspective compares the individuals who make up the firm's customer portfolio to the stocks that make up an investment portfolio.[34] In marketing, as in investments, it's important to calculate the beta, or risk-reward value, for each portfolio item and then diversify accordingly. From this perspective, firms should assemble portfolios of negatively correlated individuals so that the financial contributions of one offset the deficits of another to maximize the portfolio's risk-adjusted lifetime value.

COMPETITIVE ADVANTAGE

Companies must not only be able to create high absolute value, but also high value relative to competitors at a sufficiently low cost. **Competitive advantage** is a company's ability to perform in one or more ways that competitors cannot or will not match. Porter urged companies to build a sustainable competitive advantage.[35] But few competitive advantages are sustainable. At best, they may be leverageable. A *leverageable advantage* is one that a company can use as a springboard to new advantages, much as Microsoft has leveraged its operating system to Microsoft Office and then to networking applications. In general, a company that hopes to endure must be in the business of continuously inventing new advantages.

Any competitive advantage must be seen by customers as a *customer advantage.* For example, if a company delivers faster than its competitors, this will not be a customer advantage if customers do not value speed. Companies must focus on building customer advantages. Then they will deliver high customer value and satisfaction, which leads to high repeat purchases and ultimately to high company profitability.

Measuring Customer Lifetime Value

The case for maximizing long-term customer profitability is captured in the concept of customer lifetime value. **Customer lifetime value (CLV)** describes the net present value of the stream of future profits expected over the customer's lifetime purchases. The company must subtract from the expected revenues the expected costs of attracting, selling, and servicing that customer, applying the appropriate discount rate (e.g., 10–20 percent depending on cost of capital and risk attitudes).

Many methods exist to measure CLV.[36] "Marketing Memo: Calculating Customer Lifetime Value" illustrates one.

CLV calculations provide a formal quantitative framework for planning customer investment and help marketers to adopt a long-term perspective. However, one challenge in applying CLV concepts is to arrive at reliable cost and revenue estimates. Marketers who use CLV concepts must also be careful not to forget the importance of short-term, brand-building marketing activities that will help to increase customer loyalty.

MARKETING MEMO • CALCULATING CUSTOMER LIFETIME VALUE

Researchers and practitioners have used many different approaches for modeling and estimating customer lifetime value (CLV). Gupta and Lehmann recommend the following formula to estimate the CLV for a not-yet-acquired customer:

$$CLV = \sum_{t=0}^{T} \frac{(p_t - c_t)r_t}{(1+i)^t} - AC \qquad (1)$$

where,

p_t = price paid by a consumer at time t,
c_t = direct cost of servicing the customer at time t,
i = discount rate or cost of capital for the firm,
r_t = probability of customer repeat buying or being "alive" at time t,
AC = acquisition cost,
T = time horizon for estimating CLV.

A key decision is what time horizon to use for estimating CLV. Typically, 3–5 years is reasonable. With this information and estimates of other variables, we can calculate CLV using spreadsheet analysis.

Gupta and Lehmann illustrate their approach by calculating the CLV of 100 customers over a 10-year period (see Table 5.1). In this example, the firm acquires 100 customers with an acquisition cost per customer of $40. Therefore, in Year 0, it spends $4,000. Some of these customers defect each year. The present value of the profits from this cohort of customers over 10 years is $13,286.52. The net CLV (after deducting acquisition costs) is $9,286.52 (net CLV) or $92.87 (net CLV per customer.)

Using an infinite time horizon avoids using an arbitrary time horizon for calculating CLV. In the case of an infinite time horizon, researchers have shown that if margins (price minus cost) and retention rates stay constant over time, then the future CLV of an existing customer simplifies to the following:

$$CLV = \sum_{t=1}^{\infty} \frac{mr^t}{(1+i)^t} = m\frac{r}{(1+i-r)} \qquad (2)$$

In other words, CLV simply becomes margin (m) times a *margin multiple* $[r/(1+i-r)]$.

Table 5.2 shows the margin multiple for various combinations of r and i. This table shows a simple way to estimate CLV of a customer. For example, when retention rate is 80 percent and discount rate is 12 percent, the margin multiple is about two-and-a-half. Therefore, the future CLV of an existing customer in this scenario is simply his annual margin multiplied by 2.5.

Table 5.2 Margin Multiple

$$\frac{r}{1+i-r}$$

Retention Rate			Discount Rate	
	10%	**12%**	**14%**	**16%**
60%	1.20	1.5	1.11	1.07
70%	1.75	1.67	1.59	1.52
80%	2.67	2.50	2.35	2.22
90%	4.50	4.09	3.75	3.46

Table 5.1 A Hypothetical Example to Illustrate CLV Calculations

	Year 0	Year 1	Year 2	Year 3	Year 4	Year 5	Year 6	Year 7	Year 8	Year 9	Year 10
Number of customers	100	90	80	72	60	48	34	23	12	6	2
Revenue per customer		100	110	120	125	130	135	140	142	143	145
Variable cost per customer		70	72	75	76	78	79	80	81	82	83
Margin per customer		30	38	45	49	52	56	60	61	61	62
Acquisition cost per customer	40										
Total cost or profit	–4,000	2,700	3,040	3,240	2,940	2,496	1,904	1,380	732	366	124
Present value	–4,000	2,454.55	2,512.40	2,434.26	2,008.06	1,549.82	1,074.76	708.16	341.48	155.22	47.81

Sources: Sunil Gupta and Donald R. Lehmann, "Models of Customer Value." In *Handbook of Marketing Decision Models*, Berend Wierenga ed. (Berlin, Germany: Springer Science and Business Media, 2007); Sunil Gupta and Donald R. Lehmann, "Customers as Assets." *Journal of Interactive Marketing*, Winter 2006, 17(1), pp. 9–24; Sunil Gupta and Donald R. Lehmann, *Managing Customers as Investments*, (Upper Saddle River, NJ: Wharton School Publishing, 2005); Peter Fader, Bruce Hardie, and Ka Lee, "RFM and CLV: Using Iso-Value Curves for Customer Base Analysis." *Journal of Marketing Research*, November 2005, 42(4), pp. 415–430; Sunil Gupta, Donald R. Lehmann, and Jennifer Ames Stuart, "Valuing Customers." *Journal of Marketing Research*, February 2004, 41(1), pp. 7–18; Werner J. Reinartz and V. Kumar, "On the Profitability of Long-Life Customers in a Noncontractual Setting: An Empirical Investigation and Implications for Marketing." *Journal of Marketing*, October 2000, 64, pp. 17–35.

Cultivating Customer Relationships

Maximizing customer value means cultivating long-term customer relationships. Companies are now moving away from wasteful mass marketing to more precision marketing designed to build strong customer relationships. Today's economy is supported by information businesses. Information has the advantages of being easy to differentiate, customize, personalize, and dispatch over networks at incredible speed.

But information cuts both ways. For instance, customers now have a quick and easy means of doing comparison shopping through sites such as BizRate, Shopping.com, and PriceGrabber.com. The Internet also facilitates communication between customers. Web sites such as Epinions and Amazon.com enable customers to share information about their experiences with various products and services.

Customer empowerment has become a way of life for many companies that have had to adjust to a shift in the power with their customer relationships. "Marketing Insight: Company Response to Customer Empowerment" describes some of the changes companies have made in their marketing practices as a result.

Customer Relationship Management (CRM)

To find out how the Coles Group handles its customer relations and provides value to its customers with various loyalty programs and other perks, visit www.pearsoned.com.au/marketingmanagementaustralia.

Customer relationship management (CRM) is the process of carefully managing detailed information about individual customers and all customer "touch points" to maximize customer loyalty. A c*ustomer touch point* is any occasion on which a customer encounters the brand and product, from actual experience to personal or mass communications to casual observation. For a hotel, the touch points include reservations, check-in and check-out, frequent-stay programs, room service, business services, exercise facilities, laundry service, restaurants, and bars. For instance, the Four Seasons relies on personal touches, such as a staff that always addresses guests by name, high-powered employees who understand the needs of sophisticated business travelers, and at least one best-in-region facility, such as a premier restaurant or spa.[38] In the Asia Pacific, excluding Japan, CRM solution spending is expected to grow to $3.8 billion by 2008, a five-year compound annual growth rate of 18.2 percent. The most sophisticated markets in terms of CRM adoption are China, India, and Australia.[39]

Customer relationship management enables companies to provide excellent real-time customer service through the effective use of individual account information. Based on what they know about each valued customer, companies can customize market offerings, services, programs, messages, and media. South Korea-based retailer 2001 Outlet, for instance, has a CRM database to identify high-value customers as well as plan and execute targeted promotions to retain these customers. CRM is important because a major driver of company profitability is the aggregate value of the company's customer base.[40]

Nintendo—This computer game company has a loyalty program where visitors to its Web site are separated into three distinct value tiers. The more engaged the user is, the higher his tier status. Tier 1 members give their name, address, and email address to become registered as "My Nintendo" members. Such users receive newsletters and are free to join its online forums. To advance to Tier 2, the "Nsider," members must register at least one purchased Nintendo product to access exclusive content online. They get complimentary collector's editions of Nintendo's latest game. Tier 2 members are tracked and measured by their level of involvement such as how often they take part in the surveys, register purchased products, post comments in forums, as well as time spent on the site. By tracking their online activity, Nintendo can classify and move an elite group of individual gamers to Tier 3 called Sage. These members are chosen, not by the amount of money they spend, but by the level of their involvement at Nintendo.com. Sage members receive premium content, help moderate forums, and are sometimes given the opportunity to preview new games. Sage members are even given their own forum, which can only be accessed by fellow Sage members. Nintendo feels that categorizing users based on behavior is important. It allows Nintendo to craft different messages to different gamers. It also uses these different loyalty levels to calculate the lifetime value of a consumer. When they know how many games a person in one level is likely to purchase, Nintendo can determine how much marketing resources is needed to get that person to the next level.[41]

MARKETING INSIGHT • COMPANY RESPONSE TO CUSTOMER EMPOWERMENT

Often seen as the flag bearer for marketing best practices, Procter & Gamble's Chairman A.G. Lafley created shock waves for marketers with his Association of National Advertisers' speech in October 2006. "The power is with the consumer," proclaimed Lafley, and "marketers and retailers are scrambling to keep up with her. Consumers are beginning in a very real sense to own our brands and participate in their creation. We need to learn to let go." In support of his contention, Lafley pointed out how a teenager had created an animated spot for Pringles snacks that was posted on YouTube; how Pantene, the hair care products company, had created a campaign that encouraged women to cut their hair and donate the clippings to make wigs for cancer patients; and how sales of Cover Girl Outlast lipstick increased 25 percent after the firm put mirrored ads in women's restrooms asking, "Is your lipstick still on?" and ran targeted 5-second TV ads with the same theme.

Other marketers have begun to advocate a "bottom-up" grassroots approach to marketing, rather than the more traditional "top-down" approach where the marketers feel they are calling the shots. Burger King has launched edgy campaigns on consumer-friendly new media such as YouTube, MySpace, video games, and iPods. Allowing the customer to take charge just makes sense for a brand whose slogan is "Have It Your Way" and whose main rival, McDonald's, already owns the more staid family market.

To provide a little more control, Yahoo! engages in "participation marketing" by tapping consumers who already like a particular brand, rather than just casting a wide net. For example, to create a new music video, Yahoo! Music asked fans of the singer Shakira to contribute video clips of themselves performing her song "Hips Don't Lie," which then provided the visual content. Reflecting the company philosophy, Yahoo! CMO Cammie Dunaway notes, "Content is no longer something you push out; content is an invitation to engage with your brand."

Even the 2007 Super Bowl, the most expensive media event on the planet, had two homemade consumer commercials. To capitalize on the buzz of user-generated content, both Frito-Lay and Chevrolet created ad contests, with the winners receiving prizes and getting their ads aired during the game telecast. Perhaps the most compelling example of the new brand world comes from master marketer Nike. As part of its *Joga Bonito* (Portuguese for "play beautiful") World Cup Sponsorship, Nike spent $100 million on a multilayered campaign. The centerpiece, however, was Joga.com, a social networking Web site available in 140 countries. One million members blogged, downloaded videos, created fan communities for their favorite players or teams, and expressed their passions on bulletin-board-type debates. Nike CEO Mark Parker sums up the new marketing equation well, "A strong relationship is created when someone joins a Nike community or invites Nike into their community."

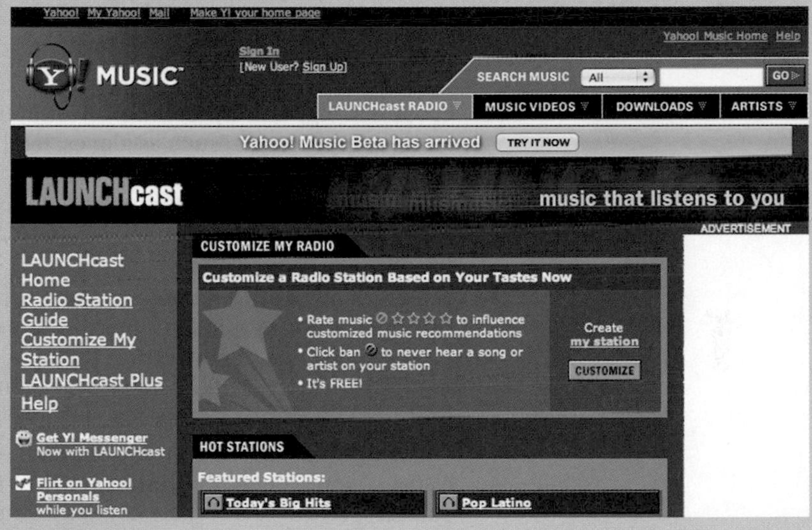

Web sites such as Yahoo! Music that empower visitors, allow them to post comments or pictures, or encourage the formation of active communities can benefit companies and customers alike.

Sources: Stuart Elliott, "Letting Consumers Control Marketing: Priceless." *New York Times*, October 9, 2006; Louise Story, "Super Bowl Glory for Amateurs with Video Cameras." *New York Times*, September 27, 2006; Todd Wasserman and Jim Edwards, "Marketers' New World Order." *BrandWeek*, October 9, 2006, pp. 4–6; Heather Green and Robert D. Hof, "Your Attention Please." *BusinessWeek*, July 24, 2006, pp. 48–53; Brian Sternberg, "The Marketing Maze." *Wall Street Journal*, July 10, 2006.

ONE-TO-ONE MARKETING

Some of the groundwork for CRM was laid by Peppers and Rogers in a series of books.[42] Peppers and Rogers outline a four-step framework for one-to-one marketing that can be adapted to CRM marketing as follows:

- **Identify your prospects and customers.** Do not go after everyone. Build, maintain, and mine a rich customer database with information derived from all the channels and customer touch points.
- **Differentiate customers in terms of (1) their needs and (2) their value to your company.** Spend proportionately more effort on the most valuable customers (MVCs). Apply activity-based costing and calculate CLV. Estimate net present value of all future profits coming from purchases, margin levels, and referrals, less customer-specific servicing costs.

- **Interact with individual customers.** It is important to improve your knowledge about their individual needs and build stronger relationships. Formulate customized offerings that are communicated in a personalized way.
- **Customize products, services, and messages to each customer.** Facilitate customer/company interaction through the company contact center and Web site.

The practice of one-to-one marketing, however, is not for every company. The required investment in information collection, hardware, and software may exceed the payout. It works best for companies that normally collect a great deal of individual customer information, carry a lot of products that can be cross-sold, carry products that need periodic replacement or upgrading, and sell products of high value.

INCREASING VALUE OF THE CUSTOMER BASE

A key driver of shareholder value is the aggregate value of the customer base. Winning companies improve the value of their customer base by excelling at strategies such as:

- **Reducing the rate of customer defection.** Selecting and training employees to be knowledgeable and friendly increases the likelihood that the inevitable shopping questions from customers will be answered satisfactorily.
- **Increasing the longevity of the customer relationship.** The more involved a customer is with the company, the more likely he or she is to stick around. Some companies treat their customers as partners—especially in business-to-business markets—soliciting their help in the design of new products or improving their customer service.
- **Enhancing the growth potential of each customer through "share-of-wallet," cross-selling, and up-selling.**[43] Harley-Davidson sells more than motorcycles and riding supplements (such as gloves, leather jackets, helmets, and sunglasses). Harley dealerships sell more than 3,000 items of clothing—some even have their own fitting rooms. Licensed goods sold by others range from the predictable (shot glasses, cue balls, and cigarette lighters) to the more surprising items (cologne, dolls, and mobile phones).
- **Making low-profit customers more profitable or terminating them.** To avoid the direct need for termination, unprofitable customers can be made to buy more or in larger quantities, forgo certain features or services, or pay higher amounts or fees. Banks, phone companies, and travel agencies are all charging for once-free services to ensure minimum customer revenue levels.
- **Focusing disproportionate effort on high-value customers.** The MVCs can be treated in a special way. Thoughtful gestures such as birthday greetings, small gifts, or invitations to special sports or arts events can send a strong signal to the customer.

Attracting and Retaining Customers

Companies seeking to expand their profits and sales have to spend considerable time and resources searching for new customers. To generate leads, the company develops ads and places them in media that will reach new prospects; it sends direct mail and makes phone calls to possible new prospects; its salespeople participate in trade shows where they might find new leads; it purchases names from list brokers; and so on.

Table 5.3 displays one analysis of some typical acquisition costs. Different types of acquisition methods can yield different types of customers with varying CLVs. One study showed that customers acquired through the offer of a 35 percent discount had about one-half the long-term value of customers acquired without any discount.[44]

REDUCING DEFECTION

It is not enough, however, to attract new customers; the company must keep them and increase their business. Too many companies suffer from high **customer churn**—high customer defection. It is like adding water to a leaking bucket. Cellular carriers, for example, are plagued with "spinners," customers who switch carriers at least three times a year looking for the best deal.

Table 5.3 Customer Acquisition Costs by Marketing Activity

Activity	Cost per New Customer	Cost per Solicitation
Personal selling	$500	$100.00
Direct mail	$115	$1.50
Telemarketing	$95	$3.30
Web site, email	$30	$0.06

1. Costs are based upon typical industry averages. Response rates are implied.
2. Actual costs vary from business to business depending on the complexity of the sales process.

Source: Justin Zohn, "Customer Acquisition Cost–A Key Marketing Metric," *National Petroleum News,* April 2003.

To reduce the defection rate, the company must:

1. **Define and measure its retention rate.** For a magazine, subscription renewal rate is a good measure of retention. For a college, it could be the first- to second-year retention rate, or the class graduation rate.
2. **Distinguish the causes of customer attrition and identify those that can be managed better.** Not much can be done about customers who leave the region or go out of business, but much can be done about those who leave because of poor service, shoddy products, or high prices.[45]
3. **Compare the lost profit equal to the customer's lifetime value from a lost customer to the costs to reduce the defection rate.** As long as the cost to discourage defection is lower than the lost profit, the company should spend the money to try to retain the customer.

Sometime such defection is due to customer variety-seeking. Pepsi, in Japan, has turned this trend to its advantage:

> **Pepsi**—In Japan where some 1,500 drinks come into the market each year, only a handful survive long enough to win a loyal following. To counter this high defection and capitalize on Japanese attraction to ***gentei*** or "limited edition," Pepsi began introducing drinks with the intention to discontinue them during the peak of their popularity. One such drink is Ice Cucumber. Within days of its introduction, clips of people drinking the pale green soda were showing up on YouTube. A couple of weeks later, all 4.8 million bottles of Ice Cucumber were sold out. But instead of ratcheting up production, Pepsi Japan discontinued the drink. It considered that the value of Ice Cucumber is that it is gone already. Previously, short-lived but successful launches included Pepsi Blue, Pepsi Red, Carnival, and Gold. These were drinks that had seen longer runs in other countries. Pepsi is aware not to overdo its ***gentei*** offerings and limits them to three or four times a year.[46]

RETENTION DYNAMICS

Figure 5.5 shows the main steps in the process of attracting and retaining customers. The starting point is everyone who might conceivably buy the product or service. These *potentials* are people or organizations who might conceivably have an interest in buying the company's product or service, but may not have the means or intention to buy. The next task is to identify which potentials are really good *prospects*—people with the motivation, ability, and opportunity to make a purchase—by interviewing them, checking on their financial standing, and so on. Marketing efforts can then concentrate on converting the prospects into *first-time customers,* and then into *repeat customers,* and then into *clients*—people to whom the company gives very special and knowledgeable treatment. The next challenge is to turn clients into *members* by starting a membership program that offers benefits to customers who join, and then turning members into *advocates,* customers who enthusiastically recommend the company and its products and services to others. The ultimate challenge is to turn advocates into *partners.*

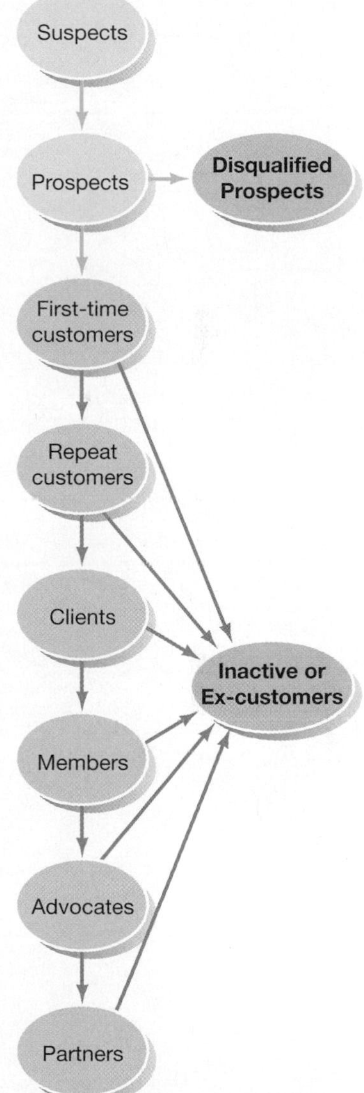

Figure 5.5 The Customer-Development Process

Source: See Jill Griffin, *Customer Loyalty: How to Earn It, How to Keep It,* (New York: Lexington Books, 1995), p. 36. Also see Murray Raphel and Neil Raphel, *Up the Loyalty Ladder: Turning Sometime Customers into Full-Time Advocates of Your Business,* (New York: Harper Business, 1995).

Unfortunately, much marketing theory and practice centers on the art of attracting new customers, rather than on retaining and cultivating existing ones. The emphasis traditionally has been on making sales rather than on building relationships; on preselling and selling rather than on caring for the customer afterward. More companies now recognize the importance of satisfying and retaining customers.

Satisfied customers constitute the company's *customer relationship capital.* If the company were to be sold, the acquiring company would pay not only for the plant and equipment and the brand name, but also for the delivered *customer base,* the number and value of the customers who would do business with the new firm. Here are some interesting facts that bear on customer retention:[47]

1. **Acquiring new customers can cost five times more than the costs involved in satisfying and retaining current customers.** It requires a great deal of effort to induce satisfied customers to switch away from their current suppliers.
2. **The average company loses 10 percent of its customers each year.**
3. **A 5 percent reduction in the customer defection rate can increase profits by 25 percent to 85 percent, depending on the industry.**
4. **The customer profit rate tends to increase over the life of the retained customer.**

Building Loyalty

Creating a strong, tight connection with the customers is the dream of any marketer and often the key to long-term marketing success. Companies that want to form strong customer bonds need to attend to a number of different considerations (see Figure 5.6). One set of researchers see retention-building activities as adding financial benefits, social benefits, or structural ties.[48] The following sections explain four important types of marketing activities that companies are using to improve loyalty and retention.

Companies that want to form strong customer bonds need to attend to the following basics:

- Get cross-departmental participation in planning and managing the customer satisfaction and retention process.
- Integrate the "Voice of the Customer" to capture their stated and unstated needs or requirements in all business decisions.
- Create superior products, services, and experiences for the target market.
- Organize and make accessible a database of information on individual customer needs, preferences, contacts, purchase frequency, and satisfaction.
- Make it easy for customers to reach appropriate company personnel and express their needs, perceptions, and complaints.
- Run award programs recognizing outstanding employees.

Figure 5.6 Forming Strong Customer Bonds

INTERACTING WITH CUSTOMERS

Listening to customers is crucial to CRM. Some companies have created an ongoing mechanism that keeps senior managers permanently plugged in to frontline customer feedback.

But listening is only part of the story. It is also important to be a customer advocate and, as much as possible, take the customers' side on issues, understanding their point of view.[49] "Marketing Memo: Creating Customer Evangelists" describes six keys to creating customers who feel so strongly about companies and brands that they go way beyond just purchasing and consuming their products and services.

DEVELOPING LOYALTY PROGRAMS

Two customer loyalty programs that companies can offer are frequency programs and club marketing programs. **Frequency programs (FPs)** are designed to provide rewards to customers who buy frequently and in substantial amounts.[50] They can help build long-term loyalty with high CLV customers, creating cross-selling opportunities in the process.

MARKETING MEMO • CREATING CUSTOMER EVANGELISTS

McConnell and Huba assert that *customer evangelists* not only buy a company's products or services but believe in them so much that they are compelled to spread the word and voluntarily recruit their friends and colleagues on the company's behalf. They studied brands such as Macintosh and Krispy Kreme that were created and sustained by customer evangelists. On their own "Church of the Customer" blog (www.churchofthecustomer.com), they offer six tips for marketing evangelism:

- **Customer plus-delta.** Understand what evangelists love by continuously gathering their input. Build-a-Bear Workshop uses a "Cub Advisory Board" in the U.S. as a feedback and decision-input body. The board is made up of twenty 8-to-12-year-olds who review new-product ideas and give a "paws up or down". Many products in the stores are customer ideas.

- **Napsterize your knowledge.** Release your own knowledge, data or intellectual property into a fast-moving distribution network. Sharing knowledge freely makes it more accessible, reducing your biggest threat: obscurity. It is liable to fall into the hands of people who will tell others about it. People talking about your knowledge increases its perceived and actual value.

- **Build the buzz.** Keep customer evangelists talking by providing them with tools, programs, and features to demonstrate their passion. Sneaker company Converse asked amateur filmmakers to submit 30-second short films that demonstrated their inspiration from the iconic brand. The best of the 1,800 submissions were showcased in the Converse Gallery Web site (conversegallery.com). Converse used the best of the best films as TV commercials. One key outcome of the gallery: sales of shoes via the Web site doubled in the month after the gallery's launch.

- **Create community.** Provide like-minded customers with the chance to meet. Paetec provides telecommunications services to hotels, universities, and other companies. It has grown into a $500 million company in 6 years, and its growth is due entirely to evangelism. Paetec's primary marketing strategy: host informal dinners around the country for customers. Current customers and key prospects are invited to dine on Paetec's tab and meet one another. No boring PowerPoint presentations here, just customers talking about their telecommunications challenges and their unfiltered experiences of being a Paetec customer. Prospects are sold on the company by other customers.

- **Make bite-size chunks.** Bite-size chunks of products and services reduce risk, improve sales cycles, and offer upfront value. Even if a customer doesn't purchase, he or she may spread favorable word of mouth. BRAND'S® Essence of Chicken, a health supplement popular among Chinese, is offered in a starter's kit where smaller bottles of the health supplement are sold to encourage first-time drinkers to try.

- **Create a cause.** Companies that strive for a higher purpose —such as supporting "freedom," as Harley-Davidson does—often find that customers, vendors, suppliers, and employees naturally root for their success. Customer evangelists crave emotional connection and validation; a well-defined cause generates emotional commitment. When your brand, product or service aspires to change the world, altruism and capitalism converge.

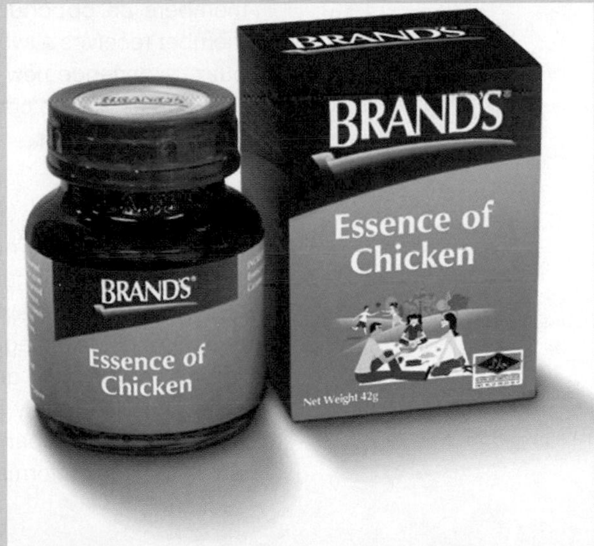

BRAND'S® Essence of Chicken is also sold in smaller bottles to encourage new buyers.

Sources: Ben McConnell and Jackie Huba, "Learning to Leverage the Lunatic Fringe." *Point*, July–August 2006, pp. 14–15; Michael Krauss, "Work to Convert Customers into Evangelists." *Marketing News*, December 15, 2006, p. 6; Ben McConnell and Jackie Huba, *Creating Customer Evangelists: How Loyal Customers Become a Loyal Sales Force*, (New York: Kaplan Business, 2003).

One of the first industries to pioneer an FP was the airline industry, which decided to offer free mileage credit to their passengers. Hotels next adopted FPs, followed by banks that issue credit cards. Today, some supermarket chains offer price club cards, which provide member customers with discounts on particular items.[51] There are also coalition FPs which allow members to accumulate and redeem credit points from multiple companies participating in the scheme.

Typically, the first company to introduce an FP gains the most benefit, especially if competitors are slow to respond. After competitors respond, FPs can become a financial burden to all the offering companies, but some companies are more efficient and creative in managing an FP. For example, airlines run tiered loyalty programs in which they offer different levels of rewards to different travelers. They may offer one frequent-flier mile for every mile flown to occasional travelers and two frequent-flier miles for every mile flown to top customers. For example, Singapore Airlines' KrisFlyer program offers its Elite Silver and Elite Gold travelers bonus miles compared to its regular flyers.

Many companies have created club membership programs. Club membership can be open to anyone who purchases a product or service, or it can be limited to an affinity group, or to those willing to pay a small fee. Although open clubs are good for building a database or snagging customers from competitors, limited membership clubs are more powerful long-term loyalty builders. Fees and membership conditions prevent those with only a fleeting interest in a company's products from joining. These clubs attract and keep those customers who are responsible for the largest portion of business. Some highly successful clubs include the following:

PlayStation—Sony PlayStation has an interactive relationship program where intense gamers can join a club called PlayStation Underground. The club gives members an opportunity to feel that they belong to a unique subculture. Each member receives a two-disc set every quarter with which they can tap in to the latest buzz, experience new game challenges, and be the first to know about upcoming new games. It also contains interviews with game developers and shows "behind-the-scene" features.

Harley-Davidson—This motorcycle company sponsors the Harley Owners Group (H.O.G.), which now numbers 650,000 members in over 1,200 chapters. The first-time buyer of a Harley-Davidson motorcycle gets a free one-year membership. H.O.G. benefits include a magazine called *Hog Tales*, a touring handbook, emergency road service, a specially designed insurance program, theft reward service, discount hotel rates, and a Fly & Ride program enabling members to rent Harleys while on vacation. The company also maintains an extensive Web site devoted to H.O.G., which includes information on club chapters, events, and a special members-only section.[52]

PERSONALIZING MARKETING

Company personnel work on cementing social bonds with customers by individualizing and personalizing customer relationships. In essence, thoughtful companies turn their customers into clients. Donnelly, Berry, and Thompson draw this distinction:

> *Customers may be nameless to the institution; clients cannot be nameless. Customers are served as part of the mass or as part of larger segments; clients are served on an individual basis. Customers are served by anyone who happens to be available; clients are served by the professional assigned to them.*[53]

An increasingly essential ingredient for the best relationship marketing today is the right technology. Table 5.5 highlights five imperatives of CRM and shows where technology

Table 5.4 Breaking Down Customer Relationship Management: What Customer Relation Management Really Comprises

CRM Imperative				
Acquiring the right customer	Crafting the right value proposition	Instituting the best processes	Motivating employees	Learning to retain customers
You Get It When ...				
• You have identified your most valuable customers. • You have calculated your share of their wallet for your goods and services.	• You have studied what products or services your customers need today and will need tomorrow. • You have surveyed what products or services your competitors offer today and will offer tomorrow. • You have spotted what products or services you should be offering.	• You have researched the best way to deliver your products or services to customers, including the alliances you need to strike, the technologies you need to invest in, and the service capabilities you need to develop or acquire.	• You know what tools your employees need to foster customer relationships. • You have identified the HR systems you need to institute to boost employee loyalty.	• You have learned why customers defect and how to win them back. • You have analyzed what your competitors are doing to win your high-value customers. • Your senior management monitors customer defection metrics.
CRM Technology Can Help ...				
• Analyze customer revenue and cost data to identify current and future high-value customers. • Target your direct marketing efforts better.	• Capture relevant product and service behavior data. • Create new distribution channels. • Develop new pricing models. • Build communities.	• Process transactions faster. • Provide better information to the front line. • Manage logistics and the supply chain more efficiently. • Catalyze collaborative commerce.	• Align incentives and metrics. • Deploy knowledge management systems.	• Track customer defection and retention levels. • Track customer service satisfaction levels.

Source: Darrel K. Rigby, Frederick F. Reichheld, and Phil Schefter, "Avoid the Four Perils of CRM." *Harvard Business Review*, February 2002, p. 106.

fits in. GE Plastics could not target its email effectively to different customers if it were not for advances in database software. Dell Computer could not customize computer ordering for its global corporate customers without advances in Web technology. Companies are using email, Web sites, call centers, databases, and database software to foster continuous contact between company and customer.

Online companies need to make sure their attempts to create relationships with customers do not backfire, as when customers are bombarded by computer-generated recommendations that consistently miss the mark. Buy a lot of baby gifts on Amazon.com, and your personalized recommendations suddenly do not look so personal! E-tailers need to recognize the limitations of online personalization at the same time that they try harder to find technology and processes that really work.[54]

Companies are also recognizing the importance of the personal component to CRM and what happens once customers make actual contact. As business guru Jeffrey Pfeffer puts it, "the best companies build cultures in which frontline people are empowered to do what's needed to take care of the customer." He cites examples of firms such as SAS, the Scandinavian airline, which engineered a turnaround based in part on the insight that a customer's impressions of a company are formed through myriad small interactions like checking in, boarding the plane, and eating a meal.[55]

CREATING INSTITUTIONAL TIES

The company may supply customers with special equipment or computer links that help customers manage orders, payroll, and inventory. Nestlé in Asia has supported its retailers with several activities to help them in inventory management.

Nestlé—Nestlé maintains close relations with its trade partners. In Japan, it pioneered the extensively used point-of-sale merchandising activities. In Thailand, it provided supermarkets with inventory control systems such as A.C. Nielsen's Spaceman and trained them on its use.

Wunderman suggests the following ways to create institutional ties:[56]

1. **Create long-term contracts.** A newspaper subscription replaces the need to buy a newspaper each day. A 20-year mortgage replaces the need to re-borrow the money each year.
2. **Charge a lower price to consumers who buy larger supplies.** Offer lower prices to people who agree to be supplied regularly with a certain brand of toothpaste, detergent, or beer.
3. **Turn the product into a long-term service.** Daimler-Chrysler is considering selling "miles of reliable transportation" instead of cars, with the consumer able to order different cars at different times, such as a station wagon for shopping and a convertible for the weekend.

Win-Backs

Regardless of the nature of the category or how hard companies may try, some customers inevitably become inactive or drop out. The challenge is to reactivate dissatisfied customers through win-back strategies.[57] It is often easier to re-attract ex-customers (because the company knows their names and histories) than to find new ones. The key is to analyze the causes of customer defection through exit interviews and lost-customer surveys and win back only those who have strong profit potential.[58]

Customer Databases and Database Marketing

Marketers must know their customers. And to know the customer, the company must collect information and store it in a database and do database marketing: A **customer database** is an organized collection of comprehensive information about individual customers or prospects that is current, accessible, and actionable for such marketing purposes as lead generation, lead qualification, sale of a product or service, or maintenance of customer relationships. **Database marketing** is the process of building, maintaining, and using customer databases and other databases (products, suppliers, resellers) for the purpose of contacting, transacting, and building customer relationships.

Customer Databases

Many companies confuse a customer mailing list with a customer database. A **customer mailing list** is simply a set of names, addresses, and telephone numbers. A customer database contains much more information, accumulated through customer transactions, registration information, telephone queries, Web cookies, and every customer contact.

Ideally, a **customer database** contains the consumer's past purchases, demographics (age, income, family members, birthdays), psychographics (activities, interests, and opinions), mediagraphics (preferred media), and other useful information.

A **business database** ideally contains business customers' past purchases; past volumes, prices, and profits; buyer team member names and ages, birthdays, hobbies, and favorite foods; status of current contracts; an estimate of the supplier's share of the customer's business; competitive suppliers; assessment of competitive strengths and weaknesses in selling and servicing the account; and relevant buying practices, patterns, and policies.

Tata Telecom—India's Tata Telecom introduced a program called "Winning Through Customer Responsiveness" to capture a larger market share. The initiative began by rotating the organizational structure vertically so that the customer was on top and an account management team that includes sales and services was directly beneath. Each of its offices was personally visited by its vice president to garner buy-in from the rank and file. It also made better use of its CRM software. Although 60 percent of its revenue came from existing customers, Tata knew surprisingly little about their buying behavior. The company had a major database that was not shared with regional offices. Every customer order used to be faxed from the regional office to headquarters, where the information was keyed into the system. This information is now recorded in a single, centralized customer database. Every lead is prequalified by marketing and entered into the system. Regional offices now have complete access to the master customer database and can place orders directly into the system. Additionally, Tata created a central Customer Interaction Center where customers' questions are matched to a service engineer based on availability and skills required for resolution. The database tracks past resolutions and allows service engineers to search previous issues and solutions.[59]

"Breakthrough Marketing: Tesco" describes how the U.K. supermarket giant has found ways to use its database to attract and engage customers.

Data Warehouses and Data Mining

Savvy companies are capturing information every time a customer comes into contact with any of its departments. Touch points include a customer purchase, a customer-requested service call, an online query, or a mail-in rebate card. Banks and credit card companies, telephone companies, catalog marketers, and many other companies have a great deal of information about their customers, including not only addresses and phone numbers, but also their transactions and enhanced data on age, family size, income, and other demographic information.

These data are collected by the company's contact center and organized into a **data warehouse**. Company personnel can capture, query, and analyze the data. Inferences can be drawn about an individual customer's needs and responses. Telemarketers can respond to customer inquiries based on a total picture of the customer relationship.

Through **data mining**, marketing statisticians can extract useful information about individuals, trends, and segments from the mass of data.[60] Data mining involves the use of sophisticated statistical and mathematical techniques such as cluster analysis, automatic interaction detection, predictive modeling, and neural networking.[61]

Some observers believe that a proprietary database can provide a company with a significant competitive advantage as Aetna Malaysia shows:

Aetna Malaysia—Aetna Malaysia initiated a complex data integration project and a customer warehouse cutting across the traditional product silos of life, property, casualty, and health insurance. This enabled predictive customer analysis and empowered its agents to advise customers on how best to cover their insurance needs with Aetna. Agents also furnished valuable input on their customers' life events such as births, deaths, and marriages. Cross-selling and up-selling were more successful because Aetna and its agents knew more about the specific needs of individual customers. Moreover, churn rates, agent defections, and loan processing time fell.[62]

BREAKTHROUGH • MARKETING

TESCO

If you asked a customer of U.K. supermarket chain Tesco what the shopping experience there was like in the early 1980s, "customer-friendly" would probably not be the answer. Though it began upgrading its stores and product selection in 1983, Tesco continued to suffer from a reputation as a "pile it high and sell it cheap" mass-market retailer, lagging behind the more upscale market leader Sainsbury's. To gain share against Sainsbury's, Tesco needed to reverse the public perception of its stores. It decided to improve the shopping experience and highlight improvements with an image campaign to "lift us out of the mold in our particular sector," as its 1989 agency brief put it.

Between 1990 and 1992, Tesco launched 114 separate initiatives to improve the quality of its stores, including adding baby-changing rooms, stocking specialty items such as French free-range chickens, and introducing a value-priced line of products. It developed a campaign titled "Every Little Helps" to communicate these improvements with 20 ads, each focusing on a different aspect of its approach—"doing right by the customer." As a result, between 1990 and 1995, Tesco attracted 1.3 million new customers, who pushed revenues and market share steadily upward until Tesco surpassed Sainsbury's as the market leader in 1995.

Tesco then introduced an initiative that would make it a world-class example of how to build lasting relationships with customers: the Tesco Clubcard frequent-shopper program. Essentially a loyalty card that offered discounts and special offers tailored to individual shoppers, the Clubcard was also a powerful data-gathering tool enabling Tesco to understand the shopping patterns and preferences of its customers better than any competitor could. Using Clubcard data, Tesco created a unique "DNA profile" for each customer based on shopping habits. To build this profile, it classified each product purchased by a customer on a set of up to 40 dimensions, including price, size, brand, eco-friendliness, convenience, and healthiness. Based on their DNA profile, Tesco shoppers received one of four million different variations of the quarterly Clubcard statement, which contained targeted special offers and other promotions. The company also installed kiosks in its stores where Clubcard shoppers could get customized coupons.

The Clubcard data also helped Tesco run its business more efficiently. Tracking Clubcard purchases helped uncover price elasticities and set promotional schedules saving over $500 million. Tesco used customer data to determine the range of products and the nature of merchandising for each store, and even the location of new stores. Within 15 months of introduction, more than eight million Clubcards had been issued, of which five million were used regularly. The customer focus enhanced by the Clubcard helped propel Tesco to even greater success than in the early 1990s. The company's market share in the U.K. rose to 15 percent by 1999, and that year other British companies voted Tesco Britain's most admired company for the second year in a row.

In the following years, Tesco continued to apply its winning formula of using customer data to dominate the British retail landscape, moving beyond supermarkets to "big-box" retailing of general merchandise, or non-food products. Not only was Tesco providing additional convenience to consumers who preferred shopping under one roof, it was also improving its profitability. The average margin of non-food products was 9 percent, as opposed to 5 percent for food. By 2003, nearly 20 percent of Tesco's revenues came from non-food items, and the company was selling more CDs than Virgin Megastores, and its apparel line, Cherokee, was the fastest growing brand in the U.K.

Tesco also undertook extensive customer research with telephone and written surveys and customer panels to extend its lead in the grocery market. By 2005, the company had a 35 percent share of supermarket spending in the U.K., almost twice that of its nearest competitor, and a 14 percent share of total retail sales. Tesco used the same customer-centered strategy to expand overseas. In 2005, it had 648 stores outside U.K. and was the supermarket leader in Poland, Hungary, Thailand, Ireland, and Slovakia. In 2006, it was Britain's largest company and the sixth largest retailer in the world.

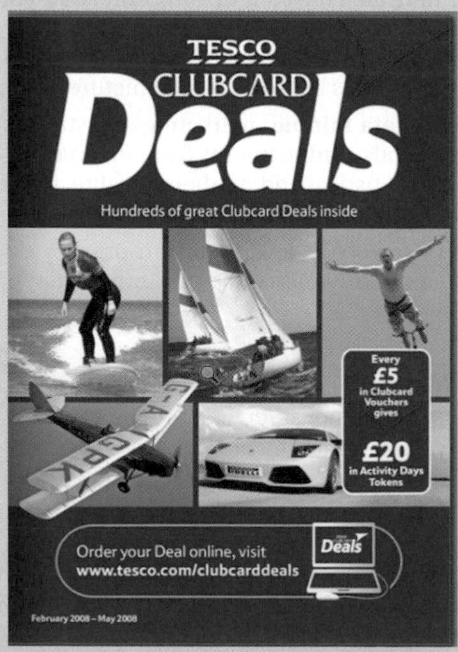

The introduction of its loyalty program, the Clubcard, was a huge success for British retailer Tesco, bringing in new customers and helping build a powerful customer database that became the springboard for further customer-centered marketing efforts.

Sources: Richard Fletcher, "Leahy Shrugs Off Talk of a 'Brain Drain'." *Sunday Times* (London), January 29, 2006; Elizabeth Rigby, "Prosperous Tesco Takes Retailing to a New Level." *Financial Times*, September 21, 2005, p. 23; Laura Cohn, "A Grocery War That's Not about Food." *BusinessWeek*, October 20, 2003, p. 30; "The Prime Minister Launches the 10th Tesco Computers for Schools Scheme." *M2 Presswire*, January 26, 2001; Ashleye Sharpe and Joanna Bamford, "Tesco Stores Ltd." (paper presented at Advertising Effectiveness Awards, 2000); Hamish Pringle and Marjorie Thompson, *Brand Spirit*, (New York: John Wiley, 1999).

USING THE DATABASE

In general, companies can use their databases in five ways:

1. ***To identify prospects*** — Many companies generate sales leads by advertising their product or service. The ads generally contain a response feature, such as a business reply card or toll-free phone number. The database is built from these responses. The company sorts through the database to identify the best prospects, then contacts them by mail, phone, or personal call in an attempt to convert them into customers.
2. ***To decide which customers should receive a particular offer*** — Companies are interested in selling, up-selling, and cross-selling their products and services. Companies set up criteria describing the ideal target customer for a particular offer. Then they search their customer databases for those who most closely resemble the ideal type. By noting response rates, a company can improve its targeting precision over time. Following a sale, it can set up an automatic sequence of activities: one week later, send a thank-you note; five weeks later, send a new offer; 10 weeks later (if customer has not responded), phone the customer and offer a special discount.
3. ***To deepen customer loyalty*** — Companies can build interest and enthusiasm by remembering customer preferences; and by sending appropriate gifts, discount coupons, and interesting reading material.
4. ***To reactivate customer purchases*** — Companies can install automatic mailing programs (automatic marketing) that send out birthday or anniversary cards, Christmas shopping reminders, or off-season promotions. The database can help the company make attractive or timely offers.
5. ***To avoid serious customer mistakes*** — A major bank confessed to a number of mistakes that it had made by not using its customer database well. In one case, the bank charged a customer a penalty for late payment on his mortgage, failing to note that he headed a company that was a major depositor in this bank. He quit the bank. In a second case, two different staff members of the bank phoned the same mortgage customer offering a home equity loan at different prices. Neither knew that the other had made the call. In a third case, a bank gave a premium customer only standard service in another country.

The Downside of Database Marketing and CRM

Having covered the good news about database marketing, we also have to cover the bad news. Four problems can deter a firm from effectively using CRM. The first is that building and maintaining a customer database requires a large investment in computer hardware, database software, analytical programs, communication links, and skilled personnel. It is difficult to collect the right data, especially to capture all the occasions of company interaction with individual customers. This problem is accentuated in Asia, where there are at least four major differences in the nature of customer relationships compared to the West:[63]

1. **Language preferences are complex but important.** For example, it is not unusual for dialects such as Hokkien to be spoken in informal settings but Mandarin to be employed more formally among the Chinese in Singapore and Malaysia. Distinguishing the proper message in the appropriate language adds richness to the relationship. However, few CRM systems have this level of intra-personal relationship tracking as a standard facility.
2. **The issue of identifying customers uniquely by name poses challenges in a racially diverse society**. Muslim names are quite long and do not always include a surname. Considerable flexibility is thus needed in the CRM system.
3. **Some jurisdictions allow for more than one marriage, and wealthy male customers may have several addresses in intricate arrangements.** Sending investment or insurance details to the wrong address can create difficulties. Linking multiple addresses, relationships, and interactions, while simultaneously maintaining discretion and privacy, is thus critical.
4. **There is also a bias against flaunting wealth and a reluctance to declare it to strangers (particularly if there is a perceived link to a government authority).** Hence, it is difficult to judge the true net worth of customers. Proxies are needed to recognize potential most valuable customers.

Building a customer database would not be worthwhile in the following cases: (1) where the product is a once-in-a-lifetime purchase (e.g., a grand piano); (2) where customers show little loyalty to a brand (i.e., there is lots of customer churn); (3) where the unit sale is very small (e.g., a candy bar); and (4) where the cost of gathering information is too high.

The second problem is the difficulty of getting everyone in the company to be customer-oriented and to use the available information. Employees find it far easier to carry on traditional transaction marketing than to practice CRM. Effective database marketing requires managing and training employees as well as dealers and suppliers.

The third problem is that not all customers want a relationship with the company, and they may resent knowing that the company has collected that much personal information about them. Marketers must be concerned about customer attitudes toward privacy and security. Online companies would be smart to explain their privacy policies, and give consumers the right not to have their information stored in a database.

A fourth problem is that the assumptions behind CRM may not always hold true.[64] For example, it may not be the case that it costs less to serve more loyal customers. High volume customers often know their value to a company and can leverage it to extract premium service and/or price discounts. Loyal customers may expect and demand more from the firm and resent any attempt by the firm to receive full or higher prices. They may also be jealous of attention lavished on other customers. When eBay began to chase big corporate customers such as IBM and Disney, some small mom-and-pop businesses who helped to build the brand felt abandoned.[65] Loyal customers may not necessarily be the best ambassadors for the brand. One study found that customers who scored high on behavioral loyalty and bought a lot of a company's products were less active word-of-mouth marketers to others than customers who scored high on attitudinal loyalty and expressed greater commitment to the firm.

Thus the benefits of database marketing do not come without heavy costs, not only in collecting the original customer data, but also in maintaining and mining them. Yet, when it works, a data warehouse yields more than it costs.

Database marketing is most frequently used by business marketers and service providers (hotels, banks, airlines, insurance, credit card, and telephone companies) that normally and easily collect a lot of customer data. Companies that are in the best position to invest in CRM are companies that do a lot of cross-selling and up-selling (e.g., banks) or companies whose customers have highly differentiated needs and are of highly differentiated value to the company. It is used less often by packaged-goods retailers and consumer packaged-goods companies, though some companies have built databases for certain brands. Businesses where the CLV is low, those who have high churn, and where there is no direct contact between the seller and the ultimate buyer may not benefit as much from CRM.

Some do not find much improvement through CRM implementation. The reasons are many: the system was poorly designed, it became too expensive, users did not make much use of it or report much benefit, and collaborators ignored the system. One set of business commentators suggested the following as the four main perils of CRM:[66] (1) implementing CRM before creating a customer strategy, (2) rolling out CRM before changing organization to match, (3) assuming more CRM technology is better, and (4) stalking, not wooing customers.

George Day concludes that one of the reasons many CRM failures occur is that companies concentrate on customer contact processes without making corresponding changes in internal structures and systems.[67] His recommendation? Change the configuration before installing CRM: "Our survey results confirm that a superior customer-relating capability has everything to do with how a business builds and manages its organization and not much to do with the CRM tools and technologies it employs." All this points to the need for each company to determine how much (and where) to invest in building and using database marketing to conduct its customer relationships.

Summary

1. Customers are value-maximizers. They form an expectation of value and act on it. Buyers will buy from the firm that they perceive to offer the highest customer-delivered value, defined as the difference between total customer value and total customer cost.
2. A buyer's satisfaction is a function of the product's perceived performance and the buyer's expectations. Recognizing that high satisfaction leads to high customer loyalty, many companies today are aiming for total customer satisfaction (TCS). For such companies, customer satisfaction is both a goal and a marketing tool.
3. Losing profitable customers can dramatically affect a firm's profits. The cost of attracting a new customer is estimated to be five times the cost of keeping a current customer happy. The key to retaining customers is relationship marketing.
4. Quality is the totality of features and characteristics of a product or service that bear on its ability to satisfy stated or implied needs. Today's companies have no choice but to implement total quality management programs if they are to remain solvent and profitable.
5. Marketing managers have two responsibilities in a quality-centered company. First, they must participate in formulating strategies and policies designed to help the company win through total quality excellence. Second, they must deliver marketing quality alongside production quality.
6. Companies are also becoming skilled in Customer Relationship Management (CRM), which focuses on meeting the individual needs of valued customers. The skill requires building a customer database and doing data mining to detect trends, segments, and individual needs.

Application

Marketing Debate—Online Versus Offline Privacy?

As more and more firms practice relationship marketing and develop customer databases, privacy issues are emerging as an important topic. Consumers and public interest groups are scrutinizing—and sometimes criticizing—the privacy policies of firms. Concerns are also being raised about potential theft of online credit card information or other potentially sensitive or confidential financial information. Others maintain that the online privacy fears are unfounded and that security issues are every bit as much a concern in the offline world. They argue that the opportunity to steal information exists virtually everywhere and that it is up to the consumer to protect his or her interests.

Take a position: (1) *Privacy is a bigger issue in the online world than the offline world* versus *privacy is no different online than offline.* (2) Consumers on the whole receive more benefit than risk from marketers knowing their personal information.

Marketing Discussion

Consider the lifetime value of customers (CLV). Choose a business and show how you would go about developing a quantitative formulation that captures the concept. How would organizations change if they totally embraced the customer equity concept and maximized CLV?

Cosmetics companies are riding on Asian women's penchant to have fair skin. Some have even entered the men's market.

Analyzing Consumer Markets

The aim of marketing is to meet and satisfy target customers' needs and wants better than competitors. Consumer behavior is the study of how individuals, groups, and organizations select, buy, use, and dispose of goods, services, ideas, or experiences to satisfy their needs and wants. Studying consumers provides clues for improving or introducing products or services, setting prices, devising channels, crafting messages, and developing other marketing activities. Marketers are always looking for emerging trends that suggest new marketing opportunities.

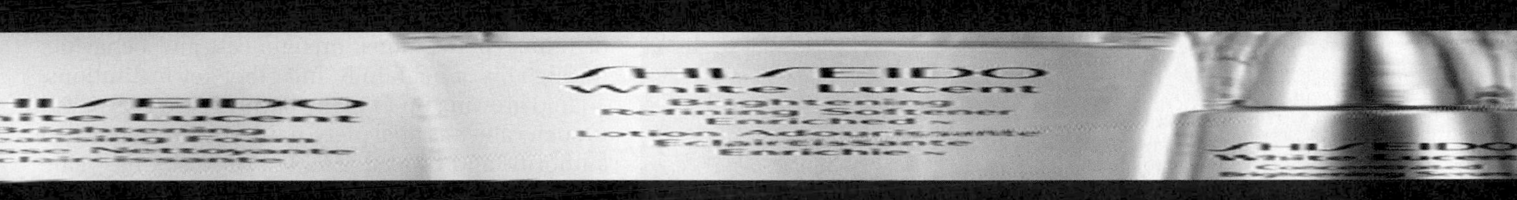

While Westerners tan to appear attractive, Asians buy products that promise to lighten their skin. Market research company Synovate found that 38 percent or more of women in Hong Kong, Korea, Malaysia, the Philippines, and Taiwan use skin whitening products. In Southeast Asia, light skin historically conveyed nobility, aristocracy, wealth, and status; while dark skin is associated with those who toiled in the fields. Only the rich could afford to stay indoors, while peasants withstood the hot sun in the rice fields. A Chinese saying goes, "One white covers up three ugliness." Another survey found that 74 percent of men in Malaysia, 68 percent in Hong Kong, and 55 percent in Taiwan say they are more attracted to women with fair complexions. The biggest market for skin whitening products is Japan, followed by China and India. Major Asian and Western cosmetic companies such as Shiseido, Olay, Chanel, and L'Oréal have jumped on the bandwagon in this growing market. Whitening ingredients have also found their way into deodorant roll-ons in Indonesia. In India, where the skin-lightening industry is worth at least $200 million, there is also skin-lightening cream for men. The Fair-and-Handsome range is endorsed by Shah Rukh Khan, one of Bollywood's biggest film stars.[1]

In this chapter, we will address the following questions:

1. How do consumer characteristics influence buying behavior?
2. What major psychological processes influence consumer responses to the marketing program?
3. How do consumers make purchasing decisions?
4. How do marketers analyze consumer decision making?

6

Successful marketing requires that companies fully connect with their customers. Adopting a holistic marketing orientation means understanding consumers—gaining a 360-degree view of both their daily lives and the changes that occur during their lifetimes. Gaining a thorough, in-depth consumer understanding helps to ensure that the right products are marketed to the right consumers in the right way. This chapter explores individual consumer buying dynamics; the next chapter explores the buying dynamics of business buyers.

What Influences Consumer Behavior?

To learn how Quebec's rich and diverse culture has led various multinational companies to adapt their campaigns, visit www.pearsoned.ca/marketingmanagementcanada.

Consumer behavior is the study of how individuals, groups, and organizations select, buy, use, and dispose of goods, services, ideas, or experiences to satisfy their needs and wants. Marketers must fully understand both the theory and reality of consumer behavior. A consumer's buying behavior is influenced by cultural, social, and personal factors. Cultural factors exert the broadest and deepest influence.

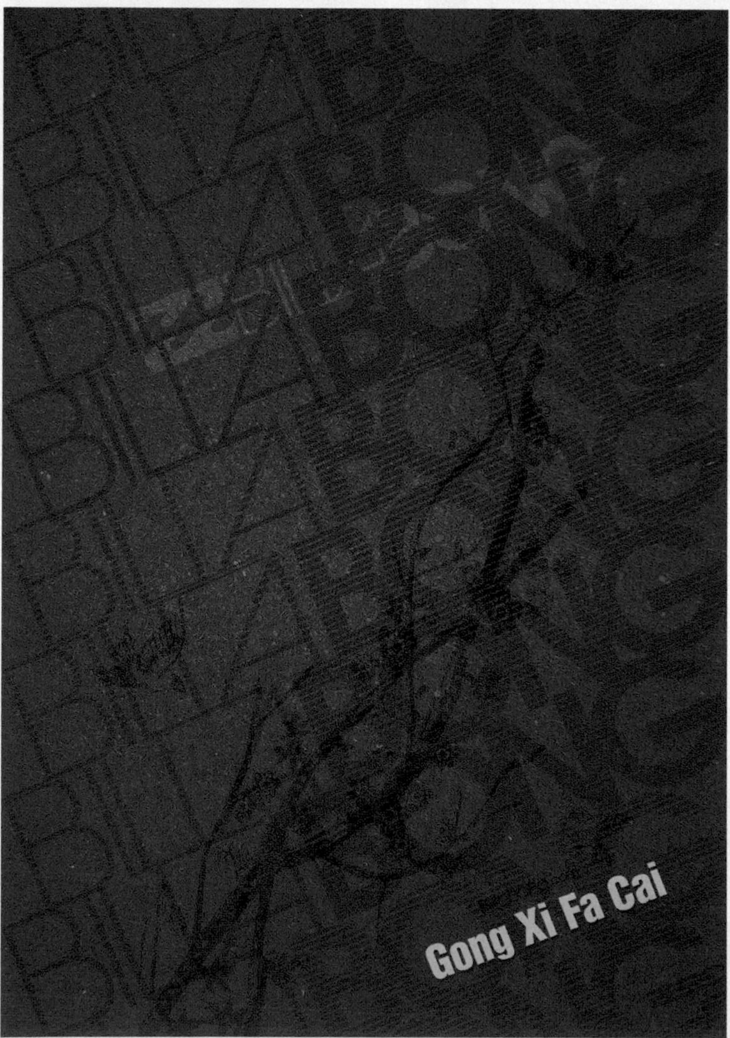

While enhancing awareness for boardsports and its brand name. Billabong is mindful to stay relevant to cultural iconic festivals. This print ad featured during the Lunar New Year helps Asian consumers, especially the Chinese, identify with Billabong.

Cultural Factors

Culture, subculture, and social class are particularly important influences on consumer buying behavior. **Culture** is the fundamental determinant of a person's wants and behavior. The growing child acquires a set of values, perceptions, preferences, and behaviors through his or her family and other key institutions. A child growing up in many parts of Asia is exposed to such values as filial piety, hard work, obedience to authority, and collectivism. For instance, the value of *krengjai,* or deference to or consideration of others, is pervasive in Thai culture.

Each culture consists of smaller **subcultures** that provide more specific identification and socialization for their members. Subcultures include nationalities, religions, racial groups, and geographic regions. When subcultures grow large and affluent enough, companies often design specialized marketing programs to serve them. *Multicultural marketing* grew out of careful marketing research, which revealed that different ethnic and demographic niches did not always respond favorably to mass marketing.

Chinese consumers, for instance, may respond differently from Indian, Malay, or Filipino consumers. To the Chinese, especially those of the Cantonese dialect group, *feng shui* (literally meaning wind water) or geomancy is important. Some Chinese avoid buying houses with the number four in the address because it sounds like, and thus connotes, "death;" while favoring the number eight as it sounds like "prosperity." The Beijing Olympics was officially opened on August 8, 2008 (8-8-08). Some Chinese even consult fortune tellers to change their names for good luck. Fortune tellers consider the person's birth date and time, astrological principles, and the five elements—metal, wood, water, fire, and earth—for a balanced, smooth life.

Disney—Disney officials consulted *feng shui* experts in building Hong Kong's Disneyland. The park faces water with mountains behind to suggest plentiful inflow of revenue and visitors, while being protected at the rear. The park's front gate was shifted 12 degrees to bring prosperity. To ensure the flow of positive energy or *chi*, Disney put a bend in the walkway from the train station to the gate. Water is heavily used in the park in the form of lakes, streams, and waterfalls placed strategically to accumulate good fortune and wealth. In kitchens, stoves are placed in lucky locations and some areas are designated "no fire zones" to balance the five elements and reduce accidents. The lucky color red frequently accents Main Street. Lucky numbers have also been incorporated throughout the theme park facilities. Disneyland Hotel's main ballroom measures 888 square meters and the chandelier in its Chinese restaurant contains 2,238 crystal lotuses, a number which sounds like the characters "easily generate wealth" in Cantonese. Both Disney hotels have no fourth floors. No clocks are sold as merchandise in Disney stores because the phrase "giving a clock" sounds the same as "going to a funeral." The park's groundbreaking and opening dates were also picked for their auspiciousness.[2]

The Disneyland Hotel in Hong Kong does not have a 4th floor as "4" sounds like "death" in Cantonese.

Virtually all human societies exhibit *social stratification*. Stratification sometimes takes the form of a caste system where the members of different castes are reared for certain roles and cannot change their caste membership. Such caste systems still operate in rural India. More frequently, it takes the form of **social classes**, relatively homogeneous and enduring divisions in a society, which are hierarchically ordered and whose members share similar values, interests, and behavior. One classic depiction of social classes defined seven ascending levels, as follows: (1) lower lowers, (2) upper lowers, (3) working class, (4) middle class, (5) upper middles, (6) lower uppers, and (7) upper uppers.[3]

Social classes have several characteristics. First, those within each class tend to behave more alike than persons from two different social classes. Social classes differ in dress, speech patterns, recreational preferences, and many other characteristics. Second, persons are perceived as occupying inferior or superior positions according to social class. Third, social class is indicated by a cluster of variables—for example, occupation, income, wealth, education, and value orientation—rather than by any single variable. Fourth, individuals can move up or down the social class ladder during their lifetimes. The extent of this mobility varies according to how rigid the social stratification is in a given society.

China's occupational classes—China has 10 distinct occupational strata. At the top of the ladder are the national leaders, followed by managers and chief executive officers. Technical professionals, businessmen, and commercial services personnel make up the middle ranks. At the lower rungs are manufacturing and agricultural workers, the jobless, and part-time urban workers. This social structure replaces the traditional agricultural-based Chinese society where laborers and peasants were once considered major economic forces. Another difference is the burgeoning middle class. Instead of the pyramid-shaped structure, an olive-shaped structure is evolving.

Social classes differ in dress and where they shop. High-end shopping malls like the Pacific Place in Hong Kong attract higher social class consumers who have the disposable income to buy high-ticket items.

Social classes show distinct product and brand preferences in many areas, including clothing, home furnishings, leisure activities, and automobiles. Social classes differ in media preferences, with upper-class consumers often preferring magazines and books and lower-class consumers often preferring television. Even within a media category such as TV, upper-class consumers tend to prefer news and drama, and lower-class consumers tend to prefer soap operas and sports programs. There are also language differences among the social classes. Advertising copy and dialogue must ring true to the targeted social class.

Social Factors

In addition to cultural factors, a consumer's behavior is influenced by such social factors as reference groups, family, and social roles and statuses.

REFERENCE GROUPS

A person's **reference groups** consist of all the groups that have a direct (face-to-face) or indirect influence on his/her attitudes or behavior. Groups having a direct influence on a person are called **membership groups**. Some membership groups are **primary groups**, such as family, friends, neighbors, and co-workers, those with whom the person interacts fairly continuously and informally. People also belong to **secondary groups**, such as religious, professional, and trade-union groups, which tend to be more formal and require less continuous interaction.

People are significantly influenced by their reference groups in at least three ways. Reference groups expose an individual to new behaviors and lifestyles, and influence attitudes and self-concept; they create pressures for conformity that may affect actual product and brand choices. People are also influenced by groups to which they do not belong. **Aspirational groups** are those a person hopes to join; **dissociative groups** are those whose values or behavior an individual rejects.

Manufacturers of products and brands where group influence is strong must determine how to reach and influence opinion leaders in these reference groups. An **opinion leader** is the person in informal, product-related communications who offers advice or information about a specific product or product category, such as which of several brands is best or how a particular product may be used.[4] Marketers try to reach opinion leaders by identifying demographic and psychographic characteristics associated with opinion leadership, identifying the media read by opinion leaders, and directing messages at opinion leaders. In Japan, high school girls have often been credited with creating the buzz that makes products such as Shiseido's Neuve nail polish a big hit.[5]

FAMILY

The family is the most important consumer buying organization in society, and family members constitute the most influential primary reference group.[6] We can distinguish between two families in the buyer's life. The **family of orientation** consists of parents and siblings. From parents, a person acquires an orientation toward religion, politics, and economics, and a sense of personal ambition, self-worth, and love.[7] Even if the buyer no longer interacts very much with his or her parents, their influence on behavior can be significant. In Asia, where parents live with grown children, their influence can be substantial. A more direct influence on everyday buying behavior is the **family of procreation**—namely, one's spouse and children.

Marketers are interested in the roles and relative influence of family members in the purchase of a large variety of products and services. These roles vary widely in different countries and social classes. For example, among traditional Chinese and Japanese households, it is not uncommon for the husband to give his wife his pay packet as she manages the family's expenditure. In contrast, India is a patriarchal society where the husband makes the most decisions. Given women's increasing wealth and income-generating ability, household purchasing patterns are gradually changing in Asia. Thus marketers of products traditionally purchased by men are now thinking about women as possible buyers:

In Asia, the family is a strong reference group, influencing members on numerous aspects of their daily life.

Korean car makers Korean car makers are taking women more seriously as they represent 30 percent of domestic sales. Hyundai has introduced the Sonata Elegance Special, a female-oriented version of its flagship mid-sized sedan. To provide a more feminine touch to its cars, Kia Motors focuses on fashionable appearances. For its sports-utility vehicle, it offers a variety of unique colors such as Hawaiian Blue and Coffee Brown, with primary colors for the interior. Daewoo's Lacetti model features a telescopic steering column which enables drivers to adjust the column length for comfort. This feature is particularly useful to women as they are generally shorter than men.[8]

Indeed, women are becoming an economic force in Asia. In China, women are at the forefront of consumer spending. Urban women are spending more of their hard-earned cash on personal travel and related recreational activities, dining out, shopping, as well as buying cars and pursuing urban leisure lifestyles. Their spending will help to determine which foreign brands will succeed in China. Analysts say that Chinese women are particularly susceptible to advertising by foreign brands like Louis Vuitton.[9] In India, Hindustan Unilever launched the Fair & Lovely Foundation to economically empower women and avail them with opportunities for education and skills training.

Men and women may respond differently to marketing messages.[10] One study showed that women valued connections and relationships with family and friends and placed a high priority on people. Men, on the other hand, related more to competition and placed a high priority on action.

Another shift in buying patterns is an increase in the amount of dollars spent and the direct and indirect influence wielded by children and teens.[11] Direct influence describes children's hints, requests, and demands—"I want to go to McDonald's." Indirect influence means that parents know the brands, product choices, and preferences of their children without hints or outright requests. One research study showed that teenagers were playing a more active role than before in helping parents choose a car, audio/video equipment, or a vacation spot.[12] "Marketing Insight: China's Young Consumers" gives an idea of what marketers can encounter in this rapidly transforming growth market.

MARKETING INSIGHT • CHINA'S YOUNG CONSUMERS

Numbering nearly 417 million, China's youths aged between 5 and 24 are the only child in their families. As such, they exert significant influence on household purchase and consumption. The "six pockets, one mouth" syndrome is emblematic of their pampering by parents and four grandparents. Their index of influence on family spending on "25 commonly purchased household items" has been estimated to be about 68 percent, above the 60 percent for U.S. children. Gong, Li, and Li have identified the following trends that have contributed to the cultural transformation of China's youth:

1. ***The rise of individuality*** — Traditional Chinese culture emphasizes balance, moderation, and harmony; characteristics that suggest a "cult of restraint." Consumption conformity is expected to preserve group harmony. Recent social and economic changes in China have inspired individuality, especially among the young. The dismantling of the iron rice bowl system has forced young Chinese to look after their own well-being. They are also more focused on their personal wants, needs, and rights than the older generations. This is best manifested in the proliferation of street fashion, from skater wear to shocking blond hair to Hello Kitty paraphernalia.
2. ***New media habits*** — Traditionally, the Chinese have relied on word-of-mouth communication from group and family members for product information. Such information is considered more credible than mass commercial sources and minimizes the risk of losing face. However, China's young have been exposed to advertising. Television is now found in over 90 percent of Chinese households and has become the most important commercial source for obtaining product information. The Internet is another new medium, with about 55 percent of Chinese netizens below the age of 24.
3. ***Brand and status consciousness*** — While thrift was valued in traditional Chinese consumption culture out of the Confucian emphasis on modesty and humility, brand and status consciousness have emerged as prepurchase evaluative criteria among the young. Chinese youths are becoming more pragmatic, educated, and cosmopolitan. Their independence and confidence, coupled with the rise of individuality, has fueled their desire for things that express these traits. Western brands are preferred over local ones as they appeal to high status consciousness. Luxury goods are no longer symbols of wasteful decadence but achievements of initiative and drive.
4. ***Capitalism and credit cards*** — Arising from the Confucian value of "living properly," Chinese have been taught to live within their means and avoid running into debt. Borrowing money is widely seen as shameful. The government has now reduced housing and health care subsidies and encouraged state-run banks to provide major loans. The Bank of China has a special loan to help young couples acquire durables and cover educational expenses. The idea of leveraging one's credit and employment to buy bigger and better things is increasingly accepted. China's young now appreciate the many facets of monetary value, and are more comfortable in using credit.
5. ***Consumer power*** — The traditional reluctance of Chinese consumers to complain is rooted in Confucian teachings that it is not wise to hold too tightly to what one has obtained or lost, as well as the belief in *yuan* or destiny, the predetermined relations with other individuals and things beyond one's control. Product failure is thus attributed to fate, rather than to the manufacturer. Economic reform has led Chinese youths to look after their rights and self-interests. They demand the same quality products marketed by MNCs elsewhere in China. The Chinese Consumers' Association was formed in 1984, and the Law on Protecting Consumers' Rights and Interests was effected in 1994. This emerging consumer society has witnessed an explosion of complaints, including lawsuits against McDonald's, Hilton, Volkswagen, and Toshiba.

Gong, Li, and Li discuss several marketing implications arising from these trends. First, numerous opportunities exist in the Chinese youth market such as credit verification services, given the explosive demand for credit cards among the young. Offering innovative financing services for purchases of high-ticket items may also be fruitful. MNCs may also redraw their global segmentation strategies to include China's youths who share a convergence of consumption behaviors with those in developed economies. MNCs may also leverage country-of-origin effects in their marketing communications and sourcing strategies. They should also develop customer satisfaction programs as these are rare in China and offer a differentiation opportunity. Brand images should also be built creatively using both conventional TV advertising as well as via the Internet and corporate sponsorship of youth programs. MNCs may also engage in line extensions of products currently targeted at the high end of the market to China's youths. Multibrand strategies may be considered to create brand exclusivity for this segment. Last, businesses should also keep parents in mind while targeting China's youth. Although weakening, parental influence is still strong and messages should appeal to parents as well.

Source: Wen Gong, Zhan G. Li, and Tiger Li, "Marketing to China's Youth: A Cultural Transformation Perspective." *Business Horizons,* 2004, 47(6), pp. 41–50.

Marketers use many channels of communication to reach kids, including such media as Nickelodeon, Cartoon Network, or the Disney Channel on TV.

Disney Channel—After being considered an unprofitable stepchild of the Disney empire, the Disney Channel has become the company's cash cow solely from its ability to reach the underserved "tween market"—the 8- to 14-year-olds—and leverage its success through Disney's other divisions. Disney has also identified international growth as one of its key strategic initiatives. Hence, in Asia, it has expanded into countries such as India, Korea, Taiwan, Singapore, Thailand, Vietnam, and Cambodia. Disney Channel is the most watched pay-TV kids channel in Asia. It also launched a series of six animated tales based on Asian folklore. Titled ***Legends of the Ring of Fire,*** it is part of Disney's effort to provide more localized content for its Asian audience. Its two other TV brands, Playhouse Disney Channel and Toon Disney, have also been launched in Asia.[13]

The *Lizzie McGuire* and *The Legends of the Ring of Fire* programs demonstrates how powerful television can be in reaching children, and marketers are using television to target children at younger ages than ever before. By the time children are around 2 years old, they can often recognize characters, logos, and specific brands. Marketers are tapping into that audience with product tie-ins, placed at a child's eye level, on just about everything—from Scooby-Doo vitamins to Disney Princesses toothbrushes.

Today companies are also likely to use the Internet to show products to children and to solicit personal information from them, offering freebies in exchange. Many have come under fire for this practice and for not clearly differentiating ads from games or entertainment. In China and Hong Kong, there is concern over businesses like Internet cafés offering online games targeting children. Numerous kids devote long hours at a stretch playing games on computer terminals against parental objections.

ROLES AND STATUSES

A person participates in many groups—family, clubs, and organizations. The person's position in each group can be defined in terms of role and status. A **role** consists of the activities a person is expected to perform. Each role carries a **status.** A senior vice president of marketing has more status than a sales manager, and a sales manager has more status than an office clerk. People choose products that reflect and communicate their role and actual or desired status in society. Company presidents often drive Mercedes, wear expensive suits, and drink XO cognac. Marketers must be aware of the status symbol potential of products and brands.

Like the family, roles and statuses in Asia are undergoing gradual changes as well. Such changes are reflected in ads featuring men in formerly traditional women's roles and smart-looking women in the workplace. Nevertheless, Asia's hierarchical society still emphasizes the relative position of an individual in a group context. Thus the concept of *mianzi* or "face," requiring individuals to abide by social norms, is vital among the Chinese (see "Marketing Insight: Face-Saving and the Chinese Consumer").

Personal Factors

A buyer's decisions are also influenced by personal characteristics. These include the buyer's age and stage in the life cycle; occupation and economic circumstances; personality and self-concept; and lifestyle and values. Because many of these characteristics have a very direct impact on consumer behavior, it is important for marketers to follow them closely.

AGE AND STAGE IN THE LIFE CYCLE

People buy different goods and services over a lifetime. Taste in food, clothes, furniture, and recreation is often age-related.

MARKETING INSIGHT • FACE-SAVING AND THE CHINESE CONSUMER

In Chinese culture, there are two types of "face." *Lian* (臉) is the confidence of the society on an individual's moral character, while *mianzi* (面子) is the prestige accorded through success and ostentation. Saving one's face is important to traditional Chinese. This has implications on consumer behavior:

- ***Influence of referent others*** — To accord respect to others and give them their *mianzi*, Chinese consumers heed the advice given by others, particularly opinion leaders. Complying with the social norm also preserves the consumer's *lian* as such behavior demonstrates one's willingness to be with the majority.
- ***Ostentatious living*** — The *mianzi* factor also suggests that Chinese are sensitive to their hierarchical position in social structures. To enhance and protect one's social standing, Chinese engage in ostentatious activities such as driving Mercedes-Benzes, throwing lavish banquets, and donning brand-name items.
- ***Fewer complaints*** — Chinese consumers are also less likely to complain when dissatisfied with a purchase. To complain is to make the other party lose his *lian* because he sold a poor product. The complainant also loses his *lian* because he is admitting that he had been taken in. Instead, harmony is strived for.
- ***Comparative advertising*** — Chinese are uncomfortable with comparative ads because they are shameless with bravado and put down the other brand. This is considered an insult to the moral character of the advertised brand. The brand therefore does not deserve honor (*meiyou mianzi* or "has no face").
- ***Negotiation*** — Chinese are also likely to cover up mistakes made. Thus during negotiations, it would be impolite to identify mistakes made by a Chinese counterpart. Also, as a face-saving strategy, Chinese businesses usually use a mediator during negotiations to protect their prestige.

Given the relatively strict code in school, Japanese youths sometimes rebel with more unique expressions of themselves in their out-of-school clothes and lifestyles.

Japanese teenagers—Japan is seeing a rising number of high school dropouts who believe that school life restricts their personal lifestyle. Such teenagers want to dye their hair fire-engine red, wear the latest street fashion which includes tutus over pants, and play in a band. They quit school because the strict discipline in schools is not compatible with what they want at this stage of their life cycle.

Consumption is also shaped by the *family life-cycle* and the number, age, and gender of people in the household at any point in time. Some households in Asia are increasingly fragmented—the traditional family with a husband, wife and kids makes up a smaller percentage of total households than before. In addition, *psychological* life-cycle stages may matter. Adults experience certain "passages" or "transformations" as they go through life.[14]

Marketers should also consider *critical life events or transitions*—marriage, childbirth, illness, relocation, divorce, career change, widowhood—as giving rise to new needs. These should alert service providers—banks, lawyers, and insurance agents—to ways they can help.[15]

OCCUPATION AND ECONOMIC CIRCUMSTANCES

Occupation also influences consumption patterns. A blue-collar worker will buy work clothes, work shoes, and lunchboxes. A company president will buy dress suits, air travel, and country club memberships. Marketers try to identify the occupational groups that have above-average interest in their products and services. A company can even tailor its products for certain occupational groups: computer software companies, for example, design different products for brand managers, engineers, lawyers, and physicians.

Product choice is greatly affected by economic circumstances: spendable income (level, stability, and time pattern), savings and assets (including the percentage that is liquid), debts, borrowing power, and attitudes toward spending and saving. Purchasing discretionary items on credit has risen in Asia. For example, while visitors to China 20 years ago had a hard time explaining what a credit card was, the majority of Chinese businesspeople now carry it around. While luxury goods makers such as Gucci, Prada, and Louis Vuitton are typically vulnerable to economic downturns, their sales in Japan were sustained and a secondary market for their used bags flourished. Nonetheless, if economic indicators point to a recession, marketers can take steps to redesign, reposition, and reprice their products or introduce or increase the emphasis on discount brands so that they can continue to offer value to target customers.

Louis Vuitton has been doing well in Asia as the region flourishes. Following its success in Japan, Louis Vuitton is opening more stores like this one in Hong Kong and others in Singapore.

PERSONALITY AND SELF-CONCEPT

Each person has personality characteristics that influence his or her buying behavior. **Personality** is a set of distinguishing human psychological traits that lead to relatively consistent and enduring responses to environmental stimuli. Personality is often described in terms of such traits as self-confidence, dominance, autonomy, deference, sociability, defensiveness, and adaptability.[16] Personality can be a useful variable in analyzing consumer brand choices. The idea is that brands also have personalities, and consumers are likely to choose brands whose personalities match their own. We define **brand personality** as the specific mix of human traits that may be attributed to a particular brand.

Aaker conducted research into brand personalities and identified the following seven brand personalities:[17]

1. ***Sincerity*** (down-to-earth, honest, wholesome, and cheerful) — For example, Hello Kitty
2. ***Excitement*** (daring, spirited, imaginative, and up-to-date) — For example, MTV
3. ***Competence*** (reliable, intelligent, and successful) — For example, Sony

4. ***Sophistication*** (upper-class and charming) — For example, Shiseido
5. ***Ruggedness*** (outdoorsy and tough) — For example, Timberland
6. ***Passion*** (emotional intensity, spirituality, and mysticism) — For example, Zara
7. ***Peacefulness*** (harmony, balance, and natural) — For example, Yamaha

The implication is that these brands will attract persons who are high on the same personality traits. A brand personality may have several attributes: Levi's suggests a personality that is youthful, rebellious, authentic, and American. The company utilizes product features, services, and image making to transmit the product's personality.

A cross-cultural study exploring the generalizability of Aaker's scale outside the United States found that three of the five factors applied in Japan and Spain, but a "peacefulness" dimension replaced "ruggedness" both in Japan and Spain, and a "passion" dimension emerged in Spain instead of "competency."[18] Research on brand personality in Korea revealed two culture-specific factors—passive likeableness and ascendancy—reflecting the importance of Confucian values in Korea's social and economic systems.[19]

Consumers often choose and use brands that have a brand personality consistent with their own *actual self-concept* (how one views oneself), although in some cases the match may be based on consumer's *ideal self-concept* (how one would like to view oneself) or even *others' self-concept* (how one thinks others see one) rather than actual self-image.[20] These effects may also be more pronounced for publicly consumed products as compared to privately consumed goods.[21] However, consumers who are high "self-monitors"—that is, sensitive to how others see them—are more likely to choose brands whose personalities fit the consumption situation.[22]

LIFESTYLE AND VALUES

People from the same subculture, social class, and occupation may lead quite different lifestyles. Members of India's so-called Gen Next spend most of their money on personal clothing and accessories, food, entertainment, and consumer durables as well as on exotic holidays in India and abroad. Luxury cars and shiny motorbikes are the most sought-after status symbols among these newly prosperous young people, most of whom work in India's burgeoning IT sector. Harley-Davidson has set its sights on the Indian market, and Levi Strauss India (Pvt.) Ltd., a subsidiary of the U.S.-based clothing giant, regards India as one of the fastest-growing markets for Levi's in the world.[23]

A **lifestyle** is a person's pattern of living in the world as expressed in activities, interests, and opinions. Lifestyle portrays the "whole person" interacting with his or her environment. Marketers search for relationships between their products and lifestyle groups. For example, a computer manufacturer might find that most computer buyers are achievement-oriented. The marketer may then aim the brand more clearly at the achiever lifestyle. Marketers are always uncovering new trends in consumer lifestyles. Here are two Asian examples:

Hong Kong's fast-food lifestyle—According to A.C. Nielsen's I-Scan Impulse, an electronic consumer panel, fast-food shops account for 20 percent of Hong Kong's total out-of-home dining market, with Western food chains surpassing Chinese chains in penetration (88 vs 80 percent), and enjoying equal share of trade in value terms (29 vs 30 percent). Most Hong Kongers patronize fast-food shops seven times a month. Over 1 in 10 Hong Kongers patronize fast-food outlets at least five times a week, with an average spending of $370. One-third of heavy fast-food shoppers are middle-income, mature working men. Their total spending on fast-food and frequency of visits are twice as much as the average fast-food diner. McDonald's is by far the most popular fast-food chain, accounting for one-fifth of total store numbers, followed by Café de Coral with 11 percent and Maxim at 7 percent.[24]

Many eateries such as Café de Coral are benefiting from the trend among Hong Kongers, particularly the men, to eat out.

Chinese men—With their sculpted bodies, moisturized skin, and fitted suits, Chinese men are taking an increasing interest in their looks and in fashion, to appeal to women, clients, and bosses. Cosmetic makers have noted this trend. L'Oréal Shanghai holds that although the male market is not very important, it is definitely progressing. Mandom, a Japanese company, successfully tested 16 products from its Gatsby line of male beauty products in China. Another beneficiary of this lifestyle trend is the male plastic surgery market. The most sought-after operations for Chinese men are facelifts, removal of eye bags, and inflation of chest muscles.[25]

Lifestyles are shaped partly by whether consumers are *money-constrained* or *time-constrained.* Companies aiming to serve money-constrained consumers will create lower-cost products and services. Local brands usually fill this need in many emerging markets, while their foreign counterparts target more affluent consumers. "Breakthrough Marketing: IKEA" outlines IKEA's global success formula of appealing to price-conscious shoppers in the furniture market.

Consumers who experience time famine are prone to **multitasking**, that is, doing two or more things at the same time. They will phone or eat while driving, or bicycle to work to get exercise. They will also pay others to perform tasks because time is more important than money. They may prefer eating buns to congee because they are quicker. Companies aiming to serve them will create convenient products and services for this group. Much of the wireless revolution is fueled by the multitasking trend. Some mobile phones allow users to talk while Web browsing over Wi-Fi and conducting business via Bluetooth.

In some categories, notably food processing, companies targeting time-constrained consumers need to be aware that these consumers seek the illusion that they are not

BREAKTHROUGH • MARKETING

IKEA

Swedish furniture retailer IKEA excels at appealing to price-conscious shoppers around the world with stylish items carefully selected for each country's market.

IKEA was founded in 1943 by a 17-year-old Swede named Ingvar Kamprad. The company, which initially sold pens, Christmas cards, and seeds from a shed on Kamprad's family farm, eventually grew into a retail titan in home furnishings and a global cultural phenomenon, what *BusinessWeek* called a "one-stop sanctuary for coolness" and "the quintessential cult brand."

IKEA inspires remarkable levels of devotion from its customers, who visit in numbers that average 1.1 million per day. In Malaysia, IKEA had a massive clear-out of its old Kuala Lumpur store before moving to new premises. The sale was supposed to last a month, but after two weeks, the event was over—there was nothing left to sell. At the new store, which measures 36,000 square meters, it took the crowds almost an hour to filter through a 2½ stroll past 7,000 items. In Atlanta, a contest was held to crown five winners "Ambassador of Kul" (Swedish for "fun") who, in order to collect their prizes, had to live in the IKEA store for three full days before it opened, which they gladly did.

IKEA achieved this level of success by offering a unique value proposition to consumers: leading-edge Scandinavian design at bargain prices. The company's fashionable bargains include Klippan sofas for $249, Billy bookcases for $120, and Lack side tables for $13. In Scandinavian markets, IKEA has even sold 2,500 prefabricated homes for around $45,000, depending on local housing prices. The company is able to offer such low prices in part because most items come boxed and require complete assembly at home, meaning they are easier to transport, take up less shelf space, and seldom require delivery, which reduces costs.

IKEA's mission of providing value is predicated on founder Kamprad's statement, "People have very thin wallets. We should take care of their interests." IKEA adheres to this philosophy by reducing prices across its products by 2 to 3 percent annually. Its focus on value also benefits the bottom line: IKEA enjoys 10 percent margins, higher than competitors.

Although many of its products are sold uniformly throughout the world, IKEA also caters to local tastes. In China, for example, it found that Chinese tend to spend most on their living rooms because this is where many people "show off" and entertain. Many Chinese living rooms contain a dining table as well and hence, dining room purchases are also common. Chinese spend less on kitchens because these tend to be small. Even the size of beds was modified. Initially, IKEA sold Hong Kong-sized beds, which are shorter than standard-sized beds. They soon realized that the beds were too short for mainland Chinese and switched to selling standard beds. Moreover, the concept of do-it-yourself (DIY) is new to the Chinese. While elsewhere, IKEA stores are open relatively far out in the suburbs, in China, they are located near public transportation lines because only 20 percent have cars. IKEA also offers local home delivery and assembly services for a fee. Such customizations are predicated on research.

IKEA has evolved into a retail empire with about 240 stores in 35 countries and revenue of nearly $27 billion in 2007 and still has excellent growth opportunities. Its Asia sales have doubled and are expected to triple its contribution to total revenue in 5 to 6 years.

Sources: Kerry Capell, "IKEA: How the Swedish Retailer Became a Global Cult Brand." *BusinessWeek,* November 14, 2005, p. 96; "Need a Home to Go with That Sofa?" BusinessWeek, November 14, 2005, p. 106; <www.ikea.com>; Jonathan Kent, "IKEA's Appeal Spreads to Asia." *BBC News Online,* August 17, 2003; Paula Miller "IKEA with Chinese Characteristics." *The China Business Review Online,* July–August 2004; Kirby Chen, "Update 1- Interview – IKEA Asia Revenue Contribution to Triple." *Reuters,* August 31, 2007.

operating within time constraints. The food processing industry labels those who seek both convenience and some involvement in the cooking process: the "convenience involvement segment."[26] Similarly, consider the Japanese fondness for "no-fuss" and virtual pets:

Pet ownership—In Tokyo, sales of "no-fuss" pets including shrimps, ants, and plankton are increasing. At Tokyo Hands, a DIY chain store, the most popular item at one time was Holo Holo, a palm-sized vertical plastic box that comes with five miniscule red shrimps, a decorative twig, and white sand. The shrimps need no feeding, washing, or petting. They feed off the algae on the tank surface. When one shrimp dies, it is eaten by the other shrimp. Holo Holo was a hit among Japanese men in their 20s and 30s who do not have the space and time to keep conventional pets. The Japanese have long had a fondness for undemanding companions such as the virtual pet Tamagotchi and palm-sized toy animals with microchip personalities.[27]

Consumer decisions are also influenced by **core values**, the belief systems that underlie consumer attitudes and behaviors. Core values go much deeper than behavior or attitude, and determine, at a basic level, people's choices and desires over the long-term. Marketers who target consumers on the basis of their values believe that by appealing to people's inner selves, it is possible to influence their outer selves—their purchase behavior.

Key Psychological Processes

The starting point for understanding consumer behavior is the stimulus-response model shown in Figure 6.1. Marketing and environmental stimuli enter the consumer's consciousness. A set of psychological processes combine with certain consumer characteristics to result in decision processes and purchase decisions. The marketer's task is to understand what happens in the consumer's consciousness between the arrival of the outside marketing stimuli and the ultimate purchase decisions. Four key psychological processes—motivation, perception, learning, and memory—fundamentally influence consumer responses to the various marketing stimuli.

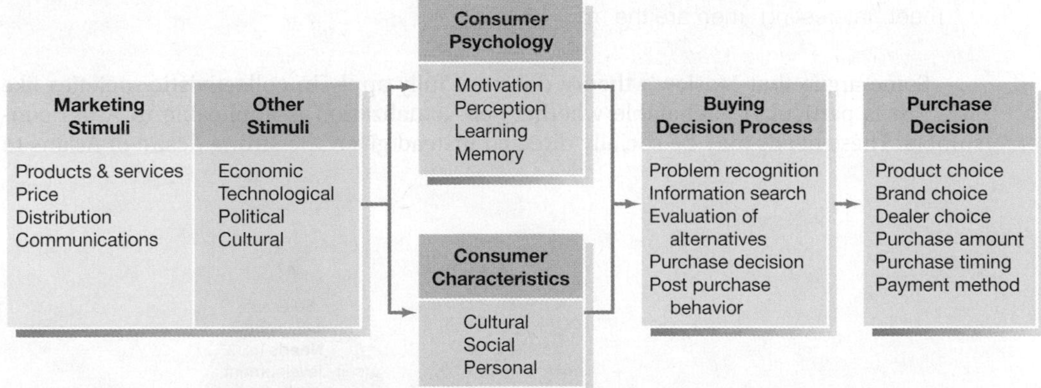

Figure 6.1 Model of Consumer Behavior

Motivation: Freud, Maslow, Herzberg

A person has many needs at any given time. Some needs are *biogenic*, arising from physiological states of tension such as hunger, thirst, or discomfort. Other needs are *psychogenic*, arising from psychological states of tension such as the need for recognition, esteem, or belonging. A need becomes a motive when it is aroused to a sufficient level of intensity. A **motive** is a need that is sufficiently pressing to drive the person to act.

Three of the best-known theories of human motivation—those of Sigmund Freud, Abraham Maslow, and Frederick Herzberg—carry quite different implications for consumer analysis and marketing strategy.

FREUD'S THEORY

Sigmund Freud assumed that the psychological forces shaping people's behavior are largely unconscious, and that a person cannot fully understand his or her own motivations. When a person examines specific brands, he or she will react not only to their stated capabilities, but also to other, less conscious cues. Shape, size, weight, material, color, and brand name can all trigger certain associations and emotions. A technique called *laddering* can be used to trace a person's motivations from the stated instrumental ones to the more terminal ones. Then the marketer can decide at what level to develop the message and appeal.[28]

Motivation researchers often collect "in-depth interviews" with a few dozen consumers to uncover deeper motives triggered by a product. They use various *projective techniques* such as word association, sentence completion, picture interpretation, and role playing. Many of these techniques were pioneered by Ernest Dichter, a Viennese psychologist.[29]

MASLOW'S THEORY

Abraham Maslow sought to explain why people are driven by particular needs at particular times.[30] Why does one person spend considerable time and energy on personal safety and another on pursuing the high opinion of others? Maslow's answer is that human needs are arranged in a hierarchy, from the most pressing to the least pressing. In order of importance, they are physiological needs, safety needs, social needs, esteem needs, and self-actualization needs (see Figure 6.2). People will try to satisfy their most important needs first. When a person succeeds in satisfying an important need, he or she will then try to satisfy the next-most-important need. For example, a starving man (need 1) will not take an interest in the latest happenings in the art world (need 5), nor in how he is viewed by others (need 3 or 4), nor even in whether he is breathing clean air (need 2); but when he has enough food and water, the next-most-important need will become salient.

Maslow's theory helps marketers understand how various products fit into the plans, goals, and lives of consumers. Here is an Asian example:

> **Japan's phone clubs**—Telephone clubs, or *terekura* (*tere* for telephone and *kura* for club), are a multibillion dollar industry in Japan. Men pay a fee to book a small room in the club where they get phone calls. Women call a toll-free line that allows them to talk to over 50,000 men. These clubs are popular because they fulfill a social need. Bored housewives wanting to kill time and lonely singles wanting to meet "interesting" men are the main callers.[31]

Some argue that Maslow's theory does not fully apply in collectivistic societies like Asia.[32] It is particularly debatable whether self-actualization is applicable to Asian consumers. These needs may be socially directed instead given the strong desire of Asians to

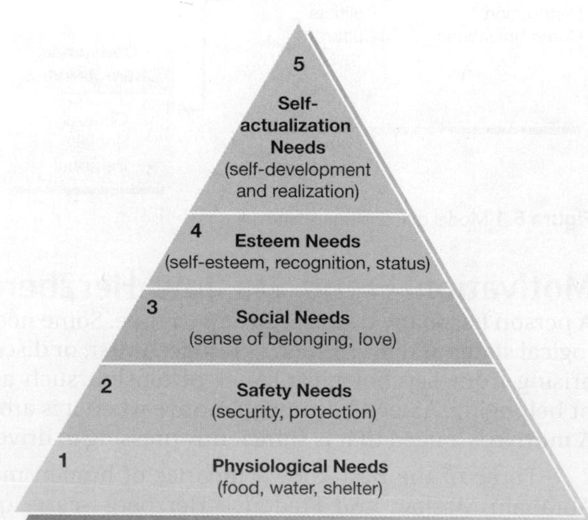

Figure 6.2 Maslow's Hierarchy of Needs

Source: A. H. Maslow, *Motivation and Personality*, 2nd ed., (Upper Saddle River, NJ: Prentice Hall, 1970). Reprinted by permission of Prentice Hall Inc.

enhance their image and position through contributions to society. Three types of socially directed needs may be considered the most important for Asians:

- ***Affiliation***— This is the acceptance of an individual as a member of a group. Consumers seeking this need will tend to conform to group norms.
- ***Admiration***— Once affiliation needs are satisfied, admiration is sought. This is respect from group members, which is earned through acts.
- ***Status***— This is esteem received from the society at large. Unlike admiration which tends to be at a more intimate level, status requires the regard of outsiders.

HERZBERG'S THEORY

Frederick Herzberg developed a two-factor theory that distinguishes *dissatisfiers* (factors that cause dissatisfaction) and *satisfiers* (factors that cause satisfaction).[33] The absence of dissatisfiers is not enough; satisfiers must be present to motivate a purchase. For example, a computer that does not come with a warranty would be a dissatisfier. Yet the presence of a product warranty may not act as a satisfier or motivator of a purchase, because it is not a source of intrinsic satisfaction. Ease of use may be a satisfier.

Herzberg's theory has two implications. First, sellers should do their best to avoid dissatisfiers (for example, a poor training manual or a poor service policy). Although these things will not sell a product, they might easily unsell it. Second, the seller should identify the major satisfiers or motivators of purchase in the market and then supply them. These satisfiers will make the major difference as to which brand the customer buys.

Japanese tourists—Bargain-hunting Japanese tourists visiting Asian countries consider the three Ks in deciding which country they visit. While cost is important, these hygiene factors weigh high on the dissatisfier list should they fail to make the grade. *Kitanai*, or dirty: Does the country have poor sanitation in restaurants and toilets? *Kakkowarui*, or unsophisticated: Is it too rural without enough modern amenities? *Kowai*, or scary: Are there high instances of murder, mugging, and infectious diseases? *Kowai* appears to have become more salient immediately following the terrorist events of September 11, 2001. Japanese tourists refrained from visiting U.S. destinations such as Hawaii in favor of Tokyo Disneyland. Even travel to Asia Pacific destinations slumped despite the heavy discounts offered by Japanese travel agencies.

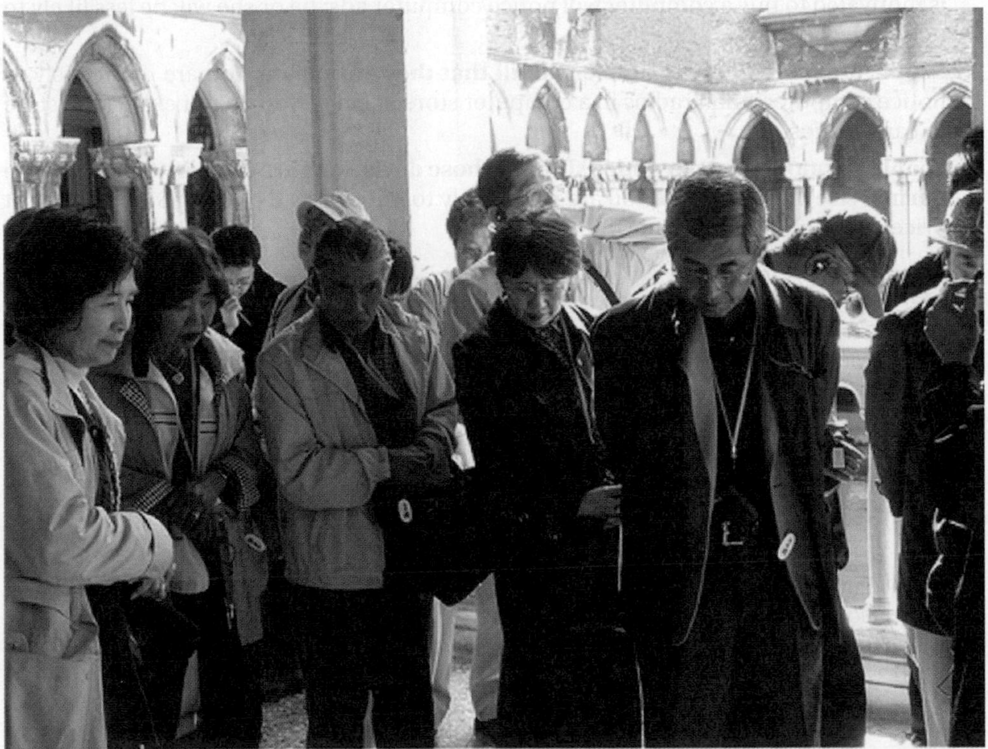

Japanese tourists have concerns about a destination that may make them dissatisfied with the travel. These are whether the destination is clean, modern, and safe.

Perception

A motivated person is ready to act. How the motivated person actually acts is influenced by his or her view or perception of the situation. **Perception** is the process by which an individual selects, organizes, and interprets information inputs to create a meaningful picture of the world.[34] Perception depends not only on the physical stimuli, but also on the stimuli's relation to the surrounding field and on conditions within the individual. The key point is that perceptions can vary widely among individuals exposed to the same reality. One person might perceive a fast-talking salesperson as aggressive and insincere; another, as intelligent and helpful. Each will respond differently to the salesperson. In marketing, perceptions are more important than the reality, as it is perceptions that will affect consumers' actual behavior.

Made-in-China image—Chinese brands such as Haier and Lenovo are making inroads in the international arena. While as late as 1998, brands from China were not clearly positioned against any specific characteristic, one survey showed that Chinese-made products were perceived to be associated with three characteristics: "for Chinese," "practical," and "value for money." However, the product recalls involving Chinese-made products in 2007 has dealt a serious blow to the "Made-in-China" name. Nonetheless, brand consulting company Interbrand says that consumers still perceive Chinese brands as "a good value," though few labeled them as "safe," "high quality," "prestigious," or "luxurious."[35]

People can emerge with different perceptions of the same object because of three perceptual processes: selective attention, selective distortion, and selective retention.

SELECTIVE ATTENTION

Consumers are exposed to numerous ads or brand communications everyday. Because they cannot possibly attend to all of these, most stimuli will be screened out—a process called **selective attention**. Selective attention means that marketers have to work hard to attract consumers' notice. The real challenge is to explain which stimuli people will notice. Here are some findings:

1. **People are more likely to notice stimuli that relate to a current need.** A person who is motivated to buy a computer will notice computer ads; he or she will be less likely to notice DVD ads.
2. **People are more likely to notice stimuli that they anticipate.** You are more likely to notice computers than radios in a computer store because you do not expect the store to carry radios.
3. **People are more likely to notice stimuli whose deviations are large in relation to the normal size of the stimuli.** You are more likely to notice an ad offering $100 off the list price of a computer than one offering $5 off.

Lenovo—The Beijing Olympics was an opportunity for sponsored brands to be noticed. As its top sponsor, Lenovo capitalized on this mega event with a marketing blitz to launch a new line of desktop computers, called Kai Tian, targeted at Olympic organizers and business executives. Says Alice Li, vice-president for Olympics Marketing at Lenovo, "The Olympics are a golden opportunity for us. Within China, we already have high brand awareness. But outside China, we still need to build our brand." To establish more visibility, Lenovo hustled for the right to design the Olympic torch. The Lenovo Olympic torch is shaped to resemble a Chinese scroll. The torch was carried to 20 countries before it arrived in Beijing. To increase the marketing payoff, Lenovo organized an online contest with Google's YouTube to choose three international torchbearers for the China portion of the torch relay. Lenovo also sold a limited edition notebook PC with design elements of the Olympic torch.[36]

Lenovo is one of the sponsors for the Beijing Olympic Games. It won the right to design the Olympic torch. This design was also used on its notebook PC. Sponsorship of such a mega event enhances consumer attention to the brand.

Although people screen out much of the surrounding stimuli, they are influenced by unexpected stimuli, such as sudden offers in the mail, over the phone, or from a salesperson. Marketers may attempt to promote their offers intrusively to bypass selective attention filters.

SELECTIVE DISTORTION

Even noticed stimuli do not always come across in the way the senders intended. **Selective distortion** is the tendency to interpret information in a way that will fit our preconceptions. Consumers will often distort information to be consistent with prior brand and product beliefs.[37]

A stark demonstration of the power of consumer brand beliefs is the typical result of product sampling tests. In "blind" taste tests, one group of consumers samples a product without knowing which brand it is, whereas another group of consumers samples the product knowing which brand it is. Invariably, differences arise in the opinions of the two groups despite the fact that the two groups are *literally consuming exactly the same product!*

When consumers report different opinions between branded and unbranded versions of identical products, it must be the case that the brand and product beliefs, created by whatever means (e.g., past experiences, marketing activity for the brand, etc.), have somehow changed their product perceptions. Examples of branded differences can be found with virtually every type of product. For example, one study found that consumers were equally split in their preference for Diet Coke versus Diet Pepsi when tasting both on a blind basis.[38] When tasting the branded versions, however, consumers preferred Diet Coke by 65 percent and Diet Pepsi by only 23 percent (with the remainder seeing no difference).

Selective distortion can work to the advantage of marketers with strong brands when consumers distort neutral or ambiguous brand information to make it more positive. In other words, beer may seem to taste better, a car may seem to drive more smoothly, the wait in a bank line may seem shorter, and so on, depending on the particular brands involved.

SELECTIVE RETENTION

People will fail to register much information to which they are exposed in memory, but will tend to retain information that supports their attitudes and beliefs. Because of **selective retention**, we are likely to remember good points about a product we like and forget good points about competing products. Selective retention again works to the advantage of strong brands. It also explains why marketers need to use repetition in sending messages to their target market—to make sure their message is not overlooked.

SUBLIMINAL PERCEPTION

The selective perception mechanisms require active engagement and thought by consumers. A topic that has fascinated armchair marketers for ages is **subliminal perception**. The argument is that marketers embed covert, subliminal messages in ads or packages. While consumers are not consciously aware of them, these messages can affect their behavior. Although it is clear many subtle subconscious effects can exist with consumer processing,[39] no evidence supports the notion that marketers can systematically control consumers at that level.[40]

Learning

When people act, they learn. **Learning** involves changes in an individual's behavior arising from experience. Most human behavior is learned. Learning theorists believe that learning is produced through the interplay of drives, stimuli, cues, responses, and reinforcement.

A **drive** is a strong internal stimulus impelling action. **Cues** are minor stimuli that determine when, where, and how a person responds. Suppose you buy a Lenovo computer. If your experience is rewarding, your response to computers and Lenovo will be positively reinforced. Later on, when you want to buy a printer, you may assume that because Lenovo makes good computers, Lenovo also makes good printers. In other words, you *generalize* your response to similar stimuli. A countertendency to generalization is discrimination. **Discrimination** means that the person has learned to recognize differences in sets of similar stimuli and can adjust responses accordingly.

Matsushita—Matsushita, an electronic appliance pioneer in China, learnt that Chinese consumers are becoming more discriminating. Initially, Matsushita sold Chinese consumers a basic version of Japan-made products. But as the Chinese grow increasingly affluent and aware of global trends, they become more demanding, while local companies such as Haier launched cheaper microwaves and television sets. Says Tetsu Kimoto, president of Matsushita's China arm, "We've entered an era where people really care about the functions, the look, and the durability. They don't just want the same thing everyone else has." So, Matsushita started to hire local engineers to come up with new models for the Chinese market.[41]

Learning theory teaches marketers that they can build demand for a product by associating it with strong drives, using motivating cues, and providing positive reinforcement. A new company can enter the market by appealing to the same drives that competitors use and by providing similar cue configurations, because buyers are more likely to transfer loyalty to similar brands (generalization); or the company might design its brand to appeal to a different set of drives and offer strong cue inducements to switch (discrimination).

De Beers—De Beers' savvy advertising and China's booming middle class has enabled China to be the world's third largest consumer for diamond jewelry after the U.S. and Japan. The idea that diamond symbolizes a lifetime of love has taken root in China, a country that traditionally prefers gold and jade. Chinese consumers have learnt to associate diamond with love, and diamond rings are now popular for weddings.[42]

Some researchers prefer more active, cognitive approaches when learning depends upon the inferences or interpretations consumers make about outcomes (was an unfavorable consumer experience due to a bad product or did the consumer fail to follow instructions properly?). The **hedonic bias** says people have a general tendency to attribute success to themselves and failure to external causes. Consumers are thus more likely to blame a product than themselves, putting pressure on marketers to carefully explicate product functions in well-designed packaging and labels, instructive ads and Web sites, and so on.

Memory

All the information and experiences individuals encounter as they go through life can end up in their long-term memory. Cognitive psychologists distinguish between **Short-Term Memory (STM)**—a temporary repository of information—and **Long-Term Memory (LTM)**—a more permanent repository.

Most widely accepted views of long-term memory structure involve some kind of associative model formulation.[43] For example, the **associative network memory model** views LTM as consisting of a set of nodes and links. *Nodes* are stored information connected by *links* that vary in strength. Any type of information—verbal, visual, abstract, or contextual—can be stored in the memory network. A spreading activation process from node to node determines the extent of retrieval and what information can actually be recalled in any given situation. When a node becomes activated because external information is being encoded (e.g., when a person reads or hears a word or phrase) or internal information is retrieved from LTM (e.g., when a person thinks about some concept), other nodes are also activated if they are sufficiently strongly associated with that node.

Consistent with the associative network memory model, consumer brand knowledge in memory can be conceptualized as consisting of a brand node in memory with a variety of linked associations. The strength and organization of these associations will be important determinants of the information that can be recalled about the brand. **Brand associations** consist of all brand-related thoughts, feelings, perceptions, images, experiences, beliefs, attitudes, and so on that become linked to the brand node.

Sangaria Oxygen Water—In Japan, bottled water with an extra shot of oxygen is the rage especially among women. With the trend towards healthier lifestyle, women associate oxygen water as an energy booster and a natural way to obtain extra oxygen molecules. To fortify such brand associations, Sangaria's bottle comes in white and has O_2 written boldly on it.

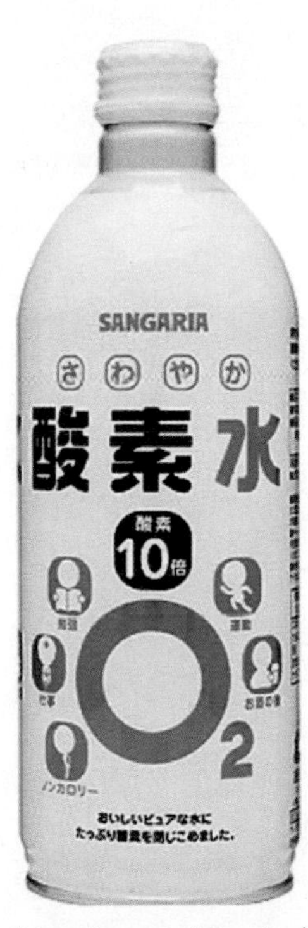

Sangaria associates itself as oxygen water by having the scientific notation for oxygen (O_2) clearly written on the bottle.

Marketing can be seen as making sure that consumers have the right types of product and service experiences such that the right brand knowledge structures are created and maintained in memory.

Chinese brands in India—Shortly after India began dropping its import barriers in the late 1990s, low-priced Chinese toys, batteries, and other consumer goods flooded the market at a steep discount from local offerings. However, stories began to circulate of defective Chinese products, such as batteries losing their charge after a single use. Konka and TCL tried to sell their products cheaply as well, reinforcing the reputation that Chinese brands are substandard. "Indian consumers believed that China was a technologically backward country," says Richie Liu, director of TCL India. Haier is determined not to repeat these early mistakes. Rather than stressing affordability, Haier is positioning its TV sets, refrigerators, and air-conditioners as premium quality with prices on par or in some cases higher than those of its competitors. This approach has been used successfully in India by LG and Samsung.[44]

Companies such as Procter & Gamble like to create mental maps of consumers that depict their knowledge of a particular brand in terms of the key associations that are likely to be triggered in a marketing setting and their relative strength, favorability, and uniqueness to consumers. Figure 6.3 displays a very simple mental map highlighting brand beliefs for a hypothetical consumer for the Haier brand.

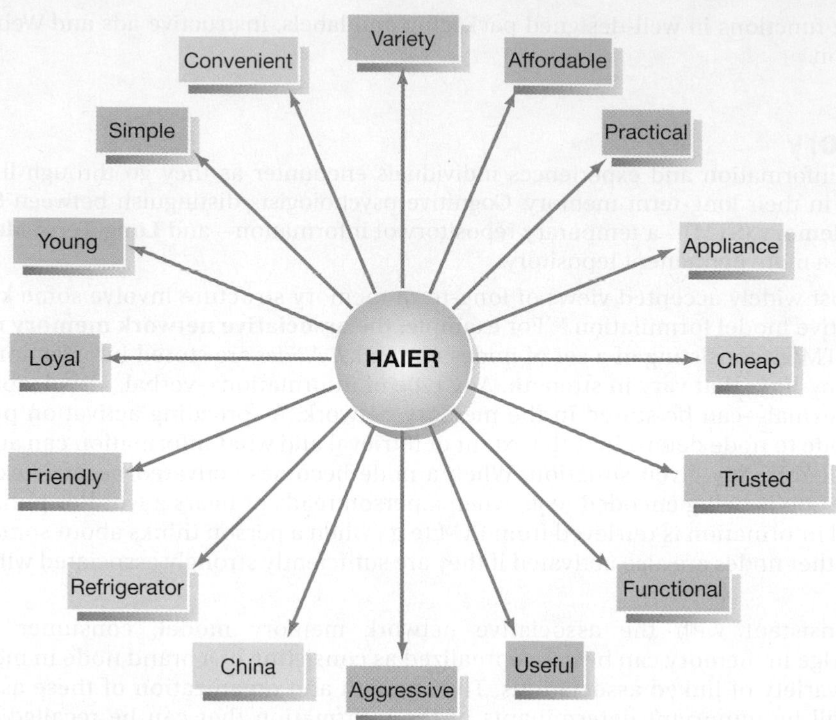

Figure 6.3 Hypothetical Haier Mental Map

MEMORY PROCESSES

Memory is a very constructive process because we do not remember information and events completely and accurately. Often we remember bits and pieces and fill in the rest based upon whatever else we know.

Memory encoding refers to how and where information gets into memory. The strength of the resulting association depends on how much we process the information at encoding (how much we think about it, for instance) and in what way.[45]

In general, the more attention placed on the meaning of information during encoding, the stronger the resulting associations in memory will be.[46] When a consumer actively thinks about and "elaborates" on the significance of product or service information, stronger associations are created in memory. Another key determinant of the strength of a newly formed association will be the content, organization, and strength of existing brand associations in memory. It will be easier for consumers to create an association to new information when extensive, relevant knowledge structures already exist in memory. One reason why personal experiences create such strong brand associations is that information about the product is likely to be related to existing knowledge.

The ease with which new information can be integrated into established knowledge structures depends on its simplicity, vividness, and concreteness. Repeated exposures to information, too, provide greater opportunity for processing and thus the potential for stronger associations. However, recent advertising research in a field setting suggests that high levels of repetition for an uninvolving, unpersuasive ad is unlikely to have as much sales impact as lower levels of repetition for an involving, persuasive ad.[47]

MEMORY RETRIEVAL

Memory retrieval refers to how information gets out of memory. According to the associative network memory model, the strength of a brand association increases both the likelihood that that information will be accessible and the ease with which it can be recalled by "spreading activation." Successful recall of brand information by consumers does not depend only on the initial strength of that information in memory. Three factors are particularly important.

First, the presence of *other* product information in memory can produce interference effects. It may cause the information to be either overlooked or confused. One challenge in a category crowded with many competitors—for example, airlines, consumer electronics, and food and beverage companies—is that consumers may mix up brands.

Second, the time since exposure to information at encoding affects the strength of a new association—the longer the time delay, the weaker the association. The time elapsed since the last exposure opportunity, however, has been shown generally to produce only gradual decay. Cognitive psychologists believe that memory is extremely durable, so that once information becomes stored in memory, its strength of association decays very slowly.[48]

Third, information may be "available" in memory (i.e., potentially recallable) but may not be "accessible" (i.e., unable to be recalled) without the proper retrieval cues or reminders. The particular associations for a brand that "come to mind" depend on the context in which the brand is considered. The more cues linked to a piece of information, however, the greater the likelihood that the information can be recalled. The effectiveness of retrieval cues is one reason why marketing *inside* a supermarket or any retail store is so critical—in terms of the actual product packaging, the use of in-store mini-billboard displays, and so on. The information they contain and the reminders they provide of advertising or other information already conveyed outside the store will be prime determinants of consumer decision making.

Pepsi—Under a new branding strategy, Pepsi is introducing a new can and bottle designs every few weeks with plans to sell 20 or more new different ones annually in every market. Pepsi has already started selling the new packages in China, Australia, and the U.S. This departure from marketing convention comes as Pepsi believes that consumer attention span is getting shorter and consumers are faced with a proliferation of brands competing for their time. Pepsi intends such cans and bottles as advertising vehicles to remind consumers of the brand, and not just containers for its drinks.[49]

Pepsi is introducing new can and bottle designs as advertising vehicles to keep top-of-mind awareness for the brand, and not just containers for its drink.

The Buying Decision Process: The Five-Stage Model

These basic psychological processes play an important role in understanding how consumers actually make their buying decisions. Marketers must understand every facet of consumer behavior. Table 6.1 provides a list of some key consumer behavior questions in terms of "who, what, when, where, how, and why." Smart companies try to fully understand the

Table 6.1 Understanding Consumer Behavior

• Who buys our product or service?
• Who makes the decision to buy the product?
• Who influences the decision to buy the product?
• How is the purchase decision made? Who assumes what role?
• What does the customer buy? What needs must be satisfied?
• Why do customers buy a particular brand?
• Where do they go or look to buy the product or service?
• When do they buy? Any seasonality factors?
• How is our product perceived by customers?
• What are customers' attitudes toward our product?
• What social factors might influence the purchase decision?
• Do customers' lifestyle influence their decisions?
• How do personal or demographic factors influence the purchase decision?

Source: Based on a list from George Belch and Michael Belch, *Advertising and Communication Management,* 6th ed., (Homewood, IL: Irwin, 2003).

customers' buying decision process—all their experiences in learning, choosing, using, and even disposing of a product.[50] Honda engineers took videos of shoppers loading groceries into car trunks to observe their frustrations and generate possible design solutions.

Marketing scholars have developed a "stage model" of the buying decision process (see Figure 6.4). The consumer passes through five stages: problem recognition, information search, evaluation of alternatives, purchase decision, and postpurchase behavior. Clearly, the buying process starts long before the actual purchase and has consequences long afterward.[51]

But consumers do not always pass through all five stages in buying a product. They may skip or reverse some stages. A woman buying her regular brand of toothpaste goes directly from the need for toothpaste to the purchase decision, skipping information search and evaluation. The model in Figure 6.4 provides a good frame of reference, however, because it captures the full range of considerations that arise when a consumer faces a highly involving new purchase.[52]

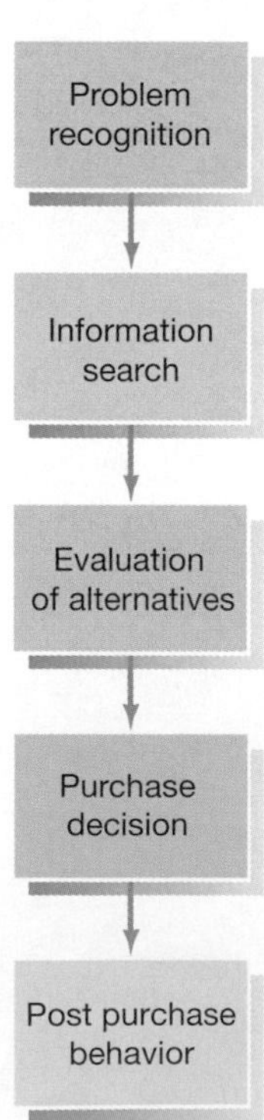

Figure 6.4 Five-Stage Model of the Consumer Buying Process

Problem Recognition

The buying process starts when the buyer recognizes a problem or need. The need can be triggered by internal or external stimuli. With an internal stimulus, one of the person's normal needs—hunger, thirst, sex—rises to a threshold level and becomes a drive; or a need can be aroused by an external stimulus. A person may admire a neighbor's new car or see a television ad for a Thai vacation, which triggers thoughts about the possibility of making a purchase.

Marketers need to identify the circumstances that trigger a particular need by gathering information from a number of consumers. They can then develop marketing strategies that trigger consumer interest. This is particularly important with discretionary purchases such as luxury goods, vacation packages, and entertainment options. Consumer motivation may need to be increased so that a potential purchase is even given serious consideration.

Information Search

An aroused consumer will be inclined to search for more information. We can distinguish between two levels of arousal. The milder search state is called *heightened attention.* At this level, a person simply becomes more receptive to information about a product. At the next level, the person may enter an *active information search*: looking for reading material, phoning friends, going online, and visiting stores to learn about the product.

INFORMATION SOURCES

Of key interest to the marketer are the major information sources to which the consumer will turn to and the relative influence each will have on the subsequent purchase decision. These information sources fall into four groups:

- ***Personal***— Family, friends, neighbors, acquaintances.
- ***Commercial***— Advertising, Web sites, salespersons, dealers, packaging, displays.
- ***Public***— Mass media, consumer-rating organizations.
- ***Experiential***— Handling, examining, using the product.

The relative amount and influence of these sources vary with the product category and the buyer's characteristics. Generally speaking, the consumer receives the most information about a product from commercial sources—that is, marketer-dominated sources. However, the most effective information often comes from personal sources or public sources that are independent authorities. Each information source performs a different function in influencing the buying decision. Commercial sources normally perform an information function, whereas personal sources perform a legitimizing or evaluation function. For example, physicians often learn of new drugs from commercial sources but turn to other doctors for evaluations.

SEARCH DYNAMICS

Through gathering information, the consumer learns about competing brands and their features. The first box in Figure 6.5 shows the *total set* of brands available to the consumer. The individual consumer will come to know only a subset of these brands (*awareness set*). Some brands will meet initial buying criteria (*consideration set*). As the consumer gathers more information, only a few will remain as strong contenders (*choice set*). The consumer makes a final choice from this set.[53]

Marketers need to identify the hierarchy of attributes that guide consumer decision making in order to understand different competitive forces and how these various sets get formed. This process of identifying the hierarchy is called **market partitioning**. Years ago, most car buyers first decided on the manufacturer and then on one of its car divisions (*brand-dominant hierarchy*). A buyer might favor General Motors cars and, within this set, Pontiac. Today, many buyers decide first on the nation from which they want to buy a car (*nation-dominant hierarchy*). Buyers may first decide they want to buy a Japanese car, then Toyota, and then the Corolla model of Toyota.

The hierarchy of attributes also can reveal customer segments. Buyers who first decide on price are price dominant; those who first decide on the type of car (sports, passenger, station wagon) are type dominant; those who first decide on the car brand are brand dominant. Type/price/brand-dominant consumers make up a segment; quality/service/type buyers make up another. Each segment may have distinct demographics, psychographics, and mediagraphics and different awareness, consideration, and choice sets.[54]

Figure 6.5 makes it clear that a company must strategize to get its brand into the prospect's awareness set, consideration set, and choice set. Food companies might work with

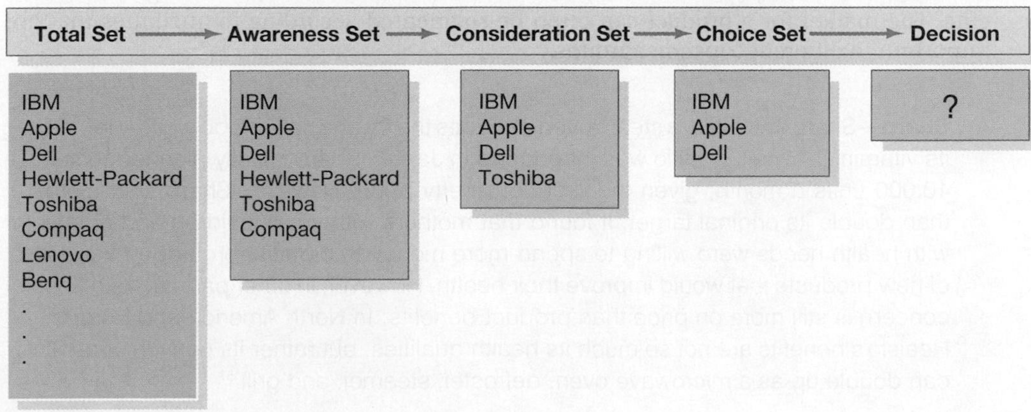

Figure 6.5 Successive Sets Involved in Consumer Decision Making

supermarkets, for instance, in changing the way they display products. If a store-owner arranges shampoo first by brand (like Lux and Kao) and then by hair type within each brand, consumers will tend to select their shampoo for varying hair types from the same brand. However, if the shampoo had been displayed with all those for dry hair together, then all those for dandruff control, and so forth, consumers would probably choose the type of shampoo they want first, and then choose which brand name they would most like for that hair type. Australian supermarkets arrange meats by the way they might be cooked, and stores use more descriptive labels, like "a 10-minute herbed beef roast." The result is that Australians buy a greater variety of meats than Americans, who choose from meats laid out by animal type—beef, chicken, pork, and so on.[55]

The company must also identify the other brands in the consumer's choice set so that it can plan the appropriate competitive appeals. In addition, the company should identify the consumer's information sources and evaluate their relative importance. Consumers should be asked how they first heard about the brand, what information came later, and the relative importance of the different sources. The answers will help the company prepare effective communications for the target market.

Evaluation of Alternatives

How does the consumer process competitive brand information and make a final value judgment? No single process is used by all consumers or by one consumer in all buying situations. There are several processes, the most current models of which see the process as cognitively-oriented. That is, they see the consumer as forming judgments largely on a conscious and rational basis.

Some basic concepts will help us understand consumer evaluation processes: First, the consumer is trying to satisfy a need. Second, the consumer is looking for certain benefits from the product solution. Third, the consumer sees each product as a bundle of attributes with varying abilities for delivering the benefits sought to satisfy this need. The attributes of interest to buyers vary by product. For example:

1. ***Cameras***— Picture sharpness, camera speed, camera size, price.
2. ***Hotels***— Location, cleanliness, atmosphere, price.
3. ***Tires***— Safety, tread life, ride quality, price.

Chinese brand evaluation—Middle-income Chinese cite three critical factors in brand evaluation—trust in its quality, a positive impact on health, and customer care. They are becoming more sophisticated and less concerned with price. When asked whether they would buy a local or foreign brand, preferences diverged based on product. Chinese consumers prefer local brands for food, toiletries, and household items. International brands rate higher for consumer electronics and home-improvement items. For clothing, European brands are seen as more fashionable than Chinese or American brands.[56]

Consumers will pay the most attention to attributes that deliver the sought-after benefits. The market for a product can often be segmented according to attributes that are important to different consumer groups.

Sharp—Sharp's Healsio, a steam oven, reduces the fat and salt in food while keeping its vitamin C. When Healsio was introduced in Japan, Sharp initially planned to sell 10,000 units a month, given the product's hefty price. However, Sharp sold more than double its original target. It found that mothers with small children and elders with health needs were willing to spend more money to benefit from added values of new products that would improve their health. However, in other parts of Asia, the concern is still more on price than product benefits. In North America and Europe, Healsio's benefits are not so much its health qualities, but rather its convenience. It can double up as a microwave oven, defroster, steamer, and grill.[57]

BELIEFS AND ATTITUDES

Through experience and learning, people acquire beliefs and attitudes. These in turn influence buying behavior. A **belief** is a descriptive thought that a person holds about something. People's beliefs about the attributes and benefits of a product or brand influence their buying decisions. Just as important as beliefs are attitudes. An **attitude** is a person's enduring favorable or unfavorable evaluation, emotional feeling, and action tendencies toward some object or idea.[58] People have attitudes toward almost everything: religion, politics, clothes, music, food.

Attitudes put people into a frame of mind: liking or disliking an object, moving toward or away from it. Attitudes lead people to behave in a fairly consistent way toward similar objects. Because attitudes economize on energy and thought, they can be very difficult to change. A company is well-advised to fit its product into existing attitudes rather than to try to change attitudes. Here is an example of an organization that used ad campaigns to remind consumers of their attitudes, with handsome results.

California Milk Processor Board—After a 20-year decline in milk consumption among Californians, the state's milk processors formed the California Milk Processor Board (CMPB) in 1993 to get people to drink more milk. The ad agency commissioned by the CMPB developed a novel approach to pitching milk's benefits. Research had shown that most consumers already believed milk was good for them. So the campaign would remind consumers of the inconvenience and annoyance of running out of milk, which became known as "milk deprivation." The "Got Milk?" tagline served to remind consumers to make sure they had milk in their refrigerators. Sales volume declined 1.67 percent in the year before the campaign's launch. A year after the launch, sales volume increased 1.07 percent. The "Got Milk?" campaign and tagline have since been used nationwide in the U.S. The ad campaign continues to pay strong dividends. For 2002 and the first half of 2003, milk sales in California, where it is centered, increased roughly 1.5 percent, whereas sales in the rest of the U.S. remained flat.[59]

9 essential nutrients
in every easy-to-open
bottle.
got milk?

A "Got Milk" ad from the very successful campaign features China star Zhang Ziyi from the film *Crouching Tiger, Hidden Dragon.*

EXPECTANCY-VALUE MODEL

The consumer arrives at attitudes (judgments, preferences) toward various brands through an attribute evaluation procedure.[60] He or she develops a set of beliefs about where each brand stands on each attribute. The **expectancy-value model** of attitude formation posits that consumers evaluate products and services by combining their brand beliefs—the positives and negatives—according to importance.

Suppose Yishan has narrowed her choice set to four laptop computers (A, B, C, D). Assume that she is interested in four attributes: memory capacity, graphics capability, size and weight, and price. Table 6.2 shows her beliefs about how each brand rates on the four attributes. If one computer dominated the others on all the criteria, we could predict that

Yishan would choose it. But, as is often the case, her choice set consists of brands that vary in their appeal. If Yishan wants the best memory capacity, she should buy A; if she wants the best graphics capability, she should buy B; and so on.

Table 6.2 A Consumer's Brand Beliefs about Computers

Computer	Attribute			
	Memory Capacity	Graphics Capacity	Size and Weight	Price
A	10	8	6	4
B	8	9	8	3
C	6	8	10	5
D	4	3	7	8

Note: Each attribute is rated from 0 to 10, where 10 represents the highest level on that attribute. Price, however, is indexed in a reverse manner, with a 10 representing the lowest price, because a consumer prefers a low price to a high price.

Most buyers consider several attributes in their purchase decision. If we knew the weights that Yishan attaches to the four attributes, we could more reliably predict her computer choice. Suppose Yishan assigned 40 percent of the importance to the computer's memory capacity, 30 percent to graphics capability, 20 percent to size and weight, and 10 percent to price. To find Yishan's perceived value for each computer, according to the expectancy-value model, we multiply her weights by her beliefs about each computer's attributes. This computation leads to the following perceived values:

$$\text{Computer A} = 0.4(10) + 0.3(8) + 0.2(6) + 0.1(4) = 8.0$$
$$\text{Computer B} = 0.4(8) + 0.3(9) + 0.2(8) + 0.1(3) = 7.8$$
$$\text{Computer C} = 0.4(6) + 0.3(8) + 0.2(10) + 0.1(5) = 7.3$$
$$\text{Computer D} = 0.4(4) + 0.3(3) + 0.2(7) + 0.1(8) = 4.7$$

An expectancy-model formulation would predict that Yishan will favor computer A, which (at 8.0) has the highest perceived value.[61]

Suppose most computer buyers form their preferences the same way. Knowing this, a computer manufacturer can do a number of things to influence buyer decisions. The marketer of computer B, for example, could apply the following strategies to stimulate greater interest in brand B:

- **Redesign the computer.** This technique is called real repositioning.
- **Alter beliefs about the brand.** This technique is called psychological repositioning.
- **Alter beliefs about competitors' brands.** This strategy, called competitive depositioning, makes sense when buyers mistakenly believe a competitor's brand has more quality than it actually has.
- **Alter the importance weights.** The marketer could try to persuade buyers to attach more importance to the attributes in which the brand excels.
- **Call attention to neglected attributes.** The marketer could draw buyers' attention to neglected attributes, such as styling or processing speed.
- **Shift the buyer's ideals.** The marketer could try to persuade buyers to change their ideal levels for one or more attributes.[62]

Purchase Decisions

In the evaluation stage, the consumer forms preferences among the brands in the choice set. The consumer may also form an intention to buy the most preferred brand. In executing a purchase intention, the consumer may make up to five sub-decisions: *brand* (brand A), *dealer* (dealer 2), *quantity* (one computer), *timing* (weekend), and *payment method* (credit card).

NONCOMPENSATORY MODELS OF CONSUMER CHOICE

The expectancy-value model is a compensatory model in that perceived good things for a product can help to overcome perceived bad things. But consumers may not want to invest so much time and energy to evaluate brands. They often take "mental shortcuts" that involve various simplifying *choice heuristics*.

With **noncompensatory models** of consumer choice, positive and negative attribute considerations do not necessarily net out. Evaluating attributes more in isolation makes decision making easier for a consumer, but also increases the likelihood that the person would have made a different choice if he or she had deliberated in greater detail. We highlight three such choice heuristics here.

1. With the **conjunctive heuristic**, the consumer sets a minimum acceptable cutoff level for each attribute and chooses the first alternative that meets the minimum standard for all attributes. For example, if Yishan decided that all attributes had to be rated at least a 5, she would choose computer C.
2. With the **lexicographic heuristic**, the consumer chooses the best brand on the basis of its perceived most important attribute (here, memory capacity). With this decision rule, Yishan would choose computer A.
3. With the **elimination-by-aspects heuristic**, the consumer compares brands on an attribute selected probabilistically—where the probability of choosing an attribute is positively related to its importance—and brands are eliminated if they do not meet minimum acceptable cutoff levels.

Characteristics of the person (e.g., brand or product knowledge), the purchase decision task and setting (e.g., number and similarity of brand choices and time pressure involved), and social context (e.g., need for justification to a peer or boss) may affect if and how choice heuristics are used.[63]

Consumers do not necessarily adopt only one type of choice rule in making purchase decisions. In some cases, they adopt a phased decision strategy that combines two or more decision rules. For example, they might use a noncompensatory decision rule such as the conjunctive heuristic to reduce the number of brand choices to a more manageable number and then evaluate the remaining brands using a compensatory model. The Intel Inside campaign made the brand the first cutoff for many consumers who would only buy a PC with an Intel chip. PC makers like IBM and Dell had little choice but to support Intel.

INTERVENING FACTORS

Even if consumers form brand evaluations, two general factors can intervene between the purchase intention and the purchase decision (see Figure 6.6).[64] The first factor is the *attitudes of others*. The extent to which another person's attitude reduces the preference for an alternative depends on two things: (1) the intensity of the other person's negative attitude toward the consumer's preferred alternative and (2) the consumer's motivation to comply with the other person's wishes.[65] The more intense the other person's negativism and the closer the other person is to the consumer, the more the consumer will adjust his or her purchase intention. The converse is also true: A buyer's preference for a brand will increase if someone he or she respects favors the same brand strongly.

Related to the attitudes of others is the role played by infomediaries who publish their evaluations. Examples include *Consumer Reports*, which provides unbiased expert reviews of all types of products and services; professional movie, book, and music reviewers; customer reviews of books and music on Amazon.com; and the increasing number of chat rooms where people discuss products, services, and companies.

The second factor is *unanticipated situational factors* that may erupt to change the purchase intention. Yishan might lose her job, some other purchase might become more urgent, or a store salesperson may turn her off. Preferences and even purchase intentions are not completely reliable predictors of purchase behavior.

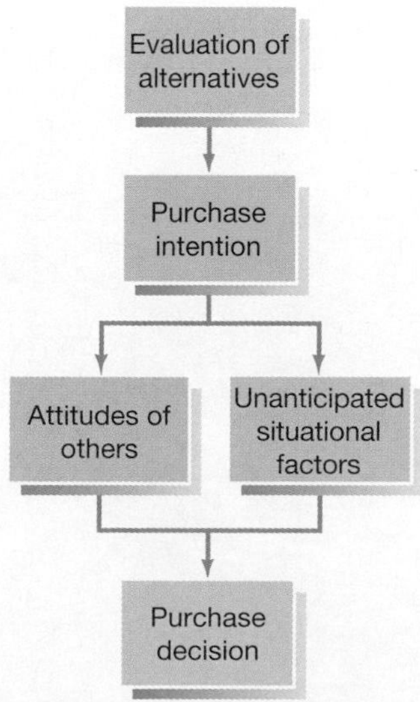

Figure 6.6 Steps Between Evaluation of Alternatives and a Purchase Decision

A consumer's decision to modify, postpone, or avoid a purchase decision is heavily influenced by *perceived risk*.[66] There are many different types of risks that consumers may perceive in buying and consuming a product:

1. ***Functional risk***—The product does not perform up to expectations.
2. ***Physical risk***—The product poses a threat to the physical well-being or health of the user or others.
3. ***Financial risk***—The product is not worth the price paid.
4. ***Social risk***—The product results in embarrassment from others.
5. ***Psychological risk***—The product affects the mental well-being of the user.
6. ***Time risk***—The failure of the product results in an opportunity cost of finding another satisfactory product.

The amount of perceived risk varies with the amount of money at stake, the amount of attribute uncertainty, and the amount of consumer self-confidence. Consumers develop routines for reducing risk, such as decision avoidance, information gathering from friends, and preference for national brand names and warranties. Marketers must understand the factors that provoke a feeling of risk in consumers and provide information and support to reduce perceived risk.

Postpurchase Behavior

After the purchase, the consumer might experience dissonance that stems from noticing certain disquieting features or hearing favorable things about other brands, and will be alert to information that supports his or her decision. Marketing communications should supply beliefs and evaluations that reinforce the consumer's choice and help him or her feel good about the brand.

The marketer's job therefore does not end with the purchase. Marketers must monitor postpurchase satisfaction, postpurchase actions, and postpurchase product uses.

POSTPURCHASE SATISFACTION

What determines customer satisfaction with a purchase? Satisfaction is a function of the closeness between expectations and the product's perceived performance.[67] If performance falls short of expectations, the consumer is *disappointed*; if it meets expectations, the consumer is *satisfied*; if it exceeds expectations, the consumer is *delighted*. These feelings make a difference in whether the customer buys the product again and talks favorably or unfavorably about it to others.

Consumers form their expectations on the basis of messages received from sellers, friends, and other information sources. The larger the gap between expectations and performance, the greater the dissatisfaction. Here the consumer's coping style comes into play. Some consumers magnify the gap when the product is not perfect, and they are highly dissatisfied; others minimize the gap and are less dissatisfied.[68]

The importance of postpurchase satisfaction suggests that product claims must truthfully represent the product's likely performance. Some sellers might even understate performance levels so that consumers experience higher-than-expected satisfaction with the product.

POSTPURCHASE ACTIONS

If the consumer is satisfied, he or she will exhibit a higher probability of purchasing the product again. On the other hand, dissatisfied consumers may abandon or return the product. They may seek information that confirms its high value. They may take public action by complaining to the company, going to a lawyer, or complaining to other groups (such as business, private, or government agencies). Private actions include making a decision to stop buying the product (*exit option*) or warning friends (*voice option*).[69] In all these cases, the seller has done a poor job of satisfying the customer.[70]

Chapter 5 described CRM programs designed to build long-term brand loyalty. Postpurchase communications to buyers have been shown to result in fewer product returns and order cancellations.[71] For example, computer companies can send a letter to new owners congratulating them on having selected a fine computer. They can place ads showing satisfied brand owners. They can solicit customer suggestions for improvements and list the location of available services. They can write intelligible instruction booklets. They can send owners a magazine containing articles describing new computer applications. In addition, they can provide good channels for speedy redress of customer grievances. Here is an example of a successful customer satisfaction program in China:

> **KFC**—KFC implemented a Customer Mania training program in China designed to make everyone in the company "maniacs" about their customers through its operational principles, CHAMPS—Cleanliness, Hospitality, Accuracy, Maintenance, Product, and Speed. "YES! My customers are important to me!", "YES! My customers are my job!", and "YES! I can solve any issues you have!" are some slogans used as part of an all-out effort to meet and exceed customer expectations.[72]

POSTPURCHASE USE AND DISPOSAL

Marketers should also monitor how buyers use and dispose of the product (see Figure 6.7). A key driver of sales frequency is product consumption rate—the more quickly buyers consume a product, the sooner they may be back in the market to repurchase it.

One opportunity to increase frequency of product use is when consumer's perceptions of their usage differ from the reality. Consumers may fail to replace products with relatively short life spans in a timely manner because of a tendency to underestimate product life.[73] One strategy to speed up replacement is to tie the act of replacing the product to a certain holiday, event, or time of year.

For example, several services run promotions tied in with the lunar festive season (e.g., curtain cleaning services). Another strategy might be to provide consumers with better information on either: (1) when the product was first used or would need to be replaced or (2) the current level of performance. For example, toothbrushes have color indicators on their bristles to indicate when they are too worn. Perhaps the simplest way to increase usage is when actual usage of a product is less than optimal or recommended. In this case, consumers must be persuaded of the merits of more regular usage, and potential hurdles to increased usage must be overcome.

If consumers throw the product away, the marketer needs to know how they dispose of it, especially if it can damage the environment (as in the case with batteries, beverage

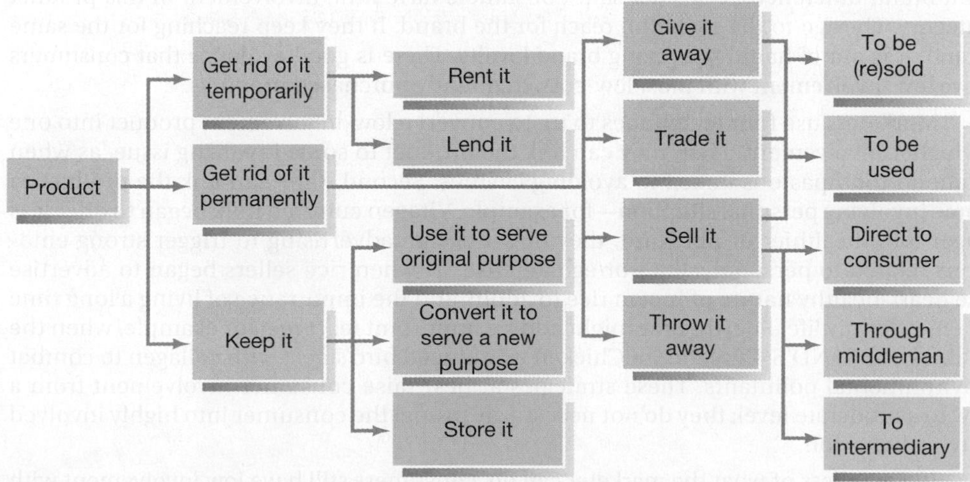

Figure 6.7 How Customers Use or Dispose of Products

Source: Jacob Jacoby, Carol K. Berning, and Thomas F. Dietvorst, "What about Disposition?" *Journal of Marketing*, July 1977, p. 23. Reprinted with permission of the American Marketing Association.

containers, and disposable diapers). Increased public awareness of recycling and ecological concerns as well as consumer complaints about having to throw away beautiful bottles led French perfume maker Rochas to think about introducing a refillable fragrance line.

Other Theories of Consumer Decision Making

The consumer decision process may not always develop in a carefully planned fashion. It is important to understand other theories and approaches to how consumers make decisions and when they might apply.

Level of Consumer Involvement

The expectancy-value model assumes a high level of involvement on the part of the consumer. **Consumer involvement** can be defined in terms of the level of engagement and active processing undertaken by the consumer in responding to a marketing stimulus, for example, from viewing an ad or evaluating a product or service.

ELABORATION LIKELIHOOD MODEL

Petty and Cacioppo's *elaboration likelihood model*, an influential model of attitude formation and change, describes how consumers make evaluations in both low- and high-involvement circumstances.[74] There are two means of persuasion with their model: The central route, where attitude formation or change involves much thought and is based on a diligent, rational consideration of the most important product or service information; and the peripheral route, where attitude formation or change involves comparatively much less thought and is a consequence of the association of a brand with either positive or negative peripheral cues. Examples of peripheral cues for consumers might be a celebrity endorsement, a credible source, or any object that engendered positive feelings.

Consumers follow the central route only if they possess sufficient *motivation, ability*, and *opportunity*. In other words, consumers must want to evaluate a brand in detail, must have the necessary brand and product or service knowledge in memory, and must be given sufficient time and the proper setting to actually do so. If any one of those three factors is lacking, consumers will tend to follow the peripheral route and consider less central, more extrinsic factors in their decisions.

LOW-INVOLVEMENT MARKETING STRATEGIES

Many products are bought under conditions of low involvement and the absence of significant brand differences. Consider salt. Consumers have little involvement in this product category. They go to the store and reach for the brand. If they keep reaching for the same brand, it is out of habit, not strong brand loyalty. There is good evidence that consumers have low involvement with most low-cost, frequently purchased products.

Marketers use four techniques to try to convert a low-involvement product into one of higher involvement. First, they can link the product to some involving issue, as when Komodo toothpaste is linked to avoiding cavities. Second, they can link the product to some involving personal situation—for example, Vitagen cultured milk began to offer less sugar for a healthier drink. Third, they might design advertising to trigger strong emotions related to personal values or ego defense, as when rice sellers began to advertise the heart-healthy nature of brown rice to adults and the importance of living a long time to enjoy family life. Fourth, they might add an important feature—for example, when the makers of BRAND'S® Essence of Chicken introduced bird's nest with collagen to combat environmental pollutants. These strategies at best raise consumer involvement from a low to a moderate level; they do not necessarily propel the consumer into highly involved buying behavior.

If, regardless of what the marketer can do, consumers still have low involvement with a purchase decision, they are likely to follow the peripheral route. Marketers must pay special attention to giving consumers one or more positive cues that they can use to justify their brand choice. Brand familiarity can be important if consumers decide to just buy the brand about which they have heard or seen the most. Frequent ad repetition, visible sponsorships, and vigorous PR are all ways to enhance brand familiarity. Other peripheral cues can also be used. A beloved celebrity endorser, attractive packaging, or an appealing promotion might tip the balance in favor of the brand.[75]

VARIETY-SEEKING BUYING BEHAVIOR

Some buying situations are characterized by low involvement but significant brand differences. Here consumers often do a lot of brand switching. Think about roasted peanuts. The consumer has some beliefs about roasted peanuts, chooses a brand of roasted peanuts without much evaluation, and evaluates the product during consumption. Next time, the consumer may reach for another brand out of a wish for a different taste. Brand switching occurs for the sake of variety rather than dissatisfaction.

The market leader and the minor brands in this product category have different marketing strategies. The market leader will try to encourage habitual buying behavior by dominating the shelf space with a variety of related but different product versions, avoiding out-of-stock conditions, and sponsoring frequent reminder advertising. Challenger firms will encourage variety seeking by offering lower prices, deals, coupons, free samples, and advertising that tries to break the consumer's purchase and consumption cycle and presents reasons for trying something new.

Decision Heuristics and Biases

We've seen that consumers do not always process information or make decisions in a deliberate, rational manner. "Marketing Insight: How Consumers Really Make Decisions" highlights how consumers make decisions.

Behavioral decision theorists have identified many different heuristics and biases in everyday consumer decision making. They come into play when consumers forecast the likelihood of future outcomes or events.[76]

1. **The *availability heuristic*** — Consumers base their predictions on the quickness and ease with which a particular example of an outcome comes to mind. If an example comes to mind too easily, consumers might overestimate the likelihood of the outcome or event happening. For example, a recent product failure may lead a consumer to inflate the likelihood of a future product failure and make him or her more inclined to purchase a product warranty.
2. **The *representativeness heuristic*** — Consumers base their predictions on how representative or similar the outcome is to other examples. One reason that package appearances may be so similar for different brands in the same product category is that they want to be seen as representative of the category as a whole.
3. **The *anchoring and adjustment heuristic*** — Consumers arrive at an initial judgment and then make adjustments of that first impression based on additional information. For services marketers, it is critical to make a strong first impression to establish a favorable anchor so that subsequent experiences are interpreted in a more favorable light.

Note that marketing managers also may use heuristics and be subject to biases in their decision making. "Marketing Memo: Decision Traps" reveals 10 common mistakes managers make in their decisions.

Mental Accounting

Researchers have found that consumers use mental accounting when they handle their money.[77] **Mental accounting** refers to the manner by which consumers code, categorize, and evaluate financial outcomes of choices. Formally, it has been defined in terms of, "The tendency to categorize *funds* or items of value even though there is no logical *basis* for the categorization, for example, individuals often segregate their savings into separate accounts to meet different goals even though funds from any of the accounts can be applied to any of the goals."[78]

For example, assume you spend $50 to buy a ticket to see a concert.[79] As you arrive at the show, you realize you've lost your ticket. You may be unsure about purchasing another

MARKETING INSIGHT • HOW CONSUMERS REALLY MAKE DECISIONS

One of the most active academic research areas in marketing is behavioral decision theory (BDT). Researchers have uncovered many fascinating influences and outcomes in consumer decision making, often challenging predictions from economic theory and assumptions about rationality.

- Consumers are more likely to choose an alternative (a home bread bakery) after a relatively inferior option (a slightly better but significantly more expensive bakery) is added to the choice set.
- Consumers are more likely to choose an alternative that appears to be a compromise in the particular choice set under consideration.
- The choices that consumers make influence their assessment of their own tastes.
- Shifting attention to one of two considered alternatives tends to enhance the perceived attractiveness and choice probability of that alternative.
- The manner in which consumers compare products that vary in terms of price and perceived quality (features, brand name) and the way those products are displayed in the store (by brand or by model type) affect their willingness to pay more for additional features or a better-known brand.
- Consumers who think about the possibility that their purchase decisions will turn out to be wrong are more likely to choose better-known brands.
- Consumers for whom possible feelings of regret are made more relevant are more likely to choose a product that is currently on sale rather than wait for a better sale or buy a higher-priced item.
- Consumers' choices are influenced by subtle (and theoretically inconsequential) changes in the way alternatives are described.
- Consumers who make purchases for later consumption appear to make systematic errors in predicting their future preferences.
- Consumers' predictions of their future tastes are not accurate—they do not really know how they will feel after consuming the same flavor of yogurt or ice cream several times.
- Consumers often overestimate the duration of their overall emotional reactions to future events (moves, financial windfalls, outcomes of sporting events).
- Consumers often overestimate their future consumption, especially if there is limited availability (which may explain why some gums have higher sales when availability is limited to several months per year than when they are offered year-round).
- In anticipating future consumption opportunities, consumers often assume they will want or need more variety than they actually do.
- Consumers are less likely to choose alternatives with product features or promotional premiums that have little or no value, even when these features and premiums are optional (like the opportunity to purchase a Collector's Plate) and do not reduce the actual value of the product in any way.
- Consumers are less likely to choose products selected by other consumers for reasons that they find irrelevant, even though these other reasons would not suggest anything positive or negative about the products' values.
- Consumers' interpretations and evaluations of past experiences are greatly influenced by the ending and trend of events. A positive event at the end of a service experience can color later reflections and evaluations of the experience as a whole.

What all these and other studies reinforce is that consumer behavior is very constructive and that the context of decisions really matter. Understanding how these effects show up in the marketplace can be crucial for marketers.

Sources: For an overview of some issues involved, see James R. Bettman, Mary Frances Luce, and John W. Payne, "Constructive Consumer Choice Processes." *Journal of Consumer Research,* December 1998, 25, pp. 187–217; and Itamar Simonson, "Getting Closer to Your Customers by Understanding How They Make Choices." *California Management Review,* Summer 1993, 35, pp. 68–84. For examples of classic studies in this area, see some of the following: Dan Ariely and Ziv Carmon, "Gestalt Characteristics of Experiences: The Defining Features of Summarized Events." *Journal of Behavioral Decision Making,* April 2000, 13(2), pp. 191–201; Ravi Dhar and Klaus Wertenbroch,"Consumer Choice between Hedonic and Utilitarian Goods." *Journal of Marketing Research,* February 2000, 37, pp. 60–71; Itamar Simonson and Amos Tversky, "Choice in Context: Tradeoff Contrast and Extremeness Aversion." *Journal of Marketing Research,* August 1992, 29, pp. 281–95; Itamar Simonson, "The Effects of Purchase Quantity and Timing on Variety-Seeking Behavior." *Journal of Marketing Research,* May 1990, 27, pp. 150–62.

ticket for $50. Assume, on the other hand, that you realized you had lost $50 on the way to buy the ticket. You might be much more likely to go ahead and buy the ticket anyway. Although the amount lost in each case was the same—$50—the reactions were very different. In the first case, you may have mentally allocated $50 for going to a concert. Buying another ticket would therefore exceed your mental concert budget. In the second case, the money that was lost did not belong to any account, so the mental concert budget had not yet been exceeded.

MARKETING MEMO • DECISION TRAPS

In *Decision Traps*, Russo and Schoemaker reveal the 10 most common mistakes managers make in their decisions.

1. ***Plunging in*** — Beginning to gather information and reach conclusions without taking a few minutes to think about the crux of the issue you're facing or to think through how you believe decisions like this one should be made.
2. ***Frame blindness*** — Setting out to solve the wrong problem because you've created a mental framework for your decision, with little thought, that causes you to overlook the best options or lose sight of important objectives.
3. ***Lack of frame control*** — Failing to consciously define the problem in more ways than one or being unduly influenced by the frames of others.
4. ***Overconfidence in your judgment*** — Failing to collect key factual information because you are too sure of your assumptions and opinions.
5. ***Shortsighted shortcuts*** — Relying inappropriately on "rules of thumb" such as implicitly trusting the most readily available information or anchoring too much on convenient facts.
6. ***Shooting from the hip*** — Believing you can keep straight in your head all the information you've discovered, and therefore "winging it" rather than following a systematic procedure when making the final choice.
7. ***Group failure*** — Assuming that with many smart people involved, good choices will follow automatically, and therefore failing to manage the group decision making process.
8. ***Fooling yourself about feedback*** — Failing to interpret the evidence from past outcomes for what it really says, either because you are protecting your ego or because you are tricked by hindsight effects.
9. ***Not keeping track*** — Assuming that experience will make its lessons available automatically, and therefore failing to keep systematic records to track the results of your decisions and failing to analyze these results in ways that reveal their key lessons.
10. ***Failure to audit your decision process*** — Failing to create an organized approach to understanding your own decision making, so you remain constantly exposed to all the other nine decision traps.

Sources: J. Edward Russo and Paul J. H. Schoemaker, *Decision Traps: Ten Barriers to Brilliant Decision Making and How to Overcome Them,* (New York: Doubleday, 1990). See also J. Edward Russo and Paul J. H. Schoemaker, *Winning Decisions: Getting It Right the First Time,* (New York: Doubleday, 2001).

According to Thaler, mental accounting is based on a set of key core principles:

1. **Consumers tend to segregate gains.** When a seller has a product with more than one positive dimension, it is desirable to have each dimension evaluated separately. Listing multiple benefits of a large industrial product, for example, can make the sum of the parts seem greater than the whole.
2. **Consumers tend to integrate losses.** Marketers have a distinct advantage in selling something if its cost can be added to another large purchase. House buyers are more inclined to view additional expenditures favorably given the high price of buying a house.
3. **Consumers tend to integrate smaller losses with larger gains.** The "cancellation" principle might explain why withholding taxes taken from monthly paychecks are less aversive than large lump sum tax payments—they are more likely to be absorbed by the larger pay amount.
4. **Consumers tend to segregate small gains from large losses.** The "silver lining" principle might explain the popularity of rebates on big ticket purchases such as cars.

The principles of mental accounting are derived in part from prospect theory. **Prospect theory** maintains that consumers frame decision alternatives in terms of gains and losses according to a value function. Consumers are generally loss-averse. They tend to over-weight very low probabilities and underweight very high probabilities.

Profiling the Customer Buying Decision Process

How can marketers learn about the stages in the buying process for their product? They can think about how they themselves would act (*introspective method*). They can interview a small number of recent purchasers, asking them to recall the events leading to their purchase (*retrospective method*). They can locate consumers who plan to buy the product and ask them to think out loud about going through the buying process (*prospective method*); or they can ask consumers to describe the ideal way to buy the product (*prescriptive method*). Each method yields a picture of the steps in the process.

Trying to understand the customer's behavior in connection with a product has been called mapping the customer's *consumption system*,[80] *customer activity cycle*,[81] or *customer scenario*.[82] This can be done for such activity clusters as doing laundry, preparing for a wedding, or buying a car. For example, buying a car involves a cluster of activities, including choosing the car, financing the purchase, buying insurance, buying accessories, and so on.

Summary

1. Consumer behavior is influenced by three factors: cultural (culture, subculture, and social class); social (reference groups, family, and social roles and statuses); and personal (age, stage in the life cycle, occupation, economic circumstances, lifestyle, personality, and self-concept). Research into all these factors can provide marketers with clues to reach and serve consumers more effectively.
2. Four main psychological processes affect consumer behavior: motivation, perception, learning, and memory.
3. To understand how consumers actually make buying decisions, marketers must identify who makes and has input into the buying decision; people can be initiators, influencers, deciders, buyers, or users. Different marketing campaigns might be targeted at each type of person.
4. The typical buying process consists of the following sequence of events: problem recognition, information search, evaluation of alternatives, purchase decision, and postpurchase behavior. The marketers' job is to understand the behavior at each stage. The attitudes of others, unanticipated situational factors, and perceived risk may all affect the decision to buy, as will consumers' levels of postpurchase satisfaction and postpurchase actions on the part of the company.
5. Consumers are constructive decision makers and subject to many contextual influences. Consumers often exhibit low involvement in their decisions, using many heuristics as a result.

Application

Marketing Debate—Is Target Marketing Ever Bad?

As marketers increasingly develop marketing programs tailored to certain target market segments in Asia, some critics have denounced these efforts as exploitative. Examples include marketing cigarettes and alcohol to less-educated Asians, and employing Asian women as clichéd stereotypes and depicting them inappropriately in ads. Others counter that targeting and positioning is critical to marketing in Asia and that these marketing programs are attempts to be relevant to a specific consumer group.

Take a position: *Target marketing in Asia is exploitative* versus *Target marketing in Asia is a sound business practice.*

Marketing Discussion—What are Your Mental Accounts?

What mental accounts do you have in your mind about purchasing products or services? Do you have any rules you employ in spending money? Are they different from what other people do? Do you follow Thaler's four principles in reacting to gains and losses?

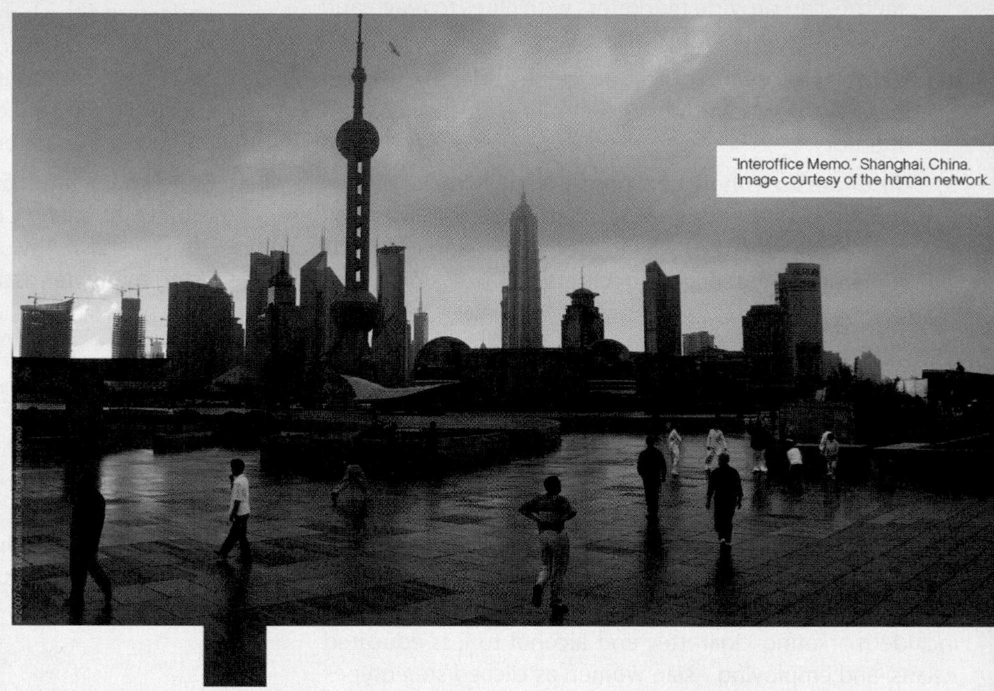

"Interoffice Memo." Shanghai, China.
Image courtesy of the human network.

Now the Shanghai meeting comes to you. Welcome to TelePresence. Where you can meet face-to-face, no matter where you are. Real life. In real time. With the touc of a button. Where you can get more work done. In less time. And reduce your impact on the environment in the process. See the big picture at cisco.com/telepresenc

welcome to
the human network. CISCO

Network equipment manufacturer Cisco discovered that about a third of the firms in the small to midsize segment of its market account for about 75 percent of total networking expenditures, pointing the way to a lucrative growth opportunity.

7 Analyzing Business Markets

Business organizations do not only sell. They also buy vast quantities of raw materials, manufactured components, plant and equipment, supplies, and business services. To create and capture value, sellers need to understand these organizations' needs, resources, policies, and buying procedures.

Cisco, the network communications equipment manufacturer that leads the market in the switches and routers for directing traffic on the Internet, sought growth by directing considerable research and marketing resources at an underserved market: Small and Midsize Business (SMB) customers, which the company defined as businesses with fewer than 250 employees.[1] To better understand buyer behavior, Cisco conducted customer research that segmented the overall SMB market into four tiers by networking expenditure and purchase patterns. Tier-1 and tier-2 companies, who view networking as the core of their business, make up 30 percent of the SMB space, but account for 75 percent of total networking expenditures. Tier-3 and tier-4 companies make up 70 percent of the market, but are hesitant to invest heavily in networking technology. Based on this understanding of the market, Cisco was able to target these segments with products and services designed specifically for them. It developed a program called the "Smart Business Roadmap" that matched common business issues faced by SMB customer types with long-term technology solutions. One of these solutions was Linksys One, a hosted communications service offering telephone, video, data, and Internet networking on one high-speed connection that debuted in 2005. Overall, Cisco raised its R&D budget for the SMB market to $2 billion and directed 40 percent of its total marketing expenditure toward this market. The program generated 22 percent growth in Cisco's business with SMBs.

In this chapter, we will address the following questions:

1. What is the business market, and how does it differ from the consumer market?
2. What buying situations do organizational buyers face?
3. Who participates in the business-to-business buying process?
4. How do business buyers make their decisions?
5. How can companies build strong relationships with business customers?
6. How do institutional buyers and government agencies do their buying?

Some of the world's most valuable brands belong to business marketers: DuPont, FedEx, GE, Hewlett-Packard, IBM, Intel, and Siemens. Some notable Asian business marketers are Huawei Technologies, Nippon Steel, Taiwan Semiconductor, and Tata Consultancy Services. Much of basic marketing also applies to business marketers. They need to embrace holistic marketing principles, such as building strong relationships with their customers, just like any marketer. But there are some unique considerations in selling to other businesses.[2] In this chapter, we will highlight some of the crucial differences for marketing in business markets.

What is Organizational Buying?

Webster and Wind define **organizational buying** as the decision making process by which formal organizations establish the need for purchased products and services and identify, evaluate, and choose among alternative brands and suppliers.[3]

The Business Market Versus the Consumer Market

The **business market** consists of all the organizations that acquire goods and services used in the production of other products or services that are sold, rented, or supplied to others. The major industries making up the business market are agriculture, forestry, and fisheries; mining; manufacturing; construction; transportation; communication; public utilities; banking, finance, and insurance; distribution; and services.

More dollars and items are involved in sales to business buyers than to consumers. Consider the process of producing and selling a simple pair of shoes. Hide dealers must sell hides to tanners, who sell leather to shoe manufacturers, who sell shoes to wholesalers, who sell shoes to retailers, who finally sell them to consumers. Each party in the supply chain also has to buy many other goods and services.

Business markets have several characteristics that contrast sharply with those of consumer markets:

- ***Fewer, larger buyers*** — The business marketer normally deals with far fewer, much larger buyers than the consumer marketer does. The fate of Bridgestone Tire Company and other automotive part suppliers depends on getting contracts from a few major auto-makers. A few large buyers do most of the purchasing in such industries as aircraft engines and defense weapons. However, it should be noted that as a slowing economy has put a stranglehold on large corporations' purchasing departments, the small and midsize business market is offering new opportunities for suppliers.[4] "Marketing Insight: Big Sales to Small Business" discusses this promising new B2B market.
- ***Close supplier-customer relationship*** — Because of the smaller customer base and the importance and power of the larger customers, suppliers are frequently expected to customize their offerings to individual business customer needs. Honda sends its engineers to suppliers' plants to scrutinize operations and achieve savings in operating costs that are split between Honda and its suppliers. Business buyers often select suppliers who also buy from them. An example would be a paper manufacturer that purchases chemicals from a chemical company that buys a considerable amount of its paper.
- ***Professional purchasing*** — Business goods are often purchased by trained purchasing agents, who must follow their organization's purchasing policies, constraints, and requirements. Many of the buying instruments—for example, requests for quotations, proposals, and purchase contracts—are not typically found in consumer buying.
- ***Multiple buying influences*** — More people typically influence business buying decisions. Buying committees consisting of technical experts and even senior management are common in the purchase of major goods. Business marketers have to send well-trained sales representatives and sales teams to deal with the well-trained buyers.

MARKETING INSIGHT • BIG SALES TO SMALL BUSINESS

Business owners represent not only a sweet spot for eBay but also for IBM, American Express, Microsoft, and other large companies. These ventures need capital equipment, technology, supplies, and services. Around the world, the B2B market is growing. Here's how some companies are reaching it:

- With its new suite of run-your-business software, **Microsoft** is counting on sales to 45 million small to midsize businesses worldwide to add $10 billion to its annual revenue by 2010. Even with all its cash, Microsoft can't afford to send reps to all of them. Instead, Microsoft is using 24,000 independent computer consulting companies known as value-added resellers. It has also added 300 sales managers to help educate and support both resellers and customers.
- **IBM** counts small to midsize businesses as 20 percent of its business and has launched Express, a line of hardware, software services, and financing for this market. IBM sells through regional reps as well as independent software vendors and resellers, and it supports its small-midsize push with millions of dollars in advertising annually. Ads include TV spots and print ads in publications such as *Inc*. IBM partners non-profits to reach certain minority segments.
- **American Express** has been steadily adding new features to its credit card for small business, which some small companies use to cover hundreds of thousands of dollars a month in cash needs. In addition to its credit card, American Express has been expanding its leading operations for small business. It has created a small business network called OPEN <www.openamericanexpress.com> to bring together various services, Web tools, and discount programs with other giants like ExxonMobil, Dell, and FedEx. With OPEN, American Express not only allows customers to save money on common expenses, but also encourages them to do much of their recordkeeping on its Web site.

Yet while small to midsize businesses present a huge opportunity, they also present huge challenges. The market is large and fragmented by industry, size, and number of years in operation. And once you reach them, it's hard to persuade them to buy. Small business owners are notably averse to long-range planning and have an "I'll buy it when I need it" decision making style. Here are some guidelines for selling to small businesses:

- **Don't lump small and midsize businesses together.** There's a big gap between $1 million in revenue and $50 million or between a start-up with 10 employees and a more mature business with 100. IBM customizes its small and midsize business portal <www.ibm.com/businesscenter/us> with call-me or text-chat buttons that are connected to products for different market segments.
- **Do keep it simple.** Simplicity means one point of contact with a supplier for all service problems or one single bill for all services and products.
- **Do use the Internet.** In its research on buying patterns of small business owners, Hewlett-Packard found that these time-strapped decision makers prefer to buy, or at least research, products and services online. To that end, HP has designed a site targeted at small and midsize businesses and pulls business owners to the site through extensive advertising, direct mail, email campaigns, catalogs, and events. IBM prospects via eBay by selling refurbished or phased-out equipment on its new B2B site. About 80 percent of IBM's equipment is sold to small businesses that are new to IBM—half of which have agreed to receive calls with other offers.
- **Don't forget about direct contact.** Even if a small business owner's first point of contact is via the Internet, you still need to offer phone or face time.
- **Do provide support after the sale.** Small businesses want partners, not pitchmen.
- **Do your homework.** The realities of small or midsize business management are different from those of a large corporation. Microsoft created a small fictional executive research firm, Southridge, and baseball-style trading cards of its key decision makers to help its employees tie sales strategies to small business realities.
- **Don't waste their time.** This is a corollary to doing your homework. Being prepared by understanding their business needs and constraints is critical before engaging small business owners. It also means referrals are far superior to cold calls.

Sources: Based on Barnaby J. Feder, "When Goliath Comes Knocking on David's Door." *New York Times*, May 6, 2003, p. G13; Jay Greene, "Small Biz: Microsoft's Next Big Thing?" *BusinessWeek* April 21, 2003, pp. 72–73; Jennifer Gilbert, "Small But Mighty." *Sales and Marketing Management*, January 2004, pp. 30–35; Verne Kopytoff, "Businesses Click on eBay." *San Francisco Chronicle*, July 28, 2003, p. E1; Matt Krantz, "Firms Jump on the eBay Wagon." *USA Today* May 3, 2004, pp. 1B, 2B.

- ***Multiple sales calls*** — Because more people are involved in the selling process, it takes multiple sales calls to win most business orders, and some sales cycles can take years. A study by McGraw-Hill found that it takes four to four-and-a-half calls to close an average industrial sale. In the case of capital equipment sales for large projects, it may take multiple attempts to fund a project, and the sales cycle—between quoting a job and delivering the product—is often measured in years.[5]
- ***Derived demand*** — The demand for business goods is ultimately derived from the demand for consumer goods. Thus the business marketer must closely monitor the buying patterns of ultimate consumers. For instance, auto-makers in China are driving the boom in the demand for rubber, aluminum, copper, and galvanized steel.

As incomes grow, mainland consumers have pushed car sales to record levels, thus driving the demand for these goods.

- ***Inelastic demand*** — The total demand for many business goods and services is inelastic—that is, not much affected by price changes. Shoe manufacturers are not going to buy much more leather if the price of leather falls, nor will they buy much less if the price rises, unless they can find satisfactory substitutes. Demand is especially inelastic in the short run because producers cannot make quick changes in production methods. Demand is also inelastic for business goods that represent a small percentage of the item's total cost, such as shoelaces.
- ***Fluctuating demand*** — The demand for business goods and services tends to be more volatile than that for consumer goods and services. A given percentage increase in consumer demand can lead to a much larger percentage increase in the demand for plant and equipment necessary to produce the additional output. Economists refer to this as the *acceleration effect.* Sometimes a rise of only 10 percent in consumer demand can cause as much as a 200 percent rise in business demand for products in the next period; a 10 percent fall in consumer demand may cause a complete collapse in business demand.
- ***Geographically concentrated buyers*** — Business buyers tend to be concentrated in certain regions. The geographical concentration of producers helps to reduce selling costs. At the same time, business marketers need to monitor regional shifts of certain industries.
- ***Direct purchasing*** — Business buyers often buy directly from manufacturers rather than through intermediaries, especially items that are technically complex or expensive (such as mainframes or aircraft).

Buying Situations

The business buyer faces many decisions in making a purchase. The number of decisions depends on the buying situation: complexity of the problem being solved, newness of the buying requirement, number of people involved, and time required. Robinson and others distinguish three types of buying situations: the straight rebuy, modified rebuy, and new task.[6]

STRAIGHT REBUY

In a straight rebuy, the purchasing department re-orders on a routine basis and chooses from suppliers on an approved list. The suppliers make an effort to maintain product and service quality and often propose automatic re-ordering systems to save time. "Out-suppliers" attempt to offer something new or to exploit dissatisfaction with a current supplier. Out-suppliers try to get a small order and then enlarge their purchase share over time.

MODIFIED REBUY

The buyer wants to modify product specifications, prices, delivery requirements, or other terms. The modified rebuy usually involves additional participants on both sides. The in-suppliers become nervous and have to protect the account. The out-suppliers see an opportunity to propose a better offer to gain some business.

NEW TASK

A purchaser buys a product or service for the first time (e.g., office building, new security system). The greater the cost or risk, the larger the number of participants and the greater their information gathering—and therefore the longer the time needed to make a decision.[7]

The business buyer makes the fewest decisions in the straight rebuy situation and the most in the new-task situation. Over time, new-task situations become straight rebuys and routine purchase behavior. New-task buying passes through several stages: awareness, interest, evaluation, trial, and adoption.[8] The effectiveness of communication tools varies at each stage. The mass media are most important during the initial awareness stage; salespeople have their greatest impact at the interest stage; and technical sources are the most important during the evaluation stage.

In the new-task situation, the buyer must determine product specifications, price limits, delivery terms and times, service terms, payment terms, order quantities, acceptable suppliers, and the selected supplier. Different participants influence each decision, and the order in which these decisions are made varies.

Because of the complicated selling involved, many companies use a *missionary sales force* consisting of their most effective salespeople. The brand promise and the manufacturer's brand name recognition will be important in establishing trust and the customer's willingness to consider change. The marketer also tries to reach as many key participants as possible and provides helpful information and assistance.

Once a customer is acquired, in-suppliers are continually seeking ways to add value to their market offer to facilitate rebuys. Often they do this by providing customized information to customers.

Customers considering spending large amounts on a single transaction for big-ticket goods and services want all the information they can get. One way to entice new buyers is to create a customer reference program in which satisfied existing customers collaborate with the company's sales and marketing department by agreeing to serve as references.

Systems Buying and Selling

Many business buyers prefer to buy a total solution to a problem from one seller. Called *systems buying*, this practice originated with government purchases of major weapons and communications systems. The government would solicit bids from *prime contractors*, who assembled the package or system. The contractor who was awarded the contract would be responsible for bidding out and assembling the system's subcomponents from *second-tier contractors*. The prime contractor would thus provide a turnkey solution, so-called because the buyer simply had to turn one key to get the job done.

YTL Corporation—When the Malaysian government first privatized infrastructural development projects, businesses could own and grow what they built. YTL, a construction company, was incentivized to introduce the turnkey concept in Malaysia. It designed, raised funding for, and built hospitals, universities, residential properties, high-rise office buildings, industrial facilities, and other infrastructural projects throughout the country. YTL later developed two power plants and a high-speed rail service in Malaysia also on a turnkey basis.

Sellers have increasingly recognized that buyers like to purchase in this way, and many have adopted systems selling as a marketing tool. One variant of systems selling is *systems contracting*, where a single supplier provides the buyer with his or her entire requirement of MRO (maintenance, repair, operating) supplies. During the contract period, the supplier manages the customer's inventory. For example, Shell Oil manages the oil inventory of many of its business customers and knows when it requires replenishment. The customer benefits from reduced procurement and management costs, and from price protection over the term of the contract. The seller benefits from lower operating costs because of a steady demand and reduced paperwork.

Systems selling is a key industrial marketing strategy in bidding to build large-scale industrial projects, such as dams, steel factories, irrigation systems, sanitation systems, pipelines, utilities, and even new towns. Project engineering firms must compete on price, quality, reliability, and other attributes to win contracts. Consider the following example.

Japan and Indonesia—The Indonesian government requested bids to build a cement factory near Jakarta. A U.S. firm's proposal included choosing the site, designing the cement factory, hiring the construction crew, assembling the materials and equipment, and turning over the finished factory to the Indonesian government. A Japanese firm's proposal included all of these services, plus hiring and training the workers to run the factory, exporting the cement through its trading companies, and using the cement to build roads and new office buildings in Jakarta. Although, the Japanese proposal involved more money, it won the contract. Clearly, the Japanese viewed the problem not just as one of building a cement factory (the narrow view of systems selling) but as one of contributing to Indonesia's economic development. They took the broadest view of the customer's needs. This is true systems selling.

Participants in the Business Buying Process

Who buys the trillions of dollars' worth of goods and services needed by business organizations? Purchasing agents are influential in straight-rebuy and modified-rebuy situations, whereas other department personnel are more influential in new-task situations. Engineering personnel usually have a major influence in selecting product components, and purchasing agents dominate in selecting suppliers.[9]

The Buying Center

Webster and Wind call the decision making unit of a buying organization *the buying center*. It is composed of "all those individuals and groups who participate in the purchasing decision making process, who share some common goals and the risks arising from the decisions."[10] The buying center includes all members of the organization who play any of seven roles in the purchasing decision process.[11]

1. ***Initiators*** — Users or others in the organization who request that something be purchased.
2. ***Users*** — Those who will use the product or service. In many cases, the users initiate the buying proposal and help define the product requirements.
3. ***Influencers*** — People who influence the buying decision. They often help define specifications and also provide information for evaluating alternatives. Technical personnel are particularly important influencers.
4. ***Deciders*** — People who decide on product requirements or on suppliers.
5. ***Approvers*** — People who authorize the proposed actions of deciders or buyers.
6. ***Buyers*** — People who have formal authority to select the supplier and arrange the purchase terms. Buyers may help shape product specifications, but they play their major role in selecting vendors and negotiating. In more complex purchases, the buyers might include high-level managers.
7. ***Gatekeepers*** — People who have the power to prevent sellers or information from reaching members of the buying center. For example, purchasing agents, receptionists, and telephone operators may prevent salespersons from contacting users or deciders.

Several individuals can occupy a given role (such as user or influencer), and the individual may occupy multiple roles.[12] A purchasing manager often occupies simultaneously the roles of buyer, influencer, and gatekeeper: He or she can determine which sales reps can call on other people in the organization, what budget and other constraints to place on the purchase; and which firm will actually get the business, even though others (deciders) might select two or more potential vendors who can meet the company's requirements.

The typical buying center has a minimum of five or six members and often has dozens. The buying center may include people outside the target customer organization, such as government officials, consultants, technical advisors, and other members of the marketing channel.

Buying Center Influences

Buying centers usually include several participants with differing interests, authority, status, and persuasiveness. Each member of the buying center is likely to give priority to very different decision criteria. For example, engineering personnel may be concerned primarily with maximizing the actual performance of the product; production personnel may be concerned mainly with ease of use and reliability of supply; financial personnel may focus on the economics of the purchase; purchasing personnel may be concerned with operating and replacement costs; union officials may emphasize safety issues, and so on.

Business buyers also have personal motivations, perceptions, and preferences, that are influenced by the buyer's age, income, education, job position, personality, attitudes toward risk, and culture. Buyers definitely exhibit different buying styles. There are "keep-it-simple" buyers, "own-expert" buyers, "want-the-best" buyers, and "want-everything-done" buyers. Some younger, highly educated buyers are computer experts who conduct rigorous analyses of competitive proposals before choosing a supplier. Other buyers are "toughies" from the old school and pit the competing sellers against one another.

Webster cautions that ultimately, individuals, not organizations, make purchasing decisions.[13] Individuals are motivated by their own needs and perceptions to maximize the rewards (pay, advancement, recognition, and feelings of achievement) offered by the organization. Personal needs "motivate" the behavior of individuals but organizational needs "legitimize" the buying decision process and its outcomes. People are not buying "products." They are buying solutions to two problems: the organization's economic and strategic problem and their own personal "problem" of obtaining individual achievement and reward. In this sense, industrial buying decisions are both "rational" and "emotional," as they serve both the organization's and the individual's needs.[14]

Buying Center Targeting

To target their efforts properly, business marketers have to figure out: Who are the major decision participants? What decisions do they influence? What is their level of influence? What evaluation criteria do they use? Consider the following example:

> *A company sells non-woven disposable surgical gowns to hospitals. The hospital personnel who participate in this buying decision include the purchasing manager, the operating-room administrator, and the surgeons. The purchasing manager analyzes whether the hospital should buy disposable gowns or reusable gowns. If the findings favor disposable gowns, then the operating-room administrator compares various competitors' products and prices and makes a choice. This administrator considers absorbency, antiseptic quality, design, and cost, and normally buys the brand that meets the functional requirements at the lowest cost. Surgeons influence the decision retroactively by reporting their satisfaction with the particular brand.*

The business marketer is not likely to know exactly what kind of group dynamics take place during the decision process, although whatever information he or she can obtain about personalities and interpersonal factors is useful.

Small sellers concentrate on reaching the *key buying influencers.* Larger sellers go for *multilevel in-depth selling* to reach as many participants as possible. Their salespeople virtually "live" with high-volume customers. Companies will have to rely more heavily on their communication programs to reach hidden buying influences and keep current customers informed.[15]

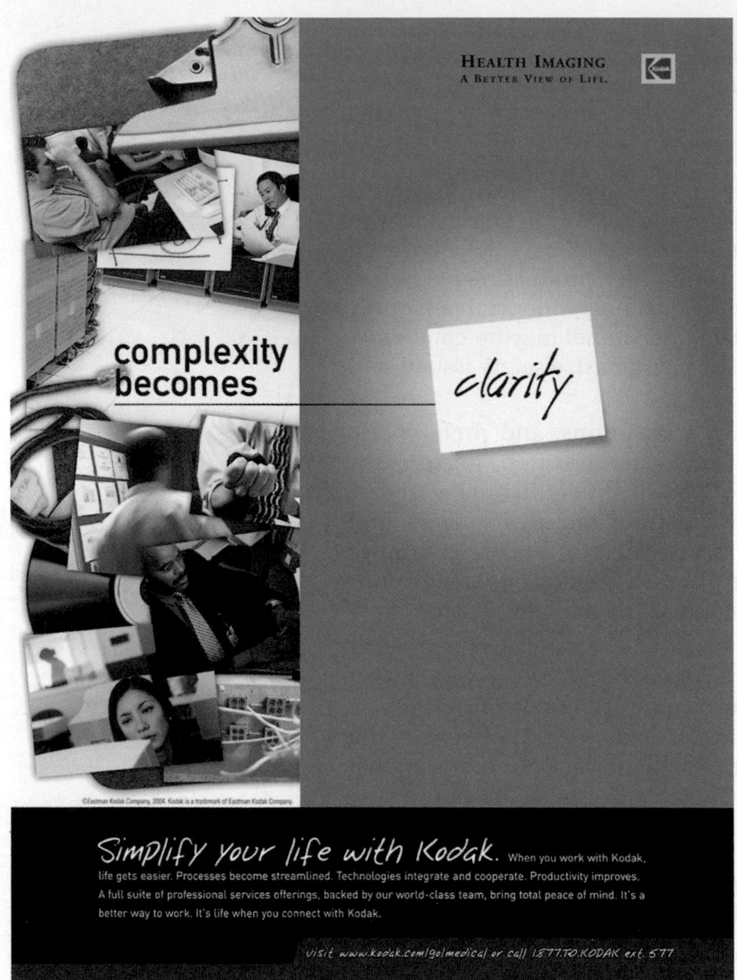

HEALTH IMAGING
A BETTER VIEW OF LIFE.
complexity becomes
clarity
©Eastman Kodak Company, 2004. Kodak is a trademark of Eastman Kodak Company
Simplify your life with Kodak. When you work with Kodak, life gets easier. Processes become streamlined. Technologies integrate and cooperate. Productivity improves. A full suite of professional services offerings, backed by our world-class team, bring total peace of mind. It's a better way to work. It's life when you connect with Kodak.
visit www.kodak.com/go/medical or call 1.877.TO.KODAK ext. 577

A Kodak ad that targets hospital administrators by offering services that streamline processes, integrate technologies, and improve productivity.

Business marketers must periodically review their assumptions about buying center participants. For years, Kodak sold X-ray film to hospital lab technicians. When its research indicated that professional administrators were increasingly making purchasing decisions, Kodak revised its marketing strategy and developed new advertising to reach out to these decision makers.

In defining target segments, four types of business customers can often be identified, with corresponding marketing implications.

1. ***Price-oriented customers*** (transactional selling) — Price is everything.
2. ***Solution-oriented customers*** (consultative selling) — They want low prices but will respond to arguments about lower total cost or more dependable supply or service.
3. ***Gold-standard customers*** (quality selling) — They want the best performance in terms of product quality, assistance, reliable delivery, etc.
4. ***Strategic value customers*** (enterprise selling) — They want a fairly permanent sole-supplier relationship with your company.

Some companies are willing to handle price-oriented buyers by setting a lower price, but establishing restrictive conditions: (1) limiting the quantity that can be purchased; (2) no refunds; (3) no adjustments; and (4) no services.[16]

Risk and gain sharing can be used to offset requested price reductions from customers. For example, say Medline, a hospital supplier, signs an agreement with Kaohsiung Hospital promising $350,000 in savings over the first 18 months in exchange for a tenfold increase of the hospital's share of supplies. If Medline achieves less than this promised savings, it will make up the difference. If Medline achieves substantially more than this promise, it participates in the extra savings. To make such arrangements work, the supplier must be willing to assist the customer to build a historical database, reach an agreement for measuring benefits and costs, and devise a dispute resolution mechanism.

Solution selling can also alleviate price pressure by enhancing customer revenues, decreasing customer risks, and reducing customer costs.

Cummins—This producer of diesel engines and power generators was a market leader in the high-horsepower end of the Indian market, but only a marginal player in the large and rapidly growing low-horsepower market, where buyers such as small retailers, regional hospitals, and farmers demand different features. Farmers, for instance, want engines protected from dirt, while noise is a bigger issue for hospitals. The solution was to modify the products by modularizing them into a series of smaller engines that can be combined with add-ons to customize for different segments. By modularizing the products, Cummins increased production runs of common components, thus keeping overall costs low. This appealed to customers who have tailor-made products at reduced costs. Distributors were also pleased as they need not source for these add-ons themselves. Cost of ownership and cost of sales in the channel are thus decreased.[17]

The Purchasing/Procurement Process

In principle, business buyers seek to obtain the highest benefit package (economic, technical, service, and social) in relation to a market offering's costs. A business buyer's incentive to purchase will be greater in proportion to the ratio of perceived benefits to costs. The marketer's task is to construct a profitable offering that delivers superior customer value to the target buyers.

Purchasing Orientations

In the past, purchasing departments occupied a low position in the management hierarchy, despite often managing more than half the company's costs. Recent competitive pressures have led many companies to upgrade their purchasing departments and elevate administrators to vice presidential rank.

These new, more strategically-oriented purchasing departments seek the best value from fewer and better suppliers. Some multinationals have even elevated them to "strategic supply departments" with responsibility for global sourcing and partnering.

The upgrading of purchasing means that business marketers must upgrade their sales personnel to match the higher caliber of the business buyers. Formally, we can distinguish three company purchasing orientations:[18]

- ***Buying orientation*** — The purchaser's focus is short-term and tactical. Buyers are rewarded on their ability to obtain the lowest price from suppliers for the given level of quality and availability. Buyers use two tactics: *commoditization*, where they imply that the product is a commodity and care only about price; and *multisourcing*, where they use several sources and make them compete for shares of the company's purchases.
- ***Procurement orientation*** — Here buyers simultaneously seek quality improvements and cost reductions. Buyers develop collaborative relationships with major suppliers and seek savings through better management of acquisition, conversion, and disposal costs. They encourage early supplier involvement in materials handling, inventory levels, just-in-time management, and even product design. They negotiate long-term contracts with major suppliers to ensure the timely flow of materials. They work closely with their manufacturing group on Materials Requirement Planning (MRP) to make sure supplies arrive on time.
- ***Supply chain management orientation*** — Here purchasing's role is further broadened to become a more strategic, value-adding operation. Purchasing executives at the firm work with marketing and other company executives to build a seamless supply chain management system from the purchase of raw materials to the on-time arrival of finished goods to the end users.

Types of Purchasing Processes

Marketers need to understand how business purchasing departments work. These departments purchase many types of products, and the purchasing process will vary depending on the types of products involved. Kraljic distinguished four product-related purchasing processes:[19]

1. ***Routine products*** — These products have low value and cost to the customer and involve little risk (e.g., office supplies). Customers will seek the lowest price and emphasize routine ordering. Suppliers will offer to standardize and consolidate orders.
2. ***Leverage products*** — These products have high value and cost to the customer but involve little risk of supply (e.g., engine pistons) because many companies make them. The supplier knows that the customer will compare market offerings and costs, and it needs to show that its offering minimizes the customer's total cost.
3. ***Strategic products*** — These products have high value and cost to the customer and also involve high risk (e.g., mainframe computers). The customer will want a well-known and trusted supplier and be willing to pay more than the average price. The supplier

should seek strategic alliances that take the form of early supplier involvement, co-development programs, and co-investment.

4. ***Bottleneck products*** — These products have low value and cost to the customer but they involve some risk (e.g., spare parts). The customer will want a supplier who can guarantee a steady supply of reliable products. The supplier should propose standard parts and offer a tracking system, delivery on demand, and a help desk.

Purchasing Organization and Administration

Most purchasing professionals describe their jobs as more strategic, technical, team-oriented, and involving more responsibility than ever before. Sixty-one percent of buyers surveyed said the buying group was more involved in new-product design and development than it was five years ago; and more than half of the buyers participate in cross-functional teams, with suppliers well-represented.[20]

In multidivisional companies, most purchasing is carried out by separate divisions. However, some companies have started to centralize purchasing. Headquarters identifies materials purchased by several divisions and buys them centrally, thereby gaining more purchasing clout. The individual divisions can buy from another source if they can get a better deal, but in general, centralized purchasing produces substantial savings. For the business marketer, this development means dealing with fewer and higher-level buyers and using a national account sales group to deal with large corporate buyers. At the same time, companies are decentralizing some purchasing operations by empowering employees to purchase small-ticket items such as special binders, coffeemakers, or Lunar New Year decorations.

Stages in the Buying Process

At this point, we are ready to describe the general stages in the business buying decision process. Robinson and Associates have identified eight stages and called them *buyphases*.[21] The stages are shown in Table 7.1. This model is called the *buygrid framework*.

Table 7.1 describes the buying stages involved in a new-task buying situation. In modified-rebuy or straight-rebuy situations, some stages are compressed or bypassed. For example, in a straight-rebuy situation, the buyer normally has a favorite supplier or a ranked list of suppliers. Thus the supplier search and proposal solicitation stages would be skipped.

The eight-stage buyphase model describes the major steps in the business buying process. Tracing out a buyflow map can provide many clues to the business marketer. A buyflow map for the purchase of a packaging machine in Japan is shown in Figure 7.1. The numbers within the icons are defined at the right. The italicized numbers between icons show the flow of events. Over 20 people in the purchasing company were involved, including the production manager and staff, new-product committee, company laboratory, marketing

Table 7.1 Buygrid Framework: Major Stages (Buyphases) of the Industrial Buying Process in Relation to Major Buying Situations (Buyclasses)

		Buyclasses		
		New-Task	**Modified-Rebuy**	**Straight-Rebuy**
Buyphases	1. Problem recognition	Yes	Maybe	No
	2. General need description	Yes	Maybe	No
	3. Product specification	Yes	Yes	Yes
	4. Supplier search	Yes	Maybe	No
	5. Proposal solicitation	Yes	Maybe	No
	6. Supplier selection	Yes	Maybe	No
	7. Order-routine specification	Yes	Maybe	No
	8. Performance review	Yes	Yes	Yes

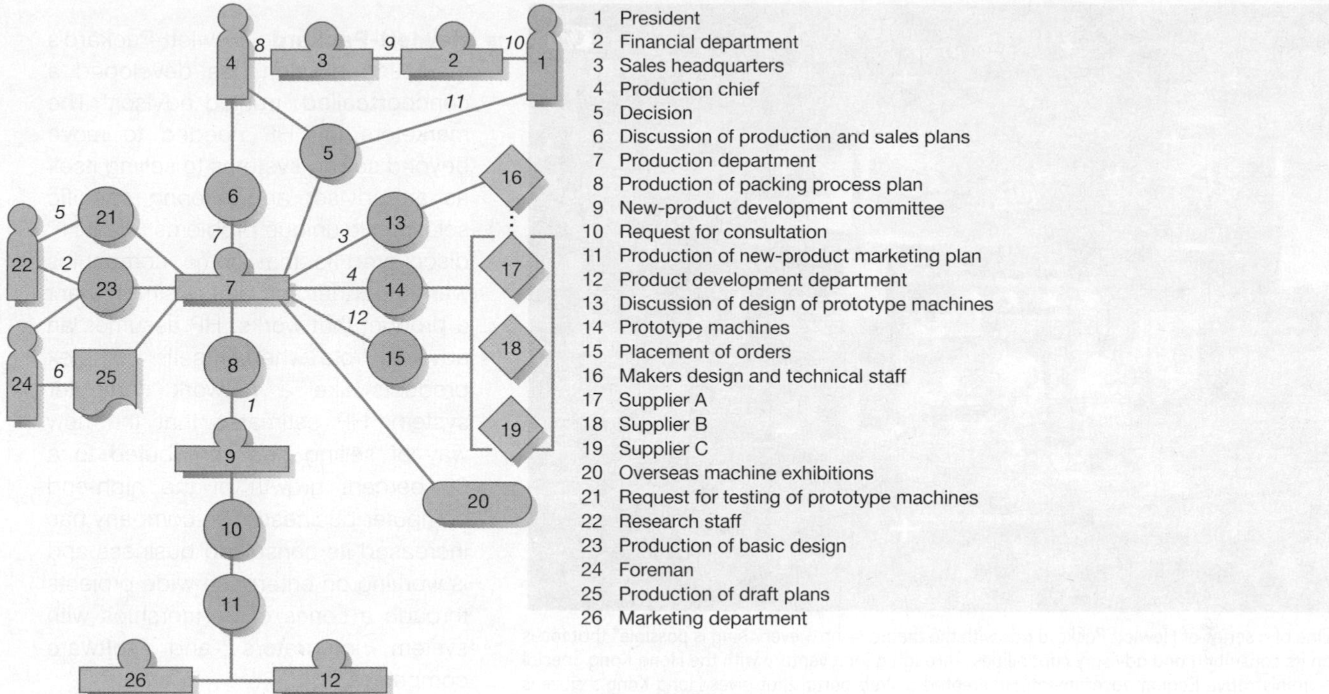

Figure 7.1 Organizational Buying Behavior in Japan: Packaging-Machine Purchase Process

Source: "Japanese Firms Use Unique Buying Behavior." *The Japan Economic Journal,* December 23, 1980, p. 29. Reprinted by permission.

department, and the department for market development. The entire decision making process took 121 days. There are important considerations in each of the eight stages.

Problem Recognition

The buying process begins when someone in the company recognizes a problem or need that can be met by acquiring a good or service. The recognition can be triggered by internal or external stimuli. Internally, some common events lead to problem recognition. The company decides to develop a new product and needs new equipment and materials. A machine breaks down and requires new parts. Purchased material turns out to be unsatisfactory, and the company searches for another supplier. A purchasing manager senses an opportunity to obtain lower prices or better quality. Externally, the buyer may get new ideas at a trade show, see an ad, or receive a call from a sales representative who offers a better product or a lower price. Business marketers can stimulate problem recognition by direct mail, telemarketing, and calling on prospects.

Zoom Technologies—Zoom Technologies has the Zoom, Hayes, and Global Village brands under its umbrella. For its Hayes product line, the company uses a "soft" technology approach in developing Asian markets like China. Each time it adds a new product, it translates all the literature and manuals, and organizes a round of conferences or seminars about the new technology. The conferences focus on providing information on how to use the products and better understand the technology.

General Need Description and Product Specification

Next, the buyer determines the needed item's general characteristics and required quantity. For standard items, this is simple. For complex items, the buyer will work with others—engineers, users—to define characteristics like reliability, durability, or price. Business marketers can help by describing how their products meet or even exceed the buyer's needs. Here is an example of how a supplier is using value-added services to gain a competitive edge.

One of a series of Hewlett Packard ads with the theme "+ hp = everything is possible" that focus on its consulting and advisory capabilities. Through a joint venture with the Hong Kong Special Administrative Region government, HP created a Web portal that gives Hong Kong's citizens 24-hour access to government services.

Hewlett-Packard—Hewlett-Packard's marketing division has developed a concept called "trusted advisor." The marketers felt HP needed to move beyond selling systems to selling itself as an advisor and offering specific solutions to unique problems. What HP discovered is that some companies want a partner and others simply want a product that works. HP assumes an advisory role when it sells complex products like a network computer system. HP estimates that the new way of selling has contributed to a 60 percent growth of the high-end computer business. The company has increased its consulting business and is working on enterprise-wide projects through a series of partnerships with system integrators and software companies.[22]

The buying organization now develops the item's technical specifications. Often, the company will assign a product-value-analysis engineering team to the project. *Product Value Analysis* (PVA) is an approach to cost reduction in which components are studied to determine if they can be redesigned or standardized or made by cheaper methods of production. The PVA team will examine the high-cost components in a given product. The team will also identify overdesigned components that last longer than the product itself. Tightly written specifications will allow the buyer to refuse components that are too expensive or that fail to meet specified standards. Suppliers can use PVA as a tool for positioning themselves to win an account.

Supplier Search

The buyer next tries to identify the most appropriate suppliers through trade directories, contacts with other companies, trade advertisements, trade shows, and the Internet.[23] The move to Internet purchasing has far-reaching implications for suppliers and will change the shape of purchasing for years to come (see "Marketing Insight: The Business-to-Business (B2B) Cyberbuying Bazaar").

B2B marketing needs to be adapted to fit the special needs of the Asian business environment. Asian companies must learn from the development of B2B e-commerce in the U.S. One lesson is that marketplaces launched by big industrial incumbents have the greatest likelihood of success, especially for industries with only a few large buyers or suppliers. "Marketing Insight: The Asian B2B Environment" describes the differences and adaptations needed for B2B e-commerce success in Asia.

E-Procurement

Web sites are organized around two types of e-hubs: *vertical hubs* centered on industries (plastics, steel, chemicals, paper) and *functional hubs* (logistics, media buying, advertising, energy management). Here is an example of an Asian vertical hub:

Global Sources—Global Sources Garments & Textiles Online was launched to help international buyers trade more effectively with apparel manufacturers in China, India, and other supply markets. Global Sources helps trading partners reduce uncertainty and maximize trade opportunities, especially after the lifting of trade quotas in China. It provides reliable and current supplier and product information as well as reviews the capabilities of qualified suppliers.[24]

MARKETING INSIGHT • THE BUSINESS-TO-BUSINESS (B2B) CYBERBUYING BAZAAR

With the growth of consumer online shopping, it is easy to lose sight of one of the most significant trends in e-commerce: the growth of business-to-business e-procurement. In addition to posting their own Web pages on the Internet, companies have established intranets for employees to communicate with one another, and extranets to link a company's communications and data with regular suppliers and distributors.

So far, most of the products businesses are buying electronically are MRO (maintenance, repair, and operations) materials and travel and entertainment services. MRO materials make up 30 percent of business purchases, and the transaction costs for order processing are high, which means there is a huge incentive to streamline the process.

Many brick-and-mortar companies have expanded their online presence by building their business-to-business operations and targeting small businesses. The companies that now purchase over the Internet are utilizing electronic marketplaces that are popping up in several forms:

- ***Catalog sites*** — Companies can order thousands of items through electronic catalogs distributed by e-procurement software. For example, Samsung Corporation's online trading catalog contains over 1,000 products in such diverse categories as chemicals, steel, and textiles.
- ***Vertical markets*** — Companies buying industrial products such as plastics, steel, or chemicals, or services such as logistics or media can go to specialized Web sites (called e-hubs). For example, Plastics.com allows plastics buyers to search for the best prices from the thousands of plastics sellers.
- ***"Pure Play" auction sites*** — These are online marketplaces such as eBay, BayanTrade, and Alibaba that could not have been realized without the Internet and for which no business model existed before their formation.
- ***Spot (or exchange) markets*** — On spot electronic markets, prices change by the minute. For example, ChemConnect is an online exchange for buyers and sellers of bulk chemicals such as benzene.
- ***Private exchanges*** — Hewlett-Packard, IBM, and Wal-Mart operate private exchanges to link with specially invited groups of suppliers and partners over the Web.
- ***Barter markets*** — In these markets, participants offer to trade goods or services.
- ***Buying alliances*** — Several companies buying the same goods join together to form purchasing consortia and gain deeper discounts on volume purchases. For example, Transora is a buying alliance formed by Coca-Cola, Sara Lee, Kraft, PepsiCo, Gillette, and Procter & Gamble.

Online business buying offers several advantages: it shaves transaction costs for both buyers and suppliers, reduces time between order and delivery, consolidates purchasing systems, and forges more intimate relationships between partners and buyers. In Asia, an added advantage is increased transparency, since employees cannot now channel business to favored suppliers in return for kickbacks. On the downside, online business buying may erode supplier-buyer loyalty and create potential security problems. Businesses also face a technological dilemma because no single system yet dominates.

Sources: Robert Yoegel, "The Evolution of B-to-B Selling on the 'Net'." *Target Marketing,* August 1998, p. 34; Andy Reinhardt, "Extranets: Log On, Link Up, Save Big." *BusinessWeek,* June 22, 1998, p. 134; "To Byte the Hand that Feeds." *Economist,* June 17, pp. 61–62; John Evan Frook, "Buying Behemoth--By Shifting $5B in Spending To Extranets, GE Could Ignite a Development Frenzy." *Internetweek,* August 17, 1998, p. 1; Nicole Harris, "Private Exchanges May Allow B-to-B Commerce to Thrive After All." *Wall Street Journal,* March 16, 2001, pp. B1, B4; Olga Kharif, "B2B, Take 2." *BusinessWeek,* November 25, 2003; George S. Day, Adam J. Fein, and Gregg Ruppersberger, "Shakeouts in Digital Markets: Lessons from B2B Exchanges." *California Management Review,* Winter 2003, 45(2), pp. 131–151; Julia Angwin, "Top Online Chemical Exchange is Unlikely Success Story." *Wall Street Journal,* January 8, 2004, p. A15.

In addition to using these Web sites, companies can do e-procurement in other ways:

- ***Set up direct extranet links to major suppliers*** — A company can set up extranet links to its major suppliers. For example, it can set up a direct e-procurement account, and its employees can make their purchases this way.
- ***Form buying alliances*** — Several companies in the petrochemical industry from China, Indonesia, South Korea, Taiwan, and Thailand formed an alliance called Chem-Cross to gain economies of scale in making purchases as well as to provide services such as stock-keeping, financing, insurance, and transportation.
- ***Set up company buying sites*** — Canon's procurement Web site contains its corporate procurement philosophy, fundamental procurement policies, procurement procedures, green procurement activities, a public quote site, and a suppliers proposal site.

MARKETING INSIGHT • THE ASIAN B2B ENVIRONMENT

Companies building B2B marketplaces in Asia have to address and adapt to the Asian business environment:

- **Manufacturing dominates.** Asia is the workshop of the world. Manufacturers buy more "direct" goods used in the final products rather than "indirect" goods that contribute to the product but are not a part of it. In Asia, direct goods account for 80 percent of the total business purchases, compared to 60 percent in the U.S. Trade in direct goods is harder to move online than trade in indirect goods, as the former needs to be tailored to suit a particular production process.

  Thus to gain liquidity, B2B markets serving Asian industries need to target direct goods early. Online marketplaces can begin with simple, standard commodities before moving to complex, engineered goods. Digital asset-management software that allows buyers and sellers to transfer engineering designs and specifications will be required. In industries with few buyers, large savings by purchasing direct goods online will be an incentive. South Korea's B2B online auctions in the chemical industry have yielded savings of 10 to 15 percent. BeXcom, an Asian B2B technology provider, has developed flourishing online marketplaces in the petrochemicals and food industries.

- **Less efficient supply chains.** Distribution and logistics account for a larger percentage of cost in Asia than in Europe and the U.S. There are usually three or four intermediaries between each seller and buyer in Asia compared to one or two in Europe.

  Online marketplaces can make supply chains in Asia more efficient by improving communications between the links and by obviating the need for so many links. Li & Fung works with a number of specialist spinners, knitters, weavers, dyers, sewers, and printers, as well as with wholesalers, retailers, and customers for finished goods. Instead of owning them in a traditional, vertically integrated structure, Li & Fung has leveraged Web technology to manage a multitude of production sites. Each link knows what to produce and when.

- **Less well-developed infrastructure.** The e-commerce infrastructure in Asia lags behind that of the U.S. Most Asian countries lack an efficient online payment system. There are few third-party logistics providers and the mechanisms for managing suppliers' credit risk and protecting against defaulting debtors are not well-developed. Information on the finances of companies involved is also scarce.

  Asian marketplaces can fill this void by going beyond the matchmaker role between buyers and sellers. For example, NECX is a consumer electronics marketplace that provides inventory management, financial settlement, and global logistics management services as well as quality assurance checks on Asian suppliers.

- **Smaller markets.** B2B markets targeting any single Asian country are unlikely to attract enough home demand for success. To combat the problem of small home markets, Asian B2B marketplaces need to target users in bigger Asian regions and in developed countries. Chinese B2B Web site Alibaba.com had global aspirations from the outset, targeting SMEs worldwide. Its business model focuses on removing the disadvantages SMEs face when conducting international trade. Alibaba has an English-language Web site catering to international merchants seeking Chinese products to import. It also operates a Chinese-language site which serves buyers and sellers interested in the domestic China trade. Its third Web site, Taobao, is free for individuals to trade through fixed-price or auction transactions. Yahoo! bought a 35 percent stake in Alibaba for US$1 billion in 2005 to expand its exposure in China. Regional players in the same industry can also gain scale by collaborating to form a vertical B2B marketplace as the petrochemical buyers and sellers in China, Indonesia, Korea, Taiwan, and Thailand did when they formed ChemCross, a petrochemical marketplace.

Sources: Rajat K. Dhawan, Ramesh Mangaleswaran, Asutosh Padhi, Shirish Sankhe, Karsten Schween, and Paresh Viash, "The Asian Difference in B2B." *McKinsey Quarterly*, 2000, 4, p. 38; Mylene Mangalindan, "Yahoo is in Talks to Buy Alibaba.com Stake." *Asian Wall Street Journal*, August 10, 2005, p. A3.

Moving into e-procurement involves more than acquiring software; it requires changing purchasing strategy and structure. However, the benefits are many: Aggregating purchases across multiple departments gains larger, centrally negotiated volume discounts. There is less buying of substandard goods from outside the approved list of suppliers, and a smaller purchasing staff is required.

The supplier's task is to get listed in major online catalogs or services, develop a strong advertising and promotion program, and build a good reputation in the marketplace. This often means creating a well-designed and easy-to-use Web site.

Hewlett-Packard—In 2003, Hewlett-Packard Co. was named number 1 in *B2B* magazine's annual ranking of the top B2B Web sites. The site <www.hp.com> was launched after HP's merger with Compaq Computer and has 2.5 million pages and roughly 1,900 site areas. The challenge for HP was to integrate this enormous amount of information and present it coherently. Upon entering the site, users can click directly into their customer segment and search for information by product or by solution or click into a product category. The site allows companies to create customized catalogs for frequently purchased products, set up automatic approval routing for orders, and conduct end-to-end transaction processing. To strengthen relationships with customers, HP.com features Flash demos that show how to use the site, e-newsletters, live chats with sales reps, online classes, and real-time customer support. HP's Web efforts are paying off big: roughly 55 percent of the company's total sales come from the Web site.[25]

Suppliers who lack the required production capacity or suffer from a poor reputation will be rejected. Those who qualify may be visited by the buyer's agents, who will examine the suppliers' manufacturing facilities and meet their personnel. After evaluating each company, the buyer will end up with a shortlist of qualified suppliers. Many professional buyers have forced suppliers to change their marketing to increase their likelihood of making the cut.

Proposal Solicitation

The buyer next invites qualified suppliers to submit proposals. If the item is complex or expensive, the buyer will require a detailed written proposal from each qualified supplier. After evaluating the proposals, the buyer will invite a few suppliers to make formal presentations.

Business marketers must be skilled in researching, writing, and presenting proposals. Written proposals should be marketing documents that describe value and benefits in customer terms. Oral presentations should inspire confidence, and position the company's capabilities and resources so that they stand out from the competition. Consider the hurdles that Xerox has set up in qualifying suppliers.

Xerox—Xerox qualifies only suppliers who meet the ISO 9000 quality standards, but to win the company's top award—certification status—a supplier must first complete the Xerox Multinational Supplier Quality Survey. The survey requires the supplier to issue a quality assurance manual, to adhere to continuous improvement principles, and to demonstrate effective systems implementation. Once qualified, a supplier must participate in Xerox's Continuous Supplier Involvement process: the two companies work together to create specifications for quality, cost, delivery times, and process capability. The final step toward certification requires a supplier to undergo additional, rigorous quality training and an evaluation based on the same criteria as the Malcolm Baldridge National Quality Award. Not surprisingly, only 176 suppliers worldwide have achieved the 95 percent rating required for certification as a Xerox supplier.[26]

Supplier Selection

Before selecting a supplier, the buying center will specify desired supplier attributes and indicate their relative importance. To rate and identify the most attractive suppliers, buying centers often use a supplier-evaluation model such as the one shown in Table 7.2.

Table 7.2 An Example of Vendor Analysis

Attributes	Importance weights			Rating Scale	
		Poor (1)	Fair (2)	Good (3)	Excellent (4)
Price	0.30				X
Supplier reputation	0.20			X	
Product reliability	0.30				X
Service reliability	0.10		X		
Supplier flexibility	0.10			X	
Total score: 0.30(4) + 0.20(3) + 0.30(4) + 0.10(2) + 0.10(3) = 3.5					

Business marketers need to do a better job of understanding how business buyers arrive at their valuations.[27] Researchers have found that business marketers employed eight different *Customer Value Assessment* (CVA) methods to assess customer value. Companies tended to use the simpler methods, although the more sophisticated ones promise to produce a more accurate picture of the customer perceived value (see "Marketing Memo: Developing Compelling Customer Value Propositions").

MARKETING MEMO • DEVELOPING COMPELLING CUSTOMER VALUE PROPOSITIONS

To command price premiums in competitive B2B markets, firms must create compelling customer value propositions. The first step is to research the customer. Here are a number of productive research methods:

1. ***Internal engineering assessment*** — Company engineers use laboratory tests to estimate the product's performance characteristics. However, this ignores the fact that in different applications, the product will have different economic value.
2. ***Field value-in-use assessment*** — Customers are interviewed about cost elements associated with using the new-product offering compared to an incumbent product. The task is to assess how much each element is worth to the buyer.
3. ***Focus-group value assessment*** — Customers in a focus group are asked what value they would put on potential market offerings.
4. ***Direct survey questions*** — Customers are asked to place a direct dollar value on one or more changes in the market offering.
5. ***Conjoint analysis*** — Customers are asked to rank their preference for alternative market offerings or concepts. Statistical analysis is used to estimate the implicit value placed on each attribute.
6. ***Benchmarks*** — Customers are shown a "benchmark" offering and then a new market offering. They are asked how much more they would pay for the new offering or how much less they would pay if certain features were removed from the benchmark offering.
7. ***Compositional approach*** — Customers are asked to attach a monetary value to each of three alternative levels of a given attribute. This is repeated for other attributes. The values are then added together for any offer configuration.
8. ***Importance ratings*** — Customers are asked to rate the importance of different attributes and the supplier firms, performance on these attributes.

Having done this research, you can specify the customer value proposition, following a number of important principles. First, clearly substantiate value claims by concretely specifying the differences between your offerings and those of competitors on the dimensions that matter most to the customer. For example, Rockwell Automation determined the cost savings customers would realize from purchasing its pump solution instead of a competitor's by using industry-standard metrics of functionality and performance: kilowatt-hours spent, number of operating hours per year, and dollars per killowatt-hour. Also, make the financial implications obvious.

Second, document the value delivered by creating written accounts of costs savings or added value that existing customers have actually captured by using your offerings. Chemical producer Akzo Nobel conducted a two-week pilot on a production reactor at a prospective customer's facility to document points-of-parity and points-of-difference of its high-purity metal organics product.

Finally, make sure the customer value proposition is well implemented within the company, the train and reward employees for developing a compelling one. Quaker Chemical conducts training programs for its managers that include a competition to develop the best proposals.

Sources: James C. Anderson, James A. Narus, and Wouter van Rossum, "Customer Value Propositions in Business Markets." *Harvard Business Review,* March 2006, pp. 2–10; James C. Anderson and James A. Narus, "Business Marketing: Understanding What Customers Value." *Harvard Business Review,* November 1998, pp. 53–65; James C. Anderson, and James A. Narus, "Capturing the Value of Supplementary Services." *Harvard Business Review,* January 1995, pp. 75–83; James C. Anderson, Dipak C. Jain, and Pradeep K. Chintagunta, "A customer Value Assessment in Business Markets: A State-of-Practice." *Journal of Business-to-Business Marketing,* January 1993, 1(1), pp. 3–29.

The choice and importance of different attributes varies with the type of buying situation.[28] Delivery reliability, price, and supplier reputation are important for routine-order products. For procedural-problem products, such as a copying machine, the three most important attributes are technical service, supplier flexibility, and product reliability. For political-problem products that stir rivalries in the organization (such as the choice of a computer system), the most important attributes are price, supplier reputation, product reliability, service reliability, and supplier flexibility.

OVERCOMING PRICE PRESSURES

The buying center may attempt to negotiate with preferred suppliers for better prices and terms before making the final selection. Despite moves toward strategic sourcing, partnering, and participation in cross-functional teams, buyers still spend a large chunk of their time haggling with suppliers on price, particularly in emerging Asian countries.

Marketers can counter the request for a lower price in a number of ways. They may be able to show evidence that the "total cost of ownership," that is, the "life-cycle cost" of using their product is lower than that of competitors' products. They can also cite the value of the services the buyer now receives, especially if those services are superior to those offered by competitors.

NUMBER OF SUPPLIERS

As a part of the buyer selection process, buying centers must decide how many suppliers to use. Companies like Nissan and Motorola are increasingly reducing the number of suppliers. These companies want their chosen suppliers to be responsible for a larger component system; they want them to achieve continuous quality and performance improvement while at the same time lowering the supply price each year by a given percentage. These companies expect their suppliers to work closely with them during product development, and they value their suggestions. There is even a trend toward single sourcing.

Xilinx—Xilinx is a global leader in programmatic logic technology. It has a large requirement for semiconductors, but the semiconductor market is highly volatile, and products can be in short supply during peak demand periods. To ensure that its demand for semiconductors is satisfied, Xilinx invested $150 million toward building a new fabrication plant for Taiwan's United Microelectronics, in return for a 25 percent stake in the company. For this, United Microelectronics commits to meeting Xilinx's needs through its existing facilities.

Companies that use multiple sources often cite the threat of a labor strike as the biggest deterrent to single sourcing. Another reason companies may be reluctant to use a single source is they fear they will become too comfortable in the relationship and lose their competitive edge.

Order-Routine Specification

After selecting suppliers, the buyer negotiates the final order, listing the technical specifications, the quantity needed, the expected time of delivery, return policies, warranties, and so on. Many industrial buyers lease heavy equipment like machinery and trucks. The lessee gains a number of advantages: conserving capital, getting the latest products, receiving better service, and some tax advantages. The lessor often ends up with a larger net income and the chance to sell to customers who could not afford outright purchase.

Buyers are moving toward blanket contracts rather than periodic purchase orders for maintenance, repair, and operating items. A blanket contract establishes a long-term relationship in which the supplier promises to resupply the buyer as needed, at agreed-upon prices, over a specified period of time. Because the stock is held by the seller, blanket contracts are sometimes called *stockless purchase plans*. The buyer's computer automatically sends an order to the seller when stock is needed. This system locks suppliers in tighter with the buyer and makes it difficult for out-suppliers to break in unless the buyer becomes dissatisfied with the in-supplier's prices, quality, or service.

Companies that fear a shortage of key materials are willing to buy and hold large inventories. They will sign long-term contracts with suppliers to ensure a steady flow of materials. Major companies regard long-term supply planning as a major responsibility of their purchasing managers. For example, Toyota may want to buy from fewer suppliers who are willing to locate close to its plants and produce high-quality components. In addition, business marketers are using the Internet to set up extranets with important customers to facilitate and lower the cost of transactions. The customers enter orders directly on the computer, and these orders are automatically transmitted to the supplier. Some companies go further and shift the ordering responsibility to their suppliers in systems called *vendor-managed inventory*. These suppliers are privy to the customer's inventory levels and take responsibility to replenish it automatically through *continuous replenishment programs*.

Performance Review

The buyer periodically reviews the performance of the chosen supplier(s). Three methods are commonly used. The buyer may contact the end users and ask for their evaluations; the buyer may rate the supplier on several criteria using a weighted score method; or the buyer might aggregate the cost of poor performance to come up with adjusted costs of purchase, including price. The performance review may lead the buyer to continue, modify, or end a supplier relationship.

Many companies have set up incentive systems to reward purchasing managers for good buying performance, in much the same way that sales personnel receive bonuses for good selling performance. These systems are leading purchasing managers to increase pressure on sellers for the best terms.

Managing Business-to-Business Customer Relationships

To improve effectiveness and efficiency, business suppliers and customers are exploring different ways to manage their relationships. Closer relationships are driven in part by trends related to supply chain management, early supplier involvement, purchasing alliances, and so on.[29] Cultivating the right relationships with business is paramount with any holistic marketing program. A master at business-to-business marketing is GE, as chronicled in "Breakthrough Marketing: General Electric." "Marketing Insight: Rules of Social and Business Etiquette" shows how business relationships are handled in Asia.

Foreign companies would do well to understand that many Asian countries are deeply rooted in Confucian values and ideology. When hiring, for instance, school affiliation and age are important factors that are considered besides merit. The relationships among individuals cultivated through affiliation to the same school, region, or family create strong societal ties that bind these individuals to their communities, and in turn extend to a sense of obligation to the workplace. Confucian influence is implied in many Asian organizations—they are more hierarchical rather than matrix in structure. This means that finding a functional expert tends to be relatively more difficult as executives are rotated across divisions. Consensus decision making is also well entrenched in Asia, with few responsibilities allocated to junior executives. Finally, title is regarded highly in Asia. With title comes respect and "face" which matter a lot in Asian society.[30]

The Benefits of Vertical Coordination

Much research has advocated greater vertical coordination between buying partners and sellers so that they transcend mere transactions to engage in activities that create more value for both parties. Building trust between parties is often seen as one prerequisite to healthy long-term relationships.[31] "Marketing Insight: Establishing Corporate Trust and Credibility" identifies some key dimensions of those concepts. Consider the mutual benefits from the following arrangement.

BREAKTHROUGH • MARKETING

GENERAL ELECTRIC

GE is made up of six major divisions that operate in areas as diverse as home appliances, jet engines, security systems, wind turbines, and financial services. The company is so large that if each of its six business units were ranked separately, all would appear in the *Fortune* 500. If GE were a country, it would be one of the 50 largest, ahead of Finland, Israel, and Ireland.

Founded by Thomas Edison as the Edison Electric Light Company in 1878, GE was an early pioneer in light bulbs and electrical appliances. It also served the electrical needs of various industries, such as transportation, utilities, manufacturing, and broadcasting.

In 2003, GE faced a new challenge: how to promote its diversified brand globally with a unified message. Its major new campaign, called "Imagination at Work," highlighted its renewed focus on innovation and new technology. The award-winning campaign promoted units such as GE Aircraft Engines, GE Medical Systems, and GE Plastics, focusing on the breadth of GE's product offerings. GE spends some $150 million on corporate advertising—a large expenditure, but one that creates efficiencies by focusing on the core GE brand. The goal was to unify these divisions under the GE brand while giving them a voice. "When you're a company like ours, with 11 different businesses, brand is really important in pulling the identity of the company together," said former Chief Marketing Officer Beth Comstock. "Integration was important in communicating the brand across the organization and to all of our constituents."

The new integrated campaign got results. "Research indicates GE is now being associated with attributes such as being high-tech, leading-edge, innovative, contemporary, and creative," said Judy Hu, GE's general manager for global advertising and branding. Just as encouraging, survey respondents still associate GE with some of its traditional attributes, such as being trustworthy and reliable.

In 2005, the company extended the campaign with its next initiative, "Ecomagination," which highlighted the company's efforts to develop environmentally friendly "green" technologies. It leveraged the "Imagination" tagline again with a 2006 campaign called "Health-Care Re-Imagined" that featured innovative GE health-care products for detecting, preventing, and curing diseases.

While the campaign unites all GE business units, GE's success rests on its ability to understand the business market and the business buying process, putting itself in the shoes of its business customers. Consider its approach to pricing its aircraft engines. GE is aware that purchasing an aircraft engine is a multi million-dollar expenditure. And it doesn't end with the purchase of the engine—customers (airlines) face substantial maintenance costs to meet FAA guidelines and ensure reliability of the engines. So in 1999, GE pioneered a new pricing option. The concept, called "Power by the Hour," gives customers an opportunity to pay a fixed fee each time they run the engine. In return, GE performs all the maintenance and guarantees the engine's reliability. When demand for air travel is uncertain, GE gives its customers a lower cost of ownership.

This kind of B2B marketing savvy helped GE cement its top position in the *Financial Times* "World's Most Respected Companies" survey for six consecutive years. Its understanding of the business markets, its way of doing business, and its brand marketing have kept GE's brand equity growing. Indeed, its brand equity was valued at $51.6 billion in the 2007 Interbrand/*BusinessWeek* ranking of the top 100 Global Brands, placing it fourth among all brands. "The GE brand is what connects us all and makes us so much better than the parts," Comstock said.

Sources: Geoffrey Colvin, "What Makes GE Great?" *Fortune*, March 6, 2006, pp. 90–104; Thomas A. Stewart, "Growth as a Process." *Harvard Business Review*, June 2006, pp. 60–70; Kathryn Kranhold, "The Immelt Era, Five Years Old, Transforms GE." *Wall Street Journal*, September 11, 2006; Daniel Fisher, "GE Turns Green." *Forbes*, August 15, 2005, pp. 80–85; John A. Byrne, "Jeff Immelt." *Fast Company*, July 2005, pp. 60–65.

MARKETING INSIGHT • RULES OF SOCIAL AND BUSINESS ETIQUETTE

Here are some rules of social and business etiquette that marketers should understand when doing business in Asian countries:

- ***China*** — Not letting others lose "face" or esteem is important to the Chinese. This can be achieved by being polite, not doing anything that can be regarded as insulting, and being firm graciously. The Chinese are sensitive about relationships with foreigners. Patience is also crucial as many things take a long time to process in China. The most important ingredient of a business relationship with a foreigner is trust and confidence in you as a person.
- ***India*** — Indians are gracious business hosts and are quite informal and relaxed in their approach to business negotiations. They greet with hands folded, *namaste*. Except for formal dinners and special meetings, chief executives of companies generally conduct business in casual dress. Although Indians are tolerant people who will overlook many a social *faux pas* or misunderstanding on the basis that you are a foreign guest in their country, any belittling of their country or culture, or outward display of arrogance and condescension, is likely to alienate them and possibly terminate the relationship. Indians do not operate with stopwatch precision. Appointments are generally approximate timings as the difficulties of getting through congested traffic may cause delays. Conversely, drop-in visits by foreign businesspeople are equally acceptable.
- ***Indonesia*** — Indonesians are friendly, soft-spoken, and conservative in dress and behavior. Thus avoid raising your voice or displaying displeasure as embarrassing anyone in public is an insult. When an Indonesian laughs, it may sometimes be to cover feelings of embarrassment or anger as well as amusement. Indonesians like to work with people they know. Therefore, to succeed in business, a high profile is needed by attending social and business functions.
- ***Japan*** — Most Japanese businesspeople know what will be discussed at a meeting, how everyone feels about it, and how it will affect their business before they even get there. The purpose of a meeting is to reach consensus. A flexible agenda is necessary so that discussions flow more freely. There is a ritual to the exchange of business cards. Cards are presented with both hands and facing the recipient so that they can be easily read. Examine carefully each business card you receive to show interest. It is impolite to write anything on somebody else's card. Diplomacy is required in gift-giving. It is a ritual in Japan and a way to show business contacts your appreciation of their time and assistance.
- ***Korea*** — Be sensitive to Korea's historical animosity toward Japan. Koreans do not like foreigners to assume that their culture is the same as Japan's. However, Koreans respect Japanese business acumen, and, like the Japanese, still observe Confucian ethics based on respect for authority and the primacy of the group over the individual. A lot of drinking and eating is involved in doing business. Do not be afraid to let your hair down at business social functions, even though Koreans may appear reserved and staid during negotiations. Despite the international trend and new attitudes of its younger generation, Korea is still a male-dominated society. This may affect how a female executive is treated on a business trip.
- ***Malaysia*** — Expect some bureaucratic red tape especially when dealing with government departments, although the private sector tends to be more efficient. Malaysians are easy-going, relaxed, and informal. Politeness is very important in all social and business interactions. When a business associate visits, the Malaysian will offer tea or coffee, and it is polite to accept and take a few sips when invited to drink. When accepting something from someone, it is polite to stoop a little and accept with both hands. Public demonstrations of affection such as hugging and touching are considered bad manners. Do not wear black, white, or navy blue at weddings as these are colors of mourning. At royal functions, avoid wearing yellow which is a color associated with royalty.
- ***Philippines*** — Filipinos are not known to hold appointments sacred. However, they are among the most hospitable people in the world. They place great emphasis on personal relations. *Pakikisama* or a sense of camaraderie, consideration, and sensitivity is important for a successful business relationship. Impersonal goals are meaningless to Filipinos. As such, frequent meetings, consultations, and correspondence are necessary to establish and maintain relationships. It is also not fruitful to be formal and businesslike all the time. Filipinos are influenced by traditional values. *Utang na loob* is a lifelong sense of obligation for an important favor granted. *Amor propio*, or pride, is similar to the concept of "face" in other Asian societies. Patience, sensitivity, and persistence are important in business. There is a tendency to reach decisions indirectly or through a third party. Sometimes, important decisions are made even before a meeting to avoid disagreement.
- ***Taiwan*** — Promptness is not regarded as important. Instead, it is *how* the time is spent that counts. Time should allow for informal conversation, getting to know your family, and extended dining. Business relationships are built on *guanxi*. The personal bond or contact is thus important. Hence, whenever possible, it is best to seek a mutual acquaintance for an introduction to a potential business associate. Protocol is valued. Sending a senior representative of your firm to make a personal call on a relatively small company in Taiwan will confer a good deal of face and help establish relations on a good footing. The Taiwanese consider splitting a bill the ultimate *faux pas*. Be prepared to make a show of paying and be gracious of your "failure" when the host pays. At dinners, you will be asked to *gan bei*—literally, "empty your glass"—the equivalent of "cheers." Getting mildly drunk is no loss of face and can go toward creating a pleasant ambience.

(Continued ...)

MARKETING INSIGHT • RULES OF SOCIAL AND BUSINESS ETIQUETTE

(Continued ...)

- ***Thailand*** — An important quality in Thai business is to have fun. If a transaction is not enjoyable, then the Thai businessperson will think there is something wrong with it. Therefore, you must look as if you are enjoying both your job and your negotiations. Another challenge is to correctly pronounce the names of your Thai associates such as Amatakulchai or Chantasakuldrong. Getting their names right enhances their respect for you and improves your chances of success. Thais are also mindful about cleanliness and neatness. Thus personal appearance, presentation materials, and products must be handled professionally.

Sources: Teresa C. Morrison, Wayne A. Conaway, and Joseph J. Douress, *Dun & Bradstreet's Guide to Doing Business Around the World*, (New York: Prentice Hall, 1997); "Tips, Tricks and Pitfalls to Avoid When Doing Business in the Tough But Lucrative Korean Market." *Business America*, June 1997, p. 7; *Negotiating in Asia*, 1991, Hong Kong: Trade Media Ltd., Asian Sources Group of Trade Journals; "Business Etiquette–Indonesia." *Rapport Quarterly*, October 1995, p. 2.

MARKETING INSIGHT • ESTABLISHING CORPORATE TRUST AND CREDIBILITY

Strong bonds and relationships between firms depend on their perceived credibility. *Corporate credibility* refers to the extent to which customers believe that a firm can design and deliver products and services that satisfy their needs and wants. Corporate credibility relates to the reputation that a firm has achieved in the marketplace and is the foundation for a strong relationship. It is difficult for a firm to develop strong ties with another firm unless it is seen as highly credible.

Corporate credibility, in turn, depends on three factors:

- ***Corporate expertise*** — The extent to which a company is seen as able to make and sell products or conduct services.
- ***Corporate trustworthiness*** — The extent to which a company is seen as motivated to be honest, dependable, and sensitive to customer needs.
- ***Corporate likability*** — The extent to which a company is seen as likable, attractive, prestigious, dynamic, etc.

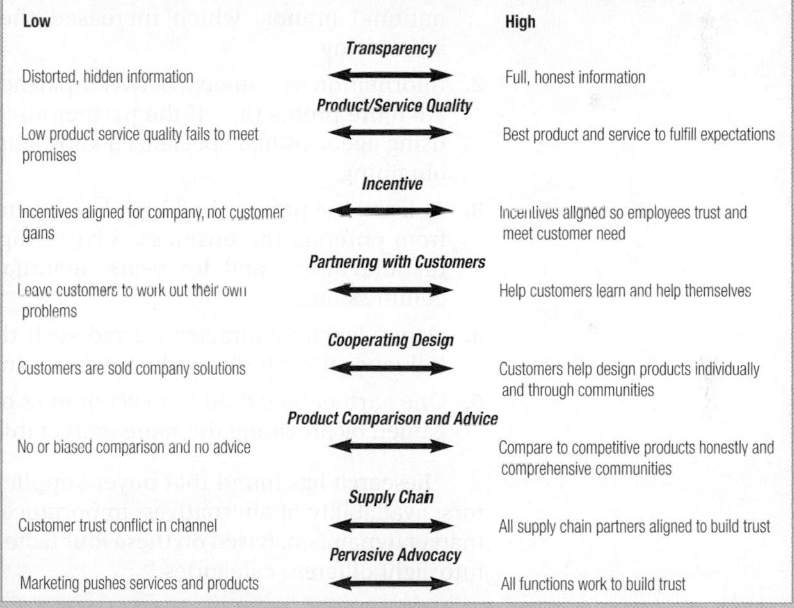

Figure 7.2 Trust Dimensions

Source: Glen Urban, "Where Are You Positioned On the Trust Dimensions?" *Don't Just Relate–Advocate. A Blueprint for Profit in the Era of Customer Power*, (Wharton School Publishers, 2005) p. 99.

In other words, a credible firm is seen as being good at what it does; it keeps its customers' best interests in mind and is enjoyable to work with.

Trust is a particularly important determinant of credibility and a firm's relationships with other firms. Trust is reflected in the willingness and confidence of a firm to rely on a business partner. A number of interpersonal and interorganizational factors affect trust in a business-to-business relationship, such as the perceived competence, integrity, honesty, and benevolence of the firm. Trust will be affected by personal interactions between employees of a firm as well as opinions about the company as a whole, and perceptions of trust will evolve with more experience with a company. Figure 7.2 provides a summary of some core dimensions of trust.

Trust can be especially tricky in online settings, and firms often impose more stringent requirements on their online business partners. Business buyers worry that they won't get products of the right quality delivered to the right place at the right time. Sellers worry about getting paid on time—or at all—and how much credit they should extend. Some firms are using tools such as automated credit-checking applications and online trust services to help determine the credibility of trading partners.

Sources: Robert M. Morgan and Shelby D. Hunt, "The Commitment-Trust Theory of Relationship Marketing." *Journal of Marketing,* 1994, 58(3), pp. 20-38; Christine Moorman, Rohit Deshpandé, and Gerald Zaltman, "Factors Affecting Trust in Market Research Relationships." *Journal of Marketing,* January 1993, 57, pp. 81-101; Kevin Lane Keller and David A. Aaker, "Corporate-Level Marketing: The Impact of Credibility on a Company's Brand Extensions." *Corporate Reputation Review,* August 1, 1998, pp. 356-378; Bob Violino, "Building B2B Trust." *Computerworld,* June 17, 2002, p. 32; Richard E. Plank, David A. Reid, and Ellen Bolman Pullins, "Perceived Trust in Business-to-Business Sales: A New Measure." *Journal of Personal Selling and Sales Management,* Summer 1999, 19(3), pp. 61-72.

Motoman Inc. and Stillwater Technologies—Motoman Inc., a leading supplier of industry robotic systems, and Stillwater Technologies, a contract tooling and machinery company and a key supplier to Motoman, are tightly integrated. Not only do they occupy office and machinery space in the same facility, they also share a common lobby, conference room, employee cafeteria, and have linked their telephone and computer systems. Aside from the benefit of short delivery distances, employees of both companies have ready access to one another and can share ideas on improving quality and reducing costs. This close relationship has opened the door to new opportunities. Both companies had been doing work for Honda, who suggested that they collaborate on systems projects. This integration makes the two companies larger than they are individually.[32]

One historical study of four very different business-to-business relationships found that several factors, by affecting partner interdependence and/or environmental uncertainty, influenced the development of a relationship between business partners.[33] The relationship between advertising agencies and clients illustrates these findings:

1. In the relationship formation stage, one partner experienced substantial market growth. Manufacturers capitalizing on mass production techniques developed national brands, which increased the importance and amount of mass media advertising.
2. Information asymmetry between partners was such that a partnership would generate more profits than if the partner attempted to invade the other firm's area. Advertising agencies had specialized knowledge that their clients would have had difficulty obtaining.
3. At least one partner had high barriers to entry that would prevent the other partner from entering the business. Advertising agencies could not easily become national manufacturers, and for years, manufacturers were not eligible to receive media commissions.
4. Dependence asymmetry existed such that one partner was more able to control or influence the other's conduct. Advertising agencies had control over media access.
5. One partner benefited from economies of scale related to the relationship. Ad agencies gained by providing the same market information to multiple clients.

Research has found that buyer-supplier relationships differed according to four factors: availability of alternatives; importance of supply; complexity of supply; and supply market dynamism. Based on these four factors, they classified buyer-supplier relationships into eight different categories:[34]

1. ***Basic buying and selling***— Relatively simple, routine exchanges with moderately high levels of cooperation and information exchange.
2. ***Bare bones*** — Similar to basic buying and selling but more adaptation by the seller and less cooperation and information exchange.
3. ***Contractual transaction***—Generally low levels of trust, cooperation, and interaction; exchange is defined by a formal contract.
4. ***Customer supply*** — Traditional custom supply situation where competition rather than cooperation is the dominant form of governance.
5. ***Cooperative systems*** — Although coupled closely in operational ways, neither party demonstrates structural commitment through legal means or adaptation approaches.
6. ***Collaborative***— Much trust and commitment leading to true partnership.
7. ***Mutually adaptive***— Much relationship-specific adaptation for buyer and seller, but without necessarily strong trust or cooperation.
8. ***Customer is king***— Although bonded by a close, cooperative relationship, the seller adapts to meet the customer's needs without expecting much adaptation or change on the part of the customer in exchange.

Some firms find that their needs can be satisfied with fairly basic supplier performance. They do not want or require a close relationship with a supplier. Alternatively, some suppliers may not find it worth their while to invest in customers with limited growth potential. One study found that the closest relationships between customer and suppliers arose when the supply was important to the customer and when there were procurement obstacles such as complex purchase requirements and few alternative suppliers.[35] Another study suggested that greater vertical coordination between buyer and seller through information exchange and planning is usually necessary only when high environmental uncertainty exists and specific investments are modest.[36]

Business Relationships: Risks and Opportunism

To understand how Dome Coffee worked its business relationships to grow its operations from Australia to an international presence, visit www.pearsoned.com.au/marketingmanagementaustralia.

Researchers have noted that in establishing a customer-supplier relationship, there is tension between safeguarding and adaptation. Vertical coordination can facilitate stronger customer-seller ties but at the same time may increase the risk to the customer's and supplier's specific investments. *Specific investments* are those expenditures tailored to a particular company and value chain partner (e.g., investments in company-specific training, equipment, and operating procedures or systems).[37] Specific investments help firms grow profits and achieve their positioning.[38] Consider the following example:

Li & Fung—Hong Kong's largest export trading company has transformed itself from being a regional buying agent to a supply chain manager of clothing. Initially, Li & Fung leveraged its knowledge of the region in buying for large U.S. retail chains like The Limited, as its knowledge of which textile quotas have been used up and where to obtain alternative supplies was important. Later, its customers began to ask Li & Fung to develop production programs based on the sketches of their designers. Li & Fung researched the market on different types of yarn and dye swatches and matched the colors to these sketches. Buyers would then assess and modify Li & Fung's prototypes. Li & Fung creates an entire program for each individual customer by specifying the product mix and production schedule. It contracts for all the supplies, works with factories to plan and monitor production, and coordinates the logistics to ensure on-time delivery. For example, to fulfill an order of 10,000 garments from a European retailer, Li & Fung may buy yarn from Korea and have it woven and dyed in Taiwan. Then, based on quota considerations and labor conditions, it may ship these raw materials to manufacture the garments in Thailand. To ensure quick delivery, it may divide the order across five Thai factories. Effectively, Li & Fung is customizing the value chain to best meet their customers' needs.[39]

Specific investments, however, also entail considerable risk to both customer and supplier. Transaction theory from economics maintains that because these investments are partially sunk, they lock in the firms that make the investments to a particular relationship. Sensitive cost and process information may need to be exchanged. A buyer may be vulnerable to holdup because of switching costs; a supplier may be more vulnerable to holdup in future contracts because of dedicated assets and/or expropriation of technology/knowledge.[40] Consider the following example:

Acer—This Taiwanese company started out being a contract manufacturer for computer makers like Unisys and Texas Instruments. As its knowledge and experience grew, Acer began to make and market its own PC brand as well. Customers complained that having both businesses caused much conflict of interest. If Acer made a certain notebook computer for, say, IBM, this Acer-made IBM-branded notebook would be competing for the consumer's attention next to a similar, but cheaper, Acer-branded model. Acer customers were also concerned that by giving Acer their business, they would be subsidizing Acer's own-brand products which directly competed against themselves. There was also the risk that intellectual property from its clients could be exploited by Acer's brand-name operations. Thus Acer spun off its contract manufacturing arm into another company called Wistron and reduced its share in this business to 30 percent.[41]

When buyers cannot easily monitor supplier performance, the supplier might shirk or cheat and not deliver the expected value. *Opportunism* can be thought of as "some form of cheating or undersupply relative to an implicit or explicit contract."[42] It may involve blatant self-interest and deliberate misrepresentation that violates contractual agreements.

Opportunism is a concern because firms must devote resources to control and monitor, that otherwise could be allocated to more productive purposes. Contracts may become inadequate to govern supplier transactions when supplier opportunism becomes difficult to detect; as firms make specific investments in assets that cannot be used elsewhere; and as contingencies are harder to anticipate.

Customers and suppliers are more likely to form a joint venture (versus a simple contract) when the supplier's degree of asset specificity is high, monitoring the supplier's behavior is difficult, and the supplier has a poor reputation.[43] When a supplier has a good reputation, for example, it is more likely to avoid opportunism to protect this valuable intangible asset.

The presence of a significant future time horizon and/or strong solidarity norms so that customers and suppliers are willing to strive for joint benefits can cause a shift in the effect of specific investments, from expropriation (increased opportunism on the receiver's part) to bonding (reduced opportunism).[44]

Relationship Marketing in the *Keiretsu* and *Chaebol*

No discussion of B2B marketing in Asia is complete without mentioning two unique organizational forms—the Japanese *keiretsu* and the Korean *chaebol*. One of the criteria that defines these industrial groups is that their members buy and sell among each other, with transactions often brokered by the trading company in the group. In general, the family-owned *chaebol* is smaller (in terms of sales, workforce, and overseas branches) and more tightly integrated than the *keiretsu*. However, as they face similar issues, the *keiretsu* is used as our expository vehicle. More specifically, the production *keiretsu* will be examined as it sets the most relevant context for B2B relationship marketing.[45]

The production *keiretsu* is characterized by the vertical integration of manufacturers and their suppliers. Large auto-makers like Toyota, Nissan, and Mitsubishi will have a group of primary subcontractors, which in turn distribute work to thousands of little firms. (Honda, which has no suppliers' organization, is a notable exception.)

All subcontractors are integrated into the manufacturer's production process, and receive extensive technological, managerial, and financial support. Subcontractors are instructed precisely on production runs, prices, and delivery schedules, which they are expected to meet. Hence, manufacturers and their subcontractors are tied by reciprocal obligation: the subcontractor to high quality and low costs; the manufacturer to providing a steady flow of financial and other resources.

Consequently, the "buy group products" mentality and reciprocal purchasing are prominent in the *keiretsu* procurement model. If one member buys from another, it can expect the other company to buy its products, although no group member would follow the "buy group" concept to the point of harming its own interest. In this way, long-term cooperative relationships are developed among member firms. Through ongoing interactions and information exchanges, *keiretsu* members build strong interdependence and social ties, and eventually, mutual trust.

However, since the collapse of Japan's bubble economy in the early 1990s, the *keiretsu* has been losing its influence. Responding to increased competition and the economic downturn in the late 1990s, many *keiretsu*-affiliated firms (*kankei kaisha*) have started expanding their businesses outside their group boundaries. Major Japanese auto-makers have increased their procurement of key components from independent suppliers (*dokuritsu kaisha*), other *keiretsu*-affiliated suppliers, and even foreign parts suppliers. For example, Denso gains only half its sales from parent company Toyota, due to increased sales to Honda and Mitsubishi.

These developments may have led to major Japanese auto-makers pursuing different supplier relationships of late. For example, Toyota has a disproportionately large number of large suppliers, with very few small-sized suppliers, while Mitsubishi has the opposite. Toyota also did not share its higher profits with its suppliers. In contrast, Nissan's suppliers did not fully share the poor performance of Nissan. It appeared that given its prolonged sales slump, Nissan had lost bargaining power to its suppliers, a situation which was reversed with the appointment of Carlos Ghosn as its CEO.

Interestingly, Western auto-makers like DaimlerChrysler are now trying to develop and maintain long-term relationships with their suppliers. Collectively, these recent trends suggest the beginning of a convergence between the supplier management polices of Japanese and Western auto-makers.

Institutional and Government Markets

Our discussion has concentrated largely on the buying behavior of profit-seeking companies. Much of what we have said also applies to the buying practices of institutional and government organizations. We now highlight certain special features of these markets.

The **institutional market** consists of schools, hospitals, nursing homes, prisons, and other institutions that must provide goods and services to people in their care. Many of these organizations are characterized by low budgets and captive clienteles. For example, hospitals have to decide what quality of food to buy for patients. The buying objective here is not profit, because the food is provided as part of the total service package; nor is cost minimization the sole objective, because poor food will cause patients to complain and hurt the hospital's reputation. The hospital purchasing agent has to search for institutional-food vendors whose quality meets or exceeds a certain minimum standard and whose prices are low. In fact, many food vendors set up a separate division to sell to institutional buyers because of these buyers' special needs and characteristics. Sin Sin, a Singaporean sauce-maker, produces, packages, and prices its sauces differently to meet the requirements of hospitals, colleges, and prisons.

In most countries, government organizations are a major buyer of goods and services. Government organizations typically require suppliers to submit bids, and normally they award the contract to the lowest bidder. In some cases, the government unit will make allowance for the supplier's superior quality or reputation for completing contracts on time.

Kuala Lumpur International Airport—The Malaysian government awarded the main contract to build the Kuala Lumpur International Airport to a consortium which included mainly Japanese firms such as Taisei, Kajima, Shimizu, and Hazema. They submitted a bid of $458 million, which was higher than the lowest bidder of $397 million. However, the consortium was awarded the contract because it was the "lowest technically acceptable and evaluated tender."

Governments will also buy on a negotiated contract basis, primarily for complex projects involving major R&D costs and risks and in cases where there is little competition. Government purchases have also been marked by kickbacks and bribery in some Asian countries (see "Marketing Insight: Government Procurement in Korea" for an example).

Meiya Power—In China, many foreign investors find that after spending hundreds of millions of dollars to seal an agreement with one arm of the government, another round of negotiation is required with another arm of the government because of shared jurisdiction and tricky regulations. Hong Kong-based consortium Meiya Power recognized this problem. While most foreign investors were targeting investments near fast-growing cities such as Shanghai and Guangzhou, Meiya Power opted to invest in underdeveloped western regions, which was advantageous as it faced less competition. By helping the central government develop the west, it was in a better political position for negotiations. Being a consortium, it enjoyed more bargaining clout with smaller provinces and greater autonomy. At the same time, it was patient not to pull the subsidiary out of China when times were bad. With China's power shortages, Meiya's business is now soaring.[46]

MARKETING INSIGHT • GOVERNMENT PROCUREMENT IN KOREA

The Public Procurement Service (PPS) in Korea is a central government organization responsible for buying goods and services and for arranging contracts for construction projects involving government facilities above certain threshold values. Four types of procurement irregularities were uncovered in its procedures:

1. ***Providing preferential treatment to certain firms during the process of establishing specifications and determining contract methods*** — The PPS was influenced by certain firms when preparing specifications, or restricting opportunities for participation in tenders by other firms. It also limited competition unnecessarily or abused the use of private contracts.
2. ***Providing preferential access to tender information at the time of making an order*** — The PPS carried summarized tender information in the government gazette but disclosed detailed information to prospective bidders in a selective and limited manner.
3. ***Applying procedures for selecting successful bidders and for conducting private contract negotiations arbitrarily*** — The PPS interpreted selection criteria, including pre-qualification, arbitrarily rather than in an open and transparent manner. It applied different negotiation prices for different prospective contractors for private contracts.
4. ***Wrongdoings of contract officers*** — There were intentional delays in placing orders, determining successful bidders, concluding contracts, and arranging payments.

To develop a more customer-centered government procurement service that was transparent, fair, efficient, and economical, several improvements were made, including:

1. Changing specific procurement specifications to more general ones.
2. Reducing the number of private contract and restricted competition tenders.
3. Actively publicizing tender information.
4. Establishing execution criteria for contract procedures to prevent arbitrary implementation.
5. Online digitizing of the procurement process through an EDI system and databases for various processes and information on suppliers.
6. Increasing officials' awareness on corruption through forums, in-office study groups, inspection teams, and public dialogues.

Source: Byungtae Kang, "Anti-Corruption Measures in the Public Procurement Service Sector in Korea." Paper Presented at the ADB/OECD Conference on Combating Corruption in the Asia-Pacific Region, (Seoul) December 11–13, 2000.

In some countries, government spending decisions are subject to public review. Hence, government organizations require considerable paperwork from suppliers, who often complain about excessive paperwork, bureaucracy, regulations, decision making delays, and frequent shifts in procurement personnel. Vendors should also pay attention to cost justification, which is a major consideration for government procurement professionals. Companies hoping to be government contractors need to help government agencies see the bottom-line impact of their offerings.

Just as companies provide government agencies with guidelines on how best to purchase and use their products, governments provide would-be suppliers with detailed guidelines describing how to sell to the government. Not following the guidelines properly and filling out forms and contracts incorrectly can create a legal nightmare.[47] Suppliers have to master the system and try to find ways to cut through the red tape. Obtaining government contacts requires an investment of time, money, and resources not unlike what is required for entering a new market overseas.

Kodak—Kodak appointed Ying Yeh, a former diplomat in the U.S. government and commercial counselor at the U.S. Embassy to China, as vice-president of its China regional operation and general manager of public affairs. With her diplomatic skills and good relationship with government officials and business circles, Yeh played a crucial role in Kodak's negotiations with the Chinese government which helped it gain approval for a $1.2 billion project.

There are many reasons why companies selling to governments have not used a marketing orientation. Government procurement policies have traditionally emphasized price, leading suppliers to invest considerable effort in bringing costs down. Where product characteristics are carefully specified, product differentiation is not a marketing factor; nor are advertising and personal selling of much consequence in winning bids.

Winning government contracts may not only be a source of revenue but also offers spillover benefits, as other businesses may follow suit in their product adoption. Linux, the software company, found that apart from large businesses and government agencies, many small and medium enterprises are also keen on adopting its offerings. The growth of Linux is expected to be particularly strong in key Asian markets where government endorsements and policies are boosting its visibility.[48]

Foreign businesses in Asia have also alleged that certain governments have favored local companies in awarding contracts. Thus tying up with an influential local business may be an effective means of penetrating the government market. Lenovo, China's leading PC maker, illustrates these points:

Lenovo—Lenovo's *guanxi* or connections has been a sore point for foreign rivals. The Chinese government's wanting to have at least one national champion in key industries has contributed to allegations that, as the government's local champion in the PC market, Lenovo enjoys a competitive advantage. Such support manifests itself in various ways. For example, the Chinese government may promote "buy local" campaigns. Consequently, Lenovo is always on the government's shortlist of vendors that companies are always urged to consider. Lenovo may also be advantaged by upstream companies in the supply chain which provide bigger discounts to Chinese businesses. This may help Lenovo underprice foreign rivals. To counter these allegations, Lenovo argues that less than 25 percent of its business comes from large corporate customers or state-owned enterprises. Nonetheless, Lenovo's customers among small- and medium-sized businesses may have chosen the brand due to its visibility in the offices of government-affiliated companies. AOL-Time Warner also selected Lenovo with its less popular portal <www.fm365.com> as its partner in a joint venture over more established private sector sites such as Netease.com, Sina.com, and Sohu.com.[49]

However, being on good terms with government officials alone may no longer suffice, even in Asia. As China shifts from a low-cost manufacturing center to an innovative market economy, foreign companies will need to develop strategic and sustainable approaches to corporate-government relationship management, beyond that of personal relationships. China's unique business situation calls for adherence to a few principles:

- **Interact with all levels of government in China.**
- **Develop relations with government** through organizations such as foreign enterprise associations, social organizations, and domestic industry associations.
- **Personal relationship or *guanxi* is not enough** in forging good relations with government.
- **There is no one-size-fits-all solution.** Business in China should be conducted by placing the operations in the hands of someone who understands Chinese issues and is familiar with government officials and structures.[50]

Finally, some companies have pursued government business by establishing separate government marketing departments. Companies such as Gateway, Kodak, and Goodyear anticipate government needs and projects, participate in the product specification phase, gather competitive intelligence, prepare bids carefully, and produce strong communications to describe and enhance their companies' reputations.

Summary

1. Organizational buying is the decision making process by which formal organizations establish the need to purchase products and services, then identify, evaluate, and choose among alternative brands and suppliers. The business market consists of organizations that acquire goods and services used to produce other products or services that are sold, rented, or supplied to others.
2. Compared to consumer markets, business markets generally have fewer and larger buyers, a closer customer–supplier relationship, and more geographically concentrated buyers. Demand in the business market is derived from demand in the consumer market and fluctuates with the business cycle. Nonetheless, the total demand for many business goods and services is quite price-inelastic. Business marketers need to be aware of the role of professional purchasers and their influencers, the need for multiple sales calls, and the importance of direct purchasing, reciprocity, and leasing.
3. The buying center is the decision making unit of a buying organization. It consists of initiators, users, influencers, deciders, approvers, buyers, and gatekeepers. To influence these parties, marketers must be aware of environmental, organizational, interpersonal, and individual factors.
4. The buying process consists of eight stages called buyphases:
   - **a.** problem recognition,
   - **b.** general need description,
   - **c.** product specification,
   - **d.** supplier search,
   - **e.** proposal solicitation,
   - **f.** supplier selection,
   - **g.** order-routine specification, and
   - **h.** performance review.
5. Business marketers must form strong bonds and relationships with their customers and provide them added value. Some customers, however, may prefer more of a transactional relationship.
6. Two unique Asian organizational settings involving B2B relationship marketing are the Japanese *keiretsu* and the Korean *chaebol*. Firms in these business groups tend to have reciprocal purchasing patterns. However, there appears to be recent convergence in the supplier management policies and those of Western manufacturers.
7. The institutional market consists of schools, hospitals, nursing homes, prisons, and other institutions that provide goods and services to people in their care. Buyers for government organizations tend to require a great deal of paperwork from their vendors and to favor open bidding and domestic companies. Suppliers must be prepared to adapt their offers to the special needs and procedures found in institutional and government markets.

Application

Marketing Debate—How Different is Business-to-Business Marketing?

Many business-to-business marketing executives lament the challenges of business-to-business marketing, maintaining that many traditional marketing concepts and principles do not apply. For a number of reasons, they assert that selling products and services to a company is fundamentally different from selling to individuals. Others disagree, claiming that marketing theory is still valid and only involves some adaptation in the marketing tactics.

Take a position: *Business-to-business marketing requires a special, unique set of marketing concepts and principles* versus *Business-to-business marketing is really not that different and the basic marketing concepts and principles apply.*

Marketing Discussion

Consider some of the consumer behavior topics from Chapter 6. How might you apply them to business-to-business settings? For example, how might non compensatory models of choice work?

PART 3

China is an attractive target market for many companies because of its huge population.

Identifying Market Segments and Targets

8

A company cannot connect with all customers in large, broad, or diverse markets. Consumers vary on many dimensions and often can be grouped according to one or more characteristics. A company needs to identify which market segments it can serve effectively. This decision requires a keen understanding of consumer behavior and careful strategic thinking. To develop the best marketing plans, managers need to understand what makes each segment unique and different.

The magnitude and wealth of older consumers, for example, should be important to many different marketers.[1] Senior consumers, those 65 and older, make up 5.7 percent of Asia's population. This segment is growing rapidly in some Asian countries. The success of China's one-child policy and the fact that more of China's increasingly well-off are choosing not to have children, are producing one of the most rapidly aging societies ever. Instead of the often used family description of "one mouth, six pockets," it will soon be "six mouths to feed and one pocket to pick up the bill." Yet, firms selling to the Chinese are focusing on the country's youths. Projections have it that by 2024, those aged over 40 will make up 58 percent of the Chinese population. These empty-nesters, whose children have left home and who, unlike their parents, have escaped low-paying state jobs, have the most purchasing power. Many have made money in China's emerging capitalist economy and are status-conscious and keen to enjoy their wealth. Older Chinese are starting to spend on pharmaceuticals and health care. Thus sales of Pfizer's cholesterol-lowering and anti-hypertension medicines are growing rapidly. To appeal to China's older generation, focus on Confucian values seems to be the key. Nestlé sells calcium-fortified milk powders through ads that encourage grown-up children to look after the health of their parents. A popular TV spot for Guibiewan, a food supplement, showed a boy eating breakfast watched by his doting father. "When I was young, everyday was like my birthday, but it seems *Baba* never had a special day," the voice-over laments. "Every father remembers his son's birthday. But how many sons know their father's? Express your respect with Guibiewan."[2]

In this chapter, we will address the following questions:

1. What are the different levels of market segmentation?
2. How can a company divide a market into segments?
3. How should a company choose the most attractive target markets?
4. What are the requirements for effective segmentation?

To compete more effectively, many companies are now embracing target marketing. Instead of scattering their marketing effort (a "shotgun" approach), they focus on those consumers they have the greatest chance of satisfying (a "rifle" approach).

Effective target marketing requires that marketers: (1) Identify and profile distinct groups of buyers who differ in their needs and preferences (market segmentation); (2) Select one or more market segments to enter (market targeting); and (3) For each target segment, establish and communicate the distinctive benefit(s) of the company's market offering (market positioning).

This chapter will focus on the first two steps. Chapter 10 discusses brand and market positioning.

Levels of Market Segmentation

The starting point for discussing segmentation is **mass marketing**. In mass marketing, the seller engages in the mass production, mass distribution, and mass promotion of one product for all buyers. Henry Ford epitomized this strategy when he offered the Model-T Ford in one color, black. Coca-Cola also practiced mass marketing when it sold only one kind of Coke in a 6.5-ounce bottle.

The argument for mass marketing is that it creates the largest potential market, which leads to the lowest costs, which in turn can lead to lower prices or higher margins. However, many critics point to the increasing splintering of the market, which makes mass marketing more difficult. The proliferation of advertising media and distribution channels is making it difficult and increasingly expensive to reach a mass audience. Whereas consumers in the past passively received whatever was broadcast on TV, empowered media users now control and shape content, thanks to the Internet and iPod. Whereas consumers once aspired to keep up with the crowd, they now prefer to stand out from the crowd. Some claim that mass marketing is dying. The rise of niche brands, product extensions, and mass customization is evidence of this.[3] Thus many companies are turning to *micromarketing* at one of four levels: segments, niches, local areas, and individuals.

Segment Marketing

A market segment consists of a group of customers who share a similar set of needs and wants. Thus, we distinguish between car buyers who are primarily seeking low-cost basic transportation, those seeking a luxurious driving experience, and those seeking driving thrills and performance. We must be careful not to confuse a *segment* and a *sector*. A car company might say that it will target young, middle-income car buyers. The problem is that young, middle-income car buyers will differ about what they want in a car. Some will want a low-cost car and others will want an expensive car. Young, middle-income car buyers are a sector, not a segment.

The marketer does not create the segments; the marketer's task is to identify the segments and decide which one(s) to target. Segment marketing offers key benefits over mass marketing. The company can presumably better design, price, communicate, and deliver the product or service to satisfy the target market. The company also can fine-tune the marketing program and activities to better reflect competitors' marketing.

Rural marketing in India—Large MNCs are fanning out into the Indian countryside, where 70 percent of its 700 million population live. Economic growth in India's agricultural sector has translated into higher income and greater sales opportunities. Half of durables and consumer goods are now sold in India's rural markets. Several manufacturers have used nontraditional marketing programs to satisfy the needs of the rural Indian market. LG Electronics offers free first aid and clean drinking water at popular religious events. It does not sell its products there. Instead, when its mobile vans go to the villages again, its logo is already familiar to the villagers and allows its salespeople easier access. It also gets petrol pump owners to display its products, tractor dealers to become its subdealers, and parks its mobile vans near *haats* to carry out product demonstrations and pick-up orders directly.

Hindustan Unilever feels that the issues of affordability, availability, awareness, and overcoming prevalent attitudes and habits need to be addressed. Hence, its vans visit villages and distribute boxes comprising a low-unit-price pack of shampoo, talcum powder, toothpaste, and skin cream. Accompanying personnel explain to consumers how to use these products. In the evenings, the vans show videos interspersed with product communication to generate product awareness and availability. HL also appoints stockists in large villages who can service smaller villages faster and more regularly. They help village-based retailers stock a larger number of products, increase their turnover, and create demand. Emulating Hindustan's "think small and keep the product simple" strategy is Britannia, which sells 2- and 6-cent "energy" biscuit packs popular among rural children. Italy's Perfetti and Spain's Agrillimon fill glass jars at village shops with hard candies selling for 0.1 cents each.

This strategy is also applied for bigger-ticket items. LG Electronics developed a special range of no-frills, user-friendly color television sets. It also introduced a regional language display menu which flashes messages in Hindi, Marathi, Bengali, and Tamil. These features make the product simple yet high-tech. As not many villagers are literate, they rely more on pictorially strong content and visuals. Philips markets a wind-up, no-battery radio for $20, Samsung a $215 refrigerator and a $175 14-inch TV, and Hero-Honda a $900 Splendour motorbike which is part of the dowry of many rural Indian brides. Services are also growing. Escotel provides mobile phone services to 500,000 subscribers in over 3,000 towns and villages, while Max New York Life markets $208 life insurance policies costing $2 in annual premiums.[4]

In rural marketing, street vendors are common, like this one in Vietnam.

However, even a segment is partly a fiction, in that not everyone wants exactly the same thing. Anderson and Narus have urged marketers to present flexible market offerings to all members of a segment.[5]

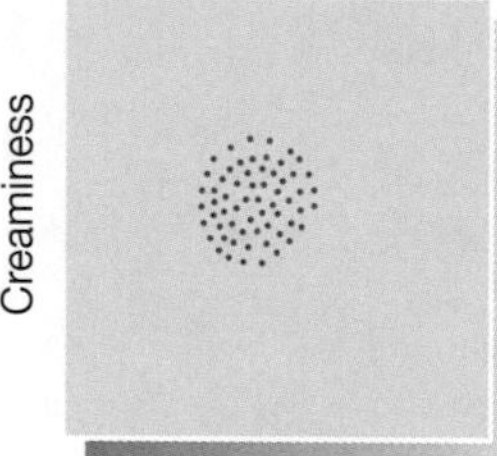

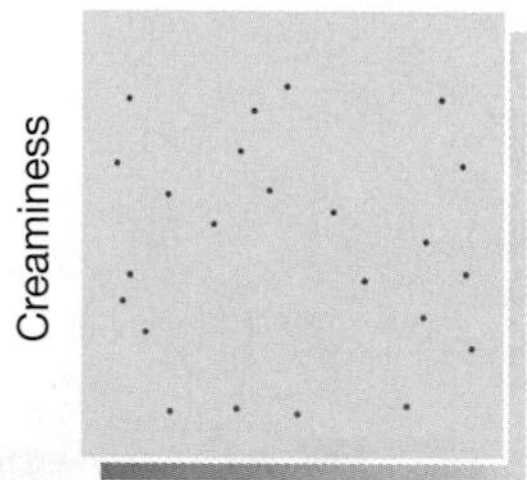

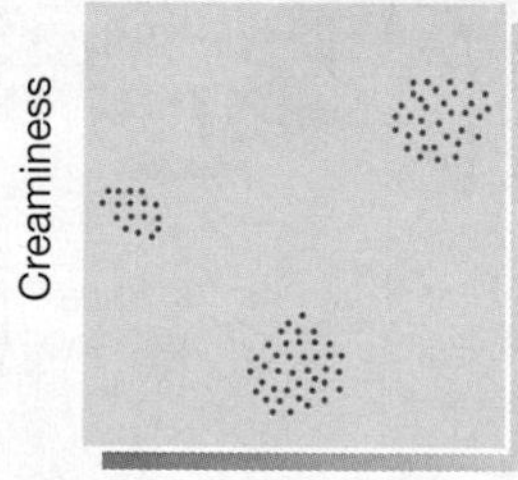

Figure 8.1 Basic Market-Preference Patterns

A **flexible market offering** consists of two parts: a *naked solution* containing the product and service elements that all segment members value, and *discretionary options* that some segment members value. Each option might carry an additional charge. For example, Malaysia budget airline AirAsia offers all economy passengers a seat. It charges economy passengers extra for food and drinks.

Market segments can be defined in many different ways. One way to carve up a market is to identify *preference segments.* Suppose ice cream buyers are asked how much they value sweetness and creaminess as two product attributes. Three different patterns can emerge.

1. ***Homogeneous preferences*** — Figure 8.1(a) shows a market where all the consumers have roughly the same preferences. The market shows no natural segments. We would predict that existing brands would be similar and cluster around the middle of the scale in both sweetness and creaminess.
2. ***Diffused preferences*** — At the other extreme, consumer preferences may be scattered throughout the space (Figure 8.1(b)), indicating that consumers vary greatly in their preferences. The first brand to enter the market is likely to position itself to appeal to the most people. A second competitor could locate next to the first brand and fight for market share, or it could locate in a corner to attract a customer group that was not satisfied with the center brand. If several brands are in the market, they are likely to position themselves throughout the space and show real differences to match differences in consumer preference.
3. ***Clustered preferences*** — The market might reveal distinct preference clusters, called *natural market segments* (Figure 8.1(c)). The first firm in this market has three options. It might position in the center, hoping to appeal to all groups. It might position in the largest market segment (*concentrated marketing*). It might develop several brands, each positioned in a different segment. If the first firm developed only one brand, competitors would enter and introduce brands in the other segments.

Later in this chapter, we will consider various ways to segment and compete in a market.

Niche Marketing

A niche is a more narrowly defined customer group seeking a distinctive mix of benefits. Marketers usually identify niches by dividing a segment into subsegments.

An attractive niche is characterized as follows: The customers in the niche have a distinct set of needs; they will pay a premium to the firm that best satisfies their needs; the niche is not likely to attract other competitors; the nicher gains certain economies through specialization; and the niche has size, profit, and growth potential. Whereas segments are fairly large and normally attract several competitors, niches are fairly small and normally attract only one or two.

Handi Network International—Handi Network International specializes in developing products that are tailored for the elderly and handicapped. It lends its expertise to large companies to help them target niche markets. For example, it has worked with Toyota to design cars that are wheelchair-accessible; it has helped Otsuka Pharmaceutical's beverage division to create a "barrier-free" vending machine with disabled users in mind; it designed an in-flight wheelchair for Japan Air System; and it created a bed with Sanyo Electric that helps a bedridden person to roll over.[6]

Larger companies, such as IBM, have lost pieces of their market to nichers. This confrontation has been labeled "guerrillas against gorillas."[7] This is happening in the online social networking market, where MySpace and Facebook are becoming mature service providers.

MySpace, FaceBook—A drop in traffic numbers has made headlines for social networking sites, MySpace and Facebook. The sites, with 130 million and 12 million users respectively, rely on advertising revenue to survive and risk losing out by trying to be all things to all people. A host of upstart social networking nichers hope to capitalize on the tendency of individuals to want to congregate with others who share their own particular passions, however arcane. For instance, there is now 1Up.com, a content-heavy social site where online gaming fanatics can trade tips, stories, opinions, and gossip. Gather.com is a social network for the so-called NPR crowd: people in the prime of their career who, unlike students, have disposable income to burn. Then there's Dogster, an ultra-niche site that has 3,500 active communities for dog owners and is already attracting scads of advertisers.[8]

Some large companies have even turned to niche marketing. Hallmark commands a 55 percent share of the $7.8 billion global greeting card market by rigorously segmenting its greeting card business. In addition to popular subbranded card lines like the humorous Shoebox Greetings, Hallmark has introduced lines targeting specific market segments. Fresh Ink targets 18- to 39-year-old women and Out of the Blue targets those who want inexpensive cards that can be sent for no reason.[9] Here is how Coca-Cola develops niches in Japan:

Coca-Cola—One of Coca-Cola's biggest challenges in Japan is finding new products that appeal to older customers. It has thus introduced drinks that claim to boost energy or have health benefits, and possibly fetch a higher price. Coke launched ***Tarumi,*** a low-calorie beverage which claims to "balance mind and body" through its blend of six minerals. *Tarumi* is Japanese for "sag unhealthily," a condition the drink intends to reverse. Another drink launched is Boco, billed as fat- and cholesterol-free.[10]

Niche marketers presumably understand their customers' needs so well that the customers willingly pay a premium for their products. Here is an Asian example:

Samsung—At the MTV Asia Awards, Thai Samsung Electronics introduced a special edition Samsung E650 slide-up mobile phone with only 3,000 units available in Thailand. Targeted at young trendsetters who love fashion and music, the MTV Asia Awards is an appropriate event to reach those aged 18–29. Further, as part of its niche marketing campaign, Samsung had a series of "see me, feel me, try me" activities at strategic locations and gatherings of hip, cool, young music lovers.[11]

As marketing efficiency increases, niches that were seemingly too small may become more profitable.[12] The low cost of setting up shop on the Internet has led to many small business start-ups aimed at niches. The recipe for Internet niching success: choose a hard-to-find product that customers do not need to see and touch. "Marketing Insight: Chasing the Long Tail" outlines how provocative the implications of Internet niching are.

Internet niching—The experience of Dan Myrick, director of *The Blair Witch Project*, illustrates what can happen when you move away from targeting the mass market. In 1999, just two years out of film school, Myrick spent eight days in the woods of Maryland shooting *The Blair Witch Project*. The crudely made film netted nearly $250 million on a $35,000 production budget, largely from audiences drawn to the movie through Myrick's Web site. Myrick has also used the Web to distribute ***The Strand,*** a series of "Webisodes" set in Venice Beach, California. He says, "The great thing about the Internet is it opens up this realm of micromarkets and I don't need an 8 or 9 or 10 Nielsen share to be a success. NBC will cancel a show if it didn't get $3 million."[13]

MARKETING INSIGHT • CHASING THE LONG TAIL

The advent of online commerce, made possible by technology and epitomized by Amazon.com, iTunes, and Netflix, has led to a shift in consumer buying patterns, according to Chris Anderson, editor-in-chief of *Wired* magazine and author of *The Long Tail*.

In most markets, the distribution of product sales conforms to a curve weighted heavily to one side—the "head"—where the bulk of sales are generated by a few products. The curve falls rapidly toward zero and hovers just above it far along the *x*-axis—the "long tail"—where the vast majority of products generate very little sales. The mass market traditionally focused on generating "hit" products that occupy the head, disdaining the low-revenue market niches comprising the tail.

Anderson asserts that as a result of consumers' embrace of the Internet as a shopping medium, the long tail harbors significantly more value than before. In fact, Anderson argues, the Internet has directly contributed to the shifting of demand "down the tail, from hits to niches" in a number of product categories, including music, books, clothing, and movies.

On his blog, Anderson boils down his argument as follows: "The Long Tail equation is simple: (1) The lower the cost of distribution, the more you can economically offer without having to predict demand; (2) The more you can offer, the greater the chance that you will be able to tap latent demand for minority tastes that was unreachable through traditional retail; and (3) Aggregate enough minority taste, and you'll often find a big new market."

Anderson identifies two aspects of Internet shopping that contribute to this shift. First, greater choice is permitted by increased inventory and variety. Given a choice between 10 hit products, consumers are forced to select one of the 10. If, however, the choice set is expanded to 1,000, then the top 10 hits will be chosen less frequently. Second, the "search costs" of finding relevant new products are lowered due to the wealth of information sources available online, the filtering of product recommendations based on user preferences that vendors can provide, and the word-of-mouth network of Internet users.

Anderson sees the long tail effect as particularly pronounced in media, a category that's historically hit-driven but that benefits enormously from these two aspects of online shopping. He points to the success of niche media properties such as the book *Touching the Void*, the band My Chemical Romance, and the documentary film *Capturing the Friedmans*, which all benefited from the choice and information-organization aspects of Internet shopping to achieve greater success than was expected.

The Long Tail thesis was also supported in two studies that measured the tail in online versus off-line book selling and clothing retail. The book-selling study concluded that the increased product variety offered by online bookstores increased consumer welfare by $731 million to $1.03 billion in 2000. In the case of online clothing retail, the study found that consumers who used both online and catalog channels of a midsize retailer purchased a more even distribution of products than through the catalog.

New consumer buying patterns, aided by the Internet, are highlighting the revenue potential of "the long tail" of the market, where many seemingly niche products can find broader success. My Chemical Romance is an example of a hit band that emerged from this "long tail."

The same companies that compete in the business of creating hits are beginning to develop ways to evolve niche successes in the long tail. For example, when the Universal Music Group released 3,000 out-of-print European recordings in download-only digital format on the Internet, it generated 250,000 individual downloads of the songs. After this encouraging start, Universal planned to eventually release more than 100,000 out-of-print recordings. In a press release, Universal even stated, "Overall, these results lend weight to author Chris Anderson's The Long Tail theory."

Yet companies like Universal may soon face additional competition from unconventional sources. Anderson predicts that as a result of the proliferation of free user-generated content, the variety popularized by YouTube, the end of the long tail where this content resides will be a "nonmonetary economy."

Others have countered that, especially in entertainment, the "head" where the hits are concentrated is valuable to consumers, not only to the content creators. It's been argued that most hits are popular because they are of high quality and that the majority of products and services making up the long tail originate from a small concentration of "long-tail aggregators"—sites such as Amazon, eBay, iTunes, and Netflix. This observation challenges the premise that old business paradigms have changed as much as Anderson suggests.

Sources: Chris Anderson, *The Long Tail*, (New York: Hyperion); "Reading the Tail." interview with Chris Anderson, *Wired*, July 8, 2006, p.30; "Wag the Dog: What the Long Tail Will Do." *Economist*, July 8, 2006, p.77; Erik Brynjolfsson, Yu "Jeffrey" Hu, and Michael D. Smith, "From Niches to Riches: Anatomy of a Long Tail." *MIT Sloan Management Review*, Summer 2006, p.67; John Cassidy, "Going Long." *New Yorker*, July 10, 2006, <www.longtail.com>

Local Marketing

Target marketing is leading to marketing programs tailored to the needs and wants of local customer groups (trading areas, neighborhoods, even individual stores). Local marketing is particularly important in countries with strong regional differences. For example, there are 55 ethnic minorities comprising some 9 percent of China's 1.3 billion consumers. China has four municipalities (Beijing, Tianjin, Shanghai, and Chongqing), over 20 provinces (e.g., Hebei, Shanxi, Liaoning, Heilongjiang, Anhui, Fujian, Henan, Hunan, Hubei, Guangdong, Sichuan, and Yunnan), five autonomous regions (Inner Mongolia, Tibet, Guangxi Zhuang, Ningxia Hui, and Xinjiang Uygur), and two Special Administrative Regions (Hong Kong and Macau).

China's regional differences—Because of China's vast land mass and varied population, it is riddled with regional differences. Beijing residents are seen as the Chinese with the most pride and to whom face matters most. Those in Tianjin are viewed as conservatives who prefer to keep a low profile. Shanghainese are noted for their shrewdness in business dealings, and together with those from Guangdong, tend to speak the loudest. In contrast, Suzhou residents are viewed as soft-spoken. Hubei people are regarded as survivors, being descended from those who lived through numerous battles for strategic control over the Yangtze and Han rivers. Sichuanese are equally tough and seem to get the best jobs in any student cohort. People from Shandong and the northeastern provinces of Heilongjiang, Jilin, and Liaoning are regarded as straightforward, kind, and cooperative.[14]

Local marketing reflects a growing trend called grassroots marketing. Marketing activities concentrate on getting as close and personally relevant to individual customers as possible. Much of Nike's initial success has been attributed to the ability to engage target consumers through grassroots marketing such as sponsorship of local school teams, expert-conducted clinics, and provision of shoes, clothing, and equipment. "Breakthrough Marketing: HSBC" profiles another success story.

Those who favor localized marketing see national advertising as wasteful because it is too "arm's length" and fails to address local needs. Those against local marketing argue that it drives up manufacturing and marketing costs by reducing economies of scale. Logistical problems are magnified. A brand's overall image might be diluted if the product and message are different in different localities.

Unilever—One of Unilever's strengths, its strong roots in local markets, has turned into its biggest weakness. Unilever's local managers have become too autonomous in its strategic decisions, leading to duplication of corporate structures. For some markets, its attention to such local details works well. For instance, Indian women often oil their hair before washing it. Hence, Western shampoos that do not remove the oil have not sold well. Unilever reformulated its shampoo in India to great success. However, in China and Hong Kong, where hair and washing habits are almost identical, Unilever also used different formulations in both markets. Sometimes, Unilever would vary the packaging and marketing in similar markets even for commoditized products such as deodorants. Says Simon Clift, its chief marketing officer, "We tend to exaggerate complexity." Unilever is making itself slimmer and more efficient by trimming its staff and closing down some factories and regional centers.[15]

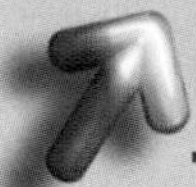

BREAKTHROUGH • MARKETING

HSBC

Originally called the Hong Kong and Shanghai Banking Corporation Limited, HSBC wants to be known as the "world's local bank." This tagline reflects HSBC's positioning as a globe-spanning financial institution with a unique focus on serving local markets. HSBC was established in 1865 to finance the growing trade between China and the U.K. It's now the second-largest bank in the world. Despite serving over 100 million customers through 9,500 branches in 79 countries, the bank works hard to maintain a local presence and local knowledge in each area. Its fundamental operating strategy is to remain close to its customers. As HSBC chairman Sir John Bond said, "Our position as the world's local bank enables us to approach each country uniquely, blending local knowledge with a worldwide operating platform."

Ads for the "World's Local Bank" campaign depicted the way two different cultures interpret the same objects or events. One TV spot showed a U.S. businessman hitting a hole-in-one during a round in Japan with his Japanese counterparts. He is surprised to find that rather than paying for a round of drinks in the clubhouse as in the U.S., by Japanese custom he must buy expensive gifts for his playing partners. The ad shows a subsequent round, with the Japanese players sporting expensive-looking new clothes and watches. The commercial closes with the U.S. player aiming his tee shot into the trees, only to have it ricochet directly into the hole. Ads for the campaign differed by region, where, according to the ad agency, "Each country has developed its own variations on the initial idea."

HSBC demonstrated its local knowledge with marketing efforts dedicated to specific locations. For example, in 2005 it set out to prove to jaded New Yorkers that the London-based financial behemoth was a bank with local knowledge. The company held a "New York City's Most Knowledgeable Cabbie" contest, in which the winning cabbie got paid to drive an HSBC-branded BankCab full-time for a year. HSBC customers could win, too. Any customer showing an HSBC bankcard, checkbook, or bank statement was able to get a free ride in the BankCab. HSBC also ran an integrated campaign highlighting the diversity of New Yorkers, which appeared on subways, taxis, bus shelters, kiosks, coffee cups, and a Times Square billboard, as well as print, radio, and TV.

More than 8,000 miles away, HSBC undertook a two-part "Support Hong Kong" campaign to revitalize the local economy hit hard by the 2003 SARS outbreak. First, HSBC delayed interest payments for personal-loan customers who worked in industries most affected by SARS (cinemas, hotels, restaurants, and travel agencies). Second, the bank offered discounts and rebates for HSBC credit card users when they shopped and dined out. More than 1,500 local merchants participated in the promotion.

HSBC also targets consumer niches with unique products and services. For example, it found a little-known product area growing at 125 percent a year: pet insurance. The bank now distributes nationwide pet insurance to its depositors through its HSBC Insurance agency. In Malaysia, HSBC offered a "smart card" and no-frills credit cards to the underserved student segment and targeted high-value customers with special "Premium Centers" bank branches.

The bank pulls its worldwide businesses together under a single global brand with the "world's local bank" slogan. The aim is to link its international size with close relationships in each of the countries in which it operates. HSBC spends $600 million annually on global marketing, which it consolidated in 2004 under the WPP group of agencies. Going forward, it will be seeking to leverage its position as the "World's Local Bank" to improve on its $13.6 billion brand value, which placed it 23rd on the 2007 Interbrand/*BusinessWeek* global brand rankings.

Sources: Carrick Mollenkamp "HSBC Stumbles in Bid to Become Global Deal Maker." *Wall Street Journal,* October 5, 2006; Kate Nicholson, "HSBC Aims to Appear Global Yet Approachable." *Campaign,* December 2, 2005, p. 15; Deborah Orr, "New Ledger" *Forbes,* March 1, 2004, pp. 72–73; "HSBC's Global Marketing Head Explains Review Decision." *Adweek,* January 19, 2003; "Now Your Customers Can Afford to Take Fido to the Vet." *Bank Marketing*, December, p. 47; Kenneth Hein, "HSBC Bank Rides the Coattails of Chatty Cabbies." *Brandweek,* December 1, 2003, p. 30; Sir John Bond and Stephen Green, "HSBC Strategic Overview." presentation to investors November 27, 2003; "Lafferty Retail Banking Awards 2003." *Retail Banker International*, November 27, pp. 4–5; "Ideas that Work." *Bank Marketing*, November 2003, p. 10; "HSBC Enters the Global Branding Big League." *Bank Marketing International*, August, pp. 1–2; Normandy Madden, "HSBC Rolls out Post-SARS Effort." *Advertising Age,* June 16, 2003, p. 12. <www.hsbc.com>.

Individual Marketing

The ultimate level of segmentation leads to "segments of one," "customized marketing," or "one-to-one marketing."[16] Today customers are taking more individual initiative in determining what and how to buy. they log onto the Internet; look up information and evaluations of product or service offers; dialogue with suppliers, users, and product critics; and in many cases, design the product they want.

Wind and Rangaswamy see the a movement toward "customerizing" the firm.[17] **Customerization** combines operationally driven mass customization with customized marketing in a way that empowers consumers to design the product and service offering of their choice. The firm no longer requires prior information about the customer, nor does the firm need to own manufacturing. The firm provides a platform and tools and "rents" out to customers the means to design their own products. A company is customerized when it is able to respond to individual customers by customizing its products, services, and messages on a one-to-one basis.[18]

Customization is certainly not for every company: It may be very difficult to implement for complex products such as automobiles. Customization can raise the cost of goods by more than the customer is willing to pay. Some customers do not know what they want until they see actual products. Customers cannot cancel the order after the company has started to work on the product. The product may be hard to repair and have little sales value.

Bases for Segmenting Consumer Markets

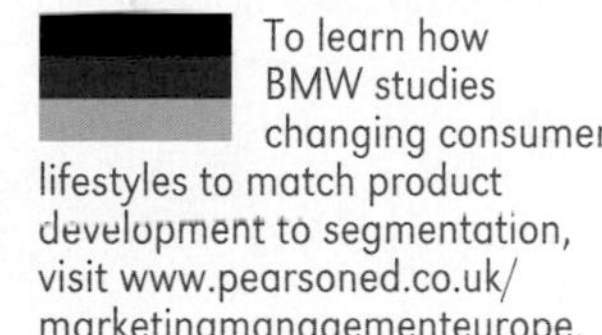

To learn how BMW studies changing consumer lifestyles to match product development to segmentation, visit www.pearsoned.co.uk/marketingmanagementeurope.

Two broad groups of variables are used to segment consumer markets. Some researchers try to form segments by looking at descriptive characteristics: geographic, demographic, and psychographic. Then they examine whether these customer segments exhibit different needs or product responses. For example, they might examine the differing attitudes of "professionals," "blue collars," and other groups toward, say, "safety" as a car benefit.

Other researchers try to form segments by looking at "behavioral" considerations, such as consumer responses to benefits, use occasions, or brands. Once the segments are formed, the researcher sees whether different characteristics are associated with each consumer-response segment. For example, the researcher might examine whether people who want "quality" rather than "low price" in buying an automobile differ in their geographic, demographic, and psychographic makeup.

Regardless of which type of segmentation scheme is employed, the key is that the marketing program can be profitably adjusted to recognize customer differences. The major segmentation variables—geographic, demographic, psychographic, and behavioral segmentation—are summarized in Table 8.1.

Geographic Segmentation

Geographic segmentation calls for dividing the market into different geographical units such as nations, states, regions, counties, cities, or neighborhoods. The company can operate in one or a few areas, or operate in all but pay attention to local variations.

Procter & Gamble—In China, P&G's customer research managers discovered that while low prices help sales in villages, it is also important to develop products that hew to cultural traditions. Thus urban Chinese pay more than $1 for Crest toothpaste with exotic flavors such as Icy Mountain Spring and Morning Lotus Fragrance; while those in the villages prefer 50-cent Crest Salt White since many rural Chinese believe that salt whitens teeth. Such geographic segmentation is also practiced for its Olay moisturizing cream, Tide detergent, Rejoice shampoo, and Pampers diapers.[19]

Table 8.1 Major Segment Variables for Consumer Markets

Geographic	
Region	Municipalities, Provinces, Special Administrative Regions, etc. (China)
City or metro size	Under 5,000; 5,000–19,000; 20,000–49,000; 50,000–99,000; 100,000–249,000; 250,000–499,000; 500,000–999,000; 1,000,000–3,999,000; 4,000,000 or over
Density	Urban, suburban, rural
Climate	Tropical; subtropical; temperate
Demographic	
Age	Under 6, 6–11, 12–19, 20–34, 35–49, 50–64, 65+
Family size	1–2, 3–4, 5+
Family life cycle	Nuclear; small extended; large extended
Gender	Male, female
Annual Income	Under $5,000, $5000–9,000; $10,000–$14,000; $15,000–$19,000; $20,000–$29,000; $30,000–$49,000; $50,000–$99,000; $100,000 and over
Occupation	Professionals, managers, executives, and businesspeople (PMEBs); craftspeople; forepersons; operatives; farmers; retired; students; homemakers; unemployed
Education	None; elementary education; secondary education; diploma level; undergraduate; postgraduate
Religion	Buddhist; Catholic; Hindu; Muslim; Protestant; Taoist; other; none
Race	Mongolian, Manchu, Tartar, Zhuang, Hui, Tibetan, Miao, Yi, etc. (China)
Nationality	Chinese; Indian; Indonesian; Japanese; Malaysian; Filipino; Korean; Vietnamese; Singaporean; Thai; other
Social class	Lower lowers, upper lowers, working class, middle class, upper middles, lower uppers, upper uppers
Psychographic	
Lifestyle	Culture-oriented, sports-oriented, outdoor-oriented
Personality	
Behavioral	Compulsive, gregarious, authoritarian, ambitious
Occasions	Regular occasion, special occasion
Benefits	Quality, service, economy, speed
User status	Non-user, ex-user, potential user, first-time user, regular user
Usage rate	Light user, medium user, heavy user
Loyalty status	None, medium, strong, absolute
Readiness stage	Unaware, aware, informed, interested, desirous, intending to buy
Attitude toward product	Enthusiastic, positive, indifferent, negative, hostile

More and more, regional marketing means marketing right down to a specific district.[20] Some companies use mapping software to show the geographic locations of their customers. The software may show a retailer that most of his customers are within only a 20-kilometer radius of his store, and further concentrated with certain areas. By mapping the densest areas, the retailer can resort to *customer cloning*, assuming that the best prospects live where most of his customers come from. Here is an example from Hong Kong:

CR Asia—CR Asia runs the Circle K convenience shops in Hong Kong. Information technology helps it to stay abreast of the buying habits of the 350,000 consumers who purchase items from its shops daily. The company has an $8-million information hub with 20 servers at its headquarters. Traditional cash registers have been replaced with scanners, allowing for data mining. This technology helps sales staff to identify what customers want at different shops and stock their shelves accordingly. Circle K can profile its shops based on the demographics and nationalities of its customers. Hence, a store in Stanley, a sedate village on the south side of Hong Kong which attracts many expatriates and tourists, sells Heineken and Häagen-Dazs ice cream; while those in working-class housing estates are stocked with San Miguel beer, which costs half the price of Heineken, and a modestly priced, nonpremium Dreyer's ice cream.[21]

Some approaches combine geographic data with demographic data to yield even richer descriptions of consumers and neighborhoods. Called geoclustering, it captures the increasing diversity of the population.

Demographic Segmentation

In demographic segmentation, the market is divided into groups on the basis of variables such as age, family size, family life cycle, gender, income, occupation, education, religion, race, generation, nationality, and social class. There are two reasons for the popularity of demographic variables to distinguish customer groups. First, consumer needs, wants, and usage rates and product and brand preferences are often associated with demographic variables. Second, demographic variables are easier to measure. Even when the target market is described in nondemographic terms (say, a personality type), the link back to demographic characteristics is needed to estimate the size of the market and the media that should be used to reach it efficiently.

Here is how certain demographic variables have been used to segment markets.

AGE AND LIFE-CYCLE STAGE

Consumer wants and abilities change with age. Toothpaste brands such as Crest and Colgate offer three main lines of products to target kids, adults, and older consumers. Age segmentation can be even more refined. Pampers divides its market into prenatal, newborn (0–1 month), infant (2–5 months), cruiser (6–12 months), toddler (13–18 months), explorer (19–23 months), and preschooler (24 months+).

Sangaria—This Japanese beverage company introduced ***Kodomo no Nomimono*** ("Kids' Drink"), a non-alcoholic fruit juice that comes in dark brown bottles and pours like a golden lager with a foamy head. Sangaria and some small beverage producers market the soft drinks as a near-beer for elementary school kids or for young women who do not like alcohol but are anxious that a teetotaler will miss all the fun.

Nevertheless, age and life-cycle can be tricky variables.[22] In some cases, the target market for products may be the psychologically young. For example, Honda tried to target 21-year-olds with its boxy Element, which company officials described as a 'dorm room on wheels." So many baby boomers were attracted to the car's ads depicting sexy college kids partying near the car at a beach. However, the average age of buyers turned out to be 42! With baby boomers seeking to stay young, Honda decided that the lines between age groups were getting blurred. When it was ready to launch a new subcompact called the Fit, Honda deliberately targeted Gen Y buyers as well as their empty-nest parents.[23]

To market the new FIT model, Honda used what it had learned from the launch of the Element—that baby boomers hanging on to their youthful image were just as interested in the stylish new cars as the original target audience, 21-year-old drivers.

LIFE STAGE

Persons in the same part of the life cycle may differ in their life stage. **Life stage** defines a person's major concern, such as going through a divorce, going into a second marriage, taking care of an older parent, deciding to cohabit with another person, deciding to buy a new home, and so on. These life stages present opportunities for marketers who can help people cope with their major concerns.

GENDER

Men and women tend to have different attitudinal and behavioral orientations, based partly on genetic make-up and partly on socialization. For example, women tend to be more communal-minded and men tend to be more self-expressive and goal-directed; women tend to take in more of the data in their immediate environment; while men tend to focus on the part of the environment that helps them achieve a goal. A research study examining how men and women shop found that men often need to be invited to touch a product, while women are likely to pick it up without prompting. Men often like to read product information; women may relate to a product on a more personal level.[24]

Gender differentiation has long been applied in clothing, hairstyling, cosmetics, and magazines. Shiseido has built a $6 billion business selling beauty products to women. Some products have been positioned as more masculine or feminine. Gillette's Venus is the most successful female shaving line ever, with over 70 percent of the market, and has appropriate product design, packaging, and advertising cues to reinforce a female image. However, men are increasingly an important segment to cosmetics companies.

The beauty industry in Japan—Japanese women continue to sustain the beauty business. Tokyo's fashionable Marunouchi business district has seen beauty outlets sprouting. One such outlet, Café de Make-up, specifically targets office ladies. It offers them an orange seat, a cup of coffee, a choice of five colors of nail polish or lipstick, the services of a beauty advisor, and a chance to apply make-up at leisure at a vanity table for a low price of 500 yen. Men are also a fast-growing segment in the beauty market. Mandom, Japan's Number 2 maker of men's cosmetics, says that sales of face care products like cleansing gels, toning lotions, and mud packs are strong and growing. One explanation for this is the slew of boyish, clean-cut actors and pop singers who have become the rage among young Japanese women. These celebrities have been engaged as endorsers of more and more beauty products.

But it's not enough to tout a product as masculine or feminine. Hypersegmentation is now occurring within both male and female personal care segments. Unilever earned kudos by targeting women who do not look like, or aspire to look like, fashion models, with its award-winning "Dove Campaign for Real Beauty":

Dove—Dove's Campaign for Real Beauty features women of all shapes, sizes, and colors posing proudly in their underwear. The company claims that the ad series, developed by Ogilvy & Mather, was not just a vehicle to sell more soap but "aims to change the status quo and offer in its place a broader, healthier, more democratic view of beauty." Across Asia, it found that less than 3 percent of women think they are beautiful. They would rather describe themselves as "simple or natural" or "average or normal." While Asian women felt that humor and happiness, dignity and confidence, kindness, intelligence, and wisdom are more important than sex appeal or youth in terms of feeling beautiful, they were still beholden to youth when it comes to looking beautiful. Sparked by the results of the study, Dove decided to provoke discussion and initiate debate on what really is beautiful. It is debunking beauty stereotypes and widening the definition of beauty.[25]

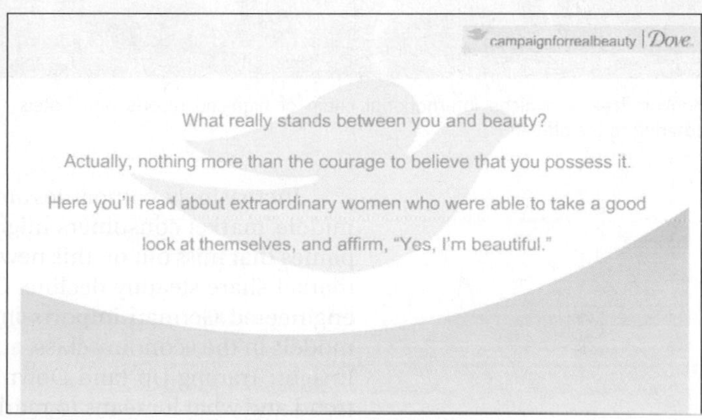

Dove's campaign for Real Beauty tries to debunk beauty stereotypes and offer a "broader, healthier, more democratic view of beauty."

Some traditionally more male-oriented markets, such as the automobile industry, are beginning to recognize gender segmentation, changing how they design and sell cars. Several Korean car manufacturers have designed cars specifically for women. Banks are also finding women a lucrative segment in Japan.

The home mortgage industry in Japan—Banks in Japan discovered that women are a "safe" and lucrative segment. Their default rate is lower than that of salarymen that banks traditionally targeted. Suruga Bank marketed Sonet, a mortgage program targeting at women, and found that not only were there less default cases, but women were also willing to pay higher rates for flexibility in mortgage financing and payment. Chuo Mitsui Trust introduced an Exerina mortgage loan that features discounted rates for pregnant women, while Resona Bank offered customized home loans and money-management courses for women, and Tokyo Star Bank included lunchtime and after-work seminars for women in its marketing of its Star One mortgage.[26]

INCOME

Income segmentation is a long-standing practice in such product and service categories as automobiles, clothing, cosmetics, financial services, and travel.

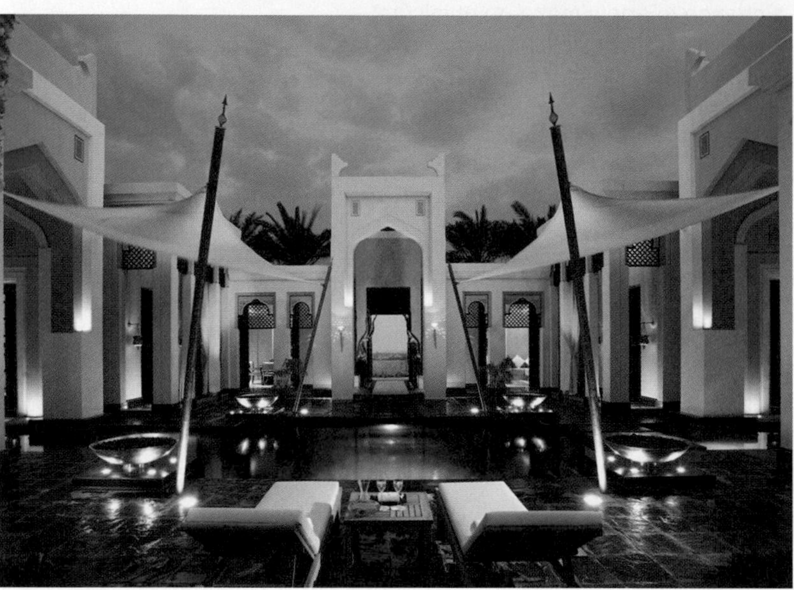

Banyan Tree is a niche international chain of high-end resorts and hotels catering to the affluent.

Banyan Tree—Singapore's Banyan Tree, famous for its upmarket pampering with a distinctive Asian touch, won a deal to run a seven-to-eight star multi-million dollar spa resort in Bahrain, where money is no object to guests. Set in a lush oasis, next to Bahrain's Formula One motor-racing circuit and a wildlife reserve, the spa resort has been billed as the ultimate in exclusivity and luxury. Catering to the "blank check" segment, the spa resort will have 78 villas designed to look like Bedouin tents. To deliver the ultimate level of privacy, guests, if they wish, can be kept away from view of other guests.[27]

Increasingly, companies are finding that their markets are "hourglass-shaped" as some middle-market consumers migrate toward both discount *and* premium products.[28] Companies that miss out on this new market risk being "trapped in the middle" and seeing their market share steadily decline. General Motors was caught in the middle, between highly engineered German imports in the luxury market and high-value Japanese and Korean models in the economy class, and has seen its market share continually slide.[29] "Marketing Insight: Trading Up (and Down): The New Consumer" describes the factors creating this trend and what it means to marketers.

GENERATION

Each generation is profoundly influenced by the times in which it grows up—the music, movies, politics, and defining events of that period. Demographers call these groups *cohorts*. Members of a cohort share the same major cultural, political, and economic experiences. They have similar outlooks and values. Marketers often advertise to a cohort group by using the icons and images prominent in their experiences. "Marketing Insight: Marketing to Generation Y" provides insight into that key age cohort.

Generation segmentation has been used by both advertising agencies and marketers in Asia. Ogilvy & Mather conducted a survey of 7,000 educated young consumers in seven Asian countries (Hong Kong, Indonesia, Malaysia, the Philippines, Singapore, Taiwan, and Thailand). From this survey, the ad agency identified an Asian version of Generation X and labeled it GENIE or the GENeration who Independently Engage. GENIEs have little respect for social structures. However, they are neither rebels against society nor consumed by materialism. While they enjoy the good life, they still value family ties and hard work. GENIEs also want to be part of society with some freedom of expression.[30] Similarly, ad agency Leo Burnett found that generation segmentation works in China:

MARKETING INSIGHT • TRADING UP (AND DOWN): THE NEW CONSUMER

A new pattern in consumer behavior has emerged in recent years, according to Michael Silverstein and Neil Fiske, the authors of *Trading Up*. In unprecedented numbers, middle-market consumers are periodically trading up to what is called "New Luxury" products and services "that possess higher levels of quality, taste, and aspiration than other goods in the category but are not so expensive as to be out of reach." For example, these consumer might trade up to an imported French wine, use a premium skin cream, or stay in a luxury hotel for a few nights on vacation, depending on the emotional benefits gained in the trade.

The authors identify a number of broad demographic and cultural explanations for the trend. In general, people have more money to spend than in years past. More women are entering the workforce and are commanding higher salaries than before. They feel entitled to spend the money they earn. As baby boomers find themselves with empty nests, as adults continue to marry later and divorce more often, the consumer has fewer mouths to feed. Finally, consumers today are better educated and more comfortable analyzing and satisfying their emotional needs, which New Luxury goods often target. As a result, the authors assert, the consumer has been transformed into "a sophisticated and discerning consumer with high aspirations and substantial buying power and clout."

Thanks to the trading-up trend, New Luxury goods sell at higher volumes than traditional luxury goods, although priced higher than conventional mid-market items. The authors identify three main types of New Luxury products:

- **Accessible superpremium products** such as Victoria's Secret underwear and Kettle gourmet potato chips carry a significant premium over middle-market brands, yet consumers can readily trade up to them because they are relatively low-ticket items in affordable categories.
- **Old Luxury brand extensions** extend historically high-priced brands down-market while retaining their cachet, such as the Mercedes-Benz C-class and the American Express Blue card.
- **Masstige goods** such as Kiehl's skin care, are priced between average middle-market brands and superpremium Old Luxury brands. They are "always based on emotions, and consumers have a much stronger emotional engagement with them than with other goods."

The authors note that to trade up on the brands that offered these emotional benefits, consumers often "trade down" by shopping at discounters such as Wal-Mart and Costco for staple items or goods that confer no emotional benefit but still deliver quality and functionality. The new consumer is also "part martyr and part hedonist," who willingly sacrifices on a number of purchases to experience enhanced benefits from a handful of others.

Silverstein reasons that with the trading-up segment of the market expected to rise, and trading-down segment predicted to grow, the firms that succeed will offer one of two kinds of value: New Luxury or Treasure Hunting. The remaining firms, which occupy the middle market, will continue to see their market share shrink as they get "trapped in the middle." Silverstein argues that most middle-market companies do not offer the economic, functional, and emotional value that modern consumers are searching for. Brands that offer opportunities to trade up, such as Coach and Victoria's Secret, or to trade down, such as IKEA, are optimally positioned to deliver the value that modern consumers seek.

Sources: Michael J. Silverstein, *Treasure Hunt: Inside the Mind of the New Consumer,* (New York: Portfolio, 2006); Jeff Cioletti, "Movin' on Up." *BeverageWorld*, June 2006, p. 20.; Michael J. Silverstein and Neil Fiske, *Trading Up: The New American Luxury,* (New York: Portfolio, 2003).

Leo Burnett—In its Consumer Quest Survey, Leo Burnett found that in China, the "Open Generation" (those aged 18–34) strives for such qualities as having a sense of accomplishment, being committed to a loving relationship, and finding inner harmony. They are more willing to sacrifice pay for time off. Their parents, called the Elder Generation, emphasize values such as setting a good example for their children, working for the good of the country, and having national pride. While the Open Generation of China shares similar tastes in music and fashion with the Gen Xers in the U.S., critical differences remain. Whereas Xers and their Baby Boomer parents share many of the same values toward work, family, and society, their Chinese counterparts have a huge experiential gap between the two generations. While the Elder Generation had to endure the Communist Revolution and the Cultural Revolution, the Open Generation of China grew up in relative political stability since the late 1970s. They have also witnessed tremendous economic change and increasing social openness with the increased availability of Western ideas, products, and culture.[31]

MARKETING INSIGHT • MARKETING TO GENERATION Y

In the U.S., they're dubbed "Echo Boomers" or "Generation Y." They grew up during times of economic abundance followed by years of economic recession. Their world was defined by long years of national calm and peace disrupted by events like 9/11. They have been "wired" almost from birth—playing computer games, navigating the Web, downloading music, connecting with friends via instant messaging and cell phones. They have a sense of entitlement and abundance from having grown up during the economic boom and being pampered by their Boomer parents. They are selective, confident, and also impatient. They "want what they want when they want it"—and they often get it by using plastic, potentially going into credit card debt.

The forces that have shaped the Gen Y cohort are important to marketers because Generation Y is the force that will shape consumer and business markets for years to come. Born between 1977 and 1994, Generation Y is three times the size of Generation X. Roughly 78 million Americans belong to this group, the largest generational cohort in American history. Their spending power is estimated at $187 billion annually. When you also factor in career growth, household and family formation, and multiply by another 53 years of life expectancy, you're in the $10 trillion range in consumer spending over the lifespan of today's 21-year-old Americans.

It's not surprising, then, that market researchers and advertisers are racing to get a bead on Gen Y's buying behavior. Because they are often turned off by overt branding practices and a "hard sell," marketers have tried many different approaches to reach and persuade Generation Y.

1. ***Online buzz*** — Rock band Foo Fighters created a digital street team that sends targeted email blasts to members who "get the latest news, exclusive audio/video sneak previews, tons of chances to win great Foo Fighters prizes, and become part of the Foo Fighters Family."

2. ***Student ambassadors*** — Red Bull enlists college students as Red Bull Student Brand Managers to distribute samples, research drinking trends, design on-campus marketing initiatives, and write stories for student newspapers.

3. ***Unconventional sports*** — Dodge automobiles sponsors the World Dodgeball Association, which is taking the sport "to a new level by emphasizing teamwork, strategy, and skill."

4. ***Cool events*** — The U.S. Open of Surfing attracted sponsors such as Honda, Philips Electronics and, O'Neill Clothing, originators of the first wet suit. Spring break in Florida has been the place for the launch of such products as Old Spice Cool Contact Refreshment Towels and Calvin Klein's CK swimwear line.

5. ***Computer games*** — Product placement is not restricted to movies or TV: Mountain Dew, Oakley, and Harley-Davidson all made deals to put logos on Tony Hawk's Pro Skater 3 from Activision.

6. ***Videos*** — Burton snowboard ensures that its boards and riders are clearly visible in any videos that are shot.

7. ***Street teams*** — As part of an anti-smoking crusade, The American Legacy hires teens as the "Truth Squad" to hand out T-shirts, bandanas, and dog tags at teen-targeted events.

Even more intriguing is a recent book authored by 17-year-old American Michael Stanat. Entitled *China's Generation Y,* Stanat's book was based on extensive research sponsored by New York's SIS International Research and CBC Market Research, Shanghai. The book investigates the strengths and weaknesses, dreams and goals, marketing dos and don'ts, and threats and opportunities of this generation of Chinese consumers. Some of the interesting facts uncovered include:

1. China's Gen Y comprises approximately 200 million Chinese aged between 15 and 25.

2. About 20 million Chinese attain teenage age annually.

3. Each year, four times as many Chinese study engineering than Americans, jeopardizing the U.S.'s scientific and technological superiority.

4. China's Gen Y are significantly more entrepreneurial and capitalistic than their parents, and with market reform, can more easily become entrepreneurs.

5. They are far more connected to the Internet and by mobile phones than any other generation in China.

6. Gen Yers consume 50 percent or more of family expenditure in some major Chinese cities.

7. They generally know more about Westerners than Westerners know about them.

Sources: J. M. Lawrence, "Trends: X-ed Out: Gen Y Takes Over." *Boston Herald,* February 2, 1999, p. 243; Martha Irvine, "Labels Don't Fit Us, Gen Y Insists." *Denver Post,* April 9, 2001, p. A9; Anonymous, "Gen Y and the Future of Mall Retailing." *American Demographics*, December 2002/January 2003, pp. J1-J4; Michael J. Weiss, "To Be about to Be." *American Demographics*, September 2003, pp. 28-36; John Leo, "The Good-News Generation." *U.S. News & World Report,* November 3, 2003, p. 60; Kelly Pate, "Not 'X,' but 'Y' Marks the Spot: Young Generation a Marketing Target." *Denver Post*, August 17, 2003, p. K1; Bruce Hororitz, "GenY: A Tough Crowd to Sell." *USA Today*, April 22, 2002, pp. 1B-2B; Bruce Hororitz, "Marketers Revel with Spring Breakers." *USA Today*, March 12, 2002, p. 3B; <www.chinageny.com>; Michael Stanat, *China's Generation Y: Understanding the Future Leaders of the World's Next Superpower*, (Paramus, NJ: Homa & Sekey, 2005).

Based on this study, McDonald's adapted its ads that are targeted at its China market:

McDonald's—A McDonald's ad in the U.S. called "Bad Hair Day" did not work in China. The ad featured a pair of mother and daughter acting more like friends than mother and daughter. Instead, McDonald's more successful ads in China focused more on families and the generations working together in a new world, rather than emphasizing a modern relationship between parent and child. One ad thus showed a grandparent eating French fries with chopsticks.

Meredith, Schewe, and Karlovich developed a framework called the Lifestage Analytic Matrix which combines information on cohorts, life stages, physiographics, emotional effects, and socioeconomics in analyzing a segment or individual.[32] For example, two individuals from the same cohort may differ in their *life stages* (getting married, having children), *physiographics* (coping with hair loss, menopause, arthritis, or osteoporosis), *emotional effects* (nostalgia for the past, wanting experiences instead of things), or *socioeconomics* (losing a job, receiving an inheritance). The authors believe this analysis will lead to more efficient targeting and messages.

SOCIAL CLASS

Social class has a strong influence on preference in cars, clothing, home furnishings, leisure activities, reading habits, and retailers. Many companies design products and services for specific social classes. The tastes of social classes change with the years. The 1990s were about greed and ostentation for the upper classes. Affluent tastes now run more conservatively, although luxury goods makers such as Coach, Tiffany, Burberry, TAG Heuer, and Louis Vuitton still successfully sell to those seeking the good life.[33]

Psychographic Segmentation

Psychographics is the science of using psychology and demographics to better understand consumers. In *psychographic segmentation*, buyers are divided into different groups on the basis of lifestyle or personality or values. People within the same demographic group can exhibit very different psychographic profiles.

One of the most popular commercially available classification systems based on psychographic measurements is SRI Consulting Business Intelligence's (SRIC-BI) VALS™ framework. VALS classifies adults into eight primary groups based on personality traits and key demographics. The segmentation system is based on responses to a questionnaire featuring four demographic and 35 attitudinal questions. The VALS system is continually updated with new data from more than 80,000 surveys per year[34] (see Figure 8.2).

The main dimensions of the VALS segmentation framework are consumer motivation (the horizontal dimension) and consumer resources (the vertical dimension). Consumers are inspired by one of three primary motivations: ideals, achievement, and self-expression. Those primarily motivated by ideals are guided by knowledge and principles. Those motivated by achievement look for products and services that demonstrate success to their peers. Consumers whose motivation is self-expression desire social or physical activity, variety, and risk. Personality traits such as energy, self-confidence, intellectualism, novelty seeking, innovativeness, impulsiveness, leadership, and vanity—in conjunction with key demographics—determine an individual's resources. Different levels of resources enhance or constrain a person's expression of his primary motivation.

The four groups with higher resources are:

1. ***Innovators*** — Successful, sophisticated, active, and "take-charge" people with high self-esteem. Purchases often reflect cultivated tastes for relatively upscale, niche-oriented products and services.
2. ***Thinkers*** — Mature, satisfied, and reflective people who are motivated by ideals and value order, knowledge, and responsibility. Favor durability, functionality, and value in products.

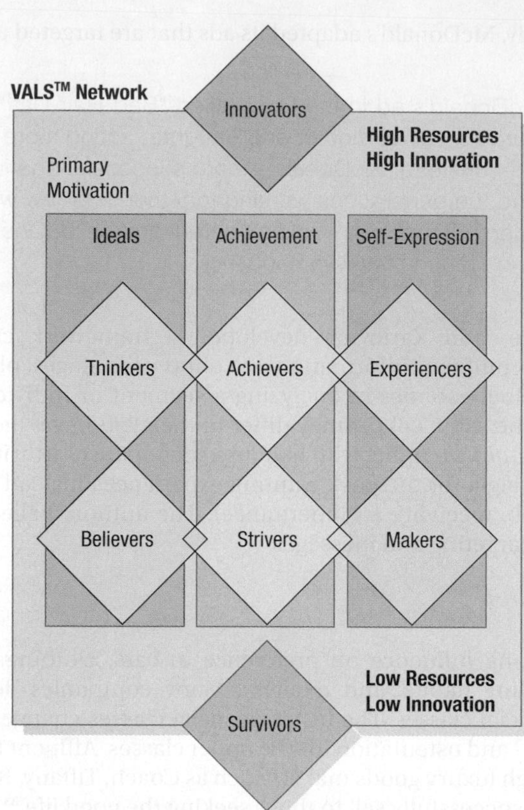

Figure 8.2 The VALS Segementation System: An 8-Part Typology

Source: © 2004 by SR2 Consulting Business Intelligence. All rights reserved. Used with permission.

3. ***Achievers*** — Successful career- and work-oriented people who value consensus and stability. Favor established and prestige products that demonstrate success to their peers.
4. ***Experiencers*** — Young, enthusiastic, and impulsive people who seek variety and excitement. Spend a comparatively high proportion of income on fashion, entertainment, and socializing.

The major tendencies of the four groups with lower resources are:

1. ***Believers*** — Conservative, conventional, and traditional people with concrete beliefs. Favor familiar and established products and are loyal to established brands.
2. ***Strivers*** — Trendy and fun-loving people who seek approval of others but are resource-constrained. Favor stylish products that emulate the purchases of those with greater material wealth.
3. ***Makers*** — Practical, self-sufficient, traditional, and family-oriented people who focus on their work and home context. Favor basic products with a practical or functional purpose.
4. ***Strugglers*** — Elderly, resigned, and passive people who are concerned about change. Loyal to their favorite brands.

You can find out which VALS type you are at SRIC-BI's Web site (www.sric-bi.com).

Psychographic segmentation schemes are often customized by culture. The Japanese version of VALS (Japan-VALS™) employs two key dimensions: life orientation (traditional ways, occupations, innovation, and self-expression) and attitudes to social change (sustaining, pragmatic, adapting, and innovating). Based on these dimensions, Japanese society can be divided into 10 segments:[35]

1. ***Integrators*** — These consumers are active, inquisitive, trend-leading, informed, and affluent. They travel frequently and are exposed to a wide range of media.
2. ***Self Innovators and Self Adopters*** — These consumers desire personal experience, fashionable display, social activities, daring ideas, and exciting, graphic entertainment.

3. ***Ryoshiki Innovators and Ryoshiki Adapters*** — These consumers are guided by their concern for their home, family, and social status. They are generally accomplished in their education and profession. (*Ryoshiki* means "good values.")
4. ***Tradition Innovators and Tradition Adapters*** — These consumers adhere to traditional religions and customs, prefer long-familiar home furnishings and dress, and hold conservative social opinions.
5. ***High Pragmatics and Low Pragmatics*** — These consumers are not very active and not well-informed, have few interests and seem flexible and even uncommitted in their lifestyle choices.
6. ***Sustainers*** — These consumers lack money, youth, and high education. They dislike innovation and are typically oriented to sustaining the past.

Behavioral Segmentation

In behavioral segmentation, buyers are divided into groups on the basis of their knowledge of, attitude toward, use of, or response to a product.

DECISION ROLES

It is easy to identify the buyer for many products. Men normally choose their shaving equipment, and women choose their pantyhose. Even here marketers must be careful in making their targeting decisions, because buying roles change. When ICI, the giant British chemical company, discovered that women made 60 percent of the decisions on the brand of household paint, it decided to advertise its Dulux brand to attract women.

People play five roles in a buying decision: *initiator, influencer, decider, buyer,* and *user.* For example, assume a wife initiates a purchase by requesting a new treadmill for her birthday. The husband may then seek information from many sources, including his best friend who has a treadmill and is a key influencer in what models to consider. After presenting the alternative choices to his wife, he then purchases her preferred model which, as it turns out, ends up being used by the entire family. Different people are playing different roles, but all are crucial in the decision process and ultimate consumer satisfaction.

BEHAVIORAL VARIABLES

Many marketers believe that behavioral variables—occasions, benefits, user status, usage rate, loyalty status, buyer-readiness stage, and attitude—are the best starting points for constructing market segments.

Occasions

Occasions can be defined in terms of the time of day, week, month, year or in terms of other well-defined temporal aspects of a consumer's life. Buyers can be distinguished according to the occasions when they develop a need, purchase a product, or use a product. For example, air travel is triggered by occasions related to business, vacation, or family. Occasion segmentation can help firms expand product usage.

Marketers can also try to extend activities associated with certain holidays to other times of the year. For instance, while Christmas, Mother's Day, and Valentine's Day are major gift-giving holidays, these and other holidays account for just over half of the gifters' budgets. That leaves the rest available throughout the year for occasion-driven gift-giving: birthdays, weddings, anniversaries, housewarming, and new babies.[36] The Japanese are arguably the most prolific in establishing occasions for marketing purposes:

Anniversaries in Japan—Anniversaries or *kinenbi* abound on the Japanese calendar. In November alone, there is Sushi Day, Dogs Day, Records Day, Handkerchief Day, Toilet Day, Elevator Day, Soccer Day, Jewelry Day, Peanut Day, Western Dress Day, Kimono Day, *Kamaboko* (fish cake) Day, Kelp Day, Japanese Chess Day, Fur Day, Married Couples Day, and Eating Out Day. These anniversaries are generally aimed at creating an occasion to promote a variety of products and institutions. For example, on Movies Day each December 1st, cinemas traditionally discount their tickets to promote attendance. Japanese retailers created White Day on March 14th for men to respond to the gifts they receive from their female friends on Valentine's Day. Premiums are offered at bowling alleys every June 22nd, Bowling Day. Indeed, the Japan Kinenbi Association publishes a newsletter highlighting forthcoming special occasions, compiles a register of *kinenbi* in the country, and provides consultation for organizations seeking a unique day of their own. As Japanese celebrate many other traditional festivals, they are receptive to new special occasions that give them an opportunity to think about the environment around them.[37]

Coca-Cola—Coke's consumer research in Japan discovered that half of young, working males skip breakfast, suggesting a new segment for beverages. Coke recognized that these young Japanese men cannot get through the morning without drinking something and introduced Pocket Dr., a drink which includes vitamins and minerals. Coke is also exploring other nutritional drinks that can serve as an instant breakfast on the run.[38]

Benefits

Buyers can be classified according to the benefits they seek. Even car drivers who want to stop for gas may seek different benefits. Through its research, Mobil identified five different benefit segments and their sizes:

1. ***Road Warriors*** — Premium products and quality service (16 percent).
2. ***Generation F*** — Fast fuel, fast service, and fast food (27 percent).
3. ***True Blues*** — Branded products and reliable service (16 percent).
4. ***Home Bodies*** — Convenience (21 percent).
5. ***Price Shoppers*** — Low price (20 percent).

Surprisingly, although gasoline is largely a commodity, price shoppers constituted only 20 percent of the buyers. Mobil decided to focus on the less price-sensitive segments and rolled out *Friendly Serve*: cleaner property, bathrooms, better lighting, well-stocked stores, and friendlier personnel. Although Mobil charged $0.02 per gallon more than its competitors, sales increased by 20–25 percent.[39]

Here is another example of benefit segmentation:

Honda—Honda is repositioning itself to be the Volvo of Asia. It is pushing safety as a major selling point. In 2003, it opened a $30 million test facility in Ohio and is now offering more premium safety devices as standard equipment. In Japan, Honda has a computer installed in every car that automatically activates the brakes if the sensors detect an imminent crash. Its Legend sedan has an infrared night vision screen that pops up on the dash and can outline human forms in the darkness. By 2007, Honda plans to make anti-lock brakes and side-curtain airbags standard equipment on all models sold in the U.S. By 2010, Honda will design the front end of all its vehicles to absorb more of the impact of a crash, and do less damage to the other driver's car.[40]

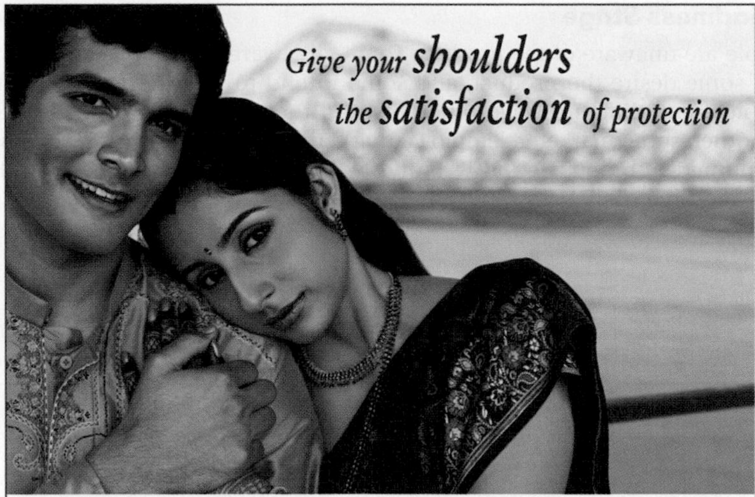
Give your shoulders
the satisfaction of protection

Be it for love or security, in good times or bad, it is always your able shoulders that your family instinctively seeks to lean on. Nobody understands this better than us and works harder to give you the true satisfaction of knowing that you have both protected and provided for all their tomorrows.

So, no matter what your long term objectives, be it your child's education, wealth creation or a worry free retirement; you can rest assured that they will be realized in our safe hands. We look forward to hear from you and being the shoulder that you can lean on, even as your family finds comfort in yours.

ICICI PRUDENTIAL
LIFE INSURANCE

We cover you. At every step in life.

sms LIFE to 7827* or call your advisor

Mumbai: 9892577766, Rest of Maharashtra: 98904 47766, Delhi: 98181 77766, Gujarat: 98982 77766, Andhra Pradesh: 98495 77766, Karnataka: 98455 77766, Chennai: 98408 77766, Kerala: 98954 77766, Kolkata: 98313 77766, Punjab: 98159 77766, U.P.(E): 99352 77766, U.P.(W): 98973 07766 or call your advisor.

Insurance is the subject matter of the solicitation. ICICI Prudential Life Insurance Company limited. *Available in select cities only. Terms & conditions apply.

Different insurance plans offer different coverage benefits. This ad by ICICI Prudential provides insurance benefits for the family.

User Status

Markets can be segmented into non-users, ex-users, potential users, first-time users, and regular users of a product. Blood banks cannot rely only on regular donors to supply blood; they must also recruit new first-time donors and contact ex-donors. Each will require a different marketing strategy. Included in the potential user group are consumers who will become users in connection with some life stage or life event. Mothers-to-be are potential users who will turn into heavy users. Producers of infant products and services learn their names and shower them with products and ads to capture a share of their future purchases. Market-share leaders tend to focus on attracting potential users because they have the most to gain. Smaller firms focus on trying to attract current users away from the market leader.

Usage Rate

Markets can be segmented into light, medium, and heavy product users. Heavy users are often a small percentage of the market but account for a high percentage of total consumption. For example, heavy beer drinkers account for 87 percent of the beer consumed—almost seven times as much as the light beer drinkers. Marketers would rather attract one heavy user than several light users. However, a potential problem is that heavy users are often either extremely loyal to one brand, or never stay loyal to a brand and are always looking for the lowest price.

Buyer-Readiness Stage

Some people are unaware of the product, some are aware, some are informed, some are interested, some desire the product, and some intend to buy. To help characterize how many people are at different stages and how well they have converted people from one stage to another, some marketers employ a marketing funnel. Figure 8.3 displays a funnel for two hypothetical brands, A and B. Brand B performs poorly compared to Brand A at converting one-time triers to more recent triers.

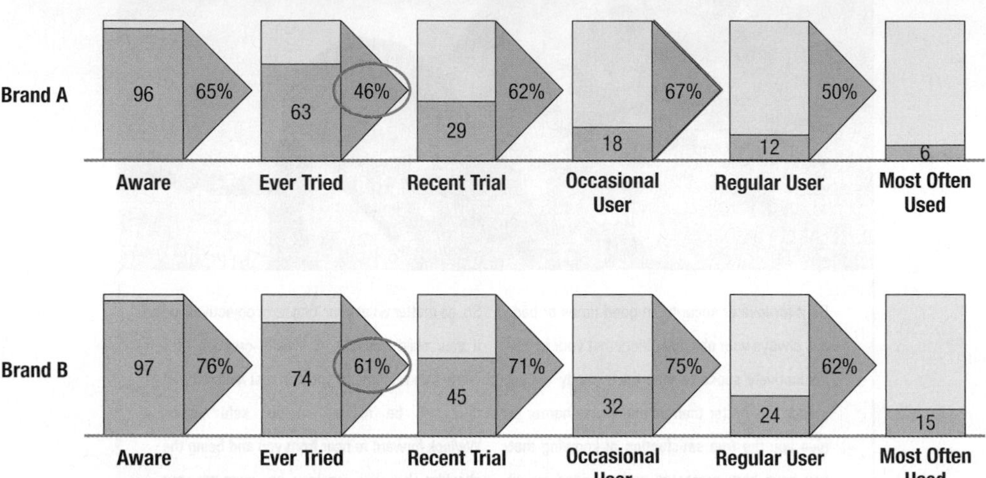

Figure 8.3 Brand Funnel

The relative numbers of consumers at different stages make a big difference in designing the marketing program. Suppose a health agency wants to encourage women to have an annual Pap test to detect cervical cancer. At the beginning, most women may be unaware of the Pap test. The marketing effort should go into awareness-building advertising using a simple message. Later, the advertising should dramatize the benefits of the Pap test and the risks of not taking it. A special offer of a free health examination might motivate women to actually sign up for the test.

> **Disney**—Disney felt that it had to prepare the Chinese public well before the opening of its theme park in Hong Kong. Jay Rasulo, president of Walt Disney Parks & Resorts, said, "For the first time, we'll be opening in a market where not all of our guests will know us well. The brand recognition is high, but the depth of storytelling isn't there." To fill this void, Disney mounted a grassroots brand-building campaign and experimented with novel marketing techniques. It teamed up with the 70 million-member Communist Youth League in China to host a series of sessions billed to aid reading skills and creativity. Disney performers toured half a dozen "children's palaces" in Guangdong province, telling stories using the Disney characters and encouraging children to draw pictures of Mickey Mouse.[41]

Loyalty Status

Buyers can be divided into four groups according to brand loyalty status:

1. ***Hard-core loyals***— Consumers who buy only one brand all the time.
2. ***Split loyals***— Consumers who are loyal to two or three brands.
3. ***Shifting loyals***— Consumers who shift loyalty from one brand to another.
4. ***Switchers***— Consumers who show no loyalty to any brand.[42]

A company can learn a great deal by analyzing the degrees of brand loyalty: (1) By studying its hard-core loyals, the company can identify its products' strengths; (2) By studying its split loyals, the company can pinpoint which brands are most competitive with its own; and (3) By looking at customers who are shifting away from its brand, the company can learn about its marketing weaknesses and attempt to correct them.

Companies selling in a market dominated by switchers may have to rely more on price-cutting. If mistreated, switchers can also turn on the company. One caution: What appear to be brand-loyal purchase patterns may reflect habit, indifference, a low price, a high switching cost, or the non-availability of other brands.

Fickle Chinese consumers—While marketers have observed that the "cool" factor is the key to unlocking Chinese consumption, they have noticed that these consumers are very fickle and loyalty to a single brand virtually does not exist. Chinese consumers are more focused on brands compared to their Western counterparts. They want brands that give them added status and not because they necessarily like them. Says Tom Doctoroff, Greater China CEO of advertising agency JWT, "There are a lot of things that are making money but nobody has established such a loyal franchise that there is absolute loyalty to that brand. I get lots of studies that say people switch a lot."[43]

Attitude

Five attitude groups can be found in a market: enthusiastic, positive, indifferent, negative, and hostile. Door-to-door workers in a political campaign use voter attitude to determine how much time to spend with that voter. They thank enthusiastic voters and remind them to vote; they reinforce those who are positively disposed; they try to win the votes of indifferent voters; they spend no time trying to change the attitudes of negative and hostile voters.

Combining different behavioral bases can help to provide a more comprehensive and cohesive view of a market and its segments. Figure 8.4 depicts one possible way to break down a target market by various behavioral segmentation bases.

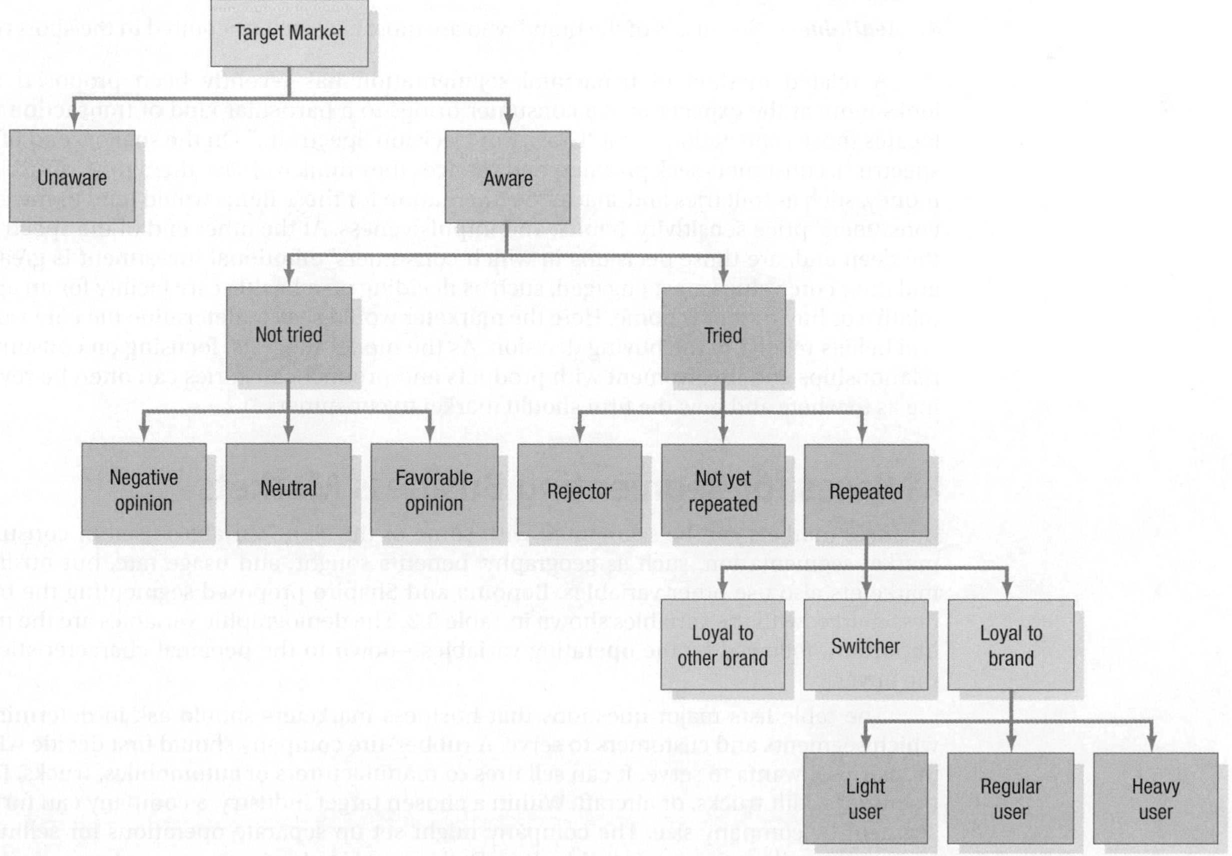

Figure 8.4 Behavioral Segmentation Breakdown

THE CONVERSION MODEL

The Conversion Model has been developed to measure the strength of the psychological commitment between brands and consumers and their openness to change.[44] To determine the ease with which a consumer can be converted to another choice, the model assesses commitment based on factors such as consumer attitudes toward and satisfaction with current brand choices in a category and the importance of the decision to select a brand in the category.[45]

The model segments *users* of a brand into four groups based on strength of commitment, from low to high, as follows:

1. ***Convertible***— Users who are most likely to defect.
2. ***Shallow***— Consumers who are uncommitted to the brand and could switch. Some are actively considering alternatives.
3. ***Average***— Consumers who are also committed to the brand they are using, but not as strongly. They are unlikely to switch brands in the short-term.
4. ***Entrenched***— Consumers who are strongly committed to the brand they are currently using. They are highly unlikely to switch brands in the foreseeable future.

The model also classifies *non-users* of a brand into four other groups based on their "balance of disposition" and openness to trying the brand, from low to high, as follows:

1. ***Strongly Unavailable***— Non-users who are unlikely to switch to the brand. Their preference lies strongly with their current brands.
2. ***Weakly Unavailable*** — Non-users who are not available to the brand because their preference lies with their current brand, although not strongly.
3. ***Ambivalent***— Non-users who are as attracted to the brand as they are to their current brands.
4. ***Available***— Non-users of the brand who are most likely to be acquired in the short run.

A related method of behavioral segmentation has recently been proposed that looks more at the expectations a consumer brings to a particular kind of transaction and locates those expectations on a "Gravity of Decision Spectrum." On the shallow end of the spectrum, consumers seek products and services they think will save them time, effort, and money, such as toiletries and snacks. Segmentation for these items would tend to measure consumers' price sensitivity, habits, and impulsiveness. At the other end of the spectrum, the deep end, are those decisions in which consumers' emotional investment is greatest and their core values most engaged, such as deciding on a health-care facility for an aging relative or buying a new home. Here the marketer would seek to determine the core values and beliefs related to the buying decision. As the model suggests, focusing on consumer's relationships and involvement with products and product categories can often be revealing as to where and how the firm should market to consumers.[46]

Bases for Segmenting Business Markets

Business markets can be segmented with some of the same variables used in consumer market segmentation, such as geography, benefits sought, and usage rate, but business marketers also use other variables. Bonoma and Shapiro proposed segmenting the business market with the variables shown in Table 8.2. The demographic variables are the most important, followed by the operating variables—down to the personal characteristics of the buyer.

The table lists major questions that business marketers should ask in determining which segments and customers to serve. A rubber-tire company should first decide which industries it wants to serve. It can sell tires to manufacturers of automobiles, trucks, farm tractors, forklift trucks, or aircraft. Within a chosen target industry, a company can further segment by company size. The company might set up separate operations for selling to large and small customers. Consider how Dell is organized.

Table 8.2 Major Segmentation Variables for Business Markets

Demographic Characteristics
1. *Industry:* Which industries should we serve?
2. *Company size:* What size companies should we serve?
3. *Location:* What geographical areas should we serve?
Operating Variables
4. *Technology:* What customer technologies should we focus on?
5. *User or non-user status:* Should we serve heavy users, medium users, light users, or non-users?
6. *Customer capabilities:* Should we serve customers needing many or few services?
Purchasing Approaches
7. *Purchasing-function organization:* Should we serve companies with highly centralized or decentralized purchasing organizations?
8. *Power structure:* Should we serve companies that are engineering dominated, financially dominated, and so on?
9. *Nature of existing relationships:* Should we serve companies with which we have strong relationships or simply go after the most desirable companies?
10. *General purchase policies:* Should we serve companies that prefer leasing? Service contracts? Systems purchases? Sealed bidding?
11. *Purchasing criteria:* Should we serve companies that are seeking quality? Service? Price?
Situational Factors
12. *Urgency:* Should we serve companies that need quick and sudden delivery or service?
13. *Specific application:* Should we focus on certain applications of our product rather than all applications?
14. *Size of order:* Should we focus on large or small orders?
Personal Characteristics
15. *Buyer-seller similarity:* Should we serve companies whose people and values are similar to ours?
16. *Attitudes toward risk:* Should we serve risk-taking or risk-avoiding customers?
17. *Loyalty:* Should we serve companies that show high loyalty to their suppliers?

Source: Adapted from Thomas V. Bonoma and Benson P. Shapiro. *Segmenting the Industrial Market,* (Lexington, MA: Lexington Books, 1983).

Dell—Dell is divided into two direct sales divisions: one sells to consumers and small businesses; another manages the company's corporate accounts. Three key segments are included under the corporate accounts umbrella: the enterprise group (*Fortune* 500 companies), large corporate accounts (multinational companies in what would be the *Fortune* 501–2000 range), and preferred accounts (medium businesses with 200–2,000 employees).

Within a given target industry and customer size, a company can segment further by purchase criteria. For example, government laboratories need low prices and service contracts for scientific equipment; university laboratories need equipment that requires little service; and industrial laboratories need equipment that is highly reliable and accurate.

Business marketers generally identify segments through a sequential process. Consider an aluminum company: The company first undertook macrosegmentation. It looked at which end-use market to serve: automobile, residential, or beverage containers. It chose the residential market, and it needed to determine the most attractive product application: semifinished material, building components, or aluminum mobile homes. Deciding to focus on building components, it considered the best customer size and chose large customers. The second stage consisted of microsegmentation. The company distinguished among customers buying on price, service, or quality. Because the aluminum company had a high-service profile, it decided to concentrate on the service-motivated segment of the market.

Marketing Targeting

Once the firm has identified its market-segment opportunities, it has to decide how many and which ones to target. Marketers are increasingly combining several variables in an effort to identify smaller, better-defined target groups. Thus a bank may not only identify a group of wealthy retired adults, but within that group distinguish several segments depending on current income, assets, savings, and risk preferences. This has led some market researchers to advocate a *needs-based market segmentation approach.* Roger Best proposed the seven-step approach shown in Table 8.3.

Table 8.3 Steps in the Segmentation Process

		Description
1.	Needs-Based Segmentation	Group customers into segments based on similar needs and benefits sought by customer in solving a particular consumption problem.
2.	Segment Identification	For each needs-based segment, determine which demographics, lifestyles, and usage behaviors make the segment distinct and identifiable (actionable).
3.	Segment Attractiveness	Using predetermined segment attractiveness criteria (such as market growth, competitive intensity, and market access), determine the overall attractiveness of each segment.
4.	Segment Profitability	Determine segment profitability.
5.	Segment Positioning	For each segment, create a value proposition and product-price positioning strategy based on that segment's unique customer needs and characteristics.
6.	Segment "Acid Test"	Create "segment storyboards" to test the attractiveness of each segment's positioning strategy.
7.	Marketing-Mix Strategy	Expand segment positioning strategy to include all aspects of the marketing mix: product, price, promotion, and place.

Source: Adapted from Robert J. Best. *Market-Based Management,* (Upper Saddle River NJ: Prentice Hall, 2000).

Effective Segmentation Criteria

Not all segmentation schemes are useful. For example, table salt buyers could be divided into long-haired and short-haired customers, but hair length is irrelevant to the purchase of salt. Further, if all salt buyers buy the same amount of salt each month, believe all salt is the same, and would pay only one price for salt, this market would be minimally segmentable from a marketing point of view.

To be useful, market segments must rate favorably on five key criteria:

- ***Measurable*** — The size, purchasing power, and characteristics of the segments can be measured.
- ***Substantial*** — The segments are large and profitable enough to serve. A segment should be the largest possible homogeneous group worth going after with a tailored marketing program. For example, it would not pay for an automobile manufacturer to develop cars for people who are under four feet tall.
- ***Accessible*** — The segments can be effectively reached and served.

- ***Differentiable*** — The segments are conceptually distinguishable and respond differently to different marketing-mix elements and programs. If married and unmarried women respond similarly to a sale on perfume, they do not constitute separate segments.
- ***Actionable*** — Effective programs can be formulated for attracting and serving the segments.

Evaluating and Selecting the Market Segments

In evaluating different market segments, the firm must look at two factors: the segment's overall attractiveness and the company's objectives and resources. How well does a potential segment score on the five criteria? Does a potential segment have characteristics that make it generally attractive, such as size, growth, profitability, scale economies, and low risk? Does investing in the segment make sense given the firm's objectives, competencies, and resources? Some attractive segments may not mesh with the company's long-run objectives, or the company may lack one or more necessary competencies to offer superior value.

After evaluating different segments, the company can consider five patterns of target market selection, shown in Figure 8.5.

Single-segment Concentration

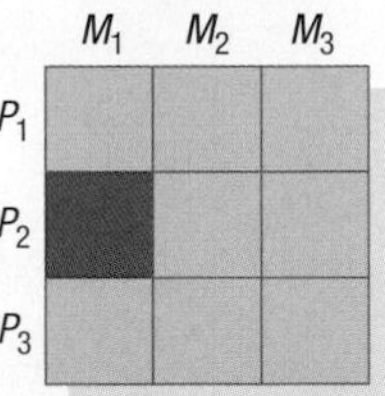

Selective Specialization

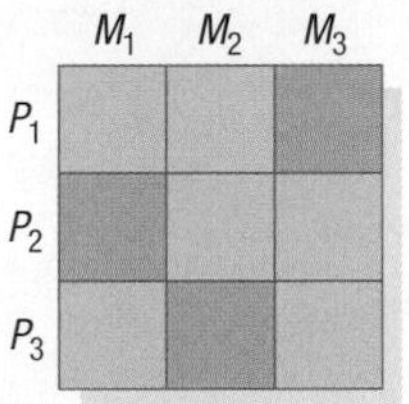

Product Specialization

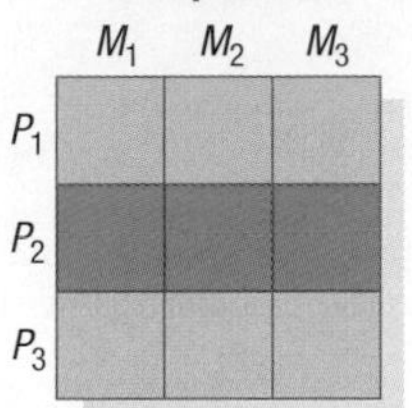

Market Specialization

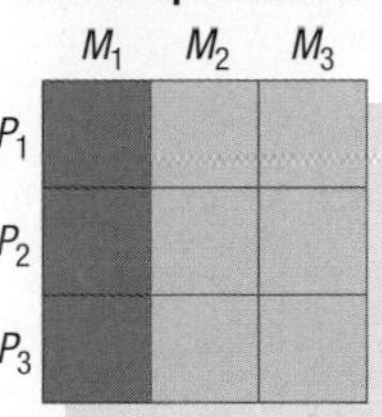

Full Market Coverage

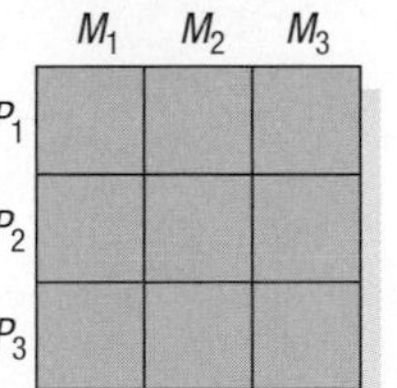

P = Product M = Market

Figure 8.5 Five Patterns of Target Market Selection

Source: Adapted from Derek F. Abell, *Defining the Business: The Starting Point of Strategic Planning*, (Upper Saddle River, NJ: Prentice Hall, 1980), chapter 8, pp. 192–196.

SINGLE-SEGMENT CONCENTRATION

Volkswagen concentrates on the small-car market and Porsche on the sports car market. Through concentrated marketing, the firm gains a strong knowledge of the segment's needs and achieves a strong market presence. Further, the firm enjoys operating economies through specializing its production, distribution, and promotion. If it captures segment leadership, the firm can earn a high return on its investment.

Tiger Motorcyles—Thai entrepreneur Piti Manomaiphibul's Tiger motorcycles are giving Japanese giants Honda, Suzuki, and Yamaha a run for their money in Thailand's lucrative motorcycle market. Tiger's bikes are targeted at a segment that Japanese producers have overlooked—the thrifty, yet style-conscious, rural rider. When Piti went to Vietnam, he saw Chinese makers of cheap motorcycles seizing nearly 70 percent of the market from Japanese producers. He decided to make a mid-priced bike as good as the Japanese and much better than the Chinese. Tiger is positioned against Japanese brands on two of the latter's weak spots—cost and design. Tiger motorbikes are produced at 20 percent less than Japanese bikes without sacrificing quality. Among its models are Ozone 3, a basic model aimed at rural student riders, a high-performance bike for riders who crave powerful but affordable bikes, and Nano, a minimotorcyle for children.[47]

However, there are risks. A particular market segment can turn sour or a competitor may invade the segment: when digital camera technology took off, Polaroid's earnings fell sharply. For these reasons, many companies prefer to operate in more than one segment. If a company selects more than one segment to serve, it should pay close attention to segment interrelationships on the cost, performance, and technology side. A company carrying fixed costs (sales force, store outlets) can add products to absorb and share some costs. The sales force will sell additional products, and a fast-food outlet will offer additional menu items. Economies of scope can be just as important as economies of scale.

Companies can try to operate in super-segments rather than in isolated segments. A **super-segment** is a set of segments sharing some exploitable similarity. For example, many symphony orchestras target people who have broad cultural interests, rather than only those who regularly attend concerts.

Selective Specialization

A firm selects a number of segments, each objectively attractive and appropriate. There may be little or no synergy among the segments, but each promises to be a moneymaker. This multi-segment strategy has the advantage of diversifying the firm's risk. When Procter

& Gamble launched Crest Whitestrips, initial target segments included newly engaged women, brides-to-be as well as gay males.

Product Specialization

The firm makes a certain product that it sells to several different market segments. An example would be a microscope manufacturer who sells to university, government, and commercial laboratories. The firm makes different microscopes for the different customer groups and builds a strong reputation in the specific product area. The downside risk is that the product may be supplanted by an entirely new technology.

Market Specialization

The firm concentrates on serving many needs of a particular customer group. An example would be a firm that sells an assortment of products only to university laboratories. The firm gains a strong reputation in serving this customer group and becomes a channel for additional products the customer group can use. The downside risk is that the customer group may suffer budget cuts or shrink in size.

Full Market Coverage

The firm attempts to serve all customer groups with all the products they might need. Only very large firms such as IBM (computer market), Toyota (vehicle market), and Coca-Cola (non-alcoholic beverage market) can undertake a full market coverage strategy. Large firms can cover a whole market in two broad ways: through undifferentiated marketing or differentiated marketing.

In *undifferentiated marketing*, the firm ignores segment differences and goes after the whole market with one offer. It designs a product and a marketing program that will appeal to the broadest number of buyers. It relies on mass distribution and advertising. It aims to endow the product with a superior image. Undifferentiated marketing is "the marketing counterpart to standardization and mass production in manufacturing."[48] The narrow product line keeps down costs of research and development, production, inventory, transportation, marketing research, advertising, and product management. The undifferentiated advertising program keeps down advertising costs. Presumably, the company can turn its lower costs into lower prices to win the price-sensitive segment of the market.

In *differentiated marketing*, the firm operates in several market segments and designs different products for each segment. Cosmetics firm Estée Lauder markets brands that appeal to women (and men) of different tastes: The flagship brand, the original Estée Lauder, appeals to older consumers; Clinique caters to middle-aged women; M.A.C. to youthful hipsters; Aveda to aromatherapy enthusiasts; and Origins to eco-conscious consumers who want cosmetics made from natural ingredients.[49]

Lenovo—China's IT service market is estimated to grow by leaps and bounds. To capitalize on this, Lenovo differentiated its retail channel to reach consumer and business customers. It doubled its chain of 1+1 Special Shops to more than 500 stores aimed at consumers. It also established a chain of about 400 commercial IT specialty shops, aimed at business customers. In so doing, Lenovo can sell bundled products like Internet services with hardware. It can also identify those customers, especially small and midsize businesses, who might buy additional services. Lenovo has two departments working on its service business—one on bundling, the other offering after-sale services such as systems integration.[50]

Differentiated marketing typically creates more total sales than undifferentiated marketing. However, it also increases the costs of doing business. Because differentiated marketing leads to both higher sales and higher costs, nothing general can be said about the profitability of this strategy. Companies should be cautious about oversegmenting their markets. If this happens, they may want to turn to *countersegmentation* to broaden the customer base. For example, Johnson & Johnson broadened its target market for its baby shampoo to include adults. Smith Kline Beecham launched its Aquafresh toothpaste to attract three benefit segments simultaneously: those seeking fresh breath, whiter teeth, and cavity protection.

Additional Considerations

Two other considerations must be taken into account in evaluating and selecting segments: segment-by-segment invasion plans and ethical choice of market targets.

SEGMENT-BY-SEGMENT INVASION PLANS

A company would be wise to enter one segment at a time. Competitors must not know to what segment(s) the firm will move next. Segment-by-segment invasion plans are illustrated in Figure 8.6. Three firms, A, B, and C, have specialized in adapting computer systems to the needs of airlines, railroads, and trucking companies. Company A meets all the computer needs of airlines. Company B sells large computer systems to all three transportation sectors. Company C sells personal computers to trucking companies.

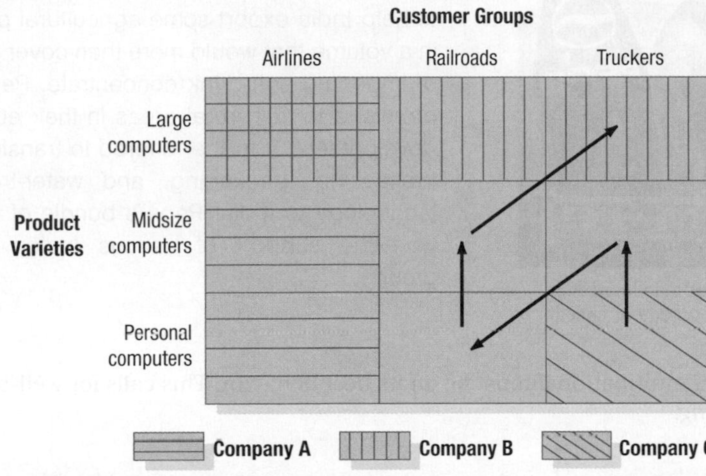

Figure 8.6 Segment-by-Segment Invasion Plan

Where should company C move next? Arrows have been added to the chart to show the planned sequence of segment invasions. Company C will next offer midsize computers to trucking companies. Then, to allay company B's concern about losing some large computer business with trucking companies, C's next move will be to sell personal computers to railroads. Later, C will offer midsize computers to railroads. Finally, it may launch a full-scale attack on company B's large computer position in trucking companies. Of course, C's hidden planned moves are provisional in that much depends on competitors' segment moves and responses.

Unfortunately, too many companies fail to develop a long-term invasion plan. PepsiCo is an exception. It first attacked Coca-Cola in the grocery market, then in the vending-machine market, then in the fast-food market, and so on. Japanese firms also plot their invasion sequence. They first gain a foothold in a market, then enter new segments with products. Toyota began by introducing small cars (Tercel, Corolla), then expanded into midsize cars (Camry, Avalon), and finally into luxury cars (Lexus).

Hyundai—In the U.S., Hyundai is gaining rave reviews as it improves the quality of its vehicles. The Sonata was recently rated as the most reliable car in America, according to *Consumer Reports*, and is selling well. Hyundai started by focusing on two segments—the midsize sedan market with the Sonata, and the sports utility vehicle market with the Santa Fe. It then considered using Kia as an alternative brand, with models that have a younger, sportier image. Following this the segments get trickier. Pick-up trucks are one possibility, but American buyers tend to be loyal to domestic brands. Hyundai has so far given hybrid engine cars a miss. That leaves luxury cars. Hyundai's management has hinted that more upmarket products will appear in the next few years.[51]

A company's invasion plans can be thwarted when it confronts blocked markets. The invader must then figure out a way to break in. The problem of entering blocked markets calls for a megamarketing approach. **Megamarketing** is the strategic coordination of economic, psychological, political, and public relations skills, to gain the cooperation of a number of parties in order to enter or operate in a given market. Pepsi used megamarketing to enter the Indian market.

A Pepsi ad from India. To enter the Indian market, Pepsi used megamarketing. With the aid of an Indian business group, it offered a package of benefits that gained its acceptance.

PepsiCo—After Coca-Cola left India, Pepsi worked with an Indian business group to gain government approval for its entry, over the objections of domestic soft drink companies and anti-multinational legislators. Pepsi offered to help India export some agricultural products in a volume that would more than cover the cost of importing soft-drink concentrate. Pepsi also promised to help rural areas in their economic development. It further offered to transfer food-processing, packaging, and water-treatment technology to India. Pepsi's bundle of benefits won the support of various Indian interest groups.

Once in, a multinational must be on its best behavior. This calls for well-thought-out *civic positioning.*

Hewlett-Packard—Hewlett-Packard positions itself as a company implementing "e-inclusion,"—the attempt to help bring the benefits of technology to the poor. Toward that end, HP began a three-year project designed to create jobs, improve education, and provide better access to government services in the Indian state of Kuppam. Working with the local government, as well as a branch of HP Labs based in India, the company provided the rural poor with access to government records, schools, health information, crop prices, and so forth. Its hope is to stimulate small, tech-based businesses. Not only does this build goodwill and the HP brand in India, but it also helps the company discover new, profitable lines of business.[52]

ETHICAL CHOICE OF MARKET TARGETS

Market targeting sometimes generates public controversy.[53] The public is concerned when marketers take unfair advantage of vulnerable groups (such as children) or disadvantaged groups (such as rural poor people), or promote potentially harmful products. The fast-food industry has been heavily criticized for marketing efforts directed toward children. Critics worry that high-powered appeals presented through the mouths of lovable animated characters will overwhelm children's defenses and lead them to want such products. Toy marketers have been similarly criticized.

China's pharmaceutical market—In China, practically all drugs are available over the counter, and can be bought without the need for prescriptions or medical advice. The Chinese, long used to the slow effects of traditional herbal medicines, are taking Western antibiotics and painkillers without being aware of their side effects. Differences in race and diet make many of these prescription medicines unsuitable for the Chinese. While authorities have cracked down on misleading advertisements by domestic manufacturers promoting miracle cures, there still exist numerous illegal medicine wholesalers.

Cigarettes—In Indonesia, locally manufactured clove-scented ***kretek*** cigarettes have, for a long time, been promoted as "good for your cough" or "clears your voice" to the young. However, it was found that ***kretek*** cigarettes have higher percentage amounts of tar and nicotine compared to other brands such as Japan's Mild Seven and Thailand's Krongthip. Anti-smoking advocates have called for more responsible marketing. Sampoerna, one of the top ***kretek*** makers, has since published estimates of tar and nicotine levels for its own and competing brands, hoping to attract smokers to its mild brand.

Not all attempts to target children, minorities, or other special segments draw criticism. Colgate-Palmolive's Colgate Junior toothpaste has special features designed to get children to brush longer and more often. Thus the issue is not who is targeted, but rather, how and for what. Socially responsible marketing calls for targeting that serves not only the company's interests, but also the interests of those targeted.

Summary

1. Target marketing involves three activities: market segmentation, market targeting, and market positioning.
2. Markets can be targeted at four levels: segments, niches, local areas, and individuals. Market segments are large identifiable groups within a market. A niche is a more narrowly defined group. Marketers appeal to local markets through grassroots marketing for trading areas, neighborhoods, and even individual stores.
3. More companies now practice individual and mass customization. The future is likely to see more self-marketing, a form of marketing in which individual consumers take the initiative in designing products and brands.
4. There are two bases for segmenting consumer markets: consumer characteristics and consumer responses. The major segmentation variables for consumer markets are geographic, demographic, psychographic, and behavioral. These variables can be used singly or in combination.
5. Business marketers use all these variables along with operating variables, purchasing approaches, and situational factors.
6. To be useful, market segments must be measurable, substantial, accessible, differentiable, and actionable.
7. A firm has to evaluate the various segments and decide how many and which ones to target: a single segment, several segments, a specific product, a specific market, or the full market. If it serves the full market, it must choose between differentiated and undifferentiated marketing. Firms must also monitor segment relationships, and seek economies of scope and the potential for marketing to super-segments. They should develop segment-by-segment invasion plans.
8. Marketers must choose target markets in a socially responsible manner.

Application

Marketing Debate—Is Mass Marketing Dead?

With marketers increasingly adopting more and more refined market segmentation schemes—fueled by the Internet and other customization efforts—some critics claim that mass marketing is dead. Others counter that there will always be room for large brands that employ marketing programs targeting the mass market.

Take a position: *Mass marketing is dead* versus *Mass marketing is still a viable way to build a profitable brand.*

Marketing Discussion—Descriptive versus Behavioral Market Segmentation Schemes

Think of various product categories. How would you classify yourself in terms of the various segmentation schemes? How would marketing be more or less effective for you depending on the segment involved? How would you contrast demographic versus behavioral segment schemes? Which ones do you think would be most effective for marketers trying to sell to you?

PART 4

Building Strong Brands

Google's founders, Larry Page and Sergey Brin.

9

Creating Brand Equity

Building a strong brand requires careful planning and a great deal of long-term investment. At the heart of a successful brand is a great product or service, backed by creatively designed and executed marketing. One of the hottest brands around is Google.

Founded in 1998 by two Stanford University Ph.D. students, search engine Google receives 200 million search requests daily. The company has turned a profit by focusing on searches alone and not adding other services, as was the case with many other portals. By focusing on plain text, avoiding ads, and using sophisticated search algorithms, Google provides fast and reliable service. Google makes money from paid listings relevant to a searcher's query, as well as licensing its technology to firms such as AOL and the *Washington Post*. In perhaps the ultimate sign of success, the brand is now often used as a verb—"to google" is to search online. Based on a public poll of the brand that had made the most impact in their lives, Google was ranked 20th by Interbrand branding consultants in its 2007 Best Global Brands study, with a brand value of $17.8 billion, up from $12.4 billion in 2006. This success has not gone unnoticed and has led to strong competitive responses from industry giant Microsoft. Indeed, Microsoft's bid for Yahoo! is an attempt to snuff Google from the online advertising business.[1]

In this chapter, we will address the following questions:

1. What is a brand and how does branding work?
2. What is brand equity?
3. How is brand equity built, measured, and managed?
4. What are the important decisions in developing a branding strategy?

over-330-year-old Tong Ren Tang, Eu Yan Sang, Tiger Balm, Boh Tea, and Jim Thompson Silk. Interestingly, China's State Internal Trade Bureau has awarded some 1,000 outfits like Tong Ren Tang with the status of Time-Honored Brands.

2. ***Acquired assets*** — These refer to a branding opportunity on the back of an identity that enjoys strong credibility. Asia's reputation for quality personal services and hospitality is an area where a global Asian hotel brand can emerge. Examples include the Oriental and Taj Hotels. Overseas Filipino contract workers comprise another promising branding avenue, given that 4.2 million of them are working abroad in some 146 countries, producing foreign exchange earnings of over $12 billion annually. India's expertise in IT can also be branded globally. Its software companies—Wipro, Infosys, and Tata Consultancy Services—have the best potential in this regard.
3. ***Potential assets*** — These refer to the building of a global Asian brand from scratch. Mexico is not famous for its beer heritage but Corona, a Mexican brand, is now well-known internationally. Many famous Japanese brands today were developed through this most difficult route. Such mainland businesses as Haier (appliances), Lenovo (PCs), and Tsingtao (beer) have the potential to become China's global brands.[22]
4. ***Combining acquired assets with potential assets*** — This hybrid approach may be achievable in the arts and entertainment industry by leveraging Asia's extraordinary history. Thus the Shanghai Theater Circus could be the next Cirque du Soleil, and Bombay Universal Picture could be the biggest producer of Western-style dramas worldwide. Asian fabric design, Asian cuisine, and even Asian success in popular sports could yield a fruitful basket of global Asian brands.

Nevertheless, numerous challenges confront Asian businesses hoping to emulate the success of their Japanese counterparts in building global brands today (see "Marketing Memo: A Checklist for Developing Global Asian Brands"). For example, the concept of Chinese brands has been evolving through the 1990s, and several leading domestic players are trying to establish international brands. Some feel that China needs a Sony, a company that stands for high quality and that produces many innovations. However, building a global brand takes time, money, marketing savvy, and international management talent, as Tsingtao's example shows:

Tsingtao—China's best-known brand overseas has a small ad budget of about $2 million for its U.S. market, mainly funded by its distributor there. Foreign exchange restrictions limit state-owned enterprises to re-invest no more than 5 percent of their total export sales on brand promotions abroad. Still, Tsingtao managed to capture 12 percent of Taiwan's beer market within months of its launch by reaching 50,000 local restaurants, pubs, convenience stores, and even betel nut vendors. Tsingtao's brewing method is similar to that of Taiwanese beer. Moreover, its TV commercial showing a bottle of Tsingtao being passed around by a group of Japanese tourists surrounding a dancing and singing *geisha* downplayed its Chinese connections. It enabled the beer to sell in the southern and rural regions of Taiwan where many old Taiwanese are deeply molded by Japanese influence and are thus more receptive to a Japanese image. The ad also appeals to young Taiwanese, many of whom are crazy over almost anything Japanese. By first half of 2005, Tsingtao's revenue was $614 million and profits were $20 million, up 15 percent and 10 percent, respectively for the same period of last year. Under its slogan, "Enthusiasm Everywhere," Tsingtao is now leveraging on its German heritage, close ties with Anheuser-Busch, and reputation as China's oldest beer to build up its image overseas. Its key challenges are the growing competition at home and overseas sales being largely limited to Chinese eateries.[23]

MARKETING MEMO • A CHECKLIST FOR DEVELOPING GLOBAL ASIAN BRANDS

Batey developed the following checklist of fundamentals for "an owner of a popular discretionary Asian brand" wishing to develop it into a "global power brand":

1. Do you see marketing as the dominant driver in your quest for global fame?
2. Do you consider your brand your most valuable financial asset?
3. Have you a brand strategy that you believe will take your brand into the global premier league?
4. Have you marketing staff with the experience and ambition to match your global ambition?
5. Do you have creative marketing communications resources and talents?
6. Do you plan to retain firm control of your global brand strategy and the quality/focus of your marketing programs worldwide?
7. Do you plan to embrace R&D and regular product enhancements with a passion?
8. Have you the financial resources needed to seriously compete in the global power brand game?

Source: Adapted from Ian Batey, *Asian Branding: A Great Way to Fly*, (Singapore: Prentice Hall, 2002), p. 54.

Brand Equity Models

Although there is agreement about basic principles, a number of models of brand equity offer some different perspectives. Here we briefly highlight four of the more established ones.

BRAND ASSET VALUATOR

Advertising agency Young and Rubicam (Y&R) developed a model of brand equity called Brand Asset Valuator (BAV). Based on research with almost 200,000 consumers in 40 countries, BAV provides comparative measures of the brand equity of thousands of brands across hundreds of different categories. There are four key components or pillars of brand equity according to BAV:

- ***Differentiation*** — This measures the degree to which a brand is seen as different from others.
- ***Relevance*** — This measures the breadth of a brand's appeal.
- ***Esteem*** — This measures how well the brand is regarded and respected.
- ***Knowledge*** — This measures how familiar and intimate consumers are with a brand.

Differentiation and Relevance combine to determine *Brand Strength.* These two pillars point to the brand's future value, rather than just reflecting its past. Esteem and Knowledge together create *Brand Stature,* which is more of a "report card" on past performance.

Examining the relationships among these four dimensions—a brand's "pillar pattern"—reveals much about its current and future status. Brand Strength and Brand Stature can be combined to form a Power Grid that depicts the stages in the cycle of brand development—each with its characteristic pillar patterns—in successive quadrants (see Figure 9.1). New brands, just after they are launched, show low levels on all four pillars. Strong new brands tend to show higher levels of Differentiation than Relevance, while both Esteem and Knowledge are lower still. Leadership brands show high levels on all four pillars. Finally, declining brands show high knowledge—evidence of past performance—relative to a lower level of Esteem, and even lower Relevance and Differentiation.

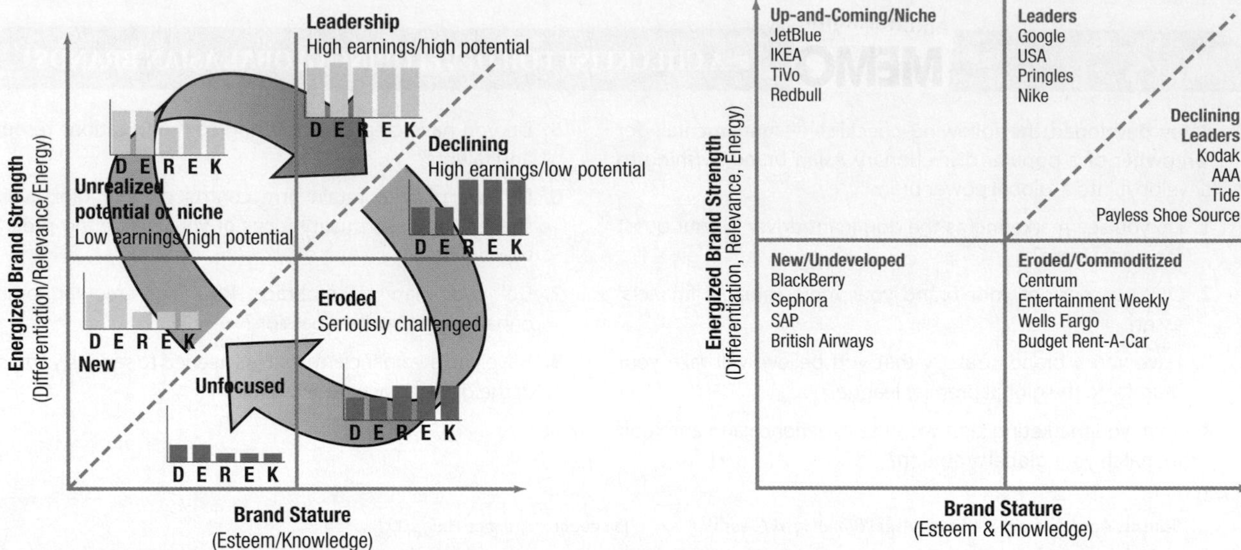

Figure 9.1 BAV Power Grid

AAKER MODEL

Aaker views brand equity as a set of five categories of brand assets and liabilities linked to a brand that add to or subtract from the value provided by a product or service to a firm and/or to that firm's customers. These categories of brand assets are: (1) brand loyalty, (2) brand awareness, (3) perceived quality, (4) brand associations, and (5) other proprietary assets such as patents, trademarks, and channel relationships.

According to Aaker, a particularly important concept for building brand equity is *brand identity*—the unique set of brand associations that represent what the brand stands for and promises to customers.[24] Aaker sees brand identity as consisting of 12 dimensions organized around four perspectives: *brand-as-product* (product scope, product attributes, quality/value, uses, users, country of origin); *brand-as-organization* (organizational attributes, local versus global); *brand-as-person* (brand personality, brand–customer relationships); and *brand-as-symbol* (visual imagery/metaphors and brand heritage).

Aaker also conceptualizes brand identity as including a core and an extended identity. The core identity—the central, timeless essence of the brand—is most likely to remain constant as the brand travels to new markets and products. The extended identity includes various brand identity elements, organized into cohesive and meaningful groups.

BRANDZ

Marketing research consultants Millward Brown and WPP have developed the BRANDZ model of brand strength, at the heart of which is the BrandDynamics pyramid. According to this model, brand building involves a sequential series of steps, where each step is contingent upon successfully accomplishing the previous step (see Figure 9.2). The objectives at each step, in ascending order, are as follows:

- ***Presence*** — Do I know about it?
- ***Relevance*** — Does it offer me something?
- ***Performance*** — Can it deliver?
- ***Advantage*** — Does it offer something better than others?
- ***Bonding*** — Nothing else beats it.

"Bonded" consumers, those at the top level of the pyramid, build stronger relationships with the brand and spend more of their category expenditures on the brand than those at lower levels of the pyramid. More consumers, however, will be found at the lower levels. The challenge for marketers is to develop activities and programs that help consumers move up the pyramid.

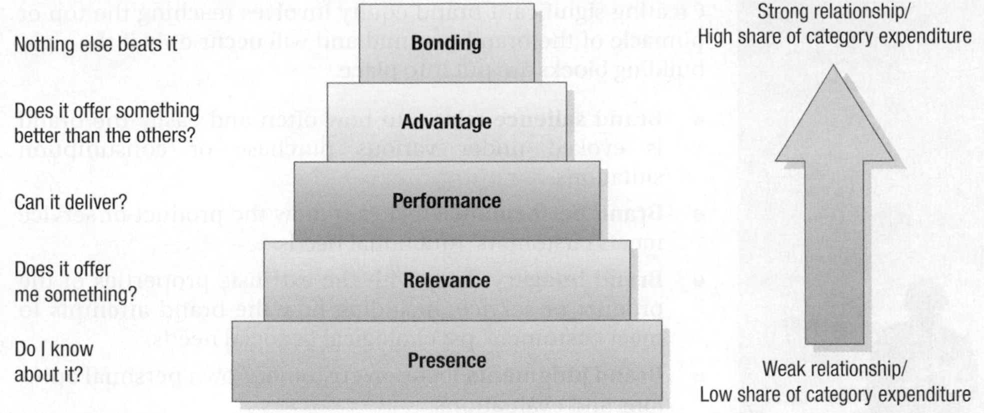

Figure 9.2 BrandDynamics™ Pyramid

Source: BrandDynamics™ Pyramid. Reprinted by permission of MillwardBrown.

BRAND RESONANCE

The brand resonance model also views brand building as an ascending, sequential series of steps, from bottom to top: (1) ensuring identification of the brand with customers and an association of the brand in customers' minds with a specific product class or customer need; (2) firmly establishing the totality of brand meaning in the minds of customers by strategically linking a host of tangible and intangible brand associations; (3) eliciting the proper customer responses in terms of brand-related judgment and feelings; and (4) converting brand response to create an intense, active loyalty relationship between customers and the brand.

According to this model, enacting the four steps involves establishing six "brand building blocks" with customers. These brand building blocks can be assembled in terms of a brand pyramid, as illustrated in Figure 9.3. The model emphasizes the duality of brands—the rational route to brand building is the left-hand side of the pyramid, whereas the emotional route is the right-hand side.[25]

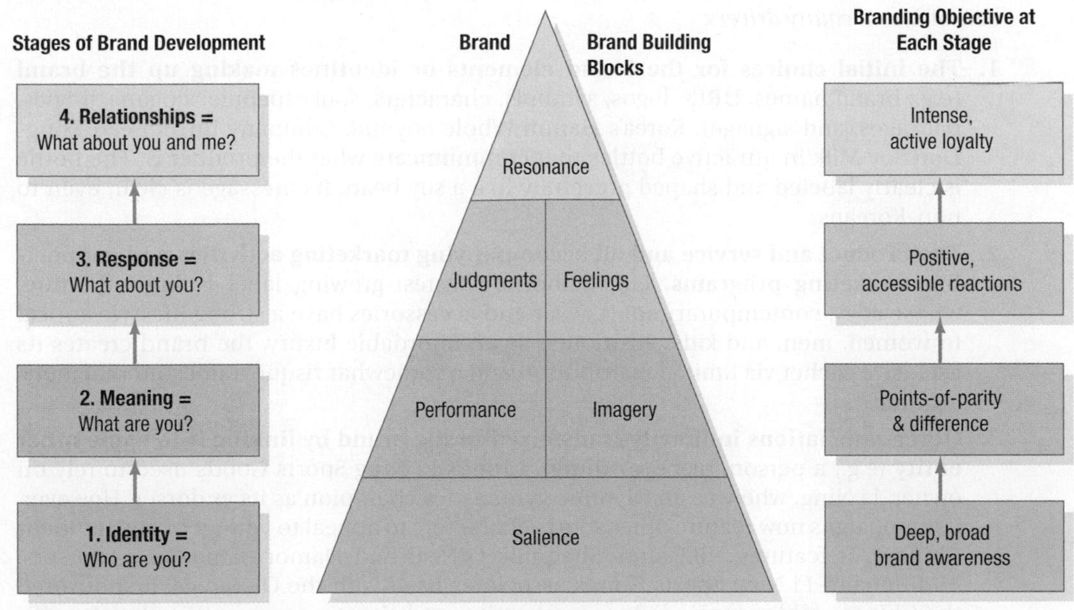

Figure 9.3 Brand Resonance Pyramid

MasterCard is an example of a brand with duality, as it emphasizes both the rational advantage to the credit card, through its acceptance at establishments worldwide, and the emotional advantage through its award-winning "priceless" advertising campaign, which shows people buying items to reach a certain goal. The goal itself—a feeling, an accomplishment or other intangible—is "priceless" ("There are some things money can't buy, for everything else, there's MasterCard.").

MasterCard appeals to "the head and the heart" in its long-running "Priceless" ad campaign.

Creating significant brand equity involves reaching the top or pinnacle of the brand pyramid and will occur only if the right building blocks are put into place.

- **Brand salience** relates to how often and easily the brand is evoked under various purchase or consumption situations.
- **Brand performance** relates to how the product or service meets customers' functional needs.
- **Brand imagery** deals with the extrinsic properties of the product or service, including how the brand attempts to meet customers' psychological or social needs.
- **Brand judgments** focus on customers' own personal opinions and evaluations.
- **Brand feelings** are customers' emotional responses and reactions toward the brand.
- **Brand resonance** refers to the nature of the relationship that customers have with the brand and the extent to which customers feel that they are "in sync" with the brand.

Resonance is characterized in terms of the intensity or depth of the psychological bond customers have with the brand, as well as the level of activity engendered by this loyalty. Examples of brands with high resonance include Harley-Davidson, Apple, and eBay.

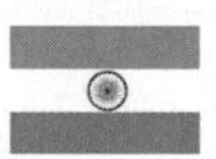

To learn how Indian leather goods brand Hidesign has used a well-designed and creative branding strategy to distinguish itself as a leading name in leather goods, visit www.pearsoned.co.in/pkotler.

Building Brand Equity

Marketers build brand equity by creating the right brand knowledge structures with the right consumers. This process depends on *all* brand-related contacts—whether marketer-initiated or not. From a marketing management perspective, however, there are three main sets of *brand equity drivers*:

1. **The initial choices for the brand elements or identities making up the brand** (e.g., brand names, URLs, logos, symbols, characters, spokespeople, slogans, jingles, packages, and signage). Korea's Hanmi Whole Soymilk Company introduced Kong-Doo Soy Milk in attractive bottles that communicate what the product is. The bottle is clearly labeled and shaped gracefully like a soy bean. Its message is clear, even to non-Koreans.
2. **The product and service and all accompanying marketing activities and supporting marketing programs.** Liz Claiborne's fastest-growing label is Juicy Couture, whose edgy, contemporary sportswear and accessories have a strong lifestyle appeal to women, men, and kids. Positioned as an affordable luxury, the brand creates its exclusive cachet via limited distribution and a somewhat risqué name and rebellious attitude.[26]
3. **Other associations indirectly transferred to the brand by linking it to some other entity** (e.g., a person, place, or thing). China's Li Ning Sports Goods used to rely on owner, Li Ning, who was an Olympic gymnastics champion as its endorser. However, its campaigns now feature other sports characters to appeal to younger, more affluent Chinese. It features NBA stars Shaquille O'Neal and Damon James as endorsers. Additionally, Li Ning Sports Goods associates itself with the Olympics. It sponsored the Chinese table tennis, diving, gymnastics, and shooting teams. It is also the official sportswear provider for the Spanish 2008 Olympic delegation. Such associations augur well for Li Ning. An Interbrand survey showed that sporting goods, along with electronics, mobile phones, and automotive, was one of 10 categories where overseas marketing executives predict within five years "a Chinese brand will be a leader outside of China."[27]

Choosing Brand Elements

Brand elements are those trademarkable devices that serve to identify and differentiate the brand. Most strong brands employ multiple brand elements. Nike has the distinctive Swoosh logo, the empowering "Just Do It" slogan, and the mythological "Nike" name based on the winged goddess of victory.

Google—In 1998, Google founders, Larry Page and Sergey Brin, decided to dump their fledgling search engine's working name—BackRub—for something shorter and simpler. "We spent a lot of time on the name ... because we figured that it would be important for people to be able to remember it," recalled Page. They eventually settled on "googol" (a Math term for 10 to the 100th power). However, they misspelled the word while checking to see whether that Internet domain was available for registration. It turned out that "google.com" was available but not googol.com. The rest is history.[28]

Brand elements can be chosen to build as much brand equity as possible. The test of the brand-building ability of these elements is what consumers would think or feel about the product if they only knew about the brand element. A brand element that contributes positively to brand equity, for example, would be one where consumers assumed or inferred certain valued associations or responses. Based on its name alone, a consumer might expect ColorStay lipsticks to be long-lasting and Vitagen cultured milk drinks to be healthful.

BRAND ELEMENT CHOICE CRITERIA

There are six criteria in choosing brand elements (as well as more specific choice considerations in each case). The first three (memorable, meaningful, and likeable) can be characterized as "brand building" in terms of how brand equity can be built through the judicious choice of a brand element. The latter three (transferable, adaptable, and protectible) are more "defensive" and are concerned with how the brand equity contained in a brand element can be leveraged and preserved in the face of different opportunities and constraints.

1. ***Memorable*** — How easily is the brand element recalled? How easily recognized? Is this true at both purchase and consumption? Short brand names such as Qoo and Kao can help, particularly in much of Asia where English is not the first language. Brand names that are multisyllabic and hard to pronounce (e.g., Häagen-Dazs) may require more time to learn and heavier promotion before they become part of the consumer's lexicon. Moreover, while plosive consonants (e.g., *b, c, d, g, k,* and *t*) may add strength to the sound of brand names in the West (e.g., Tic Tac), they may not be suitable where Chinese dialects are concerned. Nasal sounds (e.g., *nan, yin,* and *yang*) are commonplace in Cantonese, while in Mandarin, the *shoo* and *shur* sounds dominate.

Moreover, the brand name should also *look* distinctive to be memorable in Asia. Several Asian languages are not alphabet-based. Chinese, for example, uses about 50,000 ideographs composed of strokes. The Chinese also consider a name a work of art, and the art of writing (*shu fa* or calligraphy) has a long tradition. Thus the writing of a brand name is very important. It should be appealing and unique as it can function as a logo or trademark. Volkswagen has used calligraphy in its ads while Cathay Pacific uses it for its logo.

Volkswagen—Volkswagen ads for its jeep in Shanghai contain words meaning "value," "solid," and "dependable," written by famous Chinese calligraphers. In one ad, a calligraphy stroke was used as an imaginary slope that the jeep had to climb, creating a highly memorable interactive image.

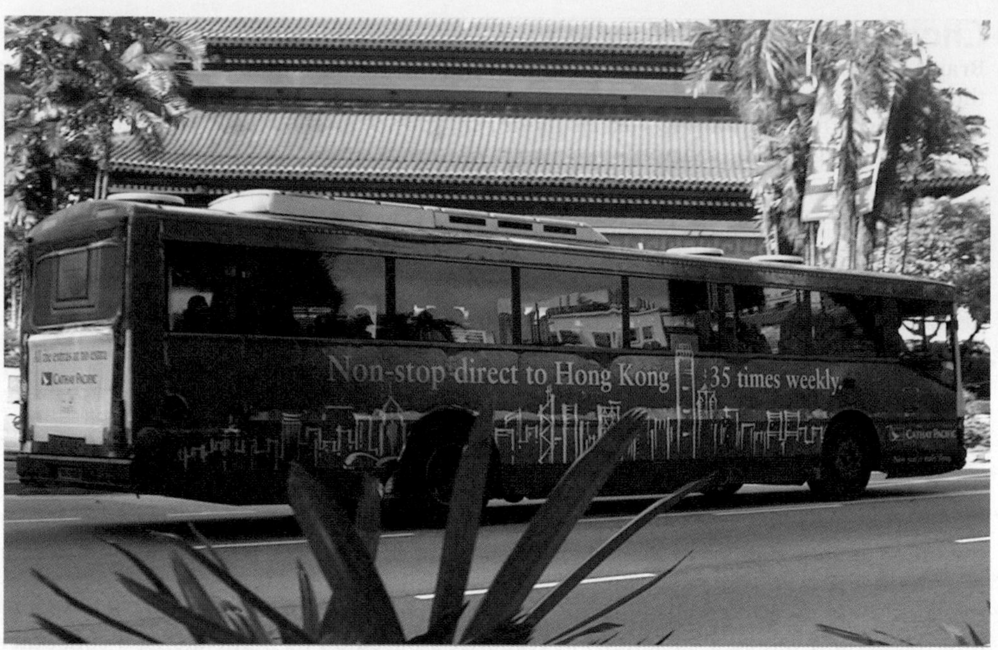

Cathay Pacific uses Chinese calligraphy for its brushwing logo and in its ad visuals to suggest its "Heart of Asia" heritage. This photo shows a Cathay Pacific bus ad promoting Hong Kong as a destination.

2. ***Meaningful*** — To what extent is the brand element credible and suggestive of the corresponding category? Does it suggest something about a product ingredient or the type of person who might use the brand? Consider the inherent meaning in names such as Sharp and Walkman. In contrast, the following brand name was misleading:

Dindings Poultry Processing—In Malaysia, Dindings Poultry Processing marketed a new product offering, calling it "Nuget Sayuran" or Vegetable Nugget. However, an ingredient label in small print stated that the product contained chicken meat. Upon receiving complaints from consumers, the company decided to change its name to "Vegetable Chicken Nugget" instead.

Meaningfulness should be interpreted in the values and lifestyle that consumers seek. A good example is Calvin Klein's fragrance CKin2u.

Calvin Klein—Its fragrance CKin2u is a clever code meant to be decipherable only by its target audience of Generation Y with its text message-influenced lexicon. According to Lori Singer, vice president of global marketing for Calvin Klein, this was a way to talk to Generation Y and "that meant embracing the media and communities they consume."[29]

Some marketers believe that an Asian name is a liability when used in certain product categories as it is suggestive of poor quality or low class when compared with Western brands. For example, some Asian fashion businesses have adopted Western names (e.g., Bonia handbags of Malaysia) or Western-sounding names (e.g., Hong Kong's Goldlion is pronounced *gold-lyon*), while others hide or downplay their national origins.

More generally, prudent marketers in the Asia Pacific should probe folklore, taboos, superstitious and religious connotations conveyed by colors, numbers, or symbols where these form part of a brand name. One aspect of symbolism is the concept of a lucky name. Pepsi-Cola (meaning "hundred happy things") is a lucky name in Chinese, while Volvo's 164 and 264 models were less popular with the Chinese as the number four signifies death. To appeal to the Chinese, Ericsson mobile phone models used to end with the digit 8 (e.g., T8, T18, T28) as it suggests prosperity.

The multitude of languages compounds the challenge of developing a brand name that has positive meaning across cultures. Barbie is a poor name for a doll in Malay-speaking countries as it sounds like the word for pork in Malay, a taboo meat for Muslims. Many Western companies in Asia have translated their names by sound (e.g., Ford), without considering the Asian name's meaning; or by meaning (e.g., General Electric) without considering how the name sounds in different languages. Problems may occur for companies who localize their existing name via transliteration. For example, Kanebo when pronounced by Hokkien speakers in Malaysia and Singapore literally means "having sex with your mother."

Not only is each Chinese character inherently meaningful, each part of the character (called radicals) is also meaningful. Thus marketers must analyze the connotations and meanings of their brand names at multiple levels. In addition, there are more homonyms in Asian than Western languages. Given their tonal nature, the same phonetic pronunciation may have different meanings depending on how the word is pronounced. For example, the word "gong" has at least nine distinct characters with equally distinct meanings in Chinese (*work, bow, public, meritorious service, attack, supply, palace, respectful,* and a surname). Consumers may mistakenly ascribe the brand name with a character of a different tone. Marketers must ensure that such tonal confusions do not occur particularly in oral communications by radio or salespeople.

Hyatt—When Hyatt Hotel entered China, it realized that the name "Hyatt" does not translate easily and confers no meaning, as most Chinese are unfamiliar with American brands. To develop its Chinese brand equity, it used the name *Yue* (悦) which means "imperial," a characteristic that many rich Chinese aspire to be. The organization then came up with courtly variations to match its subbrands: *Kai Yue* (凯悦), *Jun Yue* (君悦), and *Bo Yue* (柏悦) for the Regency, Grand, and Park Hyatt hotels, respectively.[30]

Omnicom—Omnicom exercised great consideration in its choice of a Chinese name. Frank Chen, CEO of Interbrand China said, 'Omnicom is a great name in English, but difficult to pronounce for non-native English speakers.' Hence, Interbrand was engaged to search for a Chinese name that would translate well across seven different Chinese dialects as well as capture the spirit of cooperation and scale of Omnicom's business implied by its English name. The result was *Hong Meng* (宏盟), which directly translated into English, means "magnificent alliance."[31]

Biotherm—This French skincare brand goes by the Chinese name pronounced as *Bee Er Chuen* in most Asian markets with the exception of China. China's cosmetics market is dominated by foreign brands and Biotherm wanted to highlight its international status with its name *Bee Oh Chuen* (碧欧泉), where the middle character *Oh* (欧) refers to Europe.[32]

While some Asian countries have multiple dialects (e.g., China and India), others have multiple writing systems with different historical precedents and cultural implications. For example, Japan has four writing systems: the Chinese-character based *kanji,* two phonemic systems (*hiragana* and *katakana*), and the Western alphabet system, *romaji.* Brand names written in a particular system carry certain associations related to that system. Brands in the oldest system, *kanji,* are perceived to be traditional. Hence, *kanji* is suitable for traditional products like tea. The most modern system, *katakana,* may be more suited for high-tech products as it was introduced in Japan for foreign loan words. It is also appropriate for foreign products and products associated with foreign lifestyles. *Hiragana,* written by a courtesan, has a more feminine image suitable for beauty products, hair salons, and kimono stores.

Tamagotchi—Bandai, the makers of Tamagotchi, the virtual pet, selected the ***hiragana*** writing system to brand its product. The name means "cute egg watch" (from ***tamago,*** the everyday Japanese word for egg, and the suffix ***chi***, for "small" and "cute"). Given that female teenagers were being targeted and the product's emotional, high-touch rather than high-tech nature, ***hiragana*** was considered the appropriate system.

3. ***Likeable***— How aesthetically appealing do consumers find the brand element? Is it inherently likeable visually, verbally, and in other ways? Concrete brand names such as Sunkist, Bluebird, and Head & Shoulders evoke much imagery. The Chinese name for Fuji/Xerox Shagaku, a handheld copier, fits its image well. The name, written in Chinese characters, means "picture" and "fun," suggests that it possesses the qualities of an affectionate pet name. Similarly, Zaitun (a female Islamic name) was selected for a range of locally produced toiletries in Malaysia to give a cultural dimension and associative value (purity) to the products. In contrast, the Chinese Web site, Sina.com, stirred controversy as it invoked strong negative memories of the atrocities that the Japanese inflicted on the Chinese during World War II. Consumers criticized that "sina" sounded very similar to "ci na," the Japanese word for China during the war. Further, "ci na" was still being used by right-wing Japanese to address people from China and therefore was a name with political overtones.

4. ***Transferable***—Can the brand element be used to introduce new products in the same or different categories? To what extent does the brand element add to brand equity across geographic boundaries and market segments?

   Often companies enter one Asian market after another. Such companies are likely to choose a name suited for one market but not for the next. For example, Johnson & Johnson wound up with two names in the same culture. In Hong Kong, *zhuang sheng* (meaning "feudal lord") was used. As this traditional upper-class association was considered inappropriate in socialist China, *qiang sheng* ("active life") was employed there.

   Using an existing corporate or brand name may be considered more consistent on a regional basis. This works for original, alphabetic names which are short and catchy such as 3M, IBM, and M&M. However, consumers in many Asian markets (e.g., China) are still unfamiliar with Western names and spellings. Thus judicious use of proper names is essential. For example, Britain's Derwent Valley Foods selected the brand name "Phineas Fogg" for a line of fine foods. While educated Westerners might know of its origins and associations, many Asians would not.

   The experience of Robert Bosch, a German vehicle-parts and electrical appliance firm, in selecting an appropriate name for the China and Hong Kong markets is instructive of a pan-Asian approach to branding. It wanted a Chinese name that sounded like Bosch when pronounced in both Mandarin and Cantonese; that had positive meanings related to its core business or organizational image; that had no negative sound associations; and that was distinctive from other corporate names so as not to violate trademark infringement regulations. Eventually, it selected a name (*bo shi* in Mandarin and *bok sai* in Cantonese) which had favorable connotations as it could be interpreted as "winning all over the world."

5. ***Adaptable*** — How adaptable and updatable is the brand element? As many Asian brands modernize, their elements need to be adaptable and yet retain the traditional values of the brand.

Dutch Baby—Dutch Baby began producing and marketing its milk products in Malaysia in 1965. It has a reputation of being "Malaysia's Milk Specialist" and changed its name to Dutch Lady in 2000, a name it was often referred to by customers and retailers. Management felt the new name harnessed the strength of its brand in the market, was more recognizable, and reflected a modern image.[33]

6. ***Protectible***— How legally protectible is the brand element? How competitively protectible? Can it be easily copied? It is important that names that become synonymous with product categories—such as Kleenex, Scotch Tape, and Xerox—retain their trademark rights and not become generic. It is not uncommon for multinationals entering new Asian markets to discover that their brand name has already been registered in that country. For example,

Marushin Foods, a Japanese food processing company, had registered the names of Mac and Burger prior to McDonald's arrival in Japan in 1971. It took McDonald's three years to finally register its trademark in Japan.

Further, differences arise in international trademark laws between Asia and the West. In the U.S. and some European countries, trademark ownership is based on prior use. However, in some Asian countries, the trademark is deemed to be the property, and owned by, the registering party, and therefore can be sold. Astute Asian entrepreneurs have profited from locally registering established foreign brand names. Foreign companies seeking to invest in Asia should thus ensure their brand name and trademark are registered in the Asian country of interest. For example, Starbucks in China ran into intellectual property disputes because a local coffee shop in Shanghai, U-Like Coffee, had registered the pinyin spelling of the company's name "*xing ba ke*" before Starbucks got round to doing so.[34] U-Like Coffee's logo and store design are also similar to Starbucks. Starbucks has since won the legal tussle. Other Asian companies have chosen names close to their Western competitors. Johnson & Johnson lost its lawsuit in China to protect its Carefree sanitary napkin trademark against a local company registered as Careful.[35]

In China, local coffee shop, U-Like Coffee, copied Starbucks, from its Chinese name to logo and store design. Starbucks sued and won.

Many firms strive to build a unique brand name that eventually will become intimately identified with the product category. Examples are Kleenex, Scotch Tape, and Post-it notes. In 1994, Federal Express officially shortened its marketing identity to FedEx, a term that has become a synonym for "to ship overnight." However, their very success may threaten the exclusive rights to the name. Xerox now represents a product category (copier machines) rather than the company that makes it. Thus in 1994, Xerox changed its marketing identity to "The Document Company Xerox" to better communicate its leadership as an office-systems marketer, not just a copier manufacturer.

Given the rapid growth of the global marketplace, Asian companies should choose brand names that work outside the region. Just as foreign businesses must be cognizant of Asian aspects of brand naming, Asian companies should select names that are meaningful and pronounceable in other languages as they expand outside the region. Otherwise, they will find that they cannot use their names when they go abroad.

Lenovo—The name of China's largest technology company, Legend, was picked in 1984 by its founders who were then students and engineers at a Beijing technical institute. Since then, 40 other subbrands, including Happy Family for a software line, and 1+1 for a retail chain, emerged over the years. In 2001, it hired consulting firm Interpublic to find a new name and rationalize its subbrands. The result? The number of subbrands and product names was cut to 19 and a list of attributes was created that it hoped to impart to future customers. Because the company sells many products besides PCs, Legend's old logo, which had a caricature of a floppy disk, needed an update. Interpublic presented Legend with about 250 new English names, including many that began with "L" to associate with the company's existing names. Legend's top 20 executives picked five finalists from a list of 25 candidates that had been vetted in many languages and trademark registries. From these five, Lenovo stood out because it could be trademarked in most countries and was easy to pronounce and spell. The company's Chinese name, ***Lian Xiang,*** which means "imagination," was not changed.[36]

Asian companies often face the problem that their domestic brand is not well known overseas, or their name may be associated with poor quality or image abroad. In addition to building their own names overseas, some Asian businesses overcome this problem by buying established foreign businesses and their brand names. Consider the following Chinese examples:

China Bicycle—By the 1990s, this leading global bicycle manufacturer was selling bicycles that were popular in Europe and the U.S. However, many Westerners had not heard of China Bicycle. To overcome low consumer awareness, the company bought a U.S.-based importer and distributor that owned the Diamond Back brand name in 1990. Today, a third of China Bicycle's exports carry the Diamond Back name.

Pearl River Piano—To enhance its global brand name recognition, the company bought a mature German brand, Ritmüller, in 1999, to complement its own Pearl River brand.

DEVELOPING BRAND ELEMENTS

In creating a brand, marketers have many choices of brand elements to identify their products. Before, companies chose brand names by generating a list of possible names, debating their merits, eliminating all but a few, testing them with target consumers, and making a final choice.[37] Today, many companies hire a marketing research firm to develop and test names. These companies use human brainstorming sessions and vast computer databases, cataloged by association, sounds, and other qualities. Name-research procedures include *association tests* (what images come to mind?), *learning tests* (how easily is the name pronounced?), *memory tests* (how well is the name remembered?), and *preference tests* (which names are preferred?). Of course, the firm must also conduct searches to make sure the chosen name has not already been registered. The whole process requires substantial financial investment. Asian companies have also been known to refer to books that interpret the "fate" of a name. Fortune tellers may be consulted as well—a practice many Westerners believe to be irrational.

Brand elements can play a number of brand-building roles. If consumers do not examine much information in making their product decisions, brand elements should be easily recognized and recalled, and inherently descriptive and persuasive. Memorable or meaningful brand elements can reduce the burden on marketing communications to build awareness and link brand associations. The different associations that arise from the likeability and appeal of brand elements may also play a critical role in the equity of a brand. The tiger in Exxon reinforces the image of power for the company's gas.

Brand names are not the only important brand element. Often, the less concrete brand benefits are, as is typical of service businesses, the more important it is that brand elements capture the brand's intangible characteristics. One such element is the logo, which can visually represent the brand's core benefits, and which can also transcend geographic boundaries more than verbal elements. For example, Cathay Pacific's graceful brushwing logo conveys an image of personal, Asian service.

A powerful—but sometimes overlooked—brand element is slogans. Like brand names, slogans are an extremely efficient means to build brand equity. Slogans can function as useful "hooks" or "handles" to help consumers grasp what the brand is and what makes it special. They are an indispensable means of summarizing and translating the intent of a marketing program. Think of the inherent brand meaning in slogans such as "A Great Way to Fly" (Singapore Airlines) and "Connecting People" (Nokia).

Avis—A classic case of a company using a slogan to build brand equity is that of Avis's long-running "We Try Harder" ad campaign. In 1963 when the campaign was developed, Avis was losing money and widely considered the number 2 car rental company next to market leader Hertz. When account executives from DDB ad agency met with Avis managers, they asked: "What can you do that we can say you do better than your competitors?" An Avis manager replied, "We try harder because we have to." Someone at DDB wrote this down and it became the heart of the campaign. Avis was hesitant to air the campaign not only because of its blunt, break-the-rules honesty, but also because the company had to deliver on that promise. Yet, by creating buy-in on "We Try Harder" from all Avis employees, especially its frontline employees at the rental desks, the company was able to create a company culture and brand image out of an advertising slogan.[38]

Designing Holistic Marketing Activities

Although the judicious choice of brand elements and secondary associations can make important contributions to building brand equity, the primary input comes from the product or service and supporting marketing activities.

Brands are not built by advertising alone. Customers come to know a brand through a range of contacts and touch points: personal observation and use, word of mouth, interactions with company personnel, online or telephone experiences, and payment transactions. A **brand contact** can be defined as any information-bearing experience a customer or prospect has with the brand, the product category, or the market that relates to the marketer's product or service.[39] Any of these experiences can be positive or negative. The company must put as much effort into managing these experiences as it does in producing its ads.[40] For instance, the Eslite Bookstore in Kaohsiung has a huge central space surrounded by columns. It provides the experience of being a "temple of knowledge" where readers come not only to buy books but to read and think about philosophical and humanistic issues.

Marketers are creating brand contacts and building brand equity through many avenues, such as clubs and consumer communities, trade shows, event marketing, sponsorship, factory visits, public relations and press releases, and social cause marketing. Regardless of the particular tools or approaches they choose, holistic marketers emphasize three important new themes in designing brand-building marketing programs: personalization, integration, and internalization.

PERSONALIZATION

The rapid expansion of the Internet has created opportunities to personalize marketing.[41] Marketers are increasingly abandoning mass-market practices for new approaches that call for merchants to know their customers by name. To adapt to the increased consumer desire for personalization, marketers have embraced concepts such as experiential marketing, one-to-one marketing, and permission marketing. Chapter 5 summarized some of these concepts; "Marketing Insight: Applying Permission Marketing" highlights key principles with that particular approach.

From a branding standpoint, these concepts are about getting consumers more actively involved with a brand by creating an intense, active relationship. *Personalizing marketing* is about making sure that the brand and its marketing is as relevant as possible to as many customers as possible—a challenge, given that no two customers are ever identical. Fournier's research into the nature of relationships held by consumers with their

MARKETING INSIGHT • APPLYING PERMISSION MARKETING

Permission marketing, the practice of marketing to consumers only after gaining their express permission, is a tool companies can use to break through clutter and build customer loyalty. With the help of large databases and advanced software, companies can store gigabytes of customer data and send targeted, personalized marketing messages to customers.

Godin, a pioneer in the technique, maintains that marketers can no longer use "interruption marketing" via mass media campaigns. Marketers can develop stronger consumer relationships by respecting consumers' wishes and sending messages only when they express a willingness to become more involved with the brand. According to Godin, effective permission marketing works because it is "anticipated, personal, and relevant."

Godin identifies five steps to effective permission marketing:

1. Offer the prospect an incentive to volunteer (e.g., free sample, sales promotion, or contest).
2. Offer the interested prospect a curriculum over time that teaches the consumer about the product or service.
3. Reinforce the incentive to guarantee that the prospect maintains the permission.
4. Offer additional incentives to get more permission from the consumer.
5. Over time, leverage the permission to change consumer behavior toward profits.

Permission marketing does have drawbacks. One is that it presumes consumers, to some extent, "know what they want." But in many cases, consumers have undefined, ambiguous, or conflicting preferences. In applying permission marketing, consumers may need to be given assistance in forming and conveying their preferences. "Participatory marketing" may be a more appropriate concept because marketers and consumers need to work together to find out how the firm can best satisfy consumers.

Sources: Seth Godin, *Permission Marketing: Turning Strangers into Friends, and Friends into Customers*, (New York: Simon & Schuster, 1999); Susan Fournier, Susan Dobscha, and David Mick, "Preventing the Premature Death of Relationship Marketing." *Harvard Business Review*, January-February 1998, pp. 42–51.

brands may be useful in this regard. Fournier uncovered a variety of brand relationships ranging from committed partnerships (e.g., a consumer so involved with his bicycle brand that he becomes an advocate for it) to enslavement (e.g., a consumer who is unhappy with her local cable supplier but has no alternative source for the service).[42]

Fournier's findings have particular relevance in Asia, given the premium placed on relationships in the region. Thus brand management in Asia may involve companies understanding, developing, and managing *brand relationships* with their customers.[43] Consider a typical household purchase of 300 products. Few Asian consumers are likely to want that many relationships with their suppliers. As reflected in the B2B world of the *keiretsu*, *chaebol*, and Chinese family networks, they may be more interested in a smaller number of deeper and wider brand relationships than a larger number of specific ones. Thus five or six brand relationships (e.g., one each for financial services, health care, and household products) may be preferred. Creating a brand relationship for a customer may thus involve partnering with other companies to meet a full set of customer needs. A co-branded service mark—encompassing, for example, toothpaste, mouthwash, dentists, and dental insurance—can promote this effectively.

As Asian marketers manage brand relationships, they will face the problem outsiders confront in a Confucian society: to allow one supplier to become a trusted agent upon whom all business is entrusted requires a friend in Asia, not an outsider. Peppers and Rogers introduce *brand-driven customer relationship management* to describe this concept, where relationships cannot be easily created without first establishing the relative positions for the brand and the customer. From a Confucian perspective, this involves developing a brand personality that allows the consumer to fit the brand into her social hierarchy, to know how the brand can be expected to behave, and how it relates to others in the hierarchy. Once this is established, customer relationship management techniques can be applied within the social expectations of appropriate marketing behavior.

For example, as Asian cultures tend to be communal, Asians do not typically join single-purpose groups as individuals. This implies that CRM projects attempting to appeal to the individual's need to belong may not be as effective. Thus affinity credit cards associated with non-profit causes are more successful in Western countries than in Asia, where customers have preferred cards that provide personal rewards.

However, the opportunity exists to increase a sense of prestige for important customer groups as part of a CRM program by providing preferential treatment within a group or a clan. A program that allows multiple group members to collectively build up points toward large family events like weddings may be more effective. Brand-driven CRM programs in Asia thus require more information to be captured on the customer's group and family membership than in an individualistic society like the U.S.

Moreover, Asian cultures will respond to different service processes, perceiving this as part of the overall brand relationship, not just the tangible rewards associated from frequent purchase discounts. For example, high-value customers of Korean department stores are not only given access to private lounges, they also have their shopping done for them by store staff while they relax, which is something only some Western luxury stores like Neiman Marcus provide.

Finally, given the need for brand relationship management in Asia, companies may have to transform the role of their product managers. Such a context necessitates a company being engaged in a two-way brand relationship with its customers. It must be aware of its customers, learn from them, and find solutions for them. Thus the role of a *relationship brand manager* is to find products for customers, instead of finding customers for their products.

INTEGRATION

One implication of these new marketing approaches is that the traditional "marketing mix" concept and the notion of the "4 Ps" may not adequately describe modern marketing programs. **Integrating marketing** is about mixing and matching marketing activities to maximize their individual and collective effects.[44] As part of integrated marketing, marketers need a variety of different marketing activities that reinforce the brand promise.

Integration is especially critical with marketing communications. From the perspective of brand building, all communication options should be evaluated in terms of ability to affect brand equity. Each communication option can be judged on the effectiveness and efficiency with which it affects brand awareness and with which it creates, maintains, or strengthens brand image.

> **China fashion**—Few people, both in China and overseas, recognize names such as Exception de Mixmind, Jefen, or Farina Z. These are creations of China's top fashion designers. As the world's biggest textile manufacturer, China still lacks name brands of its own. Factories in China churn out clothes for many international brands, but none of its designers have gained international recognition. Brand recognition is also low domestically because department stores in China, unlike those overseas, do not want to take risks and purchase clothes from designers. Instead, they rent space to them to sell their clothes. This forces designers to fork out money to rent the space, which few are willing to do. Further, nouveau riche Chinese consumers, exposed to overseas goods through travel and imports, prefer foreign brands.[45]

Let us distinguish between brand identity and image. *Identity* is the way a company aims to identify or position itself or its product. *Image* is the way the public actually perceives them. For the right image to be established in the minds of consumers, the marketer must convey brand identity through every available communication vehicle and brand contact. Identity should be diffused in ads, annual reports, brochures, catalogs, packaging, company stationery, and business cards. If "IBM means service," this message must be expressed in symbols, colors and slogans, atmosphere, events, and employee behavior. Although it is fast becoming an economic powerhouse, China is late in the game when it comes to developing these aspects of branding—both image and identity—but some Chinese companies are learning fast.

> **Haier**—If one company can subvert China's old reputation for producing low-cost but shoddy products, it is the white-goods manufacturer Haier (pronounced ***higher***). Adopting the strategy of successful Japanese and Korean companies, Haier concentrated on building a big market at home and then going on the offensive overseas. Since entering the U.S. market in 1999, it has become the top-selling brand of compact refrigerators, the kind in college dorm rooms. Yet, the company had to rely on innovation to get past a reputation for producing me-too products. The product that really got Haier noticed was a free-standing home wine cooler—a more convenient way of storing wine for the growing number of wine aficionados. Another way Haier is going for a more premium-priced image is by producing a line of eco-friendly, technology-rich appliances, priced at $600–$1,500, compared with the $200–$300 range of its white goods. Its Genesis top-loading washing machine and a dishwasher with a particle sensor to detect when plates are clean and an automatic shutoff to save energy are some of its offerings.[46]

Haier is a Chinese company that is building a market overseas. It is the top-selling brand of compact refrigerators.

INTERNALIZATION

Marketers must now "walk the talk" to deliver the brand promise. They must adopt an *internal* perspective to consider what steps to take to be sure employees and marketing partners appreciate and understand basic branding notions, and how they can help or hurt brand equity.[47] **Internal branding** is activities and processes that help to inform and inspire employees.[48] An up-to-date, deep understanding of the brand and its promise by all employees is critical for service companies and retailers.

Brand bonding occurs when customers experience the company as delivering on its brand promise. All of the customers' contacts with company employees and company communications must be positive. *The brand promise will not be delivered unless everyone in the company lives the brand.* One of the most potent influences on brand perception is the experience customers have with company personnel. For example, the in-flight service provided by the Singapore Girl is a critical ingredient of Singapore Airlines' branding success.

When employees care about and believe in the brand, they are motivated to work harder and feel greater loyalty to the firm. Some important principles for internal branding are:[49]

1. ***Choose the right moment***—Turning points are ideal opportunities to capture employees' attention and imagination. BP found that after it ran an internal branding campaign to accompany its external repositioning, "Beyond petroleum," most employees were positive about the new brand and thought the company was going in the right direction.
2. ***Link internal and external marketing***— Internal and external messages must match. IBM's e-business campaign not only helped to change public perceptions of the company in the marketplace, it also sent a signal to employees that IBM was determined to be a leader in the use of Internet technology.
3. ***Bring the brand alive for employees*** — A professional branding campaign should be based on marketing research and supervised by the marketing department. Internal communications should be informative and energizing. To improve employee morale, Miller Brewing has tapped into its brewing heritage to generate some pride and passion.

Leveraging Secondary Association

The third and final way to build brand equity is, in effect, to "borrow" it. That is, brand associations may themselves be linked to other entities that have their own associations, creating "secondary" brand associations. In other words, brand equity may be created by linking the brand to other information in memory that conveys meaning to consumers (see Figure 9.4).

The brand may be linked to certain source factors, such as the company (through branding strategies), countries or other geographical regions (through identification of product origin), and channels of distribution (through channel strategy); as well as to other brands (through ingredient or cobranding), characters (through licensing), spokespeople

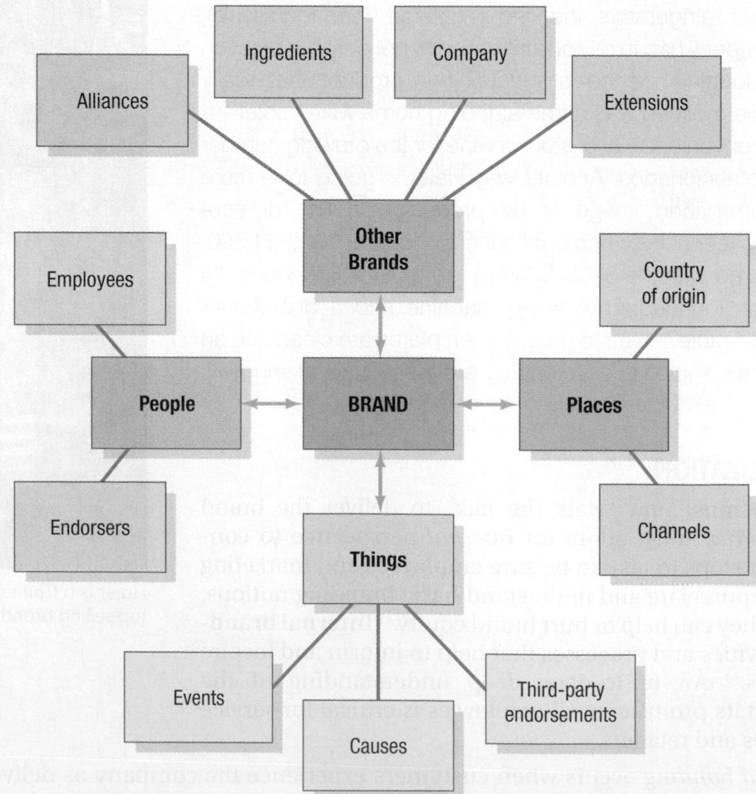

Figure 9.4 Secondary Sources of Brand Knowledge

(through endorsements), sporting or cultural events (through sponsorship), or some other third-party sources (through awards or reviews).

For example, assume Evensun—a Taiwanese Original Equipment Manufacturer (OEM) of inline skates and protection gear—decided to introduce a new inline skate called "Topdog." In creating the marketing program to support the new Topdog inline skate, the company could attempt to leverage secondary brand knowledge in several different ways:

- **Leverage associations to the corporate brand** by "subbranding" the product, calling it "Topdog by Evensun." Consumers' evaluations of the new product would be influenced by how they felt about Evensun and how they felt that such knowledge predicted the quality of an Evensun inline skate. Given its status as an OEM, this approach may not be advisable, as the Evensun name is not well recognized.
- **Try to rely on its Taiwanese origins,** but such a geographical location would seem to have little relevance to skating.
- **Try to sell through popular skate shops** in the hope that their credibility would "rub off" on the Topdog brand.
- **Attempt to co-brand** by identifying a strong ingredient brand for its fiberglass materials.
- **Attempt to find one or more top professional inline skaters** to endorse the inline skate or choose to sponsor a skating competition.
- **Attempt to secure and publicize favorable ratings** from third-party sources like leading inline skating magazines.

Thus, independent of the associations created by the inline skate itself, its brand name, or any other aspects of the marketing program, Evensun can build equity by linking the brand to these other entities.

Measuring Brand Equity

Given that the power of a brand resides in the minds of consumers and how it changes their response to marketing, there are two basic approaches to measuring brand equity. An *indirect* approach assesses potential sources of brand equity by identifying and tracking consumer brand knowledge structures. A *direct* approach assesses the actual impact of brand knowledge on consumer response to different aspects of the marketing. "Marketing Insight: The Brand Value Chain" shows how the two measurement approaches can be linked.

The two general approaches are complementary, and marketers can employ both. In other words, for brand equity to perform a useful strategic function and guide marketing decisions, it is important for marketers to (1) fully understand the sources of brand equity and how they affect outcomes of interest, as well as (2) how these sources and outcomes change, if at all, over time. Brand audits are important for the former; brand tracking is important for the latter.

KFC—A study comparing the brand image of KFC in China and in the U.S. showed that young Chinese consumers tended to rate KFC more favorably than their American counterparts. KFC was rated better on providing a healthy, well-balanced meal; efficient and courteous staff; and more attractive advertising. Brand identity impressions were also observed to be correlated with overall customer satisfaction and with future patronage intentions.[50]

A **brand audit** is a consumer-focused series of procedures to assess the health of the brand, uncover its sources of brand equity, and suggest ways to improve and leverage its equity.

Marketers should conduct a brand audit whenever they consider important shifts in strategic direction. Conducting brand audits on a regular basis (e.g., annually) allows marketers to keep their fingers on the pulse of their brands so that they can manage them more proactively and responsively. Audits are particularly useful background for managers as they set up their marketing plans.

MARKETING INSIGHT • THE BRAND VALUE CHAIN

The **brand value chain** is a structured approach to assessing the sources and outcomes of brand equity and the manner in which marketing activities create brand value (see Figure 9.5). It is based on several basic premises.

The brand value creation process begins when the firm invests in a marketing program targeting actual or potential customers. Any marketing program investment that can be attributed to brand value development, either intentional or not, falls into this category—product research, development, and design; trade or intermediary support; and marketing communications.

The marketing activity associated with the program affects the customer "mind-set" with respect to the brand. The issue is, in what ways have customers been changed as a result of the marketing program? This mind-set, across a broad group of customers, then results in certain outcomes for the brand in terms of how it performs in the marketplace. This is the collective impact of individual customer actions regarding how much and when they purchase, the price that they pay, and so on. Finally, the investment community considers market performance and other factors such as replacement cost and purchase price in acquisitions to arrive at an assessment of shareholder value in general and the value of a brand in particular.

The model also assumes that a number of linking factors intervene between these stages and determine the extent to which value created at one stage transfers to the next stage. Three sets of multipliers moderate the transfer between the marketing program and the subsequent three value stages—the program multiplier, the customer multiplier, and the market multiplier. The program multiplier determines the ability of the marketing program to affect the customer mind-set and is a function of the quality of the program investment. The customer multiplier determines the extent to which value created in the minds of customers affects market performance. This result depends on contextual factors external to the customer. Three such factors are competitive superiority (how effective is the quantity and quality of the marketing investment of other competing brands), channel and other intermediary support (how much brand reinforcement and selling effort is being put forth by various marketing partners), and customer size and profile (how many and what types of customers, profitable or not, are attracted to the brand). The market multiplier determines the extent to which the value shown by the market performance of a brand is manifested in shareholder value. It depends, in part, on the actions of financial analysts and investors.

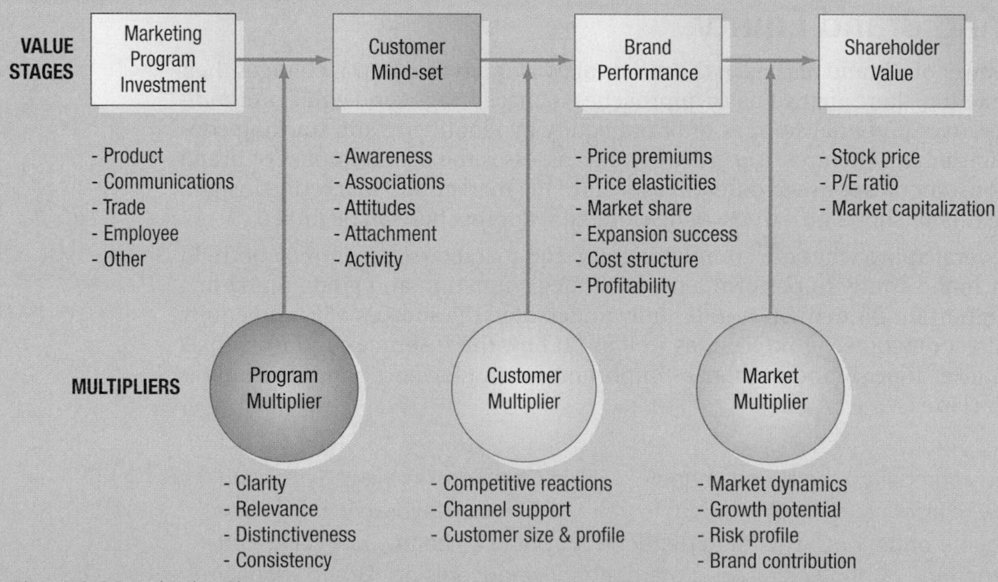

Figure 9.5 Brand Value Chain

Source: Kevin Lane Keller, *Strategic Brand Management,* 3rd ed., (Upper Saddle River, NJ: Prentice Hall, 2008). Reproduced by permission of Pearson Education, Inc. Upper Saddle River, New Jersey.

Sources: Kevin Lane Keller and Don Lehmann, "How Do Brands Create Value." *Marketing Management,* May/June 2003, pp. 27-31. See also Rajendra K. Srivastava, Tasadduq A. Shervani, and Liam Fahey, "Market-Based Assets and Shareholder Value." *Journal of Marketing,* 1998, 62(1), pp. 2-18; and M.J. Epstein and R.A. Westbrook, "Linking Actions to Profits in Strategic Decision Making." *MIT Sloan Management Review,* Spring 2001, pp. 39-49. In terms of related empirical insights, see Manoj K. Agrawal and Vithala Rao "An Empirical Comparison of Consumer-Based Measures of Brand Equity." *Marketing Letters,* 1996, 7(3), pp. 237-247, and Walfried Lassar, Banwari Mittal, and Arun Sharma, "Measuring Customer-Based Brand Equity." *Journal of Consumer Marketing,* 1995, 12(4), pp. 11-19.

Brand-tracking studies collect quantitative data from consumers on a routine basis over time to provide marketers with consistent, baseline information about how their brands and marketing programs are performing on key dimensions. Tracking studies are a means of understanding where, how much, and in what ways brand value is being created, to facilitate day-to-day decision making.

Brand Valuation

Brand equity needs to be distinguished from **brand valuation**, which involves estimating the total financial value of the brand.

Table 9.2 displays the world's most valuable brands in 2007 according to one ranking. With these well-known companies, brand value is typically over half of their total company market capitalization. John Stuart, cofounder of Quaker Oats, said: "If this business were split up, I would give you the land and bricks and mortar, and I would take the brands and trademarks, and I would fare better than you." U.S. companies do not list brand equity on their balance sheets because of the arbitrariness of the estimate. However, brand equity is given a value by some companies in the U.K., Hong Kong, and Australia. "Marketing Insight: What is a Brand Worth?" reviews one popular valuation approach, based in part on the price premium the brand commands times the extra volume it moves over an average brand.[51]

Table 9.2 The World's 10 Most Valuable Brands

Rank	Brand	2007 Brand Value (Billions)
1	Coca-Cola	$65.32
2	Microsoft	$58.71
3	IBM	$57.01
4	GE	$51.57
5	Nokia	$33.70
6	Toyota	$32.07
7	Intel	$30.95
8	McDonald's	$29.40
9	Disney	$29.21
10	Mercedes-Benz	$24.84

Source: "The 100 Top Brands." *BusinessWeek*, August 6, 2007, pp. 59-64.

Managing Brand Equity

Effective brand management requires a long-term view of marketing decisions. Because consumer responses to marketing activity depend on what they know and remember about a brand, short-term marketing actions, by changing brand knowledge, necessarily increase or decrease the success of future marketing actions. Additionally, a long-term view results in proactive strategies designed to maintain and enhance customer-based brand equity over time in the face of external changes in the marketing environment and internal changes in a firm's marketing goals and programs.

Brand Reinforcement

As the company's major enduring asset, a brand needs to be carefully managed so that its value does not depreciate. Many brand leaders of 70 years ago are still today's brand leaders: Kodak, Coca-Cola, and Campbell Soup, but only by constantly striving to improve their products, services, and marketing. Comparable long-lived Asian brands include Mikimoto pearls, Poh Chai pills, and San Miguel beer.

Brand equity is reinforced by marketing actions that consistently convey the meaning of the brand to consumers in terms of: (1) What products the brand represents; what core benefits it supplies; and what needs it satisfies; as well as (2) How the brand makes those products superior and which strong, favorable, and unique brand associations should exist

MARKETING INSIGHT • WHAT IS A BRAND WORTH?

Top brand valuation firm Interbrand has developed a model to formally estimate the dollar value of a brand. Interbrand defines Brand Value as the net present value of the earnings a brand is expected to generate in the future and believes both marketing and financial analyses are equally important in determining the value of a brand. Its process follows the following five steps (see Figure 9.6 for a schematic overview):

1. ***Market segmentation*** — The first step in the Brand Valuation process is to divide the market(s) in which the brand is sold into mutually exclusive segments of customers that help to determine the variances in the brand's economic value.
2. ***Financial analysis*** — Interbrand assesses purchase price, volume, and frequency to help calculate accurate forecasts of future brand sales and revenues. Specifically, Interbrand performs a detailed review of the brand's equities, industry and customer trends, and historic financial performance across each segment. Once it has established Branded Revenues, it deducts all associated operating costs to derive earnings before interest and tax (EBIT). It also deducts the appropriate taxes and a charge for the capital employed to operate the underlying business, leaving intangible earnings, that is, the earnings attributed to the intangible assets of the business.
3. ***Role of branding*** — Interbrand next attributes a proportion of intangible earnings to the brand in each market segment, by first identifying the various drivers of demand, then determining the degree to which the brand directly influences each. The Role of Branding assessment is based on market research, client workshops, and interviews and represents the percentage of intangible earnings the brand generates. Multiplying the Role of Branding by Intangible Earnings yields brand earnings.
4. ***Brand strength*** — Interbrand then assesses the brand's strength profile to determine the likelihood that the brand will realize forecast earnings. This step relies on competitive benchmarking and a structured evaluation of the brand's market, stability, leadership position, growth trend, support, geographic footprint, and ability to be legally protected. For each segment, Interbrand applies industry and brand equity metrics to determine a risk premium for the brand. The company's analysts derive the overall brand discount rate by adding a brand-risk premium to the risk-free rate, represented by the yield on government bonds. The brand discount rate, applied to the brand earnings forecast, yields the net present value of the brand earnings. The stronger the brand, the lower the discount rate, and vice versa.
5. ***Brand value calculation*** — Brand value is the net present value (NPV) of the forecast brand earnings, discounted by the brand discount rate. The NPV calculation comprises both the forecast period and the period beyond, reflecting the ability of brands to continue generating future earnings.

Increasingly, Interbrand uses brand value assessments as a dynamic, strategic tool to identify and maximize return on brand investment across a whole host of areas.

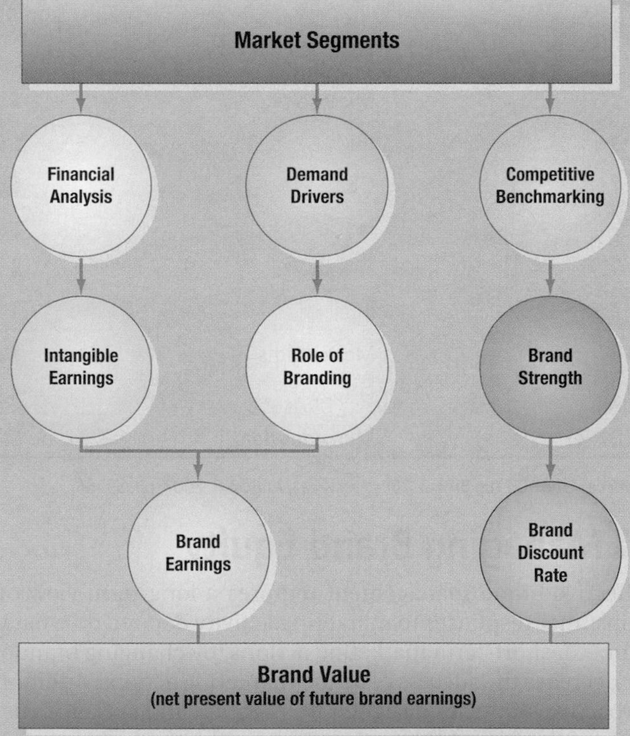

Figure 9.6 Interbrand Brand Valuation Method

Sources: Interbrand, the Interbrand Brand Glossary, and Jeff Swystun.

in the minds of consumers. Nivea, one of Europe's strongest brands, has expanded its scope from a skin cream brand to a skin care and personal care brand through carefully designed and implemented brand extensions reinforcing the Nivea brand promise of "mild," "gentle," and "caring" in a broader arena.

Reinforcing brand equity requires innovation and relevance throughout the marketing program. Marketers must introduce new products and conduct new marketing activities that truly satisfy their target markets. The brand must always be moving forward in the right direction. Marketing must always find new and compelling offerings and ways to market them. Brands that fail to do so find that their market leadership dwindles or even disappears. Unfortunately, many Asian companies have mismanaged their brands for a variety of reasons. In the quest for ever increasing profits, some Asian brands become distracted and lose focus. Their owners venture into unrelated activities for short-term gains (e.g., property). Underinvestment and neglect have also caused many erstwhile popular Asian brands in such product categories as athletic shoes, patent medicines, underwear, and cosmetics to fade into oblivion.

Sometimes, it is the heavy financial cost in investing in a brand that deters Asian companies from putting a more concerted effort. China's TCL Corp., one of the world's largest television makers, tried to establish itself in the West but gave up in 2003. Instead, TCL formed a joint venture with Thomson of France to produce TV sets under the Thomson and RCA labels for the European and U.S. markets. TCL's chief financial officer, Vincent Yan, said, "Unless you're Samsung, and you make tons of money from other activities, you can go into a market and incur a huge loss with a brand. We are not in that position."[52]

An important consideration in reinforcing brands is the consistency of the marketing support the brand receives, in terms of both amount and kind. Consistency does not mean uniformity and no changes: many tactical changes may be necessary to maintain the strategic thrust and direction of the brand. Unless there is some change in the marketing environment, however, there is little need to deviate from a successful positioning. In such cases, sources of brand equity should be vigorously preserved and defended.

Volvo—To woo a different audience, Volvo automobiles drifted away from its heritage of safety in the late 1990s to push driving fun, speed, and performance. Purchased by Ford in 1999, the company dropped its ReVOLVOlution-themed ad campaign for the brand and went back to its roots to revive sagging sales. Volvo's positioning was updated, however, to convey "active safety" to transcend the brand's boxy, sturdy "passive safety" image. With product introductions that maximized safety but that still encompassed style, performance, and luxury, Volvo's sales set records in 2003.[53]

In managing brand equity, it is important to recognize the trade-offs between those marketing activities that fortify the brand and reinforce its meaning and those that attempt to leverage or borrow from existing brand equity to reap some financial benefit.[54] At some point, failure to reinforce the brand will diminish brand awareness and weaken brand image.

Brand Revitalization

Changes in consumer tastes and preferences, the emergence of new competitors or new technology, or any new development in the marketing environment could potentially affect the fortunes of a brand. In virtually every product category, there are examples of once prominent and admired brands that have fallen on hard times or, in some cases, disappeared.[55] Nevertheless, a number of these brands have managed to make impressive comebacks in recent years, as marketers have breathed new life into their customer franchises. Asian brands such as Tiger Balm have seen their brand fortunes successfully turned around to varying degrees.

Reversing a fading brand's fortunes requires either that it "returns to its roots" and lost sources of brand equity are restored or that new sources of brand equity are established. Regardless of which approach is taken, brands on the comeback trail have to make more "revolutionary" than "evolutionary" changes.

Often, the first place to look in turning around the fortunes of a brand is to understand what its sources of brand equity were. Are positive associations losing their strength or uniqueness? Have negative associations become linked to the brand? Decisions must then be made on whether to retain the same positioning or to create a new positioning and, if so, which positioning to adopt. Consider the following "modern with a traditional twist" repositioning of Eu Yan Sang, a Chinese medicine business:

Eu Yan Sang—Eu Yan Sang (EYS) was established in 1879. Its claim to fame was Bak Foong Yun, a pill said to enhance beauty and once a staple in Hong Kong. However, EYS saw a stagnation of its customer base during the 1980s. Market research found that EYS main customers were middle-aged housewives. To expand its market to include younger people, professionals, and men, EYS re-styled its stores to look more modern, featuring better lighting and more customer-friendly products. It put up information panels in shops and handed out brochures informing people about the uses and properties of its products. It expanded distribution by selling via major supermarket chains, pharmacies, and health food stores. EYS also repackaged its products to make them more convenient to use by offering ready-prepared products. Infusions such as ginseng were ground and packed into teabags that could be prepared in 10 minutes rather than the several hours as traditionally needed. In all, EYS now makes more than 150 products and offers over 1,000 Chinese herbs. Recently, it expanded beyond the scope of traditional Chinese medicine (TCM) to include packaged health-food products such as bottled bird's nest, soups, and other dietary supplements. It also markets over 20 spa products based on Chinese herbal formulations under the brand name Zing. EYS believes that the future of health care lies in integrative medicine combining the best of natural therapies and Western medical practices. Thus it opened an integrative medicine center in Sydney. Besides Western-trained doctors, the center also has a TCM practitioner, a homeopath, and other natural therapy practitioners. EYS now has more than 60 retail branches in Hong Kong, Malaysia, and Singapore. It also has over 5,000 wholesalers and distributors worldwide carrying its products. EYS has set up a cybershop which allows consumers worldwide to buy its products.

The Bak Foong pill still remains a major stalwart as part of Eu Yan Sang's product line, especially after having undergone a packaging revamp to appeal to a more modern audience.

Sometimes the actual marketing program is the source of the problem because it fails to deliver on the brand promise. Then, a "back to basics" strategy may make sense, as it did for Harley-Davidson.

Harley-Davidson—Founded in 1903 in Milwaukee, Wisconsin, Harley-Davidson has twice narrowly escaped bankruptcy but is today one of the most-recognized motor vehicle brands in the world. In dire financial straits in the 1980s, it desperately licensed its name for such ill-advised ventures as Harley-Davidson cigarettes and wine coolers. Although consumers loved the brand, sales were depressed by product quality problems. Harley's return to greatness was begun by improving manufacturing processes. Harley also developed a strong brand community in the form of an owners' club, called the Harley Owners Group (H.O.G), which sponsors bike rallies, charity rides, and other motorcycle events. Harley-Davidson has continued to promote its brand with grassroots marketing efforts and finds itself in the enviable position of having consumer demand exceed what it can supply.

Harley-Davidson recovered from a brush with bankruptcy and revitalized its brand with a renewed commitment to quality and to grassroots marketing efforts that appeal to its image-conscious customers.

There is obviously a continuum involved with revitalization strategies, with pure "back to basics" at one end and pure "re-invention" at the other end. Many revitalizations combine elements of both strategies.

Devising a Branding Strategy

The **branding strategy** for a firm reflects the number and nature of common and distinctive brand elements applied to the different products sold by the firm. In other words, devising a branding strategy involves deciding the nature of new and existing brand elements to be applied to new and existing products.

Deciding how to brand new products is especially critical. When a firm introduces a new product, it has three main choices:

1. It can develop new brand elements for the new product.
2. It can apply some of its existing brand elements.
3. It can use a combination of new and existing brand elements.

When a firm uses an established brand to introduce a new product, it is called a **brand extension**. When a new brand is combined with an existing brand, the brand extension can also be called a **subbrand**, as with Adobe Acrobat software, Toyota Camry automobiles, and American Express Blue cards. An existing brand that gives birth to a brand extension is referred to as the **parent brand**. If the parent brand is already associated with multiple products through brand extensions, then it may also be called a **family brand**.

Brand extensions can be broadly classified into two general categories:[56] In a **line extension**, the parent brand is used to brand a new product that targets a new market segment within a product category currently served by the parent brand, such as through new flavors, forms, colors, added ingredients, and package sizes. Many companies entering China have adapted to local tastes by introducing new flavors and new ingredients. Unilever in China has introduced jasmine iced tea, Colgate-Palmolive came up with jasmine soap, and Procter & Gamble even has jasmine Crest toothpaste. McDonald's line of fast-food items includes red bean sundaes, while Pepsi's Frito-Lay bags Peking duck-flavored potato chips. When Heinz found out that Chinese do not know much about oats but are familiar with whitebait, which is traditionally fed to Chinese babies, it extended its product line by adding a whitebait-flavored oatmeal baby food. One reason for such line extensions when entering new markets is to reduce the amount of education needed. For instance, in the hair care market, the average shampoo product is a big purchase for many Chinese consumers. Hence, marketers such as Procter & Gamble use ingredients that are intuitive to people. P&G launched a ginseng version of its Rejoice shampoo which shoppers think could improve their hair shine over time just as ginseng supposedly heals the body with repeated use.[57]

Hello Kitty has been licensed to many products including credit cards, toasters, purses, confectionery, and UNO card games.

In a **category extension**, the parent brand is used to enter a different product category from that currently served by the parent brand. Honda has used its company name to cover such different products as automobiles, motorcycles, snowblowers, lawnmowers, marine engines, and snowmobiles. This allows Honda to advertise that it can fit "six Hondas in a two-car garage." Sharp, the leader in flat-panel TV, also lends its name to a variety of products such as cell phones, solar power, and white goods.

A **brand line** consists of all products—original as well as line and category extensions—sold under a particular brand. A **brand mix** (or brand assortment) is the set of all brand lines that a particular seller makes available to buyers. Many companies are now introducing **branded variants**, which are specific brand lines supplied to specific retailers or distribution channels. They result from the pressure retailers put on manufacturers to provide distinctive offerings. A camera company may supply its low-end cameras to mass merchandisers while limiting its higher-priced items to specialty camera shops.[58]

A **licensed product** is one whose brand name has been licensed to other manufacturers who actually make the product. Corporations have seized on licensing to push the company name and image across a wide range of products. Sanrio's Hello Kitty has been licensed to products ranging from credit cards to toasters.

Branding Decision

The first branding strategy decision is whether to develop a brand name for a product. Today, branding is such a strong force that hardly anything goes unbranded.

Assuming a firm decides to brand its products or services, it must then choose which brand names to use. Four general strategies are often used:

1. ***Individual names***—This policy is followed by Procter & Gamble (Head & Shoulders, Pantene, Rejoice). A major advantage of an individual-names strategy is that the company does not tie its reputation to the products. If the product fails or appears to have low quality, the company's name or image is not hurt. Companies often use different brand names for different quality lines within the same product class. Singapore Airlines named its regional air carrier SilkAir in part to protect the equity of the Singapore Airlines brand.[59]
2. ***Blanket family names***—This policy is followed by Hitachi. A blanket family name also has advantages. Development cost is less because there is no need for "name" research or heavy advertising expenditures to create brand-name recognition. Further, sales of the new product are likely to be strong if the manufacturer's name is good. Moreover, the tendency that Asians like to know who they buy from supports this approach (as well as the use of corporate names with individual product names). Hence, family and corporate brands are more evident in Asia than in the West. Kao markets everything from facepacks to detergent under its own name. Even Procter & Gamble, which uses individual names for its products, inserts its corporate logo and slogan ("Making your life better") at the end of its Asian ads to raise awareness of the company in the region.
3. ***Separate family names for all products***—This policy is followed by Matsushita (Panasonic for audio-visual products and National for household goods). If a company produces quite different products, it is not desirable to use one blanket family name. Companies often invent different family names for different quality lines within the same product class. When Toyota introduced high-end luxury cars, it used Lexus.
4. ***Corporate name combined with individual product names***—This subbranding policy is followed by Sony (Sony Bravia, Sony Walkman, Sony Vaio, Sony PlayStation), Honda, and Hewlett-Packard. The company name legitimizes, and the individual name individualizes, the new product.

Individual and blanket names are sometimes referred to as a "house of brands" and a "branded house," respectively, and can be seen as representing two ends of a brand relationship continuum, with the latter two strategies as being in between and combinations of the two. Although firms rarely adopt a pure example of any of the four strategies, deciding which general strategy to emphasize depends on several factors, as evidenced by Table 9.3.

Table 9.3 Selecting a Brand Relationship Spectrum Position

Towards a Branded House	Towards a House of Brands
Does the parent brand contribute to the offering by adding:	**Is there a compelling need for a separate brand because it will:**
• Associations enhancing the value proposition?	• Create and own an association?
• Credibility through organizational associations?	• Represent a new, different offering?
• Visibility?	• Retain/capture customer/brand bond?
• Communication efficiencies?	• Deal with channel conflict?
Will the master brand be strengthened associating with the new offering?	**Will the business support a new brand by name?**

Source: Adapted from David A. Aaker and Erich Joachimsthaler, *Brand Leadership,* (New York: Free Press, 2000), p. 120, Figure 4-6.

Two key components of virtually any branding strategy are brand extensions and brand portfolios.

Brand Extensions

Recognizing that one of their most valuable assets is their brands, many firms have decided to leverage that asset by introducing a host of new products under some of their strongest brand names. Most new products are in fact line extensions—typically 80 to 90 percent in any one year. Moreover, many of the most successful new products, as rated by various sources, are extensions (e.g., Microsoft Xbox video game system, Apple iPod digital music player, and Nokia 6800 mobile phone). Nevertheless, many new products are introduced each year as new brands (e.g., TiVo digital video recorders, and Mini automobiles).

ADVANTAGES OF BRAND EXTENSIONS

Two main advantages of brand extensions are that they can facilitate new product acceptance, as well as provide positive feedback to the parent brand and company.

Improved Odds of New-Product Success

Consumers can make inferences and form expectations of the likely composition and performance of a new product based on what they already know about the parent brand itself and the extent to which they feel this information is relevant to the new product.[60] For example, when Sony introduced a new personal computer tailored for multimedia applications, Vaio, consumers may have been more likely to feel comfortable with its anticipated performance because of their experience with and knowledge of other Sony products. Here is an Indian example:

DCW Home Products—Mumbai-based DCW Home Products has a strong brand (Captain Cook) for its salt product, and extended that to its flour line. The company found that most Indian housewives crushed their wheat grain into flour at neighborhood grinding mills. Research showed that consumers would buy a ready-made, healthy flour if one were available. Focus group studies reported that consumers were reassured by the Captain Cook name as it had come to denote quality. Indeed, the main purchase criteria of Indian housewives were found to be credibility and quality of the grain source, followed by the desire that their cooking be appreciated by their husbands.[61]

By setting up positive expectations, extensions reduce risk.[62] Because of the potentially increased consumer demand resulting from introducing a new product as an extension, it also may be easier to convince retailers to stock and promote a brand extension. From a marketing communications perspective, an introductory campaign for an extension does not have to create awareness of both the brand and the new product but instead can concentrate on the new product itself.[63]

Extensions can thus result in reduced costs of the introductory launch campaign. They also can avoid the difficulty—and expense—of coming up with a new name. Extensions allow for packaging and labeling efficiencies. Similar or virtually identical packages and labels for extensions can result in lower production costs and, if coordinated properly, more prominence in the retail store by creating a "billboard" effect. By offering consumers a portfolio of brand variants within a product category, consumers who need a change—because of boredom, satiation, or whatever—can switch to a different product type without having to leave the brand family.

Business-to-business companies are even finding that brand extensions are a powerful way to enter consumer markets, as these two name brand rubber companies discovered.

Groupe Michelin, Goodyear—Both Groupe Michelin and Goodyear, known primarily for their rubber tires, have launched a number of brand extensions in recent years. Although Michelin's extensions have mainly been in the auto accessories area—from inflation- and pressure-monitoring goods to automotive floor mats—its sports and leisure category now has the potential to overtake the auto accessories line. So far its brand extensions fall into three categories: (1) automotive and cycle-related products, (2) footwear, apparel, accessories, and equipment for work, sports, and leisure, and (3) personal accessories—gifts and collectibles promoting Michelin culture and heritage featuring Bibendum, the trademark "Michelin Man." Like Michelin, Goodyear has a category of products closely aligned to the automotive industry—such as jack stands and auto repair tools, but it, too, has branched out into consumer areas. The company is selling its own line of cleaning wipes for windows and upholstery, mechanic's gloves, and garden hose nozzles, among other products.[64]

Positive Feedback Effects

Besides facilitating acceptance of new products, brand extensions can also provide feedback benefits.[65] They can help clarify the meaning of a brand and its core brand values or improve consumer perceptions of the credibility of the company behind the extension.

Line extensions can renew interest and liking for the brand and benefit the parent brand by expanding market coverage. Kimberly-Clark's Kleenex unit has a goal of getting facial tissue in every room of the home. This philosophy has led to a wide variety of Kleenex facial tissues and packaging, including scented, ultra-soft, and lotion-impregnated tissues. Nikon has successfully extended its leadership in camera lenses to eyewear lenses. One benefit of a successful extension is that it may also serve as the basis for subsequent extensions. During the 1970s and 1980s, Billabong established its brand credibility with the young surfing community as a designer and producer of quality surf apparel. This success permitted it to extend into other youth-oriented areas, such as snowboarding and skateboarding.

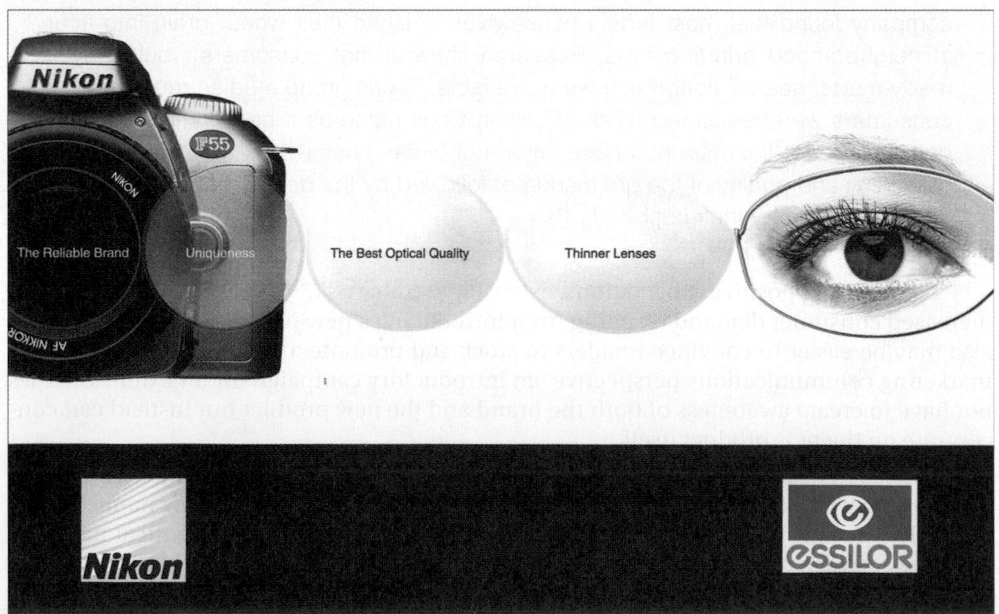

In an alliance with Essilor, Nikon has extended its expertise in camera lenses to eyewear lenses. It hopes consumers will infer that its eyewear lenses are as reliable as its camera lenses.

DISADVANTAGES OF BRAND EXTENSIONS

On the downside, line extensions may cause the brand name to not be as strongly identified with any one product.[66] Ries and Trout call this the "line-extension trap."[67] By linking its brand to mainstream food products such as mashed potatoes, powdered milk, soups, and beverages, Cadbury ran the risk of losing its more specific meaning as a chocolates and candy brand.[68] **Brand dilution** occurs when consumers no longer associate a brand with a specific product or highly similar products and start thinking less of the brand.

If a firm launches extensions consumers deem inappropriate, they may question the integrity and competence of the brand. Different varieties of line extensions may confuse and perhaps even frustrate consumers: which version of the product is the "right one" for them? As a result, they may reject new extensions for "tried and true" favorites or all-purpose versions. Retailers have to reject many new products and brands because they do not have the shelf or display space for them.

The worst possible scenario with an extension is that not only does it fail, but it harms the parent brand image in the process. Fortunately, such events are rare. "Marketing failures," where insufficient consumers were attracted to a brand, are typically much less damaging than "product failures," where the brand fundamentally fails to live up to its promise. Even then, product failures dilute brand equity only when the extension is seen as very similar to the parent brand.

Even if sales of a brand extension are high and meet targets, it is possible that this revenue may have resulted from consumers switching to the extension from existing product offerings of the parent brand—in effect *cannibalizing* the parent brand. Intra-brand shifts in sales may not necessarily be so undesirable, as they can be thought of as a form of *preemptive cannibalization.* In other words, consumers might have switched to a competing brand instead of the line extension if it had not been introduced into the category. Tide laundry detergent maintains its same market share because of the sales contributions of the various line extensions (scented and unscented powder, tablet, liquid, and other forms).

One easily overlooked disadvantage to brand extensions is that by introducing a new product as a brand extension, the firm forgoes the chance to create a new brand with its own unique image and equity. Consider the advantages to Disney of having introduced more adult-oriented Touchstone films; and to Levi's of having introduced casual Dockers pants.

SUCCESS CHARACTERISTICS

A potential new product extension for a brand must be judged by how effectively it leverages existing brand equity from the parent brand to the new product, as well as how effectively the extension, in turn, contributes to the equity of the parent brand.[69] Crest White Strips leveraged the strong reputation of Crest and dental care to provide reassurance in the teeth-whitening arena, while also reinforcing its dental authority image. The most important consideration with extensions is that there is "fit" in the minds of consumers. Consumers may see a basis of fit for an extension in many ways—common physical attributes, usage situations, or user types.

Figure 9.7 lists a number of academic research findings on brand extensions.[70] One major mistake in evaluating extension opportunities is failing to take *all* of consumers' brand knowledge structures into account. Often marketers mistakenly focus on one or perhaps a few brand associations as a potential basis of fit and ignore other, possibly more important, associations in the process.

BIC—The French company Societe Bic, by emphasizing inexpensive, disposable products, was able to create markets for nonrefillable ballpoint pens in the late 1950s; disposable cigarette lighters in the early 1970s; and disposable razors in the early 1980s. It unsuccessfully tried the same strategy in marketing Bic perfumes in the U.S. and Europe in 1989. The perfumes—two for women ("Nuit" and "Jour") and two for men ("Bic for Men" and "Bic Sport for Men")—were packaged in quarter-ounce glass spray bottles that looked like fat cigarette lighters and sold for $5 each. The products were displayed on racks at checkout counters throughout Bic's extensive distribution channels. At the time, a Bic spokeswoman described the new products as extensions of the Bic heritage—"high quality at affordable prices, convenient to purchase, and convenient to use." The brand extension was launched with a $20 million advertising and promotion campaign containing images of stylish people enjoying themselves with the perfume and using the tagline, "Paris In Your Pocket." Nevertheless, Bic was unable to overcome its lack of cachet and negative image associations, and the extension was a failure.[71]

Academics have studied brand extensions closely. Here is a summary of some of their key research findings.

- Successful brand extensions occur when the parent brand is seen as having favorable associations and there is a perception of fit between the parent brand and the extension product.
- There are many bases of fit: product-related attributes and benefits, as well as nonproduct-related attributes and benefits related to common usage situations or user types.
- Depending on consumer knowledge of the categories, perceptions of fit may be based on technical or manufacturing commonalties or more surface considerations such as necessary or situational complementarity.
- High-quality brands stretch farther than average-quality brands, although both types of brands have boundaries.
- A brand that is seen as prototypical of a product category can be difficult to extend outside the category.
- Concrete attribute associations tend to be more difficult to extend than abstract benefit associations.
- Consumers may transfer associations that are positive in the original product class but become negative in the extension context.
- Consumers may infer negative associations about an extension, perhaps even based on other inferred positive associations.
- It can be difficult to extend into a product class that is seen as easy to make.
- A successful extension can not only contribute to the parent brand image but also enable a brand to be extended even farther.
- An unsuccessful extension hurts the parent brand only when there is a strong basis of fit between the two.
- An unsuccessful extension does not prevent a firm from "backtracking" and introducing a more-similar extension.
- Vertical extensions can be difficult and often require subbranding strategies.
- The most effective advertising strategy for an extension emphasizes information about the extension (rather than reminders about the parent brand).

Figure 9.7 Research Insights on Brand Extensions

Source: Kevin Lane Keller, Strategic Brand Management, 3rd ed. (Upper Saddle River, NJ: Prentice Hall, 2008). Reproduced by permission of Pearson Education, Inc., Upper Saddle River, NJ.

Brand Portfolios

All brands have boundaries—a brand can only be stretched so far. Multiple brands are often necessary to pursue multiple market segments. Any one brand is not viewed equally favorably by all the different market segments that the firm would like to target. Some other reasons for introducing multiple brands in a category include:[72]

1. To increase shelf presence and retailer dependence in the store.
2. To attract consumers seeking variety who may otherwise have switched to another brand.
3. To increase internal competition within the firm.
4. To yield economies of scale in advertising, sales, merchandising, and physical distribution.

The **brand portfolio** is the set of all brands and brand lines a particular firm offers for sale to buyers in a particular category. Different brands may be designed and marketed to appeal to different market segments.

Armani—Armani has set out to create a product line differentiated by style, luxury, customization, and price to compete in three distinct price tiers. In the most expensive Tier I, it sells Giorgio Armani and Giorgio Armani Privé, which are custom-made runway couture products that sell for thousands of dollars. In the more moderately priced Tier II, it offers Emporio Armani, young and modern with more affordable prices, as well as the informal Armani jeans that focus on technology and ecology. In the lower-priced Tier III, the firm sells the more youthful and street-savvy translation of Armani style, A|X Armani Exchange, at retail locations in cities and suburban malls.

Armani's line of luxury clothing is differentiated to appeal to three distinct price tiers, each with different styles and levels of luxury and customization.

The hallmark of an optimal brand portfolio is the ability of each brand in it to maximize equity in combination with all the other brands in it. Marketers generally need to trade off market coverage with costs and profitability. If they can increase profits by dropping brands, a portfolio is too big; if they can increase profits by *adding* brands, it is not big enough. The basic principle in designing a brand portfolio is to *maximize market coverage,* so that no potential customers are being ignored, but to *minimize brand overlap,* so brands are not competing for customer approval. Each brand should be clearly differentiated and appealing to a sizable enough marketing segment to justify its marketing and production costs.[73]

Marketers carefully monitor brand portfolios over time to identify weak brands and kill unprofitable ones.[74] Brand lines with poorly differentiated brands are likely to be characterized by much cannibalization and require pruning.[75] Investors can choose among thousands of financial plans. Students can choose among hundreds of business schools. For the seller, this spells hypercompetition. For the buyer, it may mean too much choice.

Brands can also play a number of specific roles as part of a portfolio.

FLANKERS

Flanker or "fighter" brands are positioned with respect to competitors' brands so that more important (and more profitable) *flagship brands* can retain their desired positioning. For example, Singapore Airlines launched Tiger Airways to counter competition in the discount airline market. In designing these fighter brands, marketers must walk a fine line. Fighter brands must not be so attractive that they take sales away from their higher-priced comparison brands or referents. At the same time, if fighter brands are seen as connected to other brands in the portfolio in any way (e.g., by virtue of a common branding strategy), then fighter brands must not be designed so cheaply such that they reflect poorly on these other brands.

CASH COWS

Some brands may be kept around despite dwindling sales because they still manage to hold on to a sufficient number of customers and maintain their profitability with virtually no marketing support. These "cash cow" brands can be effectively "milked" by capitalizing on their reservoir of existing brand equity. For example, despite the fact that technological advances have moved much of its market to the newer Mach III brand of razors, Gillette still sells the older Trac II, Atra, and Sensor brands. Because withdrawing these brands may not necessarily result in customers switching to another Gillette brand, it may be more profitable for Gillette to keep them in its brand portfolio for razor blades.

LOW-END ENTRY-LEVEL

The role of a relatively low-priced brand in the brand portfolio is often to attract customers to the brand franchise. Retailers like to feature these "traffic builders" because they are able to "trade up" customers to a higher-priced brand. For example, BMW introduced certain models into its 3-series automobiles in part to bring new customers into the brand franchise with the hope of "moving them up" to higher-priced models when they later decide to trade in their cars.

HIGH-END PRESTIGE

The role of a relatively high-priced brand in the brand family often is to add prestige and credibility to the entire portfolio. Thus Lexus' prestige contributes to Toyota's positive image.

Customer Equity

Brand equity should be a top priority for any organization. "Marketing Memo: Twenty-First-Century Branding" offers some contemporary perspectives on enduring brand leadership.

Finally, we can relate brand equity to one other important marketing concept, **customer equity.** The aim of customer relationship management (CRM) is to produce high customer equity.[76] Although we can calculate it in different ways, one definition of customer equity is "the sum of lifetime values of all customers."[77] As Chapter 5 reviewed, customer lifetime value is affected by revenue and cost considerations related to customer acquisition, retention, and cross-selling.[78]

- **Acquisition** is affected by the number of prospects, the acquisition probability of a prospect, and acquisition spending per prospect.
- **Retention** is influenced by the retention rate and retention spending level.
- **Add-on spending** is a function of the efficiency of add-on selling, the number of add-on selling offers given to existing customers, and the response rate to new offers.

The brand equity and customer equity perspectives certainly share many common themes.[79] Both emphasize the importance of customer loyalty and the notion that value is created by having as many customers as possible pay as high a price as possible.

As they have been put into practice, however, the two perspectives emphasize different things. The customer equity perspective focuses on bottom-line financial value. Its clear benefit is its quantifiable measures of financial performance. But it offers limited guidance for go-to-market strategies. It largely ignores some of the important advantages of creating a strong brand, such as the ability to attract higher-quality employees; elicit stronger support from channel and supply chain partners; create growth opportunities through line and category extensions and licensing. The customer equity approach can overlook the "option value" of brands and their potential to affect future revenues and costs. It does not always fully account for competitive moves and countermoves, or for social network effects, word-of-mouth, and customer-to-customer recommendations.

MARKETING MEMO • 21ST CENTURY BRANDING

One of the most successful marketers of the last 15 years, Bedbury played a key role in the rise of both Nike and Starbucks. In his insightful book, *A New Brand World*, he offers the following branding principles:

1. **Relying on brand awareness has become marketing fool's gold** — Smart brands are more concerned with brand relevance and brand resonance.
2. **You have to know it before you can grow it** — Most brands do not know who they are, where they have been, and where they are going.
3. **Always remember the Spandex rule of brand expansion** — Just because you can doesn't mean you should.
4. **Great brands establish enduring customer relationships** — They have more to do with emotions and trust than with footwear cushioning or the way a coffee bean is roasted.
5. **Everything matters** — Even your restroom.
6. **All brands need good parents** — Unfortunately, most brands come from troubled homes.
7. **Big is no excuse for being bad** — Truly great brands use their superhuman powers for good and place people and principles before profits.
8. **Relevance, simplicity, and humanity** — Rather than technology, these will distinguish brands in the future.

Source: Scott Bedbury, *A New Brand World,* (New York: Viking Press, 2002).

Brand equity, on the other hand, tends to emphasize strategic issues in managing brands and creating and leveraging brand awareness and image with customers. It provides much practical guidance for specific marketing activities. With a focus on brands, however, managers do not always develop detailed customer analyses in terms of the brand equity they achieve or the resulting long-term profitability they create.[80] Brand equity approaches could benefit from sharper segmentation schemes afforded by customer-level analyses and more consideration of how to develop personalized, customized marketing programs for individual customers—whether individuals or organizations such as retailers. There are generally fewer financial considerations put into play with brand equity than with customer equity.

Nevertheless, both brand equity and customer equity matter. There are no brands without customers and no customers without brands. Brands serve as the "bait" that retailers and other channel intermediaries use to attract customers from whom they extract value. Customers serve as the tangible profit engine for brands to monetize their brand value.

Summary

1. A brand is a name, term, sign, symbol, or design, or some combination of these elements, intended to identify the goods and services of one seller or group of sellers and to differentiate them from those of competitors. The different components of a brand—brand names, logos, symbols, package designs, and so on—are brand elements.
2. Brands offer a number of benefits to customers and firms. Brands are valuable intangible assets that need to be managed carefully. The key to branding is that consumers perceive differences among brands in a product category.
3. Brand equity should be defined in terms of marketing effects uniquely attributable to a brand. That is, brand equity relates to the fact that different outcomes result in the marketing of a product or service because of its brand, as compared to the results if that same product or service was not identified by that brand.
4. Building brand equity depends on three main factors: (1) the initial choices for the brand elements or identities making up the brand; (2) the way the brand is integrated into the supporting marketing program; and (3) the associations indirectly transferred to the brand by linking the brand to some other entity (e.g., the company, country of origin, channel of distribution, or another brand).
5. To be managed well, brand equity needs to be measured. Brand audits measure "where the brand has been," and tracking studies measure "where the brand is now" and whether marketing programs are having the intended effects.
6. A branding strategy for a firm identifies which brand elements a firm chooses to apply across the various products it sells. In a brand extension, a firm uses an established brand name to introduce a new product. Potential extensions must be judged by how effectively they leverage existing brand equity to a new product, as well as how effectively the extension, in turn, contributes to the equity of the existing parent brand.
7. Brands can play different roles within the brand portfolio. Brands may expand coverage, provide protection, extend an image, or fulfill a variety of other roles for the firm. Each brand name product must have a well-defined positioning. In that way, brands can maximize coverage and minimize overlap and thus optimize the portfolio.
8. Customer equity is a complementary concept to brand equity that reflects the sum of lifetime values of all customers for a brand.

Application

Marketing Debate—Are Line Extensions Good or Bad?

Some critics vigorously denounce the practice of brand extensions, as they feel that too often companies lose focus and consumers become confused. Other experts maintain that brand extensions are a critical growth strategy and source of revenue for the firm.

Take a position: *Brand extensions can endanger brands* versus *Brand extensions are an important brand growth strategy.*

Marketing Discussion

How can you relate the different models of brand equity presented in the chapter? How are they similar? How are they different? Can you construct a brand equity model that incorporates the best aspects of each model?

Victoria's Secret has become a success by developing and protecting a new position in the marketplace.

Crafting the Brand Positioning

10

No company can win if its products and offerings resemble every other product and offering. Companies must pursue relevant positioning and differentiation. As part of the strategic brand management process, each company and offering must represent a distinctive big idea in the mind of the target market.

Victoria's Secret, purchased by Limited Brands in 1982, has become one of the most identifiable brands in retailing through skillful marketing of women's clothing, lingerie, and beauty products. Most U.S. women a generation ago did their underwear shopping in department stores and owned few items that could be considered "lingerie." After witnessing women buying expensive lingerie as fashion items from small boutiques in Europe, Limited Brands founder Leslie Wexner felt a similar store model could work on a mass scale in the U.S., though it was unlike anything the average shopper would have encountered amid the bland racks at department stores. Wexner, however, had reason to believe that U.S. women would relish the opportunity to have a European-style lingerie shopping experience. "Women need underwear, but women want lingerie," he observed. Wexner's assumption proved correct: A little more than a decade after he bought the business, Victoria's Secret's average customer bought 8–10 bras per year, compared with the national average of two. To enhance its upscale reputation and glamorous appeal, the brand is endorsed by high-profile supermodels in ads and fashion shows. Since 1985, Victoria's Secret has delivered 25 percent annual sales growth, selling through its stores, catalogs, and company Web site, posting $3.7 billion in revenues in 2007. It has since opened a store in Hong Kong.[1]

In this chapter, we will address the following questions:

1. How can a firm choose and communicate an effective positioning in the market?
2. How are brands differentiated?
3. What marketing strategies are appropriate at each stage of the product life cycle?
4. What are the implications of market evolution for marketing strategies?

As the success of Victoria's Secret demonstrates, a company can reap the benefits of carving out a unique position in the marketplace. But circumstances often dictate that companies reformulate their marketing strategies and offerings several times. Economic conditions change, competitors launch new assaults, and products pass through new stages of buyer interest and requirements. Marketers must develop strategies for each stage in the product's life cycle. The goal is to extend the product's life and profitability, keeping in mind that products do not last forever. This chapter explores specific ways a company can effectively position and differentiate its offerings to achieve a competitive advantage throughout the life cycle of a product or an offering.

To understand how the U.K. enterprise Nice Group has used a positioning strategy to succeed in China, visit www.pearsoned-asia.com/marketingmanagementchina.

Developing and Communicating a Positioning Strategy

All marketing strategy is built on STP—Segmentation, Targeting, and Positioning. A company discovers different needs and groups in the marketplace, targets those needs and groups that it can satisfy in a superior way, and then positions its offering so that the target market recognizes the company's distinctive offering and image. If a company does a poor job of positioning, the market will be confused. Such confusion may arise following rebranding exercises as well as after corporate mergers and acquisitions. These situations thus require careful handling to address, prevent, or minimize confusion and alienation. Consider Pacific Century Cyberworks:[2]

Pacific Century CyberWorks—Following its acquisition of Cable & Wireless HKT in 2000, Pacific Century CyberWorks (PCCW) decided to redefine its identity. Cable & Wireless HKT was known as Hong Kong Telecom (HKT) until its British-based parent, Cable & Wireless (C&W), conducted its own global rebranding exercise in June 1999, just eight months before the acquisition. Initially, the postmerger company was to be known as PCCW-HKT. PCCW's adviser, Interbrand, stated that HKT's long-standing brand represented familiarity, trust, and reliability and that it would be unwise to jeopardize this brand equity by changing its name. However, "HKT" was later dropped from its English name. In Chinese, the company has adopted a new four-character name starting with the last two characters of HKT's name followed by the first two of PCCW's. The English literal translation is Telecom Pacific Century. PCCW also launched a new logo comprising 12 geometric grids in seven colors symbolizing the company's "forward movement" and "solidarity."

Positioning is the act of designing the company's offering and image to occupy a distinctive place in the mind of the target market. The goal is to locate the brand in the minds of consumers to maximize the potential benefit to the firm. A good brand positioning helps guide marketing strategy by clarifying the brand's essence, what goals it helps the consumer achieve, and how it does so in a unique way. The result of positioning is the successful creation of a *customer-focused value proposition,* a cogent reason why the target market should buy the product. Table 10.1 shows how two companies—Volvo and Top detergent—defined their value proposition given their target customers, benefits, and prices.

Table 10.1 Examples of Value Propositions Demand States and Marketing Tasks

Company and Product	Target Customers	Benefits	Price	Value Proposition
Volvo (station wagon)	Safety-conscious "upscale"	Durability and safety	20 percent premium	The safest, most durable wagon in which families your family can ride
Top (laundry detergent)	Environmentally protective consumers	Eco-friendly and high performance cleaning	10 percent premium	A plant-based detergent that is eco-friendly and keeps your clothes clean

Oregon Scientific—This flagship brand of Hong Kong-based IDT International is positioned to be the Starbucks of the electronics world. Its founder, Raymond Chan, hopes Oregon Scientific will stand out in Asia with its midpriced lifestyle offering. It has teamed up with French guru designer, Philippe Starck, to produce a series of funky devices that tell time, temperature, humidity, and the phases of the moon, and includes an alarm clock with a harmonic piano tone. It has also signed an agreement to cobrand Ferrari electronics. Distribution-wise, it has opened over 230 retail outlets in the region, mostly in high-end department stores. It has three large concept stores in Shanghai and Hong Kong in the most exclusive retail space. On the personnel front, Chan has hired executives from Mont Blanc, Versace, and L'Oréal to run the business.[3]

Positioning requires that similarities and differences between brands be defined and communicated. Specifically, deciding on a positioning requires determining a frame of reference by identifying the target market and the competition, and identifying the ideal points-of-parity (POPs) and points-of-difference (PODs) brand associations. "Breakthrough Marketing: Shanda Interactive Entertainment" chronicles how Shanda has successfully positioned itself against other online gamers in China.

Competitive Frame of Reference

A starting point in defining a competitive frame of reference for a brand positioning is to determine **category membership**—the products or sets of products with which a brand competes and which function as close substitutes. As we discuss in Chapter 11, competitive analysis will consider a whole host of factors—including the resources, capabilities, and likely intentions of various other firms—in choosing those markets where consumers can be profitably serviced.

Target market decisions are often a key determinant of the competitive frame of reference. Deciding to target a certain type of consumer can define the nature of competition because certain firms have decided to target that segment in the past (or plan to do so in the future), or consumers in that segment may already look to certain brands in their purchase decisions. Determining the proper competitive frame of reference requires understanding consumer behavior and the consideration sets consumers use in making brand choices.

Points-of-Parity and Points-of-Difference

Once the competitive frame of reference for positioning has been fixed by defining the customer target market and nature of competition, marketers can define the appropriate PODs and POPs associations.[4]

POINTS-OF-DIFFERENCE

PODs are attributes or benefits consumers strongly associate with a brand, positively evaluate, and believe that they could not find to the same extent with a competitive brand. Strong, favorable, and unique brand associations that make up PODs may be based on virtually any type of attribute or benefit. Examples are Apple (*design*), Nike (*performance*), and Lexus (*quality*). Creating strong, favorable, and unique associations as PODs is a real challenge, but essential in terms of competitive brand positioning.

POINTS-OF-PARITY

POPs, in contrast, are associations that are not necessarily unique to the brand but may in fact be shared with other brands. These types of associations come in two basic forms: category and competitive.

BREAKTHROUGH • MARKETING

SHANDA INTERACTIVE ENTERTAINMENT

Shanda Interactive Entertainment, one of China's largest online gaming companies, was established in 2001. Founder Tianqiao Chen forked out $300,000 to a South Korean company for the Chinese rights to Legend of Mir II. To counter piracy, Chen gave the software away and got players to buy time on Shanda's servers. For as little as 3 cents an hour, they could interact and compete. Within two months, Shanda became profitable. Revenues doubled every year on average. In the third quarter of 2007, it registered a 66 percent increase in profits after the company gained users by introducing new characters and weapons to existing titles.

Online role-playing games offer China's youth an escape from the limited entertainment avenues provided by state-run TV stations and poor quality imitations of Western movies. For many, it is an escape from reality itself. Teenage boys and young men log on to Shanda's games and assume the identities of warriors, monks, and magicians to kill monsters and each other.

There are over 40 million online game players in China. In 2006, Shanda commanded 22.28 percent of the market, followed by Netease at 22.19 percent. Analysts estimate China's online gaming population to hit 84.6 million by 2012, with regular subscribers totaling 50 million.

Such growth has attracted competition, something that Shanda had not known for the first four years of its existence, when its games were China's most popular. In 2005, Netease's Fantasy Westward Journey became China's most popular online game. It also recently launched its first 3D game, Tian Xia 2. Netease is considered as one of China's Best 20 brands because it is considered "cool" among online gamers. Another rival, The9, has a runaway success in World of Warcraft and is upgrading it to Burning Crusade. "The competition to acquire the games is increasing," says Chen, "but the demographics remain fixed. If we want to keep Shanda growing very quickly, we have to expand, to broaden our demographics."

To keep ahead of the market, Shanda is increasing its portfolio. Included are a fantasy cartoon game and a new 3D role-playing game to compete with World of Warcraft. It's World of Legend and Legend of Mir are growing and showing strong momentum. This is due in part to Shanda's "free-to-play" model for both games where revenue is generated from users who buy weapons and other tools to enhance their characters. In contrast, The9's World of Warcraft employs a pay-per-hour model, though it is beginning to have a free-to-play model with an online role-playing game.

Shanda is also working on its customer service. Clerks at Shanda's customer-service center in Shanghai handle cases of lost passwords and theft of virtual equipment by hackers. Some customers travel over 800 miles to resolve their problems. Shanda also has 300 telephone operators who field an average of 8,000 calls and respond to 10,000 email messages daily. "Online gaming is not a product, it's a service," says Chen. "The first month we got profitable, we invested in the call center." Shanda has also made it easier for gamers to access its games by selling prepaid cards online, through Internet cafés, and at convenience stores. It has 317,000 distribution points around China. In 77 cities, Shanda promises to deliver new cards within three hours to dealers who have sold out their supply.

Moreover, Shanda technicians monitor real-time digital graphs tracking how many users are logged on to its games. It has 15,000 servers in 65 cities that can accommodate as many as 5.9 million users. "A lot of people think that whoever has the hottest product will be the winner," says Donglei Zhou, head of investor relations. "But it's really not. It's who has the most stable platform."

Shanda is also diversifying away from online games. It bought several companies operating beyond the realm of online gaming. These include Digital-Red, a provider of games for mobile phones, and Qidian, a literature Web site. Digital Red produces games that can be played on mobile phones and has developed a mobile entertainment platform called Game-V. Should Shanda make Game-V its mobile game publishing platform, it would compete directly with Magic Box, the game platform of China Mobile, China's largest mobile operator.

Shanda also acquired 19.5 percent of Sina.com, China's premier Internet portal and news site, as a strategic move to diversify its portfolio. It is partnering Baidu, one of China's top search engines, and is teaming up with Universal Music to offer digital downloads. Shanda has also teamed up with EachNet, eBay's Chinese subsidiary. Shanda players often swap virtual accessories such as clothing, weapons, and jewelry to win games. The EachNet tie-up gives them a place to trade these items. EachNet will provide a system to verify that these are real, authenticated items from Shanda. In return, EachNet has agreed to buy ads on Shanda's site.

Shanda also launched a home entertainment strategy to expand its business to other platforms. While there are about 40 million online game players, there are 370 million households with televisions. Hence, penetration into the TV

(Continued ...)

(Continued ...)

platform is a focus of Shanda's home entertainment strategy. It introduced a new set-top box designed to bring the Internet to China's TVs. To Chen, a marriage of broadband with TV could bring Shanda to those who might not frequent a cybercafé or use a home PC. The box features a jack for ADSL, a cable for TV, and the promise of piping the Internet—and Shanda's products—directly into the living room. Thus Shanda has lined up 48 content providers to offer a wide variety of entertainment products appealing to multiple segments. Chen envisions teens playing fantasy games, parents playing educational games with their children, grandparents playing chess or mahjong online, and families singing *karaoke* in front of their TV sets. "Maybe you can't overcome the piracy problem on the content side," Chen says, "but you can control the channel side and charge for it."

Finally, Shanda is pushing its games overseas by entering into license and distribution agreements in Vietnam, Hong Kong, and Macau.

Sources: "Shanda Buys Large Stake in Sina Portal." *People's Daily Online*, February 21, 2005; "CHL Signs Marketing Agreement with Shanda." <www.chinatechnews.com>, September 29, 2005; "Shanda Sets Sights on TV Platform." <www.china.org.cn>, April 21, 2005; "Shanda Eyes Mobile Phone Gaming Market." *People's Daily Online*, November 11, 2004; Stephan Faris, "Shanda's Got a New Game." *Fortune*, October 17, 2005, pp. 94–99; Bruce Einhorn and Ihlwan Moon, "Playing for Keeps—Online." *BusinessWeek*, November 15, 2004, pp. 38–39; Bruce Einhorn, "No Time to Play Games." *BusinessWeek*, July 11, 2005, pp. 52–53; Elias Glenn, "Tencent Looks Set to Take China Lead." *Weekend Standard*, November 26–27, 2005, p. A5; Brian Bremner, "BW's 20 Best Chinese Brands." *BusinessWeek*, August 28, 2006; Elias Glenn, "Turf Wars." *The Standard*, April 16, 2007; "Shanda Pushes Games Overseas." <www.chinatechnews.com>, June 11, 2007; Paul Waide, "China's Online Gamers Suit Up." <www.marketwatch.com>, August 26, 2007; John Liu, "Shanda's Profit Jumps 66 Percent." *International Herald Tribune*, November 28, 2007; "China's Online Gaming Population Exceeds 40 million." <www.chinadaily.com.cn>, January 16, 2008.

Category POPs are associations consumers view as essential to be a legitimate and credible offering within a certain product or service category. In other words, they represent necessary—but not necessarily sufficient—conditions for brand choice. Consumers might not consider a travel agency truly a travel agency unless it is able to make air and hotel reservations, provide advice about leisure packages, and offer various ticket payment and delivery options. Category POPs may change over time due to technological advances, legal developments, or consumer trends, but they are the "greens fees" to play the marketing game.

Competitive POPs are associations designed to negate competitors' PODs. If, in the eyes of consumers, the brand can "break even" in those areas where the competitors are trying to find an advantage *and* can achieve advantages in other areas, the brand should be in a strong—and perhaps unbeatable—competitive position.

POINTS-OF-PARITY VERSUS POINTS-OF-DIFFERENCE

To achieve a POP on a particular attribute or benefit, a sufficient number of consumers must believe that the brand is "good enough" on that dimension. There is a "zone" or "range of tolerance or acceptance" with POPs. The brand does not literally have to be seen as equal to competitors, but consumers must feel that the brand does well enough on that particular attribute or benefit. If consumers feel that way, they may be willing to base their evaluations and decisions on other factors potentially more favorable to the brand. A light beer presumably would never taste as good as a full-strength beer, but it would have to taste close enough to be able to effectively compete. For Asian brands, achieving POPs may be no mean feat, given rapid changes in the competitive landscape. For example, with the opening of China's retail market to foreign players, local stores are faced with declining store loyalty and sales. The pressure to be at least on par on some attributes is greatest in coastal cities like Shanghai, where consumers are more sophisticated and have greater store choice.[5]

With PODs, the brand must demonstrate clear superiority. Consumers must be convinced that Louis Vuitton has the most stylish handbags, Energizer is the longest-lasting battery, Toyota offers the most reliable car, and Tiger Beer is the best tasting beer. Often, the key to positioning is not so much in achieving a POD as in achieving POPs!

Visa versus American Express—Visa's POD in the credit card category is that it is the most widely available card, which underscores the category's main benefit of convenience. In contrast, American Express has built its equity by highlighting the prestige associated with the use of its card. Having established their PODs, Visa and American Express now compete by attempting to blunt each other's advantage to create POPs. Visa offers gold and platinum cards to enhance the prestige of its brand and advertises "It's Everywhere You Want to Be" in settings that reinforce exclusivity and acceptability. American Express has substantially increased the number of vendors that accept its cards and created other value enhancements through its "Make Life Rewarding" program.

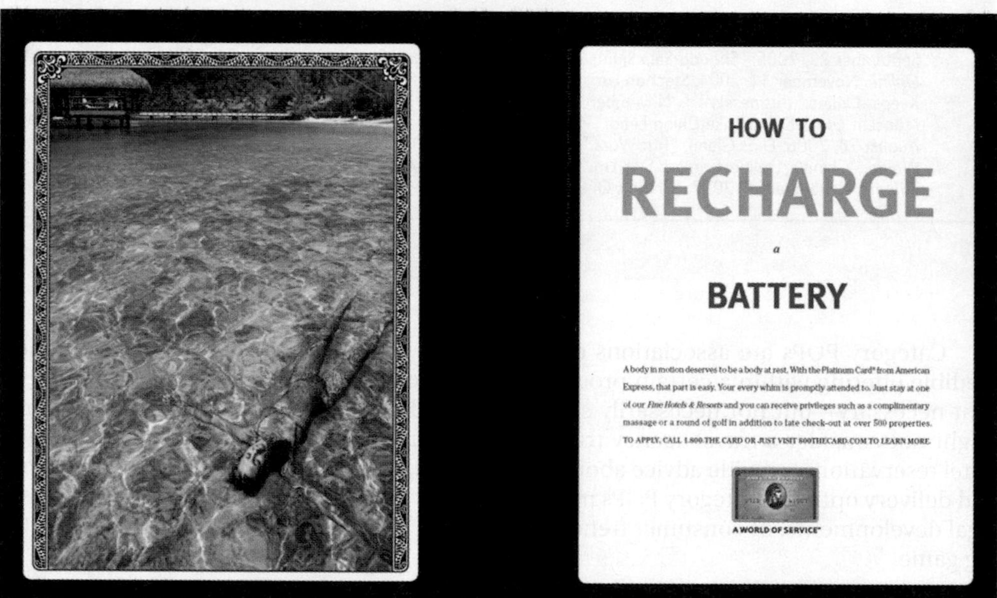

American Express built its credit card brand with appeals based on prestige and now defends itself against Visa and other competitors by increasing the number of vendors that accept the card.

Establishing Category Membership

Target customers are aware that Shiseido is a leading brand of cosmetics, Toyota is a leading car maker, Singapore Airlines is a leading airline, and so on. Often, however, marketers must inform consumers of a brand's category membership. Perhaps the most obvious situation is the introduction of new products, especially when the category membership is not apparent.

Category membership can be a special problem for high-tech products. There are also situations where consumers know a brand's category membership, but may not be convinced that the brand is a valid member of the category. For example, consumers may be aware that Canon produces digital cameras, but they may not be certain whether Canon cameras are in the same class with Sony and Nikon. In this instance, Canon might find it useful to reinforce category membership.

Brands are sometimes affiliated with categories in which they do not hold membership. This approach is one way to highlight a brand's POD, providing that consumers know the brand's actual membership. With this approach, however, it is important that consumers understand what the brand stands for, and not just what it is *not*. It is important to not be trapped between categories. The Konica e-mini M digital camera and MP3 player was marketed as the "four-in-one entertainment solution" but suffered from functional deficiencies in each of its product applications and languished in the marketplace.[6]

The typical approach to positioning is to inform consumers of a brand's membership before stating its POD. Presumably, consumers need to know what a product is and what function it serves before deciding whether it dominates the brands against which it competes. For new products, initial advertising often concentrates on creating brand awareness and subsequent advertising attempts to craft the brand image.

STRADDLE POSITIONING

Occasionally, a company will try to straddle two frames of reference:

BMW—When BMW first made a strong competitive push into the U.S. market in the early 1980s, it positioned the brand as being the only automobile that offered both luxury *and* performance. At that time, American luxury cars were seen by many as lacking performance, and American performance cars were seen as lacking luxury. By relying on the design of its cars, its German heritage, and other aspects of a well-conceived marketing program, BMW simultaneously achieved: (1) a POD on luxury and a POP on performance relative to performance cars: and (2) a POD on performance and a POP on luxury relative to luxury cars. The clever slogan "The Ultimate Driving Machine" effectively captured the newly created umbrella category—luxury performance cars.

While a straddle positioning often is attractive as a means of reconciling potentially conflicting consumer goals, it also carries an extra burden. If the POP and POD with respect to both categories are not credible, the brand may not be viewed as a legitimate player in either category. Many early PDAs that unsuccessfully tried to straddle categories ranging from pagers to laptop computers provide a vivid illustration of this risk.

There are three main ways to convey a brand's category membership:

1. ***Announcing category benefits***— To reassure consumers that a brand will deliver on the fundamental reason for using a category, benefits are frequently used to announce category membership. Thus industrial tools might claim to have durability and cold remedies might announce their efficacy. A chicken stock cube might attain membership in the seasoning category by claiming the benefit of great taste and support this benefit claim by possessing high-quality ingredients (performance) or by showing users delighting in its consumption (imagery).
2. ***Comparing to exemplars***—Well-known, noteworthy brands in a category can also be used to specify category membership. When Tommy Hilfiger was an unknown, advertising announced his membership as a great American designer by associating him with Calvin Klein and Perry Ellis, who were recognized members of that category.
3. ***Relying on the product descriptor***— The product descriptor that follows the brand name is often a concise means of conveying category origin. Ford Motor Co., invested more than $1 billion on a radical new 2004 model named the X-Trainer, which combines the attributes of an SUV, a minivan, and a station wagon. To communicate its unique position—and to avoid association with its Explorer and Country Squire models—the vehicle is designated a "sports wagon."[7]

Choosing POPs and PODs

POPs are driven by the needs of category membership (to create category POPs) and the necessity of negating competitors' PODs (to create competitive POPs). In choosing PODs, two important considerations are that consumers find the POD desirable and that the firm has the capabilities to deliver on the POD. As Table 10.2 shows, desirability and deliverability can be each judged on three criteria.

Marketers must decide at which level(s) to anchor the brand's PODs. At the lowest level are the *brand attributes,* at the next level are the *brand's benefits,* and at the top are the *brand's values.* Thus marketers of Dove soap can talk about its attribute of one-quarter cleansing cream; or its benefit of softer skin; or its value, being more attractive. Attributes are typically the least desirable level to position. First, the buyer is more interested in benefits. Second, competitors can easily copy attributes. Third, the current attributes may become less desirable.

Wahaha's Future Cola played on nationalistic sentiments for a brighter future as a distinctive positioning strategy.

Research has shown, however, that brands can sometimes be successfully differentiated on seemingly irrelevant attributes *if* consumers infer the proper benefit.[8] "Marketing Memo: Writing a Positioning Statement" outlines how positioning can be expressed formally.

Creating POPs and PODs

One common difficulty in creating a strong competitive brand positioning is that many of the attributes or benefits that make up the POPs and PODs are negatively correlated. If consumers rate the brand highly on one particular attribute or benefit, they also rate it poorly on another important attribute. For example, it might be difficult to position a brand as "inexpensive" and at the same time assert that it is "of the highest quality." Table 10.3 displays some other examples of negatively correlated attributes and benefits. Moreover, individual attributes and benefits often have positive *and* negative aspects. For example, consider a long-lived brand that is seen as having a great deal of heritage. Heritage could suggest experience, wisdom, and expertise. In contrast, it could also easily be seen as a negative: it might imply being old-fashioned and not up-to-date.

Table 10.2 Judging Desirability and Deliverability for Points-of-Difference

Desirability Criteria	Deliverability Criteria
Relevance	**Feasibility**
Target consumers must find the POD personally relevant and important. • The Westin Stamford hotel in Singapore advertised that it was the world's tallest hotel, but a hotel's height is not important to many tourists. • Procter & Gamble leverages on four different points of relevance in the detergent market: superior cleaning (Tide), fragrance (Gain), color protection (Cheer), and stain fighting (ERA). These PODs are relevant to different groups of customers.	The product design and marketing offering must support the desired association. Does communicating the desired association require real changes to the product itself, or just perceptual shifts in the way the consumer thinks of the product or brand? The latter is typically easier. • Haier tries to break away from its lower-end niche of small refrigerators into higher-end products with better margins. Its key challenge is to convince overseas retailers and consumers that it can make quality appliances. • Geely attempts to move upmarket while maintaining low sticker prices for its cars. To do so, it has to overcome its low quality image first in China, then abroad.
Distinctiveness	**Communicability**
Target consumers must find the POD distinctive and superior. • Feichang Cola was launched in China by Wahaha in a crowded soft drink market that included Coca-Cola. Positioned as Future Cola, it used the tagline, "Future Will be Better" and was promoted with a campaign that played heavily on nationalistic sentiments.	Consumers must be given a compelling reason and understandable rationale as to why the brand can deliver the desired benefit. What factual, verifiable evidence or "proof points" can ensure consumers will actually believe in the brand and its desired associations? • Substantiators often come in the form of patented, branded ingredients, such as Nivea Wrinkle Control Crème with Q10 coenzyme or Herbal Essences hair conditioner with Hawafena.
Believability	**Sustainability**
Target consumers must find the POD believable and credible. A brand must offer a compelling reason for choosing it over the other options. • Mountain Dew may argue that it is more energizing than other soft drinks and support this claim by noting that it has a higher level of caffeine. • Chanel No. 5 perfume may claim to be the quintessential elegant French perfume and support this claim by noting the long association between Chanel and haute couture.	The firm must be sufficiently committed and willing to devote enough resources to create an enduring positioning. Is the positioning pre-emptive, defensible, and difficult to attack? Can the favorability of a brand association be reinforced and strengthened over time? • It is generally easier for market leaders such as Visa and SAP, whose positioning is based in part on demonstrable product or service performance, to sustain their positioning than for market leaders such as Fendi, Prada, and Hermés, whose positioning is based on fashion and is thus subject to the whims of a more fickle market.

MARKETING MEMO • WRITING A POSITIONING STATEMENT

To communicate a company or brand positioning, marketing plans often include a *positioning statement.* The statement should follow the form: To *(target group and need)* our *(Brand)* is *(concept)* that *(POD)*. For example: "To *busy professionals who need to stay organized, Palm Pilot* is *an electronic organizer* that *allows you to back up files on your PC more easily and reliably than competitive products.*" Sometimes the positioning statement is more detailed:

> *Mountain Dew:* To young, active soft-drink consumers who have little time for sleep, Mountain Dew is the soft drink that gives you more energy than any other brand because it has the highest level of caffeine. With Mountain Dew, you can stay alert and keep going even when you have not been able to get a good night's sleep.

Note that the positioning first states the product's membership in a category (e.g., Mountain Dew is a soft drink) and then shows its POD from other members of the group (e.g., has more caffeine). The product's membership in the category suggests the POPs that it might have with other products in the category, but the case for the product rests on its PODs. Sometimes the marketer will put the product in a surprisingly different category before indicating the points-of-difference.

Sources: Bobby J. Calder and Steven J. Reagan, "Brand Design." In *Kellogg on Marketing,* Dawn Iacobucci, ed., (New York: John Wiley, 2001), p. 61; Alice M. Tybout and Brian Sternthal, "Brand Positioning." In *Kellogg on Marketing,* Dawn Iacobucci, ed., (New York: John Wiley, 2001), p. 54.

Table 10.3 Examples of Negatively Correlated Attributes and Benefits

Low Price vs. High Quality	Powerful vs. Safe
Taste vs. Low Calories	Strong vs. Refined
Nutritious vs. Good Tasting	Ubiquitous vs. Exclusive
Efficacious vs. Mild	Varied vs. Simple

Burberry Ltd—In recent years, the trademark Burberry plaid has become one of the world's most recognizable symbols. From its staid place on Burberry raincoats, the plaid began showing up on dog collars, taffeta dresses, bikinis, on gear worn by British soccer hooligans, and unfortunately, on an increasing number of counterfeit goods. This integral part of Burberry's heritage, called "the check" by those in the fashion industry, had suddenly become a liability due to overexposure. Consequently, Burberry's sales are sluggish and its CEO, Angela Ahrendt, attempted to jump-start sales growth in numerous ways. For one, she studied Burberry's 150-year history to create new brand symbols, such as an equestrian-knight logo that was trademarked by the company in 1901. Handbags will allude to the brand's tradition as a trench coat maker by featuring leather belt buckles or the quilt pattern that lined Burberry's outerwear. The other tactic Ahrendt is pushing is to invest aggressively in selling Burberry accessories—handbags, shoes, scarves, and belts—rather than apparel, which now accounts for 75 percent of the company's sales. Not only do these accessories have higher profit margins, but they are also less exposed than clothing to changes in fashion. Burberry is also doing away with lower-end products such as stadium hats and scarves. Originally, these were aimed at winning younger shoppers who would trade up later on. But Burberry decided they undermined the brand name and were too easy for counterfeiters to copy. In 2007, Burberry's brand value jumped 16 percent. With its brand on the mend, Burberry is branching into jewelry.[9]

Unfortunately, consumers typically want to maximize *both* attributes and benefits. Much of the art and science of marketing is dealing with trade-offs, and positioning is no different. The best approach clearly is to develop a product or service that performs well on both dimensions. BMW was able to establish its "luxury and performance" straddle positioning due in large part to product design and the fact that the car was seen as both luxurious and high-performance.

Some marketers have adopted other approaches to address attribute or benefit trade-offs: launching two different marketing campaigns, each one devoted to a different brand attribute or benefit; linking themselves to any kind of entity (person, place, or thing) that possesses the right kind of equity as a means to establish an attribute or benefit as a POP or POD; and even attempting to convince consumers that the negative relationship between attributes and benefits, if they consider it differently, is in fact positive.

Differentiation Strategies

To avoid the commodity trap, marketers must start with the belief that you can differentiate anything (see "Marketing Memo: How to Derive Fresh Consumer Insights to Differentiate Products and Services"). **Competitive advantage** is a company's ability to perform in one or more ways that competitors cannot or will not match. Porter urged companies to build a sustainable competitive advantage.[10] But few competitive advantages are sustainable. At best, they may be leverageable. A *leverageable advantage* is one that a company can use as a springboard to new advantages, much as Microsoft has leveraged its operating system to Microsoft Office and then to networking applications. In general, a company that hopes to endure must be in the business of continuously inventing new advantages.

Customers must see any competitive advantage as a *customer advantage.* For example, if a company delivers faster than its competitors, it would not be a customer advantage if customers do not value speed. Select Comfort has made a splash in the mattress industry with its Sleep Number beds, which allows consumers to adjust the support and fit of the mattress for optimal comfort with a simple numbering index.[11] Companies must also focus on building customer advantages.[12] Then they will deliver high customer value and satisfaction, which leads to high repeat purchases and ultimately to high company profitability.

Marketers can differentiate brands on the basis of many variables. Southwest Airlines is a good example.

MARKETING MEMO • HOW TO DERIVE FRESH CONSUMER INSIGHTS TO DIFFERENTIATE PRODUCTS AND SERVICES

MacMillan and McGrath argue that if companies examine customers' entire experience with a product or service—the consumption chain—they can uncover opportunities to position their offerings in ways that neither they nor their competitors thought possible. They list a set of questions marketers can use to help them identify new, consumer-based PODs.

- How do people become aware of their need for your product and service?
- How do consumers find your offering?
- How do consumers make their final selection?
- How do consumers order and purchase your product or service?
- What happens when your product or service is delivered?
- How is your product installed?
- How is your product or service paid for?
- How is your product stored?
- How is your product moved around?
- What is the consumer really using your product for?
- What help do consumers need when they use your product?
- What about returns or exchanges?
- How is your product repaired or serviced?
- What happens when your product is disposed of or no longer used?

Source: Ian C. MacMillan and Rita Gunther McGrath, "Discovering New Points of Differentiation." *Harvard Business Review*, July–August 1997, pp. 133–145.

Southwest Airlines—The Dallas-based carrier Southwest Airlines carved its niche in short-haul flights with low prices, reliable service, and a healthy sense of humor. Southwest keeps costs low by offering only basic in-flight service (no meals, no movies) and rapid turnaround at the gates to keep the planes in the air. But Southwest knew it could not differentiate on price alone, because competitors could try to muscle into the market with their own cheaper fares. So it has also distinguished itself as a "fun" airline, noted for humorous in-flight commentary from pilots and cabin crew members. Another popular feature of Southwest flights is the first-come, first-served open seating: Passengers are given numbered cards based on when they arrive at the gate. Southwest is now the largest airline in the U.S. in terms of passengers flown and holds the distinction of being the only low-fare airline to achieve long-term success.[13]

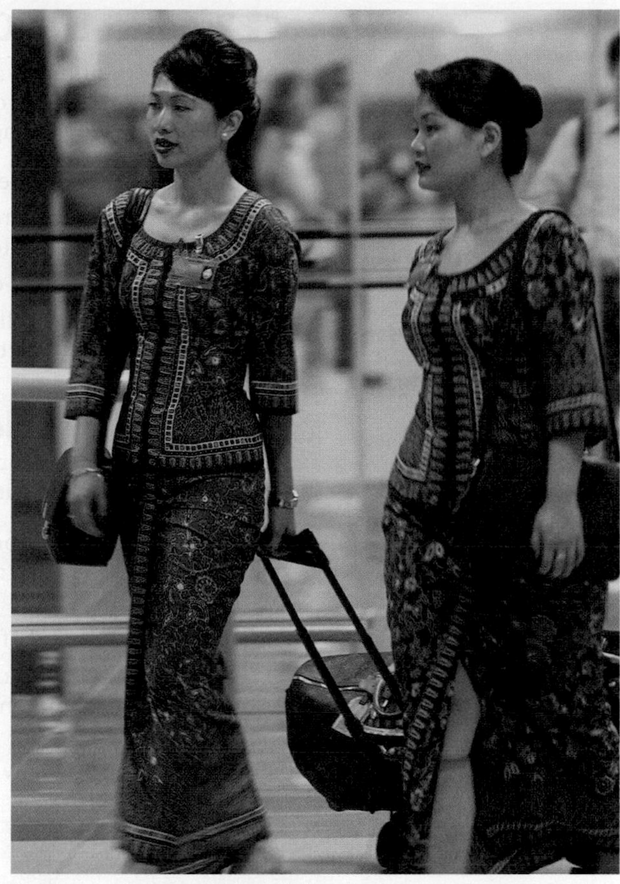

Becoming a Singapore Airlines flight attendant is not easy as company requirements are strict. But Singapore Airlines has a worldwide reputation for excellent service, built largely on the customer relations skills of its flight attendants.

The obvious means of differentiation, and often most compelling ones to consumers, relate to aspects of the product and service (reviewed in Chapters 12 and 13). Swatch offers colorful, fashionable watches. Subway differentiates itself in terms of healthy sandwiches as an alternative to fast food. In competitive markets, however, firms may need to go beyond these. Consider these other dimensions, among the many that a company can use to differentiate its market offerings:

- ***Personnel differentiation***—Companies can have better trained employees. Singapore Airlines is well-regarded in large part because of its flight attendants.
- ***Channel differentiation***—Companies can more effectively and efficiently design their distribution channels' coverage, expertise, and performance. In Asia, Dell targets both the business and the consumer markets using direct marketing. Unlike its competitors—IBM and Hewlett-Packard, who depend largely on resellers—in China, Dell targets chief information officers of Chinese state-owned enterprises, emphasizing speed, convenience, and service in its customer relationship. Its salespeople are paid similar salaries and commissions as those in Hong Kong and the U.S.[14]
- ***Image differentiation***—Companies can craft powerful, compelling images. The primary explanation for Marlboro's extraordinary worldwide market share (around 30 percent) is that Marlboro's "macho cowboy" image has struck a responsive chord with much of the cigarette-smoking public. Wine and liquor companies also work hard to develop distinctive images for their brands. Even a seller's physical space can be a powerful image generator. Hyatt Regency hotels developed a distinctive image through its atrium lobbies.

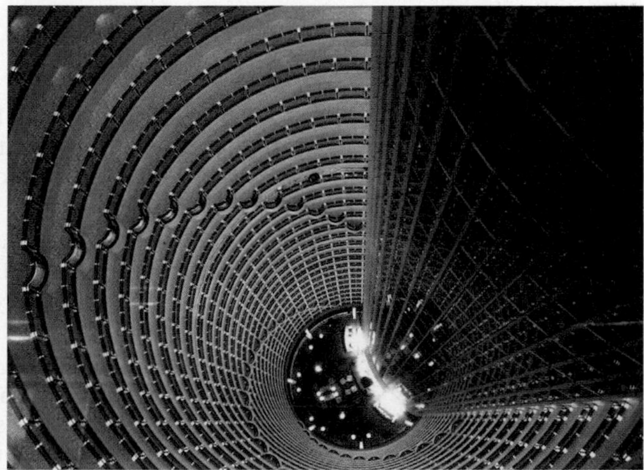

Using image differentiation, Grand Hyatt hotels have distinctive atrium lobbies.

Product Life-Cycle Marketing Strategies

A company's positioning and differentiation strategy must change as the product, market, and competitors change over the *Product Life Cycle* (PLC). To say that a product has a life cycle is to assert four things:

1. Products have a limited life.
2. Product sales pass through distinct stages, each posing different challenges, opportunities, and problems to the seller.
3. Profits rise and fall at different stages of the PLC.
4. Products require different marketing, financial, manufacturing, purchasing, and human resource strategies in each life-cycle stage.

Product Life Cycles

Most PLC curves are portrayed as bell-shaped (see Figure 10.1). This curve is typically divided into four stages: introduction, growth, maturity, and decline.[15]

1. ***Introduction*** — A period of slow sales growth as the product is introduced in the market. Profits are nonexistent because of the heavy expenses of product introduction.
2. ***Growth***— A period of rapid market acceptance and substantial profit improvement.
3. ***Maturity*** — A slowdown in sales growth because the product has achieved acceptance by most potential buyers. Profits stabilize or decline because of increased competition.
4. ***Decline***— Sales show a downward drift and profits erode.

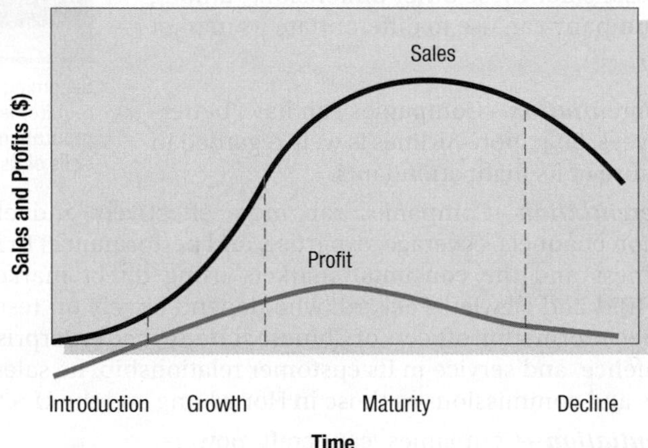

Figure 10.1 Sales and Profit Life Cycles

The PLC concept can be used to analyze a product category (television), a product form (flat screen), a product (plasma), or a brand (Pioneer). Not all products exhibit a bell-shaped PLC.[16] Three common alternate patterns are shown in Figure 10.2.

Figure 10.2(a) shows a *growth-slump-maturity pattern*, often characteristic of small kitchen appliances such as hand-held mixers and bread makers. Sales grow rapidly when the product is first introduced and then fall to a "petrified" level that is sustained by late adopters buying the product for the first time and early adopters replacing the product.

The *cycle-recycle pattern* in Figure 10.2(b) often describes the sales of new drugs. The pharmaceutical company aggressively promotes its new drug, and this produces the first cycle. Later, sales start declining and the company gives the drug another promotion push, which produces a second cycle (usually of smaller magnitude and duration).[17]

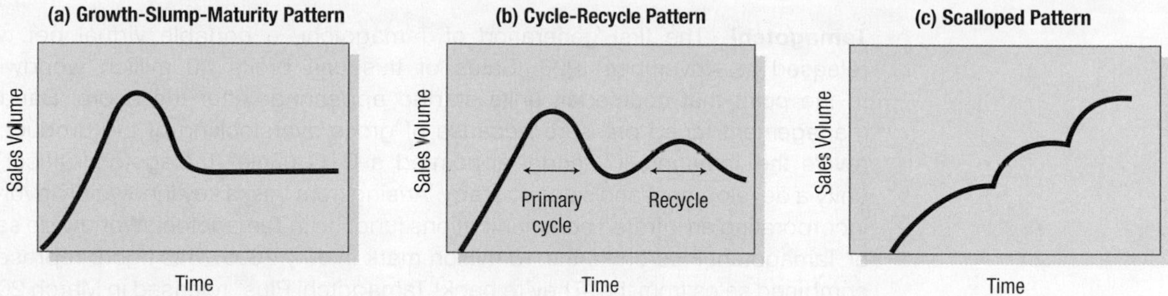

Figure 10.2 Common Product Life-Cycle Patterns

Another common pattern is the *scalloped* PLC in Figure 10.2(c). Here sales pass through a succession of life cycles based on the discovery of new product characteristics, uses, or users. For example, the sales of nylon show a scalloped pattern because of the many new uses—parachutes, hosiery, shirts, carpeting, boat sails, automobile tires—that continue to be discovered over time.[18]

Style, Fashion, and Fad Life Cycles

We need to distinguish three special categories of PLCs—styles, fashions, and fads (Figure 10.3). A *style* is a basic and distinctive mode of expression appearing in a field of human endeavor. Styles appear in homes (colonial, ranch, Tudor); clothing (formal, casual, funky); and art (realistic, surrealistic, abstract). A style can last for generations, and go in and out of vogue. A *fashion* is a currently accepted or popular style in a given field. Fashions pass through four stages: distinctiveness, emulation, mass-fashion, and decline.[19]

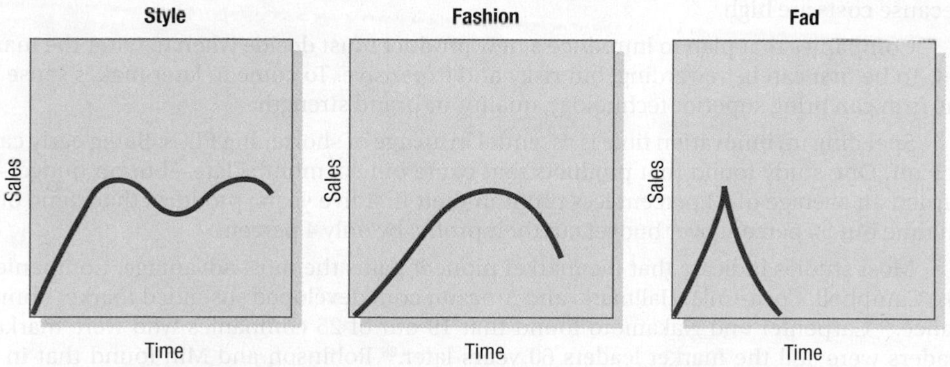

Figure 10.3 Style, Fashion, and Fad Life Cycles

The length of a fashion cycle is hard to predict. One viewpoint is that fashions end because they represent a purchase compromise, and consumers start looking for missing attributes.[20] For example, as automobiles become smaller, they become less comfortable, and then a growing number of buyers start wanting larger cars. Further, too many consumers adopt the fashion, thus turning others away. Another observation is that the length of a particular fashion cycle depends on the extent to which the fashion meets a genuine need, is consistent with other trends in the society, satisfies societal norms and values, and does not exceed technological limits as it develops.[21]

Fads are fashions that come quickly into public view, are adopted with great zeal, peak early, and decline very fast. Their acceptance cycle is short, and they tend to attract only a limited following of those who are searching for excitement or want to distinguish themselves from others. Fads do not survive because they do not normally satisfy a strong need. The marketing winners are those who recognize fads early and leverage them into products with staying power. Here is a success story of a company that managed to extend a fad's lifespan:

Tamagotchi—The first generation of Tamagotchi, a portable virtual pet, was released in November 1996. Sales of this unit broke 40 million worldwide, to the point that counterfeit units started appearing. After the boom, Bandai's management faced pressure because of gross overstocking of the product. To revive the Tamagotchi, Bandai appointed a CTO (Chief Tamagotchi Officer) to unify a development and sales strategy. Arising from this, a key innovation involved incorporating an infrared communications function in Tamagotchi. Worldwide sales of Tamagotchi Plus broke the 10 million mark in July 2005. This figure represents combined sales from the "They're back! Tamagotchi Plus" released in March 2004, and "Yuwai Keitai Kaitsu! Tamagotchi Plus," released in November 2004. English versions of Tamagotchi Plus were introduced in 44 European and Asian countries in 2004. A recent survey found that what elementary school children enjoyed most were communication games and exchanging gifts with their friends—benefits provided by Tamagotchi Plus.[22]

Marketing Strategies: Introduction Stage and the Pioneer Advantage

Because it takes time to roll out a new product, work out the technical problems, fill dealer pipelines, and gain consumer acceptance, sales growth tends to be slow at this stage.[23] Sales of expensive new products such as high-definition TV are slowed by additional factors such as product complexity and fewer potential buyers.

Profits are negative or low in the introduction stage. Promotional expenditures are at their highest ratio to sales because of the need to (1) inform potential consumers; (2) induce product trial; and (3) secure distribution in retail outlets.[24] Firms focus on those buyers who are the most ready to buy, usually higher-income groups. Prices tend to be high because costs are high.

Companies that plan to introduce a new product must decide when to enter the market. To be first can be rewarding, but risky and expensive. To come in later makes sense if the firm can bring superior technology, quality, or brand strength.

Speeding up innovation time is essential in an age of shortening PLCs. Being early can pay off. One study found that products that came out six months late—but on budget—earned an average of 33 percent less profit in their first five years; products that came out on time but 50 percent over budget cut their profits by only 4 percent.

Most studies indicate that the market pioneer gains the most advantage. Companies like Campbell, Coca-Cola, Hallmark, and Amazon.com developed sustained market dominance.[25] Carpenter and Nakamoto found that 19 out of 25 companies who were market leaders were still the market leaders 60 years later.[26] Robinson and Min found that in a sample of industrial goods businesses, 66 percent of pioneers survived at least 10 years, versus 48 percent of the early followers.[27]

What are the sources of the pioneer's advantage?[28] Early users will recall the pioneer's brand name if the product satisfies them. The pioneer's brand also establishes the attributes the product class should possess. The pioneer's brand normally aims at the middle of the market and so captures more users. Customer inertia also plays a role; and there are producer advantages: economies of scale, technological leadership, patents, ownership of scarce assets, and other barriers to entry. Pioneers can have more effective marketing spending and enjoy higher rates of consumer repeat purchases. An alert pioneer can maintain its leadership indefinitely by pursuing various strategies.[29]

Pioneering appears to be advantageous in Asia. Studies in China suggest that early entrants had superior sales growth and higher asset turnover but faced greater operational risks and achieved lower returns on their investments than later entrants. These findings imply that pioneers in emerging Asian markets should exploit first-mover advantages (market expansion and asset efficiency) while mitigating its disadvantages (risk and cost effects). They can adopt pre-emptive strategies such as patents, fill positioning gaps in the marketplace, minimize technological leakage to rivals by retaining employees, track the evolution of customer needs while being willing to cannibalize, and maintain operational flexibility. Market followers may enter through a niche to avoid confronting pioneers, acquire a pioneer that has yet to achieve its potential, and reduce risks by learning from how pioneers deal with governments, suppliers, customers, and other stakeholders in the value chain.[30]

However, the pioneer advantage is not inevitable.[31] Look at the fate of Netscape (Web browser) and Reynolds (ballpoint pens), market pioneers who were overtaken by later entrants. Consider General Motors and Volkswagen in China:

General Motors and Volkswagen—General Motors (GM) and Volkswagen (VW) were one of the earliest entrants in the China auto market. GM formed its Shanghai joint venture in 1997, while VW arrived in 1984. They quickly dominated the market. However, they are now trounced by latecomers such as Hyundai and Honda. Led by the success of its Elantra compact, Hyundai's unit sales soared by 156 percent in the first quarter of 2005 over the same period the year before. Honda sold 76 percent more cars as buyers snapped up its Fit model. Local car maker, Chery, saw its sales climb by 42 percent, led by the success of its QQ model. Meanwhile, GM's market share tumbled to less than 10 percent in 2007. VW's market share tumbled from 40 percent in 2001 to 18.6 percent in 2006. The latecomers were more attuned to making affordable, smaller cars, with comparable quality that Chinese consumers wanted. Before Hyundai launched Elantra, it sent 20 engineers and marketing experts to find out what buyers were looking for. Chery, one of Chinese largest automakers, saw its sales increased more than eightfold over the past five years. However, as first movers, GM and VW benefited from high tariffs that kept out imports and allowed them to milk the market for immense profits. But this also meant that they avoided necessary cost cutting. Moreover, most of GM and VW sales were then to state-owned companies that did not worry too much about prices. Today, most buyers are individuals who want the best deal. GM has responded by introducing no-interest loans in 2007 to gain advantage over the competition. VW stemmed its drop in market share by adding new models and cutting prices. While it had initially announced that it would not build more plants in China, VW has since announced that it would expand production because of rising sales.[32]

Schnaars studied 28 industries where the imitators surpassed the innovators.[33] He found several weaknesses among the failing pioneers, including new products that were too crude, were improperly positioned, or appeared before there was strong demand; product-development costs that exhausted the innovator's resources; a lack of resources to compete against larger firms entering; and managerial incompetence or unhealthy complacency. Successful imitators thrived by offering lower prices, improving the product more continuously, or using brute market power to overtake the pioneer. None of the companies that now dominate in the manufacture of personal computers—including Dell and Gateway—were first movers.[34]

Golder and Tellis raise further doubts about the pioneer advantage.[35] They distinguish between an *inventor* (first to develop patents in a new-product category), a *product pioneer* (first to develop a working model), and a *market pioneer* (first to sell in the new-product category). They also include non-surviving pioneers in their sample. They conclude that although pioneers may still have an advantage, a larger number of market pioneers fail than has been reported and a larger number of early market leaders (though not pioneers) succeed. Examples of later entrants overtaking market pioneers are IBM over Sperry in mainframe computers, Matsushita over Sony in VCRs, and GE over EMI in CAT scan equipment.

In a more recent study, Tellis and Golder identify the following five factors as underpinning long-term market leadership: vision of a mass market, persistence, relentless innovation, financial commitment, and asset leverage.[36] Other research has highlighted the importance of the novelty of the product innovation.[37] When a pioneer starts a market with a really new product, survival can be very challenging. In contrast, when the market is started by an incremental innovation, as was the case with MP3 players with video capabilities, pioneers' survival rates are much higher.

The pioneer should visualize the various product markets it could initially enter, knowing that it cannot enter all of them at once. Suppose market-segmentation analysis reveals the product market segments shown in Figure 10.4. The pioneer should analyze the profit potential of each product market singly and in combination and decide on a market expansion path. Thus the pioneer in Figure 10.4 plans first to enter product market P_1M_1, then move the product into a second market (P_1M_2), then surprise the competition by developing a second product for the second market (P_2M_2), then take the second product back into the first market (P_2M_1), and then launch a third product for the first market (P_3M_1). If this game plan works, the pioneer firm will own a good part of the first two segments and serve them with two or three products.

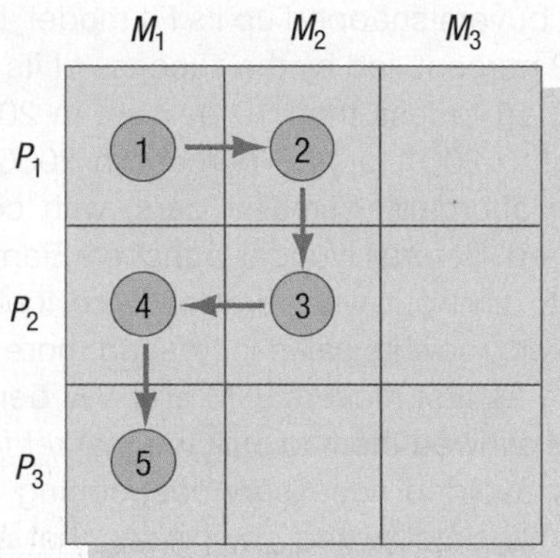

Figure 10.4 Long-Range Product Market Expansion Strategy (P_i = Product i; M_j = Market j)

Marketing Strategies: Growth Stage

The growth stage is marked by a rapid climb in sales. Early adopters like the product, and additional consumers start buying it. New competitors enter, attracted by the opportunities. They introduce new product features and expand distribution.

Prices remain where they are or fall slightly, depending on how fast demand increases. Companies maintain their promotional expenditures at the same or at a slightly increased level to meet competition and to continue to educate the market. Sales rise much faster than promotional expenditures, causing a welcome decline in the promotion-sales ratio. Profits increase during this stage as promotion costs are spread over a larger volume and unit manufacturing costs fall faster than price declines owing to the producer learning effect. Firms have to watch for a change from an accelerating to a decelerating rate of growth to prepare new strategies.

During this stage, the firm uses several strategies to sustain rapid market growth:

- It improves product quality and adds new product features and improved styling.
- It adds new models and flanker products (i.e., products of different sizes, flavors, and so forth that protect the main product).
- It enters new market segments.
- It increases its distribution coverage and enters new distribution channels.
- It shifts from product-awareness advertising to product-preference advertising.
- It lowers prices to attract the next layer of price-sensitive buyers.

These market expansion strategies strengthen the firm's competitive position. Consider how Yahoo! has fueled growth.

Yahoo!—Founded in 1994 by Web-surfing Stanford University grad students, Yahoo! has become the number-one place to be on the Web, averaging 129 million unique visitors a month, representing almost 80 percent of the online population. The company grew into more than just a search engine; it became a portal, offering a full-blown package of information and services, from email to online shopping malls. Yahoo!'s revenues, which exceeded $6 billion in 2006, come from a number of sources—banner ads, paid search, subscriptions for services such as personals, and broadband services. Yahoo!'s $1.6 billion acquisition of Overture Services, a key paid-search competitor of Google, helped strengthen its claim as a one-stop shop for advertisers. Subsequent years have seen many additional acquisitions to expand the company's online capabilities and services, including online social event calendar Upcoming.org, online video editing site Jumpcut, and online social contest site bix.com. Yahoo! also continued to grow globally with strong emphasis on Europe and Asia, helped in part by the acquisition of Kelkoo, a European comparison-shopping site, for $579 million and 46 percent of Alibaba, a Chinese e-commerce company, for $1 billion. Recently, Microsoft tried to acquire Yahoo! to boost its competitive edge over Google.[38]

A firm in the growth stage faces a trade-off between high market share and high current profit. By spending money on product improvement, promotion, and distribution, it can capture a dominant position. It forgoes maximum current profit hoping to make even greater profits in the next stage.

Marketing Strategies: Maturity Stage

At some point, the rate of sales growth will slow, and the product will enter a stage of relative maturity. This stage normally lasts longer than the previous stages and poses big challenges to marketing management. *Many products are in the maturity stage of the life cycle, and most marketing managers cope with the problem of marketing the mature product.*

The maturity stage divides into three phases: growth, stable, and decaying maturity. In the first phase, the sales growth rate starts to decline. There are no new distribution channels to fill. New competitive forces emerge (see "Marketing Insight: Competitive Category Dynamics"). In the second phase, sales flatten on a per capita basis because of market saturation. Most potential consumers have tried the product, and future sales are governed by population growth and replacement demand. In the third phase, decaying maturity, the absolute level of sales starts to decline, and customers begin switching to other products.

The sales slowdown creates overcapacity in the industry, which leads to intensified competition. Competitors scramble to find niches. They engage in frequent markdowns. They increase advertising and trade and consumer promotion. They increase R&D budgets to develop product improvements and line extensions. They make deals to supply private brands. A shakeout begins, and weaker competitors withdraw. The industry eventually consists of well-entrenched competitors whose basic drive is to gain or maintain market share.

Dominating the industry are a few giant firms—perhaps a quality leader, a service leader, and a cost leader—that serve the whole market and make their profits mainly through high volume and lower costs. Surrounding these dominant firms is a multitude of market nichers, including market specialists, product specialists, and customizing firms. The issue facing a firm in a mature market is whether to struggle to become one of the "big three" and achieve profits through high volume and low cost, or to pursue a niching strategy and achieve profits through low volume and a high margin.

Sometimes, however, the market will become polarized between low- and high-end segments, and the firms in the middle see their market share steadily erode. Here is how Swedish appliance manufacturer, Electrolux, has coped with this situation.

MARKETING INSIGHT • COMPETITIVE CATEGORY DYNAMICS

Aaker notes that because new categories can represent strategically important threats or opportunities, marketers must be very attentive to the forces that drive their emergence. He cites seven such dynamics that result in new categories.

1. ***A new product or service dimension expands the boundaries of an existing category*** — In Japan, the "always-on-the-move" trend among teenagers led Coca-Cola to design a screw-top can for Coke and Fanta. As Japanese youths are always on the go and talking on the phone, having an opened pull-tab can while walking or talking is not considered hygienic. Coca-Cola modified the product to give it a screw-top. A new subcategory had been created in which other soda drinks using conventional pull tabs became irrelevant.
2. ***A new product or set of products carves out a fresh niche in an existing category*** — The energy-bar market created by PowerBar ultimately fragmented into a variety of subcategories, including those directed at specific segments (such as Luna bars for women) and some possessing specific attributes (such as the protein-associated Balance and the calorie-control bar Pria). Each represented a subcategory for which the original PowerBar was not relevant.
3. ***A new competitor devises a way to bundle existing categories into a supercategory*** — In the late 1990s, Siebel created Internet-based customer relationship management software by pulling together a host of applications, including customer loyalty programs, customer acquisition, call centers, customer service, customer contact, and sales force automation. In doing so, Siebel rendered irrelevant, for some customers, the more specialized application programs of competitors.
4. ***A new competitor repositions existing products or services to create an original category*** — In the U.K., Ford positioned its Galaxy minivan in relation to first-class air travel — comfortable enough to be suitable for busy executives. By highlighting attributes far different from those that would appeal to a buyer looking for a family vehicle, the auto-maker created a new minivan subcategory.
5. ***Customer needs propel a new product category or subcategory*** — Dual trends—wellness and the use of herbs and natural supplements—have supported a huge new beverage category, healthy refreshment beverages. It now contains a host of subcategories, including enhanced teas, fruit drinks, soy-based drinks, and specialty waters. Coca-Cola is creating new drinks with health benefits. In a joint venture with Shiseido, Coca-Cola launched a drink, Body Style Water, flavored with fragrances thought to activate the fat-burning process.
6. ***A new technology leads the development of a product category or subcategory*** — Asahi reshaped the Japanese beer market by introducing an innovative brewing process that reduced "body" and bitterness while increasing alcohol content. Its new product, Asahi Super Dry, had a very different taste from that of other Japanese lagers and generated a new category, dry beer. As a result, Kirin, for decades the leading brand with a dominant 60 percent share of market, suddenly was not relevant for the many customers attracted to the new category. Asahi became the market leader.
7. ***A company exploits changing technologies to invent a new category*** — TiVo Inc. created a new category for home television viewing by combining the personal video player, a computer hard drive, and an electronic program guide, changing the way people watch television. Any new entrant must define itself with respect to TiVo.

Sources: Adapted from David A. Aaker, "The Relevance of Brand Relevance." *Strategy+Business*, Summer 2004, 35, pp. 1-10. See also David A. Aaker, *Brand Portfolio Strategy: Creating Relevance, Differentiation, Energy, Leverage, and Clarity*, (New York: Free Press, 2004).

Electrolux AB—In 2002, Electrolux began facing a rapidly polarizing appliance market. At one end, low-cost Asian companies such as Haier, LG, and Samsung were applying downward price pressure. At the other end, premium competitors such as Bosch, Sub-Zero, and Viking were continuing to grow at the expense of the middle-of-the-road brands. Electrolux's CEO Hans Stråberg, who took over the reins just as the middle was dropping out of the market, decided to escape the middle by rethinking Electrolux's customers' wants and needs. For instance, rather than accept the stratification between low and high, Stråberg segmented the market according to the lifestyle and purchasing patterns of about 20 different types of consumers—"20 product positions" as he calls them. Electrolux now successfully markets its steam ovens to health-oriented consumers, for example, and its compact dishwashers, originally developed for smaller kitchens, to a broader consumer segment interested in washing dishes more often. To companies finding themselves stuck in the middle of a mature market, Stråberg offers these words of advice: "Start with consumers and understand what their latent needs are and what problems they experience ... then put the puzzle together yourself to discover what people really want to have. Henry Ford is supposed to have said, 'If I had asked people what they really wanted, I would have made faster horses' or something like that. You need to figure out what people really want, although they can't express it."[39]

Some companies abandon weaker products to concentrate on more profitable and new products. Yet many mature markets and old products may still have potential. Industries widely thought to be mature—autos, motorcycles, television, watches, cameras—were proved otherwise by the Japanese, who found ways to offer new value to customers. Seemingly moribund brands like Ovaltine have achieved sales revivals through the exercise of marketing imagination. The popularity of Tiger Balm in the re-emerging traditional Chinese medicine market is an example.

Tiger Balm—This external medication for pain relief is based on a formula that originated and was used in the imperial courts of China. The founder's two sons, Boon Haw (meaning gentle tiger) and Boon Par (meaning gentle leopard) refined the formula, employing their knowledge of Chinese and Western medicines, and marketed it under the Tiger Balm name. Early marketing efforts included driving a "tiger car" painted with gold and black stripes and topped with a mock tiger's head on the hood to generate awareness. Tiger Balm's unique logo (a springing tiger), and distinct packaging (a hexagonal glass jar containing an official-looking imitation paper seal) made it stand out from its competitors. However, the brand lost momentum in the 1970s due to a tussle for corporate control. In the early 1990s, Tiger Balm was revived by new management at Haw Par Corporation. Haw Par aggressively advertised Tiger Balm in Asia by leveraging on its heritage. It also introduced Tiger Medical Plaster, Tiger Muscle Rub, and Tiger Liniment to expand its product line. A new variant, Tiger Balm Soft, was launched to target active young consumers. This topical analgesic contains a light herbal fragrance and a soft texture. Tiger Balm is now distributed in over 100 countries in Africa, the U.S., Asia, Australasia, Europe, and the Middle East. It is also available online from such sites as Costco in the U.S., Wellcome in Hong Kong, and Wellbeing in the U.K.[40]

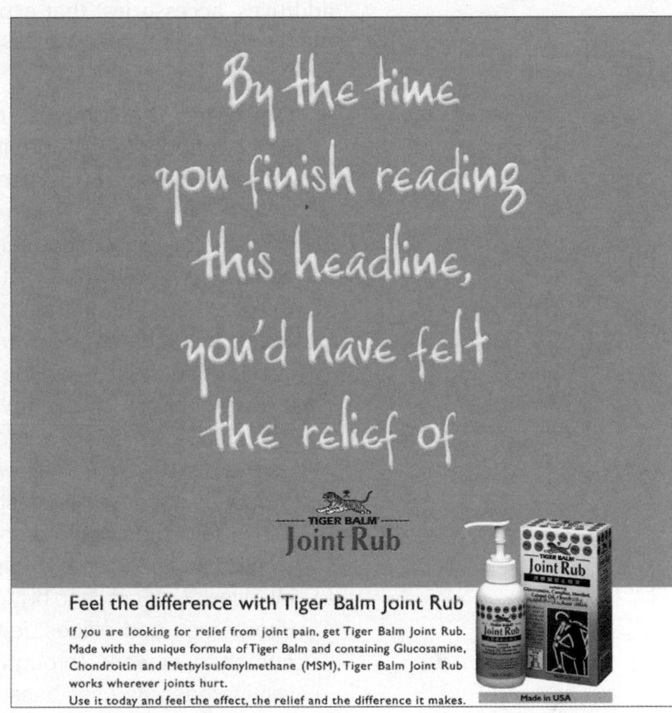

Tiger Balm revived its popularity with the constant introduction of new products.

MARKET MODIFICATION

A company might try to expand the market for its mature brand by working with the two factors that make up sales volume: Volume = number of brand users × usage rate per user, as in Table 10.4.

Table 10.4 Alternative Ways to Increase Sales Volume

Expand the Number of Brand Users	Increase the Usage Rates Among Users
• **Convert non-users.** The key to the growth of air freight service is the constant search for new users to whom air carriers can demonstrate the benefits of using air freight rather than ground transportation. • **Enter new market segments.** Johnson & Johnson promoted its baby shampoo to adults. • **Attract competitors' customers.** Pepsi is always tempting Coke drinkers to switch.	• **Have consumers use the product on more occasions.** Eat Indomie instant noodles for breakfast. • **Have consumers use more of the product on each occasion.** Drink a larger glass of soy bean milk. • **Have consumers use the product in new ways.** Use Tums antacid as a calcium supplement.[41]

PRODUCT MODIFICATION

Managers also try to stimulate sales by modifying the product's characteristics through quality improvement, feature improvement, or style improvement.

Quality improvement aims at increasing the product's functional performance. A manufacturer can often overtake its competition by launching a "new and improved" product. Grocery manufacturers call this a "plus launch" and promote a new additive or advertise something as "stronger," "bigger," or "better." This strategy is effective to the extent that the quality is improved, buyers accept the claim of improved quality, and a sufficient number of buyers will pay for higher quality.

Feature improvement aims at adding new features (for example, size, weight, materials, additives, accessories) that expand the product's performance, versatility, safety, or convenience. Thus NTT DoCoMo has improved the features of its i-mode service to stimulate sales.

DoCoMo—The Japanese mobile-phone market is nearly saturated. NTT DoCoMo, which introduced i-mode, is embarking on a feature improvement strategy to grow data traffic. Some 80 percent of its customer base are either not using the data service at all or only slightly. To increase usage of its data service, DoCoMo is pushing visual communication services such as video phones and live video streaming. For instance, some women may not want to pick up a video phone call when they are not wearing makeup. So, the first connection will be established by voice, and when they are ready, they can switch over to video phone. An avatar, such as a cartoon character, can be used to replace the receiver until she is ready. DoCoMo has also introduced phones that can double up as credit cards. This is an improvement over its handsets with FeliCa chips—tiny radios that send out a signal when the phone is placed near a sensor—which allow subscribers to pay for drinks at vending machines, buy groceries at convenience stores, or gain entry to clubs and cinemas. Turning phones into credit cards would dramatically expand their use. Previously, FeliCa phones have worked as debit cards. Despite its struggle with 3G, DoCoMo has moved forward and invested in 4G technology. It hopes that with this feature, it can replace wired links into homes and offices, letting users access a single network whether from home, commute, or work. Through these feature improvements, DoCoMo hopes that i-mode will increase its user base of 45 million in Japan, and subsequently its five million customers in such markets as Australia, France, and Taiwan.[42]

The feature improvement strategy has several advantages. New features build the company's image as an innovator and win the loyalty of market segments that value these features. They provide an opportunity for free publicity and they generate sales force and distributor enthusiasm. The chief disadvantage is that feature improvements are easily imitated; unless there is a permanent gain from being first, the feature improvement might not pay off in the long run.[43]

Style improvement aims at increasing the product's aesthetic appeal. The periodic introduction of new car models is largely about style competition, as is the introduction of new packaging for consumer products. A style strategy might give the product a unique market identity. Yet style competition has problems. First, it is difficult to predict whether people—and which people—will like a new style. Second, a style change usually requires discontinuing the old style, and the company risks losing customers.

Coca-Cola—Battered by competition from the sweeter Pepsi-Cola, Coca-Cola decided in 1985 to replace its old formula with a sweeter variation, dubbed the New Coke. Coca-Cola spent $4 million on market research. Blind taste tests showed that Coke drinkers preferred the new, sweeter formula, but the launch of New Coke provoked a national uproar. Market researchers had measured the taste but had failed to measure the emotional attachment consumers had to Coca-Cola. There were angry letters, formal protests, and even lawsuit threats, to force the retention of "The Real Thing." Ten weeks later, the company withdrew New Coke and reintroduced its century-old formula as "Classic Coke," giving the old formula even stronger status in the marketplace.

MARKETING PROGRAM MODIFICATION

Product managers might also try to stimulate sales by modifying other marketing program elements. They should ask the following questions:

- ***Price***—Would a price cut attract new buyers? If so, should the list price be lowered, or should prices be lowered through price specials, volume or early-purchase discounts, freight cost absorption, or easier credit terms? Or would it be better to raise the price to signal higher quality?
- ***Distribution***—Can the company obtain more product support and display in existing outlets? Can more outlets be penetrated? Can the company introduce the product into new distribution channels?
- ***Advertising***—Should advertising expenditures be increased? Should the message or copy be changed? Should the media mix be changed? Should the timing, frequency, or size of ads be changed?
- ***Sales promotion***—Should the company step up sales promotion—trade deals, cents-off coupons, rebates, warranties, gifts, and contests?
- ***Personal selling***—Should the number or quality of salespeople be increased? Should the basis for sales force specialization be changed? Should sales territories be revised? Should sales force incentives be revised? Can sales-call planning be improved?
- ***Services***—Can the company speed up delivery? Can it extend more technical assistance to customers? Can it extend more credit?

Marketing Strategies: Decline Stage

Sales decline for several reasons, including technological advances, shifts in consumer tastes, and increased competition. All lead to overcapacity, increased price-cutting, and profit erosion. The decline might be slow, as in the case of sewing machines; or rapid, as in the case of the 5.25-inch floppy disks. Sales may plunge to zero, or they may petrify at a low level. Here is a Chinese example regarding bicycles.

Flying Pigeon—In the early 1980s, Flying Pigeon was China's biggest bike builder. Its 20-kilogram one-speed models were the pride of workers nationwide. There was a multi-year waiting list to get one, and even then, good *guanxi* or connections were needed. At the peak of its life cycle, Flying Pigeon sold three million bikes, all of them black. Times have changed. There are more cars on the road that make bikes a poor cousin. There were less than six bike makers in the 1980s, but now, there are over 300. Flying Pigeon knows that the era of basic black is gone for good. Its bikes now come in 300 models and many colors. They are advertised and sold in more outlets, including supermarkets.[44]

As sales and profits decline, some firms withdraw from the market. Those remaining may reduce the number of products they offer. They may withdraw from smaller market segments and weaker trade channels, and they may cut their promotion budgets and reduce prices further.

Unfortunately, most companies have not developed a policy for handling aging products. A product's lifespan may be prolonged because the task of putting it to death is unpleasant. In Asia, Chinese managers may be reluctant to acknowledge poor performance of a product line, especially if it is one they had endorsed. These products are likely to persist in Chinese-run companies as a matter of *mianzi* or face. Logic may also play a role. Management believes that product sales will improve when the economy improves, or when the marketing strategy is revised, or when the product is improved; or the weak product may be retained because of its alleged contribution to the sales of the company's other products; or its revenue may cover out-of-pocket costs, even if it is not turning a profit.

Unless strong reasons for retention exist, carrying a weak product is very costly to the firm—and not just by the amount of uncovered overhead and profit: there are many hidden costs. Weak products often consume a disproportionate amount of management's time; require frequent price and inventory adjustments; generally involve short production runs despite expensive setup times; require both advertising and sales force attention that might be better used to make the healthy products more profitable; and can dilute the company's image. The biggest cost might well lie in the future. Failing to eliminate weak products delays the aggressive search for replacement products. The weak products create a lopsided product mix, long on yesterday's breadwinners and short on tomorrow's.

In handling aging products, a company faces several tasks and decisions. The first task is to establish a system for identifying weak products. Many companies appoint a product-review committee with representatives from marketing, R&D, manufacturing, and finance. The controller's office supplies data for each product showing trends in market size, market share, prices, costs, and profits. A computer program then analyzes this information. The managers responsible for dubious products fill out rating forms showing where they think sales and profits will go, with and without any changes in marketing strategy. The product-review committee makes a recommendation for each product—leave it alone, modify its marketing strategy, or drop it.[45]

Some firms abandon declining markets earlier than others. Much depends on the presence and height of exit barriers in the industry.[46] The lower the exit barriers, the easier it is for firms to leave the industry, and the more tempting it is for the remaining firms to stay and attract the withdrawing firms' customers. For example, Procter & Gamble stayed in the declining liquid-soap business and improved its profits as others withdrew.

The appropriate strategy also depends on the industry's relative attractiveness and the company's competitive strength in that industry. A company that is in an unattractive industry but possesses competitive strength should consider shrinking selectively. A company that is in an attractive industry and has competitive strength should consider strengthening its investment.

If the company were choosing between harvesting and divesting, its strategies would be quite different. *Harvesting* calls for gradually reducing a product or business's costs while trying to maintain sales. The first step is to cut R&D costs and plant and equipment investment. The company might also reduce product quality, sales force size, marginal services, and advertising expenditures. It would try to cut these costs without letting customers, competitors, and employees know what is happening. Harvesting is an ethically ambivalent strategy, and it is also difficult to execute. Yet many mature products warrant this strategy. Harvesting can substantially increase the company's current cash flow.[47]

Companies that successfully restage or rejuvenate a mature product often do so by adding value to the original product. Consider the experience of Yamaha, the dominant producer of pianos.

Yamaha—When Yamaha controlled 40 percent of the global brand piano market, total demand was sliding by 10 percent a year. Rather than giving up on selling pianos, Yamaha closely examined the market and found that the majority of pianos purchased sit around idle and neglected, without being tuned regularly. It seemed that many people owned pianos, but few were playing them. People did not want to invest the time that it takes to master the instrument. Yamaha then decided to develop a sophisticated combination of digital and optical technology that can play performance pieces just like the way professional pianists do. The advent of the digital piano has revived the piano industry and increased the market for piano maintenance as well.

When a company decides to drop a product, it faces further decisions. If the product has strong distribution and residual goodwill, the company can probably sell it to another firm. If the company cannot find any buyers, it must decide whether to liquidate the brand quickly or slowly. It must also decide on how much inventory and service to maintain for past customers.

Evidence on the Product Life-Cycle Concept

Based on the above discussion, Table 10.5 summarizes the characteristics, marketing objectives, and marketing strategies of the four stages of the PLC. The PLC concept helps marketers interpret product and market dynamics, conduct planning and control, and do forecasting. One recent research study of 30 product categories unearthed a number of interesting findings concerning the PLC:[48]

Table 10.5 Summary of Product Life-Cycle Characteristics, Objectives, and Strategies

	Introduction	Growth	Maturity	Decline
Characteristics				
Sales	Low sales	Rapidly rising sales	Peak sales	Declining sales
Costs	High cost per customer	Average cost per customer	Low cost per customer	Low cost per customer
Profits	Negative	Rising profits	High profits	Declining profits
Customers	Innovators	Early adopters	Middle majority	Laggards
Competitors	Few	Growing number	Stable number beginning to decline	Declining number
Marketing Objectives	Create product awareness and trial	Maximize market share	Maximize profit while defending market share	Reduce expenditure and milk the brand
Strategies				
Product	Offer a basic product	Offer product extensions, service, warranty	Diversify brands	Phase out weak items and models
Price	Charge cost-plus	Price to penetrate market	Price to match or beat competitors'	Cut price
Distribution	Build selective distribution	Build intensive distribution	Build more intensive distribution	Go selective: phase out unprofitable outlets
Advertising	Build product awareness among early adopters and dealers	Build awareness and interest	Stress brand differences and benefits	Reduce to level needed to retain hard-core loyals
Sales Promotion	Use heavy sales promotion to entice trial	Reduce to take advantage of heavy consumer demand	Increase to encourage brand switching	Reduce to minimal level

Sources: Chester R. Wasson, *Dynamic Competitive Strategy and Product Life Cycles*, (Austin, TX: Austin Press, 1978); John A. Weber, "Planning Corporate Growth with Inverted Product Life Cycles." *Long Range Planning*, October 1976, pp. 12-29; Peter Doyle, "The Realities of the Product Life Cycle." *Quarterly Review of Marketing*, Summer 1976.

- **New consumer durables show a distinct takeoff**, after which sales increase by roughly 45 percent a year, but also show a distinct slowdown, when sales decline by roughly 15 percent a year.
- **Slowdown occurs at 34 percent penetration on average**, well before the majority of households own a new product.
- **The growth stage lasts a little over eight years** and does not seem to shorten over time.
- **Informational cascades exist, meaning that people are more likely to adopt over time if others already have**, instead of by making careful product evaluations. One implication, however, is that product categories with large sales increases at takeoff tend to have larger sales decline at slowdown.

Critique of the Product Life-Cycle Concept

PLC theory has its share of critics. They claim that life-cycle patterns are too variable in shape and duration to be generalized, and that marketers can seldom tell what stage their product is in. A product may appear to be mature when actually it has reached a plateau prior to another upsurge. Critics also charge that, rather than an inevitable course that sales must follow, the PLC pattern is the self-fulfilling result of marketing strategies and that skillful marketing can in fact lead to continued growth.[49] Marketing Memo: "How to Build a Breakaway Brand" provides 10 rules for long-term marketing success.

MARKETING MEMO • HOW TO BUILD A BREAKAWAY BRAND

Kelly and Silverstein define a *breakaway brand* as one that stands out, not just in its own product category but from all other brands, and that achieves significant results in the marketplace. Here is a summary of their 10 tips for building a breakaway brand:

1. **Make a commitment.** Your entire organization, from the top down, needs to make a commitment to build and support a breakaway brand. Get your company behind developing new products that have breakaway attributes.
2. **Get a "chief" behind it.** Few breakaway branding initiatives have a chance of success without the enthusiastic support of your CEO, COO, or CMO. A senior executive at your company must play the role of brand visionary, brand champion, and brand architect.
3. **Find your brand truth.** Ultimately, the DNA of your breakaway brand is its brand truth. It is what defines and differentiates every breakaway brand. It is the single most important weapon a brand will ever have in the battle for increased awareness, profitability, market share, and even share price.
4. **Target a winning mindset.** The winning mind-set is the potent, aspirational, shared "view of life" among all core audience segments. It becomes the filter through which all of your advertising and promotional activities should flow.
5. **Create a category of one.** To be a breakaway brand, your brand needs not only to stand apart from others in its own category but also to transcend categories and open a defining gap between itself and its competitors. Then it becomes a category of one.
6. **Demand a great campaign.** Great campaigns are a team sport—they require a partnership between you and your agency to create a campaign that breaks away. Never compromise on a campaign, because without a great campaign, your breakaway brand can fizzle.
7. **Tirelessly integrate.** Integration is the name of the game. Depending on the audience you're trying to reach, your campaign might integrate both network and cable TV, print and online advertising, direct mail, email, radio, and nontraditional media—from street marketing to publicity stunts to contests.
8. **Take risks.** Today, 80 percent of brands are merely treading water in a sea of gray. Only 20 percent are making waves. You can't afford to have your product sink in the sea—and that may mean taking a calculated risk or two—or three—to ensure your brand rises above the others.
9. **Accelerate new-product development.** Nothing is more important than differentiating a product in the marketplace—but the only way to rise above me-too branding is to innovate and do something different and unique with the product. It may mean throwing away an old product brand and reinventing it. Or it may mean starting from scratch.
10. **Invest as if your brand depends on it.** Building a breakaway brand is serious business, so it takes a serious business investment. Invest in the product, of course—but also in the packaging and a smart integrated marketing campaign. Invest wisely ... as if your brand depends on it.

Source: Adapted from Francis J. Kelly III and Barry Silverstein, *The Breakaway Brand*, (New York: McGraw-Hill, 2005).

Market Evolution

Because the PLC focuses on what is happening to a particular product or brand rather than on what is happening to the overall market, it yields a product-oriented rather than a market-oriented picture. Firms need to visualize a *market's* evolutionary path as it is affected by new needs, competitors, technology, channels, and other developments.[50]

In the course of a product's or brand's existence, its positioning must change to keep pace with market developments. Consider the case of Lego.

LEGO Group—LEGO Group, the Danish toy company, enjoyed a 72 percent global market share of the construction toy market; but children were spending more of their spare time with video games, computers, and television and less time with traditional toys. Lego recognized the need to change or expand its market space. It redefined its market space as "family edutainment," which included toys, education, interactive technology, software, computers, and consumer electronics. All involved exercising the mind and having fun. Part of LEGO Group's plan is to capture an increasing share of customer spending as children become young adults and then parents.

Like products, markets evolve through four stages: emergence, growth, maturity, and decline.

EMERGENCE

Before a market materializes, it exists as a latent market. For example, for centuries people have wanted faster means of calculation. The market satisfied this need with abacuses, slide rules, and large adding machines. Suppose an entrepreneur recognizes this need and imagines a technological solution in the form of a small, handheld electronic calculator. He now has to determine the product attributes, including physical size and number of mathematical functions. Because he is market-oriented, he interviews potential buyers and finds that target customers vary greatly in their preferences. Some want a four-function calculator (adding, subtracting, multiplying, and dividing) and others want more functions (calculating percentages, square roots, and logs). Some want a small handheld calculator and others want a large one. This type of market, in which buyer preferences scatter evenly, is called a *diffused-preference market.*

The entrepreneur's problem is to design an optimal product for this market. He or she has three options:

1. The new product can be designed to meet the preferences of one of the corners of the market (*a single-niche strategy*).
2. Two or more products can be simultaneously launched to capture two or more parts of the market (*a multiple-niche strategy*).
3. The new product can be designed for the middle of the market (*a mass-market strategy*).

For small firms, a single-niche market strategy makes the most sense. A small firm does not have the resources for capturing and holding the mass market. A large firm might go after the mass market by designing a product that is medium in size and number of functions. Assume that the pioneer firm is large and designs its product for the mass market. On launching the product, the *emergence* stage begins.[51]

GROWTH

If the new product sells well, new firms will enter the market, ushering in a *market-growth stage.* Where will a second firm enter the market, assuming that the first firm established itself in the center? If the second firm is small, it is likely to avoid head-on competition with the pioneer and to launch its brand in one of the market corners. If the second firm is large, it might launch its brand in the center against the pioneer. The two firms can easily end up sharing the mass market. Or a large second firm can implement a multiple-niche strategy and surround and box in the pioneer.

MATURITY

Eventually, the competitors cover and serve all the major market segments and the market enters the *maturity stage.* In fact, they go further and invade each other's segments, reducing everyone's profits in the process. As market growth slows down, the market

(a) Market-fragmentation Stage

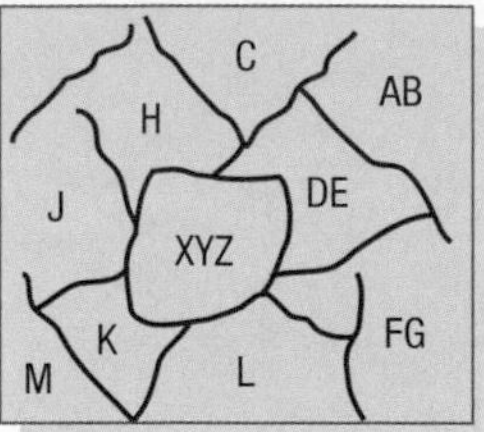

(b) Market-consolidation Stage

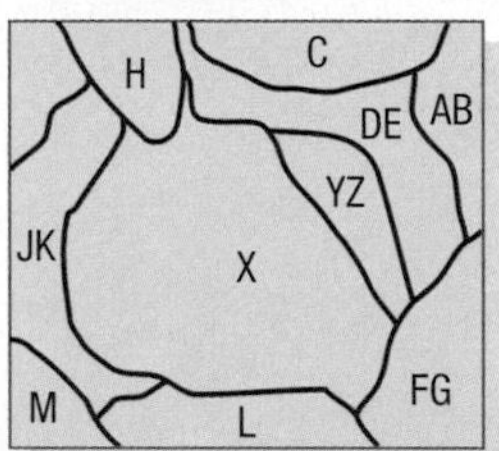

Figure 10.5 Market-fragmentation and Market-consolidation Stages

splits into finer segments and high *market fragmentation* occurs. This situation is illustrated in Figure 10.5(a) where the letters represent different companies supplying various segments. Note that two segments are unserved because they are too small to yield a profit.

Market fragmentation is often followed by a *market consolidation* caused by the emergence of a new attribute that has strong appeal. This situation is illustrated in Figure 10.5(b) and the expansive size of the X territory.

However, even a consolidated market condition will not last. Other companies will copy a successful brand, and the market will eventually splinter again. Mature markets swing between fragmentation and consolidation. The fragmentation is brought about by competition, and the consolidation is brought about by innovation. Consider the evolution of the sanitary napkin market in Asia.

Sanitary napkin market—Originally, most Asian women used cloth wads to absorb their menstrual flow. A consumer goods company looking for new markets introduced sanitary pads to compete with cloth wads. This development crystallized a latent market. Other sanitary pad makers entered and expanded the market. The number of brands proliferated and created market fragmentation. Industry overcapacity led manufacturers to search for new features. One manufacturer, hearing consumers complain that sanitary pads were not secure, introduced pads using a membrane to better prevent leakage and increased its market share. This market consolidation did not last long because competitors came out with their own versions of the same product. The market fragmented again. Then another manufacturer introduced a stick-on version of the product. It was soon copied. Currently, the market for sanitary pads include heavy versus light day pads, night wear pads, contoured pads to fit the body curvature snugly, and highly absorbent thin pads for heavy flows. The use of tampons, once considered taboo in conservative Asian market, is becoming increasingly acceptable. Thus sanitary pads evolved from a single product to one with various absorbencies, strengths, and applications. Market evolution was driven by the forces of innovation and competition.

DECLINE

Eventually, demand for the present products will begin to decrease, and the market will enter the *decline stage*. Either society's total need level declines or a new technology replaces the old. For example, shifts in tradition and a trend toward cremation have caused casket makers and funeral homes to reconsider how to conduct their business.[52]

Summary

1. Deciding on positioning requires determining a frame of reference — by identifying the target market and the nature of the competition—and the ideal POPs and PODs brand associations. Determining the proper competitive frame of reference depends on understanding consumer behavior and the considerations consumers use in making brand choices.
2. PODs are those associations unique to the brand that are also strongly held and favorably evaluated by consumers. POPs are those associations not necessarily unique to the brand but perhaps shared with other brands. Category POP associations are associations consumers view as being necessary to a legitimate and credible product offering within a certain category. Competitive POP associations are those associations designed to negate competitors' PODs.
3. The key to competitive advantage is product differentiation. A market offering can be differentiated along five dimensions: product (form, features, performance quality, conformance quality, durability, reliability, repairability, style, design); services (ease of order, delivery, installation, customer training, customer consulting, maintenance and repair, miscellaneous services); personnel, channel, or image (symbols, media, atmosphere, and events).
4. Because economic conditions change and competitive activity varies, companies normally find it necessary to reformulate their marketing strategy several times during a product's life cycle. Technologies, product forms, and brands also exhibit life cycles with distinct stages. The general sequence of stages in any life cycle is introduction, growth, maturity, and decline. Many products today are in the maturity stage.
5. Each stage of the PLC calls for different marketing strategies. The introduction stage is marked by slow growth and minimal profits. If successful, the product enters a growth stage marked by rapid sales growth and increasing profits. There follows a maturity stage in which sales growth slows and profits stabilize. Finally, the product enters a decline stage. The company's task is to identify the truly weak products; develop a strategy for each one; and phase out weak products in a way that minimizes the hardship to company profits, employees, and customers.
6. Like products, markets evolve through four stages: emergence, growth, maturity, and decline.

Application

Marketing Debate—Do Brands Have Finite Lives?

Often, after a brand begins to slip in the marketplace or disappears altogether, commentators observe, "all brands have their day." Their rationale is that all brands, in some sense, have a finite life and cannot be expected to be leaders forever. Other experts contend, however, that brands can live forever, and their long-term success depends on the skill and insight of the marketers involved.

Take a position: *Brands cannot be expected to last forever* versus *There is no reason for a brand to ever become obsolete.*

Marketing Discussion

Identify other negatively correlated attributes and benefits not included in Table 10.3. What strategies do firms use to try to position themselves on the basis of pairs of attributes and benefits?

The battle for the high-definition DVD industry standard saw Sony edging out Toshiba.

11 Dealing with Competition

Building strong brands requires a keen understanding of competition, and competition grows more intense every year. New competition is coming from all directions—from global competitors eager to grow sales in new markets; from online competitors seeking cost-efficient ways to expand distribution; from private label and store brands designed to provide low-price alternatives; and from brand extensions from strong mega-brands leveraging their strengths to move into new categories. Consider how competition has intensified in the personal computer market.

The DVD battle between Toshiba and Sony is reminiscent of the VHS versus Beta fight in the early 1980s. Many consumers were eager to see which technology emerged as the industry standard. Sony's Blu-ray was backed by Disney, 20th Century Fox, MGM, Dell, Panasonic, and Philips. Toshiba's HD DVD was backed by Paramount, Universal Pictures, Microsoft, Sanyo, and NEC. Both Blu-ray and HD are high-definition DVDs, the successor to ordinary DVDs that show pictures only in standard definition. However, Blu-ray and HD involved different hardware and were not compatible with each other. Thus consumers had to decide which system to invest in. Eventually, Toshiba lost the battle because it lacked a retail presence in many markets. It did not bring on board some of the China vendors, and it also failed to develop the European and Asian markets. Toshiba announced that it would cease developing, manufacturing, and marketing HD DVDs, effectively ending the long-running battle with Blu-ray for a dominant high-definition format.[1]

In this chapter, we will address the following questions:

1. How do marketers identify primary competitors?
2. How should we analyze competitors' strategies, objectives, strengths, and weaknesses?
3. How can market leaders expand the total market and defend market share?
4. How should market challengers attack market leaders?
5. How can market followers or nichers compete effectively?

To effectively devise and implement the best possible brand positioning strategies, companies must pay keen attention to their competitors.[2] Markets have become too competitive to just focus on the consumer alone. This chapter examines the role competition plays and how marketers can best manage their brands depending on their market position.

Competitive Forces

Porter has identified five forces that determine the intrinsic long-run attractiveness of a market or market segment: industry competitors, potential entrants, substitutes, buyers, and suppliers. His model is shown in Figure 11.1. The threats these forces pose are as follows:

1. ***Threat of intense segment rivalry***— A segment is unattractive if it already contains numerous, strong, or aggressive competitors. It is even more unattractive if it is stable or declining, if plant capacity additions are done in large increments, if fixed costs are high, if exit barriers are high, or if competitors have high stakes in staying in the segment. These conditions will lead to frequent price wars, advertising battles, and new-product introductions, and will make it expensive to compete. Consider the following Japanese examples:

> **Japanese car makers**—Japan's long-suffering automobile market saw several cash-poor manufacturers such as Isuzu and Mitsubishi struggling in a slow growth industry. Although there are some signs of recovery with demand for pricier and larger cars such as Toyota's redesigned Crown, the long-term demographic trend of an aging population is not a recipe for growth. Hence, production has leveled and car makers are safeguarding their market share. Most Japanese car makers find it tough as Toyota owns 50 percent of the domestic market and effectively sets prices for all car categories. Pressure on smaller car makers has intensified as Toyota has a healthy pipeline of new models. In 2007, Toyota introduced a new vehicle in Japan every month since May. To offset soft domestic sales, Toyota, Honda, and Nissan are boosting exports, streamlining production, and building factories overseas.[3]

2. ***Threat of new entrants*** — The most attractive segment is one in which entry barriers are high and exit barriers are low.[4] Few new firms can enter the industry, and poor-performing firms can easily exit. When both entry and exit barriers are high, profit

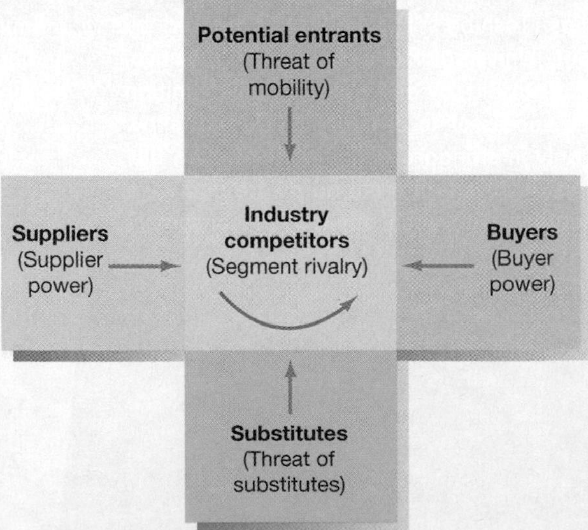

Figure 11.1 Five Forces Determining Segment Structural Attractiveness

Source: Adapted with permission of The Free Press, a Division of Simon & Schuster Adult Publishing Group, from *Competitive Advantage: Creating and Sustaining Superior Performance* by Michael E. Porter. Copyright © 1985, 1998 by Michael E. Porter. All rights reserved.

potential is high, but firms face more risk because poorer-performing firms stay in and fight it out. When both entry and exit barriers are low, firms easily enter and leave the industry, and the returns are stable and low. The worst case is when entry barriers are low and exit barriers are high: here firms enter during good times but find it hard to leave during bad times. The result is chronic overcapacity and depressed earnings for all.

3. ***Threat of substitute products*** — A segment is unattractive when there are actual or potential substitutes for the product. Substitutes place a limit on prices and on profits. The company has to monitor price trends closely. If technology advances or competition increases in these substitute industries, prices and profits in the segment are likely to fall. Full-service airlines such as Cathay Pacific, Qantas, and Singapore Airlines have seen profitability threatened by the rise of budget air travel.
4. ***Threat of buyers' growing bargaining power*** — A segment is unattractive if buyers possess strong or growing bargaining power. The rise of retail giants may suggest that the potential profitability of packaged good companies will become curtailed. Buyers' bargaining power grows when they become more concentrated or organized, when the product represents a significant fraction of the buyers' costs, when the product is undifferentiated, when the buyers' switching costs are low, when buyers are price sensitive because of low profits, or when buyers can integrate upstream. To protect themselves, sellers might select buyers who have the least power to negotiate or switch suppliers. A better defense consists of developing superior offers that strong buyers cannot refuse.
5. ***Threat of suppliers' growing bargaining power*** — A segment is unattractive if the company's suppliers are able to raise prices or reduce quantity supplied. Oil companies such as ExxonMobil, Shell, and Chevron-Texaco are at the mercy of the amount of oil reserves and the actions of oil supplying cartels like OPEC. Suppliers tend to be powerful when they are concentrated or organized, when there are few substitutes, when the supplied product is an important input, when the costs of switching suppliers are high, and when the suppliers can integrate downstream. The best defenses are to build win–win relations with suppliers or use multiple supply sources.

Identifying Competitors

It would seem a simple task for a company to identify its competitors. Pizza Hut knows that Domino's is its major competitor; and Toyota knows that the Nissan Cefiro is the major competitor for its Camry. However, the range of a company's actual and potential competitors can actually be much broader. And a company is more likely to be hurt by emerging competitors or new technologies than by current competitors.

Pizza war in India—A heated battle between Pizza Hut and Domino's pizza is brewing in Bangalore. Both brands have customized to local flavors with plenty of chilli flakes, ketchup, and other condiments. However, competition is intense as both are adding 50 stores a year—quadruple the average in other markets. Both also claim to be the market leader—Pizza Hut for casual dining, and Domino's for delivery. Pizza is big business in India because of its similarity to India's native cuisine. Unlike Chinese and Japanese, Indians eat leavened bread (*naan*) and a popular version is like garlic bread, the most often ordered side dish at both Pizza Hut and Domino's. Cheese is also ubiquitous in India's northern cuisine. Tomatoes are also prevalent in the cuisine.[5]

In recent years, for instance, a number of new "emerging giants" have arisen from developing countries, and these nimble competitors are not only competing with multinationals on their home turf but also becoming global forces in their own right. They have gained competitive advantage by exploiting their knowledge about local factors of production—capital and talent—and supply chains in order to build world-class businesses.

Indian software & services companies—Tata Consultancy Services, Infosys Technologies, Wipro, and Satyam Computer Services, all of India, have succeeded in catering to the global demand for software and services, even triumphing against multinational software service providers such as Accenture and EDS. These multinationals have a hard time sorting out talent in a market where the level of people's skills and the quality of educational institutions vary dramatically. Indian companies know their way around the human resources market and are hiring educated, skilled engineers and technical graduates at salaries much lower than those that similar employees in developed markets earn. Even as the talent in urban centers such as Bangalore and Delhi gets scarce, the Indian companies will keep their competitive advantage by knowing how to find qualified employees in Indian's second-tier cities.[6]

Inventec—Taiwan-based Inventec has become one of the world's largest manufacturers of notebook computers, PCs, and servers, also by exploiting its knowledge of local factors of production. It makes products in China and supplies them to giants such as Hewlett-Packard and Toshiba and also makes cell phones and MP3 players for other multinational customers. Inventec's customers get the low cost of manufacturing products in China without investing in factories there, and they can also use China's talented software and hardware professionals. It would not be long, however, before Inventec begins competing directly with its own customers; it has already started selling computers in Taiwan and China under its own retail brand name.[7]

We can examine competition from both an industry and a marketing point of view.[8] An **industry** is a group of firms that offer a product or class of products that are close substitutes for one another. Marketers classify industries according to number of sellers; degree of product differentiation; presence or absence of entry, mobility, and exit barriers; cost structure; degree of vertical integration; and degree of globalization.

Using the market approach, we define *competitors* as companies that satisfy the same customer need. For example, a customer who buys a word-processing package really wants "writing ability"—a need that can also be satisfied by pencils, pens, or typewriters. Marketers must overcome "marketing myopia" and stop defining competition in traditional category and industry terms.[9] Coca-Cola, focused on its soft-drink business, missed seeing the market for coffee bars and fresh-fruit-juice bars that eventually impinged on its soft-drink business.

The market concept of competition reveals a broader set of actual and potential competitors than competition defined in just product category terms. Rayport and Jaworski suggest profiling a company's direct and indirect competitors by mapping the buyer's steps in obtaining and using the product. This type of analysis highlights both the opportunities and the challenges a company faces.[10] "Marketing Insight: High Growth Through Value Innovation" describes how firms can tap into new markets that minimizes competition from others.

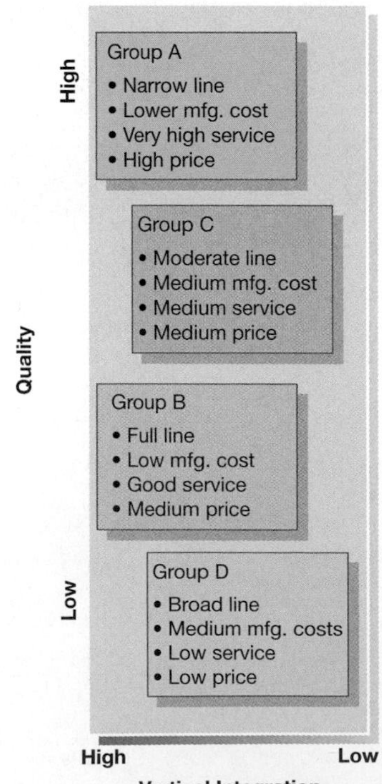

Figure 11.2 Strategic Groups in the Major Appliance Industry

Analyzing Competitors

Once a company identifies its primary competitors, it must ascertain their strategies, objectives, strengths, and weaknesses.

Strategies

A group of firms following the same strategy in a given target market is called a **strategic group.**[11] Suppose a company wants to enter the major appliance industry. What is its strategic group? It develops the chart shown in Figure 11.2 and discovers four strategic groups

MARKETING INSIGHT • HIGH GROWTH THROUGH VALUE INNOVATION

Kim and Mauborgne believe that too many firms engage in "red-ocean thinking"—seeking bloody, head-to-head battles with competitors based largely on incremental improvements in cost, quality, or both. They advocate engaging instead in "blue-ocean thinking" by creating products and services for which there are no direct competitors. Their belief is that instead of searching within the conventional boundaries of industry competition, managers should look beyond those boundaries to find unoccupied market positions that represent real value innovation.

The authors cite as one example Bert Claeys, a Belgian movie theater operator, and its introduction of the 25-screen, 7,600-seat Kinepolis megaplex. Despite an industry slump, Kineoplis has thrived on a unique combination of features, such as ample, safe, and free parking; large screens and state-of-the-art sound and projection equipment; and roomy, comfortable, oversized seats with unobstructed views. Through smart planning and economies of scale, Bert Claeys creates Kinepolis's unique cinema experience at a lower cost.

This is classic blue-ocean thinking—designing creative business ventures to positively affect both a company's cost structure and its value proposition to consumers. Cost savings result from eliminating and reducing the factors affecting traditional industry competition; value to consumers comes from introducing factors the industry has never before offered. Over time, costs drop even more as superior value leads to higher sales volume, and that generates economies of scale.

We can offer other examples of marketers that exhibit unconventional, blue-ocean thinking:

- Southwest Airlines created an airline that offers reliable, fun, and convenient service at a low cost.
- Callaway Golf designed "Big Bertha," a golf club with a large head and expanded sweet spot that helped golfers frustrated by the difficulty of hitting a golf ball squarely.
- Cirque du Soleil reinvented circus as a higher form of entertainment by eliminating high-cost elements such as animals and enhancing the theatrical experience instead.

Kim and Mauborgne propose four crucial questions for marketers to ask themselves in guiding blue-ocean thinking and creating value innovation:

1. Which of the factors that our industry takes for granted should we eliminate?
2. Which factors should we reduce well *below* the industry's standard?
3. Which factors should we raise well *above* the industry's standard?
4. Which factors should we create that the industry has never offered?

They maintain that the most successful blue-ocean thinkers took advantage of all three platforms on which value innovation can take place: *physical product*; *service* including maintenance, customer service, warranties and training for distributors and retailers; and *delivery*, meaning channels and logistics. Figure 11.3 summarizes key principles driving the successful formulation and execution of blue-ocean strategy.

FORMULATION PRINCIPLES

a. Reconstruct market boundaries
- Look across alternative industries
- Look across strategic groups within industries
- Look across chain of buyers
- Look across complementary product and service offerings
- Look across functional or emotional appeal to buyers
- Look across time

b. Focus on the big picture not the numbers

c. Reach beyond existing demand

d. Get the strategic sequence right
- Is there buyer utility?
- Is the price acceptable?
- Can we attain target cost?
- What are the adoption challenges?

EXECUTION PRINCIPLES

a. Overcome key organizational hurdles
- Cognitive hurdle
- Resource hurdle
- Motivational hurdle
- Political hurdle

b. Build execution into strategy

Figure 11.3 Key Principles of Blue-Ocean Strategy

Sources: W. Chan Kim and Renée Mauborgne, *Blue-Ocean Strategy: How to Create Uncontested Market Space and Make the Competition Irrelevant,* (Cambridge, MA: Harvard Business School Press, 2005); W. Chan Kim and Renée Mauborgne, "Creating New Market Space." *Harvard Business Review*, January–February 1999; W. Chan Kim and Renée Mauborgne, "Value Innovation: The Strategic Logic of High Growth." *Harvard Business Review*, January–February 1997.

based on product quality and level of vertical integration. Group A has one competitor, group B has three, group C has four, and group D has two. Important insights emerge from this exercise. First, the height of the entry barriers differs for each group. Second, if the company successfully enters a group, the members of that group become its key competitors.

Objectives

Once a company has identified its main competitors and their strategies, it must ask: What is each competitor seeking in the marketplace? What drives each competitor's behavior? Many factors shape a competitor's objectives, including size, history, current management, and financial situation. If the competitor is a division of a larger company, it is important to know whether the parent company is running it for growth, profits, or milking it.[12]

One useful initial assumption is that competitors strive to maximize profits. However, companies differ in the emphasis they put on short-term versus long-term profits. Many U.S. firms have been criticized for operating on a short-run model, largely because current performance is judged by stockholders who might lose confidence, sell their stock, and cause the company's cost of capital to rise. Japanese firms operate largely on a market-share-maximization model. They receive much of their funds from banks at a lower interest rate and in the past have readily accepted lower profits. An alternative assumption is that each competitor pursues some mix of objectives: current profitability, market-share growth, cash flow, technological leadership, or service leadership.

Nike and Adidas—In the run up to the Beijing Olympic Games, a shoe war has started. China is one of the largest emerging markets and a top focus for shoemakers fighting to get market share. Adidas is the official sponsor of the Olympics, reportedly paying $80 million for the sponsorship position. Besides this, its marketing blitz includes opening an average of two stores a day in China. The objective of the sponsorship is to help put it in the number 1 position in China by 2008, a coveted spot held by Nike. Nike, on the other hand, is maintaining its leadership by sponsoring 22 of the 28 competing Chinese federations. One of China's most promising athletes, Liu Xiang, a hurdler, wears its trademark Swoosh.[13]

Finally, a company must monitor competitors' expansion plans. Figure 11.4 shows a product-market battlefield map for the personal computer industry. Dell, which began as a strong force in selling PCs to individual users, is now a key player in the commercial and industrial market. Other incumbents may try to set up mobility barriers to Dell's further expansion.

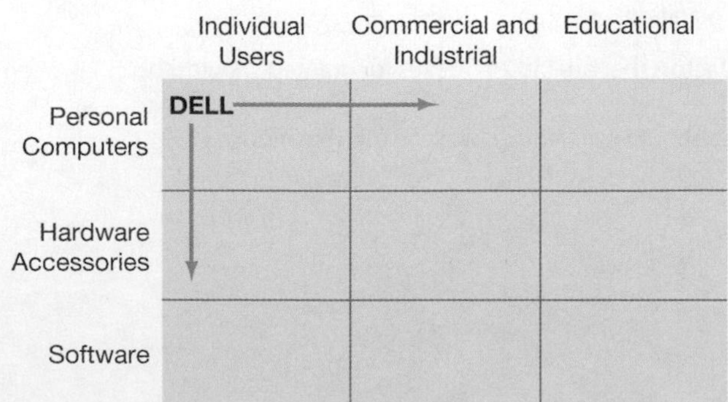

Figure 11.4 A Competitor's Expansion Plans

Strengths and Weaknesses

A company needs to gather information on each competitor's strengths and weaknesses. Table 11.1 shows the results of a company survey that asked customers to rate its three competitors, A, B, and C, on five attributes. Competitor A turns out to be well-known and respected for producing high-quality products sold by a good sales force. Competitor A is poor at providing product availability and technical assistance. Competitor B is good across the board and excellent in product availability and sales force. Competitor C rates poor to fair on most attributes. This suggests that the company could attack Competitor A on product availability and technical assistance and Competitor C on almost anything, but should not attack B, which has no glaring weaknesses.

Table 11.1 Customers' Ratings of Competitors on Key Success Factors

	Customer Awareness	Product Quality	Product Availability	Technical Assistance	Sales Force
Competitor A	E	E	P	P	G
Competitor B	G	G	E	G	E
Competitor C	F	P	G	F	F

Note: E = excellent, G = good, F = fair, P = poor.

In general, a company should monitor three variables when analyzing competitors:

1. ***Share of market*** — The competitor's share of the target market.
2. ***Share of mind*** — The percentage of customers who named the competitor in responding to the statement "Name the first company that comes to mind in this industry."
3. ***Share of heart*** — The percentage of customers who named the competitor in responding to the statement "Name the company from which you would prefer to buy the product."

There is an interesting relationship among these three measures. Table 11.2 shows the numbers for these three measures for the three competitors listed in Table 11.1. Competitor A enjoys the highest market share but is slipping. Its mind share and heart share are also slipping, probably because it is not providing good product availability and technical assistance. Competitor B is steadily gaining market share, probably due to strategies that are increasing its mind share and heart share. Competitor C seems to be stuck at a low level of market share, mind share, and heart share, probably because of its poor product and marketing attributes. We could generalize as follows: *Companies that make steady gains in mind share and heart share will inevitably make gains in market share and profitability.*

Table 11.2 Market Share, Mind Share, and Heart Share

	Market Share (%)			Mind Share (%)			Heart Share (%)		
	2006	2007	2008	2006	2007	2008	2006	2007	2008
Competitor A	50%	47%	44%	60%	58%	54%	45%	42%	39%
Competitor B	30%	34%	37%	30%	31%	35%	44%	47%	53%
Competitor C	20%	19%	19%	10%	11%	11%	11%	11%	8%

To improve market share, many companies benchmark their most successful competitors, as well as world-class performers. The technique and its benefits are described in "Marketing Memo: Benchmarking to Improve Competitive Performance."

MARKETING MEMO • BENCHMARKING TO IMPROVE COMPETITIVE PERFORMANCE

Benchmarking is the art of learning from companies that perform certain tasks better than other companies. There can be as much as a ten-fold difference in the quality, speed, and cost performance of a world-class company and an average company. The aim of benchmarking is to copy or improve on "best practices," either within an industry or across industries. Benchmarking involves seven steps:

1. Determine which functions to benchmark.
2. Identify the key performance variables to measure.
3. Identify the best-in-class companies.
4. Measure performance of best-in-class companies.
5. Measure the company's performance.
6. Specify programs and actions to close the gap.
7. Implement and monitor results.

How can companies identify best-practice companies? A good starting point is asking customers, suppliers, and distributors whom they rate as doing the best job. In addition, some consulting firms have built voluminous files on best practices. PriceWaterhouseCoopers has a Global Best Practices Knowledge Base documenting breakthrough thinking at world-class companies. This data can be accessed at their Web site <www.globalbestpractices.com.>

Sources: <www.benchmarking.org>; Patricia O'Connell, "Bringing Innovation to the Home of Six Sigma." *BusinessWeek*, August 1, 2005; John E. Prescott, Stephen H. Miller, and The Society of Competitive Intelligence Professionals, *Proven Strategies in Competitive Intelligence: Lessons from the Trenches,* (New York: John Wiley, 2001); Robert Hiebeler, Thomas B. Kelly, and Charles Ketteman, *Best Practices: Building Your Business with Customer-Focused Solutions,* (New York: Arthur Andersen/Simon & Schuster, 1998); Michael Hope, "Contrast and Compare." *Marketing,* August 28, 1997, pp. 11–13.

Selecting Competitors

After the company has conducted customer value analysis and examined competitors carefully, it can focus its attack on one of the following classes of competitors: strong versus weak, close versus distant, and "good" versus "bad."

- **Strong versus weak.** Most companies aim their shots at weak competitors, because this requires fewer resources per share point gained. Yet, the firm should also compete with strong competitors to keep up with the best. Even strong competitors have some weaknesses.
- **Close versus distant.** Most companies compete with competitors who resemble them the most. Toyota competes with Honda, not with Ferrari. Yet companies should also recognize distant competitors. Coca-Cola states that its number one competitor is tap water, not Pepsi. Museums now worry about theme parks and malls, rather than other museums.
- **"Good" versus "bad".** Every industry contains "good" and "bad" competitors.[14] Good competitors play by the industry's rules; they set prices in reasonable relation to costs; and they favor a healthy industry. Bad competitors try to buy share rather than earn it; they take large risks; they invest in overcapacity; and they upset industrial equilibrium. A company may find it necessary to attack its bad competitors to reduce or end their dysfunctional practices.

Selecting Customers

As part of the competitive analysis, firms must evaluate its customer base and think about which customers it is willing to lose and which it wants to retain. One way to divide up the customer base is in terms of whether a customer is valuable and vulnerable, creating a grid of four segments as a result; see Table 11.3. Each segment suggests different competitive activities.[15]

Table 11.3 Customer Selection Grid

	Vulnerable	Not Vulnerable
Valuable	These customers are profitable but not completely happy with the company. Find out and address their sources of vulnerability to **retain them**.	These customers are loyal and profitable. Don't take them for granted but **maintain margins** and reap the benefits of their satisfaction.
Not Valuable	These customers are likely to defect. Let them go or even **encourage their departure**.	These unprofitable customers are happy. Try to **make them valuable or vulnerable**.

Source: John H. Roberts, "Defensive Marketing: How a Strong Incumbent Can Protect Its Position." *Harvard Business Review*, November 2005, p. 156.

Australian telephone company, Telstra, conducted this type of segment analysis and developed a series of "Flex-Plan" products designed to retain the Valuable/Vulnerables but without losing the margin it realized on the Valuable/Not Vulnerables. The Flex Plans had a subscription fee but offered significant net savings. Because Valuable/Vulnerables were highly involved with the category, they were able to see how they could benefit from such plans, but Valuable/Not Vulnerable regarded the plans as unnecessary. As a result, the plans achieved the desired goals.

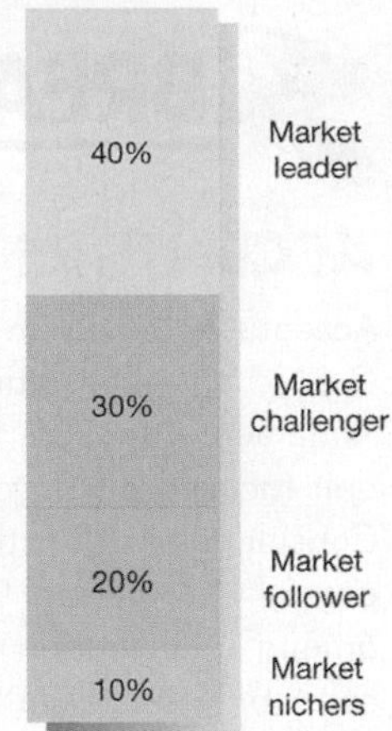

Figure 11.5 Hypothetical Market Structure

Competitive Strategies for Market Leaders

We can gain further insight by classifying firms by the roles they play in the target market: leader, challenger, follower, or nicher. Suppose a market is occupied by the firms shown in Figure 11.5. Forty percent of the market is in the hands of a *market leader;* another 30 percent is in the hands of a *market challenger;* another 20 percent is in the hands of a *market follower,* a firm that is willing to maintain its market share and not rock the boat. The remaining 10 percent is in the hands of *market nichers,* firms that serve small market segments not being served by larger firms.

Many industries contain one firm that is the acknowledged market leader. This firm has the largest market share in the relevant product market, and usually leads the other firms in price changes, new-product introductions, distribution coverage, and promotional intensity. Some well-known market leaders are Microsoft (computer software), Intel (microprocessors), McDonald's (fast food), Gillette (razor blades), and Visa (credit cards). "Breakthrough Marketing: Accenture" summarizes how that firm has attained and maintained market leadership.

Although marketers assume well-known brands are distinctive in consumers' minds, unless a dominant firm enjoys a legal monopoly, it must maintain constant vigilance. A product innovation may come along and hurt the leader; a competitor might unexpectedly find a fresh new marketing angle or commit to a major marketing investment; or the leader might find its cost structure spiraling upward. One well-known brand and market leader that lost its way is Gap.

Gap—Nowadays when people think about Gap, they do not think of hip, contemporary clothes. They think quite literally, of a "gap"—what is missing from the company's 1,295 stores. Young people will be quick to tell you that the missing ingredient is a unique style. In an era when small niche fashion brands—Coach, Juicy Couture, Tahari, Laundry—have risen to success in U.S. retailing, Gap has continued to push timeless, simple, and some would say bland, casual clothing. The main problem is that Gap does not have a target customer but tries to appeal to everyone, from newborn babies to teenagers to senior citizens. "If you stand for everything in fashion today, you stand for nothing," says Paul R. Charron, the former chief executive of Liz Claiborne, who revitalized that ailing clothing company by buying Juicy Couture and Lucky Brand. By not being vigilant about responding to (or better, yet, envisioning) the changing retailing scene, Gap has seen sales fall dramatically. Sales at stores open at least a year have fallen or remained stagnant for 28 of the past 30 months. Still, the former leading brand is planning a number of strategies to get it out of the doldrums. Among them are selling other-branded merchandise inside its stores (as it used to sell Levi's and now sells Converse), shrinking the number of stores to cut back on overexposure, and focusing on a narrower group of consumers with clothing tailored to meet their needs.[16]

The Gap brand has become diluted in an effort to appeal to too-broad a market base, and the company plans several strategies to refocus it.

BREAKTHROUGH • MARKETING

ACCENTURE

Accenture began in 1942 as Adminstrative Accounting Group, the consulting arm of accounting firm Arthur Andersen. In 1989, it launched as a separate business unit focused on IT consulting bearing the name Andersen Consulting. At that time, though it was earning $1 billion annually, Andersen Consulting had low brand awareness among information technology consultancies and was commonly mistaken for its accounting corporate parent. To build its brand and separate itself from the accounting firm with which it shared a name, Andersen Consulting launched the first large-scale advertising campaign in the professional services area. By the end of the decade, it was the world's largest management and technology consulting organization.

In 2000, following arbitration against its former parent, Andersen Consulting was granted its full independence from Arthur Andersen—but at the price of relinquishing the Andersen name. Andersen Consulting was given three months to find a name that was trademarkable in 47 countries, effective and inoffensive in over 200 languages, and acceptable to employees and clients—and that corresponded with an available URL. The effort that followed was one of the largest—and most successful—rebranding campaigns in corporate history.

As luck would have it, the company's new name came from a consultant at the company's Oslo office, who submitted "Accenture" as part of an internal name-generation initiative dubbed "Brandstorming." The consultant coined the Accenture name because it rhymed with "adventure" and connoted an "accent on the future." The name also retained the "Ac" of the original Andersen Consulting name (echoing the Ac.com Web site), which would help the firm retain some of its former brand equity. On midnight, December 31, 2000, Andersen Consulting officially adopted the Accenture name and launched a global marketing campaign targeting senior executives at Accenture's clients and prospects, all Accenture Partners and employees, the media, leading industry analysts, potential recruits, and academia.

The results of the advertising, marketing, and communications campaigns were quick and impressive. Overall, the number of firms considering purchasing Accenture's services increased by 350 percent. Accenture's brand equity increased 11 percent. Awareness of Accenture's breadth and depth of services achieved 96 percent of its previous level. Globally, awareness of Accenture as a provider of management and technology consulting services was 76 percent of the former Andersen Consulting levels. These results enabled Accenture to successfully complete a $1.7 billion IPO in July 2001.

In 2002, Accenture unveiled a new positioning to reflect its new role as a partner to aid execution of strategy, summarized succinctly by the tagline "Innovation Delivered." This tagline was supported by the statement, "From innovation to execution, Accenture helps accelerate your vision." Accenture surveyed senior executives from different industries and countries and confirmed that they saw inability to execute and deliver on ideas as the number-one barrier to success.

Accenture saw its differentiator as the ability both to provide innovative ideas—ideas grounded in business processes as well as IT—and to execute them. Competitors such as McKinsey were seen as highly specialized at developing strategy, whereas other competitors such as IBM were seen as highly skilled with technological implementation. Accenture wanted to be seen as excelling at both. Ian Watmore, Accenture's U.K. chief, explained the need to have both strategy and execution: "Unless you can provide both transformational consulting and outsourcing capability, you're not going to win. Clients expect both."

In 2002, the business climate changed. After the dot-com crash and the economic downturn, innovation was no longer enough. Executives wanted bottom-line results. Accenture built upon the "Innovation Delivered" theme when it announced its new "High Performance Delivered" tagline in late 2003, featuring golfer Tiger Woods as the spokesperson. As part of its new commitment to helping clients achieve their business objectives, Accenture introduced a policy whereby many of its contracts contained incentives that it realized only if specific business targets were met. For instance, a contract with British travel agent Thomas Cook was structured such that Accenture's bonus depended on five metrics, including a cost-cutting one. In 2004, 30 percent of the company's contracts contained such incentives. The company's focus on improving the performance and results of its clients proved beneficial to the bottom line: 2007 revenues grew 25 percent to $21.45 billion.

Sources: <www.accenture.com>; "Lessons Learned from Top Firms' Marketing Blunders." *Management Consultant International*, December 2003, p. 1; Sean Callahan, "Tiger Tees Off in New Accenture Campaign." *B to B*, October 13, 2003, p. 3; "Inside Accenture's Biggest UK Client," *Management Consultant International*, October 2003, pp. 1–3; "Accenture's Results Highlight Weakness of Consulting Market." *Management Consultant International*, October 2003, pp. 8–10; "Accenture Re-Branding Wins UK Plaudits." *Management Consultant International*, October 2002, p. 5; <www.wikinvest.com/stock/accenture_(ACN)>.

In many industries, a discount competitor has entered and undercut the leader's prices. "Marketing Insight: When Your Competitor Delivers More for Less" describes how leaders can respond to an aggressive competitive price discounter.

MARKETING INSIGHT • WHEN YOUR COMPETITOR DELIVERS MORE FOR LESS

Companies offering the powerful combination of low prices and high quality are capturing the hearts and wallets of consumers all over the world, including Asia. In the airline industry, budget airlines have debuted in Asia and have proven to give full-service airlines a run for their money. AirAsia, Jetstar Asia, Tiger Airways, and Bangkok Air are transforming the way consumers fly.

The market share gains of value-based players give their higher-priced rivals definite cause for alarm. After years of near-exclusive sway over all but the most discount-minded consumers, many mainstream companies now face steep cost disadvantages and lack the product and service superiority that once set them apart from low-priced competitors. Today, as value-driven companies in a growing number of industries move from competing solely on price to catching up on attributes such as quality, service, and convenience, traditional players rightly feel threatened.

To compete with value-based rivals, mainstream companies must reconsider the perennial routes to business success: keeping costs in line, finding sources of differentiation, and managing prices effectively. Succeeding in value-based markets requires infusing these timeless strategies with greater intensity and focus and then executing them flawlessly. Differentiation, for example, becomes less about the abstract goal of rising above competitive clutter and more about identifying opportunities left open by the value players' business models. Effective pricing means waging a transaction-by-transaction perception battle to win over consumers predisposed to believe that value-oriented competitors are always cheaper.

Competitive outcomes will be determined, as always, on the ground—in product aisles, merchandising displays, process rethinks, and pricing stickers. When it comes to value-based competition, traditional players can't afford to drop a stitch. Value-driven competitors have changed the expectations of consumers about the trade-off between quality and price. This shift is gathering momentum, placing a new premium on—and adding new twists to—the old imperatives of differentiation and execution.

Differentiation

To counter value-based players, it will be necessary to focus on areas where their business models give other companies room to maneuver. For example, instead of trying to compete on price, a value retailer might emphasize convenience across all elements of its business. This could involve rapid expansion to make its stores ubiquitous, and placing them in convenient locations with easy parking. In addition, in-store layouts can be designed to speed consumers in and out, placing key categories such as convenience foods and one-hour photo services near the front. Simple telephone and online preordering systems can be implemented, along with drive-through windows at stores.

Execution

Value-based markets also place a premium on execution, particularly in prices and costs. Kmart's disastrous experience trying to compete head-on with Wal-Mart highlights the difficulty of challenging value leaders on their own terms. Matching or even beating a value player's prices—as Kmart briefly did—won't necessarily win the battle of consumer perceptions against companies with reputations for the lowest prices. Value players tend to price frequently purchased, easy-to-compare products and services aggressively and make up for lost margins by charging more for higher-end offerings. Focused advertising to showcase "special buys" and the use of simple, prominent signage enable retailers to get credit for the value they offer and will probably become an ever more visible feature of the competitive landscape.

Ultimately, the ability to offer even selectively competitive prices depends on keeping costs in line. Continual improvement is necessary, suggesting an increasing role, in a variety of industries. For example, Toyota's lean manufacturing methods aim to reduce costs and improve quality constantly and simultaneously. In financial services, banks have used lean techniques to speed check processing and mortgage approvals and to improve call-center performance. Lean operations will probably emerge in more industries. Companies have no choice—those that fail to take out costs constantly may perish.

Source: Adapted from Robert J. Frank, Jeffrey P. George, and Laxman Narasimhan, "When Your Competitor Delivers More for Less." *McKinsey Quarterly*, Winter 2004, pp. 48-59.

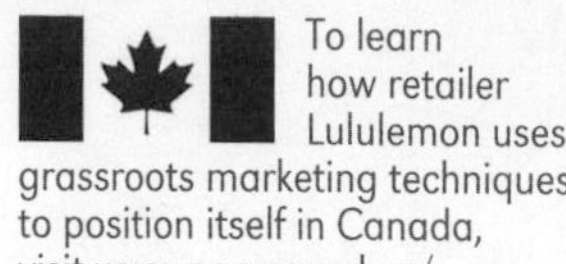

To learn how retailer Lululemon uses grassroots marketing techniques to position itself in Canada, visit www.pearsoned.ca/marketingmanagementcanada.

Expanding the Total Market

The dominant firm normally gains the most when the total market expands. If Indonesians increase their consumption of instant noodles, Indomie stands to gain the most because it is the market leader in instant noodles. If Indomie can convince more Indonesians to eat instant noodles, or to eat more packets of it during a meal, or to eat it for breakfast, lunch, dinner, as well as a snack, Indomie will benefit considerably. In general, the market leader should look for new customers or more usage from existing customers.

NEW CUSTOMERS

Every product class has the potential of attracting buyers who are unaware of the product or who are resisting it because of price or lack of certain features. A company can search for new users among three groups: those who might use it but do not *(market-penetration strategy)*, those who have never used it *(new-market segment strategy)*, or those who live elsewhere *(geographical-expansion strategy)*.

Starbucks Coffee is one of the best-known brands in the world. Starbucks sells a cup of coffee for $3 while the store next door can only get $1. Its popular café latte costs $4. Starbucks has more than 15,000 locations worldwide, and its annual revenue for 2007 topped $9.8 billion. Its corporate Web site gives a peek into its multipronged approach to growth.[17]

Starbucks introduced a new line of premium tea produced by Tazo Tea Company, a Starbucks subsidary, to attract new customers.

Starbucks—Starbucks purchases and roasts high-quality whole bean coffees and sells them along with fresh, rich-brewed, Italian style espresso beverages, a variety of pastries and confections, and coffee-related accessories and equipment—primarily through its company-operated retail stores. In addition, Starbucks sells whole bean coffees through a specialty sales group and supermarkets. Additionally, Starbucks produces and sells bottled Frappuccino® coffee drinks and a line of premium ice creams through its joint venture partnerships and offers a line of innovative premium teas produced by its wholly owned subsidiary, Tazo Tea Company. The company's objective is to establish Starbucks as the most recognized and respected brand in the world. To achieve this goal, the company plans to grow its specialty sales and other operations, and selectively pursue opportunities to leverage the Starbucks brand through the introduction of new products and the development of new distribution channels.

MORE USAGE

Usage can be increased by increasing the amount, level, or frequency of consumption.

Increasing the *amount* of consumption can sometimes be done through packaging or product design. Larger package sizes have been shown to increase the amount of product that consumers use at one time.[18] "Impulse" consumption products such as soft drinks and snacks find that usage increases when the product is made more available.

In contrast, increasing *frequency* of use involves either (1) identifying additional opportunities to use the brand in the same basic way; or (2) identifying completely new and different ways to use the brand. In some cases, the product may be seen as useful only in certain places and at certain times, especially if it has strong brand associations to particular usage situations or user types.

To generate additional usage opportunities, a marketing program can communicate the appropriateness and advantages of using the brand more frequently in new or existing situations and/or remind consumers to actually use the brand as close as possible to those situations. For example, the wine industry can try to convince consumers that wine is a "casual, everyday libation to be drunk like bottled water, beer or soda."[19]

Another potential opportunity to increase frequency of use is when consumers' perceptions of their usage differs from the reality of their usage. For many products with relatively short lifespans, consumers may fail to replace the product in a timely manner because of a tendency to overestimate the length of productive usage.[20] One strategy to speed up product replacement is to tie the act of replacing the product to a certain holiday, event, or time of year. Another strategy might be to provide consumers with better information on either: (1) when the product was first used or would need to be replaced; or (2) the current level of product performance. Each Gillette Mach3 cartridge features a blue stripe that slowly fades with repeated use. After about a dozen shaves, it fades away, signaling the user to move on to the next cartridge.

The second approach is to identify completely new and different applications. For example, food product companies have long advertised new recipes that use their branded products in entirely different ways. Lee Kum Kee, a Hong Kong-based manufacturer of Chinese sauces, provides recipes on what dishes to cook using its sauces.

Product development can spur new uses. Chewing gum manufacturers are exploring ways to make "nutraceutical" products as a cheap, effective delivery mechanism for medicine. The majority of Adam's chewing gums (number 2 in the world) claim health benefits. Aquafresh and Arm & Hammer are two dental gums that both achieved some success.[21]

Defending Market Share

While trying to expand total market size, the dominant firm must continuously defend its current business. The leader is like a large elephant being attacked by a swarm of bees. Sony must constantly guard against Panasonic; Nokia against Samsung mobile phones; Kodak against Fuji film.[22] Sometimes the competitor is domestic; sometimes it is foreign.

What can the market leader do to defend its terrain? The most constructive response is *continuous innovation*. The leader leads the industry in developing new product and customer services, distribution effectiveness, and cost cutting. It keeps increasing its competitive strength and value to customers.

Consider how Caterpillar has become dominant in the construction-equipment industry despite charging a premium price and being challenged by a number of able competitors, including John Deere, Komatsu, and Hitachi. Several policies combine to explain Caterpillar's success:[23]

- ***Premium performance*** — Caterpillar produces high-quality equipment known for its reliability and durability—key buyer considerations in the choice of heavy industrial equipment.
- ***Extensive and efficient dealership system*** — Caterpillar maintains the largest number of independent construction-equipment dealers in the industry, all of whom carry a complete line of Caterpillar equipment.
- ***Superior service*** — Caterpillar has built a worldwide parts and service system second to none in the industry.
- ***Full-line strategy*** — Caterpillar produces a full line of construction equipment to enable customers to do one-stop buying.
- ***Good financing*** — Caterpillar provides a wide range of financial terms for customers who buy its equipment.

In satisfying customer needs, a distinction can be drawn between responsive marketing, anticipative marketing, and creative marketing. A *responsive* marketer finds a stated need and fills it. An *anticipative* marketer looks ahead into what needs customers may have in the near future. A *creative* marketer discovers and produces solutions customers did not ask for but to which they enthusiastically respond. Sony exemplifies creative marketing.

Akio Morita and an early Walkman, Morita refused to abandon his idea for a portable cassette player, saying Sony doesn't serve markets, Sony creates markets. And he was certainly right: by the 20th anniversary of the Walkman, Sony had sold over 250 million units.

Sony—Sony has introduced many successful new products that customers never asked for or even thought were possible: Walkmans, VCRs, video cameras, CDs. Sony is a ***market-driving firm,*** not just a market-driven firm. Akio Morita, its founder, once proclaimed that Sony doesn't serve markets; Sony creates markets.[24] The Walkman is a classic example: In the late 1970s, Akio Morita was working on a pet project that would revolutionize the way people listened to music: a portable cassette player he called the Walkman. Engineers at the company insisted there was little demand for such a product, but Morita refused to part with his vision. By the 20th anniversary of the Walkman, Sony had sold over 250 million in nearly 100 different models.[25]

Twenty centuries ago, in a treatise called *The Art of War*, the famed Chinese military strategist, Sun Tzu, told his warriors: "One does not rely on the enemy not attacking, but on the fact that he himself is unassailable" (see "Marketing Insight: *Sun Tzu Bing Fa*: Modern Strategy Insights from Ancient China"). The leader of continuous innovation applies the military principle of the offensive: the commander exercises initiative, sets the pace, and exploits enemy weaknesses.

MARKETING INSIGHT • *SUN TZU BING FA*: MODERN STRATEGY INSIGHTS FROM ANCIENT CHINA

In Chinese, the phrase military strategy comprises *Bing* ("兵; soldier") and *Fa* ("法; doctrine"), which can be translated to mean "the art of war." This is the title of Sun Tzu's classic treatise, written in the 4th century B.C.

The Chinese expression *Shang Chang Ru Zhan Chang* (商场如战场) is translated to mean: "The marketplace is a battlefield." This is how some Asians view success or failure in business. From an Asian perspective, the outcome of a family business directly influences the family's survival and well-being. As the family is the key unit of a nation, its performance affects the nation's survival and well-being. Thus many Asians treat business competition as life-and-death warfare.

A key principle articulated by Sun Tzu concerns the need for careful strategic planning. He wrote, "With careful and detailed planning, one can win; with careless and less detailed planning, one cannot win. How much less chance of victory has one who does not plan at all! From the way planning is done beforehand, one can predict victory or defeat." Relatedly, Sun Tzu emphasized the importance of avoiding bloody conflicts as much as possible: "To subdue the enemy without fighting is the supreme excellence." This is possible through a meticulous assessment of the strengths and weaknesses of one's company *and* one's competitors, as well as the market environment: "If you know your enemy and know yourself, you need not fear the result of a hundred battles. If you know yourself but not the enemy, for every victory gained, you will also suffer a defeat. If you know neither your enemy nor yourself, you will succumb in every battle .... Know the terrain, know the weather, and your victory will be complete."

Sun Tzu further described the necessity of appraising seven elements:

- ***Moral influence*** — This refers to how people who support their ruler are willing to fight through the pitfalls of war. Thus managers must formulate a common corporate goal to be shared by all employees, so that everyone will perceive themselves as members of the same group. A successful manager should be able to mobilize subordinates to work as a team. The company will then be able to "fight as one man" (同心; *tongxin*) in competition with others.
- ***Ability of generals*** — A good general should possess five qualities: wisdom (智; *zhi*), sincerity (诚; *cheng*), benevolence (仁; *ren*), courage (勇; *yong*), and strictness (严; *yan*). Thus corporate leaders should have the following qualities: broad knowledge with ability to identify business trends and opportunities; ability to establish mutual trust between management and employees; ability to delegate power, while knowing how to tolerate employees' unavoidable mistakes; understanding the problems of subordinates and caring for their welfare; avoiding harassment from trifles; boldness to make risky decisions, while not making hasty or reckless ones; and ability to mete out punishment decisively and fairly. Sun Tzu stressed the importance of a broadly defined generalship for leaders as opposed to merely their technical backgrounds. In many Asian companies, a manager's general qualities are often viewed as more important than technical qualifications.
- ***Climate and terrain*** — Climate refers to conditions which represent an uncontrollable aspect of military situations. However, a good general knows how to use

(Continued ...)

MARKETING INSIGHT • *SUN TZU BING FA*: MODERN STRATEGY INSIGHTS FROM ANCIENT CHINA

(*Continued*...)

these components advantageously, choosing the right time to fight, and turning bad weather to the disadvantage of the enemy. Likewise, marketers have to grapple with the "business climate." These include political situations, economic cycles, investment climate, and other related social and cultural factors such as changes in demographics and consumer attitudes. To be competitive, a company must capitalize on environmental changes and formulate its strategies accordingly. Managers must be able to adapt strategies for environmental constraints, select the best time, and turn these conditions into advantages. An import substitution policy, for example, may hamper market entry, but at the same time may provide opportunities for investment, which can result in access to a closed market.

Terrain refers to the area for military operations. While the geographical features of the battlefield are largely uncontrollable variables, the chosen ground for fighting is. In business, therefore, a company must decide which place to manufacture and which market to target. The location should be selected according to its needs. For example, if it needs to tap cheap labor, it should move its operations to a developing country.

- ***Strength*** — Strength is relative: "In war, numbers alone confer no advantage. If one does not advance by force recklessly, is able to concentrate his military power through a correct assessment of the enemy situation, and enjoys the full support of his men, that would suffice." Thus there is no absolute superiority or inferiority in competition. What matters is knowing where one's competitive edge lies, and when, where, and how to engage in competition. Organization size may seem to provide an advantage for major enterprises, but it can also lead to bureaucracy and low efficiency. Indeed, many recent corporate restructuring exercises have aimed to downsize operations to pursue niche strategies and to be more nimble in seizing market opportunities. A small enterprise must be able to concentrate its resources, deceive its competitors by hiding its real strengths, and use market intelligence to obtain information on its competitors. Thus smaller Asian firms, having benefited from technologies through all possible channels, have become tough competitors within a short time.
- ***Doctrine*** — This element stresses the importance of rules and regulations, designation of ranks, allocation of responsibilities, and organizational structure. There is a need to delegate the necessary power to one's subordinates and to maintain a good balance between an authoritarian leader and unorganized decentralization. Thus managers should have sufficient power to coordinate their strategies. Adequate empowerment to carry out various assignments is also preferred.
- ***Training*** — Training is essential for ensuring success. If soldiers do not know how to follow signals, they cannot act accordingly. Companies with well-trained employees can thus operate with greater organizational efficiency and effectiveness. Investment in a variety of training programs is a hallmark of successful business enterprises worldwide.
- ***Discipline*** — A good army always has stringent discipline, which it can achieve with an efficient reward-and-punishment system. Soldiers must be treated with humanity but kept under close control. Orders should be consistently carried out under strict supervision. Thus a company with an effective disciplinary system will be geared toward higher performance. When employees are well aware of what they will receive, they will perform accordingly.

Operational Guidelines

At the operational level, Sun Tzu advocates some principles and rules for offence and defence which businesses may find useful:

- **Short war.** "Let your great object be victory, not lengthy compaigns. Rapidity is the essence of war." Thus planning should be well-conceived, but implementation of plans should be swift and decisive.
- **Concentration.** "Keep your forces concentrated, while the enemy must be divided." Clearly, this is an endorsement of target marketing.
- **Deception and surprise.** "All warfare is based on deception; take advantage of the enemy's unreadiness, make your way by unguarded routes, and attack unguarded spots." This advocates the identification and targeting of new markets with potential ignored by one's competitors.
- **Initiative.** "The clever combatant imposes his will on the enemy, but does not allow the enemy's will to be imposed on him." This advocates engaging competitors on one's terms, rather than those of the competitor.
- **Attack weakness.** "In war, the way is to avoid what is strong and to strike what is weak." This supports the flank and bypass attack strategies by market challengers against market leaders.
- **Flexibility.** "Just as water retains no shape, so in warfare there are no constant conditions. The soldier works out his victory in relation to the foe whom he is facing, and does not repeat the tactics which have gained him one victory, but lets his methods be regulated by the infinite variety of circumstances." Marketers must thus cope with change and adapt quickly. This principle also favors the use of adaptive selling to canned presentations.

Limitations

Despite these insights, not all of Sun Tzu's ideas can be applied in a business context. For example, he tended to exaggerate the role of the leader while downgrading that of the soldiers: "Although soldiers are not very smart, they are most easily moved." Moreover, business is an act of construction, while war is one of destruction.

Sources: Sun Tzu, *The Art of War*, (London: Oxford University Press, 1963); Min Chen, "Sun Tzu's Strategic Thinking and Contemporary Business." *Business Horizons*, March-April, 1994, pp. 42-48; Chuniu Wu, "Sun Tzu's Art of War in Modern Perspective." *Business Times* (Singapore), ISEAS Trends Section, September 24-25, 1994, p. III.

Even when it does not launch offensives, the market leader must not leave any major flanks exposed. It must consider carefully which terrains are important to defend, even at a loss, and which can be surrendered.[26] The aim of defensive strategy is to reduce the probability of attack, divert attacks to less threatening areas, and lessen their intensity. The defender's speed of response can make an important difference in the profit consequences. A dominant firm can use the six defense strategies summarized in Figure 11.6.[27]

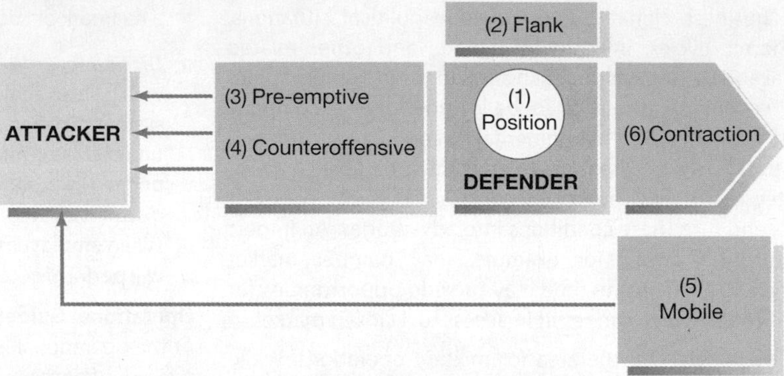

Figure 11.6 Six Types of Defense Strategies

POSITION DEFENSE

Position defense involves occupying the most desirable market space in the minds of the consumer, making the brand almost impregnable, like Fab laundry detergent with cleaning; Colgate toothpaste with cavity prevention; and Pampers diapers with dryness.

President Chain Store—Taiwanese retail company, President, through its chain of 7-Eleven convenience stores, sells its own brand of frozen foods, milk, hot dogs, cooking oil, and just about every major food group to make itself a complete food retailer. Further, it regularly introduces new products. President first introduced black tea, then tea with milk, followed by honey tea, *oolong* tea, and green tea. Juices, instant noodles, dairy products, and carbonated beverages also undergo similar permutations.

FLANK DEFENSE

Although position defense is important, the market leader should also erect outposts to protect a weak front or possibly serve as an invasion base for counterattack.

Heublein—When Heublein's brand Smirnoff, which had 23 percent of the U.S. vodka market, was attacked by low-priced competitor Wolfschmidt, Heublein actually *raised* the price and put the increased revenue into advertising. At the same time, Heublein introduced another brand, Relska, to compete with Wolfschmidt and still another, Popov, to sell for less than Wolfschmidt. This strategy effectively bracketed Wolfschmidt and protected Smirnoff's flanks.

Shiseido—Shiseido's main focus in China is to make-over its upmarket Auprés brand, launched in 1994 specifically for the Chinese market. To cater to rising purchasing power among Chinese consumers, it repackaged the Auprés line by adding a deluxe version and a men's skincare line called JS. It also emphasized its attention to service by offering a special counter in department stores where customers can freely sample cosmetics—something that is still quite uncommon in China. Additionally, Shiseido is pushing its lower end non-prestige cosmetic brands such as Za and Pure Mild in China.[28]

PRE-EMPTIVE DEFENSE

A more aggressive maneuver is to attack *before* the enemy starts its offense. Alasdair Morrison, Jardine Matheson's *taipan*, summed it well when he said, "If you own $8 billion worth of real estate in Hong Kong, two of the territory's major hotels, and Asia's leading merchant bank, if you are number one like we are, you've got to keep investing to stay number one." Similarly, when Toyota's Hiroshi Okuda took over the helm as the first president to come from outside the Toyoda family, he said, "What should a company do when everyone else thinks it is best in the business? Try harder."

Singapore Airlines—To fortify its position as the premier Asian airline, SIA is the first airline to fly the double-decker super-jumbo Airbus aircraft known as A380. The 555-seat juggernaut jet enables the airline to take a larger number of passengers on long-haul routes at a lower operating cost per seat. The services that SIA offers on these jets are aimed to give an unprecedented flying experience, setting new standards for the airline industry. Already, SIA offers sleeper bed seats (branded SpaceBed) in business class and has been a pioneer in introducing such innovative inflight entertainment services as multi-player electronic games including chess and mahjong.

A company can launch a pre-emptive defense in several ways. It can wage guerrilla action across the market—hitting one competitor here, another there—and keep everyone off balance; or it can try to achieve a grand market envelopment. It can introduce a stream of new products, making sure to precede them with *preannouncements*—deliberate communications regarding future actions.[29] Preannouncements can signal to competitors that they will have to fight to gain market share.[30] If Microsoft announces a new product development plan, smaller firms may choose to concentrate their development efforts in other directions to avoid head-to-head competition. Some high-tech firms have even been accused of engaging in "vaporware"—preannouncing products that miss delivery dates or are not even ever introduced.[31]

COUNTEROFFENSIVE DEFENSE

When attacked, most market leaders will respond with a counterattack. Counterattacks can take many forms. In a *counteroffensive*, the leader can meet the attacker frontally or hit its flank or launch a pincer movement. An effective counterattack is to invade the attacker's main territory so that it will have to pull back to defend the territory.

DoCoMo—This company has dominated the Japanese cell phone market, especially when it rolled out i-mode that allowed users to email, shop, and bank online through their cell phones. DoCoMo had twice the market share of its next rival, KDDI. However, KDDI started to make inroads when DoCoMo's 3G offering was less than impressive. Consumers liked KDDI's slower but less buggy data offering called AU. They were impressed with its sleek handsets, longer-lasting batteries, and fun services such as easy video mail and song downloads. KDDI also offered a fixed-rate monthly tariff for unlimited use of AU's data services. Not to be outdone, DoCoMo counterattacked by expanding the network coverage of its 3G service—FOMA (Freedom of Mobile Multimedia Access). It also started offering a monthly fixed rate similar to KDDI's. This represents a major shift for DoCoMo, which grew its i-mode business by charging users based on the amount of data they send. DoCoMo is also going beyond wireless communications. It has teamed up with Sony to offer phones with "smart cards" that will allow DoCoMo users to use their phones to buy items such as train and cinema tickets or restaurant meals by passing the phone through a sensor device.[32]

Another common form of counteroffensive is the exercise of economic or political clout. The leader may try to crush a competitor by subsidizing lower prices for the vulnerable product with revenue from its more profitable products; or may prematurely announce that a product upgrade will be available, to prevent customers from buying the competitor's product; or may lobby legislators to take political action to inhibit or cripple the competition.

Unilever China—In streamlining its Chinese operations into a single holding company based in Shanghai, Dutch company Unilever faced problems when seven of its Chinese partners did not want to swap their stakes in various joint ventures for minority shares in the resulting entity. A Dutch minister lobbied Shanghai officials to support Unilever's consolidation plans. Unilever also approached then Chinese premier and Shanghai's ex-mayor, Zhu Rongji, arguing that only one foreign personal products company could have a strong position in China. It was either Unilever, based in Shanghai, or another company based in Guangzhou (Procter & Gamble). Zhu Rongji endorsed the plan and subsequently influenced four of the Chinese partners, who were connected to the Shanghai municipal government. Unilever was thus successful and later announced the formation of its holding company.[33]

MOBILE DEFENSE

In mobile defense, the leader stretches its domain over new territories that can serve as future centers for defense and offense through market broadening and market diversification. *Market broadening* involves shifting focus from the current product to the underlying generic need. The company gets involved in R&D across the whole range of technology associated with that need. Thus "petroleum" companies sought to recast themselves into "energy" companies. Implicitly, this change demanded that they dip their research fingers into the oil, coal, nuclear, hydroelectric, and chemical industries.

GoodBaby—This Chinese company makes about a third of all baby strollers sold in the U.S. and more than half of children's bicycles, as well as car seats, playpens, bassinets, and other kids' products marketed under such names as Geoby, Cosco, Safety 1st, Huffy, and Schwinn. In China, Goodbaby's products have more than 80 percent market share. However, despite growth opportunities both at home and abroad, it faces the threat of market liberalization with China's entry into the World Trade Organization. Hence, Goodbaby plans to enter the retail business by expanding its product lines to include disposable diapers and infant/children's clothing. It has over 1,100 Chinese patents in about 30 countries. In the diaper market, it faces stiff competition from market leaders Pampers and Huggies. As Goodbaby is not able to leverage its stroller distribution network to market its diapers, it has to establish new distributor relationships. Therefore, its diapers are priced 15 percent below that of the two leading brands. The clothing market has its own set of challenges. Goodbaby is negotiating with Oshkosh and Nike to create co-branded products for China as there are low entry barriers for foreign competition. Goodbaby also has licensing agreements with Disney and manufacturing relationships with Wal-Mart, Sears, and other U.S. companies. It plans to open up to 5,000 stores in Chinese middle-class suburbs and city centers, selling infant and toddler clothes, diapers, strollers, sippy cups and other products. This broadening is aimed at increasing Goodbaby's domestic profit margins, since the stores will eliminate middlemen costs. However, the move is risky as Goodbaby has no retailing experience and may alienate its existing retailers. The market may also not be ready for so many shops dedicated to selling such products.[34]

Market diversification involves shifting into unrelated industries. When tobacco companies like Reynolds and Philip Morris acknowledged the growing curbs on cigarette smoking, they were not content with position defense or even with looking for cigarette substitutes. Instead they moved quickly into new industries, such as beer, liquor, soft drinks, and frozen foods. Below is a Japanese example.

Ajinomoto—This Japanese company, best known for commercializing a seasoning based on monosodium glutamate, specializes in amino acid-derived products. It is now trying to build a global franchise by extending its expertise to other products. In the animal feed market, Ajinomoto produces amino acid-based feedstock additives for cattle and poultry; as well as lysine, a feed additive to fatten livestock, to meet the increasing demand for meat from the emerging middle-class in China. In the consumer market, it sells an array of instant soups, pasta dishes, edible oils, and frozen foods. It has also introduced Amino Vital, a health supplement drink in the U.S. This drink has become the rage among professional athletes, and Ajinomoto is working on penetrating the market of amateur athletes as well.[35]

CONTRACTION DEFENSE

Large companies sometimes recognize that they can no longer defend all of their territory. The best course of action then appears to be *planned contraction* (also called *strategic withdrawal*): giving up weaker territories and reassigning resources to stronger territories. Diageo acquired most of Seagram's brands in 2001 and spun off Pillsbury and Burger King so it could concentrate on powerhouse alcoholic beverage brands such as Smirnoff vodka, J&B scotch, and Tanqueray gin.[36]

Expanding Market Share

Market leaders can improve their profitability by increasing their market share. In some markets, one share point is worth tens of millions of dollars. No wonder normal competition has turned into marketing warfare, as the following Chinese example illustrates.

Harbin Brewery—Harbin Brewery, one of China's largest brewers, was caught in a beer brawl between Anheuser-Busch and SABMiller. The former bought a 29 percent stake in Harbin Beer and the reaction from SABMiller was swift. It launched a hostile takeover bid to protect its existing 29 percent stake in Harbin Beer. Eventually, SABMiller dropped its $550 million bid after Anheuser-Busch launched a $720 million counteroffer. Both global beer makers are interested in Harbin Beer because they want to expand their market share and have a bigger bite of the China market. With $6 billion sales in 2003, China is the world's second biggest beer market, after the U.S., and many observers reckon that it will surpass the U.S. by the end of the decade. Other international breweries are following suit. Belgium's Interbrew bought several breweries near Shanghai to capture a prominent position in China's two richest provinces, Guangdong and Zhejiang, while Scottish and Newcastle have a stake in Chongqing Breweries.[37]

However, gaining increased share in the served market does not automatically produce higher profits—especially for labor-intensive service companies that may not experience many economies of scale. Much depends on the company's strategy.

Because the cost of buying higher market share may far exceed its revenue value, a company should consider four factors before pursuing increased market share:

- **The possibility of provoking antitrust action in some countries such as the U.S., as in the recent investigations of Microsoft and Intel.** Jealous competitors are likely to cry "monopoly" if a dominant firm makes further inroads. This rise in risk would diminish the attractiveness of pushing market share gains too far.

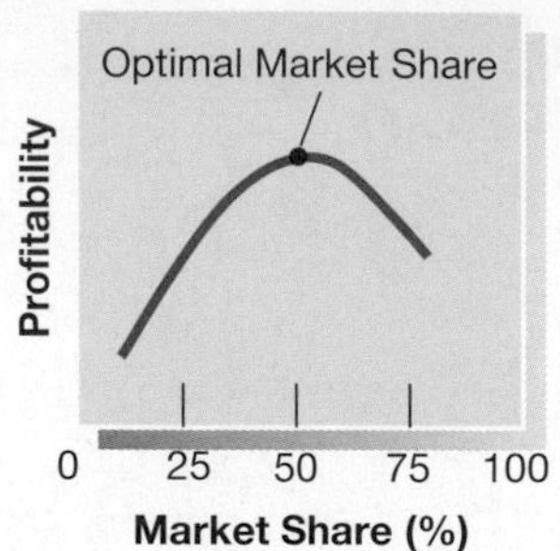

Figure 11.7 The Concept of Optimal Market Share

- **Economic cost.** Figure 11.7 shows that profitability might fall with further market-share gains after some level. In the illustration, the firm's *optimal market share* is 50 percent. The cost of gaining further market share might exceed the value. The "holdout" customers may dislike the company, be loyal to competitive suppliers, have unique needs, or prefer dealing with smaller suppliers. The cost of legal work, public relations, and lobbying rises with market share. Pushing for higher market share is less justified when there are few scale or experience economies, unattractive market segments exist, buyers want multiple sources of supply, and exit barriers are high. Some market leaders have even increased profitability by selectively decreasing market share in weaker areas.[38]
- **Pursuing the wrong marketing-mix strategy.** Companies that cut prices more deeply than competitors typically do not achieve significant gains, as enough rivals meet the price cuts and others offer other values so that buyers do not switch. Competitive rivalry and price cutting have been shown to be most intense in industries with high fixed costs, high inventory costs, and stagnant primary demand, such as steel, auto, paper, and chemicals.[39] Companies successfully gaining share typically outperform competitors in three areas: new-product activity, relative product quality, and marketing expenditures.[40]
- **The effect of increased market share on actual and perceived quality.**[41] Too many customers can put a strain on the firm's resources, hurting product value and service delivery. Some online companies experienced growing pains when its customer base expanded, resulting in system outages and access problems. Consumers may also infer that "bigger is not better" and assume that growth will lead to a deterioration of quality. If "exclusivity" is a key brand benefit, existing customers may resent additional new customers.

Other Competitive Strategies

Firms that occupy second, third, and lower ranks in an industry are often called runner-up, or trailing firms. Some, such as Colgate, Nissan, Sharp, Avis, and PepsiCo, are quite large in their own right. These firms can adopt one of two postures. They can attack the leader and other competitors in an aggressive bid for further market share (market challengers), or they can play ball and not "rock the boat" (market followers).

Market-Challenger Strategies

Many market challengers have gained ground or even overtaken the leader. Toyota today produces more cars than General Motors. Challengers like Airbus set high aspirations, leveraging their resources while the market leader often runs the business as usual. Now let's examine the competitive attack strategies available to market challengers.

DEFINING THE STRATEGIC OBJECTIVE AND OPPONENT(S)

A market challenger must first define its strategic objective. Most aim to increase market share. The challenger must decide whom to attack:

- **It can attack the market leader.** This is a high-risk but potentially high-payoff strategy and makes good sense if the leader is not serving the market well. The alternative strategy is to out-innovate the leader across the whole segment. Xerox wrested the copy market from 3M by developing a better copying process. Later, Canon grabbed a large chunk of Xerox's market by introducing desk copiers.

Samsung—This electronics firm wants to wrest the world's biggest chipmaker position from Intel. Since 2004, Samsung is making headway in some key areas: flash memory and processors for mobile gadgets such as cell phones, digital cameras, and MP3 players. Its success lies in the potential of demand tipping from the PC toward portable devices, and Samsung feels that mobile products will fuel the industry's future growth. It jumped from 10th position in 2003 to second to Intel in 2007 in the chip business.[42]

- **It can attack firms of its own size that are not doing the job and are underfinanced.** These firms have aging products, are charging excessive prices, or are not satisfying customers in other ways.
- **It can attack small local and regional firms.** Several major banks grew to their present size by gobbling up smaller rivals.

If the attacking company goes after the market leader, its objective might be to gain a certain share. If the attacking company goes after a small local company, its objective might be to drive that company out of existence.

CHOOSING A GENERAL ATTACK STRATEGY

Given clear opponents and objectives, what attack options are available? We can distinguish among five attack strategies: frontal, flank, encirclement, bypass, and guerilla attacks.

Frontal Attack

In a pure *frontal attack*, the attacker matches its opponent's product, advertising, price, and distribution. The principle of force says that the side with the greater manpower (resources) will win. A modified frontal attack, such as cutting price vis-à-vis the opponent's, can work if the market leader does not retaliate and if the competitor convinces the market that its product is equal to the leader's.

Apple—Apple's introduction of its iTunes music store and downloading software is a watershed in digital music. Its iPods can play MP3s and its iTunes is equally compatible with PCs and Macintosh computers, opening its potential market to the broadest possible audience of computer users. These innovations humbled Sony, whose Walkman once dominated the "portable music" market. In contrast, Sony performed dismally. It was slow to create a service that would enable its customers to buy music legally. It developed several nondescript portable music players—among which the Network Walkman does not provide good and popular music selections—and a digital music download service, Sony Connect, that few people adopt because it loads too slowly and does not play MP3s.[43]

Flank Attack

An enemy's weak spots are natural targets. A *flank attack* can be directed along two strategic dimensions—segmental and geographic. The segmental attack involves serving uncovered market needs, as Japanese auto-makers did when they developed more fuel-efficient cars. In a geographic attack, the challenger spots areas where the opponent is underperforming.

Wahaha—This Chinese beverage maker grew its market by focusing on less developed markets in China and avoiding head-on confrontations with PepsiCo and Coca-Cola Co. It is now a big force in provincial capitals like Kunming, Yunnan. Wahaha has a significant advantage in second-tier markets, which includes most of rural China.[44]

A flanking strategy is another name for identifying shifts in market segments that are causing gaps to develop, then rushing in to fill the gaps and develop them into strong segments. Flanking is in the best tradition of modern marketing, which holds that the purpose of marketing is to discover needs and satisfy them. Flank attacks are particularly attractive to a challenger with fewer resources than its opponent and are much more likely to be successful than frontal attacks.

Search engines—Given Google's 45 percent share of the Internet search business, it might seem foolhardy for anybody to challenge it. A frontal attack on Google would mean building a better mousetrap—in this case a better search algorithm. Yet, a handful of smaller search companies are mounting flank attacks on Google, and they are confident they will be able to swipe some of the search giant's market share. The flank these small companies are attacking is the one missing element in Google's searches: human intelligence and its ability to reason and contextualize. Jim Wales, cofounder of Wikipedia, the collaborative Internet encyclopedia, plans to create an open-source search engine called Wikia that uses human deduction as well as a machine-driven algorithm. Wales figures that humans are better at weeding out spam search results. ChaCha employs a similar strategy and has thrived in Korea, where Google has made few inroads. ChaCha, founded by MIT research scientist Scott A. Jones, uses 25,000 part- and full-time employees who can offer guided searches in real time. Anyone who has ever "googled" a topic and come up with thousands of Web pages, only of a handful of which are truly helpful, can see how guided search might be an attractive offering. ChaCha's human-guided searches can offer a smaller set of focused and relevant results. The expense of using human guides might be daunting, but ChaCha has managed to bring in 10,000 guides a month at $5 to $10 an hour; it offers them a financial incentive for bringing in others. For its part, Wikia plans to use thousands of volunteers, building on the model of its successful all-volunteer-run Wikipedia.[45]

Encirclement Attack

The encirclement maneuver is an attempt to capture a wide slice of the enemy's territory through a "blitz." It involves launching a grand offensive on several fronts. Encirclement makes sense when the challenger commands superior resources and believes a swift encirclement will break the opponent's will. In making a stand against arch rival Microsoft, Sun Microsystems licensed its Java software to hundreds of companies and millions of software developers for all sorts of consumer devices. As consumer electronics products began to go digital, Java started appearing in a wide range of gadgets.

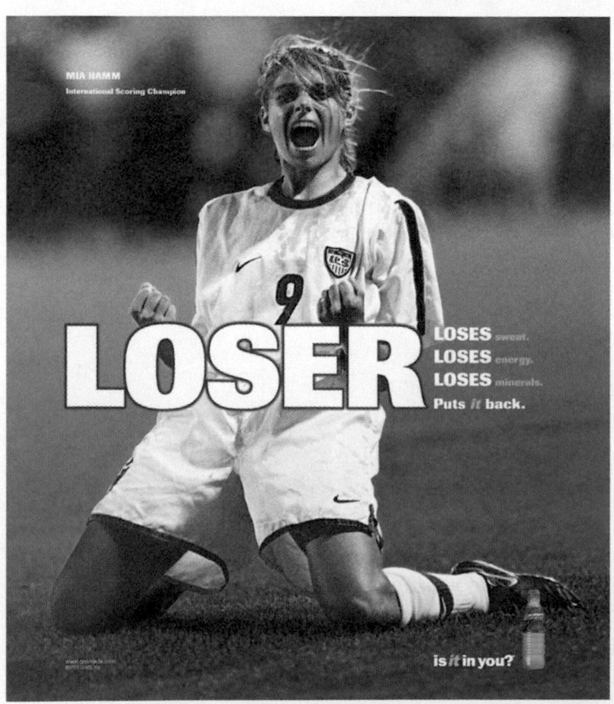

A Gatorade ad with the soccer star Mia Hamm. In a bypass strategy against Coca-Cola, Pepsi bought the Quaker Oats Company, owner of Gatorade Thirst Quenchers, which has a much larger share of the sports drink market than Coca-Cola's Powerade.

Bypass Attack

The most indirect assault strategy is the *bypass*. It means bypassing the enemy and attacking easier markets to broaden one's resource base. This strategy offers three lines of approach: diversifying into unrelated products, diversifying into new geographical markets, and leapfrogging into new technologies to supplant existing products. Pepsi used a bypass strategy against Coke by: (1) aggressively rolling out Aquafina bottled water nationally in 1997 before Coke launched its Dasani brand; (2) purchasing orange juice giant Tropicana for $3.3 billion in 1998, which owned almost twice the market share of Coca-Cola's Minute Maid; and (3) purchasing The Quaker Oats Company, owner of market leader Gatorade sports drink, for $14 billion in 2000.[46]

Technological leapfrogging is a bypass strategy practiced in high-tech industries. The challenger patiently researches and develops the next technology and launches an attack, shifting the battleground to its territory, where it has an advantage. Nintendo's successful attack in the video-game market was precisely about wresting market share by introducing a superior technology and redefining the "competitive space." Then Sega/Genesis did the same with more advanced technology, and by 2002, Sony's Playstation has grabbed the technological lead to gain almost 60 percent of the video-game market.[47] Presently, Nintendo is challenging the market with its Wii. Challenger Google used technological leapfrogging to overtake Yahoo! and become the market leader in search engines.

Guerrilla Warfare

Guerrilla warfare consists of waging small, intermittent attacks to harass and demoralize the opponent and eventually secure permanent footholds. The guerrilla challenger uses both conventional and unconventional means of attack. These include selective price cuts, intense promotional blitzes, and occasional legal action.

Normally, guerrilla warfare is practiced by a smaller firm against a larger one. The smaller firm launches a barrage of attacks in random corners of the larger opponent's market in a manner calculated to weaken the opponent's market power. Military dogma holds that a continual stream of minor attacks usually creates more cumulative impact, disorganization, and confusion in the enemy than a few major attacks. A guerrilla campaign can be expensive, although admittedly less expensive than a frontal, encirclement, or flank attack. Guerrilla warfare is more a preparation for war than a war itself. Ultimately, it must be backed by a stronger attack if the challenger hopes to beat the opponent.

CHOOSING A SPECIFIC ATTACK STRATEGY

The challenger must go beyond the five broad strategies and develop more specific strategies. Any aspect of the marketing program can serve as the basis for attack, such as lower-priced or disconnected products, new or improved products and services, a wider variety of offerings, and innovative distribution strategies.

A challenger's success depends on combining several strategies to improve its position over time. Here is what Samsung did.

Samsung—Samsung has used many challenger strategies to take on Japanese manufacturers and outsell them across a wide range of products. Like many other Asian companies, Samsung used to stress volume and market domination rather than profitability. Yet during the Asian financial crisis of the late 1990s, when other Korean *chaebol* collapsed beneath a mountain of debt, Samsung took a different tack. It cut costs and placed new emphasis on manufacturing flexibility, which allows its consumer electronics goods to go from project phase to store shelves within six months. It also began a serious focus on innovation, using technological leapfrogging to produce state-of-the-art cell phone handsets that are big sellers not only across Asia but also in Europe and the U.S.[48]

"Marketing Memo: Making Smaller Better" provides some additional tips for challenger brands.

MARKETING MEMO • MAKING SMALLER BETTER

Morgan offers eight suggestions of how small brands can better compete:

1. ***Break with your immediate past*** — Don't be afraid to ask "dumb" questions to challenge convention and view your brand differently.
2. ***Build a "lighthouse identity"*** — Establish values and communicate who and why you are (e.g., Apple).
3. ***Assume thought leadership of the category*** — Break convention in terms of representation (what you say about yourself), where you say it (medium), and experience (what you do beyond talk).
4. ***Create symbols of re-evaluation*** — A rocket uses half of its fuel in the first mile to break loose from the gravitational pull—you may need to polarize people.
5. ***Sacrifice*** — Focus your target, message, reach and frequency, distribution, and line extensions and recognize that less can be more.
6. ***Overcommit*** — Although you may do fewer things, do "big" things when you do them.
7. ***Use publicity and advertising to enter popular culture*** — Unconventional communications can get people talking.
8. ***Be idea-centered, not consumer centered*** — Sustain challenger momentum by not losing sight of what the brand is about and can be, and redefine marketing support and the center of the company to reflect this vision.

Source: Adam Morgan, *Eating the Big Fish: How Challenger Brands Can Compete Against Brand Leaders,* (New York: John Wiley, 1999).

Market-Follower Strategies

Some years ago, Theodore Levitt wrote an article entitled "Innovative Imitation," in which he argued that a strategy of *product imitation* might be as profitable as a strategy of *product innovation*.[49] The innovator bears the expense of developing the new product, getting it into distribution, and informing and educating the market. The reward for all this work and risk is normally market leadership. However, another firm can come along and copy or improve on the new product. Although it probably will not overtake the leader, the follower can achieve high profits because it did not bear any of the innovation expense.

Many companies prefer to follow rather than challenge the market leader. Patterns of "conscious parallelism" are common in capital-intensive, homogeneous-product industries, such as steel, fertilizers, and chemicals. The opportunities for product differentiation and image differentiation are low; service quality is often comparable; and price sensitivity runs high. The mood in these industries is against short-run grabs for market share because that strategy only provokes retaliation. Most firms decide against stealing one another's customers. Instead, they present similar offers to buyers, usually by copying the leader. Market shares show high stability.

This is not to say that market followers lack strategies. A market follower must know how to hold current customers and win a fair share of new customers. Each follower tries to bring distinctive advantages to its target market—location, services, financing. Because the follower is often a major target of attack by challengers, it must keep its manufacturing costs low and its product quality and services high. It must also enter new markets as they open up. The follower has to define a growth path, but one that does not invite competitive retaliation. Four broad strategies can be distinguished:

- ***Counterfeiter*** — The counterfeiter duplicates the leader's product and package and sells it on the black market or through disreputable dealers. Music record firms, Louis Vuitton, and Rolex have been plagued with the counterfeiter problem, especially in Asia (see "Marketing Insight: Counteracting Counterfeiting" for details).

iPhones—Fake iPhones made their debut in Asia before Apple introduced them in this region in 2008. In Taipei, iPhone knockoffs can be bought at two-thirds the legitimate price. Demand for iPhones is so hot that counterfeiters claim they cannot ignore it. Counterfeiters designed the fakes from pictures posted on the Internet even before Apple unveiled the iPhone in January 2007. The fakes are advertised on the Internet. While the counterfeits resemble iPhones, they do not use Apple software. Says one counterfeit manufacturer, "It's the exterior we are imitating. If customers want functions, we can offer more and better functions than the real phone."[50]

- ***Cloner*** — The cloner emulates the leader's products, name, and packaging, with slight variations. For example, Glico Pocky chocolate stick snacks has a look-alike in Giant Chocky; Oreo chocolate sandwich cookies in Rodeo; Tsingtao (青島) beer in Tsingitao (青一島) and Tsingsuntao (青山島). In the computer business, clones are a fact of life.
- ***Imitator*** — The imitator copies some things from the leader but maintains differentiation in terms of packaging, advertising, pricing, or location. The leader does not mind the imitator as long as the imitator does not attack the leader aggressively.
- ***Adapter*** — The adapter takes the leader's products and adapts or improves them. The adapter may choose to sell to different markets, but often the adapter grows into the future challenger, as many Japanese firms have done after adapting and improving products developed elsewhere.

What does a follower earn? Normally, less than the leader. For example, a study of food processing companies showed the largest firm averaging a 16 percent return on investment; the number 2 firm, 6 percent; the number 3 firm, –1 percent, and the number 4 firm, –6 percent. In this case, only the top two firms have profits. No wonder Jack Welch, former CEO of GE, told his business units that each must reach the number 1 or number 2 position in its market or else! Followership is often not a rewarding path.

MARKETING INSIGHT • COUNTERACTING COUNTERFEITING

The combined price of a genuine Hermés wallet, a Louis Vuitton black "epi" leather knapsack, and a watch, belt, pair of glasses, pair of pants, and pair of sandals from Gucci would amount to $5,109 in Hong Kong boutiques. In Shenzhen, the fake editions of these items would cost a total of $150. Counterfeit goods account for 3 to 4 percent of world trade, amounting to a $350-billion a year industry. Counterfeiting is among the world's fastest-growing and most lucrative businesses. Fake Duracell batteries and Oral-B toothpaste are sold in the U.S., while fake Head & Shoulders shampoo is available in the Middle East and Eastern Europe—all made in China. A third of Japanese companies said imitations of their products were China-made, followed by South Korea with 18.1 percent, and Taiwan with 17.6 percent.

Two technological trends have emerged in counterfeiting: the use of the Internet to sell pirated products and the proliferation of cheap high-tech equipment that facilitates better-quality reproduction of original material. With its ease of access, large audience, and potential for anonymity, the Internet provides an ideal platform for counterfeiters. For example, there are at least 160 Web sites offering "genuine" Chanel products even though Chanel does not sell any of its products on the Internet. Textile piracy has grown in sophistication as the Internet has made it easier to copy branded goods. Digital technology has also facilitated the production of imitation CDs of the same quality as the original. It costs only five cents to produce a pirated version of a hit CD which is then sold in Asia for 40 to 50 times that amount. Improved technology has also helped counterfeiters design large-scale integration chips for calculators and LCDs.

The fight against piracy is hampered by public perception that counterfeiting is a low grade victimless crime. Thus a Hong Kong government billboard campaign tried to appeal to consumers' conscience by declaring, "You are what you wear. Get real." Yet, counterfeit aircraft and auto parts, medical equipment, birth control pills, and even vodka have been known to threaten lives. Moreover, with the increase in quality of counterfeit products, some consumers who once rejected fakes are now clamoring for them and boasting about the source and cost of their purchases.

What can marketers do to combat counterfeiters? Here are some strategies:

- **Do nothing.** Sometimes taking action may offend an otherwise congenial Asian partner or local markets may view the Western firm as being heavy-handed.
- **Team up with other brands to fund the cost of working with local governments to raid producers and sellers of fakes.** Examples: Comite Colberg, an association of 75 French luxury brands, the Business Software Alliance, and the Beijing-based Quality Brands Protection Committee which includes Compaq, Anheuser Busch, J&J, Philip Morris, and Prada.
- **Lobby home governments.** Thus the U.S. government has placed Indonesia on its "priority watch list" for intellectual property rights violations which may impact Jakarta's ability to attract investments, particularly in high-tech sectors. Other Asian nations similarly affected include the Philippines and Taiwan. This may motivate more consistent enforcement of intellectual property laws in the region. The Taiwan Anti-piracy Alliance is lobbying its government to make piracy a prosecutable crime without the need for complaints from victims.
- **Develop in-house anti-fraud squads.** Reebok and Nike send teams of undercover agents on training courses that teach them to recognize their company's goods from fakes and to identify culprits.
- **Engage investigative agencies.** Firms in the consumer electronics and entertainment industry have engaged such agencies to identify counterfeiters, their distribution channels, and their manufacturing sites for authorities to take action. Casio hired private investigators to monitor counterfeits at major export promotion fairs and nip large-lot transactions in the bud.
- **Accelerate R&D efforts.** Continually improving product performance and bettering the price/value offering creates a moving target for pirates. Canon is developing calculators with more functions and higher quality more quickly.
- **Use high-tech labeling like special inks and dyes, holograms, and electronic signatures.** Australia had a leading athlete donate DNA which was then incorporated into special ink used in official products sold at the Sydney Olympic Games.
- **Advertise to end-users.** A pull strategy may be employed to persuade consumers that the real product is superior to pirated brands thus devaluing the latter's status.
- **Form partnerships.** "If you can't beat 'em, join 'em." While Yamaha failed to combat imitation motorbikes by complaining to the Chinese authorities and placing newspaper ads condemning the practice, Honda decided to partner a Hainan company that prospered by making fake Honda bikes. The Sundrio Honda Motorcycle Company now produces low-priced bikes for the Chinese market.

Yamaha's plight highlights the serious challenges that remain in the fight against counterfeiting in Asia. For example, in China, local branches of such regulatory bodies as the Administration for Industry and Commerce and the Quality and Technical Supervisory Bureaus are willing to get tough. However, counterfeiters are seldom handed over for criminal prosecution partly because officials may then be unable to extract bribes from the pirates. Some pirates are as organized and large as MNCs. Given their size, they can not only produce more and better quality fakes, but are also harder to dismantle. Ironically, things may improve when counterfeiters start to target local Chinese brands.

Sources: Joanne Lee-Young, "Counterfeit Culture." *Asian Wall Street Journal*, March 10, 2000, pp. P1–P4; Robert Tilley, "The Brand Name Bandits." *Asia-Inc*, December 2000–January 2001; Robert Go, "Copyright Piracy a Threat to Indonesia's Recovery." *Sunday Times* (Singapore), May 5, 2002, p. 15; Hau Boon Lai, "Copycats: If You Can't Beat 'Em." *Sunday Times* (Singapore), May 5, 2002, p. 31; Dexter Roberts, "Clear Sailing for Pirates." *BusinessWeek Asian Edition*, July 8, 2002, p. 27; "Anti-Piracy Alliance Founded in Taiwan." *Asia Pulse*, August 13, 2002; Sachiko Hirao, "Japanese Firms Fight Back against Chinese Copies." *Japan Times*, August 10, 2002; Clifford Schultz II and Ben Saporito, "Protecting Intellectual Property: Strategies and Recommendations to Deter Counterfeiting and Brand Piracy in Global Markets." *Columbia Journal of World Business*, Spring 1996, 31, pp. 18–28.

At Berjaya Times Square in Kuala Lumpur, Malaysia, Dairy Queen is located on one floor, while its imitator, Dairy King, is located on the same spot on the next floor.

Market-Nicher Strategies

An alternative to being a follower in a large market is to be a leader in a small market, or niche. Smaller firms normally avoid competing with larger firms by targeting small markets of little or no interest to the larger firms. Here is an example.

> **Logitech International**—Logitech has become a $2.1-billion global success story by making every variation of computer mouse imaginable. The company turns out mice for left- and right-handed people, cordless mice that use radio waves, mice shaped like real mice for children, and 3-D mice that let the user appear to move behind screen objects. It sells to OEMs as well as via its own brand at retail. Its global dominance in the mouse category enabled the company to expand into other computer peripherals, such as PC headsets, PC gaming peripherals, and Webcams.[51]

Firms with low shares of the total market can be highly profitable through smart niching. Such companies tend to offer high value, charge a premium price, achieve lower manufacturing costs, and shape a strong corporate culture and vision.

In a study of hundreds of business units, the Strategic Planning Institute found that the return on investment averaged 27 percent in smaller markets, but only 11 percent in larger markets.[52] Why is niching so profitable? The main reason is that the market nicher ends up knowing the target customers so well that it meets their needs better than other firms selling to this niche casually. As a result, the nicher can charge a substantial price over costs. The nicher achieves *high margin,* whereas the mass-marketer achieves *high volume.*

Nichers have three tasks: creating niches, expanding niches, and protecting niches. Niching carries a major risk in that the market niche might dry up or be attacked. The company is then stuck with highly specialized resources that may not have high-value alternative uses.

Because niches can weaken, the firm must continually create new ones. "Marketing Memo: Niche Specialist Roles" outlines some options. The firm should "stick to its niching" but not necessarily to its niche. That is why *multiple niching* is preferable to *single niching.* By developing strength in two or more niches, the company increases its chances for survival.

Firms entering a market should aim at a niche initially rather than the whole market (see "Marketing Memo: Strategies for Entering Markets Held by Incumbent Firms"). Consider Virgin Mobile:

MARKETING MEMO • NICHE SPECIALIST ROLES

The key idea in successful nichemanship is specialization. Here are some possible niche roles:

- ***End-user specialist*** — The firm specializes in serving one type of end-use customer. For example, a *value-added reseller (VAR)* customizes the computer hardware and software for specific customer segments and earns a price premium in the process.
- ***Vertical-level specialist*** — The firm specializes at some vertical level of the production-distribution value chain. A copper firm may concentrate on producing raw copper, copper components, or finished copper products.
- ***Customer-size specialist*** — The firm concentrates on selling to either small, medium-sized, or large customers. Many nichers specialize in serving small customers who are neglected by the majors.
- ***Specific-customer specialist*** — The firm limits its selling to one or a few customers. *Keiretsu* suppliers may sell their entire output to a single company, such as Matsushita.
- ***Geographic specialist*** — The firm sells only in a certain locality, region, or area of the world.
- ***Product or product-line specialist*** — The firm carries or produces only one product line or product. Hanjaya Mandala Sampoerna produces *kretek*, a clove-scented cigarette favored by most Indonesian smokers. Its main brand, Dji Sam Soe (a Chinese dialect for "Two, Three, Four"), is hand-rolled by thousands of employees in East Java. The company also offers machine-rolled and low-tar brands such as A Mild. In 2005, Sampoerna was acquired by Philip Morris International, the international operating company of the Altria Group.
- ***Product-feature specialist*** — The firm specializes in producing a certain type of product or product feature.
- ***Job-shop specialist*** — The firm customizes its products for individual customers.
- ***Quality-price specialist*** — The firm operates at the low- or high-quality ends of the market. Hewlett-Packard specializes in the high-quality, high-price end of the hand-calculator market.
- ***Service specialist*** — The firm offers one or more services not available from other firms. An example would be a bank that takes loan requests over the phone and hand-delivers the money to the customer.
- ***Channel specialist*** — The firm specializes in serving only one channel of distribution. For example, a soft-drink company decides to make a very large-sized soft drink available only at gas stations.

MARKETING MEMO • STRATEGIES FOR ENTERING MARKETS HELD BY INCUMBENT FIRMS

Carpenter and Nakamoto examined strategies for launching a new product into a market dominated by one brand, such as Kleenex or FedEx. (These brands, which include many market pioneers, are particularly difficult to attack because many are the standard against which others are judged.) They identified four strategies that have good profit potential in this situation:

1. ***Differentiation*** — Positioning away from the dominant brand with a comparable or premium price and heavy advertising spending to establish the new brand as a credible alternative. Example: Honda's motorcycle challenges Harley-Davidson.
2. ***Challenger*** — Positioning close to the dominant brand with heavy advertising spending and comparable or premium price to challenge the dominant brand as the category standard. Example: Pepsi competing against Coke.
3. ***Niche*** — Positioning away from the dominant brand with a high price and a low advertising budget to exploit a profitable niche. Example: Brands of toothpaste for smokers and those with sensitive gums competing against Crest.
4. ***Premium*** — Positioning near the dominant brand with little advertising spending but a premium price to move "up market" relative to the dominant brand. Examples: Godiva chocolate and Häagen-Dazs ice cream competing against standard brands.

Sources: Gregory S. Carpenter and Kent Nakamoto, "Competitive Strategies for Late Entry into a Market with a Dominant Brand." *Management Science*, October 1990, pp. 1268–1278; Gregory S. Carpenter and Kent Nakamoto, "The Impact of Consumer Preference Formation on Marketing Objectives and Competitive Second Mover Strategies." *Journal of Consumer Psychology*, 1996, 5(4), pp. 325-358; Venkatesh Shankar, Gregory Carpenter, and Lakshman Krishnamurthi, "Late Mover Advantage: How Innovative Late Entrants Outsell Pioneers." *Journal of Marketing Research*, February 1998, 35, pp. 54–70.

Virgin Mobile—While Virgin is a big player in music, air travel, and other industries, it is the new kid on the block in the wireless business. Yet, rather than launching a frontal attack on big names, Virgin Mobile is targeting young phone users and was the first wireless company to expressly target this group. Virgin Mobile offers one of the simplest prepaid plans around with no contracts and no hidden fees. The company touts cool features such as a "rescue ring" to escape a boring date or the voice of Isaac Hayes or Grandpa Munster for the greeting. And, to emphasize that the phone plan has "nothing to hide," Virgin runs provocative ads featuring nude actors. CEO Richard Branson himself even showed up half-naked in New York's Times Square to kick off the company's 50–50 joint venture with Sprint PCS Group. The niching strategy seems to be working in some markets.[53]

Balancing Customer and Competitor Orientations

We have stressed the importance of a company's positioning itself competitively as a market leader, challenger, follower, or nicher. Yet a company must not spend all its time focusing on competitors.

Competitor-Centered Companies

A *competitor-centered company* sets its course as follows:

SITUATION

- Competitor W is going all out to crush us in Kuala Lumpur.
- Competitor X is improving its distribution coverage in Jakarta and hurting our sales.
- Competitor Y has cut its price in Hong Kong, and we lost three share points.
- Competitor Z has introduced a new service feature in Taipei, and we are losing sales.

REACTIONS

- We will withdraw from the Kuala Lumpur market because we cannot afford to fight this battle.
- We will increase our advertising expenditure in Jakarta.
- We will meet competitor Y's price cut in Hong Kong.
- We will increase our sales promotion budget in Taipei.

This kind of planning has some pluses and minuses. On the positive side, the company develops a fighter orientation. It trains its marketers to be on constant alert, to watch for weaknesses in its competitors' and its own position. On the negative side, the company is too reactive. Rather than formulating and executing a consistent, customer-oriented strategy, it determines its moves based on its competitors' moves. It does not move toward its own goals. It does not know where it will end up, because so much depends on what its competitors do.

Customer-Centered Companies

A *customer-centered company* focuses more on customer developments in formulating its strategies.

SITUATION

- The total market is growing at 4 percent annually.
- The quality-sensitive segment is growing at 8 percent annually.
- The deal-prone customer segment is also growing fast, but these customers do not stay with any supplier very long.
- A growing number of customers have expressed an interest in a 24-hour hotline, which no one in the industry offers.

REACTIONS

- We will focus more effort on reaching and satisfying the quality segment of the market. We will buy better components, improve quality control, and shift our advertising theme to quality.
- We will avoid cutting prices and making deals because we do not want the kind of customer that buys this way.
- We will install a 24-hour hotline if it looks promising.

Clearly, the customer-centered company is in a better position to identify new opportunities and set a course that promises to deliver long-run profits. By monitoring customer needs, it can decide which customer groups and emerging needs are the most important to serve, given its resources and objectives. Jeff Bezos, founder of Amazon.com, strongly favors a customer-centered orientation: "Amazon.com's mantra has been that we were going to obsess over our customer and not our competitors. We watch our competitors, learn from them, see the things that they were doing good for customers and copy those things as much as we can. But we were never going to obsess over them."[54]

Summary

1. To prepare an effective marketing strategy, a company must study competitors as well as actual and potential customers. Companies need to identify competitors' strategies, objectives, strengths, and weaknesses.
2. A company's closest competitors are those seeking to satisfy the same customers and needs and making similar offers. A company should also pay attention to latent competitors, who may offer new or other ways to satisfy the same needs. A company should identify competitors by using both industry and market-based analyses.
3. A market leader has the largest market share in the relevant product market. To remain dominant, the leader looks for ways to expand total market demand, attempts to protect its current market share, and perhaps tries to increase its market share.
4. A market challenger attacks the market leader and other competitors in an aggressive bid for more market share. Challengers can choose from five types of general attack; challengers must also choose specific attack strategies.
5. A market follower is a runner-up firm that is willing to maintain its market share and not rock the boat. A follower can play the role of counterfeiter, cloner, imitator, or adapter.
6. A market nicher serves small market segments not being served by larger firms. The key to nichemanship is specialization. Nichers develop offerings to fully meet a certain group of customer's needs, commanding a premium price in the process.
7. As important as a competitive orientation is in today's global markets, companies should not overdo the emphasis on competitors. They should maintain a good balance of consumer and competitor monitoring.

Application

Marketing Debate—How Do You Attack a Category Leader?

Attacking a leader is always difficult. Some strategists recommend attacking a leader "head-on" by targeting its strengths. Other strategists disagree and recommend flanking and attempting to avoid the leader's strengths.

Take a position: *The best way to challenge a leader is to attack its strengths* versus *The best way to attack a leader is to avoid a head-on assault and to adopt a flanking strategy.*

Marketing Discussion

Pick an industry. Classify firms according to the four different roles they might play: leader, challenger, follower, and nicher. How would you characterize the nature of competition? Do the firms follow the principles described in the chapter?

PART 5

Shaping the Market Offerings

High-performance equipment backed by superior sales and service functions are at the heart of Caterpillar's successful product strategy.

12 Setting Product Strategy

At the heart of a great brand is a great product. Product is a key element in the market offering. Market leaders generally offer products and services of superior quality.

Caterpillar has become a leading firm by maximizing total customer value in the construction equipment industry, despite challenges from a number of able competitors, such as John Deere, J.I. Case, Komatsu, Volvo, and Hitachi. First, Caterpillar produces high-performance equipment known for its reliability and durability—key purchase considerations in the choice of heavy industrial equipment. The firm also makes it easy for customers to find the right product by providing a full line of construction equipment and offering a wide range of financial terms. Caterpillar maintains the largest number of independent construction-equipment dealers in the industry. These dealers all carry a complete line of Caterpillar products and are typically better trained and perform more reliably than competitors' dealers. Caterpillar has also built a worldwide parts and service system second to none in the industry.Customers recognize all the value that Caterpillar creates in its offerings, allowing the firm to command a premium price in the marketplace.[1]

In this chapter, we will address the following questions:

1. What are the characteristics of products, and how do marketers classify products?
2. How can companies differentiate products?
3. How can a company build and manage its product mix and product lines?
4. How can companies combine products to create strong co-brands or ingredient brands?
5. How can companies use packaging, labeling, warranties, and guarantees as marketing tools?

Marketing planning begins with formulating an offering to meet target customers' needs or wants. The customer will judge the offering by three basic elements: product features and quality, services mix and quality, and price (see Figure 12.1). In this chapter, we examine product; in Chapter 13, services; and in Chapter 14, prices. All three elements must be meshed into a competitively attractive offering.

Value-based prices

Attractiveness of the market offering

Product features and quality

Services mix and quality

Figure 12.1 Components of the Market Offering

Product Characteristics and Classifications

Many people think that a product is a tangible offering, but a product can be more than that. A **product** is anything that can be offered to a market to satisfy a want or need. Products that are marketed include physical goods, services, experiences, events, persons, places, properties, organizations, information, and ideas.

Product Levels: The Customer Value Hierarchy

In planning its market offering, the marketer needs to address five product levels (see Figure 12.2).[2] Each level adds more customer value, and the five constitute a **customer value hierarchy**.

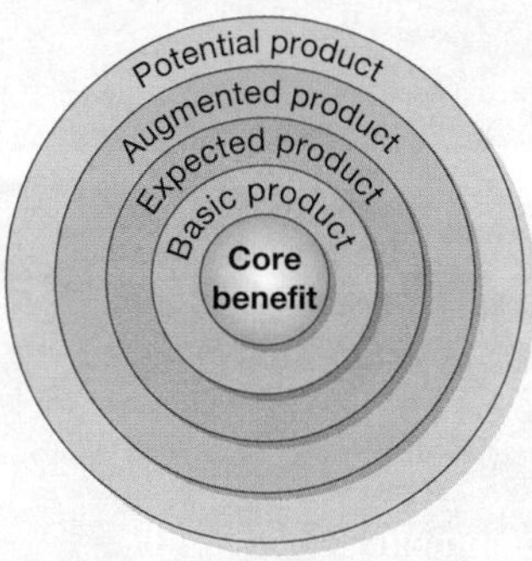

Figure 12.2 Five Product Levels

- The fundamental level is the **core benefit**: the service or benefit the customer is really buying. A hotel guest is buying "rest and sleep." A woman buying cosmetics is buying "hope." Marketers must see themselves as benefit providers.
- At the second level, the marketer has to turn the core benefit into a **basic product**. Thus a hotel room includes a bed, bathroom, towels, desk, dresser, and closet.
- At the third level, the marketer prepares an **expected product**, a set of attributes and conditions buyers normally expect when they purchase this product. Hotel guests expect a clean bed, fresh towels, working lamps, and a relative degree of quiet. Because most hotels can meet this minimum expectation, the traveler normally will settle for whichever hotel is most convenient or least expensive. In developing countries and emerging markets, however, competition takes place mostly at the expected product level.
- At the fourth level, the marketer prepares an **augmented product** that exceeds customer expectations. In developed countries, brand positioning and competition take place at this level. For example, several top Malaysian hotels offer sunshine-and-surgery packages, including full medical check-ups, to attract foreigners seeking treatment there. Here's one on Japanese fashion:

Japanese fashion—The Japanese are devising a variety of novel defences against crime. Fashion is augmented as an anti-crime novelty. One is the "vending machine skirt." With a deft motion, the front of a skirt reveals a sheet printed in bright red with a soft drink logo partly visible. By holding the sheet fully open and stepping to the side of the road, a woman walking alone could camouflage herself to shake off pursuers. Another is the "manhole bag," a purse that can hide one's valuables by unfolding to look like a round sewer cover. When laid on the street with the wallet still inside, unwitting thieves may mistake it for an ordinary manhole.[3]

- At the fifth level stands the **potential product**, which encompasses all the possible augmentations and transformations the product or offering might undergo in the future. Here is where companies search for new ways to satisfy customers and distinguish their offer. For instance, consider the rapid growth of Internet-connected phones, which offer businesses possibilities of engaging in m-commerce (mobile commerce):

NTT DoCoMo—In Japan, about two million teens carry DoCoMo's i-mode cell phones. They view ***manga*** cartoons, ***haiku*** poetry, and pictures of snow falling on the Hokkaido mountains. They spend much time sending and receiving instant messages from friends. They can also use their phones to order goods by scanning a list of several thousand companies that sell things. A DoCoMo subscriber wanting a new pair of running shoes can look up shoes, then Nike, then style and size, and order a pair of shoes. The subscriber's address is in the system and the shoes will be sent to the 7-Eleven store nearest his home or office. The subscriber can pick up the shoes at that store or pay the store to deliver the shoes. Each month, the subscriber receives a bill from NTT listing the subscriber fee, the usage fee, and the cost of all the transactions. The subscriber can then pay the bill at the nearest 7-Eleven store.[4]

Differentiation arises and competition increasingly occurs on the basis of product augmentation, which also leads the marketer to look at the user's total **consumption system**: the way the user performs the tasks of getting and using products and related services.[5]

Each augmentation adds cost, however and augmented benefits soon become expected benefits and necessary points-of-parity. Today's hotel guests expect cable or satellite television with a remote control and high-speed Internet access or two phone lines. This means competitors will have to search for still other features and benefits (see "Marketing Insight: Metamarkets and Metamediaries").

As some companies raise the price of their augmented product, some competitors offer a "stripped-down" version at a much lower price. Thus alongside the growth of fine hotels like Bangkok's The Oriental and Hoi An's Nam Hai Resort, we see the emergence of budget hotels and lower-cost hotels catering to clients who simply want the basic product.

MARKETING INSIGHT • METAMARKETS AND METAMEDIARIES

There are some products whose purchase necessitates other purchases. The new-automobile market is a good example of a "metamarket." The consumer chooses an automobile but also must buy insurance from an insurance company and often must get a loan from a bank. A smart auto company or auto dealer would make all three purchases easy for the buyer by partnering with an insurance company and a bank. Such an auto dealer is performing as a "metamediary."

The wedding market is also a metamarket. The bride and groom need a bridal gown and tuxedo respectively, a chapel, a hotel for the wedding, a caterer, and possibly a wedding consultant. Here the wedding dress seller or the wedding consultant might perform as a wedding metamediary.

Metamarkets are the result of marketers observing the total consumption system and "packaging" a system that simplifies carrying out these related product/service activities. Sawhney defines a metamarket as "a set of products and services that consumers need to perform a ***cognitively related*** set of activities. Other metamarkets that are organized around major assets or major life events include:

- Buying a home.
- Giving birth to a child.
- Getting a divorce.
- Planning a vacation.

Source: Adapted from Mohan Sawhney, "Rethinking Marketing and Mediation in the Networked Economy." Winning Strategies for E-Commerce Lecture at the Kellogg School of Management, April 7–10, 1999.

Product Classifications

Marketers have traditionally classified products on the basis of durability, tangibility, and use (consumer or industrial). Each product type has an appropriate marketing-mix strategy.[6]

DURABILITY AND TANGIBILITY

Products can be classified into three groups, according to durability and tangibility:

1. ***Non-durable goods*** — These are tangible goods normally consumed in one or a few uses, like beer and soap. Because these goods are consumed quickly and purchased frequently, the appropriate strategy is to make them available in many locations, charge only a small markup, and advertise heavily to induce trial and build preference.
2. ***Durable goods*** — These are tangible goods that normally survive many uses: refrigerators, machine tools, and clothing. Durable products normally require more personal selling and service, command a higher margin, and require more seller guarantees.
3. ***Services*** — These are intangible, inseparable, variable, and perishable products. As a result, they normally require more quality control, supplier credibility, and adaptability. Examples include haircuts, legal advice, and appliance repairs.

CONSUMER-GOODS CLASSIFICATION

The vast array of goods consumers buy can be classified on the basis of shopping habits. We can distinguish among convenience, shopping, specialty, and unsought goods.

The consumer usually purchases **convenience goods** frequently, immediately, and with a minimum of effort. Examples include tobacco products, soaps, and newspapers. Convenience goods can be further divided. *Staples* are goods consumers purchase on a regular basis. A buyer might routinely purchase Maggi ketchup, Colgate toothpaste, and Nissin instant noodles. *Impulse goods* are purchased without any planning or search effort. Candy bars and magazines are impulse goods. *Emergency goods* are purchased when a need is urgent—umbrellas during a rainstorm, boots and shovels during the first winter snowstorm. Manufacturers of impulse and emergency goods will place them in those outlets where consumers are likely to experience an urge or compelling need to make a purchase.

Shopping goods are goods that the consumer, in the process of selection and purchase, characteristically compares on such bases as suitability, quality, price, and style. Examples include furniture, clothing, used cars, and major appliances. Shopping goods can be further divided. *Homogeneous shopping goods* are similar in quality but different enough in price to justify shopping comparisons. *Heterogeneous shopping goods* differ in product features and services that may be more important than price. The seller of heterogeneous shopping goods carries a wide assortment to satisfy individual tastes and must have well-trained salespeople to inform and advise customers.

Specialty goods have unique characteristics or brand identification for which a sufficient number of buyers are willing to make a special purchasing effort. Examples include cars, stereo components, photographic equipment, and men's suits. A Mercedes is a specialty good because interested buyers will travel far to buy one. Specialty goods do not involve making comparisons; buyers invest time only to reach dealers carrying the wanted products. Dealers do not need convenient locations, although they must let prospective buyers know their locations.

Unsought goods are those the consumer does not know about or does not normally think of buying. The classic examples of known but unsought goods are life insurance, funeral services, and encyclopedias. Unsought goods require advertising and personal-selling support.

INDUSTRIAL-GOODS CLASSIFICATION

Industrial goods can be classified in terms of how they enter the production process and their relative costliness. We can distinguish three groups of industrial goods: materials and parts, capital items, and supplies and business services. **Materials and parts** are goods that enter the manufacturer's product completely. They fall into two classes: raw materials and manufactured materials and parts. *Raw materials* fall into two major groups: *farm products* (e.g., wheat, livestock, fruits, and vegetables) and *natural products* (e.g., fish, timber, and crude petroleum). Farm products are supplied by many producers, who turn them over to marketing intermediaries, who provide assembly, grading, storage, transportation, and selling services. Their perishable and seasonal nature gives rise to special marketing practices. Their commodity character results in relatively little advertising and promotional activity, with some exceptions. At times, commodity groups will launch campaigns to promote their products—eggs, milk, and wheat. Some producers brand their products—Dole pineapples and Sunkist oranges. This trend has spread to China.

Chinese farm brands—For decades, Chinese farmers never bothered to brand their produce. However, things changed with the registration of famous brands of nearly 1,000 varieties of such farm products as rice, wheat, mushrooms, chickens, oranges, apples, garlic, and crabs. Branded farm produce typically fetches a price premium and sells better than non-branded alternatives. Dangyuan pears from Anhui province sell well and are priced 30 percent higher than generic pears. Farmers are also not hesitant to protect their interest through legal procedures. For instance, Zhao Baoquan has threatened to sue anyone selling fake Shanhua mushrooms.

Natural products are limited in supply. They usually have great bulk and low unit value and must be moved from producer to user. Fewer and larger producers often market them directly to industrial users. Because the users depend on these materials, long-term supply contracts are common. The homogeneity of natural materials limits the amount of demand-creation activity. Price and delivery reliability are the major factors influencing the selection of suppliers.

Manufactured materials and parts fall into two categories: component materials (iron, yarn, cement, wires) and component parts (small motors, tires, castings). *Component materials* are usually fabricated further—pig iron is made into steel, and yarn is woven into cloth. The standardized nature of component materials usually means that price and supplier reliability are key purchase factors. *Component parts* enter the finished product with no further change in form, as when small motors are put into vacuum cleaners, and tires are put on automobiles. Most manufactured materials and parts are sold directly to industrial users. Price and service are major marketing considerations, and branding and advertising tend to be less important.

Capital items are long-lasting goods that facilitate developing or managing the finished product. They include two groups: installations and equipment. *Installations* consist of buildings (factories, offices) and heavy equipment (generators, drill presses, mainframe computers, elevators). Installations are major purchases. They are usually bought directly from the producer, with the typical sale preceded by a long negotiation period. The producer's sales force includes technical personnel. Producers have to be willing to design to specification and to supply postsale services. Advertising is much less important than personal selling.

Equipment comprises portable factory equipment and tools (hand tools, lift trucks) and office equipment (personal computers, desks). These types of equipment do not become part of a finished product. They have a shorter life than installations but a longer life than operating supplies. Although some equipment manufacturers sell direct, more often they use intermediaries, because the market is geographically dispersed, the buyers are numerous, and the orders are small. Quality, features, price, and service are major considerations. The sales force tends to be more important than advertising, although the latter can be used effectively.

Supplies and business services are short-term goods and services that facilitate developing or managing the finished product. Supplies are of two kinds: *maintenance and repair items* (paint, nails, brooms), and *operating supplies* (lubricants, coal, writing paper, pencils). Together, they go under the name of MRO goods. Supplies are the equivalent of convenience goods; they are usually purchased with minimum effort on a straight rebuy basis. They are normally marketed through intermediaries because of their low unit value and the great number and geographic dispersion of customers. Price and service are important considerations, because suppliers are standardized and brand preference is not high.

Business services include *maintenance and repair services* (window cleaning, copier repair), and *business advisory services* (legal, management consulting, advertising). Maintenance and repair services are usually supplied under contract by small producers or are available from the manufacturers of the original equipment. Business advisory services are usually purchased on the basis of the supplier's reputation and staff.

Differentiation

To be branded, products must be differentiated. Physical products vary in their potential for differentiation. At one extreme, we find products that allow little variation: eggs, aspirin, and steel. Yet even here, some differentiation is possible: Seng Choon eggs, Bayer aspirin, and India's Tata Steel have carved out distinct identities in their categories. Kao makes household cleaners such as Magiclean and Quickle, each with a separate brand identity. At the other extreme are products capable of high differentiation, such as automobiles, commercial buildings, and furniture. Here the seller faces an abundance of design parameters, including form, features, performance quality, conformance quality, durability, reliability, repairability, and style.[7]

Product Differentiation

FORM

Many products can be differentiated in **form**—the size, shape, or physical structure of a product. Consider the many possible forms taken by products such as aspirin. Although aspirin is essentially a commodity, it can be differentiated by dosage, size, shape, color, coating, or action time.

Pantene—Previously, Pantene offered consumer benefits based on hair type. For example, damaged hair can be repaired to become healthy hair. However, Pantene soon found that differentiation based on hair type was not meaningful to Asian consumers. "Curls," for instance, was not relevant to most Asians. Few understood what "sheer volume" means. Hence, with its "Reborn" campaign launched in Thailand, Indonesia, the Philippines, Malaysia, Singapore, Vietnam, and India, Pantene created differentiation based on form that was meaningful to Asian women—Smooth & Silky, Volume & Fullness, and a Classic Clean range comprising Balance Clean, Lively Clean, and AntiDandruff. Whatever choice the consumer made, Pantene promised to make the consumer's hair look "reborn."[8]

FEATURES

Most products can be offered with varying **features** that supplement its basic function. A company can identify and select appropriate new features by surveying recent buyers and then calculating *customer value* vs. *company cost* for each potential feature. The company should also consider how many people want each feature, how long it would take to introduce each feature, and whether competitors could easily copy the feature. Companies must also think in terms of feature bundles or packages. Auto companies often manufacture cars at several "trim levels." This lowers manufacturing and inventory costs. Each company must decide whether to offer feature customization at a higher cost or a few standard packages at a lower cost.

Nissan—With Japan's auto market in a slump, Nissan's designers identified two potential target groups—young urban women who want a small, eco-friendly vehicle for city commuting and young men who desire a car for hanging out together. It learned that young women liked driving better if they had a car that was easy to park and removes the stress of city driving. Hence, Nissan designed a three-seat electric car with a bubble-like rotating cabin that is capable of driving sideways to slip easily into a parking space. The car, called Pivo 2, also provides driving directions in a soothing voice to reduce stress. For the second target market of young men desiring for a car to hang out together, Nissan developed the Round Box. This compact convertible concept car features an interior that feels like a sports bar with gadgets that can be used by a group. It has a large touchscreen, interactive display that the driver and all passengers can use. Its navigation system also allows passengers to search for a restaurant and send directions to it on the driver's display.[9]

CUSTOMIZATION

Marketers can differentiate products by making them customized to an individual. As companies have grown proficient at gathering information about individual customers and business partners (suppliers, distributors, retailers), and as their factories are being designed more flexibly, they have increased their ability to individualize market offerings, messages, and media. **Mass customization** is the ability of a company to meet each customer's requirements—to prepare on a mass basis individually-designed products, services, programs, and communications.[10]

Although Levi's was among the first clothing manufacturers to introduce custom jeans, other players have introduced mass customization into other markets. About 60 percent of the 40,000 Minis that BMW sells in the United States each year are customized.[11] Lego has embraced mass customization from the start.

Lego—In a sense, Lego of Billund, Denmark, has always been mass customized. Every child who has ever had a set of the most basic Legos has built his or her own unique and amazing creations, brick by plastic brick. However, in 2005, Lego set up The Lego Factory, which, as it says on the company Web site, "lets you design, share, and build your very own custom Lego products." Using Lego's freely downloadable Digital Designer Software, customers can create any structure. The creations can exist—and be shared with other enthusiasts—solely online or, if customers want to build it, the software tabulates the pieces required and sends an order to Lego's Enfield, Connecticut, warehouse. The employees there put all the pieces into a box and send it off. Not only do Lego Factory customers have the pride of building their own creations, but they can also earn royalties if Lego decides the design is good enough to put in its own catalog. Some of the most creative models: a rendering of the Danish parliament building and of M.C. Escher's *Another World.* And in 2006, The Lego Factory initiated a design competition in which eight contestants compete to be profiled on the Lego Factory Web site along with their creations.[12]

PERFORMANCE QUALITY

Most products are established at one of four performance levels: low, average, high, or superior. **Performance quality** is the level at which the product's primary characteristics operate. Firms should not necessarily design the highest performance level possible. The manufacturer must design a performance level appropriate to the target market and competitors' performance levels. A company must also manage performance quality through time. Continuously improving the product can produce the high returns and market share. Lowering quality in an attempt to cut costs often has dire consequences.

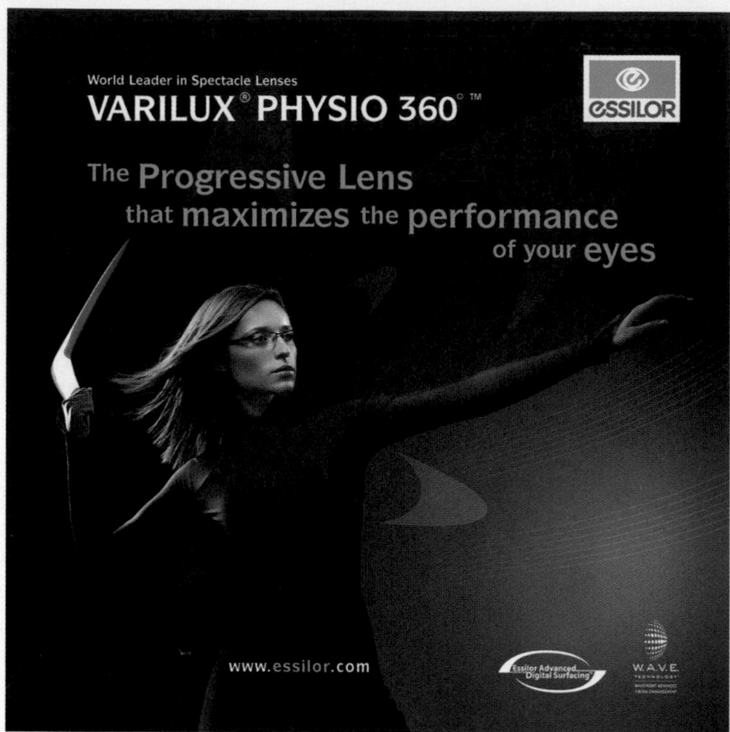
World Leader in Spectacle Lenses
VARILUX® PHYSIO 360° ™
ESSILOR
The Progressive Lens
that maximizes the performance
of your eyes
www.essilor.com
Essilor Advanced Digital Surfacing
W.A.V.E.

As part of its performance quality, Essilor introduced Varilux Physio 360°, the first progressive lens to use technology that was used in laser surgery and advanced astronomy for sharper vision and great looks.

Essilor—Lens maker, Essilor, is continuously improving on its product offerings. It introduced a new lens called Varilux Physio 360° in Singapore in 2007, targeted at the well-heeled graying population. This state-of-the-art progressive lens is the first to use Waterfront Advanced Vision Enhancement (WAVE) technology to offer high-resolution vision. WAVE technology is used in laser surgery and advanced astronomy. Essilor applies this technology to its lens by reshaping the entire beam of light passing through a lens. This eliminates irregularities entering the pupil, giving the wearer high resolution images and better vision. For far distance vision, there is enhanced contrast. For intermediate vision, the new lens offers wider vision area and thus enables easier focus when working on the computer. For handling near tasks, the lens allows comfortable posture. Together, sharper vision is achieved while enhancing the looks of the wearer. These benefits are sought by its target market of an aging population with high discretionary income.

CONFORMANCE QUALITY

Buyers expect products to have a high **conformance quality**, which is the degree to which all the produced units are identical and meet the promised specifications. Suppose a Porsche 911 is designed to accelerate to 150 kilometers per hour within 10 seconds. If every Porsche 911 coming off the assembly line does this, the model is said to have high conformance quality. The problem with low conformance quality is that the product will disappoint some buyers.

DURABILITY

Durability, a measure of the product's expected operating life under natural or stressful conditions, is a valued attribute for certain products. Buyers will generally pay more for vehicles and kitchen appliances that have a reputation for being long-lasting. However, this rule is subject to some qualifications. The extra price must not be excessive. Further, the product must not be subject to rapid technological obsolescence, as is the case with personal computers and video cameras.

RELIABILITY

Buyers normally will pay a premium for more reliable products. **Reliability** is a measure of the probability that a product will not malfunction or fail within a specified time period. National, which manufactures major home appliances, has an outstanding reputation for creating reliable appliances. "Breakthrough Marketing: Toyota" describes how that company has excelled at making and selling high-quality, dependable automobiles.

REPAIRABILITY

Repairability is a measure of the ease of fixing a product when it malfunctions or fails. Ideal repairability would exist if users could fix the product themselves with little cost in money or time. Some products include a diagnostic feature that allows service people to correct a problem over the telephone or advise the user how to correct it. Many computer hardware and software companies offer technical support over the phone, by fax or email, or by real-time "chat" online.

BREAKTHROUGH • MARKETING

TOYOTA

Toyota may have gotten its start in automaking by being a fast follower, but it is now the innovator. In 1936, Toyota admitted following Chrysler's landmark Airflow and patterning its engine after a 1933 Chevrolet engine. But by 2000, when it introduced the first hybrid electric-gasoline car, the Prius, Toyota was the leader. In 2002, when the second-generation Prius hit showrooms, dealers received 10,000 orders before the car was even available; GM followed with an announcement that it would enter the hybrid market with models of its own.

Toyota offers a full line of cars for the U.S. market, from family sedans to sport utility vehicles to trucks to minivans. Toyota also has products for different price points, from lower-cost Scions to mid-priced Camrys to the luxury Lexus. Designing these different products means listening to different customers, building the cars they want, and then crafting the marketing to reinforce each make's image. For example, Toyota spent four years carefully listening to teens before launching the Scion for first-time car buyers. It learned, for instance, that Scion's target age group of 16- to 21-year-olds wanted personalization. To meet that preference, Toyota builds the car "mono-spec" at the factory with just one well-equipped trim level but lets customers at dealerships choose from over 40 customization elements, from stereo components to wheels and even floor mats. Toyota markets the Scion at music events and will have showrooms where "young people feel comfortable hanging out and not a place where they just go stare at a car," said Scion vice president Jim Letz.

In contrast, Toyota's marketing strategy for the Lexus line focuses on perfection. The tagline for the global strategy is "Passionate Pursuit of Perfection." Dealerships offer white-glove treatment. Toyota markets Lexus globally and understands that each country defines perfection differently. In the United States, for example, perfection and luxury mean comfort, size, and dependability. In Europe, luxury means attention to detail and brand heritage. Therefore, although the core of Lexus marketing is similar (a consistent Lexus visual vocabulary, logo, font, and overall communication), the advertising varies by country.

A big reason behind Toyota's success is its manufacturing. Toyota's combination of manufacturing speed and flexibility is world class. It is the master of lean manufacturing and continuous improvement. Its plants can make as many as eight different models at the same time, which brings Toyota huge increases in productivity and market responsiveness. And it relentlessly innovates. A typical Toyota assembly line makes thousands of operational changes in the course of a single year. Toyota employees see their purpose as threefold: making cars, making cars better, and teaching everyone how to make cars better. The company encourages problem

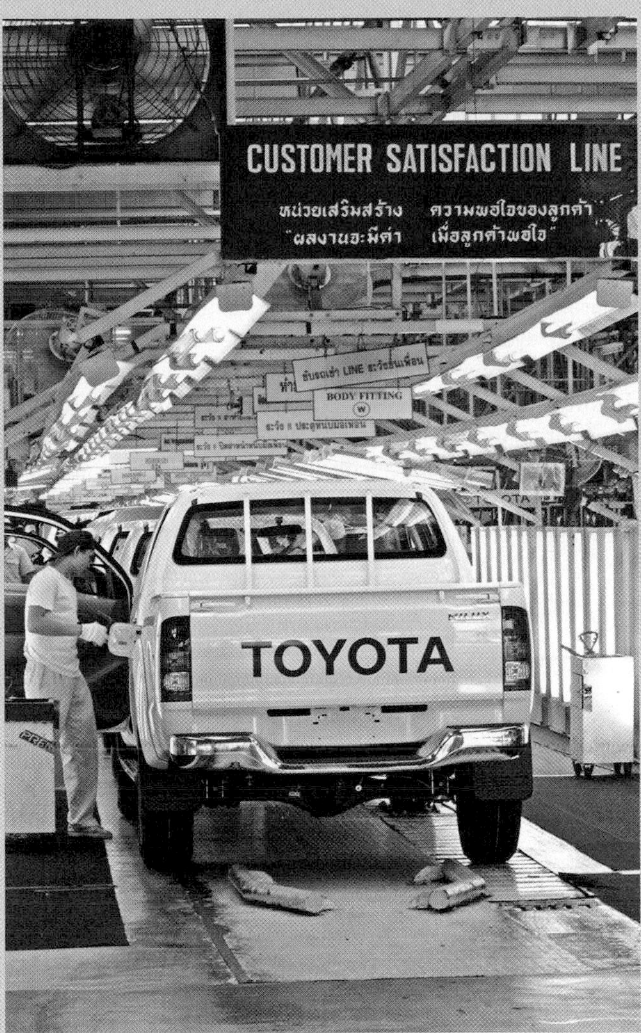

Toyota's product strategy is built on innovation and agility and has recently vaulted the firm into the number-one spot in the industry for the first time.

solving, always looking to improve the process by which it improves all other processes.

Toyota is integrating its assembly plants around the world into a single giant network. The plants will customize cars for local markets and be able to shift production quickly to satisfy any surges in demand from markets worldwide. With a manufacturing network, Toyota can build a wide variety of models much more inexpensively. That means Toyota will be able to fill market niches as they emerge without building whole new assembly operations. "If there's a market or market segment where they aren't present, they go there," said Tatsuo Yoshida, auto analyst at Deutsche Securities Ltd. And with consumers being increasingly fickle about what they want in a car, such market agility gives Toyota a huge competitive edge.

(Continued ...)

BREAKTHROUGH • MARKETING

(Continued ...)

In 2006, Toyota earned over $11 billion—more than all other major automakers *combined*. It now produces 50 percent more automobiles than it did in 2001, and 60 percent of the cars Toyota sells in North America are made here. In the first quarter of 2007, it edged past General Motors to become the world's largest carmaker, and its market cap of $110 billion is more than that of GM, Ford, and DaimlerChrysler combined. In 2007, Toyota reported a 13.3 percent growth in revenue despite the severe business environment. It attributed this to its growth strategy of utilizing every opportunity across the full product line-up and all regions. This includes a plug-in hybrid car which Toyota announced it will introduce by 2010. As part of its environmental movement, Toyota is also developing a new hybrid-electric car specifically for its Lexus division.

With such lofty ambitions, Toyota is targeting China as a key market of the future. Preoccupied with its efforts in the U.S., Toyota is a late entrant to China. However, it has surpassed Nissan and Honda as the top-selling Japanese car there. In 2007, it sold over 430,000 cars. Although the Chinese government supports clean, fuel-efficient vehicles, many Japanese manufacturers are hesitant to take leading technologies to China for fear their intellectual property will be stolen. And Chinese consumers aren't exactly clamoring for higher-priced environmentally-friendly cars. It's reported that of the 430,000 hybrids made, less than 400 were manufactured in the China plant. Despite this, Toyota announced boldly that it will manufacture its Camry-hybrid to China by 2010.

Sources: Martin Zimmerman, "Toyota's First Quarter Global Sales Beat GM's Preliminary Numbers." *Los Angeles Times*, April 24, 2007; Charles Fishman, "No Satisfaction at Toyota." *Fast Company*, December 2006–January 2007, pp. 82–90; Stuart F. Brown, "Toyota's Global Body Shop." *Fortune*, February 9, 2004, p. 120; James B. Treece, "Ford Down; Toyota Aims for No. 1," *Automotive News*, February 2, 2004, p.1; Brian Bemner and Chester Dawson, "Can Anything Stop Toyota?" *BusinessWeek*, November 17, 2003, pp. 114–22; "Toyota Announces Record Third Quarter Operating Results." *JCN Newswires*, February 5, 2008; Micheline Maynard, "Toyota Will Offer a Plug-In Hybrid by 2010." *New York Times*, January 14, 2008; "Toyota Camry Hybrids in China." *Grayline*, July 1, 2008; and <www.toyota.com.>

STYLE

Style describes the product's look and feel to the buyer. Car buyers pay a premium for Jaguars because of their extraordinary look. Aesthetics play a key role in such brands as Absolut vodka, Apple computers, Montblanc pens, Samsung cell phones, and Harley-Davidson motorcycles.[13] Style has the advantage of creating distinctiveness that is difficult to copy. On the negative side, strong style does not always mean high performance. A car may look sensational but spend a lot of time in the repair shop.

In Asia, there is a widespread interest in and demand for aesthetic products—i.e., those that have an attractive look, touch, feel, and attention to detail. In particular, three aesthetic principles may be useful in guiding style decisions in Asia:[14]

1. ***Complexity and decoration*** — Asians love the display of multiple forms, shapes, and colors. This feature is most pronounced in Chinese, Thai, Malay, and Indonesian aesthetics.
2. ***Balancing various aesthetic elements*** — Harmony in aesthetic expression is viewed as a particularly important goal.
3. ***Naturalism*** — In China, symbols and displays of natural objects such as mountains, rivers, dragons, and phoenixes are frequently found in packaging, advertising, and on logos (e.g., Dragonair and Tiger Beer). In Japan, gardens, trees, and flowers are objects of aesthetic symbolism.

Under style differentiation, packaging is a major weapon, especially in food products, cosmetics, toiletries, and small consumer appliances. The package provides the buyer's first encounter with the product and is capable of either turning the buyer on or off.

Knorr—When Knorr launched its bouillon cubes in Vietnam, its Thai-made product packaging had Vietnamese and English-language copy even though most Vietnamese did not speak English at that time. It felt that too much local packaging would discourage consumers who equate "quality" with "foreign," while an entirely foreign product might also be rejected as one that has been "dumped" on the market.

Design

As competition intensifies, design offers a potent way to differentiate and position a company's products and services.[15] In increasingly fast-paced markets, price and technology are not enough. Design is the factor that will often give a company its competitive edge. **Design** is the totality of features that affects how a product looks and functions in terms of customer requirements.

Design is particularly important in making and marketing retail services, apparel, packaged goods, and durable equipment. All the qualities we have discussed are design parameters. The designer has to figure out how much to invest in form, feature development, performance, conformance, durability, reliability, repairability, and style. To the company, a well-designed product is one that is easy to manufacture and distribute. To the customer, a well-designed product is one that is pleasant to look at and easy to open, install, use, repair, and dispose of. The designer has to take all these factors into account.

The arguments for good design are particularly compelling for smaller consumer products companies and start-ups that do not have big advertising dollars. Indeed, most of the creative products in Japanese entertainment and fashion are started by small businesses that license their work to large companies. Here is a small U.S. business that has leveraged Japanese pop culture in its design for profit:

Ugly Dolls—This is a line of $30 fabric dolls cocreated by David Horvath, an American commercial artist who grew up playing with Japanese video games and robot dolls that his ad executive father brought home from Japan. These whimsical figures were inspired by Horvath's early look at Japanese cartoons, toys, and comics. They appeal to American teens who are fans of Japanese pop culture such as ***anime***, the distinctive Japanese-style cartoons with wide-eyed characters. Some 60,000 Ugly Toys are now sold a month in stores from Barneys New York to specialized Asian culture boutiques like Giant Robot. "We get people from America looking for Ugly Dolls because they think it's this cool thing from Japan," Horvath says. "This cool thing is from Brooklyn."[16]

As the Ugly Dolls example illustrates, Japanese design and style are being exported to the West.[17] *Anime* is a growing trend in the U.S., influencing how toys, cartoons, comics, video games, and movies look. Japanese kids have collected small dolls for years, even buying them in vending machines. Now, American versions like Disney's Cuties and Mattel's Shorties, inspired by Japanese animation, are in. Toyota, for example, had a hit among younger drivers with its Scion xB in the U.S. and Japan because of its distinctly boxy wagon. In the luxury goods market, Burberry and Bottega Veneta have turned to Japan as a source of inspiration. Juha Christensen, president of mobile and devices at software maker, Macromedia, always stops by Akihabara, Tokyo's electronics district, on his business trips to Japan. "Japan is a great place to look at to find the trends we will see here in two to three years," says Christensen.

Japan out-spends many other industrial countries on design. Forced to compete with lower-cost products from China and Korea, Japanese designers have differentiated their products by adding a bigger element of design and fashion. Sony's view is that designers are like lighthouse keepers for the engineer, who is like a ship. The engineer can go anywhere with his technology but does not know which direction to take. Hence, the lighthouse keeper must guide the ships. Together with Korea's Samsung, Sony has won the Industrial Design Excellence Awards (IDEA) for making design the heart of their product-development strategies. "Marketing Insight: Design as a Powerful Marketing Tool" describes some successes and failures in design.

Services Differentiation

When the physical product cannot easily be differentiated, the key to competitive success may lie in adding valued services and improving their quality. The main service differentiators are ordering ease, delivery, installation, customer training, customer consulting, and maintenance and repair.

MARKETING INSIGHT • DESIGN AS A POWERFUL MARKETING TOOL

Manufacturers, service providers, and retailers seek new designs to create differentiation and establish a more complete connection with consumers. Holistic marketers recognize the emotional power of design and the importance to consumers of how things look and feel. Design is now more fully integrated into the marketing management process. Here are some examples:

- When **Samsung**'s CEO Jong-Yong Yun saw that its products did not stand out in design compared to Sony's, he started to emphasize design. Samsung hired U.S. design firm IDEO to help develop a computer monitor. It also set up the Innovative Design Lab of Samsung (IDS), an in-house school where promising designers can study under experts from the Art Center College of Design, one of the top U.S. design schools. Samsung designers are also dispatched to Egypt, India, Paris, Frankfurt, New York, and Washington to tour museums, visit icons of modern architecture, and explore ruins. Some spend a few months at fashion houses, cosmetics specialists, and design consultancies to stay current with what is happening in other industries. Samsung's designers have also broken through the barrier of Korea's traditional Confucian hierarchies. Located close to the headquarters, Samsung's design center has no dress code, younger staffers can dye their hair green or pink, and everyone is encouraged to speak up and challenge their superiors.
- Sweden's **IKEA** has become a top furniture retailer in part through its ability to design and manufacture inexpensive furniture that doesn't seem cheap.
- Another Scandinavian company, Finland's **Nokia,** is credited with taking a little black blob with tiny buttons and turning it into an object of desire. Nokia was the first to introduce user-changeable covers for cell phones; the first to have elliptical-shaped, soft, and friendly forms; and the first with big screens. In the early 1990s, Nokia controlled only 12 percent of the global market for cell phones. Today, it is the world leader in handsets, with 38 percent of the market.

With an increasingly visually-oriented culture, translating brand meaning and positioning through design is critical. "In a crowded marketplace," writes Virginia Postrel in *The Substance of Style*, "aesthetics is often the only way to make a product stand out." Design can shift consumer perceptions to make brand experiences more rewarding. Consider the lengths Boeing went to make its 777 airplane seem roomier and more comfortable. Raised center bins, side luggage bins, divider panels, gently arched ceilings, and raised seats make the aircraft interior seem bigger. As one design engineer noted, "If we do our jobs, people don't realize what we have done. They just say they feel more comfortable."

Designers sometimes put a human face—literally—on their products. The Porsche Boxster's bulges and curves can be seen as suggestive of muscle; the Apple iMac was thought by one designer to be "a head stuck to a body via a long skinny arm"; and Microsoft's optical mouse can be seen as an outstretched hand. When Frog Design set out to make a Disney cordless phone for kids, it wanted the design to live up to the famed Disney imagery. After exhaustive study, Frog defined the composite elements of a Disney character and applied it to the phone. The eyes were interpreted in terms of the LCD screen and were made as big as possible; the torso was interpreted in terms of the housing of the phone and was S-shaped, with a roundness in the top front and bottom back; and the feet were interpreted in terms of the base and charger stand, which used built-up plastic to emulate a sock pushed up around an ankle.

A bad design can also ruin a product's prospects. Sony's e-Villa Internet appliance was intended to allow consumers to have Internet access from their kitchen. But at nearly 14.5 kilograms and 40 centimeters, the mammoth product was so awkward and heavy that the owner's manual recommended customers use their legs, not their back, to pick it up. The product was eventually withdrawn after three months.

Sources: Frank Nuovo, "A Call for Fashion." *Fast Company*, June 2004, p. 52; Bobbie Gossage, "Strategies: Designing Success." *Inc. Magazine*, May 2004, pp. 27–29; Jim Hopkins, "When the Devil is in the Design." *USA Today*, December 31, 2001, p. 3B; J. Lynn Lunsford and Daniel Michaels, "Masters of Illusion." *Wall Street Journal*, November 25, 2002, pp. B1, B5; Jerome Kathman, "Building Leadership Brands By Design." *Brandweek*, December 1, 2003, p. 20; Bob Parks, "Deconstructing Cute." *Business 2.0*, December 2002/January 2003, pp. 47–50; Lisa Margonelli, "How IKEA Designs Its Sexy Price Tags." *Business 2.0*, October 2002, pp. 106–112; David Rocks, and Moon Ihlwan, "Samsung Design." *BusinessWeek*, November 29, 2004, pp. 44–49.

ORDERING EASE

Ordering ease refers to how easy it is for the customer to place an order with the company. Baxter Healthcare has eased the ordering process by supplying hospitals with computer terminals through which they send orders directly to Baxter. Many banks now provide home banking software to help customers get information and do transactions more efficiently. Consumers are now able to order and receive groceries without going to the supermarket.

DELIVERY

Delivery refers to how well the product or service is delivered to the customer. It includes speed, accuracy, and care attending the delivery process. Today's customers have grown to expect delivery speed: pizza delivered in one-half hour, film developed in one hour, eyeglasses made in one hour, cars lubricated in 15 minutes. Giordano has a computerized *Quick Response System* (QRS) that links the information systems of its suppliers, manufacturing plants, distribution centers, and retailing outlets.

INSTALLATION

Installation refers to the work done to make a product operational in its planned location. Buyers of heavy equipment expect good installation service. Differentiating at this point in the consumption chain is particularly important for companies with complex products. Ease-of-installation becomes a true selling point, especially when the target market is technology novices.

CUSTOMER TRAINING

Customer training refers to training the customer's employees to use the vendor's equipment properly and efficiently. General Electric not only sells and installs expensive X-ray equipment in hospitals; it also gives extensive training to users of this equipment. McDonald's requires its new franchisees to attend Hamburger University for two weeks to learn how to manage the franchise properly.

CUSTOMER CONSULTING

Customer consulting refers to data, information systems, and advice services that the seller offers to buyers.

Systems consultancy in China—IBM and Hewlett-Packard offer service networks that provide their Asian customers with technical advice and long-term systems consultancy. Hence, IBM and HP have had a considerable head start in more complex sales such as nationwide technology projects initiated by the Chinese government. To their own disadvantage, competitors like Dell lagged in developing such programs in China, choosing to target more tech-savvy Chinese businesses such as China Pacific Insurance which require less consulting assistance.[18]

MAINTENANCE AND REPAIR

Maintenance and repair describes the service program for helping customers keep purchased products in good working order. Hewlett-Packard offers online technical support, or "e-support," for their customers. In the event of a service problem, customers can use various online tools to find a solution. Those aware of the specific problem can search an online database for fixes; those unaware can use diagnostic software that finds the problem and searches the online database for an automatic fix. Customers can also seek online help from a technician.[19]

RETURNS

Although product returns are undoubtedly a nuisance to customers, manufacturers, retailers, and distributors alike, they are also an unavoidable reality of doing business, especially with online purchases. Although the average return rate for online sales is roughly 5 percent, return and exchange policies are estimated to serve as a deterrent for one-third to one-half of online buyers. The cost of processing a return can be two to three times that of an outbound shipment, totaling an average of $30–$35 for items bought on the Internet.

Costco Wholesale Corp.—Costco's ultragenerous return policy was perhaps the cushiest in the retail electronics business. Until recently, a customer could buy an expensive plasma TV, use it indefinitely, and take it back any time. Then he or she could use the refund to buy a newer model—often at a cheaper price. However, what was the customer's gain was Costco's loss. The membership warehouse chain ended up losing "tens of millions of dollars" annually with this policy. In early 2007, Costco cut its return policy for electronics to (a still generous) 90 days in California with a subsequent rollout nationwide. Some customers, who had come to rely on the trust and generosity embodied in Costco's return policy, vowed to shop for electronics elsewhere. Yet, most realized the good times had to come to a halt. To Costco's credit, it is now offering more technical support for installing and operating the electronics it sells; the company had discovered that most returns were due not to problems with the items so much as customers' inability to set up today's very complicated electronic devices. And with the exception of electronics and computers—which now must be returned within six months—all other Costco items can still be returned for any reason at any time.[20]

We can think of product returns in two ways:[21]

- ***Controllable returns*** — These from problems, difficulties, or errors of the seller or customer and can mostly be eliminated with proper strategies and programs by the company or its supply chain partners. Improved handling or storage, better packaging, and improved transportation and forward logistics can eliminate problems before they happen.
- ***Uncontrollable returns*** — These cannot be eliminated by the company in the short-run through any of these means.

One basic returns strategy that companies can adopt is to attempt to eliminate the root causes of controllable returns while at the same time developing processes for handling uncontrollable product returns. The goal of a product return strategy is to have fewer products returned and a higher percentage of returns that can go back into the distribution pipeline to be sold again.

Product and Brand Relationships

Each product can be related to other products.

The Product Hierarchy

The product hierarchy stretches from basic needs to particular items that satisfy those needs. We can identify six levels of the product hierarchy (using life insurance as an example):

1. ***Need family*** — The core need that underlies the existence of a product family. For example, security.
2. ***Product family*** — All the product classes that can satisfy a core need with reasonable effectiveness. For example, savings and income.
3. ***Product class*** — A group of products within the product family recognized as having a certain functional coherence. Also known as product category. For example, financial instruments.
4. ***Product line*** — A group of products within a product class that are closely related because they perform a similar function, are sold to the same customer groups, are marketed through the same outlets or channels, or fall within given price ranges. A product line may be composed of different brands or a single family brand or individual brand that has been line extended. For example, life insurance.
5. ***Product type*** — A group of items within a product line that share one of several possible forms of the product. For example, term life.
6. ***Item (also called stockkeeping unit or product variant)*** — A distinct unit within a brand or product line distinguishable by size, price, appearance, or some other attribute. For example: Prudential renewable term life insurance.

To read about French carmarker Renault and its strategy for pursuing international growth, visit www.pearsoned.co.uk/marketingmanagementeurope.

Product Systems and Mixes

A **product system** is a group of diverse but related items that function in a compatible manner. For example, PalmOne handheld and smartphone product lines come with attachable products including headsets, cameras, keyboards, presentation projectors, e-books, MP3 players, and voice recorders. A **product mix** (also called a **product assortment**) is the set of all products and items a particular seller offers for sale. A product mix consists of various product lines. NEC's product mix consists of communication products and computer products. Panasonic's product lines include digital audiovisual products, cell phones, car navigation equipment, and home appliances. At the National University of Singapore, there are separate academic deans for the medical school, law school, business school, engineering faculty, arts and social science faculty, and computer science school.

A company's product mix has a certain width, length, depth, and consistency. These concepts are illustrated in Table 12.1 for selected Lion consumer products from Japan.

- The **width** of a product mix refers to how many different product lines the company carries. Table 12.1 shows a product-mix width of five lines. (In fact, Lion produces many additional lines.)

Table 12.1 Product-Mix Width and Product-Line Length for Lion Products

	Product-Mix Width				
	Toothpaste	**Shampoo**	**Soaps**	**Laundry Detergents**	**Dishwashing Detergents**
Product Line Length	Clinica	Shokubutsu-Monotari	Shokubutsu-Monogatari	Top	Charmy
	Dentor			Heyaboshi	
	Prime	Soft-in-One	Kireikirei	Blue Dia	
	Hitect	Free & Free Damage Aid		Acron	

- The **length** of a product mix refers to the total number of items in the mix. In Table 12.1, it is 14. We can also talk about the average length of a line. This is obtained by dividing the total length (here 14) by the number of lines (here 5), or an average product length of 2.8.
- The **depth** of a product mix refers to how many variants are offered of each product in the line. If Top laundry detergent comes in two scents (lemon and regular), two formulations (liquid and powder), and two additives (with or without bleach), Top has a depth of eight as there are eight distinct variants. The average depth of a product mix can be calculated by averaging the number of variants within the brand groups.
- The **consistency** of the product mix refers to how closely related the various product lines are in end use, production requirements, distribution channels, or some other way. Lion's product lines are consistent insofar as they are consumer goods that go through the same distribution channels. The lines are less consistent insofar as they perform different functions for buyers.

These four product-mix dimensions permit the company to expand its business in four ways. It can add new product lines, thus widening its product mix. It can lengthen each product line. It can add more product variants to each product and deepen its product mix. Finally, a company can pursue more product-line consistency. To make these product and brand decisions, it is useful to conduct product-line analysis.

Product-Line Analysis

In offering a product line, companies normally develop a basic platform and modules that can be added to meet different customer requirements. Car manufacturers build their cars around a basic platform. Homebuilders show a model home to which additional features can be added. This modular approach enables the company to offer variety while lowering production costs.

Product-line managers need to know the sales and profits of each item in their line to determine which items to build, maintain, harvest, or divest.[22] They also need to understand each product line's market profile.

SALES AND PROFITS

Figure 12.3 shows a sales and profit report for a five-item product line. The first item accounts for 50 percent of total sales and 30 percent of total profits. The first two items account for 80 percent of total sales and 60 percent of total profits. If these two items were suddenly hurt by a competitor, the line's sales and profitability could collapse. These items must be carefully monitored and protected. At the other end, the last item delivers only 5 percent of the product line's sales and profits. The product-line manager may consider dropping this item unless it has strong growth potential.

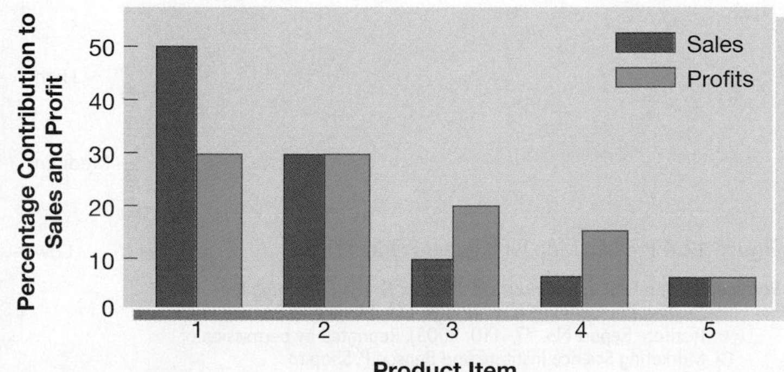

Figure 12.3 Product-Item Contributions to a Product Line's Total Sales and Profits

Every company's product portfolio contains products with different margins. Supermarkets make almost no margin on bread and milk; reasonable margins on canned and frozen foods; and even better margins on flowers, ethnic food lines, and freshly baked goods. A local telephone company makes different margins on its core telephone service, call waiting, caller ID, and voice mail.

A company can classify its products into four types that yield different gross margins, depending on sales volume and promotion. To illustrate with laptop computers:

- ***Core products*** — Basic laptop computers that produce high sales volume and are heavily promoted but with low margins because they are viewed as undifferentiated commodities.
- ***Staples*** — Items with lower sales volume and no promotion, such as faster CPUs or bigger memories. These yield a somewhat higher margin.
- ***Specialties*** — Items with lower sales volume but which might be highly promoted, such as digital movie-making equipment; or might generate income for services, such as personal delivery, installation, or onsite training.
- ***Convenience items*** — Peripheral items that sell in high volume but receive less promotion, such as computer monitors, printers, upscale video or sound cards, and software. Consumers tend to buy them where they buy the original equipment because it is more convenient than making further shopping trips. These items can carry higher margins.

The main point is that companies should recognize that these items differ in their potential for being priced higher or advertised more as ways to increase their sales, margins, or both.[23]

MARKET PROFILE

The product-line manager must review how the line is positioned against competitors' lines. Consider paper company X with a paperboard product line.[24] Two paperboard attributes are weight and finish quality. Paper weight is usually offered at standard levels of 90, 120, 150, and 180 weight. Finish quality is offered at low, medium, and high levels. Figure 12.4 shows the location of the various product-line items of company X and four competitors, A, B, C, and D. Competitor A sells two product items in the extra-high weight class ranging from medium to low finish quality. Competitor B sells four items that vary in weight and finish quality. Competitor C sells three items in which the greater the weight, the greater the finish quality. Competitor D sells three items, all lightweight but varying in finish quality. Company X offers three items that vary in weight and finish quality.

The product map shows which competitors' items are competing against company X's items. For example, company X's low-weight, medium-quality paper competes against competitor D's and B's papers, but its high-weight, medium-quality paper has no direct competitor. The map also reveals possible locations for new items. No manufacturer offers a high-weight, low-quality paper. If company X estimates a strong unmet demand and can produce and price this paper at low cost, it could consider adding this item to its line.

Another benefit of product mapping is that it identifies market segments. Figure 12.4 shows the types of paper, by weight and quality, preferred by the general printing industry, the point-of-purchase display industry, and the office-supply industry. The map shows that

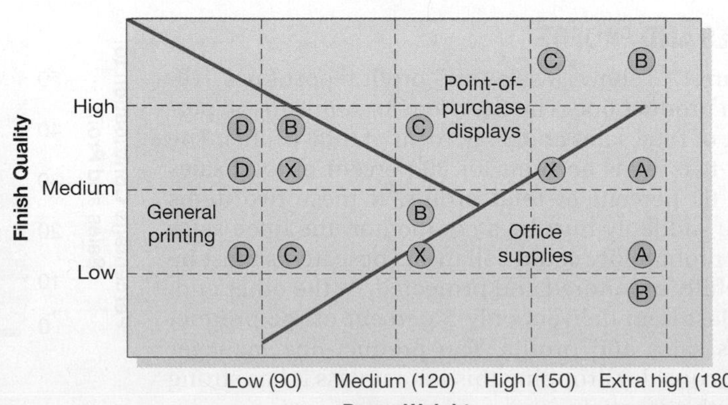

Figure 12.4 Product Map for a Paper-Product Line

Source: Benson P. Shapiro, *Industrial Product Policy: Managing the Existing Product Line*, (Cambridge, MA: Marketing Science Institute Report No. 77–110, 2003). Reprinted by permission of Marketing Science Institute and Benson P. Shapiro.

company X is well positioned to serve the needs of the general printing industry but is less effective in serving the other two industries.

Product-line analysis provides information for two key decision areas—product-line length and product-mix pricing.

Product-Line Length

Company objectives influence product-line length. One objective is to create a product line to induce upselling: thus Nissan would like to move customers up from the Sunny to Cefiro to Infiniti. A different objective is to create a product line that facilitates cross-selling: Hewlett-Packard sells printers as well as computers. Still another objective is to create a product line that protects against economic ups and downs: Electrolux offers white goods such as refrigerators, dishwashers, and vacuum cleaners under different brand names in the discount, middle market, and premium segments, in part in case the economy moves up or down.[25] Companies seeking high market share and market growth will generally carry longer product lines. Companies that emphasize high profitability will carry shorter lines consisting of carefully chosen items.

Product lines tend to lengthen over time. Excess manufacturing capacity puts pressure on the product-line manager to develop new items. The sales force and distributors also pressure the company for a more complete product line to satisfy customers. But as items are added, costs rise: design and engineering costs, inventory-carrying costs, manufacturing-changeover costs, order-processing costs, transportation costs, and new-item promotional costs. Eventually, someone calls a halt: Top management may stop development because of insufficient funds or manufacturing capacity. The controller may call for a study of money-losing items. A pattern of product-line growth followed by massive pruning may repeat itself many times. Increasingly, consumers are growing weary of dense product lines, over-extended brands, and feature-laden products (see "Marketing Insight: When Less Is More").

A company lengthens its product line in two ways: by line stretching and line filling.

LINE STRETCHING

Every company's product line covers a certain part of the total possible range. For example, BMW automobiles are located in the upper price range of the automobile market. **Line stretching** occurs when a company lengthens its product line beyond its current range. The company can stretch its line down-market, up-market, or both ways.

Down-Market Stretch

A company may want to introduce a lower-priced line for any of three reasons:

1. The company may notice strong growth opportunities as mass retailers such as Wal-Mart, Carrefour, and others attract a growing number of shoppers who want value-priced goods.
2. The company may wish to tie up lower-end competitors who might otherwise try to move up-market. If the company has been attacked by a low-end competitor, it often decides to counterattack by entering the low end of the market. Mercedes introduced the A-Class model after Toyota entered the higher end with the Lexus.
3. The company may find that its market is stagnating or declining. Seiko and Citizen watches introduced lower-end watches. Seiko introduced Alba in Asia and the Pulsar in the U.S., while Citizen offered Adec.

A company faces a number of naming choices in deciding to move down-market. Sony, for example, faced three choices:

1. Use the name Sony on all of its offerings. (Sony did this.)
2. Introduce lower-priced offerings using a subbrand name, such as Sony Value Line. The risks are that the Sony name loses some of its quality image and that some Sony buyers might switch to the lower-priced offerings.
3. Introduce the lower-priced offerings under a different name, without mentioning Sony; but Sony would have to spend a lot of money to build up the new brand name, and the

MARKETING INSIGHT • WHEN LESS IS MORE

Although many consumers find the notion of having more choices appealing, the reality is that consumers can sometimes be overwhelmed by the choices involved. With thousands of new products introduced each year, consumers find it harder and harder to successfully navigate through store aisles. One study found that the average shopper spent 40 seconds or more in the supermarket soda aisle, compared to 25 seconds six or seven years ago. Another research study showed that although consumers expressed greater interest in shopping with a larger assortment of 24 different flavored jams than a smaller assortment of 6, they were 10 times more likely to actually make a selection with the smaller assortment.

Marketers are learning through sometimes painful experience that product lines can get too long, or products can become just too complicated.

Although consumers with well-defined preferences may benefit from more differentiated products that offer specific benefits to better suit their needs, too much product choice may be a source of frustration, confusion, and regret for other consumers. Product proliferation has another downside. Exposing the customer to constant product changes and introductions may nudge them into reconsidering their choices, resulting in their switching to a competitor's product as a result.

And not all the new choices may be winners anyway, as Nestlé found out with its KitKat bars, among the best-selling candy bars in the United Kingdom since they were invented there in the 1930s. To increase sales in 2004, the company rolled out a vast array of new flavors. The summer saw the launch of strawberries and cream, passion fruit and mango, and red berry versions; with winter came Christmas pudding, tiramisu (with real wine and marscapone), and low-carb versions. The new flavors were a disaster—the tastes were too sweet and unusual for many—and even worse, some consumers could not find the classic KitKat bars among all the new varieties. An ill-timed switch from the classic slogan, "Have a Break, Have a KitKat," did not help, and sales dropped 18 percent as a result. The new flavors were then discontinued.

Smart marketers are also realizing that it's not just the product lines that are making consumer heads spin—many products themselves are just too complicated for the average consumer. Royal Philips Electronics learned its lesson when the company asked 100 top managers to take various Philips electronic products home one weekend and see whether they could make them work. The number of executives who returned frustrated and angry spoke volumes about the challenges the ordinary consumer faced. A Yankee Group research study in 2004 reinforces this fact: almost a third of all home-networking products sold that year were returned because the consumer could not get them to work; almost half of potential digital camera buyers were delaying their purchase because they thought the products were too complicated; and about a quarter of consumers thought they already owned an HDTV (they did not). Philips launched an initiative in September 2004 with a goal to make technology simpler, backed by a $100 million ad campaign "Sense and Simplicity."

Sources: Deborah Ball, "Flavor Experiment for KitKat Leaves Nestlé with a Bad Taste." *Wall Street Journal*, July 6, 2006; Barry Schwartz, *The Paradox of Choice: Why More Is Less*, (New York: Harper Collins Ecco, 2004); Frisco Endt, "It Is Rocket Science." *Newsweek*, October 18, 2004, p. E8; Alexander Chernev, "When More Is Less and Less Is More: The Role of Ideal Point Availability and Assortment in Choice." *Journal of Consumer Research*, September 2003, 30, pp. 170–183; Sheena S. Iyengar and Mark R. Lepper, "When Choice Is Demotivating: Can One Desire Too Much of a Good Thing?" *Journal of Personality and Social Psychology*, December 2000, 79(6), pp. 995–1006; Ravi Dhar, "Consumer Preference for a No-Choice Option." *Journal of Consumer Research*, September 1997, 27, pp. 233–248.

mass merchants may not even accept a brand that lacks the Sony name. Sony did this by acquiring Aiwa.

Moving down-market carries risks. Kodak introduced Kodak Funtime film to counter lower-priced brands, but it did not price Kodak Funtime low enough to match the lower-priced film. It also found some of its regular customers buying Funtime, so it was cannibalizing its core brand. It withdrew the product. In contrast, Mercedes successfully introduced its C-Class cars at $30,000 without injuring its ability to sell other Mercedes cars for $100,000 and up. Below are two Asian examples:

> **Cathay Pacific and Singapore Airlines**—Both Cathay Pacific and Singapore Airlines have regional carriers (Dragonair and SilkAir respectively). A low-cost local carrier is better equipped than its stately long-haul parent to pioneer short-haul routes into Asia's emerging markets. Although both have business class sections, neither has first class. Dragonair gives Cathay Pacific a chance to build a local brand distinct from its parent. One of its selling points is the poor safety record of Chinese airlines which ply domestic routes in the mainland. Dragonair serves routes from Hong Kong to various Chinese cities. Singapore Airlines also has a stake in a budget airline, Tiger Airways, that offers a single class and no-frills service to meet the threat of discount airlines like Malaysia's AirAsia.

Up-Market Stretch

Companies may wish to enter the high end of the market for more growth, higher margins, or simply to position themselves as full-line manufacturers. Many markets have spawned surprising upscale segments: Starbucks in coffee, Häagen-Dazs in ice cream, and Evian in bottled water. The leading Japanese auto companies have each introduced an upscale automobile: Toyota's Lexus, Nissan's Infiniti, and Honda's Acura. Note that they invented entirely new names rather than using or including their own names, because consumers may not have given the brand "permission" to stretch upward at the time when those different lines where introduced.

Other companies have included their own name in moving up-market. General Electric introduced the GE Profile brand for its large appliance offerings in the upscale market. Some brands have used modifiers to signal a noticeable, although presumably not dramatic, quality improvement, such as Ultra Dry Pampers and Extra Strength Tylenol.

Two-Way Stretch

Companies serving the middle market might decide to stretch their line in both directions. Toyota has a two-way stretch of its product line. Alongside its midrange Corolla model, it added the Camry to serve the upper end of the car market, and the Vios to serve the compact car market. It also introduced the Lexus as a premium offering for the luxury car segment. Thus the Lexus aims to attract top managers; the Camry, the middle managers; the Corolla, junior managers; and the Vios, first-time car buyers with low budgets. The major risk with this strategy is that some car buyers will trade down to lower-priced models if they perceive few differences between the models. But it is still better for Toyota to capture its customers who move downward than to lose them to competitors. In addition, to minimize its association with Toyota, and hence the risks of cannibalization, Lexus was not launched under the Toyota name. It also has its own distribution arrangements apart from the other Toyota models.

LINE FILLING

A product line can also be lengthened by adding more items within the present range. There are several motives for *line filling*: reaching for incremental profits, trying to satisfy dealers who complain about lost sales because of missing items in the line, trying to utilize excess capacity, trying to be the leading full-line company, and trying to plug holes to keep out competitors.

> **Hyundai and Kia**—Korean auto-maker Hyundai and its sister company, Kia, have launched an extensive line filling strategy to appeal to more buyers in the U.S. Kia, which produced two models in 1999, plans to have at least 11 models by the end of 2010. The brand already has such upscale wheels as the Amanti sedan and four-wheel-drive Sorento SUV in showrooms. Hyundai unleashed its "24/7" plan with the introduction of seven models over 24 months, including the lowest- and highest-end sedans in its lineup. It also has a new version of its flagship Sonata midsize sedan, which it considers to be competitive against the Honda Accord and Toyota Camry. Both divisions say their buyer bases are moving upscale along with their product lines. "In 2000, the average Kia buyer paid $12,000. Five years later, the average sale is more than $20,000," says Peter Butterfield, CEO of Kia Motors America. The brands are reaching more customers, such as former BMW and Lexus owners.[26]

Line filling is overdone if it results in self-cannibalization and customer confusion. The company needs to differentiate each item in the consumer's mind. Each item should possess a *just-noticeable difference.* According to Weber's law, customers are more attuned to relative than to absolute difference.[27] They will perceive the difference between boards 1 and 2 meters long but not between boards 29 and 30 centimeters long. The company should also check that the proposed item meets a market need and is not being added simply to satisfy an internal need.

LINE MODERNIZATION, FEATURING, AND PRUNING

Product lines need to be modernized. A company's machine tools might have a 1970s look and lose out to newer-styled competitors' lines. The issue is whether to overhaul the line piecemeal or all at once. A piecemeal approach allows the company to see how customers and dealers take to the new style. It is also less draining on the company's cash flow, but it allows competitors to see changes and to start redesigning their own lines.

In rapidly changing product markets, modernization is continuous. Companies plan improvements to encourage customer migration to higher-valued, higher-priced items. Microprocessor companies such as Intel and software companies such as Microsoft, continually introduce more advanced versions of their products. A major issue is timing improvements so they do not appear too early (damaging sales of the current line) or too late (after the competition has established a strong reputation for more advanced equipment).

The product-line manager typically selects one or a few items in the line to feature. Toshiba may announce a special low-priced washing machine to attract customers. At other times, managers will feature a high-end item to lend prestige to the product line. Sometimes a company finds one end of its line selling well and the other end selling poorly. The company may try to boost demand for the slower sellers, especially if they are produced in a factory that is idled by lack of demand; but it could be counter-argued that the company should promote items that sell well rather than try to prop up weak items.

Product-line managers must periodically review the line for deadwood that is depressing profits. The weak items can be identified through sales and cost analysis. Pruning is also done when the company is short of production capacity. Companies typically shorten their product lines in periods of tight demand and lengthen their lines in periods of slow demand.

> **Haier**—In an attempt to reward creativity, Haier appears to have gone overboard. It allowed every engineer the freedom to design and build his own products. In 2004, Haier had 96 products in 15,100 specifications, including a fridge that pickles Korean *kimchee* cabbage and a washing machine that also cleans sweet potatoes. Most of these variants add more to production costs and complexity than sales. Haier also moved beyond producing white goods to computers, cell phones, and even interior design and pharmaceuticals. It appears that product-line pruning is needed.[28]

In 1999, Unilever announced its "Path to Growth" program designed to get the most value from its brand portfolio by eliminating three-quarters of its 1,600 distinct brands by 2003.[29] More than 90 percent of its profits came from just 400 brands, prompting Unilever cochairman Niall FitzGerald to liken the brand reduction to weeding a garden, so "the light and air get in to the blooms which are likely to grow the best." The company retained global brands such as Lipton, as well as regional brands and "local jewels" such as Persil, the leading detergent in the United Kingdom. In Asia, the leading brands Unilever carries are Knorr, Lipton, Mazola, Skippy, and Best Foods. Unilever extended its Knorr brand portfolio to include Asian flavors such as Thai *tom yam, tepung goring* (Indian spices for frying), *tepung rangup berempah* (for crispy frying), and *ikan bilis* (anchovies).

Pruning slow-selling brands from product lines often benefits the brands that are left, such as Unilever's bestsellers including Knorr's *ikan bilis* (anchovies) stock in Asia.

Multibrand companies all over the world are attempting to optimize their brand portfolios. In many cases, this has led to a greater focus on core brand growth and to concentrating energy and resources on the biggest and most established brands. Hasbro has designated a set of core toy brands, including GI Joe, Transformers, and My Little Pony, to emphasize in its marketing. P&G's "back to basics strategy" concentrated on its brands with over $1 billion in revenue, such as Tide, Crest, Pampers, and Pringles. Every product in a product line must play a role, as must any brand in the brand portfolio.

Volkswagen—Volkswagen has four different brands to manage in its European portfolio. Initially, Audi and Seat had a sporty image and VW and Skoda had a family-car image. Audi and VW were in a higher price-quality tier than their respective counterparts. Skoda and Seat with their basic spartan interiors and utilitarian engine performance were clearly differentiated. With the goal of reducing costs, streamlining part/systems designs, and eliminating redundancies, Volkswagen upgraded the Seat and Skoda brands. Once viewed as subpar products by European consumers, Skoda and Seat have captured market share with splashy interiors, a full array of safety systems, and reliable powertrains borrowed from Volkswagen. The danger, of course, is that by borrowing from its upper-echelon Audi and Volkswagen products, Volkswagen may have diluted their cachet. Frugal European automotive consumers may convince themselves that a Seat or Skoda is almost identical to its VW sister, at several thousand euros less.[30]

Product-Mix Pricing

Chapter 14 describes pricing concepts, strategies, and tactics in detail, but it is useful to consider some basic product-mix pricing issues here. Price-setting logic must be modified when the product is part of a product-mix. In this case, the firm searches for a set of prices that maximizes profits on the total mix. Pricing is difficult because the various products have demand and cost interrelationships and are subject to different degrees of competition.

We can distinguish six situations involving product-mix pricing: product-line pricing, optional-feature pricing, captive-product pricing, two-part pricing, by-product pricing, and product-bundling pricing.

PRODUCT-LINE PRICING

Companies normally develop product lines rather than single products and introduce price steps.

In many lines of trade, sellers use well-established price points for the products in their line. A men's clothing store might carry men's suits at three price levels: $200, $400, and $600. Customers will associate low-, average-, and high-quality suits with the three price points. The seller's task is to establish perceived-quality differences that justify the price differences.

Procter & Gamble—P&G feels that the key to the Asian market is to tailor its products to the pockets and needs of low-income consumers. Given that there are many low-income Asian consumers, P&G had to rethink its business model to provide products of quality but affordable to consumers with lower incomes. In India, it introduced cheaper Pampers by developing a bikini design to suit India's tropical heat as well as pockets. Thus Pampers offers different disposable diapers at various price levels depending on product features.[31]

OPTIONAL-FEATURE PRICING

Many companies offer optional products, features, and services along with their main product. The automobile buyer can order electric window controls, light dimmers, and an extended warranty. Pricing is a sticky problem, because companies must decide which items to include in the standard price and which to offer as options.

Restaurants face a similar pricing problem. Customers can often order liquor in addition to the meal. Many restaurants price their liquor high and their food low. The food revenue covers costs, and the liquor produces the profit. This explains why servers often press hard to get customers to order drinks. Other restaurants price their liquor low and food high to draw in a drinking crowd.

CAPTIVE-PRODUCT PRICING

Some products require the use of ancillary, or **captive**, **products**. Manufacturers of razors, digital phones, and cameras often price them low and set high markups on razor blades, monthly subscription, and film, respectively. A phone company may give a cell phone free if the person commits to buying two years of phone service.

There is a danger in pricing the captive product too high in the aftermarket. Caterpillar, for example, makes high profits in the aftermarket by pricing its parts and service high. This practice has given rise to "pirates," who counterfeit the parts and sell them to mechanics who install them, sometimes without passing on the cost savings to customers. Meanwhile, Caterpillar loses sales.[32]

TWO-PART PRICING

Service firms often engage in **two-part pricing**, consisting of a fixed fee plus a variable usage fee. Telephone users pay a minimum monthly fee plus charges for calls beyond a certain area. Amusement parks charge an admission fee plus fees for rides over a certain minimum. The service firm faces a problem similar to captive-product pricing—namely, how much to charge for the basic service and how much for the variable usage. The fixed fee should be low enough to induce purchase of the service; the profit can then be made on the usage fees.

BY-PRODUCT PRICING

The production of certain goods—meats, petroleum products, and other chemicals—often results in by-products. If the by-products have value to a customer group, they should be priced on their value. Any income earned on the by-products will make it easier for the company to charge a lower price on its main product if competition forces it to do so.

Golden Hope Plantations—Malaysia's Golden Hope used to burn old rubber trees after their productive life. It now cuts down old trees and uses the wood to supply fast-growing markets for rubber wood furniture, parquet flooring, and particle and Medium-Density Fiber (MDF) boards. From the MDF business alone, Golden Hope generates pre-tax profits which are more than five times that for rubber per hectare each year. It is doing the same for its palm oil plantations. Disposing of the waste from palm oil production was a headache. It now turns the waste into fiber for making MDF boards, stuffing for car seats, and bedding for medicinal use.

PRODUCT-BUNDLING PRICING

Sellers often bundle products and features. **Pure bundling** occurs when a firm only offers its products as a bundle. Artists Management Group will sign up a "hot" actor if the film company will also accept other talents that it represents (directors, writers, scripts). This is a form of *tied-in sales*. In **mixed bundling**, the seller offers goods both individually and in bundles. When offering a mixed bundle, the seller normally charges less for the bundle than if the items were purchased separately. An auto manufacturer might offer an option package at less than the cost of buying all the options separately. A theater company will price a season subscription at less than the cost of buying all the performances separately. Because customers may not have planned to buy all the components, the savings on the price bundle must be substantial enough to induce them to buy the bundle.[33]

Some customers will want less than the whole bundle. Suppose a medical equipment supplier's offer includes free delivery and training. A particular customer might ask to forgo the free delivery and training in exchange for a lower price. The customer is asking the seller to "unbundle" or "rebundle" its offer. If a supplier saves $100 by not supplying delivery and reduces the customer's price by $80, the supplier has kept the customer happy while increasing its profit by $20.

Studies have shown that as promotional activity increases on individual items in the bundle, buyers perceive less savings on the bundle and are less apt to pay for the bundle. This research has offered the following three suggested guidelines for correctly implementing a bundling strategy:[34]

- **Do not promote individual products in a package as frequently and cheaply as the bundle.** The bundle price should be much lower than the sum of individual products or the consumer will not perceive its attractiveness.
- **Limit promotions to a single item in the mix if you still want to promote individual products.** Or alternate promotions, one after another, to avoid conflicting promotions.
- **If you decide to offer large rebates on individual products, it must be the absolute exception** and done with discretion. Otherwise, the consumer uses the price of individual products as an external reference for the bundle, which then loses value.

Co-Branding and Ingredient Branding

CO-BRANDING

Products are often combined with products from other companies in various ways. A rising phenomenon is the emergence of **co-branding**—also called dual branding or brand bundling—in which two or more well-known existing brands are combined into a joint product and/or marketed together in some fashion.[35] One form of co-branding is *same-company co-branding*, as when Lion advertises Mama Lemon dishwashing detergent together with Top laundry detergent. Still another form is *joint venture co-branding*, as in the case of General Electric and Hitachi light bulbs in Japan. There is *multiple-sponsor co-branding*, as in the case of Taligent, a technological alliance of Apple, IBM, and Motorola.[36] Finally, there is *retail co-branding* where two retail establishments, such as fast food restaurants, use the same location as a way to optimize both space and profits. For example, Kasikornbank in Thailand has Starbucks located in its branches to optimize the space as well as build on each other's image.

A Starbucks outlet at a Kasikornbank branch in Bangkok, Thailand.

The main advantage to co-branding is that a product may be convincingly positioned by virtue of the multiple brands involved. Co-branding can generate greater sales from the existing target market as well as open additional opportunities with new consumers and channels. Co-branding also can reduce the cost of product introduction because two well-known images are combined, accelerating potential adoption. And co-branding may be a valuable means to learn about consumers and how other companies approach them. Companies within the automotive industry have reaped all of these benefits of co-branding.

Coca-Cola and L'Oréal—Coca-Cola and L'Oréal partnered to create a new health-and-beauty beverage to be launched in 2008. Called Lumaé, the nutraceutical drink is a tea-based ready-to-drink beverage containing ingredients that helps women care for their skin. Lumaé targets active, influential, image-conscious women who embrace health and wellness. Coke is interested in marketing and distributing Lumaé like a beauty brand instead of a soft drink.[37]

The potential disadvantages of co-branding are the risks and lack of control from becoming aligned with another brand in the minds of consumers. Consumer expectations about the level of involvement and commitment with co-brands are likely to be high, so unsatisfactory performance could have negative repercussions for the brands involved. If the other brand has entered into a number of co-branding arrangements, there may be a risk that overexposure will dilute the transfer of any association. It may also result in a lack of focus on existing brands.

A necessary condition for co-branding success is that the two brands separately have brand equity—adequate brand awareness and a sufficiently positive brand image. The most important requirement is that there is a logical fit between the two brands such that the combined brand or marketing activity maximizes the advantages of the individual brands while minimizing the disadvantages. Research shows that consumers are more apt to perceive co-brands favorably if the two brands are complementary rather than similar.[38] For example, Sony Ericsson mobile phones leverage Sony's strength in consumer electronics and marketing, and Ericsson's expertise in wireless technology.

Besides these strategic considerations, co-branding ventures must be entered into and executed carefully. There must be the right kind of fit in values, capabilities, and goals, in addition to an appropriate balance of brand equity. There must be detailed plans to legalize contracts, make financial arrangements, and coordinate marketing programs. As one executive at Nabisco put it, "Giving away your brand is a lot like giving away your child—you want to make sure everything is perfect." The financial arrangement between brands may vary, although one common approach involves a licensing fee and royalty from the brand more involved in the production process.

Brand alliances involve a number of decisions:[39] What capabilities do you not have? What resource constraints are you faced with (people, time, money, etc.)? What growth goals or revenue needs do you have? In assessing a joint branding opportunity, a number of questions need to be asked. Is it a profitable business venture? How does it help to maintain or strengthen brand equity? Is there any possible risk of dilution of brand equity? Does it offer any extrinsic advantages (e.g., learning opportunities)?

INGREDIENT BRANDING

Ingredient branding is a special case of co-branding. It involves creating brand equity for materials, components, or parts that are necessarily contained within other branded products. Some successful ingredient brands include Dolby noise reduction, Gore-Tex water-resistant fibers, and Scotchgard fabrics.

An interesting take on ingredient branding is "selfbranding" in which companies advertise and even trademark their own branded ingredients. For instance, Westin Hotels advertises its "Heavenly Bed" and "Heavenly Shower," and Tide announces that it contains the scent of "Everfresh" bath soap, an ingredient it developed. If you can do it well, it makes much more sense to self brand ingredients because you have more control and can develop the ingredient to suit your purposes.[40]

Ingredient brands attempt to create sufficient awareness and preference for their product such that consumers will not buy a "host" product that does not contain the ingredient. DuPont has achieved success marketing its products as ingredient brands.

DuPont—Over the years, DuPont has introduced a number of innovative products, such as Corian® solid surface material, for use in markets ranging from apparel to aerospace. Many of these products, such as Lycra® and Stainmaster® fabrics, Teflon® coating, and Kevlar® fiber, became household names as ingredient brands in consumer products manufactured by other companies. Several recent ingredient brands include Supro® isolated soy proteins used in food products and RiboPrinter® genetic fingerprinting technology.[41]

Many manufacturers make components or materials that enter into final branded products, but whose individual identity normally gets lost. One of the few component branders who have succeeded in building a separate identity is Intel. Intel's consumer-directed brand campaign convinced many personal computer buyers to buy only computer brands with "Intel Inside." As a result, major PC manufacturers—IBM, Dell, and Compaq—purchase their chips from Intel at a premium price rather than buy equivalent chips from an unknown supplier. Most component manufacturers, however, would find it difficult to create a successful ingredient brand. "Marketing Memo: Making Ingredient Branding Work" outlines the characteristics of successful ingredient branding.

Packaging, Labeling, Warranties and Guarantees

Most physical products have to be packaged and labeled. Some packages—such as the Coke bottle and the L'eggs container—are world famous. Many marketers have called packaging a fifth P, along with price, product, place, and promotion. Most marketers, however, treat packaging and labeling as an element of product strategy. Warranties and guarantees can also be an important part of the product strategy which often appear on the package.

MARKETING MEMO • MAKING INGREDIENT BRANDING WORK

What are the requirements for success for ingredient branding?

1. **Consumers must perceive that the ingredient matters** to the performance and success of the end product. Ideally, this intrinsic value is easily visible or experienced.
2. **Consumers must be convinced that not all ingredient brands are the same** and that the ingredient is superior.
3. **A distinctive symbol or logo must clearly signal to consumers** that the host product contains the ingredient. Ideally, the symbol or logo would function like a "seal" and would be simple and versatile and credibly communicate quality and confidence.
4. **A coordinated "pull" and "push" program must help consumers understand the importance and advantages of the branded ingredient.** Channel members must offer full support. Often this will involve consumer advertising and promotions and—sometimes in collaboration with manufacturers—retail merchandising and promotion programs.

Sources: Kevin Lane Keller, *Strategic Brand Management*, 3rd ed., (Upper Saddle River, NJ: Prentice-Hall, 2007); Paul F. Nunes, Stephen F. Dull, and Patrick D. Lynch, "When Two Brands are Better Than One." *Outlook*, 2003, 1, pp. 14–23.

Packaging

We define **packaging** as all the activities of designing and producing the container for a product. Packages might include up to three levels of material. Flower by Kenzo perfume is in a bottle (*primary package*) that is in a cardboard box (*secondary package*) that is in a corrugated box (*shipping package*) containing six dozen boxes of Flower bottles.

Well-designed packages can create convenience and promotional value. We must include packaging as a styling weapon, especially in food products, cosmetics, toiletries, and small consumer appliances. The package is the buyer's first encounter with the product and is capable of turning the buyer on or off. Here is an Asian example:

Health Food Enterprises—Most packaging for herbal medicines in China use traditional designs with very earthy colors such as brown or yellow. Health Food Enterprises wanted a rich-looking package that reflected its costly contents. The company's shark cartilage capsules sell for as much as $64 per bottle of 100 capsules. It thus introduced a series of elegant gold-trim packages in royal blue, jade green, and purple.

Various factors have contributed to the growing use of packaging as a marketing tool:

- ***Self-service*** — More products are being sold on a self-service basis. In a supermarket which may stock 15,000 items, a typical shopper passes by some 300 items per minute. Given that as much as half of all purchases are made on impulse, the effective package must perform many of the sales tasks: attract attention, describe the product's features, create consumer confidence, and make a favorable overall impression.
- ***Consumer affluence*** — Rising consumer affluence means consumers are willing to pay a little more for the convenience, appearance, dependability, and prestige of better packages.
- ***Company and brand image*** — Packages contribute to instant recognition of the company or brand. Future Cola's cans are designed to project a modern image.
- ***Innovation opportunity*** — Innovative packaging can bring large benefits to consumers and profits to producers. Companies are incorporating unique materials and features such as resealable spouts and openings.
- ***Protecting intellectual property rights*** — In some Asian countries like China, many MNCs and some well-known local companies want packaging that is difficult to copy. Unusual package shapes and complicated printing techniques such as embossing can help deter counterfeiters.

Developing an effective package requires a number of decisions. From the perspective of both the firm and consumers, packaging must achieve a number of objectives:[42]

1. Identify the brand.
2. Convey descriptive and persuasive information.
3. Facilitate product transportation and protection.
4. Assist at-home storage.
5. Aid product consumption.

To achieve the marketing objectives for the brand and satisfy the desires of consumers, the aesthetic and functional components of packaging must be chosen correctly. Aesthetic considerations relate to a package's size and shape, material, color, text and graphics. Color must be carefully chosen: blue is cool and serene, red is active and lively, yellow is medicinal and weak, pastel colors are feminine and dark colors are masculine. Functionally, structural design is crucial. For example, packaging innovations with food products over the years have resulted in packages becoming resealable, tamper-proof, and more convenient to use (easy-to-hold, easy-to-open, or squeezable). Changes in canning have made vegetables crunchier, and special wraps have extended the life of refrigerated food.[43]

The various packaging elements must be harmonized. The packaging elements must also be harmonized with decisions on pricing, advertising, and other parts of the marketing program. Packaging changes can have immediate impact on sales.

After packaging is designed, it must be tested. *Engineering tests* are conducted to ensure that the package stands up under normal conditions; *visual tests*, to ensure that the script is legible and the colors harmonious; *dealer tests*, to ensure that dealers find the packages attractive and easy to handle; and *consumer tests*, to ensure favorable consumer response.

Developing effective packaging may cost several hundred thousand dollars and take several months to complete. Companies must pay attention to growing environmental and safety concerns about packaging. Shortages of paper, aluminum, and other materials suggest that marketers should try to reduce packaging. Many packages end up as broken bottles and crumpled cans littering the streets and countryside. Packaging creates a major problem for solid waste disposal, requiring huge amounts of labor and energy. Fortunately, some companies have gone "green."

Labeling

Sellers must label products. The label may be a simple tag attached to the product or an elaborately designed graphic that is part of the package. The label might carry only the brand name or a great deal of information. Even if the seller prefers a simple label, the law may require additional information.

Labels perform several functions. First, the label *identifies* the product or brand—for instance, the name Sunkist stamped on oranges. The label might also *grade* the product as when Thai fragrant rice is grade labeled 100 percent Long Grain or 100 percent Broken A1 Extra Super. The label might *describe* the product: who made it, where it was made, when it was made, what it contains, how it is to be used, and how to use it safely. Finally, the label might *promote* the product through attractive graphics. For example, when American direct investment company Asimco bought Five Star, then an 80-year old state-owned factory in Beijing, it repackaged the beer brand and sold it at a premium price. The new packaging projects a trendy image of a foreign brand with a Chinese name. New technology allows for 360-degree shrink-wrapped labels to surround containers with bright graphics and accommodate more on-pack product information, replacing paper labels glued onto cans and bottles.[44]

Labels eventually become out-moded and need freshening up. The label on Milkmaid condensed milk has been redone several times with graded changes each time. The Two Girls cosmetic brand, popular in Hong Kong decades ago, was revamped with a fashionable yet nostalgic look reminiscent of old Shanghai to compete with the likes of Revlon and Chanel for the attention of young, affluent Chinese females. Companies with labels that have become icons need to tread very carefully when initiating a redesign:

Campbell Soup Company—The Campbell Soup Company has estimated that the average American shopper sees its familiar red-and-white can 76 times a year, creating the equivalent of millions of dollars worth of advertising. Its label is such an icon that pop artist Andy Warhol immortalized it in one of his silk screens in the 1960s. The original Campbell's Soup label—with its scripted name and signature red-and-white—was designed in 1898, and the company did not redesign it until more than a century later, in 1999. To make the label more contemporary and easier for customers to find individual soups, Campbell made the famous script logo smaller and featured a photo of a steaming bowl of the soup flavor inside. The company also put nutritional information on the packaging, serving suggestions, quick dinner ideas, and colored bands that identify the six subgroups of condensed soup, i.e., creams, broths, etc.[45]

In Asia, instances of imitative packaging exist. For example, the popular U.S. cookie brand, Oreo, had a lookalike made in Indonesia called Rodeo. However, packaging and labeling laws, and their enforcement, vary from country to country in the region. As Asian countries develop, they are likely to embrace stricter labeling standards. For example, additional labeling laws may require *open dating* (to describe product freshness), *unit pricing* (to state the product cost in standard measurement units), *grade labeling* (to rate the quality level of certain consumer goods), and *percentage labeling* (to show the percentage of each important ingredient).

Warranties and Guarantees

All sellers are legally responsible for fulfilling a buyer's normal or reasonable expectations. Warranties are formal statements of expected product performance by the manufacturer. Products under warranty can be returned to the manufacturer or designated repair center for repair, replacement, or refund. Warranties, whether expressed or implied, are legally enforceable.

Mitsubishi—To counter consumer perceptions that Mitsubishi lags behind competitors in quality, the company offered a new 10-year, 100,000-mile Powertrain warranty in North America, replacing its seven-year, 60,000-mile warranty. Mitsubishi hopes that the new longer-term warranty will signal to consumers that the company has confidence in the quality and reliability of its vehicles.[46]

Many sellers offer either general guarantees or specific guarantees.[47] A company such as Kao promises general or complete satisfaction without being more specific: "If you are not satisfied for any reason, return for replacement, exchange, or refund." Other companies offer specific guarantees and in some cases, extraordinary guarantees:

- FedEx won its place in the minds and hearts of mailers by promising next-day delivery "absolutely, positively by 10:30 a.m."
- A.T. Cross guarantees its Cross pens and pencils for life. The customer mails the pen to A.T. Cross (mailing envelopes are provided at stores selling its products), and the pen is repaired or replaced at no charge.

Guarantees reduce the buyer's perceived risk. They suggest that the product is of high quality and that the company and its service performance are dependable. All this enables the company to charge a higher price than a competitor who is not offering an equivalent guarantee.

Guarantees are most effective in two situations. The first is where the company or the product is not well-known. For example, a company might sell a liquid claiming to remove the toughest spots. A "money-back guarantee if not satisfied" would provide buyers with some confidence in purchasing the product. The second situation is where the product's quality is superior to the competition. The company can gain by guaranteeing superior performance, knowing that competitors cannot match its guarantee.

Summary

1. Product is the first and most important element of the marketing mix. Product strategy calls for making coordinated decisions on product mixes, product lines, brands, and packaging and labeling.
2. In planning its market offering, the marketer needs to think through the five levels of the product: the core benefit, the basic product, the expected product, the augmented product, and the potential product, which encompasses all the augmentations and transformations the product might ultimately undergo.
3. Products can be classified in several ways. In terms of durability and reliability, products can be nondurable goods, durable goods, or services. In the consumer-goods category, products are convenience goods (staples, impulse goods, emergency goods), shopping goods (homogeneous and heterogeneous), specialty goods, or unsought goods. In the industrial-goods category, products fall into one of three categories: materials and parts (raw materials and manufactured materials and parts), capital items (installations and equipment), or supplies and business services (operating supplies, maintenance and repair items, maintenance and repair services, and business advisory services).
4. Brands can be differentiated on the basis of a number of different product or service dimensions: product form, features, performance, conformance, durability, reliability, repairability, style, and design, as well as such service dimensions as ordering ease, delivery, installation, customer training, customer consulting, and maintenance and repair.
5. Most companies sell more than one product. A product mix can be classified according to width, length, depth, and consistency. These four dimensions are the tools for developing the company's marketing strategy and deciding which product lines to grow, maintain, harvest, and divest. To analyze a product line and decide how many resources should be invested in that line, product-line managers need to look at sales and profits and market profile.
6. A company can change the product component of its marketing mix by lengthening its product via line stretching (down-market, up-market, or both) or line filling; by modernizing its products; by featuring certain products; and by pruning its products to eliminate the least profitable.
7. Brands are often sold or marketed jointly with other brands. Ingredient brands and co-brands can add value assuming they have equity and are perceived as fitting appropriately.
8. Physical products have to be packaged and labeled. Well-designed packages can create convenience value for customers and promotional value for producers. In effect, they can act as "five-second commercials" for the product. Warranties and guarantees can offer further assurance to consumers.

Application

Marketing Debate—Are Line Extensions Good or Bad?

The "form versus function" debate applies in many arenas, including marketing. Some marketers believe that product performance is the end all and be all. Other marketers maintain that the looks, feel and other design elements of products are what really make the difference.

Take a position: *Product functionality is the key to brand success* versus *Product design is the key to brand success.*

Marketing Discussion

Consider the different means of differentiating products and services. Which ones have the most impact on your choices? Why? Can you think of certain brands that excel on a number of these different means of differentiation?

PART 5

Bumrungrad International Hospital in Bangkok is a premier destination for tourists seeking medical services.

Designing and Managing Services 13

As companies find it increasingly harder to differentiate their physical products, they turn to service differentiation. Many books point out the significant profitability of companies that manage to deliver superior service.[1] Companies seek to develop a reputation for superior performance in on-time delivery, better and faster answering of inquiries, and quicker resolution of complaints. Service becomes the mantra. An excellent Asian example of how the growth of services has changed the face of business is Thailand's Bumrungrad International Hospital.

Bangkok is one of the world's premier destinations for health tourism. Leading the way is Bumrungrad International. Established in 1981, Bumrungrad, which means "care for the people," set itself apart from the rest of Bangkok's health tourism industry by hiring not only experienced foreign doctors but also foreign management expertise. At its helm is Curt Schneider, an American who reshaped and repackaged the hospital into an international brand. He has turned Bumrungrad into a hospital that balances clinical care with teaching and research that keeps the hospital, and its staff and doctors, at the top of their game. Offering lower cost with comparable quality, Bumrungrad saw its enrolment of patients increasing. Serving over a million patients annually, over 400,000 are foreigners with American, Japanese, and British patients forming the bulk of its foreign clientele. It gets over 200 emails in 17 languages daily and usually responds within a day. Today, the 550-bed Bumrungrad is extending its expertise in health care management overseas. It has taken a 43 percent stake in Manila's Asian Hospital and a 49 percent stake in a new Dubai hospital currently under construction.[2]

In this chapter, we will address the following questions:

1. How do we define and classify services, and how do they differ from goods?
2. How do we market services?
3. How can we improve service quality?
4. How do services marketers create strong brands?
5. How can goods marketers improve customer-support services?

Service businesses increasingly fuel the world economy. Because understanding the special nature of services and what that means to marketers is critical, we systematically analyze services and how to market them most effectively in this chapter.

The Nature of Services

One of the megatrends of recent years has been the phenomenal growth of services. In Asia, the service sector makes up 40 percent (in Indonesia) to 85 percent (in Hong Kong) of the various countries' GDP.[3] This percentage has been increasing over the years in most Asian countries. For instance, the biggest gains in recent years for U.S. companies operating in China come from wholesale and retail trade, finance, and insurance; not manufacturing.[4] Several reasons account for this—rising levels of income and education, an aging population requiring more services, and more women in the labor force, thus requiring more home and recreational services. Hence, there is a growing interest in the special challenges and opportunities in the marketing of services in Asia.

Service Industries are Everywhere

The *government sector*, with its courts, employment services, hospitals, loan agencies, military services, police and fire departments, postal service, regulatory agencies, and schools, is in the service business. The *private non-profit sector*, with its museums, charities, churches, colleges, foundations, and hospitals, is in the service business. A good part of the *business sector*, with its airlines, banks, hotels, insurance companies, law firms, management consulting firms, medical practices, motion-picture companies, plumbing-repair companies, and real estate firms, is in the service business. Many workers in the *manufacturing sector*, such as computer operators, accountants, and legal staff, are really service providers. In fact, they make up a "service factory" providing services to the "goods factory." And those in the *retail sector*, such as cashiers, clerks, salespeople, and customer service representatives, are also providing a service.

We define a service as follows: a **service** is any act or performance that one party can offer to another that is essentially intangible and does not result in the ownership of anything. Its production may or may not be tied to a physical product.

Manufacturers, distributors, and retailers can provide value-added services or simply excellent customer service to differentiate themselves, as in the following example:

Lexus and Toyota—To operate effectively in the lucrative but highly competitive luxury automobile market, Lexus is committed to making sure its customers have another car at their disposal if theirs happens to be in the shop. When Lexus had to recall the RX330 in 2006, it gave its inconvenienced customers a free iPod Nano. When customers balked about the price and value of early scheduled maintenance, Lexus implemented a new system that cut the average appointment time in half. In a survey on service quality conducted by *BusinessWeek* in 2007, Lexus was ranked 4th while its sister company, Toyota, was ranked 50th. The value-added services that Lexus provides include paying for some postwarranty repairs to keep loyal customers happy and setting up a live chat room on its Web site to handle queries from possible buyers, complaints from customers, and even address auto service issues. Toyota also differentiates itself in the service it provides. In China, it has rolled out sophisticated dealership software that monitors sales people's contact with customers. To ease customer concerns over counterfeit parts, a big issue in China, Toyota has installed glass windows overlooking repair shops to highlight its transparency.[5]

Many pure service firms are using the Internet to reach customers. A little surfing on the Web will turn up a large number of virtual service providers. For example, the Central Radio and Television University, based in Beijing, set up Provincial Radio and Television

Universities in provinces and municipalities to enroll students by broadcasting basic and specialized courses, supporting these courses with printed teaching materials.

Categories of Service Mix

The service component can be a minor or a major part of the total offering. Five categories of offerings can be distinguished:

1. ***Pure tangible good*** — The offering consists primarily of a tangible good such as soap, toothpaste, or salt. No services accompany the product.
2. ***Tangible good with accompanying services*** — The offering consists of a tangible good accompanied by one or more services. Levitt observes that "the more technologically sophisticated the generic product (e.g., cars and computers), the more dependent are its sales on the quality and availability of its accompanying customer services (e.g., display rooms, delivery, repairs and maintenance, application aids, operator training, installation advice, warranty fulfillment)."[6]
3. ***Hybrid***— The offering consists of equal parts of goods and services. For example, people patronize restaurants for both food and service.
4. ***Major service with accompanying minor goods and services*** — The offering consists of a major service along with additional services or supporting goods. For example, airline passengers buy transportation. The trip includes some tangibles, such as food and drinks, a ticket stub, and an airline magazine. The service requires a capital-intensive good—an airplane—for its realization, but the primary item is a service.
5. ***Pure service*** — The offering consists primarily of a service. Examples include babysitting, physiotherapy, and massage.

Because of this varying goods-to-service mix, it is difficult to generalize about services without further distinctions. Here are some additional distinctions that can be helpful:

- Services vary on whether they are ***equipment-based*** (automated car washes, vending machines) or ***people-based*** (window washing, accounting services). People-based services vary by whether they are provided by unskilled, skilled, or professional workers.
- Service companies can choose among different ***processes*** to deliver their service. Restaurants have developed such different formats as cafeteria-style, fast-food, buffet, and table service.
- Some services require the ***client's presence*** and some do not. Brain surgery involves the client's presence; a car repair does not. If the client must be present, the service provider has to be considerate of his or her needs. Thus beauty salon operators will invest in decor, play background music, and converse with their clients.
- Services differ on whether they meet a ***personal need*** (personal services) or a ***business need*** (business services). Service providers typically develop different marketing programs for personal and business markets.
- Service providers differ in their ***objectives*** (profit or non-profit) and ***ownership*** (private or public). These two characteristics, when crossed, produce four quite different types of organizations. The marketing programs of a private investor hospital will differ from those of a private charity hospital or a profit-making cosmetic surgery hospital.[7]

The nature of the service mix also has implications for how consumers evaluate quality. Figure 13.1 shows various products and services according to difficulty of evaluation.[8] At the left are goods high in *search qualities*—that is, characteristics the buyer can evaluate before purchase. In the middle are goods and services high in *experience qualities*—characteristics the buyer can evaluate after purchase. At the right are goods and services high in *credence qualities*—characteristics the buyer normally finds hard to evaluate even after consumption.[9]

Because services are generally high in experience and credence qualities, there is more risk in purchase. This has several consequences. First, service consumers generally rely on word of mouth rather than advertising. Second, they rely heavily on price, personnel, and physical cues to judge quality. Third, they are highly loyal to service providers who satisfy them. Fourth, because of the switching costs involved, much consumer inertia can exist. It can be challenging to entice a customer away from a competitor.

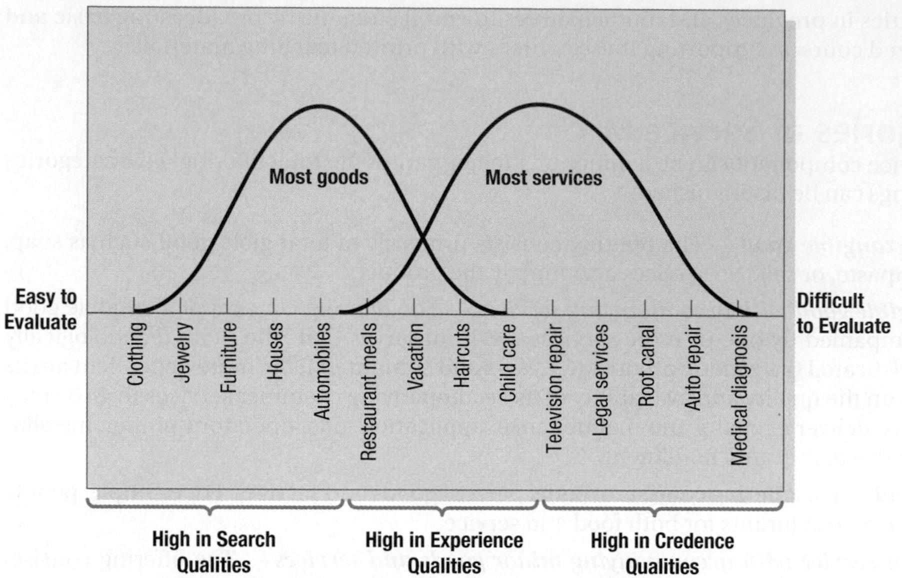

Figure 13.1 Continuum of Evaluation for Different Types of Products

Source: Valarie A. Zeithaml, "How Consumer Evaluation Processes Differ between Goods and Services." In *Marketing of Services*, J. Donnelly and W.R. George, eds., (Chicago, IL: American Marketing Association, 1981). Reprinted with permission of the American Marketing Association.

Distinctive Characteristics of Services

Services have four distinctive characteristics that greatly affect the design of marketing programs: *intangibility, inseparability, variability,* and *perishability.*

INTANGIBILITY

Unlike physical products, services cannot be seen, tasted, felt, heard, or smelled before they are bought. The person getting a face-lift cannot see the results before the purchase, and the patient in the psychiatrist's office cannot know the exact outcome.

To reduce uncertainty, buyers will look for evidence of quality. They will draw inferences about quality from the place, people, equipment, communication material, symbols, and price that they see. Therefore, the service provider's task is to "manage the evidence," to "tangibilize the intangible."[10] Whereas product marketers are challenged to add abstract ideas, service marketers are challenged to add physical evidence and imagery to abstract offers. Consider these Asian airline slogans: "Smooth as Silk" (Thai Airways); "Where You are the Maharajah" (Air India).

Service companies can try to demonstrate their service quality through *physical evidence* and *presentation.*[11] A hotel will develop a look and style of dealing with customers that realizes its intended customer value proposition, whether it is cleanliness, speed, or some other benefit.

Indian Airlines—In India, airlines such as Kingfisher and SpiceJet focused on the young, leggy flight attendants in tight skirts and heels. On the other hand, flight attendants at Indian Airlines are dressed in ***saris***, traditional Indian costumes. Given the increased competition, Indian Airlines has grounded some employees for putting on too much weight. It claims that it is selecting the best ambassadors to represent the national carrier. It argues that thinner employees are more agile and better equipped to tackle terrorist incidents and other emergencies. "When passengers are held captive inside the aeroplane staring at the flight crew for hours, they form an opinion of the airline. It's a cosmetic issue, but it's crucial," said a company lawyer. He added, "Staff need to be fit enough to control guys who are trying to take over the flight. Weight is an indication of fitness."[12]

Suppose a bank wants to position itself as the "fast" bank. It could make this positioning strategy tangible through a number of marketing tools:

1. ***Place***— The exterior and interior should have clean lines. The layout of the desks and the traffic flow should be planned carefully. Waiting lines should not get overly long.
2. ***People***— Personnel should be busy. There should be a sufficient number of employees to manage the workload.
3. ***Equipment***— Computers, copying machines, desks should be and look "state of the art."
4. ***Communication material***— Printed materials—text and photos—should suggest efficiency and speed.
5. ***Symbols***— The name and symbol should suggest fast service.
6. ***Price***— The bank could advertise that it will deposit $5 in the account of any customer who waits in line for more than five minutes.

Service marketers must be able to transform intangible services into concrete benefits. Consider Chinatrust Commercial Bank:

Chinatrust Commercial Bank—Taiwan's largest bank believes in the use of electronic services to benefit customers and the bank. Its customer-to-teller transaction costs $1.44 each. An ATM transaction costs 72 cents, while an Internet transaction costs 14 cents. Internet banking is seen as a way to contain costs. Online banking also allows the bank to build a profile of its customers and each transaction can be used as an opportunity to market additional services to them. To ensure security, Chinatrust uses a one-megabit encryption code for Internet transactions. Feedback from customers is that they find it easier than going to the bank. They can obtain loans, check their balances, and even purchase mutual funds over the Internet. The service also allows a variety of updating services. Chinatrust is proud that in eight months, it has done what has taken the U.S. banking industry 30 years to do with the Internet.[13]

Their intangibility implies that services may be more difficult to imitate. This is especially important in environments where intellectual-property protection is lacking. Here's an example:

Yum Brands—Yum Brands operates the KFC fast-food chain. In 2004, Yum's KFC operations in China topped $100 million in operating profit, making China the firm's second most profitable market after the U.S. KFC has 1,100 outlets in China, about twice as many as its main competitor, McDonald's. KFC succeeded in part because it offers a bright, clean dining environment. It sells ambience, not just chicken.[14]

To aid in "tangibilizing the intangible," Carbone and Haeckel propose a set of concepts called *customer experience engineering.*[15] Companies must first develop a clear picture of what they want the customer's perception of an experience to be and then design a consistent set of *performance and context clues* to support that experience. In the case of a bank, whether the teller dispensed the right amount of cash is a performance clue; a context clue is whether the teller was properly dressed. The context clues in a bank are delivered by people (*humanics*) and things (*mechanics*). The company assembles the clues in an *experience blueprint,* a pictorial representation of the various clues. To the extent possible, the clues should address all five senses. The Walt Disney Company is a master at developing *experience blueprints* in its theme parks.[16]

Shangri-La Hotel is another master at blueprinting its experience.

At Tokyo DisneySea, children are eager to experience the pleasure of meeting and taking pictures with their favorite Disney characters.

The Shangri-La Hotel in Hong Kong. Its training programs are focused on inculcating Asian values and customs.

Shangri-La Hotel—This Hong Kong-based hotel is venturing into new markets on both sides of the Pacific. The challenge it faces is in instilling important elements of its service culture to a different environment. Shangri-La's training programs are focused on and developed from Asian values and customs. Its philosophy, "Asian Hospitality from Caring People," is described in five core values—Respect, Humility, Courtesy, Sincerity, and Helpfulness. A Shangri-La guest is to be treated like someone who comes to your home. Shangri-La must show the guest that he is valued and that he is welcome. Shangri-La also has to show its sincere appreciation to its guests for having chosen the hotel. A one-year "cascading process" involving communication of these values from top management to other employees was instituted. At the corporate level, four processes—check-in/check-out, customer feedback with research tools, easy-to-do business, and de-bureaucratization—were identified. Four hotels were assigned to improve and test run these processes. The processes were then blueprinted and implemented in all Shangri-La Hotels.[17]

INSEPARABILITY

Services are typically produced and consumed simultaneously. This is not true of physical goods, which are manufactured, put into inventory, distributed through multiple resellers, and consumed later. If a person renders the service, then the provider is part of the service. Because the client is also present as the service is produced, provider—client interaction is a special feature of services marketing.

For entertainment and professional services, buyers are very interested in the specific provider. It is not the same action comedy when it features Jet Li if Jackie Chan was unavailable. When clients have strong provider preferences, price is raised to ration the preferred provider's limited time.

Several strategies exist for getting around this limitation. The service provider can learn to work with larger groups. Thus group counseling may be offered instead of individual counseling. The service provider can also learn to work faster, spending less time with each client and seeing more clients. A doctor may spend 30 more-efficient minutes with each patient instead of 50 less-structured minutes and see more patients. The service organization can train more service providers and build up client confidence. Performance arts groups employ understudies and traveling troupes in addition to their core set of performers.

VARIABILITY

Because they depend on who provides them and when and where they are provided, services are highly variable. Some doctors have an excellent bedside manner; others are less patient with their patients. Some surgeons are very successful in performing a certain operation; others are not. Service buyers are aware of this variability and often talk to others before selecting a service provider. Here are three steps service firms can take to increase quality control.

1. **Invest in good hiring and training procedures.** Recruiting the right employees and providing them with excellent training is crucial, regardless of whether employees are

competence, a caring attitude, responsiveness, initiative, problem-solving ability, and goodwill. Service companies such as FedEx and Marriott empower their frontline personnel to spend up to $100 to resolve a customer problem. Singapore Airlines (SIA) has stringent hiring criteria where over 90 percent of flight attendant applicants are rejected. Successful applicants go through a thorough and rigorous training program which has been so successful that SIA established the Service Quality Center to provide service training and consulting to over 700 organizations.

2. **Standardize the service-performance process throughout the organization.** This is done by preparing a *service blueprint* that depicts events and processes in a flowchart, with the objective of recognizing potential fail points. Figure 13.2 shows a service blueprint for a floral-delivery organization.[18] The customer's experience is limited to dialing the phone, making choices, and placing an order. Behind the scenes, the floral organization gathers the flowers, places them in a vase, delivers them, and collects payment. Any one of these activities can be done well or poorly.

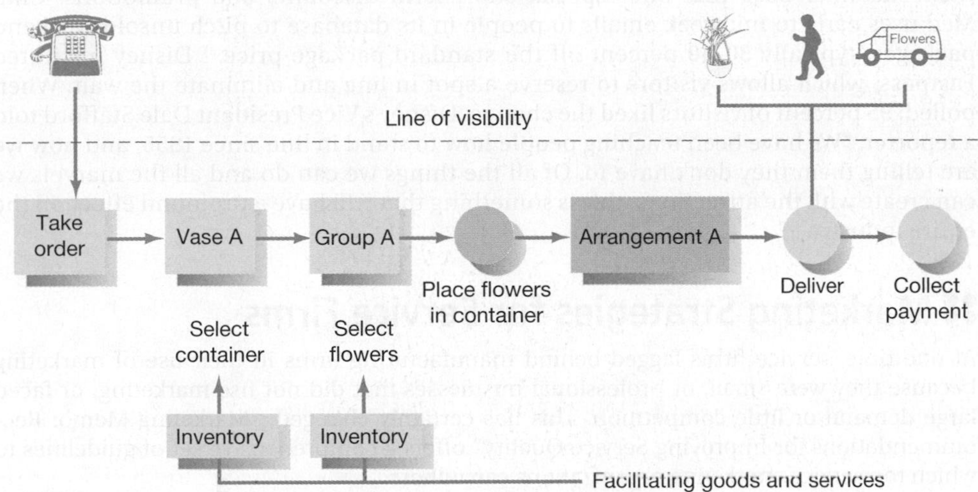

Figure 13.2 A Service-Performance-Process Map: A Floral-Delivery Organization

Source: Adapted from G. Lynn Shostack, "Service Positioning Through Structural Change." *Journal of Marketing*, January 1987, p. 39. Reprinted with permission of the American Marketing Association.

3. **Monitor customer satisfaction.** Employ suggestion and complaint systems, customer surveys, and comparison shopping. Citibank checks continuously on measures of ART (accuracy, responsiveness, and timeliness). Firms can also develop customer information databases and systems to permit more personalized, customized service.[19]

PERISHABILITY

Services cannot be stored. Perishability is not a problem when demand is steady. When demand fluctuates, service firms have problems. For example, public transportation companies have to own much more equipment because of rush-hour demand than if demand were even throughout the day. Some doctors charge patients for missed appointments because the service value exists only at that point.

Several strategies can produce a better match between demand and supply in a service business.[20] On the demand side:

- ***Differential pricing*** — This will shift some demand from peak to off-peak periods. Examples include weekday movie prices and weekend discount prices for car rentals.
- ***Nonpeak demand*** — This can be cultivated. The Night Safari in Singapore provides tourists with a night-time attraction, while most places are competing during the day.
- ***Complementary services*** — These services can be developed to provide alternatives to waiting customers, such as cocktail lounges in restaurants and automatic teller machines in banks.
- ***Reservation systems*** — These are a way to manage the demand level. Airlines, hotels, and physicians employ them extensively.

On the supply side:

- ***Part-time employees*** — They can be hired to serve peak demand. Colleges add part-time teachers when enrollment goes up, and restaurants call in part-time servers when needed.
- ***Peak-time efficiency*** — These routines can be introduced. Employees perform only essential tasks during peak periods. Nurses assist physicians during busy periods.
- ***Increased consumer participation*** — This can be encouraged. Consumers fill out their own medical records or bag their own groceries.
- ***Shared services*** — These can be developed. Several hospitals can share medical equipment purchases.
- ***Facilities for future expansion*** — These can be developed. An amusement park buys surrounding land for later development.

Many airlines, hotels, and resorts have email alerts to self-selected segments of their customer base that offer special short-term discounts and promotions. Club Med uses early to midweek emails to people in its database to pitch unsold weekend packages, typically 30–40 percent off the standard package price.[21] Disney instituted Fastpass, which allows visitors to reserve a spot in line and eliminate the wait. When polled, 95 percent of visitors liked the change. Disney's Vice President Dale Stafford told a reporter, "We have been teaching people how to stand in line since 1955, and now we are telling them they don't have to. Of all the things we can do and all the marvels we can create with the attractions, this is something that will have a profound effect on the entire industry."[22]

Marketing Strategies for Service Firms

At one time, service firms lagged behind manufacturing firms in their use of marketing because they were small, or professional businesses that did not use marketing, or faced large demand or little competition. This has certainly changed. "Marketing Memo: Recommendations for Improving Service Quality" offers a comprehensive set of guidelines to which top service-marketing organizations can adhere.

A Shifting Customer Relationship

Not all Asian companies, however, have invested in providing superior service, at least not across the region and not to all customers. Japan is often held up as the icon of service in Asia. Politeness, courtesy, and attention to detail are some of the hallmarks of Japanese culture. You are greeted by voices from every corner when you enter a restaurant and thanked again when you leave. All goods, regardless of value, are beautifully and intricately wrapped and presented. Standards and guidelines are religiously followed for a consistent service delivery. However, such strict adherence to guidelines is also their shortcoming, resulting in the loss of initiative from frontline staff and the reluctance of managers to empower the front-line for fear of lowering standards. "Marketing Insight: The Japanese Philosophy of Service" examines how the Japanese view service as an integral part of the product offering.

In contrast, China is an infant in the service quality game. Most frontline staff are not aware of and not exposed to the concept of quality service. In Indonesia, Malaysia, the Philippines, and Thailand, service quality is generally a concept familiar only to those working in the tourism industry, where frontline staff are very warm, easy-going, and congenial. Although they may not demonstrate the same professional finesse in handling customers as the Japanese, they make up for it by their enthusiasm.

Technology has also impacted the nature of the customer relationship. In the past, service companies held out a welcoming hand to all customers. However, with much more data on individuals, companies can classify their customers into profit tiers. So service is not uniform for all customers. Airlines, hotels, and banks all pamper good customers. Big spenders get special discounts, promotional offers, and lots of special service. The rest of their customers get higher fees, stripped-down service, and at best a voice message to answer inquiries.

MARKETING MEMO • RECOMMENDATIONS FOR IMPROVING SERVICE QUALITY

Pioneers in conducting academic service research, Berry, Parasuraman, and Zeithaml, offer 10 lessons that they maintain are essential for improving service quality across service industries.

1. ***Listening*** — Understand what customers really want through continuous learning about the expectations and perceptions of customers and non-customers (for instance, by means of a service-quality information system).
2. ***Reliability*** — Reliability is the single most important dimension of service quality and must be a service priority.
3. ***Basic service*** — Service companies must deliver the basics and do what they are supposed to do—keep promises, use common sense, listen to customers, keep customers informed, and be determined to deliver value to customers.
4. ***Service design*** — Develop a holistic view of the service while managing its many details.
5. ***Recovery*** — To satisfy customers who encounter a service problem, service companies should encourage customers to complain (and make it easy for them to do so), respond quickly and personally, and develop a problem-resolution system.
6. ***Surprising customers*** — Although reliability is the most important dimension in *meeting* customers' service expectations, process dimensions such as assurance, responsiveness, and empathy are most important in *exceeding* customer expectations, for example, by surprising them with uncommon swiftness, grace, courtesy, competence, commitment, and understanding.
7. ***Fair play*** — Service companies must make special efforts to *be* fair, and to *demonstrate* fairness, to customers and employees.
8. ***Teamwork*** — Teamwork is what enables large organizations to deliver service with care and attentiveness by improving employee motivation and capabilities.
9. ***Employee research*** — Marketers should conduct research with employees to reveal why service problems occur and what companies must do to solve problems.
10. ***Servant leadership*** — Quality service comes from inspired leadership throughout the organization; from excellent service-system design; from the effective use of information and technology; and from a slow-to-change, invisible, all-powerful, internal force called corporate culture.

Sources: Leonard L. Berry, A. Parasuraman, and Valarie A. Zeithaml, "Ten Lessons for Improving Service Quality." *MSI Reports Working Paper Series, No.03-001* (Cambridge, MA: Marketing Science Institute, 2003), pp. 61–82. See also, Leonard L. Berry's books, *On Great Service: A Framework for Action,* (New York: Free Press, 2006) and *Discovering the Soul of Service,* (New York: Free Press, 1999), as well as his articles, Leonard L. Berry, Venkatesh Shankar, Janet Parish, Susan Cadwallader, and Thomas Dotzel, "Creating New Markets through Service Innovation." *Sloan Management Review*, Winter 2006, pp. 56–63; Leonard L. Berry, Stephan H. Haeckel, and Lewis P. Carbone, "How to Lead the Customer Experience." *Marketing Management*, January–February 2003, pp. 18–23; and Leonard L. Berry, Kathleen Seiders, and Dhruv Grewal, "Understanding Service Convenience." *Journal of Marketing*, July 2002, pp. 1–17.

MARKETING INSIGHT • THE JAPANESE PHILOSOPHY OF SERVICE

Customer service, product quality, and after-sales service are the three pillars of marketing in Japan. Japanese companies pay great attention to researching what customers want. In the U.S., the customer is always right. In Japan, *okyakusama wa kamisama desu*—"the customer is God". Thus Japanese companies are well attuned to their customers' special needs (*anshin* which means "trust from the heart"), particularly since Japanese customers expect prompt service and availability of a full line of parts for any major purchase. Japanese want to feel comfortable and "in touch" with their suppliers and business partners—a human dimension to business. Therefore, *anshin* requires that a company understands the customer's needs and oblige to his demands. This takes time and close relations. Two-way obligations between customers and suppliers are built over the years and extend to social activities such as attending weddings.

The concern for quality service is derived from the concept of *giri*, which imbues Japanese employees with a deep sense of duty to fulfill their obligations to their supervisors and their customers. In Japan's hierarchical society, the vendor's caste is a full step below the customer's. In fact, the vendor's very existence is treated as justified by the customer. Hence, a successful vendor is mindful that no matter how unique his product, or how huge his market share, he has to solve his customer's problem attentively.

Japanese obsession with quality stems from two cultural values, *wa*, harmony, and *on*, obligation. To the Japanese, within everything there is an inherent state of perfection and harmony. This means that in providing service, perfection is the only reasonable standard, all else falls short and there is disharmony. Since disharmony is undesirable, obligation is needed to restore harmony. If one knows of a way to reach a state of harmony, one is obliged to pursue it.

To illustrate Japanese thoroughness in providing excellent service, consider their ventures into the automobile industry

(*Continued...*)

MARKETING INSIGHT • **THE JAPANESE PHILOSOPHY OF SERVICE**

(Continued ...)

in the Middle East. Japanese motor vehicle manufacturers saw the potential in an expanding Middle East market not only for automobiles but also spare parts, gas station equipment, tires, repair-shop tools, and mechanical services. They began training auto mechanics all over the region. Toyota, Nissan, and Honda announced plans to help Libya set up service shops in 44 towns and cities. Toyota sent three experts to Libya to give technical advice on building a repair shop in Tripoli, and Libyans went to Japan for training in motor-servicing techniques. Honda also sent auto experts to Libya, while Nissan trained mechanics at its service centers in Athens and in Japan. Japanese automakers are counting on the service market not only to provide a lucrative sideline to the main business of selling cars but also to boost Middle East demand for Japanese vehicles. The reasoning goes like this: if Middle East mechanics are trained to service Japanese cars, then people in the market for new cars are more likely to choose a brand they know they can have repaired locally. That is strategy!

Sources: James C. Morgan and J. Jeffrey Morgan, *Cracking the Japanese Market,* (New York: The Free Press, 1991); Paul A. Herbig and Frederick Palumbo, "Serving the Aftermarket in Japan and the United States." *Industrial Marketing Management*, November 1993, pp. 339-346.

Financial services giants have installed special software that tells them—in an instant—when a lucrative customer is on the phone. Such systems immediately send the call ahead of dozens—even hundreds—of other callers who must wait while the big spender gets special attention.[23]

This shift from a customer service democracy to a meritocracy is also a response to lower profit margins resulting from customers becoming more price-driven and less loyal. Companies are now driven to seek ways to squeeze more profit out of the different customer tiers.

Hewlett-Packard tries to respond to every email query within an hour, and usually answers within 10 minutes. The firm monitors its email centers minute by minute to ensure it meets its service-quality standards. Because of its successful email service centers, HP received 25 percent fewer calls to its call center between 2005 and 2006. Email volume rose, improving profits because an email response costs HP 60 percent less than a phone call.

Email response must be implemented properly to be effective.[24] One expert believes companies should (1) send an automated reply to tell customers when a more complete answer will arrive (ideally within 24 hours); (2) ensure the subject line always contains the company name; (3) make the message easy to scan for relevant information; and (4) give customers an easy way to respond with follow-up questions.[25]

PROFIT TIERS

Firms have decided to raise fees and lower service to those customers who barely pay their way and to coddle big spenders to retain their patronage as long as possible. Customers in high-profit tiers get special discounts, promotional offers, and lots of special service; customers in lower-profit tiers may get more fees, stripped-down service, and voice messages to process their inquiries.

Companies that provide differentiated levels of service, however, must be careful about claiming superior service—the customers who receive poor treatment will badmouth the company and injure its reputation. Delivering services that maximize both customer satisfaction and company profitability can be challenging. "Breakthrough Marketing: Southwest Airlines" describes how that spunky airline took on the big boys and succeeded.

CUSTOMER EMPOWERMENT

Customers are becoming more sophisticated about buying product-support services and are pressing for "services unbundling." They may want separate prices for each service element and the right to select the elements they want. Customers also

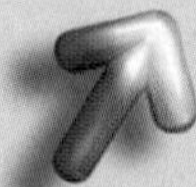

BREAKTHROUGH•MARKETING

SOUTHWEST AIRLINES

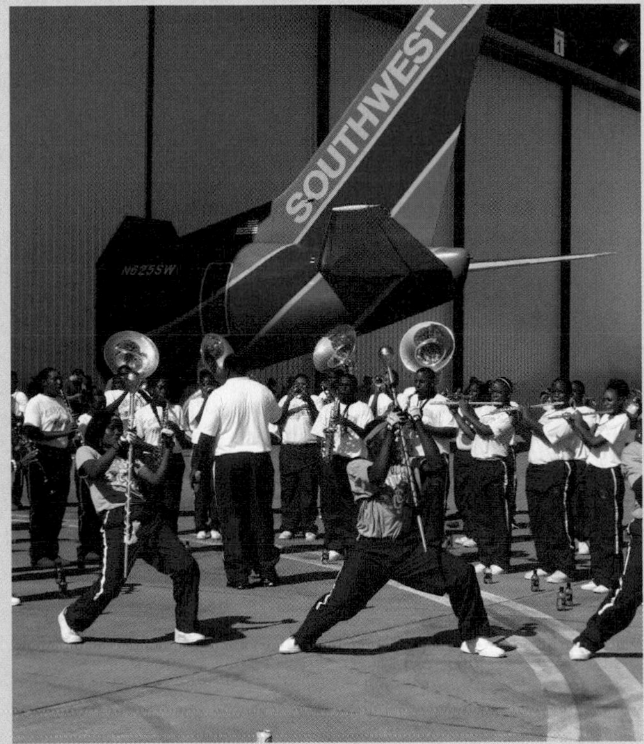

Southwest Airlines consistently delivers on its promise of low fares by paring costs and maintaining the spirit of fun that characterized its own low-budget start.

Southwest Airlines entered the airline industry in 1971 with little money, but lots of personality. Marketing itself as the LUV airline, the company featured a bright red heart as its first logo. In the 1970s, flight attendants in red-orange hot pants served Love Bites (peanuts) and Love Potions (drinks). With little money for advertising in the early days, Southwest relied on its outrageous antics to generate word-of-mouth advertising.

Later ads showcased Southwest's low fares, frequent flights, on-time arrivals, and top safety record. Throughout all the advertising, the spirit of fun pervaded. For example, one TV spot showed a small bag of peanuts with the words, "This is what our meals look like at Southwest Airlines. ... It's also what our fares look like." Southwest used ads with humor to poke fun at itself and to convey its personality.

Southwest can offer low fares because it streamlines operations. For example, it flies only Boeing 737s, which saves time and money because training is simplified for pilots, flight attendants, and mechanics; and management can substitute aircraft, reschedule flight crews, or transfer mechanics quickly. Southwest also bucks the traditional hub-and-spoke system and offers only point-to-point service; it chooses to fly to smaller airports that have lower gate fees and less congestion, which speeds aircraft turnaround. Southwest's 15–20-minute turnaround time from flight landing to departure is half the industry average, giving it better asset utilization (it flies more flights and more passengers per plane per day).

Southwest grows by entering new markets that are overpriced and underserved by current airlines. The company believes it can bring fares down by one-third to one-half whenever it enters a new market, and it grows the market in every city it serves by making flying affordable to people who previously could not afford to fly. Southwest currently serves 65 cities in 30 states.

Even though Southwest is a low-cost airline, it has pioneered many additional services and programs such as same-day freight service, senior discounts, Fun Fares, and Fun Packs. Despite Southwest's reputation for low fares and no-frills service, the company wins the hearts of customers. It consistently ranks at the top of lists of customer service for airlines, yet the average price of a flight is $87. Southwest has been ranked by *Fortune* magazine as the U.S.'s most admired airline since 1997, as its fifth-most admired corporation in 2007, and as one of the top five best places to work. Southwest's financial results also shine: The company has been profitable for 34 straight years. It has been the only airline to report profits every quarter since September 11, 2001, and one of the few that has had no layoffs amid a travel slump created by the slow economy and the threat of terrorism.

Although the hot pants are long gone, the LUVing spirit remains at the heart of Southwest. The company's stock symbol on the NYSE is LUV and red hearts can be found everywhere across the company. These symbols embody the Southwest spirit of employees "caring about themselves, each other, and Southwest's customers." "Our fares can be matched; our airplanes and routes can be copied. But we pride ourselves on our customer service," said Sherry Phelps, director of corporate employment. That is why Southwest looks for and hires people who generate enthusiasm. In fact, having a sense of humor is a selection criteria it uses for hiring. As one employee explained, "We can train you to do any job, but we can't give you the right spirit." And the feeling is reciprocated. When Southwest needed to close reservation centers in three cities in 2004, it did not fire a single employee but rather paid for relocation and commuting expenses.

Sources: Barney Gimbel, "Southwest's New Flight Plan." *Fortune*, May 16, 2005, pp. 93-98; Melanie Trottman, "Destination: Philadelphia." *Wall Street Journal*, May 4, 2004; Andy Serwer, "Southwest Airlines: The Hottest Thing in the Sky." *Fortune*, March 8, 2004; Colleen Barrett, "Fasten Your Seat Belts." *Adweek*, January 26, 2004, p. 17; "Southwest May Not Be No.1, but It Sure Looks Like the Leader." *Airline Financial News*, November 24, 2003; Eva Kaplan-Leiserson, "Strategic Service." *Training and Development*, November 2003, pp. 14-16; <www.southwest.com>.

increasingly dislike having to deal with a multitude of service providers handling different types of equipment. Some third-party service organizations now service a greater range of equipment.

Most important, the Internet has empowered customers by letting them vent their rage about bad service—or reward good service—and have their comments beamed around the world with a mouse click.[26] Ninety percent of angry customers reported that they shared their story with a friend. Now, they can share their stories with strangers via the Internet, or "word of mouth on steroids" as some say. With a few clicks on the PlanetFeedback Web site, shoppers can send an email complaint, compliment, suggestion, or question directly to a company with the option to post comments publicly at the site as well.

Most companies respond quickly, some within an hour. More important than simply responding to a disgruntled customer, however, is preventing dissatisfaction from occurring in the future. That may mean simply taking the time to nurture customer relationships and give customers attention from a real person. Columbia Records spent $10 million to improve its call center, and customers who phone the company can now "opt out" to reach an operator at any point in their call.

JetBlue—CEO David Neeleman set the bar high for responding to enraged customers after the company's drastic Valentine's Day failure of 2007. During storms in New York City, JetBlue left hundreds of passengers stranded aboard grounded aircraft—some for longer than nine hours—and cancelled more than 1,000 flights. JetBlue had built its reputation on being a more responsive, humane company in an era of minimal services and maximal delays for airline passengers. Hence, CEO Neeleman knew he had to act fast to stem another kind of storm: a whirlwind of customer defections. Within 24 hours, Neeleman had placed full-page ads in newspapers nationwide in which he personally responded to JetBlue's debacle. "We are sorry and embarrassed," the ads declared, "But most of all we are deeply sorry." Along with the heartfelt apology, JetBlue gave concrete reparations to passengers. Neeleman announced a new "customer bill of rights" that promises passengers travel credits for excessive waits. For instance, passengers who are unable to disembark from an arriving flight for three hours or more will receive vouchers worth the full value of their round-trip ticket. Waiting for as little as 30 minutes will bring smaller amounts. JetBlue will also hand out vouchers for the full amount of passengers' round trips if a flight is cancelled within 12 hours of a scheduled departure. The apology, backed by concrete benefits for the angry and inconvenienced passengers, netted kudos for the company from both the business press and JetBlue's own true-blue customers. Neeleman eventually stepped down as CEO though, as new management was brought in to address some of the growth challenges the airlines faced.[27]

CO-PRODUCTION

The reality is that customers do not merely purchase and use services, they play an active role in the delivery of that service every step of the way.[28] Their words and actions affect the quality of their service experiences and those of others, and the productivity of frontline employees. One study estimated that one-third of all service problems are caused by the customer.[29] With an increasing shift to self-service technologies, we can expect this percentage to rise.

Preventing service failures from ever happening to begin with is crucial, as service recovery is always challenging. One of the biggest problems is attribution—customers will often feel that the firm is at fault or, even if not, that it is still responsible for righting any wrongs. Unfortunately, although many firms have well-designed and executed procedures to deal with their own failures, they find that managing customer failures is much more difficult.

Figure 13.3 displays the four broad categories of root causes for customer failures, although there often are multiple causes at work. Solutions come in all forms, as illustrated by some of the following examples:[30]

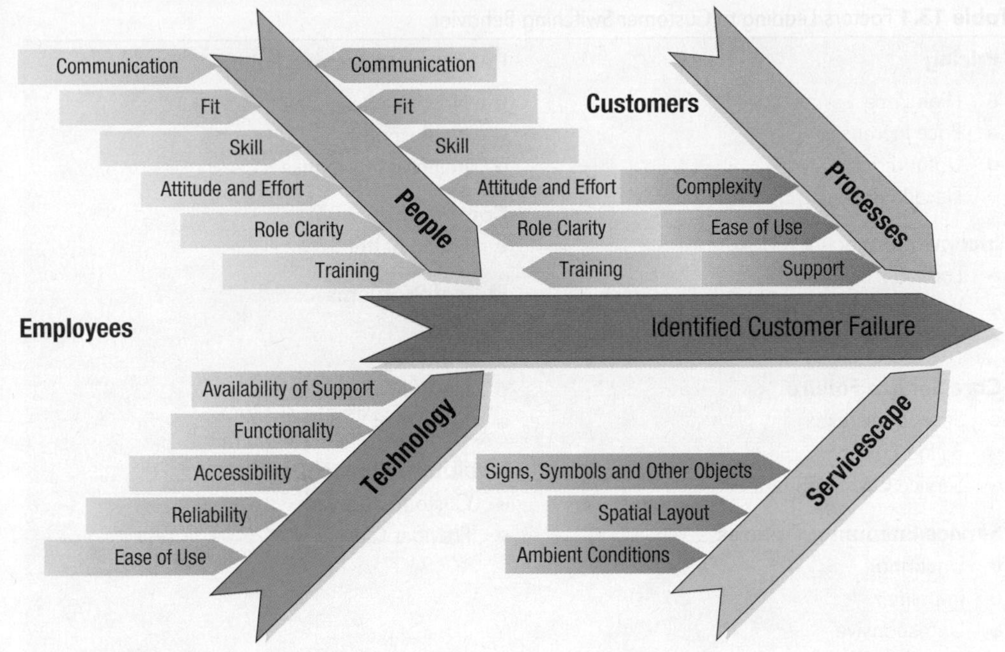

Figure 13.3 Root Causes of Customer Failure

Source: Stephen Tax, Mark Colgate, and David Bowen, *MIT Sloan Management Review,* Spring 2006, pp. 30–38.

1. **Redesign processes and redefine customer roles to simplify service encounters.** One of the keys to the success of some DVD rental stores is that they charge a flat fee and allow customers to return DVDs by mail at their leisure, giving customers greater control and flexibility.
2. **Incorporate the right technology to aid employees and customers.** Some companies keep a virtual copy of purchase information in case customers are unable to produce a receipt needed for a return.
3. **Create high-performance customers by enhancing their role clarity, motivation, and ability.** Some automobile companies coaches novice buyers about proper vehicle maintenance. Insurance companies may remind policyholders to suspend their car insurance when they are stationed overseas for a long period of time. Or insurance companies may offer integrated health management services to employers, or provide instant incentives to employees, such as a 20 percent reduction in their contribution to health insurance premiums, to get them to participate in various health programs.
4. **Encourage "customer citizenship" where customers help customers.** At golf courses, players can not only follow the rules by playing and behaving appropriately, they can encourage others to do so.

Holistic Marketing for Services

Because service encounters are complex interactions affected by multiple elements, adopting a holistic marketing perspective is especially important. The service outcome, and whether or not people will remain loyal to a service provider, is influenced by a host of variables. One study identified more than 800 critical behaviors that cause customers to switch services.[31] These behaviors fall into one of eight categories (see Table 13.1).

Holistic marketing for services requires external, internal, and interactive marketing (see Figure 13.4).[32] *External marketing* describes the normal work of preparing, pricing, distributing, and promoting the service to customers. *Internal marketing* describes training and motivating employees to serve customers well. Berry

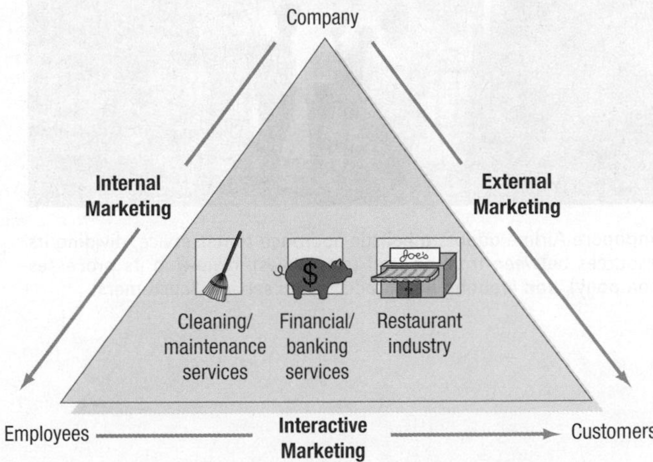

Figure 13.4 Three Types of Marketing in Service Industries

Table 13.1 Factors Leading to Customer Switching Behavior

Pricing	Response to Service Failure
• High Price • Price Increases • Unfair Pricing • Deceptive Pricing	• Negative Response • No Response • Reluctant Response
Inconvenience	**Competition**
• Location/Hours • Wait for Appointment • Wait for Service	• Found Better Service
Core Service Failure	**Ethical Problems**
• Service Mistakes • Billing Errors • Service Catastrophe	• Cheat • Hard Sell • Unsafe • Conflict of Interest
Service Encounter Failures	**Involuntary Switching**
• Uncaring • Impolite • Unresponsive • Unknowledgeable	• Customer Moved • Provider Closed

Source: Susan M. Keaveney, "Customer Switching Behavior in Service Industries: An Exploratory Study." *Journal of Marketing*, April 1995, pp. 71–82. Copyright © 1995 American Marketing Association. Used with permission.

has argued that the most important contribution the marketing department can make is to be "exceptionally clever in getting everyone else in the organization to practice marketing."[33]

Singapore Airline adopts a holistic approach to its service, dividing its resources between training staff (employees), reviewing its processes (company), and creating new products and services (customers).

Singapore Airlines (SIA)—Singapore Airlines is consistently recognized as the world's "best" airline in large part due to its stellar efforts at internal marketing. SIA strives to create a "wow effect" and regularly surprises its customers. It does this by listening intensely and constantly identifying opportunities generated by customer feedback. Some examples of this are SIA's new lighter, more nutritious fare and its in-flight email service. SIA places a high emphasis on training. Its latest initiative, called "Transforming Customer Service (TCS)," involves staff in five key operational areas: cabin crew, engineering, ground services, flight operations and sales support. The TCS culture is embedded in all management training, company-wide. TCS also uses a 40-30-30 rule in its holistic approach to people, processes, and products: 40 percent of resources go to training and invigorating staff, 30 percent is spent on reviewing process and procedures, and the last 30 percent on creating new product and service ideas. In 2007, with its innovatively designed Boeing 777-300 ERS and Airbus A380 planes, SIA set new standards of comforts in all classes of service, from eight private minirooms in first class to wider seats, AC power supplies, and USB ports in economy.[34]

Interactive marketing describes the employees' skill in serving the client. Clients judge service not only by its *technical quality* (e.g., was the surgery successful?) but also by its *functional quality* (e.g., did the surgeon show concern and inspire confidence?).[35] Technology has great power to make service workers more productive.[36] However, companies must avoid pushing productivity so hard that they reduce perceived quality. Some methods lead to too much standardization. Service providers must deliver "high-touch" and not just "high-tech."[37]

Mount Elizabeth Hospital (MEH)—This Singapore hospital believes that in nursing care, the clinical skills of its medical staff and the attitudes of its hospital employees are key to high-quality assessments by patients. Thus MEH embarked on internal marketing, training programs, and reward systems. It studied the high patient contact points and found that the hospital's lowest-paid, least-educated individuals usually had the most patient and visitor contact. MEH then placed greater emphasis on hiring practices, job development, and training for these positions. The role of the front office clerk was redesigned and its job requirements were elevated to those of a hotel front office. Existing personnel were sent for training to upgrade their skills. Personnel with required skills were hired and pay scales were adjusted.[38]

The "high-touch" aspect of service delivery is particularly evident in Asia, where service styles tend to be more people-oriented than in the West.[39] In Asia, even consumers of low-cost services expect a relatively high level of service. Most Asian countries are characterized by relatively large power distances that reflect social hierarchies. Chinese culture, for example, focuses on courteous rituals that encourage individuals to maintain the hierarchical social order. In such cultures, the lower social status of service employees requires them to provide customers with high levels of service.

Moreover, while Western cultures endorse explicit, direct, and unambiguous communications, Asians place greater emphasis on the quality of interpersonal relationship and interaction between employee and customer. Western customers may prefer efficient delivery even if that delivery is impersonal. However, to Asians, the personal characteristics of the service provider are important. Asian customers find it awkward to be served by an older person unless the person is the owner. Efficiency and time-savings are less important than personal attention. Asian consumers' expectations of personalized service are thus higher than Western consumers. For example, Japanese consumers expect their automobile vendors to remind them when service is due, pick up their vehicle, return it to their home after servicing it, and provide a replacement car if needed. This is routinely expected as it is available from all domestic suppliers. In contrast, such service would be considered exceptional and highly personal in the U.S.

Thus *customization* rather than *standardization* is the key in Asian services marketing. Rather than focusing on schedules, number of destinations, baggage handling, and frequent-flier programs, Asian airlines position themselves primarily on providing superior in-flight service. For example, when Virgin Atlantic engaged Cathay Pacific in a price war on the profitable Hong Kong-London route, the latter responded with "in-flight service enhancements."[40] Here is another example.

United Airlines—United spent a huge amount on advertising with its slogan "Fly the Friendly Skies." However, many Asian passengers were not impressed by the "friendliness" of United's U.S. crew on its Asian flights. After some deliberation, the airline decided to hire local, younger, and more enthusiastic staff members. Customer service satisfaction soon increased on its trans-Pacific flights.

Within Asia, what constitutes personalized service also varies by culture and the competitive state of the market. Regional marketers should thus analyze the meaning of service attributes across different Asian markets. For example, Singaporean and Taiwanese consumers perceived banks' provision of 24-hour access to their accounts by the Internet or phone as offering personalized service, while those from Korea and Hong Kong evaluated the same attribute as providing service reliability.[41]

A second dimension of Asian service pertains to **service ritualization**. Asian customers value the ritualistic aspects of service. These include the movement, pose, and look of the service personnel. This ritualistic element is most prominent in Japan, where every salesperson is trained in elaborate gift-wrapping techniques. Japanese women speak in a higher-pitched voice in customer-contact situations than in private situations. In top hotels, the bell-boys accompany the guests to the departing bus or car and wait till the guests have left. Even in fast-food outlets, ritualized service is quite common in Japan.[42]

Takashimaya—In New York, Takashimaya Department Store has received rave reviews for its calm ambience and service. Its in-store display is considered artfully decorated compared to the chaotic displays in most department stores. Further, its gift wrapping, a service ritual in Japan, and customer service are highly regarded, making Takashimaya a great place to find unique gifts.[43]

Haier is the preferred brand in China for household appliances—a result of providing its customers with quality service. To learn about the successful service strategies that propelled this company to its current position, visit www.pearsoned-asia.com/marketingmanagementchina.

Managing Service Quality

The service quality of a firm is tested at each service encounter. If retail clerks are bored, cannot answer simple questions, or are conversing with each other while customers are waiting, customers will think twice about doing business with that seller again.

Customer Expectations

Customers form service expectations from many sources, such as past experiences, word of mouth, and advertising. In general, customers compare the *perceived service* with the *expected service*.[44] If the perceived service falls below the expected service, customers are disappointed. If the perceived service meets or exceeds their expectations, they are apt to use the provider again. Successful companies add benefits to their offering that not only *satisfy* customers but also surprise and *delight* them. Delighting customers is a matter of exceeding expectations.

Ritz-Carlton Hotels—Ritz-Carlton Hotels' legendary service starts with 100 hours of training annually for every employee. The company empowers employees to make decisions and spend money to solve customer-service issues. Guestrooms are exhaustively reviewed every 90 days and guaranteed to be defect-free, check-in time has been cut in half, and special programs created for family travelers and weddings. It is perhaps no surprise that Ritz-Carlton was the first two-time winner of the Malcolm Baldridge National Quality Award.[45]

Chinese tea houses—With tea houses becoming popular both in China and in overseas Chinese markets, many tea shops are finding new ways to attract customers. In Hangzhou, performances of tea art are shown. Instead of merely pouring the drink into many cups, waiters and waitresses are engaging in stunts such as bending over backwards to serve the traditional Chinese beverage to delight customers.[46]

Parasuraman, Zeithaml, and Berry formulated a service-quality model that highlights the main requirements for delivering high service quality.[47] The model, shown in Figure 13.5, identifies five gaps that cause unsuccessful delivery:

1. ***Gap between consumer expectation and management perception*** — Management does not always correctly perceive what customers want. Hospital administrators may think that patients want better food, but patients may be more concerned with nurse responsiveness.
2. ***Gap between management perception and service-quality specification*** — Management might correctly perceive customers' wants but not set a performance standard. Hospital administrators may tell the nurses to give "fast" service without specifying it in minutes.
3. ***Gap between service-quality specifications and service delivery*** — Personnel might be poorly trained, or incapable or unwilling to meet the standard; or they may be held to conflicting standards, such as taking time to listen to customers and serving them fast.

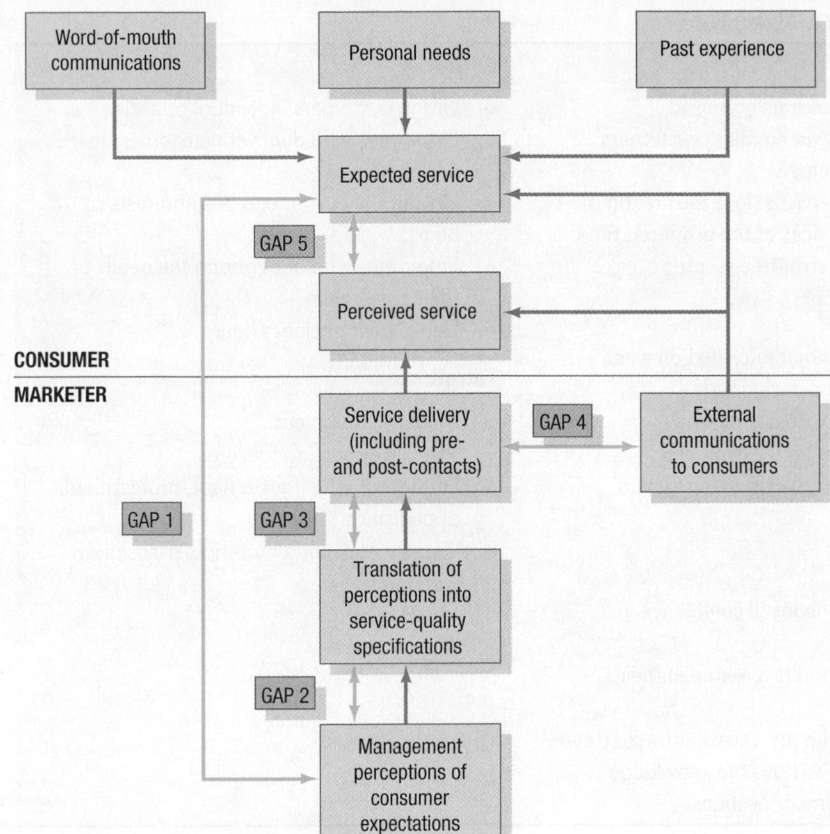

Figure 13.5 Service-Quality Model

Source: A Parasuraman, Valarie A. Zeithaml, and Leonard L. Berry, "A Conceptual Model of Service Quality and Its Implications for Future Research." *Journal of Marketing*, Fall 1985, p. 44. Reprinted with permission of the American Marketing Association. This model is more fully discussed or elaborated in Valarie Zeithaml, Mary Jo Bitner, and Dwayne D. Gremler, *Services Marketing: Integrating Customer Focus across the Firm*, 4th ed., (New York: Mc Graw-Hill, 2006).

4. ***Gap between service delivery and external communications***— Consumer expectations are affected by statements made by company representatives and ads. If a hospital brochure shows a beautiful room, but the patient arrives and finds the room to be cheap and tacky-looking, external communications have distorted the customer's expectations.
5. ***Gap between perceived service and expected service***— This gap occurs when the consumer misperceives the service quality. The physician may keep visiting the patient to show care, but the patient may interpret this as an indication that something really is wrong.

Based on this service-quality model, these researchers identified the following five determinants of service quality, in order of importance.[48]

1. ***Reliability***— The ability to perform the promised service dependably and accurately.
2. ***Responsiveness***— The willingness to help customers and to provide prompt service.
3. ***Assurance***— The knowledge and courtesy of employees and their ability to convey trust and confidence.
4. ***Empathy***— The provision of caring, individualized attention to customers.
5. ***Tangibles***— The appearance of physical facilities, equipment, personnel, and communication materials.

Based on these five factors, the researchers developed the 21-item SERVQUAL scale (see Table 13.2).[49] They also note that there is a *zone of tolerance* or range where consumer perceptions on a service dimension would be deemed satisfactory, anchored by the minimum level consumers would be willing to accept and the level that customers believe can and should be delivered.

"Marketing Insight: The Role of Expectations on Service Quality Perceptions" describes important recent research on services marketing. "Marketing Memo: Assessing E-Service Quality" reviews models of online service quality.

Table 13.2 SERVQUAL Attributes

Reliability

- Providing service as promised
- Dependability in handling customers' service problems
- Performing services right the first time
- Providing services at the promised time
- Maintaining error-free records

Responsiveness

- Keeping customer informed on when services will be performed
- Prompt service to customers
- Willingness to help customers
- Readiness to respond to customers' requests

Assurance

- Employees who instill confidence in customers
- Making customers feel safe in their transactions
- Employees who are consistently courteous
- Employees who have the knowledge to answer customer questions

Empathy

- Giving customers individual attention
- Employees who deal with customers in a caring fashion
- Having the customer's best interests at heart
- Employees who understand the needs of their customers
- Convenient business hours

Tangibles

- Modern equipment
- Visually appealing facilities
- Employees who have a neat, professional appearance
- Visually appealing materials associated with the service

Source: A Parasuraman, Valarie A. Zeithaml, and Leonard L. Berry, "A Conceptual Model of Service Quality and Its Implications for Future Research." *Journal of Marketing,* Fall 1985, pp. 41–50. Reprinted by permission of American Marketing Association.

MARKETING INSIGHT • THE ROLE OF EXPECTATIONS ON SERVICE QUALITY PERCEPTIONS

The Parasuraman, Ziethaml, and Berry service-quality model highlights some of the gaps that cause unsuccessful service delivery. Subsequent research has extended the model to incorporate additional considerations. Boulding, Kalra, Staelin, and Zeithaml have developed a dynamic process model of service quality. The model is based on the premise that customer perceptions and expectations of service quality change over time, but at any one point in time are a function of prior expectations of what *will* and what *should* happen during the service encounter, as well as the *actual* service delivered during the last contact. The researcher's empirically-tested model contends that the two different types of expectations have opposing effects on perceptions of service quality.

1. **Increasing customer expectations of what the firm will deliver** can lead to improved perceptions of overall service quality.
2. **Decreasing customer expectations of what the firm should deliver** can lead to improved perceptions of overall service quality.

Much work has validated the role of expectations in consumer's interpretations and evaluations of the service encounter and the relationship they adopt with a firm over time. Consumers are often forward-looking regarding their decision to keep or switch from a service relationship. Any marketing activity that affects current or expected future usage can help to solidify a service relationship.

With continuously provided services, such as public utilities, health care, financial services, computing services, insurance and other professional, membership, or subscription services, customers have been observed to mentally calculate their *payment equity*—the perceived fairness of the level of economic benefits derived from service usage in relation to the level of economic costs. Payment costs typically consist of some combination of an initial payment such as a membership fee or retainer; a fixed, periodic fee such as a monthly service charge; and a variable fee such as usage-based charges. Payment benefits depend on current payment and usage levels. The perceived fairness of the exchange determines service satisfaction and future usage. In other words, it is as if customers ask themselves, "Am I using this service enough, given what I pay for it?" Customers may be satisfied even with low usage *if* that is their expectation.

There can be a dark side to long-term service relationships. For example, with an ad agency, the client may feel that over time, the agency loses objectivity and becomes stale in its thinking or begins to take advantage of the relationship.

Sources: William Boulding, Ajay Kalra, Richard Staelin, and Valarie A. Zeithaml, "A Dynamic Model of Service Quality: From Expectations to Behavioral Intentions." *Journal of Marketing Research*, February 1993, 30, pp. 7–27; Katherine N. Lemon, Tiffany Barnett White, and Russell S. Winer, "Dynamic Customer Relationship Management: Incorporating Future Considerations into the Service Retention Decision." *Journal of Marketing*, January 2002, 6, pp. 1–14; Ruth N. Bolton and Katherine N. Lemon, "A Dynamic Model of Customers' Usage of Services: Usage as an Antecedent and Consequence of Satisfaction." *Journal of Marketing*, May 1999, 36, pp. 171–186; Kent Grayson and Tim Ambler, "The Dark Side of Long-Term Relationships in Marketing Services." *Journal of Marketing Research*, February 1999, 36, pp. 132–141.

MARKETING MEMO • ASSESSING E-SERVICE QUALITY

Zeithaml, Parasuraman, and Malhotra define online service quality as the extent to which a Web site facilitates efficient and effective shopping, purchasing, and delivery. They identified 11 dimensions of perceived e-service quality: access, ease of navigation, efficiency, flexibility, reliability, personalization, security/privacy, responsiveness, assurance/trust, site aesthetics, and price knowledge. Some of these service-quality dimensions were the same online as offline, but some specific underlying attributes were different. Different dimensions emerged with e-service quality too. They also found that empathy did not seem to be as important online, unless there were service problems. Core dimensions of regular service quality were efficiency, fulfillment, reliability, and privacy; core dimensions of service recovery were responsiveness, compensation, and real-time access to help.

Wolfinbarger and Gilly developed a reduced scale of online service quality with four key dimensions: reliability/fulfillment, Web site design, security/privacy, and customer service. The researchers interpret their study findings to suggest that the most basic building blocks of a "compelling online experience" are reliability and outstanding Web site functionality in terms of time savings, easy transactions, good selection, in-depth information, and the "right level" of personalization. Their 14-item scale is displayed here:

Reliability/Fulfillment

- The product that came was represented accurately by the Web site.
- You get what you ordered from this Web site.
- The product is delivered within the time promised by the company.

Web Site Design

- This Web site provides in-depth information.
- The site does not waste my time.
- It is quick and easy to complete a transaction at this Web site.
- The level of personalization at this site is about right, not too much or too little.
- This Web site has a good selection.

Security/Privacy

- I feel that my privacy is protected at this site.
- I feel safe in my transactions with this Web site.
- This Web site has adequate security transactions.

Customer Service

- The company is willing and ready to respond to customer needs.
- When you have a problem, the Web site shows a sincere interest in solving it.
- Inquiries are answered promptly.

Sources: Valarie A. Zeithaml, A. Parsu Parasuraman, and Arvind Malhotra, "A Conceptual Framework for Understanding e-Service Quality: Implications for Future Research and Managerial Practice." *Marketing Science Institute Working Paper*, Report No. 00-115, 2000; Mary Wolfinbarger and Mary C. Gilly, ".comQ: Dimensionalizing, Measuring, and Predicting Quality of the E-tail Experience." *Marketing Science Institute Working Paper*, Report No. 02-100, 2002.

Best Practices of Service-Quality Management

Various studies have shown that well-managed service companies share the following common practices: a strategic concept, a history of top-management commitment to quality, high standards, self-service technologies, systems for monitoring service performance and customer complaints, and an emphasis on employee satisfaction.

STRATEGIC CONCEPT

Top service companies are "customer obsessed." They have a clear sense of their target customers and their needs. They have developed a distinctive strategy for satisfying these needs. While most brokerage firms chase after an older, wealthier customer base, online brokers E*Trade targets younger customers who are technologically savvy and self-sufficient but largely ignored by other firms. As CEO Christos Cotsakos observes, "There's this whole generation that's very computer-literate, that's building wealth and looking for solutions that aren't like their grandfathers'. If we can identify with this new class of individuals and provide them with the best value, we think we can own that space."[50]

TOP-MANAGEMENT COMMITMENT

Companies such as Singapore Airlines, Giordano, Marriott, and Disney have a thorough commitment to service quality. Their managements look not only at financial performance on a monthly basis, but also at service performance. Each McDonald's outlet is continually assessed on its conformance to QSCV: quality, service, cleanliness, and value. See "Marketing Memo: The Seven Deadly Sins of Service Management" for Giordano's perspective on this issue.

HIGH STANDARDS

The best service providers set high service-quality standards. Citibank aims to answer phone calls within 10 seconds and customer letters within two days. The standards must be set *appropriately* high. A 98 percent accuracy standard may sound good, but it would result in FedEx losing 64,000 packages a day; six misspelled words on each page of a book; and 400,000 mis-filled prescriptions daily in the U.S. One can distinguish between companies offering "merely good" service and those offering "breakthrough" service, aimed at being 100 percent defect-free.[51]

Asian airports—Asian airports are steeped in providing superb service. Hong Kong International Airport was named the World's Best Airport in 2007 and was praised for its efficiency, consistency, and quality of service delivered across its frontline staff areas. Seoul Incheon Airport and Singapore Changi Airport shared the second spot. Hong Kong Airport excelled in airport dining, duty-free shopping, security processing, baggage delivery, cleanliness, leisure amenities, and staff friendliness. Incheon Airport did well in keeping the terminals clean and washrooms clean, and as an airport for transit. Changi Airport was praised for its smooth immigration processing, duty-free shopping, airport dining, leisure amenities, and as an airport for transit. Other Asian airports that did well were Kuala Lumpur International Airport (ranked 5th) and Kansai International Airport (ranked 9th). In a separate award, the Airports Council International ranked Incheon Airport no. 1, followed by Kuala Lumpur Airport and Singapore Changi Airport. Incheon Airport was commended for delivering quality airport service and seeing itself as part of the overall tourism value chain. The commitment is given very high priority politically as well as operationally by the airport.[52]

Asian airports are known for providing excellent services. Singapore's Changi Airport is consistently ranked in the top three for international airports.

A service company can differentiate itself by designing a better and faster delivery system. There are three levels of differentiation.[53] The first is *reliability:* some suppliers are more reliable in their on-time delivery, order completeness, and order-cycle time. The second is *resilience:* some suppliers are better at handling emergencies, product recalls, and answering inquiries. The third is *innovativeness*: some suppliers create better information systems and, introduce bar coding and mixed pallets to help the customer.

Many distribution experts say that a company's money would be better spent on improving delivery performance than on advertising. They say that superior service performance is a more effective differentiator than image expenditures. Further, it is harder for a competitor to duplicate a superior distribution system than to copy an advertising campaign.

MARKETING MEMO • THE SEVEN DEADLY SINS OF SERVICE MANAGEMENT

Giordano is arguably Asia's most successful home-grown clothing retail chain. Outstanding service is a cornerstone for Giordano's success. Peter Lau, its chairman and CEO, outlined seven cardinal errors top management of service businesses should note and avoid:

1. ***Short-sightedness*** — Instead of calculating the immediate economic return of each service initiative, Giordano focuses on its long-term cumulative benefits.
2. ***Unhappy frontliners*** — Unhappy staff will result in unhappy customers. Giordano offers its staff a 1.5-day holiday weekly and constant attitude training.
3. ***Bloated management ego*** — Most managers believe they know more than their staff and customers. Giordano believes in sharing information. Every morning, store briefings are held and the *Giordano Morning Post* faxed to all stores listing each shop's sales and which items sell well. Customer feedback is collected and rewarded regularly. Giordano also has a mystery shopper program.
4. ***Absence of customer-friendly policies*** — Most companies have procedures designed for selfprotection. Giordano's procedures facilitate customer satisfaction. Its exchange and refund policies, usually no questions asked, are liberal. Staff are empowered to implement these policies to the best of their judgment.
5. ***Training for short-term returns rather than for character-building*** — Most companies do not have holistic people-development programs. Giordano employees are given not only sales training, but also personal growth workshops. Training costs per employee average $700 annually. Employees spend 34 hours a year in training. A two-year management trainee program has also been implemented.
6. ***Management does not walk the talk*** — Most managers fail to lead by example. All Giordano senior managers frequent its stores to communicate with sales staff and customers. Company policies apply to all employees equally, with no added privilege given to anyone.
7. ***Complacency*** — Most companies are satisfied with the status quo. Giordano seeks to constantly improve its processes for anticipating and fulfilling customer demands. To stay abreast of fashion trends, for example, its New York design studio sends the latest in fashion basics from the U.S. via the Internet to Giordano's Hong Kong head office.

Source: Peter Lau, "The Seven Deadly Sins of Service Management." In *Asian Business Wisdom: From Deals to Dot.coms*, Dinna Louis C. Dayao, ed., (Singapore: John Wiley, 2001), pp. 203–207.

Bank of Asia—This is one of Thailand's smallest banks but believes it can become one of the country's biggest through a ubiquitous automated teller machine (ATM) network. Bank of Asia found that the average bank customer withdraws cash two and a half times a week but does not like going to branches to collect the money. Hence, it is bringing banking to consumers by expanding its ATM network to places which consumers frequent such as Shell gas stations, shopping malls, hospitals, colleges, and McDonald's outlets. The bank also recognizes that ATMs are more effective at dispensing than collecting cash. Thus its staff are located at some ATMs in Shell stations and shopping malls to steer customers to the nearest branch. To woo customers from other banks, it printed promotions on the back of its ATM slips, a move later imitated by its bigger local rivals.[54]

"Marketing Insight: Developing Customer Interface Systems" discusses how service marketers must re-engineer their customer interface systems for optimal efficiency and effectiveness.

SELF-SERVICE TECHNOLOGIES (SSTS)

As with products, consumers value convenience in services.[55] Many person-to-person service interactions are being replaced by self-service technologies.[56] To the traditional vending machines we can add ATMs, self-pumping at gas stations, self-checkout at hotels, self-ticket purchasing on the Internet, and self-customization of products on the Internet.

Not all SSTs improve service quality, but they can make service transactions more accurate, convenient, and faster. Obviously they can also reduce costs. IBM saved $2 billion by shifting 99 million service telephone calls online.[57] Every company needs to think about improving its service using SSTs.

MARKETING INSIGHT • DEVELOPING CUSTOMER INTERFACE SYSTEMS

Marketing academics and consultants Rayport and Jaworski define a *customer-service interface* as any place at which a company seeks to manage a relationship with a customer, whether through people, technology, or some combination of the two. They believe that to deliver high levels of customer-perceived value, any interface should excel on four dimensions:

- ***Physical presence and appearance*** — Be on the scene in sufficient numbers and presentable in appearance. At the Oriental Hotel, the frontline staff is differentiated on appearance as uniformed, clean-cut, businesslike, courteous, individual, and authentic.
- ***Cognition*** — Be able to recognize patterns, draw intelligent conclusions, and communicate articulately. At Giordano, salespeople are skilled at recognizing and rewarding the store's best customers with appropriate service and attention.
- ***Emotion or attitude*** — Be respectful and attentive, displaying brand-consistent personality attributes, and emotionally calibrated with the customer. Southwest Airlines' flight crew's sense of humor and positive dispositions enhance passengers' travel experience.
- ***Connectedness*** — Remain well connected to other resources important to the customer's experience. Oriental, Giordano, and Singapore Airlines coordinate communications and activities to provide a holistic, positive experience.

Rayport and Jaworski believe companies are facing a crisis in customer interaction and relationship management. Although many companies serve customers through a broad array of interfaces, from retail sales clerks to Web sites to voice-response telephone systems, these more often constitute an interface *collection*, not an actual interface *system*, as the whole set does not add up to the sum of its parts in its ability to provide superior service and build strong customer relationships. Rising complexity and costs, and customer dissatisfaction can result. Networked technologies, however, such as Web sites, kiosks, interactive voice-response units, vending machines, and touch screens let managers successfully introduce machines into front office roles that have long been held by humans. Here is one example they note:

- Borders deployed Title Sleuth self-service kiosks to take the burden of title searches off its employees. The three hundred machines handle up to 1.2 million customer searches per week, and customers using these machines spend 50 percent more per store visit and generate 20 percent more special-order sales.

According to Rayport and Jaworski, successfully integrating technology into the work force requires a comprehensive reengineering of the front office to identify what people do best, what machines do best, and how to deploy them separately and together. Managers can take the following steps in conducting a service interface re-engineering project:

1. **Understand the experience customers want.** Do customers seek information, advice, social exchange, affirmation, anonymity, discretion, efficiency, or something else? What interactions and relationships will shape those experiences? What are the implications of these experiences for the firm's own goals and objectives?
2. **Understand the potential of technology.** What is the effectiveness and efficiency of possible technology? What new roles can technology assume?
3. **Match the interface type to the task.** Should the interface be people-dominant, machine-dominant, or a hybrid of the two? What are the associated costs and customer outcomes?
4. **Put work in its right place.** Should services be provided proximally (in stores or on-site) or remotely (through network connections to customers or operations off-site)?
5. **Optimize performance across the system.** Whereas most customers use multiple channels, is the interface system able to capitalize on the economic potential of each?

Sources: Jeffrey F. Rayport and Bernard J. Jaworski, *Best Face Forward,* (Boston, MA: Harvard Business School Press, 2005); Jeffrey F. Rayport, Bernard J. Jaworski, and Ellie J. Kyung, "Best Face Forward." *Journal of Interactive Marketing*, Autumn 2005, 19, pp. 67–80; Jeffrey F. Rayport and Bernard J. Jaworski, "Best Face Forward." *Harvard Business Review*, December 2004, 82, pp. 47–58.

Some companies have found that the biggest obstacle is not the technology itself, but convincing customers to use it, especially for the first time. Customers must have a clear sense of their roles in the SST process, must see a clear benefit to SST, and must feel they have the ability to actually use it.[58] Singapore Airlines has been successfully in getting its passengers to check in and choose their seats online. It also has some success in getting customers travelling without checked in baggage to print their own boarding passes by displaying this self-service facility prominently in its Web site.

MONITORING SYSTEMS

Top firms audit service performance, both their own and competitors, on a regular basis. They collect *voice of the customer (VOC) measurements* to probe customer satisfiers and dissatisfiers. They use comparison shopping, ghost shopping, customer surveys, suggestion and complaint forms, service audit teams, and letters to the president.

Mystery shopping—the use of undercover shoppers who are paid to report back to the company—is used by fast-food chains, gas stations, and large government agencies to pinpoint and fix customer service problems.

Services can be judged on *customer importance* and *company performance. Importance-performance analysis* is used to rate the various elements of the service bundle and identify what actions are required. Table 13.3 shows how customers rated 14 service elements (attributes) of an automobile dealer's service department on importance and performance. For example, "Job done right the first time" (attribute 1) received a mean importance rating of 3.83 and a mean performance rating of 2.63, indicating that customers felt it was highly important but not performed well.

Table 13.3 Customer Importance and Performance Ratings for an Auto Dealership

Attribute Number	Attribute Description	Mean Importance Rating[a]	Mean Performance Rating[b]
1	Job done right the first time	3.83	2.63
2	Fast action on complaints	3.63	2.73
3	Prompt warranty work	3.60	3.15
4	Able to do any job needed	3.56	3.00
5	Service available when needed	3.41	3.05
6	Courteous and friendly service	3.41	3.29
7	Car ready when promised	3.38	3.03
8	Perform only necessary work	3.37	3.11
9	Low prices on service	3.29	2.00
10	Clean up after service work	3.27	3.02
11	Convenient to home	2.52	2.25
12	Convenient to work	2.43	2.49
13	Courtesy buses and cars	2.37	2.35
14	Send out maintenance notices	2.05	3.33

[a] Ratings obtained from a four-point scale of "extremely important" (4), "important" (3), "slightly important" (2), and "not important" (1).

[b] Ratings obtained from a four-point scale of "excellent" (4), "good" (3), "fair" (2), and "poor" (1). A "no basis for judgment" category was also provided.

The ratings of the 14 elements are displayed in Figure 13.6 and divided into four sections. Quadrant A shows important service elements that are not being performed at the desired levels; they include elements 1, 2, and 9. The dealer should concentrate on improving the service department's performance on these elements. Quadrant B shows important service elements that are being performed well; the company needs to maintain the high performance. Quadrant C shows minor service elements that are being delivered in a mediocre way but do not need any attention. Quadrant D shows that a minor service element, "Send out maintenance notices," is being performed in an excellent manner. Perhaps the company should spend less on sending out maintenance notices and use the savings to improve performance on important elements. The analysis can be enhanced by checking on the competitors' performance levels on each element.[59]

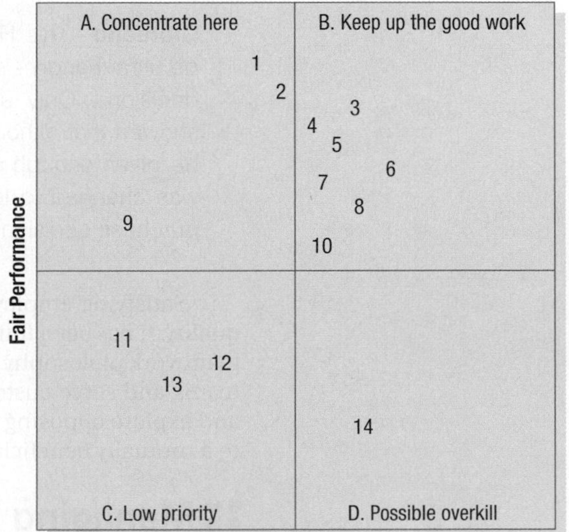

Figure 13.6 Importance-Performance Analysis

SATISFYING CUSTOMER COMPLAINTS

Every complaint is a gift if handled well. Companies that encourage disappointed customers to complain—and also empower employees to remedy the situation on the spot—have been shown to achieve higher revenues and greater profits than companies that do not have a systematic approach for addressing service failures.[60] Pizza Hut prints its toll-free number on all pizza boxes. When a customer complains, Pizza Hut sends voice mail to the store manager, who must call the customer within 48 hours and resolve the complaint. Hyatt Hotels also gets high marks on many of these criteria.

Getting frontline employees to adopt *extra-role behaviors* and to advocate the interests and image of the firm to consumers, as well as take initiative and engage in conscientious behavior in dealing with customers, can be a critical asset in handling complaints. Research has shown that customers evaluate complaint incidents in terms of the outcomes they receive, the procedures used to arrive at those outcomes, and the nature of the interpersonal treatment during the process. Companies also are increasing the quality of their *call centers* and their *customer-service representatives* (CSRs).

Handling phone calls more efficiently can improve service, reduce complaints, and extend customer longevity. Yet more often than not the problem is not poor quality but that customers are asked to use an automated voice-response system instead of interacting with a customer-service representative.

SATISFYING EMPLOYEES AS WELL AS CUSTOMERS

Excellent service companies know that positive employee attitudes will promote stronger customer loyalty.

Instilling a strong customer orientation in employees can also increase their job satisfaction and commitment, especially if they're in service settings that allow for a high degree of customer-contact time. Employees thrive in customer-contact positions when they have an internal drive to (1) pamper customers; (2) accurately read customer needs; (3) develop a personal relationship with customers; and (4) deliver quality service to solve customers' problems.[61] Some companies have observed a high correlation between customer satisfaction, employee satisfaction, and store profitability.

Given the importance of positive employee attitudes, service companies must attract the best employees they can find. They need to market a career rather than just a job. They must design a sound training program and provide support and rewards for good performance. They can use the intranet, internal newsletters, daily reminders, and employee roundtables to reinforce customer-centered attitudes. Some Asian companies, especially Chinese state firms, lack employees who are customer-oriented. Thus they have recruited foreign talent at middle- to top-management levels. For example, Shenzhen-based Ping An Insurance has been hiring several Taiwanese insurance professionals to improve its operations.[62]

Yet a company must be careful in training its employees not to be too friendly as the following example shows.

Giordano—This Hong Kong-based clothing chain used to train its sales clerks to be ultra-friendly—so friendly that they rarely left customers alone to make purchase decisions. Only after many complaints did Giordano conduct new studies that showed that although the customers liked smiling sales clerks, they also wanted to be given enough privacy to enjoy their shopping experience. Hence, their training was changed to teach sales clerks to give customers more privacy to make their purchase decisions.[63]

Satisfying employees may also involve organizational changes in instituting service quality. It has been found in China and Singapore that service companies with a cooperative teamwork philosophy were able to allow their employees to work collaboratively with other teams and serve customers better. Although the employees express their feelings directly and explore opposing views, they were able to use the best ideas from each team and agree to a mutually beneficial, high-quality solution.[64]

Managing Service Brands

Some of the world's strongest brands are services—consider financial service leaders such as Citibank, American Express, and HSBC; and airlines such as Singapore Airlines, Cathay Pacific, and Japan Airlines. As with any brand, service brands must be skillful at differentiating themselves and developing appropriate brand strategies.

Differentiating Services

Service marketers frequently complain about the difficulty of differentiating their services. The deregulation of several major service industries—communications, transportation, energy, banking—has resulted in intense price competition. To the extent that customers view a service as fairly homogeneous, they care less about the provider than the price.

Service offerings, however, can be differentiated in many ways. The offering can include innovative features. What the customer expects is called the *primary service package.* The provider can add *secondary service features* to the package. In the airline industry, various carriers have introduced such secondary service features as movies, merchandise for sale, air-to-ground telephone service, and frequent-flier reward programs. Mandarin Oriental has hotel rooms for high-tech travelers who need accommodations that will support computers, fax machines, and email. Conversely, other service providers are adding a human element to combat competition from online businesses. Below are examples of how Japanese banks are providing more services to woo the retail market.

Japanese retail banking—Retail bank customers in Japan have long been subjected to unhelpful tellers, a poor selection of financial products at uncompetitive rates, and ATMs that shut down after 6 p.m. Now, after the success of Citibank and HSBC, Japanese banks are wooing retail customers. Mitsubishi Tokyo Financial Group has opened a one-stop financial supermarket offering banking, insurance, and securities. It has also set up a "retail academy" to improve branch employees' customer-service skills. It is also the first in Japan to introduce biometric ATM machines that scan customer palms to provide account access. Mizuho Financial Group has booths where customers can consult securities staff at other bank branches via video phone service. It is also expanding its lending businesses through tie-ups with Credit Saison, a credit card company, and Orient Corp., a consumer finance firm.[65]

Sometimes the company achieves differentiation through the sheer range of its service offerings and the success of its cross-selling efforts. The major challenge is that most service offerings and innovations are easily copied. Still, the company that regularly introduces innovations will gain a succession of temporary advantages over competitors.

Alexandra Hospital—Hospitals throughout Asia are facing increasing pressure to raise the quality of healthcare with limited resources. In a collaboration with Cisco Systems and Fujitsu Asia, Alexandra Hospital in Singapore introduced the Clinical Connection Suite to innovate the hospital and provide better service. This IT system enables healthcare professionals at Alexandra to diagnose, treat, and advise patients within the shortest time and at the lowest possible cost. For a start, a "just in time" approach to bed management reduces waiting times for beds and increases efficiency in the utilization of beds. Says Teng Lit Liak, Chief Executive Officer of Alexandra Hospital, "It is our aim to get a patient who needs admission into a hospital bed within minutes rather than making him or her wait for hours.[66]

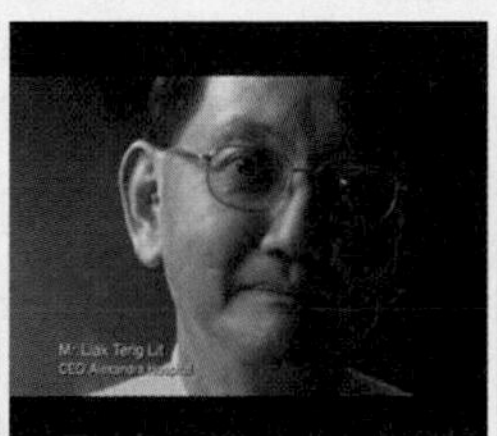
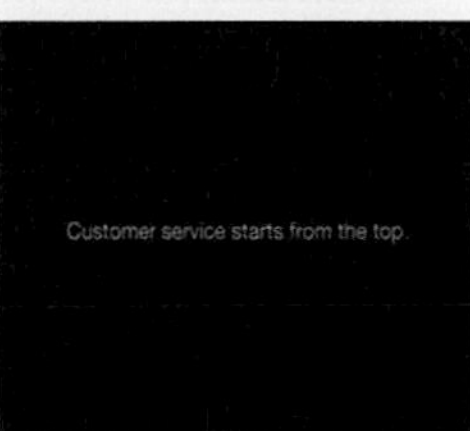

In a collaboration with Cisco Systems and Fujitsu Asia, Alexandra Hospital in Singapore introduced the Clinical Connection Suite to provide better service to patients.

Creativity and innovation is as vital in services as in any industry. There are always ways to improve the customer experience. When a group of hospitality and travel industry experts convened late in 2006 to share their insights into what the ideal 2025 hotel might look like, their visions suggested a totally transformed service experience. One idea, turning hotels into retails showrooms where guests can try out and buy displayed items, was later adopted by chains such as Hyatt Hotels. Some of the other ideas have yet to be implemented and may take more time, but they help point out how achieving service excellence is a never-ending process:[67]

1. Kinetic corridors could light up with a blanket of stars and illuminated signs to provide guests with an easy relaxing entry to their rooms.
2. A multipurpose bed could be flipped over to create more work surfaces or rise all the way up to be a ceiling panel.
3. A multitask chair could be equipped with reading lights, fold-up tablet tray tables, integrated speakers near the ears, and a muscle massager.

Developing Brand Strategies for Services

Developing brand strategies for a service brand requires special attention to choosing brand elements, establishing image dimensions, and devising the branding strategy.

CHOOSING BRAND ELEMENTS

The intangibility of services has implications for the choice of brand elements. Because service decisions and arrangements are often made away from the actual service location itself (e.g., at home or at work), brand recall becomes critically important. In such cases, an easy-to-remember brand name is critical.

Other brand elements—logos, symbols, characters, and slogans—can also "pick up the slack" and complement the brand name to build brand awareness and brand image. These other brand elements often attempt to make the service and some of its key benefits more tangible, concrete, and real—e.g., the "smiling maharaja" of Air India, and the "Singapore Girl" of Singapore Airlines.

Because a physical product does not exist, the physical facilities of the service provider—its primary and secondary signage, environmental design and reception area, apparel, collateral material, and so on—are especially important. All aspects of the service delivery process can be branded, which is why Singapore Airlines is concerned about the appearance of its flight attendants; and why UPS has developed such strong equity with the brown color of its trucks.

ESTABLISHING IMAGE DIMENSIONS

Organizational associations—such as perceptions about the people who make up the organization and who provide the service—are likely to be particularly important brand associations that may affect evaluations of service quality directly or indirectly. One particularly important association is company credibility and perceived expertise, trustworthiness, and likeability.

Service firms must therefore design marketing communication and information programs to develop their brand personality and help consumers learn more about the brand than the information they get from service encounters alone.

Mandarin Oriental Hotel—This Hong Kong-based chain of luxury hotels employed its logo—the fan—in a recent global ad campaign. The campaign featured a series of celebrities, such as Martin Sheen, Michelle Yeoh, Whoopi Goldberg, Elle Macpherson, and Lance Armstrong, under the tagline "He/She's a fan." The celebrities regularly stay at the hotel and consider themselves its fans. The ads refer readers to the hotel chain's Web site for more information on why each celebrity is a fan of the hotel. The ads were placed in such international lifestyle, travel, and fashion magazines as ***The New Yorker***, ***Vanity Fair***, ***Architectural Digest***, ***Harper's & Queen***, and ***Forbes Global***.

DEVISING BRANDING STRATEGY

Finally, services also must consider developing a brand hierarchy and brand portfolio that permits positioning and targeting of different market segments. Classes of service can be branded vertically on the basis of price and quality. Vertical extensions often require sub-branding strategies where the corporate name is combined with an individual brand name or modifier. In the hotel and airlines industries, brand lines and portfolios have been created by brand extension and introductions. For example, frequent-flier programs of most airlines have been branded, such as Evergreen Club (EVA Airways), Krisflyer (Singapore Airlines), and Marco Polo Club (Cathay Pacific). The circus Cirque du Soleil has adopted a very strict branding strategy.[68]

Cirque du Soleil— In its 25-year history, Cirque du Soleil (French for "circus of the sun") has continually broken loose from circus convention. It takes traditional ingredients such as trapeze artists, clowns, muscle men, and contortionists and places them in a nontraditional setting with lavish costumes, New Age music, and spectacular stage designs. And it eliminates other commonly observed elements—there are no animals. Each production is loosely tied together with a theme such as "a tribute to the nomadic soul" (*Varekai*) or "a phantasmagoria of urban life" (*Saltimbanco*). The group has grown from its Quebec street-performance roots to become a half-billion dollar enterprise with 3,000 employees on four continents entertaining audiences of millions annually. Part of the success is a company culture that encourages artistic creativity and innovation and carefully safeguards the brand (see Figure 13.7). Each new production is created in-house—roughly one a year—and is unique: There are no duplicate touring companies. In addition to using a varied mix of media and local promotion, an extensive interactive email program to its million-plus-member Cirque Club creates an online community of fans—20–30 percent of all ticket sales for touring shows come from club members. The Cirque du Soleil brand has expanded to encompass a record label, a retail operation, and resident productions in Las Vegas (five in all), Orlando, and Tokyo.

Cirque du Soleil's branding strategy includes spectacular themed performances by circus players with elaborate costumes and New Age music—and no animals. Each touring production is unique; there are no duplicate casts, protecting the brand from overexposure and easy imitation.

1. **Cast teams for creative conflict.** Cirque officials generally make sure there's a mix of nationalities and viewpoints when they draft a creative team. Then they lock creators in a room with the instructions, "Don't come out till you have something great."
2. **Always shoot for the triple somersault.** Cirque's founder, Guy Laliberte, is famous for asking his people to stretch beyond the great to the jaw-dropping. "It is a commitment to a degree of sophistication and performance that distinguishes Cirque du Soleil productions from their less demanding peers," says coach Boris Verkhovsky.
3. **Recruit the near-great.** Elite athletes who just missed the national team generally have the same work ethic, the same tricks, and nearly the same skills as medal winners. The difference: They still have something to prove, and they're rarely prima donnas.
4. **Push the envelope—at the interview.** Cirque scouts routinely ask candidates to do something unexpected at their audition: Climb a rope... then sing a song when you get to the top ("Happy Birthday" is forbidden). It is a good way to find talent that's multidimensional and comfortable improvising, not to mention a great character test.
5. **Do not be greedy.** Cirque limits its show production to one a year. It believes that to have fun creating shows and pushing the boundaries, one show a year is good enough. It does not want to jeopardize quality. If there's no creative challenge, it will not do a deal, regardless of the financial impact.
6. **Protect creative teams from business pressures.** The creative teams are isolated from the Cirque du Soleil "machine." The creative teams need to eat and breathe their show. Keeping them away from day-to-day operations protects them from business pressures.

Figure 13.7 Flying High Without a Net: Cirque du Soleil's Formula for Creative Success

Source: Linda Tischler, "Join the Circus." *Fast Company*, July 2005, pp. 53–58. Reprinted by permission of Fast Company via Copyright clearance center.

Managing Product Support Services

No less important are product-based industries that must provide a service bundle. Manufacturers of equipment—small appliances, office machines, tractors, mainframes, airplanes—all have to provide *product support services.* Product support service is becoming a major battleground for competitive advantage. Chapter 12 described how products could be augmented with key service differentiators—ordering ease, delivery, installation, customer training, customer consulting, and maintenance and repair. Some companies like Caterpillar make over half their profits from these services. In the global marketplace, companies that make a good product but provide poor local service support are seriously disadvantaged. Firms that provide high-quality service outperform their less service-oriented competitors.

Identifying and Satisfying Customer Needs

The company must define customer needs carefully in designing a service support program. Customers have three specific worries:[69]

- **They worry about reliability and *failure frequency.*** A farmer may tolerate a combine that will break down once a year, but not two or three times a year.
- **They worry about *downtime.*** The longer the downtime, the higher the cost. The customer counts on the seller's *service dependability*—the seller's ability to fix the machine quickly, or at least provide a loaner.[70]
- **They worry about *out-of-pocket costs.*** How much does the customer have to spend on regular maintenance and repair costs?

A buyer takes all these factors into consideration in choosing a vendor. The buyer tries to estimate the **life-cycle cost**, which is the product's purchase cost plus the discounted cost of maintenance and repair less the discounted salvage value. Buyers ask for hard data in choosing among vendors.

The importance of reliability, service dependability, and maintenance vary. A one-computer office will need higher product reliability and faster repair service than an office where other computers are available if one breaks down. An airline needs 100 percent reliability in the air. Where reliability is important, manufacturers or service providers can offer guarantees to promote sales.

To provide the best support, a manufacturer must identify the services customers value most and their relative importance. For expensive equipment, manufacturers offer *facilitating services* such as installation, staff training, maintenance and repair services, and financing. They may also add *value-augmenting services,* which include warranties, guarantees, and trade-in allowances.

IBM—In Asia, IBM launched its Global Asset Recovery Solutions program to give companies a secure and cost-effective way to retire hardware they no longer need. Although it is the customers' responsibility to clean up their hard disk, IBM adds another layer of precaution by cleaning them again when they receive these used machines. It scrubs the hard disks with a secure data disposal process approved by such government agencies as the FBI.[71]

A manufacturer can offer and charge for product support services in different ways. One specialty organic-chemical company provides a standard offering plus a basic level of services. If the customer wants additional services, it can pay extra or increase its annual purchases to a higher level, in which case additional services would be included. As another alternative, many companies offer *service contracts* (also called *extended warranties*), in which sellers agree to provide free maintenance and repair services for a specified period of time at a specified contract price.

Postsale Service Strategy

The quality of customer service departments varies greatly. At one extreme are departments that simply transfer customer calls to the appropriate person or department for action, with little follow-up. At the other extreme are departments eager to receive customer requests, suggestions, and even complaints and handle them expeditiously.

In providing service, most companies progress through a series of stages. Manufacturers usually start out by running their own parts-and-service departments. They want to stay close to the equipment and know its problems. They also find it expensive and time-consuming to train others, and discover that they can make good money running the parts-and-service business. As long as they are the only supplier of the needed parts, they can charge a premium price. In fact, many equipment manufacturers price their equipment low and compensate by charging high prices for parts and service. (This explains why competitors manufacture the same or similar parts and sell them to customers or intermediaries for less.)

Over time, manufacturers switch more maintenance and repair service to authorized distributors and dealers. These intermediaries are closer to customers, operate in more locations, and can offer quicker service. Manufacturers still make a profit on the parts but leave the servicing profit to intermediaries. Still later, independent service firms emerge. They typically offer a lower price or faster service than the manufacturer or authorized intermediaries.

THE CUSTOMER-SERVICE IMPERATIVE

Customer service choices are increasing rapidly, holding down prices and profits on service. Equipment manufacturers increasingly have to figure out how to make money on their equipment, independent of service contracts. Some new car warranties now cover 200,000 kilometers before servicing. The increase in disposable or never-fail equipment makes customers less inclined to pay from 2–10 percent of the purchase price every year for a service. Some large customers handle their own maintenance and repair. A company with several hundred personal computers, printers, and related equipment might find it cheaper to have its own service personnel on site. These companies typically press the manufacturer for a lower price, because they are providing their own services.

Summary

1. A service is any act or performance that one party can offer to another that is essentially intangible and does not result in the ownership of anything. It may or may not be tied to a physical product.
2. Services are intangible, inseparable, variable, and perishable. Each characteristic poses challenges and requires certain strategies. Marketers must find ways to give tangibility to intangibles; to increase the productivity of service providers; to increase and standardize the quality of the service provided; and to match the supply of services with market demand.
3. Service industries used to lag behind manufacturing firms in adopting and using marketing concepts and tools, but this situation has now changed. Service marketing must be done holistically: It calls not only for external marketing but also for internal marketing to motivate employees and interactive marketing to emphasize the importance of both "high-tech" and "high-touch."
4. Customers' expectations play a critical role in their service experiences and evaluations. Companies must manage service quality by understanding the effects of each service encounter.
5. Top service companies excel at the following practices: a strategic concept, a history of top-management commitment to quality, high standards, self-service technologies, systems for monitoring service performance and customer complaints, and an emphasis on employee satisfaction.
6. To brand a service organization effectively, the company must differentiate its brand through primary and secondary service features and develop appropriate brand strategies. Effective branding programs for services often employ multiple brand elements. They also develop brand hierarchies and portfolios and establish image dimensions to reinforce or complement service offerings.
7. Even product-based companies must provide postpurchase service. To provide the best support, a manufacturer must identify the services customers value most and their relative importance. The service mix includes both presale services (facilitating and value-augmenting services) and postsale services (customer service departments, repair and maintenance services).

Application

Marketing Debate—Is Service Marketing Different From Product Marketing?

Some services marketers vehemently maintain that services marketing is fundamentally different from product marketing and that different skills are involved. Some traditional product marketers disagree, saying "good marketing is good marketing."

Take a position: *Product and services marketing are fundamentally different* versus *Product and services marketing are highly related.*

Marketing Discussion

Colleges, universities and other educational institutions can be classified as service organizations. How can you apply the marketing principles developed in this chapter to your school? Do you have any advice as to how they could become better service marketers?

PART 5

Gillette's Fusion Power razor commands a premium price and about 70 percent of the global market

Developing Pricing Strategies and Programs

14

Price is the one element of the marketing mix that produces revenue; the other elements produce costs. Prices are perhaps the easiest element of the marketing program to adjust; product features, channels, and even promotion take more time. Price also communicates to the market the company's intended value positioning of its product or brand. A well-designed and marketed product can command a price premium and reap big profits. Consider Gillette.

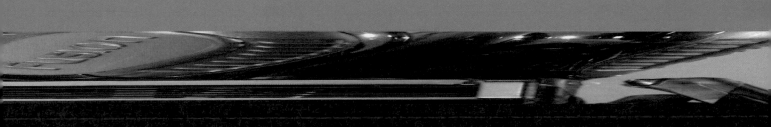

Gillette has a tradition of product innovation, beginning with the invention of the safety razor by King C. Gillette in 1901. Subsequent product breakthroughs include the first twin-blade shaving system, Trac II, in 1971; the first razor with a pivoting head, Atra, in 1977; the first razor with spring-mounted twin blades, Sensor, in 1989; and the first triple-blade system, Mach3, in 1998. January 2006 saw the launch of the "best shave on the planet" with the six-bladed Fusion—five blades in the front for regular shaving and one in the back for trimming—in both power and non-power versions. Gillette conducts exhaustive consumer research in designing its new products and markets aggressively to spread the word. Gillette spent over $1.2 billion on research and development after the Mach3 was introduced. About 9,000 men tested potential new products and preferred the new Fusion razor by a two-to-one margin over the older Mach3 varieties. To back the introduction, Procter & Gamble, which acquired Gillette in 2005 for $57 billion (a record five times sales), spent $200 million in the United States and over $1 billion worldwide. The payoff? Gillette enjoys enormous market leadership in the razors and blades categories, owning roughly 70 percent of the global market. Gillette also commands sizable price premiums. Refills for the Fusion Power cost $14 for a four-pack, compared to $5.29 for a 5-pack of Sensor Excel. All this adds up to significant, sustained profitability for corporate owner P&G.[1]

In this chapter, we will address the following questions:

1. How do consumers process and evaluate prices?
2. How should a company set prices initially for products or services?
3. How should a company adapt prices to meet varying circumstances and opportunities?
4. When should a company initiate a price change?
5. How should a company respond to a competitor's price change?

The Gillette example reveals the power of pricing. Pricing decisions are complex and difficult. Holistic marketers must take into account many factors in making pricing decisions—the company, the customers, the competition, and the marketing environment. Pricing decisions must be consistent with the firm's marketing strategy, target markets, and brand positionings. In this chapter, we provide concepts and tools to facilitate the setting of initial prices and adjusting prices over time and markets.

Understanding Pricing

Price is not just a number on a tag or an item. Price comes in many forms and performs many functions. Rent, tuition, fares, fees, rates, tolls, retainers, wages, and commissions all may in some way be the price you pay for some good or service. It's also made up of many components. If you buy a new car, the sticker price may be adjusted by rebates and dealer incentives. Some firms allow for payment through multiple forms, such as $129 plus 25,000 frequent flier miles from an airline loyalty program.[2]

Throughout most of history, prices were set by negotiation between buyers and sellers. "Bargaining" is still prevalent in many parts of Asia today. Setting one price for all buyers is a relatively modern idea in the region, a trend which emerged with the development of large-scale retailing.

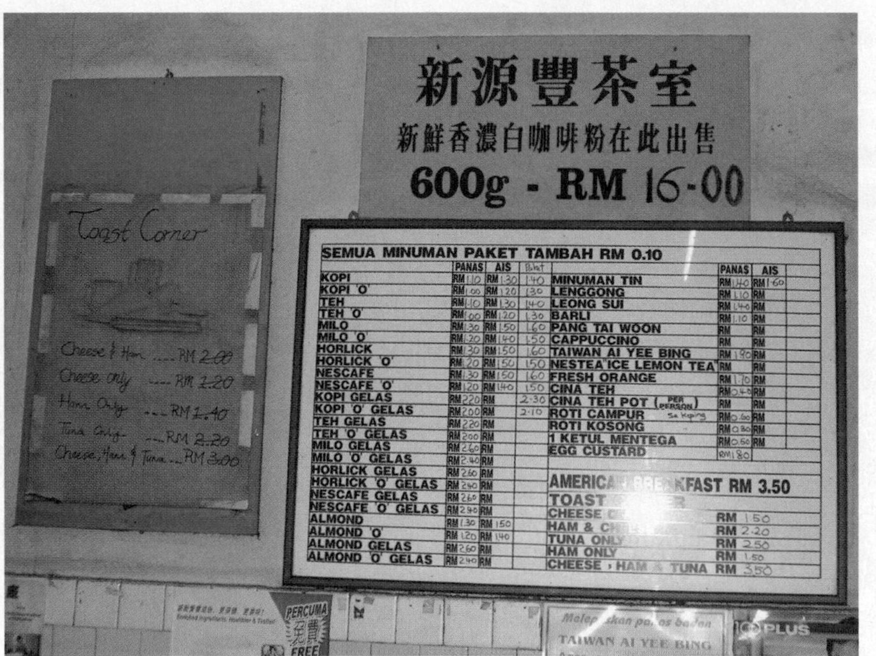

In more traditional shops such as this coffee shop in Malaysia, the menu and prices are posted on the wall. Sometimes, they are even handwritten on a wall mirror.

Traditionally, price has operated as the major determinant of buyer choice. This is still the case in poorer nations, among poorer groups, and with commodity-type products. Although non-price factors have become more important in recent decades, price still remains one of the most important elements determining market share and profitability in Asia for several reasons. First, buyers are accorded higher status in Chinese and Japanese culture. As Asian business culture places much importance on status, this status difference allows buyers to do better than sellers relative to societies like the U.S., where the status of buyers is less important.[3] Economic factors also impact price. With the rising oil prices, there is considerable upward pressure on prices. As consumers' real incomes stagnated, they experienced diminishing expectations and shopped more carefully. The result was a marketplace characterized by higher prices and more cautious consumers.

A Changing Pricing Environment

Pricing practices have changed significantly in recent years. Many firms are bucking the low-price trend and have been successful in trading consumers up to more expensive products and services by combining unique product formulations with engaging marketing campaigns. Even products in fiercely competitive supermarket categories have been able to enjoy price hikes for the right new offerings. Procter & Gamble launched Crest Pro-Health toothpaste at a 50 percent premium over other premium toothpastes, as well as

Olay Definity mass-market skin care line with a $25-plus price point that rivaled the lower end of department store brands. Rival Unilever has struck gold with Axe deodorants, which have pushed prices in the category to over $4. Even Coca-Cola has been able to find higher price points, introducing the Coke Blak line extension at about $2 per 8-ounce bottle, or roughly twice what it could receive for 2 liters of regular Coke.[4]

Today, the Internet is also partially reversing the fixed pricing trend. As one industry observer noted, "We are moving toward a very sophisticated economy. It's kind of an arms race between merchant technology and consumer technology."[5] Here is a list of how the Internet allows sellers to discriminate between buyers, and buyers to discriminate between sellers.[6]

Buyers can:

- ***Get instant price comparisons from thousands of vendors*** — Customer can compare the prices of the same product offered by various stores on PriceScan.com. Intelligent shopping agents ("bots") take price comparison a step further and seek out products, prices, and reviews from hundreds if not thousands of merchants.
- ***Name their price and have it met*** — On Priceline.com, the customer states the price he wants to pay for an airline ticket, hotel, or rental car, and Priceline checks whether any seller is willing to meet that price. Volume-aggregating sites combine the orders of many customers and press the supplier for a deeper discount.
- ***Get products free*** — Open Source, the free software movement that started with Linux, will erode margins for any company creating software. The biggest challenge confronting Microsoft, Oracle, IBM, and other major software producer is: How do you compete with programs that can be had for free? "Marketing Insight: Giving It All Away" describes how different firms have been successful with essentially free offerings.

Sellers can:

- ***Monitor customer behavior and tailor offers to individuals*** — GE Lighting, which gets 55,000 pricing requests a year, has Web programs that evaluate 300 factors that go into a pricing quote, such as past sales data and discounts, so it can reduce processing time from up to 30 days to 6 hours.
- ***Give certain customers access to special prices*** — CDNOW, an online vendor of music albums, emails certain buyers a special Web site address with lower prices. Business marketers are already using extranets to get a precise handle on inventory, costs, and demand at any given moment in order to adjust prices instantly.

Both buyers and sellers can:

- ***Negotiate prices in online auctions and exchanges*** — Want to sell hundreds of excess and slightly worn widgets? Post a sale on eBay. Want to purchase vintage kimono fabric? Go to www.ichiroya.com.

Among the marketers attempting to swim against the trend toward low prices is Coca-Cola with its Coke Blak.

How Companies Price

Companies do their pricing in various ways. In small companies, prices are often set by the boss. In large companies, pricing is handled by division and product-line managers. Even here, top management sets general pricing objectives and policies and often approves the prices proposed by lower levels of management. In industries where pricing is a key factor (aerospace, airlines, and oil companies), companies will often establish a pricing department to set or assist others in determining appropriate prices. This department reports to the marketing department, finance department, or top management. Others who exert an influence on pricing include sales managers, production managers, finance managers, and accountants.

Executives complain that pricing is a big headache—and one that is getting worse by the day. Many companies do not handle pricing well, throwing up their hands with "strategies" like this: "We determine our costs and take our industry's traditional margins." Other common mistakes are: price is not revised often enough to capitalize on market changes; price is set independent of the rest of the marketing mix rather than as an intrinsic element of market-positioning strategy; and price is not varied enough for different product items, market segments, distribution channels, and purchase occasions.

MARKETING INSIGHT • GIVING IT ALL AWAY

Giving away products for free via sampling has been a successful marketing tactic for years. Estée Lauder gave free samples of cosmetics to celebrities, and organizers at awards shows to this day like to lavish award winners with extensive free items or gifts known as "swag." Other manufacturers, such as Gillette and Hewlett-Packard have built their business model around selling the host product essentially at cost and making money on the sale of necessary supplies, such as razor blades and printer ink.

With the advent of the Internet, software companies began to adopt similar practices. Adobe gave away PDF Reader for free in 1994, as did Macromedia with its Shockwave player in 1995. In the process, the software became the industry standard, but the firms really made their money selling the product's authoring software. More recently, a number of Internet start-ups such as MySpace and Skype have all achieved some success with a "freemium" strategy—free online services with a premium component. Venture capitalists and entrepreneurs believe that successful online freemium strategies of this kind depend on a number of factors (see Figure 14.1).

Off-line, other firms are also adopting freemium-type strategies. In Europe, profits for discount air carrier Ryanair have been sky-high thanks to its revolutionary business model. The secret? Founder Michael O'Leary thinks like a retailer, charging for almost everything but the seat itself:

1. **A quarter of Ryanair's seats are free.** O'Leary wants to double that within five years, with the ultimate goal of all seats for free. Passengers pay only taxes and fees of about \$10–\$24, with an average one-way fare of roughly \$52.
2. **Passengers pay extra for basically everything else on the flight:** checked luggage (\$9.50 per bag); snacks (\$5.50 for a hot dog, \$4.50 for chicken soup; and \$3.50 for water); and bus or train transportation into town from the far-flung airports that Ryanair uses (\$24).
3. **Flight attendants sell a variety of merchandise,** including digital cameras (\$137.50) and iPocket MP3 players (\$165). Onboard gambling and cell phone service are projected new revenue sources.
4. **Seats do not recline, window shades and seat-back pockets have been removed, and there is no entertainment.** Seat-back trays now carry ads, and the exteriors of the planes are giant billboards for Vodafone Group, Jaguar, Hertz, and others.
5. **More than 98 percent of tickets are sold online.** The Web site also offers travel insurance, hotels, ski packages, and car rentals.
6. **Only Boeing 737–800 jets are flown to reduce maintenance, and flight crews buy their own uniforms.**

Ryanair wants to earn revenue on everything but the seats on its airplanes. In addition to charging passengers for baggage and snacks and eliminating frills like entertainment and reclining seats, the carrier sells ad space on the interior and exterior of its planes. This Ryanair Boeing 737 is painted in a special sponsored Vodaphone color scheme.

The formula works for Ryanair's customers, and the airline flies 42 million passengers annually to 127 cities. All the extras add up to 15 perent of revenue. Ryanair enjoys net margins of 18 percent, which are more than double the 7 percent margins Southwest has achieved. Some U.S. airlines have taken notice. Fellow discount carrier Spirit Airlines has begun to charge for checking bags and all drinks; and even non-discount carriers such as American, Northwest, and Delta have begun to charge extra for aisle seats, headsets, and snacks.

Sources: Peter J. Howe, "The Next Pinch: Fees to Check Bags." *Boston Globe,* March 8, 2007; Katherine Heires, "Why It Pays to Give Away the Store." *Business 2.0,* October 2006: pp. 36–37; Kerry Capel, "Wal-Mart with Wings." *BusinessWeek,* November 27, 2006: pp. 44–45; Matthew Maier, "A Radical Fix for Airlines: Make Flying Free." *Business 2.0,* April 2006: pp. 32–34; Gary Stoller, "Would You Like Some Golf Balls with That Ticket." *USA Today,* October 30, 1996.

Others have a different attitude: They use price as a key strategic tool. These "power pricers" have discovered the highly leveraged effect of price on the bottom line.[7] They customize prices and offerings based on segment value and costs.

The importance of pricing for profitability was demonstrated in a study by McKinsey which concluded that a 1 percent improvement in price created an improvement in operating profit of 11.1 percent. In contrast, 1 percent improvements in variable cost, volume, and fixed cost produced profit improvements, respectively, of only 7.8 percent, 3.3 percent, and 2.3 percent.

Figure 14.1 Guidelines for a Successful Freemium Strategy

1. **Have a product or service that truly stands out.** Its performance, ease of use, and reliability should be superior to those of current offerings.
2. **Know your up-selling plan from the beginning.** Before you even go into beta, make sure you have at least one paid, add-on premium service up your sleeve. Better yet, have more than one.
3. **Once you have decided that a product will be given away for free, don't change your mind.** "The fundamental 'what's for free' and 'what's for pay' divide needs to be set early," says Adeo Ressi, CEO of Game Trust, a start-up that hosts 45 free games and sells enhancements online. If you make changes, Ressi says, you risk alienating customers accustomed to getting your product for free.
4. **Access to your product should be just one click away.** The fewer time-consuming plug-ins, downloads, and registration forms required, the better. Otherwise people may get bored or frustrated and abort.
5. **Make sure the major bugs have been exterminated.** Your product can be in beta, Rimer says, but not "so much in beta that it does not work well."
6. **Harness the collective intelligence of your users.** Måårten Mickos, CEO of mySQL, says customer suggestions can help speed up product improvements or inspire ideas for premium services.
7. **Keep improving the product to give users more reasons to stick with it.** "The reality is that offering a product for free can be far riskier than if you actually charged for your product," says Howard Anderson, a lecturer at the MIT Entrepreneurship Center. "Only one in 10 companies will succeed at pulling this off."
8. **Identify a range of revenue sources.** The Epocrates service, which offers medical professionals both free and premium access to reference material via PDAs, does not charge just for the premium information. It also charges fees to pharmaceutical firms for surveys it conducts of Epocrates customers. Similarly, MySQL makes money from customer service as well as from fees charged to firms that redistribute the software.
9. **Timing is everything.** Make sure that revenue from your premium service soon covers the cost of your free service. Otherwise, cut your losses and move on to the next start-up.

Sources: Peter J. Howe, "The Next Pinch: Fees to Check Bags," *Boston Globe*, March 8, 2007; Katherine Heires, "Why It Pays to Give Away the Store," *Business 2.0* (October 2006): 36–37; Kerry Capel, "'Wal-Mart with Wings,'" *BusinessWeek*, November 27, 2006, pp. 44–45; Matthew Maier, "A Radical Fix for Airlines: Make Flying Free," *Business 2.0* (April 2006): 32–34; Gary Stoller, "Would You Like Some Golf Balls with That Ticket," *USA Today*, October 30,1996.

Effectively designing and implementing pricing strategies requires a thorough understanding of consumer pricing psychology and a systematic approach to setting, adapting, and changing prices.

Consumer Psychology and Pricing

Many economists assume that consumers are "price takers" and accept prices at "face value" or as given. Marketers recognize that consumers often actively process price information, interpreting prices in terms of their knowledge from prior purchasing experience, formal communications (advertising, sales calls, and brochures), informal communications (friends, colleagues, or family members), and point-of-purchase or online resources.[8] Purchase decisions are based on how consumers perceive prices and what they consider to be the current actual price—*not* the marketer's stated price. They may have a lower price threshold below which prices may signal inferior or unacceptable quality, as well as an upper price threshold above which prices are prohibitive and seen as not worth the money. The following example helps illustrate the large part consumer psychology plays in determining three different prices for essentially the same item: a black T-shirt.

Armani, Gap, H&M—The black T-shirt for women looks pretty ordinary. In fact, it is not that different from the black T-shirt sold by Gap and by Swedish discount clothing chain, H&M. Yet the black Armani T-shirt costs $275.00, whereas the Gap item costs $14.90 and the H&M one $7.90. Customers who purchase the Armani T-shirt are paying for a T-shirt made of 70 percent nylon, 25 percent polyester, and 5 percent Elastine, whereas the Gap and H&M shirts are made mainly of cotton. True, the Armani T is a bit more stylishly cut than the other two and sports a "Made in Italy" label, but how does it command a $275 price tag? A luxury brand, Armani is primarily known for its suits, handbags, and evening gowns that it sells for thousands of dollars. In that context, it can hardly sell its T-shirts for $15 or even $100. And because there aren't many takers for $275 T-shirts, Armani does not make many, thus further enhancing the appeal for status seekers who like the idea of having a "limited edition" T-shirt. "Value is not only quality, function, utility, channel of distribution," says Arnold Aronson, managing director of retail strategies for Kurt Salmon Associates and former CEO of Saks Fifth Avenue; it is also a customer's perception of a brand's luxury connotations.[9]

Understanding how consumers arrive at their perceptions of prices is an important marketing priority. Here we consider three key topics—reference prices, price-quality inferences, and price endings.

REFERENCE PRICES

Research has shown that although consumers may have fairly good knowledge of the range of prices involved, surprisingly few can recall specific prices of products accurately.[10] However, consumers often employ **reference prices** when examining prices. Thus consumers often compare an observed price to an internal reference price (pricing information from memory) or an external frame of reference (such as a posted "regular retail price").[11]

All types of reference prices are possible (see Table 14.1). Sellers often attempt to manipulate reference prices. For example, a seller can situate its product among expensive products to imply that it belongs in the same class. Department stores will display women's apparel in separate departments differentiated by price; dresses found in the more expensive department are assumed to be of better quality.

Table 14.1 Possible Consumer Reference Prices

- "Fair price" (what the product should cost)
- Typical price
- Last price paid
- Upper-bound price (reservation price or what most consumers would pay)
- Lower-bound price (lower threshold price or the least consumers would pay)
- Competitor prices
- Expected future price
- Usual discounted price

Source: Adapted from Russell S. Winer, "Behavioral Perspectives on Pricing: Buyer's Subjective Perceptions of Price Revisited." In Timothy Devinney, ed., *Issues in Pricing: Theory and Research*, (Lexington, MA: Lexington Books, 1988), pp. 35–57.

Reference-price thinking is also encouraged by stating a high manufacturer's suggested price, or by indicating that the product was priced much higher originally, or by pointing to a competitor's high price.[12]

Consumer electronics—On JVC's Web site, the manufacturer's suggested retail price often bears no relationship to what you would be charged by a retailer for the same item. For instance, for a model of mini-digital video camcorder that doubles as a digital still camera, JVC suggests a certain retail price, while at a retail store, the same camcorder is sold at a lower price. Compared with other consumer items, from clothing to cars to furniture to toothbrushes, the gap between the prices routinely quoted by manufacturer and retailer in consumer electronics is large. One explanation is that electronic companies are training consumers to think they are getting some discount. A product manager for Olympus, primarily known for its cameras, defends the practice by saying that the high manufacturer's suggested retail price is a psychological tool, a reference price that makes people see they are getting something of value for less than top price. Regardless of how inflated—and how perplexing—manufacturers' suggested retail prices are, everyone usually winds up happy. Manufacturers, like JVC or Olympus, get their sales. Retailers get buyers to think they are getting a bargain, and consumers get gadgets they want at prices they think are good.[13]

High reference prices in the consumer electronics industry have trained consumers to gravitate toward "sale" prices.

When consumers evoke one or more of these frames of reference, their perceived price can vary from the stated price.[14] Research on reference prices has found that "unpleasant surprises"—when perceived price is lower than the stated price—can have a greater impact on purchase likelihood than pleasant surprises.[15] Consumer expectations can also play a key role in price response. In the case of Internet auction sites, such as eBay, when consumers know similar goods will be available in future auctions, they will bid less in the current auction.[16]

Clever marketers try to frame the price to signal the best value possible. For example, a relatively more expensive item can be seen as less expensive by breaking the price down into smaller units. A $500 annual membership may be seen as more expensive than "under $50 a month" even if the totals are the same.[17]

PRICE-QUALITY INFERENCES

Many consumers use price as an indicator of quality. Image pricing is especially effective with ego-sensitive products such as perfumes and expensive cars. A $100 bottle of perfume might contain $10 worth of scent, but gift givers pay $100 to communicate their high regard for the receiver.

Price and quality perceptions of cars interact.[18] Higher-priced cars are perceived to possess high quality. Higher-quality cars are likewise perceived to be higher priced than they actually are. When alternative information about true quality is available, price becomes a less significant indicator of quality. When this information is not available, price acts as a signal of quality.

Some brands adopt scarcity as a means to signify quality and justify premium pricing. Luxury-goods makers of watches, jewelry, perfume, and other products often emphasize exclusivity in their communication messages and channel strategies. For luxury-goods customers who desire uniqueness, demand may actually increase with higher prices, as they may believe that fewer other customers will be able to afford to purchase the product.[19]

Tiffany & Co.—For its entire history, Tiffany's name has connoted diamonds and luxury. Yet, in the late 1990s during the stock market boom, there emerged the notion of "affordable luxuries." Tiffany seized the moment by creating a line of cheaper silver jewelry, and its "Return to Tiffany" silver bracelet became a must-have item for teens of a certain set. Sales skyrocketed after the introduction of the "Return to Tiffany" collection, rising 67 percent from 1997 to 2002, with earnings more than doubling over the same time. But the rise in sales of cheaper silver jewelry brought on both an image and a pricing crisis for the company: What if all those teens who bought Tiffany charm bracelets grew up to think of Tiffany's only as a place where they got the jewelry of their girlhood? Starting in 2002, the company began hiking prices again. (The Return to Tiffany bracelet has gone from $110 to $175—a price increase of 30 percent from 2001.) At the same time, the company launched higher-end collections, renovated stores to feature expensive items that would appeal to more mature buyers, and expanded agressively into new cities and shopping malls. When the slowdown came in 2005—with earnings and the stock price plunging—sales of items over $20,000 and $50,000 began growing and now lead the company in terms of growth. Still, the firm must be ever careful about diluting its high-end appeal. As one customer says of Tiffany's jewelry, "You used to aspire to be able to buy something at Tiffany, but now it's not that special anymore."[20]

For years the link between price and quality was what made Tiffany special. The luxury jeweler has recently tried to broaden its appeal to ever-younger consumers but must safeguard its high-end image.

PRICE ENDINGS

Many sellers believe that prices should end in an odd number. Many customers see a stereo amplifier priced at $299 instead of $300 as a price in the $200 range rather than $300 range. Research has shown that consumers tend to process prices in a "left-to-right" manner rather than by rounding.[21] Price encoding in this fashion is important if there is a mental price break at the higher, rounded price. Another explanation for "9" endings is that they convey the notion of a discount or bargain, suggesting that if a company wants a high-price image, it should avoid the odd-ending tactic.[22] One study even showed that demand actually increased one-third by *raising* the price of a dress from $34 to $39, but demand was unchanged when prices increased from $34 to $44.[23]

In Asia, sellers may also be affected by buyer superstitions in pricing their products. Thus Chinese restaurants in Hong Kong, Malaysia, and Singapore are known for setting prices ending with the lucky number eight (e.g., $888 per table). In 2004, Bentley sold three ultra-luxury Mulliners to buyers in China for 8.88 million yuan ($1.07 million) each.[24]

Prices that end with "0" and "5" are also common as they are thought to be easier for consumers to process and retrieve from memory.[25] "Sale" signs next to prices have been shown to spur demand, but only if not overused: Total category sales are highest when some, but not all, items in a category have sale signs; past a certain point, use of additional sale signs will cause total category sales to fall.[26]

Pricing cues such as sale signs and prices that end in 9 become less effective the more they are employed. They are more influential when consumers' price knowledge is poor, when they purchase the item infrequently or are new to the category, and when product designs vary over time, prices vary seasonally, or quality or sizes vary across stores.[27] Limited availability (for example, "three days only") also can spur sales among consumers actively shopping for a product.[28]

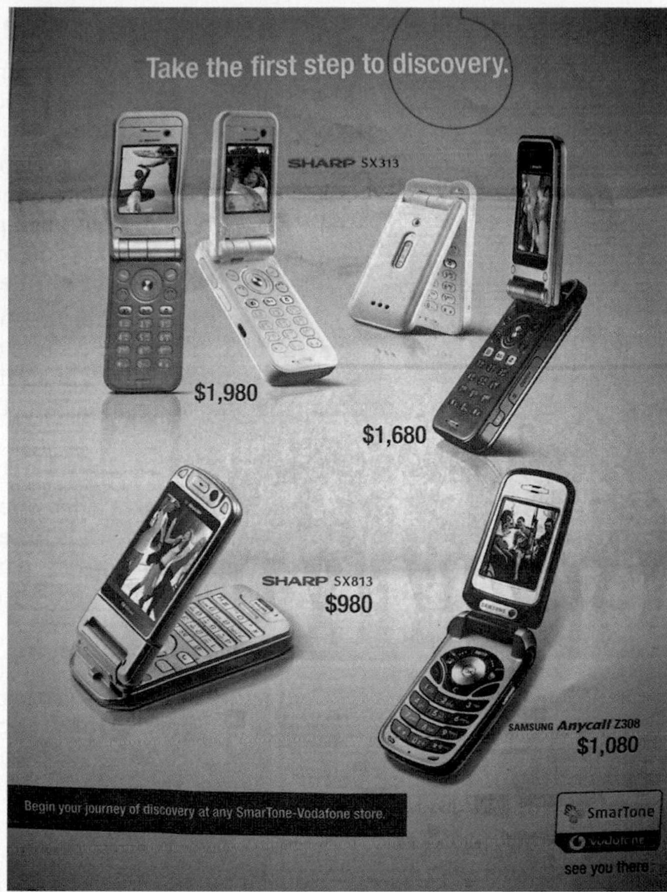

SmarTone Vodafone in Hong Kong prices its mobile phones with auspicious numbers such as "6," "8," and "9" which sound like "longevity", "prosperity," and "sufficiency" respectively in Cantonese.

Psychological pricing: What does the price suggest about the product and buying situation?

Setting the Price

A firm must set a price for the first time when it develops a new product, when it introduces its regular product into a new distribution channel or geographical area, and when it enters bids on new contract work. The firm must decide where to position its product on quality and price.

Most markets have three to five price points or tiers. Marriott Hotels is good at developing different brands for different price points: Marriott Vacation Club—Vacation Villas (highest price), Marriott Marquis (high price), Marriott (high-medium price), Renaissance (medium-high price), Courtyard (medium price), Towne Place Suites (medium-low price), and Fairfield Inn (low price). Consumers often rank brands according to these price tiers in a category.[29]

The firm must consider many factors in setting its pricing policy.[30] Let us look in some detail at a six-step procedure: (1) selecting the pricing objective; (2) determining demand; (3) estimating costs; (4) analyzing competitors' costs, prices, and offers; (5) selecting a pricing method; and (6) selecting the final price.

Step 1: Selecting the Pricing Objective

The company first decides where it wants to position its market offering. The clearer a firm's objectives, the easier it is to set price. A company can pursue any of five major objectives through pricing: survival, maximum current profit, maximum market share, maximum market skimming, or product-quality leadership.

SURVIVAL

Companies pursue *survival* as their major objective if they are plagued with overcapacity, intense competition, or changing consumer wants. As long as prices cover variable costs and some fixed costs, the company stays in business. Survival is a short-run objective; in the long-run, the firm must learn how to add value or face extinction.

MAXIMUM CURRENT PROFIT

Many companies try to set a price that will *maximize current profits*. They estimate the demand and costs associated with alternative prices and choose the price that produces maximum current profit, cash flow, or rate of return on investment. This strategy assumes that the firm has knowledge of its demand and cost functions; in reality, these are difficult to estimate. In emphasizing current performance, the company may sacrifice long-run performance by ignoring the effects of other marketing-mix variables, competitors' reactions, and legal restraints on price.

MAXIMUM MARKET SHARE

Some companies want to *maximize their market share*. They believe that a higher sales volume will lead to lower unit costs and higher long-run profit. They set the lowest price, assuming the market is price-sensitive.

Lenovo—In 2005, Lenovo launched the Think Center E Series aimed at the fast-growing small and midsize business segment. At an entry price of $379, the systems are preloaded with crash and recovery software. Lenovo managers have promised that the company would remain competitive with Dell, which has made low pricing a hallmark of its most recent PC market share push.[31]

Toyota—For years, Toyota resisted incentives because it did not want to give up profits and damage its brand. Then, a weak yen and strong models enabled it to gain market share without closing big deals. However, with the strengthening of the yen and stiffer price competition, Toyota raised incentives on a range of vehicles. It cut $1,000 off the Corolla and $3,400 off the Tundra truck. These juicy deals in 2004 helped Toyota win U.S. market share, but eroded profits. However, unlike the American cars that give generous discounts, Toyota shows more restraint. For instance, instead of giving more cash rebate on a minivan, Toyota gave consumers a $1,000 boost by combining a small price cut with free options.[32]

The following conditions favor setting a low price: (1) The market is highly price sensitive, and a low price stimulates market growth without cannibalizing sales of existing products; (2) production and distribution costs fall with accumulated production experience; and (3) a low price discourages actual and potential competition.

IKEA—IKEA is using market-penetration pricing to get a lock on China's surging market for home furnishings. When the Swedish home furnishings giant opened its first store in Beijing in 2002, shoppers would come in mainly to take advantage of the air-conditioning and the decorating ideas on display. Outside the store, shops were selling copies of IKEA's furniture designs at a fraction of IKEA's prices. The only way for IKEA to lure China's price-sensitive and frugal customers was to drastically slash its prices. By stocking its Chinese stores with Chinese-made products, IKEA has been able to slash prices as low as 70 percent below its own prices outside China. The move has worked. Customers are taking their low-priced goods to the check-out counters in droves, and IKEA is building its largest store in the world—aside from the flagship store in Stockholm—in Beijing. Western brands in China usually price products such as make-up and running shoes 20 percent to 30 percent higher than in their other markets, both to make up for China's high import taxes and to give their products added cachet. But with a 43 percent market share in China's homewares segment alone, IKEA is proving that it pays to buck a pricing trend.[33]

IKEA used a price penetration strategy in China to dovetail with its price-sensitive and frugal customers. This has proved to be successful.

MAXIMUM MARKET SKIMMING

Companies unveiling a new technology favor setting high prices to *maximize market skimming*. Sony is a frequent practitioner of **market-skimming pricing**, where prices start high and are slowly lowered over time.

Sony—When Sony introduced the world's first High-Definition Television (HDTV) to the Japanese market in 1990, it was priced at $43,000 so that Sony could "skim" the maximum amount of revenue from the various segments of the market. The price dropped steadily through the years—a 28-inch HDTV cost just over $6,000 in 1993 and a 40-inch HDTV cost about $1,200 in 2007.

This strategy can be fatal, however, if a worthy competitor decides to price low. When Philips, the Dutch electronics manufacturer, priced its video-disc players to make a profit on each player, Japanese competitors priced low and succeeded in building their market share rapidly, which in turn pushed down their costs substantially.

Market skimming makes sense under the following conditions: (1) A sufficient number of buyers have a high current demand; (2) the unit costs of producing a small volume are not so high that they cancel the advantage of charging what the traffic will bear; (3) the high initial price does not attract more competitors to the market; and (4) the high price communicates the image of a superior product.

PRODUCT-QUALITY LEADERSHIP

A company might aim to be the *product-quality leader* in the market. Many brands strive to be "affordable luxuries"—products or services characterized by high levels of perceived quality, taste, and status with a price just high enough not to be out of consumers' reach. Brands such as Starbucks coffee, Victoria's Secret lingerie, and Mercedes cars have been able to position themselves as quality leaders in their category, combining quality, luxury, and premium prices with an intensely loyal customer base.[34]

Samsung—Samsung built its image as a product-quality leader in China by launching high-end consumer electronics and appliances. This included selling its top-of-the-line digital phones, MP3 players, and projection TVs which were then priced up to $2,400. Samsung also has a growing business selling high-end displays used in notebook PCs. It has also moved up-market in conventional appliances such as refrigerators and washing machines. Its cell phones exemplify Samsung's thrust to be perceived as a product-quality leader. When its A-288 handset was launched, it sold 300,000 units, mainly to young professional women in China's major cities. Samsung expects its high-end products to account for 70 percent of its Chinese sales as it launches a new generation of digital devices with China as its top priority.[35]

OTHER OBJECTIVES

Non-profit and public organizations may have other pricing objectives. A university aims for *partial cost recovery,* knowing that it must rely on private gifts and public grants to cover the remaining costs. A non-profit hospital may aim for full cost recovery in its pricing. A non-profit theater company may price its productions to fill the maximum number of theater seats. A social service agency may set a service price geared to client income.

Whatever the specific objective, businesses that use price as a strategic tool will profit more than those who simply let costs or the market determine their pricing.

Step 2: Determining Demand

Each price will lead to a different level of demand and therefore have a different impact on a company's marketing objectives. The relation between alternative prices and the resulting current demand is captured in a demand curve (see Figure 14.2). Typically, demand and

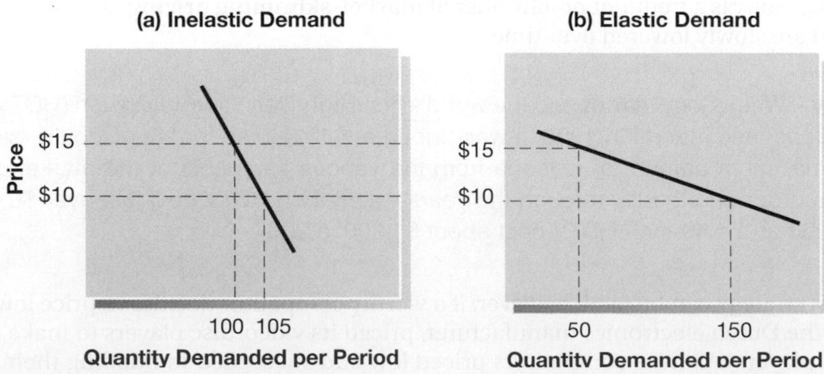

Figure 14.2 Inelastic and Elastic Demand

price are inversely related: the higher the price, the lower the demand. For prestige goods, the demand curve sometimes slopes upward. A perfume company raised its price and sold more perfume rather than less! Some consumers take the higher price to signify a better product. However, if the price is too high, the level of demand may fall.

PRICE SENSITIVITY

The demand curve shows the market's probable purchase quantity at alternative prices. It sums the reactions of many individuals who have different price sensitivities. The first step in estimating demand is to understand what affects price sensitivity. Generally, customers are most price-sensitive to products that cost a lot or are bought frequently. They are less price-sensitive to low-cost items or items they buy infrequently. They are also less price-sensitive when price is only a small part of the total cost of obtaining, operating, and servicing the product over its lifetime. A seller can charge a higher price than competitors and still get the business if the company can convince the customer that it offers the lowest *total cost of ownership*.

Clearly, companies prefer customers who are less price sensitive. Table 14.2 lists some characteristics that are associated with decreased price sensitivity. On the other hand, the Internet has the potential to increase customers' price sensitivity. Although the Internet increases the opportunity for price-sensitive buyers to find and favor lower-price sites, many buyers may not be that price-sensitive. A McKinsey study found that 89 percent of a sample of Internet customers visited only one book site, 84 percent visited only one toy site, and 81 percent visited only one music site, which indicates that there is less price-comparison shopping taking place on the Internet than is possible.

Table 14.2 Factors Leading to Less Price Sensitivity

- The product is more distinctive.
- Buyers are less aware of substitutes.
- Buyers cannot easily compare the quality of substitutes.
- The expenditure is a smaller part of the buyer's total income.
- The expenditure is small compared to the total cost of the end product.
- Part of the cost is borne by another party.
- The product is used in conjunction with assets previously bought.
- The product is assumed to have more quality, prestige, or exclusiveness.
- Buyers cannot store the product.

Source: Adapted from Thomas T. Nagle and Reed K. Holden, *The Strategy and Tactics of Pricing*, 4th ed., (Upper Saddle River, NJ: Prentice Hall, 2006), chapter 4.

Companies need to understand the price-sensitivity of their customers and prospects and the trade-offs people are willing to make between price and product characteristics. Consider the following Taiwanese example:

UTStarcom—Taiwan-born Hong Liang Lu started UTStarcom, a telecommunications gear supplier, using the Personal Access System (PAS) developed in Japan. PAS uses phones that offer wireless calling. But unlike cellular systems, PAS allows users to send and receive calls only from a limited area and does not offer roaming. Despite these constraints, it has become a runaway success. Nicknamed "Little Smart," UTStarcom is a popular alternative to the underserved segment of price-sensitive blue-collar workers who do not travel much and hence, have no need for roaming. By combining UTStarcom gear with existing infrastructure, it costs half the price of regular cellular systems. There is also no charge for incoming calls and outgoing calls cost only a quarter of normal cellular rates.[36]

Asian consumers generally tend to be price-sensitive and are pragmatic shoppers, particularly for private consumption goods.[37] Three factors contribute to Asians' price consciousness. First, Asia's collectivistic orientation places greater value on personal relationships than on material goods. This leads to greater pragmatism in buying products for private consumption. Second, Asians have a habit of frugality, which stems from a lack of social welfare outside of the family. This encourages wealth accumulation within the family. Indeed, household savings in China, Taiwan, Japan, and Singapore are among the highest in the world. Third, Asians have been known for their sophistication with money handling, especially in southern China and the mercantile overseas Chinese communities. Thus money, while not hoarded, is also not wasted.

Such price consciousness impacts Asian shopping behavior, which in turn affects pricing practices. One study in southern California found that Chinese consumers engaged in more information search on products and prices than U.S. consumers. This demand for lower prices was reflected in the lower prices for comparable products charged by Chinese supermarkets in America. Such differences in price behaviors and their consequences should be greater in Asia, given that the Chinese consumers in the study had been acculturated to American society. However, Asian shoppers are status-conscious and less frugal for public consumption goods, especially gifts. Social recognition and social norms of reciprocity contribute to the importance of the symbolic meaning of such products. Status goods and high prices symbolize the importance of the relationship that the gift giver has with the recipient.

ESTIMATING DEMAND CURVES

Most companies make some attempt to measure their demand curves using several different methods.

- **Surveys** can explore how many units consumers would buy at different proposed prices, although there is always the chance that they might understate their purchase intentions at higher prices to discourage the company from setting higher prices.
- **Price experiments** can vary the prices of different products in a store or charge different prices for the same product in similar territories to see how the change affects sales. Another approach is to use the Internet. An e-business could test the impact of a 5 percent price increase by quoting a higher price to every 40th visitor to compare the purchase response. However, it must do this carefully and not alienate customers.[38]
- **Statistical analysis** of past prices, quantities sold, and other factors can reveal their relationships. The data can be longitudinal (over time) or cross-sectional (different locations at the same time). Building the appropriate model and fitting the data with the proper statistical techniques calls for considerable skill.

Advances in database management have improved marketers' abilities to optimize pricing. A New York-based pharmacy chain uncovered a new strategy by analyzing its data—set the price markup on diapers as a function of a child's age. Making the newborn's sizes more expensive and big-kids pull-ups cheaper boosted the chain's baby care revenue by 27 percent.

In measuring the priçe-demand relationship, the market researcher must account for various factors that will influence demand. The competitor's response will make a difference. Also, if the company changes other marketing-mix factors besides price, the effect of the price change itself will be hard to isolate.

Car purchases in China—Chinese drivers are still very price-sensitive, despite increased affluence, as auto-makers have yet to establish strong brand images in China. An A.C. Nielsen survey showed that price is the key for Chinese car buyers, with value-for-money accounting for 36 percent of the purchase decision process compared to only 17 percent for brand awareness. Price will continue to be an important factor as long as car manufacturers fail to forge relationships with their customers. Car sales dropped in 2004 and auto-makers cut prices with sluggish demand. General Motors slashed $5,000 from the sticker price of its midsize Buick Regal sedan to $35,900, while Volkswagen cut prices on seven models by as much as 11 percent. Hyundai also announced across-the-board price cuts of 10 percent. However, these cuts had an unintended effect. Many customers waited for even deeper discounts, thus hurting the overall market.[39]

Nagle presents an excellent summary of the various methods for estimating price sensitivity and demand.[40]

PRICE ELASTICITY OF DEMAND

Marketers need to know how responsive, or elastic, demand would be to a change in price. Consider the two demand curves in Figure 14.2. With demand curve (a), a price increase from $10 to $15 leads to a relatively small decline in demand from 105 to 100. With demand curve (b), the same price increase leads to a substantial drop in demand from 150 to 50. If demand hardly changes with a small change in price, we say the demand is *inelastic*. If demand changes considerably, demand is *elastic*. The higher the elasticity, the greater the volume growth resulting from a 1 percent price reduction.

Demand is likely to be less elastic when: (1) there are few or no substitutes or competitors; (2) buyers do not readily notice the higher price; (3) buyers are slow to change their buying habits; and (4) buyers think the higher prices are justified. If demand is elastic, sellers will consider lowering the price. A lower price will produce more total revenue. This makes sense as long as the costs of producing and selling more units do not increase disproportionately.[41]

Price elasticity depends on the magnitude and direction of the contemplated price change. It may be negligible with a small price change and substantial with a large price change. It may differ for a price cut versus a price increase, and there may be a *price indifference band* within which price changes have little or no effect. A McKinsey pricing study estimated that the price indifference band can range as large as 17 percent for mouthwash, 13 percent for batteries, 9 percent for small appliances, and 2 percent for certificates of deposit.

Finally, long-run price elasticity may differ from short-run elasticity. Buyers may continue to buy from a current supplier after a price increase, but they may eventually switch suppliers. Here demand is more elastic in the long run than in the short run, or the reverse may happen: buyers may drop a supplier after being notified of a price increase but return later. The distinction between short-run and long-run elasticity means that sellers will not know the total effect of a price change until time passes.

One comprehensive study reviewing a 40-year period of academic research projects that investigated price elasticity yielded a number of interesting findings:[42]

- The average price elasticity across all products, markets, and time periods studied was −2.62.
- Price elasticity magnitudes were higher for durable goods than for other goods, and higher for products in the introduction/growth stages of the product life cycle than in the mature/decline stages.
- Inflation led to substantially higher price elasticities, especially in the short run.
- Promotional price elasticities were higher than actual price elasticities in the short run (although the reverse was true in the long run).
- Price elasticities were higher at the individual item or SKU level than at the overall brand level.

Step 3: Estimating Costs

Demand sets a ceiling on the price the company can charge for its product. Costs set the floor. The company wants to charge a price that covers its cost of producing, distributing, and selling the product, including a fair return for its effort and risk. Yet, when companies price products to cover full costs, the net result is not always profitability.

TYPES OF COSTS AND LEVELS OF PRODUCTION

A company's costs take two forms, fixed and variable. **Fixed costs** (also known as **overhead**) are costs that do not vary with production or sales revenue. A company must pay bills each month for rent, heat, interest, salaries, and so on, regardless of output.

Variable costs vary directly with the level of production. For example, each Casio calculator involves a cost of plastic, microprocessor chips, packaging, etc. These costs tend to be constant per unit produced. They are called variable because their total varies with the number of units produced.

Total costs consist of the sum of the fixed and variable costs for any given level of production. **Average cost** is the cost per unit at that level of production; it is equal to total costs divided by production. Management wants to charge a price that will at least cover the total production costs at a given level of production.

To price intelligently, management needs to know how its costs vary with different levels of production. Take the case in which a company such as Casio has built a fixed-size plant to produce 1,000 calculators a day. The cost per unit is high if few units are produced per day. As production approaches 1,000 units per day, the average cost falls because the fixed costs are spread over more units. Short-run average cost increases after 1,000 units, because the plant becomes inefficient: workers have to line up for machines, machines break down more often, and workers get in each other's way (see Figure 14.3(a)).

If Casio believes it can sell 2,000 units per day, it should consider building a larger plant. The plant will use more efficient machinery and work arrangements, and the unit cost of producing 2,000 units per day will be less than the unit cost of producing 1,000 units per day. This is shown in the Long-Run Average Cost curve (LRAC) in Figure 14.3(b). In fact, a 3,000-capacity plant would be even more efficient according to Figure 14.3(b), but a 4,000-daily production plant would be less efficient because of increasing diseconomies of scale: There are too many workers to manage, and paperwork slows things down. Figure 14.3(b) indicates that a 3,000-daily production plant is the optimal size if demand is strong enough to support this level of production.

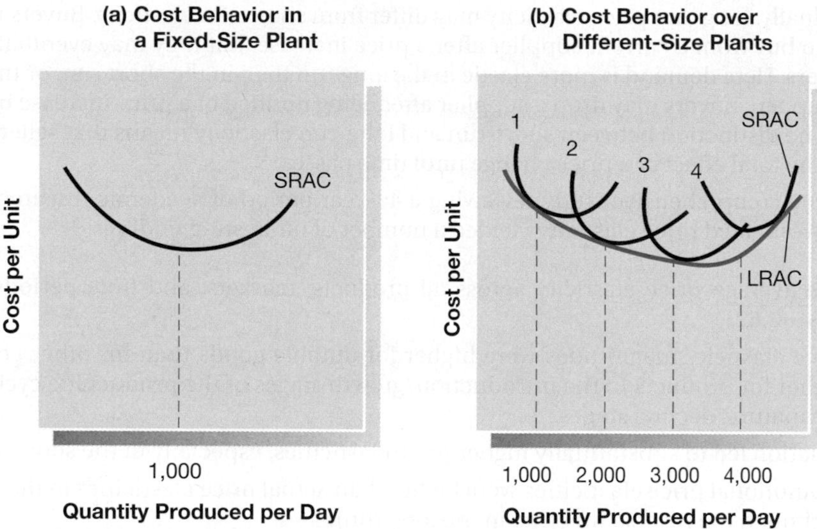

Figure 14.3 Cost per Unit at Different Levels of Production per Period

ACCUMULATED PRODUCTION

Suppose Casio runs a plant that produces 3,000 calculators per day. As Casio gains experience producing calculators, its methods improve. Workers learn shortcuts, materials flow more smoothly, and procurement costs fall. The result, as Figure 14.4 shows, is that average cost falls with accumulated production experience. Thus the average cost of producing the first 100,000 calculators is $10 per calculator. When the company has produced the first 200,000 calculators, the average cost has fallen to $9. After its accumulated production experience doubles again to 400,000, the average cost is $8. This decline in the average cost with accumulated production experience is called the **experience curve** or **learning curve**.

Now suppose three firms compete in this industry, Casio, A, and B. Casio is the lowest-cost producer at $8, having produced 400,000 units in the past. If all three firms sell the calculator for $10, Casio makes $2 profit per unit, A makes $1 per unit, and B breaks even. The smart move for Casio would be to lower its price to $9. This will drive B out of

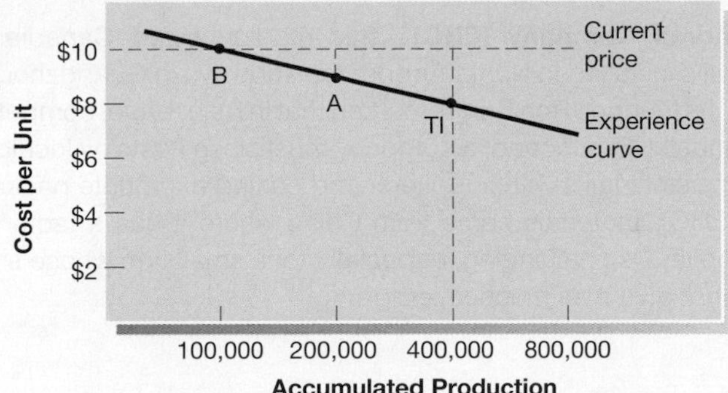

Figure 14.4 Cost per Unit as a Function of Accumulated Production: The Experience Curve

the market, and even A may consider leaving. Casio will pick up the business that would have gone to B (and possibly A). Further, price-sensitive customers will enter the market at the lower price. As production increases beyond 4,00,000 units, Casio's costs will drop still further and faster and more than restore its profits, even at a price of $9. Casio has used this aggressive pricing strategy repeatedly to gain market share and drive others out of the industry.

Experience-curve pricing, nevertheless, carries major risks. Aggressive pricing might give the product a cheap image. The strategy also assumes that competitors are weak followers. It leads the company into building more plants to meet demand, while a competitor innovates a lower-cost technology. The market leader is now stuck with the old technology.

Most experience-curve pricing has focused on manufacturing costs, but all costs, including marketing costs, can be improved on. If three firms are each investing a large sum of money in telemarketing, the firm that has used it the longest might achieve the lowest costs. This firm can charge a little less for its product and still earn the same return, all other costs being equal.[43]

ACTIVITY-BASED COST ACCOUNTING

Today's companies try to adapt their offers and terms to different buyers. A manufacturer, for example, will negotiate different terms with different retail chains. One retailer may want daily delivery (to keep inventory lower) while another may accept twice-a-week delivery to get a lower price. The manufacturer's costs will differ with each chain, and so will its profits. To estimate the real profitability of dealing with different retailers, the manufacturer needs to use **Activity-Based Cost (ABC) accounting** instead of standard cost accounting.[44]

ABC accounting tries to identify the real costs associated with serving each customer. It allocates indirect costs like clerical costs, office expenses, supplies, etc. to the activities that use them, rather than in some proportion to direct costs. Both variable and overhead costs are tagged back to each customer. Companies that fail to measure their costs correctly are not measuring their profit correctly and are likely to misallocate their marketing effort. The key to effectively employing ABC is to define and judge "activities" properly. One proposed time-based solution calculates the cost of one minute of overhead and then decides how much of this cost each activity uses.[45]

TARGET COSTING

Costs change with production scale and experience. They can also change as a result of a concentrated effort by designers, engineers, and purchasing agents to reduce them through **target costing.**[46] The Japanese use this method. Market research is employed to establish a new product's desired functions and the price at which the product will sell, given its appeal and competitors' prices. Deducting the desired profit margin from this price leaves the target cost that must be achieved. Each cost element—design, engineering, manufacturing, sales—must be examined and different ways to bring down costs must be considered. The objective is to bring the final cost projections into the target cost range. If this is not possible, it may be necessary to stop developing the product because it could not sell for the target price and make the target profit.

Escalator Handrail Company (EHC)—This medium-sized Canadian company supplies handrails installed in Narita Airport, the subways in Guangzhou, Shanghai, and Singapore. Its founder, Ron Ball, remarked that in Asia, brutal competition means prices fall continually. To succeed, a company must slash costs by localizing supply, maintaining consistent links with suppliers, and cutting expatriate packages. Some 60 percent of EHC's materials come from China where it has a factory. However, developing suppliers is challenging, especially for a small firm whose smaller scale of orders does not give it as much leverage.[47]

Step 4: Analyzing Competitors' Costs, Prices, and Offers

Within the range of possible prices determined by market demand and company costs, the firm must take competitors' costs, prices, and possible price reactions into account. The firm should first consider the nearest competitor's price. If the firm's offer contains features not offered by the nearest competitor, their worth to the customer should be evaluated and added to the competitor's price. If the competitor's offer contains some features not offered by the firm, their worth to the customer should be evaluated and subtracted from the firm's price. Now the firm can decide whether it can charge more, the same, or less than the competitor. Consider the fast-food market in the Philippines:

Jollibee and McDonald's—Jollibee follows Western fast-food business models, but sells food suited to Filipino tastes. Jollibee's outlets are clean and well-lighted like McDonald's and operate with the same efficiency. Similar to Disney, it spends 4 percent of its gross sales on advertising. During the Asian crisis, Jollibee offered value meals at different price points so that no matter what the consumer's budget, it had something delicious to offer. The crisis drew new customers as high-income families cut spending, some switching from gourmet restaurants to fast food. Jollibee responded by holding price increases at 8.5 percent to McDonald's 10 percent when the country's inflation rate was 9.7 percent. McDonald's, which started its Philippine operations three years after Jollibee was set up, is playing catch-up. McDonald's aim is to reach not only Westernized urbanites, but also the much larger middle and lower classes, which is Jollibee's main customer base. It has started selling Pinoyburger, a juicier and sweeter product similar to Jollibee's Yumburger. However, its profit margin is 0.4 percent relative to Jollibee's 6.1 percent as it has to import much of its ingredients. McDonald's share of the fast-food market is 20 percent, while Jollibee's is over 50 percent.[48]

The introduction of any price or the change of any existing price can provoke a response from customers, competitors, distributors, suppliers, and even government. Competitors are most likely to react when the number of firms are few, the product is homogeneous, and buyers are highly informed. Competitor reactions can be a special problem when these firms have a strong value proposition. Zantac ulcer medication was able to take share away from market pioneer Tagamet and command a price premium in the process because of its performance advantages—fewer drug interactions and side effects and more convenient dosing.[49]

How can a firm anticipate a competitor's reactions? One way is to assume the competitor reacts in the standard way to a price being set or changed. Another is to assume the competitor treats each price difference or change as a fresh challenge and reacts according to self-interest at the time. Now the company will need to research the competitor's current financial situation, recent sales, customer loyalty, and corporate objectives. If the competitor has a market share objective, it is likely to match price differences or changes.[50] If it has a profit-maximization objective, it may react by increasing the advertising budget or improving product quality.

The problem is complicated because the competitor can put different interpretations on lowered prices or a price cut: that the company is trying to steal the market, that the company is doing poorly and trying to boost its sales, or that the company wants the whole industry to reduce prices to stimulate total demand.

Step 5: Selecting a Pricing Method

Given customers' demand schedule, the cost function, and competitors' prices—the company is now ready to select a price. Figure 14.5 summarizes the three major considerations in price setting. Costs set a floor to the price. Competitors' prices and the price of substitutes provide an orienting point. Customers' assessment of unique features establishes the price ceiling.

Companies select a pricing method that includes one or more of these three considerations. We will examine six price-setting methods: markup pricing, target-return pricing, perceived-value pricing, value pricing, going-rate pricing, and auction-type pricing.

Figure 14.5 The Three Cs Model for Price Setting

MARKUP PRICING

The most elementary pricing method is to add a standard **markup** to the product's cost. Construction companies submit job bids by estimating the total project cost and adding a standard markup for profit. Lawyers and accountants typically price by adding a standard markup on their time and costs.

Suppose a toaster manufacturer has the following costs and sales expectations:

Variable cost per unit	\$10
Fixed cost	\$300,000
Expected unit sales	50,000

The manufacturer's unit cost is given by:

$$\text{Unit cost} = \text{variable cost} + \frac{\text{fixed cost}}{\text{unit sales}} = \$10 + \frac{\$300{,}000}{50{,}000} = \$16$$

Now assume the manufacturer wants to earn a 20 percent markup on sales. The manufacturer's markup price is given by:

$$\text{Markup price} = \frac{\text{unit cost}}{(1 - \text{desired return on sales})} = \frac{\$16}{1 - 0.2} = \$20$$

The manufacturer would charge dealers \$20 per toaster and make a profit of \$4 per unit. The dealers in turn will markup the toaster. If dealers want to earn 50 percent on their selling price, they will markup the toaster to \$40. This is equivalent to a cost markup of 100 percent. Markups are generally higher on seasonal items (to cover the risk of not selling), specialty items, slower-moving items, items with high storage and handling costs, and demand-inelastic items, such as prescription drugs.

Does the use of standard markups make logical sense? Generally, no. Any pricing method that ignores current demand, perceived value, and competition is not likely to lead to the optimal price. Markup pricing works only if the marked-up price actually brings in the expected level of sales.

Companies introducing a new product often price it high, hoping to recover their costs as rapidly as possible. But this strategy could be fatal if a competitor is pricing low. This happened to Philips when pricing its video-disc players. Philips wanted to make a profit on each player. Japanese competitors priced low and succeeded in building their market share rapidly, which in turn pushed down their costs substantially.

Still, markup pricing remains popular. First, sellers can determine costs much more easily than they can estimate demand. By tying the price to cost, sellers simplify the pricing task. Second, where all firms in the industry use this pricing method, prices tend to be similar. Price competition is therefore minimized. Third, many people feel that cost-plus pricing is fairer to both buyers and sellers. Sellers do not take advantage of buyers when the latter's demand becomes acute, and sellers earn a fair return on investment.

TARGET-RETURN PRICING

In **target-return pricing**, the firm determines the price that would yield its target rate of Return On Investment (ROI). Target pricing is used by General Motors, which prices its automobiles to achieve a 15–20 percent ROI. This method is also used by public utilities, which need to make a fair return on investment.

Suppose the toaster manufacturer has invested $1 million in the business and wants to set a price to earn a 20 percent ROI, specifically $200,000. The target-return price is given by the following formula:

$$\text{Target-return price} = \text{unit cost} + \frac{\text{desired return} \times \text{invested capital}}{\text{unit sales}}$$

$$= \$16 + \frac{0.2 \times 1{,}000{,}000}{50{,}000} = \$20$$

The manufacturer will realize 20 percent ROI provided its costs and estimated sales turn out to be accurate. But what if sales do not reach 50,000 units? The manufacturer can prepare a break-even chart to learn what would happen at other sales levels (see Figure 14.6). Fixed costs are $300,000 regardless of sales volume. Variable costs, not shown in the figure, rise with volume. Total costs equal the sum of fixed costs and variable costs. The total revenue curve starts at zero and rises with each unit sold.

The total revenue and total cost curves cross at 30,000 units. This is the break-even volume. It can be verified by the following formula:

$$\text{Break-even volume} = \frac{\text{fixed cost}}{(\text{price} - \text{variable cost})} = \frac{\$300{,}000}{\$20 - \$10} = 30{,}000$$

The manufacturer, of course, is hoping that the market will buy 50,000 units at $20, in which case it earns $200,000 on its $1 million investment, but much depends on price elasticity and competitors' prices. Unfortunately, target-return pricing tends to ignore these considerations. The manufacturer needs to consider different prices and estimate their probable impacts on sales volume and profits. The manufacturer should also search for ways to lower its fixed or variable costs, because lower costs will decrease its required break-even volume.

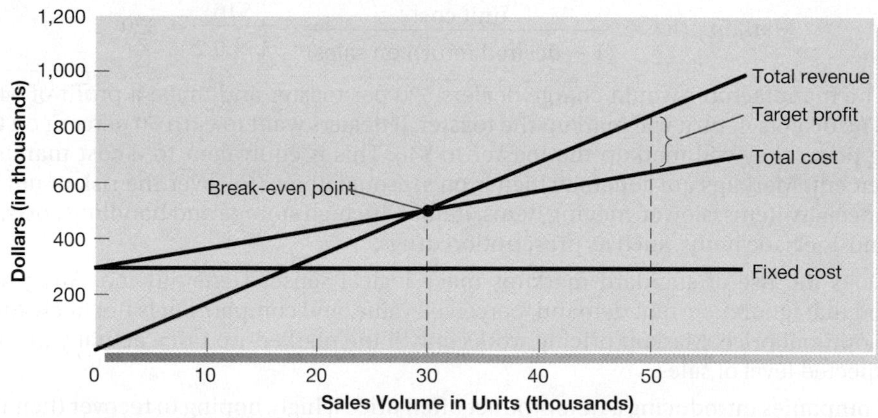

Figure 14.6 Break-Even Chart for Determining Target-Return Price and Break-Even Volume

PERCEIVED-VALUE PRICING

An increasing number of companies base their price on the customer's **perceived value**. They must deliver the value promised by their value proposition, and the customer must perceive this value. They use the other marketing-mix elements, such as advertising and sales force, to communicate and enhance perceived value in buyers' minds.[51]

Perceived value comprises several elements, such as the buyer's image of the product performance, the channel deliverables, the warranty quality, customer support, and softer attributes such as the supplier's reputation, trustworthiness, and esteem. Further, each potential customer places different weights on these different elements, with the result that some will be *price buyers,* others will be *value buyers,* and still others will be *loyal buyers.* Companies need different strategies for these three groups. For price buyers, companies need to offer stripped-down products and reduced services. For value buyers, companies must keep innovating new value and aggressively reaffirming their value. For loyal buyers, companies must invest in relationship building and customer intimacy.

Caterpillar uses perceived value to set prices on its construction equipment. It might price its tractor at $100,000, although a similar competitor's tractor might be priced at $90,000. When a prospective customer asks a Caterpillar dealer why he should pay $10,000 more for the Caterpillar tractor, the dealer answers:

$90,000	is the tractor's price if it is only equivalent to the competitor's tractor
$7,000	is the price premium for Caterpillar's superior durability
$6,000	is the price premium for Caterpillar's superior reliability
$5,000	is the price premium for Caterpillar's superior service
$2,000	is the price premium for Caterpillar's longer warranty on parts
$110,000	is the normal price to cover Caterpillar's superior value
−$10,000	discount
$100,000	final price

The Caterpillar dealer is able to indicate why Caterpillar's tractor delivers more value than the competitor's. Although the customer is asked to pay a $10,000 premium, he is actually getting $20,000 extra value! He chooses the Caterpillar tractor because he is convinced that its lifetime operating costs will be lower.

Yet even when a company claims that its offering delivers more total value, not all customers will respond positively. There is always a segment of buyers who care only about the price. There are other buyers who suspect that the company is exaggerating its product quality and services. One company installed its software system in one or two plants operated by a company. The substantial and well-documented cost savings convinced the customer to buy the software for its other plants.

The key to perceived-value pricing is to deliver more value than the competitor and to demonstrate this to prospective buyers. Basically, a company needs to understand the customer's decision making process. The company can try to determine the value of its offering in several ways: managerial judgments within the company, value of similar products, focus groups, surveys, experimentation, analysis of historical data, and conjoint analysis.[52]

VALUE PRICING

In recent years, several companies have adopted **value pricing**: they win loyal customers by charging a fairly low price for a high-quality offering. Among the best practitioners of value pricing are IKEA and budget airlines such as AirAsia.

Value pricing is not a matter of simply setting lower prices; it involves re-engineering the company's operations to become a low-cost producer without sacrificing quality, and lowering prices significantly to attract a large number of value-conscious customers.

Toyota—In 2000, Toyota engaged in a cost-cutting program called Construction of Cost Competitiveness for the 21st Century (CCC21) and was successful in saving the auto-maker $10 billion over a five-year time frame. It helped Toyota cut procurement costs by nearly a third. As the program wound down, Toyota looked at other ways to reduce costs including cutting steel parts in cars from 610 to 500 to deal with the soaring cost of steel, forcing some component makers to meet or beat rock-bottom prices offered by suppliers in China, and buying from more parts manufacturers not affiliated with Toyota's *keiretsu*.[53]

An important type of value pricing is **Everyday Low Pricing** (EDLP), which takes place at the retail level. A retailer who holds to an EDLP pricing policy charges a constant low price with little or no price promotions and special sales. These constant prices eliminate week-to-week price uncertainty and can be contrasted to the "high-low" pricing of promotion-oriented competitors. In **high-low pricing**, the retailer charges higher prices on an everyday basis but then runs frequent promotions in which prices are temporarily lowered below the EDLP level.[54] The two different pricing strategies have been shown to affect consumer price judgments—deep discounts (EDLP) can lead to lower perceived prices by consumers over time than frequent, shallow discounts (high-low), even if the actual averages are the same.[55]

Some retailers have even based their marketing strategy around what could be called *extreme* everyday low pricing. Partly fueled by an economic downturn, once unfashionable "dollar stores" are gaining in popularity, such as the following 100-yen store chain in Japan.

Daiso—Hirotake Yano created a retail trend in Japan when he opened a chain of 100-yen shops. Although Japanese are brand-conscious and are willing to pay two or three times more for brand names, the recession in the 1990s has younger Japanese coming to grips with the concepts of value and discount shopping. Everything in the 2,300 Daiso stores sells at 100 yen, including utensils, cosmetics and accessories, CDs, stationery, and handicrafts. The larger stores carry 1,500 types of cosmetics, 500 varieties of necklaces, 500 kinds of folders, and 85 different scissors. There are also items that would normally cost 10 or 20 times more, including collapsible umbrellas, leather gloves, personal digital assistants, and watches. These bargains have attracted many buyers, giving Daiso annual sales of more than 200 billion yen. Daiso's success has also spurred other merchants, like some big supermarkets, to launch 88-yen shops.[56]

Daiso is a Japanese chain that sells items at 100 yen. It has expanded to various Asian countries. In Singapore, Daiso prices its products at S$2.

The most important reason retailers adopt EDLP is that constant sales and promotions are costly and have eroded consumer confidence in the credibility of everyday shelf prices. Consumers also have less time and patience for such time-honored traditions as watching for supermarket specials and clipping coupons. Yet, there is no denying that promotions create excitement and draw shoppers. For this reason, EDLP is not a guarantee of success. As supermarkets face heightened competition, many find that the key to drawing shoppers is using a combination of high-low and everyday low pricing strategies, with increased advertising and promotions.[57]

GOING-RATE PRICING

In **going-rate pricing**, the firm bases its price largely on competitors' prices. The firm might charge the same, more, or less than major competitor(s). In oligopolistic industries that sell a commodity such as steel, paper, or fertilizer, firms normally charge the same price. The smaller firms "follow the leader," changing their prices when the market leader's prices change rather than when their own demand or costs change. Some firms may charge a slight premium or slight discount, but they preserve the amount of difference. Thus minor gasoline retailers usually charge a few cents less per gallon than the major oil companies, without letting the difference increase or decrease.

Going-rate pricing is quite popular. Where costs are difficult to measure or competitive response is uncertain, firms feel that the going price is a good solution because it is thought to reflect the industry's collective wisdom.

AUCTION-TYPE PRICING

Auction-type pricing is growing more popular, especially with the growth of the Internet. "Breakthrough Marketing: eBay" describes the ascent of that wildly successful Internet company. There are over 2,000 electronic marketplaces selling everything from pigs to used vehicles to cargo to chemicals. One major use of auctions is to dispose of excess inventories or used goods. Companies need to be aware of the three major types of auctions and their separate pricing procedures.

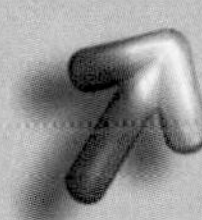

BREAKTHROUGH • MARKETING

EBAY

Pierre Omidayar created eBay to help his girlfriend sell her Pez candy dispenser collection. Soon eBay grew into a broader site where consumers could auction collectibles like baseball cards and Barbie dolls. The momentum continued, with sellers posting new and unusual items, and customers looking for everyday products from used furniture to new digital cameras. Small businesses discovered that eBay was an efficient way to reach consumers and other businesses. Large companies saw eBay as an opportunity to sell bulk lots of unsold inventory.

By 2003, eBay was transacting $23 billion in worldwide sales in 23 merchandise categories. The site has 62 million registered users and receives 43 million unique visitors a month. Yet, eBay itself does not buy any inventory or own the products on its site. It earns its money by collecting a fee for the auction listing, plus a commission when the sale is complete.

eBay constantly creates new categories of merchandise for buyers and businesses. One such category is used cars. Traditionally, used cars were sold locally in the U.S., but eBay Motors created a national used-car marketplace that is now one of eBay's largest segments. Given the reputation of used car salespeople, how could anyone trust a seemingly anonymous car seller in a distant location? eBay Motors created such trust-building elements as online reputation ratings of buyers and sellers; an escrow service for holding funds until the car is delivered; fraud-protection warranty of up to $20,000; and a network of available third-party inspectors. In any given month (such as April 2003), eight million customers visit the eBay Motors site. Each auction gets an average of 7–8 bids. Roughly 75 percent of cars sold on the site are sold across state lines.

Although eBay began as an auction site, it evolved to also offer a fixed-price "buy it now" option to buyers who did not want to wait for an auction and were willing to pay the price set by the seller. For years, buyers and sellers used eBay as an informal guide to market value. eBay became the de facto arbiter of price. A consumer or businessperson who wanted to know the "going price" for anything from a copier to a new DVD player checked on eBay. Companies with a new product design who wanted to test its consumer appeal and pricing could try it out on eBay. In late 2003, eBay began selling sales price data on thousands of goods auctioned on the site. PGA.com, for example, uses eBay's data to set market values for more than 2,000 models of used golf clubs.

eBay is also positioning itself to be a global giant. Asia represents a major opportunity for eBay. Over $2 billion

(Continued ...)

(Continued ...)

worth of goods were sold in Asia over eBay in 2004, an 80 percent growth over 2003. "We believe we can grow our Asian business at least 50 percent a year compounded over the next three years, probably longer," says Jae H. Lee, eBay's Asia Pacific chief. "We enable people who can't sell through traditional retail channels by providing them with an easy-to-use marketplace that gets them in touch with the end-buyer who is willing to pay the highest price for their goods," says Lee. "What could be better than that?"

Thus in Chinese provinces, women's groups are selling everything from textiles to handicraft, bypassing half a dozen middlemen and getting prices they'd never dreamed of. In South Korea, where a highway was being built near Seoul, a community of street shops feared for their business while construction was underway. eBay stepped in to help them sell their goods. However, sellers cannot trade dutiable items like imported luxury cars, although they could sell cars over eBay locally, like in the U.S., since there are no duties involved. Outright fraud in Asia represents less than 0.1 percent of transactions in 2004. "The place is as safe as it can be," says Lee. Like in the U.S., eBay operates its PayPal system in Asia, which bills the buyer's credit card in the currency of his choice. It also has both fixed-priced sales and auctions. In Asia, fixed-priced sale is a big portion of eBay's business, with mainly in-season goods like cameras, electronic items, cell phones, computer gear, and garments being sold. In South Korea, fixed-priced items make up 60 percent of sales. However, in China, collectibles are more likely to be auctioned while in-season goods are sold at fixed prices.

For now, eBay Asia has a presence in South Korea, China, Hong Kong, Singapore, the Philippines, Malaysia, and India. Purchasing power and Internet penetration are keys to eBay's growth in the region. South Korea accounts for nearly half of all Asian revenues for eBay, with China running a close second. Even some of the more mature markets in Asia like Hong Kong and Singapore are fairly large businesses for eBay, although unlike South Korea, where people are generally buying and selling locally, they are driven mainly by cross-border trading. Singaporeans sell collectibles to Europeans or Americans rather than to their neighbors.

Given its attractive business, eBay has attracted numerous competitors. Among the biggest is Yahoo! In Asia, Yahoo! is still the dominant player in Japan and Taiwan and is trying to give eBay a run for its money in China. Yahoo! Japan has done well because it started as a joint venture with Softbank, whose backing was instrumental in its success. eBay closed its Japanese operations in early 2002. "Yahoo!, having first-mover advantage, did very well in Japan," concedes Lee. "We retreated from Japan but we are learning to get back in. It's the biggest country in Asia in terms of purchasing power. We need to be there."

eBay is also looking at rolling out its portals in other Asian markets like Thailand, Indonesia, and Vietnam. "Our aim is to have an eBay flag flying in almost every major country in Asia in, say, five years," says Lee. Most of the expansion in Asia will be through greenfield projects rather than acquisitions. "If there is a market where there is a strong established local player and it makes sense for us, we may do an acquisition but that's highly unlikely because we believe our brand name in Asia is now strong enough to carry us through in the smaller markets of Asia," he adds.

The next challenge for eBay in Asia is to convince the region that much of its usual buying and selling ought to be done online. How long would it take before selling things over the Internet becomes the norm in Asia? Lee says in Japan and South Korea, it is already mainstream. "We have housewives and older people, not just young geeks, selling or buying stuff regularly. If we were a department store, we'd probably be the second-largest in Korea, based on how much we are selling," he adds. Still, eBay has to overcome a maze of legal problems. Avnish Bajaj, its India head, was recently arrested when it was reported that someone was trying to sell a porn clip of two teens having sex at a prominent New Delhi high school. "Unbeknownst to us, someone in India put up a pornographic video for sale. It's almost like arresting the owner of a mall for some transaction in a mall," he remarked.

In China, eBay faces stiff competition from local rival Taobao.com. Taobao is a subsidiary of Chinese e-commerce firm Alibaba, partly owned by Yahoo!. eBay's share in the Chinese consumer-to-consumer e-commerce market in 2006 was 15.4 percent, down from 29.1 percent in 2005. In contrast, Taobao's share has increased to 82 percent and Paipai.com, the online trading arm of Tencent, the largest Chinese instant messaging firm, is third with 2.7 percent market share.

eBay's pricing revolution gives customers control all over the world. Customers choose the price they want to pay. At the same time, eBay's efficiency and wide reach lets sellers worldwide make good margins. eBay charges a listing fee and a commission that ranges from 1 to 5 percent. Merchants report profit margins of 40 percent. Of the thousands of Internet auction sites, eBay is the largest and was profitable from the start. It netted $4.55 billion in 2005 and expects to hit $5.7 billion in revenue in 2006. Not bad for a company that does not actually sell anything.

Sources: Betsy Streisand, "Make New Sales, but Keep the Old." *U.S. News and World Report*, February 16, 2004, p. 40; "Booting Online." *Economist*, January 24, 2004, p. 30; David Kirkpatrick, "Why 'Bottom Up' Is On Its Way Up." *Fortune*, January 26, 2004; Adam Lashinsky, "5: There's No Stopping eBay." *Fortune*, February 23, 2004, p. 78; Assif Shameen, "eBay takes on Asia." *Asia Inc.*, March 2005, pp. 26–30; <www.investor.ebay.com/financial.cfm>, accessed on January 18, 2006; Mayumi Negishi, "EBay, Yahoo Japan to Link Up Auction Services." *Reuters News*, December 4, 2007, <www.global.factiva.com.libproxy1.nus.edu.sg/ha/default.aspx> accessed on April 1, 2008; Liu Baijia, "US Giant eBay Loses Ground to TaoBao." *China Daily*, April 17, 2007.

- **English auctions (ascending bids) — one seller and many buyers.** On sites such as Yahoo! and eBay, the seller puts up an item and bidders raise the offer price until the top price is reached. English auctions are being used today for selling antiques, cattle, real estate, and used equipment and vehicles.
- **Dutch auctions (descending bids) — one seller and many buyers, or one buyer and many sellers.** In the first kind, an auctioneer announces a high price for a product and then slowly decreases the price until a bidder accepts the price. In the other, the buyer announces something that he wants to buy and then potential sellers compete to get the sale by offering the lowest price. Each seller sees what the last bid is and decides whether to go lower.
- **Sealed-bid auctions — would-be suppliers can submit only one bid and cannot know the other bids.** A supplier will not bid below its cost but cannot bid too high for fear of losing the job. The net effect of these two pulls can be described in terms of the bid's *expected profit.* Using expected profit for setting price makes sense for the seller that makes many bids. The seller who bids only occasionally or who needs a particular contract badly will not find it advantageous to use expected profit. This criterion does not distinguish between a $1,000 profit with a 0.10 probability and a $125 profit with a 0.80 probability. Yet the firm that wants to keep production going would prefer the second contract to the first.

As more and more firms use online auctions for industrial buying, they need to recognize the possible effects it can have on their suppliers. If the increased savings a firm obtains in an online auction translates into decreased margins for an incumbent supplier, the supplier may feel the firm is opportunistically squeezing out price concessions.[58] Online auctions with a large number of bidders, greater economic stakes, and less visibility in pricing have been shown to result in greater overall satisfaction, more positive future expectations, and fewer perceptions of opportunism.

Step 6: Selecting the Final Price

Pricing methods narrow the range from which the company must select its final price. In selecting that price, the company must consider additional factors, including the impact of other marketing activities, company pricing policies, gain-and-risk-sharing pricing, and the impact of price on other parties.

IMPACT OF OTHER MARKETING ACTIVITIES

The final price must take into account the brand's quality and advertising relative to the competition. In a classic study, Farris and Reibstein examined the relationships among relative price, relative quality, and relative advertising for 227 consumer businesses, and found the following:

- **Brands with average relative quality but high relative advertising budgets could charge premium prices.** Consumers apparently were willing to pay higher prices for known products than for unknown products.
- **Brands with high relative quality and high relative advertising obtained the highest prices.** Conversely, brands with low quality and low advertising charged the lowest prices.
- **The positive relationship between high prices and high advertising held most strongly in the later stages of the product life cycle for market leaders.**[59]

These findings suggest that price is not as important as quality and other benefits in the market offering. One study asked consumers to rate the importance of price and other attributes in using online retailing. Only 19 percent cared about price; far more cared about customer support (65 percent), on-time delivery (58 percent), and product shipping and handling (49 percent).[60]

COMPANY PRICING POLICIES

The price must be consistent with company pricing policies. At the same time, companies are not averse to establishing pricing penalties under certain circumstances.[61]

Airlines charge those who change their reservations on discount tickets. Banks charge fees for too many withdrawals in a month or for early withdrawal of a certificate of deposit. Car rental companies charge penalties for no-shows for specialty vehicles. Although these policies are often justifiable, they must be used judiciously so as not to unnecessarily alienate customers (see "Marketing Insight: Stealth Price Increases").

Many companies set up a pricing department to develop policies and establish or approve decisions. The aim is to ensure that salespeople quote prices that are reasonable to customers and profitable to the company. Dell Computer has developed innovative pricing techniques.

Dell—Dell uses a high-tech "cost-forecasting" system that enables it to scale its selling prices[62] based on consumer demand and the company's own costs. The company instituted this flexible pricing model in 2001 to maximize its margins during the economic slowdown. Dell managers get cost information from suppliers, which they then combine with knowledge about profit targets, delivery dates, and competition to set prices for business segments. On any given day, the same computer might sell at different prices depending on whether the purchaser is a government, small business, or home PC buyer. The cost-forecasting system helped Dell increase its profits.[63]

GAIN-AND-RISK-SHARING PRICING

Buyers may resist accepting a seller's proposal because of a high perceived level of risk. The seller has the option of offering to absorb part or all of the risk if he does not deliver the full promised value. Consider the following:

Thomson 800—This condominium project was launched in Singapore during the Asian economic crisis by Hong Kong magnate Ka Shing Li. To encourage purchases during the bleak period, the developer guaranteed new buyers a 10 percent capital appreciation over five years. If the price fell by more than 10 percent at the end of that period, buyers would be paid the difference between the purchase price and the valuation price.

MARKETING INSIGHT • STEALTH PRICE INCREASES

With consumers resisting higher prices, companies are trying to figure out how to increase revenue without really raising prices. Increasingly, the solution has been through the addition of fees for what had once been free features. Such small additional charges can add up to a substantial source of revenue.

Fees for consumers who pay bills online, bounce checks, or use ATMs bring banks an estimated $30 billion annually in the U.S., while credit card late payments exceed $10 billion. The telecommunications industry has been aggressive at adding fees for setup, change-of-service, service termination, directory assistance, regulatory assessment, number portability, and cable hookup and equipment, costing consumers billions of dollars. Even governments have their own array of fees, fines, and penalties to raise revenue.

This use of fees has several implications. Given that list prices stay fixed, they may result in inflation being understated. They also make it harder for consumers to compare competitive offerings.

Companies justify the extra fees as the only fair and viable way to cover expenses without losing customers. Many argue that it makes sense to charge a premium for added services that cost more to provide, rather than charge all customers the same amount regardless of whether or not they use the extra service. Breaking out charges and fees according to the services involved is seen as a way to keep the basic costs low. Companies also use fees as a means to weed out unprofitable customers or change their behavior. Some airlines now charge passengers for paper tickets and for excess baggage.

Ultimately, the viability of extra fees will be decided in the marketplace and by the willingness of consumers to vote with their wallets and pay the fees or vote with their feet and move on.

Source: Adapted from Michael Arndt, "Fees! Fees! Fees!" *BusinessWeek*, September 29, 2003, pp. 99–104; "The Price is Wrong." *Economist*, May 25, 2002, pp. 59–60.

IMPACT OF PRICE ON OTHER PARTIES

Management must also consider the reactions of other parties to the contemplated price.[64] How will distributors and dealers feel about it? If they do not make enough profit, they may not choose to bring the product to market. Will the sales force be willing to sell at that price? How will competitors react? Will suppliers raise their prices when they see the company's price? Will the government intervene and prevent this price from being charged?

Adapting the Price

Companies usually do not set a single price, but rather a pricing structure that reflects variations in geographical demand and costs, market-segment requirements, purchase timing, order levels, delivery frequency, guarantees, service contracts, and other factors. As a result of discounts, allowances, and promotional support, a company rarely realizes the same profit from each unit of a product that it sells. Here we will examine several price-adaptation strategies: geographical pricing, price discounts and allowances, promotional pricing, and differentiated pricing.

Geographical Pricing (Cash, Countertrade, Barter)

In geographical pricing, the company decides how to price its products to different customers in different locations and countries.

Procter & Gamble—China is P&G's sixth-largest market, yet two-thirds of China's population earns less than $25 per month. So in 2003, P&G developed a tiered pricing initiative to help compete against cheaper local brands while still protecting the value of its global brands. P&G introduced a 320-gram bag of Tide Clean White for 23 cents, compared with 33 cents for 350 grams of Tide Triple Action. The Clean White version does not offer such benefits as stain removal and fragrance, but it costs less to make and, according to P&G, outperforms every other brand at that price level.[65]

Procter & Gamble sets different prices for different customers in different locations, often by making slight changes in the product. Clean White, for instance, is the lower-priced version of its detergent for the Chinese market and lacks stain removal ingredients and fragrance.

Should the company charge higher prices to distant customers to cover the higher shipping costs or a lower price to win additional business? How should exchange rates and the strength of different currencies be accounted for?

Another issue is how to get paid. This issue is critical when buyers lack sufficient hard currency to pay for their purchases. Many buyers want to offer other items in payment, a practice known as **countertrade**. Countertrade may account for 15–25 percent of world trade and takes several forms[66]: barter, compensation deals, buyback agreements, and offset.

- ***Barter*** — The direct exchange of goods, with no money and no third party involved. Malaysia's TV3 station once offered barter trade agreements to advertisers reluctant to pay cash for airtime to promote their products and services. TV3 received bungalows, condominiums, and mobile phones in lieu of cash.
- ***Compensation deal*** — The seller receives some percentage of the payment in cash and the rest in products. Malaysia signed an agreement with Moscow to purchase fighter planes valued at $500 million, to be paid over five years partly with $95 million worth of palm oil.
- ***Buyback arrangement*** — The seller sells a plant, equipment, or technology to another country and agrees to accept as partial payment products manufactured with the supplied equipment. A U.S. chemical company built a plant for an Indian company and accepted partial payment in cash and the remainder in chemicals manufactured at the plant.
- ***Offset*** — The seller receives full payment in cash but agrees to spend a substantial amount of the money in that country within a stated time period. Offset usually involves technology transfer, co-production investment, licensing, and subcontracting. A South Korean Ministry of National Defense deal with McDonnell Douglas included aircraft assembled from McDonnell Douglas kits by Samsung Aerospace and aircraft manufactured under license by Samsung.
- ***Public-Private Partnership (PPP)*** — This complex form of countertrade typically involves multiple parties. A Chinese construction firm bidding to build a hydro-electric dam for the Malaysian government offers to procure Middle East investors to set up, by way of foreign direct investment, an aluminum smelting plant near the dam site if it gets the job. Many global companies who engage in such complex deals have in-house countertrade departments. Other companies rely on barter houses and countertrade specialists (see "Marketing Memo: Guidelines for Countertraders").

MARKETING MEMO • GUIDELINES FOR COUNTERTRADERS

Sellers engaging in countertrade must evaluate the risks involved, select a product to receive in countertrade, pick a trading company if they have no in-house countertrade department, and formulate countertrade contracts. Dan West, president of West Trade International, provides some useful guidelines in this connection:

- ***Evaluating countertrade risks*** — First, determine if the government or only private businesses are involved; if the latter, identify them and check their reputations and credit information with third parties. Second, conduct preliminary research by visiting the country to establish initial contact, preferably in person. Third, check the ownership of banks that might be in the transaction chain. Fourth, consider engaging a country agent who knows the key players, the market, and the regulations. Fifth, check the import and export tariffs of the country. Sixth, determine if a third party will assume the risk if you have to market the product. Seventh, establish whether there is a market for the product being countertraded through market research; if possible, buy back something that you can use internally to simplify the transaction (see next point).
- ***Selecting a product to receive in countertrade*** — First, check your raw material needs when choosing a product to countertrade; if the product is something you can use internally, it is possible a new raw-material source has been found. Second, strive for flexibility of choice in the products you receive and obtain the maximum number of countries in which the product can be sold. Third, reserve the right to inspect the goods before shipment. Fourth, examine pricing at the world level so that prices of the products are not grossly inflated. Fifth, avoid products that have numerous marketing and distribution limitations. Sixth, look for high value, low volume products that ideally do not take up much space, weigh little, and are worth a lot of money.
- ***Picking a trading company*** — For companies without in-house countertrade departments, selecting a good trading company is important for success. First, examine the strength of the trading company (e.g., its knowledge about a particular foreign company or country, or product or industry), its track record (e.g., ability to close a deal); ask for references and check them; check their financial resources. Second, check the trading company's commitment to countertrade (e.g., its personnel, degree of marketing assistance it can provide).
- ***Formulating a countertrade contract*** — Aside from the standard sales and purchasing contracts, there is a protocol agreement to be formulated which ties the other contracts together and defines the terms of the countertrade transaction. The protocol agreement should include: an overall statement of what is expected of the parties; effective date the contract begins and ends; obligation of the parties involved; contract value; payment terms; choice of goods; time available to complete the countertrade; term of commitment; liquidated damages for non-completion; marketing limitations regarding sale of the product(s) to other countries or companies; and ability to transfer countertrade commitment to another company for execution of the deal.

Source: Adapted from Dan West, "Countertrade." *Business Credit*, April 2002, 104(4/1).

Price Discounts and Allowances

Most companies will adjust their list price and give discounts and allowances for early payment, volume purchases, and off-season buying (see Table 14.3).[67] Companies must do this carefully or find that their profits are much less than planned.[68]

Table 14.3 Price Discounts and Allowances

Cash Discount:	A price reduction to buyers who pay bills promptly. A typical example is "2/10, net 30," which means that payment is due within 30 days and that the buyer can deduct 2 percent by paying the bill within 10 days.
Quantity Discount:	A price reduction to those who buy large volumes. A typical example is "$10 per unit for less than 100 units; $9 per unit for 100 or more units." Quantity discounts must be offered equally to all customers and must not exceed the cost savings to the seller. They can be offered on each order placed or on the number of units ordered over a given period.
Functional Discount:	Discount (also called *trade discount*) offered by a manufacturer to trade-channel members if they will perform certain functions, such as selling, storing, and recordkeeping. Manufacturers must offer the same functional discounts within each channel.
Seasonal Discount:	A price reduction to those who buy merchandise or services out of season. Hotels, motels, and airlines offer seasonal discounts in slow selling periods.
Allowance:	An extra payment designed to gain reseller participation in special programs. *Trade-in allowances* are granted for turning in an old item when buying a new one. *Promotional allowances* reward dealers for participating in advertising and sales support programs.

Discount pricing has become the modus operandi of many companies offering both products and services. Some product categories tend to self-destruct by always being on sale. Salespeople, in particular, are quick to give discounts to close a sale. But word can get around fast that the company's list price is "soft," and discounting becomes the norm. The discounts undermine the value perceptions of the offerings.

Some companies in an overcapacity situation are tempted to give discounts or even begin to supply a retailer with a store brand version of their product at a deep discount. However, because the store brand is priced lower, it may start making inroads on the manufacturer's brand. Manufacturers should consider the implications of supplying products at a discount to retailers as they may end up losing long-run profits in trying to meet short-run volume goals.

Airline industry in India—The opening of India's aviation sector saw several new flights and routes, leading to a price war. One sector that has seen sharp price cuts is the busy India-U.S. routes. Direct flights are being offered by Jet Airways, Delta, Continental Airlines, and American Airlines. The price war started when Jet Airways and Delta offered its non-stop Mumbai-New York economy flight at $1,000 compared to the usual $2,000. With such keen competition and loss of monopoly status, state-owned Air India was compelled to cut its price. The price war is expected to spread to other flights. As is, Jet Airways offered its Mumbai-Brussels-Newark economy flight from $500 to $1,000. The Southeast Asia sectors have also seen fare cuts, especially with domestic carriers such as Air Deccan and Kingfisher launching their international operations.[69]

People with higher incomes and higher product involvement willingly pay more for features, customer service, quality, added convenience, and the brand name. So it can be a mistake for a strong, distinctive brand to plunge into price discounting to respond to low-price attacks.[70] At the same time, discounting can be a useful tool if the company can gain concessions in return, such as when the customer agrees to sign a three-year contract, is willing to order electronically, thus saving the company money, or agrees to buy in large quantities.

Sales management needs to monitor the proportion of customers receiving discounts, the average discount, and the particular salespeople who are over-relying on discounting. Higher levels of management should conduct a **net price analysis** to arrive at the "real price" of their offering. The real price is affected not only by discounts, but by many other expenses (see promotional pricing below) that reduce the realized price: Suppose the company's list price is $3,000. The average discount is $300. The company's promotional spending averages $450 (15 percent of the list price). Co-op advertising money of $150 is given to retailers to back the product. The company's net price is $2,100, not $3,000.

Promotional Pricing

Companies can use several pricing techniques to stimulate early purchase:

- ***Loss-leader pricing*** — Supermarkets and department stores often drop the price on well-known brands to stimulate additional store traffic. This pays if the revenue on the additional sales compensates for the lower margins on the loss-leader items. Manufacturers of loss-leader brands typically object because this practice can dilute the brand image and bring complaints from retailers who charge the list price.
- ***Special-event pricing*** — Sellers will establish special prices in certain seasons to draw more customers. Every December, there are back-to-school sales.
- ***Cash rebates*** — Auto companies and other consumer-goods companies offer cash rebates to encourage purchase of the manufacturers' products within a specified time period. Rebates can help clear inventories without cutting the stated list price.
- ***Low-interest financing*** — Instead of cutting its price, the company can offer customers low-interest financing. Automakers have even announced no-interest financing to attract customers.
- ***Longer payment terms*** — Sellers, especially mortgage banks and auto companies, stretch loans over longer periods and thus lower the monthly payments. Consumers often worry less about the cost (i.e., the interest rate) of a loan and more about whether they can afford the monthly payment.
- ***Warranties and service contracts*** — Companies can promote sales by adding a free or low-cost warranty or service contract.
- ***Psychological discounting*** — This strategy involves setting an artificially high price and then offering the product at substantial savings; for example, "Was $359, now $299."

Promotional-pricing strategies are often a zero-sum game. If they work, competitors copy them and they lose their effectiveness. If they do not work, they waste money that could have been put into other marketing tools, such as building up product quality and service or strengthening product image through advertising.

Differentiated Pricing

Companies often adjust their basic price to accommodate differences in customers, products, locations, and so on.

Price discrimination occurs when a company sells a product or service at two or more prices that do not reflect a proportional difference in costs. In first-degree price discrimination, the seller charges a separate price to each customer depending on the intensity of his or her demand. In second-degree price discrimination, the seller charges less to buyers who buy a larger volume. In third-degree price discrimination, the seller charges different amounts to different classes of buyers, as in the following cases:

- ***Customer-segment pricing*** — Different customer groups are charged different prices for the same product or service. For example, public buses often charge a lower admission fee to students and senior citizens.
- ***Product-form pricing*** — Different versions of the product are priced differently but not proportionately to their respective costs. Evian prices a 48-ounce bottle of its mineral water at $2. It takes the same water and packages 1.7 ounces in a moisturizer spray for $6. Through product-form pricing, Evian manages to charge $3 an ounce in one form and about $.04 an ounce in another.
- ***Image pricing*** — Some companies price the same product at two different levels based on image differences. A perfume manufacturer can put the perfume in one bottle, give it

a name and image, and price it at $10 an ounce. It can put the same perfume in another bottle with a different name and image and price it at $30 an ounce.

- ***Channel pricing***— Coca-Cola carries a different price depending on whether it is purchased in a fine restaurant, a fast-food restaurant, or a vending machine.
- ***Location pricing***— The same product is priced differently at different locations even though the cost of offering at each location is the same. A theater varies its seat prices according to audience preferences for different locations.
- ***Time pricing***— Prices are varied by season, day, or hour. Public utilities vary energy rates to commercial users by time of day and weekend versus weekday. Restaurants charge less to "early bird" customers. Hotels charge less on weekends.

The airline and hospitality industries use yield management systems and **yield pricing**, by which they offer discounted but limited early purchases, higher-priced late purchases, and the lowest rates on unsold inventory just before it expires.[71] Airlines charge different fares to passengers on the same flight, depending on the seating class; the time of day (morning or night coach); the day of the week (workday or weekend); the season; the person's company, past business, or status (children, senior citizen); and so on.

The phenomenon of offering different pricing schedules to different consumers and dynamically adjusting prices is exploding.[72] Many companies are using software packages that provide real-time controlled tests of actual consumer response to different pricing schedules. Constant price variation, however, can be tricky where consumer relationships are concerned. Research shows it tends to work best in situations where there's no bond between the buyer and the seller. One way to make it work is to offer customers a unique bundle of products and services to meet their needs precisely, making it harder for them to make price comparisons.

The tactic most companies favor, however, is to use variable prices as a reward for good behavior rather than as a penalty. For instance, shipping company APL Inc. rewards customers who can better predict how much cargo space they will need with cheaper rates for booking early. Customers are also getting savvier about how to avoid buyer's remorse from overpaying. They are changing their buying behavior to accommodate the new realities of dynamic pricing—where prices vary frequently by channels, products, customers, and time.

Most consumers are probably not even aware of the degree to which they are the targets of discriminatory pricing. For instance, catalog retailers like Victoria's Secret routinely send out catalogs that sell identical goods except at different prices. Consumers who live in a more free-spending zip code may see only the higher prices.

Some forms of price discrimination (in which sellers offer different price terms to different people within the same trade group) are illegal. However, price discrimination is legal if the seller can prove that its costs are different when selling different volumes or different qualities of the same product to different retailers. Predatory pricing—selling below cost with the intention of destroying competition—is unlawful.[73] Even if legal, some differentiated pricing may meet with a hostile reaction. Coca-Cola considered raising its vending machine soda prices on hot days using wireless technology, and lowering the price on cold days. Customers so disliked the idea that Coke abandoned it.

For price discrimination to work, certain conditions must exist. First, the market must be segmentable and the segments must show different intensities of demand. Second, members in the lower-price segment must not be able to resell the product to the higher-price segment. Third, competitors must not be able to undersell the firm in the higher-price segment. Fourth, the cost of segmenting and policing the market must not exceed the extra revenue derived from price discrimination. Fifth, the practice must not breed customer resentment and ill will. Sixth, the particular form of price discrimination must not be illegal.[74]

Initiating and Responding to Price Changes

Companies often face situations where they may need to cut or raise prices.

Initiating Price Cuts

Several circumstances might lead a firm to cut prices. One is excess plant capacity: The firm needs additional business and cannot generate it through increased sales effort, product improvement, or other measures. It may resort to aggressive pricing, but in initiating a price cut, the company may trigger a price war.

European low-cost airlines such Sterling and SAS have different views on their respective future pricing strategies. To learn more, visit www.pearsoned.co.uk/marketingmanagementeurope.

Cutting prices to keep customers or beat competitors often encourages customers to demand price concessions, however, and trains salespeople to offer them.[75] A price-cutting strategy involves possible traps:

- ***Low-quality trap***— Consumers will assume that the quality is low.
- ***Fragile-market-share trap*** — A low price buys market share but not market loyalty. The same customers will shift to any lower-priced firm that comes along.
- ***Shallow-pockets trap***— The higher-priced competitors may cut their prices and may have longer staying power because of deeper cash reserves.
- ***Price-war trap***— Competitors respond by lowering their prices even more, triggering a price war.

Customers often question the motivation behind price changes.[76] They may assume the item is about to be replaced by a new model; the item is faulty and is not selling well; the firm is in financial trouble; the price will come down even further; or the quality has been reduced. The firm must monitor these attributions carefully.

Initiating Price Increases

A successful price increase can raise profits considerably. For example, if the company's profit margin is 3 percent of sales, a 1 percent price increase will increase profits by 33 percent if sales volume is unaffected. This situation is illustrated in Table 14.4. The assumption is that a company charged $10 and sold 100 units and had costs of $970, leaving a profit of $30, or 3 percent on sales. By raising its price by 10 cents (1 percent price increase), it boosted its profits by 33 percent, assuming the same sales volume.

Table 14.4 Profits Before and After a Price Increase

	Before	After	
Price	$10	$10.10	(a 1-percent price increase)
Units sold	100	100	
Revenue	$1,000	$1,010	
Costs	$970	$970	
Profit	$30	$40	(a $33\frac{1}{3}$-percent profit increase)

A major circumstance provoking price increases is *cost inflation.* Rising costs unmatched by productivity gains squeeze profit margins and lead companies to regular rounds of price increases. Companies often raise their prices by more than the cost increase, in anticipation of further inflation or government price controls, in a practice called *anticipatory pricing.*

Another factor leading to price increases is overdemand. When a company cannot supply all of its customers, it can raise its prices, ration supplies to customers, or both. The price can be increased in the following ways. Each has a different impact on buyers.

- ***Delayed quotation pricing***— The company does not set a final price until the product is finished or delivered. This pricing is prevalent in industries with long production lead times, such as industrial construction and heavy equipment.
- ***Escalator clauses***— The company requires the customer to pay today's price and all or part of any inflation increase that takes place before delivery. An escalator clause bases price increases on some specified price index. Escalator clauses are found in contracts for major industrial projects, like aircraft construction and bridge building.
- ***Unbundling***— The company maintains its price but removes or prices separately one or more elements that were part of the former offer, such as free delivery or installation. Car companies sometimes add anti-lock brakes and passenger-side airbags as supplementary extras to their vehicles.
- ***Reduction of discounts***— The company instructs its sales force not to offer its normal cash and quantity discounts.

Although there is always a chance that a price increase can carry some positive meanings to customers—for example, that the item is "hot" and represents an unusually good value—consumers generally dislike higher prices. In passing price increases on to customers, the company must avoid looking like a price gouger.[77] Companies also need to think of who will bear the brunt of increased prices. Customer memories are long, and they can turn against companies they perceive as price gougers.

Although strong brands can command price premiums, the premiums cannot be excessive. Price hikes without corresponding investments in the value of the brand increases vulnerability to lower-priced competition. Consumers may be willing to "trade down" because they no longer can justify to themselves that the higher priced brand is worth it.

Several techniques help consumers avoid sticker shock and a hostile reaction when prices rise: one is that a sense of fairness must surround any price increase, and customers must be given advance notice so they can do forward buying or shop around. Sharp price increases need to be explained in understandable terms. Making low-visibility price moves first is also a good technique: eliminating discounts, increasing minimum order sizes, and curtailing production of low-margin products are some examples; and contracts or bids for long-term projects should contain escalator clauses based on such factors as increases in recognized national price indexes.[78]

Given strong consumer resistance to price hikes, marketers go to great lengths to find alternative approaches that will allow them to avoid increasing prices when they otherwise would have done so. Here are a few popular ones.

- Shrinking the amount of product instead of raising the price. (Hershey Foods maintained its candy bar price but trimmed its size. Nestlé maintained its size but raised the price.)
- Substituting less-expensive materials or ingredients. (Many candy bar companies substituted synthetic chocolate for real chocolate to fight price increases in cocoa.)
- Reducing or removing product features.
- Removing or reducing product services, such as installation or free delivery.
- Using less-expensive packaging material or larger package sizes.
- Reducing the number of sizes and models offered.
- Creating new economy brands. (Supermarkets such as Cold Storage and Park 'N Shop sell house brands that are cheaper than national brands.)

Responding to Competitors' Price Changes

How should a firm respond to a price cut initiated by a competitor? In markets characterized by high product homogeneity, the firm should search for ways to enhance its augmented product. If it cannot find any, it will have to meet the price reduction. If the competitor raises its price in a homogeneous product market, other firms might not match it unless the increase will benefit the industry as a whole. Then the leader will have to roll back the increase.

In non-homogeneous product markets, a firm has more latitude. It needs to consider the following issues: (1) Why did the competitor change the price? Was it to steal the market, utilize excess capacity, meet changing cost conditions, or lead an industry-wide price change? (2) Does the competitor plan to make the price change temporary or permanent? (3) What will happen to the company's market share and profits if it does not respond? Are other companies going to respond? (4) What are the competitor's and other firms' responses likely to be to each possible reaction?

Market leaders frequently face aggressive price cutting by smaller firms trying to build market share. Using price, Fuji attacks Kodak and Hyundai attacks Toyota. Price cuts can also be used to attack another industry as the following example shows.

Softbank's Yahoo! BB—High-speed Internet access from Softbank's Yahoo! BB is getting cheaper and is becoming a hit in Japan. In June 2005, some 4.5 million Japanese signed up with this Internet service provider. At \$30–\$40 a month for broadband running at 50 megabits a second, it is considered a bargain. Calls among Yahoo! BB customers are free and calls to others in Japan cost a maximum of 7 cents for three minutes. This is cheaper than the 35 cents that rival NTT charges for its traditional telecommunications network. Additionally, for an extra \$10 a month, Softbank Yahoo! BB customers get BBTV which includes 24 television channels, plus on-demand videos for \$3 per movie, or 30 films a month for \$8.[79]

Brand leaders also face lower-priced, private-store brands. The brand leader can respond in several ways. "Marketing Memo: How to Fight Low-Cost Rivals" highlights some possible responses.

MARKETING MEMO • HOW TO FIGHT LOW-COST RIVALS

Kumar studied 50 incumbents and 25 low-cost businesses to better understand the threats posed by disruptive, low-cost competitors. He notes that successful price warriors, such as Germany's Aldi supermarkets, India's Aravind Eye Hospitals, and Israel's Teva Pharmacueticals, are changing the nature of competition all over the world by employing several key tactics, such as focusing on just one or a few consumer segments, delivering the basic product or providing one benefit better than rivals do, and backing low prices with superefficient operations.

Kumar believes ignoring low-cost rivals is a mistake, because they eventually force companies to vacate entire market segments. He does not see price wars as the answer either: slashing prices usually lowers profits for incumbents without driving the low-cost entrants out of business. In the race to the bottom, he says, the challengers always come out ahead of the incumbents. Instead, he offers three possible responses that will vary in their success depending on different factors, as outlined in Figure 14.7.

The first approach to competing against cut-price players is to differentiate the product or service through various means:

- Design cool products (Apple; Bang & Olufsen)
- Continually innovate (Gillette; 3M)
- Offer unique product mix (Sharper Image; Whole Foods)
- Brand a community (Harley-Davidson; Red Bull)
- Sell experiences (Four Seasons; Starbucks)

Kumar cautions that three conditions will determine the success of a differentiation response:

1. **Companies must not use differentiation tactics in isolation.** Bang & Olufsen has competed effectively against low-cost electronics manufacturers in part because of its strong design capabilities, but also because the company continually introduces new products, cultivates an upscale brand image, and supports modern-looking retail outlets.
2. **Companies must be able to persuade consumers to pay for added benefits.** Charging a small premium for greater services or benefits, as Target and Walgreen have done, can be a powerful defense.
3. **Companies must first bring costs and benefits in line.** Hewlett-Packard's resurgence in the PC industry can be

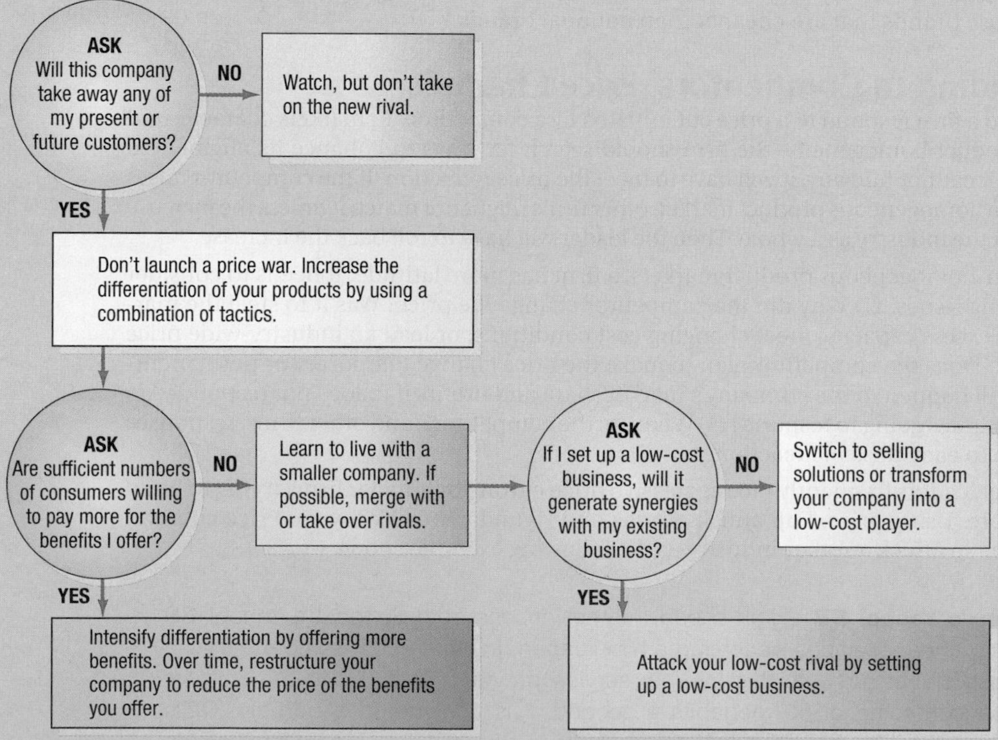

Figure 14.7 A Framework for Responding to Low-cost Rivals

(Continued ...)

MARKETING MEMO • HOW TO FIGHT LOW-COST RIVALS

(Continued ...)

attributed in part to its success in cutting Dell's cost advantage from 20 percent to 10 percent.

Kumar cautions that unless sizable numbers of consumers demand additional benefits, companies may need to yield some markets to price warriors. For example, British Airways has relinquished some short-haul routes to low-cost rivals easyJet and Ryanair. Kumar also believes strategies that help an incumbent firm coexist with low-cost rivals can work initially, but over the long haul, consumers migrate to low-cost options as they become more familiar with them.

Another approach that many companies have tried in responding to low-cost competitors is to introduce a low-cost venture themselves. Citing the failure of no-frills second carriers such as Continental Lite, Delta's Song, KLM's Buzz, SAS's Snowflake, and United's Shuttle, however, Kumar asserts that companies should set up low-cost operations only if (1) the traditional operation will become more competitive as a result; and (2) the new business will derive some advantages that it would not have gained as an independent entity.

A dual strategy succeeds only if companies can generate synergies between the existing businesses and the new ventures, as financial service providers HSBC and ING did. The low-cost venture most likely includes a unique brand name or identity, adequate resources, and a willingness to endure some cannibalization between the two businesses.

If there are no synergies between traditional and low-cost businesses, companies should consider two other options: They can switch from selling products to selling solutions, or even convert themselves into low-cost players. In the former approach, Kumar believes that by offering products and services as an integrated package, companies can expand the segment of the market that is willing to pay more for additional benefits. Selling solutions requires managing customers' processes and increasing their revenues or lowering their costs and risks.

And if all else fails, the best solution may be re-invention as a low-cost player. After all, as noted above, Ryanair was an unprofitable, high-cost traditional airline before it completely—and quite successfully—transformed itself into a low-cost carrier.

Source: Nirmalya Kumar, "Strategies to Fight Low-Cost Rivals." *Harvard Business Review,* December 2006, pp. 104–112.

An extended analysis of alternatives may not always be feasible when the attack occurs. The company may have to react decisively within hours or days, especially in those industries where price changes occur with some frequency and where it is important to react quickly, such as the meatpacking, lumber, or oil industries. It would make better sense to anticipate possible competitors' price changes and prepare contingent responses.

Summary

1. Despite the increased role of non-price factors in modern marketing, price remains a critical element of the marketing mix. Price is the only one of the four Ps that produces revenue; the others produce costs.
2. In setting pricing policy, a company follows a six-step procedure. It selects its pricing objective. It estimates the demand curve, the probable quantities it will sell at each possible price. It estimates how its costs vary at different levels of output, at different levels of accumulated production experience, and for differentiated marketing offers. It examines competitors' costs, prices, and offers. It selects a pricing method. It selects the final price.
3. Companies do not usually set a single price, but rather a pricing structure that reflects variations in geographical demand and costs, market-segment requirements, purchase timing, order levels, and other factors. Several price-adaptation strategies are available: (1) geographical pricing; (2) price discounts and allowances; (3) promotional pricing; and (4) discriminatory pricing.
4. After developing pricing strategies, firms often face situations in which they need to change prices. A price decrease might be brought about by excess plant capacity, declining market share, a desire to dominate the market through lower costs, or economic recession. A price increase might be brought about by cost inflation or overdemand. Companies must carefully manage customer perceptions in raising prices.
5. Companies must anticipate competitor price changes and prepare contingent responses. A number of responses are possible in terms of maintaining or changing price or quality.
6. The firm facing a competitor's price change must try to understand the competitor's intent and the likely duration of the change. Strategy often depends on whether a firm is producing homogeneous or non-homogeneous products. Market leaders attacked by lower-priced competitors can choose to maintain price, raise the perceived quality of their product, reduce price, increase price and improve quality, or launch a low-priced fighter line.

Application

Marketing Debate—Is the Right Price A Fair Price?

Prices are often set to satisfy demand or to reflect the premium that consumers are willing to pay for a product or service. Some critics shudder, however, at the thought of $2 bottles of water, $150 running shoes, and $500 concert tickets.

Take a position: *Prices should reflect the value that consumers are willing to pay* versus *Prices should primarily just reflect the cost involved in making a product or service.*

Marketing Discussion

Think of the various pricing methods—markup pricing, target-return pricing, perceived value-pricing, value pricing, going-rate pricing, and auction-type pricing. As a consumer, which method do you personally prefer to deal with. Why? If the average price were to stay the same, which would you prefer: (1) for firms to set one price and not deviate or (2) to employ slightly higher prices most of the year, but slightly lower discounted prices or specials for certain occasions.

Delivering Value

Pacific Andes coordinates a value network of fish suppliers and distributors for the China market.

Designing and Managing Marketing Channels and Value Networks

15

Successful value creation needs successful value delivery. Holistic marketers are increasingly taking a value network view of their businesses. Instead of limiting their focus to their immediate suppliers, distributors, and customers, they are examining the whole supply chain that links raw materials, components, and manufactured goods and show how they move toward the final consumers. Companies are looking at their suppliers' suppliers upstream and at their distributors' customers downstream. They are looking at customer segments and considering a wide range of different possible means to sell, distribute, and service their offerings.

Pacific Andes, a Hong Kong-based company, runs one of the world's largest frozen-fish businesses. This company was initially engaged in shrimp trading. However, when its farm in mainland China failed to deliver, the company had to source from different suppliers. This also prompted management to transform the business by selling into China, and by leveraging China's lower labor costs in reprocessing products for export. The product identified was the Alaskan pollock, a fish abundant in Russian waters and used for pet food. However, when McDonald's decided on using pollock for its products, the market took off and, inevitably, competition increased. To stay ahead, Pacific Andes employed a bartering strategy, underwriting Russian shipyard construction and repair work. With the Russian economy shaky, boat owners agreed, and cheap fish flowed. Pacific Andes then struck more pay dirt when it decided to meet the Russian boats at sea with its own vessels. This reduced waste, and transportation and logistics costs; and harvested fish faster for processing than its competitors. However, the Asian economic crisis forced the company to close down 35 distribution centers in China, sell off much of its Pacific fleet, and tell suppliers that the practice of advanced payments was discontinued. It was then that Pacific Andes developed a "just-in-time" scheme, where customers were given 12- or 24-month contracts for the exclusive supply of fish on a weekly basis, and according to their needs. This meant that customers could reduce their inventory and storage costs. Business began growing again, and the company invested in building new factories in China. It also acquired a controlling stake in China Fisheries, a mainland company with a large fleet of deep sea fishing vessels, to be less dependent on external supply sources.[1]

In this chapter, we will address the following questions:

1. What is a marketing channel system and value network?
2. What work do marketing channels perform?
3. How should channels be designed?
4. What decisions do companies face in managing their channels?
5. How should companies integrate channels and manage channel conflict?
6. What are the key issues with e-commerce?

Companies today must build and manage a continuously evolving value network. In this chapter, we consider strategic and tactical issues with marketing channels and value networks. We will examine marketing channel issues from the perspective of retailers, wholesalers, and physical distribution agencies in the next chapter.

Marketing Channels and Value Networks

Most producers do not sell their goods directly to the final users; between them stands a set of intermediaries performing a variety of functions. These intermediaries constitute a marketing channel (also called a trade channel or distribution channel). Formally, **marketing channels** are sets of interdependent organizations involved in the process of making a product or service available for use or consumption. They are the set of pathways a product or service follows after production, culminating in purchase and use by the final end-user.[2]

Some intermediaries—such as wholesalers and retailers—buy, take title to, and resell the merchandise; they are called *merchants.* Others—brokers, manufacturers' representatives, sales agents—search for customers and may negotiate on the producer's behalf but do not take title to the goods; they are called *agents.* Still others—transportation companies, independent warehouses, banks, advertising agencies—assist in the distribution process but neither take title to goods nor negotiate purchases or sales; they are called *facilitators.*

To learn how the use of marketing channels have helped rejuvenate the indigenous U.S. toy manufacturing industry, visit wps.prenhall.com/bp_kotler_mm_13/.

The Importance of Channels

A **marketing channel system** is the particular set of marketing channels employed by a firm. Decisions about the marketing channel system are among the most critical facing management. In the U.S., channel members collectively earn margins that account for 30–50 percent of the ultimate selling price. In contrast, advertising typically accounts for less than 5–7 percent of the final price.[3] Marketing channels also represent a substantial opportunity cost. Converting potential buyers into profitable orders is one of the chief roles of marketing channels. Marketing channels must not just *serve* markets, they must also *make* markets.[4]

The channels chosen affect all other marketing decisions. The company's pricing depends on whether it uses mass merchandisers or high-quality boutiques. The firm's sales force and advertising decisions depend on how much training and motivation dealers need. In addition, channel decisions involve relatively long-term commitments to other firms as well as a set of policies and procedures. When an auto-maker signs up independent dealers to sell its automobiles, the auto-maker cannot buy them out the next day and replace them with company-owned outlets.[5]

In managing its intermediaries, the firm must decide how much effort to devote to push versus pull marketing. A **push strategy** involves the manufacturer using its sales force and trade promotion money to induce intermediaries to carry, promote, and sell the product to end-users. Push strategy is appropriate where there is low brand loyalty in a category, brand choice is made in the store, the product is an impulse item, and product benefits are well understood. A **pull strategy** involves the manufacturer using advertising and promotion to induce consumers to ask intermediaries for the product, thus inducing the intermediaries to order it. Pull strategy is appropriate when there is high brand loyalty and high involvement in the category, when people perceive differences between brands, and when people choose the brand before they go to the store. Top marketing companies such as Nike, Sony, and Coca-Cola skillfully employ both push and pull strategies.

Channel Development

A new firm typically starts as a local operation selling in a limited market, using existing intermediaries. The number of such intermediaries is apt to be limited: a few manufacturers' sales agents, a few wholesalers, several established retailers, a few trucking companies, and a few warehouses. Deciding on the best channels might not be a problem. The problem might be to convince the available intermediaries to handle the firm's line.

If the firm is successful, it might branch into new markets and use different channels in different markets. In smaller markets, the firm might sell directly to retailers; in larger markets, it might sell through distributors. In rural areas, it might work with general-goods merchants; in urban areas, with limited-line merchants. In one part of the country, it might grant exclusive franchises; in another, it might sell through all outlets willing to handle the merchandise. In one country, it might use international sales agents; in another, it might partner with a local firm.[6] In short, the channel system evolves in response to local opportunities and conditions. Consider some of the challenges Dell has encountered in recent years.

Dell—Dell revolutionized the personal computer category by selling products directly to customers via the telephone and later the Internet, rather than through retailers or resellers. Customers could custom design the exact PC they wanted, and rigorous cost cutting allowed for low everyday prices. Sound like a winning formula? It was for almost two decades. But 2006 saw the company encounter a number of problems that led to a steep stock price decline. First, re-invigorated competitors such as Hewlett-Packard narrowed the gap in productivity and price. Always focused more on the business market, Dell struggled to sell effectively to the consumer market. A shift in consumer preferences to buy in retail stores as opposed to buying direct did not help, but self-inflicted damage from an ultra-efficient supply chain model that squeezed costs—and quality—out of customer service was perhaps the most painful. Managers evaluated call center employees primarily on how long they stayed on each call—a recipe for disaster as scores of customers felt their problems were ignored or not properly handled. A lack of R&D spending that hindered new-product development and led to a lack of differentiation did not help either. Clearly, Dell was entering a new chapter in its history that would require a fundamental rethinking of its channel strategy and its marketing approach as a whole.[7]

Hybrid Channels

Today's successful companies are also multiplying the number of "go-to-market" or **hybrid channels** in any one market area:

- Following its acquisition of IBM's PC division, Lenovo Australia will retain IBM's brand name and existing channel for its corporate customers. The channel is a three-tier model involving selling directly to large accounts and large resellers, and through three distributors for smaller accounts. It will develop the Lenovo brand for its consumer business, and is deciding on whether to sell direct to retailers or go through distributors.[8]
- Hewlett-Packard revamped its Asian channel strategy to allow customers to request products shipped directly from its factory. HP now offers configure-to-order products in Korea, Malaysia, Singapore, Taiwan, and Thailand. Customers still have to make such orders with the channels. HP thus leverages on its channels to reach its targeted customers, while reducing 50 percent of delivery time.[9]

- Singapore Airlines has travel agencies to sell its tickets, but customers can also buy directly from SIA over the phone (called electronic ticketing) or from its Web site.

Companies that manage hybrid channels must make sure these channels work well together and match each target customer's preferred ways of doing business. Customers expect *channel integration*, characterized by the following features:

- The ability to order a product online and pick it up at a convenient retail location.
- The ability to return an online-ordered product to a nearby store of the retailer.
- The right to receive discounts based on total online and offline purchases.

Understanding Customer Needs

Consumers may choose the channels they prefer based on a number of factors: the price, product assortment, and convenience of a channel option, as well as their own particular shopping goals (economic, social, or experiential).[10] As with products, segmentation exists, and marketers employing different types of channels must be aware that different consumers have different needs during the purchase process.

Nunes and Cespedes argue that in many markets, buyers fall into one of four categories.[11]

1. ***Habitual shoppers*** — Purchase from the same places in the same manner over time.
2. ***High value deal seekers*** — Know their needs and "channel surf" a great deal before buying at the lowest possible price.
3. ***Variety-loving shoppers*** — Gather information in many channels, take advantage of high-touch services and then buy in their favorite channel, regardless of price.
4. ***High-involvement shoppers*** — Gather information in all channels, make their purchase in a low-cost channel, but take advantage of customer support from a high-touch channel.

The same consumer may choose to use different channels for different functions in making a purchase. A consumer may choose to browse through a catalog before visiting a store or take a test drive at a dealer before ordering a car online.

Consumers may seek different types of channels depending on the particular types of goods involved. Some consumers are willing to "trade up" to retailers offering higher-end goods such as TAG Heuer watches; these same consumers are also willing to "trade down" to discount retailers to buy private label paper towels.

Value Networks

A supply chain view of a firm sees markets as destination points and amounts to a linear view of the flow. However, the company should first think of the target market and then design the supply chain backward from that point. This view has been called **demand chain planning**. Schultz says: "A demand chain management approach does not just push things through the system. It emphasizes what solutions consumers are looking for, not what products we are trying to sell them." He suggested that the traditional marketing "four Ps" be replaced by a new acronym, SIVA, which stands for solutions, information, value, and access.[12]

An even broader view sees a company at the center of a **value network**—a system of partnerships and alliances that a firm creates to source, augment, and deliver its offerings. A value network includes a firm's suppliers and its suppliers' suppliers and its immediate customers and their end-customers. The value network includes valued relations with others such as university researchers and government approval agencies. A company needs to orchestrate these parties to enable it to deliver superior value to the target market.

Demand chain planning yields several insights. First, the company can estimate whether more money is made upstream or downstream, in case it might want to integrate backward or forward. Second, the company is more aware of disturbances anywhere in the supply chain that might cause costs, prices, or supplies to change suddenly. Third, companies can go online with their business partners to carry on faster and more accurate communications, transactions, and payments to reduce costs, speed up information, and increase accuracy. With the Internet, companies are forming more numerous and complex relationships with other firms.

PCH International—Outsourcing in China can be a risky proposition with unreliable business partners. Product quality, reliability, and ontime delivery vary widely. Shenzhen-based PCH International has been successful in managing supply chains for the electronics business. It allows customers to track products directly from the source, providing names, addresses, and photos of supplier plants on an exclusive intranet, and facilitating visits by end-users to source factories. The intranet lets customers track suppliers' inventories, capacity, and even raw materials so that they can better plan production schedules. Such transparency and information sharing has helped the supply chain to be as efficient as a vertically integrated relationship.[13]

Managing value networks has required companies to make increasing investments in Information Technology (IT) and software. They have invited such software firms as SAP and Oracle to design comprehensive *Enterprise Resource Planning* (ERP) systems to manage cash flow, manufacturing, human resources, purchasing, and other major functions within a unified framework. They hope to break up department silos and carry out core business processes more seamlessly. In most cases, however, companies are still a long way from truly comprehensive ERP systems.

Marketers, for their part, have traditionally focused on the side of the value network that looks toward the customer. In the future, they will increasingly participate in and influence their companies' upstream activities and become network managers, not only product and customer managers.

The Role of Marketing Channels

Why would a producer delegate some of the selling job to intermediaries? Delegation means relinquishing some control over how and to whom the products are sold. Producers do gain several advantages by using intermediaries:

- **They may lack the financial resources to carry out direct marketing.** For example, Toyota has 308 car dealers selling its cars in 5,800 outlets in Japan alone. Even Toyota would be hard-pressed to raise the cash to buy out its dealers.
- **They can often earn a greater return by increasing investment in their main business.** If a company earns a 20 percent rate of return on manufacturing and a 10 percent return on retailing, it does not make sense to do its own retailing.
- **In some cases direct marketing simply is not feasible.** Wrigley's would not find it practical to establish small retail gum shops throughout the world or to sell gum by mail order. It would have to sell gum along with many other small products and would end up in the drugstore and grocery store business. Wrigley's finds it easier to work through the extensive network of privately-owned distribution organizations.

Intermediaries normally achieve superior efficiency in making goods widely available and accessible to target markets. Through their contacts, experience, specialization, and

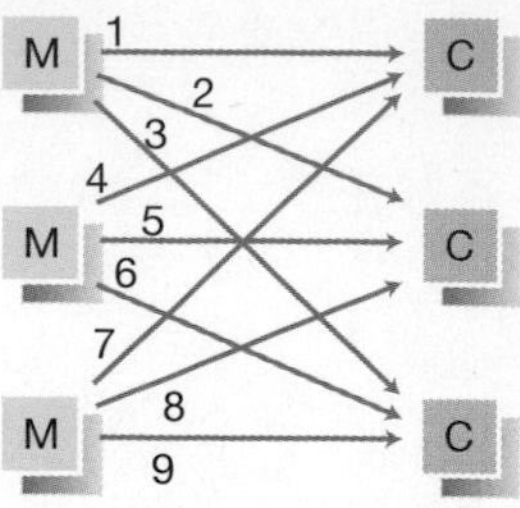

(a) Number of Contacts
M x C = 3 x 3 = 9

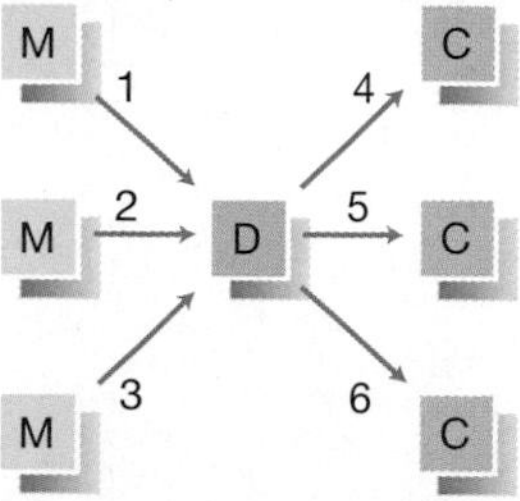

(b) Number of Contacts
M + C = 3 + 3 = 6

M = Manufacturer
C = Customer
D = Distributor

Figure 15.1 How a Distributor Increases Efficiency

scale of operation, intermediaries usually offer the firm more than it can achieve on its own. According to Stern and his colleagues:

> *Intermediaries smooth the flow of goods and services... This procedure is necessary in order to bridge the discrepancy between the assortment of goods and services generated by the producer and the assortment demanded by the consumer. The discrepancy results from the fact that manufacturers typically produce a large quantity of a limited variety of goods, whereas consumers usually desire only a limited quantity of a wide variety of goods.*[14]

Figure 15.1 shows one major source of cost savings using intermediaries. Part (a) shows three producers, each using direct marketing to reach three customers. This system requires nine different contacts. Part (b) shows the three producers working through one distributor, who contacts the three customers. This system requires only six contacts. In this way, intermediaries reduce the number of contacts and the work.

Channel Functions and Flows

A marketing channel performs the work of moving goods from producers to consumers. It overcomes the time, place, and possession gaps that separate goods and services from those who need or want them. Members of the marketing channel perform a number of key functions (see Table 15.1).

Table 15.1 Channel Member Functions

- Gather information about potential and current customers, competitors, and other actors and forces in the marketing environment.
- Develop and disseminate persuasive communications to stimulate purchasing.
- Reach agreements on price and other terms so that transfer of ownership or possession can be effected.
- Place orders with manufacturers.
- Acquire the funds to finance inventories at different levels in the marketing channel.
- Assume risks connected with carrying out channel work.
- Provide for the successive storage and movement of physical products.
- Provide for buyers' payment of their bills through banks and other financial institutions.
- Oversee actual transfer of ownership from one organization or person to another.

Some functions (physical, title, promotion) constitute a *forward flow* of activity from the company to the customer; other functions (ordering and payment) constitute a *backward flow* from customers to the company. Still others (information, negotiation, finance, and risk taking) occur in both directions. Five flows are illustrated in Figure 15.2 for the marketing of forklift trucks. If these flows were superimposed in one diagram, the tremendous complexity of even simple marketing channels would be apparent. A manufacturer selling a physical product and services might require three channels: a *sales channel*, a *delivery channel*, and a *service channel*.

The question is not *whether* various channel functions need to be performed—they must be—but rather, *who* is to perform them. All channel functions have three things in common: they use up scarce resources; they can often be performed better through specialization; and they can be shifted among channel members. When the manufacturer shifts some functions to intermediaries, the producer's costs and prices are lower, but the intermediary must add a charge to cover its work. If the intermediaries are more efficient than the manufacturer, prices to consumers should be lower. If consumers perform some functions themselves, they should enjoy even lower prices.

Marketing functions, then, are more basic than the institutions that perform them at any given time. Changes in channel institutions largely reflect the discovery of more efficient ways to combine or separate the economic functions that provide assortments of goods to target customers, as the following Asian examples show:

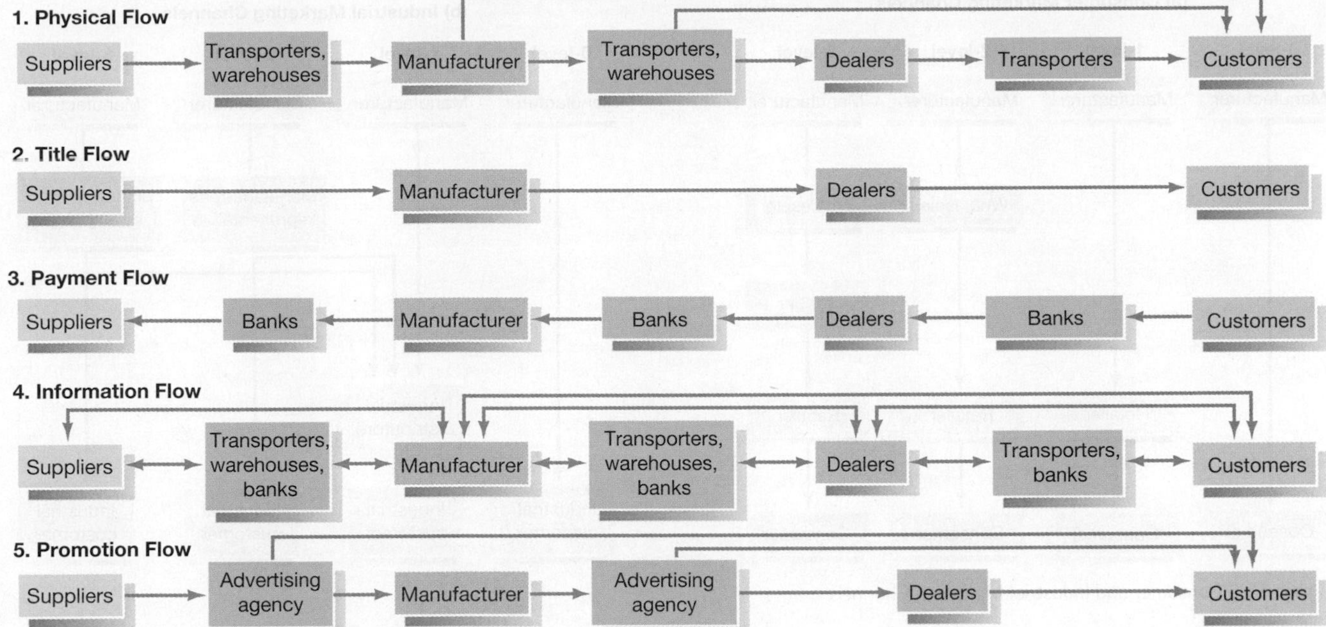

Figure 15.2 Five Marketing Tools for the Marketing Channel for Forklift Trucks

Kraft—To keep logistics costs down and improve efficiency, Kraft consolidated its distribution centers in China. After taking over Nabisco's China operations, it gradually reduced the number of such centers from 13 in 2001 to five in 2004. The main cost of a distribution center lies in inventory maintenance, especially in a market like China where market demand fluctuates and the inventory level must be kept down. With a more efficient and consolidated distribution network, Kraft managed to cut its operational costs in China by 5–10 percent.[15]

Nippon Lever—Nippon Lever uses three distribution channels—one each for detergents, consumer foods, and industrial foods. A difficulty it faces is the different wholesalers for each of their brands. At the wholesale level, there is much specialization and very little synergy. Despite the differing routes and intermediaries through which Nippon Lever deals, its consumer products are reassembled at the retail level, to be sold primarily in supermarkets. To service its distribution system, Nippon Lever has three separate sales forces—two consumer, and one industrial. Within the consumer foods sales force, there is some specialization on a number of client companies, but the firm takes advantage of opportunities in the distribution sector to eliminate specialization by its salespeople. In the retail area, there is some synergy because salespeople talk to any single retailer about most of Nippon Lever's products, something which cannot be said of its wholesale sales effort. The retail salespeople negotiate mainly with retail headquarters. In addition, Nippon Lever has a merchandising force that supports its sales effort to supermarkets.[16]

Channel Levels

The producer and the final customer are part of every channel. We will use the number of intermediary levels to designate the length of a channel. Figure 15.3(a) illustrates several consumer-goods marketing channels of different lengths.

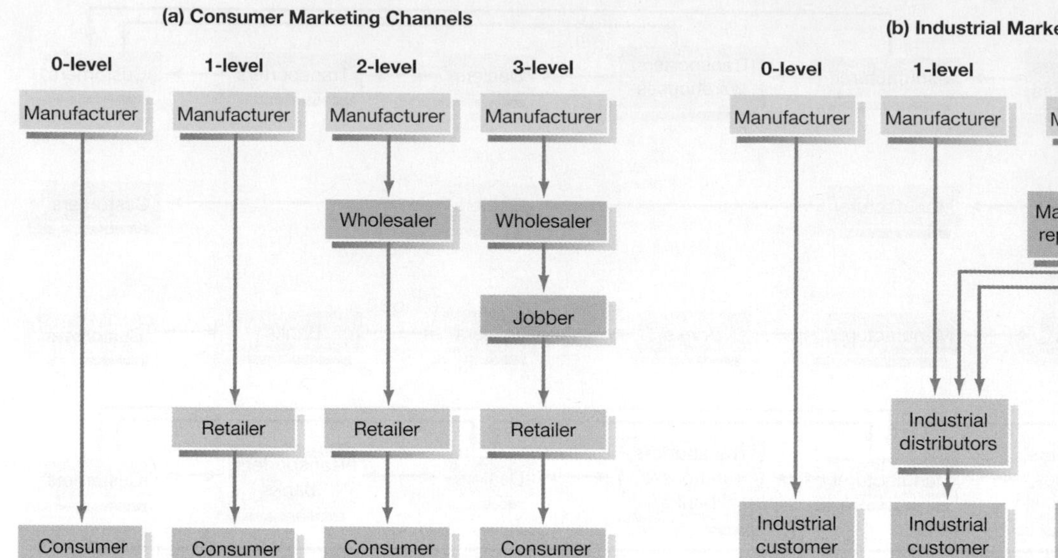

Figure 15.3 Consumer and Industrial Marketing Channels

A **zero-level channel** (also called a **direct-marketing channel**) consists of a manufacturer selling directly to the final customer. The major examples are door-to-door sales, home parties, mail order, telemarketing, TV selling, Internet selling, and manufacturer-owned stores. Avon sales representatives sell cosmetics door-to-door; and Tupperware representatives sell kitchen goods through home parties.

A *one-level channel* contains one selling intermediary, such as a retailer. A *two-level channel* contains two intermediaries. In consumer markets, these are typically a wholesaler and a retailer. A *three-level channel* contains three intermediaries. In the meatpacking industry, wholesalers sell to jobbers, who sell to small retailers. In Japan, food distribution may involve as many as six levels. From the producer's point of view, obtaining information about end-users and exercising control becomes more difficult as the number of channel levels increases. Moreover, physical distribution is slower and profit margins are lower with longer channels. Still, companies like Wrigley's persevere in China despite these challenges given the large commercial opportunity there:

Wrigley's—This U.S. chewing gum brand, manufactured in China, travels through a complex distribution structure. It includes trucks, ships, more trucks, and the small-scale distribution performed by single distributors on bicycles and carts. It takes months for the product to reach its final retail locations. Instead of being able to negotiate national-level contracts with broad-based retail chains, Wrigley's salespeople visit individual kiosk owners in cities like Shanghai to encourage the stocking and sales of its gum.[17]

Figure 15.3(b) shows channels commonly used in industrial marketing. An industrial-goods manufacturer can use its sales force to sell directly to industrial customers; or it can sell to industrial distributors, who sell to the industrial customers; or it can sell through manufacturer's representatives or its own sales branches directly to industrial customers, or indirectly to industrial customers through industrial distributors. Zero-, one-, and two-level marketing channels are quite common.

Channels normally describe a forward movement of products from source to user. One can also talk about *reverse-flow channels.* They are important in the following cases: (1) to reuse products or containers (such as refillable chemical-carrying drums); (2) to refurbish products (such as circuit boards or computers) for resale; (3) to recycle products (such as paper); and (4) to dispose of products and packaging (waste products). Several intermediaries play a role in reverse-flow channels, including manufacturers' redemption centers, community groups, traditional intermediaries such as soft-drink intermediaries, trash-collection specialists, recycling centers, trash-recycling brokers, and central-processing warehousing.[18]

Service Sector Channels

Marketing channels are not limited to the distribution of physical goods. Producers of services and ideas also face the problem of making their output available and accessible to target populations. Schools develop "educational-dissemination systems" and hospitals develop "health-delivery systems." These institutions must figure out agencies and locations for reaching a population spread out over an area.

As the Internet and other technologies advance, service industries such as airlines, hospitality, banking, insurance, stockbroking, and travel are operating through new channels. For example, cross-selling opportunities have motivated several mergers and acquisitions in the financial sector worldwide. Banks have bought stakes in insurance companies and stockbroking houses to exploit their distribution channels and maximize the merged companies' products worldwide.

Marketing channels also keep changing in "person" marketing. Besides live and programmed entertainment, entertainers, musicians, and other artists can reach prospective and existing fans online in many ways—via their own Web sites, social community sites such as MySpace, and third-party Web sites. Even legendary former Beatle Paul McCartney decided to end his 45-year relationship with music conglomerate EMI to launch his new album, *Memory Almost Full*, in June 2007 as the debut release from Hear Music, a record label cofounded by Starbucks, to be sold at the company's coffee shops, as well as record stores and on iTunes.[19] Politicians also must choose a mix of channels—mass media, rallies, coffee hours, spot TV ads, direct mail, billboards, faxes, email, blogs, podcasts, Web sites—for delivering their messages to voters.[20]

Channel-Design Decisions

Designing a marketing channel system involves analyzing customer needs, establishing channel objectives, identifying major channel alternatives, and evaluating major channel alternatives.

Analyzing Customers' Desired Service Output Levels

In designing the marketing channel, the marketer must understand the service output levels desired by target customers. Channels produce five service outputs:

1. ***Lot size*** — The number of units the channel permits a typical customer to purchase on one occasion. In buying cars for its fleet, Hertz prefers a channel from which it can buy a large lot size; a household wants a channel that permits buying a lot size of one.
2. ***Waiting and delivery time*** — The average time customers of that channel wait for receipt of the goods. Customers increasingly prefer faster delivery channels.
3. ***Spatial convenience*** — The degree to which the marketing channel makes it easy for customers to purchase the product.
4. ***Product variety*** — The assortment breadth provided by the marketing channel. Normally, customers prefer a greater assortment because more choices increase the chance of finding what they need.
5. ***Service backup*** — The add-on services (credit, delivery, installation, repairs) provided by the channel. The greater the service backup, the greater the work provided by the channel.[21]

The marketing-channel designer knows that providing greater service outputs means increased channel costs and higher prices for customers. Different customers have different service needs. The success of discount stores indicates that many consumers are willing to accept smaller service outputs if they can save money.

Establishing Objectives and Constraints

Channel objectives should be stated in terms of targeted service output levels. Under competitive conditions, channel institutions should arrange their functional tasks to minimize total channel costs and still provide desired levels of service outputs.[22] Usually, planners can identify several market segments that want different service levels. Effective planning requires determining which market segments to serve and the best channels for each.

Channel objectives vary with product characteristics. Perishable products require more direct marketing. Bulky products, such as building materials, require channels that minimize the shipping distance and the amount of handling. Non-standard products, such as custom-built machinery and specialized business forms, are sold directly by company sales representatives. Products requiring installation or maintenance services, such as heating and cooling systems, are usually sold and maintained by the company or by franchised dealers. High-unit-value products such as generators and turbines are often sold through a company sales force rather than intermediaries.

Channel design must take into account the strengths and weaknesses of different types of intermediaries. For example, manufacturers' reps are able to contact customers at a low cost per customer because the total cost is shared by several clients, but the selling effort per customer is less intense than if company sales reps did the selling. Channel design is also influenced by competitors' channels.

Dell—To cut distribution costs, Dell set up its China Customer Center (CCC) in Xiamen and applied its direct model to China. Products are made-to-order within three to four days, and upgraded systems can be delivered within a week. Dell also has direct sales and technical support operations. It launched toll-free sales and technical-support telephone numbers to provide immediate local-language assistance to customers. The Xiamen operation employs about 500 people. Around 200 are "outside sales" staff, engaged in door-to-door visits, and looking after corporate customers. The remainder work at the CCC and includes engineers, production staff, and "inside sales" staff. The latter are engaged in taking online and telephone orders.[23]

Channel design must adapt to the larger environment. Four environmental issues bear consideration in Asia:

1. ***The underdevelopment of infrastructure in Asia's larger emerging markets*** — Many intermediaries in Asia's emerging markets are mom-and-pop operations with limited scope for expansion. It is costly to physically supply the goods, largely because these countries lack organized, centralized delivery and transportation networks. Indeed goods, particularly foodstuffs, are often not handled according to internationally accepted standards. Consequently, a distribution channel model based on developed-country experiences must be modified to work in Asia. Even so, it may be less profitable and optimal than desired:

Sara Lee—With its 27 provinces and scattered islands, Indonesia stretches 5,120 kilometers from east to west, and 2,000 kilometers from north to south. Despite the development of supermarkets, mini-markets, department stores, and modern shopping centers in major cities, traditional forms of retailing still dominate distribution in the country, perhaps because 70 percent of Indonesia's total population is rural. Such traditional forms as street hawkers and small roadside stalls make up the bulk of the value of goods transacted in Jakarta. The problems are compounded for Sara Lee's frozen food products targeted at higher-end consumers in Jakarta (the relatively small affluent customer base with refrigerators at home). Sara Lee's licensing arrangement with national distributors is a less-than-adequate alternative to building up its own transportation fleet and frozen-storage facilities, and few retail outlets possess freezers. Moreover, some outlets turn the freezers off overnight.[24]

An infrastructure-related problem is the scarcity of market research information to assist in formulating distribution strategies. For example, no exact figures are available for the total number of distribution outlets in Indonesia. Estimates range from 200,000–1.5 million, although 400,000 is the consensus figure. Retail spending statistics are difficult to compile with some exceptions (e.g., Taiwan's frozen food industry which has an active trade press). The reason may lie in the way people shop in many Asian countries. Much buying is done in informal and unregulated markets and bazaars. For example, it is estimated that two-thirds of Indonesians buy daily from *pasars* (roadside stalls selling produce and locally manufactured goods). This purchase pattern rules out tracking to the extent of the U.S. supermarket chains, where nation-wide sales can be calculated weekly. The only way to track a product is to ask as many local distributors as possible to report their sales. The reporting inaccuracies and lag time make fine-tuning a product's distribution to a given market a long process.[25]

2. ***Economic factors***— During the Asian economic crisis, some Western MNCs were either interested in buying their regional distributors, switching partners before their competitors, or bypassing their intermediaries. Buying distributors made financial sense as the crisis had made Asian distributors cheaper and more attractive to purchase. Bypassing intermediaries would enable MNCs to move their goods to market using shorter channels more quickly. Also, the economic turmoil increased the risks of leaving critical interaction with customers to a third party. In some cases, local distributors collapsed, while others, though they managed to survive, did not have the financial strength to maintain acceptable marketing or service standards. This compromised customer loyalty and brand image.[26]

BMW and DaimlerChrysler—In Thailand, BMW set up a subsidiary to handle distribution and manage its dealers as it found that its partners did not have sufficient funds or ability to maintain its high standards. It also provided marketing and financial support to its distributors elsewhere in the region. In Indonesia, BMW kept down the price of spare parts despite the effects of the plunging rupiah to show responsibility to its customers. Similarly, DaimlerChrysler found its Thai Mercedes-Benz dealers engaged in a price war that was triggered by the recession. Some dealers were also providing substandard customer service. Hence, it set up a new distribution and marketing operation under its own control.

3. ***Legal regulations and restrictions***— Government regulations and practices can result in distribution difficulties. This can be seen most notably in Japan.[27] Until 1992, the Japanese Large Scale Retail Store Law of 1974 prevented stores occupying more than 1,500 square meters of floor space from opening without filing a complicated set of paperwork and securing the permission of their neighbors. The application process could take as long as 10 years, and failure was common as incumbent retailers in the area were unlikely to welcome a larger competitor. This law has resulted in small-sized stores which has led to many inefficiencies and high costs in the overall retail structure. Other Japanese legal restrictions include a Ministry of Transportation prohibition on ticket sales outside a registered travel office which affects the travel and banking industries; and a Ministry of Finance rule that limits banking business to banking hours.

   However, the granting of liquor licenses was liberalized in 2000. In 1996, the system regulating rice sales was changed to permit greater participation, with registration procedures further simplified in 1999. Since 1999, general retail stores and convenience stores have been allowed to sell medical supplies that were previously limited to licensed pharmacies. The use of self-service pumps by gas stations was permitted in 1998. These deregulatory measures enable greater flexibility in channel choice in Japan.

4. ***Consumer lifestyle and population density***— Hong Kong is an island with an area of 1,034 square kilometers and a fairly affluent population of over six million. However, given its very high population density (almost 6,000 people per square kilometer), few residents own cars. Most use the city's excellent public transportation system. Thus Wal-Mart's warehouse-style hypermarket, called Value Club, was a failure there. Hongkongers could not easily travel to and from the store on the subway carrying large packages of dry goods and paper products even though these were offered at low unit prices. Nor could they store these quantities in their small apartments. Their lifestyle

was more suited to daily grocery shopping in a neighborhood store that facilitated the stocking of small quantities of household groceries for the family.[28]

Given the dynamic nature of the Asian environment, manufacturers should be keenly aware of changes that may impact their distribution strategy. Perhaps the most important change anticipated is the simplification of the distribution system. In addition, Asian nations like China and South Korea have revised tax laws and selectively liberalized their distribution industry to allow foreign participation. The entry of foreign retailers should upgrade the standards of, and increase competition in, the distribution industry in these countries. The increased purchasing power of larger retail chains and manufacturers' developing of their own distribution systems to tap the growing Asian market are expected to diminish the role of the wholesaler in the region. As distributors begin to handle fewer product lines, specialization will be more common, thus reducing the potential for channel conflict. Physical distribution should be improved as investments in infrastructure begin to pay off.

Identifying Major Channel Alternatives

Companies can choose from a wide variety of channels for reaching customers—from sales forces to agents, distributors, dealers, direct mail, telemarketing, and the Internet. Each channel has unique strengths as well as weaknesses. Sales forces can handle complex products and transactions, but they are expensive. The Internet is much less expensive, but it cannot handle complex products. Distributors can create sales, but the company loses direct contact with customers.

The problem is further complicated by the fact that most companies now use a mix of channels. Each channel hopefully reaches a different segment of buyers and delivers the right products to each at the least cost. When this does not happen, there is usually channel conflict and excessive cost.

A channel alternative is described by three elements: the types of available business intermediaries, the number of intermediaries needed, and the terms and responsibilities of each channel member.

TYPES OF INTERMEDIARIES

A firm needs to identify the types of intermediaries available to carry on its channel work.

For example, a test-equipment manufacturer developed an audio device for detecting poor mechanical connections in machines with moving parts. Company executives felt this product would sell in all industries where electric, combustion, or steam engines were used, such as aviation, automobiles, railroads, food canning, construction, and oil. The sales force was small. The problem was how to reach these diverse industries effectively. The following alternatives were identified:

- **Expand the company's direct sales force**. Assign sales representatives to contact all prospects in an area, or develop separate sales forces for the different industries.
- **Hire manufacturers' agents** in different regions or end-user industries to sell the new equipment.
- **Find distributors** in the different regions or end-user industries that will buy and carry the device. Give them exclusive distribution, adequate margins, product training, and promotional support.

Table 15.2 lists channel alternatives identified by a consumer electronics company that produces cellular car phones.

Companies should search for innovative marketing channels. For example, to achieve wider distribution, Asian banks may follow Bank One in the U.S. by using Avon sales representatives to market their credit cards.[29]

Sometimes a company chooses an unconventional channel because of the difficulty or cost of working with the dominant channel. The advantage is that the company will encounter less competition during the initial move into this channel. Avon chose door-to-door selling because it was not able to break into regular department stores. The company made more money than most firms selling through department stores. Unconventional channels are also used to stay ahead of intense competition.

Table 15.2 Channels Alternatives for a Cellular Car Phone Maker

- The company could sell its car phones to automobile manufacturers to be installed as original equipment.
- The company could sell its car phones to auto dealers.
- The company could sell its car phones to retail automotive-equipment dealers through a direct sales force or through distributors.
- The company could sell its car phones to car phone specialist dealers through a direct sales force or dealers.
- The company could sell its car phones through mail-order catalogs.
- The company could sell its car phones through mass merchandisers such as Carrefour and Giant.

AirAsia—With increased competition and rising costs, Malaysian budget airline AirAsia is the first airline in the world to offer a full booking system via mobile phone. Customers anywhere in the world can use their mobile phones to access AirAsia's Web pages directly and make flight bookings at any time. It hopes to win more customers who have mobile phones but may not have easy access to the Internet. This unconventional channel also reduces AirAsia's operating costs by cutting out travel agents and sales offices.[30]

Perhaps the most unique type of intermediary in Asia is the trading house. Asian nations have a higher dependency on export trade for their survival. Thus there tends to be more dynamic trading activity and far greater experience in foreign trade among Far Eastern economies than Western nations. The channel modes developed in the West are not always adequate in capturing the complex interactions in the import-export trade of Far Eastern countries. These trading houses, called horizontal *keiretsu* in Japan and *hong* in Hong Kong, function basically as matchmakers between potential buyers and sellers. Examples of trading houses are Japan's Mitsubishi Corporation and Hong Kong's Jardine Strategic.

Trading houses provide both parties with negotiating opportunities and participate in the negotiations as mediators, sometimes representing the exporter, and other times, the importer. The degree of assistance provided varies depending on exporter-importer characteristics. Less experienced importers are given more assistance than more experienced ones by the importer-assisting section of the trading house. Similarly, less experienced exporters are given more assistance than more experienced ones by the exporter-assisting section of the trading house.[31]

NUMBER OF INTERMEDIARIES

Companies must decide on the number of intermediaries to use at each channel level. Three strategies are available: exclusive distribution, selective distribution, and intensive distribution.

Exclusive distribution means severely limiting the number of intermediaries. It is used when the producer wants to maintain control over the service level and outputs offered by the resellers. Often it involves *exclusive dealing* arrangements. By granting exclusive distribution, the producer hopes to obtain more dedicated and knowledgeable selling. It requires greater partnership between seller and reseller and is used in the distribution of new automobiles, some major appliances, and some women's apparel brands. When Italian designer label Gucci found its image severely tarnished by overexposure from licensing and discount stores, it ended contracts with third-party suppliers and opened its own stores.[32] Exclusive deals between suppliers and retailers are becoming a mainstay for specialists looking for an edge in a business world increasingly driven by price.[33] For example, at one time, Disney Consumer Products gave Wal-Mart a six-month exclusive on sales of toys and merchandise from its Kim Possible franchise.

Selective distribution involves the use of more than a few but less than all of the intermediaries who are willing to carry a particular product. It is used by established companies and by new companies seeking distributors. The company does not have to worry about too many outlets; it can gain adequate market coverage with more control and less cost than intensive distribution. Disney is a good example of selective distribution.

Disney—Disney sells its videos through five main channels: movie rental stores; the company's proprietary retail stores, called Disney Stores; retail stores like Takashimaya and Isetan; online retailers like Amazon.com and Disney's own online Disney Stores; the Disney catalog; and other catalog sellers. These varied channels afford Disney maximum market coverage, and enable the company to offer its videos at a number of price points.[34]

Intensive distribution consists of the manufacturer placing the goods or services in as many outlets as possible. This strategy is generally used for items such as tobacco products, soap, snack foods, and gum—products for which the consumer requires a great deal of location convenience. In China, popular outlets like wet markets, convenience stores, and supermarkets are situated within 10 minutes' walking distance from consumers' homes. In Indonesia, Unilever has built a network of nearly 20,000 distributors and two million retailers—including bicycle-powered ice cream carts and roadside stands that cover the far-flung corners of the island nation.

M-Link Asia—Thailand's M-Link Asia, a telecommunication equipment company, beefed up its retail distribution network to set up more M Shop outlets to focus on after-sale and value-added services. This is in response to a change in their business model, following operators' decisions to unlock their access codes. With handset margins shrinking, operators are focusing on selling their SIM cards which can be used with handsets purchased from any source. As a result, M-Link needed stronger distribution channels to increase handset sales.[35]

Manufacturers are constantly tempted to move from exclusive or selective distribution to more intensive distribution to increase coverage and sales. This strategy may help in the short term, but often hurts long-term performance. Intensive distribution increases product and service availability but may also result in retailers competing aggressively. If price wars ensue, retailer profitability may also decline, potentially dampening retailer interest in supporting the product and harming brand equity.

TERMS AND RESPONSIBILITIES OF CHANNEL MEMBERS

The producer must determine the rights and responsibilities of participating channel members. Each channel member must be treated respectfully and given the opportunity to be profitable.[36] The main elements in the "trade-relations mix" are price policies, conditions of sale, territorial rights, and specific services to be performed by each party.

- ***Price policy***— This calls for the producer to establish a price list and schedule of discounts and allowances that intermediaries see as equitable and sufficient.
- ***Conditions of sale***— They refer to payment terms and producer guarantees. Most producers grant cash discounts to distributors for early payment. Producers might also guarantee distributors against defective merchandise or price declines. A guarantee against price declines gives distributors an incentive to buy larger quantities.
- ***Distributors' territorial rights*** — They define the distributors' territories and the terms under which the producer will enfranchise other distributors. Distributors normally expect to receive full credit for all sales in their territory, whether or not they did the selling.
- ***Mutual services and responsibilities***— They must be carefully spelled out, especially in franchised and exclusive-agency channels. McDonald's provides franchisees with a building, promotional support, a record-keeping system, training, and general administrative and technical assistance. In turn, franchisees are expected to satisfy company standards regarding physical facilities, cooperate with new promotional programs, furnish requested information, and buy supplies from specified vendors.

Evaluating the Major Alternatives

Each channel alternative needs to be evaluated against economic, control, and adaptive criteria.

ECONOMIC CRITERIA

Each channel alternative will produce a different level of sales and costs. Figure 15.4 shows how six different sales channels stack up in terms of the value added per sale and the cost per transaction. For example, in selling industrial products costing between $2,000 and $5,000, the cost per transaction has been estimated as $500 (field sales), $200 (distributors), $50 (telesales), and $10 (Internet). Banks claim that in selling retail banking services, the cost per transaction is $2 (teller), $.50 (ATM), and $.10 (Internet). Clearly, sellers would try to replace high-cost channels with low-cost channels when the value added per sale was sufficient. The lower-cost channels tend to be low-touch channels. This is not important in ordering commodity items, but buyers who are shopping for more complex products may prefer high-touch channels such as salespeople.

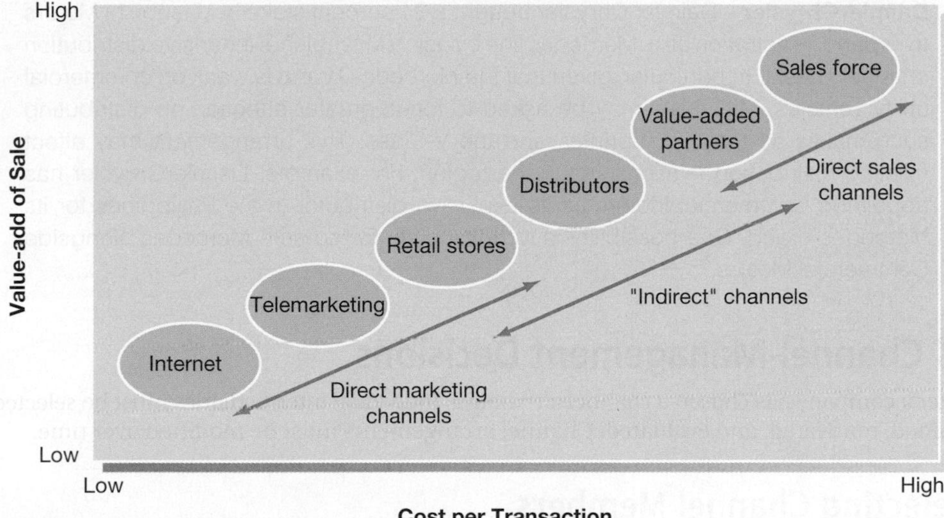

Figure 15.4 The Value Adds versus Costs of Different Channels
Source: Oxford Associates, adapted from Dr. Rowland T. Moriarty, Cubex Corp.

When sellers discover a convenient lower-cost channel, they try to get their customers to use it. The company may reward customers for switching. Many airlines initially gave bonus frequent flier mileage awards when customers booked reservations online. Other companies may raise the fees on customers using their higher-cost channels to get them to switch. Companies that are successful in switching their customers to lower-cost channels, assuming no loss of sales or deterioration in service quality, will gain a **channel advantage**.[37]

The first step is to determine whether a company sales force or a sales agency will produce more sales. Most marketing managers believe that a company sales force will sell more. They concentrate on the company's products; they are better trained to sell those products; they are more aggressive because their future depends on the company's success; and they are more successful because many customers prefer to deal directly with the company. However, the sales agency could conceivably sell more. First, the agency has 30 representatives, not just 10. This sales force might be just as aggressive as a direct sales force, depending on the commission level. Some customers prefer dealing with agents who represent several manufacturers rather than with salespersons from one company; and the agency has extensive contacts and marketplace knowledge, whereas a company sales force would need to build these from scratch.

The next step is to estimate the costs of selling different volumes through each channel. The cost schedules are shown in Figure 15.5. The fixed costs of engaging a sales agency are lower than those of establishing a company sales office, but costs rise faster through an agency because sales agents get a larger commission than company salespeople. The final step is comparing sales and costs. As Figure 15.5 shows, there is one sales level (S_B) at which

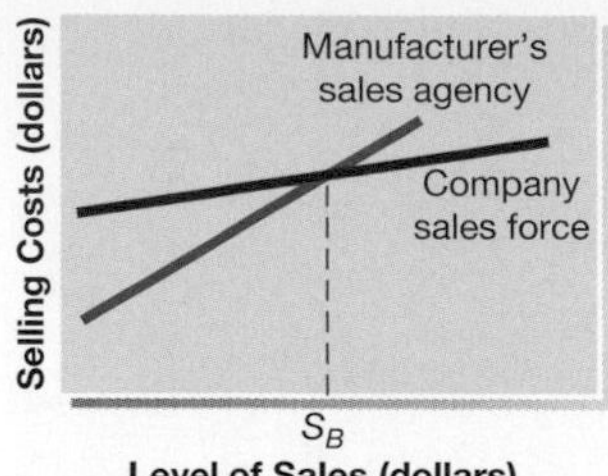

Figure 15.5 Break-even Cost Chart for the Choice Between a Company Sales Force and a Manufacturer's Sales Agency

selling costs are the same for the two channels. The sales agency is thus the better channel for any sales volume below S_B, and the company sales branch is better at any volume above S_B. Given this information, it is not surprising that sales agents tend to be used by smaller firms, or by large firms in smaller territories where the volume is low.

CONTROL AND ADAPTIVE CRITERIA

Using a sales agency poses a control problem. A sales agency is an independent firm seeking to maximize its profits. Agents may concentrate on the customers who buy the most, not necessarily those who buy the manufacturer's goods. Further, agents might not master the technical details of the company's product or handle its promotion materials effectively.

To develop a channel, members must make some degree of commitment to each other for a specified period of time. Yet these commitments invariably lead to a decrease in the producer's ability to respond to a changing marketplace. In rapidly changing, volatile, or uncertain product markets, the producer needs channel structures and policies that provide high adaptability.

DaimlerChrysler—Daimler Chrysler bought a 34 percent stake in Mitsubishi Motors to expand penetration of its Mercedes line by using Mitsubishi's extensive distribution channel in Asia. In particular, given that the Mercedes brand is weak on commercial utility vehicles, Mitsubishi may be asked to focus greater attention on distributing such makes as the Vito, Sprinter, and the V-Class. This arrangement may affect existing distribution relationships in the region. For example, DaimlerChrysler has appointed Commercial Motors as its exclusive distributor in the Philippines for its Mercedes brand. One possibility is for Mitsubishi to "co-sell" Mercedes alongside Commercial Motors.[38]

Channel-Management Decisions

After a company has chosen a channel alternative, individual intermediaries must be selected, trained, motivated, and evaluated. Channel arrangements must be modified over time.

Selecting Channel Members

Companies need to select their channel members carefully. To customers, the channels are the company. Consider the negative impression customers would get of McDonald's, Crystal Jade Restaurant, or Toyota if one or more of their outlets or dealers consistently appeared dirty, inefficient, or unpleasant.

Epson—Japan's Epson Corporation, a leading manufacturer of computer printers, decided to add computers to its product line. Unhappy with its current distributors and not trusting their ability to sell to new types of retail outlets, Epson quietly recruited new distributors. It appointed Hergenrather, a recruiting company, to search for applicants who: (1) have two-step distribution experience (factory to distributor to dealer); (2) are willing and able to set up their own distributorships; (3) will handle only Epson products but may stock other companies' software; (4) will hire a training manager and run a fully equipped service center. Successful applicants will each be offered a $80,000 yearly salary plus bonus and $375,000 to help them set up the business. They will also obtain equity in the business by investing $25,000. Hergenrather used the Yellow Pages to get the names of existing distributors and contacted their second-in-command managers. It arranged interviews and, after much work, produced a list of highly qualified individuals, from which it chose the 12 most qualified candidates. Epson's existing distributors were given a 90-day termination notice. Despite these measures, Epson never succeeded as a computer manufacturer.[39]

To facilitate channel member selection, producers should determine what characteristics distinguish the better intermediaries. They should evaluate the number of years in business, other lines carried, growth and profit record, financial strength, cooperativeness, and service reputation. If the intermediaries are sales agents, producers should evaluate the number and character of other lines carried and the size and quality of the sales force. If the intermediaries are department stores that want exclusive distribution, the producer should evaluate locations, future growth potential, and type of clientele.

Training and Motivating Channel Members

A company needs to view its intermediaries in the same way it views its end-users. It needs to determine intermediaries' needs and construct a channel positioning such that its channel offering is tailored to provide superior value to these intermediaries.

Stimulating channel members to top performance starts with understanding their needs and wants. The company should provide training programs, market research programs, and other capability-building programs to improve intermediaries' performance. The company must constantly communicate its view that the intermediaries are partners in a joint effort to satisfy end-users of the product.

> **Microsoft**—Microsoft recognizes its distributors in various Asian markets with an array of annual awards, taking out full-page color ads in local newspapers to announce and thank the prize winners. There are awards for Partner of the Year, Distributor (Finished Goods) of the Year, Distributor (Original Equipment Manufacturer) of the Year, Large Account Reseller of the Year, Small-Medium Enterprise Partner of the Year, Certified Partner Excellence, Marketing Excellence, Certified Technical Education Center of the Year, and Retail Center of the Year.

Producers vary greatly in skill in managing distributors. **Channel power** can be defined as the ability to alter channel members' behavior resulting in actions they would not have taken otherwise.[40] Manufacturers can draw on the following types of power to elicit cooperation:

- ***Coercive power*** — A manufacturer threatens to withdraw a resource or terminate a relationship if intermediaries fail to cooperate. This power can be effective, but its exercise produces resentment and can generate conflict and lead the intermediaries to organize countervailing power.
- ***Reward power***— The manufacturer offers intermediaries an extra benefit for performing specific acts or functions. Reward power typically produces better results than coercive power, but can be overrated. The intermediaries may come to expect a reward every time the manufacturer wants a certain behavior to occur.
- ***Legitimate power***— The manufacturer requests a behavior that is warranted under the contract. As long as the intermediaries view the manufacturer as a legitimate leader, legitimate power works.
- ***Expert power*** — The manufacturer has special knowledge that the intermediaries value. However, once the expertise is passed on to the intermediaries, this power weakens. The manufacturer must continue to develop new expertise so that the intermediaries will want to continue cooperating.
- ***Referent power*** — The manufacturer is so highly respected that intermediaries are proud to be associated with it. Companies such as McDonald's, Singapore Airlines, and Sony have high referent power.

Coercive and reward power are objectively observable; legitimate, expert, and referent power are more subjective and dependent on the ability and willingness of parties to recognize them.

Most producers see gaining intermediaries' cooperation as a huge challenge.[41] They often use positive motivators, such as higher margins, special deals, premiums, cooperative advertising allowances, display allowances, and sales contests. At times they will apply negative sanctions, such as threatening to reduce margins, slow down delivery, or terminate the relationship. The weakness of this approach is that the producer is using crude, stimulus-response thinking.

Samsung—Loyal mobile phone distributors are key to Samsung's success in China. Margins for its sales agents can be almost double of other brands' as Samsung's prices are higher. However, if distributors are caught unloading phones cheaply, they are cut off to prevent image dilution.[42]

More sophisticated companies try to forge a long-term partnership with distributors. The manufacturer clearly communicates what it wants from its distributors in the way of market coverage, inventory levels, marketing development, account solicitation, technical advice and services, and marketing information. The manufacturer seeks distributor agreement with these policies and may introduce a compensation plan for adhering to the policies. In Asia, Del Monte and Procter & Gamble are two companies with excellent distributor-relations planning.

Del Monte—Del Monte in the Philippines has a policy geared toward reaching smaller retail outlets. As part of the Cash Van project, distributors are encouraged to carry Del Monte brands to neighborhood stores and groceries through a series of incentives which includes a cost-free acquisition plan for the vans. Results saw the distribution percentage of Del Monte pineapple juice increasing from 43 to 78 percent, and its tomato sauce market share jumped from 13 to 89 percent in three years.

Procter & Gamble—In Japan, P&G established a National Accounts Division to foster closer relationships with its dealers. Its sales force provides retail coverage from corporate headquarters to the retail stores with direct linkage to the supplying wholesalers. It increased call frequency to the larger outlets, while working through its wholesalers to manage the balance of the retail trade. To rationalize its wholesale network, P&G selected a small number of about 50 core wholesalers to be given geographical priority, supplemented by an additional 100 specially selected firms to round out the geographical coverage and ensure that all major chains and trade types were covered. P&G works closely with its network of chosen wholesalers in a strategic alliance that competes on equal footing with the distribution systems utilized by its competitors in Japan.

Evaluating Channel Members

Producers must periodically evaluate intermediaries' performance against such standards as sales-quota attainment, average inventory levels, customer delivery time, treatment of damaged and lost goods, and cooperation in promotional and training programs. A producer will occasionally discover that it is paying too much to particular intermediaries for what they are actually doing. One manufacturer that was compensating a distributor for holding inventories found that the inventories were actually held in a public warehouse at its expense. Producers should set up functional discounts in which they pay specified amounts for the trade channel's performance of each agreed-upon service. Underperformers need to be counseled, retrained, motivated, or terminated.

Kraft—In China, Kraft used to team up only with the largest logistics company in each region. However, as Kraft was not one of its largest clients, it experienced delays of up to two days when there was a shortage of vehicles. This led Kraft to engage mid-sized logistics companies like P.G. Logistics who consider Kraft their most important client, thus according Kraft priority attention.[43]

Modifying Channel Design and Arrangements

A producer must periodically review and modify its channel arrangements. Modification becomes necessary when the distribution channel is not working as planned, consumer buying patterns change, the market expands, new competition arises, innovative distribution channels emerge, and the product moves into later stages in the product life cycle.

Gap—Gap was a former client of Hong Kong-based trading company Li & Fung, which provided sourcing services for it. Hansel Wong, vice president of Gap International Sourcing, recognizes that Li & Fung is "quite widespread in terms of sourcing channels" and also has the people to run it. Nevertheless, Gap ended its relationship with Li & Fung in the late 1980s and now handles its own sourcing. "When you expect to grow, you want to plant your seeds in rich soil, rather than leaving it to a third party," Wong explains.[44]

No marketing channel will remain effective over the whole product life cycle. Early buyers might be willing to pay for high value-added channels, but later buyers will switch to lower-cost channels. Small office copiers were first sold by manufacturers' direct sales forces, later through office equipment dealers, still later through mass merchandisers, and now by mail-order firms and Internet marketers.

In competitive markets with low entry barriers, the optimal channel structure will inevitably change over time. The change could involve adding or dropping individual channel members, adding or dropping particular market channels, or developing a totally new way to sell goods. Consider Apple.

Apple Stores—When Apple stores were launched in 2001, many critics questioned their prospects and *BusinessWeek* published an article titled, "Sorry Steve, Here's Why Apple Stores Won't Work." Fast-forward five years, and Apple was celebrating the launch of its spectacular new Manhattan showcase store. With over 175 locations and annual sales per square foot of $4,032—compared to Tiffany's $2,666, Best Buy's $930, and Saks' $362—Apple stores were an unqualified success. Opened because of the company's frustration with its poor retail presentation by others, the stores sell Apple products exclusively and target tech-savvy customers with in-store product presentations and workshops; a full line of Apple products, software, and accessories; and a "Genius Bar" staffed by Apple specialists who provide technical support often free of charge. Although the move upset existing retailers, Apple has worked hard to smooth relationships, in part justifying the decision to add its own stores as a natural evolution of its already existing online sales channel.[45]

To preserve its channel relationship, Apple has justified the opening of hundreds of its own retail stores as a natural extension of its online sales channel. The stores have proven extremely profitable too.

Adding or dropping individual channel members requires an incremental analysis. What would the firm's profits look like with and without this intermediary? An automobile manufacturer's decision to drop a dealer requires subtracting the dealer's sales and estimating the possible sales loss or gain to the manufacturer's other dealers. Sometimes a producer considers dropping all intermediaries whose sales are below a certain amount.

The most difficult decision involves revising the overall channel strategy.[46] Distribution channels clearly become outmoded, and a gap arises between the existing distribution system and the ideal system that would satisfy target customers' needs and desires (see "Marketing Memo: Designing a Customer-Driven Distribution System"). Examples abound: Avon's door-to-door system for selling cosmetics had to be modified as more women entered the workforce, and IBM's exclusive reliance on a field sales force was also modified with the introduction of low-priced personal computers.

MARKETING MEMO • DESIGNING A CUSTOMER-DRIVEN DISTRIBUTION SYSTEM

Stern and his colleagues have outlined an excellent framework, called Customer-Driven Distribution System Design, for moving a poorly functioning distribution system closer to a customer's ideal system. Companies have to reduce the gaps between the service outputs that target customers' desires, those the existing channel system delivers, and those management thinks are feasible within the existing constraints. Six steps are involved:

1. Research target customers' value perceptions, needs, and desires regarding channel service outputs.
2. Examine the performance of the company's and competitors' existing distribution systems in relation to customer desires.
3. Find service output gaps that need corrective action.
4. Identify major constraints that will limit possible corrective actions.
5. Design a "management-bounded" channel solution.
6. Implement the reconfigured distribution system.

Source: Anne T. Coughlan, Erin Anderson, Louis W. Stern, and Adel I. El-Ansary. *Marketing Channels*, 7th ed., (Upper Saddle River, NJ: Prentice Hall, 2005).

Channel Integration and Systems

Distribution channels do not stand still. New wholesaling and retailing institutions emerge, and new channel systems evolve. We will look at the recent growth of vertical, horizontal, and multichannel marketing systems; the next section examines how these systems cooperate, conflict, and compete.

Vertical Marketing Systems

One of the most significant recent channel developments is the rise of vertical marketing systems. A **conventional marketing channel** comprises an independent producer, wholesaler(s), and retailer(s). Each is a separate business seeking to maximize its own profits, even if this goal reduces profit for the system as a whole. No channel member has complete or substantial control over other members.

A **vertical marketing system (VMS)**, by contrast, comprises the producer, wholesaler(s), and retailer(s) acting as a unified system. One channel member, the *channel captain*, owns the others or franchises them or has so much power that they all cooperate. "Marketing Insight: The Importance of Channel Stewards" provides some perspective on how *channel stewards*, a closely related concept, should work.

LG—LG has outsmarted its foreign and local rivals in India, cornering 30 percent of the air-conditioner market, over 20 percent of the washing machine and color TV business, and beating rivals such as Whirlpool, Sony, and Samsung. It used its brand power to be a channel captain. It reversed the Indian tradition of giving 30- to 45-day credit on goods. If dealers failed to pay on time, they would lose LG's business. This gave dealers an incentive to promote LG products and it gave LG enough cash flow to demand discounts from suppliers.[47]

MARKETING INSIGHT • THE IMPORTANCE OF CHANNEL STEWARDS

Rangan believes that companies should adopt a new approach to going to market—channel stewardship. He defines **channel stewardship** as the ability of a given participant in a distribution channel—a steward—to create a go-to-market strategy that simultaneously addresses customers' best interests and drives profits for all channel partners. A channel steward might be the maker of the product or service (such as Procter & Gamble or Singapore Airlines); the maker of a key component (such as microchip maker Intel); the supplier or assembler (such as Dell); or the distributor or retailer (such as Wal-Mart). Within a company, Rangan notes the stewardship function might reside with the CEO, a top manager, or a team of senior managers.

The concept of channel stewardship is meant to appeal to any organization in the distribution channel that wants to bring a disciplined approach to channel strategy. An effective channel steward considers the channel from the customer's point of view. With that view in mind, the steward then advocates for change among all participants, transforming disparate entities into partners having a common purpose.

Channel stewardship has two important outcomes. One is to expand value for the steward's customers and increase the size of the market or existing customers' purchases through the channel in the process. A second outcome is to create a more tightly woven, and yet adaptable, channel where valuable members are suitably rewarded and the less valuable members are weeded out.

Rangan outlines three key disciplines of channel management:

1. **Mapping** is undertaken at an industry level to gain a sense of what the key determinants of channel strategy are and how they are evolving. It gives an idea of current best practices and gaps, and it projects what the future requirements might be.
2. **Building and editing** is an assessment of the producer's own channels with a view to identifying any deficits in meeting customers' needs and/or competitive best practices.
3. **Aligning and influencing** closes the gaps and works out a compensation package in tune with effort and performance for channel members that add or could add value.

Rangan maintains that the beauty of the channel stewardship discipline is that it works at the level of customer needs and not at the level of channel institutions. As a result, channel managers can evolve and change their fulfillment of customer needs without having to change channel structure all at once. An evolutionary approach to channel change, it requires constant monitoring, learning, and adaptation, but all in the best interests of customers, channel partners, and the channel steward.

Source: Adapted from V. Kasturi Rangan. *Transforming Your Go-to-Market Strategy: The Three Disciplines of Channel Management,* (Boston: Harvard Business School Press, 2006).

VMSs arose as a result of strong channel members' attempts to control channel behavior and eliminate the conflict that results when independent members pursue their own objectives. VMSs achieve economies through size, bargaining power, and elimination of duplicated services. There are three types of VMS: corporate, administered, and contractual.

CORPORATE VMS

A *corporate VMS* combines successive stages of production and distribution under single ownership. Toyota is a good example of backward corporate vertical integration as it holds equity stakes in key suppliers. In contrast, sales-distribution *keiretsu* involves forward vertical integration from the factory to retail outlets. Matsushita Electric Industrial Company owns local sales companies which in turn control some 25,000 *keiretsu* retail stores, mass-sales stores of consumer electronics, department stores, and chain stores. Such *keiretsu* is declining as retail stores increase sales costs and weaken product planning and development. Thus Japanese manufacturers are reducing the number of owned retail outlets to concentrate on the most productive stores, while improving relations with mass retailers.[48]

ADMINISTERED VMS

An *administered VMS* coordinates successive stages of production and distribution through the size and power of one of the members. Manufacturers of a dominant brand are able to secure strong trade cooperation and support from resellers. Thus Johnson & Johnson and L'Oréal are able to command high levels of cooperation from their resellers regarding displays, shelf space, promotions, and price policies.

The most advanced supply-distributor arrangement for administered VMS involves **distribution programming**, which can be defined as building a planned, professionally managed, vertical marketing system that meets the needs of both manufacturer and distributors. The manufacturer establishes a department within the company called *distributor-relations planning.* Its job is to identify distributor needs and build up merchandising programs to help each distributor operate as efficiently as possible. This department and the distributors jointly plan merchandising goals, inventory levels, space and visual merchandising plans, sales-training requirements, and advertising and promotion plans. The aim is to convert the distributors from thinking that they make their money primarily on the buying side (through tough negotiation with the manufacturer) to seeing that they make their money on the selling side (by being part of a sophisticated, vertical marketing system).

CONTRACTUAL VMS

A *contractual VMS* consists of independent firms at different levels of production and distribution integrating their programs on a contractual basis to obtain more economies or sales impact than they could achieve alone. Johnston and Lawrence call them "Value-Adding Partnerships" (VAPs).[49] Contractual VMSs now constitute one of the most significant developments in the economy. They are of three types:

1. ***Wholesaler-sponsored voluntary chains*** — Wholesalers organize voluntary chains of independent retailers to help them compete with large chain organizations. The wholesaler develops a program in which independent retailers standardize their selling practices and achieve buying economies that enable the group to compete effectively with chain organizations.
2. ***Retailer cooperatives*** — Retailers take the initiative and organize a new business entity to carry on wholesaling and possibly some production. Members concentrate their purchases through the retailer co-op and plan their advertising jointly. Profits are passed back to members in proportion to their purchases. Non-member retailers can also buy through the co-op but do not share in the profits. In Korea, major supermarket chains including Lucky, Kosco, and Life have a joint procurement system for buying agricultural products from farmers to lower their costs and place them in a better bargaining position relative to imports.
3. ***Franchise organizations*** — A channel member called a *franchisor* might link several successive stages in the production-distribution process. Franchising has been the fastest-growing retailing development in recent years. Although the basic idea is an old one, some forms of franchising are quite new.

   The traditional system is the *manufacturer-sponsored retailer franchise.* Toyota, for example, licenses dealers to sell its cars. The dealers are independent businesspeople who agree to meet specified conditions of sales and services. Another is the *manufacturer-sponsored wholesaler franchise.* Coca-Cola, for example, licenses bottlers (wholesalers) in various markets who buy its syrup concentrate and then carbonate, bottle, and sell it to retailers in local markets. A newer system is the *service-firm-sponsored retailer franchise.* A service firm organizes a whole system for bringing its service efficiently to consumers. Examples are found in the car rental business (Avis, Hertz) and fast-food-service business (McDonald's, Burger King).

THE NEW COMPETITION IN RETAILING

Many independent retailers that have not joined VMSs have developed specialty stores that serve special market segments. The result is a polarization in retailing between large vertical marketing organizations and independent specialty stores, which creates a problem for manufacturers. They are strongly tied to independent intermediaries, but must eventually realign themselves with the high-growth vertical marketing systems on less attractive terms. Further, vertical marketing systems constantly threaten to bypass large manufacturers and set up their own manufacturing. *The new competition in retailing is no longer between independent business units but between whole systems of centrally programmed networks (corporate, administered, and contractual) competing against one another to achieve the best cost economies and customer response.*

Horizontal Marketing Systems

Another channel development is the **horizontal marketing system**, in which two or more unrelated companies put together resources or programs to exploit an emerging marketing opportunity. Some supermarket chains have arrangements with local banks to offer in-store banking. Each company lacks the capital, know-how, production, or marketing resources to venture alone, or it is afraid of the risk. The companies might work with each other on a temporary or permanent basis or create a joint venture company. For instance, as demand for private flights increases, Skyjet International, a private-jet company, teamed up with Qatar Airways and Air China to offer private-jet connections primarily in Asia and the Middle East.[50]

In Japan, small companies benefit from horizontal marketing systems in the form of *yugoka. Yugoka* refers to the amalgamation of companies in different industries to obtain better business results through the pooling of various management resources. This is achieved through strategic alliances in the form of cooperatives, joint ventures, or mergers. The benefits derived from being part of a *yugoka* include exchange of information on market and technology, and participation in joint development of new products and services.[51]

Multichannel Marketing Systems

Once, many companies sold to a single market through a single channel. Today, with the proliferation of customer segments and channel possibilities, more companies have adopted multichannel marketing. **Multichannel marketing** occurs when a single firm uses two or more marketing channels to reach one or more customer segments. An **integrated marketing channel system** is one in which the strategies and tactics of selling through one channel reflect the strategies and tactics of selling through other channels.

Coca-Cola—Coca-Cola serves mainland consumers through various channels in different parts of China. The use of a Direct Store Delivery (DSD) system involving sales centers, a sales staff, and delivery trucks is increasing in China. However, it is unlikely to be the mainstay of Coca-Cola's distribution system in China due to difficulties in managing the operation, establishing financial control, tracking sales, and the cost in renting warehouses, buying trucks, and hiring staff. Thus Coca-Cola is establishing entrepreneurial distribution partners who sell its brands to retailers and small wholesalers for a small fee. These one-person enterprises know the demand conditions in local villages and can advise how Coca-Cola products can be distributed to them. There are also independent small and large wholesalers holding inventories of its brands, selling them directly to retailers or to another tier of wholesalers. Some are state-owned enterprises in various stages of restructuring. Distribution stakeholders also include many local retailers, restaurants, and other enterprises that can reach final consumers.[52]

Coke approached some Chinese neighborhood committees to sell its products. These committees are made up of pensioners who serve as socialist guardians. They have proven to be useful vehicles for building brand awareness.

"Marketing Memo: Multichannel Shopping Checklist" offers some concrete advice on channel integration of online and offline channels.

MARKETING MEMO • MULTICHANNEL SHOPPING CHECKLIST

An e-commerce consulting firm sent mystery shoppers to visit retail locations of 16 e-tailers in the U.S. to test their claims of an integrated shopping experience in the online/retail returns process. Overall, the study found that 44 percent of in-store returns of merchandise purchased online required a store manager to override the retail system in order to accept the return. In response to this and several other inadequacies revealed by the study, the e-tailing group created a "Best of Breed Multichannel Shopping Checklist" to help marketers better integrate online and offline channels:

- Train all store associates on processes for online merchandise returns.
- List your company's toll free number on the Web homepage, and be sure your customer-service hours of operation are easily accessible.
- Provide an information center that is easy to navigate and includes contact information, FAQs, guarantees, return policies, and tips for first-time customers.
- Implement a store locator feature that includes store locations, hours, and events.
- Make store pickup for purchases an option and include real-time inventory levels, where applicable.
- Post the store's weekly circular online for a more complete multichannel experience.
- Offer gift certificates that can be redeemed online and offline.
- Send e-mail notifications of the order, shipping, and return credit; include a reminder of the returns process in notifications as well as a link to your store locator.
- Supply all pertinent/compatible information for store return of merchandise on the packing slip or invoice.

Source: Excerpted from Hallie Mummert, "Multichannel Marketers Earn a 'C+' on Returns." *Target Marketing*, October 2003, p. 158.

By adding more channels, companies can gain three important benefits. The first is increased market coverage. The second is lower channel cost—selling by phone rather than personal visits to small customers. The third is more customized selling—adding a technical sales force to sell more complex equipment. The gains from adding new channels come at a price, however. New channels typically introduce conflict and control problems. Two or more channels may end up competing for the same customers. The new channels may be more independent and make cooperation more difficult.

Clearly, companies need to think through their channel architecture. They must determine which channels should perform which functions. Figure 15.6 shows a simple grid to help make channel architecture decisions. The grid consists of major marketing channels (as rows) and the major channel tasks that must be completed (as columns).[53]

The grid illustrates why using only one channel is not efficient. Consider using only a direct sales force. A salesperson would have to find leads, qualify them, presell, close the sale, provide service, and manage account growth. It's more efficient for the company to perform the earlier tasks, leaving the salesperson to invest his or her costly time primarily in closing the sale. The company's marketing department would run a preselling campaign informing prospects about the company's products through advertising, direct mail, and telemarketing; generate leads through telemarketing, direct mail, advertising, and trade shows; and qualify leads into hot, warm, and cool. The salesperson comes to the prospect when the prospect is ready to talk business. This multichannel architecture optimizes coverage, customization, and control while minimizing cost and conflict.

Companies should use different channels for selling to different size customers. A company can use its direct sales force to sell to large customers, telemarketing to sell to midsized customers, and distributors to sell to small customers; but these gains can be compromised by an increased level of conflict over who has account ownership. For example, territory-based sales representatives may want credit for all sales in their territories, regardless of the marketing channel used.

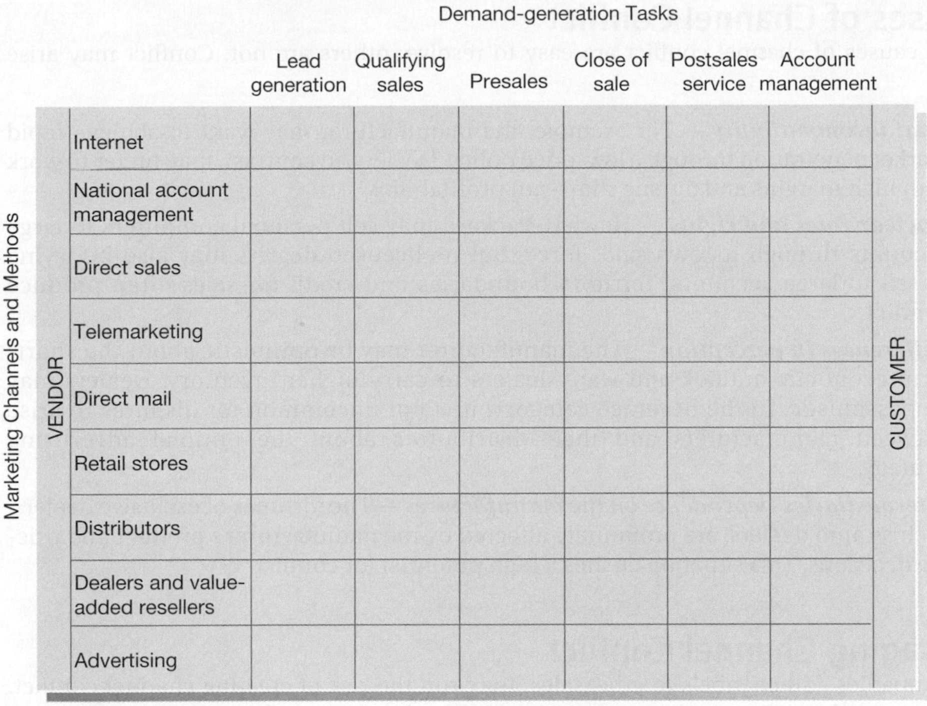

	Lead generation	Qualifying sales	Presales	Close of sale	Postsales service	Account management
Internet						
National account management						
Direct sales						
Telemarketing						
Direct mail						
Retail stores						
Distributors						
Dealers and value-added resellers						
Advertising						

Demand-generation Tasks; Marketing Channels and Methods; VENDOR; CUSTOMER

Figure 15.6 The Hybrid Grid

Source: Rowland T. Moriarty and Ursula Moran, "Marketing Hybrid Marketing Systems." *Harvard Business Review*, November–December 1990, p. 150.

Conflict, Cooperation, and Competition

No matter how well channels are designed and managed, there will be some conflict, if for no other reason than the interests of independent business entities do not always coincide. **Channel conflict** is generated when one channel member's actions prevent the channel from achieving its goal. **Channel coordination** occurs when channel members are brought together to advance the goals of the channel, as opposed to their own potentially incompatible goals.[54] Here we examine three questions: What types of conflict arise in channels? What causes channel conflict? What can be done to resolve conflict situations?

Types of Conflict and Competition

Suppose a manufacturer sets up a vertical channel consisting of wholesalers and retailers. The manufacturer hopes for channel cooperation that will produce greater profits for each channel member. Yet vertical, horizontal, and multichannel conflict can occur.

Vertical channel conflict means conflict between different levels within the same channel. For example, a company may come into conflict with its dealers when enforcing policies on service, advertising, and pricing. An example of the latter is Japanese discount retailers selling Shiseido products below the company's recommended price.

Horizontal channel conflict involves conflict between members at the same level within the channel. For instance, some Pizza Hut franchisees may complain about other Pizza Hut franchisees cheating on ingredients, providing poor service, and hurting the overall Pizza Hut image.

Multichannel conflict exists when the manufacturer has established two or more channels that sell to the same market. Multichannel conflict is likely to be especially intense when the members of one channel get a lower price (based on larger volume purchases) or work with a lower margin. A key question was whether the sales gains from the big retail chains would offset the loss from the dealer defections.[55]

Causes of Channel Conflict

Some causes of channel conflict are easy to resolve, others are not. Conflict may arise from:

- ***Goal incompatibility*** — For example, the manufacturer may want to achieve rapid market penetration through a low-price policy. Dealers, in contrast, may prefer to work with high margins and pursue short-run profitability.
- ***Unclear roles and rights*** — Hewlett-Packard may sell personal computers to large accounts through its own sales force, but its licensed dealers may also be trying to sell to large accounts. Territory boundaries and credit for sales often produce conflict.
- ***Differences in perception*** — The manufacturer may be optimistic about the short-term economic outlook and want dealers to carry higher inventory. Dealers may be pessimistic. In the beverage category, it is not uncommon for disputes to arise between manufacturers and their distributors about the optimal advertising strategy.
- ***Intermediaries' dependence on the manufacturer*** — The fortunes of exclusive dealers, such as auto dealers, are profoundly affected by the manufacturer's product and pricing decisions. This situation creates a high potential for conflict.

Managing Channel Conflict

As companies add channels to grow sales, they run the risk of creating channel conflict. Some channel conflict can be constructive and lead to better adaptation to a changing environment, but too much is dysfunctional. The challenge is not to eliminate conflict but to manage it better.

There are several mechanisms for effective conflict management.[56] One is the adoption of superordinate goals. Channel members come to an agreement on the fundamental goal they are jointly seeking, whether it is survival, market share, high quality, or customer satisfaction. They usually do this when the channel faces an outside threat, such as a more efficient competing channel, an adverse piece of legislation, or a shift in consumer desires.

A useful step is to exchange persons between two or more channel levels. Toyota executives work for a short time in some dealerships, and some dealership owners might work in Toyota's dealer policy department. Hopefully, the participants will grow to appreciate the other's point of view.

Co-optation is an effort by one organization to win the support of the leaders of another organization by including them in advisory councils, boards of directors, and the like. As long as the initiating organization treats the leaders seriously and listens to their opinions, co-optation can reduce conflict, but the initiating organization may have to compromise its policies and plans to win their support.

When conflict is chronic or acute, the parties may have to resort to diplomacy, mediation, or arbitration. *Diplomacy* takes place when each side sends a person or group to meet with its counterpart to resolve the conflict. *Mediation* means resorting to a neutral third party who is skilled in conciliating the two parties' interests. *Arbitration* occurs when the two parties agree to present their arguments to one or more arbitrators and accept the arbitration decision.

Dilution and Cannibalization

Marketers must also be careful not to dilute their brands through inappropriate channels. This is especially a concern with luxury brands whose images are often built on the basis of exclusivity and personalized service. The images of brands such as Calvin Klein and Tommy Hilfiger took a hit when they sold too many of their products in discount channels. Coach has worked hard to avoid diluting its image.

Coach—Handbag maker Coach's sustained double-digit growth through 2004–2005 was the result of some timely product introductions, but also a well-designed expansion in channels. As it turned out, the fastest-growing segment of Coach's business was factory outlets selling discontinued or older styles at 25 percent discounts. The company manages its channels carefully, however, and seeks to keep discount shoppers separate from more upscale and profitable clientele. Coach maintains full price in its 199 regular stores and does not discount. Merchandise that does not sell is not reduced in price but instead is sent to factory outlets located at least 96 kilometers away. As evidence of the firm's success in distinguishing the two channels, the average full-price shopper (a 35-year-old, college-educated, and single or newly married working woman) is very different from the average factory outlet shopper (a 45-year-old, college-educated married woman who buys 80 percent of her Coach purchases from outlets).[57]

Coach avoids brand dilution while enjoying multichannel distribution by keeping its full-price store shoppers separate from its discount shoppers, even locating its factory outlets a minimum of 96 kilometers from its retail store.

To help tap into affluent shoppers who work long hours and have little time to shop, high-end fashion brands such as Dior, Louis Vuitton, and Fendi have unveiled e-commerce sites. These luxury makers also see their Web sites as a way for customers to research items before walking into a store and a means to help combat fakes sold over the Internet. Given the lengths these brands go to pamper their customers in their stores—doormen, glasses of champagne, extravagant surroundings—they have had to work hard to provide a high-quality experience online.[58]

Legal and Ethical Issues in Channel Relations

For the most part, companies are legally free to develop whatever channel arrangements suit them. In fact, laws typically seek to prevent companies from using exclusionary tactics that might keep competitors from using a channel. Here we briefly consider the legality of certain practices, including tying agreements, dealers' rights, exclusive dealing, and exclusive territories.

Manufacturers of a strong brand sometimes sell it to dealers only if they will take some or all of the rest of the line. This practice is called full-line forcing. Such **tying agreements** are not necessarily illegal, but may violate laws in certain countries if they tend to lessen competition substantially.

Manufacturers are free to select their dealers, but their right to terminate dealers can be somewhat restricted in some countries. In general, sellers can drop dealers "for cause," but they cannot drop dealers if, for example, the dealers refuse to cooperate in a doubtful legal arrangement, such as exclusive dealing or tying agreements. Asian dealers are particularly perturbed at principals who terminate distribution agreements after the dealers have developed the market, and who then want to reap the benefits for themselves.

Many manufacturers like to develop exclusive channels for their products. A strategy in which the seller allows only certain outlets to carry its products is called **exclusive distribution**, and when the seller requires that these dealers not handle competitors' products, this is called **exclusive dealing**. Both parties benefit from exclusive arrangements: The seller obtains more loyal and dependable outlets, and the dealers obtain a steady source of supply of special products and stronger seller support. Exclusive arrangements are legal if they do not substantially lessen competition or tend to create a monopoly, and when both parties enter into the agreement voluntarily.

Exclusive dealing often includes exclusive territorial agreements. The producer may agree not to sell to other dealers in a given area, or the buyer may agree to sell only in its own territory. The first practice increases dealer enthusiasm and commitment. It is also perfectly legal—a seller has no legal obligation to sell through more outlets than it wishes. The second practice, whereby the producer tries to keep a dealer from selling outside its territory, has become a major issue in some countries.

Specifically, the issue relates to the practice of **gray marketing** or parallel importing. This involves the sale of authorized, branded products through unauthorized channels. While counterfeiting (or black marketing) is illegal, gray marketing is in many cases legal and occurs frequently in Asia.[59] The major suppliers of parallel imports include authorized intermediaries (often in other markets), professional arbitragers like trading houses, and manufacturers (either through their headquarters or foreign divisions).[60]

Four factors motivate the growth of gray marketing:[61]

1. **Differential pricing to different channel members may lead to a distributor over-ordering to obtain a discount and then selling off the excess to unauthorized channels.**
2. **Manufacturers may price differently to different geographic markets due to differences in tax, exchange rates, or price sensitivity.** This enables parallel importers to buy from the cheapest source worldwide and, in some cases like China, smuggle the goods to avoid duty. This provides a cost advantage to parallel importers over authorized dealers who must bear the cost of advertising and promotion.
3. **Products may be sold through high-service, high-price channels, providing an opportunity to introduce gray markets through discount retailers.** Japanese discount chain Jonan Denki takes employees on post-Christmas European shopping trips to legally purchase large quantities of luxury brands for sale in its stores.
4. **The development of emerging markets and worldwide trade liberalization create incentives for firms to capitalize on their brand equity and volume potential** by offering similar products across different countries. However, this leads to substantial price variation across nations due to differences in exchange rates, purchasing power, and supply-side factors (e.g., distribution and servicing).

Manufacturers may stop parallel importing by taking legal action where possible, checking their own order-processing procedures, keeping track of their products, and limiting differential pricing policies to reduce or prevent arbitrage opportunities.[62] They may also police their distributors, raise their prices to lower-cost intermediaries, or alter product or service features for different channels.

However, the costs and benefits of gray marketing should be considered before taking any action. Manufacturers tolerate gray marketing when (1) violations are difficult to detect or document; (2) the potential for one channel to free-ride on another member is low; (3) the product is mature; and (4) the parallel importer is a high-performing dealer loyal to the manufacturer rather than one which carries competing brands in the manufacturer's product category.[63]

Some manufacturers actually welcome gray markets as these increase their coverage in emerging markets, pressure authorized channels to compete harder, and avail the product to price-sensitive consumers. This occurs for hard liquor, cigarettes, and other fast-moving consumer goods in China, Indonesia, and Vietnam. While ethically questionable, the objective is to achieve a substantial market share and brand recognition with products sold relatively cheaply from the non-payment of customs duties. Such manufacturers can also simultaneously reap the benefit from the image of an imported brand with perceived superior quality.[64]

E-Commerce Marketing Practices

E-business describes the use of electronic means and platforms to conduct a company's business.[65] **E-commerce** means that the company or site offers to transact or facilitate the selling of products and services online. E-commerce has given rise in turn to e-purchasing and e-marketing. **E-purchasing** means companies decide to purchase goods, services, and information from various online suppliers. Smart e-purchasing has already saved companies millions of dollars. **E-marketing** describes company efforts to inform, communicate, promote, and sell its products and services over the Internet. The *e* term is also used in terms such as e-finance, e-learning, and e-service. But as someone observed, the *e* will eventually be dropped when most business practice is online.

We can distinguish between **pure-click** companies, those that have launched a Web site without any previous existence as a firm, and **brick-and-click** companies, existing companies that have added an online site for information and/or e-commerce.

Pure-Click Companies

There are several kinds of pure-click companies: search engines, Internet Service Providers (ISPs), commerce sites, transaction sites, content sites, and enabler sites. Commerce sites sell all types of products and services, notably books, music, toys, insurance, stocks, clothes, financial services, and so on. Among the most prominent commerce sites are Amazon and eBay.

The Internet is most useful for products and services when the shopper seeks greater ordering convenience (e.g., books and music) or lower cost (e.g., stock trading or news reading). It is also useful when buyers need information about product features and prices (e.g., automobiles or computers). The Internet is less useful for products that must be touched or examined in advance. But even this has exceptions. For example, many people order precious stones from Thai Web site, Thaigem.com.

Thaigem.com—Thaigem, a Thai online jewelry company, claims to be the vendor of 90 percent of gems sold online worldwide. Its Web site contains over 400 varieties of gemstones displayed in 800,000 images. The gems range from Sri Lankan amber-green actnolite to Cambodian blue-green zircon. The site also contains a comprehensive set of buyers' guides on a large variety of gemstones, which enable customers to buy by birthstone, and information on the numerous countries from which Thaigem obtains its gems. Thaigem has over 1.5 million hits monthly. The site is well known among consumers, hobbyists, geologists, and merchants surfing for a bargain. Thaigem also stands out for its clear English and painless navigation. As Professional Jeweler commented, Thaigem is "wonderfully organized, easy to use and full of great [jewelry] and gemstones at reasonable prices ... one of the nicest and most fun [jewelry] sites around." Thaigem has since launched a Japanese site, and has Chinese- and Japanese-speaking staff. It offers 24-hour customer service by email and phone. U.S. customers can call a toll-free number that is routed to Thailand. Customers can also chat with a representative online and instantly receive a transcript.[66]

"Breakthrough Marketing: Amazon.com" describes the quintessential online retailer.

Consumer surveys suggest that the most significant inhibitors of online shopping are the absence of pleasurable experiences, social interaction, and personal consultation with a company representative.[67] Firms are responding. Some companies use live online chat to give potential customers immediate advice about products for sale on their Web sites. Another benefit of providing live sales assistance is the ability to sell additional items. When a representative is involved in the sale, the average amount per order is typically higher. B2B marketers also need to put a human face on their e-commerce presence, and some are doing so by taking advantage of Web 2.0 technologies such as virtual environments, blogs, online videos, and click-to-chat.

Cisco Systems—Cisco is experimenting with a variety of Web 2.0 applications such as posting videos of its "human network" campaign on YouTube, holding analyst briefings in the virtual world of Second Life, and especially using click-to-chat. "The single biggest home run we've achieved in the last month is click-to-chat," said Michael Metz, Cisco's senior director of Web marketing and strategy. When users, who tend to be small-business customers, click on a button in the technical portion of Cisco's Web site, they are connected to a call center representative who helps them solve their problem. Then Cisco added a more sales-oriented click-to-chat feature. If a user comes back to a product page several times to look at a particular item, a chat box comes up saying, "Can we help you with product X?" So-called proactive chat enabled Cisco to improve its lead conversion rate by 50 percent in just the first three months.[68]

BREAKTHROUGH • MARKETING

AMAZON.COM

Founded by Jeff Bezos, Amazon.com started as the "world's largest bookstore" in 1995. A virtual bookstore that physically owned no books, Amazon.com promised to revolutionize retailing. Although some may debate whether that was accomplished, Bezos clearly blazed an e-commerce trail of innovations that many have studied and followed.

Amazon.com set out to create personalized storefronts for each customer by providing more useful information and more choices than could be found in your typical neighborhood bookstore. Readers can review books and evaluate them on a one- to five-star rating system, and browsers can rate which reviews are helpful and which are not. Amazon.com's personal recommendation service aggregates data on buying patterns to infer who might like which book. The site offers peeks into books' contents, index, and beginning pages with a "search inside the book" feature that lets customers search the entire text of 120,000 books—about as many titles as are in a Barnes & Noble bookstore. Amazon.com's one-click shopping lets buyers make purchases with one click.

Amazon.com also established itself as an electronic marketplace by enabling merchants of all kinds to sell items on Amazon.com. It powers and operates retail Web sites for the NBA and Marks & Spencer. Amazon.com derives about 40 percent of its sales from its million-plus affiliates called "Associates," independent sellers or businesses that receive commissions for referring to the Amazon.com site customers who then make a purchase.

To overcome the lag between purchase and delivery of product, Amazon.com has offered fast, inexpensive shipping. For a $79 annual fee, Amazon.com Prime offers unlimited free express shipping for most items. Amazon.com has also diversified its product lines into DVDs, music CDs, computer software, video games, electronics, apparel, furniture, food, toys, and more. It has established separate Web sites in Canada, the United Kingdom, Germany, Austria, France, China, and Japan and moved into the black in 2003. Revenue exceeded $14.84 billion in 2007.

One key to Amazon.com's success in all these different ventures was a willingness to invest in the latest Internet technology to make shopping online faster, easier, and more personally rewarding. The Amazon.com Web project, launched in 2002, opened up its databases to more than 65,000 programmers and businesses that, in turn, have built moneymaking Web sites, new online shopping interfaces, and innovative services for Amazon.com's 800,000 or so active sellers. One application was a service, ScoutPal, that turned cell phones into mobile bar-code scanners.

Amazon.com's next move? The firm is spending heavily on development to allow consumers to download video, music, and books. As Bezos wrote in his letter to shareholders in 1997, which he reprinted in Amazon.com's 2005 annual report, "It's all about the long term."

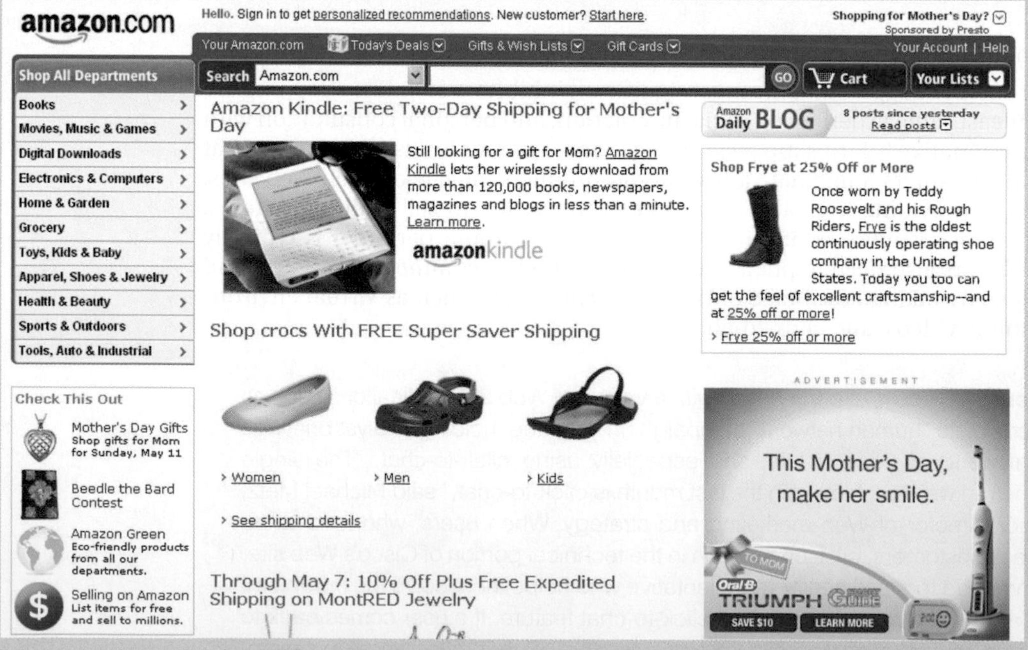

Amazon.com began as "the world's largest bookstore" and has gone on to become the quintessential online retailer, selling goods of all kinds and offering reviews, recommendations, and other customizing features on its Web site.

Sources: "Click to Download." *Economist*, August 19, 2006, pp. 57–58; Robert D. Hof, "Jeff Bezos' Risky Bet." *BusinessWeek*, November 13, 2006, Erick Schonfield, "The Great Giveaway." *Business 2.0*, April 2005, pp. 80–86; Elizabeth West, "Who's Next?" *Potentials*, February 2004, pp. 7–8; Robert D. Hof, "The Wizard of Web Retailing." *BusinessWeek*, December 20, 2004, pp. 18; Chris Taylor, "Smart Library." *Time*, November 17, 2003, p. 68; <biz.yahoo.com/bw/080130/20080130006013.html>, accessed on April 10, 2008.

To increase the entertainment and information value and the customer satisfaction from Web-based shopping experiences, some firms are employing *avatars,* graphical representations of virtual, animated characters that can act as company representatives. Avatars can provide a more interpersonal shopping experience by serving as identification figures, as personal shopping assistants, as Web site guides, or as conversation partners. Research has shown that avatars can enhance the effectiveness of a Web-based sales channel, especially if they are seen as expert or attractive.[69]

Ensuring security and privacy online remains important. Customers must find the Web site trustworthy, even if it represents an already highly credible offline firm such as Kodak. Investments in Web site design and processes can help reassure customers sensitive to online risk.[70] A study by A.C. Nielsen showed that customers tend to stick to what they know when it comes to online shopping.[71] Some 60 percent of online shoppers say they buy mostly from the same site, suggesting that online shoppers are uniquely loyal. One in four relied on personal recommendations. Online retailers are also trying new technologies, such as blogs, social networks, and mobile marketing, to attract new shoppers.

Although the popular press has given the most attention to Business-to-Consumer (B2C) Web sites, even more activity is being conducted on Business-to-Business (B2B) sites. These are changing the supplier–customer relationship in profound ways. Firms are using B2B auction sites, spot exchanges, online product catalogs, barter sites, and other online resources to obtain better prices.

The purpose of B2B sites is to make markets more efficient. In the past, buyers exerted a lot of effort to gather information on worldwide suppliers. With the Internet, buyers have easy access to a great deal of information. They can get information from: (1) supplier Web sites; (2) *infomediaries,* third parties that add value by aggregating information about alternatives; (3) *market makers,* third parties that create markets linking buyers and sellers; and (4) *customer communities,* Web sites where buyers can swap stories about suppliers' products and services.[72] The largest of the B2B market makers, Alibaba, is homegrown in China, a country where businesses have faced decades of Communist antipathy to private enterprise.

Alibaba is the largest online B2B marketplace. It is homegrown in China, a country where businesses have faced decades of Communist antipathy to private enterprise.

Alibaba—The brainchild of 42-year-old Jack Ma, Alibaba has become the world's largest online B2B marketplace, Asia's most popular online auction site, and now, with its acquisition of Yahoo! China, the 12th most popular Web site in the world. At its heart are two B2B Web sites, alibaba.com and china.alibaba.com. The former is a marketplace for companies around the globe to buy and sell in English, and the latter is a domestic Chinese marketplace. Whereas Alibaba's rivals, such as Commerce One, were founded with the goal of slashing procurement costs, the Chinese powerhouse has a more nationalist agenda: to build markets for China's vast number of small and medium-sized businesses. Alibaba enables them to both trade with each other and link to global supply chains. Of his focus on SMEs, Jack Ma says, "We are interested in catching shrimp, not the whales. When you catch the shrimp, then you will also catch the whales." European importers are particularly drawn to the "shrimp" in Alibaba's B2B net, in large part because Alibaba has set up a system by which businesses can easily establish trust. When membership in Alibaba's B2B exchange was free, members complained, "I don't trust this guy!" says Jack Ma, so he set up TrustPass, in which users pay Alibaba a fee to hire a third party that verifies them. Users must have five people vouch for them and provide a list of all their certificates/business licenses. Finally, anyone on Alibaba who has done business with a user is encouraged to comment on the firm, in the same way buyers comment on sellers in Amazon.com's or eBay's marketplace. This feature was not very common in the online B2B world, but Alibaba has made it a standard. Businesses are even starting to print "TrustPass" on their business cards, a true sign of Alibaba's B2B credibility.[73]

The net impact of these mechanisms is to make prices more transparent.[74] In the case of undifferentiated products, price pressure will increase. For highly differentiated products, buyers will gain a better picture of the items' true value. Suppliers of superior products will be able to offset price transparency with value transparency; suppliers of undifferentiated products will need to drive down their costs in order to compete.

Brick-and-Click Companies

Many brick-and-mortar companies have agonized over whether to add an online e-commerce channel. Many companies moved quickly to open Web sites describing their businesses but resisted adding e-commerce to their sites. These include Compaq and Barnes & Noble. They felt that selling their products or services online would produce channel conflict—they would be competing with their offline retailers, agents, or own stores.[75]

Adding an e-commerce channel creates the threat of a backlash from retailers, brokers, agents, and other intermediaries. The question is how to sell both through intermediaries and online. There are at least three strategies for trying to gain acceptance from intermediaries: (1) offer different brands or products on the Internet; (2) offer the offline partners higher commissions to cushion the negative impact on sales; and (3) take orders on the Web site but have retailers deliver and collect payment.

Harley-Davidson—Given that Harley sells more than $500 million worth of parts and accessories to its loyal followers, an online venture was an obvious next step to generate even more revenue. However, Harley needed to avoid the wrath of its dealers who benefited from the high margins on those sales. Harley's solution was to send customers seeking to buy accessories online to the company's Web site. Before they can buy anything, they are prompted to select a participating Harley-Davidson dealer. When the customer places the order, it is transmitted to the selected dealer for fulfillment, ensuring that the dealer still remains the focal point of the customer experience. Dealers, in turn, had to agree to a number of standards, such as checking for orders twice a day and shipping orders promptly. The Web site now gets over a million visitors a month.[76]

Ultimately, companies may need to decide whether to drop some or all of their retailers and go direct. Banks, however, have found that despite the convenience of online services, some customers still prefer to conduct certain transactions at the bank itself. Thus most new checking and savings accounts are still opened in physical bank branches.[77] "Marketing Insight: E-Tailing Lessons for the Asia Pacific" documents key lessons for success from businesses involved with retail e-commerce in the region.

M-Commerce

Consumers and businesspeople no longer need to be near a computer to send and receive information. All they need is a cell phone or Personal Digital Assistant (PDA). While they're on the move, they can connect to the Internet to check stock prices, the weather, and sports scores; send and receive email messages; and place online orders. A whole field called *telematics* places wireless Internet-connected computers in the dashboards of cars and trucks, and makes more home appliances (such as computers) wireless so they can be used anywhere in or near the home. Many see a big future in what is now called *m-commerce* (*m* for mobile).[78]

Consider the fast growth of Internet-connected phones. In Japan, millions of teenagers carry DoCoMo phones available from NTT (Nippon Telephone and Telegraph). They can also use their phones to order goods. Each month, the subscriber receives a bill from NTT listing the monthly subscriber fee, the usage fee, and the cost of all the transactions. The person can then pay the bill at the nearest Seven–Eleven store.

MARKETING INSIGHT • E-TAILING LESSONS FOR THE ASIA PACIFIC

The Boston Consulting Group conducted nearly 500 in-depth interviews of businesses involved in retail e-commerce in the Asia Pacific. Here are the 10 key lessons for regional success drawn from the project:

1. **Convert visitors to buyers.** As Asian customers are more attuned to interpersonal transactions, it is critical for regional Web sites to build trust and credibility. South Korea's Hansol CS leveraged its reputation as a leading mail-order business for online success. It implemented a real-time system that confirmed customer orders almost immediately, a delivery tracking system, and a promise of rapid delivery backed by customer compensation for late fulfillment.
2. **Learn from customers daily.** As e-business is rapidly evolving, quick response to the changing mix of customers, their behavior, and their choices is necessary. Online surveys and data mining techniques are useful to obtain insights into online consumer behavior. China's Stockstar.com is a successful finance portal with a large and loyal user base. Its online survey progressed from obtaining demographic information to preference data regarding the site's services. Focus groups were also employed to augment the findings.
3. **Build the brand and offer customer service.** Beyond getting the basics right, e-tailers should introduce functions that engage consumers, such as chat rooms and customer product reviews. South Korea's Kyobo Books has leveraged a strong offline brand to build a loyal online customer base by creating a strong reader community through hosting interactive chat rooms and promoting other book-related social events.
4. **Address offline compromises.** E-tailers should explore where traditional shopping experiences leave consumers dissatisfied and exploit them. General Motors in Taiwan started to sell cars online in 1999. Noticing that the offline auto buying experience fell short on convenience, GM enhanced its site's convenience by designing a virtual online test drive and offering door-to-door delivery of a test-drive vehicle.
5. **Form partnerships.** Creating everything internally is unlikely and undesirable for most e-tailers. Hence, content and service providers can form partnerships with promising Asian e-tailers, rendering their capabilities, industry experience, and fixed assets for mutual benefit. 7dream.com is a Japanese joint venture whose partners include Seven-Eleven, NEC, Nomura Research Institute (NRI), and Sony. NEC designs and operates the site and produces the multimedia terminals, NRI houses the servers and data center, Sony furnishes music data downloading for the Minidisc platform and other technologies, and Seven-Eleven provides its retail expertise and extensive store network.
6. **Create defensibility.** Successful e-tailing should avoid easily replicated "me-too" business models. Leading designer labels such as Dolce & Gabbana and Helmut Lang face the problem of how to sell their leftover merchandise. Opening up their own outlets can undermine sales at existing stores and dilute their brand image. Most end up selling to big discounters, losing control over how and where their products are sold. Thus Internet sites like Yoox allow luxury brands to offload last season's merchandise without diluting their brands or cannibalizing sales at existing stores. Setting up their own single-brand e-tailing sites may not be cost efficient as there would not be enough sales volume to enable them to offer the steep discounts that Yoox does.
7. **Target new communities.** New communities, free of geographic constraints, form rapidly on the Internet. They are defined by interest (e.g., golfers), experience (e.g., frequent travelers), and culture (e.g., overseas Chinese). Businesses can thus use the Web to reach groups previously closed to them, particularly in smaller Asian markets. A stamp collector in Tawau in East Malaysia realized that there were international collectors interested in North Borneo stamps when he offered them for sale on eBay. He has turned his hobby into a small Internet business.
8. **Secure early options.** Businesses must balance between seeking out potential growth areas and rushing into a market before it is ready. They should build flexibility in their business models which allow rapid movement into new categories or markets when the opportunity arises. The Spot is an umbrella brand for multiproduct specialist sites in Australia. By creating new Spot sites (e.g., ToySpot, BookSpot, CDSpot) the company can gain quick results in these categories before competitors emerge.
9. **Create a scaleable and flexible supply chain.** Strong supply chain capability powers successful e-businesses. Many systems are manual and paper-based in developing Asian countries, and are thus not scaleable to handle demand growth. Thus time and money must be spent to improve supply chains. Businesses should encourage their partners (e.g., courier services) to enhance their internal processes.
10. **Get talent.** Successful online operations require a wide range of capabilities. Beyond technical competence, skills are needed in management, business development, partnership formation, sales and marketing, fund raising, and corporate finance. All Asian markets are short of such expertise. Offering nontraditional compensation, a flexible working environment, and an entrepreneurial atmosphere help encourage creativity and retain employees.

Sources: David C. Michael, Greg Sutherland, and Scott R. Ohman, "E-Tailing in Asia Pacific." In Siew Meng Leong, Swee Hoon Ang, and Chin Tiong Tan, eds., *Marketing in the New Asia,* (Singapore: McGraw-Hill, 2001), pp. 327–339; Kerry Capell, "Who Cares If It's Not the Latest." *BusinessWeek Asian Edition*, December 30, 2002, p. 23.

The potential market opportunities for location-based services are enormous. Imagine some not-too-distant possibilities:

- Getting a Coke by pointing and clicking the phone at a vending machine. The bottle drops down and an appropriate amount is deducted from your bank account.
- Using the phone to search for a nearby restaurant that meets the criteria you entered.
- Watching stock prices on the phone while sitting in the restaurant and deciding to place a purchase order.
- Clicking the phone to pay the bill for your meal.
- Coming home and clicking a combination of keys on the phone to open your door.

Some see positive benefits, such as locating people making emergency calls or checking on the whereabouts of children late at night. Others worry about privacy issues. What if an employer learns that an employee is being treated for AIDS at a local clinic, or a wife finds her husband is out clubbing? Like so many new technologies, location-based services have potential for good or harm and ultimately will warrant public scrutiny and regulation.

Summary

1. Most producers do not sell their goods directly to final users. Between producers and final users stands one or more marketing channels, a host of marketing intermediaries performing a variety of functions.
2. Marketing-channel decisions are among the most critical decisions facing management. The company's chosen channel(s) profoundly affect all other marketing decisions.
3. Companies use intermediaries when they lack the financial resources to carry out direct marketing, when direct marketing is not feasible, and when they can earn more by doing so. The most important functions performed by intermediaries are information, promotion, negotiation, ordering, financing, risk taking, physical possession, payment, and title.
4. Manufacturers have many alternatives for reaching a market. They can sell direct or use one-, two-, or three-level channels. Deciding which type(s) of channel to use calls for analyzing customer needs, establishing channel objectives, and identifying and evaluating the major alternatives, including the types and numbers of intermediaries involved in the channel.
5. Effective channel management calls for selecting intermediaries and training and motivating them. The goal is to build a long-term partnership that will be profitable for all channel members.
6. Marketing channels are characterized by continuous and sometimes dramatic change. Three of the most important trends are the growth of vertical marketing systems, horizontal marketing systems, and multichannel marketing systems.
7. All marketing channels have the potential for conflict and competition resulting from such sources as goal incompatibility, poorly defined roles and rights, perceptual differences, and interdependent relationships. Companies can manage conflict by striving for superordinate goals, exchanging people among two or more channel levels, co-opting the support of leaders in different parts of the channel, and encouraging joint membership in and between trade associations.
8. Channel arrangements are up to the company, but there are certain legal and ethical issues to be considered with regard to practices such as exclusive dealing or territories, tying agreements, and dealers' rights. Businesses in Asia must grapple with the prevalent practice of gray marketing or the sale of authorized goods via unauthorized channels. They must weigh the costs and benefits of parallel importing before taking action.
9. E-commerce has grown in importance as companies have adopted "brick-and-click" channel systems. Channel integration must recognize the distinctive strengths of online and offline selling and maximize their joint contributions.

Application

Marketing Debate—Does It Matter Where You Are Sold?

Some marketers feel that the image of the particular channel in which they sell their products does not matter—all that matters is that the right customers shop there and the product is displayed in the right way. Others maintain that channel images—such as a retail store—can be critical and must be consistent with the image of the product.

Take a position: *Channel images do not really affect the brand images of the products they sell that much* versus *Channel images must be consistent with the brand image.*

Marketing Discussion

Think of your favorite retailers. How have they integrated their channel system? How would you like their channels to be integrated? Do you use multiple channels from them? Why?

Zara's nimble retailing model enables new fashions to be brought from drawing board to selling floor in a matter of weeks and be sold at full price.

Managing Retailing, Wholesaling, and Logistics

16

In the previous chapter, we examined marketing intermediaries from the viewpoint of manufacturers who wanted to build and manage marketing channels. In this chapter, we view these intermediaries—retailers, wholesalers, and logistical organizations—as requiring and forging their own marketing strategies. Intermediaries must strive for marketing excellence like any company or suffer the consequences.

Spain's Zara has become Europe's leading apparel retailer in recent years by adopting a different retail model. The firm's strategy is to give customers a lot of variety at affordable prices. It can make 20,000 different items in a year, about triple what The Gap would do. Zara distributes all its merchandise, regardless of origin, from Spain and is willing to experience occasional shortages to preserve an image of exclusivity. Unlike some other retailers, Zara does not spend lavish amounts of money on advertising or on deals with designers. Instead it invests more in its store locations. Zara places its stores—over 90 percent of which it owns—in heavily trafficked, high-end retail zones. These practices help it to sell more at full price—85 percent of its merchandise—than the industry average of 60 percent. By controlling all aspects of the supply chain, Zara can take an idea and make it a reality on the store floor in about five weeks, compared to the months needed by a typical clothing manufacturer.[1]

In this chapter, we will address the following questions:

1. What major types of marketing intermediaries occupy this sector?
2. What marketing decisions do these marketing intermediaries make?
3. What are the major trends with marketing intermediaries?

But while "fast-forward" retailers such as Zara, Sweden's H&M, Spain's Mango, and Britain's Topshop have thrived in recent years, others such as the U.S.'s Gap have struggled. Many of the more successful intermediaries use strategic planning, advanced information systems, and sophisticated marketing tools. They measure performance more on a return-on-investment basis than on a profit-margin basis. They segment their markets, improve their market targeting and positioning, and aggressively pursue market expansion and diversification strategies. In this chapter, we consider marketing excellence in retailing, wholesaling, and logistics.

Retailing

Retailers use strategic planning, advanced information systems, and sophisticated marketing tools to beat the competition. They measure performance more on a return-on-investment basis than on a profit-margin basis. They segment their markets, improve their market targeting and positioning, and aggressively pursue market expansion and diversification strategies. In this chapter, we consider marketing excellence in retailing, wholesaling, and logistics.

Retailing includes all the activities involved in selling goods or services directly to final consumers for personal, nonbusiness use. A **retailer** or **retail store** is any business enterprise whose sales volume comes primarily from retailing.

Any organization selling to final consumers—whether it is a manufacturer, wholesaler, or retailer—is doing retailing. It does not matter *how* the goods or services are sold (by person, mail, telephone, vending machine, or Internet) or *where* they are sold (in a store, on the street, or in the consumer's home).

Types of Retailers

Consumers today can shop for goods and services in a wide variety of retail organizations. There are store retailers, non-store retailers, and retail organizations. Perhaps the best-known type of retailer is the department store. Japanese department stores such as Takashimaya and Mitsukoshi attract millions of shoppers each year. These stores feature art galleries, restaurants, cooking classes, and children's playgrounds.

Department stores are the best-known type of retailers. Japan's Takashimaya attracts millions each year with special offerings such as art galleries, playgrounds, and restaurants.

Table 16.1 Major Retailer Types

Specialty store: Narrow product line. E.g., The Body Shop.
Department store: Several product lines. E.g., Isetan.
Supermarket: Large, low-cost, low-margin, high-volume, self-service store designed to meet total needs for food and household products. E.g., Wellcome.
Convenience store: Small store in residential area, often open 24/7, limited line of high-turnover convenience products plus takeout. E.g., 7-Eleven.
Discount store: Standard or specialty merchandise; low-price, low-margin, high-volume stores. E.g., Wal-Mart.
Off-price retailer: Leftover goods, overruns, irregular merchandise sold at less than retail. E.g., Reject Shop.
Superstore: Huge selling space, routinely purchased food and household items, plus services (laundry, shoe repair, dry cleaning, and check cashing). Category killer (deep assortment in one category) such as Toys "R" Us; hypermarket (huge stores that combine supermarket, discount, and warehouse retailing) such as Carrefour.
Catalog showroom: Broad selection of high-markup, fast-moving, brand-name goods sold by catalog at discount. Customers pick up merchandise at the store.

Retail-store types pass through stages of growth and decline that can be described as the *retail life cycle.*[2] A type emerges, enjoys a period of accelerated growth, reaches maturity, and then declines. The most important retail-store types are described in Table 16.1.

LEVELS OF SERVICE

The *wheel-of-retailing* hypothesis explains one reason that new store types emerge.[3] Conventional retail stores typically increase their services and raise their prices to cover the costs. These higher costs provide an opportunity for new store forms to offer lower prices and less service. New store types meet widely different consumer preferences for service levels and specific services.

Retailers can position themselves as offering one of four levels of service:

1. ***Self-service***— Self-service is the cornerstone of all discount operations. Many customers are willing to carry out their own locate-compare-select process to save money. A.C. Nielsen found that all across Asia except the Philippines, modern self-service outlets are gaining a significant share of trade compared to traditional trade. In particular, the growth has been significant in China, Indonesia, and Korea.[4]
2. ***Self-selection***— Customers find their own goods, although they can ask for assistance.
3. ***Limited service*** — These retailers carry more shopping goods, and customers need more information and assistance. The stores also offer services (such as credit and merchandise-return privileges).
4. ***Full service***— Salespeople are ready to assist in every phase of the locate-compare-select process. Customers who like to be waited on prefer this type of store. The high staffing cost, along with the higher proportion of specialty goods and slower-moving items and the many services, results in high-cost retailing.

By combining these different service levels with different assortment breadths, we can distinguish the four broad positioning strategies available to retailers, as shown in Figure 16.1:

1. ***Takashimaya***— Stores that feature a broad product assortment and high value added. Stores in this quadrant pay close attention to store design, product quality, service, and image. Their profit margin is high, and if they are fortunate enough to have high volume, they will be very profitable.
2. ***Shanghai Tang***— Stores that feature a narrow product assortment and high value added. Such stores cultivate an exclusive image and tend to operate on a high margin and low volume.

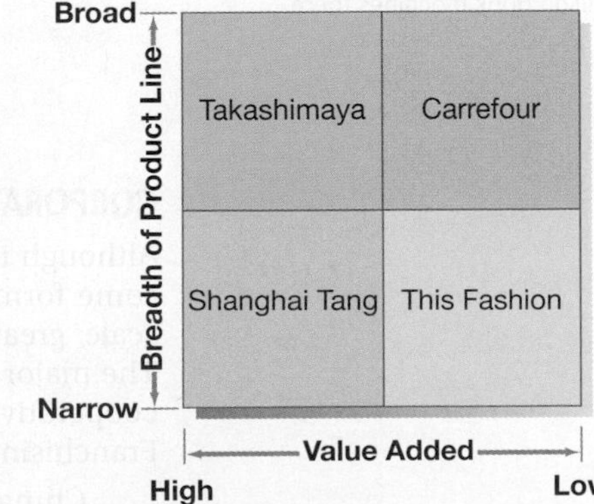

Figure 16.1 Retail Positioning Map

Source: Adapted from William T. Gregor and Eileen M. Friars, *Money Merchandising: Retail Revolution in Consumer Financial Service* (Cambridge, MA: The MAC Group, 1982).

3. ***This Fashion*** — Stores that feature a narrow line and low value added. Such stores keep their costs and prices low by centralizing buying, merchandising, advertising, and distribution.
4. ***Carrefour*** — Stores that feature a broad line and low value added. They focus on keeping prices low so that they have an image of being a place for good buys. They make up for low margins by high volume.

Although the overwhelming bulk of goods and services is sold through stores, *non-store retailing* has been growing much faster than store retailing. Non-store retailing falls into four major categories: direct selling, direct marketing (which includes telemarketing and Internet selling), automatic vending, and buying services:

Vending machines are an effective distribution system in Japan. Products sold through vending machines range from the usual soft drinks, beers, and cigarettes to more exotic items such as hot instant noodles and eggs. Coca-Cola alone operates more than a million drink machines there.

1. **Direct selling** (also called *multilevel selling, network marketing*) involves companies selling door-to-door or at home sales parties. Avon, Tupperware, and Mary Kay Cosmetics are sold one-to-many: a salesperson goes to the home of a host who has invited friends; the salesperson demonstrates the products and takes orders. Pioneered by Amway, the multilevel (network) marketing sales system consists of recruiting independent businesspeople who act as distributors. The distributor's compensation includes a percentage of sales of those the distributor recruits as well as earnings on direct sales to customers.
2. **Direct marketing** has roots in direct-mail and catalog marketing; it includes *telemarketing, television direct-response marketing,* and *electronic shopping.* Sales through direct marketing are highest within Asia in Japan, although home shopping TV channels are gaining popularity in Korea and Taiwan (see "Marketing Insight: Enhancing Online Shopping in Asia").
3. **Automatic vending** is used for a variety of merchandise, including impulse goods like cigarettes, soft drinks, coffee, candy, newspapers, magazines, and other products like hosiery, cosmetics, hot food, condoms, and paperbacks. Vending machines are found in factories, offices, large retail stores, gasoline stations, hotels, restaurants, and many other places. They offer 24-hour selling, self-service, and merchandise that is always fresh. Japan has the most vending machines per person. These reliable, high-tech machines allow consumers to buy products ranging from blue jeans to expensive lunches. The machines take orders directly from DoCoMo mobile phones, the cost to be charged against the customer's prepaid account. Coca-Cola has over one million vending machines in Japan yielding annual sales of $50 billion—twice that of the U.S.
4. **Buying service** is a storeless retailer serving a specific clientele—usually employees of large organizations—who are entitled to buy from a list of retailers that have agreed to give discounts in return for membership.

CORPORATE RETAILING

Although many retail stores are independently owned, an increasing number are part of some form of **corporate retailing.** Corporate retail organizations achieve economies of scale, greater purchasing power, wider brand recognition, and better-trained employees. The major types of corporate retailing—corporate chain stores, voluntary chains, retailer cooperatives, franchises, and merchandising conglomerates—are described in Table 16.2. Franchising is described in detail in "Marketing Insight: Franchise Fever in Asia."

China has the world's largest number of franchise stores, with more than 2,000 brands and over 120,000 outlets. In Shanghai alone, there are 16,000 franchise chain stores. The franchise business model has been adopted in nearly 50 sectors, including convenience stores, education, and training.[5]

MARKETING INSIGHT • ENHANCING ONLINE SHOPPING IN ASIA

Customers continue to validate the concept of e-commerce with their wallets in the more developed Asian countries. An A.C. Nielsen's study of online shoppers showed that the world's most avid Internet shoppers hail from South Korea—99 percent of Internet users in South Korea have shopped online. Japanese was second with 97 percent. Koreans are also the most frequent online shoppers with 79 percent of such Internet users having made a purchase online in the last month. Being style-savvy, a whopping 70 percent of South Korean online shoppers had bought clothing, accessories, and shoes online in the last three months.

E-commerce sites harbor such advantages over brick-and-mortar retailers as ease of use, product research and comparison tools, large inventories and better selection, and in-home purchasing. In contrast, brick-and-mortar retailers have several natural advantages over e-tailers, such as providing the traditional shopping experience; customer loyalty and trust; products shoppers can actually see, touch, and test; real-life customer service, and no delivery lag-time for small or medium-sized purchases. Brick-and-mortar retailers also have the potential for cross-marketing, and blending online and offline operations.

A synthesis of the physical and virtual retail model leveraging the best of both worlds seems to be underway. Thus Internet shopping in Taiwan saw marked growth after e-commerce sites started tying up with 24-hour convenience stores. Buyers could receive their products faster than through the mail, and they can sometimes return defective goods through the store. Stores could also collect payment for those buyers who worry about paying via the Internet. The major purchasers tend to be housewives who find Web shopping convenient. Reflecting this, Web sites featuring women's fashion, cosmetics, baby-care products, and travel are seeing the fastest e-buying growth.

In Korea, LG combines the strengths of its home shopping network, cybermall, and mail-order business. Its 24-hour TV shopping channel prices items up to a third cheaper than department stores. Its cybermall leverages on this channel, luring online shoppers with slick TV footage of its latest products that can be downloaded via Korea's broadband connections. Complemented by its mail-order business, LG's retail unit targets consumers who want goods delivered to their homes. Delivery costs are minimal as nearly half of Korea's families live in apartment blocks.

Some Asian brick-and-mortar retailers are adding Internet content to their physical stores. Japan's Lawson chain installed online computer terminals in all of its over 7,000 convenience stores. Customers can sign on for free, browse through the online catalog, and place an order on the shopping network called Loppi. Popular offerings include sporting event and concert tickets, computer game software, and music CDs. Bigger-ticket items such as discount tours have also been promoted online. Loppi is online shopping with a twist, since most purchases are still in cash at the register to preserve Lawson's face-to-face contact with its customers. Shoppers sign on at the easy-to-use terminal, select a product, and receive a paper receipt which they take to the cash register to pay with cash or a house Visa credit card. Products like Pokemon toys are delivered to the store a few days later for customer pick-up, while large items like computers or perishable items like flowers are home delivered. The Loppi system has allowed Lawson to add nearly 1,000 new items without the need for inventory; important in a country with expensive property and distribution problems. It has also expanded the market for other products such as fresh flowers, which is now sold year-round instead of only in May, prior to Mother's Day.

However, the initial uptake of e-tailing is lower in Hong Kong and Singapore, whose compact island geographies are custom-built for off-line shopping. Thus online retailing must add even more value to convince shoppers in these countries. Indeed, some successful brick-and-mortar Hong Kong retailers like Giordano have Web sites that are pedestrian in design, minimally stocked, and offering no real deals. Giordano believes e-tailing is unproven and generally unprofitable, given the large and continuous investment needed to maintain a leading edge Web site. Moreover, it believes that Asia is a region where logistics pose real problems that hinder successful Web retailing. Finally, the majority of Asian consumers still shop off-line. If brick-and-mortar retailers like Giordano continue to find innovative ways to attract and retain customers, the proportion of online retail sales may well be lower.

Sources: "Trends in Online Shopping: A Global Nielsen Consumer Report." *A.C. Nielsen Report*, February 2008; "Traditional Retailers Dominate Global e-Shopping." *A.C. Nielsen Insights Asia Pacific,* April 2001, pp. 4–5; Moon Ihlwan, "A Gold Mine Called Home Shopping." *BusinessWeek Asian Edition,* November 5, 2001, p. 21; Sui Noi Goh, "Stay-home Mothers Getting Hooked on e-Shopping." *Sunday Times* (Singapore), July 28, 2002; "IBM: E-Business Means Big Business for Japanese Convenience Store." *M2 Presswire,* July 21, 1999; "Saying No to Net Losses." *Asiaweek,* October 15, 1999, p. 69.

MARKETING INSIGHT • FRANCHISE FEVER IN ASIA

Franchising is the most common route to becoming an entrepreneur. It is nearly impossible to drive down the streets of major Asian capitals without seeing a McDonald's, a Starbucks, or a Hard Rock Café.

How does a franchising system work? In a franchising system, individual *franchisees* are a tightly knit group of enterprises whose systematic operations are planned, directed, and controlled by the operation's innovator, called a *franchiser*. Franchises are distinguished by three characteristics:

1. **The franchiser owns a trade or service mark and licenses it to franchisees in return for royalty payments.**
2. **The franchisee pays for the right to be part of the system.** Start-up costs include rental and lease equipment and fixtures, and usually a regular license fee. McDonald's franchisees may invest as much as $1.6 million in total start-up costs and fees. The franchisee then pays McDonald's a certain percentage of sales plus a monthly rent to the landlord.
3. **The franchiser provides its franchisees with a system for doing business.** McDonald's requires franchisees to attend "Hamburger University" for three weeks to learn how to manage the business. Franchisees must follow certain procedures in buying materials.

Franchising is mutually beneficial to both franchiser and franchisee. Among the benefits reaped by franchisers are the motivation and hard work of employees who are entrepreneurs rather than "hired hands," the franchisees' familiarity with local communities and conditions, and the enormous purchasing power of the franchiser. Franchisees benefit from buying into a business with a well-known and accepted brand name. They find it easier to borrow money from financial institutions, and they receive support in areas ranging from marketing and advertising to site selection and staffing.

Three new directions in franchising may deliver both franchiser growth and franchisee earnings. First, strategic alliances are being developed among major outside corporations. Fuji USA arranged with Moto Photo, a one-hour photo developer, to carry its film. Fuji won instant market penetration through Moto Photo's 400 locations, and Moto Photo franchisees enjoyed Fuji's name recognition and advertising reach.

Second, non-traditional locations are being increasingly used to site franchises. Franchises are opening in airports, sports stadiums, college campuses, hospitals, casinos, theme parks, and convention halls all over Asia.

Third, Western franchisers who face saturated domestic markets are turning toward Asia for growth. In China, franchise sales volume takes up only 5 percent of the national retail sales, compared to the world average of more than 40 percent. Under an effective management, sales volume of franchises has grown at an annual growth rate of 40 percent, ahead of the retail sector's 10 percent average. Moreover, franchised stores can expand at an amazing speed. Some 60 percent start operations in less than two months from when they were established. For example, Lanzhou-based Malan Noodle Fastfood set up more than 300 outlets within a year.

The Beijing Olympic Games in 2008 saw a mushrooming of franchise operations. The Fatburger restaurant chain and Auntie Anne's Pretzels opened to capitalize on the demand.

Critical to franchise success is identifying the right Asian partner and understanding local conditions. Domino's (pizza) was brought to Japan by master franchisee Ernest Higa who owns 106 stores with combined sales of $140 million. Part of Higa's success can be attributed to adapting Domino's product to the Japanese market, where presentation is key. Higa meticulously charted the placement of pizza toppings and made cutmark perforations in the boxes for perfectly uniform sizes.

In contrast, Pizza Hut's experience in Thailand provided its parent company Tricon some lessons in managing a global network of ambitious franchisees. It had sold franchise rights to Bill Heinecke for $5,000 in 1980 when pizza was unheard of in Thailand, and cheese was not a popular part of the diet. Yet by 1999, Heinecke had built a chain of 116 restaurants and Thailand became one of Pizza Hut's 10 largest international markets. However, Heinecke's desire to become a franchisee for an Australian chicken chain clashed with Tricon's rule that none of its franchisees could compete with its other brands (KFC in this case). In 2000, the two sides settled a contentious legal battle by agreeing that Heinecke could keep his pizza outlets and rebrand them. Since then, Tricon opened over 80 Pizza Huts in Thailand, often placing them close to its rival.

From an Asian perspective, franchising provides Asian entrepreneurs opportunities for regionalizing proven brands and business processes from the West in addition to, or instead of, trying to build their own brands. Hong Kong-based Dairy Farm, which runs supermarkets, holds the franchise for IKEA in Hong Kong and Taiwan. More established Asian entrepreneurs obtain master franchises for the entire region and sub-license their rights to others. For instance, the franchisor for 7-Eleven Taiwan also holds the franchise to Starbucks. Some like Singapore's franchisee of ice cream parlor chain Swensen's even go so far as to become bigger than the original franchiser. 7-Eleven Japan even acquired its U.S. franchiser.

Asian entrepreneurs are also setting up their own franchise systems. Japan's Circle K can be found in Hong Kong, while Jollibee has franchises throughout Asia and the Middle East. Smaller Asian businesses also see franchising as a major growth engine. Propelled by the Singapore government's initiatives to export businesses and business concepts, small- and medium-sized enterprises like Kinderland children's music school have franchised their operations regionally.

Sources: "Franchising—A Marriage of System Member." In Sidney Levy, George Frerichs, and Howard Gordon, eds., *Marketing Managers Handbook*, 3rd ed., (Chicago: Dartnell, 1994), pp. 919-934; Richard Gibson, "Even 'Copycat' Businesses Require Creativity and Flexibility." *Wall Street Journal Online*, March 2004; <http://www.entrepreneur.com>; Brian O'Keefe, "What do KFC and Pizza Hut Conjure Up Abroad? Are They American Symbols? Or Have They Become Global?" *Fortune*, November 26, 2001, pp. 60-66; "Global Franchising 2002." *Straits Times* (Singapore), September 18, 2002, pp. L11-L12, L14; Amy Cortese, "Before the Olympics, a Parade of Companies." *New York Times*, March 30, 2003.

Table 16.2 Major Types of Corporate Retail Organizations

Corporate chain store: Two or more outlets owned and controlled, employing central buying and merchandising, and selling similar lines of merchandise. E.g., Giordano.
Voluntary chain: A wholesaler-sponsored group of independent retailers engaged in bulk buying and common merchandising. E.g., Independent Grocers Alliance.
Retailer cooperative: Independent retailers using a central buying organization and joint promotion efforts. E.g., Associated Grocers.
Consumer cooperative: A retail firm owned by its customers. Members contribute money to open their own store, vote on its policies, elect a group to manage it, and receive dividends. E.g. Singapore's NTUC offers child care, dental care, taxi service, supermarket, and pharmaceutical and insurance services.
Franchise organization: Contractual association between a franchiser and franchisees, popular in a number of product and service areas. E.g., Jollibee.
Merchandising conglomerate: A corporation that combines several diversified retailing lines and forms under central ownership, with some integration of distribution and management. E.g., Dairy Farm operates the Wellcome supermarket chain in Hong Kong and Taiwan, Mannings and 7-Eleven stores in Hong Kong and Shenzhen, and Giant hypermarkets in India, Indonesia, Malaysia, and Singapore. It also has interests in the Maxim's food outlets and cake shops in Hong Kong; the Cold Storage chain in Malaysia and Singapore; and Health and Glow drug stores and Foodworld Supermarkets in India; among others.

The New Retail Environment

In the past, retailers secured customer loyalty by offering convenient locations, special or unique assortments of goods, greater or better services than competitors, and store credit cards. All this has changed. Today, brands such as Ralph Lauren Polo, Calvin Klein, and Levi's are found in department stores, in their own shops, in merchandise outlets, and in off-price discount stores. In their drive for volume, manufacturers have placed their branded goods everywhere. The result is that retail-store assortments have grown more alike.

Service differentiation also has eroded. Many department stores have trimmed services, and many discounters have increased services. Customers have become smarter shoppers. They do not want to pay more for identical brands, especially when service differences have diminished; nor do they need credit from a particular store, as bank credit cards are becoming more widely accepted.

Here are some retail developments that are changing the way consumers buy, and manufacturers and retailers sell.

1. ***New retail forms and combinations*** — Some supermarkets include bank branches. Bookstores feature coffee shops. Gas stations include food stores. Shopping malls and bus and train stations have peddlers' carts in their aisles. Some retailers are experimenting with limited-time-only stores called "pop-ups" that let retailers promote brands, reach seasonal shoppers for a few weeks in busy areas, and create buzz.
2. ***Growth of intertype competition*** — Different types of stores—discount stores, catalog showrooms, department stores—all compete for the same consumers by carrying the same type of merchandise. Retailers that have helped shoppers to be economically cautious, to simplify their increasingly busy and complicated lives and provide an emotional connection are the winners in the new retailing landscape of the 21st century.[6]
3. ***Competition between store-based and nonstore-based retailing*** — Consumers now receive sales offers through direct mail letters and catalogs, and over television, computers, and telephones. These nonstore-based retailers are taking business away from store-based retailers. Some store-based retailers see online retailing as a definite threat.

4. ***Growth of giant retailers*** — Through their superior information systems, logistical systems, and buying power, giant retailers are able to deliver good service and immense volumes of products at appealing prices to masses of consumers. They are crowding out smaller manufacturers who cannot deliver enough quantity and even dictating to the most powerful manufacturers what to make, how to price and promote, when and how to ship, and even how to improve production and management. Manufacturers need these accounts; otherwise they would lose 10–30 percent of the market.

   Some giant retailers are *category killers* that concentrate on one product category. Toys "R" Us concentrates on toys. Others are *supercenters* that combine grocery items with a huge selection of non-food merchandise (Giant, Wal-Mart, and Carrefour). The supercenter is becoming popular in Asia.

Big Bazaar—In India, a retail revolution has taken place. The mom-and-pop neighborhood stores that have, for decades, dominated the retail scene, are slowly giving way to modern trade channels. Big Bazaar is the Indian version of Wal-Mart and the modern Indian family's favorite store. This discount hypermarket stocks everything from peanuts and avocados to mops and crockery. It is constantly jam-packed. While foreign competition such as Wal-Mart and Carrefour is barred from Indian retail, local retail stores and malls are expected to grow from 3 percent of the market in 2004 to 9 percent in 2010. One reason for the growth of modern retail is that 60 percent of India is under the age of 30, and young Indians have an affinity for modern shopping.[7]

5. ***The traditional trade is alive and well*** — Despite the growth of modern retailing in Asia, traditional retail formats are still abundant in many parts of the region. Four Asian countries still have over 6,000 grocery stores per million population: India, the Philippines, Sri Lanka, and Indonesia. In Southeast Asia, 75 percent of the urban population continues to use the retail trade regularly, with the exception of Singapore. In many of these countries, shoppers are using the traditional trade frequently, particularly for impulse goods. With the exception of Korea and Japan, Asian shoppers still use wet markets as their main source of fresh food, with the vast majority using them three to five times weekly.[8] Traditional stores continue to remain in demand because of their convenient locations, fresh food, and appeal to the small basket and low income shoppers.[9]

Floating markets in Thailand are typical of how mobile traditional retailers are in location. The floating market sells a wide range of products, including fruits, handbags, and cooked food.

Wet markets such as this in Vietnam sell fresh vegetables and meat.

6. ***Growing investment in technology*** — Retailers are using computers to produce better forecasts, control inventory costs, order electronically from suppliers, send email between stores, and even sell to customers within stores. They are adopting checkout scanning systems,[10] electronic funds transfer, electronic data interchange,[11] in-store television, store traffic radar systems,[12] and improved merchandise-handling systems.
7. ***Global presence of major retailers*** — Retailers with unique formats and strong brand positioning are increasingly appearing in other countries.[13] Retailers such as McDonald's, Carrefour, IKEA, and Toys "R" Us have become globally prominent. Among Asian retailers, the Japanese have the longest and largest international presence. Japanese retailers have been used as a channel to market Japanese consumer goods to foreign buyers, serve Japanese tourists and expatriates abroad, and enable the Japanese to study customer behavior first-hand. For example, department-store chains like Daimaru, Takashimaya, Isetan, and Sogo have long featured on the regional retail scene. With China's entry into the WTO, foreign retailers are expanding their operations there. While they had bought or leased properties that suited their specific needs in the past, market liberalization has allowed them to buy local shopping chains as prime property becomes more scarce. B&Q, a home improvement store owned by Britain's Kingfisher, bought five Chinese stores that hold a franchise from U.S. retailer PriceSmart, while Britain's Tesco bought half of the Hymall chain.[14]
8. ***Upgrading of Asian retailers*** — Some Asian retailers are reacting strongly to the entry of foreign players. Larger Asian department stores have established their own hypermarkets and discount outlets as a defensive strategy against foreign chains. Malaysia's Metrojaya has Cosmart, Indonesia's Matahari has Mega M, Thailand's Central Retail Group has Cencar, Korea's Shinsegae has E-Mart, China's Lianhua has Nonggongshang, and Taiwan's Ta-Tung Group has Save and Safe hypermarkets. Such home-grown stores offer clean, cheap, and convenient shopping similar to that offered by foreign rivals. With government subsidies and local connections, some in China can be set up for half or even a third of the cost borne by their foreign counterparts.[15] Across Asia, there are five countries where hypermarkets/large format stores are the dominant format in urban areas—China, Korea, Malaysia, Taiwan, and Thailand. Thailand has the highest proportion of loyal hypermarket shoppers in Asia.[16]

   Small- and medium-sized Asian retailers have upgraded their marketing knowledge and skills to better serve their customers, or have merged or exited the market. Investment in technology, product specialization, and developing strong supplier alliances are used to promote micromarketing, cut costs, and improve distribution efficiency. In China, many mainland retailers are forming collective buying groups with businesses like Hualian Bai Huo in Tianjin and Shanghai to gain economies of scale and more efficient distribution. Once full liberalization occurs in China's retail market, competition is expected to intensify further, followed by a substantial shakeout.

Marketing Decisions

We will examine retailers' marketing decisions in target market, product assortment and procurement, services and store atmosphere, price, communication, and location.

In the highly competitive grocery retailing industry, what's one of the hottest marketing strategies for ensuring success? To learn how San Antonio-based retailer, H-E-B has managed to challenge national retailers, visit wps.prenhall.com/bp_kotler_mm_13/.

TARGET MARKET

Until the target market is defined and profiled, the retailer cannot make consistent decisions on product assortment, store decor, advertising messages and media, price, and service levels. Some retailers have not only defined their target markets quite well, but are also slicing the market into finer segments and introducing new lines of stores to provide a more relevant set of offerings to exploit niche markets. Consider Giordano:

Giordano—This retail apparel conglomerate practices target marketing. Its Giordano stores emphasize value-for-money casual clothes and accessories in basic but colorful styles and excellent customer service. Giordano's sensible, versatile, and stylish clothes offer austerity-minded consumers guilt-free shopping. It replicates fashion-forward looks, getting affordable versions of the latest street-culture-inspired styles quickly to its over 1,800 stores in 30 Asia Pacific and Middle Eastern countries. It has since launched Giordano Junior, Giordano Ladies, and BlueStar targeting different segments. Giordano Junior is a 60-store chain in Korea, Taiwan, and Singapore. It targets modern parents with children aged 3–12 who desire shopping ease. Its wide selection allows parents to mix and match clothes for their children. Safety is also incorporated into the clothes' designs. For example, buttons have lock stitching to reduce choking hazards. The 30-store Giordano Ladies chain, mostly in Hong Kong, Taiwan, and China, targets young trendy women who like personalized service. Clothes at Giordano Ladies stores are pricier and more stylish than at Giordano stores. Staff are trained to memorize the names of regular customers and recall their past purchases. Offering magazines for reading in comfortable resting areas, this chain has appealed to several Hong Kong starlets. The BlueStar stores, mainly found in Hong Kong, China, and Taiwan, feature budget clothes 30 percent cheaper than the Giordano line. The chain caters to discount shoppers that the main Giordano brand no longer wants to be aligned with. In Hong Kong, it attracts new immigrants from China. In Shanghai, it is called BlueNavy.[17]

PRODUCT ASSORTMENT

The retailer's product assortment must match the target market's shopping expectations. Consider Tsutaya:

Tsutaya—Tsutaya is Japan's largest retailer of movies, recorded music, and game software. It represents the fashion and culture that appeal to Japanese youth. Both Microsoft and Sony chose Tsutaya's flagship Tokyo store—an eight-storey emporium located in the youth-oriented district of Shibuya—to launch major products like Xbox and PlayStation2. The most popular of its nearly 1,100 shops, many of them franchises, offer movie theaters and Starbucks coffee. Its online presence boosts Tsutaya's image as a vendor of youth culture. Tsutaya Online is the leading e-commerce site in Japan and is a very popular destination on NTT's i-mode mobile Internet service. Some 2.4 million users regularly log on to conduct searches and order movie and music titles. Tsutaya sends out discount coupons online to increase store sales. It also boasts 16.4 million loyalty card members, 35 percent of whom are in their twenties. Tsutaya was one of the first Japanese businesses to install an electronic system to track inventory and customers. The system can analyze trends hourly at each store. It also tracks demographics, consumer tastes, and other data in every major urban district. Tsutaya uses such information in its product assortment and store location decisions.[18]

The retailer has to decide on product-assortment *breadth* and *depth*. A restaurant can offer a narrow and shallow assortment (small lunch counters), a narrow and deep assortment (delicatessen), a broad and shallow assortment (coffeeshop), or a broad and deep assortment (food court). Some retailers are located in specialized locations catering to a narrow assortment such as the Electronic Street in Tokyo that sells only electronic products. Table 16.3 provides an illustration of how Borders developed category assortment within a section of its stores.

Table 16.3 Retail Category Management

Step	What It Means	How Borders Applied It
1. Define the category.	Decide where you draw the line between product categories. For example, do your customers view alcohol and soft drinks as one beverage category, or should you manage them separately?	Named the cookbook section Food and Cooking because consumers expected to see books on nutrition there as well.
2. Figure out its role.	Determine how the category fits into the whole store. For example, "destination" categories lure folks in, so they get maximum marketing push, whereas "fill-ins" carry a minimal assortment.	Decided to make Food and Cooking a destination category.
3. Assess performance.	Analyze sales data from A.C. Nielsen, Information Resources Inc., and others. Identify opportunities.	Learned that cookbooks sell faster than expected during holiday. Responded by creating gift promotions.
4. Set goals.	Agree on the category's objectives, including sales, profit, and average-transaction targets, as well as customer satisfaction levels.	Aimed to grow cookbook sales faster than the store average and to grab market share from competition.
5. Choose the audience.	Sharpen your focus within the category for maximum effect.	Decided to go after repeat buyers. "Since 30 percent of shoppers buy 70 percent of the cookbooks sold, we are aiming at the enthusiast," says Borders' chief marketing officer Mike Spinozzi.
6. Figure out tactics.	Decide the best product selection, promotion merchandising, and pricing to achieve the category's goals.	Gave more prominent displays to books by celebrity chefs like Mario Batali. Created a more approachable product selection by reducing the number of titles on certain subjects.
7. Implement the plan.	Set the timetable and execute the tactics.	Introduced changes to its cooking sections as of November 2002.

Source: Andrew Raskin, "Who's Minding the Store?" *Business 2.0,* February 2003, p. 73.

The real challenge begins after defining the store's product assortment, and that is to develop a product-differentiation strategy. Here are some possibilities:

- **Feature exclusive national brands that are not available at competing retailers.** Robinsons in Singapore carries exclusive lines such as Fenn Wright Manson, Principles, Kaliko, Precis, and Tuzzi.
- **Feature mostly private branded merchandise.** Benetton, Gap, and Giordano design most of the clothes carried in their stores. Many supermarket and convenience chains carry private branded merchandise. Japanese retailer Ryoshin Keikaku's Mujirushi Ryohin stores—meaning "no label, good product"—have been particularly successful in private labeling. Mujirushi (Muji for short) clothes, food, and household products are designed in-house in a narrow range of natural colors. Aside from its minimalist-looking stores in Japan, Britain, France, Hong Kong, and Singapore, Muji products are also sold in New York's Museum of Modern Art.[19]
- **Feature blockbuster distinctive merchandise events.** Isetan may run month-long shows featuring the goods of another country, such as France, throughout the store.
- **Feature surprise or ever-changing merchandise.** Off-price apparel retailer Reject Shop offers surprise assortments of overstocks and closeouts.

Stores selling mobile phones and cameras along Tokyo's Electronic Street, a specialized location for such electronic products.

Reject Shop from Malaysia's Metrojaya has surprise assortments of overstocks at discounted prices.

- **Feature the latest or newest merchandise first.** Zara sells hip clothing merchandise to young women, catching trends to launch new products months before traditional competitors.
- **Offer merchandise customizing services.** The Imperial Tailors department of Shanghai Tang features a team of Shanghainese tailors who make exquisitely detailed clothing to customer specifications.
- **Offer a highly targeted assortment.** Retail stores may carry goods just for taller men, expectant mothers, or larger women. There are garment stores as well as food and grocery outlets in Hong Kong specifically catering to the 240,000 Filipino, Thai, and Indonesian domestic helpers there.[20]

PROCUREMENT

After deciding on the product-assortment strategy, the retailer must establish merchandise sources, policies, and practices. In the corporate headquarters of a supermarket chain, specialist buyers (sometimes called *merchandise managers*) are responsible for developing brand assortments and listening to salespersons' presentations. In some chains, buyers have the authority to accept or reject new items. In other chains, they are limited to screening "obvious rejects" and "obvious accepts;" they bring other items to the buying committee for approval. Even when an item is accepted by a chain-store buying committee, individual stores in the chain may not carry it. About one-third of the items must be stocked and about two-thirds are stocked at the discretion of each store manager.

Manufacturers face a major challenge trying to get new items onto store shelves. They offer supermarkets new items, but these can be rejected by the supermarkets. Manufacturers need to know the acceptance criteria used by buyers, buying committees, and store managers. A.C. Nielsen interviewed store managers and found that they are most influenced (in order of importance) by strong evidence of consumer acceptance, a well-designed advertising and sales-promotion plan, and generous financial incentives to the trade.

Wal-Mart—Wal-Mart's global procurement headquarters is located in Shenzhen. Suppliers go to Wal-Mart's "negotiations center," take a number, and wait for an audience with Wal-Mart's buyers or quality inspectors. Wal-Mart is trying to replace the Chinese business culture built on personal relationships with its own modern supply network built on information technology. Many Chinese manufacturers noted that Wal-Mart people "used calculators," did not want to be entertained in expensive restaurants, and were sticklers for quality, deadlines, and price. They also found that if their goods are not selling, they are shown the door, unless they have used Wal-Mart's software to analyze the market and can propose alternatives. In 2004, Wal-Mart spent $18 billion on merchandise from Chinese suppliers, accounting for 35 percent of China's exports. If Wal-Mart were a country, it would be China's sixth-largest export market.[21]

Retailers are rapidly improving their skills in demand forecasting, merchandise selection, stock control, space allocation, and display. In more developed cities, they are using computers to track inventory, compute economic order quantities, order goods, and analyze dollars spent on vendors and products. Supermarket chains are using scanner data to manage their merchandise mix on a store-by-store basis and soon all stores will probably be using "smart tags" to track goods, in real time, as they move from factories to supermarkets to shopping baskets. Smart tags are based on inexpensive versions of Radio Frequency Identification (RFID) tracking technology. RFID systems comprise readers and "smart tags"—microchips attached to antennas. When a tag nears a reader, it broadcasts the information in the chip. Smart tags contain unique numbers to identify products and to provide a means to look up detailed additional information stored in the computer.

For more on the possible uses—and abuses—of this technology, see "Marketing Insight: Making Labels Smarter."

When retailers study the economics of buying and selling individual products, they typically find that a third of their square footage is being tied up by products that do not make an economic profit (above the cost of capital) for the store. Another third of the space is typically allocated to product categories that have break-even economics. And the final third of space actually creates more than 100 percent of the economic profit. Yet, most retailers are unaware of which third of their products is generating the profit.[22]

Stores are using **Direct Product Profitability (DPP)** to measure a product's handling costs (receiving, moving to storage, paperwork, selecting, checking, loading, and space cost) from the time it reaches the warehouse until a customer buys it in the retail store. Resellers who have adopted DPP learn to their surprise that the gross margin on a product often bears little relation to the direct product profit. Some high-volume products may have such high handling costs that they are less profitable and deserve less shelf space than low-volume products. Clearly, vendors are facing increasingly sophisticated retailers.

MARKETING INSIGHT • MAKING LABELS SMARTER

In April 2004, several pallets of toilet paper arrived at a Wal-Mart distribution center. This mundane event actually heralded a revolution in retailing technology. With a small electronic tag affixed to each crate of Kimberly-Clark goods, the toilet tissue announced its own arrival to the distribution center at the same time that a computer checked that the crates were those from Kimberly-Clark's plant. If any crates were missing, the computer would issue an alert.

Radio Frequency Identification (RFID) or "smart" tags have been around for decades. However, Wal-Mart's widespread adoption could make them as common as bar codes. Indeed, Wal-Mart stunned the retailing world when it demanded its top 100 suppliers implement RFID technology. And what Wal-Mart demands, suppliers *do*, saving the mega-retailer as much as $8 billion a year. Here's a snapshot of how RFID will change the business landscape.

A key rationale for RFID tags is that retailers can alert manufacturers before shelves go bare, and consumer goods manufacturers can further perfect their supply chain so that they don't produce or distribute too few or too many goods. Gillette maintains that retailers and consumer goods firms lose around $30 billion a year from being out-of-stock on crucial items. Gillette is using smart tags to let store owners know that they need to reorder more stock, as well as to provide alerts if a large decrease from a shelf may be the result of shoplifting. Gillette also is using smart tags to improve logistics and shipping from factories versus traditional bar code scanning. IBM consultants assert that smart tags can shrink inventories by 5–25 percent.

Gillette isn't alone. Coca-Cola is embedding RFID readers in 200,000 of its one million vending machines in Japan to allow consumers to buy a Coke using wallet phones with RFID chips. Dutch bookseller Selexyz is tagging every title it stocks after a pilot study showed a 25 percent increase in sales. RFID-tagged books make for easier inventory control, consumer search, and checkout at the register.

The ability to link product IDs with databases containing the life histories and whereabouts of products makes RFID useful for preventing counterfeiting and even ensuring food and drug safety. A food company could program a system to alert plant managers when cases of meat sit too long unrefrigerated. Widespread tagging of medicines can also keep counterfeit pharmaceuticals from entering the market. Some retailers are using RFID to prevent shoplifting.

In Korea, RFID is being rolled out progressively. Phones with RFID are gradually being produced. The government has allocated the 900-megahertz frequency for the phone applications as well as logistics tracking purposes. The Korean Defense Ministry has announced that it is utilizing the chips to track supplies of bullets and grenades, while its National Veterinary Research and Quarantine Service intends to attach RFID tags to imported beef to better handle emergency situations such as outbreaks of mad cow disease.

Although a potential boon to marketers, smart tags raise issues of consumer privacy. Consider tagged medications. Electronic readers in office buildings might detect the type of medication carried by employees—an invasion of privacy. What about RFID-enabled customer loyalty cards that encode all sorts of personal and financial data? Some public-interest groups in the U.S. have called for strict public-notification rules, the right to demand deactivation of the tag when people leave stores, and overall limits on the technology's use until privacy concerns have been better addressed. Privacy advocates have ample time to organize. So far the price of RFID technology is too prohibitive to tag individual items. At a price of 25–50 cents per tag, it is not yet worth it to put them on every can of soda or tube of toothpaste.

Sources: Christine Y. Chen, "Wal-Mart Drives a New Tech Boom." *Fortune,* June 28, 2004, pp. 202; Rana Foroohar, "The Future of Shopping." *Newsweek,* June 7, 2004, p. 74; Jonathan Krim, "Embedding Their Hopes in RFID, Tagging Technology Promises Efficiency but Raises Privacy Issue." *Washington Post,* June 23, 2004, p.E.01; Barbara Rose, "Smart-Tag Wave About to Wash over Retailing." *Chicago Tribune,* April 18, 2004, p. 5; "The Best Thing Since Bar Code." *Economist,* February 8, 2003, pp. 57–58; Moon Ihlwan, Cliff Edwards, and Peter Burrows, "Honing Its Digital Game." *BusinessWeek,* July 18, 2005, pp. 16–18; Mary Catherine O'Conner, "Gillette Fuses RFID with Product Launch." *RFID Journal,* March 27, 2006.

To better differentiate themselves and generate consumer interest, some luxury retailers are attempting to make their stores and merchandise more varied. Burberry sells umbrellas in its distinctive plaid design only in Japan and customized trench coats only in New York.[23]

PRICES

Prices are a key positioning factor and must be decided in relation to the target market, the product-and-service assortment mix, and the competition. All retailers would like to achieve high volumes and high gross margins. They would like high *Turns* × *Earns*, but the two usually do not go together. Most retailers fall into the *high-markup, lower-volume* group (fine specialty stores) or the *low-markup, higher-volume* group (mass merchandisers and discount stores).

Retailers must also pay attention to pricing tactics. Most retailers will put low prices on some items to serve as traffic builders or loss leaders. They will run storewide sales. They will plan markdowns on slower-moving merchandise.

As Chapter 14 notes, some retailers such as Wal-Mart are using Everyday Low Pricing (EDLP). EDLP could lead to lower advertising costs, greater pricing stability, a stronger image of fairness and reliability, and, under certain circumstances, higher retail profits than Hi-Lo pricing.[24]

SERVICES

The services mix is a key tool for differentiating one store from another. Retailers must decide on the *services mix* to offer customers:

- Prepurchase services include accepting telephone and mail orders, advertising, window and interior display, fitting rooms, shopping hours, fashion shows, and trade-ins.
- Postpurchase services include shipping and delivery, gift wrapping, adjustments and returns, alterations and tailoring, installations, and engraving.
- Ancillary services include general information, check cashing, parking, restaurants, repairs, interior decorating, credit, rest rooms, and baby-attendant service.

Retailers also need to consider differentiating based on unerringly reliable customer service. Pressed by discounters and by shoppers who are increasingly indifferent about brands, retailers are rediscovering the usefulness of customer service as a point of differentiation, whether it is face-to-face, across phone lines, or even via a technological innovation.

STORE ATMOSPHERE

Every store has a physical layout that makes it difficult or easy to move around. Every store has a "look." The store must embody a planned atmosphere that suits the target market and draws consumers toward purchase (see "Marketing Memo: Helping Stores to Sell"). The Mall of Emirates in Dubai features ski slopes even though Dubai is snow-free.

STORE ACTIVITIES AND EXPERIENCES

The growth of e-commerce has forced traditional brick-and-mortar retailers to respond. In addition to their natural advantages, such as products that shoppers can actually see, touch, and test, real-life customer service, and no delivery lag time for small- or medium-sized purchases, they also provide a shopping experience as a strong differentiator.[25]

To entice Internet-savvy consumers to visit their stores, real-life retailers are developing new services and promotions. The change in strategy can be noticed in practices as simple as calling each shopper a "guest" (as many stores are beginning to do) or as grandiose as building an indoor amusement park. Here is a Malaysian example:

MARKETING MEMO • HELPING STORES TO SELL

In the pursuit of higher sales volume, retailers are studying their store environments for ways to improve the shopper experience. Paco Underhill is managing director of the retail consultant Envirosell Inc., whose clients include McDonald's, Starbucks, Estée Lauder, Citibank, Gap, and Burger King. He offers the following advice for fine-tuning retail space in order to keep shoppers spending:

- **Attract shoppers and keep them in the store.** The amount of time shoppers spend in a store is perhaps the single most important factor in determining how much they will buy. To increase shopping time, give shoppers a sense of community; recognize them in some way, manner, or form; give them ways to deal with their accessories, such as husbands and children; and keep an environment that is both familiar and fresh each time they come in.
- **Honor the "transition zone."** On entering a store, people need to slow down and sort out the stimuli, which means they will likely be moving too fast to respond positively to signs, merchandise, or sales clerks in the zone they cross before making that transition. Make sure there are clear sight lines. Create a focal point for information within the store.
- **Don't make them hunt.** Put the most popular products up front to reward busy shoppers and encourage leisurely shoppers to look more.
- **Make merchandise available to the reach and touch.** It is hard to overemphasize the importance of customers' hands. A store can offer the finest, cheapest, sexiest goods, but if the shopper cannot reach or pick them up, much of their appeal can be lost.
- **Note that men do not ask questions.** Men always move faster than women do through a store's aisles. In many settings, it is hard to get them to look at anything they had not intended to buy. Men also do not like asking where things are. If a man cannot find the section he is looking for, he will wheel about once or twice, then leave the store without ever asking for help.
- **Remember women need space.** A shopper, especially a woman, is far less likely to buy an item if her derriere is brushed, even lightly, by another customer when she is looking at a display. Keeping aisles wide and clear is crucial.
- **Make checkout easy.** Be sure to have the right high-margin goods near cash registers to satisfy impulse shoppers. And people love to buy candy when they check out—so satisfy their sweet tooth.

Some of Underhill's additional words of wisdom for modern retailers include: (1) develop expertise in the mature market; (2) sell both to and through your customer; (3) localize your presence; (4) extend your brand—use your history better; (5) build on the Internet-to-phone-to-store connection; (6) find your customers where they are; (7) refine the details of each point of sale; and (8) go undercover as your reality check.

Sources: Paco Underhill, *Call of the Mall: The Geography of Shopping*, (New York: Simon & Schuster, 2004); Paco Underhill, *Why We Buy: The Science of Shopping*, (New York: Simon & Schuster, 1999). See also Kenneth Hein, "Shopping Guru Ses Death of Detergent Aisle." *Brandweek*, March 27, 2006, p. 11; "Monday Keynote: Why They Buy." *Loupe Online*, 15 (Fall); Bob Parks, "5 Rules of Great Design." *Business 2.0*, March 2003, pp. 47–49; Keith Hammonds, "How We Sell." *Fast Company*, November 1999, p. 294; <www.envirosell.com>.

Berjaya Times Square—This megamall is regarded as the "mother of all malls" in Kuala Lumpur, Malaysia. It is located at the edge of the Bukit Bintang shopping district, a prime area for shoppers. The mall boasts 7.5 million square feet of built-up area comprising 3.45 million square feet of retail space for over 1,000 retail outlets. It also has a food and entertainment center, a 1.75-million square foot hotel and service suites, and a 380,000-square foot indoor theme park. The theme park offers thrill rides in its Cosmos World, including a 800-meter long roller coaster and a 30-meter high Spinning Star. To complement these attractions, Berjaya Times Square also features a Retailtainment Zone called 'Graffiti Street,' designated for entertainment-based merchandise, games, toys, adventure sports gear, and other specialty retailers. There is also a zone catering to kids called 'Kidz Town,' which is filled with toy stores and other children-related retail outlets.

At Berjaya Times Square, retailtainment in the form of Cosmo's World, a theme park, provides shoppers entertainment in a retail setting.

A Japanese restaurant with a display case showing plastic models of its dishes to communicate their price and look.

There has been a marked rise in establishments that provide a place for people to congregate, such as cafés, juice bars, bookshops, and brew pubs. Kinokuniya Bookstore has a café in some of its stores.

COMMUNICATION

Retailers use a wide range of communication tools to generate traffic and purchases. They place ads, run special sales, issue money-saving coupons, and run frequent shopper-reward programs, in-store food sampling, and coupons on shelves or at checkout points. In Shanghai, "live" models are used by some retailers in window displays to attract attention. In Japan, restaurants display plastic models of their dishes in window casings to communicate how the dishes look and their prices. Each retailer must use communications that support and reinforce its image positioning. They must carefully train salespeople to greet customers, interpret their needs, and handle complaints. Off-price retailers will arrange their merchandise to promote the idea of bargains and large savings, while conserving on service and sales assistance.

Jollibee—This Filipino fast-food chain has beaten McDonald's in its game in the Philippines. Its mascot, a jolly bee, was chosen because it epitomized the Filipino spirit of light-hearted, everyday happiness. Like Filipino working folk, the bee hops around and produces sweet things for life, and is happy even though it is busy. The staff at Jollibee greet customers with a gesture adopted from the sign language of the deaf—a vertical stroke for "bee" and hands shoveling towards the heart for "happy." They also address customers as "sir" and "mom," which is a casual and respectful greeting in the Philippines.[26]

LOCATION

Retailers are accustomed to saying that the three keys to success are "location, location, and location." Department store chains, oil companies, and fast-food franchisers exercise great care in selecting locations. The problem breaks down into selecting regions of the country in which to open outlets, then particular cities, and then particular sites. A supermarket chain might decide to operate in Thailand; in the cities of Bangkok and Chiangmai; and in six locations, mostly suburban, within the Bangkok area.

Tokyo's Shinjuku district is full of shops and offices. Rents are steep because of the high traffic.

Retailers can locate their stores in the central business district, a regional shopping center, a community shopping center, a shopping strip, or within a larger store:

- ***Central business districts*** — This is the oldest and most heavily trafficked city area, often known as "downtown." Store and office rents are normally high. As Asia becomes more saturated with shopping malls, some retailers are branching out to less competitive suburban locations from downtown areas to obtain lower rent and to reach out to new segments.
- ***Regional shopping centers*** — These are large suburban malls containing 40–200 stores. Typically, malls feature one or two anchor stores, such as Isetan or Parkson Grand, and numerous smaller stores, many under franchise operation. Malls are attractive because of generous parking, one-stop shopping, restaurants, and recreational facilities.

- ***Community shopping centers*** — These are smaller malls with one anchor store and 20–40 smaller stores.
- ***Strip malls* (also called *shopping strips*)** — These contain a cluster of stores, usually housed in one long building, serving a neighborhood's needs for groceries, hardware, laundry, shoe repair, and dry cleaning. They usually serve people who live nearby.
- ***A location within a larger store*** — Certain well-known retailers—McDonald's, Starbucks, Dunkin' Donuts—locate new, smaller units as concession space within larger stores or operations, such as airports, schools, or department stores.

Given the relationship between high traffic and high rents, retailers must decide on the most advantageous locations for their outlets. They can use various methods to assess locations, including traffic count, surveys of consumer shopping habits, and analysis of competitive locations.[27] Several models for site location have also been formulated.[28]

Retailers can assess a particular store's sales effectiveness by looking at four indicators: (1) number of people passing by on an average day; (2) percentage who enter the store; (3) percentage of those entering who buy; and (4) average amount spent per sale.

Nanjing Road—How does Shanghai's Nanjing Road fare relative to Paris' Champs-Elysées, London's Oxford Street, Tokyo's Ginza, and Chicago's Michigan Avenue? According to a McKinsey study, there are six characteristics of world-class retail districts. It must have a rich history, distinctive architecture and retail formats, diverse commercial functions ranging from retail to culture and entertainment, exciting anchor tenants, convenient public infrastructure and a pleasant environment, and a strong public-private partnership. Nanjing Road has a rich history, being the former site of Shanghai's racetrack, and Park Hotel, Chairman Mao's favorite place. It also has a Concession-era marketplace for carpet peddlers and clairvoyants. Architecturally, elegant 1930s buildings and some Art Deco mansions from the Concession period can be found. The public transportation is fairly good and the government plays a strong role in rejuvenating the place. However, Nanjing Road fares poorly in attracting diversity, being predominantly department store-based, with the tenants (which are mostly state-owned enterprises) engaged in aging business formats. Nonetheless, Nanjing Road attracts the highest traffic (800,000 people on a weekday, two million on a weekend) compared to Champs-Elysées (500,000 to 700,000), Oxford Street (500,000), Ginza (250,000), and Michigan Avenue (120,000 to 210,000).[29]

Besides the main cities, some retailers may also consider establishing themselves in provincial cities to capitalize on potential growth. In countries such as China, where interest in logo-emblazoned fashion is high, luxury shops are opening stores even outside Beijing and Shanghai as the following example illustrates.

Luxury boutiques in China—The world's largest luxury brand, Louis Vuitton, opened its 338th boutique in Qingdao, a Chinese sea resort best known for its Tsingtao beer. Luxury brands are beginning their push into the provinces, to cities like Dalian, Chengdu, Xi'an, Hangzhou, and Qingdao. Rolling out products and hiring teams in secondary cities signals a company's conviction that there is serious profit potential. Experts say that China is the best thing to happen to luxury companies' bottom lines since Japan in the 1980s. According to a Louis Vuitton spokesman, affluent Chinese tourists are already spending more than Japanese tourists. Given its rapidly evolving environment, anticipating retail location is challenging. Vuitton has opted for hotel locations because hotel groups are financially stable partners and allow brands more control over the look of their boutiques than shopping malls. They also guarantee minimum traffic levels of target customers. In contrast, Gucci and Prada have a different strategy. In Hangzhou, they share part of a new, smart-looking store built by Lane Crawford, a Hong Kong department store. However, the entrance to the Gucci store is littered with paper and smells of French fries as McDonald's has moved next door.[30]

Suntec City, a major retail and office complex in Singapore, has a Fountain of Wealth that signifies good luck to its tenants and shoppers.

"Breakthrough Marketing: Wal-Mart" discusses the retailer's foray into Asia and the marketing decisions it had to make.

Aside from these practical considerations, many retailers in Asia also employ *feng shui* (literally meaning wind and water) in locating their retail outlets as well as in conducting other marketing activities. This refers to the use of geomancy and is discussed in more detail in "Marketing Insight: *Feng Shui* and Its Application to Retailing and Marketing in the Far East."

Private Labels

A growing trend and major marketing decision for retailers concerns private labels. A **private label brand** (also called reseller, store, house, or distributor brand) is one retailers and wholesalers develop. Retailers such as Benetton, The Body Shop, and Giordano carry mostly own-brand merchandise. Taiwan's Uni-President chain carries its own private labels such as Q instant noodle mix, AB yoghurt, and Chai Li Won tea drinks.

Some experts believe that 50 percent is the natural limit for carrying private brands because (1) consumers prefer certain national brands; and (2) many product categories are not feasible or attractive on a private-brand basis.

Private label penetration remains low across all Asian countries, even in countries where shopper awareness of house brands is high (85–95 percent).[31] In Hong Kong, Korea, Singapore, and Thailand, the percentage of shoppers who actually buy any private label is typically only 30–50 percent. The only two countries where more than half of urban shoppers claim to buy private label are Singapore (56 percent) and Korea (53 percent). Taiwan is the least developed market with only 27 percent of shoppers claiming to purchase private label products. According to an A.C. Nielsen survey of 38 markets in 14 product areas, three Asian markets were among markets showing the most rapid growth in sales of private label products: Thailand, Korea, and Singapore.[32]

Role of Private Labels

Why do intermediaries sponsor their own brands? First, they are more profitable. Intermediaries search for manufacturers with excess capacity who will produce the private label at a low cost. Other costs, such as R&D, advertising, sales promotion, and physical distribution are also much lower. This means that the private brander can charge a lower price and yet make a higher profit margin. Second, retailers develop exclusive store brands to differentiate themselves from competitors. For example, some domestic retailers in China have launched private labels as part of their strategy of fighting back against foreign competitors.

> **China Resources Enterprise (CRE)**—This chain operates more than 1,700 supermarkets and hypermarkets, including China Resources Vanguard stores. To fight against the likes of Carrefour and Wal-Mart, it has rolled out more than 60 private label products, including bottled water, shampoo, and body lotion. To build loyalty, it has a frequent shopper program where discounts are given. It has also sought to improve management by raiding managers from foreign chains. Half of the middle and senior managers in CRE's retail units have worked at foreign-owned stores.[33]

BREAKTHROUGH MARKETING

WAL-MART

Wal-Mart Stores, Inc. is the largest retailer in the world, with sales of $351.1 billion in 2007, 1.9 million employees, and 6,500 stores in 14 countries. Its foray into Asia has been successful in China, but less so in Japan and Hong Kong.

In China, part of Wal-Mart's expansion strategy is to look inland, where provincial governments have been aggressively wooing foreign investors. Despite their lower-per-capita incomes, inland cities can be more attractive than coastal locations. Fewer families buy cars, and many continue to live in low-cost, state-subsidized housing, leaving them with more disposable income. At Nanchang, Wal-Mart's sales per customer are about 90 percent of those in coastal cities. Joe Hatfield, CEO of Wal-Mart Asia, predicts that roughly half of Wal-Mart's growth in China will come from inland cities in future. In 2008, there were 97 Wal-Mart Supercenters, three SAM's Clubs, two neighborhood markets, and 101 Trust-Mart hypermarkets in China.

However, competition is keen for Wal-Mart in China. It competes with state-run chains such as Brilliance, China's largest retailer. In most Chinese cities, municipal governments control prime real estate, giving the edge to state-owned retailers. Foreign competitors like Carrefour are also no pushover. Carrefour entered China a year after Wal-Mart but has grown more rapidly. Carrefour forged alliances with local Chinese governments to circumvent many of Beijing's restrictions. It is China's largest foreign retailer and vows to match Wal-Mart's expansion store for store.

Wal-Mart keeps a close eye on its rivals. CEO Hatfield says, "You have to get out there and ask, 'What are our competitors doing that we're not?' You have to be hungry for new knowledge everyday." His pursuit of local knowledge produced differences in the look and feel of Wal-Mart stores in China. Chinese customers tend to shop by foot, and live in smaller apartments with smaller refrigerators. So they shop more frequently and buy in smaller quantities. Thus Wal-Mart devotes much floor space to food. Perishable products are prominently displayed and are stocked in a multitude of shapes, colors, and flavors. Another distinction is that Chinese customers like to examine the merchandise before buying, demanding that staff not only take a fitted sheet out of the plastic but also demonstrate it on an actual bed. They also like clamor. Managers can induce sales by restacking an item noisily in the middle of the floor. At most Supercenters, the best-selling items are $1-freshly prepared lunches comprising two meats, two vegetables, rice, and a cup of hot soup. Another innovation involves "retailtainment." Stores provide space for local school groups to perform, and organize daily activities for the elderly. Residents are welcomed to linger and enjoy the free air-conditioning.

One similarity though is the obsession with *tian tian ping jia*—everyday low prices: $8 for men's dress slacks, including alterations, $4.80 for dress shoes, DVD players for $23.97, and inline skates for $11. The products are often displayed with signs declaring the value of the discount obtained from suppliers by Wal-Mart buyers.

In Hong Kong, its Value Club hypermarket failed as non-car driving Hongkongers' lifestyles and small apartments were more suited to daily grocery shopping at neighborhood stores. To enter Japan, Wal-Mart bought a controlling stake in Seiyu department store. Since then, Seiyu's revenues and profits have been declining, as Wal-Mart has yet to articulate a clear strategy for its acquisition. Seiyu remains far from offering the storewide, permanent low prices characteristic of Wal-Mart. Seiyu has not been able to cut costs enough to allow it to offer the low prices to keep customers coming back. It offers a handful of weekly specials but otherwise keep prices relatively high—contrary to Wal-Mart's EDLP. One reason is that Japanese customers associate low prices with low quality and are suspicious when a retailer offers products at a much lower price. It is also difficult for Seiyu to take more costs out of its supply chain. Japanese consumers buy more fresh produce than shoppers elsewhere, making lowering costs tough. They also traditionally shop almost everyday, preferably at small convenience stores than at large lower-priced retailers.

Sources: William J. Holstein, "Why Wal-Mart Can't Find Happiness in Japan." *Fortune,* July 27, 2007; Jerry Useem, "Should We Admire Wal-Mart?" *Fortune,* March 8, 2004, pp. 118–121; *Wal-Mart China Fact Sheet*, March 2008, <www.walmart.com>; "Wal-Mart Opens First Store in Guizhou." *Business Daily Update,* May 31, 2004; "Japan's Seiyu Opens Wal-Mart Style Supermarket." April 2004, <www.retail-merchandise.com>; Ian Rowley, "Can Wal-Mart Woo Japan?" *BusinessWeek,* May 10, 2004; Rafael Nam and James Brooke, "Japan Gets a Taste of Wal-Mart." *New York Times,* late edition (East Coast), May 11, 2004, p. W1; Clay Chandler, "The Great Wal-Mart of China." *Fortune,* July 25, 2005, pp. 60–68; Andrew Browne and Kathy Chen, "Boom Echoes in China's Interior." *Wall Street Journal,* October 17, 2005, pp. 22–23; Ian Rowley, "Japan Isn't Buying the Wal-Mart Idea." *BusinessWeek,* February 28, 2005, pp. 24–25.

MARKETING INSIGHT • *FENG SHUI* AND ITS APPLICATION TO RETAILING AND MARKETING IN THE FAR EAST

Marketers in Asia have come to recognize that the supernatural attracts many Asians. Many folklores, taboos, and superstitious and religious connotations by colors, numbers, and symbols exist in Asia today. Marketers should thus capitalize on Asians' beliefs in the supernatural strategically.

Feng shui is a particularly good example. Widely applied in Chinese culture but also in Japan and Vietnam, it means "wind and water." It refers to the ancient art of geomancy—a calculated assessment of the most favorable conditions for any venture. It is believed that Man's destiny could be enhanced if there is a correct alignment of the environment's *chi* (invisible energy) with the human *chi*. Thus *feng shui* involves the art of placing things, ranging from the orientation of buildings to the furnishing of the interiors, to influence the *chi* of a site. Excellent living conditions contribute to good health, which in turn leads to success and prosperity. In Kuala Lumpur, for instance, the headquarters of Malaysian Airline System, Promet, and MUI were placed so that there was harmony and neutrality among the surrounding buildings. Objects used in the practice of *feng shui* include bright colors and/or light refracting surfaces such as mirrors, crystals, chimes and bells; living objects such as fountains; and heavy objects like rocks and sculptures.

Some general guidelines of *feng shui* include where the front door of a business should face for a favorable orientation. A law firm, a medical center, a trading company, or a shipping firm should face north or east, while a north or southeast facing is appropriate for saloons and retail stores. According to *feng shui*, an ideal retail shop is a corner plot with a cater-cornered entrance to draw in maximum *chi* and business. The entrance area should also be clear of obstacles or trees "to give the life forces a clear path to the house." If the entrance is too small, *feng shui* would suggest mirrored or reflective panels be added on either side of the opening. Crystal chandeliers are said to activate the *chi* and distribute it around the shop. Plants can be used to block off sharp corner projections. They help to allow the *chi* to rise and circulate, giving a growing, lively feeling to the space.

In addition, to have good *feng shui*, the building must face the water and be flanked by the mountains. It should also not block the view of the mountain spirits. Thus several major Hong Kong offices, such as the headquarters of HSBC, have see-through lobbies to keep the spirits happy. In contrast, sharp angles give off bad *feng shui*. This explains why the Bank of China in Hong Kong is perceived as having bad luck by many people. Similarly, The Gateway in Singapore has two triangular towers; its sharp edges and jutting points are traditionally considered inauspicious. However, to compensate, The Gateway has a northeast-southwest facing which is ideal in Singapore. The building's sharp edges thus slice through oncoming winds to reduce their power.

As *feng shui* also incorporates numerology, addresses and opening dates must be carefully chosen. The numbers 2, 5, 6, 8, 9, and 10 are deemed lucky, but not 4 which connotes death; while the letter A is favored over C (which sounds like death), F (for failure), and X (because it denotes something is wrong). To compensate for its bad geomancy, the Bank of China opened its doors in Hong Kong on August 8, 1988 (8/8/88), as the number eight connotes becoming rich. Similarly, the Beijing Olympics opened on August 8, 2008 (8/8/08) for auspiciousness.

Feng shui is big business in Asia. A company which consults an expert geomancer, and publicizes it, signals to its customers and employees that it cares for their prosperity and well-being. Hong Kong International Airport, for instance, engaged geomancy experts for advice to ward off evil and incorporated *feng shui* considerations in its design. Western firms in the region have also come to use *feng shui*. J. Walter Thompson, for example, has retained a *feng shui* expert in Hong Kong who visits its offices periodically and is consulted before major presentations. The practice has also spread around the world. City planners in Vancouver reportedly consulted a geomancy expert as have executives at Motorola Semiconductor in Phoenix.

Sources: Bernd H. Schmitt and Yigang Pan, "Managing Corporate and Brand Identities in the Asia-Pacific Region." *California Management Review*, Summer 1994, pp. 32-48; Martin M. Pegler, "The Art of *Feng Shui* in Visual Merchandising." *Retail Asia*, January/February 1996, pp. 37-40; and "*Feng Shui* Check for HK Airport." *Straits Times* (Singapore), November 12, 1996, p. 4; Swee Hoon Ang, "Chinese Consumers' Perception of Alpha-Numeric Brand Names." *Journal of Consumer Marketing*, 1997, 14(3), pp. 220-233; Thomas Kramer and Lauren Block, "Conscious and Nonconscious Components of Superstitious Beliefs in Judgment and Decision Making." *Journal of Consumer Research*, April 2008, 34, pp. 783-793.

In some cases, there has even been a return to "no branding" of certain staple consumer goods and pharmaceuticals. Carrefour, the originator of the French hypermarket, introduced a line of "no brands" in its stores in the early 1970s. Today, Japanese retailer Mujirushi Ryohin has taken Carrefours' strategy a step further by successfully defining its stores with the no-brand concept.

Mujirushi Ryohin—Mujirushi Ryohin's full name translates into "no-brand quality products." The Japanese retailer, known simply as "Muji," has become a huge success, with 387 outlets in 15 countries, including 34 in Europe. Until recently, it has been known in the United States only through products carried in the New York Museum of Modern Art store—an $8 aluminum business card holder and $42 collapsible speakers. But the no-brand retailer—which carries 7,000 products ranging from $4.00 socks to $115,000 prefab homes—is opening a 5,000-square-foot store in mid-town Manhattan. Its biggest challenge will be deciding what to charge for its wares. In Japan, low prices are a huge part of Muji's appeal. Another challenge will be to stay true to its no-brand ethos. Muji's intended audience is young 20 to 30-year-olds who are tired of in-your-face logos and designer goods. But its sleek, functional postindustrial products will probably seem anything but generic to U.S. consumers. Muji's products resonate with the minimalism of Japan's gardens and haiku poetry, and this is how the company will differentiate itself among the competition and—whether it wants to or not—become an identifiable brand.[34]

Generics are unbranded, plainly packaged, less expensive versions of common products such as soy sauce, paper towels, and canned fruits. They offer standard or lower quality at a price that may be as much as 20–40 percent lower than nationally advertised brands and 10–20 percent lower than retailer private label brands. The lower price of generics is made possible by lower-quality ingredients, lower-cost labeling and packaging, and minimal advertising.

The Private Label Threat

In the confrontation between manufacturers' and private brands, retailers have many advantages and increasing market power. Because shelf space is scarce, many supermarkets now charge a *slotting fee* for accepting a new brand, to cover the cost of listing and stocking it. Retailers also charge for special display space and in-store advertising space. They typically give more prominent display to their own brands and make sure they are well-stocked. Retailers are now building better quality into their store brands.

The growing power of store brands is not the only factor weakening national brands. Consumers are more price-sensitive. They are noting better quality as competing manufacturers and national retailers copy and duplicate the qualities of the best brands. The continuous barrage of coupons and price specials has trained a generation of shoppers to buy on price. The fact that companies have reduced advertising to 30 percent of their total promotion budget has weakened their brand equity. The endless stream of brand extensions and line extensions has blurred brand identity and led to a confusing amount of product proliferation.

Manufacturers have reacted to the private label threat, in part, by spending substantial amounts of money on consumer-directed advertising and promotion to maintain strong brand preference. The prices have to be somewhat higher to cover the higher promotion cost. At the same time, mass distributors pressure manufacturers to put more promotional money into trade allowances and deals if they want adequate shelf space. Once manufacturers start giving in, they have less to spend on advertising and consumer promotion, and their brand leadership spirals down. This is the national brand manufacturers' dilemma.

To maintain their power, leading brand marketers should invest in heavy and continuous R&D to bring out new brands, line extensions, features, and quality improvements. They must sustain a strong "pull" advertising program to maintain high consumer brand recognition and preference. They must find ways to partner with major mass distributors in a joint search for logistical economies and competitive strategies that produce savings.

Cutting all unnecessary costs allows national brands to command a price premium, although it cannot exceed the value perceptions of consumers.[35] "Marketing Memo: How to Compete Against Store Brands" reflects on the severity of the private-label challenge and what leading brand marketers must do in response.[36]

MARKETING MEMO • HOW TO COMPETE AGAINST STORE BRANDS

Steenkamp and Kumar have identified what they feel are the most successful strategies for launching, leveraging, and competing against store brands. Based on extensive research, Kumar and Steenkamp begin their analysis with a number of observations of the sometimes surprising realities of private labels in the marketplace.

- **Private labels are ubiquitous.** Currently, store brands are present in over 95 percent of consumer packaged-goods categories and have made huge inroads in a variety of other industries, from apparel to books, from financial services to pharmaceuticals.
- **Consumers accept private labels.** Two-thirds of consumers around the world believe that "supermarket-owned brands are a good alternative to other brands."
- **Private-label buyers come from all socioeconomic strata.** It is considered "smart" shopping to purchase private-label products of comparable quality for a much lower price, rather than being "ripped off" by high-priced manufacturer brands.
- **Private labels are not a recessionary phenomenon.** Part of private-label growth in a recession is permanent, caused by consumer learning. As consumers learn about the improved quality of private labels in recessions, a significant proportion of them remain loyal to private labels, even after the necessity to save money is over.
- **Consumer loyalty shifts from manufacturers to retailers.** Consumers are becoming first and foremost loyal to a specific retailer.
- **Profits flow from manufacturers to retailers.** Between 1996 and 2003, U.S. retailers gained five share points of the combined manufacturer and retailer profit pool and more than 50 percent of the system profit growth.

Steenkamp and Kumar believe manufacturer brands must accept these new private-label realities and respond aggressively. They offer four key sets of strategic recommendations for manufacturers to compete against or collaborate with private labels.

- **Fight selectively** where manufacturers can win against private labels and add value for consumers, retailers, and shareholders. This is typically where the brand is one or two in the category or occupying a premium niche position.
- **Partner effectively** by seeking win-win relationships with retailers through strategies that complement the retailer's private labels.
- **Innovate brilliantly** with new products to help beat private labels. Continuously launching incremental new products keeps the manufacturer brands looking fresh, but this must be punctuated by periodically launching radical new products.
- **Create winning value propositions** by imbuing brands with symbolic imagery as well as functional quality that beats private labels. Too many manufacturer brands have let private labels equal and sometimes better them on functional quality. In addition, to have a winning value proposition, the pricing needs to be monitored closely to ensure that perceived benefits are equal to the price premium.

Sources: Jan-Benedict E.M. Steenkamp and Nirmalya Kumar, *Private Label Strategy: How to Meet the Store-Brand Challenge*, (Boston: Harvard Business School Press, 2007).

Wholesaling

Wholesaling includes all the activities involved in selling goods or services to those who buy for resale or business use. Wholesaling excludes manufacturers and farmers because they are engaged primarily in production, and it excludes retailers. Wholesalers (also called *distributors*) differ from retailers in a number of ways. First, wholesalers pay less attention to promotion, atmosphere, and location because they are dealing with business customers rather than final consumers. Second, wholesale transactions are usually larger than retail transactions, and wholesalers usually cover a larger trade area than retailers. Third, the government deals with wholesalers and retailers differently in terms of legal regulations and taxes.

Why are wholesalers used at all? Why do manufacturers not sell directly to retailers or final consumers? In general, wholesalers are used when they are more efficient in performing one or more of the following functions:

- ***Selling and promoting***— Wholesalers' sales forces help manufacturers reach many small business customers at a relatively low cost. Wholesalers have more contacts, and often buyers trust wholesalers more than they trust a distant manufacturer.
- ***Buying and assortment building***— Wholesalers are able to select items and build the assortments their customers need, saving the customers considerable work.
- ***Bulk breaking***— Wholesalers achieve savings for their customers through buying in large carload lots and breaking the bulk into smaller units.

- ***Warehousing*** — Wholesalers hold inventories, thereby reducing inventory costs and risks to suppliers and customers.
- ***Transportation*** — Wholesalers can often provide quicker delivery to buyers because they are closer to the buyers.
- ***Financing*** — Wholesalers finance customers by granting credit, and finance suppliers by ordering early and paying bills on time.
- ***Risk bearing*** — Wholesalers absorb some risk by taking title and bearing the cost of theft, damage, spoilage, and obsolescence.
- ***Market information*** — Wholesalers supply information to suppliers and customers regarding competitors' activities, new products, price developments, and so on.
- ***Management services and counseling*** — Wholesalers often help retailers improve their operations by training sales clerks, helping with store layouts and displays, and setting up accounting and inventory-control systems. They may help industrial customers by offering training and technical services.

Trends in Wholesaling

Manufacturers always have the option of bypassing wholesalers or replacing inefficient wholesalers with better ones. Manufacturers' major complaints against wholesalers are as follows: they do not aggressively promote the manufacturer's product line, and act more like order takers; they do not carry enough inventory and therefore fail to fill customers' orders fast enough; they do not supply the manufacturer with up-to-date market, customer, and competitive information; they do not attract high-caliber managers and bring down their own costs; and they charge too much for their services.

Some large manufacturers and retailers moved aggressively into direct buying programs. Savvy wholesalers then began to re-engineer their businesses. Successful wholesaler-distributors adapted their services to meet their suppliers' and target customers' changing needs. They recognized that they had to add value to the channel. They also had to reduce their operating costs by investing in more advanced materials-handling technology, information systems, and the Internet. Some have even gone into the retail business as the following example shows.

H.P. France NY—When Japan-based H.P. France NY, operator of 43 stores across Asia and Europe, arrived in the U.S., it planned for the first time to institute both a retail and wholesale platform. The result was Destination—a sleek, lofty boutique in Manhattan's Meatpacking District. Upstairs, a wholesale showroom houses about six up-and-coming European and Japanese accessories brands such as Jacques Le Corre, Minima Moralia, and Nneuhs. It feels that with a showroom, it can reach a wider audience, the public.

Narus and Anderson interviewed leading industrial distributors and identified four ways they strengthened their relationships with manufacturers: (1) They sought a clear agreement with their manufacturers about their expected functions in the marketing channel; (2) They gained insight into the manufacturers' requirements by visiting their plants and attending manufacturer association conventions and trade shows; (3) They fulfilled their commitments to the manufacturer by meeting the volume targets, paying bills promptly, and feeding back customer information to their manufacturers; and (4) They identified and offered value-added services to help their suppliers.[37]

Asian wholesalers are also beginning to reap the benefits of strengthened relationships with their principals.

Coca-Cola—Many of Coca-Cola's wholesalers in China have worked with the beverage company for 10–15 years, although their scale and scope have evolved over time. They were distributors for other manufacturers earlier in their relationship with Coca-Cola. One partner in Xinmi had businesses that included fast food and audio/visual equipment. Recognizing the business potential for developing a Coca-Cola delivery network in Xinmi and confident of its future with the company, the partner is now solely committed to selling Coca-Cola. Similarly, a small wholesaler in Jiangsu has expanded his sales network given his relationship with Coca-Cola. In return, he credits Coca-Cola for equipping him with business management skills for a modern market economy. His association with Coca-Cola also enhanced the image and profitability of his business.[38]

The wholesaling industry remains vulnerable to one of the most enduring trends—fierce resistance to price increases and the winnowing out of suppliers based on cost and quality. The trend toward vertical integration, in which manufacturers try to control or own their intermediaries, is still strong.

Market Logistics

Physical distribution starts at the factory. Managers choose a set of warehouses (stocking points) and transportation carriers that will deliver the goods to final destinations in the desired time or at the lowest total cost. Physical distribution has now been expanded into the broader concept of **Supply Chain Management (SCM).** Supply chain management starts before physical distribution: it involves procuring the right inputs (raw materials, components, and capital equipment); converting them efficiently into finished products; and dispatching them to the final destinations. An even broader perspective calls for studying how the company's suppliers themselves obtain their inputs. The supply chain perspective can help a company identify superior suppliers and distributors, and help them improve productivity, which ultimately brings down the company's costs. "Marketing Insight: Toyota's Supplier Relationships" shows how Toyota successfully employs knowledge sharing to enhance relationships with its suppliers.

MARKETING INSIGHT • TOYOTA'S SUPPLIER RELATIONSHIPS

When Toyota first posted profits that exceeded the combined earnings of its three largest competitors, some experts say one reason for its superior performance lies in Toyota's relationships with its suppliers. At Toyota, three processes are the key to its successful value proposition to its suppliers—supplier associations, consulting groups, and learning teams.

The objective of the supplier association, called *kyohokai* in Japan, is to provide a regular forum for Toyota to share information with and elicit feedback from its suppliers. The association holds both general-assembly meetings (bimonthly) and topic committee meetings (monthly or bimonthly). The former allows high-level sharing of knowledge regarding production plans, policies, and market trends within the supplier network. The latter allows more frequent interactions on cost, quality, safety, and social activities. For example, the quality committee picks a theme for the year, such as "eliminating supplier design defects," and meets bimonthly to share knowledge on that topic.

Toyota also provides expert consultants to assist its suppliers. The Operations Management Consulting Division (OMCD) acquires, stores, and diffuses valuable production knowledge residing within the Toyota Group. It consists of six highly experienced senior executives along with 50 consultants. About 15–20 are permanent members of the OMCD, while the rest are fast-track younger individuals who deepen their knowledge of the Toyota Production System (TPS) by spending three- to five-year rotations at the OMCD. Toyota sends these in-house experts to suppliers, sometimes months at a time, to help them solve problems implementing the TPS. Toyota does not charge for its consultants' time, instead making the OMCD a resource available to all its members.

Finally, Toyota organizes voluntary learning groups called *jishuken* among its key suppliers. With the help of an OMCD consultant, the teams spend months addressing problems in each member's plant. *Jishuken* are an advanced knowledge-sharing mechanism in Japan through which members learn as a group, exploring new ideas and applications of TPS. The team then transfers lessons learnt to Toyota through the supplier network.

These processes have evolved Toyota into a knowledge-sharing network and provided a vehicle for a shared identity among Toyota suppliers. Instead of merely bilateral ties between Toyota and each of its suppliers, suppliers began to form ties with each other. These multilateral relationships facilitate the flow of knowledge so that members are able to learn much faster than rival, nonparticipating suppliers.

Sources: Jeffrey H. Dyer and Nile W. Hatch, "Using Supplier Networks to Learn Faster." *MIT Sloan Management Review,* Spring 2004, 45(3), pp. 57–63.

Market logistics involves planning the infrastructure to meet demand, then implementing and controlling the physical flows of materials and final goods from points of origin to points of use, to meet customer requirements at a profit.

Market logistics represent a major challenge for distributors in Asia. Geographic distances, population density, and supporting infrastructure impact market access and logistics efficiency. At one extreme, Hong Kong and Singapore are small, with concentrated populations served by sound infrastructure. In contrast, China's vast and often unfriendly geography hinders the development of an effective transportation network. Total spending on logistics makes up at least 15 percent of China's GDP compared to less than 10 percent in the U.S. Logistics operations account for more than 90 percent of the time taken to get products on to shelves and make up 20 percent of the cost of goods. However, with China now a member of the WTO, logistics operators have much to look forward to. Trade will be boosted as more shipping lines and air-cargo carriers serve China. Greater outsourcing of logistics services is likely to occur. The market share of third-party logistics providers will increase as logistics giants set up operations in China. Currently, third-party logistics providers have a penetration rate of 2 percent of China's overall logistics business compared to the 8 percent of U.S. and 10 percent of Europe's.[39]

Market logistics planning has four steps:[40]

1. Deciding on the company's value proposition to its customers. (What on-time delivery standard should be offered? What levels should be attained in ordering and billing accuracy?)
2. Deciding on the best channel design and network strategy for reaching the customers. (Should the company serve customers directly or through intermediaries? What products to source from which manufacturing facilities? How many warehouses to maintain and where should they be located?)
3. Developing operational excellence in sales forecasting, warehouse management, transportation management, and materials management.
4. Implementing the solution with the best information systems, equipment, policies, and procedures.

Market logistics leads to an examination of the most efficient way to deliver value:

- A software company normally sees its challenge as producing and packaging software disks and manuals, then shipping them to wholesalers—who ship them to retailers, who sell them to customers. Customers bring the software package to home or office and download the software onto a hard drive. Market logistics would look at two superior delivery systems. The first involves ordering the software to be downloaded onto the customer's hard drive. The second system allows software to be loaded onto a computer by the computer manufacturer. Both solutions eliminate the need for printing, packaging, shipping, and stocking millions of disks and manuals. The same solutions are available for distributing music, newspapers, video games, films, and other products that deliver voice, text, data, or images.
- The IKEA Retailers, franchisees of the world-famous IKEA concept for retail sale of furniture and home furnishings, are able to sell good-quality furniture and home furnishings at 20 percent less than competitors. The cost savings stem from several sources: (1) The IKEA Retailers buy in such large volume that they get lower prices; (2) the furniture and home furnishings are designed in "knockdown" form and shipped flat at a much lower transportation cost; (3) the customer drives the furniture home, which saves delivery cost; and (4) the customer assembles the furniture. The IKEA concept works on a low markup and high volume.

Integrated Logistics Systems

The market logistics task calls for **Integrated Logistics Systems (ILS)**, involving materials management, material flow systems, and physical distribution, abetted by information technology (IT). Third-party suppliers, such as FedEx Logistics Services, often participate in designing or managing these systems. Volvo, working with FedEx, set up a warehouse in Memphis with a complete stock of truck parts. A dealer, needing a part in an emergency, phones a toll-free number, and the part is flown out the same day and delivered that night either at the airport or at the dealer's office or even at the roadside repair site. Here is an Asian example involving Hong Kong-based Li & Fung:

> **Li & Fung**—Li & Fung offers MNC clients like Avon, The Limited, Tesco, and Reebok, everything from buying raw materials to planning production and monitoring manufacturing. It orchestrates the production, comes up with samples, and feeds them information. Its full-service sourcing network includes every Asian country and stretches to South Africa and Mexico. To service Avon, Li & Fung has a dedicated Avon division that develops, sources, and delivers 300–400 products a year to Avon units in North America, Australia, Germany, Japan, China, and Britain. The cycle begins nine months to a year prior to launch when Avon develops new products in line with marketing themes while Li & Fung estimates consumer demand in each market. Six to eight months prior to launch, Li & Fung determines what goes into the product and the cheapest way to make it. Three to five months before launch, Li & Fung selects the raw material suppliers and assembly points, performs quality control, and organizes export documentation and shipping. This enables Avon to showcase the products at sales-representative conferences and sell the product via catalog and direct sales channels to consumers one to three months before the launch.[41]

Information systems play a critical role in managing market logistics, especially computers, point-of-sale terminals, uniform product bar codes, satellite tracking, Electronic Data Interchange (EDI), and Electronic Funds Transfer (EFT). These developments have shortened the order-cycle time, reduced clerical labor, reduced the error rate in documents, and provided improved control of operations. They have enabled companies to make promises such as "the product will be at dock 25 at 10:00 a.m. tomorrow," and control this promise through information.

Market logistics involves several activities. The first is sales forecasting, on the basis of which the company schedules distribution, production, and inventory levels. Production plans indicate the materials the purchasing department must order. These materials arrive through inbound transportation, enter the receiving area, and are stored in raw-material inventory. Raw materials are converted into finished goods. Finished-goods inventory is the link between customer orders and manufacturing activity. Customers' orders draw down the finished-goods inventory level, and manufacturing activity builds it up. Finished goods flow off the assembly line and pass through packaging, in-plant warehousing, shipping-room processing, outbound transportation, field warehousing, and customer delivery and servicing.

Management has become concerned about the total cost of market logistics, which can amount to 30–40 percent of the product's cost. Lower market-logistics costs will permit lower prices, yield higher profit margins, or both. Even though the cost of market logistics can be high, a well-planned program can be a potent tool in competitive marketing. Companies can attract additional customers by offering better service, faster cycle time, or lower prices through market-logistics improvements.

Market-Logistics Objectives

Many companies state their market-logistics objective as "getting the right goods to the right places at the right time for the least cost." Unfortunately, this objective provides little practical guidance. No system can simultaneously maximize customer service and minimize distribution cost. Maximum customer service implies large inventories, premium transportation, and multiple warehouses, all of which raise market-logistics costs.

A company cannot achieve market-logistics efficiency by asking each market-logistics manager to minimize his or her own logistics costs. Market-logistics costs interact and are often negatively related. For example:

- The traffic manager favors rail shipment over air shipment because rail costs less. However, because the railroads are slower, rail shipment ties up working capital longer, delays customer payment, and might cause customers to buy from competitors who offer faster service.

- The shipping department uses cheap containers to minimize shipping costs. Cheaper containers lead to a higher rate of damaged goods and customer ill-will.
- The inventory manager favors low inventories. This increases stockouts, back orders, paperwork, special production runs, and high-cost fast-freight shipments.

Given that market-logistics activities involve strong trade-offs, decisions must be made on a total system basis. The starting point is to study what customers require and what competitors are offering. Customers are interested in on-time delivery, supplier willingness to meet emergency needs, careful handling of merchandise, supplier willingness to take back defective goods and resupply them quickly.

The company ultimately has to establish some promise to the market. Coca-Cola wants to "put Coke within an arm's length of desire." Some companies define standards for each service factor. One appliance manufacturer has established the following service standards: to deliver at least 95 percent of the dealer's orders within seven days of order receipt, to fill the dealer's orders with 99 percent accuracy, to answer dealer inquiries on order status within three hours, and to ensure that damage to merchandise in transit does not exceed 1 percent.

Given the market-logistics objectives, the company must design a system that will minimize the cost of achieving these objectives. Each possible market-logistics system will lead to the following cost:

$$M = T + FW + VW + S$$

where, M is total market-logistics cost of proposed system, T is total freight cost of proposed system, FW is total fixed warehouse cost of proposed system, VW is total variable warehouse costs (including inventory) of proposed system, and S is total cost of lost sales due to average delivery delay under proposed system.

Choosing a market-logistics system calls for examining the total cost (M) associated with different proposed systems and selecting the system that minimizes it. If it is hard to measure S, the company should aim to minimize $T + FW + VW$ for a target level of customer service.

Market-Logistics Decisions

Four major decisions must be made with regard to market logistics: (1) How should orders be handled? (order processing); (2) Where should stocks be located? (warehousing); (3) How much stock should be held? (inventory); and (4) How should goods be shipped? (transportation).

ORDER PROCESSING

Most companies today are trying to shorten the *order-to-payment cycle*—that is, the elapsed time between an order's receipt, delivery, and payment. This cycle involves many steps, including order transmission by the salesperson, order entry and customer credit check, inventory and production scheduling, order and invoice shipment, and receipt of payment. The longer this cycle takes, the lower the customer's satisfaction and the lower the company's profits. Salespeople may be slow in sending in orders and use inefficient communications; these orders may pile up on the desk of order processors while they wait for credit department approval and inventory availability information from the warehouse.

Companies need to prepare criteria for the Perfect Order. Suppose the customer expects on-time delivery, order completeness, picking accuracy, and billing accuracy. Suppose the supplier has a 70 percent chance of delivering all four of these perfectly on any order. Then the probability that the supplier will fulfill perfect orders five times in a row to that customer would be $0.70^5 = 0.168$. The customer's series of disappointments is likely to lead him to drop this supplier. A 70 percent standard is not good enough.

Changi International Airport Services—Changi International Airport Services (CIAS) prepares inflight meals for airlines such as Air France, KLM, and Lufthansa. It has introduced a wireless system that improves in-flight meal ordering and catering. Called Wireless Meal Ordering, the system equips airline representatives with PDAs which directly connect them by wireless networking technology to CIAS's back-end computer system. When passenger numbers change, or when there are last-minute requests for special meals, airline reps can make changes on the fly. In the past, miscommunications arose when airline reps had to write down the new orders and place phone calls to CIAS's kitchen. The PDA can also be used to broadcast urgent messages, such as change of flight details, to airline reps and CIAS staff.[42]

WAREHOUSING

Every company has to store finished goods until they are sold, because production and consumption cycles rarely match. The storage function helps to smooth discrepancies between production and quantities desired by the market. The company must decide on the number of inventory stocking locations. While more stocking locations means that goods can be delivered to customers more quickly, it also means higher warehousing and inventory costs. To reduce warehousing and inventory duplication costs, the company might centralize its inventory in one place and use fast transportation to fulfill orders. After National Semiconductor shut down its six storage warehouses and set up a central distribution warehouse in Singapore, its standard delivery time decreased by 47 percent, its distribution costs fell 2.5 percent, and its sales increased 34 percent.[43]

Some inventory is kept at or near the plant, and the rest is located in warehouses in other locations. The company might own private warehouses and also rent space in public warehouses. *Storage warehouses* store goods for moderate-to-long periods of time. *Distribution warehouses* receive goods from various company plants and suppliers and move them out as soon as possible. *Automated warehouses* employ advanced materials-handling systems under the control of a central computer.

Some warehouses are now taking on activities formerly done in the plant. These include assembly, packaging, and constructing promotional displays. "Postponing" finalization of the offering can achieve savings in costs and finer matching of offerings to demand.

INVENTORY

Inventory levels represent a major cost. Salespeople would like their companies to carry enough stock to fill all customer orders immediately. However, this is not cost-effective. *Inventory cost increases at an accelerating rate as the customer service level approaches* 100 *percent.* Management needs to know how much sales and profits would increase as a result of carrying larger inventories and promising faster order fulfillment times, and then make a decision.

Inventory decision making involves knowing when to order and how much to order. As inventory draws down, management must know at what stock level to place a new order. This stock level is called the *order (reorder) point.* An order point of 20 means reordering is required when the stock falls to 20 units. The order point should balance the risks of stockout against the costs of overstock. The other decision is how much to order. The larger the quantity ordered, the less frequently an order has to be placed. The company needs to balance order-processing costs and inventory-carrying costs. *Order-processing costs* for a manufacturer consist of *setup costs* and *running costs* (operating costs when production is running) for the item. If setup costs are low, the manufacturer can produce the item often, and the average cost per item is stable and equal to the running costs. If setup costs are high, however, the manufacturer can reduce the average cost per unit by producing a long run and carrying more inventories.

Order-processing costs must be compared with *inventory-carrying costs.* The larger the average stock carried, the higher the inventory-carrying costs. These carrying costs include storage charges, cost of capital, taxes and insurance, and depreciation and obsolescence. Carrying costs might run as high as 30 percent of inventory value. This means that marketing managers who want their companies to carry larger inventories need to show that the larger inventories would produce incremental gross profit to exceed incremental carrying costs.

The optimal order quantity can be determined by observing how order-processing costs and inventory-carrying costs sum up at different order levels. Figure 16.2 shows that the order-processing cost per unit decreases with the number of units ordered because the order costs are spread over more units. Inventory-carrying charges per unit increase with the number of units ordered because each unit remains longer in inventory. The two cost curves are summed vertically into a total-cost curve. The lowest point on the total-cost curve is projected down on the horizontal axis to find the optimal order quantity Q^*.[44]

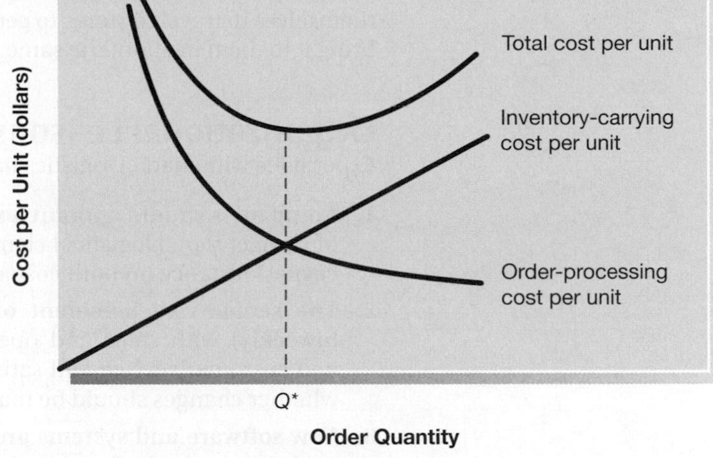

Figure 16.2 Determining Optimal Order Quantity

Companies are reducing their inventory costs by treating inventory items differently. They are positioning inventory items according to risk and opportunity. They distinguish between bottleneck items (high-risk, low-opportunity), critical items (high-risk, high-opportunity), commodities (low-risk, high-opportunity), and nuisance items (low-risk, low-opportunity).[45] They are also keeping slow-moving items in a central location while carrying fast-moving items in warehouses closer to customers.

The ultimate answer to carrying *near-zero inventory* is to build for order, not for stock. Sony calls it SOMA, "sell-one, make-one." Dell, for example, gets the customer to order a computer and pay for it in advance. Then Dell uses the customer's money to pay suppliers to ship the necessary components. As long as customers do not need the item immediately, everyone can save money.

Some retailers are using eBay to unload excess inventory. Several big chains have set up "eBay Stores," Web pages devoted to their merchandise. They use the pages to auction off an assortment of items ranging from overstock goods to returned, reconditioned or slightly damaged products. By cutting out the traditional liquidator middleman, retailers can make 60–80 cents on the dollar as opposed to 10 cents on the dollar.

TRANSPORTATION

Marketers need to be concerned with transportation decisions. Transportation choices will affect product pricing, on-time delivery performance, and the condition of the goods when they arrive, all of which affect customer satisfaction.

In shipping goods to its warehouses, dealers, and customers, the company can choose among five transportation modes: rail, air, truck, waterway, and pipeline. Shippers consider such criteria as speed, frequency, dependability, capability, availability, traceability, and cost. For speed, air, rail, and truck are the prime contenders. If the goal is low cost, then it is water and pipeline.

Shippers are increasingly combining two or more transportation modes, thanks to containerization. **Containerization** consists of putting the goods in boxes or trailers that are easy to transfer between two transportation modes. *Piggyback* describes the use of rail and trucks; *fishyback*, water and trucks; *trainship*, water and rail; and *airtruck*, air and trucks. Each coordinated mode offers specific advantages. For example, piggyback is cheaper than trucking alone, yet provides flexibility and convenience.

In deciding on transportation modes, shippers can choose from private, contract, and common carriers. If the shipper owns its own truck or air fleet, the shipper becomes a *private carrier*. A *contract carrier* is an independent organization selling transportation services to others on a contract basis. A *common carrier* provides services between predetermined points on a scheduled basis and is available to all shippers at standard rates.

Today billions of dollars are being invested to develop "last-mile delivery systems" to bring products to homes within a short delivery period. Domino's Pizza organized its franchised stores to be in locations where it could promise to deliver hot pizzas to homes within one-half hour. Consumers may soon think twice about whether they should exert themselves to travel to stores to get their food, videos, or clothes or simply ask the stores to bring it to them in about the same amount of time.

Organizational Lessons

Experience with market logistics has taught executives three major lessons:

1. **Companies should appoint a senior vice president of logistics** to be the single point of contact for all logistical elements. This executive should be accountable for logistical performance on both cost and customer-satisfaction criteria.
2. **The senior vice president of logistics should hold periodic meetings (weekly, biweekly)** with sales and operations people to review inventory, operating costs, and customer service and satisfaction, as well as to consider market conditions and whether changes should be made in production schedules.
3. **New software and systems are the key** to achieving competitively superior logistics performance in the future.

Market-logistics strategies must be derived from business strategies, rather than solely from cost considerations. The logistics system must be information-intensive and establish electronic links among all the significant parties. Finally, the company should set its logistics goals to match or exceed competitors' service standards and should involve members of all relevant teams in the planning process.

Asahi Breweries—When Asahi Breweries decided to make freshness a key selling point in its marketing plan, it overhauled its entire inventory and delivery system. Now, trucks arriving at warehouses are directed to a specific dock by a computer, which also generates the correct merchandise order. The benefits extend beyond the goal of shipping all beer within five days of production. In aiming to promote the product's freshness, Asahi ended up speeding up operations at every level and subsequently derived dramatic cost reductions. For instance, it cut its inventory from 3 days to 1.8 days, thus freeing up working capital.[46]

What happens if a firm's market logistics are not set up properly? Kodak launched a national advertising campaign for a new instant camera before it had delivered enough cameras to the stores. Customers found that it was not available and bought Polaroid cameras instead.

Today's stronger demands for logistical support from large customers will increase suppliers' costs. Customers want more frequent deliveries so that they do not have to carry as much inventory. They want a shorter order-cycle time, which means that suppliers will have to carry high in-stock availability. Customers often want direct store delivery rather than shipments to distribution centers. They want mixed pallets rather than separate pallets. They want tighter promised delivery times. They may want custom packaging, price tagging, and display building.

Suppliers cannot reject many of these requests, but at least they can set up different logistical programs with different service levels and customer charges. Smart companies will adjust their offerings to each major customer's requirements. The company's trade group will set up *differentiated distribution* by offering different bundled service programs for different customers.

Summary

1. Retailing includes all the activities involved in selling goods or services directly to final consumers for personal, non-business use. Retailers can be understood in terms of store retailing, non-store retailing, and retail organizations.
2. Like products, retail-store types pass through stages of growth and decline. As existing stores offer more services to remain competitive, costs and prices go up, which opens the door to new retail forms that offer a mix of merchandise and services at lower prices. The major types of retail stores are specialty stores; department stores; supermarkets; convenience stores; discount stores; off-price retailers (factory outlets, independent off-price retailers, and warehouse clubs); superstores (combination stores and supermarkets); and catalog showrooms.
3. Although most goods and services are sold through stores, non-store retailing has been growing. The major types of non-store retailing are direct selling (one-to-one selling, one-to-many-party selling, and multilevel network marketing); direct marketing (which includes e-commerce and Internet retailing); automatic vending; and buying services.
4. Although many retail stores are independently owned, an increasing number are falling under some form of corporate retailing. Retail organizations achieve many economies of scale, such as greater purchasing power, wider brand recognition, and better-trained employees. The major types of corporate retailing are corporate chain stores, voluntary chains, retailer cooperatives, consumer cooperatives, franchise organizations, and merchandising conglomerates.
5. Like all marketers, retailers must prepare marketing plans that include decisions on target markets, product assortment and procurement, services and store atmosphere, price, promotion, and place. These decisions must take into account major trends, such as new retail forms and combinations, growth of intertype retail competition, competition between store-based and non-store-based retailing, growth of giant retailers, growing investment in technology, and global presence of major retailers.
6. Wholesaling includes all the activities involved in selling goods or services to those who buy for resale or business use. Wholesalers can perform functions better and more cost-effectively than the manufacturer can. These functions include selling and promoting, buying and assortment building, bulk breaking, warehousing, transportation, financing, risk bearing, dissemination of market information, and provision of management services and consulting.
7. There are four types of wholesalers: merchant wholesalers; brokers and agents; manufacturers' and retailers' sales branches, sales offices, and purchasing offices; and miscellaneous wholesalers such as agricultural assemblers and auction companies.
8. Like retailers, wholesalers must decide on target markets, product assortment and services, price, promotion, and place. The most successful wholesalers are those who adapt their services to meet suppliers' and target customers' needs.
9. Producers of physical products and services must decide on market logistics—the best way to store and move goods and services to market destinations, to coordinate the activities of suppliers, purchasing agents, manufacturers, marketers, channel members, and customers. Major gains in logistical efficiency have come from advances in information technology.

Application

Marketing Debate—Should National Brand Manufacturers Also Supply Private Label Brands?

One controversial move by some marketers of major brands is to supply private label makers. For example, Ralston-Purina and Heinz have admitted to supplying products—sometimes lower in quality—to be used for private labels. However, other marketers criticize this "if you can't beat them, join them" strategy, maintaining that these actions, if revealed, may create confusion or even reinforce a perception by consumers that all brands in a category are essentially the same.

Take a position: *Manufacturers should feel free to sell private labels as a source of revenue* versus *National manufacturers should never get involved with private labels.*

Marketing Discussion

Think of your favorite stores. What is it that they do that encourages your loyalty? What do you like about the in-store experience?

PART 7

Communicating Value

The "Evolution" ad video, transforming an ordinary-looking woman's face into the image of a supermodel, was just one of the creative marketing communications that sparked Dove's recent shift in marketing strategy.

Designing and Managing Integrated Marketing Communications

17

Modern marketing calls for more than developing a good product, pricing it attractively, and making it accessible. Companies must also communicate with present and potential stakeholders, and the general public. For most companies, the question is not whether to communicate but rather what to say, how to say it, to whom, and how often. But communications gets harder as more companies clamor to grab the consumer's increasingly divided attention. To effectively reach and influence target markets, holistic marketers are creatively employing multiple forms of communications.[1]

Dove has been a Unilever stalwart for decades, backed by traditional advertising touting the brand's benefit of one-quarter moisturizing cream and exhorting women to take the seven-day Dove test to discover its effects. A significant shift in strategy occurred for Dove in 2003 with the launch of the Real Beauty campaign, which celebrates "real women" of all shapes, sizes, ages, and colors. The campaign arose from research revealing that only 2 percent of women worldwide considered themselves beautiful. In Asia, the campaign featured flat-chested Asian women, women with gray hair or freckles—not traditional models. The ads promoted Dove skin products such as Intensive Firming Cream, Lotion, and Body Wash. The multimedia campaign was thoroughly integrated. Traditional TV and print ads were combined with all forms of new media, such as real-time voting for models on mobile phones and tabulated displays of results on giant billboards. PR was dialed up; paid media was dialed down. The Internet was crucial for creating a dialogue with women. A Web site was launched and supplemented with ad videos. The Dove "Evolution" video showed a rapid-motion view of an ordinary-looking woman transformed by makeup artists, hairdressers, lighting, and digital retouching to look like a model. When it was uploaded to YouTube by Dove's ad agency Ogilvy & Mather, it was an instant viral hit, drawing 2.5 million views. Although the campaign sparked much debate, it was credited with boosting Dove sales and share in every country in which it was launched. It received the Grand Effie for the most effective marketing campaign in 2006 from the American Marketing Association.[2]

In this chapter, we will address the following questions:

1. What is the role of marketing communication?
2. How do marketing comunications work?
3. What are the major steps in developing effective communication?
4. What is the communications mix and how should it be set?
5. What is an integrated marketing communications program?

Marketing communications can have a huge payoff. This chapter describes how communications work and what marketing communications can do for a company. It also addresses how holistic marketers combine and integrate marketing communications. Chapter 18 examines the different forms of mass (non-personal) communications (advertising, sales promotion, events and experiences, and public relations and publicity); while Chapter 19 examines the different forms of personal communications (direct marketing, including e-commerce and personal selling).

The Role of Marketing Communications

Marketing communications is the means by which firms attempt to inform, persuade, and remind consumers—directly or indirectly—about the products and brands that they sell. In a sense, marketing communications represents the "voice" of the brand and is a way to establish a dialogue and build relationships with consumers.

Marketing communications performs many functions for consumers. Consumers can be told or shown how and why a product is used, by what kind of person, and where and when; consumers can learn about who makes the product and what the company and brand stand for; and consumers can be given an incentive or reward for trial or usage. Marketing communications allows companies to link their brands to other people, places, events, brands, experiences, feelings, and things. Marketing communications can contribute to brand equity by establishing the brand in memory and crafting a brand image.

Marketing Communications and Brand Equity

Although marketing communications can play a number of crucial roles, they must do so in an increasingly tough communication environment. Technology and other factors have profoundly changed the way consumers process communications, and even whether they choose to process them. The rapid diffusion of powerful broadband Internet connections, ad-skipping digital video recorders, multipurpose mobile phones, and portable music and video players have forced marketers to rethink a number of their traditional practices.[3] These dramatic changes have eroded the effectiveness of the mass media.[4]

While some marketers flee traditional media, they still encounter challenges. Commercial clutter is rampant, and it seems the more consumers tune out marketing appeals, the more marketers try to dial them up. In the U.S., the average city dweller is exposed to 3,000 to 5,000 ad messages a day. In Asia, city dwellers are similarly bombarded with communications stimuli. In Japan, train straps bear the name and picture of advertised watches. Even commercial aircraft is not spared. AirAsia, Malaysia's budget airline, has an alliance with English football club Manchester United (MU). Its Red Devil Airbus is painted in MU's official all-red strip with the club's renowned personalities such as Sir Alex Ferguson, Wayne Rooney, Cristiano Ronaldo, and Park Ji Sung.[5] With ads in almost every medium and form on the rise, some consumers feel they are becoming increasingly invasive.[6]

In this new communication environment, although advertising is often a central element of a marketing communications program, it is usually not the only one—or even the most important one—in terms of building brand equity and driving sales. Consider how Nike chose to introduce the latest version of its successful line of sneakers endorsed by basketball star LeBron James:

A wide range of marketing activities supported the traditional advertising in Nike's campaign introducing a new line of sneakers endorsed by basketball star LeBron James.

Nike Air Zoom LeBron IV—Nike's launch of the new version of its shoe line was supported by a wide range of traditional and non-traditional communications that included the first episode of *Sports Center* on ESPN to be sponsored by a single advertiser; the distribution of 400,000 copies of DVDs about the making of the shoe and the ad campaign; saturation advertising on espn.com, mtv.com, and other Web sites; a "pop-up retail store" in Manhattan; video clips appearing as short programs on the MTV2 cable network; and a retro-chic neon billboard near Madison Square Garden that showed a continuously dunking Mr. James. The campaign also featured television ads and online video featuring James as "the LeBrons," characters who represent four sides of his personality and who first appeared in ads for the Nike Air Zoom LeBron III shoe the previous year, as well as print ads.[7]

MARKETING COMMUNICATIONS MIX

The **marketing communications** mix consists of six major modes of communication:[8]

1. ***Advertising*** — Any paid form of non-personal presentation and promotion of ideas, goods, or services by an identified sponsor.
2. ***Sales promotion*** — A variety of short-term incentives to encourage trial or purchase of a product or service.
3. ***Events and experiences*** — Company-sponsored activities and programs designed to create daily or special brand-related interactions.
4. ***Public relations and publicity*** — A variety of programs designed to promote or protect a company's image or its individual products.
5. ***Direct marketing*** — Use of mail, telephone, fax, email, or the Internet to communicate directly with or solicit response or dialogue from specific customers and prospects.
6. ***Personal selling*** — Face-to-face interaction with one or more prospective purchasers for the purpose of making presentations, answering questions, and procuring orders.

Table 17.1 lists numerous communication platforms. Company communication goes beyond those specific platforms. The product's styling and price, the shape and color of the package, the salesperson's manner and dress, the store decor, the company's stationery—all communicate something to buyers. Every *brand contact* delivers an impression that can strengthen or weaken a customer's view of the company.

As Figure 17.1 shows, marketing communication activities contribute to brand equity in many ways: by creating awareness of the brand; linking the right associations to the brand image in consumers' memory; eliciting positive brand judgments or feelings; and/or facilitating a stronger consumer-brand connection.

Table 17.1 Common Communication Platforms

Advertising	Sales Promotion	Events/ Experiences	Public Relations & Publicity	Personal Selling	Direct Marketing
Print and broadcast ads	Contests, games, sweepstakes, lotteries	Sports	Press kits	Sales presentations	Catalogs
Packaging—outers	Premiums and gifts	Entertainment	Speeches	Sales meetings	Mailings
Packaging inserts	Samples	Festivals	Seminars	Incentive programs	Telemarketing
Motion pictures	Fairs and trade shows	Arts	Annual reports	Samples	Electronic shopping
Brochures and booklets	Exhibits	Causes	Charitable donations	Fairs and trade shows	TV shopping
Posters and leaflets	Demonstrations	Factory tours	Sponsorships		Fax mail
Directories	Coupons	Company museums	Publications		Email
Reprints of ads	Rebates	Street activities	Community relations		Voice mail
Billboards	Low-interest financing		Lobbying		
Display signs	Entertainment		Identity media		
Point-of-purchase displays	Trade-in allowances		Company magazine		
Audiovisual materials	Continuity programs				
Symbols and logos	Tie-ins				
Videotapes and CD-ROMs					

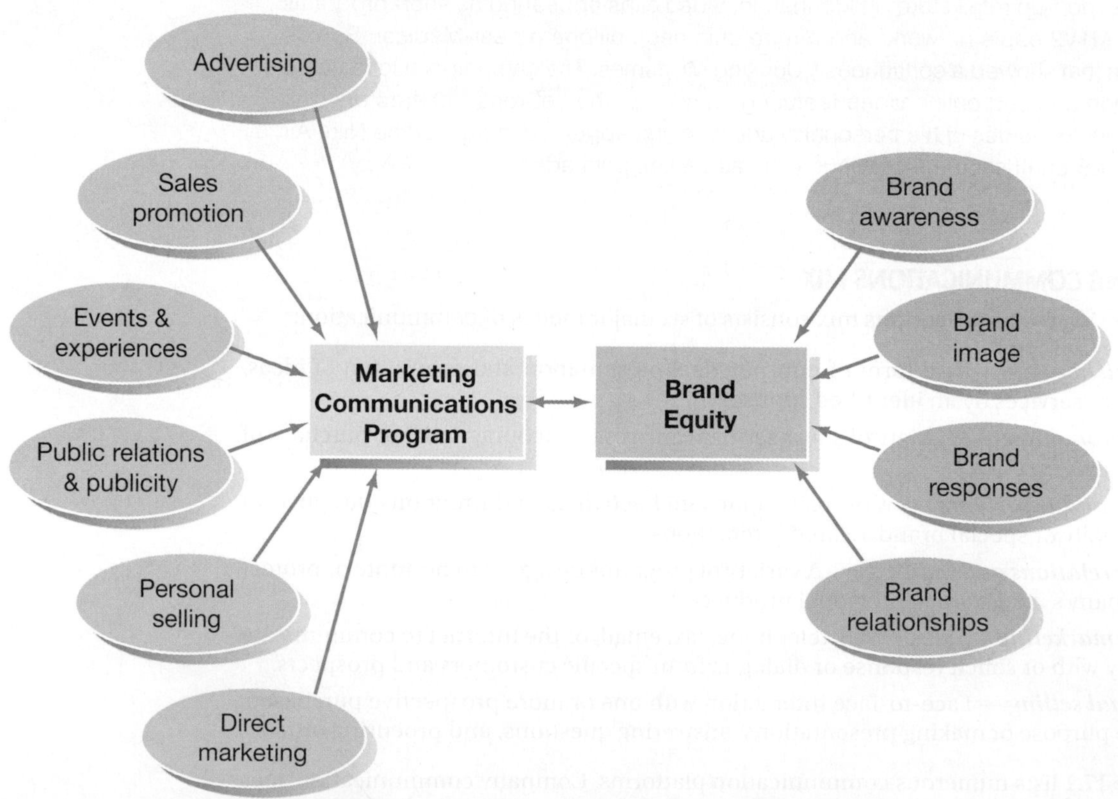

Figure 17.1 Integrating Marketing Communications to Build Brand Equity

MARKETING COMMUNICATION EFFECTS

The manner in which brand associations are formed does not matter. In other words, if a consumer has an equally strong, favorable, and unique brand association of Subaru with the concepts "outdoors," "active," and "rugged" because of exposure to a TV ad that shows the car driving over rugged terrain at different times of the year, or because Subaru sponsors ski, kayak, and mountain bike events, the impact in terms of Subaru's brand equity should be identical.

But these marketing communications activities must be integrated to deliver a consistent message and achieve the strategic positioning. The starting point in planning marketing communications is an audit of all the potential interactions that customers in the target market may have with the company and all its products and services. For example, someone interested in purchasing a new laptop computer might talk to others, see television ads, read articles, look for information on the Internet, and look at laptops in a store.

Marketers need to assess which experiences and impressions will have the most influence at each stage of the buying process. This understanding will help them allocate communications dollars more efficiently and design and implement the right communications programs. Armed with these insights, marketers can judge marketing communications according to its ability to affect experiences and impressions, build brand equity, and drive brand sales. For example, how well does a proposed ad campaign contribute to awareness or to creating, maintaining, or strengthening brand associations? Does a sponsorship cause consumers to have more favorable brand judgments and feelings? To what extent does a promotion encourage consumers to buy more of a product? At what price premium?

Nike—Nike has "a history of making controversial ads," says former VP Charlie Denson. Such ads have made its brand stand out from its competitors, which is particularly crucial in Asia. For example, in Singapore where graffiti is not allowed, it plastered over 700 bus terminals with graffiti-like posters of basketball star LeBron James. Nike went ahead despite being warned by Henry Goh, the sales and marketing director of Clear Channel, which owns the bus terminals. Clear Channel received over 50 complaints from angry adult commuters. However, older people are not the target market for Nike. "We heard that teenagers liked it so much they tried to take some of the posters off the bus shelters as souvenirs," Goh adds. Similarly, Nike spokeswoman Shelley Peng says that its ads, while upsetting older mainland consumers, are popular with Chinese teens.[9]

From the perspective of building brand equity, marketers should be "media neutral" and evaluate *all* the different possible communication options according to effectiveness criteria (how well does it work) as well as efficiency considerations (how much does it cost). This broad view of brand-building activities is especially relevant when marketers are considering strategies to improve brand awareness.[10]

Anything that causes the consumer to notice and pay attention to the brand—such as sponsorship and out-of-home advertising—can increase brand awareness, at least in terms of brand recognition. To enhance brand recall, however, more intense and elaborate processing may be necessary, so that stronger brand links to the product category or consumer needs are established to improve memory performance.

Motorola—As part of its brand differentiation efforts in China, Motorola supported Project Hope, launched by the Chinese Education Ministry, by building many elementary schools in the most remote and poorest rural areas, donating computers to middle and high schools, and establishing Motorola Scholarships with leading Chinese universities. Motorola received highly favorable publicity and media coverage, and enhanced its image among young Chinese consumers.[11]

The Communication Process Models

Marketers should understand the fundamental elements of effective communication. Two models are useful: a macromodel and a micromodel.

MACROMODEL OF THE COMMUNICATION PROCESS

Figure 17.2 shows a macro communication model with nine elements. Two elements represent the major parties in a communication—*sender* and *receiver*. Two represent the major communication tools—*message* and *media*. Four represent major communication functions—*encoding, decoding, response,* and *feedback*. The last element in the system is *noise* (random and competing messages that may interfere with the intended communication).[12]

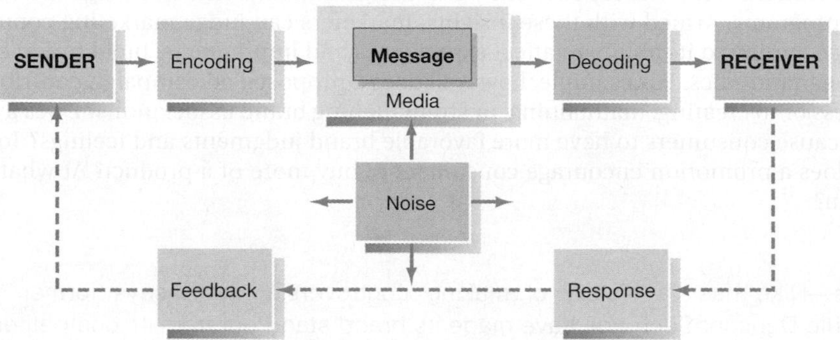

Figure 17.2 Elements in the Communication Process

The model emphasizes the key factors in effective communication. Senders must know what audiences they want to reach and what responses they want to get. They must encode their messages so that the target audience can decode them. They must transmit the message through media that reach the target audience and develop feedback channels to monitor the responses. The more the sender's field of experience overlaps with that of the receiver, the more effective the message is likely to be.

Note that selective attention, distortion, and retention processes—concepts first introduced in Chapter 6—may be operating during communication.

MICROMODEL OF CONSUMER RESPONSES

Micromodels of marketing communications concentrate on consumers' specific responses to communications. Figure 17.3 summarizes four classic *response hierarchy models.*

These models assume that the buyer passes through a cognitive, affective, and behavioral stage, in that order. This "learn-feel-do" sequence is appropriate when the audience has high involvement with a product category perceived to have high differentiation, as in purchasing an automobile or house. An alternative sequence, "do-feel-learn," is relevant when the audience has high involvement but perceives little or no differentiation within the product category, as in purchasing an airline ticket or personal computer. A third sequence, "learn-do-feel," is relevant when the audience has low involvement and perceives little differentiation within the product category, as in purchasing salt or batteries. By choosing the right sequence, the marketer can do a better job of planning communications.[13]

Here we will assume that the buyer has high involvement with the product category and perceives high differentiation within the category. We will illustrate the *hierarchy-of-effects model* (in the second column of Figure 17.3).

- ***Awareness***— If most of the target audience is unaware of the object, the communicator's task is to build awareness. For instance, in China, car dealers are generally not involved in direct selling. Hence, car manufacturers rely heavily on advertising to raise brand

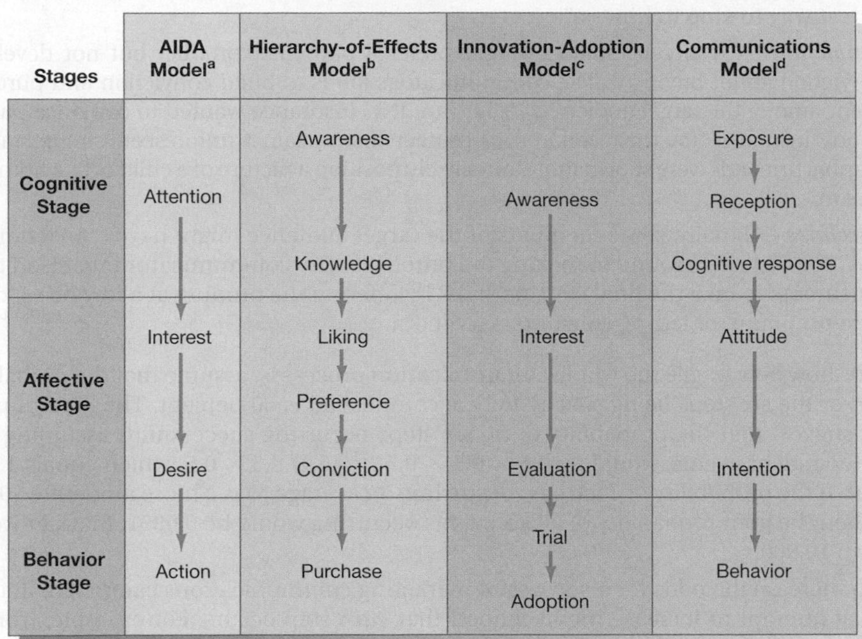

Figure 17.3 Response Hierarchy Models

Sources: [a]E. K. Strong, *The Psychology of Selling* (New York: McGraw-Hill, 1925): 9; [b]Robert J. Lavidge and Gary A. Steiner, "A Model for Predictive Measurements of Advertising Effectiveness," *Journal of Marketing* (October 1961): 61; [c]Everett M. Rogers, *Diffusion of Innovation*, 5th ed., (New York: The Free Press, 1995); [d]various sources.

awareness and influence consumer decision. Says A.C. Nielsen China, "Brand awareness is the essential indicator of brand health, although not the only one." A.C. Nielsen found that high media spending does not necessarily relate to high brand awareness. Volkswagen has the highest brand awareness. But locally-produced cars have greater awareness in Beijing than in Shanghai and Guangzhou because there are more private car owners in Beijing while the latter cities have a substantial number of corporate car owners.[14]

- ***Knowledge*** — The target audience might have brand awareness but not know much more. When the Clear Blue home pregnancy test kit was launched in Hong Kong, a simple approach was used to show how easy it was to use this relatively new product. The main space in the print ad was devoted to two Chinese characters—one meaning "yes," (有) and the other meaning "no" (冇). The characters are similar, with "yes" having two horizontal lines through the central square in the character. The lines are colored blue, giving potential customers a direct message of how the test works. The lines imply double happiness—a great joy for the pregnant woman as well as the family expecting the arrival of the baby.
- ***Liking*** — If target members know the brand, how do they feel about it? Good public relations calls for "good deeds followed by good words." Shanghai beer brand Reeb ("beer" spelt backwards) showed a TV commercial depicting everyday city scenes which touched the hearts of Shanghainese.
- ***Preference*** — The target audience might like the product but not prefer it to others. In this case, the communicator must try to build consumer preference by comparing quality, value, performance, and other features to likely competitors. To create preference for 999 Ointment in China, a print ad was created using typography that works only for Chinese characters. The nine characters can be read from left to right, right to left, top to bottom, or bottom to top. Regardless of the direction in which the ad was processed, the characters read "Itchiness stops fast," "Stops itchiness fast," or

"Fast stopping itchiness." The idea was "however you look at it, 999 Ointment is the fastest way to stop itchiness."

- ***Conviction*** — A target audience might prefer a particular product but not develop a conviction about buying it. The communicator's job is to build conviction and purchase intent among the target audience. In Taiwan, ING Insurance wanted to convince parents to buy insurance for their children to protect them against unforeseen circumstances. Graphic print ads were shown that strategically position a picture of a child over a homeless person.
- ***Purchase*** — Finally, some members of the target audience might have conviction but may not quite get around to making the purchase. The communicator must lead these consumers to take the final step, perhaps by offering the product at a low price, offering a premium, or letting consumers try it out.

To show how fragile the whole communication process is, assume that the probability of *each* of the six steps being successfully accomplished is 50 percent. The laws of probability suggest that the probability of *all* six steps occurring successfully, assuming they are independent events, would be $0.5 \times 0.5 \times 0.5 \times 0.5 \times 0.5 \times 0.5$, which equals 1.5625 percent. If the probability of each step occurring, on average, was a more moderate 10 percent, then the joint probability of all six events occurring would be 0.0001. In other words, only 1 in 10,000!

To increase the odds for a successful marketing communications campaign, marketers must attempt to increase the likelihood that *each* step occurs. For example, from an advertising standpoint, the ideal ad campaign would ensure that:

1. The right consumer is exposed to the right message at the right place and at the right time.
2. The ad causes the consumer to pay attention to it but does not distract from the intended message.
3. The ad properly reflects the consumer's level of understanding about the product and the brand.
4. The ad correctly positions the brand in terms of desirable and deliverable points-of-difference and points-of-parity.
5. The ad motivates consumers to consider purchase of the brand.
6. The ad creates strong brand associations to all of these stored communication effects so that they can have an effect when consumers are considering making a purchase.

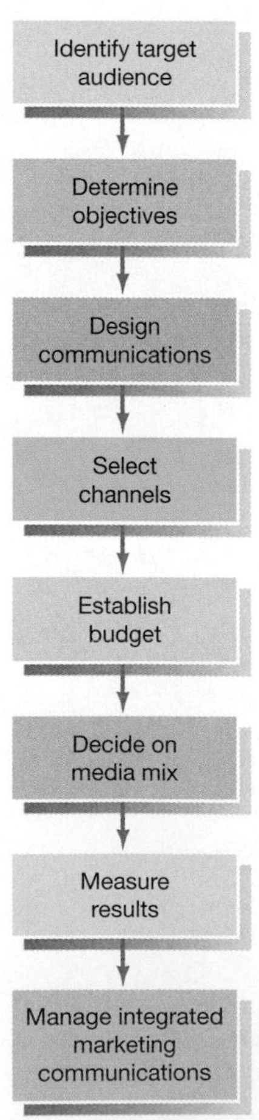

Figure 17.4 Steps in Developing Effective Communications

Developing Effective Communications

Figure 17.4 shows the eight steps in developing effective communications. We begin with the basics: identifying the target audience, determining the objectives, designing the communications, selecting the channels, and establishing the budget.

Identify the Target Audience

The process must start with a clear target audience in mind: potential buyers of the company's products, current users, deciders, or influencers; individuals, groups, particular publics, or the general public. The target audience is a critical influence on the communicator's decisions on what to say, how to say it, when to say it, where to say it, and to whom to say it.

The target audience can potentially be profiled in terms of any of the market segments identified in Chapter 8. It is often useful to define a target audience in terms of usage and loyalty. Is the target new to the category or a current user? Is the target loyal to the brand, loyal to a competitor, or someone who switches between brands? If the target is a brand user, is he or she a heavy or light user? Communication strategy will differ depending on the usage and loyalty involved. We can also conduct *image analysis* to provide further insight by profiling target audience in terms of brand knowledge.

Za—Japanese make-up brand, Za, underwent a complete facelift in Bangkok. After a long courtship with Thai teens and failing to live up to sales and profit expectations, Za targeted the 20- to 30-year olds. In addition to a logo change, the advertising carried a more mature "Be Beautiful Today" tagline instead of the younger "Be Sparkling, Be Yourself" slogan. It also featured Asian models to make the brand more relevant to Thai consumers. Through market research, Za found that older consumers were more concerned with health and skincare. Hence, its proportion of skincare products increased 30–50 percent. Additionally, the target group was interested in whitening products. Its campaign initially focused on PR and outdoor ads, and marketing of the whitening products was achieved through point-of-sales advertising, road shows, and sampling exercises at office buildings in Bangkok.[15]

Design the Communications

Formulating the communications to achieve the desired response will require solving three problems: *what to say* (message strategy), *how to say it* (creative strategy), and *who should say it* (message source).

MESSAGE STRATEGY

In determining message strategy, management searches for appeals, themes, or ideas that will tie into the brand positioning and help to establish points-of-parity or points-of-difference. Some of these may be related directly to product or service performance (the quality, economy, or value of the brand) whereas others may relate to more extrinsic considerations (the brand as being contemporary, popular, or traditional).

Maloney saw buyers as expecting one of four types of reward from a product: rational, sensory, social, or ego satisfaction.[16] Buyers might visualize these rewards from results-of-use experience, product-in-use experience, or incidental-to-use experience. Crossing the four types of rewards with the three types of experience generates 12 types of messages. For example, the appeal "gets clothes cleaner" is a rational-reward promise following results-of-use experience. The phrase "real beer taste in a great light beer" is a sensory-reward promise connected with product-in-use experience.

It is widely believed that industrial buyers are most responsive to performance messages. They are knowledgeable about the product, trained to recognize value, and accountable to others for their choices. Consumers, when they buy certain big-ticket items, also tend to gather information and estimate benefits.

CREATIVE STRATEGY

Communications effectiveness depends on how a message is being expressed as well as the content of the message itself. An ineffective communication may mean that the wrong message was used or the right message was just being expressed poorly. *Creative strategies* are how marketers translate their messages into a specific communication. Creative strategies can be broadly classified as involving either "informational" or "transformational" appeals.[17] These two general categories each encompass several different specific creative approaches.

Informational Appeals

An *informational appeal* elaborates on product or service attributes or benefits. Examples in advertising are problem-solution ads (Panadol stops headache pain quickly), product demonstration ads (Kao's Family Kyukyutto dishwashing detergent's sparkling squeaky-clean finish upon rinsing), product comparison ads (SingTel offers better mobile coverage than M1), and testimonials from unknown or celebrity endorsers (NBA star Yao Ming pitching for Reebok). Informational appeals assume very rational processing of the communication on the part of the consumer. Logic and reason rule.

Hovland's research has shed much light on informational appeals and their relation to such issues as conclusion drawing, one- versus two-sided arguments, and order of argument presentation. Some early experiments supported stating conclusions for the audience. Subsequent research, however, indicates that the best ads ask questions and allow readers and viewers to form their own conclusions.[18] If Honda had hammered away that the Element was for young people, this strong definition might have blocked older age groups from buying it. Some stimulus ambiguity can lead to a broader market definition and more spontaneous purchases.

You would think that one-sided presentations that praise a product would be more effective than two-sided arguments that also mention shortcomings. Yet two-sided messages may be more appropriate, especially when negative associations must be overcome. Examples include "Heinz Ketchup is slow good" and "Listerine tastes bad twice a day."[19] Two-sided messages are more effective with more educated audiences and those who are initially opposed.[20]

Finally, the order in which arguments are presented is important.[21] For a one-sided message, presenting the strongest argument first has the advantage of arousing attention and interest. This is important in media where the audience often does not attend to the whole message. With a captive audience, a climactic presentation might be more effective. For a two-sided message, if the audience is initially opposed, the communicator might start with the other side's argument and conclude with his or her strongest argument.[22]

Transformational Appeals

A *transformational appeal* elaborates on a non-product related benefit or image. It might depict what kind of person uses a brand or what kind of experience results from using the brand (soft shiny hair when using Lux shampoo). Transformational appeals often attempt to stir up emotions that will motivate purchase.

Communicators use negative appeals such as fear, guilt, and shame to get people to do things (brush their teeth, have an annual health checkup) or stop doing things (smoking, alcohol abuse, overeating). Fear appeals work best when they are not too strong. Further, fear appeals work better when source credibility is high and when the communication promises to relieve, in a believable and efficient way, the fear it arouses.[23]

Messages are most persuasive when they are moderately discrepant with what the audience believes. Messages that state only what the audience already believes at best only reinforce beliefs, and if the messages are too discrepant, they will be counter-argued and disbelieved.

Kraft—In its Singapore campaign for cheese singles titled, "The Body Builder for Kids," Kraft gave a clever twist to the common belief that cheese helps build strong bones. It used normal daily interactions between a parent and child and flipped their places. The unusual switch drew attention to an otherwise common belief. For example, one ad showed a father returning home from work and being swung up in the air by the child. This is a creative way to reinforce the message that Kraft Cheese Singles strengthens children.

KRAFT THE BODY BUILDER FOR KIDS
Kraft Singapore used unexpected visuals to draw attention to the message that Kraft Cheese Singles is "the Body Builder for Kids."

Communicators also use positive emotional appeals such as humor, love, pride, and joy. Motivational or "borrowed interest" devices—such as the presence of cute babies, frisky puppies, popular music, or provocative sex appeals—are often employed to attract consumer attention and raise their involvement with an ad. Borrowed interest techniques are thought to be necessary in the tough new media environment characterized by low involvement consumer processing and much competing ad and programming clutter. British singer Sting made a lucrative deal with Ford as part of the company's efforts to reach consumers aged 35 and above. In an ad for Jaguar, he was shown being driven around in the car while his hit single, "Desert Rose," played in the background.[24]

Although these borrowed interest approaches can attract attention and create more liking and belief in the sponsor, they may also detract from comprehension, wear out their welcome fast, and overshadow the product.[25] Attention-getting tactics are often *too* effective and distract from brand or product claims. Thus one challenge in arriving at the best creative strategy is figuring out how to "break through the clutter" to attract the attention of consumers—but still be able to deliver the intended message.

The magic to advertising is to bring concepts on a piece of paper to life in the minds of the consumer target. In a print ad, the communicator has to decide on headline, copy, illustration, and color. For a radio message, the communicator has to choose words, voice qualities, and vocalizations. If the message is to be carried on television or in person, all these elements plus body language (non-verbal clues) have to be planned. Presenters have to pay attention to facial expressions, gestures, dress, posture, and hairstyle. If the message is carried by the product or its packaging, the communicator has to pay attention to color, texture, scent, size, and shape.

Every detail matters. Think how the legendary ad taglines listed on the right were able to bring to life the brand themes listed on the left.

Brand Theme	Ad Tagline
• Our hamburgers are bigger.	• Where's the Beef? (Wendy's restaurants)
• We don't rent as many cars, so we have to do more for our customers.	• We Try Harder (Avis auto rental)
• 7-Up is not a cola.	• The Un-Cola (7-Up)

MESSAGE SOURCE

Many communications do not use a source beyond the company itself. Others use known or unknown people. Messages delivered by attractive or popular sources can potentially achieve higher attention and recall, which is why advertisers often use celebrities as spokespeople. Celebrities are likely to be effective when they personify a key product attribute. Zhang Ziyi's attention to perfection in the soup served in a restaurant did this for Visa; and Gong Li's beauty did this for Osim's health supplement brand Nourish Refine.

Osim used Chinese actress Gong Li to promote its health supplement, Nourish Refine.

What is important is the spokesperson's credibility. Pharmaceutical companies want doctors to testify about product benefits because doctors have high credibility. Anti-drug crusaders will use ex-drug addicts because they have higher credibility. What factors underlie source credibility? The three most often identified are expertise, trustworthiness, and likability.[26] *Expertise* is the specialized knowledge the communicator possesses to back the claim. *Trustworthiness* is related to how objective and honest the source is perceived to be. Friends are trusted more than strangers or salespeople, and people who are not paid to endorse a product are viewed as more trustworthy than people who are paid.[27] *Likability* describes the source's attractiveness. Qualities like candor, humor, and naturalness make a source more likable. The most highly credible source would be a person who scores high on all three dimensions. Often, celebrities like Yao Ming are used to endorse products, sometimes to great effect:

Yao Ming—This 2.3-meter tall basketball player is the symbol of the Chinese renaissance and its determination to compete on a world stage. Yao is so well-liked that he is a multiple-product endorser. A Gatorade ad featuring Yao, Derek Jeter, and Peyton Manning was rated the highest ever in likeability among consumers in Gatorade's history. Among others, Yao has a sponsorship deal with Reebok, and pitches for McDonald's and Visa for the Beijing Olympics. Appealing to audiences in both East and West, Yao is a tremendous global asset.[28]

"Marketing Insight: Celebrity Endorsements as a Strategy" focuses on the use of testimonials, while "Marketing Insight: Collectivism, Consensus Appeals, and Credibility" discusses the impact of Asia's predominantly collectivistic orientation on message design in the region.

MARKETING INSIGHT • CELEBRITY ENDORSEMENTS AS A STRATEGY

A well-chosen celebrity can draw attention to a product or brand, as when Hong Kong actress Bernice Liu showed how she slimmed down thanks to Marie France Bodyline; or, the celebrity's mystique can transfer to the brand—Yao Ming entertains with his basketball skills in a Gatorade ad.

The choice of the celebrity is critical. The celebrity should have high recognition, high positive affect, and high appropriateness to the product. Andy Lau has high recognition but may not appeal to all. Jackie Chan has high recognition and high positive affect but may not be appropriate for advertising personal hygiene products. Singers Jay Chou and Rain, and Korean film stars Bae Yong-Joon and Jeon Ji-Hyun may successfully advertise many products because they have extremely high ratings for familiarity and likability (known as the Q factor in the entertainment industry).

Athletes are commonly employed to endorse athletic products, beverages, and apparel. China basketball star Yao Ming is one of the hottest stars in television commercials in the U.S. He has appeared in campaigns for Apple Computers and Visa, and has deals with Gatorade, McDonald's, and Garmin. He is used not only to push the brands but also to create brand awareness in regions that these companies are penetrating, namely, China. In India where cricket is the national sport, stars such as Sachin Tendulkar are sought by ESPN-Star and Hero Honda to be their endorser.

Celebrities can play a more strategic role for their brands, not only endorsing a product but also helping design, position, and sell merchandise and services. Since signing Tiger Woods in 1996, Nike has seen its share of the golf ball market jump 1–6 percent. Woods has played a key role in developing a series of golf products and apparel that Nike has periodically altered to reflect his changing personality and design tastes.

Using celebrities poses certain risks. The celebrity might hold out for a larger fee at contract renewal time or withdraw. Just as can happen with movies and records, celebrity campaigns can sometimes be an expensive flop. Pepsi chose to drop star endorsers Britney Spears and Beyoncé Knowles, whose personalities may have been too overpowering for the brand, to focus on promoting occasions that go well with drinking Pepsi.

The celebrity might lose popularity or, even worse, get caught in a scandal or embarrassing situation. McDonald's chose not to renew a $12 million annual contract with basketball star Kobe Bryant after accusations of rape. Model Kate Moss was dropped from several endorsements when her drug addiction came to light.

Sources: Irving Rein, Philip Kotler, and Martin Scoller, *The Making and Marketing of Professionals into Celebrities,* (Chicago: NTC Business Books, 1997); Greg Johnson, "Woods' Cautious Approach to the Green." *Los Angeles Times*, July 26, 2000, p. A1; Theresa Howard, "Pepsi Takes Some Fizz Off Vanilla Rival." *USA Today*, November 16, 2003; Keith Naughton, "The Soft Sell." *Newsweek*, February 2, 2004, pp. 46–47; Betsy Cummings, "Star Power." *Sales and Marketing Management*, April 2001, pp. 52–59; Chris Isidore, "Yo! Yao Stands Alone." *CNNMoney*, February 28, 2003; "Yao Ming Signs New Endorsement." *People's Daily Online*, April 14, 2005.

If a person has a positive attitude toward a source and a message, or a negative attitude toward both, a state of *congruity* is said to exist. What happens if the person holds one attitude toward the source and the opposite toward the message? Suppose a consumer hears a likable celebrity praise a brand that she dislikes? Osgood and Tannenbaum say that *attitude change will take place in the direction of increasing the amount of congruity between the two evaluations.*[29] The consumer will end up respecting the celebrity somewhat less or respecting the brand somewhat more. If she encounters the same celebrity praising other disliked brands, she will eventually develop a negative

MARKETING INSIGHT • COLLECTIVISM, CONSENSUS APPEALS, AND CREDIBILITY

Individualism–collectivism is perhaps the most central dimension in cultural variability identified in cross-cultural research. Members of individualistic cultures (e.g., Western countries such as the U.S., Canada, and Australia) tend to hold an independent view of the self that emphasizes separateness, internal attributes, and the uniqueness of individuals. In contrast, members of collectivistic cultures (e.g., Asian countries such as Hong Kong, Taiwan, and Japan) tend to hold an interdependent view of the self that emphasizes connectedness, social context, and relationships.

In collectivistic cultures, the opinions of others or group norms are emphasized. Consensual decision making is thus characteristic of many Japanese corporations. Similarly, collectivistic Asian consumers prefer consensus appeals containing information involving others' opinions about or evaluations of an object. One study found that ads employing appeals that emphasize individualistic benefits were more persuasive in the U.S. than in Korea. In contrast, ads emphasizing family or in-group benefits were more persuasive in Korea than in the U.S. Given Asians' more interdependent orientation, consensus information may be perceived as being more diagnostic (i.e., important) and more accessible (i.e., readily retrieved from memory).

The thoughts, desires, and opinions of in-group members or significant, respected individuals are also considered to be more important by consumers in collectivistic than individualistic cultures. Thus expert and trustworthy sources may be considered more credible by collectivistic Asian than individualistic Western consumers. In contrast, no credibility differences in source attractiveness and likeability have been found across cultures, as these factors are unrelated to individualism–collectivism.

Sources: Jennifer L. Aaker and Durairaj Maheswaran, "The Effect of Cultural Orientation on Persuasion." *Journal of Consumer Research*, December 1997, pp. 315–328; Sang-Pil Han and Sharon Shavitt, "Persuasion and Culture: Advertising Appeals in Individualistic and Collectivistic Societies." *Journal of Experimental Social Psychology*, July 1994, pp. 326–350; Harry C. Triandis, "The Self and Behavior in Differing Cultural Contexts." *Psychological Review*, July 1989, pp. 506–552; Jennifer Aaker, "Accessibility or Diagnosticity? Disentangling the Influence of Culture on Persuasion Processes and Attitudes." *Journal of Consumer Research*, March 2000, pp. 340–357.

view of the celebrity and maintain her negative attitude toward the brands. The **principle of congruity** implies that communicators can use their good image to reduce some negative feelings toward a brand but, in the process, might lose some esteem with the audience.

GLOBAL ADAPTATIONS

Multinational companies wrestle with a number of challenges in developing global communications programs: They must decide whether the product is appropriate for a country. They must make sure the market segment they address is both legal and customary. They must decide if the style of the ad is acceptable, and they must decide whether ads should be created at headquarters or locally.[30]

1. **Product** — Many products are restricted or forbidden in certain parts of the world. Beer, wine, and spirits cannot be advertised or sold in Muslim countries. Tobacco products are subject to strict regulation in many countries.[31]
2. **Market segment** — In some countries like Norway and Sweden, no TV ads may be directed at children under 12.
3. **Style** — Comparative ads, while acceptable and even common in the U.S. and Canada, are less commonly used in Singapore, unacceptable in Japan, and illegal in India. PepsiCo had a comparative taste test ad in Japan that was refused by many TV stations and eventually led to a lawsuit (see "Marketing Insight: Comparative Advertising in Asia").
4. **Local or Global** — Today, more and more multinational companies are attempting to build a global brand image by using the same advertising in all markets. For example, HSBC launched a global advertising campaign called "The World's Local Bank" to brand itself as a bank that understands the intricacies of dealing with different cultures worldwide, and is thus able to serve its global customers better. Its research showed that compared to its competitors, which often had a distinctive national tone—Citibank is American, Barclays is British, and Deutsche Bank is German—HSBC was often described as the foreign bank or as an international bank. This has given HSBC's global brand an edge as a bank that does not offer the same products and services in every market.[32]

HSBC's "The World's Local Bank" campaign positions itself as a bank that understands cultural differences and hence, is able to serve its global customers better.

MARKETING INSIGHT • COMPARATIVE ADVERTISING IN ASIA

Comparative advertising takes different forms. Some are direct, identifying and comparing against the competitor. Others are more subtle, relying on image through the use of wit, humor, and visual elements to degrade the competition. In more individualistic societies like the U.S., comparative ads that highlight the superiority of the target brand are seen as more effective. Although its use in Asia is increasing, comparative advertising is still not well received among more traditional Asians. These collectivistic consumers are concerned with the loss of face involved in the public disparagement of rival brands in such ads.

In Philippines' first comparative ad, Mirinda claimed that taste tests showed more consumers preferred it to Royal Tru Orange. The latter complained and threatened to pull their ads from any media that carried Mirinda's claims. Comparative advertising was then banned in less than a year. Similarly, comparative advertising is often shunned in Japan as companies try to project a friend-next-door image of reliability and plainness. In Thailand, direct comparative advertising is non-existent as it is considered too "in-your-face." Moreover, as Thais tend to sympathize with the underdog, comparative advertising may well backfire. When used, comparative ads have a humorous slant. Thus Pepsi's comparative ad is effective in Thailand. It portrayed Coke drinkers as dull and boring, while Pepsi consumers are more vibrant and "hearty party" types.

Under China's Law Against Unfair Competition, advertisers cannot promote their products by defaming the credibility of another product by means other than confirmed scientific theory; exaggerate by means of comparison a flaw in a similar product; or use the message or logo of a competitor to benefit by association. Reeb beer used ads obliquely attacking Suntory, saying it is unnecessary to use spring water to brew beer. (Suntory's cans advertised the beer as being "Brewed with natural mineral water.") The city administrative bureau fined Shanghai Mila, Reeb's producer, for libel and ordered it to publicly apologize to Suntory.

Under what circumstances would comparative advertising be effective in Asia? Comparative advertising is likely to be more persuasive when the target audience consists mainly of the "me" generation who are more interested in how the brand benefits them than in what others think. When a brand can actually identify strong reasons why the target consumer should buy it in preference to others, comparative advertising can be used to highlight its clear superiority. Finesse is favored over logic and reason as Asians prefer more subtle and sophisticated comparisons to degrade competition.

Sources: Beting Laygo Dolor, "Comparative Advertising." *Manila Standard* (Philippines), October 9, 2002; Ken Belson, "Only Japan's Wealthy Welcome at This Bank." *New York Times*, March 3, 2002, p. 5; "China–Tiger's Fire!" *Media and Marketing Europe*, December 31, 2001; Xu Fang, "Suntory Beats Back Rival's Libelous Ads." *Shanghai Daily* (China), November 10, 1999; "Comparing Commercials." *Bangkok Post* (Thailand), May 28, 2001. For an excellent summary of comparative advertising research in general, see Dhruv Grewal, Sukumar Kavanoor, and James Barnes, "Comparative versus Noncomparative Advertising: A Meta-Analysis." *Journal of Marketing*, October 1997, pp. 1–15.

The management of marketing communications programs in Asia is accentuated when it must be coordinated pan-regionally. One study found more than half of the companies surveyed practice centralized decision making for ads regarding branding, coupled with local execution. At Compaq, for instance, strategic decisions are "100 percent out of Houston. But tactical ones are made by country because speed is of the essence" to react quickly to changing market conditions. A rare proponent for decentralization is Microsoft where advertising decisions are left very much to the discretion of the individual offices. Unilever is also at the extreme with a "glocal" strategy where local decisions are made regarding advertising.[33] Purely centralized strategies are less common. However, some businesses like L'Oréal employ a global approach with centralized decision making and a high degree of marketing communications standardization.[34]

Overall, regulatory, political, economic, infrastructural, and cultural variations across Asia must be considered in managing pan-regional marketing communications programs and messages:

- ***Regulations*** — Promoting certain products like alcohol and tobacco are restricted in Muslim countries in Asia. China has restrictive censorship rules for TV and radio advertising; the words "the best" are banned, as are ads that "violate social customs" or present women in "improper ways." Sometimes a company is required to change the manner in which it sells its products. Avon China was forced to open retail stores after the Chinese government banned direct selling. New advertising and promotion campaigns repositioned Avon as a retailer, rather than a direct marketer.[35]
- ***Politics*** — Companies may get caught in the middle of a sensitive political issue. Coca-Cola ran a campaign in mainland China featuring popular female Taiwanese singer A-Mei as an endorser for Sprite. Authorities in China blacklisted the star after she sang Taiwan's national anthem at the inauguration of the island's new president. Coca-Cola had to replace all television, print, and radio advertising that used her voice.[36] Asian markets are perceived to vary in their level of political risk. For example, China is viewed as being a higher risk but more attractive market than Singapore. Generally, the higher a market's political risk, the greater the need for marketing communications adaptation to satisfy local requirements.[37]
- ***Economics*** — The level of "ad literacy" varies as a function of economic development in the region. Simple, product- or user-oriented advertising emphasizing concrete, utilitarian, and functional appeals may be more effective in emerging Asian markets, while more sophisticated approaches using hedonistic, image- and lifestyle-oriented approaches are employed in developed Asian nations. Thus marketing communications in markets like Vietnam, India, and Indonesia aim to educate and inform consumers regarding what the product is, how it is used, and what its benefits are, while those in markets like Hong Kong, Taiwan, and Korea focus more on having and doing.[38] However, as regional economies develop, greater brand competition will occur where more identical offerings would have to be differentiated by image. Direct and straightforward appeals may work only for rural consumers who are faced with fewer brand choices, while urban consumers become more brand- and ad-savvy. For example, a Leo Burnett study of 500 consumers in China's five largest cities found urban consumers preferring more subtle executions that rely on humor and irony, and which do not talk down to them. Understandably, a Haier commercial did not go down well in the following focus group research:

Haier—The home appliance company was advertising a giant TV and included a stream of blurbs for the TV, one of which was about receiving email over the tube. A surfer rides the waves between skyscrapers, his wash leaving an "@" in the water. In a focus group interview, a Beijing woman remarked that the ad was "too direct." "There's this guy talking, telling me about the product, showing me some images. Yeah, we get it, we understand it—but we don't like it."[39]

- ***Infrastructure*** — Differences in marketing infrastructure such as media, ad agencies, and production facilities affect the feasibility of standardizing marketing communications. The availability of media in Asian markets and their relative levels of importance to target segments affect the transfer of communications strategy from one market to another. Media cost differences may cause standardization to be economically infeasible. For example, on a relative basis, Singapore has a limited number of advertising media, while it is difficult for businesses in China to determine which media reaches the target consumer at the best reach, frequency, and cost.[40]

- ***Culture*** — Most Asian countries have high-context (i.e., diffuse) cultures. This allows marketing communications to employ more symbolic and implicit messages across the region. However, for consumers to infer the same meaning from such messages, a high degree of homogeneity must exist in the society. This is the case in Japan and Korea, but is less so in Southeast Asia whose people come from more varied ethnic backgrounds. In Japan, for example, there is extensive use of short, 15-second TV commercials which leave viewers to draw their own conclusions. Japanese ads are also well-known for their dreamlike style of advertising where messages are so elusive and esoteric that they say nothing about the product.[41] Such symbolism deliberately flatters the audience because the ability to understand the ad is an indication of sophistication.[42] An ad by Japanese department store, Seibu, showed a picture of a six-month old baby swimming with his eyes wide open in clear blue water. The caption read: "Discovering Yourself."

Select the Communications Channels

Selecting efficient channels to carry the message becomes more difficult as channels of communication become more fragmented and cluttered. Communications channels may be personal and nonpersonal. Within each are many subchannels.

PERSONAL COMMUNICATION CHANNELS

Personal communication channels involve two or more persons communicating directly face-to-face, person-to-audience, over the telephone, or through email. Instant messaging and independent sites to collect consumer reviews are another means of growing importance in recent years. Personal communication channels derive their effectiveness through individualized presentation and feedback.

A further distinction can be drawn among advocate, expert, and social communication channels. *Advocate channels* consist of company salespeople contacting buyers in the target market. *Expert channels* consist of independent experts making statements to target buyers. *Social channels* consist of neighbors, friends, family members, and associates talking to target buyers.

Burson-Marsteller and Roper Starch Worldwide found that one influential person's word of mouth tends to affect the buying attitudes of two other people, on average. However, that circle of influence jumps to eight online. There is considerable consumer-to-consumer communication on the Web on a whole range of subjects. Online visitors increasingly create product information, not just consume it. They join Internet interest groups to share information, so that "word of Web" is joining "word of mouth" as an important buying influence. One pervasive Web-based communication channel is the blog. "A blog is where a person is responsible for talking about a range of things, for example, what new products are being developed, or 'Hey, we heard this from our customers.' It's written conversationally and is not so static," says Susannah Gardner, author of *Buzz Marketing with Blogs for Dummies*. Realizing their impact, businesses have jumped on the blogwagon to better connect with the public.

Words about good companies travel fast; words about bad companies travel even faster. As one marketer noted, "You don't need to reach two million people to let them know about a new product—you just need to reach the right 2,000 people in the right way and they will help you reach two million."[43]

Mister Donut—This doughnut chain created a stir in Taiwan when it first opened for business, attracting both the uninitiated and long-time doughnut lovers. Although Mister Donut relied on nothing but word of mouth to promote itself—no ads were placed on TV or in newspapers—people waited for hours, in the rain and cold weather, to buy the doughnuts. Mister Donut had to limit the number of doughnuts each customer could purchase per visit and employ interns to regulate lines and maintain order. Unlike other doughnut shops, Mister Donut offers breakfast pastries tailored to Asian preferences. Its doughnuts are not as sweet and are made from imported Japanese ingredients.[44]

Personal influence carries especially great weight in two situations. One is with products that are expensive, risky, or purchased infrequently. The other is where the product suggests something about the user's status or taste. People often ask others for a recommendation for a doctor, plumber, hotel, lawyer, accountant, architect, insurance agent, interior decorator, or financial consultant. If we have confidence in the recommendation, we normally act on the referral. In such cases, the recommender has potentially benefited the service provider as well as the service seeker. Service providers clearly have a strong interest in building referral sources.

NON-PERSONAL COMMUNICATION CHANNELS

Non-personal channels are communications directed to more than one person and include media, sales promotions, events, and publicity.

- **Media** consist of print media (newspapers and magazines), broadcast media (radio and television), network media (telephone, cable, satellite, wireless), electronic media (audiotape, videotape, videodisc, CD-ROM, Web page); and display media (billboards, signs, posters). Most non-personal messages come through paid media. Christian Dior launched its Dior Addict cosmetic line through email and direct mail in Hong Kong.
- **Sales promotions** consist of consumer promotion (such as samples, coupons, and premiums); trade promotion (such as advertising and display allowances); and business and sales-force promotion (contests for sales reps).
- **Events and experiences** include sports, arts, entertainment, and cause events as well as less formal activities that create novel brand interactions with consumers.
- **Public relations** include communications directed internally to employees of the company or externally to consumers, other firms, the government, and media.

Much of the recent growth of non-personal channels has been with events and experiences. A company can build its brand image through creating or sponsoring events. Event marketers who once favored sports events are now using other venues such as art museums, zoos, or ice shows to entertain clients and employees. Visa is an active sponsor of the Olympics; Caltex sponsors golf tournaments; and Heineken sponsors sports events. When Samsung wanted to refashion its image from a low-end electronics maker to a leader of the digital age creating digital convergence products, its "DigitAll Experience" global advertising campaign included sports sponsorship:

Samsung—Samsung has been an official Olympics partner since 1997. It also extended its sponsorship to the Beijing Olympics. The global agreement includes sponsoring 199 National Olympic Committees, and positioning Samsung as a worldwide official partner for wireless communication equipment. Samsung is also a sponsor of the Chelsea soccer club for five years from 2005. In addition to the phrase, "Samsung Mobile" appearing on Chelsea players' jerseys, the deal gives Samsung exclusivity with Chelsea in product categories such as mobile phones, audio visual products, white goods, and IT equipment.[45]

Companies are searching for better ways to quantify the benefits of sponsorship and are demanding greater accountability from event owners and organizers. Companies can also create events designed to surprise the public and create a buzz. Many amount to guerrilla marketing tactics. For example, Driver 2, a car-chase video game, arranged for a convoy of 20 car wrecks with smoke pouring from their engines to crawl through Manhattan and Los Angeles to attract attention to the new game.

The increased use of attention-getting events is a response to the fragmentation of media: Consumers can turn to hundreds of cable channels, thousands of magazine titles, and millions of Internet pages. Events can create attention, although whether they have a lasting effect on brand awareness, knowledge, or preference will vary considerably, depending on the quality of the product, the event itself, and its execution.

INTEGRATION OF COMMUNICATIONS CHANNELS

Although personal communication is often more effective than mass communication, the mass media might be the major means of stimulating personal communication. Mass communications affect personal attitudes and behavior through a two-step process. Ideas often flow from radio, television, and print to opinion leaders and from these to the less media-involved population groups. This two-step flow has several implications. First, the influence of mass media on public opinion is not as direct, powerful, and automatic as supposed. It is mediated by opinion leaders, people whose opinions are sought or who carry their opinions to others. Second, the two-step flow challenges the notion that consumption styles are primarily influenced by a "trickle-down" or "trickle-up" effect from mass media. People interact primarily within their own social groups and acquire ideas from opinion leaders in their groups. Third, two-step communication suggests that mass communicators should direct messages specifically to opinion leaders and let them carry the message to others. The automobile Mini developed a clever communication strategy to get people talking and driving.

Mini—The tiny Mini automobile was sold for only seven years in the U.S., during the 1960s, before it was withdrawn due to stiff emission regulations. In March 2002, BMW decided to relaunch a new, modernized Mini Cooper in the U.S., targeting hip city dwellers who wanted a cool, fun, small car for under $20,000. With only $20 million to spend on the introduction, the Mini marketers decided to launch a guerrilla communications campaign featuring non-traditional uses of billboards, posters, print ads, and grassroots efforts, and no TV ads. The Mini was stacked on top of three Ford Excursion SUVs and driven around national auto shows and 21 major cities. The car showed up in other unusual places, such as inside a sports stadium as seats and inside Playboy as a centerfold. Text-only billboards proclaimed: "THE SUV BACKLASH OFFICIALLY STARTS NOW," "GOLIATH LOST," and "XXL-XL-L-M-S-MINI." Many communications were linked to a cleverly designed Web site that provided necessary product information. The imaginative campaign resulted in a buyer waiting list that was six months long in spring 2002. And Mini hasn't stopped innovating. Using RFID technology, it began to deliver custom messages in January 2007 to Mini owners in four cities on digital signs the company calls "talking billboards." Its 2006 "covert" print campaign, which challenged Mini owners to solve various puzzles in ads, won Grand Prize among the coveted MPA Kelly Awards for excellence and effectiveness in magazine ads, partly because it deepened brand engagement to 21 percent, its highest level ever, and increased online chat 75 percent.[46]

Establish the Total Marketing Communications Budget

One of the most difficult marketing decisions is determining how much to spend on promotion. John Wanamaker, the department-store magnate, once said, "I know that half of my advertising is wasted, but I don't know which half."

Industries and companies vary considerably in how much they spend on promotion. Expenditures might be 30–50 percent of sales in the cosmetics industry and 5–10 percent in the industrial-equipment industry. Within a given industry, there are low- and high-spending companies.

How do companies decide on the promotion budget? We will describe four common methods: the affordable method, percentage-of-sales method, competitive-parity method, and objective-and-task method.

AFFORDABLE METHOD

Many companies set the promotion budget at what they think the company can afford. The affordable method completely ignores the role of promotion as an investment and the immediate impact of promotion on sales volume. It leads to an uncertain annual budget, which makes long-range planning difficult.

PERCENTAGE-OF-SALES METHOD

Many companies set promotion expenditures at a specified percentage of sales (either current or anticipated) or of the sales price. Automobile companies typically budget a fixed percentage for promotion based on the planned car price. Oil companies set the appropriation at a fraction of a cent for each liter of gasoline sold under their own label.

Supporters of the percentage-of-sales method see a number of advantages. First, promotion expenditures will vary with what the company can "afford." This satisfies financial managers, who believe that expenses should be closely related to the movement of corporate sales over the business cycle. Second, it encourages management to think of the relationship among promotion cost, selling price, and profit per unit. Third, it encourages stability when competing firms spend approximately the same percentage of their sales on promotion.

Despite these advantages, the percentage-of-sales method has little to justify it. It views sales as the determiner of promotion rather than as the result. It leads to a budget set by the availability of funds rather than by market opportunities. It discourages experimentation with countercyclical promotion or aggressive spending. Dependence on year-to-year sales fluctuations interferes with long-range planning. There is no logical basis for choosing the specific percentage, except what has been done in the past or what competitors are doing. Finally, it does not encourage building the promotion budget by determining what each product and territory deserves.

COMPETITIVE-PARITY METHOD

Some companies set their promotion budget to achieve share-of-voice parity with competitors. Two arguments are made in support of the competitive-parity method. One is that competitors' expenditures represent the collective wisdom of the industry. The other is that maintaining competitive parity prevents promotion wars. Neither argument is valid. There are no grounds for believing that competitors know better. Company reputations, resources, opportunities, and objectives differ so much that promotion budgets are hardly a guide. Further, there is no evidence that budgets based on competitive parity discourage promotional wars.

OBJECTIVE-AND-TASK METHOD

The objective-and-task method calls upon marketers to develop promotion budgets by defining specific objectives, determining the tasks that must be performed to achieve these objectives, and estimating the costs of performing these tasks. The sum of these costs is the proposed promotion budget.

For example, suppose Pocari wants to introduce a new natural energy drink called Xburst for the casual athlete.[47]

1. **Establish the market share goal.** The company estimates 50 million potential users and sets a target of attracting 8 percent of the market—that is, four million users.
2. **Determine the percentage of the market that should be reached by advertising.** The advertiser hopes to reach 80 percent (40 million prospects) with the advertising message.
3. **Determine the percentage of aware prospects that should be persuaded to try the brand.** The advertiser would be pleased if 25 percent of aware prospects (10 million) tried Xburst. This is because it estimates that 40 percent of all triers, or four million people, would become loyal users. This is the market goal.
4. **Determine the number of advertising impressions per 1 percent trial rate.** The advertiser estimates that 40 advertising impressions (exposures) for every 1 percent of the population would bring about a 25 percent trial rate.
5. **Determine the number of gross rating points that would have to be purchased.** A gross rating point is one exposure to 1 percent of the target population. Because the company wants to achieve 40 exposures to 80 percent of the population, it will want to buy 3,200 gross rating points.
6. **Determine the necessary advertising budget on the basis of the average cost of buying a gross rating point.** To expose 1 percent of the target population to one impression costs an average of \$3,277. Therefore, 3,200 gross rating points would cost \$10,486,400 (= \$3,277 × 3,200) in the introductory year.

The objective-and-task method has the advantage of requiring management to spell out its assumptions about the relationship among dollars spent, exposure levels, trial rates, and regular usage.

A major question is how much weight marketing communications should receive in relation to alternatives such as product improvement, lower prices, or better service. The answer depends on where the company's products are in their life cycles, whether they are commodities or highly differentiable products, whether they are routinely needed or have to be "sold," and other considerations. Marketing communication budgets tend to be higher when there is low channel support, much change in the marketing program over time, many hard-to-reach customers, more complex customer decision making, differentiated products and non-homogeneous customer needs, and frequent product purchases in small quantities.[48]

In theory, the total communications budget should be established so that the marginal profit from the last communication dollar just equals the marginal profit from the last dollar in the best non-communication use. Implementing this principle, however, is not easy.

Deciding on the Marketing Communications Mix

Companies must allocate the marketing communications budget over the six major modes of communication—advertising, sales promotion, public relations and publicity, events and experiences, personal selling, and direct marketing.

Within the same industry, companies can differ considerably in their media and channel choices. Avon concentrates its promotional funds on personal selling, whereas Revlon spends heavily on advertising. "Breakthrough Marketing: Intel" shows how the company has used a variety of communication vehicles to turn their sales fortunes around.

Companies are always searching for ways to gain efficiency by replacing one promotional tool with others. Many companies are replacing some field sales activity with ads, direct mail, and telemarketing. One auto dealer dismissed his five salespeople and cut his prices, and sales exploded. Companies are shifting advertising funds into sales promotion. "Marketing Insight: Marketing Communications and the Urban Chinese Consumer" reports some recent research findings on the advertising and promotional attitudes of mainland consumers.

The substitutability among communications tools also implies that marketing functions need to be coordinated as the following OCBC example illustrates.

Ambient display of balls at parks

OCBC—OCBC is one of the major local banks in Singapore. It launched a "Stay Curious" campaign to trigger curiosity from the public of its product and service innovations, and to engage the public in a new and refreshing way. The various communications elements were coordinated to promote a consistent message. It had copy printed upside-down for the launch print ad, interactive ad icons on Web pages, peep-hole and light-up panel posters at shopping malls and bus shelters, and ambient display of balls with quotes on curiosity at parks. For TV commercials, OCBC leveraged on everyday things such as the slinky toy to reflect how curiosity can spark discoveries.

A slinky toy is seen moving down a flight of stairs.

It stops when it arrives on the landing next to a stack of books.

MVO: **When you have an unstoppable urge to explore,**

Magically it begins climbing up the books.

you can overcome anything.

Super: STAY CURIOUS

Logo: Q and Ask OCBC lock-up

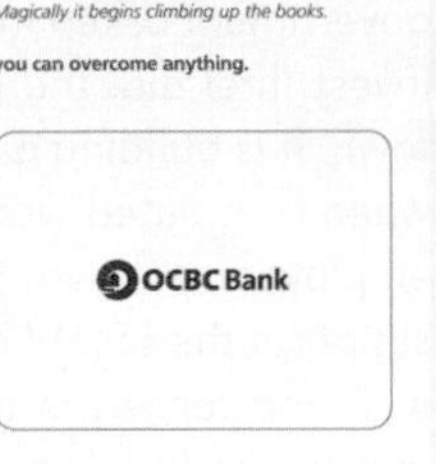

Logo: OCBC Bank

Storyboards from the television commercial "Slinky"

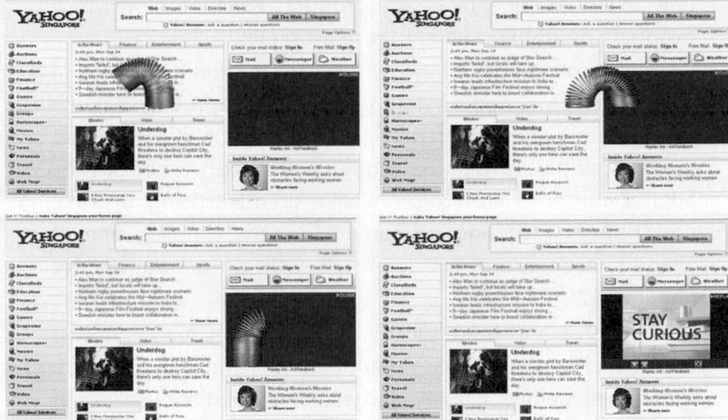

Floating Web banner with the "Slinky"

OCBC's coordinated "Stay Curious" campaign demonstrates how ambient displays, television commercials, and floating web banners can be used to deliver a synergistic message.

BREAKTHROUGH • MARKETING

INTEL

Intel makes microprocessors (or chips) found in most PCs. In the early days, Intel chips were known simply by their engineering numbers, such as "80386" or "80486." While Intel positioned its chips as the most advanced, it soon learned that numbers can't be trademarked. Rivals launched their own "486" chips, and Intel could not distinguish itself from the competition. Worse, Intel's products were hidden from consumers inside PCs. With an unseen, untrademarked product, Intel had trouble convincing consumers to pay more for its high-performance chips.

Intel's response was a marketing campaign that created history. It chose a trademarkable name (Pentium) and launched a marketing campaign to build awareness of the Intel brand. "Intel Inside" was Intel's effort to get its name outside of the PC and into consumers' minds.

Intel used an innovative cooperative scheme to extend the reach of its campaign. It would help computer makers, who used Intel processors, to advertise their PCs if the makers also included the Intel logo in their ads. Intel also gave computer manufacturers a rebate on Intel chips if they agreed to place an "Intel Inside" sticker on the outside of their PCs and laptops.

Simultaneously with the cooperative ads, Intel began its own ad program to familiarize consumers with the Intel name. The "Intel Inside" campaign changed Intel's image from a chip maker to a quality standard-bearer. The ads that included the Intel Inside logo were designed to create confidence in consumers that purchasing a PC with an Intel chip was both a safe and technologically sound choice.

Intel continues its integrated campaigns to this day. For example, when launching its Centrino mobile platform, Intel began with TV ads that aired in 12 countries. The ads include the animated logo and now familiar five-note brand signature melody. Print, online, and outdoor advertising followed shortly thereafter. Print ads ran in magazines and featured ads that targeted that magazine. For instance, an ad appearing in a sports magazine showed the logo in the center of a tennis racquet with the tagline "High performance laptop. No strings attached."

Simultaneously, Intel held a "One Unwired Day" event that took place in major cities such as New York, Chicago, San Francisco, and Seattle. In addition to allowing free trial Wi-Fi access, each city held festival events that included live music, product demonstrations, and prize giveaways. Intel also set up free access demonstration sites (with wireless Centrino-powered laptops) in areas frequented by road warriors, such as San Francisco's airport. To boost interest in mobile computing, it partnered Zagat Survey to produce a mini-guide inserted into *The New Yorker* that identified more than 50 "Wi-Fi Hotspots"—namely restaurants and hotels—in the "One Unwired Day" cities. Finally, Intel ran online ads on Web sites such as CNET and Weather.com. Yahoo! created a Wi-Fi Center Web site co-sponsored by Intel and featuring Centrino advertising.

Going forward, Intel will aggressively target opportunities outside of its traditional revenue stream in PCs. It will be moving beyond "Intel Inside" to "Intel Everywhere"—Intel chips in every type of digital device, from mobile phones to flat-panel TVs to portable video players and wireless home networks, even medical diagnostic gear. Intel is targeting 10 new product areas for its chips. If the new markets take off, they'll increase demand for PCs and services, bringing

(Continued ...)

(Continued ...)

new revenues for Intel's core products even if its own new products do not succeed in these markets.

Intel is also expanding globally. Its marketing efforts in Asia are exemplified by its aggressive drive in China. Each "Meet Intel" seminar, featuring an array of PCs powered by Intel chips, attracts as many as 800 corporate clients. Such seminars follow after weeks of advertising in local newspapers targeting consumers directly. Intel is one of China's largest foreign advertisers, with an annual budget of some $20 million.

An example of Intel's savvy marketing in China is how it entered Chengdu. With a population of six million, Chengdu ranks well behind China's largest and most industrialized cities. But, it is home to some of China's top engineering schools, making it a promising source of highly skilled labor—and PC buyers. Intel experienced it first-hand in 1998 when it held a PC party on the streets of Chengdu. The event turned out to be one of the biggest ever—more than 400,000 people showed up. Most important, as part of its "go west" campaign targeting foreign investors, China's national government asked Intel to invest in building up Chengdu. And invest Intel did, the results of which can be seen all around town. It is building a large chip-testing plant in the city, which when completed would make Intel one of the largest private employers in town. Intel sponsors after-school projects and supports the local I-café, one of the biggest gathering spots in China for teens to play computer games. It is spending millions to blanket the city in advertising. Intel ads are on local TV, billboards, placards in hotels and at the airport, and on nearly every surface in the city's largest computer store.

Sources: Cliff Edwards, "Intel Everywhere?" *BusinessWeek,* 56(7), March 8, 2004; Scott Van Camp, "ReadMe.1st." *Brandweek,* 17(1), February 23, 2004; "How to Become a Superbrand." *Marketing*, January 8, 2004, p. 15; Roger Slavens, "Pam Pollace, VP-Director, Corporate Marketing Group, Intel Corp." *B to B*, December 8, 2003, p. 19; Kenneth Hein, "Study: New Brand Names Not Making their Mark." *Brandweek,* 12(1), December 8, 2003; Heather Clancy, "Intel Thinking Outside The Box." *Computer Reseller News*, November 24, 2003, p. 14; Cynthia L. Webb, "A Chip Off the Old Recovery?", 2003, <Washingtonpost.com>, (accessed on October 15, 2003); "Intel Launches Second Phase of Centrino Ads." *Technology Advertising and Branding Report*, October 6, 2003, David Kirkpatrick, "At Intel, Speed Isn't Everything." *Fortune*, February 9, 2004, p. 34; Fred Vogelstein, "How Intel Got Inside." *Fortune*, October 4, 2004, pp. 73-78.

MARKETING INSIGHT • MARKETING COMMUNICATIONS AND THE URBAN CHINESE CONSUMER

How do Chinese consumers feel about advertising? Compared to American consumers, urban Chinese consumers have similar, if not somewhat more favorable, attitudes toward advertising. A study found that, in general, more liked than disliked advertising (49 versus 20 percent). However, 45 percent felt that there was too much advertising. Almost 70 percent felt that advertising was informative, while 24 percent felt it insulted their intelligence. They often used ad information to help them make purchasing decisions, although only one in four was confident when using such information. Given that alternative sources of information to aid purchase decisions are relatively scarce in China, even those with less confidence in ad information (70 percent did not trust advertising) found it necessary to use it. Unlike the U.S. where consumers with lower education and lower income are relatively more likely to enjoy advertising, it is the better educated Chinese consumers who have more favorable attitudes toward advertising, enjoying it more and holding more positive beliefs about it.

Given the general favorable sentiments towards advertising, it pays for marketers to research their target markets and understand the type of advertising and promotional tools that will appeal most effectively to them. Research costs account 5–7 percent of an ad agency's revenue in China, higher than 1–2 percent regionwide. Consumer research in China need not follow the conventional ways of information gathering. For example, Leo Burnett found that Chinese youths were too timid to participate fully in focus groups. Thus to study fashion-conscious youth, Leo Burnett gave each a stylish notebook, a disposable camera, and Post-it notes. After two weeks, the notebooks were collected. The findings were stunning. They read like intimate diary entries that gave the marketers insights into what youths considered as fashion and their hopes for the future. Grey Worldwide had executives from its client, Danone, spend a weekend with different Chinese families to observe how they cook, eat, and shop at the local market.

A.C. Nielsen categorized urban Chinese consumers into five groups, each with different advertising and promotion preferences:

- The **Adventurous** have high aspirations and want to go ahead. They are always eager to try new things, buy the latest fashions, and possess cutting-edge gadgets, rather than live frugally. Advertising that associates the brand with role models such as celebrities appeals most to them.
- The **Worker Bees** believe strongly in quality and are willing to pay for high-quality brands. They work hard, coming into the office early and leaving late, and try make as much money as fast as possible. For such consumers, editorials in magazines and peer endorsement are more effective.
- The **Value Hunters** seek the best bargains and are willing to wait to achieve the best value for money. Such consumers are deal-prone, waiting till sale time to buy a top brand. Effective tools are likely to be sales offering discounts and buy-one-get-one promotions.
- The **Herds** look for products with everyday value. They believe that the more a product is advertised, the better its quality. They are thus vulnerable to the influence of ads, especially TV commercials.
- The **Laggards** are conservative and find saving difficult. They are brand-conscious but do not discriminate between local and foreign brand names. They favor promotional tools that emphasize the inherent value of the brand.

Sources: Dongsheng Zhou, Weijiong Zhang, and Ilan Vertinsky, "Advertising Trends in Urban China." *Journal of Advertising Research,* 2002, 42(3), pp. 73–83; Gabriel Kahn, "Ad Companies Seek New Ways to Chart Changes in China." *Asian Wall Street Journal*, April 25, 2002; Li Xue Ying, "Capturing China's Huge Consumer Market." *Straits Times* (Singapore), December 7, 2002, p. A3.

Characteristics of the Marketing Communications Mix

Each communication tool has its own unique characteristics and costs.

ADVERTISING

Advertising can be used to build up a long-term image for a product (Coca-Cola ads) or trigger quick sales (an Isetan ad for a weekend sale). Advertising can efficiently reach geographically dispersed buyers. Certain forms of advertising (TV) can require a large budget, whereas other forms (radio) need less. Just the presence of advertising might have an effect on sales: consumers might believe that a heavily advertised brand must offer "good value."[49] Because of the many forms and uses of advertising, it is difficult to make generalizations.[50] Yet the following qualities can be noted:

1. ***Pervasiveness*** — Advertising permits the seller to repeat a message many times. It also allows the buyer to receive and compare the messages of various competitors. Large-scale advertising says something positive about the seller's size, power, and success.
2. ***Amplified expressiveness*** — Advertising provides opportunities for dramatizing the company and its products through the artful use of print, sound, and color.
3. ***Impersonality*** — The audience does not feel obligated to pay attention or respond to advertising. Advertising is a monologue in front of, not a dialogue with, the audience.

SALES PROMOTION

Companies use sales promotion tools—coupons, contests, premiums, and the like—to draw a stronger and quicker buyer response. Sales promotion can be used for short-run effects such as to highlight product offers and boost sagging sales. Sales promotion tools offer three distinctive benefits:

1. ***Communication*** — They gain attention and may lead the consumer to the product.
2. ***Incentive*** — They incorporate some concession, inducement, or contribution that gives value to the consumer.
3. ***Invitation*** — They include a distinct invitation to engage in the transaction now.

PUBLIC RELATIONS AND PUBLICITY

Marketers tend to underuse public relations, yet a well-thought-out program coordinated with the other communications-mix elements can be extremely effective. The appeal of public relations and publicity is based on three distinctive qualities:

1. ***High credibility*** — News stories and features are more authentic and credible to readers than ads.
2. ***Ability to catch buyers off guard*** — Public relations can reach prospects who prefer to avoid salespeople and advertisements.
3. ***Dramatization*** — Public relations have the potential for dramatizing a company or product.

EVENTS AND EXPERIENCES

There are many advantages to events and experiences:

1. ***Relevant*** — A well-chosen event or experience can be seen as highly relevant as the consumer gets personally involved.
2. ***Involving*** — Given its live, real-time quality, consumers can find events and experiences more actively engaging.
3. ***Implicit*** — Events are more of an indirect "soft sell."

DIRECT AND INTERACTIVE MARKETING

Direct and interactive marketing takes many forms—over the phone, online, or in person. They share three distinctive characteristics. Direct and interactive marketing messages are:

1. ***Customized*** — The message can be prepared to appeal to the addressed individual.
2. ***Up-to-date*** — A message can be prepared very quickly.
3. ***Interactive*** — The message can be changed depending on the person's response.

WORD-OF-MOUTH MARKETING

Word of mouth also takes many forms online or off-line. Three noteworthy characteristics are:

1. ***Credible*** — Because people trust others they know and respect, word of mouth can be highly influential.
2. ***Personal*** — Word of mouth can be a very intimate dialogue that reflects personal facts, opinions, and experiences.
3. ***Timely*** — It occurs when people want it to and when they are most interested, and it often follows noteworthy or meaningful events or experiences.

PERSONAL SELLING

Personal selling is the most effective tool at later stages of the buying process, particularly in building up buyer preference, conviction, and action. Personal selling has three distinctive qualities:

1. ***Personal interaction*** — Personal selling involves an immediate and interactive relationship between two or more persons. Each party is able to observe the other's reactions.
2. ***Cultivation*** — Personal selling permits all kinds of relationships to spring up, ranging from a matter-of-fact selling relationship to a deep personal friendship.
3. ***Response*** — Personal selling makes the buyer feel under some obligation for having listened to the sales talk.

Factors in Setting the Marketing Communications Mix

Companies must consider several factors in developing their communications mix: type of product market, consumer readiness to make a purchase, and stage in the product life cycle. Also important is the company's market rank.

TYPE OF PRODUCT MARKET

Communications-mix allocations vary between consumer and business markets. Consumer marketers tend to spend comparatively more on sales promotion and advertising; business marketers tend to spend comparatively more on personal selling. In general, personal selling is used more with complex, expensive, and risky goods and in markets with fewer and larger sellers (hence, business markets).

Although advertising is used less than sales calls in business markets, it still plays a significant role:

- Advertising can provide an introduction to the company and its products.
- If the product has new features, advertising can explain them.
- Reminder advertising is more economical than sales calls.
- Advertisements offering brochures and carrying the company's phone number are an effective way to generate leads for sales representatives.
- Sales representatives can use tear sheets of the company's ads to legitimize their company and products.
- Advertising can remind customers of how to use the product and reassure them about their purchase.

Several studies have underscored advertising's role in business markets. Advertising combined with personal selling can increase sales over what would have resulted if there had been no advertising.[51] Corporate advertising can improve a company's reputation and improve the sales force's chances of getting a favorable first hearing and early adoption of the product.[52]

Personal selling can also make a strong contribution in consumer-goods marketing. Some consumer marketers use the sales force mainly to collect weekly orders from dealers and to see that sufficient stock is on the shelf. Yet an effectively trained company sales force can make four important contributions:

1. ***Increase stock position*** — Sales representatives can persuade dealers to take more stock and devote more shelf space to the company's brand.
2. ***Enthusiasm building*** — Sales representatives can build dealer enthusiasm by dramatizing planned advertising and sales-promotion backup.
3. ***Missionary selling*** — Sales representatives can sign up more dealers.
4. ***Key account management*** — Sales representatives can take responsibility for growing business with the most important accounts.

BUYER-READINESS STAGE

Communication tools vary in cost-effectiveness at different stages of buyer readiness. Figure 17.5 shows the relative cost effectiveness of three communication tools. Advertising and publicity play the most important roles in the awareness-building stage. Customer comprehension is primarily affected by advertising and personal selling. Customer conviction is influenced mostly by personal selling. Closing the sale is influenced mostly by personal selling and sales promotion. Reordering is also affected mostly by personal selling and sales promotion, and somewhat by reminder advertising.

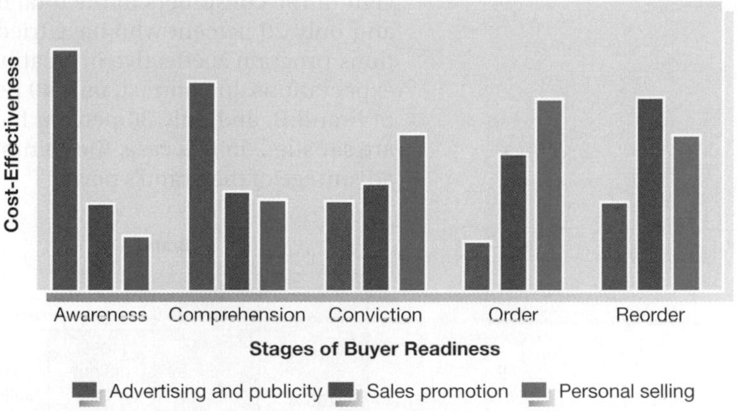

Figure 17.5 Cost-Effectiveness of Three Different Communication Tools at Different Buyer-Readiness Stages

PRODUCT LIFE-CYCLE STAGE

Communication tools also vary in cost-effectiveness at different stages of the product life cycle. In the introduction stage, advertising and publicity have the highest cost-effectiveness, followed by personal selling to gain distribution coverage and sales promotion to induce trial. In the growth stage, demand has its own momentum through word of mouth. In the maturity stage, sales promotion, advertising, and personal selling all grow more important, in that order. In the decline stage, sales promotion continues strong, advertising and publicity are reduced, and salespeople give the product only minimal attention.

Measuring Communications Results

Senior managers want to know the *outcomes* and *revenues* resulting from their communications investments. Too often, however, their communications directors supply only *outputs* and *expenses:* press clipping counts, numbers of ads placed, media costs. In fairness, the communications directors try to translate outputs into intermediate outputs such as reach and frequency, recall and recognition scores, persuasion changes, and cost-per-thousand calculations. Ultimately, behavior change measures capture the real payoff.

After implementing the communications plan, the communications director must measure its impact on the target audience. Members of the target audience are asked whether they recognize or recall the message, how many times they saw it, what points they recall, how they felt about the message, and their previous and current attitudes toward the product and the company. The communicator should also collect behavioral measures of audience response, such as how many people bought the product, liked it, and talked to others about it.

Agro Asia (Double A)—Given the low interest in the product category, Thai photocopying paper manufacturer Agro Asia organized a regional campaign to increase brand awareness. It used a wacky tone to illustrate Double A's "no paper jam" benefit to differentiate itself from its rivals, HP, Fuji, and Xerox. Called "Paper Jams Drive People Crazy," it parodies formulaic shampoo commercials. The commercial opens with a woman standing at a photocopying machine, stroking her hair while she waits for a printout. She notices dandruff and a male TV presenter-like character appears with a bottle of shampoo in hand. The presenter tells the woman that the "scalp is like a piece of jammed paper with no natural nutrients." The presenter is stopped in mid-sentence as the woman has a fit because the machine has jammed yet again. The supporting print campaign featured image of screaming office workers imposed onto giant balls of crumpled paper. Increase of brand awareness ranged 70–97 percent in Hong Kong, Malaysia, Singapore, and Thailand where Double A is sold.[53]

Figure 17.6 provides an example of good feedback measurement. We find that 80 percent of the consumers in the total market are aware of brand A, 60 percent have tried it, and only 20 percent who have tried it are satisfied. This indicates that the communications program is effective in creating awareness, but the product fails to meet consumer expectations. In contrast, only 40 percent of the consumers in the total market are aware of brand B, and only 30 percent have tried it, but 80 percent of those who have tried it are satisfied. In this case, the communications program needs to be strengthened to take advantage of the brand's power.

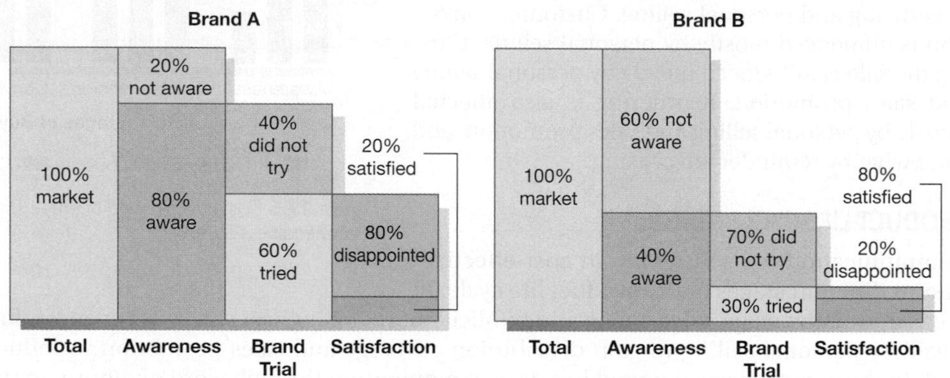

Figure 17.6 Current Consumer States for Two Brands

Managing the Integrated Marketing Communications Process

As defined by the American Association of Advertising Agencies, **Integrated Marketing Communications (IMC)** is a concept of marketing communications planning that recognizes the added value of a comprehensive plan. Such a plan evaluates the strategic roles of a variety of communications disciplines—for example, general advertising, direct response, sales promotion, and public relations—and combines these disciplines to provide clarity, consistency, and maximum impact through the seamless integration of messages.

Unfortunately, many companies still rely on one or two communication tools. This practice persists in spite of the fragmenting of mass markets into a multitude of mini markets, each requiring its own approach; the proliferation of new types of media; and the growing sophistication of consumers. The wide range of communication tools, messages, and audiences makes it imperative that companies move toward integrated marketing communications. Companies must adopt a "360-degree view" of consumers to fully understand all the different ways that communications can affect consumer behavior in their daily lives.

Here are two successful examples of integrated marketing communication programs.

Accenture—Forced to change its company name from Andersen Consulting after an arbitrator's decision, Accenture developed a rebranding campaign that utilized a fully integrated communications program. By January 2001, television, print, Internet, and poster ads featuring the Accenture name had appeared in each of 48 different countries where the company did business. Between January and March 2001, over 6,000 television commercials spots and 1,000 print ads were run in global markets. In Australia, the company placed a "cover wrap" on the magazine ***Business Review Weekly*** and advertised on bus stops and park benches in Sydney's business district. It placed large-scale outdoor ads in Milan's Oberdan Square and coated 10 taxis in London with Accenture signage. The January 2001 Accenture World Match Play Championship allowed the company to run some 300 commercials in its international markets and 100 commercials in the U.S., plus print advertisements in major newspapers, business periodicals, and golf magazines in the U.S. Additional high-profile global advertising sponsorship opportunities included the Formula 1 Racing Series, several European skiing events, the Six Nations Rugby tournament, the Asian PGA tour, the World Soccer Dream Match in Japan, and the Italian Football Championship.

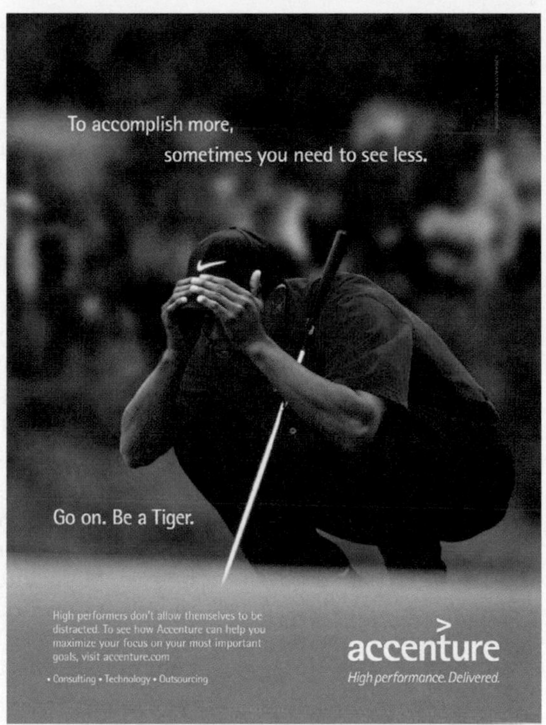

One of a series of Tiger Woods ads that was part of the Accenture rebranding campaign.

Coordinating Media

Media coordination can occur across and within media types. Personal and non-personal communication channels should be combined to achieve maximum impact. Imagine a marketer using a single tool in a "one-shot" effort to reach and sell a prospect. An example of a *single-vehicle, single-stage campaign* is a one-time mailing offering a cookware item. A *single-vehicle, multiple-stage campaign* would involve successive mailings to the same prospect. Magazine publishers, for example, send about four renewal notices to a household before giving up. A more powerful approach is the *multiple-vehicle, multiple-stage campaign*. Consider the following sequence in Figure 17.7.

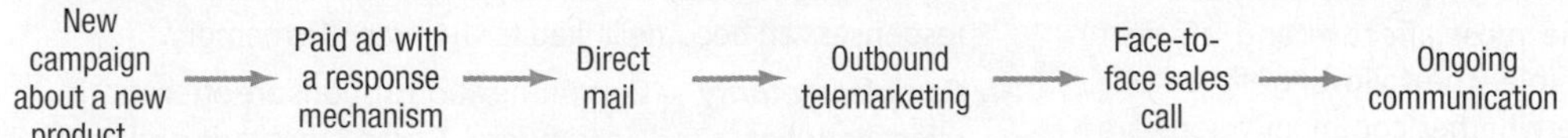

Figure 17.7 Example of Multiple-Vehicle, Multiple-Stage Communication Campaign

Multiple media deployed within a tightly defined time frame can increase message reach and impact. For a Citibank campaign to market home equity loans, instead of using only "mail plus an 800 number," Citibank used "mail plus coupon plus 800 number plus outbound telemarketing plus print advertising." Although the second campaign was more expensive, it resulted in a 15 percent increase in the number of new accounts compared with direct mail alone.[54]

Research has also shown that promotions can be more effective when combined with advertising.[55] The awareness and attitudes created by advertising campaigns can improve the success of more direct sales pitches. Many companies are coordinating their online and off-line communication activities. Advertisers who bought television advertising may also buy ad space on the station's Web sites.[56] Listing URL Web addresses in ads (especially print) and on packages allows people to more fully explore a company's products, find store locations and get more product or service information.

Pepsi has been highly successful in linking its online and off-line efforts. In 2001, Pepsi and Yahoo! joined forces for an online promotion that increased sales 5 percent at a cost of about one-fifth of the previous mail-in promotion. During the promotion, Pepsi displayed the portal's logo on 1.5 billion cans while Yahoo! created a co-branded PepsiStuff.com e-commerce site where visitors could redeem points from bottle caps for prizes ranging from electronic goods to concert tickets.[57] When Dutch financial services firm ING Group launched its brand in the U.S., TV and print ads were paired with online ads. In one campaign on financial news sites, all the "ings" in the news text turned orange—matching ING's corporate colors.[58]

Even if consumers do not order online, they can use Web sites in ways that drive them into stores to buy. Some Web sites serve as a research tool for consumers, as customers look online first before going into the store.

To learn how Indian business and government leaders put together an elaborate marketing and PR effort to showcase India as an attractive place for business, go to www.pearsoned.co.in/pkotler.

IMPLEMENTING IMC

Integrated marketing communications has been slow to take hold for several reasons. Large companies often employ several communications specialists to work with their brand managers who may know comparatively little about the other communication tools. Further complicating matters is that many global companies use a large number of ad agencies located in different countries and serving different divisions, resulting in uncoordinated communications and image diffusion.

However, a few large agencies have now substantially improved their integrated offerings. To facilitate one-stop shopping, major ad agencies have acquired promotion agencies, public relations firms, package-design consultancies, Web site developers, and direct mail houses. Many international clients have opted to put a substantial portion of their communications work through one agency. An example is IBM turning all of its advertising over to Ogilvy to attain uniform branding. The result is integrated and more effective marketing communications and a much lower total communications cost.

Integrated marketing communications can produce stronger message consistency and greater sales impact. It forces management to think about every way the customer comes in contact with the company, how the company communicates its positioning, the relative importance of each vehicle, and timing issues. It gives someone the responsibility—where none existed before—to unify the company's brand images and messages as they come through thousands of company activities. IMC should improve the company's ability to reach the right customers with the right messages at the right time and in the right place.[59] "Marketing Memo: How Integrated is Your IMC Program?" provides some guidelines.

MARKETING MEMO • HOW INTEGRATED IS YOUR IMC PROGRAM?

In assessing the collective impact of an IMC program, the overriding goal is to create the most effective and efficient communications program possible. The following six criteria can be used to help determine whether communications are truly integrated.

- ***Coverage*** — Coverage is the proportion of the audience reached by each communication option employed, as well as how much overlap exists among communication options. In other words, to what extent do different communication options reach the designated target market and the same or different consumers making up that market?
- ***Contribution*** — Contribution is the inherent ability of a marketing communication to create the desired response and communication effects from consumers in the absence of exposure to any other communication option. How much does a communication affect consumer processing and build awareness, enhance image, elicit responses, and induce sales?
- ***Commonality*** — Commonality is the extent to which *common* associations are reinforced across communication options, i.e., the extent to which information conveyed by different communication options share meaning. The consistency and cohesiveness of the brand image is important because it determines how easily existing associations and responses can be recalled and how easily additional associations and responses can become linked to the brand in memory.
- ***Complementarity*** — Communication options are often more effective when used in tandem. Complementarity relates to the extent to which *different* associations and linkages are emphasized across communication options. Different brand associations may be most effectively established by capitalizing on those marketing communication options best suited to eliciting a particular consumer response or establishing a particular type of brand association.
- ***Versatility*** — In any integrated communication program, when consumers are exposed to a particular marketing communication, some will have already been exposed to other marketing communications for the brand, and some will not have had any prior exposure. Versatility refers to the extent to which a marketing communication option is robust and "works" for different groups of consumers. The ability of a marketing communication to work at two levels—effectively communicating to consumers who have or have *not* seen other communications—is critically important.
- ***Cost*** — Marketers must weigh evaluations of marketing communications on all these criteria against their cost to arrive at the most effective *and* efficient communications program.

Sources: Kevin Lane Keller, *Strategic Brand Management*, 3rd ed., (Upper Saddle River, NJ: Prentice-Hall, 2008).

IMC advocates describe it as a way of looking at the whole marketing process instead of focusing on individual parts of it. Companies such as Motorola, Xerox, and Hewlett-Packard are bringing together advertising, direct marketing, public relations, and employee communications experts to meet a few times each year for training and improved communication among them. Procter & Gamble recently revised its communications planning by requiring that each new program be formulated jointly, with its ad agency sitting together with P&G's public relations agencies, direct marketing units, promotion-merchandising firms, and Internet operations. Cerebos is an example of an Asian company that has employed IMC in implementing brand-driven customer relationship management initiatives and injecting an organization-wide customer-centric culture:

Cerebos—Since 2002, the company that manufactures and markets BRAND'S® Essence of Chicken, a traditional nutritional drink used by Asian consumers as an occasional "pick-me-up," has moved from a print-and-television advertising-centric marketing model to a consumer-centric marketing model. The growing sophistication and saturation of the health-care supplement market meant that the "one size fits all" approach of the traditional mass communications model was growing less effective in reaching consumers. Cerebos thus adopted a more customer-focused approach across the company to maintain its market leadership in China, Hong Kong, Malaysia, Singapore, Taiwan, and Thailand.

The company established a CRM infrastructure which focused on connecting with consumers. It built extensive profiles of its customers' needs and usage habits. It also gained their feedback on formulation, distribution, and packaging. Three core IMC infrastructures were developed to implement Cerebos' brand-driven CRM initiative. First, a Web site www.brandsworld.com was designed to offer health information, expert opinions, news, and updates. The site also functions as a hub for many of Brand's activities, and provides ample opportunity for two-way conversations with the brand. Second, call centers were established in each market, backed by sophisticated data-management technology, to serve as the frontline in customer service. Finally, an on-going one-to-one direct marketing communications program was initiated, mainly targeting key user groups. It was designed to keep them feeling involved and important to BRAND'S®.

As a result, today, BRAND'S® interacts with more than one million customers annually in six countries. The strong brand equity and customer loyalty built over the years through its products and CRM infrastructure have resulted in customers taking an active interest in what BRAND'S® does and providing a continuous loop of feedback to the company. This data and a foundational CRM infrastructure is better able to help Cerebos stay ahead of its competition.

Summary

1. Modern marketing calls for more than developing a good product, pricing it attractively, and making it accessible to target customers. Companies must also communicate with present and potential stakeholders, and with the general public.
2. The marketing communications mix consists of six major modes of communication: advertising, sales promotion, events and experiences, public relations and publicity, direct marketing, and personal selling.
3. The communication process consists of nine elements: sender, receiver, message, media, encoding, decoding, response, feedback, and noise. To get their messages through, marketers must encode their messages in a way that takes into account how the target audience usually decodes messages. They must also transmit the message through efficient media that reach the target audience and develop feedback channels to monitor response to the message. Consumer response to a communication can be often modeled in terms of a response hierarchy and "learn-feel-do" sequence.
4. Developing effective communications involves eight steps: (1) Identify the target audience; (2) determine the communications objectives; (3) design the communication; (4) select the communication channels; (5) establish the total communications budget; (6) decide on the communications mix; (7) measure the communications' results; and (8) manage the integrated marketing communications process.
5. In identifying the target audience, the marketer needs to close any gap that exists between current public perception and the image sought. Communications objectives may involve category need, brand awareness, brand attitude, or brand purchase intention. Formulating the communication requires solving three problems: what to say (message strategy), how to say it (creative strategy), and who should say it (message source). Communication channels may be personal (advocate, expert, and social channels) or nonpersonal (media, atmosphere, and events). The objective-and-task method of setting the promotion budget, which calls upon marketers to develop their budgets by defining specific objectives, is the most desirable.
6. In deciding on the marketing communications mix, marketers must examine the distinct advantages and costs of each communication tool and the company's market rank. They must also consider the type of product market in which they are selling, how ready consumers are to make a purchase, and the product's stage in the product life cycle. Measuring the marketing communications mix's effectiveness involves asking members of the target audience whether they recognize or recall the communication, how many times they saw it, what points they recall, how they felt about the communication, and their previous and current attitudes toward the product and the company.
7. Managing and coordinating the entire communications process calls for Integrated Marketing Communications (IMC): marketing communications planning which recognizes the added value of a comprehensive plan that evaluates the strategic roles of a variety of communications disciplines and combines these disciplines to provide clarity, consistency, and maximum impact through the seamless integration of discrete messages.

Application

Marketing Debate—Has TV Advertising Lost Power?

Long deemed the most successful medium, television advertising has received increased criticism as being too expensive and, even worse, no longer as effective as it once was. Critics maintain that consumers tune out too many ads by zipping and zapping and that it is difficult to make a strong impression. The future, claim some, is with online advertising. Supporters of TV advertising disagree, contending that the multisensory impact of TV is unsurpassed and that no other media option offers the same potential impact.

Take a position: *TV advertising has faded in importance* versus *TV advertising is still the most powerful advertising medium.*

Marketing Discussion

Pick a brand and go to its Web site. Locate as many forms of communications as you can find. Conduct an informal communications audit. What do you notice? How consistent are the different communications?

PART 7

supercute. superconfident. $800

SAYING IT WITH FASHION

PRICELESS

MasterCard

proud sponsor of the

Singapore Fashion Fe

28 March – 6 April 2

www.mastercardmoments.com/

MasterCard's *Priceless* campaign included a "Saying it with Fashion" subcampaign which consisted of advertisements and a sponsorship of the Singapore Fashion Festival.

Managing Mass Communications: Advertising, Sales Promotions, Events, and Public Relations

18

Although there has been an enormous increase in the use of personal communications by marketers in recent years due to the rapid penetration of the Internet and other factors, the fact remains that mass media, if used correctly, can still dramatically improve the fortunes of a brand or a company. Consider how MasterCard uses mass media advertising and event sponsorship to reach its target audience and make its *Priceless* campaign a success.

Mastercard's "Saying it with Fashion" advertising campaign was launched in the lead-up to the Singapore Fashion Festival 2008, in which MasterCard Worldwide was the presenting sponsor. The *Priceless®* advertising was launched under the banner of its advertising campaign "I'm Every Woman," which salutes the power and dynamism of today's Asian woman.

While the 2007 campaign called on women to show their inspired self to the world, the 2008's campaign showcased how women used fashion to express different aspects of their personality, to the extent that they are "Saying it with Fashion," the *Priceless* tagline for the advertisements. MasterCard's pre-launch focus groups revealed that the creative concept strongly resonated with women, who connected with the expression of a woman's uniqueness, as well as the juxtaposition between everyday situations and aspirations.

MasterCard has been committed to developing a deep understanding of Asian women's rapidly evolving lifestyles and how they have become an economic driving force today. It is a presenter and sponsor of some of the foremost premium global fashion events, building a strong fashion platform which reaches out to the powerful group of Asian women consumers who are estimated to have $516 billion of discretionary spending power at their command by 2014.

This campaign is among the many *Priceless* campaigns around the world. The award-winning *Priceless* campaign has appeared in 110 countries and 51 languages, and continues to provide a versatile, global platform that enables the company to reach consumers and build the MasterCard brand. The *Priceless* theme crosses cultures and geography, and is a transcendent platform for all of MasterCard's payment programs and marketing initiatives. It reinforces the message that MasterCard understands the truly important things in life.

In this chapter, we will address the following questions:

1. What steps are required in developing an advertising program?
2. How should sales promotion decisions be made?
3. What are the guidelines for effective brand-building events and experiences?
4. How can companies exploit the potential of public relations and publicity?

Marketers of all kinds are trying to come to grips with how to best use mass media in the new communications environment. In this chapter, we examine the nature and use of four mass communications tools—advertising, sales promotions, events and experiences, and public relations and publicity.

Developing and Managing an Advertising Programmme

Advertising is any paid form of non-personal presentation and promotion of ideas, goods, or services by an identified sponsor. Ads can be a cost-effective way to disseminate messages, whether to build a brand preference or to educate people.

Most companies use an outside agency to help create advertising campaigns and to select and purchase media. Today, advertising agencies are redefining themselves as *communication companies* that assist clients to improve their overall communications effectiveness by offering strategic and practical advice on many forms of communication.[1]

In developing an advertising program, marketing managers must always start by identifying the target market and buyer motives. Then they can make the five major decisions, known as "the five Ms": (1) *Mission*: What are the advertising objectives? (2) *Money*: How much can be spent? (3) *Message*: What message should be sent? (4) *Media*: What media should be used? (5) *Measurement*: How should the results be evaluated? These decisions are summarized in Figure 18.1 and described in the following sections.

Setting the Objectives

The advertising objectives must flow from prior decisions on the target market, brand positioning, and the marketing program.

An **advertising goal** (or objective) is a specific communications task and achievement level to be accomplished with a specific audience in a specific period of time:[2]

> *To increase among 30 million Indonesian car owners the number who identify the Toyota Corona as an efficient car and who are persuaded that it is reliable from 10 percent to 40 percent in one year.*

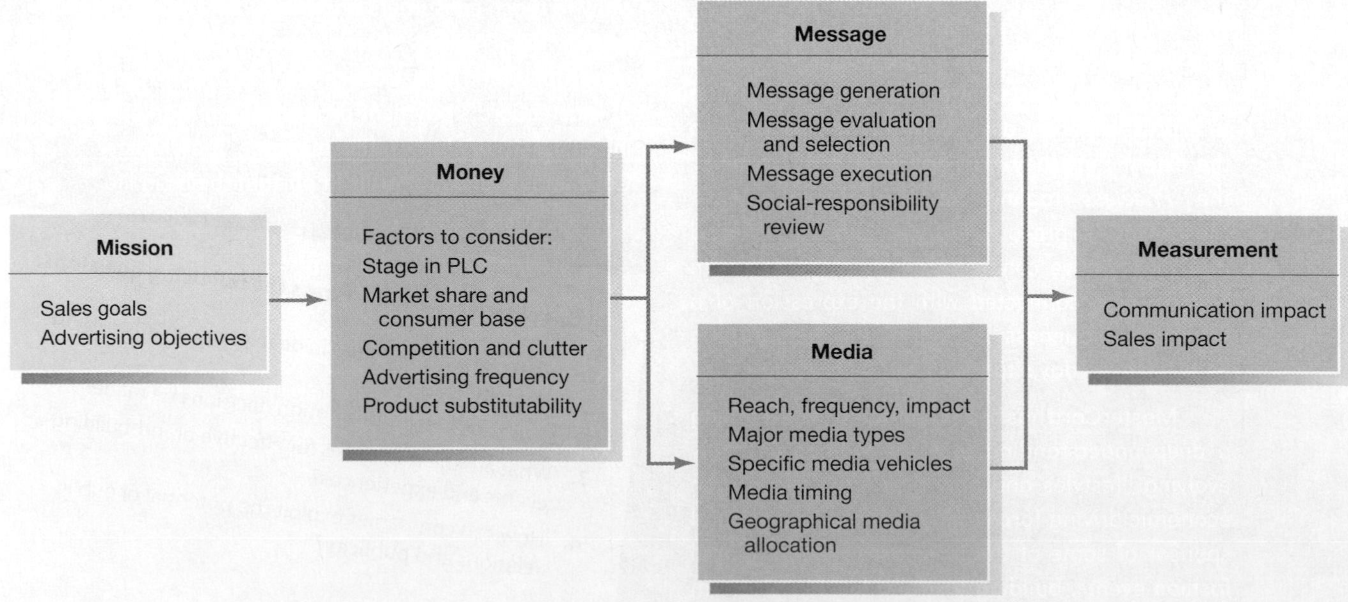

Figure 18.1 The Five Ms of Advertising

Advertising objectives can be classified according to whether their aim is to inform, persuade, remind, or reinforce. They aim at different stages in the *hierarchy-of-effects* discussed in Chapter 17.

- **Informative advertising** aims to create brand awareness and knowledge of new products or new features of existing products. In Japan, De Beers taught the "engagement ring" concept as a new expression of love in a culture accustomed to arranged marriages. Two in three Japanese brides now receive a diamond engagement ring, when previously only gold rings were exchanged. Its ads in China target young women whose mothers wore only gold and jade. The ads educate these consumers about diamonds being an enduring symbol of a bright, shared future rather than only of romantic love.[3]
- **Persuasive advertising** aims to create liking, preference, conviction, and purchase of a product or service. In India, arresting the spread of the HIV/AIDS pandemic is challenging as there is a two-way social stigma—that associated with the patient seeking such treatment as well as the clinic being promoted as one for sexually transmitted diseases. Key Clinic, a family health care center, sought to establish itself as a trusted, affordable, and accessible clinic where such treatments can be received with dignity. Its persuasive campaign included educational sessions and demonstrating that Key Clinic doctors are caring and accessible.

Key Clinic uses a persuasive campaign to encourage people who need treatment for sexually transmitted diseases to seek medical assistance at their clinics. In the top ad, the copy says "Whatever the illness, let's go the Key Clinic." In the bottom ad, a poem is used in the ad copy: "Correct or good treatment, every patient is looked after. So come and meet the doctors; Key Clinic is proud of this." The tagline, "Let's go to Key Clinic" is repeated in all the ads.

- **Reminder advertising** aims to stimulate repeat purchase of products and services. Gai Zhong Gai is a Chinese brand of calcium tablets. Given that most Chinese place highest value on low price and reliability, Gai Zhong Gai's ad used a straightforward message that emphasized these benefits. This simplistic approach and constant repetition of its message encouraged continued purchase of the brand.[4]
- **Reinforcement advertising** aims to convince current purchasers that they made the right choice. Automobile ads depicting satisfied customers enjoying special features of their new car are illustrative of reinforcement advertising.

The advertising objective should emerge from a thorough analysis of the current marketing situation. If the product class is mature, the company is the market leader, and brand usage is low, the proper objective should be to stimulate more usage. If the product class is new, the company is not the market leader, but the brand is superior to the leader, then the proper objective is to convince the market of the brand's superiority.

Deciding on the Advertising Budget

How does a company know if it is spending the right amount? Some critics charge that large consumer packaged-goods firms tend to overspend on advertising as a form of insurance against not spending enough, and that industrial companies underestimate the power of company and product image building, and tend to underspend.[5]

Although advertising is treated as a current expense, part of it is really an investment in building brand equity. When $5 million is spent on capital equipment, the equipment may be treated as a five-year depreciable asset and only one-fifth of the cost is written off in the first year. When $5 million is spent on advertising to launch a new product, the entire cost must be written off in the first year. This reduces the company's reported profit and therefore limits the number of new-product launches a company can undertake in any one year.

FACTORS AFFECTING BUDGET DECISIONS

Here are five specific factors to consider when setting the advertising budget:[6]

1. ***Stage in the product life cycle*** — New products typically receive large advertising budgets to build awareness and to gain consumer trial. Established brands are usually supported with lower advertising budgets as a ratio to sales.[7]
2. ***Market share and consumer base*** — High-market-share brands usually require less advertising expenditure as a percentage of sales to maintain share. To build share by increasing market size requires larger expenditures.
3. ***Competition and clutter*** — In a market with many competitors and high advertising spending, a brand must advertise more heavily to be known. Even simple clutter from ads not directly competing with the brand creates a need for heavier advertising.
4. ***Advertising frequency*** — The number of repetitions needed to put across the brand's message to consumers has an important impact on the advertising budget.
5. ***Product substitutability*** — Brands in less well-differentiated or commodity-like product classes (beer, soft drinks, banks, and airlines) require heavy advertising to establish a differential image.

In one study of budget allocation, Low and Mohr found that managers allocate less to advertising as brands move to the more mature phase of the product life cycle; when a brand is well-differentiated from the competition; when managers are rewarded on short-term results; as retailers gain more power; and when managers have less experience with the company.[8]

ADVERTISING ELASTICITY

The predominant response function for advertising is often concave but can be S-shaped.[9] When consumer response is S-shaped, some positive amount of advertising is necessary to generate any sales impact, but sales increases eventually flatten out.[10]

One classic study found that increasing TV advertising budget had a measurable effect on sales only half the time. The success rate was higher on new products or line extensions than on established brands, and when there were changes in copy or in media strategy (such as an expanded target market). When advertising was successful in increasing sales, its impact lasted up to two years after peak spending. Moreover, the long-term incremental sales generated were approximately double the incremental sales observed in the first year of an advertising spending increase.[11]

Other studies reinforce these conclusions. One study found that advertising often did not increase sales for mature brands or categories in decline. A review of academic research found that advertising elasticities were estimated to be higher for new products (0.3) than for established products (0.1).[12]

Developing the Advertising Campaign

In designing and evaluating an ad campaign, it is important to distinguish the *message strategy* or positioning of an ad—*what* the ad attempts to convey about the brand—and its *creative strategy*—*how* the ad expresses the brand claims. So designing effective advertising campaigns is both an art and a science. Consider the following example:

Singapore Ministry of Health—An award-winning Chinese-language print ad by the Singapore Ministry of Health for its dental hygiene campaign treated readers to a rather incongruous message. At first glance, the ad did not appear to have anything to do with dental health. It was a tongue twister. The tagline in small print read, "Try saying that without your real teeth." Chinese-speaking readers loved the ad.[13]

Chinese Characters	Meaning	Pronunciation
十四是十四	14 is 14	*Shi si shi shi si*
四十是四十	40 is 40	*Si shi shi si shi*
十四不是四十	14 is not 40	*Shi si bu shi si shi*
四十不是十四	40 is not 14	*Si shi bu shi shi si*

To develop a message strategy, advertisers go through three steps: message generation and evaluation, creative development and execution, and social responsibility review.

MESSAGE GENERATION AND EVALUATION

It is important to generate fresh insights and avoid using the same appeals and positions as others. If automobile ads all show the same thing—a car driving at high speed on a curved mountain road or across a desert, they will only establish a weak link between the brand and the message. Advertisers are always seeking "the big idea" that connects with consumers rationally and emotionally, sharply distinguishes the brand from its competitors, and is broad and flexible enough to translate to different media, markets, and time periods.[14]

A good ad normally focuses on one or two core selling propositions. As part of refining the brand positioning, the advertiser should conduct market research to determine which appeal works best with its target audience. Once they find an effective appeal, advertisers should prepare a *creative brief*, typically covering one or two pages. This is an elaboration of the *positioning statement* and includes: key message, target audience, communication objectives (to do, to know, to believe), key brand benefits, support for the brand promise, and media.

How many alternative ad themes should the advertiser create before making a choice? The more ads created, the higher is the probability of finding an excellent one. Fortunately, the expense of creating rough ads is rapidly falling due to computers. An ad agency's creative department can compose many alternative ads in a short time by drawing from computer files containing still and video images.

Marketers can also cut the cost of creative dramatically by using consumers as their creative team, a strategy sometimes called "open source" or "crowdsourcing." However, as the following examples show, this technique can be pure genius or a regrettable failure.

L'Oréal—An in-house-produced ad for cosmetics giant L'Oréal would typically run $164,000 for a 30-second TV spot. Yet, the company took its inspiration from Current TV, a cable TV channel where user-generated content, in the form of 5-minute segments on any topic, is the programming norm. When Current TV opened up the creative process to commercials, L'Oréal became a Current TV sponsor and paid for an ad produced by someone using the handle "spicytuna." The price tag was a mere $1,000, but you wouldn't know it from the high-concept ad, which featured a Japanese paper fan unfolding across the TV screen. Hidden under the fan was a woman's white-painted face, and when the fan folded up entirely, the face reappeared but with electric-looking green eye shadow. When the ad faded to black, a tagline appeared, "Find color in confidence. L'Oréal Paris."[15]

Other marketers caution that the open-source model does not work for every company or every product. Consumer-generated ads may backfire as it did for Chevrolet.

General Motors—In 2006, Chevy directed customers to a special Web site and invited them to create ads for the 2007 Tahoe SUV. The site, <www.chevyapprentice.com>, was a partnership with the popular TV show, *The Apprentice*, and it allowed apprentice creative directors to choose from a dozen short video clips and almost as many soundtracks and to write their own copy. The ads would then be entered in a contest. But the campaign backfired when Chevy decided to make the spots viral, giving them as much exposure as possible without vetting them first. Instead of singing the Tahoe's praises, many of the spots lambasted Chevy for producing a gas-guzzling contributor to global warming. One said, "This powerful V8 engine only gets 15 miles to the gallon. In a world of limited national resources, you don't need GPS to see where this road is going." One analyst said of the fiasco, "Brands need to be smarter about empowering their brand advocates. In the case of Chevy Tahoe, what you really want to do is take consumers who are most devoted to your product and put them behind the wheel."[16]

An intimate knowledge of the local culture is important to develop a suitable theme. Leveraging its superior understanding of the Chinese market, a local ad agency beat four multinational ad agencies for the Electrolux account:

Electrolux—Chinese ad agency East West proposed an ad featuring Electrolux appliances, including a stove-top fan, whisking away billows of smoke from a stove. The happy owner then picks up a sledgehammer and knocks down the wall between her kitchen and the living room. This theme resonated the way Chinese chefs cook and the deep desire of many Chinese for space and freedom. The idea, says Hong Yan, co-owner of East West, is that like society, "the kitchen is open."[17]

However, Chinese ad agencies are normally not as specialized as their counterparts in developed countries.[18] Chinese firms also believe that they understand the market better than ad agencies. Consequently, Chinese clients tend to dominate the campaign development process while ad agencies mainly perform the technical tasks.[19]

Some ad agencies in Asia have implemented "disaster checks" before their campaigns go live to make sure that they are not blinded to a political sore spot. Toyota, for instance, has established a "supervisory system" for its marketing—a public relations officer in charge of its Chinese office.[20] "Marketing Insight: Advertising Guidelines for Modern Asia" outlines some considerations when advertising in Asia.

MARKETING INSIGHT • ADVERTISING GUIDELINES FOR MODERN ASIA

As Asian markets become more sophisticated, so too will regional advertising. Jim Aitchison, who has worked in Asian advertising for over 20 years, gave the following insights about advertising in the region:

- **There is no such thing as a "typical" Asian campaign.** Generally, most are visually, not verbally led, consistent with the logographic nature of many Asian languages. The best have well-focused singular themes and present their messages in a fresh, different manner.
- **There is no such thing as a "typical" Asian consumer.** Each market has its own personality. The different experiences and exposures have produced people with different perspectives. However, this does not mean that advertising has to be crude and simplistic to "reach" to everyone. There are sufficient similarities to unite rather than divide regional audiences.
- **The best work adheres to the universal truths of advertising.** The universal truths of advertising—singularity of proposition, simplicity of expression, and relevance of message—still apply. Regional campaigns that span different cultures, languages, and social and economic development work best when they contain some magic element of surprise or difference. Lateral thinking is also more evident now in Asia than 10 or 20 years ago. Simplistic, condescending creativity is becoming less evident. Thus younger and better educated Chinese want ads to be less direct and more subtle, and prefer ads that allow them to draw inferences about the brand.
- **The best work is true to its own culture.** The best Asian ads do not ape the West. They speak with their own voice for their brands. Malaysia's Petronas ads are uniquely, passionately Malaysian. Hong Kong's Swipe commercial featuring an old man famous for his anti-British graffiti cleaning his own graffiti with the brand was pure local satire. The best ideas go beyond mere language and style. They reflect deep characteristics of people and come from real life.
- **Humor appears to be a successful tool in Asia.** While Thai advertising has been famous for its sense of humor, other Asian markets are appearing to be more willing to sell with a smile. The humor is also more piquant when it reflects some quirk of its local culture or society. Amul's poster ads in India constantly satirize the Indian government or world events.
- **Asians respond to beautiful executions and craft.** The ads by Singapore Airlines bear testimony that beautifully crafted strategic work, expressing relevant, truthful brand ideas work. Another is Singapore Telecoms' (SingTel) anniversary ad campaign that featured well-executed appropriate messages of how ordinary Singaporeans value the telecommunications company. One showed a handicapped person communicating via the email services provided by SingTel, while another showed how a man misses his best friend (a dog) and communicated to it by phone.

Source: Jim Aitchison, *How Asia Advertises,* (Singapore: John Wiley, 2002).

CREATIVE DEVELOPMENT AND EXECUTION

The ad's impact depends not only on what is said, but often more important, on how it is said. Execution can be decisive. Every advertising medium has specific advantages and disadvantages. Here, we review television, radio, and print advertising media.

Television Ads

Television is generally acknowledged as the most powerful advertising medium and reaches a broad spectrum of consumers. The wide reach translates to low cost per exposure. From a brand-building perspective, TV advertising has two particularly important strengths. First, it can be an effective means of vividly demonstrating product attributes and persuasively explaining their corresponding consumer benefits. Second, TV advertising can be a compelling means for dramatically portraying user and usage imagery, brand personality, and other brand intangibles.

Because of the fleeting nature of the message and the potentially distracting creative elements often found in a TV ad, product-related messages and the brand itself can be overlooked. Moreover, the numerous ads and non-programming material on television creates clutter that makes it easy for consumers to ignore or forget ads. Another important disadvantage is the high cost of production and placement.

Nevertheless, properly designed and executed TV ads can improve brand equity and affect sales and profits. Over the years, one of the most consistently successful TV advertisers has been Apple. The "1984" ad for the introduction of the Macintosh personal computer—portraying a stark Orwellian future with a feature film look—ran only once on TV but is one of the best known ads ever. In the following years, Apple successfully created

Absolut vodka ads emphasize the distinctive shape of the bottle and the personality of the magazine or city in which the ad appears. Here are ads that were developed to capture the spirit of three Asian cities: Bangkok, Beijing, and Kyoto.

awareness and image for a series of products, most recently with its acclaimed iPod ad campaign. A well-done TV commercial can still be a powerful marketing tool.

Print Ads

Print media offers a stark contrast to broadcast media. Because of its self-paced nature, magazines and newspapers can provide much detailed product information and can also effectively communicate user and usage imagery. At the same time, the static nature of the visual images in print media makes it difficult to provide dynamic presentations or demonstrations. Another disadvantage is that it can be a fairly passive medium.

The two main print media—magazines and newspapers—share many advantages and disadvantages. Although newspapers are timely and pervasive, magazines are typically more effective at building user and usage imagery. Daily newspapers tend to be used a lot for local—especially retailer—advertising. Although advertisers have some flexibility in designing and placing newspaper ads, poor reproduction quality and short shelf life can diminish their impact.

Format elements such as ad size, color, and illustration also affect a print ad's impact. A minor rearrangement of mechanical elements can improve attention-getting power. Larger ads gain more attention, though not necessarily by as much as their difference in cost. Four-color illustrations increase ad effectiveness and ad cost. New electronic eye movement studies show that consumers can be led through an ad by strategic placement of dominant elements.

Researchers studying print advertisements report that the *picture, headline*, and *copy* are important, in that order. The picture must be strong enough to draw attention. Then the headline must reinforce the picture and lead the person to read the copy. The copy itself must be engaging and the advertised brand's name must be sufficiently prominent. Even then, a really outstanding ad will be noted by less than 50 percent of the exposed audience. About 30 percent might recall the headline's main point; about 25 percent might remember the advertiser's name; and less than 10 percent will read most of the body copy. Ordinary ads do not achieve even these results.

Given how consumers process print ads, some clear managerial implications emerge, as summarized in "Marketing Memo: Print Ad Evaluation Criteria." One print ad campaign that successfully carved out a brand image is Absolut Vodka.

Absolut Vodka—Vodka is generally viewed as a commodity product, yet the level of brand preference and loyalty in the vodka market is astonishing. Most of this preference and loyalty is attributed to brand image. When the Swedish brand Absolut first entered the U.S. market, sales was a disappointing 7,000 cases. Within 12 years, sales had soared to over two million cases. It became the largest selling imported vodka in the U.S., with 65 percent of the market, thanks in large part to its marketing strategy. In the U.S. market, Absolut has aimed for sophisticated, upwardly mobile, affluent drinkers. The vodka comes in a distinctive clear bottle that is used as the centerpiece of every ad. The campaign cleverly juxtaposed a punning caption against a stylized image of the brand's distinctively shaped bottle. This campaign was carried through to Asia. For example, in "Absolut Bangkok," a silhouette of the bottle was formed by boats in the city's famed floating market.

Radio Ads

Radio is a pervasive medium. Its main advantage is flexibility—stations are more targeted, ads are relatively inexpensive to produce and place, and short closings allow for quick response. Radio is a particularly effective medium in the morning; it can also let companies achieve a balance between broad and localized market coverage.

MARKETING MEMO • PRINT AD EVALUATION CRITERIA

In addition to considering the communication strategy target market, communication objectives, and message and creative strategy, the following questions concerning executional elements should be answered affirmatively when judging print ad effectiveness:

1. Is the message clear at a glance? Can you quickly tell what the ad is about?
2. Is the benefit in the headline?
3. Does the illustration support the headline?
4. Does the first line of the copy support or explain the headline and the illustration?
5. Is the ad easy to read and follow?
6. Is the product easily identified?
7. Is the brand or sponsor clearly identified?

Source: Philip Ward Burton and Scott C. Purvis, *Which Ad Pulled Best*, 9th ed., (Lincolnwood, IL: NTC Business Books, 2002).

The obvious disadvantages of radio are the lack of visual images and the relatively passive nature of the consumer processing that results.[21] Nevertheless, radio ads can be extremely creative. Some see the lack of visual images as a plus because they feel the clever use of music, sound, and other creative devices can tap into the listener's imagination to create powerfully relevant and well-liked images.

LEGAL AND SOCIAL ISSUES

Advertisers and their agencies must be sure advertising does not overstep social and legal norms. Public policy makers have developed a substantial body of laws and regulations to govern advertising.

For example, ads using the words "most," "best," and "number one" are not allowed in China. However, such regulations vary by location. In Chengdu, ads cannot say "the most beautiful housing development" or "best value." However, in Shanghai, Beijing, and Guangzhou, these words are usually allowed.[22] The Chinese government also has regulations regarding the design, image, taste, and possible psychological impact of foreign ads on viewers of varying age groups.

Advertisers should not make false claims, such as stating that a product cures something when it does not. They must avoid false demonstrations. In some countries, it is illegal to create ads that have the capacity to deceive, even though no one may actually be deceived. For example, wall paint cannot be advertised as giving five years' protection unless it does so under typical conditions. The problem is how to tell the difference between deception and "puffery"—simple exaggerations not intended to be believed which are permitted by law.

Some marketers use bait-and-switch advertising to attract buyers under false pretenses. Suppose a seller advertises a DVD player at $149. When consumers try to buy the advertised machine, the seller cannot then refuse to sell it, downplay its features, show a faulty one, or promise unreasonable delivery dates to switch the buyer to a more expensive machine.[23]

To be socially responsible, advertisers must be careful not to offend the general public as well as any ethnic groups, racial minorities, or special-interest groups.[24] A print ad for Clinique's perfume, Elixir, showing a snake crawling over the head of an image of Buddha was taken off because it was insulting to Thais. Most Thais are Buddhists and the head is considered the most revered part of the body. In China, a Toyota ad showing two stone lions saluting a Prado SUV angered many Chinese as the lions, a traditional symbol of Chinese power, resembled those flanking the Marco Polo Bridge, the site near Beijing where the opening battle in Japan's 1937 invasion of China took place. Additionally, as Chinese words often hold multiple meanings, Prado translates into Chinese as *badao*, which also means "rule by force" or "overbearing." Toyota had to pull and apologize for the ad.[25] In Malaysia, Unilever's ad for Pond's skin lightening moisturizer showed a Malay college student using the product for a fairer complexion to get a boy's attention. The ad was deemed offensive to the darker complexioned ethnic group.[26]

In most Asian countries, sex sells, especially for beer. This picture was taken of a convenience store in Malaysia selling beer.

Sex appeals have also come under increased scrutiny.[27] Here is an ad using sex appeal that failed:

> **Boon Rawd Brewery**—Boon Rawd Brewery launched Leo Beer using billboards throughout Thailand featuring a Thai sex symbol in a skimpy outfit suggestively staring out with a bottle of Leo Beer in front of her. The campaign bombed. Said one leading adman, "Sex is not used in Thailand as it goes against our traditional Buddhist values and culture. For Thais, humor is the most powerful and effective method whether you use sex appeal or not ... If sex sells in a funny way, it will work."

Some advertisers have pushed the boundaries of responsible advertising in the region. For example, U.K.-based clothing chain French Connection used shock tactics to build its brand among Asian youths. Its FCUK campaign had its promotions pulled in Singapore. However, the ban got the company more publicity. While parents may be upset with the controversial campaign, teenagers appreciated the humor behind the sexual innuendo. Sex appeals may have to be adapted to meet the varying standards of government regulations in the region. Thus lipstick on men was refused by one government authority, revealing female underarms by another, and plunging necklines by a third.

Deciding on Media and Measuring Effectiveness

After choosing the message, the advertiser's next task is to choose media to carry it. The steps here are deciding on desired reach, frequency, and impact; choosing among major media types; selecting specific media vehicles; deciding on media timing; and deciding on geographical media allocation. Then the results of these decisions need to be evaluated.

Deciding on Reach, Frequency, and Impact

Media selection is finding the most cost-effective media to deliver the desired number and type of exposures to the target audience. What do we mean by the desired number of exposures? Presumably, the advertiser is seeking a specified advertising objective and response from the target audience—for example, a target level of product trial. The rate of product trial will depend, among other things, on the level of brand awareness. Suppose the rate of product trial increases at a diminishing rate with the level of audience awareness, as shown in Figure 18.2(a). If the advertiser seeks a product trial rate of (say) T^*, it will be necessary to achieve a brand awareness level of A^*.

The next task is to find out how many exposures, E^*, will produce an audience awareness of A^*. The effect of exposures on audience awareness depends on the exposures' reach, frequency, and impact:

- ***Reach (R)*** — The number of different persons or households exposed to a particular media schedule at least once during a specified time period.
- ***Frequency (F)*** — The number of times within the specified time period that an average person or household is exposed to the message.
- ***Impact (I)*** — The qualitative value of an exposure through a given medium (thus a cosmetic ad in *Cleo* would have a higher impact than in *Fortune* magazine).

Figure 18.2(b) shows the relationship between audience awareness and reach. Audience awareness will be greater, the higher the exposures' reach, frequency, and impact. There are important trade-offs among reach, frequency, and impact. Suppose the planner has an advertising budget of $1,000,000 and the cost per thousand exposures of average quality is $5. This means the advertiser can buy 200,000,000 exposures ($1,000,000 ÷ [$5/1,000]). If the advertiser seeks an average exposure frequency of 10, then the advertiser can reach 20,000,000 people (200,000,000 ÷ 10) with the given budget. But if the advertiser wants higher-quality media costing $10 per thousand exposures, it will be able to reach only 10,000,000 people unless it is willing to lower the desired exposure frequency.

The relationship between reach, frequency, and impact is captured in the following concepts:

- ***Total number of exposures (E)***— This is the reach times the average frequency; that is, $E = R \times F$. This measure is referred to as the gross rating points (GRP). If a given media schedule reaches 80 percent of the homes with an average exposure frequency of three, the media schedule is said to have a GRP of 240 (80 × 3). If another media schedule has a GRP of 300, it is said to have more weight, but we cannot tell how this weight breaks down into reach and frequency.
- ***Weighted number of exposures (WE)***— This is the reach times average frequency times average impact, that is $WE = R \times F \times I$.

The media planner has to figure out the most cost-effective combination of reach, frequency, and impact. Reach is most important when launching new products, flanker brands, extensions of well-known brands, or infrequently purchased brands; or going after an undefined target market. Frequency is most important where there are strong competitors, a complex story to tell, high consumer resistance, or a frequent-purchase cycle.[28]

Many advertisers believe a target audience needs a large number of exposures for the advertising to work. Others doubt the value of high frequency. They believe that after people see the same ad a few times, they either act on it, get irritated by it, or stop noticing it.[29]

Another factor arguing for repetition is that of forgetting. The job of repetition is partly to put the message back into memory. The higher the forgetting rate associated with a brand, product category, or message, the higher the warranted level of repetition. However, repetition is not enough; ads wear out and viewers tune out. Advertisers should not coast on a tired ad but insist on fresh executions by their advertising agency.

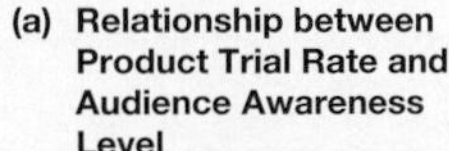

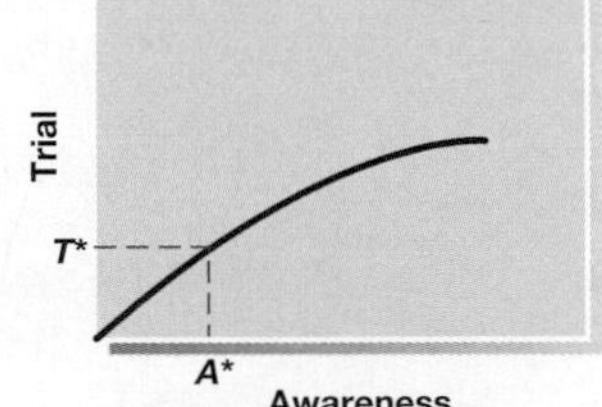

(b) Relationship between Audience Awareness Level and Exposure Reach and Frequency

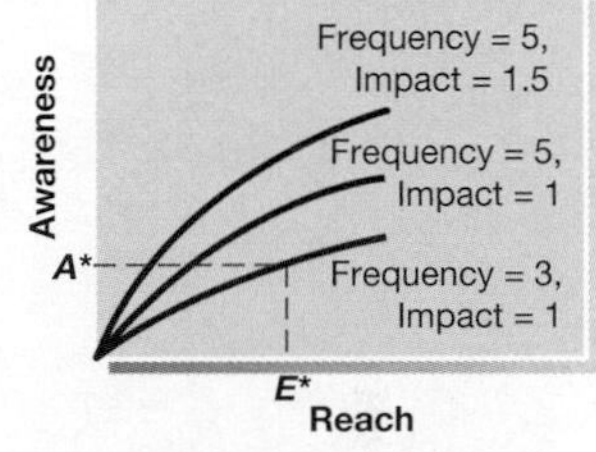

Figure 18.2 Relationship Among Trial, Awareness, and the Exposure Function

Choosing Among Major Media Types

The media planner has to know the capacity of the major advertising media types to deliver reach, frequency, and impact. The major advertising media along with their costs, advantages, and limitations are profiled in Table 18.1.

Media planners make their choices by considering the following variables:

- ***Target-audience media habits***— Radio and television are the most effective media for reaching teenagers.
- ***Product characteristics*** — Media types have different potential for demonstration, visualization, explanation, believability, and color. Women's dresses are best shown in color magazines, and cars are best demonstrated on television.
- ***Message characteristics*** — Timeliness and information content will influence media choice. A message announcing a major sale tomorrow will require radio, TV, or newspaper. A message containing a great deal of technical data might require specialized magazines or mailings.
- ***Cost***— Television is usually more expensive than radio advertising. What counts is the cost per thousand exposures.

Given the abundance of media, the planner must first decide how to allocate the budget to the major media types. Consumers are increasingly time-starved. Attention is becoming a scarce currency, and advertisers need strong devices to capture people's attention.[30]

Table 18.1 Profiles of Major Media Types

Medium	Advantages	Limitations
Newspapers	Flexibility; timeliness; good local market coverage; broad acceptance; high believability	Short life; poor reproduction quality; small "pass-along" audience
Television	Combines sight, sound, and motion; appealing to the senses; high attention; high reach	High absolute cost; high clutter; fleeting exposure; less audience selectivity
Direct mail	Audience selectivity; flexibility; no ad competition within the same medium; personalization	Relatively high cost; "junk mail" image
Radio	Mass use; high geographic and demographic selectivity; low cost	Audio presentation only; lower attention than television; non-standardized rate structures; fleeting exposure
Magazines	High geographic and demographic selectivity; credibility and prestige; high-quality reproduction; long life; good pass-along readership	Long ad purchase lead time; some waste circulation; no guarantee of position
Outdoor	Flexibility; high repeat exposure; low cost; low competition	Limited audience selectivity; creative limitations
Yellow Pages	Excellent local coverage; high believability; wide reach; low cost	High competition; long ad purchase lead time; creative limitations
Newsletters	Very high selectivity; full control; interactive opportunities; relative low costs	Costs could run away
Brochures	Flexibility; full control; can dramatize messages	Overproduction could lead to runaway costs
Telephone	Many users; opportunity to give a personal touch	Relative high cost unless volunteers are used
Internet	High selectivity; interactive possibilities; relatively low cost	Relatively new media with a low number of users in some countries

KitKat—KitKat has been successfully in garnering consumer attention both in Japan and China by associating the product with a basic emotion that its audience identified with. Through an integrated campaign of online, television, and print ads, KitKat got customers to use the chocolate bar as a stress-breaker. One spot featured students taking high-pressure exams. They pulled out the chocolate bars and broke them, not only to relieve the stress but also for luck. Overnight, sales skyrocketed. In China, KitKat employed a similar strategy by encouraging boyfriends to log into the KitKat Web site and express their love for their girlfriends. Using ads that are engaging and involving the consumer as an active participant in the campaign made the KitKat campaigns attention-grabbing.[31]

Alternative Advertising Options

In recent years, researchers have noticed reduced effectiveness due to increased commercial clutter (advertisers beaming shorter and more numerous commercials at the audience) and lower viewing owing to the growth in cable and satellite TV and DVDs/VCRs.[32]

PLACE ADVERTISING

Place advertising, also called out-of-home advertising, is a broadly defined category that captures many different alternative advertising forms. Marketers are using creative and unexpected ad placements to grab consumers' attention. The rationale often given is that marketers are better off reaching people in other environments, such as where they work, play, and, of course, shop. Some of the options available include billboards, public places, product placement, and point-of-purchase.

Billboards

Billboards have been transformed over the years and now use colorful, digitally produced graphics, backlighting, sounds, movement, and unusual—even 3-D images.[33] Adidas hoisted human billboards in Tokyo and Osaka, Japan. Two soccer players competed for shots during 15-minute matches scheduled five times a day while they and a ball dangled from ropes 12 stories above ground.[34] Billboards do not even necessarily have to stay in one place. Marketers can buy ad space on billboard-laden trucks that are driven continuously all day in selected areas.

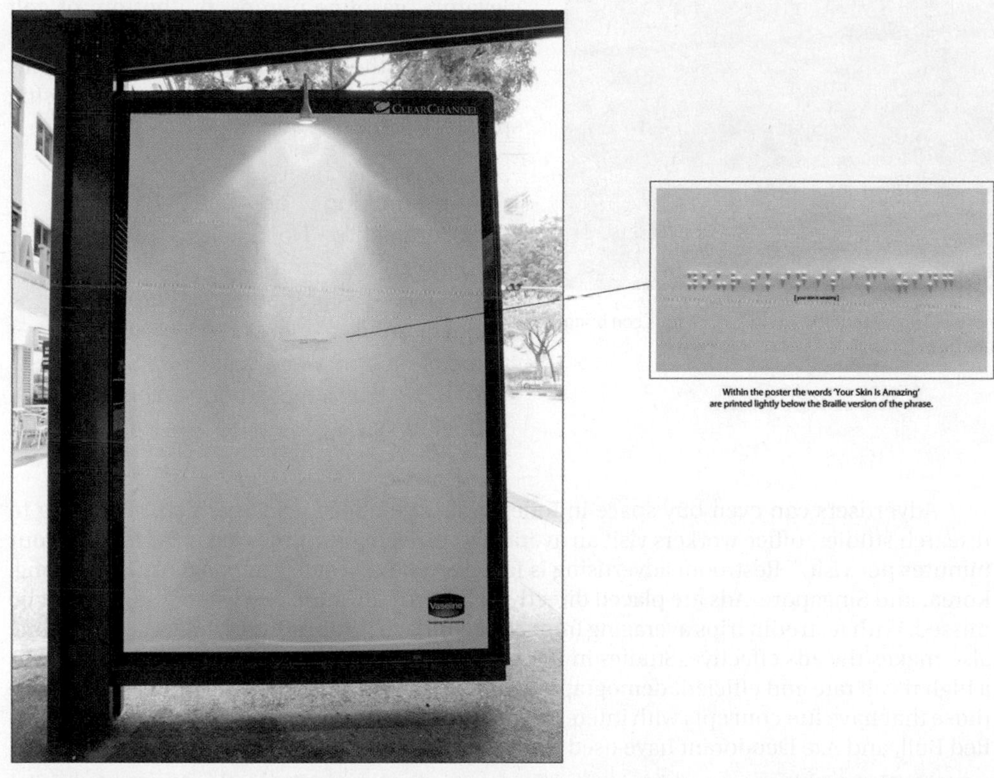
CLEARCHANNEL
Vaseline
Within the poster the words 'Your Skin Is Amazing' are printed lightly below the Braille version of the phrase.

Vaseline uses outdoor media to demonstrate how sensitive skin is. The bus shelter poster has the words "Your Skin is Amazing" printed lightly below the Braille version of the phrase. Similarly, Braille stickers that read "Your Skin is Amazing" were placed where people typically put their fingers–bus handles, trolley bars, lift buttons, arm chair handles–alerting them to the printed message.

Outdoor advertising is popular in Asia for the following reasons. The traffic jams in cities such as Bangkok, Kuala Lumpur, Shanghai, and Tokyo suggest that there is a massive captive audience. In rural areas where television and newspaper advertising is less available, billboards are used to reach the mass audience. Moreover, TV advertising rates have increased dramatically while outdoor advertising has become more cost-effective. According to Hong Kong-based Clear Media, which owns 18,000 bus shelters in 30 Chinese cities, some of its billboards are seen by 70 percent of young people five to 10 times

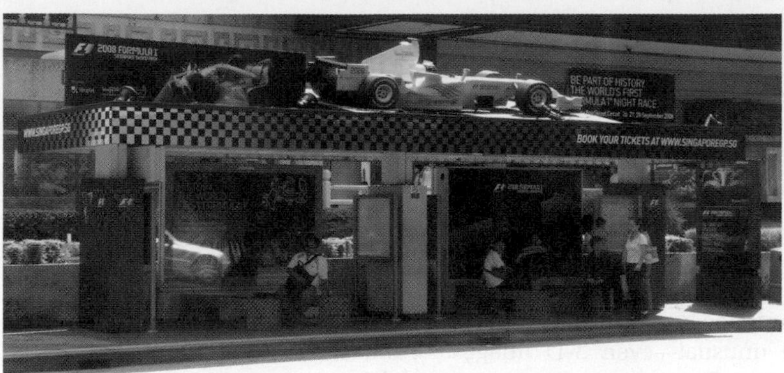

A 3-D bus stop ad announcing ticket sales for the world's first Formula1 night race in Singapore.

HSBC advertises on Kuala Lumpur's monorail to show that the world's local bank can bring people places—a tie-in to the monorail that goes through the heart of the city.

a fortnight. To reach that number on TV would be extremely expensive.[35]

Public Spaces

Advertisers are placing traditional TV and print ads in unconventional places such as movies, airlines, lounges, classrooms, sports arenas, office and hotel elevators, escalator handrails, restrooms, and other public places. Billboard-type poster ads are showing up everywhere. Transit ads on buses, subways, and commuter trains—around for years—have become a valuable way to reach working women. "Street furniture"—bus shelters, kiosks, and public areas—is another fast-growing option.

Advertisers can buy space in stadiums and arenas and on garbage cans, bicycle racks, parking meters, airport luggage carousels, elevators, gasoline pumps, the bottom of golf cups, airline snack packages, and supermarket produce in the form of tiny labels on apples and bananas. Another innovative advertising space is the road.

> **Anti-smoking ad**—The Singapore government's "No Smoking" message found its way to a space on the road. In several high-pedestrian areas, the government has imprinted on the road messages in white such as "Smoking kills 12 times more people than road accidents."

Advertisers can even buy space in toilet stalls and above urinals which, according to research studies, office workers visit an average of three to four times a day for roughly four minutes per visit.[36] Restroom advertising is fast becoming popular in Bangkok, Hong Kong, Korea, and Singapore. Ads are placed directly in front of the audience where they cannot be missed. With restroom trips averaging from 30 seconds to three minutes, high exposure time also makes the ads effective. Studies in Bangkok have shown that restroom advertising has a high recall rate and efficient demographic targeting. Ads that tend to be more effective are those that have fun concepts with interesting product or service information. Adidas, Durex, Red Bull, and Axe Deodorant have used this medium.[37]

Another public space which is used for innovative advertising is the Automated Teller Machine (ATM) as the following example shows:

> **Unilever**—In Singapore, Unilever tied up with DBS Bank to run an advertising campaign for its Wall's brand of ice cream through the bank's ATMs. An ATM user will see a screen advertisement of Wall's. DBS has the widest distribution and reach in terms of ATMs, giving it a substantial "eyeball" count that is attractive to advertisers. The placement of an ATM ad is where the consumers least expect it and gives them a new brand experience. Also, the attention of an ATM user is very focused on the screen. Hence, it is a very effective way of bringing across messages without distraction.[38]

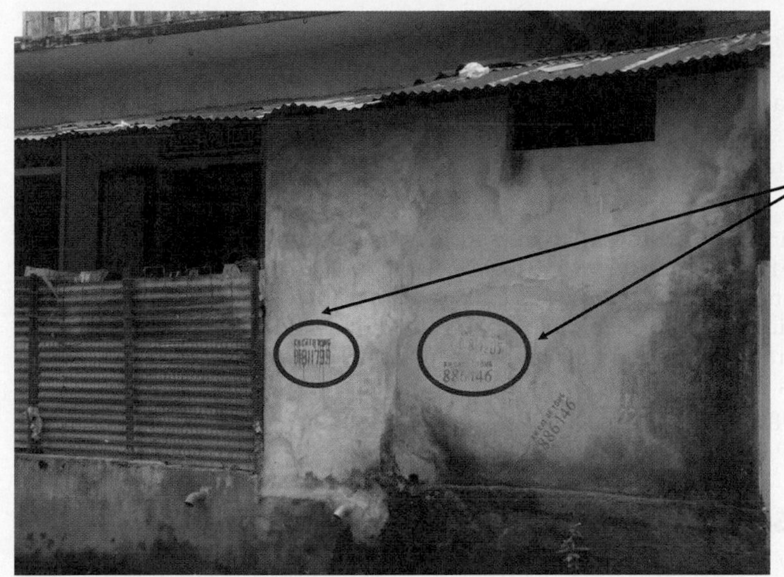
Contact numbers and brand names are stamped on walls.
In rural parts of Asia where outdoor media is not formalized, marketers have advertised freely by stamping on outside walls of houses their phone numbers and products. Here, in a Vietnamese suburb, the contact numbers and brand names can be clearly seen stamped on a house.

PRODUCT PLACEMENT

Product placement has expanded from movies to all types of TV shows. Marketers pay fees of $50,000–$100,000 and even higher so that their products make cameo appearances in movies and on television. The exact sum depends on the amount and nature of the brand exposure. Sometimes placements are the result of a larger network advertising deal, but other times they are the work of small product placement shops that maintain close ties with prop masters, set designers, and production executives.[39] Brands such as Heineken, Aston Martin, Sony, and Omega have major promotional pushes based on product placement tie-ins with the James Bond film *Casino Royale*.[40]

Some firms get product placement at no cost by supplying their products to the movie company (Nike does not pay to be in movies but often supplies shoes, jackets, bags, etc.).[41] Firms sometime just get lucky and are included in shows for plot reasons. FedEx received lots of favorable exposure from the movie *Cast Away*.[42]

In China, several broadcasters are signing up for shows where the products are the stars.[43] Entire programs are produced and branded by advertisers. The stations benefit from slick programming, minus production costs; while advertisers get the perfect channel for reaching the consumers they crave. For marketers, developing TV programs offers a way to build brands without paying the full price for expensive Chinese TV advertising whose rates have been soaring with the flourishing economy.

Lycra My Show—This talent show was one of the biggest summer hits in China. Its production was organized and funded by Vivendi's Universal Music, the Shanghai Media Group, and U.S.-based fabric company Invista's Lycra brand, along with co-sponsors Coca-Cola and Sony Ericsson. Contestants, vying to win a recording contract and career investment from Universal Music, sing their hearts out while sporting stretchy Lycra-based clothing.

Such program sponsorship is also part of a movement to integrate marketing into consumers' lives beyond traditional TV commercials, as the following example illustrates:

Home Show—British home-improvement store, B&Q, used its own TV show called the *Home Show*, produced by Frontiers Group China. Featuring home renovation tips, the show aims to build awareness for its Chinese stores. As people are purchasing homes for the first time in China, B&Q wants to be considered the top name and authority on home décor.

Marketers are finding other inventive ways to advertise during actual television broadcasts. Sports fans are familiar with the virtual logos networks add digitally to the playing field. Invisible to spectators at the event, these ads look just like painted-on logos to home viewers. Ads also appear in best-selling paperback books and movie videotapes. Written material such as annual reports, data sheets, catalogs, and newsletters increasingly carry ads. **Advertorials** are print ads that offer editorial content that reflects favorably on the brand and are difficult to distinguish from newspaper or magazine content. Many companies include advertising inserts in monthly bills. Some companies mail CDs or DVDs to prospects.

POINT-OF-PURCHASE

There are so many ways to communicate with consumers at the ***point-of-purchase*** **(P-O-P)**. In-store advertising includes ads on shopping carts, cart straps, aisles, and shelves, as well as promotion options such as in-store demonstrations, live sampling, and instant coupon machines. Some supermarkets are selling floor space for company logos and experimenting with talking shelves. P-O-P radio provides FM-style programming and commercial messages to thousands of food stores and drugstores nationwide. Programming includes a store-selected music format, consumer tips, and commercials.

The appeal of point-of-purchase advertising lies in the fact that numerous studies show that in many product categories, consumers make the bulk of their final brand decisions in the store. One study suggested that 70 percent of all buying decisions are made in the store. In-store advertising is designed to increase the number of spontaneous buying decisions.

Evaluating Alternative Media

Ads can now appear virtually anywhere consumers have a few spare minutes or even seconds and thus enough time to notice them. The main advantage of non-traditional media is that a very precise and—because of the nature of the setting involved—captive audience often can be reached in a cost-effective manner. The message must be simple and direct. In fact, outdoor advertising is often called the "15-second sell." Strategically, out-of-home advertising is often more effective at enhancing brand awareness or reinforcing brand image rather than creating new brand associations.

The challenge with non-traditional media is demonstrating its reach and effectiveness through credible, independent research. These new marketing strategies and tactics must ultimately be judged on how they contribute, directly or indirectly, to brand equity. Unique ad placements designed to break through clutter may also be perceived as invasive and obtrusive.

Consumers must be favorably affected in some way to justify the marketing expenditures for nontraditional media. There will, however, always be room for creative means of placing the brand in front of consumers. The possibilities are endless: "Marketing Insight: Playing Games with Brands" describes the emergence of yet another new media trend.

Selecting Specific Vehicles

The media planner must search for the most cost-effective vehicles within each chosen media type. These choices are critical given the high cost of producing and airing television commercials. In making choices, the planner has to rely on measurement services that provide estimates of audience size, composition, and media cost. Audience size has several possible measures:

- ***Circulation*** — The number of physical units carrying the advertising.
- ***Audience*** — The number of people exposed to the vehicle. (If the vehicle has pass-on readership, then the audience is larger than circulation.)

MARKETING INSIGHT • PLAYING GAMES WITH BRANDS

Given the explosive popularity of video games with younger consumers, many advertisers have adopted an "if you can't beat them, join them" attitude. Online games have wide appeal. Women seem to prefer puzzles and collaborative games, whereas men seem more attracted to competitive or simulation games. An "advergame" can be played on the sponsor's corporate homepage, on gaming portals, or even at restaurants.

7-Up, McDonald's, and Porsche have been featured in games. Honda developed a game that allowed players to choose a Honda and zoom around city streets plastered with Honda logos. In the first three months, 78,000 people played for an average of eight minutes. The cost-per-thousand (CPM) of $7 compared favorably to a primetime TV commercial CPM of $11.65. Marketers collect valuable customer data upon registration and often seek permission to send email.

Marketers are also playing starring roles in popular videogames. In multiplayer videogame Test Drive Unlimited, players can take a break from the races to go shopping, where they can encounter at least 10 real-world brands such as Lexus and Hawaiian Airlines. Tomb Raider's Lara Croft tools around with a Jeep Commander. Mainstream marketers such as Apple, Procter & Gamble, Toyota, and Visa are all jumping on board. Spending on in-game advertising and product placement is expected to grow from $56 million in 2005 to $730 million in 2010, with a typical cost per thousand of $30. The growing popularity of virtual communities is creating new placement opportunities for marketers. Coca-Cola, IBM, and Toyota are among the companies that have set up a virtual presence.

Sources: "Virtual Worlds Generate Real-Life Benefits for Properties, Sponsors." *IEG Sponsorship Report*, June 11, 2007, pp. 1, 8; Allison Fass, "Sex, Pranks, and Reality." *Forbes*, July 2, 2007, p. 48; Erika Brown, "Game On!" *Forbes*, July 24, 2006, pp. 84–86; David Radd, "Advergaming: You Got It." *BusinessWeek*, October 11, 2006; Stuart Elliott, "Madison's Avenue's Full-Court Pitch to Video Gamers." *New York Times*, October 16, 2005; "Women Get in the Game." <www.microsoft.com>, January 8, 2004.

Virtual communities and videogames are among the new frontiers for advertisers trying to reach young consumers. The above is a scene from Second Life.

- ***Effective audience*** — The number of people with target audience characteristics exposed to the vehicle.
- ***Effective ad-exposed audience*** — The number of people with target audience characteristics who actually saw the ad.

Media planners calculate the cost per thousand persons reached by a vehicle. If a full-page, four-color ad in *Newsweek* costs $200,000 and *Newsweek*'s estimated readership is 3.1 million people, the cost of exposing the ad to 1,000 persons is approximately $65.

The same ad in *BusinessWeek* may cost $70,000 but reach only 970,000 persons—at a cost-per-thousand of $72. The media planner ranks each magazine by cost-per-thousand and favors magazines with the lowest cost-per-thousand for reaching target consumers. The magazines themselves often put together a "reader profile" for their advertisers, summarizing the characteristics of the magazine's readers with respect to age, income, residence, marital status, and leisure activities.

Several adjustments have to be applied to the cost-per-thousand measure. First, the measure should be adjusted for *audience quality.* For a baby lotion ad, a magazine read by one million young mothers would have an exposure value of one million; if read by one million teenagers, it would have almost a zero exposure value. Second, the exposure value should be adjusted for the *audience-attention probability.* Readers of *Vogue* may pay more attention to ads than readers of *Newsweek.* A "happy" commercial placed within an upbeat television show is more likely to be effective than a downbeat commercial in the same place. Third, the exposure value should be adjusted for the magazine's *editorial quality* (prestige and believability). In addition, people are more likely to believe a TV or radio ad and to become more positively disposed toward the brand when the ad is placed within a program they like.[44] Fourth, the exposure value should be adjusted for the magazine's *ad placement policies and extra services* (such as regional or occupational editions and lead-time requirements).

Media planners are increasingly using more sophisticated measures of effectiveness and employing them in mathematical models to arrive at the best media mix. Many advertising agencies use a computer program to select the initial media and then make further improvements based on subjective factors.[45]

Media buying is complex in Asia. Indeed, China is said to have the world's most complex media market. While the U.S. has 210 television markets and fewer than 2,000 TV channels, China has over 3,000 channels and hundreds of markets, most of them based in small cities with limited audiences. There are also 1,800 radio stations, more than 1,000 newspapers, some 7,000 magazines, and numerous Internet portals with more than 59 million users, a number that is expected to surge as more Chinese can afford computers and home Internet connections. In addition, regional variations from language and business etiquette to customs and beliefs exist. While Beijing is trying to get everyone to speak standardized Chinese, non-Han people, such as Tibetans and Uighurs in the far West, speak entirely different languages. Even among the majority Han ethnic group, there are distinct dialects such as Shanghainese and Cantonese, that are unintelligible to outsiders.[46] Additionally, circulation numbers provided by media operators may not be reliable as they tend to inflate the numbers to raise their advertising rates. Information on reader profiles is also difficult to obtain and continuously changing.[47]

Deciding on Media Timing and Allocation

In choosing media, the advertiser faces both a macroscheduling and a microscheduling problem. The *macroscheduling problem* involves scheduling the advertising in relation to seasons and the business cycle. Suppose 70 percent of a product's sales occur between June and September. The firm can vary its advertising expenditures to follow the seasonal pattern, to oppose the seasonal pattern, or to be constant throughout the year.

The *microscheduling problem* calls for allocating advertising expenditures within a short period to obtain maximum impact. Suppose the firm decides to buy 30 radio spots in the month of September. Figure 18.3 shows several possible patterns. The left side shows that advertising messages for the month can be concentrated ("burst" advertising), dispersed continuously throughout the month, or dispersed intermittently. The top side shows that the advertising messages can be beamed with a level, rising, falling, or alternating frequency.

The most effective pattern depends on the communication objectives in relation to the nature of the product, target customers, distribution channels, and other marketing factors. The timing pattern should consider three factors. *Buyer turnover* expresses the rate at which new buyers enter the market; the higher this rate, the more continuous the advertising should be. *Purchase frequency* is the number of times during the period

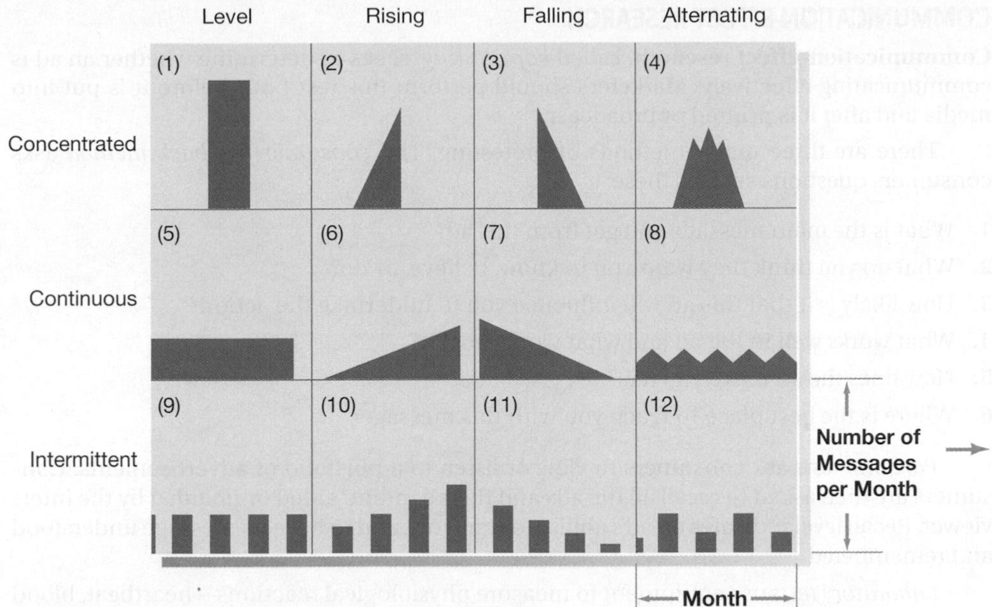

Figure 18.3 Classification of Advertising Timing Patterns

that the average buyer buys the product; the higher the purchase frequency, the more continuous the advertising should be. The *forgetting rate* is the rate at which the buyer forgets the brand; the higher the forgetting rate, the more continuous the advertising should be.

In launching a new product, the advertiser has to choose among continuity, concentration, flighting, and pulsing.

- **Continuity** is achieved by scheduling exposures evenly throughout a given period. Generally, advertisers use continuous advertising in expanding market situations, with frequently purchased items, and in tightly defined buyer categories.
- **Concentration** calls for spending all the advertising dollars in a single period. This makes sense for products with one selling season or holiday.
- **Flighting** calls for advertising for a period, followed by a period with no advertising, followed by a second period of advertising activity. It is used when funding is limited, the purchase cycle is relatively infrequent, and with seasonal items.
- **Pulsing** is continuous advertising at low-weight levels reinforced periodically by waves of heavier activity. Pulsing draws on the strength of continuous advertising and flights to create a compromise scheduling strategy.[48] Those who favor pulsing feel that the audience will learn the message more thoroughly, and money can be saved.

A company has to decide how to allocate its advertising budget over space as well as over time. The company makes "national buys" when it places ads on national TV networks or in nationally circulated magazines. It makes "spot buys" when it buys TV time in just a few markets or in regional editions of magazines. These markets are called *areas of dominant influence* (ADIs) or *designated marketing areas* (DMAs). Ads reach a market 80–140 kilometers from a city center. The company makes "local buys" when it advertises in local newspapers, radio, or outdoor sites.

Evaluating Advertising Effectiveness

Most advertisers try to measure the communication effect of an ad—that is, its potential effect on awareness, knowledge, or preference. They would also like to measure the ad's sales effect.

COMMUNICATION-EFFECT RESEARCH

Communication-effect research, called *copy testing*, seeks to determine whether an ad is communicating effectively. Marketers should perform this test both before it is put into media and after it is printed or broadcast.

There are three major methods of pretesting. The *consumer feedback method* asks consumers questions such as these:

1. What is the main message you get from this ad?
2. What do you think they want you to know, believe, or do?
3. How likely is it that this ad will influence you to undertake the action?
4. What works well in the ad and what works poorly?
5. How does the ad make you feel?
6. Where is the best place to reach you with this message?

Portfolio tests ask consumers to view or listen to a portfolio of advertisements. Consumers are then asked to recall all the ads and their content, aided or unaided by the interviewer. Recall level indicates an ad's ability to stand out and to have its message understood and remembered.

Laboratory tests use equipment to measure physiological reactions—heartbeat, blood pressure, pupil dilation, galvanic skin response, perspiration—to an ad; or consumers may be asked to turn a knob to indicate their moment-to-moment liking or interest while viewing sequenced material.[49] These tests measure attention-getting power but reveal nothing about impact on beliefs, attitudes, or intentions. Table 18.2 describes some specific advertising research techniques.

Table 18.2 Advertising Research Techniques

For Print Ads:
Starch and Gallup & Robinson, Inc., are two widely used print pretesting services. Test ads are placed in magazines, which are then circulated to consumers. These consumers are contacted later and interviewed. Recall and recognition tests are used to determine advertising effectiveness.

For Broadcast Ads:
In-home tests: A video tape is taken or downloaded into the homes of target consumers, who then view the commercials.

Trailer tests: In a trailer in a shopping center, shoppers are shown the products and given an opportunity to select a series of brands. They then view commercials and are given coupons to be used in the shopping center. Redemption rates indicate commercials' influence on purchase behavior.

Theater tests: Consumers are invited to a theater to view a potential new television series along with some commercials. Before the show begins, consumers indicate preferred brands in different categories; after the viewing, consumers again choose preferred brands. Preference changes measure the commercials' persuasive power.

On-air tests: Respondents are recruited to watch a program on a regular TV channel during the test commercial or are selected based on their having viewed the program. They are asked questions about commercial recall.

Pretest critics maintain that agencies can design ads that test well, but may not necessarily perform well in the marketplace. Proponents of ad pretesting maintain that useful diagnostic information can emerge and that pretests should not be used as the sole decision criterion anyway. Given Asia's multiracial makeup, pretests can furnish insightful information as the following example demonstrates.

Malaysia—In Malaysia, advertisers conduct ad pretests to ensure that they do not offend any racial group. The pretests routinely reflect ethnic preferences. Chinese consumers want a rational message such as how the product works, how much it costs, and so on; while Malay consumers prefer more emotional appeals.[50]

Widely acknowledged as being one of the best advertisers around, Nike is notorious for doing very little ad pretesting.

Nike—China banned a Nike commercial titled, "Chamber of Fear", showing American basketball star, LeBron James, in a battle with an animated cartoon *kungfu* master, two women in traditional Chinese attire, and a pair of dragons. The commercial was said to have violated regulations that mandate all ads in China to uphold national dignity and interest, and respect its culture. The portrayal of every Chinese character being defeated was perceived by the media authorities and the public as showing the Chinese as a useless race. Nike maintained that the company intended the commercial to send a positive message to youths to not fear anything. If Nike had conducted some pretests, it could have realized that the commercial was culturally insensitive and would not have been well-received.[51]

This Nike ad featuring American basketball sensation, LeBron James, defeating various animated figures from Chinese culture was banned for offending national dignity.

Many advertisers use posttests to assess the overall impact of a completed campaign. If a company hoped to increase brand awareness from 20 to 50 percent and succeeded in increasing it to only 30 percent, then the company is not spending enough, its ads are poor, or some other factors have been ignored.

In China, advertisers and ad agencies are beginning to think of China as a single market with many different commercial cultures, more like Europe than America. The winning ads are those that understand the differing trends best. Pre- and posttests are thus needed to understand the market as the following example illustrates.

Fanta—A Fanta TV commercial showed a Chinese high-school teacher taking a sip and rocketing gleefully into the air. Posttest results showed that the ad played better in southern China than in the north. In southern China, humor tends to be more slapstick and physical, like those in Hong Kong movies. In the north, consumers love clever wordplays, a legacy of traditional Chinese opera and verbal sparring.[52]

SALES-EFFECT RESEARCH

What sales are generated by an ad that increases brand awareness by 20 percent and brand preference by 10 percent? Advertising's sales effect is generally harder to measure than its communication effect. Sales are influenced by many factors, such as features, price, and availability, as well as competitors' actions. The fewer or more controllable these other

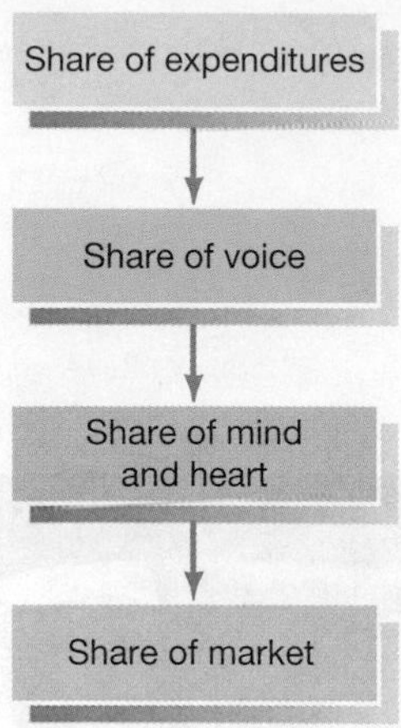

Figure 18.4 Formula for Measuring Sales Impact of Advertising

factors are, the easier it is to measure effect on sales. The sales impact is easiest to measure in direct-marketing situations and hardest to measure in brand or corporate image-building advertising.

Companies are generally interested in finding out whether they are overspending or underspending on advertising. One approach to answering this question is to work with the formulation shown in Figure 18.4.

A company's *share of advertising expenditures* produces a *share of voice* (i.e., proportion of company advertising of that product to all advertising of that product) that earns a *share of consumers' minds and hearts* and ultimately, a *share of market*.

Researchers try to measure the sales impact through analyzing historical or experimental data. The *historical approach* involves correlating past sales to past advertising expenditures using advanced statistical techniques.[53] Other researchers use an *experimental design* to measure advertising's sales impact. A growing number of researchers are striving to measure the sales effect of advertising expenditures instead of settling for communication-effect measures.[54] Millward Brown International has conducted tracking studies for years to help advertisers decide whether their advertising is benefiting their brand.[55] Another research pioneer, Nielsen, tracks commercials electronically.[56]

Sales Promotion

Sales promotion, a key ingredient in marketing campaigns, consists of a collection of incentive tools, mostly short term, designed to stimulate quicker or greater purchase of particular products or services by consumers or the trade.[57]

Whereas advertising offers a *reason* to buy, sales promotion offers an *incentive* to buy. Sales promotion includes tools for *consumer promotion* (samples, coupons, cash refund offers, prices off, premiums, prizes, patronage rewards, free trials, warranties, tie-in promotions, cross-promotions, point-of-purchase displays, and demonstrations); *trade promotion* (prices off, advertising and display allowances, and free goods); and *business* and *sales-force promotion* (trade shows and conventions, contests for sales reps, and specialty advertising).

Objectives

Sales promotion tools vary in their specific objectives. A free sample stimulates consumer trial, whereas a free management-advisory service aims at cementing a long-term relationship with a retailer.

Sellers use incentive-type promotions to attract new triers, to reward loyal customers, and to increase the repurchase rates of occasional users. Sales promotions often attract brand switchers, who are primarily looking for low price, good value, or premiums. Sales promotions generally are unlikely to turn them into loyal users, although they may be induced to make some subsequent purchases.[58] Sales promotions used in markets of high brand similarity can produce a high sales response in the short run but little permanent gain in market share. In markets of high brand dissimilarity, sales promotions may be able to alter market shares permanently. In addition to brand switching, consumers may engage in stockpiling—purchasing earlier than usual (purchase acceleration) or purchasing extra quantities.[59] But sales may then hit a post-promotion dip.[60]

A number of sales promotion benefits flow to manufacturers and consumers.[61] Sales promotions enable manufacturers to adjust to short-term variations in supply and demand. They enable manufacturers to test how high a list price they can charge, because they can always discount it. They induce consumers to try new products instead of never straying from current ones. They lead to more varied retail formats, such as the everyday-low-price store and the promotional-pricing store. For retailers, promotions may increase sales of complementary categories (DVD player promotions may help to drive DVD sales) as well as induce some store-switching by consumers.

They promote greater consumer awareness of prices. They help manufacturers sell more than they would normally sell at the list price and adapt programs to different consumer segments.

Advertising versus Promotion

Sales promotion expenditures have been increasing as a percentage of budget expenditure. Several factors contribute to this growth, particularly in consumer markets.[62] Promotion is now more accepted by top management as an effective sales tool; more product managers are qualified to use sales-promotion tools; and product managers are under greater pressure to increase current sales. In addition, the number of brands has increased; competitors use promotions frequently; many brands are seen as similar; consumers are more price-oriented; the trade has demanded more deals from manufacturers; and advertising efficiency has declined because of rising costs, media clutter, and legal restraints. These trends are also observable in an emerging market like China.

A.C. Nielsen—With increasing competition in China, promotion is seen as a critical marketing tool to attract shoppers' attention and generate sales. A.C. Nielsen found that many shopping decisions are made in-store and at point-of-purchase, rather than out-of-store. Hence, traditional marketing tools such as advertising are not enough to drive consumer loyalty or obtain a greater share of wallet for shoppers with many in-store choices. Promotions are thus at the top of many marketers' agenda. Direct monetary benefit from promotions is most preferred. This includes "Buy One Get One Free," "Price Discount," and "Bigger Volume at Same Price." Lucky draws and points for gifts are not as popular because they do not offer immediate benefits, are usually complicated in procedure, and have little chance of reaping the benefits. The Chinese look for convenient and exciting promotions, although "exciting" carries different meanings to housewives and youngsters. For housewives, exciting promotions mean more frequent promotions that come with cost savings; while youngsters associate exciting promotions with creativity and uniqueness.[63]

However, there is a danger in letting advertising take too much of a back seat to promotions, because advertising typically builds brand loyalty. The question of whether or not sales promotion weakens brand loyalty is subject to interpretation. Sales promotion, with its incessant price-offs, coupons, deals, and premiums, may devalue the product offering in buyers' minds. However, before jumping to any conclusion, we need to distinguish between price promotions and added-value promotions. Certain types of sales promotion can actually enhance brand image. The rapid growth of sales promotion media has created clutter similar to advertising clutter. Manufacturers have to find ways to rise above the clutter—for instance, by offering larger coupon-redemption values or using more dramatic point-of-purchase displays or demonstrations.

Usually, when a brand is price promoted too often, the consumer begins to devalue it and buys it mainly when it goes on sale. So there is risk in putting a well-known brand on promotion over 30 percent of the time.[64]

Dominant brands offer deals less frequently, because most deals subsidize only current users. Prior research has shown that sales promotions yield faster and more measurable responses in sales than advertising does but do not tend to yield new, long-term buyers in mature markets. Loyal brand buyers tend not to change their buying patterns as a result of competitive promotion. Advertising appears to be more effective at deepening brand loyalty.[65] Although added-value promotions can be distinguished from price promotions.[66] Certain types of sales promotions may be able to actually enhance brand image.

American Express—In the middle of Christmas shopping season, American Express ran a sales promotion at a high-traffic mall in the U.S. that swept tired shoppers off their feet, literally. The company created a 3,400-square-foot American Express Members Lounge from November 2006 to January 2007. Furnished with soft leather sofas and lamps emitting a sense of Zen-like serenity, the lounge featured a host of free amenities: stacks of magazines, premium coffee, snacks, Internet access, private restrooms, iPod charging, and even complimentary gift wrapping. Yet, not just any shopper could enter the Members Lounge. You needed to either swipe your AmEx card or fill out an application to become an AmEx cardholder. The lounge represented American Express's first promotion geared directly to consumers. With so much competing plastic, the company needs to give its brand the concrete feel of exclusivity that it strives to get across in its ads. "This is a test, our way of demonstrating why it's important to keep that card in your wallet," said AmEx's senior vice president and general manager of membership rewards for American Express.[67]

There is also evidence that price promotions do not build permanent total-category volume. One study of over 1,000 promotions concluded that only 16 percent paid off.[68] Small-share competitors find it advantageous to use sales promotion because they cannot afford to match the market leaders' large advertising budgets, nor can they obtain shelf space without offering trade allowances or stimulate consumer trial without offering incentives. Price competition is often used by a small brand seeking to enlarge its share, but it is less effective for a category leader whose growth lies in expanding the entire category.[69] The upshot is that many consumer-packaged-goods companies feel they are forced to use more sales promotion than they wish. They blame the heavy use of sales promotion for decreasing brand loyalty, increasing consumer price-sensitivity, brand-quality-image dilution, and a focus on short-run marketing planning.

Major Decisions

In using sales promotion, a company must establish its objectives, select the tools, develop the program, pretest the program, implement and control it, and evaluate the results.

ESTABLISHING OBJECTIVES

Sales promotion objectives are derived from broader promotion objectives, which are derived from more basic marketing objectives developed for the product. For consumers, objectives include encouraging purchase of larger-sized units, building trial among nonusers, and attracting switchers away from competitors' brands. Ideally, promotions with consumers would have short-run sales impact as well as long-run brand equity effects. For retailers, objectives include persuading retailers to carry new items and higher levels of inventory, encouraging off-season buying, encouraging stocking of related items, offsetting competitive promotions, building brand loyalty, and gaining entry into new retail outlets. For the sales force, objectives include encouraging support of a new product or model, encouraging more prospecting, and stimulating off-season sales.[70]

SELECTING CONSUMER PROMOTION TOOLS

The promotion planner should take into account the type of market, sales promotion objectives, competitive conditions, and each tool's cost-effectiveness.

The main consumer-promotion tools are summarized in Table 18.3. *Manufacturer promotions* include rebates, gifts to motivate purchases, and high-value trade-in credit. *Retailer promotions* include price cuts, feature advertising, retailer coupons, and retailer contests or premiums.

Table 18.3 Major Consumer Promotion Tools

Samples: Offers of a free amount of a product or service delivered door-to-door, sent in the mail, picked up in a store, attached to another product, or featured in an advertising offer.

Coupons: Certificates entitling the bearer to a stated saving on the purchase of a specific product: mailed, enclosed in other products or attached to them, or inserted in magazine and newspaper ads.

Cash Refund Offers (rebates): Provide a price reduction after purchase rather than at the retail shop: consumer sends a specified "proof of purchase" to the manufacturer who "refunds" part of the purchase price by mail.

Price Packs (cents-off deals): Offers to consumers of savings off the regular price of a product, flagged on the label or package. A *reduced-price pack* is a single package sold at a reduced price (such as two for the price of one). A *banded pack* is two related products banded together (such as a toothbrush and toothpaste).

Premiums (gifts): Merchandise offered at a relatively low cost or free as an incentive to purchase a particular product. A *with-pack premium* accompanies the product inside or on the package. A *free in-the-mail premium* is mailed to consumers who send in a proof of purchase, such as a box top or UPC code. A *self-liquidating premium* is sold below its normal retail price to consumers who request it.

Frequency Programs: Programs providing rewards related to the consumer's frequency and intensity in purchasing the company's products or services.

Prizes (contests, sweepstakes, games): *Prizes* are offers of the chance to win cash, trips, or merchandise as a result of purchasing something. A *contest* calls for consumers to submit an entry to be examined by a panel of judges who will select the best entries. A *sweepstakes* asks consumers to submit their names in a drawing. A *game* presents consumers with something every time they buy—bingo numbers, missing letters—which might help them win a prize.

Patronage Awards: Values in cash or in other forms that are proportional to patronage of a certain vendor or group of vendors.

Free Trials: Inviting prospective purchasers to try the product without cost in the hope that they will buy.

Product Warranties: Explicit or implicit promises by sellers that the product will perform as specified or that the seller will fix it or refund the customer's money during a specified period.

Tie-in Promotions: Two or more brands or companies team up on coupons, refunds, and contests to increase pulling power.

Cross-Promotions: Using one brand to advertise another noncompeting brand.

Point-of-Purchase (POP) Displays and Demonstrations: POP displays and demonstrations take place at the point-of-purchase or sale.

We can also distinguish between sales promotion tools that are *consumer franchise-building* and those that do not. The former impart a selling message along with the deal, as in the case of free samples, frequency awards, coupons when they include a selling message, and premiums when they are related to the product. Sales promotion tools that typically are not brand-building include price-off packs, consumer premiums not related to a product, contests and sweepstakes, consumer refund offers, and trade allowances.

Consumer franchise-building promotions offer the best of both worlds—they build brand equity while moving products. Here's an example of a highly effective consumer franchise-building promotion.

Body by Milk—Although almost every home has milk in the refrigerator, milk consumption by teenagers has been in decline for years. To help teens better understand and appreciate that milk helps them stay lean, toned, and healthy for the "look they want," the "Body by Milk" promotion from the National Fluid Milk Processor Promotion Board was launched in 2006. Milk moustache ads run in magazines read by teenagers featured celebrities chosen for their physiques and appeal to teenagers: soccer star David Beckham and *American Idol* winner Carrie Underwood. The campaign's interactive components included a page on MySpace and banner ads on Web sites such as Facebook and Gamezone.com. The Body by Milk Web site featured an "auction" in which visitors could bid each day for merchandise — from companies such as Adidas, the sports apparel maker and Baby Phat, a clothing maker — using bar-code or expiration-date data from milk containers. Visitors to the site could also create their own milk mustache ads. The celebrities also appeared in posters that were distributed, through school food service directors, in more than 100,000 schools, illuminating milk's new message, driving teens to bodybymilk.com for engagement in the Milk Auction. The campaign resulted in much online and off-line activity and a change in teen perceptions.[71]

Sales promotion seems most effective when used together with advertising. In one study, a price promotion alone produced only a 15 percent increase in sales volume. When combined with feature advertising, sales volume increased 19 percent; when combined with feature advertising and a point-of-purchase display, sales volume increased 24 percent.[72]

SELECTING TRADE PROMOTION TOOLS

Manufacturers use several trade promotion tools (Table 18.4). A higher proportion of the promotion pie is devoted to trade-promotion tools than to consumer promotion. Manufacturers award money to the trade (1) to persuade the retailer or wholesaler to carry the brand; (2) to persuade the retailer or wholesaler to carry more units than the normal amount; (3) to induce retailers to promote the brand by featuring, display, and price reductions; and (4) to stimulate retailers and their sales clerks to push the product.

Table 18.4 Major Trade Promotion Tools

Price-Off (off-invoice or off-list): A straight discount off the list price on each case purchased during a stated time period.

Allowance: An amount offered in return for the retailer's agreeing to feature the manufacturer's products in some way. An *advertising allowance* compensates retailers for advertising the manufacturer's product. A *display allowance* compensates them for carrying a special product display.

Free Goods: Offers of extra cases of merchandise to intermediaries who buy a certain quantity or who feature a certain flavor or size.

Source: For more information, see Betsy Spethman, "Trade Promotion Redefined." *Brandweek*, March 13, 1995, pp. 25–32.

The growing power of large retailers has increased their ability to demand trade promotion at the expense of consumer promotion and advertising.[73] These retailers depend on promotion money from the manufacturers. No manufacturer could unilaterally stop offering trade allowances without losing retailer support. The company's sales force and its brand managers are often at odds over trade promotion. The sales force says that the local retailers will not keep the company's products on the shelf unless they receive more trade promotion money, whereas the brand managers want to spend the limited funds on consumer promotion and advertising.

Coca-Cola—In China's fragmented retail industry, Coca-Cola sought the cooperation of retailers by paying some sales reps on a commission basis. This increased the number of Coke coolers and umbrellas in prime locales. The company also began conducting road shows, handing out free samples, and providing entertainment to rural customers.

Manufacturers face several challenges in managing trade promotions. First, they often find it difficult to police retailers to make sure they are doing what they agreed to do. Manufacturers are increasingly insisting on proof of performance before paying any allowances. Second, more retailers are doing *forward buying*—that is, buying a greater quantity than they can sell during the deal period. Retailers might respond to a 10-percent-off-case allowance by buying a 12-week or longer supply. The manufacturer has to schedule more production than planned and bear the costs of extra work shifts and overtime. Third, retailers are doing more diverting, buying more than needed in a region in which the manufacturer offered a deal, and shipping the surplus to their stores in nondeal regions. Manufacturers are responding by limiting the amount they will sell at a discount, or producing and delivering less than the full order to smooth production.[74]

All said, manufacturers feel that trade promotion has become a nightmare. It contains layers of deals, is complex to administer, and often leads to lost revenues.

SELECTING BUSINESS AND SALES FORCE PROMOTION TOOLS

Companies spend heavily on business and sales force promotion tools (Table 18.5). These tools are used to gather business leads, impress and reward customers, and motivate the sales force to greater effort. Companies typically develop budgets for each business promotion tool that remain fairly constant from year to year.

Table 18.5 Major Business and Sales Force Promotion Tools

Trade Shows and Conventions: Industry associations organize annual trade shows and conventions. Participating vendors expect benefits including generating new sales leads, maintaining customer contacts, introducing new products, meeting new customers, selling more to present customers, and educating customers with publications, videos, and other audiovisual materials.
Sales Contests: A sales contest aims at inducing the sales force or dealers to increase their sales results over a stated period, with prizes (money, trips, gifts, or points) going to those who succeed.
Specialty Advertising: Specialty advertising consists of useful, low-cost items bearing the company's name and address, and sometimes an advertising message that salespeople give to prospects and customers. Common items are ballpoint pens, calendars, key chains, flashlights, tote bags, and memo pads.

DEVELOPING THE PROGRAM

In planning sales promotion programs, marketers are increasingly blending several media into a total campaign concept, such as the following:

Canon—With the popularity of email and mobile mail, the Japanese practice of sending Nengajo New Year cards had begun to decline, especially among younger consumers. To reverse this trend, Canon launched the "Enjoy Photo" promotion, which targeted young women and focused on the joy and happiness of printing and sending photos. Three sisters served as "navigators" to guide users through the process. At a product launch party they showed their own digital camera photos, and ads and a Canon catalog portrayed them enjoying Nengajo printing in their daily lives. The ads contained a URL to encourage people to check out a Web site with more detail and featured minidrama movies. Canon printers also appeared in Bals Tokyo, one of the most popular home interior shops among youth in Tokyo, and Odaiba, a popular destination in Tokyo. Canon also created ties with partner hotels at major theme parks in Tokyo. These combined efforts led to an explosion of buzz, press, and Web traffic and a sharp incease in sales.[75]

In deciding to use a particular incentive, marketers have several factors to consider. First, they must determine the *size* of the incentive. A certain minimum is necessary if the promotion is to succeed. Second, the marketing manager must establish *conditions* for participation. Incentives might be offered to everyone or to select groups. Third, the marketer has to decide on the *duration* of the promotion. According to one researcher, the optimal frequency is about three weeks per quarter, and optimal duration is the length of the average purchase cycle.[76] Fourth, the marketer must choose a *distribution vehicle.* A fifteen-cents-off coupon can be distributed in the package, in stores, by mail, or in advertisements. Fifth, the marketing manager must establish the *timing* of promotion. Finally, the marketer must determine the *total sales promotion budget.* The cost of a particular promotion consists of the administrative cost (printing, mailing, and promoting the deal) and the incentive cost (cost of premium or cents-off, including redemption costs), multiplied by the expected number of units that will be sold on the deal. In the case of a coupon deal, the cost would take into account the fact that only a fraction of the consumers will redeem the coupons.

PRETESTING, IMPLEMENTING, CONTROLLING, AND EVALUATING THE PROGRAM

Although most sales promotion programs are designed on the basis of experience, pretests can determine if the tools are appropriate, the incentive size optimal, and the presentation method efficient. Consumers can be asked to rate or rank different possible deals, or trial tests can be run in limited geographic areas.

Marketing managers must prepare implementation and control plans for each individual promotion that cover lead time and sell-in time. *Lead time* is the time necessary to prepare the program prior to launching it: initial planning, design, and approval of package modifications or material to be mailed or distributed; preparation of advertising and point-of-sale materials; notification of field sales personnel; establishment of allocations for individual distributors; purchasing and printing of special premiums or packaging materials; production of advance inventories in preparation for release at a specific date; and, finally, the distribution to the retailer.[77] *Sell-in time* begins with the promotional launch and ends when approximately 95 percent of the deal merchandise is in the hands of consumers.

Manufacturers can evaluate the program using three methods: sales data, consumer surveys, and experiments. The first method involves scanner sales data. Marketers can analyze the types of people who took advantage of the promotion, what they bought before the promotion, and how they behaved later toward the brand and other brands. Did the promotion attract new triers and stimulate more purchasing by existing customers?

In general, sales promotions work best when they attract competitors' customers who then switch. If the company's product is not superior, the brand's share is likely to return to its pre-promotion level. *Consumer surveys* can be conducted to learn how many recall the promotion, what they thought of it, how many took advantage of it, and how the promotion affected subsequent brand-choice behavior.[78] Sales promotions can also be evaluated through *experiments* that vary such attributes as incentive value, duration, and distribution media. For example, coupons can be sent to half of the households in a consumer panel. Scanner data can be used to track whether the coupons led more people to buy the product and when.

There are additional costs beyond the cost of specific promotions. First, promotions might decrease long-run brand loyalty. Second, promotions can be more expensive than they appear. Some are inevitably distributed to the wrong consumers. Third, there are the costs of special production runs, extra sales force effort, and handling requirements. Finally, certain promotions irritate retailers, who may demand extra trade allowances or refuse to cooperate.[79]

Here is an example of a promotion which produced several undesired and unanticipated consequences and costs:

McDonald's—McDonald's McSnoopy campaign in Hong Kong offered buyers the plastic beagle dressed in different national costumes for 77 cents each time they purchased a set meal. Long lines gathered for the 28 dolls at McDonald's outlets. Most were adults ranging from laborers to stockbrokers who believed that the dolls were a good investment in a recession. A Tsim Sha Tsui shop even sold full sets of the dolls at $154, a markup of about 700 percent of their retail value. Daily fights were also reported in the rush for the dolls. Avid collectors also bought additional sets of the extra-value meal only to discard the food in rubbish bins once they obtained the dolls. This attracted elderly destitute to linger at McDonald's outlets hoping to land a discarded meal.

Events and Experiences

Companies also sponsor events including sports, entertainment tours and attractions, festivals, fairs, the arts, as well as cause marketing. By becoming part of a special and more personally relevant moment in consumers' lives, companies' involvement with events can broaden and deepen the relationship with their target market. Such below-the-line activities are gaining popularity in Asia as companies try to find better use for their money to achieve a higher return on investments. An event, relative to an ad, may cost less and yet allows the advertiser to interact with a captive target market.

Mengniu Dairy—In 2004, Mengniu Dairy was China's top seller of milk. It was the official provider of dairy products during Liwei Yang's long months of training to become China's first astronaut. Following Yang's success in space, Mengniu blitzed the country with ads featuring men, women, and children drinking milk—a campaign that continued even as China's second manned space flight orbits the earth. Mengniu also sponsors a TV show called *Super Voice Girl*, a local program based loosely on *American Idol*. Given the program's popularity, Mengniu has created a buzz for its yoghurt product targeted at teenage girls, the show's main audience.[80]

Daily encounters with brands may also affect consumers' brand attitudes and beliefs. *Atmospheres* are "packaged environments" that create or reinforce leanings toward product purchase. Law offices decorated with Oriental rugs and oak furniture communicate "stability" and "success."[81] A five-star hotel will use elegant chandeliers, marble columns, and other tangible signs of luxury.

Many firms are creating on-site and off-site product and brand experiences. There is Toyota City in Tokyo, Everything Coca-Cola in Las Vegas, and M&M World in Times Square in New York. Small brands, of necessity, are even more likely to take less obvious and less expensive paths in sponsorship and communications.

Events Objectives

Marketers report a number of reasons why they sponsor events:

1. ***To identify with a particular target market or lifestyle*** — Customers can be targeted geographically, demographically, psychographically, or behaviorally according to events. Events can be chosen based on attendees' attitudes and usage toward certain products or brands. Adidas is the sportswear sponsor for the 2008 Olympic Games in Beijing. This is an important sponsorship because China is a fragmented market and the Olympic Games is an event with the rare power of uniting China. Even though Nike opened its stores at a rate faster than Adidas, Adidas sales in China has skyrocketed in part because of its Olympic Games' sponsorship.[82]
2. ***To increase awareness of company or product name*** — Sponsorship often offers sustained exposure to a brand, a necessary condition to build brand recognition. By skillfully choosing sponsorship events or activities, identification with a product and thus

brand recall can also be enhanced. Volvo was one of the first automakers to sponsor golf events in China. It created the Volvo China Open and the Volvo China Tour. From close to zero sales in 1994, Volvo sales increased to $133.6 million in 2007.[83]

3. ***To create or reinforce consumer perceptions of key brand image associations*** — Events themselves have associations that help to create or reinforce brand associations. Shimano, a Japanese bike components manufacturer, was associated with seven-time Tour de France winner, Lance Armstrong. The bike ridden by Armstrong was powered by Shimano pedals and cranks and shifted by Shimano's derailleurs.
4. ***To enhance corporate image dimensions*** — Sponsorship is seen as a means to improve perceptions that the company is likable, prestigious, etc. so that consumers will credit the company and favor it in later product choices. General Electric provided multiyear funding for *Zhima Jie*, a Chinese children's TV educational program adapted from *Sesame Street*. GE believes that this sponsorship is a smart way to build brand awareness and image to increase its sales through children's influence on household purchases, and to nurture brand loyalty among future Chinese consumers.[84]
5. ***To create experiences and evoke feelings*** — The feelings engendered by an exciting or rewarding event may also indirectly link to the brand. Online activation accounts for a large portion of LG Electronics MobileComm USA's sponsorship leveraging efforts. The company uses sites such as MySpace and YouTube to extend its personality online and created its own proprietary Web site, LifeWithLG.com, as a central place for information about events and celebrity endorsers and related content for downloading.[85]
6. ***To express commitment to the community or on social issues*** — Sponsorships that involve corporate tie-ins with non-profit organizations and charities are often called cause-related marketing. Levi's awarded $285,000 to three organizations in India to help women and youth through economic development, education, and HIV/AIDS prevention programs. Children from the "poorest of the poor" are given high-quality, value-based education, nutrition, and healthcare through immunization and regular check ups. Older siblings are given vocational training, while alcoholic fathers go through detoxification programs. Indian wives, who are largely monogamous, but have no control over their husbands' behavior, are educated about reproductive health and HIV/AIDS through programs at garment factories employing female workers.[86]
7. ***To entertain key clients or reward key employees*** — Many events include lavish hospitality tents and other special services or activities which are only available for sponsors and their guests. Involving clients with the event in these and other ways can engender goodwill and establish valuable business contacts. From an employee's perspective, events can build participation and morale or be used as an incentive. Accenture sponsors the annual World Match Play Golf Championship, where it entertains its clients and woos future prospects. Its employees who attend the event can also mingle with the world's top golfers including Tiger Woods.
8. ***To permit merchandising or promotional opportunities*** — Many marketers tie in contests or sweepstakes, in-store merchandising, direct response or other marketing activities with an event. Ford produced and sponsored *Ford Maverick Beyond Infinity*, a *Survivor*-like show in China, to promote its Maverick SUV. Co-sponsors Nike and Nestlé had the contestants dressed in Nike clothing and cooling off with Nestlé drinks.

Despite these potential advantages, there are a number of potential disadvantages to sponsorship. The success of an event can be unpredictable and beyond the control of the sponsor. Although many consumers will credit sponsors for providing the financial assistance to make an event possible, some consumers may still resent the commercialization of events.

Major Decisions

Developing successful sponsored events involves choosing the appropriate events; designing the optimal sponsorship program for the event; and measuring the effects of sponsorship.[87]

CHOOSING EVENT OPPORTUNITIES

Because of the number of opportunities and their huge costs, marketers are becoming more selective about choosing sponsorship events.

The event must meet the marketing objectives and communication strategy that have been defined for the brand. The audience delivered by the event must match the target market of the brand. The event must have sufficient awareness, possess the desired image, and be capable of creating the desired effects with that target market. Consumers must make favorable attributions to the sponsor for its event involvement. An "ideal event" might be one (1) whose audience closely matches the desired target market; (2) that generates much favorable attention; (3) that is unique but not encumbered with many sponsors; (4) that lends itself to ancillary marketing activities; and (5) that reflects or enhances the brand or corporate image of the sponsor.

Nintendo—Before launching its new Wii player, Nintendo identified influential bloggers who were either mothers or members of large, multigenerational families. It hosted parties for the individual families or for groups of the mum's friends, showing them how easy the Wii was for anyone to use. Grandparents could experience the ease in handling the Wii. Together with TV news stories about Wiis in nursing homes, a lot of buzz was generated. Nintendo's Wii strategy shook the gaming industry and has set it apart from its rivals.[88]

DESIGNING SPONSORSHIP PROGRAMS

Many marketers believe that it is the marketing program accompanying an event sponsorship that ultimately determines its success. A sponsor can strategically identify itself at an event in several ways, including banners, signs, and programs. For more significant impact, sponsors typically supplement such activities with samples, prizes, advertising, retail promotions, and publicity. At least two to three times the amount of the sponsorship expenditure should be spent on related marketing activities.

Event creation is a particularly important skill in publicizing fund-raising drives for nonprofit organizations. Fund-raisers have developed a large repertoire of special events, including anniversary celebrations, art exhibits, auctions, benefit evenings, book sales, cake sales, contests, dances, dinners, fairs, fashion shows, parties in unusual places, phonathons, rummage sales, tours, and walkathons. No sooner is one type of event created, such as a walkathon, than competitors spawn new versions, such as readathons, bikeathons, and jogathons.[89]

MEASURING SPONSORSHIP ACTIVITIES

As with public relations, measurement of events is difficult. There are two basic approaches to measuring the effects of sponsorship activities: The *supply-side* method focuses on potential exposure to the brand by assessing the extent of media coverage; and the *demand-side* method focuses on reported exposure from consumers. We examine each in turn.

Supply-side methods attempt to approximate the amount of time or space devoted to media coverage of an event. For example, the number of seconds that the brand is clearly visible on a television screen or column inches of press clippings covering an event that mention the brand can be estimated. This measure of potential "impressions" is then translated into an equivalent "value" in advertising dollars according to the fees associated in actually advertising in the particular media vehicle. Some industry consultants have estimated that 30 seconds of TV logo exposure can be worth 6 to 10 or as much as 25 percent of a 30-second TV ad spot.

Although supply-side exposure methods provide quantifiable measures, their validity can be questioned. The difficulty lies in the fact that equating media coverage with advertising exposure ignores the content of the respective communications consumers receive. The advertiser uses media space and time to communicate a strategically designed message. Media coverage and telecasts only expose the brand and do not necessarily embellish its meaning in any direct way. Although some public relations professionals maintain that positive editorial coverage can be worth five to 10 times the advertising equivalency value, it is rare that sponsorship provides such favorable treatment.[90]

The "demand-side" method attempts to identify the effects sponsorship has on consumers' brand knowledge. Marketers can survey event spectators to measure sponsor recall of the event as well as resulting attitudes and intentions toward the sponsor. AT&T uses a three-pronged approach:[91]

1. ***Direct tracking of sponsorship-related promotions*** — Web data, call center data, online event statistics, and other consumer engagements.
2. ***Qualitative research*** — On-site/in-market, pre/post, and participant/non-participant, using a proprietary model for brand equity transfer and subsequent impact on purchase intent.
3. ***Quantitative analysis*** — Analytics to link sponsorship to brand awareness, sales, and retention and to optimize tactics in sponsorship activation that maximize ROI.

Creating Experiences

A large part of local, grassroots marketing is experiential marketing, which not only communicates features and benefits but also connects a product or service with unique and interesting experiences. "The idea is not to sell something, but to demonstrate how a brand can enrich a customer's life."[92] "Marketing Insight: Experiential Marketing" describes the concept of Customer Experience Management.

MARKETING INSIGHT • EXPERIENTIAL MARKETING

Through several books and papers, Schmitt has developed the concept of *Customer Experience Management (CEM)*—the process of strategically managing a customer's entire experience with a product or company. According to Schmitt, brands can help to create five different types of experiences: sense, feel, think, act, relate. In each case, Schmitt distinguishes between hard-wired and acquired experiential response levels. He maintains that marketers can provide experiences for customers through a set of experience providers.

1. ***Communications*** — advertising, public relations, annual reports, brochures, newsletters, and magalogs (a combination of a magazine and a catalog).
2. ***Visual/verbal identity*** — names, logos, signage, and transportation vehicles.
3. ***Product presence*** — product design, packaging, and point-of-sale displays.
4. ***Co-branding*** — event marketing and sponsorships, alliances and partnerships, licensing, and product placement in movies or TV.
5. ***Environments*** — retail and public spaces, trade booths, corporate buildings, office interiors, and factories.
6. ***Web sites and electronic media*** — corporate sites, product or service sites, CD-ROMs, automated emails, online advertising, and Intranets.
7. ***People*** — salespeople, customer-service representatives, technical support or repair providers, company spokepersons, and CEOs and other executives.

The CEM framework is made up of five basic steps:

1. ***Analyzing the experiential world of the customer*** — gaining insights into the sociocultural context of consumers or the business context of business customers.
2. ***Building the experiential platform*** — developing a strategy that includes the positioning for the kind of experience the brand stands for ("what"), the value proposition of what relevant experience to deliver ("why"), and the overall implementation theme that will be communicated ("how").
3. ***Designing the brand experience*** — implementing their experiential platform in the look and feel of logos and signage, packaging, and retail spaces, in advertising, collaterals, and online.
4. ***Structuring the customer interface*** — implementing the experiential platform in the dynamic and interactive interfaces including face-to-face, in stores, during sales visits, at the check-in desk of a hotel, or the e-commerce engine of a Web site.
5. ***Engaging in continuous innovation*** — implementing the experiential platform in new-product development, creative marketing events for customers, and fine-tuning the experience at every point of contact.

Schmitt cites Pret A Manger, the U.K.-based sandwich company, as an example of an attractive brand experience, customer interface, and ongoing innovation: "The Pret A Manger brand is about great tasting, handmade, natural products served by amazing people who are passionate about their work. The sandwiches and stores look appealing and attractive. The company hires only 5 percent of those who apply and only after they have worked for a day in the shop. This process ensures good fit and good teamwork." He also offers Singapore Airlines, Starbucks, and Amazon.com as outstanding provides of customer experiences.

Sources: <www.exgroup.com>; Bernd Schmitt, *Customer Experience Management: A Revolutionary Approach to Connecting with Your Customers,* (New York: John Wiley, 2003); Bernd Schmitt, David L. Rogers, and Karen Vrotsos, *There's No Business That's Not Show Business: Marketing in an Experience Culture,* (Upper Saddle River, NJ: Prentice Hall, 2003); Bernd Schmitt, *Experiential Marketing: How to Get Companies to Sense, Feel, Think, Act, and Relate to Your Company and Brands,* (New York: Free Press, 1999); Bernd Schmitt and Alex Simonson, *Marketing Aesthetics: The Strategic Management of Brands, Identity, and Image,* (New York: Free Press, 1997).

Consultants Pine and Gilmore argue that we are on the threshold of the "Experience Economy," a new economic era in which all businesses must orchestrate memorable events for their customers.[93] They assert:

- If you charge for stuff, then you are in the *commodity business*.
- If you charge for tangible things, then you are in the *goods business*.
- If you charge for the activities you perform, then you are in the *service business*.
- If you charge for the time customers spend with you, then and only then are you in the *experience* business.

Citing a range of companies from Disney to AOL, they maintain that salable experiences come in four varieties: entertainment, education, esthetic, and escapist. Consumers seem to appreciate that. One survey showed four of five respondents found participating in a live event was more engaging than all other forms of communication. The vast majority also felt experiential marketing gave them more information than other forms of communication and would make them more likely to tell others about participating in the event and be receptive to other marketing for the brand.[94]

Companies can even create a strong image by inviting prospects and customers to visit their headquarters and factories. Boeing, Ben & Jerry's, Hershey's, Yakult, and Toyota sponsor excellent company tours that draw millions of visitors a year. Companies such as Hallmark and Sony have built corporate museums at their headquarters that display their history and the drama of producing and marketing their products.

Toyota City in Odaiba, Tokyo showcases a collection of Toyota and Lexus cars. It draws millions of visitors who are interested in knowing what Toyota offers.

Public Relations

Not only must the company relate constructively to customers, suppliers, and dealers, it must also relate to a large number of interested publics. A **public** is any group that has an actual or potential interest in or impact on a company's ability to achieve its objectives. **Public relations (PR)** involve a variety of programs designed to promote or protect a company's image or its individual products.

The wise company takes concrete steps to manage successful relations with its key publics. Most companies have a public relations department that monitors the attitudes of the organization's publics and distributes information and communications to build goodwill. The best PR departments spend time counseling top management to adopt positive programs and to eliminate questionable practices so that negative publicity does not arise in the first place. They perform the following five functions:

1. ***Press relations***— Presenting news and information about the organization in the most positive light.
2. ***Product publicity***— Sponsoring efforts to publicize specific products.
3. ***Corporate communications***— Promoting understanding of the organization through internal and external communications.
4. ***Lobbying***— Dealing with legislators and government officials to promote or defeat legislation and regulation.
5. ***Counseling***— Advising management about public issues, company positions, and image during good and bad times.

As "Marketing Insight: Managing a Brand Crisis" explains, sometimes PR must spearhead marketing communication efforts to help when a brand gets into trouble.

MARKETING INSIGHT • MANAGING A BRAND CRISIS

Marketing managers must assume that at some point in time, some kind of brand crisis will arise. Diverse brands such as Perrier, Exxon Oil, Coca-Cola, and Pepsi have all experienced a potentially crippling brand crises. These may be particularly damaging if there are widespread repercussions: (1) a loss in the product's sales, (2) reduced effectiveness of its marketing activities for the product, (3) an increased sensitivity to rival firms' marketing activities,and (4) reduced effectiveness of its marketing activities on the sales of competing, unaffected brands.

In general, the more strongly brand equity and corporate image have been established—especially corporate credibility and trustworthiness—the more likely that the firm can weather the storm. Careful preparation and a well-managed crisis management program, however, are also critical. As Johnson & Johnson's nearly flawless handling of the Tylenol product-tampering incident suggests, the key to managing a crisis is that consumers see the response by the firm as both *swift* and *sincere.* Customers must feel an immediate sense that the company truly cares. Listening is not enough.

The longer it takes a firm to respond, the more likely that consumers can form negative impressions from unfavorable media coverage or word of mouth. Perhaps worse, consumers may find they don't really like the brand after all and permanently switch brands or products. Getting in front of a problem with PR, and then perhaps ads, can help avoid those problems.

Consider Coca-Cola and Pepsi in India. Weeks after allegations of pesticide contamination first surfaced, Coke and Pepsi were still struggling to win back consumer confidence. They underestimated how quickly the allegations would spiral into a nationwide scandal, misjudged the speed with which local politicians would use this as an opportunity to attack global brands, and failed to respond swiftly to quell consumer anxiety. When the allegations were made, Coke and Pepsi commissioned their own laboratories to conduct tests and decided to wait till the results came through before commenting in detail. This approach backfired as their reticence fanned consumer suspicion. They became bogged down in the technicalities of the allegations rather than focusing on winning back the emotional support of their customers.

Second, the more sincere the firm's response—public acknowledgment of the impact on consumers and willingness to take whatever steps are necessary to solve the crisis—the less likely that consumers will form negative attributions. When consumers reported finding shards of glass in some jars of its baby food, Gerber tried to reassure the public that there were no problems in its manufacturing plants but adamantly refused to have products withdrawn from food stores. After market share slumped from 66 percent to 52 percent within a couple of months, one company official admitted, "Not pulling our baby food off the shelf gave the appearance that we aren't a caring company."

Sources: Amelia Gentleman, "Coke and Pepsi Stumble in India." *International Herald Tribune,* August 23, 2006; Harald Van Heerde, Kristiaan Helsen, and Marnik G. Dekimpe, "The Impact of a Product-Harm Crisis on Marketing Effectiveness." *Marketing Science,* March-April 2007, 26, pp. 230-45; Michelle L. Roehm and Alice M. Tybout, "When Will a Brand Scandal Spill Over and How Should Competitors Respond?" *Journal of Marketing Research,* August 2006, 43, pp. 366-73; Jill Klein and Niraj Dawar, "Corporate Social Responsibility and Consumers' Attributions and Brand Evaluations in a Product-Harm Crisis." *International Journal of Research in Marketing,* September 2004, 21(3), pp. 203-17; Rohini Ahluwalia, Robert E. Burnkrant, and H. Rao Unnava, "Consumer Response to Negative Publicity: The Moderating Role of Commitment." *Journal of Marketing Research,* May 2000, 37, pp. 203-14; Niraj Dawar and Madan M. Pillutla, "The Impact of Product-Harm Crises on Brand Equity: The Moderating Role of Consumer Expectations." *Journal of Marketing Research,* May 2000, 37, pp. 215-26.

Marketing Public Relations

Many companies are turning to **marketing public relations (MPR)** to support corporate or product promotion and image making. MPR, like financial PR and community PR, serves a special constituency, the marketing department.[95]

To learn how the American Burger King franchise was started in Western Australia by a Canadian and grew to 210 outlets by 2003 before being consolidated under "Happy Jacks", visit www.pearsoned.com.au/marketingmanagementaustralia.

The old name for MPR was **publicity**, which was seen as the task of securing editorial space—as opposed to paid space—in print and broadcast media to promote or "hype" a product, service, idea, place, person, or organization. MPR goes beyond simple publicity and plays an important role in the following tasks:

- ***Assisting in the launch of new products*** — The amazing commercial success of toys such as Teenage Mutant Ninja Turtles, Mighty Morphin' Power Rangers, Beanie Babies, and Pokemons owes a great deal to clever publicity.
- ***Assisting in repositioning a mature product*** — New York City had extremely bad press in the 1970s until the "I Love New York" campaign.
- ***Building interest in a product category*** — Companies and trade associations have used MPR to rebuild interest in declining commodities such as eggs, milk, and beef, and to expand consumption of such products as tea and orange juice.
- ***Influencing specific target groups*** — McDonald's sponsors dictionaries, and encourages tree planting and recycling in Chinese communities to build goodwill.
- ***Defending products that have encountered public problems*** — PR professionals must be adept at managing crises, such as DBS's destruction of safe deposit boxes at its Hong Kong branch, and Ajinomoto's pork contamination in its Indonesian factory.
- ***Building the corporate image in a way that reflects favorably on its products*** — Akio Morita's speeches and books have helped to create an innovative image for Sony.

As the power of mass advertising weakens, marketing managers are turning to MPR to build awareness and brand knowledge for both new and established products. MPR is also effective in blanketing local communities and reaching specific groups. In several cases, MPR proved more cost-effective than advertising. Nevertheless, it must be planned jointly with advertising.[96] Marketing managers need to acquire more skill in using MPR resources. Perhaps one of the most accomplished users of MPR is Branson of the Virgin Group (see "Breakthrough Marketing: Virgin Group").

Clearly, creative public relations can affect public awareness at a fraction of the cost of advertising. The company does not pay for the space or time obtained in the media. It pays only for a staff to develop and circulate the stories and manage certain events. If the company develops an interesting story, it could be picked up by the media and be worth millions of dollars in equivalent advertising. Some experts say that consumers are five times more likely to be influenced by editorial copy than by advertising.

> **Subaru**—In the Ultimate Subaru Impreza All-Wheel Challenge held in Singapore, 120 contestants attempted to outlast each other to claim the prize of a car. Braving the elements, each contestant had to place a hand on the car continuously with the winner being the last man standing. Large crowds formed daily to view the contestants with their hands on the car. The eventual winner held out for nearly 62 hours. There was extensive and prominent radio, press, and TV coverage during and after the event. The contest stole the limelight from the Singapore Motor Show, the largest automotive event in the region, which was held around the same time. Public opinion of the contest was generally positive. While some thought it was degrading, others felt it reflected the work ethic and determination of Asians.[97]

Major Decisions in Marketing PR

In considering when and how to use MPR, management must establish the marketing objectives, choose the PR messages and vehicles, implement the plan carefully, and evaluate the results. The main tools of MPR are described in Table 18.6.[98]

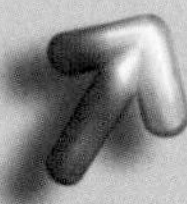

BREAKTHROUGH • MARKETING

VIRGIN GROUP

Canny marketing public relations has helped Richard Branson build an empire of successful brands under the Virgin name. Here, with actress Daryl Hannah, he peddles a blender at the 2007 Virgin Festival at Pimlico Racetrack in Baltimore to publicize the festival's efforts to incorporate the highest standards of sustainability and deliver a 'near zero waste' music experience to festival attendees.

Virgin, the brainchild of England's flamboyant iconoclast Richard Branson, vividly illustrates the power of strong traditional and non-traditional marketing communications. Branson roared onto the British stage in the 1970s with his innovative Virgin Records. He signed unknown artists no one would touch and began a marathon of publicity that continues to this day. He has since sold Virgin Records (to Thorn-EMI for nearly $1 billion in 1992) but created over 200 companies worldwide whose combined revenues exceed $5 billion.

The Virgin name—the third most respected brand in Britain—and the Branson personality help to sell diverse products and services such as planes, trains, finance, soft drinks, music, mobile phones, cars, wines, publishing, even bridal wear. Clearly, Branson can create interest in almost any business he wants by simply attaching the name "Virgin" to it. Virgin Mobile exemplifies this strategy. Branson supplies the brand and a small initial investment and takes a majority control, and big-name partners come up with the cash.

Some marketing and financial critics point out that he is diluting the brand, that it covers too many businesses. Branson has had some fumbles: Virgin Cola, Virgin Cosmetics, and Virgin Vodka have all but disappeared. Despite the diversity, all the lines connote value for money, quality, innovation, fun, and a sense of competitive challenge. The Virgin Group looks for new opportunities in markets with underserved, overcharged customers and complacent competition. Branson called these customer-hostile competitors "big bad wolves." "Wherever we find them, there is a clear opportunity area for Virgin to do a much better job than the competition. We introduce trust, innovation, and customer friendliness where they don't exist," Branson said. And once Virgin finds an opportunity, its vaunted marketing expertise kicks in.

A master of the strategic publicity stunt, Branson took on stodgy, overpriced British Airways by wearing World War I-era flying gear to announce the formation of Virgin Atlantic in 1984. The first Virgin flight took off laden with celebrities and media and equipped with a brass band, waiters from Maxim's in white tie and tails, and free-flowing champagne. The airborne party enjoyed international press coverage and millions of dollars' worth of free publicity. Branson knew that photographers have a job to do and they'd turn up at his events if he gave them a good reason.

Similarly, when Branson launched Virgin Cola in the United States in 1998, he steered an army tank down Fifth Avenue in New York, garnering interviews on each of the network morning TV shows. In 2002, he plunged into Times Square connected to a crane to announce his mobile phone business. In 2004, when introducing a line of hip techie gadgets called Virgin Pulse, Branson again took center stage, this time at a nightclub in New York City. He arrived wearing a pair of flesh-colored tights and a portable CD player to cover the family jewels.

Although Branson eschews traditional market research for a "screw it, let's do it" attitude, he stays in touch through constant customer contact. When he first set up Virgin Atlantic, he called 50 customers every month to chat and get their feedback. He appeared in airports to rub elbows with customers, and if a plane was delayed, he handed out gift certificates to a Virgin Megastore or discounts on future travel. Virgin's marketing campaigns include press and radio ads, direct mail, and point-of-sale material. Virgin Mobile, for example, rolled out a postcard advertising campaign offering consumers discounts on new phones.

To identify where listeners to Virgin's Web-based Virgin Radio reside, the company created a VIP club. Listeners join the club by giving their postal code, which then lets Virgin Radio target promotions and advertising to specific locations, just as a local radio station would. Once known as the "hippie capitalist" and now knighted by the Queen of England, Branson continues to look for new businesses and to generate publicity in his characteristic charismatic style. Remembering a friend's advice about publicity—"If you don't give them a photograph that will get them on the front page, they won't turn up at your next event"—Branson always gives them a reason.

Sources: Peter Elkind, "Branson Gets Grounded." *Fortune,* February 5, 2007, pp. 13–14; Alan Deutschman, "The Enlightenment of Richard Branson." *Fast Company,* September 2006, p. 49; Andy Serwer, "Do Branson's Profits Equal His *Joie de Vivre*?" *Fortune,* October 17, 2005, p. 57; Kerry Capell with Wendy Zellner, "Richard Branson's Next Big Adventure." *BusinessWeek,* March 8, 2004, pp. 44–45; Melanie Wells, "Red Baron." *Forbes,* July 3, 2000, pp. 151–160; Sam Hill and Glenn Rifkin, *Radical Marketing,* (New York: Harper Business, 1999); <www.virgin.com>.

Table 18.6 Major Tools in Marketing PR

Publications: Companies rely extensively on published materials to reach and influence their target markets. These include annual reports, brochures, articles, company newsletters and magazines, and audiovisual materials.
Events: Companies can draw attention to new products or other company activities by arranging special events like news conferences, seminars, outings, trade shows, exhibits, contests and competitions, and anniversaries that will reach the target publics.
Sponsorships: Companies can promote their brands and corporate name by sponsoring sports and cultural events and highly regarded causes.
News: One of the major tasks of PR professionals is to find or create favorable news about the company, its products, and its people, and get the media to accept press releases and attend press conferences.
Speeches: Increasingly, company executives must field questions from the media or give talks at trade associations or sales meetings, and these appearances can build the company's image.
Public Service Activities: Companies can build goodwill by contributing money and time to good causes.
Identity Media: Companies need a visual identity that the public immediately recognizes. The visual identity is carried by company logos, stationery, brochures, signs, business forms, business cards, buildings, uniforms, and dress codes.

ESTABLISHING OBJECTIVES

MPR can build *awareness* by placing stories in the media to bring attention to a product, service, person, organization, or idea. It can build *credibility* by communicating the message in an editorial context. It can help boost sales force and dealer enthusiasm with stories about a new product before it is launched. It can hold down *promotion cost* because MPR costs less than direct-mail and media advertising.

Kejian—Kejian, one of China's top mobile phone makers, sponsored Everton, a soccer club in the English Premier League when it had a Chinese player on its team. Televised Everton matches had attracted many mainland viewers. Kejian wanted to develop its domestic market by focusing on younger consumers who tend to like sports. Such consumers may perceive Kejian as a strong company for it to sponsor an internationally known club such as Everton. Kejian hoped the sponsorship would raise its international profile and lay the foundation for its plan to eventually go global. The sponsorship was successful. Kejian's name awareness in England and Europe increased, while its sales in China more than doubled in a year.[99]

Whereas PR practitioners reach their target public through the mass media, MPR is increasingly borrowing the techniques and technology of direct-response marketing to reach target audience members one on one.

CHOOSING MESSAGES AND VEHICLES

The MPR manager must identify or develop interesting stories about the product. Suppose a relatively unknown college wants more visibility. The MPR practitioner will search for stories. Do any faculty members have unusual backgrounds, or are any working on unusual projects? Are any new and unusual courses being taught? Are any interesting events taking place on campus? If there are no interesting stories, the MPR practitioner should propose newsworthy events the college could sponsor. Here the challenge is to create news. PR ideas include hosting major academic conventions, inviting expert or celebrity speakers, and developing news conferences. Each event is an opportunity to develop a multitude of stories directed at different audiences.

IMPLEMENTING THE PLAN AND EVALUATING RESULTS

MPR's contribution to the bottom line is difficult to measure, because it is used along with other promotional tools. The three most commonly used measures of MPR effectiveness are number of exposures; awareness, comprehension, or attitude change; and contribution to sales and profits.

The easiest measure of MPR effectiveness is the number of *exposures* carried by the media. Publicists supply the client with a clippings book showing all the media that carried news about the product and a summary statement such as the following:

> *Media coverage included 3,500 column inches of news and photographs in 350 publications with a combined circulation of 79.4 million; 2,500 minutes of air time of 290 radio stations and an estimated audience of 65 million; and 660 minutes of air time on 160 television stations with an estimated audience of 91 million. If this time and space had been purchased at advertising rates, it would have amounted to $1,047,000.*[100]

This measure is not very satisfying because it contains no indication of how many people actually read, heard, or recalled the message and what they thought afterward; nor does it contain information on the net audience reached, because publications overlap in readership. Because publicity's goal is reach, and not frequency, it would be more useful to know the number of unduplicated exposures.

A better measure is the change in product awareness, comprehension, or attitude resulting from the MPR campaign (after allowing for the effect of other promotional tools). For example, how many people recall hearing the news item? How many told others about it (a measure of word of mouth)? How many changed their minds after hearing it?

Sales-and-profit impact is the most satisfactory measure. Assume that Maggi cooking sauces saw sales increase 43 percent by the end of a campaign. However, advertising and sales promotion had also been stepped up. Suppose total sales have increased by $1,500,000, and management estimates that MPR contributed 15 percent of the total increase. Then the return on MPR investment is calculated as follows:

Total sales increase	$1,500,000
Estimated sales increase due to PR (15 percent)	225,000
Contribution margin on product sales (10 percent)	22,500
Total direct cost of MPR program	210,000
Contribution margin added by PR investment	12,500
Return on MPR investment ($12,500/$10,000)	125%

Summary 

1. Advertising is any paid form of non-personal presentation and promotion of ideas, goods, or services by an identified sponsor. Advertisers include not only business firms but also charitable, non-profit, and government agencies.
2. Developing an advertising program is a five-step process: (1) set advertising objectives; (2) establish a budget; (3) choose the advertising message and creative strategy; (4) decide on the media; and (5) evaluate communication and sales effects.
3. Sales promotion consists of a diverse collection of incentive tools, mostly short term, designed to stimulate quicker or greater purchase of particular products or services by consumers or the trade. Sales promotion includes tools for consumer promotion, trade promotion, and business and sales force promotion (trade shows and conventions, contests for sales reps, and specialty advertising). In using sales promotion, a company must establish its objectives, select the tools, develop the program, pretest the program, implement and control it, and evaluate the results.
4. Events and experiences are a means to become part of special and more personally relevant moments in consumers' lives. Involvement with events can broaden and deepen the relationship of the sponsor with its target market, but only if managed properly.
5. Public relations (PR) involve a variety of programs designed to promote or protect a company's image or its individual products. Many companies today use marketing public relations (MPR) to support the marketing department in corporate or product promotion and image making. MPR can affect public awareness at a fraction of the cost of advertising, and is often much more credible. The main tools of PR are publications, events, sponsorships, news, speeches, public service activities, and identity media.

Application

Marketing Debate—Should Marketers Test Advertising?

Advertising creatives have long lamented ad pretesting. They believe that it inhibits their creative process and results in much sameness in commercials. Marketers, on the other hand, believe that ad pretesting provides necessary checks and balances as to whether an ad campaign is being developed in a way so that it will connect with consumers and be well-received in the marketplace.

Take a position: *Ad pretesting in often an unnecessary waste of marketing dollars* versus *Ad pretesting provides an important diagnostic function for marketers as to the likely success of an ad campaign.*

Marketing Discussion

What are some of your favorite TV ads? Why? How effective are the message and creative strategies? How are they building brand equity?

PART 7

South Korea is a global leader in broadband.

Managing Personal Communications: Direct Marketing and Personal Selling

19

Today, marketing communications are increasingly seen as an interactive dialogue between the company and its customers. Making the sale to customers requires working hard and working smart. Companies must not only ask "How can we reach our customers?" but also, "How can our customers reach us?" Thanks to technological breakthroughs, people can now communicate through traditional media (newspapers, magazines, radio, telephone, television, and billboards), as well as through computers, fax machines, mobile phones, pagers, and wireless appliances. By decreasing communications costs, the new technologies have encouraged more companies to move from mass communication to more targeted communications and one-to-one dialogue.

With a 71.2 percent penetration rate and the fastest Internet access speed, South Korea leads the world in broadband. The country has the world's highest rate of video and movie-on-demand downloads. A two-hour local hit movie of the 1990s can be downloaded for 80 cents in half a minute. Similarly, TV viewers can download the previous night's news broadcast or program for as little as 40 cents. "What Apple's iTunes is doing to music in the U.S. now, broadband did to movies and TV archives in Korea a year ago," says Jae Wong Lee, CEO of Daum Corporation, Korea's largest Internet portal. Online shopping comprises nearly 12 percent of all retail sales in South Korea. Seven in 10 online Korean shoppers have bought clothing, accessories, or shoes online in the past three months. Companies like CJ Home Shopping and LG Home Shopping, which started with home shopping channels on cable TV, derive most of their revenues from online sales. About six million South Koreans have an avatar, a cartoon character that represents their network identity. When a user's avatar appears on screen, others logged to the network are alerted and can join in to play an online network game, share a video clip or audio files, do a video chat, or invite the user to watch the same on-demand video or sports game they are watching. On average, a South Korean youth has more than 70 friends in his social network site.[1]

In this chapter, we will address the following questions:

1. How can companies integrate direct marketing for competitive advantage?
2. How can companies do effective interactive marketing?
3. How can marketers best take advantage of the power of word of mouth?
4. What decisions do companies face in designing and managing a sales force?
5. How can salespeople improve their selling, negotiating, and relationship marketing skills?

Personalizing communications and creating dialogues by saying and doing the right thing to the right person at the right time is critical for marketing. In this chapter, we consider how companies personalize their marketing communications to have more of an impact. We begin by evaluating direct marketing; then we consider personal selling and the sales force.

Direct Marketing

Direct marketing is the use of consumer-direct channels to reach and deliver goods and services to customers without using marketing middlemen. These channels include direct mail, catalogs, telemarketing, interactive TV, kiosks, Web sites, and mobile devices.

Direct marketers seek a measurable response, typically a customer order. This is sometimes called **direct-order marketing**. Today, many direct marketers use direct marketing to build a long-term relationship with the customer.[2] They send birthday cards, information materials, or small premiums to certain customers. Airlines, hotels, and other businesses build strong customer relationships through frequency award programs and club programs.

Direct marketing is one of the fastest growing avenues for serving customers. Business marketers are using direct marketing to increase the productivity of their sales forces and to reduce field sales expenses. Sales through traditional direct marketing channels (catalogs, direct mail, and telemarketing) are thus growing rapidly. Direct sales include sales to the consumer market, B2B, and fund raising by charitable institutions. Figure 19.1 provides a breakdown of the various types of direct marketing.

Reflecting its growth, several large advertising agencies have acquired regional direct marketing firms or established specialized units to handle the direct marketing business in Asia. OgilvyOne bought China's BrandOne. Others like McCann-Erickson, which opened O5, have established independent agencies dedicated to providing specialized comprehensive marketing services, including direct marketing, to its clients.

The Benefits of Direct Marketing

Market demassification has resulted in an ever-increasing number of market niches. Consumers, short of time and tired of traffic and parking headaches, appreciate toll-free phone numbers and Web sites available 24 hours a day, seven days a week, and direct marketers' commitment to customer service. The growth of next-day delivery via FedEx and UPS has made ordering fast and easy. In addition, many chain stores have dropped slower-moving specialty items, creating an opportunity for direct marketers to promote these items to interested buyers.

Increased credit card penetration, especially in China and Korea, has also fuelled direct marketing. The growth of the Internet, email, mobile phones, and fax machines has made product selection and ordering much simpler. China alone boasts over 210 million Internet users in 2007.[3] The youth market in Asia seems particularly amenable to direct marketing. Many youth market-focused campaigns rely on database marketing and online clubs. In turn, these rely on interactive email campaigns and short message service (SMS) as key tools. Direct marketing is particularly well-received in developing Asian countries where, unlike mature markets, consumers have yet to be buried in "junk mail" and spam.

Heinz—To break into the Philippines market, Heinz sent 150,000 housewives in Manila samples of Heinz tomato ketchup in bright red cans. A surprising 8 percent of the recipients responded by signing on to Heinz's mailing list, even without a deadline or the offer of another freebie. A similar campaign in the U.S. might net 2 percent of recipients at best. The responses gave Heinz valuable data about young shoppers willing to switch from the Del Monte ketchup their mothers used. One reason for the high response rate is that Filipinos generally receive only a few pieces of mail a week. Thus even a random solicitation can seem special. Another reason is the relative novelty of such efforts in most of Asia. Since women have fewer mailings sent to them, they are not yet as cynical as those in the U.S.[4]

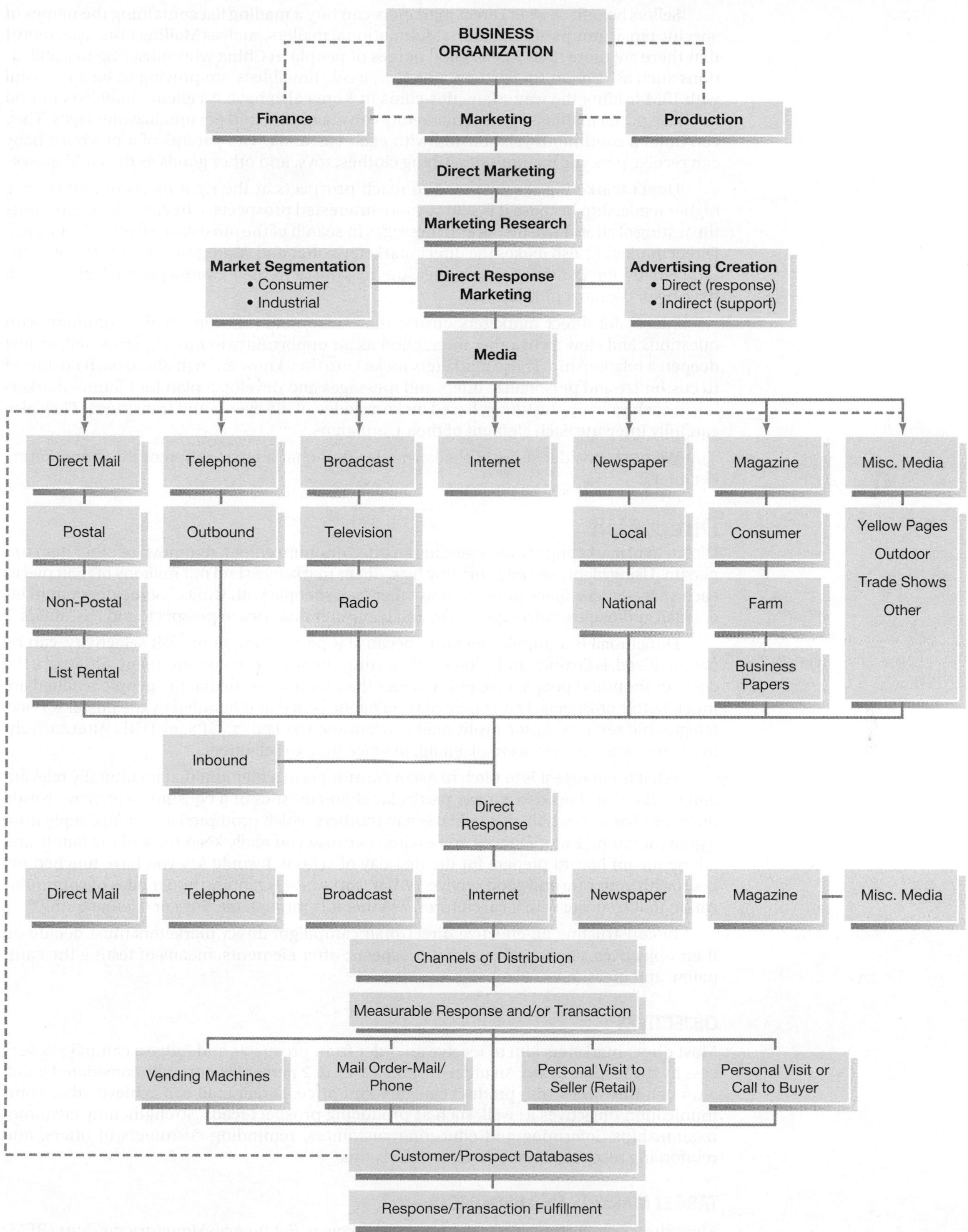

Figure 19.1 Direct Marketing Flow Chart

Source: Adapted from *Direct Marketing* magazine, 224 seventh street, Garden city, New York, 11530-5711.

Sellers benefit as well. Direct marketers can buy a mailing list containing the names of specific target groups of customers. Multinational mailers, such as Mailing Lists Asia, report that there are more than 50,000 good names of people in China who subscribe to publications such as *Economist, Fortune,* and *Newsweek.* Email lists are proving to be successful with IBM leading the way. Many dot-coms in Korea also have excellent email lists but do not have postal mailings.[5] Direct marketers can customize and personalize messages. They can build a continuous relationship with each customer. The parents of a newborn baby can receive periodic mailings describing clothes, toys, and other goods as the child grows.

Direct marketing can be timed to reach prospects at the right moment and receive higher readership because it is sent to more interested prospects. Direct marketing permits the testing of alternative media and messages in search of the most cost-effective approach. Direct marketing also makes the direct marketer's offer and strategy less visible to competitors. Finally, direct marketers can measure responses to their campaigns to decide which have been the most profitable.

Successful direct marketers ensure that customers can contact the company with questions and view a customer interaction as an opportunity to up-sell, cross-sell, or just deepen a relationship. These marketers make sure they know enough about each customer to customize and personalize offers and messages and develop a plan for lifetime marketing to each valuable customer, based on knowledge of life events and transitions. They also carefully integrate each element of their campaigns.

We next consider some of the key issues that characterize different direct marketing channels.

Direct Mail

Direct-mail marketing involves sending an offer, announcement, reminder, or other item to a person. Using highly selective mailing lists, direct marketers send out millions of mail pieces each year—letters, fliers, foldouts, and other "salespeople with wings." Some direct marketers mail audiotapes, videotapes, CDs, and computer diskettes to prospects and customers.

Direct mail is a popular medium because it permits target market selectivity, can be personalized, is flexible, and allows early testing and response measurement. Although, the cost per thousand people reached is higher than with mass media, the people reached are much better prospects. Direct mail may be paper-based and handled by the postal service, telegraphic services, or for-profit mail carriers such as FedEx, UPS, or DHL. Alternatively, marketers may employ fax mail, email, or voice mail to sell direct.

What is important is to pitch to Asian consumers in a medium that is culturally relevant and meets a local need or targets particular characteristics of a consumer segment. Nestlé once sent back-to-school tips to Malaysian mothers which prompted a favorable reply from a grateful mum, "I was shocked and excited because you really keep track of my family and advise me on how to prepare for the first day of school. I would say you have touched my heart with your care and good service." What works best is tapping into modes of communication that resonate with local cultures, whether it is through mailings or telemarketing.[6]

In constructing an effective direct-mail campaign, direct marketers must decide on their objectives, target markets, and prospects; offer elements, means of testing the campaign, and measures of campaign success.

OBJECTIVES

Most direct marketers aim to receive an order from prospects and judge a campaign's success by the response rate. An order-response rate of 2 percent is normally considered good, although this varies with product category and price. Direct mail can achieve other communication objectives as well, such as producing prospect leads, strengthening customer relationships, informing and educating customers, reminding customers of offers, and reinforcing recent customer purchase decisions.

TARGET MARKETS AND PROSPECTS

Most direct marketers apply the formula *Recency, Frequency, Monetary amount* (RFM) for rating and selecting customers. For any proposed offering, the company selects customers according to how much time has passed since their last purchase, how many times they have purchased, and how much they have spent since becoming a customer. Suppose the company is offering a leather jacket. It might make this offer to customers who made their last purchase between 30 and 60 days ago, who make three to six purchases a year, and who have spent at least $100 since becoming customers. Points are established for varying RFM levels, and each customer is scored. The higher the score, the more attractive the customer. The mailing is sent only to the most attractive customers.[7]

Prospects can also be identified based on such variables as age, sex, income, education, and previous mail-order purchases. Occasions provide a good departure point for segmentation. New parents will be in the market for baby clothes and baby toys; college freshmen will buy computers and small television sets; newlyweds will be looking for housing, furniture, appliances, and bank loans. Another useful segmentation variable is consumer lifestyle or "passion" groups, such as computer buffs, cooking buffs, and outdoor buffs.

In B2B direct marketing, the prospect is often not an individual but a group of people or a committee that includes both decision makers and multiple decision influencers. "Marketing Memo: When Your Customer is a Committee" offers tips on crafting a direct-mail campaign aimed at business buyers.

The company's best prospects are customers who have bought its products in the past. Additional names can be obtained by advertising some free offer. The direct marketer can also buy lists of names from list brokers, but these lists often have problems, including name duplication, incomplete data, and obsolete addresses. The better lists include overlays of demographic and psychographic information. Direct marketers typically buy and test a sample before buying more names from the same list. They can build their own lists by advertising a free offer and collecting responses.

MARKETING MEMO • WHEN YOUR CUSTOMER IS A COMMITTEE

One of the many advantages of database marketing and direct mail is that they allow you to tailor format, offer, and sell messages to the target audience(s). Business marketers can create a series of interrelated and reinforced mailings to decision makers and decision influencers. Here are some tips for increasing success in selling to a customer-by-committee:

- When creating lead generation and follow-up mailings, remember that most business mailings are screened once, twice, or even more before reaching your targeted audience.
- Plan and budget for a series of mailings to each of your customer-by-committee members. Timing and multiple exposures are critical in reaching these audiences.
- Whenever possible, mail to individuals by name and title. Using the title helps the in-office mail screener reroute your mailing if the individual addressed has moved on to another job.
- Do not necessarily use the same format and size for reaching all your targeted audiences. A more expensive-looking envelope may reach the president or CEO, but it may be equally effective to use a less expensive, less personal format to reach other decision influencers.
- Tell your customer-by-committee that you are communicating with others in the organization.
- Make your decision influencers feel important. They can be your biggest advocates.
- When communicating with different audiences, make sure you anticipate—and address—their individual buying objectives and objections.
- When your database or mailing lists cannot help you reach all the key people, ask the individual you are addressing to pass along your information.
- When doing a lead-generation mailing, make sure to ask for the names and titles of those who might be interested and involved in the buying decision. Enter this information into your database.
- Even though it may seem like a lot of work (and expense) to write different versions of the same letter and create different offers, there is a big payoff. The final decision maker may be interested in having a payback calculated, but others may be interested in day-to-day benefits such as safety, convenience, and time savings. Tailor your offer to your targets.

Source: Adapted from Pat Friesen, "When Your Customer Is a Committee." *Target Marketing*, August 1998, p. 40.

OFFER ELEMENTS

The offer strategy has five elements—the *product*, the *offer*, the *medium*, the *distribution method*, and the *creative strategy*.[8] Fortunately, all of these elements can be tested.

In addition to these elements, the direct-mail marketer has to decide on five components of the mailing itself: the outside envelope, sales letter, circular, reply form, and reply envelope. Here are some findings:

1. **The outside envelope will be more effective if it contains an illustration**, preferably in color, or a catchy reason to open the envelope, such as the announcement of a contest, premium, or benefit. Envelopes are more effective when they contain a colorful commemorative stamp, when the address is hand-typed or handwritten, and when the envelope differs in size or shape from standard envelopes.[9]
2. **The sales letter should use a personal salutation and start with a headline in bold type.** The letter should be printed on good-quality paper and be brief. A computer-typed letter usually outperforms a printed letter, and the presence of a pithy P.S. increases the response rate, as does the signature of someone whose title is important.
3. In most cases, **a colorful circular accompanying the letter will increase the response rate** by more than its cost.
4. **Direct mailers should feature a toll-free number and also send recipients to their Web site.** Coupons should be printed out at the Web site.
5. **The inclusion of a postage-free reply envelope will dramatically increase the response rate.**

Direct mail should be followed up by an email, which is less expensive and less intrusive than a telemarketing call.

TESTING ELEMENTS

One of the great advantages of direct marketing is the ability to test, under real marketplace conditions, different elements of an offer strategy, such as products, product features, copy platform, mailer type, envelope, prices, or mailing lists.

Response rates typically understate a campaign's long-term impact. Suppose only 2 percent of the recipients who receive a direct-mail piece advertising Samsonite luggage place an order. A much larger percentage became aware of the product (direct mail has high readership), and some percentage may have formed an intention to buy at a later date (either by mail or at a retail outlet). Further, some of them may mention Samsonite luggage to others as a result of the direct-mail piece. To derive a more comprehensive estimate of the promotion's impact, some companies are measuring direct marketing's impact on awareness, intention to buy, and word of mouth.

MEASURING CAMPAIGN SUCCESS: LIFETIME VALUE

By adding up the planned campaign costs, the direct marketer can figure out in advance the needed break-even response rate. This rate must be net of returned merchandise and bad debts. Returned merchandise can kill an otherwise effective campaign. The direct marketer needs to analyze the main causes of returned merchandise (late shipment, defective merchandise, damage in transit, not as advertised, incorrect order fulfillment).

Even when a specific campaign fails to break even in the short-run, it can still be profitable in the long run if customer lifetime is factored in (see Chapter 5). A customer's ultimate value is not revealed by a purchase response to a particular mailing. Rather, it is the expected profit made on all future purchases net of customer acquisition and maintenance costs. For an average customer, one would calculate the average customer longevity, average customer annual expenditure, and average gross margin, minus the average cost of customer acquisition and maintenance (properly discounted for the opportunity cost of money).[10]

Catalog Marketing

In catalog marketing, companies may send full-line merchandise catalogs, specialty consumer catalogs, and business catalogs, usually in print form but also sometimes as CDs, videos, or online. Avon sells cosmetics and IKEA sells furniture through catalogs. Many of these direct marketers have found that combining catalogs and Web sites can be an effective way to sell. Thousands of small businesses also issue specialty catalogs. Large businesses send catalogs to business prospects and customers.

Catalogs are a huge business in some parts of developed Asia like Japan. The Japanese have embraced mail-order catalogs from foreign retailers. Land's End Japan spends 40 percent of its operating costs in creating and mailing catalogs. Other U.S. catalog companies such as L.L. Bean, Eddie Bauer, and Patagonia have also set up operations in Japan. Within a few years, foreign catalogs—mostly from the U.S.—have won 5 percent of the $20 billion Japanese mail-order catalog market. A full 90 percent of L.L. Bean's international sales come from Japan.

L.L. Bean—L.L. Bean entered the Japanese market in 1989. From 1991, several factors helped its business. The Japanese government encouraged people to take longer vacations and the value of the yen to the dollar was very attractive. L.L. Bean started opening stores to complement its catalog business, offering high-quality merchandise aimed at specific groups, and adapted to local tastes and trends. Responding to customer feedback, it introduced a line of "Japan Fit" apparel, designed to better suit Japanese women's body types. Unlike in the U.S. where the catalogs display a wide variety of colors, L.L. Bean Japan found that a narrower selection is relevant in Japan. Spring pastels and pinks may be popular in the U.S. but in general perform poorly in Japan where earth tones are more acceptable. In 2000, with the economic recession in Japan, L.L. Bean improved its brand presentation and integrated its distribution channels for a more efficient operation. In addition to its print catalog and retail outlet sales, it has a thriving Web presence.[11]

The success of a catalog business depends on the company's ability to manage its customer lists carefully so that there is little duplication or bad debts, to control its inventory carefully, to offer quality merchandise so that returns are low, and to project a distinctive image. Some companies distinguish their catalogs by adding literary or information features, sending swatches of materials, operating a special hotline to answer questions, sending gifts to their best customers, and donating a percentage of the profits to good causes.

Telemarketing

Telemarketing is the use of the telephone and call centers to attract prospects, sell to existing customers, and provide service by taking orders and answering questions. Telemarketing helps companies increase revenue, reduce selling costs, and improve customer satisfaction.

Companies use call centers for *inbound telemarketing* (receiving calls from customers) and *outbound telemarketing* (initiating calls to prospects and customers). Telemarketing has yet to become a major direct marketing tool in Asia for several reasons: (1) it is too difficult to set up in emerging Asian economies with poor telecommunications infrastructure; (2) extensive training is required; (3) there is high staff turnover, as reliable and bright telemarketers are hard to keep given the tight labor market for their services; and (4) there are numerous multicountry complications and associated language problems.

Nonetheless, telemarketing can be used in business as well as consumer marketing. It can reduce the amount of personal selling. Telemarketing, as it improves with the use of videophones, will increasingly replace, though never eliminate, more expensive field sales calls. Salespeople have closed big sales without ever meeting the customer face-to-face in the U.S. However, the likelihood of this happening in Asia would seem to be lower given the region's greater emphasis on relationships and higher risk aversion in some countries. An example of successful telemarketing is Retin-A in the Philippines.

Retin-A—Jansenn Pharmaceutical was experiencing a low repeat-buyer rate for its Retin-A anti-wrinkle ointment in the Philippines. Marketers called buyers to explain that the ointment might cause stinging and peeling. Buyers initially thought they were allergic, not realizing that this was part of the treatment. The calls cleared the misconception. More important, the buyers were so talkative that the telemarketing force had to be doubled to deal with the long calls. After the campaign, the retention rate quadrupled.[12]

Related to telemarketing is SMS marketing, which has particular potential in emerging Asian economies with poor fixed line telecommunications infrastructure, but where consumers may be accessible via wireless means. Indeed, the Philippines are the SMS capital of the world. Despite its lower mobile phone penetration, the Philippines generates more text messages than all of Europe combined.[13] While low cost is partly responsible, a deeper cultural reason is that extended families are ubiquitous and represent an important social system in the Philippines. SMS keeps families, neighbors, and friends closely connected in a society which places a premium on social relations. As a form of m-commerce, SMS is thus used by Filipino marketers to offer a wide range of services, including daily news and soap opera updates, games, lotteries, purchasing from vending machines, and limited mobile phone banking.

However, the wide range of mobile phones available in the region makes it difficult for the industry to come up with a single compatible m-commerce solution. The wide availability of low-cost Internet services in several Asian countries like Singapore is another impediment. In addition, mobile phone operators outside Japan are reluctant to work with competitors to adopt a centralized billing and revenue-sharing arrangement that would encourage usage by consumers, fearing a "commoditization" of their networks. Finally, there is the security issue to protect wireless transactions.[14]

Public and Ethical Issues in Direct Marketing

Direct marketers and their customers usually enjoy mutually rewarding relationships. Occasionally, however, a darker side emerges:

- ***Irritation*** — Many people do not like the large number of hard-sell, direct marketing solicitations. Especially bothersome are dinnertime or late-night phone calls, poorly trained callers, and computerized calls by auto-dial recorded-message players.
- ***Unfairness*** — Some direct marketers take advantage of impulsive or less sophisticated buyers or prey on the vulnerable, especially the elderly.[15]
- ***Deception and fraud*** — Some direct marketers design mailers and write copy intended to mislead. They may exaggerate product size, performance claims, or the "retail price."
- ***Invasion of privacy*** — It seems that almost every time consumers order products by mail or telephone, enter a sweepstakes, apply for a credit card, or take out a magazine subscription, their names, addresses, and purchasing behavior may be added to several company databases. Critics worry that marketers may know too much about consumers' lives, and that they may use this knowledge to take unfair advantage.

People in the direct marketing industry are addressing the issues. They know that, left unattended, such problems will lead to increasingly negative consumer attitudes, lower response rates, and calls for greater state and federal regulation. In the final analysis, most direct marketers want the same thing consumers want: honest and well-designed marketing offers targeted only to those who appreciate hearing about the offer.

To learn how Stella Artois uses interactive marketing to succeed in Belgium, visit www.pearsoned.co.uk/marketingmanagementeurope.

Interactive Marketing

The newest channels for direct marketing are electronic.[16] The Internet provides marketers and consumers with opportunities for much greater *interaction* and *individualization*. Few marketing programs are considered complete without some type of prominent online component.

Advantages and Disadvantages of Interactive Marketing

Interactive marketing offers unique benefits.[17] Companies can send tailored messages that engage consumers by reflecting their special interests and behavior. The Internet is highly accountable and its effects can be easily traced. Online, advertisers can gauge response instantaneously by noting how many unique visitors or "UVs" click on a page or ad, how long they spend with it, where they go afterwards, and so on.[18]

The Web offers the advantage of *contextual placement* and buying ads on sites that are related to the marketer's offerings. Marketers can also place advertising based on keywords from search engines, to reach people when they've actually started the buying process. Light consumers of other media, especially television, can be reached online. The Web is especially effective at reaching people during the day. Young, high-income, high-education customers' total online media consumption exceeds that of TV.[19]

Using the Web also has disadvantages. Consumers can effectively screen out most messages. Marketers may think their ads are more effective than they are if bogus clicks are generated by software-powered Web sites. Advertisers lose some control over what consumers will do with their online messages and activity. Consumers could place a video in undesirable or unseemly places.

But many feel the pros outweigh the cons, and the Web is attracting marketers of all kinds. To capitalize on advertisers' interest, firms are rushing online services and other support to marketers. Microsoft has invested in a broad range of businesses for placing ads on the Web, video games, mobile phones and alongside Internet search results. "Breakthrough Marketing: Yahoo!" describes that company's online efforts.

For marketers of automobiles, financial services, personal computers, and telecommunications, marketing activities on the Web have become crucial. But others are quickly following. The migration of advertising from print to online is evident in China as Chinese Internet users tend to be trend-conscious, young, and relatively wealthy. Tiffany, the premium jeweler, launched a 557-page site in Chinese to woo the mainland's *nouveau riche*. Procter & Gamble set up a site pitching its beauty brands Olay, SK-II, and Hugo Boss. It also created a site to launch a youth-oriented Crest sub-brand called "Whitening Expression." It asked youths to post videos of themselves dancing with a tube of Crest in hand, and visitors to the site vote on the best act. General Motors held an online contest to choose the Chinese name for its new Chevrolet compact, giving one of the cars, the Lova, to the winner.[20]

In the U.S., Pepsi spent between 5 and 10 percent of its overall ad budget online in 2006, compared to just 1 percent in 2001, because of its cost-effectiveness.[21]

Pepsi—Pepsi North America was able to monitor its "Call upon Yoda" promotion with a Star Wars theme. In one ad, the film's green, pointy-eared Yoda floated across Yahoo!'s homepage to land in a small box near the upper right corner. Users who clicked on the ad box were taken to a Pepsi site, where they were given a chance to win a $100,000 prize. Using marketing research data, Pepsi was able to place its ads on areas of Yahoo!'s site most frequented by heavy buyers of 12-packs and 24-packs of soda, its target for the promotion. Pepsi concluded that sales to that group rose in double-digit percentages as a result of the ads. In China, Pepsi leveraged its Internet presence into widespread buzz when it challenged consumers to design ads for the company.

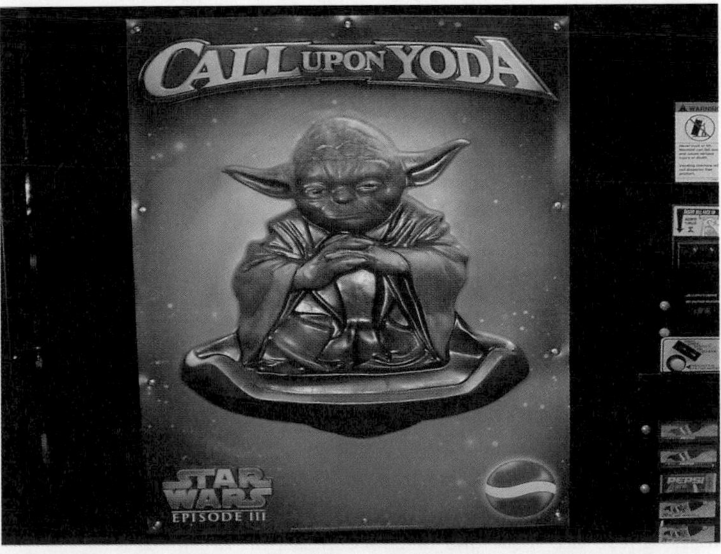

Internet technology harnessed by Yahoo! and marketing research data collected by Pepsi allowed Pepsi to reach specific targets with its recent Star Wars-themed promotion.

BREAKTHROUGH • MARKETING

YAHOO!

Yahoo! grew from a tiny upstart to a major contender in Internet media. David Filo and Jerry Yang, two computer science Ph.D. students at Stanford University, created a simple search engine in 1994, with the acronym meaning "Yet Another Hierarchical Officious Oracle." Using a homemade filing system, they catalogued sites on the newly created World Wide Web and published the directory on the Internet. At the time, Yahoo!'s search engine was unique because in addition to the standard word search features, it offered users a massive searchable index. Surfers could search for sites in broad categories like Business and Economy or Arts and Humanities. They could organize the results by country or region and look at results from within just one category.

Yahoo!'s entry into interactive marketing is to offer contextual advertising on its site. Contextual advertising means that the commercial links on a Yahoo! page are tied to the particular content on that page. It appeals to advertisers moving away from mass marketing toward more targeted approaches. Yahoo!'s new ad server creates contextual relevance, catching a consumer or decision maker reading material directly related to the advertised topic.

Yahoo!'s two main advantages over search engine rival Google are its vast array of original content and a database with information about its 133 million registered users. By knowing where searchers live and what their interests are, Yahoo! believes it can present them with more relevant search results and more focused advertising.

Yahoo! is also attracting traditional advertisers like Pepsi and Ford. For example, Yahoo!'s ad for the Ford Explorer featured sound effects simulating an engine with animation that made the Web browser appear to shake. To announce its new Ford F-150 Truck, Ford created an interactive 3-D ad and purchased roadblocks (ads that browsers must click through to reach other content) on the first day of its launch at Yahoo! as well as MSN and AOL.

Yahoo! has also created search engines for various markets worldwide. In Japan, Yahoo! is beating eBay at auctions. Unlike Yahoo! which initially charged no commission, eBay did. Hurt by the long economic slump, Japanese consumers discovered online auctions, for which they could adopt Internet nicknames to take the sting out of buying other people's stuff. The Japanese are also fans of collectibles that are ideal for online auctions. In addition, Yahoo! Japan spends 8 percent of revenue on promotions that include renting billboards in trendy Tokyo districts, opening an Internet café with Starbucks, and covering planes of a domestic airline with its logo. Recently, Yahoo! Japan expanded its online music distribution service by allowing customers to listen to selected songs in full before they decide to buy. Existing services only allow customers to listen to song samples of about 30 seconds. Yahoo! Japan expects to earn advertising revenue and commissions from song sales, while aiming to bolster traffic to its fee-based operations through the new service.

In contrast, Yahoo! is struggling in China, where there are 210 million Internet users, second only to the U.S. Yahoo! acquired 3721, the first Chinese-language search company, to complement its search site, Yisou.com. Both compete with market leader Baidu, which has the world's largest Chinese Web index and a search engine that includes MP3 music files and digital images. Yahoo!'s Chinese-language search engines rank a close second behind Baidu, with 323 million searches compared with the latter's 342 million. However, Yahoo!'s 3721 is the top Chinese keyword search engine, with 40 percent market share by revenue.

A key strength of 3721 is the relationships its sales staff had built up with advertisers. In addition, 3721 understands the local market and helped Yahoo! spruce up its Chinese site design and positioning. In December 2004, Yahoo! offered broadband subscribers a service that combined mail and instant messaging. However, its mail messenger service is tied for fifth with a 1.5 percent market share. Yahoo! also started a free email service that gives users one gigabyte of storage, four times more than what is offered for free in the U.S. The move garnered many new users but prompted both Sina and Netease to release a free email service with 1.5 gigabytes of storage. Yahoo! also developed an online Chinese auction site, <www.1pai.com> (meaning No. 1 Auction), with Sina to compete with eBay. It relocated hundreds of its U.S. servers to China to speed up the massive volume of online transactions and set up a customer service center to help with customer delivery and payment. While generating traffic, the site is not yet profitable.

As its brand recognition as a search engine has some way to go in China, Yahoo! took a 40 percent stake in Alibaba, a Chinese B2B Web site, and appointed Alibaba's founder Jack Ma to head its China operations. Ma plans to spend $350 million to rebuild Yahoo!'s brand as a search engine in China.

Sources: Saul Hansell, "The Search Engine That Isn't a Verb, Yet." *New York Times,* February 22, 2004; George Mannes, "Yahoo! Surge Points to Advertising Shift." <www.thestreet.com>, January 19, 2005; Ken Belson, Rob Hof, and Ben Elgin, "How Yahoo! Japan Beat eBay at Its Own Game." *BusinessWeek,* June 4, 2001; "Yahoo! Japan to Expand Its Online Music Service." *Reuters,* August 22, 2005; Bruce Einhorn, "U.S. Web Giants Target China." *BusinessWeek Online,* June 13, 2005; Peter S. Wang, "Tigerish Ambitions." *Asia Inc.*, March 2005, pp. 31–33; "Chinese Curiosity Driven By Baidu." *Los Angeles Times* as reported in *Straits Times*, September 10, 2005, p. 24; Jamil Andertini, "Cashed-up Alibaba Opens Fire." *South China Morning Post*, November 10, 2005, p. B1; Sara Lacy, "Carefully Clearing Yahoo!'s Clutter." *BusinessWeek*, September 19, 2005, pp. 54–56; Eric Wan, "Chinese Mainland Internet Population Tops 200 Million." January 17, 2008, <http://www.chinatechnews.com/2008/01/17/6302-chinese-mainlands-internet-population-tops-200-million/> (accessed on April 14, 2008).

Marketers must go where the customers are, and increasingly that's online. Asian youths feel that what's "hot" is spending time online (56 percent), using mobile services (49 percent), sending emails (41 percent), and using social networks (37 percent); while not "hot" includes watching TV (46 percent) and spending money on music (36 percent).[22] Customers define the rules of engagement, however, and insulate themselves with the help of agents and intermediaries if they so choose. Customers define what information they need, what offerings they're interested in, and what they're willing to pay.[23]

Online advertising was estimated at a little less than 6 percent of global ad spending in 2006, but is expected to jump to 10 percent to become a $25 billion business by 2009. Helping fuel that growth is the emergence of rich media ads that combine animation, video, and sound with interactive features.[24]

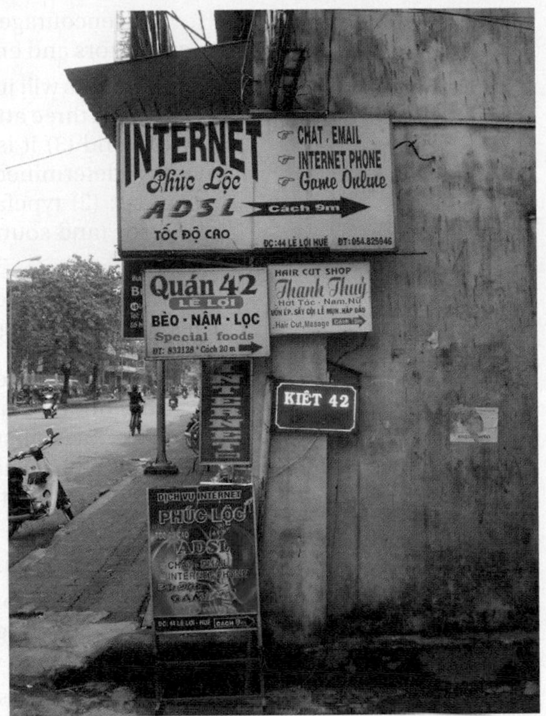

Internet cafés such as this one are a common sight in Asia even in poorer communities. Some 56 percent of Asian youths think that spending time online is "hot."

Motorola—In China, online advertising has been growing by more than 75 percent annually for the past three years. The lifestyle of Chinese youths has changed. When Motorola launched a new line of youth-oriented mobile phones, it did not advertise on TV or in the newspapers. Instead, it hired a pair of college students from Guangzhou who had become an Internet sensation with their home-made videos of themselves lip-synching Western pop songs. Motorola built an online marketing campaign in which the duo lip-synched "As Long As You Love Me" by the Backstreet Boys. The response was overwhelming. Motorola then continued with a lip-synching and song remixing competition. This garnered over 14 million page views, with the surge in traffic crashing the site at one point. Visitors cast more than 1.3 million votes to determine the winner of the contest and sales of the new phones soared. Motorola's music download site, <motomusic.com.cn>, became the most popular legal site in China and handset sales doubled.[25]

Placing Ads and Promotion Online

A company chooses which forms of interactive marketing will be most cost-effective in achieving communication and sales objectives.

WEB SITES

Companies must design Web sites that embody or express their purpose, history, products, and vision.[26] A key challenge is designing a site that's attractive on first viewing and interesting enough to encourage repeat visits.[27] Rayport and Jaworski propose that effective sites feature seven design elements they call the 7Cs (see Figure 19.2).[28]

- ***Context*** — Layout and design
- ***Content*** — Text, pictures, sound, and video the site contains
- ***Community*** — How the site enables user-to-user communication
- ***Customization*** — Site's ability to tailor itself to different users or to allow users to personalize the site
- ***Communication*** — How the site enables site-to-user, user-to-site, or two-way communication
- ***Connection*** — Degree that the site is linked to other sites
- ***Commerce*** — Site's capabilities to enable commercial transactions

Figure 19.2 Seven Key Design Elements of an Effective Web

Source: Jeffrey F. Rayport and Bernard J. Jaworski, *e-commerce,* (New York: McGraw-Hill, 2001), p. 116.

To encourage repeat visits, companies must pay special attention to context and content factors and embrace another "C"—constant change.[29]

Visitors will judge a site's performance on ease of use and physical attractiveness. Ease of use has three attributes: (1) the site downloads quickly: (2) the first page is easy to understand: and (3) it is easy to navigate to other pages that open quickly. Physical attractiveness is determined by these factors: (1) individual pages are clean and not crammed with content; (2) typefaces and font sizes are very readable; and (3) the site makes good use of color (and sound). Web sites must also be sensitive to security and privacy-protection issues.[30]

Web sites should also be designed to take into consideration cultural orientation. A study examining Japanese and U.S. Web sites found several distinct characteristics:[31]

- Given Japan's collectivistic and group-oriented behavior, its Web sites tended to feature online clubs, family themes, and links to local companies. For example, the Web sites for Fujitsu and Olympus prominently depicted features like camera clubs and news clubs. They also had links to local Web sites such as racketball associations, travel agencies, and tours for seeing cherry blossoms.
- To cater to its risk-averse culture, Japanese Web sites frequently portrayed elements of Japanese culture, tradition, harmony, and company history.
- Japan's high context culture was reflected in the Web sites' being rich in color, aesthetics, and having a general feel of tranquility. Pictures of butterflies, cherry blossoms, nature scenes, and cultural artifacts were common.
- Japanese Web sites also depicted politeness in the form of customary notes of thanks to the customers, greetings, and notes of best wishes for good health. In contrast, American Web sites emphasized more of a hard-sell approach using superlatives. They were also more informative and with a less decorative atmosphere.

MICROSITES

A **microsite** is a limited area on the Web managed and paid for by an external advertiser/company. Microsites are individual Web pages or cluster of pages that function as supplements to a primary site. They're particularly relevant for companies selling low-interest products. People rarely visit an insurance company's Web site, but the company can create a microsite on used-car sites that offers advice for buyers of used cars and at the same time a good insurance deal. Some microsites have become huge online hits.

Burger King's Subservient Chicken—To compete with McDonald's wholesome, family-friendly image, Burger King adopted a youthful, irreverent personality and menu-driven positioning via its long-time "Have It Your Way" slogan. To promote its TenderCrisp sandwich, ad agency Crispin, Porter & Bogusky created a Web site featuring a "subservient chicken," an actor dressed in a chicken costume who performed a wide range of wacky actions based on a user's typed commands—dust furniture, play air guitar, or, naturally, lay an egg! The site employed prerecorded footage but looked like an interactive Webcam. Within a week of launch, about 54 million people had checked out the chicken for an average of eight minutes. This program was designed not only to entertain and connect with target market 14- to 25-year-olds, but to it help reinforce the brand's customization message and contemporary image. Said one Burger King executive, "We're really trying to do something different and not just give consumers a straight ad over and over."[32]

SEARCH ADS

A hot growth area in interactive marketing is **paid-search** or **pay-per-click ads,** which represent 40 percent of all online ads.[33] Thirty-five percent of all searches are reportedly for products or services. The search terms serve as a proxy for the consumer's consumption interests and trigger relevant links to product or service offerings alongside search results from Google, MSN, and Yahoo!. Advertisers pay only if people click on the links, but marketers believe consumers who have already expressed interest by virtue of the search are prime prospects.

The cost per click depends on how high the link is ranked and the popularity of the keyword. Average click-through is about 2 percent, much more than for comparable online ads.[34] One Samsung executive estimated it was 50 times cheaper to reach 1,000 people online than on TV, and the company shifted 10 percent of its advertising budget to the Internet.[35] Some believe the Internet is moving from the era of search to the era of discovery, thanks to recommender sites and systems that suggest music, movies, Web sites, or whatever is meaningful to users whether they've heard of it or even ask.

DISPLAY ADS

Display ads or **banner ads** are small, rectangular boxes containing text and perhaps a picture that companies pay to place on relevant Web sites. The larger the audience, the more the placement costs.

Display ads still hold great promise compared to popular search ads. Given that Internet users spend only 5 percent of their time online actually searching for information, there are many opportunities to reach and influence consumers while they travel the Web. But ads need to be more attention getting and influential, better targeted, and more closely tracked.[36]

The emergence of behavioral targeting is allowing companies to track the online behavior of target customers to find the best match between ad and prospect. For example, if a person clicks on three Web sites related to auto insurance, then visits an unrelated site for sports or entertainment, auto insurance ads may show up on that site, in addition to the auto insurance sites. This practice ensures that ads are readily apparent for a potential customer likely to be in the market. Although critics worry about companies knowing too much about customers, Microsoft claims behavioral targeting can increase the likelihood a visitor clicks an ad by as much as 76 percent.[37]

INTERSTITIALS

Interstitials are advertisements, often with video or animation that pop up between changes on a Web site. Ads for Johnson & Johnson's Tylenol headache reliever would pop up on brokers' Web sites whenever the stock market fell by 100 points or more. Because consumers found pop-up ads intrusive and distracting, many computer users install software to block these ads.[38]

INTERNET-SPECIFIC ADS AND VIDEOS

With user-generated content sites such as YouTube, MySpace, and Google Video, consumers and advertisers can upload ads and videos to be shared virally by millions of people.

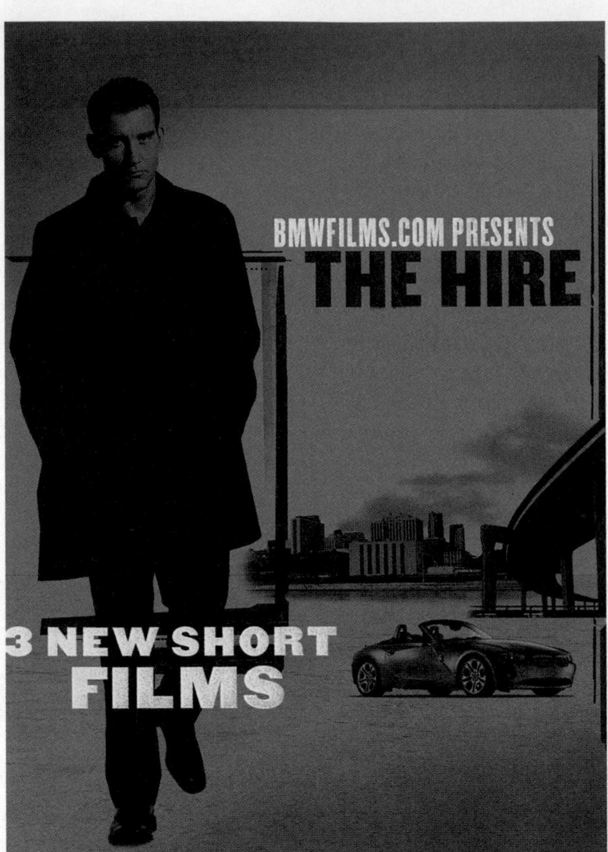

BMW's online videos had cinematic production quality and stars to match. The ads showcased various BMW models and won an enthusiastic response from consumers and film critics alike.

BMW Films—In North America, BMW is positioned as the "Ultimate Driving Machine" on the basis of its dual benefits of luxury and high performance. Beginning in 2001, it created "The Hire" series, eight short films by famous action movie directors such as John Woo, Guy Ritchie, and Ang Lee and starring celebrities such as Madonna. Each was less than 10 minutes long and could be downloaded only from a corporate Web site, <www.bmwfilms.com> and viewed on the Internet. With a budget of $3 million per film, the films were cinematic in look, but also designed to showcase the unique qualities of different BMW models. To build traffic to the site, BMW used television spots that mirrored movie trailers. The response was overwhelming. According to BMW's ad agency, 55.1 million people viewed "The Hire" series, and tremendous PR buzz resulted. Many film critics even gave the films rave reviews. And by having visitors register before downloading the films, BMW was able to collect contact information for a large number of potential buyers, many of whom were younger and not necessarily as well represented in BMW's prior marketing efforts.[39]

SPONSORSHIPS

Many companies get their name on the Internet by sponsoring special content on Web sites that carry news, financial information, and so on. **Sponsorships** are best placed in well-targeted sites that offer relevant information or service. The sponsor pays for showing the content and in turn receives acknowledgment as the sponsor of that particular service on the site.

A popular vehicle for sponsorship is *podcasts,* digital media files created for playback on portable MP3 players, laptops, or PCs. Sponsors run a 15- or 30-second audio ad at the beginning of the podcast. As podcasts are able to reach very specific market segments, analysts expect their popularity to grow.[40]

ALLIANCES

When one Internet company works with another, they end up advertising each other through **alliances** and **affiliate programs**. Amazon.com has almost one million affiliates that post its banners on their Web sites. Companies can also undertake guerrilla marketing actions to publicize their site and generate word of mouth. Companies can offer to push content and ads to targeted audiences who agree to receive them and are presumably more interested in the product or product category.

ONLINE COMMUNITIES

Many companies sponsor online communities whose members communicate through postings, instant messaging, and chat discussions about special interests related to the company's products and brands. These communities can provide companies useful, hard-to-get information.

EMAIL

Email uses only a fraction of the cost of a "d-mail," or direct mail, campaign. Microsoft spent approximately $70 million a year on paper-driven campaigns. It switched to sending out 20 million pieces of email every month at a significant savings. Consumers are besieged by emails though, and many employ spam filters. The following are some important guidelines for productive email campaigns, followed by pioneering email marketers:[41]

- **Give the customer a reason to respond.** Offer powerful incentives for reading email pitches and online ads, such as email trivia games, scavenger hunts, and instant-win sweepstakes.
- **Personalize the content of your emails.** IBM's iSource has been distributed directly to customers' office email each week, delivering only "the news they choose" in Announcements and Weekly Updates. Customers who agree to receive the newsletter select from topics listed on an interest profile.
- **Offer something the customer can't get via direct mail.** Because email campaigns can be carried out quickly, they can offer time-sensitive information. Travelocity sends frequent emails pitching last-minute cheap airfares. Club Med uses email to pitch unsold, discounted vacation packages to prospects in its database.
- **Make it easy for customers to "unsubscribe."** Online customers demand a positive exit experience. According to one study, the top 10 percent of Web users who communicate much more often online typically share their views by email with 11 friends when satisfied, but contact 17 friends when dissatisfied.[42]

To increase the effectiveness of emails, some researchers are employing "heat mapping," by which they can measure what people read on a computer screen by using cameras attached to a computer that track eye movements. One study showed that clickable graphic icons and buttons that linked to more details of a marketing offer increased click-through rates by 60 percent compared to links that used an Internet address.[43]

MOBILE MARKETING

Mobile ad spending was $2.7 billion in 2007 and is expected to grow to $19.1 billion in 2012. Most ad dollars go to text messaging, which is expected to continue to be the dominant "non-voice mobile service" over the next few years, particularly in large markets in China and India that lack 3G networks.[44]

But new dual-mode phones will make it increasingly easy to blend mobile phones with wireless Internet service. With mobile phones' ubiquitous nature and marketers' ability to personalize messages based on demographics, the appeal of mobile marketing is obvious. A study showed that Asian youths use mobile phones while commuting to kill time. Their favored content on their phones are news updates, entertainment, and music. They perceive the mobile phones as portable, personal, and private; and a cool product to have.[45]

The affordability of mobile phones and the coming of age of a generation of Japanese for whom mobile phones, more than personal computers, had been an integral part of their lives have led to the success of mobile marketing. With Japanese telecommunications companies' decision to offer unlimited transmission of packet data as part of flat monthly rates, novels are even marketed through phones as the following example shows:

Mobile phone novels—Until recently, mobile phone novels composed on phone pads and read by fans on their tiny screens were dismissed by Japanese as unworthy of the country that gave the world its first novel, *The Tale of Genji*. Now, with telecommunications service providers, including NTT DoCoMo, providing unlimited transmission of data such as text messaging, the mobile phone novel industry has flourished. In 2007, three of Japan's best-selling novels were by first-time mobile phone novelists.[46]

Some marketers are testing the waters. In the U.S., every two-minute mobile episode of Fox's *Prison Break: Proof of Innocence* starts with a 10-second message that showcases Toyota's new subcompact sedan, Yaris.[47]

Word of Mouth

Social networks, such as MySpace and Facebook, have become an important force in both business-to-consumer and business-to-business marketing.[48] A key aspect of social networks is *word of mouth* and the number and nature of conversations and communications between different parties. Consumers talk about dozens of brands each day. Although many are media and entertainment products such as movies, TV shows, and publications, food products, travel services, retail stores, and many other types of products are often mentioned.[49] And although meganetworks such as MySpace and Facebook offer the most exposure, niche social networks offer a more targeted market more likely to spread the brand message.

Companies are becoming acutely aware of the power of word of mouth. Products and brands as diverse as Hush Puppies shoes, Krispy Kreme doughnuts, and the blockbuster movie *The Passion of the Christ* were built through strong word of mouth,[50] as were companies such as Body Shop, Palm, Red Bull, Starbucks, and Amazon.com. In some cases, positive word of mouth happens organically with little advertising, but in many cases, it is managed and facilitated.[51] Word of mouth can be particularly effective for smaller businesses for whom customers may feel a more personal relationship.

Social networks in the form of online virtual communities can be a vital resource for companies. Apple has a large number of discussion groups organized by product lines and also by consumer versus professional use. These groups are customers' primary source of product information after warranties expire. Philip Morris developed a 26-million-plus database of Marlboro smokers, partly from necessity as media options dwindled due to legislative actions. It is now the primary means of marketing the brand.[52]

Here we consider how word of mouth is formed and travels.

Buzz and Viral Marketing

Some marketers highlight two particular forms of word of mouth—buzz and viral marketing.[53] *Buzz marketing* generates excitement, creates publicity, and conveys new relevant brand-related information through unexpected or even outrageous means.[54] *Viral marketing* is another form of word of mouth, or "word of mouse," that encourages consumers to pass along company-developed products and services or audio, video, or written information to others online.[55]

Agencies have been created solely to help clients create buzz. Procter & Gamble has 225,000 teens enlisted in Tremor and 600,000 mothers enrolled in Vocalpoint. Both groups are built on the premise that certain individuals want to learn about products, receive samples and coupons, share their opinions with companies, and, of course, talk up their experiences with others. P&G chooses well-connected people—the Vocalpoint moms have big social networks and generally speak to 25–30 other women during the day, compared to an average of five for other moms—and their messages carry a strong reason to share product information with a friend.[56]

Buzz and viral marketing both try to create a splash in the marketplace to showcase a brand and its noteworthy features. Some believe that viral and buzz marketing are driven more by the rules of entertainment than the rules of selling. A successful viral campaign has been characterized as "that addictive, self-propagating advertainment that lives on Web sites, blogs, mobile phones, message boards, and even in real-world stunts ...."

Campfire—A viral campaign for Sega's *Beta-7* sports video game, featuring a fictitious gamer playing the game nonstop for three months, collected 2.2 million online followers and helped Sega top sales projections by 25 percent in a category dominated by Electronic Art's ***Madden NFL***. The campaign was created by viral experts Campfire, also responsible for ***The Blair Witch Project*** campaign and Audi's A3 automobile "Art of the Heist" promotion. For Audi, Campfire staged a labyrinthine cross-country heist for a new 2006 A3 "stolen" from its Park Avenue showroom. More than 5,000,000 people tracked the heist online and through live events, resulting in 10,000 leads. Campfire designs its online promotions carefully to have multiple layers of "rabbit holes" for people with varying levels of interest: the "divers" who participate minute-by-minute; the "dippers" who casually check the message boards once a week, and the "skimmers" who accidentally read about it while surfing online.[57]

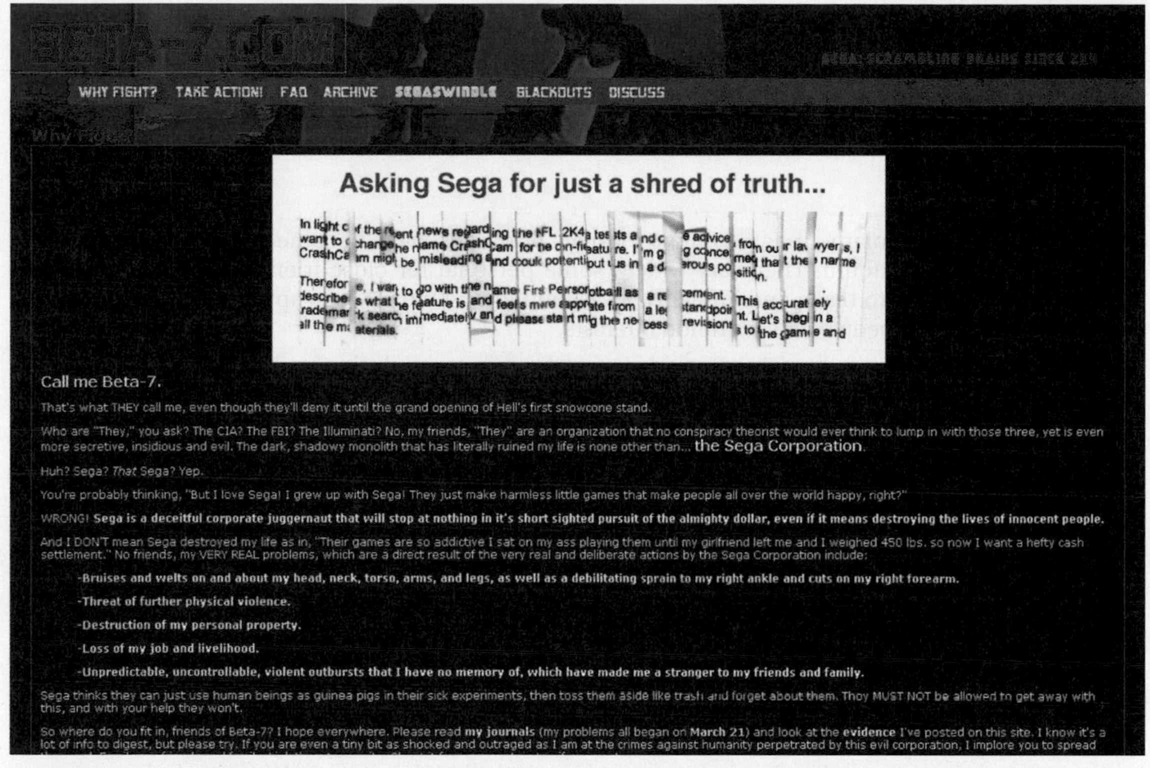

A successful viral campaign, such as the one Campfire designed for Sega's *Beta-7* sports video game, is part marketing, part entertainment.

Opinion Leaders

Communication researchers propose a social-structure view of interpersonal communication.[58] They see society as consisting of *cliques,* small groups whose members interact frequently. Clique members are similar, and their closeness facilitates effective communication but also insulates the clique from new ideas. The challenge is to create more openness so that cliques exchange information with others in the society. This openness is helped by people who function as liaisons and connect two or more cliques without belonging to either, and *bridges,* people who belong to one clique and are linked to a person in another.

There are three factors that work to ignite public interest in an idea.[59] According to the first, "The Law of the Few," three types of people help to spread an idea like an epidemic. First are *Mavens,* people knowledgeable about big and small things. Second are *Connectors,* people who know and communicate with a great number of other people. Third are *Salesmen,* who possess natural persuasive power. Any idea that catches the interest of Mavens, Connectors, and Salesmen is likely to be broadcast far and wide. The second factor is "Stickiness." An idea must be expressed so that it motivates people to act. Otherwise, "The Law of the Few" will not lead to a self-sustaining epidemic. Finally, the third factor, "The Power of Context," controls whether those spreading an idea are able to organize groups and communities around it.

One team of viral marketing experts caution that although influencers or "alphas" start trends, they are often too introspective and socially alienated to spread them. They advise marketers to cultivate "bees," hyperdevoted customers who are not just satisfied knowing about the next trend but live to spread the word.[60] Companies can take several steps to stimulate personal influence channels to work on their behalf. "Marketing Memo: How to Start a Buzz Fire" describes some techniques.

Consumers can resent personal communications if unsolicited. Some word-of-mouth tactics walk a fine line between acceptable and unethical. One controversial tactic, sometimes called *stealth marketing,* pays people to anonymously promote a product or service in public places without disclosing their financial relationship to the sponsoring firm. They may pretend they are ordinary consumers who happen to like the product, displaying, demonstrating, or talking it up in the process.

Hiring a person to go into a bar and loudly ordering a specific branded drink strikes some as inappropriate.[61] To launch its T681 mobile camera phone, Sony Ericsson hired actors dressed as tourists to approach people at tourist locations and ask to have their photo taken. Handing over the mobile phone was an opportunity to discuss its merits. Although the approach no doubt created positive benefits, some found the deception distasteful.

Blogs

Blogs, regularly updated online journals or diaries, have become an important outlet for word of mouth. They vary widely, some personal for close friends and families, others designed to reach and influence a vast audience. One obvious appeal of blogs is bringing together people with common interests.

Blog search engines provide up-to-the-minute analysis of millions of blogs to find out what's on people's minds.[62] Popular blogs are creating influential opinion leaders. Roughly a third of Internet users read blogs.[63] Although many of these consumers examine product information contained in blogs, they may still see information from corporate Web sites or a professional review site as more trustworthy.[64]

Some consumers use blogs and videos as a means of retribution and revenge on companies for bad service and faulty products. Dell's customer-service shortcomings were splashed all over the Internet through a series of "Dell Hell" postings.

Measuring the Effects of Word of Mouth[65]

Marketers are exploring a range of measures to capture word-of-mouth effects. Although 80 percent of word of mouth occurs off-line, many marketers concentrate on online effects given the ease of tracking them.

In measuring the viral success of its <jackrabbit.intuit.com> Web site designed to support new small business owners, Intuit identified blogs that either picked up stories originally posted by a few influential bloggers given a special preview, or wrote their own stories. Intuit classified each blog according to *velocity* (whether it took a month or happened in a few days), *share of voice* (how much talk occurred in the blogosphere), *voice quality* (what was said and how positive or negative it was), and *sentiment* (how meaningful the comments were).

MARKETING MEMO • HOW TO START A BUZZ FIRE

Although many word-of-mouth effects are beyond marketers' control, certain steps improve the likelihood of starting a positive buzz. Figure 19.3 displays more do's and don'ts.

- **Identify influential individuals and companies and devote extra effort to them.** In technology, influencers might be large corporate customers, industry analysts and journalists, selected policy makers, and a sampling of early adopters.
- **Supply key people with product samples.** When two pediatricians in the U.S. launched MD Moms to market baby skin care products, they liberally sampled the product to physicians and mothers hoping they would mention them on Internet message boards and parenting Web sites. The strategy worked—the company hit year one distribution goals by the end of the first month.
- **Work through community influentials such as local DJs, class presidents, and presidents of women's organizations.** When Ford introduced the Focus, it handed out cars to DJs and trendy people so they would be seen around town in them. Ford also identified 100 influential young consumers in five key marketing states and gave them cars to drive around.
- **Develop word-of-mouth referral channels to build business.** Professionals will often encourage clients to recommend their services. Some weight-loss centers find that word-of-mouth referrals from someone in the program have a huge impact on business.
- **Provide compelling information that customers want to pass along.** Companies shouldn't communicate with customers in terms better suited for a press release. Make it easy and desirable for a customer to borrow elements from an email message or blog. Information should be original and useful. Originality increases the amount of word of mouth, but usefulness determines whether it will be positive or negative.

(Continued ...)

MARKETING MEMO • HOW TO START A BUZZ FIRE

(Continued ...)

"PAY" WITH FEEDBACK

You don't need to pay cash to get someone to say something about your product—they're already doing it. Find a way to let your customers communicate with you, then listen to them and provide them real support and appreciation. They'll volunteer to help a brand that lets them be part of the process.

INSIST ON OPENNESS

Campaign success—and perhaps your company's reputation—hinges on the openness of your word-of-mouth participants. If you're creating an organized word-of-mouth program, require that your volunteers are above board.

DEMAND HONESTY

If you listen closely, you'll realize that honest opinions influence purchasing decisions more so than questionably positive opinions.

HELP CUSTOMERS TELL STORIES

Consumers place products in the context of their daily lives. If a runner's footwear helps her set a personal best in a marathon, she doesn't exclaim, "Just do it!" Rather, she talks about how the sneakers benefited her stride. In a word-of-mouth campaign for Levi's Dockers, participants described the pride of being dressed sharply at social events. Provide your customers with tools to help them share their real stories more effectively.

DON'T SCRIPT

For years marketers have delivered their messages as taglines that make every product sound perfect. Forcing word-of-mouth participants to repeat these messages is awkward and unnatural. Worse still is asking participants to repeat a marketing script of a perfect opinion that's not their own. Communicate the history, benefits, and unique attributes of your product to those who volunteer to experience and discuss it—and then get out of the way.

DON'T PLAN

Word of mouth is a spontaneous event. It can happen at anytime or anywhere—and yes, it can not happen, even when you want it to. If you try to force word of mouth to take place when it's not appropriate or comfortable, the result will no longer resemble real word of mouth. The key is to help people become more conscious of their opinions. They'll share them when others are really listening.

DON'T SELL

Odds are your company employs a trained and qualified sales force. Let them do their job . . . and let word-of-mouth volunteers do theirs. No one likes to be forcibly sold a product. We like to learn about the pros and cons and then arrive at our own decision. Your word-of-mouth volunteers are not salespeople. They are siblings, friends, coworkers, and accidental acquaintances.

DON'T IGNORE

Listening to word of mouth about your product can be like a trip to the dentist: It's uncomfortable for a moment, but the benefits last a lifetime. However difficult the feedback may be to hear, it is even more powerful to incorporate. Honest word of mouth provides you with a unique opportunity to use real opinions as an incredible feedback loop; and the more you listen and perfect your product, the better your word of mouth will become.

Figure 19.3 BzzAgent's Word-of-Mouth Do's and Don'ts

Source: Dave Balter, "Rules of the Game." *Advertising Age Point,* December 2005, pp. 22–23.

Sources: Sarit Moldovan, Jacob Goldenberg, and Amitava Chattopadhyay, "What Drives Word of Mouth? The Roles of Product Originality and Usefulness." *MSI Report No. 06-111* (Cambridge, MA: Marketing Science Institute, 2006); Karen J. Bannan, "Online Chat Is a Grapevine That Yields Precious Fruit." *New York Times*, December 25, 2006; John Batelle, "The Net of Influence." *Business 2.0*, March 2004, p. 70; Ann Meyer, "Word-of-Mouth Marketing Speaks Well for Small Business." *Chicago Tribune,* July 28, 2003; Malcolm Macalister Hall, "Selling by Stealth." *Business Life*, November 2001, pp. 51–55.

DuPont suggests possible measures such as campaign scale (how far it reached); speed (how fast it spread); share of voice in that space; share of voice in that speed; whether it achieved positive lift in sentiment; whether the message was understood; whether it was relevant; whether it had sustainability (and was not a one-shot deal); and how far it moved from its source.

Designing the Sales Force

The original and oldest form of direct marketing is the field sales call. Today most industrial companies rely heavily on a professional sales force to locate prospects, develop them into customers, and grow the business; or they hire manufacturers' representatives and agents to carry out the direct-selling task.

In addition, many consumer companies use a direct-selling force: insurance agents, stockbrokers, and distributors work for direct-sales organizations such as Avon, Amway, Mary Kay, and Nu Skin. Asia accounts for 40 percent of the world's direct-sales market.[66] Direct selling in China alone is estimated to be $1 billion annually.[67] Unlike in the U.S. and U.K. where the retailers can block their suppliers from becoming their competitors, Asia has fewer such restrictions. For example, India has many small mom-and-pop shops that have little leverage over MNCs. Hence, Hindustan Unilever has set up its own direct-selling arm to compete directly with its retailers.

Hindustan Unilever—With the direct-selling business in India worth $350 million a year, and a growing middle class, Hindustan Unilever began direct sales in 2000 with Aviance, a new line of high-end shampoos, skin creams, and cosmetics that cost about 40 percent more than Unilever brands sold in stores. Since then, its direct sales unit, called Hindustan Unilever Network, has added home, dish, laundry detergents, male grooming products, and oral care to its door-to-door line. It hopes to include health supplements and specialty foods to its direct-sales portfolio in the near future.[68]

Direct-sales companies promote the opportunities for locals, especially in Asia, to start their own new business as sales representatives. Foreign companies usually focus on big cities such as Shanghai and Beijing using mass media communications, neglecting second-tier cities. Direct sales allow local companies to reach such fringe cities. Moreover, the personal touch that direct sales can provide may alleviate perceptions by some consumers about large foreign businesses having little emotional impact in their lives.[69]

Nu Skin—Nu Skin China's CEO says, "If you took our products and placed them on a market shelf someplace, they would look very much like the other products that you would see there and it would be difficult to differentiate. But because of this one-to-one sales opportunity we have, our people can spend half an hour or an hour of spinning the bottle around and looking at the ingredients panel and explaining what these products are, or what the innovations involved in these products can do for you. And at the end of one of these sales presentations, we've got a very educated consumer and usually a very committed buyer going forward."[70]

Although no one debates the importance of the sales force in marketing programs, companies are sensitive to the high and rising costs (salaries, commissions, bonuses, travel expenses, and benefits) of maintaining a sales force. Not surprisingly, companies are trying to increase the productivity of the sales force through better selection, training, supervision, motivation, and compensation.

The term *sales representative* covers a broad range of positions. Six can be distinguished, ranging from the least to the most creative types of selling:[71]

1. ***Deliverer*** — A salesperson whose major task is product delivery (water, fuel, oil).
2. ***Order taker*** — A salesperson who acts predominantly as an inside order taker (the salesperson standing behind the counter) or outside order taker (the soap salesperson calling on the supermarket manager).

3. ***Missionary*** — A salesperson who is not expected or permitted to take an order but whose major task is to build goodwill or to educate the actual or potential user (the medical "detailer" representing an ethical pharmaceutical house).
4. ***Technician*** — A salesperson with a high level of technical knowledge (the engineering salesperson who is primarily a consultant to the client companies).
5. ***Demand creator*** — A salesperson who relies on creative methods for selling tangible products (vacuum cleaners, cleaning brushes, and household products) or intangibles (insurance, advertising services, or education).
6. ***Solution vendor*** — A salesperson whose expertise is in the solving of a customer's problem, often with a system of the company's products and services (e.g., computer and communications systems).

Sales personnel serve as the company's personal link to the customers. The sales representative is the company to many of its customers. It is the sales rep who brings back much-needed information about the customer. Therefore, the company needs to carefully consider issues in sales force design—namely, the development of sales force objectives, strategy, structure, size, and compensation (see Figure 19.4).

In some instances, companies engage both direct sales as well as set up retail stores. Nu Skin, for instance, uses a hybrid business model in China, combining its successful multilevel marketing approach with retail stores. LG's De Bon cosmetics have a direct sales force as well as beauty boutiques in Vietnam.

LG—Korean conglomerate LG employed a shrewd marketing strategy that transformed its relatively obscure cosmetics brand, De Bon, into a trendsetter in Vietnam. Rather than simply advertise, LG fuelled a Vietnamese craze for "Korean style" by sponsoring a stream of Korean family dramas and romantic comedies on state-run television. In keeping with its slogan, "The First Name in Beauty," LG also opened pristine boutiques and dispatched its sales force to offices at lunchtime to help Vietnamese primp their eyebrows and learn other beauty tricks.[72]

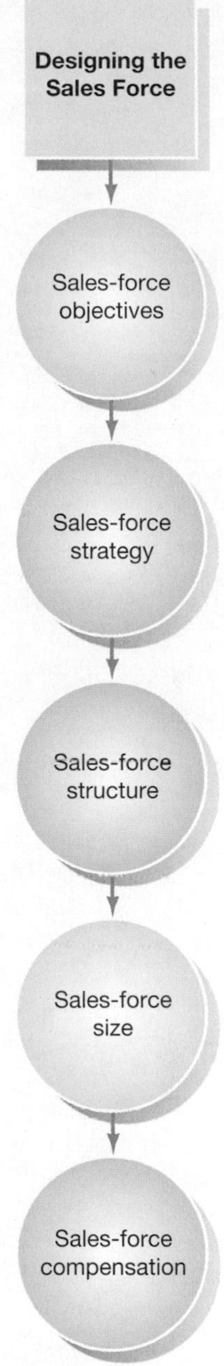

Figure 19.4 Designing a Sales Force

Sales Force Objectives and Strategy

In the past, all the sales force had to do was "sell, sell, and sell." Sales reps now need to know how to diagnose a customer's problem and propose a solution. Salespeople show a customer prospect how their company can help a customer improve profitability.

Companies need to define the specific objectives they want their sales force to achieve. For example, a company might want its sales representatives to spend 80 percent of their time with current customers and 20 percent with prospects, and 85 percent of their time on established products and 15 percent on new products. The specific allocation scheme depends on the kind of products and customers. However, regardless of the selling context, salespeople will have one or more of the following specific tasks to perform:

- ***Prospecting*** — Searching for prospects, or leads.
- ***Targeting*** — Deciding how to allocate their time among prospects and customers.
- ***Communicating*** — Communicating information about the company's products and services.
- ***Selling*** — Approaching, presenting, answering objections, and closing sales.
- ***Servicing*** — Providing various services to the customers—consulting on problems, rendering technical assistance, arranging financing, expediting delivery.
- ***Information gathering*** — Conducting market research and doing intelligence work.
- ***Allocating*** — Deciding which customers will get scarce products during product shortages.

Because of the expense, most companies are moving to the concept of a *leveraged sales force*. A sales force focuses on selling the company's more complex and customized products to large accounts, while low-end selling is done by inside salespeople and

Web ordering. Tasks such as lead generation, proposal writing, order fulfillment, and post-sale support are turned over to others. Salespeople handle fewer accounts, and are rewarded for key account growth. This is far different from expecting salespeople to sell to every possible account, which is usually the weakness of geographically based sales forces.[73]

Companies must deploy sales forces strategically so that they call on the right customers at the right time and in the right way. Today's sales representatives act as "account managers" who arrange fruitful contact between various people in the buying and selling organizations. Selling increasingly calls for teamwork requiring the support of other personnel, such as *top management*, especially when national accounts or major sales are at stake; *technical people*, who supply technical information and service to the customer before, during, or after product purchase; *customer service representatives*, who provide installation, maintenance, and other services; and an *office staff*, consisting of sales analysts, order expediters, and assistants.

To maintain a market focus, salespeople should know how to analyze sales data, measure market potential, gather market intelligence, and develop marketing strategies and plans. Sales representatives need analytical marketing skills, and these skills become especially important at the higher levels of sales management. Marketers believe that sales forces will be more effective in the long run if they understand marketing as well as selling. Too often marketing and sales are in conflict: marketers complain the sales force isn't converting leads, and the sales force complains marketing isn't generating enough leads (see Figure 19.5). Improved internal collaboration and communication between these two departments can increase revenues and profits.[74]

Once the company decides on an approach, it can use a direct or a contractual sales force. A **direct (company) sales force** consists of full- or part-time paid employees who work exclusively for the company. This sales force includes inside sales personnel who conduct business from the office using the telephone and receive visits from prospective buyers, and field sales personnel who travel and visit customers. A **contractual sales force** consists of manufacturers' reps, sales agents, and brokers who are paid a commission based on sales.

Sales: I need leads, but marketing never sends me any good leads. How am I supposed to get new business with no good leads?

Marketing: We deliver tons of leads and they just sit in the system. Why won't sales call on any of them?

Sales: I have nothing new to sell. What is marketing doing? Why can't they figure out what customers want before they give it to us? Why don't they give me anything that's easy to sell?

Marketing: Why won't sales get out and sell my new programs? How do they expect customers to place orders without sales contacts?

Sales: My people spend too much time on administration and paperwork. I need them out selling.

Marketing: We need information to get new ideas. How long does it take to type in a few words? Don't they know their own customers?

Sales: How am I going to hit my number? Marketing is a waste of time. I'd rather have more sales reps.

Marketing: How am I going to hit my number? Sales won't help and I don't have enough people to do it myself.

Figure 19.5 A Hypothetical (Dysfunctional) Sales-Marketing Exchange

Sales-Force Structure

The sales-force strategy has implications for its structure. A company that sells one product line to one end-using industry with customers in many locations would use a territorial structure. A company that sells many products to many types of customers might need a product or market structure. Some companies need a more complex structure. For example, Motorola manages four types of sales forces: (1) a strategic marketing sales force comprising technical, applications, and quality engineers and service personnel assigned to key accounts; (2) a geographic sales force calling on thousands of customers in different territories; (3) a distributor sales force calling on and coaching its distributors; and (4) an inside sales force doing telemarketing and taking orders via phone and fax.

Hewlett-Packard—When CEO Mark Hurd took the helm of a troubled Hewlett-Packard, he made it a priority to do a sales-force make-over. He's now credited with transforming HP's sales culture by radically changing its structure. Before, each salesperson was responsible for selling the entire portfolio of HP's products. Although that allowed reps to cross-sell and up-sell and streamlined things for the client, who dealt with only one rep, it was a nearly impossible task for reps and often kept them mired in administrative tasks. Hurd decentralized the sales force and divided sales between HP's three main divisions: IT for large enterprises, printers and printing, and personal computers (including laptops and handhelds). Customers' fairly linear needs mean HP can still keep things streamlined with one contact salesperson per customer. The salesperson, however, is backed up by a "virtual" sales team of specialists who deal with specific areas such as storage, software, and servers. This massive transformation couldn't have taken place without intensive sales training. For instance, a rep who sells to large global enterprise accounts is given a thorough understanding of the client industry in order to converse intelligently about it with both general business executives and IT executives.[75]

Figure 19.6 shows how a company must focus on different aspects of its sales force structure over the life cycle of the business. Hitachi Data Systems reorganized its sales team by appointing a single global executive and forming a global sales organization. The global sales team was also expanded to include sales representatives and systems engineers.[76] "Marketing Insight: Major Account Management" discusses major account management, a specialized form of sales-force structure.

	BUSINESS LIFE CYCLE STAGE			
	Start-Up	Growth	Maturity	Decline
EMPHASIS				
ROLE OF SALES FORCE AND SELLING PARTNERS	⇨⇨⇨⇨	⇨⇨	⇨	⇨⇨⇨
SIZE OF SALES FORCE	⇨⇨⇨	⇨⇨⇨⇨	⇨⇨	⇨⇨⇨⇨
DEGREE OF SPECIALIZATION	⇨	⇨⇨⇨⇨	⇨⇨⇨	⇨⇨
SALES FORCE RESOURCE ALLOCATION	⇨⇨	⇨	⇨⇨⇨⇨	⇨
UNDERLYING CUSTOMER STRATEGY	Create awareness and generate quick product uptake	Penetrate deeper into existing segments and develop new ones	Focus on efficiently serving and retaining existing customers	Emphasize efficiency, protect critical customer relationships, exit unprofitable segments

Figure 19.6 The Four Factors for a Successful Sales Force

Source: Andris Zoltners, Prabhakant Sinha, and Sally E. Lorimer, "Match Your Sales-Force Structure to Your Business Life Cycle." *Harvard Business Review*, July–August 2006, pp. 81–89.

MARKETING INSIGHT • MAJOR ACCOUNT MANAGEMENT

Major accounts (also called key accounts, national accounts, global accounts, or house accounts) are typically singled out for special attention. Important customers who have multiple divisions in many locations are offered major account contracts, which provide uniform pricing and coordinated service for all customer divisions. A major account manager (MAM) supervises field reps calling on customer plants within their territories. Large accounts are often handled by a strategic account management team with cross-functional personnel who handle all aspects of the relationship.

If a company has several such accounts, it is likely to organize a major account management division, in which the average MAM handles nine accounts. MAMs typically report to the national sales manager who reports to the vice president of marketing and sales, who in turn reports to the CEO.

Major account management is growing. As buyer concentration increases through mergers and acquisitions, fewer buyers account for a larger share of a company's sales. Many buyers are centralizing their purchases for certain items, which gives them more bargaining power. Sellers in turn need to devote more attention to these major buyers. Further, as products become more complex, more groups in the buyer's organization become involved in the purchase process. The typical salesperson might not have the skill, authority, or coverage to be effective in selling to the large buyer.

In selecting major accounts, companies look for accounts that purchase a high volume (especially of more profitable products), purchase centrally, require a high level of service in several geographic locations, may be price-sensitive, and may want a long-term partnering relationship. Major account managers have a number of duties: acting as the single point of contact; developing and growing customer business; understanding customer decision processes; identifying added-value opportunities; providing competitive intelligence; negotiating sales; and orchestrating customer service. MAMs are typically evaluated on their effectiveness in growing their share of the account's business and on their achievement of annual profit-and-sales volume goals. One MAM said, "My position must not be as a salesman, but as a 'marketing consultant' to our customers and a salesman of my company's capabilities as opposed to my company's products."

Major accounts normally receive more favorable pricing based on their purchase volume, but marketers cannot rely exclusively on this incentive to retain customer loyalty. There is always a risk that competitors can match or beat a price or that increased costs may necessitate raising prices. Many major accounts look for added value more than for a price advantage. They appreciate having a single point of dedicated contact; single billing; special warranties; EDI links; priority shipping; early information releases; customized products; and efficient maintenance, repair, and upgraded service. In addition to these practical considerations, there is the value of goodwill. Personal relationships with personnel who value the major account's business and who have a vested interest in the success of that business are compelling reasons for being a loyal customer.

Sources: S. Tubridy, "Major Account Management." In *AMA Management Handbook*, 3rd ed., John J. Hampton, ed., (New York: Amacom, 1994), pp. 3-25, 3-27; Sanjit Sengupta, Robert E. Krapfel, and Michael A. Pusateri, "The Strategic Sales Force." *Marketing Management*, Summer 1997, pp. 29-34; Robert S. Duboff and Lori Underhill Sherer, "Customized Customer Loyalty." *Marketing Management*, Summer 1997, pp. 21-27; Tricia Campbell, "Getting Top Executives to Sell." *Sales & Marketing Management*, October 1998, p. 39; "Promotion Marketer of the Decade: Wal-Mart." *Promo*, December 1, 1999; Noel Capon, *Key Account Management and Planning: The Comprehensive Handbook for Managing Your Company's Most Important Strategic Asset,* (New York: Free Press, 2001); Sallie Sherman, Joseph Sperry, and Samuel Reese, *The Seven Keys to Managing Strategic Accounts,* (New York: McGraw-Hill Trade, 2003). More information can be obtained from NAMA (National Account Management Association), <www.nasm.com>.

Sales-Force Size

Once the company clarifies its strategy and structure, it is ready to consider sales-force size. Sales representatives are one of the company's most productive and expensive assets. Increasing their number will increase both sales and costs.

Once the company establishes the number of customers it wants to reach, it can use a *workload approach* to establish sales-force size. This method consists of five steps:

1. Customers are grouped into size classes according to annual sales volume.
2. Desirable call frequencies (number of calls on an account per year) are established for each class.
3. The number of accounts in each size class is multiplied by the corresponding call frequency to arrive at the total workload for the country, in sales calls per year.
4. The average number of calls a sales representative can make per year is determined.
5. The number of sales representatives needed is determined by dividing the total annual calls required by the average annual calls made by a sales representative.

Suppose the company estimates that there are 1,000 A accounts and 2,000 B accounts. A accounts require 36 calls a year, and B accounts require 12 calls a year. The company needs a sales force that can make 60,000 sales calls a year. Suppose the average rep can make 1,000 calls a year. The company would need 60 full-time sales representatives.

Sales-Force Compensation

To attract top-quality sales reps, the company has to develop an attractive compensation package. Sales reps want income regularity, extra reward for above-average performance, and fair payment for experience and longevity. Management wants control, economy, and simplicity. Some of these objectives will conflict. No wonder compensation plans exhibit a tremendous variety from industry to industry and even within the same industry.

The company must determine the four components of sales-force compensation—a fixed amount, a variable amount, expense allowances, and benefits. The *fixed amount*, a salary, is intended to satisfy the need for income stability. The *variable amount*, which might be commissions, bonus, or profit sharing is intended to stimulate and reward effort. *Expense allowances* enable sales reps to meet the expenses involved in travel and entertaining. *Benefits*, such as paid vacations, sickness or accident benefits, pensions, and life insurance are intended to provide security and job satisfaction.

Fixed compensation receives more emphasis in jobs with a high ratio of non-selling to selling duties and in jobs where the selling task is technically complex and involves teamwork. Cultural aspects also contribute to why fixed compensation is favored over variable compensation in some Asian countries. For example, Japan's social system is based mainly on hereditary and seniority criteria. Thus salary raises are based on longevity with the company. Commission systems, if used, are tied to the combined efforts of the entire sales force, fostering the Japanese team ethic and downplaying the economic aspirations of individual salespeople.[77] In Thailand, family background determines social position. Because money confers only limited status, straight salaries are more "respectable" and desirable than larger incomes with substantial but variable commission components. Variable compensation receives more emphasis in jobs where sales are cyclical or depend on individual initiative. Ingersoll-Rand believes that "everybody cuts their own deals" in China. So it pays its compressor reps mainly on commission and has a pyramid bonus plan for its regional sales managers. Fixed and variable compensation give rise to three basic types of compensation plans—straight salary, straight commission, and combination salary and commission. Most firms use a combination of salary and commission, though the relative proportion varies widely.[78]

Straight-salary plans provide sales reps with a secure income, make them more willing to perform non-selling activities, and give them less incentive to overstock customers. From the company's perspective, they provide administrative simplicity and lower turnover. Straight-commission plans attract higher performers, provide more motivation, require less supervision, and control selling costs. However, commission plans overemphasize getting the sale rather than building the relationship. Combination plans feature the benefits of both plans while reducing their disadvantages.

With compensation plans that combine fixed and variable pay, companies may link the variable portion of a salesperson's pay to a wide variety of strategic goals. Some see a new trend toward deemphasizing volume measures in favor of factors such as gross profitability, customer satisfaction, and customer retention. For example, IBM partly rewards salespeople on the basis of customer satisfaction as measured by customer surveys.[79] Other companies are basing the rep's reward partly on a sales team's performance or even company-wide performance. This should get reps to work more closely together for the common good.

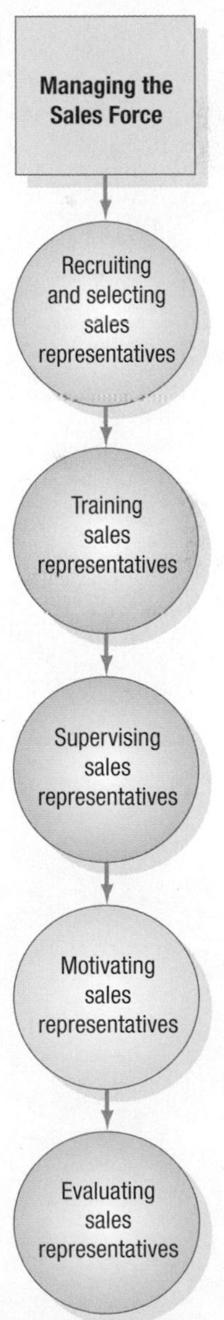

Figure 19.7 Managing the Sales Force

Managing the Sales Force

Once the company has established objectives, strategy, structure, size, and compensation, it has to recruit, select, train, supervise, motivate, and evaluate sales representatives. Various policies and procedures guide these decisions (see Figure 19.7).

Recruiting and Selecting Representatives

Central to a successful sales force is the selection of effective representatives. One survey revealed that the top 27 percent of the sales force brought in over 52 percent of the sales. Beyond differences in productivity is the great waste in hiring the wrong people. Sales force turnover leads to lost sales, costs of finding and training replacements, and often a strain on existing salespeople to pick up the slack.

Numerous studies have shown little relationship between sales performance on one hand, and background and experience variables, current status, lifestyle, attitude, personality, and skills on the other. More effective predictors have been composite tests and assessment centers that simulate the working environment so applicants are assessed in an environment similar to the one in which they would work.[80]

After management develops its selection criteria, it must recruit. The human resources department seeks applicants by soliciting names from current sales representatives, using employment agencies, placing job ads, and contacting college and other students. Culturally diverse Asian markets like India and Malaysia provide unique recruitment challenges. In India, there are 300–1,000 dialects, including more than 50 with at least a million speakers. Thus Swedish Match completely decentralized its recruitment activities to ensure not only those sales recruits speak the correct dialect(s) for the area but they are also respected members of their communities and can capitalize on personal contacts. Social class and gender biases also affect sales force selection in Asia. Sales positions are traditionally viewed as being of lower status and are male-dominated in Asian society. This also extends to perceptions of sales managers. For example, male salespeople had consistently poorer attitudes toward female sales managers than did female salespeople in China, indicating male resistance to women in sales management positions.[81]

Following recruitment, the company must select from its pool of applicants. Selection procedures can vary from a single informal interview to prolonged testing and interviewing. Many companies give sales applicants formal tests. Although test scores are only one information element in a set that includes personal characteristics, references, past employment history, and interviewer reactions, they are weighted quite heavily by such companies as IBM, Prudential, and Procter & Gamble. Gillette claims that tests have reduced turnover and correlated well with the subsequent progress of new reps in the sales organization. Yet few U.S., Japanese, or European MNCs employ quantitative testing procedures for sales selection in Asia, preferring to rely on personal characteristics, references, past employment history, and interview performance.[82] In China, few differences were found in the sales hiring practices of MNCs like 3M, Lever, Bayer, and Mitsubishi Bank, and domestic firms. Possibly, MNCs may have learned how to tailor their recruitment methods to those normally followed in China. However, MNCs reported higher usage of interview panels compared to local businesses possibly because MNCs in their early stages of expansion into other markets tend to staff their key positions with parent company nationals. Thus panel interviews are used to gain multiple assessments and reduce potential cultural biases. In contrast, domestic businesses reported higher rates of requiring sales applicants to respond to specific job situations. It may be that domestic sales managers were attempting to assess recruits' analytical and thinking abilities as a reflection of their on-the-job capability.[83]

Training and Supervising Sales Representatives

Today's customers expect salespeople to have deep product knowledge, to add ideas to improve the customer's operations, and to be efficient and reliable. These demands have required companies to make a much higher investment in sales training. Amway's sales reps in India did not have adequate product knowledge. This adversely affected the company's performance until remedial action was taken:

Amway—Amway found that many Indians perceived it as a very expensive brand meant for the premium segment. Few realized that almost all of Amway's products were concentrates. When used in the proper diluted form, the cost per use worked out to be on par with and in some cases, even lower than the nearest competitor's products. Its sales reps were not aware of this fact. Since the reps were unsure about the price-value equation of Amway's products, they could not effectively convince the consumers either. To solve this, Amway put stickers on its products which clearly indicated the number of usages. It also introduced value-for-money "*chhota* (small) packs." These measures significantly boosted sales and helped Amway shake off its super premium image. They allowed for market penetration to consumers from lower income levels.[84]

New reps may spend a few weeks to several months in training. In the U.S., the median training period is 28 weeks in industrial-products companies, 12 in service companies, and four in consumer-products companies. Training time varies with the complexity of the selling task and the type of person recruited into the sales organization.

IBM—At IBM, new reps receive extensive initial training and may spend 15 percent of their time each year in additional training. IBM has now switched 25 percent of the training from classroom to e-learning, saving a great deal of money in the process. It uses a self-study system called Info-Window that combines a personal computer and a laser videodisc. A trainee can practice sales calls with an on-screen actor who portrays a buying executive in a particular industry. The actor-buyer responds differently depending on what the trainee says.

In Asia, training time and orientation also varies by company. One study found that MNCs in China provided longer training (13 days) compared to domestic firms (8 days). Both groups based their training program needs on new product/company strategies, the sales rep's weaknesses, and environmental changes. Principal training objectives included teaching job skills and implementing the company's business strategies. However, MNCs in China devoted more time communicating market information than domestic firms, possibly to socialize sales neophtyes into a culture of free-market business practices, while domestic firms allocated more time on teaching sales procedures than MNCs.[85]

Research on sales training for new reps between MNCs and local firms in Malaysia, a multiethnic society with high levels of collectivism and power distance, yielded findings implying that MNCs tended to be more result-oriented, while local firms tended to be more cost-focused in their sales training. MNCs were also more market- and customer-oriented, while local firms were more product-oriented. Specifically: (1) MNCs reported significantly higher scores on training needs determination; (2) local companies ranked decreasing selling cost as an important sales training objective, while MNCs rated improving sales-force control to be essential; (3) MNCs spent more time on sales demonstration methods, while local businesses allocated more time for on-the-job training methods; (4) MNCs devoted more training time to communicating market information, while local firms spent more time disseminating product information; (5) MNCs allocated double the time on sales training than local firms (4.5–9.4 days); and (6) MNCs used more cross-functional sales trainers, while local firms employed more field management trainers.[86]

New methods of training are continually emerging, such as role playing and sensitivity training; the use of cassette tapes, videotapes, and CD-ROMs; and programmed learning, distance learning, and films on selling.

East Asian business practices may require adaptation of sales-training techniques. For instance, written job descriptions, a key feature of American sales management, are scarcely used in Japan. The Japanese system involves changing departments and positions every few years within a company. Thus Japanese salespeople are oriented through on-the-job training rather than through formal training or job descriptions. Indeed, even Japanese salespeople sent overseas get little more than a language course to equip them for their assignment.

Mentoring techniques are employed extensively in Japan as a personalized form of training for sales managers posted overseas. A new arrival is often "assigned" to someone in the company who knows the ropes and spends the necessary time explaining the culture and business practices of the foreign country. Returning sales staff also give talks to colleagues back at headquarters along with visiting lecturers specifically hired for this task. Sales-training sessions between instructors and trainees feature appraisals, feedback, and coaching, and are conducted with ritualistic decorum so that even the most constructive of criticism does not result in "loss of face" for sales trainees.[87]

Sales training may also serve to enhance salesperson retention. However, companies like LG's Vina Cosmetics in Vietnam have suffered from poaching by rivals. Its general director remarked that the company has become a training academy for its competitors.[88]

Companies vary in how closely they supervise sales reps. Reps paid mostly on commission generally receives less supervision. Those who are salaried and must cover definite accounts are likely to receive substantial supervision. With multilevel selling, used by Avon, Sara Lee, and others, independent distributors are also in charge of their own sales force selling company products. These independent contractors or reps are paid a commission not only on their own sales but also on the sales of people they recruit and train.[89] Supervising such reps is particularly problematic in developing Asian countries, where many salespeople may sell various products for other companies to increase their commission. Forever Living, a U.S.-based company that conducts multilevel marketing of nutritional products and cosmetics, has agents who also sell Oriflame products, a competing brand, and Prudential Life Insurance all at the same time.[90]

Sales Rep Productivity

How many calls should a company make on a particular account each year? Some research has suggested that today's sales reps are spending too much time selling to smaller, less profitable accounts when they should be focusing more of their efforts on selling to larger, more profitable accounts.[91]

NORMS FOR PROSPECT CALLS

Companies often specify how much time reps should spend prospecting for new accounts. They set up prospecting standards for a number of reasons. Left to their own devices, many reps will spend most of their time with current customers, who are known quantities. Reps can depend on them for some business, whereas a prospect might never deliver any business. Some companies rely on a missionary sales force to open new accounts.

USING SALES TIME EFFICIENTLY

Studies have shown that the best sales reps are those who manage their time effectively.[92] One planning tool is *time-and-duty analysis*, which helps reps understand how they spend their time and how they might increase their productivity. During the day, sales reps spend time planning, traveling, waiting, selling, and in administrative tasks (report writing and billing, attending sales meetings, and talking to others in the company about production, delivery, billing, sales performance, and other matters). With so many duties, it is no wonder that actual face-to-face selling time amounts to as little as 29 percent of total working time![93]

Companies are constantly seeking ways to improve sales force productivity. Their methods take the form of training sales reps in the use of "phone power," simplifying record keeping and administrative time, and using the computer and the Internet to develop call and routing plans, supply customer and competitive information, and automate the order preparation process.

To cut costs, reduce time demands on their outside sales force, and take advantage of computer and telecommunications innovations, many companies have increased the size and responsibilities of their inside sales force.[94]

Inside salespeople are of three types. *Technical support people* provide technical information and answers to customers' questions. *Sales assistants* provide clerical backup for the outside salespersons. They call ahead and confirm appointments, carry out credit checks, follow up on deliveries, and answer customers' questions. *Telemarketers* use the phone to find new leads, qualify them, and sell to them. Telemarketers can call up to 50 customers a day, compared to the four an outside salesperson can contact.

The inside sales force frees the outside reps to spend more time selling to major accounts, identifying and converting new major prospects, placing electronic ordering systems in customers' facilities, and obtaining more blanket orders and systems contracts. The inside salespeople spend more time checking inventory, following up orders, and phoning smaller accounts. The outside sales reps are paid largely on an incentive-compensation basis, and the inside reps on a salary or salary plus bonus pay.

Another breakthrough is the new high-tech equipment—desktop and laptop PCs, PDAs, videocassette recorders, videodiscs, automatic dialers, email, fax machines, teleconferencing and videophones. The salesperson has truly gone "electronic." Not only are sales and inventory information transferred much faster, but specific computer-based decision support systems on CDs have been created for sales managers and sales reps.

One of the most valuable electronic tools for the sales rep is the company Web site, and one of its most useful applications is as a prospecting tool. Company Web sites can help define the firm's relationships with individual accounts and identify those whose business warrants a personal sales call. The Web site provides an introduction to self-identified potential customers. Depending on the nature of the business, the initial order may even take place online. For more complex transactions, the site provides a way for the buyer to contact the seller.

Selling over the Internet supports relationship marketing by solving problems that do not require live intervention and thus allows more time to be spent on issues that are best addressed face-to-face.

Motivating Sales Representatives

The majority of sales reps require encouragement and special incentives. This is especially true of field selling: Reps usually work alone, their hours are irregular, and they are often away from home. They confront aggressive, competing sales reps; they have an inferior status relative to the buyer; they often do not have the authority to do what is necessary to win an account; and they sometimes lose large orders they have worked hard to obtain.[95]

Most marketers believe that the higher the salesperson's motivation, the greater the effort and the resulting performance, rewards, and satisfaction—and thus further motivation. Such thinking is based on several assumptions.

- **Sales managers must be able to convince salespeople that they can sell more by working harder or by being trained to work smarter.** This link is undermined if sales are determined largely by economic conditions or competitive actions.
- **Sales managers must be able to convince salespeople that the rewards for better performance are worth the extra effort.** This link is undermined if the rewards seem to be set arbitrarily or are too small or of the wrong kind.

To increase motivation, marketers reinforce intrinsic and extrinsic rewards of all types. One study that measured the importance of different rewards found that the reward with the highest value was pay, followed by promotion, personal growth, and sense of accomplishment.[96] The least valued rewards were liking and respect, security, and recognition. In other words, salespeople are highly motivated by pay and the chance to get ahead and satisfy their intrinsic needs, and less motivated by compliments and security. However, the researchers also found that the importance of motivators varied with demographic characteristics: Financial rewards were mostly valued by older, longer-tenured people and those who had large families. Higher-order rewards (recognition, liking and respect, sense of accomplishment) were more valued by young salespeople who were unmarried or had small families and usually more formal education.

Many companies set annual sales quotas. Quotas can be set on dollar sales, unit volume, margin, selling effort or activity, and product type. Compensation is often tied to degree of quota fulfillment. Sales quotas are developed from the annual marketing plan. The company first prepares a sales forecast that becomes the basis for planning production, workforce size, and financial requirements. Management then establishes quotas for regions and territories, which typically add up to more than the sales forecast to encourage managers and salespeople to perform at their best levels. If they fail to make their quotas, the company nevertheless might still reach its sales forecast.

Each area sales manager divides the area's quota among the area's reps. Sometimes a rep's quotas are set high, to spur extra effort, or more modestly, to build confidence. One view is that a salesperson's quota should be at least equal to the person's last year's sales plus some fraction of the difference between territory sales potential and last year's sales. The more favorably the salesperson reacts to pressure, the higher the fraction should be.

Conventional wisdom is that profits are maximized by sales reps focusing on the more important and more profitable products. Reps are not likely to achieve their quotas for established products when the company is launching several new products at the same time. The company will need to expand its sales force for new product launches.

Setting sales quotas creates problems. If the company underestimates and the sales reps easily achieve their quotas, the company has overpaid its reps. If the company overestimates sales potential, the salespeople will find it very hard to reach their quotas and be frustrated or quit. Another downside is that quotas can drive reps to get as much business as possible—often resulting in their ignoring the service side of the business. The company gains short-term results at the cost of long-term customer satisfaction.

Some companies are dropping quotas.[97] Siebel, the leading supplier of sales automation software, judges its sales reps using a number of metrics, such as customer satisfaction, repeat business, and profitable revenues. Almost 40 percent of incentive compensation is based on customers' reported satisfaction with service and product. The company's close scrutiny of the sales process leads to satisfied customers: Over 50 percent of Siebel's revenue comes from repeat business.[98] Even hard-driving Oracle has changed its approach to sales compensation.

Oracle—Finding sales flagging and customers griping, Oracle, the second-largest software company in the world, has been overhauling its sales department and practices in recent years. Its rapidly expanding capabilities, with diverse applications such as human resources, supply chain, and CRM, made its account management system difficult. One rep could no longer be responsible for selling all Oracle products to certain customers. Re-organization let reps specialize in a few particular products. To tone down the sales force's reputation as overly aggressive, Oracle changed the commission structure from a range 2–12 percent to a flat 4–6 percent and adopted a set of sales staff guidelines on how to "play nice" with partners, including channels, Independent Software Vendors (ISVs), resellers, integrators, and Value-Added Resellers (VARs). The six principles instructed sales staff to identify and work with partners in accounts and respect their positions and the value they add in those accounts. The principles were intended to address partner feedback that Oracle can and should be more predictable and reliable.[99]

Evaluating Sales Representatives

We have been describing the *feed-forward* aspects of sales supervision—how management communicates what the sales reps should be doing and how it motivates them. But good feed-forward requires good *feedback*, which means getting regular information from reps to evaluate performance.

SOURCES OF INFORMATION

The most important source of information about reps is sales reports. Additional information comes through personal observation, salesperson self-reports, customer letters and complaints, customer surveys, and conversations with other sales representatives.

Sales reports are divided between *activity plans* and *write-ups of activity results*. The best example of the former is the salesperson's work plan, which reps submit a week or month in advance. The plan describes intended calls and routing. This report forces sales reps to plan and schedule their activities and inform management of their whereabouts. It provides a basis for comparing their plans and accomplishments. Sales reps can be evaluated on their ability to "plan their work and work their plan."

Many companies require representatives to develop an annual territory marketing plan in which they outline their program for developing new accounts and increasing business from existing accounts. This type of report casts sales reps into the role of market managers and profit centers. Sales managers study these plans, make suggestions, and use them to develop sales quotas. Sales reps write up completed activities on *call reports.* Sales reps also submit expense reports, new-business reports, lost-business reports, and reports on local business and economic conditions.

These reports provide raw data from which sales managers can extract key indicators of sales performance: (1) average number of sales calls per salesperson per day; (2) average sales call time per contact; (3) average revenue per sales call; (4) average cost per sales call; (5) entertainment cost per sales call; (6) percentage of orders per hundred sales calls; (7) number of new customers per period; (8) number of lost customers per period; and (9) sales-force cost as a percentage of total sales.

FORMAL EVALUATION

The sales force's reports along with other observations supply the raw materials for evaluation. There are several approaches to conducting evaluations. One type of evaluation compares current performance to past performance. An example is shown in Table 19.1.

The sales manager can learn many things about a rep from this table. Total sales increased every year (line 3). This does not necessarily mean that the person is doing a better job. The product breakdown shows that he has been able to push the sales of product B further than the sales of product A (lines 1 and 2). According to his quotas for the two products (lines 4 and 5), his success in increasing product B sales could be at the expense of product A sales. According to gross profits (lines 6 and 7), the company earns more selling A than B. The rep might be pushing the higher volume, lower-margin product at the expense of the more profitable product. Although he increased total sales by $1,100 between 2007 and 2008 (line 3), the gross profits on total sales actually decreased by $580 (line 8).

Table 19.1 Form for Evaluating Sales Representative's Performance

Territory: East Representative: Kim Lee	2005	2006	2007	2008
1. Net sales product A	$251,300	$253,200	$270,000	$263,100
2. Net sales product B	423,200	439,200	553,900	561,900
3. Net sales total	674,500	692,400	823,900	825,000
4. Percent of quota product A	95.6	92.0	88.0	84.7
5. Percent of quota product B	120.4	122.3	134.9	130.8
6. Gross profits product A	$50,260	$50,640	$54,000	$52,620
7. Gross profits product B	42,320	43,920	55,390	56,190
8. Gross profits total	92,580	94,560	109,390	108,810
9. Sales expense	$10,200	$11,100	$11,600	$13,200
10. Sales expense to total sales (%)	1.5	1.6	1.4	1.6
11. Number of calls	1,675	1,700	1,680	1,660
12. Cost per call	$6.09	$6.53	$6.90	$7.95
13. Average number of customers	320	24	328	334
14. Number of new customers	13	14	15	20
15. Number of lost customers	8	10	11	14
16. Average sales per customer	$2,108	$2,137	$2,512	$2,470
17. Average gross profit per customer	$289	$292	$334	$326

Sales expense (line 9) shows a steady increase, although total expense as a percentage of total sales seems to be under control (line 10). The upward trend in total dollar expense does not seem to be explained by any increase in the number of calls (line 11), although it might be related to success in acquiring new customers (line 14). There is a possibility that in prospecting for new customers, this rep is neglecting present customers, as indicated by an upward trend in the annual number of lost customers (line 15).

The last two lines show the level and trend in sales and gross profits per customer. These figures become more meaningful when they are compared with overall company averages. If this rep's average gross profit per customer is lower than the company's average, he could be concentrating on the wrong customers or not spending enough time with each customer. A review of annual number of calls (line 11) shows that he might be making fewer annual calls than the average salesperson. If distances in the territory are similar to other territories, this could mean that he is not putting in a full workday, he is poor at sales planning and routing, or he spends too much time with certain accounts.

The rep might be quite effective in producing sales but not rate highly with customers. Perhaps he is slightly better than the competitors' salespeople, or his product is better, or he keeps finding new customers to replace others who do not like to deal with him. The customers' opinion of the salesperson, product, and service can be measured by mail questionnaires or telephone calls.

Evaluations can also assess the salesperson's knowledge of the company, products, customers, competitors, territory, and responsibilities. Personality characteristics can be rated, such as general manner, appearance, speech, and temperament. Research has found that, aside from sales quotas, the three next most popular methods of evaluating salespeople employed by U.S. MNCs in Asia in evaluating their sales forces were knowledge, appearance, and motivation. Possibly, these indicators require minimal monitoring and are unlikely to fluctuate over time, minimizing managerial resources on sales control. Another reason may be that U.S. subsidiaries "do as the Romans do" and tended toward qualitative factors presumably favored by Asian firms. Finally, outside of the more developed Asian countries, educational standards, commercial orientations, and personal affluence levels (which affect product knowledge, appearance, and motivation) are not uniform. These sales evaluation criteria may thus furnish valuable insights on performance in Asia rather than in the U.S.[100] The sales manager can review any problems in motivation or compliance.[101] Sales reps can provide attributions as to the success or failure of a sales call and how they would propose to improve the odds on subsequent calls. Possible explanations for their performance could be related to internal (effort, ability, and strategy) and external (task and luck) factors.[102]

Principles of Personal Selling

Personal selling is an ancient art. Effective salespersons have more than instinct; they are trained in methods of analysis and customer management. Today's companies spend hundreds of millions of dollars each year to train salespeople and transform them from passive order-takers into active order-getters. Reps are taught the SPIN method to build long-term relationships with questions such as:[103]

1. ***Situation questions*** — These ask about facts or explore the buyer's present situation. For example, "What system are you using to invoice your customers?"
2. ***Problem questions*** — These deals with problems, difficulties, and dissatisfactions the buyer is experiencing. For example, "What parts of the system create errors?"
3. ***Implication questions*** — These ask about the consequences or effects of a buyer's problems, difficulties, or dissatisfactions. For example, "How does this problem affect your people's productivity?"
4. ***Need-payoff questions*** — These ask about the value or usefulness of a proposed solution. For example, "How much would you save if our company could help reduce the errors by 80 percent?"

Most sales training programs agree on the major steps involved in any effective sales process. We show these steps in Figure 19.8 and discuss their application to industrial selling next.[104]

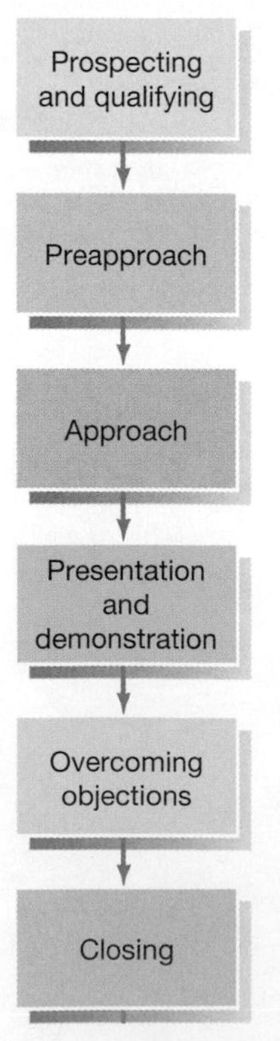

Figure 19.8 Major Steps in Effective Selling

The Seven Steps

PROSPECTING AND QUALIFYING

The first step in selling is to identify and qualify prospects. More companies are taking responsibility for finding and qualifying leads so that the salespeople can use their expensive time doing what they can do best: selling. Companies can qualify the leads by contacting them by mail or phone to assess their level of interest and financial capacity. The leads can be categorized, with "hot" prospects turned over to the field sales force and "warm" prospects turned over to the telemarketing unit for follow-up. Even then, it usually takes about four calls on a prospect to consummate a business transaction.

PREAPPROACH

The salesperson needs to learn as much as possible about the prospect company (what it needs, who is involved in the purchase decision) and its buyers (personal characteristics and buying styles). For example, top managers are typically the most important decision makers in campaign planning and ad agency selection in China. Thus ad agencies should focus their sales pitch to top managers. For the sake of being prudent, they should also recognize the importance of Chinese marketing departments who play crucial roles as influencers, buyers, and gatekeepers.[105] The salesperson should set call objectives: to qualify the prospect, gather information, make an immediate sale. Another task is to decide on the best contact approach, which might be a personal visit, a phone call, or a letter. Finally, the salesperson should plan an overall sales strategy for the account.

APPROACH

The salesperson should know how to greet the buyer to get the relationship off to a good start. The salesperson might consider wearing clothes similar to what buyers wear (for instance, in Singapore, office clothing is more casual than in Hong Kong); show courtesy and attention to the buyer; and avoid distracting mannerisms, such as staring at the customer. The opening line should be positive; for example, "Mr. Wong, I am Y.C. Ho from the ABC Company. My company and I appreciate your willingness to see me. I will do my best to make this visit profitable and worthwhile for you and your company." This opening line might be followed by key questions and active listening to understand the buyer's needs.

PRESENTATION AND DEMONSTRATION

The salesperson now tells the product "story" to the buyer, following the AIDA formula of gaining *attention,* holding *interest,* arousing *desire,* and obtaining *action.* The salesperson uses a *features, advantages, benefits,* and *value* approach (FABV). Features describe physical characteristics of a market offering, such as chip processing speeds or memory capacity. Advantages describe why the features provide an advantage to the customer. Benefits describe the economic, technical, service, and social benefits delivered by the offering. Value describes the worth (often in monetary terms) of the offering. Too often, salespeople spend too much time dwelling on product features (a product orientation) and not enough stressing the offering's benefits and value (a customer orientation).

OVERCOMING OBJECTIONS

Customers typically pose objections during the presentation or when asked for the order. *Psychological resistance* includes resistance to interference, preference for established supply sources or brands, apathy, reluctance to giving up something, unpleasant associations created by the sales rep, predetermined ideas, dislike of making decisions, and a neurotic attitude toward money. *Logical resistance* might consist of objections to the price, delivery schedule, or certain product or company characteristics.

To handle these objections, the salesperson maintains a positive approach, asks the buyer to clarify the objection, questions the buyer in a way that the buyer has to answer his or her own objection, denies the validity of the objection, or turns the objection into a reason for buying. Handling and overcoming objections is a part of the broader skills of negotiation.

One potential problem is for salespeople to give in too often when customers demand a discount. One company recognized this as a problem when its sales revenue went up by 25 percent but its profit had remained flat. The company decided to retrain its salespeople to "sell the price," rather than "sell through price." Salespeople were given richer information about each customer's sales history and behavior. They received training to recognize value-adding opportunities rather than price-cutting opportunities. As a result, the company's sales revenue climbed and so did its margins.[106]

CLOSING

Now the salesperson attempts to close the sale. Salespeople need to know how to recognize closing signs from the buyer, including physical actions, statements or comments, and questions. There are several closing techniques. They can ask for the order, recapitulate the points of agreement, offer to help the secretary write up the order, ask whether the buyer wants A or B, get the buyer to make minor choices such as the color or size, or indicate what the buyer will lose if the order is not placed now. The salesperson might offer the buyer specific inducements to close, such as a special price, an extra quantity, or a token gift.

FOLLOW-UP AND MAINTENANCE

Follow-up and maintenance are necessary if the salesperson wants to ensure customer satisfaction and repeat business. Immediately after closing, the salesperson should cement any necessary details on delivery time, purchase terms, and other matters that are important to the customer. The salesperson should schedule a follow-up call when the initial order is received to make sure there is proper installation, instruction, and servicing. This visit or call will detect any problems, assure the buyer of the salesperson's interest, and reduce any cognitive dissonance that might have arisen. The salesperson should also develop a maintenance and growth plan for the account.

Negotiation

Marketing is concerned with exchange activities and the manner in which the terms of exchange are established. In *routinized exchange*, the terms are established by administered programs of pricing and distribution. In *negotiated exchange*, price and other terms are set via bargaining behavior, in which two or more parties negotiate long-term binding agreements. Although, the price is the most frequently negotiated issue, other issues include contract completion time; quality of goods and services offered; purchase volume; responsibility for financing, risk taking, promotion, and title; and product safety.

Marketers who find themselves in bargaining situations need certain traits and skills to be effective. The most important are preparation and planning skill, knowledge of subject matter being negotiated, ability to think clearly and rapidly under pressure and uncertainty, ability to express thoughts verbally, listening skill, judgment and general intelligence, integrity, ability to persuade others, and patience.[107]

Much attention has been focused on effective negotiation styles in Asia. Both marketing research and practice have found that behaviors, comments, time orientation, social practices and etiquette considered appropriate in the corporate dealings of one country may be deemed arrogant, insensitive, overconfident, and aggressive in another. We now discuss negotiation styles and cultural norms in greater detail with particular reference to Japan, South Korea, China, and Thailand.[108]

LANGUAGE

The language of the host country is one of the most difficult challenges for an international salesperson to manage. "Give me a yes or no answer" is a highly damaging demand for most Asians. This is because of their reluctance to displease another with a negative answer and also to save them from the embarrassment of having to admit an inability. There is no word for "no" in Thailand. The Japanese either circumscribe the "no" or answer in terms of both yes and no. A joke or smile should be used to mitigate any negative situation, and indirect questions asked to obtain feedback. In contrast, Koreans are more individualistic like the Chinese. They are three times as likely as the Japanese to say "no." Koreans and Chinese use confrontation to try to control the negotiation process. Moreover, few Chinese, Korean, or Japanese speak fluent English. Thus it is prudent to write out all numbers, make time available for translation and correction, and encourage the other party to repeat the agreed upon understanding from time to time. Language training may also help salespeople negotiate more effectively in these countries. Foreign negotiators should also note that for Chinese and Koreans, the family name comes first before the given name. Correctly addressing a business partner is necessary to avoid embarrassment.

EYE CONTACT

In the U.S., salespeople tend to maintain eye contact with their prospects; failure to do so may arouse suspicion. However, maintaining eye contact may be perceived as a sign of aggression in such Asian countries as Japan, South Korea, and Taiwan.

TIME

Americans are monochronic time processors, living by schedules and deadlines. The efficient use of time is reflected in such phrases as "Time is money." In contrast, polychronic time processing is prevalent in Eastern cultures where time is viewed as unlimited and unending, as reflected by the Thai saying *mai pen rai* ("never mind, it's OK"). Sales meetings in the U.S. may begin with phrases like "Let's dispense with the preliminaries." However, in Japan, Thailand, and Korea, casual conversation precedes business matters, given the preference to develop personal ties with strangers before concluding a deal with them. It is thus important to keep adequate time reserves for negotiations.

STATUS AND TITLE

Nearly all communications in Japan occur within an elaborate and vertically organized social structure. Rarely do Japanese converse without knowing, or determining, who is above and who is below them. Two implications for negotiation arise from this. First, business cards (*meishi*) are always exchanged and carefully studied when the Japanese meet someone. Those doing business with the Japanese need business cards that explain their corporate designations. Otherwise, the Japanese would not know how to relate to this seemingly isolated individual. Second, buyer-seller relationships tend to work better when both parties are of equivalent rank, age, or seniority. The same holds for Koreans—senior Korean officials will not deal comfortably with a junior member of the other party's negotiating team, no matter how much expertise the latter may possess. Koreans are extremely sensitive about status and titles, and like the Japanese, ranks and titles are expected to be used in addressing hosts.

DECISION-MAKING STYLE

Japanese decision making demands that group members achieve agreement through consensus. *Nemawashi* holds that group commitment is stronger if the group is tightly bound. Thus negotiations must occur within an atmosphere of friendliness and cooperation in Japan. Consequently, the Japanese maintain the illusion of surface agreement until a consensus is reached. The Japanese process of consultation (*ring-seido*) could bring to the surface problems not appreciated by or known to foreign salespeople. This will require further consultations to remove obstacles. In Japan, there is no "laying one's cards on the table" until a close understanding between parties has been reached, if at all. (However, once agreement is reached its execution is quick.) Negotiators must reach agreement with all the people involved with the buying process in Japan. If not, any agreement reached may have to be renegotiated internally between one's negotiating partner and colleagues who have not been involved in talks. In Thailand, different ethnic groups conduct business differently. Often educational level and degree of international exposure will affect Thai negotiation attitudes and styles.

FLUID CONTRACTS

The establishment of personal relationships, bringing together two groups with common interests, allows the Japanese to view contracts as personal agreements that should be changed when conditions change. A change will be reciprocated in future, but contracts are seen as fluid. A change in the price of raw material will prompt a Japanese supplier to ask that the contractual price at delivery be changed, since higher costs preclude a profit. The buyer is expected to agree to the increase, if possible, on the assumption that the supplier will in the future offer discounts or preferential treatment. Similarly, Korean contracts are not merely documents stating mutual obligations and rights. They are also declarations of intentions backed by the integrity of the signatories. These intentions are more important than the contractual clauses. Hence, renegotiation and redoing of contracts are expected behaviors; Koreans do not consider a contract binding if conditions or interests change. An agreement is only good as long as the persons who negotiated are in power. A valuable ploy after the contract is signed is to perform favors for the main Korean parties so that they maintain a proprietary interest in the project. Indeed, Asians typically ask for concessions at the end of negotiations, just when you think that the process is over and agreement has been reached. In sum, where one party may view the goal of negotiation as being a signed contract, the other may use it as a process to establish a relationship. The key question is thus: "How important is this relationship, how far should I take it and what concessions should I make?"

MEDIATION

Mediation is another important aspect of negotiation in Asia. In Japan, mediators help in passing any criticisms and negative news via "letters of understanding" which can state a position or demands in more blunt terms than those proper during conversations. In Korea and China, government officials should be sought to support major ventures as such individuals still direct much of these economies. If a mediator is inconvenient, informal meetings are used to discuss formal matters. Serious discussions can thus be disguised as entertainment. This explains why the Japanese spend much of their time entertaining clients and prospects. Informal discussions at bars, suppers, and golf courses can signal disagreements that would be unwelcome in more formal settings where the Japanese do not like rude shocks. The use of mediators and informal discussions avoids potential embarrassment that may result in loss of face.

INFORMAL COMMUNICATIONS

As with the Japanese, the Chinese are often unwilling to say publicly what they may readily admit in private conversation. Thus it is also important to recognize and establish informal communications with them. For example, an interpreter may be used to exchange messages informally and thereby resolve a possible impasse that may have developed in the formal negotiation. During the negotiation phase, one of the Chinese team members will be taking extensive notes. Thus maintaining a consistent attitude is necessary. Radical changes in proposals or in negotiating strategy should be avoided. Being too flexible may signal that one is being insincere. Realism is preferred—unreasonable demands may destroy one's credibility. In the concession-making phase, try not to impose upon or overpower the Chinese partner. Concepts should be discussed in terms of equality, mutual benefit, or reciprocity.

Relationship Marketing

The principles of personal selling and negotiation we have described are largely transaction-oriented because their purpose is to close a specific sale. But in many cases the company is not seeking an immediate sale, but rather to build a long-term supplier-customer relationship. The company wants to demonstrate that it has the capabilities to serve the account's needs in a superior way. Today's customers are large and often global. They prefer suppliers who can sell and deliver a coordinated set of products and services to many locations; who can quickly solve problems that arise in different locations; and who can work closely with customer teams to improve products and processes.

Salespeople working with key customers must do more than call when they think customers might be ready to place orders. They should call or visit at other times, take customers to dinner, and make useful suggestions about the business. They should monitor key accounts, know customers' problems, and be ready to serve them in various ways.

When a relationship management program is properly implemented, the organization will begin to focus as much on managing its customers as on managing its products.

At the same time, companies should realize that while there is a strong and warranted move toward relationship marketing, it is not effective in all situations. Ultimately, companies must judge which segments and which specific customers will respond profitably to relationship management.

Relationship marketing is particularly important when dealing with Asian customers. Client-salesperson relationships are cultivated to establish trust and respect. This is because Chinese societies tend to be low-trust cultures, a value reinforced by their recent political and social history. Institutional underdevelopment also creates an uncertain and risky environment that generates low trust among people. Forming and maintaining trustworthy relationships thus form an integral aspect of the Asian cultural make-up.[109] For example, trust and creditworthiness were considered the most important priorities in the business philosophies of small Chinese firms in Hong Kong, along with strong personal and company reputation, personal and social networking[110] (see "Marketing Insight: Culture and Relationship Marketing").

Various regional terms are used to describe such relationships: *guanxi* ("good relations" or "connections") is used among the Chinese, while *wa* and *inhwa* are used among Japanese and Koreans respectively (both meaning "harmony").[111] *Guanxi* is dynamic and certain social *guanxi* is transferable. Thus if person A wants to make a request of person C with whom A has no *guanxi*, A may seek out a member of his/her own *guanxi* network (person B) who has *guanxi* with C. Given B provides A the introduction to C, a *guanxi* relationship may be established between A and C. The transferability of *guanxi* is exemplified by the statement of Chon-Phung Lim, GM of Hewlett-Packard Southeast Asia: "A person who brings a buyer and seller together is more than a middleman—he vouches for the reputation of the one he introduces. Thus strangers doing business become strangers no more."[112] An indirect social network such as classmates, friends, and colleagues can be used to promote products for salespeople without an initial direct *guanxi* network. The intensity of *guanxi*-based personal selling has been found to be positively related to profitability, market growth, and asset efficiency among foreign-invested enterprises in China.[113]

The enduring strength of *guanxi* lies in the conduct of moderately asset-specific activities such as long-term supplier relations for industrial machinery. A well-developed *guanxi* network in China can assist managers in at least three ways. First, *guanxi* provides an avenue for building sales through long-term accounts payable. Sellers benefit by providing favorable credit terms with extended payment periods resulting in concordant sales growth. Buyers benefit from more favorable cash flow circumstances and increased operational flexibility. Second, companies interested in marketing industrial and consumer goods reliant on personal selling will benefit from strong *guanxi* relationships. The Chinese partner can assist with sales contracts and distribution access, and provide commercial security for such service businesses as insurance and banking. Third, a firm needs to nurture *guanxi* relationships to keep abreast of changes in relevant policy, garner the necessary licenses, permits, and approvals, and have access to government procurement contracts.[114]

Thus salespeople in Asia try to refrain from exploiting customers in a single transaction to gain and retain their trust. They will often throw in a little something extra or do special favors such as extending credit without any formal documentation. Salespeople also market themselves before they sell their products. Without patience and effort, salespeople cannot build personal relationships with customers.[115] How can trust be established? One study found that perceived opportunistic intentions undermined the level of trust among ethnic Chinese industrial buyers and sellers in Malaysia. In contrast, it was shown that organizational trust (i.e., customer reliance on the organization's image before bestowing trust on the salesperson), strength of personal relationships, dialect fluency (which enhanced communication), and perceived similarity in cultural values contributed to increasing perceptions of trust. Such trust also dictated the probability of future interaction between the exchange parties.[116]

However, relationships must also be constantly maintained and strengthened. A good starting point is a willingness to participate and imitate. Small courtesies (e.g., attending lunches, receptions, and factory and warehouse tours, and giving follow-up presents) are essential to conducting business and reaching sales agreements. If a salesperson is in Asia for a long time, and is successful in managing to do a lot of such seemingly little things correctly, he or she will likely develop a network of useful relationships. Indeed, the quality of relationships is used as an indicator of long-term commitment of a company. Relationship

MARKETING INSIGHT • CULTURE AND RELATIONSHIP MARKETING

Trompenaars and Hampden-Turner have constructed a cultural framework focusing on the impact of cultural differences on commercial behavior. Their research was used by Peppers and Rogers in effecting CRM initiatives in non-U.S. cultures. Trompenaars and Hampden-Turner argue that Asian cultures tend to possess six characteristics which impact their commercial behavior:

1. **Particularism** — Asians tend to search for the ways many things are different. They look for exceptions, circumstances, and relations. Westerners who search for sameness and similarities using rules, codes, laws, and generalizations (called universalism), are reluctant to conduct business with friends. In contrast, Koreans are uncomfortable conducting business with persons other than friends as they feel most people will not exploit a friend.
2. **Communitarianism** — Asians emphasize cooperation, social concern, altruism, public service, and societal legacy. A communitarian society values individual achievement as originating from shared knowledge, communal values, and mutual support. Communitarian groups (families, neighborhoods, and clans) are ends to themselves. Nowhere does the divide between insiders and outsiders carry as much importance as in Asia. The family is the bulwark of communitarian business cultures, originating over 85 percent of such business.
3. **Diffuseness** — Asians are less precise in defining the constructs. They emphasize "soft" processes such as relations, patterns, connectedness, and synthesis. Diffuse thinking tends to stress the aesthetics, harmony, and closeness of relationships. Diffuse cultures are concerned with goodwill and support from customers and the willingness of customers to remain loyal in the face of difficulties. Diffuse cultures would not deny that profits are necessary, but they argue that multiple bonds with customers are the origins of profits.
4. **Ascribed Status** — Asians tend to subscribe more to ascribed than achieved status. Ascribed status is accorded because of position, a social circle, physical attributes, or birth. In Korea, age, position, education, and family background determine position in the social hierarchy. Ascribed status is connected to business enterprises that act with trust, integrity, and reputation for fair dealing. Only if you have more to lose than money (your name and admiration of family and friends) is it safe to trust you. A Japanese emperor was reputed to have said: "To lose face is everything, but to lose everything is not necessarily to lose face."
5. **Outer Direction** — Asians conceive of virtue as external to themselves in natural rhythms and the beauty of nature. Indonesia, Japan, Thailand, Malaysia, and Singapore celebrate harmonious interaction, while Korea appears less outward directed. In Japan, the environment (moods, expressions, the situation, and even silence) contains much of the message. As there is less verbalization in such cultures, they are sometimes viewed as being mysterious, intriguing, sneaky, or untrustworthy. The more vocal expressions of members of inner directed cultures are at times viewed by outer directed cultures as verbose, redundant, and insincere.
6. **Synchronous Time** — Time is not viewed as sequential but as cyclical or recurring. Synchronous people dislike waiting in line for service. They also "give time" to people important to them. Top people deserve more scope to synchronize their face-to-face engagements. Hence, they enter the room last after the juniors have assembled. Synchronization is often symbolized by bowing, nodding, or making exclamations of assent. (The Chinese and Japanese languages are also nonsequential in structure.)

These findings have two broad implications for marketing management. First, each of the six cultural dimensions which characterize Asian values emphasizes the importance of relationships in social and commercial behavior more than cultures like the U.S. Unlike the prototypical Asian culture, the U.S. emphasizes universalism, individualism, specificity, achieved status, inner-directedness, and sequential time. Thus relationship marketing is more important and challenging in Asia than in the U.S.

Second, the cultural differences between Asia and the U.S., the birthplace of customer relationship management, also necessitate modifications of CRM strategies for successful application in the region. For example, universalist cultures are more likely to view the discrimination in CRM as a surprise, as they expect everyone to be equal before the law. In contrast, particularist cultures take such treatment for granted, since social standing and ascribed status routinely produce differences in the respect people receive. The challenge is to impress Asian customers with personal service when they already expect it. Thus Japanese salespeople constantly call on good customers to receive instruction rather than just sell. Tokyo traffic is heavier on the second and fourth Fridays of every month as this is when salespeople hand-deliver invoices to their important customers. However, Asian cultures tend to be more outwardly directed. This implies Asian marketers are better at listening to customers and tend to put more options for customer consideration. This inclination to listen will be a key tool as Asian companies implement closer relationships with their customers.

Sources: Visa International (Asia Pacific) Consulting and Peppers and Rogers Group (Asia), *One to One in Retail Financial Services: Replications of U.S. Studies in Five Asian Countries*, January 2002; Charles M. Hampden-Turner, Fons Trompenaars, and David Lewis, *Building Cross-Cultural Competence: How to Create Wealth from Conflicting Values* (New Haven: Yale University Press, 2000). See also Alphons Trompenaars, Charles M. Hampden-Turner, and Fons Trompenaars, *Riding the Waves of Culture*, 2nd ed. (New York: McGraw-Hill, 1998); Alphons Trompenaars, Charles M. Hampden-Turner, and Fons Trompenaars, *21 Leaders for the 21st Century* (New York: McGraw-Hill, 2001); Charles M. Hampden-Turner and Fons Trompenaars, *Mastering the Infinite Game: How East Asian Values are Transforming Business Practices* (Oxford: Capstone Publishing, 1997).

building in Japan is so important that salespeople will spend an inordinate amount of time servicing existing customers and proportionately less time on prospecting.[117]

Finally, relationships in Asia exist at many levels: consumer relationships with brands and their corporate stables; consumer relationships with retailers; and those between channel intermediaries from manufacturer to consumer. Companies are attempting to buy into this web of relationships when entering such Asian markets as Japan. They must develop and facilitate relationships at all levels. The loss of a top salesperson with an excellent network may mean a substantial loss of sales. When Vivek Paul, CEO and arguably top salesperson of Wipro Technologies resigned, predictions were rife that the Indian tech-services company would have trouble getting new customers.[118] Time must thus be spent "getting to know people" and persuading those involved that they are likely to be worthy partners in a long-term business venture, which in addition, will almost certainly require product knowledge training and point-of-sales support materials. This recipe requires a serious consideration of sales and marketing approach and style, a growing understanding of local business etiquette, and an ability to convey the message that the company will be involved for the long run—as well as offering a sound business proposition or good sales terms.[119] As Douglas Daft, who spent 30 years living and working in Asia before becoming chairman and CEO of Coca-Cola, recently wrote:

> *"Every lasting relationship begins with respect for the individual. These must be long-term, patiently nurtured connections, which are maintained by listening to the concerns of all who are touched by one's business. Even when your target audience is measured in the billions, you must focus on a single individual—one consumer, customer, employee, or partner—at a time. Relationships are vital to earning the trust of consumers, a trust that is inviolate and is ultimately the key to continued successful growth."*[120]

Summary

1. Direct marketing is an interactive marketing system that uses one or more media to effect a measurable response or transaction at any location. Direct marketing, especially electronic marketing, is showing explosive growth.
2. Direct marketers plan campaigns by deciding on objectives, target markets and prospects, offers, and prices. This is followed by testing and establishing measures to determine the campaign's success.
3. Major channels for direct marketing include face-to-face selling, direct mail, catalog marketing, telemarketing, interactive TV, kiosks, Web sites, and mobile devices.
4. Interactive marketing provides marketers with opportunities for much greater interaction and individualization through well-designed Web sites as well as online ads and promotions.
5. Sales personnel serve as a company's link to its customers. The sales rep is the company to many of its customers, and it is the rep who brings back to the company much-needed information about the customer.
6. Designing the sales force requires decisions regarding objectives, strategy, structure, size, and compensation. Objectives may include prospecting, targeting, communicating, selling, servicing, information gathering, and allocating. Determining strategy requires choosing the most effective mix of selling approaches. Choosing the sales force structure entails dividing territories by geography, product, or market (or some combination of these). Estimating how large the sales force needs to be involves estimating the total workload and how many sales hours (and hence salespeople) will be needed. Compensating the sales force entails determining what types of salaries, commissions, bonuses, expense accounts, and benefits to give, and how much weight customer satisfaction should have in determining total compensation.
7. There are five steps involved in managing the sales force: (1) recruiting and selecting sales representatives; (2) training the representatives in sales techniques and in the company's products, policies, and customer-satisfaction orientation; (3) supervising the sales force and helping reps to use their time efficiently; (4) motivating the sales force, and balancing quotas, monetary rewards, and supplementary motivators; and (5) evaluating individual and group sales performance.
8. Effective salespeople are trained in the methods of analysis and customer management, as well as the art of sales professionalism. No approach works best in all circumstances, but most trainers agree that selling is a seven-step process: prospecting and qualifying customers, preapproach, approach, presentation and demonstration, overcoming objections, closing, and follow-up and maintenance.
9. Another aspect of selling is negotiation, the art of arriving at transaction terms that satisfy both parties. In Asia, negotiators should consider various cultural norms such as language, eye contact, status and title, decision-making style, fluid contracts, mediation, and informal communications.
10. A third aspect of personal communications is relationship marketing, which focuses on developing long-term, mutually beneficial relationships between two parties. Relationship marketing assumes greater importance in Asia given the region's cultural make-up. Cultural differences may necessitate modifications to customer relationship marketing approaches developed in the U.S. for successful application to Asia. Asian concepts like *guanxi*, *wa*, and *inhwa* are relevant to relationship marketing. Such relationships can be transferable, but take time and patience to build and maintain, and should occur at multiple levels.

Application

Marketing Debate—Are Great Salespeople Born or Made?

One difference of opinion over to sales concerns the potential impact of training versus selection in developing an effective sales force. Some observers maintain that the best salespeople are "born" and are effective due to their personalities and all the interpersonal skills they have developed over a lifetime. Others contend that application of leading-edge sales techniques can make virtually anyone a sales star.

Take a position: *The key to developing an effective sales force is selection* versus *The key to developing an effective sales force is training.*

Marketing Discussion

Pick a company and go to the Web site. How would you evaluate the Web site? How well does it score on the 7Cs design elements: Context, content, community, customization, communication, connection, and commerce?

Long-Term Growth

Johnson & Johnson knows the value of new-product development for the world of medicine. The company is moving forward on several different research and investment fronts to keep the supply of ideas coming.

Introducing New Market Offerings 20

Companies need to grow their revenue over time by developing new products and expanding into new markets. New-product development shapes the company's future: improved or replacement products will maintain or build sales. Indeed, the Chinese expression for business, *sheng yi* (生意), literally means "to give birth to ideas." Johnson & Johnson believes in new-product development.

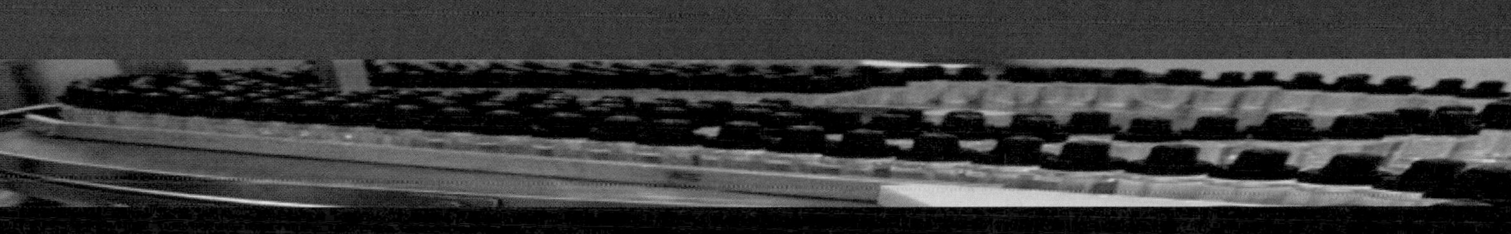

To improve the odds for new-product success in its growing medical device business, Johnson & Johnson (J&J) is making a number of changes. First, it is trying to replicate the dynamic venture-capital world within the company by creating internal start-ups that seek financing from other J&J units. Teams with a promising idea create a business plan and try to win financing from the company's venture-capital arm, Johnson & Johnson Development Corp., which has invested in outside start-ups for years, as well as from one or more of J&J's existing businesses. J&J is also pushing for greater input from doctors and insurers to provide stronger assurance that any device it introduces will be highly desirable, feasible, and cost-effective. The Ethicon-Endo unit designed new surgical clips based on discussions with physicians about the need to find ways to make surgery less invasive. J&J also put one of its most successful scientists in the newly created position of Chief Science and Technology Officer, to encourage collaboration between J&J's different businesses and to overcome the barriers that can prevail in its decentralized structure. One notable success: the $2.6 billion Cypher drug-coated stent. J&J isn't starting from scratch; with 15,000 R&D employees and an R&D budget of $6.3 billion, it has had more than its share of new-product successes through the years, but innovative companies never stand still and are always looking for new and better ways to drive new-product growth.[1]

In this chapter, we will address the following questions:

1. What challenges does a company face in developing new products and services?
2. What organizational structures and processes do managers use to manage new-product development?
3. What are the main stages in developing new products and services?
4. What is the best way to manage the new-product development process?
5. What factors affect the rate of diffusion and consumer adoption of newly launched products and services?

Marketers play a key role in the new-product process by identifying and evaluating new product ideas and working with R&D and others in every stage of development. This chapter provides a detailed analysis of the new-product development process.

New-Product Options

There are different types of new products and a variety of ways to create them.[2]

Make or Buy

A company can add new products through acquisition or development. The **acquisition** route can take three forms: (1) the company can buy other companies, (2) it can acquire patents from other companies, or (3) it can buy a license or franchise from another company. China electronic manufacturer TCL increased its presence in Europe by acquiring Alcatel, while Lenovo bought IBM's personal computer division for its branding, management expertise, and access to the U.S. market. Shanghai Automotive acquired Korea's Ssangyong Motor as part of its efforts to become a global player.[3]

The **development** route can take two forms: (1) the company can develop new products in its own laboratories, or (2) it can contract with independent researchers or new-product development firms to develop specific new products.

Types of New Products

We can identify six categories of new products:[4]

1. ***New-to-the-world products*** — New products that create an entirely new market.
2. ***New product lines*** — New products that allow a company to enter an established market for the first time.
3. ***Additions to existing product lines*** — New products that supplement established product lines (package sizes, flavors, and so on).
4. ***Improvements and revisions of existing products*** — New products that provide improved performance or greater perceived value and replace existing products. At Sony, over 80 percent of new-product activity is modifying and improving existing products.
5. ***Repositioning*** — Existing products that are targeted to new markets or market segments.
6. ***Cost reductions*** — New products that provide similar performance at lower cost.

In many categories, it is becoming increasingly difficult to identify blockbuster products that will transform a market; but continuous innovation to better satisfy consumer needs can force competitors to play catch-up.[5] Continually launching new products as brand extensions into related product categories can also broaden the brand meaning. Nike started as a running-shoe manufacturer but now competes in the sports market with all types of athletic shoes, clothing, and equipment.

Less than 10 percent of all new products are truly innovative and new to the world. These products involve the greatest cost and risk because they are new to both the company and the marketplace. Radical innovations can hurt the company's bottom line in the short run, but the good news is that success can create a greater sustainable competitive advantage than more ordinary products. Companies typically must create a strong R&D and marketing partnership to pull off a radical innovation.[6] Few reliable techniques exist for estimating demand for these innovations. Focus groups will provide some perspectives on customer interest and need, but marketers may need to use a probe-and-learn approach based on observation and feedback of early users' experiences and other means.[7]

Many high-tech firms strive for radical innovation.[8] High tech covers a wide range of industries—telecommunications, computers, consumer electronics, biotech, and software. High-tech marketers face a number of challenges in launching their products: high technological uncertainty; high market uncertainty; high competitive volatility; high investment costs; short product life cycles; and difficulty in finding funding sources for risky projects.[9]

Challenges in New-Product Development

New-product introductions have accelerated in recent years. In many industries, such as retailing, consumer goods, electronics, autos, and others, the time it takes to bring a product to market has been cut in half.[10] Luxury leather-goods maker Louis Vuitton implemented a new factory format dubbed Pégase so that it could ship fresh collections to its boutiques every six weeks—more than twice as frequently as in the past—giving customers more new looks to choose from.[11]

Japanese toiletry brand, Shokubutsu from LION Corporation, adds new variants to its body foam product line in its Singapore market with whitening, anti-bacteria, soothing, revitalizing, firming, nourishing and moisturizing qualities as part of its continuous innovation.

The Innovation Imperative

In an economy of rapid change, continuous innovation is a necessity. Highly innovative firms are able to identify and quickly seize new market opportunities. Table 20.1 lists the 2008 rankings of the top 25 globally innovative firms on the basis of a *BusinessWeek*-Boston Consulting Group survey. Innovative firms create a positive attitude toward innovation and risk taking, routinize the innovation process, practice teamwork, and allow their people to experiment and even fail.

Companies that fail to develop new products are putting themselves at risk. Their existing products are vulnerable to changing customer needs and tastes, new technologies, shortened product life cycles, and increased domestic and foreign competition. New technologies are especially threatening.

New-Product Success

Most established companies focus on *incremental innovation.* Incremental innovation can allow companies to enter new markets by tweaking products for new customers, use variations on a core product to stay one step ahead of the market, and create interim solutions for industry-wide problems. Southwest Airlines has made some notable incremental innovations.

Southwest Airlines—An airline known for bucking tradition, Southwest used incremental innovation to offset the impact of an important competitor innovation: frequent flier miles. Begun by American Airlines more than 20 years ago to boost customer loyalty, frequent flier rewards programs were soon rolled out by all the major airlines. Southwest, however, decided to tie its rewards to the number of flights taken rather than miles flown. The airline offers mainly short-haul flights for business travelers who often fly the same route over and over. The program was a big hit with this target market.[12]

Management consultant McKinsey proposed two strategies towards innovation. The "Let a thousand flowers bloom" approach encourages many raw ideas, although these tend to be incrementally innovative in nature. In contrast, the "Prune the weeds" approach generates few ideas, but these tend to be breakthrough innovations.

Most established companies focus on *incremental innovation.* Newer companies create *disruptive technologies* that are cheaper and more likely to alter the competitive space. Established companies can be slow to react or invest in these disruptive technologies because they threaten their investment. Then they suddenly find themselves facing formidable new competitors, and many fail.[13] To ensure that they do not fall into this trap, incumbent firms must carefully monitor the preferences of both customers and non-customers over time and uncover evolving, difficult-to-articulate customer needs.[14]

Table 20.1 The World's Top 25 Most Innovative Companies

2008 Rank	2007 Rank	Company	HQ Country	Revenue Growth 2004–07* (in %)	Margin Growth 2004–07* (in %)	Stock Returns 2004–07** (in %)	Most known for its Innovative... (% who think so)
1	1	APPLE	USA	47	69	83	Products (52%)
2	2	GOOGLE	USA	73	5	53	Customer Experience (26%)
3	3	TOYOTA MOTOR	Japan	12	1	15	Processes (36%)
4	4	GENERAL ELECTRIC	USA	9	1	3	Processes (43%)
5	5	MICROSOFT	USA	16	8	12	Products (26%)
6	NR	TATA GROUP	India	Private	Private	Private	Products (58%)
7	39	NINTENDO	Japan	37	4	77	Products (63%)
8	6	PROCTER & GAMBLE	USA	16	4	12	Processes (30%)
9	10	SONY	Japan	8	13	17	Products (56%)
10	13	NOKIA	Finland	20	2	35	Products (36%)
11	20	AMAZON.COM	USA	29	–11	28	Customer Experience (33%)
12	9	IBM	USA	1	11	4	Processes (31%)
13	34	RESEARCH IN MOTION	Canada	56	–1	51	Products (37%)
14	16	BMW	Germany	6	–5	11	Customer Experience (40%)
15	31	HEWLETT-PACKARD	USA	10	17	35	Processes, Business Models, and Customer Experience (27% each)
16	12	HONDA MOTOR	Japan	12	6	14	Products (40%)
17	8	WALT DISNEY	USA	6	14	7	Customer Experience (63%)
18	NR	GENERAL MOTORS	USA	–2	NA***	–11	Products (55%)
19	NR	RELIANCE INDUSTRIES	India	31	–7	94	Business Models (31%)
20	21	BOEING	USA	9	32	21	Products (63%)
21	NR	GOLDMAN SACHS GROUP	USA	30	6	28	Processes and Business Models (33% each)
22	7	3M	USA	7	5	3	Products (45%)
23	11	WAL-MART STORES	USA	10	–2	–2	Processes (48%)
24	15	TARGET	USA	11	3	0	Customer Experience (67%)
25	NR	FACEBOOK	USA	Private	Private	Private	Customer Experience (51%)

Source: "The World's Fifty Most Innovative Companies." Special Report, *BusinessWeek*, April 17, 2008.

Note: Analysis and data provided in collaboration with the innovation practice of the Boston Consulting Group and BCG-VaueScience. Reuters and Compustat were use for financial and industry date and Bloomberg for total shareholder returns.

*Compound growth rates for revenue and operating margins are based on 2004-07 fiscal year data as originally stated. Operating margin is earnings before interest and taxes as a percentage of revenue. Where possible, quarterly and semiannual data were used to bring performance for pre-June yearends closer to December, 2007. Financial figures were calculated in local currency.

**Stock returns are annualized, 12/31/04 to 12/31/07, and account for price appreciation and dividends.

***Calculating three-year compound annual growth rate for operating margins was not possible when either figure was negative.

NR = Not ranked.

Hybrid cars—The debate over hybrid cars has split the auto industry. Honda, Toyota, and Ford are betting that these vehicles, which combine an electric motor with a conventional engine, are the best way to save gas and clean up emissions. They also think that while hybrids are an interim technology; car makers will learn valuable lessons from it, helping them to develop next-generation fuel-cell vehicles. However, General Motors, DaimlerChrysler, and Nissan are less enamored with hybrid cars, believing that the technology is not likely to be profitable for years and that auto-makers should not try to impose the technology on the market. Both sides are making calculated gambles. The pro-hybrid camp is betting billions that hybrids will sell briskly enough to eventually turn a profit, while the con camp argue that hybrids are a pricey interim solution. With rising oil prices, hybrids may take off. Auto-makers quick in offering hybrids will be ahead of their rivals in amortizing the heavy investment costs. Toyota aims at one million hybrid vehicle sales per year in the early 2010s. It is working on a "plug-in" hybrid to be introduced in 2010.[15]

New-Product Failure

New-product development can be quite risky. What else can a company do to develop successful new products? Cooper and Kleinschmidt found that the number-one success factor is a unique, superior product. Such products succeed 98 percent of the time, compared to products with a moderate advantage (58 percent success) or minimal advantage (18 percent success).[16] Another key factor is a well-defined product concept. The company that carefully defines and assesses the target market, product requirements, and benefits before proceeding has a lower rate of failure. Other success factors are technological and marketing synergy, quality of execution in all stages, and market attractiveness.

Cooper and Kleinschmidt also found that domestic products designed solely for the domestic market tend to show a high failure rate, low market share, and low growth. In contrast, products designed for the world market—or at least to include neighboring countries—achieve significantly more profits, both at home and abroad. Yet only 17 percent of the products in their study were designed with an international orientation. The implication is that companies should adopt an international focus in designing and developing new products.

SED Inc.—A joint venture between Canon and Toshiba was formed to produce screens for a new kind of flat television. The result: SED, which stands for Surface-conduction Electron-emitter Display. On an SED, dark colors appear richer, while letters appearing across the screen are clearer when compared with plasma displays. The SED also uses one-third to half of the power of plasma and LCD TVs. Yet, for all of its advantages, its cost is exorbitant. The technology used to produce SEDs does not allow for mass production. It is estimated that only 75,000 SED TVs can be made a month in 2008, and 250,000 a month in 2010. By contrast, Matsushita produced 400,000 plasma TVs a month by end 2006. The superior technology also cannot accommodate smaller TV sets. SED Inc. will initially produce 50-inch TVs. Smaller sets will require more complexity and higher cost. With TV prices in a free fall, SED TVs may not be competitive against its plasma and LCD counterparts.[17]

New products continue to fail at a disturbing rate. Despite spending huge sums on R&D, most companies have low levels of innovation productivity. Up to 96 percent of all new projects fail to meet or beat targets for return on investment.[18]

New products can fail for many reasons: ignoring or misinterpreting market research; overestimating market size; high development costs; poor design; incorrect positioning, ineffective advertising, or wrong price; insufficient distribution support; and competitors who fight back hard.

Several factors also tend to hinder new-product development:

- ***Shortage of important ideas in certain areas***— There may be few ways left to improve some basic products (such as steel or detergents).
- ***Fragmented markets***— Companies have to aim their new products at smaller market segments, and this can mean lower sales and profits for each product.
- ***Social and governmental constraints***— New products have to satisfy consumer safety and environmental concerns.
- ***Cost of development***— A company typically has to generate many ideas to find just one worthy of development, and often faces high R&D, manufacturing, and marketing costs.
- ***Capital shortages***— Some companies with good ideas cannot raise the funds needed to research and launch them.
- ***Faster required development time***— Companies must learn how to compress development time by using new techniques, strategic partners, early concept tests, and advanced marketing planning.
- ***Shorter product life cycles***— When a new product is successful, rivals are quick to copy it. Sony used to enjoy a three-year lead on its new products. Now Matsushita will copy the product within months, leaving hardly enough time for Sony to recoup its investment.

Table 20.2 summarizes causes of new-product failure.

Table 20.2 Causes of New-Product Failure

1. *Market/marketing failure*
   - Small size of the potential market
   - No clear product differentiation
   - Poor positioning
   - Misunderstanding of customer needs
2. *Financial failure*
   - Low return on investment
3. *Timing failure*
   - Late in the market
   - "Too" early—market not yet developed
4. *Technical failure*
   - Product did not work
   - Bad design
5. *Organizational failure*
   - Poor fit with the organizational culture
   - Lack of organizational support
6. *Environmental failure*
   - Government regulations
   - Macroeconomic factors

Source: Dipak Jain, "Managing New-Product Development for Strategic Competitive Advantage." *Kellogg on Marketing*, Dawn Iacobucci, ed., (New York: John Wiley, 2001), p. 131.

But failure comes with the territory, and truly innovative firms accept it as part of what's needed to be successful. Many Web companies are the result of failed business ventures and experience numerous failed initiatives as they evolve their services.

Eli Lilly—Initial product failure is not always the end of the road for an idea. Recognizing that 90 percent of experimental drugs fail, Eli Lilly has established a corporate culture that looks at failure as an inevitable part of discovery, and its scientists are encouraged to look for new uses for compounds that fail at any stage in a human clinical trial. Evista was a failed contraceptive that became a $1 billion-a-year drug for osteoporosis. Stattera was unsuccessful as an antidepressant but became a top seller for attention deficit/hyperactivity disorder. One promising cardiovascular drug in development started as an asthma project.[19]

Asian companies have typically not invested heavily in long-term research because there were more lucrative and stable profits to be earned from licensing and trading. The generally hierarchical and paternalistic management style of Asian companies and society may also discourage creativity or creative people:[20] Two Chinese sayings illustrate the importance of fitting in: "It is the tall tree which catches the wind," and "It is the nail which sticks out most that gets pounded in first." Both advise employees to keep a low profile and fit in with the consensus. Creative input is also hampered because the entrepreneur has the latitude to take the initiative while others must be content with its execution. There is also a reluctance to comment on matters outside of one's assigned responsibility (see "Marketing Insight: The Effects of National Culture on New-Product Development" for a further discussion).

Organizational Arrangements

Many companies today use *customer-driven engineering* to design new products. Customer-driven engineering attaches high importance to incorporating customer preferences in the final design.

MARKETING INSIGHT • THE EFFECTS OF NATIONAL CULTURE ON NEW-PRODUCT DEVELOPMENT

Nakata and Sivakumar linked the five dimensions of national culture—individualism, power distance, masculinity, uncertainty avoidance, and Confucian dynamic—to two broad phases of the new-product development (NPD) process: initiation, which covered idea generation, screening, and concept testing; and implementation, which covered product development, test marketing, and product launch.

Individualistic societies have loose ties among members and include such countries as the U.S., Canada, and the U.K. In contrast, collectivistic nations such as Japan and Taiwan have close membership ties. Power distance is the extent to which less powerful members of organizations and institutions accept and expect that power is distributed unequally. High power distance nations include the Philippines, India, and France; while societies with low power distance include Australia, Israel, and the U.S. Masculinity is the degree to which a society is characterized by assertiveness versus nurturance (femininity). High masculine cultures include Italy and Germany; while Thailand and Sweden are low on this factor. Uncertainty avoidance centers on how societies deal with unknown aspects of the future. Countries low on this factor, such as the U.S., Hong Kong, and Singapore, work to meet basic needs, are tolerant of various behaviors, and are relatively secure. However, societies anxious over the future actively avoid risk and devise means to create a sense of control. These include France and Belgium.

Overall, countries which are individualistic and low in power distance, masculinity, and uncertainty avoidance (e.g., the U.S., U.K., and Australia) tend to facilitate the initiation stage of NPD through the kind of drive, nonconformity, and personal vision associated with product champions and key innovators, encouraging contribution of diverse ideas and efforts from persons irrespective of their positions, establishing warm and supportive climates, and through risk taking with minimal planning and controls.

In contrast, societies which are collectivistic and high in power distance, masculinity, and uncertainty avoidance (e.g., Pakistan, the Philippines, Taiwan, Thailand, and Japan) tend to facilitate the implementation phase of NPD through their emphasis on interdependence, cooperation, and unified purpose, centralized command to ensure coordinated of complex efforts, promoting goal directedness and formalization, and emphasizing risk aversion and tight planning and control.

For example, in an agreement between two pharmaceutical companies, the original technology was provided by Searle of the U.S. (initiating culture), while the development was handled by Japan's Sankyo (an implementing culture).

Finally, societies with a positive Confucian dynamic like Hong Kong, Taiwan, Japan, and South Korea, have values indicating a dynamic, future-oriented mentality such as persistence, hard work, thrift, shame, and a strong regard for relationships. Societies negative on this factor like Canada, Pakistan, and West Africa have values representing a static mentality focusing on the past and the present, such as face, reciprocation, and tradition. The positive pole of Confucian dynamism promotes NPD at the initiation and the implementation stages by emphasizing action and future possibilities, while its negative pole impedes NPD at both stages by focusing on preserving the past and present realities.

Clearly, other factors such as organizational culture may interact with national culture to affect NPD. For example, Sony is more innovative than Matsushita, although both are Japanese companies.

Source: Cheryl Nakata and K. Sivakumar, "National Culture and New Product Development: An Integrative Review." *Journal of Marketing*, January 1996, pp. 61–72.

Xerox—Xerox traditionally developed new products as many firms did in the past: come up with an idea, develop a prototype, and get some consumer feedback. When Xerox researchers first came up with the idea for a dual-engine commercial printer, they decided to first go straight to the consumer to collect feedback before even developing any prototypes. Luckily they did. Although the Xerox team thought customers would want a second engine for special purposes, the fact that the second engine would be a back-up if the main engine failed turned out to be the biggest draw. As one customer said, "If you're down, you're dead." In introducing the dual-engine Nuvera 288 Digital Perfecting System in April 2007, Xerox chief technology officer Sophie V. Vandebroek cited "customer-led innovation" as a critical driver. Xerox now believes in brainstorming, or "dreaming with the customer," by combining company experts who know technology with customers who know the "pain points" and what the most valuable product features can be. In addition, scientists and engineers are encouraged to meet face to face with customers, in some cases working on-site for a few weeks to see how customers interact with products.[21]

Xerox's popular new dual-engine printer was a response to customers' feedback on the value of a commercial printer with a back-up engine.

New-product development requires senior management to define business domains, product categories, and specific criteria. General Motors has a hefty $400 million benchmark it must apply to new car models—this is what it costs to get a new vehicle into production.[22] One company established the following acceptance criteria:

- The product can be introduced within five years.
- The product has a market potential of at least $50 million and a 15 percent growth rate.
- The product would provide at least 30 percent return on sales and 40 percent on investment.
- The product would achieve technical or market leadership.

Budgeting for New-Product Development

Senior management must decide how much to budget for new-product development. R&D outcomes are so uncertain that it is difficult to use normal investment criteria. Some companies solve this problem by financing as many projects as possible, hoping to achieve a few winners. Other companies apply a conventional percentage of sales figures or spend what the competition spends. Still other companies decide how many successful new products they need and work backward to estimate the required investment.

Table 20.3 shows how a company might calculate the cost of new-product development. The new-products manager at a large consumer-packaged-goods company reviewed the results of 64 ideas. Only one in four, or 16, passed the screening stage. It cost $1,000 to review each idea at this stage. Half of these ideas, or eight, survived the concept-testing stage, at a cost of $20,000 each. Half of these, or four, survived the product-development stage, at a cost of $200,000 each. Half of these, or two, did well in the test market, at a cost of $500,000 each. When these two ideas were launched, at a cost of $5 million each, only one was highly successful. Thus the one successful idea cost the company $5,721,000 to develop.

Table 20.3 Finding One Successful New Product (Starting with 64 New Ideas)

Stage	Number of Ideas	Pass Ratio	Cost per Product Idea	Total Cost
1. Idea screening	64	1:4	$1,000	$64,000
2. Concept testing	16	1:2	20,000	320,000
3. Product development	8	1:2	200,000	1,600,000
4. Test marketing	4	1:2	500,000	2,000,000
5. National launch	2	1:2	5,000,000	10,000,000
			$5,721,000	$13,984,000

In the process, 63 other ideas fell by the wayside. The total cost for developing one successful new product was $13,984,000. Unless the company can improve the pass ratios and reduce the costs at each stage, it will have to budget nearly $14 million for each successful new idea it hopes to find. If top management wants four successful new products in the next few years, it will have to budget at least $56 million (4 × $14 million) for new-product development.

Organizing New-Product Development

Companies handle the organizational aspect of new-product development in several ways.[23] Many companies assign responsibility for new-product ideas to *product managers.* But product managers are often so busy managing existing lines that they give little thought to new products other than line extensions. They also lack the specific skills and knowledge needed to develop and critique new products. Kraft and Johnson & Johnson have *new-product managers* who report to category managers. Some companies have a *high-level management committee* charged with reviewing and approving proposals. Large companies often establish a *new-product department* headed by a manager who has substantial authority and access to top management. The department's major responsibilities include generating and screening new ideas, working with the R&D department, and carrying out field testing and commercialization.

Adobe Systems Inc.—A developer of software solutions for graphic designers and publishers, Adobe established a task force in 2004 to identify all the obstacles company innovators faced in trying to develop new products. The team found the corporate hierarchy resisted ideas needing a new sales channel, new business model, or even new packaging, and the company had grown so large that ideas originating in branch offices were not getting a fair shake. The company then established a New Business Initiatives Group that holds quarterly Adobe Idea Champion Showcases. About 20 product managers and other employees (except top executives who are barred from the proceedings) watch as potential employee-entrepreneurs give brief presentations and Q&A sessions. The ideas are vetted by Adobe entrepreneurs-in-residence, but even one that's nixed can still get a hearing on the company's brainstorming site. Since the new initiative was formed, the event has become extremely popular within Adobe—an ***American Idol***-style way for good ideas to come to the fore.[24]

3M, Dow, and General Mills often assign new-product development work to *venture teams.* A **venture team** is a cross-functional group charged with developing a specific product or business. These "intrapreneurs" are relieved of their other duties and given a budget, a time frame, and a "skunkworks" setting. *Skunkworks* are informal workplaces, sometimes garages, where intrapreneurial teams attempt to develop new products.

Cross-functional teams can collaborate and use concurrent new-product development to push new products to market.[25] Concurrent product development resembles a rugby match rather than a relay race, with team members passing the new product back and forth as they head toward the goal.

Cross-functional teams help to ensure that engineers are not just driven to create a "better mousetrap" when potential customers do not really need or want one. Indeed, the success of new Japanese products is due in large part to utilizing cross-functional teams comprising staff from R&D, engineering, manufacturing, purchasing, finance, and marketing from the outset. Such integration is the key driver in diffusing market and customer knowledge of development and forms the foundation for technological applications valued by customers. Japanese businesses thus bring customers in at an early stage to get their views. Also, the manufacturing department plays a critical role in the early stages of product design. Providing manufacturing process information helps Japanese businesses reduce the costs of design features and the number of design changes, thus reducing development cycle-time and costs.[26]

Many companies such as 3M, Hewlett-Packard, and Lego use the *stage-gate system* to manage the innovation process.[27] The process is divided into stages, and at the end of each stage is a gate or checkpoint. The project leader, working with a cross-functional team, must bring a set of known deliverables to each gate before the project can pass to the next stage. To move from the business plan stage into product development requires a convincing market research study of consumer needs and interest, a competitive analysis, and a technical appraisal. Senior managers review the criteria at each gate to judge whether the project deserves to move to the next stage. The gatekeepers make one of four decisions: *go, kill, hold,* or *recycle.* Stage-gate systems make the innovation process visible to all involved and clarify the project leader's and team's responsibilities at each stage.[28]

The stages in the new-product development process are shown in Figure 20.1. Many firms have multiple, parallel sets of projects working through the process, each at a different stage.[29] The process can be depicted as a *funnel:* a large number of initial new-product ideas and concepts are winnowed down to a few high-potential products that are ultimately launched. But the process is not always linear. Many firms use a *spiral development process* that recognizes the value of returning to an earlier stage to make improvements before moving forward.

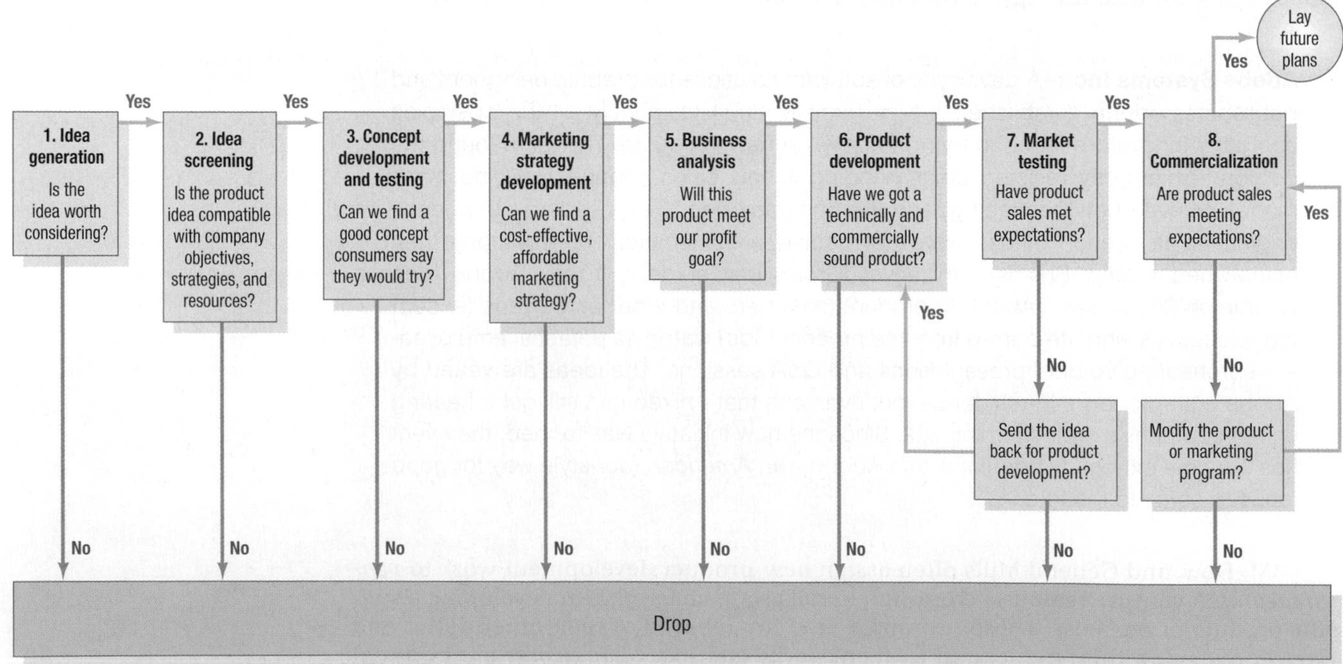

Figure 20.1 The New-Product Development Decision Process

Managing the Development Process: Ideas

Idea Generation

The new-product development process starts with the search for ideas. Some marketing experts believe that the greatest opportunities and highest leverage with new products are found by uncovering the best possible set of unmet customer needs or technological innovation.[30] New-product ideas can come from interacting with various groups and from using creativity-generating techniques (see "Marketing Memo: Ten Ways to Great New-Product Ideas").

MARKETING MEMO • TEN WAYS TO GREAT NEW-PRODUCT IDEAS

1. Run informal sessions where groups of customers meet with company engineers and designers to discuss problems and needs, and brainstorm potential solutions.
2. Allow time off—scouting time—for technical people to putter on their own pet projects. 3M allows 15 percent time off.
3. Make a customer-brainstorming session a standard feature of plant tours.
4. Survey your customers: find out what they like and dislike in your and competitors' products.
5. Undertake "fly-on-the-wall" or "camping out" research with customers.
6. Use iterative rounds: a group of customers in one room, focusing on identifying problems, and a group of your technical people in the next room, listening and brainstorming solutions. The proposed solutions are then tested immediately on the group of customers.
7. Set up a keyword search that routinely scans trade publications in multiple countries for new-product announcements.
8. Treat trade shows as intelligence missions, where you view all that is new in your industry under one roof.
9. Have your technical and marketing people visit your suppliers' labs and spend time with their technical people—find out what is new.
10. Set up an idea vault, and make it open and easily accessible. Allow employees to review the ideas and add constructively to them.

Source: Adapted from Robert Cooper, *Product Leadership: Creating and Launching Superior New Products,* (New York: Perseus Books, 1998).

INTERACTING WITH OTHERS

Encouraged by the *open innovation* movement, many firms are increasingly going outside the company to tap external sources of new ideas, including customers, scientists, competitors, employees, channel members, and top management. "Marketing Insight: P&G's New Connect-and-Develop Approach to Innovation" describes how that company has become more externally focused in its new-product development.

Customer needs and wants are the logical place to start the search. One-on-one interviews, focus group discussions, and observational research can explore product needs and reactions.

Sony—Perceived by many young Chinese as their Daddy's brand, Sony opened a design center in Shanghai. To understand the lives of young Chinese, Sony equipped 50 youths with digital cameras to document their daily lives in photographs. Using the many photos collected, Sony categorized young Chinese into seven segments, such as "Cheerful Next Generation" and "Try Harder for Life". Sony then designed a line of MP3 players in muted colors with a smooth river-rock-like appearance to appeal to trendsetters in these segments.[31]

Griffin and Hauser suggest that conducting 10–20 in-depth experiential interviews per market segment often uncovers the vast majority of customer needs.[32] But many additional approaches can be profitable (see "Marketing Memo: Seven Ways to Draw New Ideas from Your Customers").

MARKETING INSIGHT • P&G'S NEW CONNECT-AND-DEVELOP APPROACH TO INNOVATION

For fiscal years 2000–2004, Procter & Gamble's corporate profits jumped by almost 70 percent, to $9.8 billion, and revenues increased by almost 30 percent, to $51 billion. Helping fuel that growth were successful new products such as Swiffer (a sweeper for hard floor surfaces), Mr. Clean Magic Eraser (a soft cleaning pad that removes dirt and stains), and Actonel (a prescription medication for osteoporosis). In January 2005, P&G acquired Gillette for $54 billion. But to a large degree P&G's growth in recent years has been driven by what CEO A.G. Lafley calls "the core"—core markets, categories, brands, technologies, and capabilities—and innovation has been at the heart of that.

Mr. Clean Magic Eraser is one of Procter & Gamble's most recent innovations. The company has revamped the process by which it researches and develops new products, tapping more external sources than ever before.

To more effectively develop its core, P&G adopted a "connect-and-develop" model that emphasizes the pursuit of more externally sourced innovation. Twenty-five percent of new products and technologies come from outside the company; Lafley wants to raise that to 50 percent, so "half would come out of P&G labs and half would come *through* P&G labs, from the outside."

P&G collaborates with organizations and individuals around the world, systematically searching for proven technologies, packages, and products it can improve, scale up, and market, either on its own or in partnership with other companies. It has forged strong relationships with external designers, distributing product development around the world to increase what P&G calls "consumer sensing," and even bringing John Osher, who invented the successful Crest SpinBrush electric rotating toothbrush, inside the company for a period to help make it more innovative.

To focus its idea search, P&G identifies the top 10 customer needs, closely related products that could leverage or benefit from existing brand equity, and technology "game boards" that map the flow of technology adoption across different product categories. With these sources as boundaries, P&G may consult government and private labs, as well as academic and other research institutions; suppliers, retailers, competitors, development and trade partners, VC firms, and individual entrepreneurs. P&G uses online networks to reach thousands of experts worldwide.

All these connections have helped to produce 100 new products in two years. For example, new ink-jet technology for printing edible images on cakes invented by a professor in Bologona, Italy, was used to create Pringles potato chips with jokes and pictures printed on them. The product was developed two to three years faster than usual at a fraction of the cost and resulted in double-digit growth for the Pringles brand. P&G has identified three core requirements for a successful connect-and-develop strategy:

1. Never assume that "ready-to-go" ideas found outside are truly ready to go. There will always be development work to do, including risky scale-up.
2. Don't underestimate the internal resources required. You'll need a full-time, senior executive to run any connect-and-develop initiative.
3. Never launch without a mandate from the CEO. Connect and develop cannot succeed if it's cordoned off in R&D. It must be a top-down, company-wide strategy.

The connect-and-develop model certainly seems to be working for P&G. Forty-five percent of initiatives in the product-development portfolio have key elements that were discovered externally. Through connect and develop—along with improvements in other aspects of innovation related to product cost, design, and marketing—R&D productivity has increased by nearly 60 percent. The innovation success rate has more than doubled, and the cost of innovation has fallen. R&D investment as a percentage of sales is down from 4.8 percent in 2000 to 3.4 percent today. Since 2000, P&G's share price has doubled, and the company now has a portfolio of twenty-two billion-dollar brands.

Sources: Steve Hamm, "Speed Demons." *BusinessWeek*, March 27, 2006, pp. 69–76; Larry Huston and Nabil Sakkab, "Connect and Develop: Inside Procter & Gamble's New Model for Innovation." *Harvard Business Review*, March 2006, pp. 58–66; Geoff Colvin, "Lafley and Immelt: In Search of Billions." *Fortune*, December 11, 2006, pp. 70–72; Rajat Gupta and Jim Wendler, "Leading Change: An Interview with the CEO of P&G." *McKinsey Quarterly*, July 2005.

MARKETING MEMO • SEVEN WAYS TO DRAW NEW IDEAS FROM YOUR CUSTOMERS

1. **Observe how your customers are using your product**. Medtronic, a medical device company, has salespeople and market researchers regularly observe spine surgeons who use their products and competitive products, to learn how they can be improved. Similarly, GE has gathered ideas for improving CAT scanners by observing their use by skilled medical personnel.
2. **Ask your customers about their problems with your products**. Komatsu Heavy Equipment sent a group of engineers and designers to the U.S. for six months to ride with equipment drivers and learn how to make products better. Procter & Gamble, recognizing consumers were frustrated that potato chips would break and were difficult to save after opening the bag, designed Pringles to be uniform in size and encased in a tennis-ball-type can so consumers could open the can, consume a few unbroken chips, and close it again.
3. **Ask your customers about their dream products**. Ask your customers what they want your product to do, even if the ideal sounds impossible. One 70-year-old camera user told Minolta he would like the camera to make his subjects look better and not show their wrinkles and aging. In response, Minolta produced a camera with two lenses, one of which was for rendering softer images of the subjects.
4. **Use a customer advisory board to comment on your company's ideas**. Levi Strauss uses youth panels to discuss lifestyles, habits, values, and brand engagements; Cisco runs Customer Forums to improve its offerings; and Harley-Davidson solicits product ideas from its one million H.O.G. (Harley Owners Group) members.
5. **Use Web sites for new ideas**. Companies can use specialized search engines such as Technorati and Day Pop to find blogs and postings relevant to their businesses. P&G's site has *We're Listening* and *Share Your Thoughts* sections and Advisory Feedback sessions to gain advice and feedback from customers.
6. **Form a brand community of enthusiasts who discuss your product**. Harley-Davidson and Apple have strong brand enthusiasts and advocates; Sony engaged in collaborative dialogues with consumers to co-develop Sony's PlayStation 2; and LEGO draws on kids and influential adult enthusiasts for feedback on new-product concepts in early stages of development.
7. **Encourage or challenge your customers to change or improve your product**. Salesforce.com wants its users to develop and share new software applications using simple programming tools; International Flavors & Fragrances gives a toolkit to its customers to modify specific flavors, which IFF then manufactures; LSI Logic Corporation also provides customers with do-it-yourself toolkits so that customers can design their own specialized chips; and BMW posted a toolkit on its Web site to let customers develop ideas using telematics and in-car online services.

Source: Philip Kotler, "Drawing New Ideas from Your Customers." Unpublished paper, 2007.

The traditional company-centric approach to product innovation is giving way to a world in which companies cocreate products with consumers.[33] Companies are increasingly turning to "crowdsourcing" to generate new ideas or, as we saw in the previous chapter, to create consumer-generated marketing campaigns. Crowdsourcing means inviting the Internet community to help create content or software, often with prize money or a moment of glory involved. This strategy has helped create new products and companies such as the open-source encyclopedia, Wikipedia, and the hugely popular video Web site YouTube, which was purchased by Google.

Besides producing new and better ideas, co-creation can help customers feel closer to and more favorably towards the company, and to tell others of their involvement through favorable word of mouth.[34]

Lead users can be a good source of input when they innovate products without the consent or even the knowledge of the companies that produce them. Mountain bikes developed as a result of youngsters taking their bikes up to the top of a mountain and riding down. When the bikes broke, the youngsters began building more durable bikes and adding things such as motorcycle brakes, improved suspension, and accessories. The youngsters, not the companies, developed these innovations. Some companies, particularly those that want to appeal to hip young consumers, bring the lead users into their product-design process.

Technical companies can learn a great deal by studying customers who make the most advanced use of the company's products and who recognize the need for improvements before other customers do.[35] Microsoft studied 13 to 24-year-olds—the NetGen—and developed its Threedegrees software product to satisfy their instant messaging needs.[36](For the special case of high-tech products, see "Marketing Insight: Developing Successful High-Tech Products.")

Employees throughout the company can be a source of ideas for improving production, products, and services. Toyota claims its employees submit two million ideas annually (about 35 suggestions per employee), over 85 percent of which are implemented. For examples on how Japanese businesses derive new ideas from their employees, see "Marketing Insight: New-Idea Generation in Japanese Companies."

MARKETING INSIGHT • DEVELOPING SUCCESSFUL HIGH-TECH PRODUCTS

High tech covers a wide range of industries—telecommunications, computers, consumer electronics, biotech, and software. Radical innovations carry a high level of risk and typically hurt the company's bottom line at least in the short run. The good news is that success can create a greater sustainable competitive advantage than might come from more ordinary products.

One way to define the scope of high tech is by its common characteristics:

- ***High technological uncertainty*** — Scientists working on high-tech products are never sure they will function as promised and be delivered on time.
- ***High market uncertainty*** — Marketers are not sure what needs the new technology will meet. How will buyers use Interactive TV? Will hybrid cars be more popular than conventional cars?
- ***High competitive volatility*** — Will the strongest competition come from within the industry or from outside? Will competitors rewrite the rules? What products will this new technology replace?
- ***High investment cost–low variable cost*** — Many high-tech products require a large upfront investment to develop the first unit, but the costs fall rapidly on additional units. The cost of developing a new piece of software is very high, but the cost of distributing it in a CD-ROM is relatively low.
- ***Short life*** — Most high-tech products must be constantly upgraded. Competitors will often force the innovator to produce a second generation before recouping its investment on the first generation.
- ***Finding funding sources for such risky projects is not easy*** — Companies must create a strong R&D/marketing partnership to pull it off. Few reliable techniques exist for estimating demand for radical innovations. Focus groups will provide some perspectives on customer interest and need, but high-tech marketers will have to use a probe-and-learn approach based on observing early users and collecting feedback on their experiences.

High-tech marketers also face difficult questions related to the marketing mix:

- ***Product*** — What features and functions should they build into the new product? Should manufacturing be done in-house or be outsourced?
- ***Price*** — Should the price be set high? Would a low price be better to sell more quickly and go down the experience curve faster? Should the product be almost given away to accelerate adoption?
- ***Distribution*** — Is the product best sold through the company's own sales force or should it be put in the hands of agents, distributors, and dealers? Should the company start with one channel or build multiple sales channels early?
- ***Communication*** — What are the best messages to convey the basic benefits and features of the new product? What are the best media for communicating these messages? What sales-promotion incentives would drive early interest and purchase?

Source: For further ideas, see Jakki Mohr, *Marketing of High-Technology Products and Innovations*, 2nd ed., (Upper Saddle River, NJ: Prentice Hall, 2005).

MARKETING INSIGHT • NEW-IDEA GENERATION IN JAPANESE COMPANIES

Japanese companies steeped in rigid hierarchical structures and consensus management systems have employed various methods to stimulate employee creativity for generating new-product ideas. Some examples are:

- Shiseido has banned the addressing of colleagues in the traditional fashion indicating their relative rank. It also uses philosophical introspection to change corporate culture. Such themes as "Time and Space," "Expression and Language," "Beauty and Truth," and "Body and Soul," are explored through lectures, group discussions, experiential exercises, and meditation sessions.
- NEC's researchers have flexible working hours, can wear whatever they please, and even need not report to work at all if they do not want to. Outstanding researchers have their pictures displayed in the research center's Hall of Fame.
- Fujitsu allows its researchers to choose their own hours, specific interests, and apparel. Overtime pay is replaced by productivity-linked pay, and staff with good ideas are encouraged to consider spinning off venture businesses.
- Toyota claims that its employees submit two million ideas annually—about 35 suggestions per employee—and over 85 percent are implemented. The Toyota Engineering Society organizes an annual Idea Olympics. Engineers submit ideas under the categories of rides, fun, creativity, and recycling. Winning ideas are paraded in public at Toyota City in Aichi prefecture.
- Hitachi has a shadow society called the *Henjinkai* (oddball club) created to forge stronger links among its more gifted researchers. It has more than 1,200 members—all engineers with Ph.D.s earned mostly after joining Hitachi—fraternize at technical conferences, swap ideas, and informally advise Hitachi's board on important technological developments.
- Omron, a maker of electronic controls, has a monthly *juku* (cram school), to break down mind-sets. Here, mid-level employees try to think and plan as if they were 19th-century warlords, private detectives, or Formula One race car drivers.
- Fuji asks senior managers to study offbeat topics such as the history of Venice or the sociology of apes to broaden their minds and find new ideas.
- Employees of Shimizu, Japan's largest construction company, spend time playing games that force teams to tackle impossible problems such as getting back from the moon on a damaged spacecraft.

Sources: Michel Syrett, "Nurturing Ideas Pays Dividends." *Asian Business*, February 1996, pp. 20-23; Peter Gloster and James Leung, "Innovators Spearhead Global Drive by Techno Giants." *Asian Business*, May 1996, pp. 28-34; Steven V. Brull, Robert D. Hof, Julia Flynn, and Neil Gross, "Fujitsu Gets Wired." *BusinessWeek*, March 18, 1996, pp. 28-32; Neil Gross, "Inside Hitachi." *International BusinessWeek*, September 28, 1992, pp. 80-86; Emily Thornton, "Japan's Struggle to Be Creative." *Fortune* (International Edition), April 1993, pp. 40-42.

Samsung—The VIP (or Value Innovation Program) House is a dormitory with meeting rooms where groups of engineers, product managers, and researchers discuss projects such as how to decrease the thickness of conventional tube TVs. Some projects are expected to last a month, while others last as long as a year. The employees' bosses have vowed in writing to keep them in the VIP House until they have solved their particular problem. "Seventy to eighty percent of quality, cost, and delivery time is determined in the initial stages of product development," says Kyung-Han Jung, a VIP House manager. Samsung's drive to cut cost and complexity early in the design cycle is one reason why it has lower manufacturing costs, higher profit margins, quicker time to market, and more innovative products than its rivals. A mind-set change has also helped Samsung become a leader in design. While suits were the normal attire for Samsung's 12 mobile phone designers who were mostly aged over 40 decade ago, Samsung's designers are now younger and most work in jeans and sneakers. Some even have their hair tinted in pink or purple.[37]

Companies can also find good ideas by researching competitors' products and services. They can find out what customers like and dislike about competitors' products. They can buy their competitors' products, take them apart, and build better ones. Company sales representatives and intermediaries are a particularly good source of ideas. These groups have firsthand exposure to customers and are often the first to learn about competitive developments.

Top management can be another major source of ideas. Some company leaders take personal responsibility for technological innovation in their companies. Intel's Andrew Grove and Sony's late Akio Morita take personal responsibility for technological innovation in their companies. New-product ideas can also come from inventors, patent attorneys, university and commercial laboratories, industrial consultants, advertising agencies, marketing research firms, and industrial publications. However, although ideas can flow from many sources, their chances of receiving serious attention often depend on someone in the organization taking the role of product champion.

Ideas can also be generated with the involvement of academic institutions. Soya sauce maker Kikkoman chose the National University of Singapore to house its first research & development facility outside Japan. It invested in a food science and technology laboratory to develop new products and conduct research on the health benefits of Asian food and the safety of new products.[38]

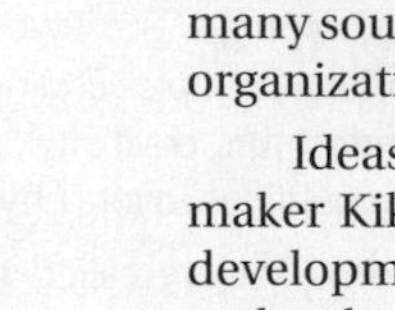
"I've got a great idea!"

"It won't work here."

"We've tried it before."

"This isn't the right time."

"It can't be done."

"It's not the way we do things."

"We've done all right without it."

"It will cost too much."
"Let's discuss it at our next meeting."

Figure 20.2 Forces Fighting New Ideas

Source: With permission of Jerold Panas, Young & Partners Inc.

CREATIVITY TECHNIQUES

Here is a sampling of techniques for stimulating creativity in individuals and groups.[39]

- ***Attribute listing***— List the attributes of an object, such as a screwdriver. Then modify each attribute, such as replacing the wooden handle with plastic, providing torque power, adding different screw heads, and so on.
- ***Forced relationships***— List several ideas and consider each one in relation to others. In designing new office furniture, for example, consider a desk, bookcase, and filing cabinet as separate ideas. One can then imagine a desk with a built-in bookcase or a desk with built-in files or a bookcase with built-in files.
- ***Morphological analysis***— Start with a problem, such as "getting something from one place to another via a powered vehicle." Now think of dimensions, such as the type of platform (cart, chair, sling, and bed), the medium (air, water, oil, and rails), and the power source (compressed air, electric motor, and magnetic fields). By listing every possible combination, one can generate many new solutions.
- ***Reverse assumption analysis***— List all the normal assumptions about an entity and then reverse them. Instead of assuming that a toy is for children, merely for entertainment, and not adaptable, reverse each assumption. Robotic pets from Japanese manufacturers did just that. The pets can provide the elderly company and monitor their health.
- ***New contexts*** — Take familiar processes, such as people-helping services, and put them into a new context. Guests at leading Asian hotels like the Shangri-La are greeted at curbside, brought to their rooms by a guest relations officer, and registered without having to go to the front desk.
- ***Mind-mapping***— Start with a thought, such as a car, write it on a piece of paper, then think of the next thought that comes up (say Hyundai), link it to car, then think of the next association (Korea), and do this with all associations that come up with each new word. Perhaps a whole new idea will materialize.

Increasingly, new product ideas arise from *lateral marketing* that combines two product concepts or ideas to create a new offering. Here are some successful examples:

- Gas station stores = gas stations + food
- Cybercafés = cafeteria + Internet
- Kinder Surprise = candy + toy
- iPod = audio + visual + portable

Idea Screening

In screening ideas, the company must avoid two types of errors. A *DROP-error* occurs when the company dismisses an otherwise good idea. It is extremely easy to find fault with other people's ideas (Figure 20.2). Some companies shudder when they look back at ideas they dismissed or breathe sighs of relief when they realize how close they came to dropping what eventually became a huge success. Sony has been humbled by several missteps. It did not anticipate the personal computer revolution or the popularity of mobile telephony. It ignored the rise of flat-panel LCD TVs, and more recently, it let Apple's iPod overtake its Walkman to become the icon of the digital music age. A DROP-error was also nearly made for the hit TV show *Friends*.

> **Friends**—The situation comedy *Friends* enjoyed a phenomenal run from 1994 to 2004. But the TV series almost wasn't shown. Its pilot episode was described as "not very entertaining, clever, or original" and was given a failing grade in an internal research report, scoring 41 out of 100. Ironically, the pilot for an earlier hit sitcom, *Seinfeld*, was also rated as "weak," although the pilot for the medical drama *ER* scored a healthy 91. Adults aged 35 and over in the sample found the *Friends* characters "smug, superficial, and self-absorbed."[40]

An idea that almost didn't get off the storyboard was the pilot for *Friends,* one of the longest-running hit comedies on television. The test episode was deemed "not very entertaining, clever, or original." Dropping an idea that later proves successful is the marketer's nightmare called a DROP-error.

A *GO-error* occurs when the company permits a poor idea to move into development and commercialization. An *absolute product failure* loses money; its sales do not cover variable costs. A *partial product failure* loses money, but its sales cover all its variable costs and some of its fixed costs. A *relative product failure* yields a profit that is less than the company's target rate of return.

> **Acer**—Taiwanese PC maker Acer had big plans for its Tablet PCs which function like laptops but also let users write with a stylus directly on the screen. The operating system was developed by Microsoft and computer manufacturers such as Acer, Fujitsu, and NEC signed up to sell the machines. Acer thought that it could sell as many as 250,000 tablets in the first year, but with only 120,000 sold, Jim Wong, president of Acer's information technology business group, could only say, "It has been a disappointment."[41]

The purpose of screening is to drop poor ideas as early as possible. The rationale is that product-development costs rise substantially with each successive development stage. Most companies require new-product ideas to be described on a standard form that can be reviewed by a new-product committee. The description states the product idea, the target market, and the competition, and roughly estimates market size, product price, development time and costs, manufacturing costs, and rate of return.

The executive committee then reviews each idea against a set of criteria. Does the product meet a need? Would it offer superior value? Can it be distinctively advertised? Does the company have the necessary know-how and capital? Will the new product deliver the expected sales volume, sales growth, and profit?

The surviving ideas can be rated using a weighted-index method like that in Table 20.4. The first column lists factors required for successful product launches, and the second column assigns importance weights. The third column scores the product idea on a scale 0–1.0, with 1.0 the highest score. The final step multiplies each factor's importance

Table 20.4 Product-Idea Rating Device

Product Success Requirements	Relative Weight (a)	Product Score (b)	Product Rating (c = a × b)
Unique or superior product	.40	.8	.32
High performance-to-cost ratio	.30	.6	.18
High marketing dollar support	.20	.7	.14
Lack of strong competition	.10	.5	.05
Total	1.00		.69[a]

[a]Rating scale: .00–.30 poor; .31–.60 fair; .61–.80 good. Minimum acceptance rate: .61.

by the product score to obtain an overall rating. In this example, the product idea scores. 69, which places it in the "good idea" level. The purpose of this basic rating device is to promote systematic evaluation and discussion. It is not supposed to make the decision for management.

As the idea moves through development, the company will constantly need to revise its estimate of the product's overall probability of success, using the following formula:

$$\text{Overall probability of success} = \text{Probability of technical completion} \times \text{Probability of commercialization given technical completion} \times \text{Probability of economic success given commercialization}$$

For example, if the three probabilities are estimated as 0.50, 0.65, and 0.74, respectively, the overall probability of success is 0.24. The company then has to judge whether this probability is high enough to warrant continued development.

Managing the Development Process: Concept to Strategy

Attractive ideas must be refined into testable product concepts. A *product idea* is a possible product the company might offer to the market. A *product concept* is an elaborated version of the idea expressed in consumer terms.

Concept Development and Testing

CONCEPT DEVELOPMENT

Let us illustrate concept development with the following situation: A large food-processing company gets the idea of producing a powder to add to milk to increase its nutritional value and taste. This is a product idea, but consumers do not buy product ideas; they buy product concepts.

(a) Product-positioning Map (Breakfast Market)

A product idea can be turned into several concepts. The first question is: who will use this product? The powder can be aimed at infants, children, teenagers, young or middle-aged adults, or older adults. Second, what primary benefit should this product provide? Taste, nutrition, refreshment, and energy? Third, when will people consume this drink? Breakfast, midmorning, lunch, midafternoon, dinner, or late evening? By answering these questions, a company can form several concepts:

- ***Concept 1*** — An instant breakfast drink for adults who want a quick nutritious breakfast without preparation.
- ***Concept 2*** — A tasty snack drink for children to drink as a midday refreshment.
- ***Concept 3*** — A health supplement for older adults to drink in the late evening before they go to bed.

Each concept represents a *category concept* that defines the product's competition. An instant breakfast drink would compete against congee, toast, *mantou*, and other breakfast alternatives. A tasty snack drink would compete against soft drinks, fruit juices, and other thirst quenchers.

(b) Brand-positioning Map (Instant Breakfast Drink Market)

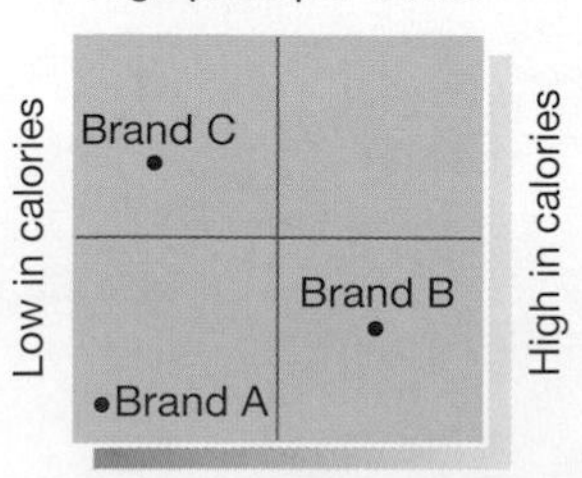

Figure 20.3 Product and Brand Positioning

Suppose the instant-breakfast-drink concept looks best. The next task is to show where this powdered product would stand in relation to other breakfast products. Figure 20.3(a) uses the two dimensions of cost and preparation time to create a *product-positioning map* for the breakfast drink. An instant breakfast drink offers low cost and quick preparation. Its nearest competitor is toast; its most distant competitor is congee. These contrasts can be utilized in communicating and promoting the concept to the market.

Next, the product concept has to be turned into a *brand concept.* Figure 20.3(b) is a brand-positioning map showing the current positions of three existing brands of instant breakfast drinks. The company needs to decide how much to charge and how calorific to make its drink. The new brand would be distinctive in the medium-price, medium-calorie market or in the high-price, high-calorie market. The company would not want to position it next to an existing brand, unless that brand is weak or inferior.

CONCEPT TESTING

Concept testing involves presenting the product concept to target consumers and getting their reactions. The concepts can be presented symbolically or physically. The more the tested concepts resemble the final product or experience, the more dependable concept testing is.

Visa—The Citibank Clear Visa Mini represents a breakthrough in card design innovation. Just 57 percent the size of a regular-sized credit card, the mini card can also be attached to a key chain. With many products such as mobile phones and laptops getting smaller to suit consumers' mobile lifestyle, Visa thought that a smaller card was in order. Before it introduced its miniature-sized card in Asia, Visa conducted an extensive focus group research among consumers aged 20–35 in five countries to test consumer reception and preference. The research results found the concept extremely well-received by consumers.[42]

In the past, creating physical prototypes was costly and time-consuming, but computer-aided design and manufacturing programs have changed that. Today firms can use *rapid prototyping* to design products (e.g., small appliances or toys) on a computer, and then produce plastic models of each. Potential consumers can view the plastic models and give their reactions.[43] Companies are also using *virtual reality* to test product concepts. Virtual reality programs use computers and sensory devices (such as gloves or goggles) to simulate reality.

Concept testing entails presenting consumers with an elaborated version of the concept. Here is the elaboration of concept one in our milk example:

Our product is a powdered mixture that is added to milk to make an instant breakfast that gives the person all the needed nutrition along with good taste and high convenience. The product would be offered in three flavors (chocolate, vanilla, and strawberry) and would come in individual packets, six to a box, at $2.49 a box.

After receiving this information, researcher measure product dimensions by having consumers respond to the following questions:

1. ***Communicability and believability***— Are the benefits clear to you and believable? If the scores are low, the concept must be refined or revised.
2. ***Need level***— Do you see this product solving a problem or filling a need for you? The stronger the need, the higher the expected consumer interest.
3. ***Gap level***— Do other products currently meet this need and satisfy you? The greater the gap, the higher the expected consumer interest. The need level can be multiplied by the gap level to produce a *need-gap score.* A high need-gap score means that the consumer sees the product as filling a strong need that is not satisfied by available alternatives.
4. ***Perceived value***— Is the price reasonable in relation to the value? The higher the perceived value, the higher the expected consumer interest.
5. ***Purchase intention***— Would you (definitely, probably, probably not, or definitely not) buy the product? This would be high for consumers who answered the previous three questions positively.
6. ***User targets, purchase occasions, purchasing frequency***— Who would use this product, and when and how often will the product be used?

Respondents' answers indicate whether the concept has a broad and strong consumer appeal, what products this new product competes against, and which consumers are the best targets. The need-gap levels and purchase-intention levels can be checked against norms for the product category to see whether the concept appears to be a winner, a long shot, or a loser. One food manufacturer rejects any concept that draws a definitely-would-buy score of less than 40 percent.

CONJOINT ANALYSIS

Consumer preferences for alternative product concepts can be measured through **conjoint analysis**, a method for deriving the utility values that consumers attach to varying levels of a product's attributes.[44] Respondents are shown different hypothetical offers formed by combining varying levels of the attributes, then asked to rank the various offers. Management can identify the most appealing offer and the estimated market share and profit the company might realize.

Green and Wind have illustrated this approach in connection with developing a new spot-removing carpet-cleaning agent for home use.[45] Suppose the new-product marketer is considering five design elements:

- Three package designs (A, B, and C).
- Three brand names (Satu, Dua, and Tiga).
- Three prices ($1.19, $1.39, and $1.59).
- A possible ISO certification (yes, no).
- A possible money-back guarantee (yes, no).

Although the researcher can form 108 possible product concepts (3 × 3 × 3 × 2 × 2), it would be too much to ask consumers to rank 108 concepts. A sample of, say, 18 contrasting product concepts can be chosen, and consumers would rank them from the most to the least preferred.

The marketer now uses a statistical program to derive the consumer's utility functions for each of the five attributes (see Figure 20.4). Utility ranges between zero and one; the higher the utility, the stronger the consumer's preference for that level of the attribute. Looking at packaging, we see that package B is the most favored, followed by C and then A (A hardly has any utility). The preferred names are Tiga, Satu, and Dua, in that order. The consumer's utility varies inversely with price. An ISO certification is preferred, but it does not add that much utility and may not be worth the effort to obtain it. A money-back guarantee is strongly preferred.

The consumer's most desired offer would be package design B, with the brand name Tiga, selling at the price of $1.19, with an ISO certification and a money-back guarantee. We can also determine the relative importance of each attribute to this consumer—the

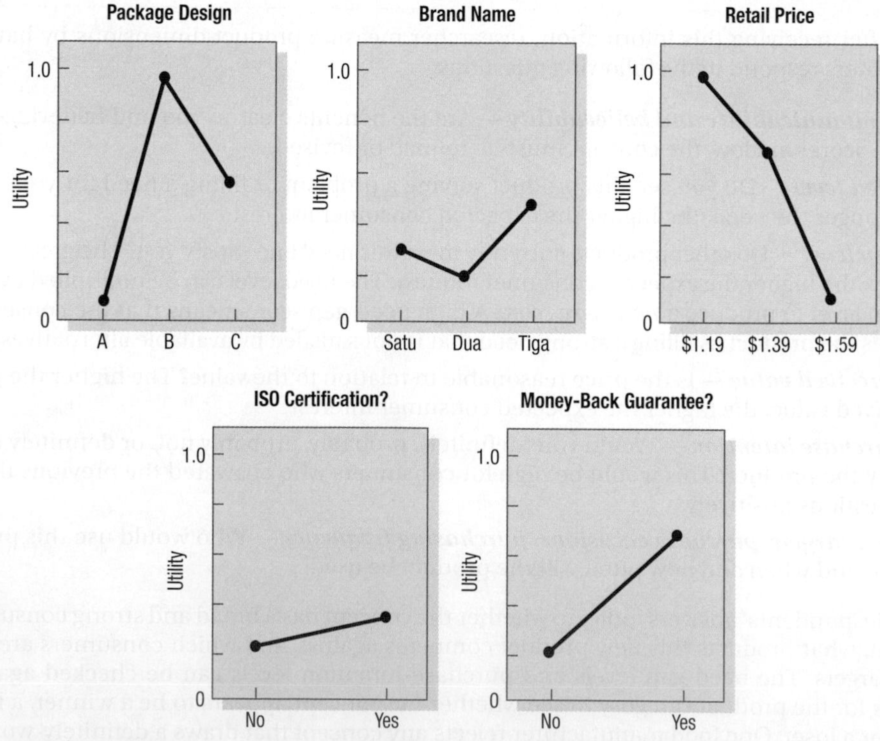

Figure 20.4 Utility Functions Based on Conjoint Analysis

difference between the highest and lowest utility level for that attribute. The greater the difference, the more important the attribute. Clearly, this consumer sees price and package design as the most important attributes, followed by money-back guarantee, brand name, and an ISO certification.

When preference data are collected from a sufficient sample of target consumers, the data can be used to estimate the market share any specific offer is likely to achieve, given any assumptions about competitive response. The company, however, may not launch the market offer that promises to gain the greatest market share because of cost considerations. The most customer-appealing offer is not always the most profitable offer to make.

Under some conditions, researchers will collect the data not with a full-profile description of each offer, but by presenting two factors at a time. For example, respondents may be shown a table with three price levels and three package types and asked which of the nine combinations they would like most, followed by which one they would prefer next, and so on. They would then be shown a further table consisting of trade-offs between two other variables. The trade-off approach may be easier to use when there are many variables and possible offers. However, it is less realistic in that respondents are focusing on only two variables at a time. Instead, adaptive conjoint analysis (ACA), a "hybrid" data collection technique that combines self-explicated importance ratings with pair wise trade-off tasks, may be used.

Marketing Strategy

Following a successful concept test, the new-product manager will develop a preliminary strategy plan for introducing the new product into the market. The plan consists of three parts. The first part describes the target market's size, structure, and behavior; the planned product positioning; and the sales, market share, and profit goals sought in the first few years:

The target market for the instant breakfast drink is families with children who are receptive to a new, convenient, nutritious, and inexpensive form of breakfast. The company's brand will be positioned at the higher-price, higher-quality end of the instant-breakfast-drink category. The company will aim initially to sell 500,000 cases or 10 percent of the market, with a loss in the first year not exceeding $1.3 million. In the second year, it will aim for 700,000 cases or 14 percent of the market, with a planned profit of $2.2 million.

The second part outlines the planned price, distribution strategy, and marketing budget for the first year:

The product will be offered in chocolate, vanilla, and strawberry in individual packets of six to a box at a retail price of $2.49 a box. There will be 48 boxes per case, and the case price to distributors will be $24. For the first two months, dealers will be offered one case free for every four cases bought, plus cooperative-advertising allowances. Free samples will be distributed door-to-door. Coupons for 20 cents off will appear in newspapers. The total sales-promotional budget will be $2.9 million. An advertising budget of $6 million, two-thirds of which will go into television and one-third into newspapers. Advertising copy will emphasize the benefit concepts of nutrition and convenience. The advertising-execution concept will revolve around a small boy who consumes the instant breakfast drink and grows strong. During the first year, $100,000 will be spent on marketing research to buy store audits and consumer-panel information to monitor market reaction and buying rates.

The third part of the marketing-strategy plan describes the long-run sales and profit goals and marketing-mix strategy over time:

The company intends to win a 25 percent market share and realize an after-tax return on investment of 12 percent. To achieve this return, product quality will start high and be improved over time through technical research. Price will initially be set at a high level and lowered gradually to expand the market and meet competition. The total promotion budget will be boosted each year by about 20 percent, with the initial advertising-sales promotion split of 65:35 evolving eventually to 50:50. Marketing research will be reduced to $60,000 per year after the first year.

Business Analysis

After management develops the product concept and marketing strategy, it can evaluate the proposal's business attractiveness. Management needs to prepare sales, cost, and profit projections to determine whether they satisfy company objectives. If they do, the concept can move to the development stage. As new information comes in, the business analysis will undergo revision and expansion.

ESTIMATING TOTAL SALES

Total estimated sales are the sum of estimated first-time sales, replacement sales, and repeat sales. Sales-estimation methods depend on whether the product is a one-time purchase (such as an engagement ring or retirement home), an infrequently purchased product, or a frequently purchased product. For one-time purchased products, sales rise at the beginning, peak, and later approach zero as the number of potential buyers is exhausted (see Figure 20.5(a)). If new buyers keep entering the market, the curve will not go down to zero.

Infrequently purchased products—such as automobiles, toasters, and industrial equipment—exhibit replacement cycles dictated by physical wearing out or by obsolescence associated with changing styles, features, and performance. Sales forecasting for this product category calls for estimating first-time sales and replacement sales separately (see Figure 20.5(b)).

Frequently purchased products, such as consumer and industrial non-durables, have product life-cycle sales resembling Figure 20.5(c). The number of first-time buyers initially increases and then decreases as fewer buyers are left (assuming a fixed population). Repeat purchases occur soon, providing that the product satisfies some buyers. The sales curve eventually falls to a plateau representing a level of steady repeat-purchase volume; by this time, the product is no longer a new product.

In estimating sales, the manager's first task is to estimate first-time purchases of the new product in each period. To estimate replacement sales, management has to research the product's *survival-age distribution*—that is, the number of units that fail in year one, two, three, and so on. The low end of the distribution indicates when the first replacement sales will take place. The actual timing will be influenced by a variety of factors. Because replacement sales are difficult to estimate before the product is in use, some manufacturers base the decision to launch a new product solely on the estimate of first-time sales.

For a frequently purchased new product, the seller has to estimate repeat sales as well as first-time sales. A high rate of repeat purchasing means that customers are satisfied; sales are likely to stay high even after all first-time purchases take place. The seller should note the percentage of repeat purchases that take place in each repeat-purchase class: those who rebuy once, twice, three times, and so on. Some products and brands are bought a few times and dropped.[46]

(a) One-time Purchased Product

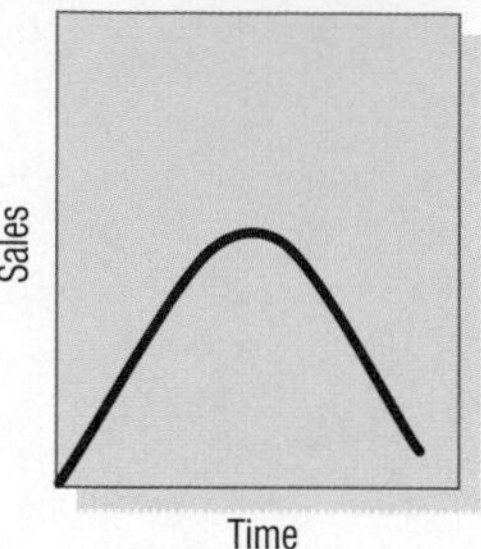

(b) Infrequently Purchased Product

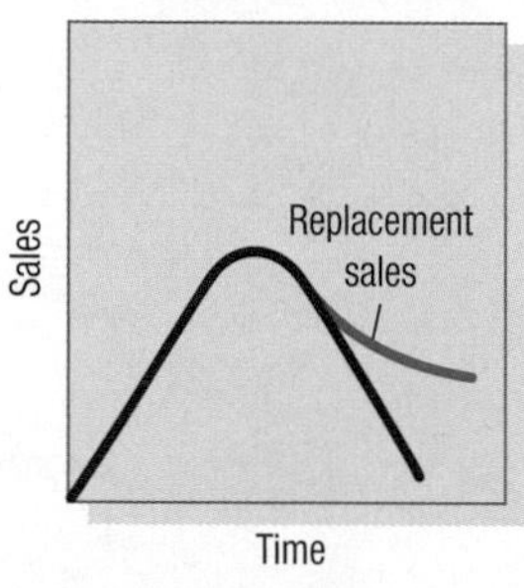

(c) Frequently Purchased Product

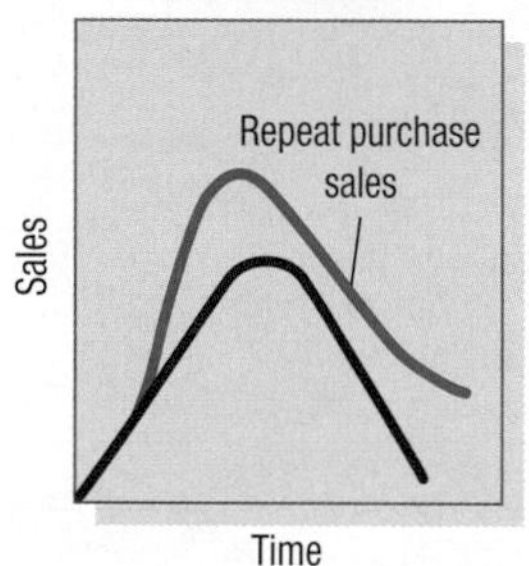

Figure 20.5 Product Life-Cycle Sales for Three Types of Products

ESTIMATING COSTS AND PROFITS

Costs are estimated by the R&D, manufacturing, marketing, and finance departments. Table 20.5 illustrates a five-year projection of sales, costs, and profits for the instant breakfast drink.

Row 1 shows the projected sales revenue over the five-year period. The company expects to sell $11,889,000 (approximately 500,000 cases at $24 per case) in the first year. Behind this sales projection is a set of assumptions about the rate of market growth, the company's market share, and the factory-realized price. *Row 2* shows the cost of goods sold, which hovers around 33 percent of sales revenue. This cost is found by estimating the average cost of labor, ingredients, and packaging per case. *Row 3* shows the expected gross margin, which is the difference between sales revenue and cost of goods sold.

Row 4 shows anticipated development costs of $3.5 million, including product-development cost, marketing-research costs, and manufacturing-development costs. *Row 5* shows the estimated marketing costs over the five-year period to cover advertising, sales promotion, and marketing research and an amount allocated for sales-force coverage and marketing administration. *Row 6* shows the allocated overhead to this new product to cover its share of the cost of executive salaries, heat, light, and so on.

Row 7, the gross contribution, is found by subtracting the preceding three costs from the gross margin. *Row 8*, the supplementary contribution, lists any change in income from

Table 20.5 Projected Five-Year Cash Flow Statement (in thousands of dollars)

	Year 0	Year 1	Year 2	Year 3	Year 4	Year 5
1. Sales revenue	$0	$11,889	$15,381	$19,654	$28,253	$32,491
2. Cost of goods sold	0	3,981	5,150	6,581	9,461	10,880
3. Gross margin	0	7,908	10,231	13,073	18,792	21,611
4. Development costs	-3,500	0	0	0	0	0
5. Marketing costs	0	8,000	6,460	8,255	11,866	13,646
6. Allocated overhead	0	1,189	1,538	1,965	2,825	3,249
7. Gross contribution	-3,500	-1,281	2,233	2,853	4,101	4,716
8. Supplementary contribution	0	0	0	0	0	0
9. Net contribution	-3,500	-1,281	2,233	2,853	4,101	4,716
10. Discounted contribution (15%)	-3,500	-1,113	1,691	1,877	2,343	2,346
11. Cumulative discounted cash flow	-3,500	-4,613	-2,922	-1,045	1,298	3,644

other company products caused by the introduction of the new product. It has two components. *Dragalong income* is additional income on other company products resulting from adding this product to the line. *Cannibalized income* is the reduced income on other company products resulting from adding this product to the line.[47] Table 20.5 assumes no supplementary contributions. *Row 9* shows the net contribution, which in this case is the same as the gross contribution. *Row 10* shows the discounted contribution—that is, the present value of each future contribution discounted at 15 percent per annum. For example, the company will not receive $4,716,000 until the fifth year. This amount is worth only $2,346,000 today if the company can earn 15 percent on its money through other investments.[48]

Finally, *Row 11* shows the cumulative discounted cash flow, which is the cumulation of the annual contributions in *Row 10*. Two things are of central interest. The first is the maximum investment exposure, which is the highest loss that the project can create. We see that the company will be in a maximum loss position of $4,613,000 in the first year. The second is the payback period, which is the time when the company recovers all of its investment, including the built-in return of 15 percent. The payback period here is approximately three and a half years. Management therefore has to decide whether to risk a maximum investment loss of $4.6 million and a possible payback period of three and a half years.

Companies use other financial measures to evaluate the merit of a new-product proposal. The simplest is **break-even analysis**, in which management estimates how many units of the product the company would have to sell to break even with the given price and cost structure. Or the estimate may be in terms of how many years it will take to break even. If management believes sales could easily reach the break-even number, it is likely to move the project into product development.

A more complex method of estimating profit is **risk analysis**. Here three estimates (optimistic, pessimistic, and most likely) are obtained for each uncertain variable affecting profitability under an assumed marketing environment and marketing strategy for the planning period. The computer simulates possible outcomes and computes a rate-of-return probability distribution showing the range of possible rates of returns and their probabilities.[49]

Managing the Development Process: Development to Commercialization

Up to now, the product has existed only as a word description, a drawing, or a prototype. This next step involves a jump in investment that dwarfs the costs incurred in the earlier stages. At this stage the company will determine whether the product idea can be translated into a technically and commercially feasible product. If it cannot, the accumulated project cost will be lost except for any useful information gained in the process.

The Virgin Group is widely admired by many in the UK for its culture of exploring new opportunities in highly competitive markets. However, many have questioned the wisdom of extending the umbrella brand with the launch of Virgin Media, set up as a rival to Rupert Murdoch's BSkyB. To learn more, visit www.pearsoned.co.uk/marketingmanagementeurope.

Product Development

The job of translating target customer requirements into a working prototype is helped by a set of methods known as *quality function deployment* (QFD). The methodology takes the list of desired *customer attributes* (CAs) generated by market research and turns them into a list of *engineering attributes* (EAs) that the engineers can use. For example, customers of a proposed truck may want a certain acceleration rate (CA). Engineers can turn this into the required horsepower and other engineering equivalents (EAs). The methodology permits measuring the trade-offs and costs of providing the customer requirements. A major contribution of QFD is that it improves communication between marketers, engineers, and the manufacturing people.[50]

PHYSICAL PROTOTYPES

The R&D department will develop one or more physical versions of the product concept. Its goal is to find a prototype that embodies the key attributes described in the product-concept statement, that performs safely under normal use and conditions, and that can be produced within the budgeted manufacturing costs. Developing and manufacturing a successful prototype can take days, weeks, months, or even years. Sophisticated virtual-reality technology is speeding the process. By designing and testing product designs through simulation, for example, companies achieve the flexibility to respond to new information and to resolve uncertainties by quickly exploring alternatives.

Boeing—Boeing designed its 777 aircraft on a totally digital basis. Engineers, designers, and more than 500 suppliers designed the aircraft on a special computer network without ever making a blueprint on paper. Its partners were connected by an extranet enabling them to communicate, share ideas, and work on the design at a distance. A computer-generated "human" could climb inside the three-dimensional design on-screen to show how difficult maintenance access would be for a live mechanic. Such computer modeling allowed engineers to spot design errors that otherwise would have remained undiscovered until a person began to work on a physical prototype. Avoiding the time and cost associated with building physical prototypes reduced development time, scrappage, and rework by 60–90 percent.[51]

Lab scientists must not only design the product's functional characteristics, but also communicate its psychological aspects through physical cues. How will consumers react to different colors, sizes, and weights? In the case of a mouthwash, a yellow color supports an "antiseptic" claim (Listerine), a red color supports a "refreshing" claim (Colgate), and a green or blue color supports a "cool" claim (Darlie). Marketers need to supply lab people with information on what attributes consumers seek and how consumers judge whether these attributes are present.

CUSTOMER TESTS

When the prototypes are ready, they must be put through rigorous functional tests and *customer tests. Alpha testing* is the name given to testing the product within the firm to see how it performs in different applications. After refining the prototype further, the company moves to *beta testing* with customers.[52] It enlists a set of customers to use the prototype and give feedback.

Consumer testing can take several forms, from bringing consumers into a laboratory to giving them samples to use in their homes. Procter & Gamble has on-site labs such as a diaper-testing center where dozens of mothers bring their babies to be studied. To develop its Cover Girl Outlast all-day lip color, P&G invited 500 women to come to its labs each morning to apply the lipstick, record their activities, and return eight hours later so it could measure remaining lip color, resulting in a product that came with a tube of glossy moisturizer that women can reapply on top of their color without having to look at a mirror. In-home placement tests are common for products ranging from ice cream flavors to new appliances.

How do we measure customer preferences? The *rank-order* method asks the consumer to rank the options. The *paired-comparison* method presents pairs of options and asks the consumer which one is preferred in each pair. The *monadic-rating* method asks the consumer to rate each product on a scale so marketers can derive the individual's preference order and levels.

Market Testing

After management is satisfied with functional and psychological performance, the product is ready to be dressed up with a brand name and packaging, and put into a market test. The new product is introduced into an authentic setting to learn how large the market is and how consumers and dealers react to handling, using, and repurchasing the product.

For example, Singapore and other Asian markets are used for market testing Coca-Cola and Disney innovations because of their ability to adapt to and adopt new ideas:

Coca-Cola—Along with Malaysia and Hawaii, Singapore is a test market for Coca-Cola's new "Style-A-Coke" shrinkwrap system. Upon purchase, customers in selected 7-Eleven stores can customize their Coke bottle by choosing from four designs on the spot at no extra cost. There is no advertising campaign for this initiative. The test markets were chosen because of their multiethnic populations. The likelihood of a regional rollout depends upon the success of these trials. Other Coca-Cola innovations test-marketed in Singapore include the cashless vending machine and a Dial-A-Coke vending machine that allows consumers to use their mobile phones to purchase cans of Coke.[53]

Disney—Walt Disney believes that tailoring its cartoon characters to Asian tastes will help boost revenues from its regional operations. Hence, Singapore is used as its test market for a new range of adapted electronic products starting with MP3 players, radios, and home appliances such as popcorn-makers. Walt Disney uses Singapore along with China and South Korea as test markets for these branded electronics which will have localized designs to suit Asian children's tastes.[54]

Some Asian businesses do not undertake market testing, believing that it is costly and might delay the launch of the product. Others feel that they are sufficiently familiar with the market to bypass this stage or fear that competitors might get wind of their new products and imitate them. However, market testing can yield valuable information about buyers, dealers, marketing program effectiveness, and market potential. The main issues are: how much market testing should be done, and what kind(s)?

The amount of market testing is influenced by the investment cost and risk on the one hand, and the time pressure and research cost on the other. High investment-high risk products, where the chance of failure is high, must be market tested; the cost of the market tests will be an insignificant percentage of the total project cost. High-risk products—those that create new-product categories (first instant breakfast drink) or have novel features (first gum-strengthening toothpaste)—warrant more market testing than modified products (another toothpaste brand).

The amount of market testing may be severely reduced if the company is under great time pressure because the season is just starting or because competitors are about to launch their brands. The company may thus prefer the risk of a product failure to the risk of losing distribution or market penetration on a highly successful product.

CONSUMER-GOODS MARKET TESTING

In testing consumer products, the company seeks to estimate four variables: *trial, first repeat, adoption,* and *purchase frequency.* The company hopes to find all these variables at high levels. In some cases, it will find many consumers trying the product but few rebuying it; or it might find high permanent adoption but low purchase frequency (as with gourmet frozen foods).

Here are four major methods of consumer-goods market testing, from the least to the most costly.

Sales-Wave Research

In *sales-wave research,* consumers who initially try the product at no cost are re-offered the product, or a competitor's product, at slightly reduced prices. They might be re-offered the product as many as three to five times (sales waves), with the company noting how many customers selected that product again and their reported level of satisfaction. Sales-wave research can also expose consumers to one or more advertising concepts to see the impact of that advertising on repeat purchase.

Sales-wave research can be implemented quickly, conducted with a fair amount of security, and carried out without final packaging and advertising. However, it does not indicate the trial rates that would be achieved with different sales-promotion incentives, because the consumers are preselected to try the product; nor does it indicate the brand's power to gain distribution and favorable shelf position.

Simulated Test Marketing

Simulated test marketing calls for finding 30–40 qualified shoppers and questioning them about brand familiarity and preferences in a specific product category. These people are then invited to a brief screening of both well-known and new commercials or print ads. One ad advertises the new product, but it is not singled out for attention. Consumers receive a small amount of money and are invited into a store where they may buy any item. The company notes how many consumers buy the new brand and competing brands. This provides a measure of the ad's relative effectiveness against competing ads in stimulating trial. Consumers are asked the reasons for their purchases or non-purchases. Those who did not buy the new brand are given a free sample. Some weeks later, they are reinterviewed by phone to determine product attitudes, usage, satisfaction, and repurchase intention and are offered an opportunity to repurchase any product.

This method gives fairly accurate results on advertising effectiveness and trial rates (and repeat rates if extended) in a much shorter time and at a fraction of the cost of using real test markets. Pretests often take only three months and may cost $250,000.[55] The results are incorporated into new-product forecasting models to project ultimate sales levels. Marketing research firms report surprisingly accurate predictions of sales levels of products that are subsequently launched in the market.[56]

Controlled Test Marketing

In this method, a research firm manages a panel of stores that will carry new products for a fee. The company with the new product specifies the number of stores and geographic locations it wants to test. The research firm delivers the product to the participating stores and controls shelf position; number of facings, displays, and point-of-purchase promotions; and pricing. Sales results can be measured through electronic scanners at the checkout. The company can also evaluate the impact of local advertising and promotions.

Controlled test marketing allows the company to test the impact of in-store factors and limited advertising on buying behavior. A sample of consumers can be interviewed later to give their impressions of the product. The company does not have to use its own sales force, give trade allowances, or "buy" distribution. However, controlled test marketing provides no information on how to sell the trade on carrying the new product. This technique also exposes the product and its features to competitors' scrutiny.

Test Markets

The ultimate way to test a new consumer product is to put it into full-blown test markets. The company chooses a few representative cities, and the sales force tries to sell the trade on carrying the product and giving it good shelf exposure. The company puts on a full advertising and promotion campaign similar to the one it would use in national marketing. Test marketing also permits testing the impact of alternative marketing plans by varying the marketing program in different cities: the cost of a full-scale test will depend on the number of test cities, the test duration, and the amount of data the company wants to collect.

Management faces several decisions:

1. ***How many test cities?*** — Most tests use between two and six cities. The greater the maximum possible loss, the greater the number of contending marketing strategies, the greater the regional differences, and the greater the chance of test-market interference by competitors, the greater the number of cities that should be used.
2. ***Which cities?*** — Each company must develop selection criteria such as having good media coverage, cooperative chain stores, and average competitive activity.
3. ***Length of test?*** — Market tests last anywhere from a few months to a year. The longer the average repurchase period, the longer the test period.
4. ***What information?*** — Warehouse shipment data will show gross inventory buying but will not indicate weekly sales at the retail level. Store audits will show retail sales and competitors' market shares but will not reveal buyer characteristics. Consumer panels will indicate which people are buying which brands and their loyalty and switching rates. Buyer surveys will yield in-depth information about consumer attitudes, usage, and satisfaction.
5. ***What action to take?*** — If the test markets show high trial and repurchase rates, the product should be launched nationally; if they show a high trial rate and a low repurchase rate, the product should be redesigned or dropped; if they show a low trial rate and a high repurchase rate, the product is satisfying but more people have to try it. This means increasing advertising and sales promotion. If trial and repurchase rates are both low, the product should be abandoned.

Despite its benefits, many companies today skip test marketing and rely on faster and more economical testing methods. Colgate-Palmolive often launches a new product in a set of small "lead countries" and keeps rolling it out if it proves successful.

BUSINESS-GOODS MARKET TESTING

Business goods can also benefit from market testing. Expensive industrial goods and new technologies will normally undergo alpha testing (within the company) and beta testing (with outside customers). During beta testing, the vendor's technical people observe how test customers use the product, a practice that often exposes unanticipated problems of safety and servicing and alerts the vendor to customer training and servicing requirements. The vendor can also observe how much value the equipment adds to the customer's operation as a clue to subsequent pricing.

The vendor will ask the test customers to express their purchase intention and other reactions after the test. Vendors must carefully interpret the beta test results because only a small number of test customers are used, they are not randomly drawn, and the tests are somewhat customized to each site. Another risk is that test customers who are unimpressed with the product may leak unfavorable reports about it.

A second common test method for business goods is to introduce the new product at trade shows. The vendor can observe how much interest buyers show in the new product, how they react to various features and terms, and how many express purchase intentions or place orders. Numerous international trade shows are conducted all over Asia in a wide variety of industries. In Taiwan alone, there are trade shows featuring semiconductor equipment and materials, textile machinery, electronic components and equipment, food machinery and technology, packaging, and woodworking machinery and supplies. However, trade shows reveal the product to competitors. Thus the vendor should be ready to launch the product soon after the trade show.

New industrial products can be tested in distributor and dealer display rooms, where they may stand next to the manufacturer's other products and possibly competitors' products. This method yields preference and pricing information in the product's normal selling atmosphere. The disadvantages are that the customers might want to place early orders that cannot be filled, and those customers who come in might not represent the target market.

Industrial manufacturers come close to using full test marketing when they give a limited supply of the product to the sales force to sell in a limited number of areas that receive promotion support and printed catalog sheets.

Commercialization

If the company goes ahead with commercialization, it will face its largest costs to date. The company will have to contract for manufacture or build or rent a full-scale manufacturing facility. Another major cost is marketing. To introduce a major new consumer packaged good into the market, the company will have to spend a hefty amount in advertising, promotion, and other communications in the first year. In the introduction of new food products, marketing expenditures typically represent about 60 percent of sales during the first year. Most new-product campaigns rely on a sequenced mix of market communication tools.

WHEN (TIMING)

In commercializing a new product, market-entry timing is critical. Suppose a company has almost completed the development work on its new product and learns that a competitor is nearing the end of its development work. The company faces three choices:

1. ***First entry*** — The first firm entering a market usually enjoys the "first mover advantages" of locking up key distributors and customers and gaining leadership. But if the product is rushed to market before it is thoroughly debugged, the first entry can backfire.
2. ***Parallel entry*** — The firm might time its entry to coincide with the competitor's entry. The market may pay more attention when two companies are advertising the new product.
3. ***Late entry*** — The firm might delay its launch until after the competitor has entered. The competitor will have borne the cost of educating the market, and its product may reveal faults the late entrant can avoid. The late entrant can also learn the size of the market.

The timing decision involves additional considerations. If a new product replaces an older product, the company might delay the introduction until the old product's stock is drawn down. If the product is seasonal, it might be delayed until the right season arrives;[57] often a product waits for a "killer application" to occur. Complicating new product launches, many companies are encountering competitive "design-arounds"—rivals are imitating inventions but making their own versions just different enough to avoid patent infringement and the need to pay royalties.

WHERE (GEOGRAPHIC STRATEGY)

The company must decide whether to launch the new product in a single locality, a region, several regions, the national market, or the international market. Most will develop a planned market rollout over time. Many companies entering China first launch their products in more affluent major coastal cities before going inland. Here is an exception:

> **ATG**—This auto components joint-venture company is located in Anqing, in Anhui province, well away from China's coastal areas. In setting up its operations and building its factory, ATG received fast and favorable treatment from local officials keen on attracting foreign investment. Local competition was also less severe. Within five years, ATG was the market leader.[58]

Company size is an important factor here. Small companies will select an attractive city and put on a blitz campaign. They will enter other cities one at a time. Large companies will introduce their product into a whole region and then move to the next region. Companies with national distribution networks will launch their new products nationally.

Most companies design new products to sell primarily in the domestic market. If the product does well, the company considers exporting to neighboring countries or the world market, redesigning if necessary. Cooper and Kleinschmidt found that domestic industrial products designed solely for the domestic market tend to show a high failure rate, low market share, and low growth. In contrast, those designed for the world market—or at least to include neighboring countries—achieve significantly more profits, both at home and abroad. Yet only 17 percent of the products in Cooper and Kleinschmidt's study were designed with an international orientation.[59] The implication is that companies should adopt an international focus in designing and developing new products. Interestingly, some of the best product ideas from the developing world have the potential for catching on everywhere, including mature markets like the U.S.

TeleVital—The founder of this company, Kishore Kumar, first developed a simple PC-based remote health-monitoring system for distant villages in his native India. Now TeleVital is marketing the technology to the U.S. Its first U.S. customer, Battle Mountain General Hospital in Nevada, could not afford patient-monitoring equipment or the people to operate it. Now it is hooking up with a hospital 100 miles away to track its patients. Said its administrator, "We in rural America can really use equipment like this."[60]

In choosing rollout markets, the major criteria are market potential, company's local reputation, cost of filling the pipeline, cost of communication media, influence of area on other areas, and competitive penetration. The presence of strong competitors will influence rollout strategy. Suppose McDonald's wants to launch a new chain of fast-food Chinese pork buns in China. One formidable competitor is strongly entrenched in eastern China. Another chain is entrenched in the west but is weak. The north is the battleground between two other chains. The south is open, but another competitive chain is planning to move in. McDonald's faces a complex decision in choosing a geographic rollout strategy.

With the Web connecting far-flung parts of the globe, competition is more likely to cross national borders. Companies are increasingly rolling out new products simultaneously across the globe, rather than nationally or even regionally. However, masterminding a global launch poses challenges.

TO WHOM (TARGET-MARKET PROSPECTS)

Within the rollout markets, the company must target its initial distribution and promotion to the best prospect groups. Presumably, the company has already profiled the prime prospects, who would ideally have the following characteristics: They would be early adopters, heavy users, and opinion leaders, and they could be reached at a low cost.[61] Few groups have all these characteristics. The company should rate the various prospect groups on these characteristics and target the best group. The aim is to generate strong sales as soon as possible to attract further prospects.

HOW (INTRODUCTORY MARKET STRATEGY)

The company must develop an action plan for introducing the new product into the rollout markets. Because new-product launches often take longer and cost more money than expected, many potentially successful offerings suffer from underfunding. It's important to allocate sufficient time and resources—but also not to overspend—as the new product gains traction in the marketplace.[62]

A master of new-product introductions, Apple Computer staged a massive marketing blitz in 1998 to launch the iMac, its re-entry into the computer PC business after a hiatus of 14 years. Five years later, Apple struck gold again with the launch of the iPod. "Breakthrough Marketing: Apple" gives the details.

To coordinate the many activities involved in launching a new product, management can use network-planning techniques such as critical path scheduling. **Critical path scheduling (CPS)** calls for developing a master chart showing the simultaneous and sequential activities that must take place to launch the product. By estimating how much time each activity takes, the planners estimate completion time for the entire project. Any delay in any activity on the critical path will cause the project to be delayed. If the launch must be completed earlier, the planner searches for ways to reduce time along the critical path.[63]

BREAKTHROUGH • MARKETING

APPLE iPod

In a few short years, the iPod MP3 music player has truly become a cultural phenomenon. Few people are without one. The iPod exemplified Apple's innovative design skills and looked, felt, and operated like no other. With the launch of iTunes Music Store, a dynamic duo of legally downloadable music and a cutting-edge portable music player caused iPod sales to skyrocket. To the delight of Apple (and the chagrin of competitor Sony), the iPod has become "the Walkman of the 21st century."

Beyond spurring sales, the iPod has been central in changing the way people listen to and use music. The shuffle feature of iPods helped people make connections between different genres of music. According to musician John Mayer, "People feel they're walking through musicology" when they use their iPods, leading them to listen to more music, and with more passion. Podcasting enables users to replace radio broadcasts and listen to DJ sets without commercial interruption. The new video, photo, and phone features have the potential to change how people interact with those media as well.

The campaign for the Apple iPod was a masterful new-product introduction that helped the product quickly achieve a dominant market share.

Apple reached this impressive state of market domination through a combination of shrewd product innovation and clever marketing. It defined a broad access point for its target market—music lovers who wanted *their* music, whenever and wherever. The marketing effort was designed to appeal to Mac fans as well as people who had not used Apple products in the past. This broader access required a shift in Apple's channel strategies.

Besides this enhanced "push" effort, Apple also developed memorable, creative "pull" advertising that helped drive the popularity of the iPod. The Silhouettes campaign ran all over the world with a message simple enough to work across cultures, portraying the iPod as cool, but not so cool as to be beyond the reach of anyone who enjoyed music. Television commercials featured people in silhouette listening to iPods and dancing in front of neon backgrounds. Similar images populated print ads, billboards, and posters. Ad text such as "*iPod. Welcome to the digital music revolution. 10,000 songs in your pocket. Mac or PC*" told the story of iPod's capabilities in a simple, appealing way.

Apple's campaign also flooded a handful of big cities such as San Francisco and Shanghai with iPod billboards, bus posters, print ads, and TV commercials that were intended to spread the message "iPod is everywhere." The brand enjoyed exceedingly strong PR, buzz, and word of mouth. Apple has continually updated the iPod and released new versions, spawning an "iPod economy" of third-party accessories and add-ons. Even though some analysts thought sales might slow, consumers have continued to snap up the music players. By April 2007, more than 100 million iPods had been sold worldwide and the iPod contributed one-third of Apple's corporate revenue. A halo effect from iPod was thought to help explain Apple's increase in market share in retail computers of more than three percentage points in recent years. With the launch of the iPod touch, revenue grew at a faster 17 percent rate in 2008. Apple hopes to repeat the success of the iPod with its launch of the iPhone 3G.

Source: Terril Yue Jones, "How Long Can the iPod Stay on Top?" *Los Angeles Times*, March 5, 2006; Beth Snyder Bulik, "Grab an Apple and a Bag of Chips." *Advertising Age*, May 23, 2005; Jay Parsons, "A Is for Apple on iPod." *Dallas Morning News*, October 6, 2005; Peter Burrows, "Rock On, iPod." *BusinessWeek*, June 7, 2004, pp. 130–31; Jay Lyman, "Mini iPod Moving Quickly, Apple Says." *TechNewsWorld*, February 26, 2004; Steven Levy, "iPod Nation." *Newsweek*, July 25, 2004; <www.apple.com>; <www.effie.org>; "Apple Computer: iPod Silhouettes." New York Marketing Association; Saul Hansell, "Can the Touch Revive Apple's iPod Sales?" <www.bits.blogs.nytimes.com>, January 22, 2008; <www.apple.com/iphone>.

The Consumer-Adoption Process

Adoption is an individual's decision to become a regular user of a product. How do potential customers learn about new products, try them, and adopt or reject them? The *consumer-adoption process* is later followed by the *consumer-loyalty process*, which is the concern of the established producer. Years ago, new-product marketers used a *mass market approach* to launch products. This approach had two main drawbacks: It called for heavy marketing expenditures, and it involved many wasted exposures. These drawbacks led to a second approach, *heavy-user target marketing*. This approach makes sense, provided that heavy users are identifiable and are early adopters. However, even within the heavy-user group, many heavy users are loyal to existing brands. New-product marketers now aim at consumers who are early adopters.

Stages in the Adoption Process

An **innovation** is any good, service, or idea that is *perceived* by someone as new. The idea may have a long history, but it is an innovation to the person who sees it as new. Innovations take time to spread through the social system. Rogers defines the **innovation diffusion process** as "the spread of a new idea from its source of invention or creation to its ultimate users or adopters."[64] The consumer-adoption process focuses on the mental process through which an individual passes from first hearing about an innovation to final adoption.[65]

Adopters of new products have been observed to move through five stages:

1. ***Awareness*** — The consumer becomes aware of the innovation but lacks information about it.
2. ***Interest*** — The consumer is stimulated to seek information about the innovation.
3. ***Evaluation*** — The consumer considers whether to try the innovation.
4. ***Trial*** — The consumer tries the innovation to improve his or her estimate of its valuc.
5. ***Adoption*** — The consumer decides to make full and regular use of the innovation.

The new-product marketer should facilitate movement through these stages. A portable electric-dishwasher manufacturer might discover that many consumers are stuck in the interest stage; they do not buy because of their uncertainty and the large investment cost. But these same consumers would be willing to use an electric dishwasher on a trial basis for a small monthly fee. The manufacturer should consider offering a trial-use plan with an option to buy.

Factors Influencing the Adoption Process

Marketers recognize the following characteristics of the adoption process: differences in individual readiness to try new products; the effect of personal influence; differing rates of adoption; and differences in organizations' readiness to try new products.

READINESS TO TRY NEW PRODUCTS AND PERSONAL INFLUENCE

Everett Rogers defines a person's level of innovativeness as "the degree to which an individual is relatively earlier in adopting new ideas than the other members of his social system." In each product area, there are pioneers and early adopters. Some people are the first to adopt new clothing fashions or new appliances; some doctors are the first to prescribe new medicines; and some farmers are the first to adopt new farming methods.[66] People can be classified into the adopter categories shown in Figure 20.6. After a slow start, an increasing number of people adopt the innovation, the number reaches a peak, and then it diminishes as fewer non-adopters remain. The five adopter groups differ in their value orientations and their motives for adopting or resisting the new product.[67]

- **Innovators** are technology enthusiasts and are venturesome and enjoy tinkering with new products and mastering their intricacies. In return for low prices, they are happy to conduct alpha and beta testing and report on early weaknesses.
- **Early adopters** are opinion leaders who carefully search for new technologies that might give them a dramatic competitive advantage. They are less price-sensitive and willing to adopt the product if given personalized solutions and good service support.

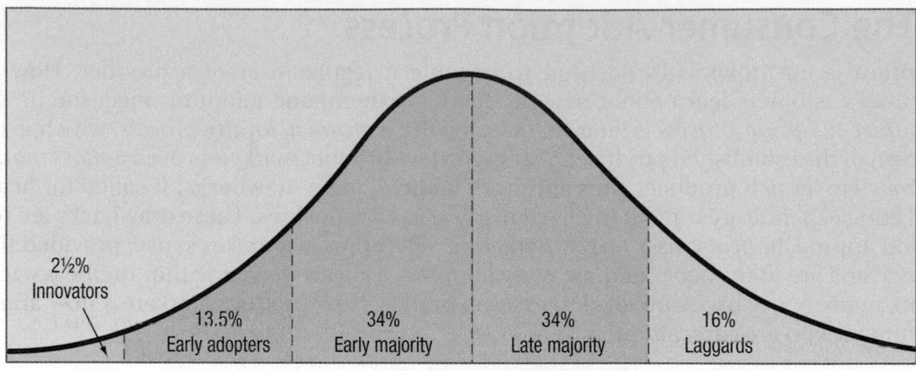

Figure 20.6 Adopter Categorization on the Basis of Relative Time of Adoption of Innovations

Source: Redrawn from Everett M. Rogers, *Diffusion of Innovation*, (New York: Free Press, 1983). Reprinted with permission of The Free Press, a Division of Simon & Schuster Adult Publishing Group, from *Diffusion of Innovation* by Everett M. Rogers. Copyright © 1962, 1971, 1983 by The Free Press. All rights reserved.

- **Early majority** are deliberate pragmatists who adopt the new technology when its benefits are proven and a lot of adoption has already taken place. They make up the mainstream market.
- **Late majority** are skeptical conservatives who are risk-averse, technology-shy, and price-sensitive.
- **Laggards** are tradition-bound and resist the innovation until they find that the status quo is no longer defensible.

Each of the five groups must be approached with a different type of marketing if the firm wants to move its innovation through the full product life cycle.[68]

Personal influence is the effect one person has on another's attitude or purchase probability. Although personal influence is an important factor, its significance is greater in some situations and for some individuals than for others. Personal influence is more important in the evaluation stage of the adoption process than in the other stages. It has more influence on late adopters than early adopters. It also is more important in risky situations. Companies often target innovators and early adopters with product rollouts.

Near-water drinks—These drinks are the rage among trendy young Japanese. Fizzy, still, sweetened with fruit juice, and enhanced with vitamins and minerals, they are priced as much as 25 percent more than plain bottled water. Until recently, Japanese "office ladies" in their 20s and 30s were important trend-setters. But as companies cut salaries and bonuses, these office workers became more reluctant to spend. Instead, teenagers have emerged as the big spenders and trend-setters. Kirin, which launched the first near-water brand Supli, believes that the way to start a trend in Japan is to get high school girls to buy the product. Its market research reveals that young women want healthy drinks that keep the sweetness of juice without the calories. This fulfills a need for a drink between tasteless tea and too-fruity sports drinks.

Asians may be more susceptible to personal influence than American consumers. Because Confucianism is part of their background, East Asians are more collectivistic and motivated toward conforming to the norms of their reference groups. The concern about not "losing face" (i.e., maintaining their social status and prestige) leads East Asians to care more deeply about others' perceptions of themselves.[69] For example, it is not unusual to find South Koreans living in the same area (e.g., an apartment building) consuming products and brands purchased from the same stores.[70] Social approval is thus more important in increasing product trial and adoption in Asia than in the U.S. Gaining acceptance for an innovation relies more on accessing the Asian consumer's referral network and utilizing positive word of mouth than in the U.S.[71]

For instance, home shopping parties have been effective in Japan as they leverage the culture's tight social structure. The success of direct selling organizations like Tupperware, Avon, and Amway in Japan, all of whom employ multilevel marketing, attests to the importance of referral networks in new-product adoption.[72] Advertising can also be employed to stimulate and simulate positive word-of-mouth.

However, the impact of personal influence varies across Asian consumers and products. High context Asian societies like Japan, South Korea, and Taiwan have homogeneous populations sharing similar cultural and socioeconomic backgrounds. The transfer of ideas occurs more frequently between individuals under these similar circumstances than, say in Singapore, where there are more subcultures. Thus the word-of-mouth effect has been found to be stronger in Japan, South Korea, and Taiwan than in the U.S. for such consumer durables as room airconditioners, washing machines, cars, refrigerators, radios, TVs, vacuum cleaners, and calculators.[73] In contrast, a Singapore study found that personal influence was less strong for such non-durables as laundry detergent and shampoo compared to the performance characteristics of these products.[74]

Similarly, a study on Internet adoption in 50 countries showed that countries high on individualism had a greater rate of Internet adoption than countries that were more collectivistic. Internet adoption also increases as power distance decreases. This means that the more exchange between people of different statuses, the greater the level of Internet adoption. Countries that tended to avoid uncertainty adopted the Internet less than those that were more inclined to embrace uncertainty. The results imply that Asian countries like Pakistan, the Philippines, Taiwan, Thailand, and Japan—which tend to be collectivistic, with higher power distance, and less tolerance for uncertainty—would have slower Internet adoption.[75]

CHARACTERISTICS OF THE INNOVATION

Some products catch on immediately (rollerblades), whereas others take a long time to gain acceptance (diesel engine autos). Five characteristics influence the rate of adoption of an innovation. We will consider them in relation to the adoption of Sony's PlayStation Portable (PSP).[76]

The first is *relative advantage*—the degree to which the innovation appears superior to existing products. The greater the perceived relative advantage of using a PSP, say, for portability and graphics, the faster it will be adopted. The PSP packs all the graphics power of the PlayStation into a sleek, battery-powered device that is built around a dazzling 10.5-cm color LCD display. The images are much sharper and brighter, and the stereo sound crisp. Besides games, it is also a portable music and movie player. The second is *compatibility*—the degree to which the innovation matches the values and experiences of the individuals. PSPs, for example, are highly compatible with avid videogamers who want convenience and all in one. Third is *complexity*—the degree to which the innovation is relatively difficult to understand or use. Sony has made it unnecessarily hard and expensive to move music, photos, and movies to and from the PSP. One has to use Sony's proprietary Memory Stick Duo flash memory cards to do so. The PSP music software also does not allow for easy sorting of tunes by artist, album, or playlist. Fourth is *divisibility*—the degree to which the innovation can be tried on a limited basis. PSPs can be sampled in a retail store or perhaps a friend's house. Fifth is *communicability*—the degree to which the beneficial results of use are observable or describable to others. The fact that PSPs have some clear advantages can help create interest and curiosity.

Other characteristics that influence the rate of adoption are cost, risk and uncertainty, scientific credibility, and social approval. The new-product marketer has to research all these factors and give the key ones maximum attention in designing the new product and its marketing program.[77]

ORGANIZATIONS' READINESS TO ADOPT INNOVATIONS

The creator of a new teaching method would want to identify innovative schools. The producer of a new piece of medical equipment would want to identify innovative hospitals. Adoption is associated with variables in the organization's environment (community progressiveness, community income), the organization itself (size, profits, and pressure to change), and the administrators (education level, age, and sophistication). Other forces come into play in trying to get a product adopted into organizations that receive the bulk of their funding from the government, such as public schools. A controversial or innovative product can be squelched by negative public opinion.

Summary

1. Once a company has segmented the market, chosen its target customer groups and identified their needs, and determined its desired market positioning, it is ready to develop and launch appropriate new products. Marketing should participate with other departments in every stage of new-product development.
2. Successful new-product development requires the company to establish an effective organization for managing the development process. Companies can choose to use product managers, new-product managers, new-product committees, new-product departments, or new-product venture teams. Increasingly, companies are adopting cross-functional teams and developing multiple product concepts.
3. Eight stages are involved in the new-product development process: idea generation, screening, concept development and testing, marketing-strategy development, business analysis, product development, market testing, and commercialization. At each stage, the company must determine whether the idea should be dropped or moved to the next stage.
4. The consumer-adoption process is the process by which customers learn about new products, try them, and adopt or reject them. Today, many marketers are targeting heavy users and early adopters of new products, because both groups can be reached by specific media and tend to be opinion leaders. The consumer-adoption process is influenced by many factors beyond the marketer's control, including consumers' and organizations' willingness to try new products, personal influences, and the characteristics of the new product or innovation.

Application

Marketing Debate—Whom Should You Target With New Products?

Some new-products experts maintain that getting close to customers through intensive research is the only way to develop successful new products. Other experts disagree and maintain that customers can't possibly provide useful feedback on what they do not know and can't provide insights that will lead to breakthrough products.

Take a position: *Consumer research is critical to new-product development* versus *Consumer research may not be all that helpful in new-product development.*

Marketing Discussion

Think about the last new product you bought. How do you think its success will be affected by the five characteristics of an innovation: relative advantage, compatibility, complexity, divisibility, and communicability?

PART 8

Nokia's global view motivates broad product lines that appeal to an array of customers and price ranges all over the world.

Tapping into Global Markets

21

With faster communication, transportation, and financial flows, the world is rapidly shrinking. Products developed in one country—Louis Vuitton purses, Mont Blanc pens, McDonald's hamburgers, Japanese sushi, Chanel suits, German BMWs—are finding enthusiastic acceptance in others. An Indonesian businessman may wear an Armani suit to meet a Hong Kong friend at a Thai restaurant, who later drives home in a car made in India to drink Japanese tea and watch an American sitcom on a Korean TV. Consider the international success of Nokia.

Nokia has made a remarkable transformation from an obscure Finnish conglomerate into the world's largest maker of mobile phones. Part of Nokia's success is due to the broad view it takes of its business, selling a wide range of products to consumers of all kinds all over the world. Nokia also takes a broad perspective on competition, viewing Apple, Sony, and Canon as threats as much as traditional rivals Motorola and Samsung. To sustain its market leadership, Nokia has launched a range of handsets, the Nseries, with advanced features such as music playing, video recording, and computing (email). But Nokia wants to be a leader in all global markets, so it cannot afford to sell just high-end products. With the bulk of industry growth coming from developing markets, Nokia has made sure its cheapest handsets are appealing—and profitable—in markets such as China, India, and Latin America. Along with a $750 handset with built-in global-positioning receivers, it also sells basic models that cost just $45. Although Nokia has struggled somewhat in North America—in part because many networks there use a different wireless standard (CDMA) than in Europe (GSM)—its global footprint is still impressive. Everyday, over 900 million people communicate on a Nokia. It sells almost the same number of handsets as the combined volume of Motorola, Samsung, and Sony Ericsson. It is the number one in each of the fastest-growing markets—China, Southeast Asia, and India—and its global sales and manufacturing are so well-honed that Nokia takes 80 percent of the industry's profit on 38 percent of the volume.[1]

In this chapter, we will address the following questions:

1. What factors should a company review before deciding to go abroad?
2. How can companies evaluate and select specific foreign markets to enter?
3. What are the major ways of entering a foreign market?
4. To what extent must the company adapt its products and marketing program to each foreign country?
5. How should the company manage and organize its international activities?

Although the opportunities for companies to enter and compete in foreign markets are significant, the risks can also be high. However, companies selling in global industries really have no choice but to internationalize their operations. In this chapter, we review the major decisions in expanding into global markets.

Competing on a Global Basis

Two hundred giant corporations, most of them larger than many national economies, have sales that in total exceed a quarter of the world's economic activity. Altria, including its main subsidiary Philip Morris, is about the same size as the economy of New Zealand and operates in over 160 countries. Some 12 percent of China's exports to the U.S. end up on Wal-Mart's shelves, and Wal-Mart's trade with China accounts for 1 percent of China's GDP.[2]

Many companies have conducted international marketing for decades—Nestlé, Shell, Sony, and Toshiba are familiar to consumers worldwide. But global competition is intensifying. But global competition is intensifying as new firms make their mark on the international stage. "Breakthrough Marketing: Samsung" describes the swift global ascent of that company.

BREAKTHROUGH • MARKETING

SAMSUNG

Korean consumer electronics giant Samsung has made a remarkable transformation, from a provider of value-priced commodity products that Original Equipment Manufacturers (OEMs) sold under their own brands, to a global marketer of premium-priced Samsung-branded consumer electronics such as flat-screen TV's, digital cameras, and cell phones. Its high-end cell phones have been a growth engine, and Samsung has released a steady stream of innovations, popularizing the PDA phone and the first cell phone with an MP3 player.

Samsung used to stress volume and market domination rather than profitability. Yet during the Asian financial crisis of the late 1990s, when other Korean *chaebol* collapsed beneath a mountain of debt, Samsung took a different tack. It cut costs and re-emphasized product quality and manufacturing flexibility, which allowed its consumer electronics to go from project phase to store shelves within six months. It also refocused on innovation, using technological leapfrogging to produce best-selling mobile handsets for Asia, Europe, and the U.S.

Samsung's success has been driven by well-designed, path-breaking products, but also by an upgrade in its brand image. From 1998 to 2006, it spent $6 billion in marketing, sponsoring the past five Olympics, running a global ad campaign themed "Imagine," and even erecting a large video screen in Times Square. Samsung views its brand message as "technology," "design," and "sensation" (human). With increasing digital convergence, it has been able to introduce a wide range of electronic products under its strong brand umbrella. The company has poured money into R&D, with a $40 billion budget for 2005–2010, and more than doubled its number of researchers between 2000 and 2006.

Its greatest sign of success, though, may be that longtime market leader Sony has been courting Samsung for joint ventures, partnering on a $2 billion state-of-the-art LCD factory in South Korea and agreeing to share 24,000 basic patents covering a range of components and production processes. Perhaps this is not surprising given that in 2005, for the first time, brand valuation experts Interband valued the Samsung brand as worth more than the Sony brand. To maintain its market leadership, however, Samsung cannot rest on its laurels and must continue to successfully expand via new products and new markets.

Sources: Moon Ihlwan, "Samsung Is Having a Sony Moment." *BusinessWeek,* July 30, 2007, p. 38; Martin Fackler, "Raising the Bar at Samsung." *New York Times,* April 25, 2006; "Brand New." *Economist,* January 15, 2005, pp. 10–11; Paticia O'Connell, "Samsung's Goal: Be Like BMW." *BusinessWeek,* August 1, 2005; Heidi Brown and Justin Doeble, "Samsung's" Next Act." *Forbes,* July 26, 2004; John Quelch and Anna Harrington, "Samsung Electronics Company: Global Marketing Operations." Harvard Business School Case 9-504-051.

Although some businesses may want to eliminate foreign competition through protective legislation, the better way to compete is to continuously improve products at home and expand into foreign markets. A global industry is an industry in which the strategic positions of competitors in major geographic or national markets are fundamentally affected by their overall global positions.[3] A global firm is a firm that operates in more than one country and captures R&D, production, logistical, marketing, and financial advantages in its costs and reputation that are not available to purely domestic competitors.

L'Oréal—This French company's skill lies in buying local cosmetics brands, giving them a facelift, and exporting them globally. In 1996, it bought a dowdy U.S. company, Maybelline, and transformed its image to a modern contemporary brand for women of all ages internationally. Japanese teens were excited over Maybelline's Wonder Curl mascara in 1999 and flocked to buy Volum' Express, its eyelash product. Maybelline's Water Shine Diamonds grew out of a failed Japanese trial run of Moisture Whip, a wet-look lipstick, in 2000. Being a little too dry for Japanese women, L'Oréal put in more moisturizing formula and renamed the product Water Shine. Water Shine became so successful in Japan that L'Oréal sold it in Asia and then worldwide. In 2000, L'Oréal formed a strategic alliance with Japanese cosmetics company Shu Uemera to learn more about how the Japanese approached cosmetics as well as participate in Shu Uemera's rapid expansion into China. It has since acquired a controlling interest in Shu Uemera. In 2003, L'Oréal bought two Chinese cosmetics brands—Yue Sai and Mininurse—and has set up its fourth R&D center in Shanghai to analyze Chinese skin and hair.[4]

However, a company need not be large to sell globally. Small- and medium-sized firms can practice global nichemanship.

Lee Kum Kee—Founded over 100 years ago, this family-owned Hong Kong food manufacturer is familiar to East Asians and to Chinese communities globally. Lee Kum Kee is used in Chinese restaurant kitchens internationally and it is widening its product line to push Chinese food culture globally. New products include single-use sauce packets and ready-made sauces in such flavors as sweet-and-sour fish, black-bean chicken, and spicy *tofu* for American and European markets. Lee Kum Kee products sell in over 60 countries and are adapted based on consumer research. The size of its single-use sauce packets was increased in Australia after it found that Australians preferred more sauce with their food. It set up a user-friendly Web site and introduced preservative-free soy sauce to attract health-conscious young professionals. Its product label was redesigned to emphasize the English "Lee Kum Kee," not the Chinese characters, as it felt that non-Chinese customers might be afraid of trying to prepare Chinese food and of pronouncing its name.[5]

For a company of any size to go global, it must make a series of decisions (see Figure 21.1). We will examine each of these decisions here.

Deciding Whether to Go Abroad

Most companies would prefer to remain domestic if their domestic market were large enough. Managers would not need to learn other languages and laws, deal with volatile

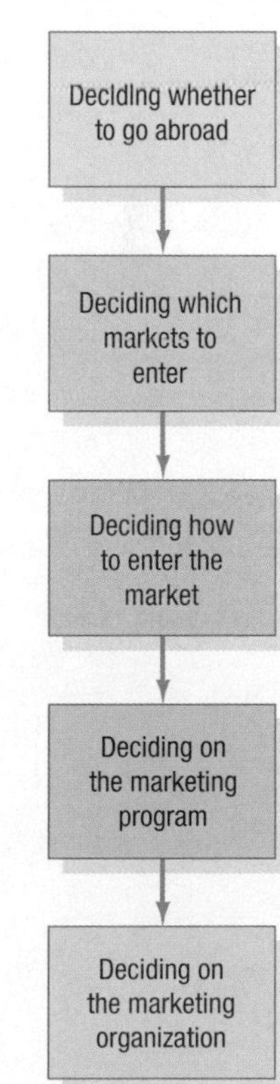

Figure 21.1
Major Decisions in International Marketing

Besides Chinese sauces, Lee Kum Kee also sells Malay sauces such as satay stir-fry sauce.

currencies, face political and legal uncertainties, or redesign their products to suit different customer needs and expectations. Business would be easier and safer. Yet several factors are drawing more and more companies into the international arena:

- The company discovers that some foreign markets present higher profit opportunities than the domestic market.
- The company needs a larger customer base to achieve economies of scale.
- The company wants to reduce its dependence on any one market.
- Global firms offering better products or lower prices can attack the company's domestic market. The company might want to counterattack these competitors in their home markets.
- The company's customers are going abroad and require international servicing.
- The company wishes to enhance its home image by succeeding elsewhere. Emerging market consumers are likely to respond more favorably to local brands which have made inroads in international markets.
- The company wishes to acquire foreign expertise and technology.

Chinese companies in Germany—There are many small Chinese companies, usually in shipping and trading, in Germany. Some Chinese companies are located in Germany to copy German technology. More than half of capital-goods companies surveyed by the German Engineering Federation reported that they have seen their products copied by foreigners, with the main offenders being Chinese product pirates. Others have acquired German companies for various reasons. Huapeng Trading acquired Welz, a maker of pressurized containers, for quicker delivery and servicing. Shenyang Machine Tool Group bought Schiess, a maker of heavy-duty lathes and boring machines, for its patents and engineering expertise.[6]

The *internationalization process* has four stages:[7]

1. No regular export activities.
2. Export via independent representatives (agents).

3. Establishment of one or more sales subsidiaries.
4. Establishment of production facilities abroad.

The first task is to get companies to move from stage 1 to stage 2. This move is helped by studying how firms make their first export decisions.[8] Most firms work with an independent agent and enter a nearby or similar country. A company then engages further agents to enter additional countries. Later, it establishes an export department to manage its agent relationships. Still later, the company replaces its agents with its own sales subsidiaries in its larger export markets. This increases the company's investment and risk, but also its earning potential.

To manage these subsidiaries, the company replaces the export department with an international department. If certain markets continue to be large and stable, or if the host country insists on local production, the company takes the next step of locating production facilities in those markets. This means a still larger commitment and still larger potential earnings. By this time, the company is operating as a multinational and is engaged in optimizing its global sourcing, financing, manufacturing, and marketing. According to some researchers, top management begins to pay more attention to global opportunities when they find that over 15 percent of revenue comes from foreign markets.[9]

Deciding Which Markets to Enter

In deciding to go abroad, the company needs to define its marketing objectives and policies. What proportion of foreign to total sales will it seek? Most companies start small when they venture abroad. Some plan to stay small; others have bigger plans. Ayal and Zif have argued that a company should enter fewer countries when:

- Market entry and market control costs are high.
- Product and communication adaptation costs are high.
- Population, income size and growth are high in the initial countries chosen.
- Dominant foreign firms can establish high barriers to entry.[10]

How Many Markets to Enter

The company must decide how many countries to enter and how fast to expand. Consider Lenovo's experience:

To learn about Billabong and how it has grown from its start selling board sports merchandise in Australia into an international brand offering many more products, visit www.pearsoned.com.au/marketingmanagementaustralia.

Lenovo—This Chinese PC maker was cautious in its international expansion plans. Many Japanese, Korean, and Taiwanese PC makers had failed in the U.S. market. So in 2002, when Lenovo (then Legend) announced plans to become an international brand, it stated that a concerted push into the U.S. would not occur within 5 to 10 years. Lenovo would first establish its brand in Southeast Asia, where it thinks its low-cost, no-frills PCs would catch on. However, in 2005, it acquired the PC business of IBM to begin its U.S. entry.[11]

A company's entry strategy typically follows one of two possible approaches: a *waterfall approach,* in which countries are gradually entered sequentially; or a *sprinkler approach,* in which many countries are entered simultaneously within a limited period of time. Increasingly, especially with technology-intensive firms, they are born global and market to the entire world right from the outset.[12]

Generally, most companies such as Matsushita, BMW, General Electric, Benetton, and The Body Shop follow the waterfall approach. It allows firms to carefully plan expansion and is less likely to strain human and financial resources. When first mover advantage is crucial and a high degree of competitive intensity prevails, the sprinkler approach is preferred, as when Microsoft introduces a new form of Windows software. The main risk is the substantial resources involved and the difficulty of planning entry strategies in so many potentially diverse markets.

The company must also decide on the types of countries to consider. Attractiveness is influenced by the product, geography, income and population, and political climate.

Developed versus Developing Markets

One of the sharpest distinctions in global marketing is between developed and developing or less mature markets such as Russia, India, and China.[13] The unmet needs of the emerging or developing world represent huge potential markets for food, clothing, shelter, consumer electronics, appliances, and other goods. Market leaders are rushing into China and India, and increasingly into the rural parts of these emerging economies.

The developed nations and the prosperous parts of developing nations account for less about 20 percent of the world's population. Is there a way for marketers to serve the other 80 percent, which has much less purchasing power? Successfully entering developing markets requires a special set of skills and plans. Consider how the following companies are pioneering ways to serve these invisible consumers:[14]

- Hindustan Unilever in India created Project Shakti in which a direct distribution network was established for hard-to-reach locales. It recruited entrepreneurial women from these villages and trained them to become distributors by providing education, advice, and products to their villages. These village women entrepreneurs, called Shakti Amma ("empowered mother"), have unique knowledge about what the village needs and which products are in demand.
- Grameen-Phone markets mobile phones to 35,000 villages in Bangladesh by hiring village women as agents who lease phone time to other villagers, one call at a time.
- An Indian-Australian car manufacturer created an affordable rural transport vehicle to compete with bullock carts rather than cars. The vehicle functions well at low speeds and carries up to two tons.

These marketers are able to capitalize on the potential of developing markets by changing their conventional marketing practices to sell their products and services more effectively.[15] It cannot be business as usual when selling into developing markets. Economic and cultural differences abound and a marketing infrastructure may barely exist.

Smaller packaging and lower sales prices is often critical in markets where incomes are limited. Unilever's 4-cent sachets of detergent and shampoo have been a big hit in rural India, where 70 percent of the country's population still lives. When Coke moved to a smaller 200 ml bottle in India, selling for 10 to 12 cents in small shops, bus-stop stalls, and roadside eateries, sales jumped.[16] A Western image can also be helpful, as Coke discovered in China. Part of its success against local cola brand Jianlibao was due to its symbolic values of modernity and affluence.[17]

Danone—In Bangladesh, French food giant Danone recently partnered with Muhammed Yunus' Nobel-prize-winning microcredit organization, Grameen Bank, to make and sell low-cost, nutritionally fortified yogurts under the brand name Shoktidoi. The joint venture will provide income to thousands of local farmers who supply the milk (and who raise cows by borrowing small amounts of money from Grameen) and to villagers who distribute the yogurt. At 8 cents per 80-gram pot, Shoktidoi will not likely net profits for Danone right now. Yet, the firm is confident tangible returns will match the intangible returns of feeding the poor. Danone has transformed Bangladesh into a laboratory in which it develops new food products for malnourished children in very poor countries, but it could also churn out new products there for mature and richer markets, all at low cost.[18]

The challenge is to think creatively about how marketing can fulfill the dreams of most of the world's population for a better standard of living. Many companies are betting that they can do that. "Marketing Insight: Spotlight on Key Asian Developing Markets" highlights some important developments in India and China.

General Motors—After launching Buick in China in 1999, GM poured over $2 billion into the region over the next five years, expanding the line up to 14 models, ranging from the $8,000 Chevrolet Spark mini-car to high-end Cadillacs. Despite fierce competition in the third largest car market, GM secured a 12.1 percent market share in 2007 and reaped sizable profits. But initial gains in the Chinese market do not necessarily spell long-term success. After investing to establish the markets, foreign pioneers in TVs and motorcycles saw domestic Chinese firms emerge as rivals. To secure and build on its gains, General Motors pledged to invest more in the region to boost capacity and build its reputation.[19]

Even entering a developed market is challenging as firms need to adapt to a different cultural environment and consumer behavior.

MARKETING INSIGHT • SPOTLIGHT ON KEY DEVELOPING ASIAN MARKETS

India

India's recent growth rate has been as explosive as its neighbor China's. Reforms in the early 1990s that significantly lowered barriers to trade and liberalized capital markets have brought booming investment and consumption. But it's not all about demand. With its large numbers of low-cost, high-IQ, English-speaking employees, India is snapping up programming and call center jobs once held by U.S. workers in a wave of outsourcing that shows no signs of stopping. By 2008, IT services and back-office work in India will swell fivefold, to a $57 billion annual export industry employing four million people and accounting for 7 percent of India's GDP.

Although India's ascent inevitably means lost jobs for U.S. white-collar workers, it also means a larger market for U.S. and Western goods—and pain for traditional Indian families. Along with training in U.S. accents and geography, India's legions of call center employees are absorbing new ideas about family, material possessions, and romance and questioning conservative traditions. They want to watch Hollywood movies, listen to Western music, chat on mobile phones, buy on credit rather than save, and eat in restaurants or cafés. They're being targeted relentlessly by companies that have waited to see India develop a Western-style consumer class.

India still struggles with poor infrastructure and highly restrictive labor laws. Its retail channel structure, although improving, still lags. The quality of public services—education, health, provision of water—is also often lacking. But all these obstacles have not prevented global firms such as Mittal, Reliance, Tata, WiPro, and Infosys from achieving varying degrees of international success.

China

China's 1.3 billion people have marketers scrambling to gain a foothold there, and competition has been heating up between domestic and international firms. Initial gains in the Chinese market didn't necessarily spell long-term success for many international firms. After investing to establish the markets, foreign pioneers in television sets and motorcycles saw domestic Chinese firms emerge as rivals. In 1995, virtually all mobile phones in China were made by global giants Nokia, Motorola, and Ericsson. Within 10 years, their market share had dropped to 60 percent. China's 2001 entry into the World Trade Organization has eased manufacturing and investment rules and modernized retail and logistics industries. Greater competition in pricing, products, and channels have resulted.

Selling in China means going beyond the big cities to the 700 million potential consumers who live in small villages, towns, and cities in the rural interior. About half of potential PC buyers live outside major cities; only one-third of overall retail revenues come from China's 24 largest cities. Rural consumers can be challenging though, as they have lower incomes, are less sophisticated buyers, and often cling to local cultural and buying habits.

Luxury cars, however, are the fastest-growing segment of the auto market thanks to China's growing ranks of millionaires and booming stock market and economy. China's emerging middle class consists of more active and more discerning consumers who demand higher-quality products. Although the mainland's population is four times that of the U.S. Chinese consumers spent just 12 percent of what U.S. consumers did in 2006.

Sources: "India on Fire." *Economist,* February 3, 2007, pp. 69–71; Joanna Slater, "Call of the West." *Wall Street Journal,* January 2, 2004; Manjeet Kripalani and Pete Engardio, "The Rise of India." *BusinessWeek,* December 8, 2003, pp. 66–76; Dexter Roberts, "Cadillac Floors It in China." *BusinessWeek,* June 4, 2007, p. 52; Bruce Einhorn, "Grudge Match in China," *BusinessWeek,* April 2, 2007, pp. 42–43; Russell Flannery, "Watch Your Back." *Forbes,* April 23, 2007, pp. 104–105; Dexter Roberts, "Cautious Consumers." *BusinessWeek,* April 30, 2007, pp. 32–34; Seung Ho Park and Wilfried R. Vanhonacker, "The Challenge for Multinational Corporations in China: Think Local, Act Global." *MIT Sloan Management Review,* May 31, 2007; Dexter Roberts, "Scrambling to Bring Crest to the Masses." *BusinessWeek,* June 25, 2007, pp. 72–73.

Toto—Toto is a market leader in Japan for high-end bath and toilet fixtures. Its Washlet, the world's first toilet equipped with automated bidet, has received rave reviews from Western tourists visiting Japan. Toto toilets also come with heated seats and automatic lids. Sensing impending market saturation at home, Toto decided to enter the U.S. However, Americans appear to lack awareness and education regarding why their bottoms need to be washed after every visit to the toilet. To address this, Toto released a series of ads in digital and print featuring naked backsides painted over with smiley faces and the tagline "Clean is Happy." However, a Times Square billboard featuring the ad drew the ire of the clergy, prompting the ad agency responsible to "cover up" the offending flesh. Toto also issued an official apology to the community.[20]

International marketers also face stiff local competition. Besides their close grasp on local tastes, such companies may also have larger distribution networks, especially in rural areas.[21] Indeed, domestic success over foreign rivals may encourage them to expand overseas.

TCL—TCL was founded in 1981 in China's southern Guangdong province. TCL started with home appliances, but its forte proved to be in TVs and cell phones. The TCL brand is one of the best recognized in China, and TCL is one of China's fastest growing companies. With its solid success at home, TCL is eyeing the international market. It acquired Thomson Electronics and formed a joint venture with Alcatel. Today, TCL is the world's largest maker of TV sets, producing about 18.5 million TVs a year. However, TCL still needs to establish its name outside China. Thus its TVs will carry the TCL brand in China and developing Asian countries, but will continue using the RCA brand in North America and the Thomson brand in Europe. Similarly, its cell phones will use the TCL brand in Asia and the Alcatel brand in Europe and Latin America.[22]

"Marketing Insight: Emerging Market Companies" describes four types of local businesses and their strategies for meeting the challenge of foreign competitors entering their home markets.

Regional Free Trade Zones

Regional economic integration—trading agreements between blocs of countries—has intensified in recent years. This development means that companies are more likely to enter entire regions at the same time. Certain countries have formed free trade zones or economic communities—groups of nations organized to work toward common goals in the regulation of international trade. Such communities include the Asia Pacific Economic Cooperation (APEC), European Union (EU), North American Free Trade Agreement (NAFTA), and Latin American free trade area (MERCOSUL).

APEC

Twenty-one Pacific Rim countries, including the NAFTA member states, Japan, and China, are working to create a pan-Pacific free trade area under the auspices of the APEC forum. There are also active attempts at regional economic integration in the Caribbean, Southeast Asia, and parts of Africa.

EU

The EU comprises 25 member countries containing over 454 million consumers and accounts for 23 percent of the world's exports. It has a common currency, the euro, and offers tremendous trade opportunities for non-European firms. However, it also poses threats as European companies will grow bigger and more competitive. The EU is also not

MARKETING INSIGHT • EMERGING MARKET COMPANIES

How can local businesses in emerging markets cope with foreign competition entering their home markets? Recent research has uncovered the strategies that four types of Emerging Market Companies (or EMCs) have adopted to this end.

1. **Dodger** — This EMC knows its assets work only at home and dodges its competition by restructuring its local assets and uses them as a competitive advantage. It may achieve this by changing the nature of the industry in which it operates, which is not an easy or inexpensive task, or by becoming extremely locally focused to out-localize its international rivals. If it feels that competition from rivals is too strong, a dodger may enter a joint venture or sell out to one of its rivals.

Shinsegae—When Korea opened its retail sector to foreign competition in 1996, the likes of Wal-Mart and Carrefour were expected to dominate local incumbents like Shinsegae. Then, Shinsegae ran a network of warehouse stores under the Costco Wholesale banner, which did not allow it to adapt its stores to suit local tastes. Costco also had veto rights over new locations. With the Asian crisis, Shinsegae's finances were decimated. In 1998, Shinsegae sold the warehouse business to Costco for $100 million. As the Korean economy poised itself for a rebound, Shinsegae reshaped its businesses around its own discount unit, E-Mart. With Korean companies selling land to survive, Shinsegae bought cheap parcels at strategic locations and started building 10 E-Marts a year. It now boasts 20 percent of Korea's warehouse stores. Before E-Mart, Koreans had limited choice and few bargains. With its buying power, E-Mart, under its motto "Economy and Everyday Low Prices," sells everything from clothes to electronics to food at prices as much as 30 percent lower than conventional outlets. Shinsegae also localized its E-Marts. Koreans preferred not to buy in bulk and never warmed to the high shelves and concrete floors of the warehouse experience. So E-Mart features the more familiar layout of a department store. It also caters to the local appetite for fresh fish and vegetables, ensuring that sushi, squid, cucumber, and spinach are restocked twice daily. By 2002, E-Mart captured nearly a third of Korea's $10 billion discount retail market, ahead of Carrefour and Magnet. Its profits grew 19-fold since 1997, while Wal-Mart did not post a profit in the three years after it entered the Korean market.

2. **Defender** — This refers to an EMC that already possesses defensible local assets. A defender erects barriers to international entry by serving local customers' needs better than international players can. Resisting the temptation to reach all customers or imitate MNCs, defenders fine-tune their offerings to the often unique needs of their customers. Successful defenders focus on consumers who appreciate the local touch and ignore those who favor global brands.

Amul—This is India's largest dairy products company. Amul has a sophisticated supply chain that incorporates 175 cooperatives involving two million people in villages across the country. Villagers would milk their cows twice daily and take their output to a village milk cooperative center. There, the milk is measured, tested, and paid for. In some villages, nearly 15 percent of the population are cooperative members. The village collection points are the beginning of a supply chain that resembles a sophisticated organization. Amul's processing plants and packaging are first-rate. Given its own low-cost sources of raw milk, Amul's cheese, ice cream, and chocolates are seizing market share from the likes of Nestlé and Unilever. Its sales of $38 million represents a growth rate of 40 percent.

3. **Extender** — This is an EMC that has defended its local market and can extend into other, similar markets. Extenders can leverage their assets most efficiently by seeking markets similar to their home base in terms of consumer preferences, geographic proximity, distribution channels, or government regulations.

Jollibee—The Philippines' fast-food leader has extended its reach by focusing on Filipinos in other countries for its international expansion. After competing successfully with such formidable MNCs as McDonald's at home, Jollibee felt its battle-tested recipes would find similar appeal in global markets. Now, 10 percent of its stores are located outside the Philippines, primarily in places with large expatriate Filipino populations such as the Middle East and Hong Kong. There are over 5,00,000 Filipinos working in the Middle East and Jollibee has established 10 restaurants there.

(Continued ...)

MARKETING INSIGHT • EMERGING MARKET COMPANIES

(Continued...)

4. **Contender** — This EMC competes in major international markets by upgrading capabilities and resources to match MNCs. The number of Asian contenders has risen steadily, particularly in commodity industries where plentiful resources or labor gives them an advantage. Success may also hinge on finding a market niche that is distinct and defensible.

These successful Asian examples illustrate the importance of strategic flexibility in response to market opportunities, a point often overlooked by regional marketers who have benefited from the protection of industry boundaries. With the onslaught of globalization in many of these markets, Asian marketers must develop a fluidity of thought and action, and realize that they can respond effectively to competition in a variety of ways.

Pearl River Piano—This state-owned Chinese company has emerged as a global player in the market for entry-level pianos. Price competition is keen, with once dominant U.S. and European players being supplanted by Yamaha and Korean companies which exploited their low labor cost to enter the market. Pearl River initially marketed pianos mainly for children of local families that benefited from China's export boom in Guangzhou. However, over a 10-year period, the company improved its product design and manufacturing efficiency through automation and computer-generated design equipment. Pearl River also brought in foreign industry executives as consultants. To learn management concepts from Japan's industry leader, it forged a $10 million joint venture with Yamaha in 1995. Pearl River now operates the largest factory in the world with a daily production of 250 pianos. Pearl River also bought a mature German brand, Ritmüller, in 1999 to complement its own brand, the same year it opened its first warehouse and sales office in the U.S. Its U.S. outfit is locally run. In 2002, Pearl River's brands were represented in 310 specialized U.S. piano shops out of a national total of 1,100, compared to none in 2000. It ships pianos in colors that fit U.S. living rooms. Its success is evident when, in 2001 as piano purchases in the U.S. fell by 12 percent to 88,000, Pearl River's shipments rose by more than 44 percent to 4,200, accounting for 5 percent of the U.S. market. Meanwhile, Pearl River has also benefited back home as pianos have caught on in China with the country becoming more affluent.

Sources: Niraj Dawar and Tony Frost, "Competing with Giants: Survival Strategies for Local Companies in Emerging Markets." *Harvard Business Review,* March-April 1999, pp. 119–129; Moon Ihlwan, "Holding Off the Wal-Marts of the World." *BusinessWeek,* January 21, 2002, p. 21; Manjeet Kripalani and Pete Engardio, "Small is Profitable." *BusinessWeek Online,* August 25, 2002; Russell Flannery, "Piano Man." *Forbes Global,* May 13, 2002, pp. 24–25; <www.amulind.com>.

a homogenous market, as companies will face 14 languages, 2,000 years of historical and cultural differences, and a host of local rules.

NAFTA

NAFTA comprises the U.S., Canada, and Mexico. This zone contains 360 million people consuming $6.7 million worth of goods and services annually.

MERCOSUL

This zone now links Brazil, Argentina, Paraguay, Uruguay, Chile, and Mexico, and may merge with NAFTA to form an all-Americas free trade area.

Evaluating Potential Markets

Yet, however much nations and regions integrate their trading policies and standards, each nation still has unique features that must be understood. A nation's readiness for different products and services and its attractiveness as a market to foreign firms depend on its economic, political-legal, and cultural environments.

Suppose a company has assembled a list of potential markets to enter. How does it choose among them? Many companies prefer to sell to neighboring countries because they understand these countries better and can control their costs more effectively.

At other times, psychic proximity determines choices. This partly explains why companies from Commonwealth countries such as Hong Kong, Malaysia, and Singapore often choose the U.K. as their springboard into the European market because they feel more comfortable with the language, laws, and culture. Indeed, psychic proximity may explain why overseas Chinese groups from Hong Kong, Indonesia, Malaysia, Singapore, Thailand, and Taiwan have committed billions of dollars in China via their public-listed companies alone. Such a strategy may have emanated from a perceived home-ground advantage for the overseas Chinese businesses. Investing in China is like going back home for overseas Chinese tycoons. Similarly, Chinese businesses may find psychic comfort in partnering overseas Chinese companies when they invest abroad.

Thailand and China—Chinese companies take their cue from overseas Chinese contacts when investing overseas. Thailand, for historical and cultural reasons, presents a friendly face to Chinese enterprises in a region long marked by suspicion of China. Most of Thailand's richest men are Thai Chinese and they are in politics. Worldbest Textile, a subsidiary of Shanghai-based state-owned enterprise, has two factories in eastern Thailand. Thailand's low labor costs and efficient financial system are other reasons for Chinese investments. Thailand's Charoen Pokphand (CP), one of the first foreign investors in China, also helps attract Chinese investment. CP is a major shareholder in Business Development Bank which helps finance medium-sized enterprises in the Shanghai region.[23]

However, companies should be careful in choosing markets according to cultural distance. Besides the fact that potentially better markets may be overlooked, it also may result in a superficial analysis of some very real differences among the countries. It may also lead to predictable marketing actions that would be a disadvantage from a competitive standpoint.[24]

Chinese construction companies—Among Asian companies, Japanese and Korean construction firms have generally dominated the large-scale infrastructure building industry. Such names as Kajima, Itochu, Ssangyong, and Shinhan are well known regionally and internationally. In contrast, Chinese construction companies, while winning contracts in mature markets like the U.S., have made their mark in less developed markets. Their lower construction costs and vast experience in selected infrastructure projects like dams have been key to this success. China is the home to almost half the world's large dams and has the know-how to build them quickly and cheaply. Thus Sinohydro is the lead partner in the Tekeze Dam Project in Ethiopia. It is also building a hydropower station in Zambia, and, with China International Water & Electric, the Merowe Dam in Sudan.[25]

It often makes sense to operate in a few of them with a deeper commitment and penetration in each. In general, a company prefers to enter countries (1) that rank high on market attractiveness, (2) that are low in market risk, and (3) in which it possesses a competitive advantage. Here is how Bechtel Corporation, the construction giant, goes about evaluating overseas markets.

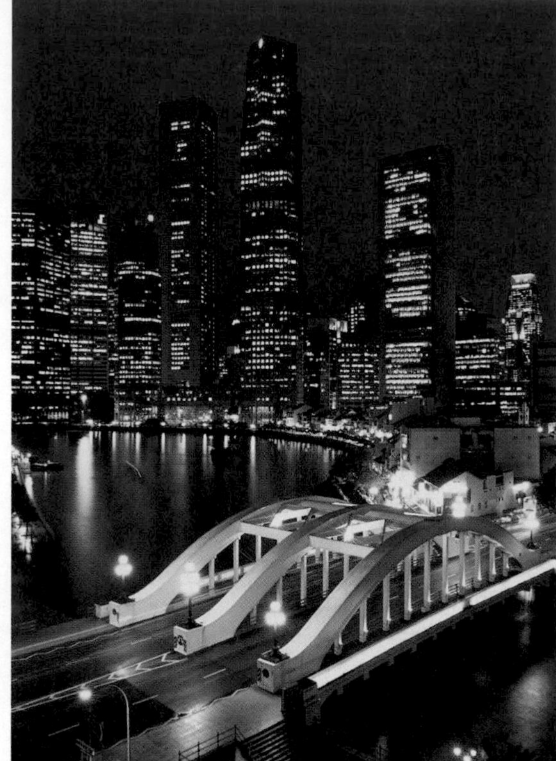

Singapore meets most but not all of Bechtel's criteria for overseas investment; its population is relatively small.

Bechtel Corporation—Bechtel provides premier technical, management, and directly related services to develop, manage, engineer, build, and operate installations for customers in nearly 60 countries worldwide. Before Bechtel ventures into new markets, the company starts with a detailed strategic market analysis. It looks at its markets and tries to determine where it should be in four or five years' time. A management team does a cost-benefit analysis that factors in the position of competitors, infrastructure, regulatory and trade barriers, and the tax situation (both corporate and individual). Ideally, the new market should be a country with an untapped need for its products or services; a quality, skilled labor pool capable of manufacturing the product; and a welcoming environment (governmental and physical).

Are there countries that meet Bechtel's requirements? Although Singapore has an educated, English-speaking labor force, basks in political stability, and encourages foreign investment, it has a small population. Although India possesses an eager, hungry-to-learn labor pool, its infrastructure creates difficulties. The team evaluating a new market must determine whether the company could earn enough on its investment to cover the risk factors or other negatives.[26]

For many businesses, China appears to provide the greatest source of marketing opportunities. For example, China has already passed the U.S. as the world's biggest user of mobile phones. "Marketing Insight: China Post-WTO," discusses the implications for marketers following the country's entry into the World Trade Organization.

MARKETING INSIGHT • CHINA POST-WTO

On September 17, 2001, China formally accepted the terms that permitted its entry into the World Trade Organization (WTO), opening up an enormous market to foreign competition while simultaneously threatening the survival of other businesses elsewhere. Selected impacts of China's entry into the WTO include:

- ***North America*** — Farmers will get a new market for grain and rice. Semiconductor, telecom-gear, and computer makers will get duty free access to China. Adverse impact will be light since the U.S. already imports most of the goods China makes.
- ***Mexico*** — Garment and shoe industries which have boomed under NAFTA will be hit hard as quotas limiting Chinese exports to the U.S. will be lifted. Also, Mexico must drop high tariffs on 1,300 Chinese products, hurting its industries.
- ***European Union*** — Imports of Chinese shoes, dishes, and kitchen utensils will rise as the EU phases out quotas. However, makers of luxury cars, telecom, and industrial equipment will benefit.
- ***South Korea*** — Exports of fabrics, industrial gear, and high-grade steel to China could swell. However, other industries could slip as MNCs flock to China.
- ***India*** — Imports from China will rise sharply as curbs are phased out on 743 Chinese products. India's garment and shoe exports could also suffer.
- ***Japan*** — Imports on a wide variety of consumer goods will grow as more Japanese manufacturers shift production to China. Equipment, vehicle, and electronics exports to China will rise.
- ***Taiwan*** — Its trade surplus with China will fall as it drops import bans on Chinese products. More production and engineering will go to China, but this will enhance the competitiveness of Taiwanese businesses.
- ***Southeast Asia*** — Thailand, the Philippines, Indonesia, and Malaysia will lose foreign investment to China. Pressure will grow to upgrade industries and workforces.

For businesses like Citicorp, China post-WTO represents a dream market. Foreign banks will be allowed to open fully-owned branches in China and take deposits in local currency. Banking is now dominated by huge state-owned institutions which have given loans to poorly run state-owned enterprises. These local banks are saddled with high levels of bad debt but

(Continued ...)

MARKETING INSIGHT • CHINA POST-WTO

(*Continued ...*)

are so entrenched and politically connected that no foreign bank will compete directly with them. However, Citicorp believes that with personal income growing rapidly for millions of Chinese, particularly those in China's more prosperous southeastern crescent, an all-out drive to market credit cards and home mortgages makes business sense.

Prior to China's entry into WTO, foreign companies cannot set up their own distribution chains, service centers, or dealer networks. This means relying on local partners. Many foreign businesses discovered that their main distributor was also the distributor for their main competitor. The WTO will change this and enable businesses like Caterpillar to penetrate the market. While China is one vast construction site, with highways, dams, buildings, and neighborhoods springing up everywhere, Caterpillar is conspicuous by its absence thus far. Its products are too expensive for Chinese buyers. The construction industry is full of small, inefficient producers who engage in aggressive price cutting. While Caterpillar will expand its locally made products, it will not be a low-price competitor in China. WTO rules will allow Caterpillar to build its own distribution networks to support its dealers and service centers across China and to change how Chinese customers think about buying its equipment from purely price considerations to productivity concerns.

However, WTO entry will not make or break any company in China. Some changes are incremental, an acceleration of liberalizing trends over the past 20 years. Even in industries where changes will be sweeping, it will take more time than the five-year WTO transition period calls for. In the auto industry, for example, "more protection" is expected for the over-120 local vehicle assemblers to preserve domestic employment. This may confirm the wisdom of such early market entrants as General Motors which now produces two models with its Chinese partner, Shanghai Auto. Under WTO rules, GM will have more flexibility in purchasing components and expanding capacity, which should improve the quality of its cars and reduce costs.

However, after the initial five-year-grace period, there are still areas where China has not opened up its trade. The Chinese government still forces foreign auto-makers operating in China to buy a certain quantity of their components from local suppliers and applies import duties on parts. This was deemed illegal by the WTO, backing complaints by the EU, the U.S., and Canada. China still accounts for about 70 percent of all counterfeit goods in the world. Restrictions regarding the distribution of foreign films, music, books, and videos still exist.

Chinese businesses will need to meet its obligations as a WTO member. Chinese firms must be responsive to competition from foreign players. The WTO will benefit such companies as state-owned Cosco, an emerging player in international shipping, as trade will expand in both directions. More adept local financial institutions like the Bank of China are already taking steps, and already have millions of "Great Wall" cards in the hands of Chinese consumers. Businesses like steel maker Angang must increase their efficiency at their plants to compete. For others like Dongfeng, an agricultural machinery group, the WTO brings mixed blessings. Most of its production lines are labor intensive and inefficient and potential foreign partners have "already married" other local players. However, more rigorous government implementation of anti-piracy laws under the WTO would enable it to protect its well-known brand now being used by other companies to sell Dongfeng's products (sometimes even under the Dongfeng name).

Sources: Bill Powell, "China's Great Step Forward." *Fortune,* September 17, 2001, pp. 29–45; Bruce Einhorn, Mark L. Clifford, Chester Dawson, Irene M. Kunii, Manjeet Kripalani, Moon Ihlwan, Dexter Roberts, Alysha Webb, and Pete Engardio, "China: Will Its Entry into the WTO Unleash New Prosperity or Further Destabilize the World Economy?" *BusinessWeek,* October 22, 2001, pp. 40–46; "China Duties on Car Parts Break Trade Law: WTO." <www.ChinaPost.com.tw>, February 15, 2008; Gordon Chang, "China vs The WTO." *New York Sun,* April 18, 2007.

Deciding How to Enter the Market

Once a company decides to target a particular country, it has to determine the best mode of entry. Its broad choices are indirect exporting, direct exporting, licensing, joint ventures, and direct investment. These five market-entry strategies are shown in Figure 21.2. Each succeeding strategy involves more commitment, risk, control, and profit potential.

Indirect and Direct Export

The normal way to get involved in an international market is through export. Companies typically start with indirect exporting—that is, they work through independent intermediaries. Domestic-based export merchants buy the manufacturer's products and then sell them abroad. Domestic-based export agents seek and negotiate foreign purchases and are paid a commission. Included in this group are trading companies. Cooperative organizations carry on exporting activities on behalf of several producers and are partly under their administrative control. They are often used by producers of primary products such

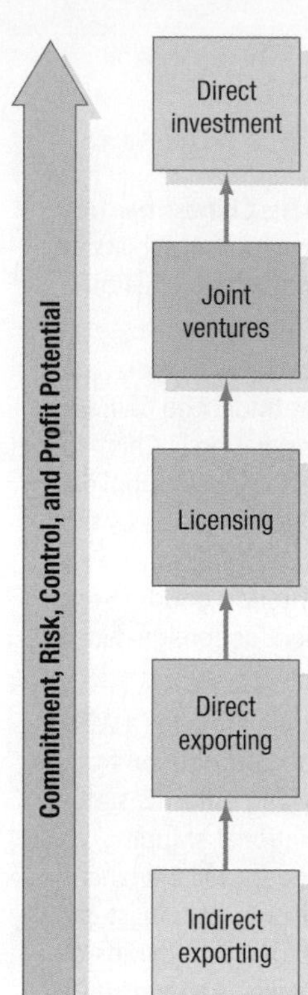

Figure 21.2 Five Modes of Entry into Foreign Markets

as fruits or nuts. Export-management companies agree to manage a company's export activities for a fee.

Indirect export has two advantages. First, there is less investment. The firm does not have to develop an export department, an overseas sales force, or a set of international contacts. Second, there is less risk: because international-marketing intermediaries bring know-how and services to the relationship, the seller will normally make fewer mistakes.

Companies eventually may decide to handle their own exports.[27] The investment and risk are somewhat greater, but so is the potential return. A company can carry on direct exporting in several ways:

- ***Domestic-based export department or division*** — This might evolve into a self-contained export department operating as a profit center.
- ***Overseas sales branch or subsidiary*** — The sales branch handles sales and distribution and might handle warehousing and promotion as well. It often serves as a display and customer service center.
- ***Traveling export sales representatives*** — Home-based sales representatives are sent abroad to find business.
- ***Foreign-based distributors or agents*** — These distributors and agents might be given exclusive rights to represent the company in that country, or only limited rights.

Many companies use exporting as a way to "test the waters" before building a plant and manufacturing a product overseas, as the following example shows:

SVA—This Shanghai-based electronics company sells plasma television sets to U.S. retail chains. When it first entered the U.S., it relied largely on distributors such as Ingram Micro and D&H Distributing. Working with such distributors helped it learn about the U.S. market before building its own overseas market capabilities. It also chose to work with distributors on trade-level promotional activities including attendance at industry conferences rather than advertising to build brand awareness. Distributors found SVA attractive because it enabled them to offer customers low-cost products. This was particularly attractive to small- and mid-size retailers competing with Wal-Mart. SVA avoided the low-end color TV market where it could meet intense competition from other Chinese companies selling on an OEM basis. Instead, it focused on upmarket products such as plasma displays and LCD monitors and TVs. It priced these products well below its Japanese and Korean competitors, but above those of manufacturers that relied solely on low prices. It also sold through Amazon.com, Buy.com, Costco, and Office Depot. Finally, it recruited U.S.-based executives to whom it gave an equity stake.[28]

Using a Global Web Strategy

With the Web, it is not even necessary to attend trade shows to show one's wares: electronic communication via the Internet is extending the reach of companies large and small, allowing them to attract new customers outside their home countries, to support existing customers who live abroad, to source from international suppliers, and to build global brand awareness.

These companies adapt their Web sites to provide country-specific content and services to their best potential international markets, ideally in the local language. The number of Internet users is rising quickly as access costs decline, local-language content increases, and infrastructure improves. Upscale U.S. retailer and cataloger The Sharper Image gets more than 25 percent of its online business from overseas customers.[29]

The Internet has become an effective means of conducting market research, and offering customers several time zones away a secure process for ordering and paying for products. "Going abroad" on the Internet does pose special challenges. The global marketer may run up against governmental or cultural restrictions. In China and Japan, credit card usage is low. Hence, adaptations are made for Internet transactions. Cash-on-delivery services are provided. Sometimes, a third party, usually a company, serves as an intermediary by paying for the goods first, and the purchaser pays the third party upon collection.

Licensing

Licensing is a simple way to become involved in international marketing. The licensor licenses a foreign company to use a manufacturing process, trademark, patent, trade secret, or other item of value for a fee or royalty. The licensor gains entry at little risk; the licensee gains production expertise or a well-known product or brand name.

Licensing has potential disadvantages. The licensor has less control over the licensee than it does over its own production and sales facilities. Further, if the licensee is very successful, the firm has given up profits; and if and when the contract ends, the company might find that it has created a competitor. To avoid this, the licensor usually supplies some proprietary ingredients or components needed in the product (as Coca-Cola does). But the best strategy is for the licensor to lead in innovation so that the licensee will continue to depend on the licensor.

In the past, licensing has generally been neglected as an entry strategy in Asia for two main reasons: (1) the belief, usually true, that local manufacturers do not possess the capability of absorbing and applying advanced technologies; and (2) the poor legal protection for foreign intellectual property in the region. However, the situation varies from country to country, with the more developed Asian nations such as Japan, Singapore, South Korea, and Taiwan being better choices for licensing. South Korea's Doosan Group, for example, has among its MNC partners, Showa Kirin Brewery, Coca-Cola, Seagrams, Anheuser Busch, Nestlé, KFC, Kodak, Oak Industries, and 3M. Also, as educational and skill levels in Asia rise, licensing will be a much more viable strategy in the region.

There are several variations on a licensing arrangement. Companies such as Hyatt and Marriott sell management contracts to owners of foreign hotels to manage these businesses for a fee. The management firm may even be given the option to purchase some share in the managed company within a stated period.

In contract manufacturing, the firm hires local manufacturers to produce the product. Contract manufacturing gives the company less control over the manufacturing process and the loss of potential profits on manufacturing. However, it offers a chance to start faster, with less risk and with the opportunity to form a partnership or buy out the local manufacturer later. Hasbro, the toy maker, has its products like GI Joe, Transformers, Mastermind, and Trivial Pursuit contract-manufactured in China, India, Macau, and Thailand.

Finally, a company can enter a foreign market through franchising, which is a more complete form of licensing. The franchiser offers a complete brand concept and operating system. In return, the franchisee invests in and pays certain fees to the franchiser. McDonald's, KFC, and Avis have entered scores of countries by franchising their retail concepts and making sure their marketing is culturally relevant.

KFC—KFC is the world's largest fast-food chicken chain, owning or franchising 12,800 outlets in about 90 countries—60 percent of them outside the U.S. KFC overcame several obstacles when it entered the Japanese market. The Japanese saw fast food as artificial, made by mechanical means, and unhealthy. To build trust in the KFC brand, advertising showed scenes depicting Colonel Sanders' beginnings in Kentucky that conveyed southern hospitality, old American tradition, and authentic home cooking. The campaign was hugely successful, and in less than eight years, KFC expanded its presence from 400 locations to more than 1,000. KFC is China's largest, oldest, and most popular quick-service restaurant chain, also with over 1,000 locations. KFC China offers such fare as an "Old Beijing Twister"—a wrap modeled after the way Peking duck is served, but with fried chicken inside. It even has a Chinese mascot—a kid-friendly character named Chicky, which the company boasts has become "the Ronald McDonald of China."[30]

KFC has tailored its approach, menu, and even mascot to appeal to Chinese tastes and has become China's fastest-growing and most popular fast-food chain.

However, international franchising may not be easy for both the franchisor and franchisee. A study of Taiwanese franchises found that the top five franchisor gripes with franchisees were: (1) not participating in marketing promotions, (2) not following the chain's business policies, (3) not accepting the chain's product prices, (4) wanting larger sales territory than it can handle, and (5) not repaying loans. The top five franchisee complaints about the franchisor were: (1) not supplying enough marketing support, (2) providing products of unsatisfactory quality, (3) store sales not meeting expectations, (4) imposing excessive restrictions on items that can be sold in the store, and (5) charging too much for goods sold in the store.[31]

Joint Ventures

Foreign investors may join with local investors to create a joint venture company in which they share ownership and control. For instance:[32]

- Shanghai Baosteel Group has a $1.4 billion joint venture steel mill in Brazil with Companhia Vale do Rio Doce, the world's largest producer of iron ore.
- Coca-Cola and Nestlé joined forces to develop the international market for "ready-to-drink" tea and coffee, which they currently sell in significant amounts in Japan.
- In India, Hindustan Unilever and Tata-owned Lakme have formed Lakme Lever to sell branded products like Elizabeth Arden, Rimmel, and Calvin Klein.

A joint venture may be necessary or desirable for economic or political reasons. The foreign firm might lack the financial, physical, or managerial resources to undertake the venture alone; or the foreign government might require joint ownership as a condition for entry. Even corporate giants need joint ventures to crack the toughest markets.

Unilever—When Unilever wanted to enter China's ice cream market, it joined forces with Sumstar, a state-owned Chinese investment company. The venture's general manager says Sumstar's help in breaking through the formidable Chinese bureaucracy was crucial in getting a high-tech ice cream plant up and running in just 12 months.[33]

"Marketing Insight: *Guanxi* and Its Application to Marketing in Greater China" discusses the nature and role of connections in Asian marketing.

MARKETING INSIGHT • *GUANXI* AND ITS APPLICATION TO MARKETING IN GREATER CHINA

Guanxi is a major dynamic in Chinese society. Literally translated, *guanxi* means "good relations" or "connections." Chinese society is particularly marked by distrust of non-family members. To overcome this distrust, the Chinese have developed family-like links more extensively than almost any other nation. And family in the Chinese context stretches from close family, to slightly distant, to more distant, embracing people who are connected to someone in one's family, to friends of family, and to all their families. The family is really a system of contacts, rather than purely an emotional unit as in the West. This system extends to classmates, to political powers, and to co-regionals who are frequently chosen as business partners. In conducting business, Chinese firms will look first to these links as bases for *guanxi*.

In general, three forms of "ritualization" foster *guanxi*:

1. ***Surname*** — The surname indicates the village that the Chinese forefathers came from. Bearing the same surname suggests a common history.
2. ***Locality*** — Coming from the same school or province would suggest a common heritage that cements a bond between parties.
3. ***Language*** — This is the oldest form of ritualization. Thailand, for instance, is dominated by the Teochew diaspora; Singapore, Penang, and Medan have the Hokkiens as the majority community; while certain cities in Sarawak, Ipoh, and Kuala Lumpur are inhabited by Hakkas.

Such *guanxi* has helped businesses flourish. For instance, the firmly established seafood network of the Teochews in Hong Kong, Malaysia, Shantou, Singapore, and Thailand has thrived for more than 100 years. The Teochews control the world trade of sharksfin.

The successful marketer is thus one who can make *guanxi* work for him or her. As the concept has overtones of an unlimited exchange of favors between two parties in a special relationship, it requires that each party be fully committed to the other. Thus marketers practicing *guanxi* must honor their obligations, be good and loyal friends, and true co-regionals. They must develop a reputation for fairness, giving their partners their due share. They do favors, can be relied on, and will reciprocate. They are fully civilized because they are fully social: a true Chinese. Hence, *guanxi* ties have to be continually reinforced; marketers who let their *guanxi* relations lapse will find that they have to deal with parties who are uninterested in their products and services.

Guanxi also helps to reduce risk. Overseas Chinese use *guanxi* in China to compensate for the relative lack of the rule of law and transparency in rules and regulations. Under such conditions, speaking the same language and sharing similar cultural bonds is a useful lubricant for marketing exchange. Moreover, *guanxi* ties should be systematically extended. One way among Chinese business people is to capitalize on their staff who leave to set up their own firms. Seed capital is provided for these individuals to get started, usually as subcontractors. In this way, *guanxi* links are spread, creating future business partners and extending the network. This network of political/economic systems is thus bound together by a shared tradition, rather than geography.

An extensive *guanxi* network also provides an excellent source of market intelligence. Indeed, one lesson the Chinese business community can teach a globalizing economy is to exploit knowledge arbitrage. This involves cross-border exchanges bringing together suppliers and technology from disparate markets to serve a third country's unmet needs. An example is Star TV, developed by Richard Li, who brought together a U.S. satellite vehicle, a rocket launcher made in China, and international expertise in broadcasting to create pan-Asia's first satellite TV station. However, the development of an ideology of economic self-interest may eventually replace the clannish constraints of traditional businesses founded on a survivor mentality and patriarchal authority. This may lead to the "Chinese Commmonwealth" being no longer exclusively Chinese.

Western firms are already trying to tap this *guanxi* network of 55 million overseas Chinese to market more effectively in Asia. General Motors capitalized on *guanxi* with local manufacturer Jin Bei in northern Shenyang, Beijing Wan Yuan Industry Corporation, and Beijing Economic Technology Investment Development Corporation to secure a foothold in the China market.

Whether *guanxi* ties can be used successfully by Chinese marketers in the West remains to be seen. The market imperfections that they can exploit in Asia tend to be smoothed out in the West where there are more transparent regulations. Still, it will be interesting to discover if the *guanxi* links with their Western partners developed in Asia can be leveraged by Chinese marketers in other parts of the world.

Finally, the cost of developing and maintaining a *guanxi* relationship may also be very high. *Guanxi* may also degenerate into corruption, nepotism, and cronyism. In some sense, its extreme abuse may have partly contributed to the Asian economic crisis in the late 1990s.

Sources: Pete Engardio, Amy Borrus, and Neil Gross, "Greater China Could be the Biggest Tiger of All." *International BusinessWeek,* September 28, 1992, pp. 37; Louis Kraar, "The New Power in Asia." *Fortune,* October 31, 1994, pp. 38–68; Matthew Montagu-Pollock, "All the Right Connections." *Asian Business,* January 1991, pp. 20–24; Kevin Hamlin, "Connections: The Key to Fast Growth." *Asia Inc,* July 1994, pp. 28–32; "Linking Asia's Ruling Families." *Business Times,* Singapore, November 5–6, 1994, p. EL5; "Linking Politics and Business." *Business Times,* Singapore, November 12–13, 1994, EL5; Christopher Kuffel, "*Guanxi*, or the Network of Power." *International Herald Tribune*, Sponsored Section, October 1994, p. 2; Jon P. Alston, "*Wa*, *Guanxi*, and *Inhwa*: Managerial Principles in Japan, China, and Korea." *Business Horizons,* March–April 1989, pp. 26–31; John Kao, "The Worldwide Web of China Business." *Harvard Business Review,* March–April 1993, pp. 24–33; Chak Yan Chang, "Three Factors Propel Chinese Network." *Straits Times,* Singapore, July 11, 1996, p. 28; Dexter Roberts and Joyce Barnathan, "Maybe *Guanxi* Isn't Everything After All." *BusinessWeek,* February 24, 1997, 17; Thomas Hon Wing Polin, "Master of *Guanxi*." *Asiaweek,* November 3, 2000, p. 40.

Asian companies have also formed joint ventures when they expand overseas. Japanese department store chain Mitsukoshi operates a joint venture called Shin Kong Mituskoshi in Taiwan and has another with Beijing Hualian Group in China. Tiger Balm, a medicated ointment brand from Singapore, partnered with Japanese pharmaceutical company, Ryukakusan to develop and market its products from Japan to other countries. It also hopes that the joint venture will provide it with window to Japanese technology and a stronger link to Japanese distribution channels.

Joint ownership has certain drawbacks. The partners might disagree over their investment, marketing, or other policies. One partner might want to re-invest earnings for growth, and the other might want to declare more dividends. Joint ownership can also prevent a multinational company from carrying out specific manufacturing and marketing policies on a worldwide basis.

France Telecom and TelecomAsia—France Telecom and Thailand's Telecom Asia formed a joint venture in 2002 to tap into Thailand's growing cell phone market. FranceTelecom's cell phone unit, Orange, was to provide marketing savvy and technological prowess, while TelecomAsia had the local knowledge and connections. However, after a traumatic two-year relationship, the joint venture fell through over competing strategic visions. Orange preferred to expand business methodically with a low-price strategy to build a broad subscriber base, while TelecomAsia wanted to push more multimedia options to lure higher-spending clientele. Some analysts contend that Thai-Western tie-ups fail because of philosophical differences—Western partners want fast returns, while Thai partners prefer to re-invest their earnings to build long-term competitive position.[34]

Foreign companies establishing joint ventures in Asia typically team up with four types of local partners:

- ***High net-worth families*** — These partners tend to have sufficient funds but usually will be reluctant to increase their initial investment and are willing to let the foreign partner run the joint venture.
- ***Relatively small companies in the same business*** — They have expertise in the field and may have government connections, but often lack capital. Such local firms are more likely to participate actively in the joint ventures.
- ***Large companies*** — They possess widespread government and corporate connections, sales and distribution networks, and sufficient capital.
- ***Government or governmental-linked companies*** — They have political connections, but may or may not have the relevant expertise or capital.

"Marketing Memo: Guidelines for Managing Joint Ventures in Asia" provides some useful information on how to manage a joint venture in Asia.

Direct Investment

The ultimate form of foreign involvement is direct ownership of foreign-based assembly or manufacturing facilities. The foreign company can buy part or full interest in a local company or build its own facilities. China National Bluestar Group bought a controlling stake in Korea's Ssangyong Motors, including its jeep and SUV maker, for a reported $1 billion to turn the company around.[35] General Motors has invested billions of dollars in auto manufacturers worldwide, such as Shanghai GM, Fiat Auto Holdings, Isuzu, Daewoo, Suzuki, Saab, Fuji Heavy Industries, and Jinbei GM Automotive Co.[36]

If the market appears large enough, foreign production facilities offer distinct advantages. First, the firm secures cost economies in the form of cheaper labor or raw materials, foreign-government investment incentives, and freight savings. Second, the firm strengthens its image in the host country because it creates jobs. Third, the firm develops a deeper relationship with government, customers, local suppliers, and distributors, enabling it to adapt its products better to the local environment. Fourth, the firm retains full control over its investment and thus can develop manufacturing

MARKETING MEMO • GUIDELINES FOR MANAGING JOINT VENTURES IN ASIA

Starting the JV

Choosing the right partner is critical. The three major elements of a good partner include compatibility, capability to contribute complementary strengths and resources, and commitment to keeping the venture going through difficult times.

Living with the JV

To make the JV work, much depends on the previous cooperation between the partners and external market conditions. Six tenets JV managers deem essential for success include:

1. **Mutual trust, particularly at senior management levels, that can carry the JV through turbulent times.**
2. **The ability to compromise—delivering ultimatums is a sure way to kill a JV.**
3. **Favorable business conditions, under which the JV can make a few mistakes without upsetting parents, and profits can be used to build up the JV's strength.**
4. **Granting the JV autonomy to help it develop.**
5. **Agreeing on the future direction and goals of the JV to facilitate compromises on difficult issues and strengthen the commitment to work together.**
6. **Building a separate culture for the JV to combine the best of both worlds,** e.g., blending Western management styles to take into account Asian preferences and practices. The colonial mentality of some international expatriates (or even Western-educated Asian managers) has been shown to reduce the full potential of the JV's employees.

Managing the Breakup

JVs last for varying lengths of time. When one partner wants to separate, it is important to institute divorce proceedings that reach an amicable settlement. Success at separation often results from JV partners:

1. **Recognizing the possibility of dissolution at the venture's outset.**
2. **Writing separation clauses into the JV contract to provide for an equitable valuation of assets** — Engaging a lawyer with expertise in legal and cultural issues or who can bring in an Asian lawyer would be useful to this end. However, in Japan and China, the lawyer is neither as ubiquitous nor as influential as he or she is in the West.
3. **Setting up transitional supplier agreements.**
4. **Recognizing the importance of communicating and dealing fairly with employees of the JV.**

Sources: Mimi Cauley de la Sierra, "Managing a Successful Global Alliance." *Business International Corporation*, New York, July 1992; Robert P. Piccus, "Strategic Alliances with Japan: Cross-Border Options for Asia/Pacific." *Business International Asia/Pacific Ltd*, Hong Kong, December 1991; David M. Reid, "Effective Marketing for Japan: The Consumer Goods Experience." *Business International Asia/Pacific Ltd*, Hong Kong, June 1991, pp. 31–39; Frederic Swierczek and Georges Hirsch, "Joint Ventures in Asia and Multicultural Management." *European Management Journal,* June 1994, pp. 197–209; D. Robert Webster, "International Joint Ventures with Pacific Rim Partners." *Business Horizons,* March–April 1989, pp. 65–71.

and marketing policies that serve its long-term international objectives. Fifth, the firm assures itself access to the market in case the host country starts insisting that locally purchased goods have domestic content.

Companies may also engage in direct investment due to the underperformance of their overseas joint ventures. Thus Wholly-Foreign Owned Enterprises (WFOEs) are becoming more evident in China. They have met only minimal resistance with authorities who are more concerned about what outside investors bring to China (jobs, technology, and foreign exchange), rather than how their deals are structured. The Chinese government particularly values investments in the priority sectors of agriculture, energy, transportation, industrial raw materials, and technology. Foreign businesses are also finding that the flexibility and managerial control of WFOEs fit well with China's current competitive situation. Motorola and General Motors have shown that WFOEs are even possible in more regulated industries such as telecommunications and automotives. However, unless the investment is valued, Chinese authorities will demand an export quota of at least 50 percent from WFOEs as a "fee" for not working with a Chinese partner.[37]

The main disadvantage of direct investment is that the firm exposes a large investment to risks such as blocked or devalued currencies, worsening markets, or expropriation. The firm will find it expensive to reduce or close down its operations, because the host country might require substantial severance pay to the employees.

Deciding on the Marketing Program

International companies must decide how much to adapt their marketing strategy to local conditions.[38] At one extreme are companies that use a globally standardized marketing mix worldwide. Standardization of the product, communication, and distribution channels promises the lowest costs. Table 21.1 summarizes some of the pros and cons of standardizing the marketing program. At the other extreme is an adapted marketing mix, where the producer adjusts the marketing program to each target market. For a discussion of the main issues, see "Marketing Insight: Global Standardization or Adaptation?"

MARKETING INSIGHT • GLOBAL STANDARDIZATION OR ADAPTATION?

The marketing concept holds that consumer needs vary and that marketing programs will be more effective when they are tailored to each target group. This also applies to foreign markets. Yet in 1983, Levitt challenged this view and supplied the intellectual rationale for global standardization: "The world is becoming a common marketplace in which people—no matter where they live—desire the same products and lifestyles."

The development of the Web, the rapid spread of cable and satellite TV around the world, and the global linking of telecommunications networks have led to a convergence of lifestyles. The convergence of needs and wants has created global markets for standardized products, particularly among the young middle class.

Levitt favors global corporations that try to sell the same product the same way to all consumers. They focus on similarities across world markets and "sensibly force suitably standardized products and services on the entire globe." These global marketers achieve economies through standardization of production, distribution, marketing, and management. They translate their efficiency into greater value for consumers by offering high quality and more reliable products at lower prices.

Coca-Cola, McDonald's, Marlboro, Nike, the NBA, and Gillette are among the companies that have successfully marketed global products. Consider Gillette: some 1.2 billion people use at least one Gillette product daily, according to the company's estimates. Gillette enjoys huge economies of scale by selling a few types of razor blades in every single market.

Many companies have tried to launch their version of a world product. Yet, most products require some adaptation. Toyota's Corolla will exhibit some differences in styling. McDonald's offers a ham and cheese "Croque McDo" in France, a variation of the French favorite croque monsieur. Coca-Cola is sweeter or less carbonated in certain countries. Rather than assuming that its domestic product can be introduced "as is" in another country, the company should review the following elements and determine which would add more revenue than cost:

- Product features
- Brand name
- Labeling
- Packaging
- Colors
- Advertising execution
- Materials
- Prices
- Sales promotion
- Advertising themes
- Advertising media

Consumer behavior can dramatically differ across markets. Take beverages. One of the highest per capita consumption of carbonated soft drinks is the U.S. with 203.9 liters per capita consumption; Italy is among the lowest. But Italy is one of the highest per capita drinkers of bottled water with 164.4 liters, whereas the U.K. is only 20 liters. For beer, Ireland and the Czech Republic lead the pack, with over 150 liters per capita, with France among the lowest at 35.9 liters.

Besides demand-side differences, supply-side differences can also prevail. Levitt's critics pointed out that flexible manufacturing techniques made it easier to produce many different product versions, tailored to particular countries. One study showed that companies made one or more marketing-mix adaptations in 80 percent of their foreign products and that the average number of adapted elements was four. So perhaps Levitt's globalization dictum should be rephrased. Global marketing, yes. Global standardization, not necessarily.

Sources: Theodore Levitt, "The Globalization of Markets." *Harvard Business Review,* May-June 1983, pp. 92–102; Bernard Wysocki Jr., "The Global Mall: In Developing Nations, Many Youths Splurge, Mainly on U.S. Goods." *Wall Street Journal,* June 26, 1997, p. A1; "What Makes a Company Great?." *Fortune,* October 26, 1998, pp. 218–226; David M. Szymanski, Sundar G. Bharadwaj, and P. Rajan Varadarajan, "Standardization versus Adaptation of International Marketing Strategy: An Empirical Investigation." *Journal of Marketing,* October 1993, pp. 1–17; "Burgers and Fries a la Francaise." *The Economist,* April 17, 2004, pp. 60-61; Johny K. Johansson, "Global Marketing: Research on Foreign Entry, Local Marketing, Global Management." In *Handbook of Marketing,* Bart Weitz and Robin Wensley, eds., (London: Sage Publications), pp. 457–483.

Table 21.1 Global Marketing Pros and Cons

Advantages
• Economies of scale in production and distrubution
• Lower marketing costs
• Power and scope
• Consistency in brand image
• Ability to leverage good ideas quickly and efficiently
• Uniformity of marketing practices
Disadvantages
• Differences in consumer needs, wants, and usage patterns for products
• Differences in consumer response to marketing-mix elements
• Difference in brand and product development and the competitive environment
• Differences in the legal environment
• Differences in marketing institutions
• Differences in administrative procedures

Although many companies have tried to launch their version of a world product, most products require at least some adaptation. Barbie dolls have flatter chests and shorter legs in Japan. Some Nissan models go by different names in some countries. Rather than assuming it can introduce its domestic product "as is" in another country, the company should review the following elements and determine which add more revenue than cost:

- Product features
- Labeling
- Colors
- Materials
- Sales promotion
- Advertising media
- Brand name
- Packaging
- Advertising execution
- Prices
- Advertising themes

Consumer behavior can dramatically differ across markets. Satisfying different consumer needs and wants can require different marketing programs. Cultural differences can often be pronounced across countries. Hofstede identifies four cultural dimensions that can differentiate countries:[39]

1. ***Individualism vs. collectivism*** — In collectivist societies, such as Japan, the self-worth of an individual is rooted more in the social system than in individual achievement.
2. ***High vs. low power distance*** — High power distance cultures tend to be less egalitarian.
3. ***Masculine vs. feminine*** — How much the culture is dominated by assertive males versus nurturing females.
4. ***Weak vs. strong uncertainty avoidance*** — How risk-tolerant or -aversive people are.

Besides demand-side differences, supply-side differences can prevail. Flexible manufacturing techniques make it easier to produce many different product versions, tailored to particular countries.

Most brands are adapted to some extent to reflect significant differences in consumer behavior, brand development, competitive forces, and the legal or political environment.[40] Even global brands undergo some changes in product features, packaging, channels, pricing, or communications in different global markets.[41] (See "Marketing Memo: The Ten Commandments of Global Branding.") Firms must make sure their message is relevant to consumers in every market.

MARKETING MEMO • THE TEN COMMANDMENTS OF GLOBAL BRANDING

For many companies, global branding has been both a blessing and a curse. A global branding program can lower marketing costs, realize greater economies of scale in production, and provide a long-term source of growth. If not designed and implemented properly, it may ignore important differences in consumer behavior and/or the competitive environment in the individual countries. These suggestions can help a company retain many of the advantages of global branding while minimizing the potential disadvantages:

1. **Understand similarities and differences in the global branding landscape.** International markets can vary in terms of brand development, consumer behavior, competitive activity, legal restrictions, and so on.
2. **Do not take shortcuts in brand-building.** Building a brand in new markets should be done from the "bottom-up," both strategically (building awareness before brand image) and tactically (creating sources of brand equity in new markets).
3. **Establish a marketing infrastructure.** A company must either build marketing infrastructure "from scratch" or adapt to existing infrastructure in other countries.
4. **Embrace integrated marketing communications.** A company must often use many forms of communication in overseas markets, not just advertising.
5. **Establish brand partnerships.** Most global brands have marketing partners in their international markets that help companies achieve advantages in distribution, profitability, and added value.
6. **Balance standardization and customization.** Some elements of a marketing program can be standardized (packaging, brand name); others typically require greater customization (distribution channels).
7. **Balance global and local control.** Companies must balance global and local control within the organization and distribute decision making between global and local managers.
8. **Establish operable guidelines.** Brand definition and guidelines must be established, communicated, and properly enforced so that marketers everywhere know what they are expected to do and not do. The goal is to set rules for how the brand should be positioned and marketed.
9. **Implement a global brand equity measurement system.** A global brand equity system is a set of research procedures designed to provide timely, accurate, and actionable information for marketers so they can make the best possible short-run tactical decisions and long-run strategic decisions.
10. **Leverage brand elements.** Proper design and implementation of brand elements (brand name and trademarked brand identifiers) can be an invaluable source of brand equity worldwide.

Source: Adapted from Kevin Lane Keller and Sanjay Sood, "The Ten Commandments of Global Branding." *Asian Journal of Marketing,* 2001, 8(2), pp. 97–108.

Tokyo Disneyland retains much Americana. This concert has a rock-and-roll theme.

Disney—When Disney launched the Euro Disney theme park outside Paris in 1992, it was criticized as being an example of American cultural imperialism. French customs and values, such as serving wine with meals, were ignored. As one Euro Disney executive noted, "When we first launched, there was the belief that it was enough to be Disney. Now we realize our guests need to be welcomed on the basis of their own culture and travel habits." Renamed Disneyland Paris, the theme park eventually became Europe's biggest tourist attraction by making changes and adding more local touches. In Japan, Tokyo Disneyland and DisneySea shows are in Japanese, but retain much Americana. As Winnie the Pooh is Japan's most popular Disney character, it is featured more prominently than Mickey Mouse. In Hong Kong, Disney incorporated Chinese *feng shui* practices in its construction of the park and hotel while retaining American culture in its shows. Hong Kong Disneyland's eight restaurants offer a variety of Asian foods, including roast pork, *dim sum,* and *laksa,* a curry noodle soup from Southeast Asia.[42]

MARKETING INSIGHT • ESTABLISHING GLOBAL SERVICE BRANDS

The world market for services is growing at double the rate of world merchandise trade. Large firms in accounting, advertising, banking, communications, construction, insurance, law, management consulting, and retailing are pursuing global expansion. American Express, Citigroup, Club Med, and Hilton are known worldwide.

Many countries, however, have erected entry barriers or regulations. Malaysia requires all TV commercials to be locally produced with local models. Many U.S. states bar foreign bank branches. At the same time, the U.S. is pressuring South Korea to open its markets to U.S. banks. The World Trade Organization, consisting of 151 countries, and the General Agreement on Tariffs and Trade (GATT), consisting of 128 countries, continue to press for more free trade in international services and other areas.

Retailers who sell books, videos, and CD-ROMs, and entertainment companies have also had to contend with a culture of censorship in countries such as China and Singapore. In Singapore, for example, book retailers must submit potentially "hot" materials to the Committee on Undesirable Publications.

Sources: Charles P. Wallace, "Charge!" *Fortune,* September 28, 1998, pp. 189–196, <www.wto.org>; Ben Dolven, "Find the Niche." *Far Eastern Economic Review,* March 26, 1998, pp. 58–59.

Product

Some types of products travel better across borders than others—food and beverage marketers have to contend with widely varying tastes.[43] "Marketing Insight: Establishing Global Service Brands" describes some of the special concerns for marketing services globally. Keegan has distinguished five adaptation strategies of product and communications to a foreign market (see Figure 21.3).[44]

Communications \ Product	Do Not Change Product	Adapt Product	Develop New Product
Do Not Change Communications	Straight extension	Product adaptation	Product invention
Adapt Communications	Communication adaptation	Dual adaptation	

Figure 21.3 Five International Product and Communication Strategies

Straight extension means introducing the product in the foreign market without any change. Straight extension is tempting because it involves no additional R&D expense, manufacturing retooling, or promotional modification; but it can be costly in the long run.

Product adaptation involves altering the product to meet local conditions or preferences. For instance, Unilever uses black sesame and ginseng in its shampoo for the China market. There are several levels of adaptation.

- **A company can produce a regional version of its product.** Finnish mobile phone superstar Nokia customized its 6100 series phone for every major market. Developers built in rudimentary voice recognition for Asia, where keyboards are a problem, and raised the ring volume so the phone could be heard on crowded Asian streets.
- **A company can produce a country version of its product.** In Japan, Mister Donut's coffee cup is smaller and lighter to fit the hand of the average Japanese consumer; even the doughnuts are a little smaller.
- **A company can produce a city version of its product**—for instance, a beer to meet Shanghai tastes or Tokyo tastes.
- **A company can produce different retailer versions of its product,** such as different coffee brews for different chain stores.

Product invention consists of creating something new. It can take two forms. Backward invention is re-introducing earlier product forms that are well adapted to a foreign country's needs. Mitsubishi transferred the technology of its older models to help develop Malaysia's Proton car. Panasonic shipped outdated cassette players when the brand was first introduced to Chinese households.

Forward invention is creating a new product to meet a need in another country. There is an enormous need in less developed countries for low-cost, high-protein foods. Toyota produces vehicles specifically designed, with the help of local employees, to suit the tastes of these markets.[45]

Levi's—Levi's learned the hard way that one size does not fit all of Asia. The Japanese are built differently from the Chinese, who are built differently from the Australians. In 2002, when it brought its new Levi's Engineered Jeans, developed in Europe, straight to the Asian market, sales did not take off. The jeans gaped at the waist of most Asian women and the leg length, which the styling made difficult to alter, was too long. Now, about 20 percent of Levi's clothes sold in Asia are original products designed in one of its regional R&D centers. Another 75 percent of its clothes are styles brought in from Europe or the U.S. but redesigned at those centers to fit Asian builds.[46]

Product invention is a costly strategy, but the payoffs can be great, particularly if a company can parlay a product innovation into other countries. In globalization's latest twist, American companies are not only inventing new products for overseas markets, but also lifting products and ideas from their international operations and bringing them home.

McDonald's—For nearly 20 years, McDonald's has achieved solid international growth, which accounts for about 60 percent of corporate profits. In McDonald's international operations, local managers and franchise operators have much say in how the business is run. The locals create a supply chain infrastructure within each country or region and everything is financed in the local currency. The strategy is to be as much a local business as possible. Much attention is placed on local customs like food tastes. McDonald's allowed its local Indonesian managers to add rice to its menu after the rupiah collapsed in 1997, which made its main imported product, french fries, much too expensive. In Seoul, the burger chain sells roast pork on a bun with garlicky soy sauce. In Taiwan, it offers rice meals in four varieties, while its Thai menu includes chicken congee and fancy omelettes with steamed rice. In India, the restaurants feature a vegetable burger with cheese. In Malaysia, the breakfast menu includes chicken porridge. In Singapore, McDonald's introduced rice burgers. McDonald's now wants to use the strategies that have made its international operations so profitable to improve its U.S. market share. It is testing a variation of the theme that "all business is local" by decentralizing marketing and decision making at home. Many decisions have been shifted closer to the marketplace, enabling quicker action to be taken. McDonald's is also trying to alleviate the strain with its franchise operators by getting to know owner operators and their concerns. A more flexible cooking system has also generated somewhat higher customer satisfaction.[47]

McDonald's in Malaysia adapts its menu to include *bubur ayam* or chicken porridge—a local favorite breakfast meal.

In launching products and services globally, certain brand elements may have to be changed. Brand slogans or ad taglines sometimes have to be changed too:[48]

- Electrolux's ad line for its vacuum cleaners in Korea was retranslated into English—"Nothing sucks like an Electrolux"—which certainly would not lure customers!
- Pepsi's "Come Alive with Pepsi" was translated as "Come out of the Grave with Pepsi" in China.

Table 21.2 lists some other famous blunders in this arena.

Table 21.2 Blunders in International Marketing

- Philips began to earn a profit in Japan only after it had reduced the size of its coffeemakers to fit into smaller Japanese kitchens and its shavers to fit smaller Japanese hands.
- Coca-Cola had to withdraw its two-liter bottle in Spain after discovering that few Spaniards owned refrigerators with large enough compartments to accommodate it.
- Procter & Gamble's Crest toothpaste initially failed in Mexico when it used the U.S. campaign. Mexicans did not care as much for the decay-prevention benefit, nor did scientifically oriented advertising appeal to them.
- General Foods squandered millions trying to introduce packaged cake mixes to Japanese consumers. The company failed to note that only 3 percent of Japanese homes were equipped with ovens.
- S. C. Johnson's wax floor polish initially failed in Japan. The wax made the floors too slippery, and Johnson had overlooked the fact that Japanese do not wear shoes in their homes.

Different standards across countries may also force businesses to adapt their products. This can add 10 to 15 percent to operating costs. For example, at one time, a company serving the Indonesian and Thai soap markets needed different production runs to manufacture soap bars. In Indonesia, weight was measured at the factory, while in Thailand, it was measured on the shelf. Evaporation during transport meant that 100-gram soap bars had to be produced at 104 grams for the Thai market.[49]

Communications

Companies can run the same marketing communications programs as used in the home market or change them for each local market, a process called communication adaptation. If it adapts both the product and the communication, the company engages in dual adaptation.

Consider the message. The company can use one message everywhere, varying only the language, name, and colors.[50] Exxon used "Put a tiger in your tank" with minor variations and gained international recognition. Colors can be changed to avoid taboos in some countries. Purple is associated with death in Myanmar and some Latin American nations; white is a mourning color in India; and green is associated with disease in Malaysia.[51]

The second possibility is to use the same theme globally but adapt the copy to each local market. Apple Computer's "Mac vs. PC," which was voted the best U.S. ad campaign of 2006 by *Adweek* magazine, features two actors bantering. One is hip-looking (Apple), the other nerdy-looking (PC). Apple dubbed the ads for Spain, France, Germany, and Italy but chose to reshoot and rescript for the United Kingdom and Japan—two important markets with unique advertising and comedy cultures. The U.K. ads followed a similar formula but tweaked the jokes to reflect British humor; the Japanese ads avoided direct comparisons and were more subtle in tone.[52]

The third approach consists of developing a global pool of ads, from which each country selects the most appropriate. Levi's uses this approach. Its global ad theme is the company's American roots. However, it lets each market choose the TV commercial that works best for that market. Thus in Indonesia, local managers selected one showing Levi's-clad teenagers cruising around in a 1960 convertible; while in Japan, Levi Strauss used American movie icons like James Dean because of Japanese obsession with American cultural heroes.

Finally, some companies allow their country managers to create country-specific ads—within guidelines. Ajinomoto, the Japanese seasoning company, used alliterative phrasing in its TV commercials to help consumers remember the product. Country managers could choose the alliterative phrasing to suit their market. For instance, in the Philippines, it is "Tak Tak;" in Indonesia, it is "Chup Chup;" and in Thailand, it is "Thae Thae." Also, in the Philippines, it is "you're sure it's pure;" and in Indonesia, "Putih dan Gurih" ("White and Delicious"). Billabong, the Australian board sports brand, feels that in Southeast Asia, it has to move away slightly from a completely standardized global approach to its marketing. While it is imperative to stick with its core values of athleticism with board sports, Billabong created a series of country-specific ads featuring a top board sport personality from each country.

Such communication adaptation may also be reflected in how companies structure their relationships with ad agencies. For example, Heineken's global brand team in Amsterdam works with three global ad agencies—Weiden + Kennedy Amsterdam, Publicis New York, and Bates Asia. However, each country is autonomous in how it manages the brand, so long as it sticks within Heineken's global strategy and brand rules.[53]

The use of media also requires international adaptation because media availability varies from country to country. Saudi Arabia does not want advertisers to use women in ads. India taxes advertising. There are also variations in regulations pertaining to advertising across borders:

Indonesia's Rahtu

Malaysia's Usher

Singapore's Firdaus

Billabong adapts its ads to the local market while adhering to its core values of athleticism in board sports. In Indonesia, its ad featured Rahtu, one of Indonesia's top 10 surfers. In Malaysia, Usher, a Billabong skater, is the winner in Bowl Competition 2008. In Singapore, the ad featured Firdaus, a Billabong skater who won the Asian X Games 2007.

Tobacco advertising—In Taiwan and South Korea, cigarette advertising is allowed in magazines only. Malaysia bans cigarette advertising and event sponsorship except for events such as its Formula One Grand Prix. China recently banned billboard cigarette advertising. At both extremes, there are no restrictions in Japan, the Philippines, and Indonesia as cigarette advertising is permitted in print, radio, and television; while in Hong Kong, Singapore, Thailand, and Vietnam, all forms of cigarette advertising and promotion are banned. Singapore and Thailand also do not allow sponsorship of programs or events by cigarette companies, and all information on market share of brands in these countries is proprietary.

Adapting creative strategies and styles to suit different Asian markets is prevalent as these markets vary in cultural orientation. In more collectivistic societies such as Hong Kong, South Korea, and Taiwan, ads tend to favor psychological over informative appeals. Another study found two broad types of reactions among upscale Chinese consumers to global and local ads.[54] One was largely driven by the desire for global cosmopolitanism and status goods for the sake of *mianzi* (face or prestige), whereas the other was motivated by a more nationalistic desire to invoke Chinese values that are seen as local in origin. Thus advertisers cannot assume that "West is best" or that seemingly straightforward Western advertising techniques will work the same way in China. One successful ad is by Yang-shengtang turtle pills. By emphasizing the Chinese cultural values of filial loyalty, care for family, and respect for the elderly, this Chinese brand created a strongly emotional positive image. Coca-Cola's success in sinicizing Sprite through the use of a Chinese Olympic diving champion is an example of success through localizing rather than globalizing advertising messages.

Marketers must also adapt sales-promotion techniques to different markets. Several Asian countries have laws preventing or limiting sales-promotion tools such as discounts, rebates, coupons, games of chance, and premiums. In Indonesia, contest winners are required to answer a question on skill so that winning is not based purely on luck. Reliance on mass media and sales promotion in developed markets tends to be based on advertising which is less expensive than face-to-face contact. However, in several emerging countries in Asia, the face-to-face method may be more economical:

Citibank—When Citibank launched its credit card in some emerging Asian countries, it found that the cost-per-customer of door-to-door sales was lower than magazine inserts, direct mail, and application forms placed on sales counters. Personal selling also allowed it to deliver more customized and interactive messages. This is important at an early stage in a product's life cycle and led to higher conversion rates than television advertising.

In developing markets, high mobile phone penetration and high text-messaging volume make mobile marketing attractive. A pioneer in China, Coca-Cola China created a national campaign asking Beijing residents to send text messages guessing the high temperature in the city every day for just over a month, for a chance to win a one-year supply of Coke products. The campaign attracted more than four million messages over the course of 35 days.[55]

Personal selling tactics may need to change too. The direct, no-nonsense approach favored in the U.S. (characterized by a "let's get down to business" and "what's in it for me" stance) may not work as well in Asia where an indirect, subtle approach can be more effective.[56] With younger, more worldly employees, however, such cultural differences may be less pronounced.

Price

Multinationals face several pricing problems when selling abroad. They must deal with price escalation, transfer prices, dumping charges, and gray markets.

Microsoft—When Microsoft entered China, the company made its first big blunder by trying to sell its Windows operating system at the same high price it commands in the developed world. Yet, pirated copies were available at rock-bottom prices. Microsoft spent the next 10 years trying to crack down on piracy in China, suing companies for using its software illegally and always losing in court. The Chinese government grew ever more mistrustful of Microsoft—even suspecting the United States was spying via the software—and put open-source Linux operating systems on all workers' PCs. So how did Microsoft become so respected in China that CEO Bill Gates is now a celebrity? For one thing, by doing a complete turnaround and tolerating piracy. "It's easier for our software to compete with Linux when there's piracy than when there's not," says Gates. Yet, the best move Microsoft made was to collaborate with the Chinese government and open a research center in Beijing, which today lures the country's top computer scientists. Rather than being known as a company that comes to China to sue people, it is regarded as a company with long-term vision.[57]

When companies sell their goods abroad, they face a price escalation problem. A Gucci handbag may sell for $120 in Italy and $240 in the U.S. Why? Gucci has to add the cost of transportation, tariffs, importer margin, wholesaler margin, and retailer margin to its factory price. Depending on these added costs as well as the currency-fluctuation risk, the product might have to sell for two to five times as much in another country to make the same profit for the manufacturer. Because the cost escalation varies from country to country, the question is how to set the prices in different countries. Companies have three choices:

1. **Set a uniform price everywhere.** Pokka might want to charge 75 cents for Pokka products everywhere in the world, but then Pokka would earn quite different profit rates in different countries. Also, this strategy would result in the price being too high in poor countries and not high enough in rich countries.
2. **Set a market-based price in each country.** Here Pokka would charge what each country could afford, but this strategy ignores differences in the actual cost from country to country. Also, it could lead to a situation in which intermediaries in low-price countries reship their Pokka products to high-price countries.
3. **Set a cost-based price in each country.** Here Pokka would use a standard markup of its costs everywhere, but this strategy might price Pokka out of the market in countries where its costs are high.

Price could be set in the context of local consumers' Purchasing Power Parity (PPP).[58] One company found that in China, the number of consumers in the $10,000–$40,000 income range was less than three million at market exchange rates, but over 80 million at the PPP rates. Companies may need to work back from PPP numbers when pricing products.

In emerging Asian countries, this may imply thin margins, but hopefully large volumes. If successful, such a strategy could drive product, packaging, distribution, and communication decisions. For example, Unilever's Lifebuoy soap, which is popular in

India and Indonesia, is priced low, made using inexpensive local ingredients and packaging, and distributed intensively. By volume, Lifebuoy is the world's largest-selling brand of soap.

Danone—From its research, Danone knows that Malaysian and Singaporean consumers are unlikely to accept a dairy product that is less than 100 percent made from milk. But to do that in China would mean that the product would have to be priced too high for a vast number of people. So, for the Chinese market, a spectrum of dairy products is offered, down to where milk is merely a minor ingredient. The price points—which affect product and packaging strategies—similarly play a critical role. The Indian price or resistance point is 10 cents, half the 25 cents for the mainland Chinese given the latter's higher average discretionary income.

Having said that, it does not necessarily imply that prices must be kept low for all emerging Asian markets. Nokia found that Asians buy the coolest, most feature-packed mobile phone they can afford and then pick the network to use it on. In contrast, U.S. consumers buy whichever phone the network gives away for a two-year contract. Hence, Nokia sells phones at a higher average price in emerging countries like China than it does in the U.S.[59]

Another problem arises when a company sets a transfer price (the price it charges another unit in the company) for goods that it ships to its foreign subsidiaries. If the company charges too high a price to a subsidiary, it may end up paying higher tariff duties, although it may pay lower income taxes in the foreign country. If the company charges too low a price to its subsidiary, it can be charged with dumping. Dumping occurs when a company charges either less than its costs or less than it charges in its home market, to enter or win a market.

Various governments are watching for abuses and often force companies to charge the arm's-length price—that is, the price charged by other competitors for the same or a similar product. Businesses also lobby governments to take action against perceived dumping by foreign, often Asian, competitors to preserve their commercial interests.

Many multinationals are plagued by the gray-market problem. The gray market consists of branded products diverted from normal or authorized distribution channels in the country of product origin or across international borders. Dealers in the low-price country find ways to sell some of their products in higher-price countries, thus earning more. Often a company finds some enterprising distributors buying more than they can sell in their own country and reshipping the goods to another country to take advantage of price differences. "Marketing Insight: Unauthorized Sales – Dealing with the Gray Market and Counterfeit Products" describes some issues with gray markets, as well as product fakes.

The Internet will also reduce price differentiation between countries. When companies sell their wares over the Internet, price will become transparent: customers can easily find out how much products sell for in different countries. Take an online training course, for instance. Whereas the price of a classroom-delivered day of training can vary significantly from the U.S. to France to Thailand, the price of an online-delivered day of training would have to be similar.[60]

Another recent global pricing challenge is that countries with overcapacity, cheap currencies, and the need to export aggressively have pushed prices down and devalued their currencies. For multinational firms, this poses challenges: sluggish demand and reluctance to pay higher prices make selling in these emerging markets difficult. Instead of lowering prices, and taking a loss, some multinationals have found more lucrative and creative means of coping.[61]

MARKETING INSIGHT • UNAUTHORIZED SALES — DEALING WITH THE GRAY MARKET AND COUNTERFEIT PRODUCTS

One of the downsides of globalization is that someone, somewhere, could be making money from your products and services, without your authorization or even knowledge. Two particularly thorny problems exist with gray markets and counterfeits.

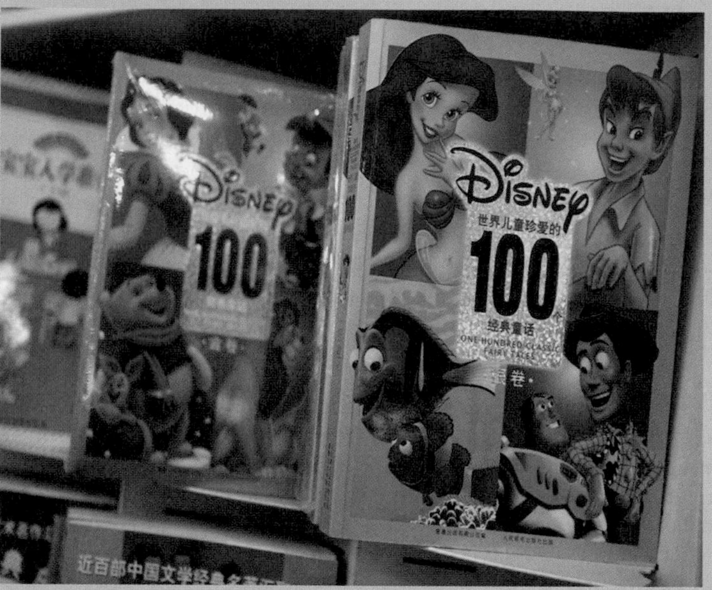

To prevent counterfeiting of its many products in China, Disney created an entire rewards program that required customers to submit proof of purchase for prizes such as a trip to Hong Kong Disneyland.

The Gray Market

Research suggests that gray market activity—sales of genuine trademarked products through distribution channels unauthorized by the manufacturer or brand owner—accounts for over $40 billion in revenue each year. Gray markets create a "free-riding problem" and make legitimate distributors' investments in supporting a manufacturer's product less productive. Gray markets also make a selective distribution system more intensive. Gray markets harm distributor relations, tarnish the manufacturer's brand equity, and undermine the integrity of the distribution channel.

Multinationals try to prevent gray markets by policing the distributors, by raising their prices to lower-cost distributors, or by altering the product characteristics or service warranties for different countries.

One research study found that gray market activity was most effectively deterred when the penalties were severe, when manufacturers were able to detect violations or mete out punishments in a timely fashion, or both.

Counterfeit Products

With the latest technology available everywhere, it's no surprise that fakes and imitations have become a major problem. Counterfeiting, estimated to cost businesses $600 billion a year, is expected to increase to $1.2 trillion by 2009. The Chinese have been prime offenders. According to U.S. Customs and Border Protection, 88 percent of all goods seized by Customs in a recent year originated in China (81 percent), Hong Kong (6 percent), or Taiwan (1 percent).

Fakes take a big bite of the profits of luxury brands such as Hermès, LVMH Moët Hennessy Louis Vuitton, Tiffany, and iPhones but faulty counterfeits can literally kill people. Mobile phones with counterfeit batteries, fake brake pads made of compressed grass trimmings, and counterfeit airline parts pose safety risks to consumers. Virtually every product is vulnerable. As one anti-counterfeit consultant observed, "If you can make it, they can fake it." Defending against counterfeiters is difficult; some observers estimate that a new security system can be just months old before counterfeiters start nibbling at sales again.

The Web has been especially problematic. One estimate put Web sales of knockoff goods from watches to pharmacueticals at $119 billion in 2007—up from $84 billion the year before. eBay has come under heavy criticism from some manufacturers. Based on a survey of thousands of items, LVMH estimated 90 percent of Louis Vuitton and Christian Dior items listed on eBay were fakes, prompting the firm to sue.

Manufacturers are fighting back online with Web-crawling software that detects fraud and automatically sends warnings to apparent violaters without the need for any human intervention. Acushnet, maker of Titleist golf clubs and balls, shut down 75 auctions of knockoff gear in one day with just one mouse click. Web-crawling technology searches for counterfeit storefronts and sales by detecting domain names similar to legitimate brands and unauthorized Web sites that plaster brand trademarks and logos all over their homepages. It also checks for keywords such as "cheap," "discount," "authentic," and "factory variants," as well as colors that products were never made in and prices that are far too low.

Some counterfeiters have been very brazen. Take Beijing's Shijingshan Amusement Park. With it's slogan, "Disneyland is Not Too Far," the park features a replica of the Magic Kingdom complete with Cinderella's castle, and staff dressed as Mickey Mouse, Minnie Mouse, Donald Duck and other Disney characters.

Dealing with counterfeits is a never-ending struggle, and firms are trying all kinds of tacks online and off-line to fight back. To combat piracy in China, Disney developed a "Disney Magical Journey" rewards program. Consumers had to peel red hologram-covered stickers off legitimate Disney products, attach them to a form with some personal details, and mail them in to enter a contest for free Disney DVDs, television sets, and a trip to Hong Kong Disneyland. In addition to raising awareness of legitimate products and developing a database of Disney-friendly Chinese consumers, the promotion helped clean up some of Disney's channels as consumers would call to alert the company to retailers that, perhaps even unknowingly, were selling product fakes.

Sources: Gray Markets: <www.agmaglobal.org>; David Blanchard, "Just in Time–How to Fix a Leaky Supply Chain." *IndustryWeek*, May 1, 2007; Kersi D. Antia, Mark E. Bergen, Shantanu Dutta, and Robert J. Fisher, "How Does Enforcement Deter Gray Market Incidence?" *Journal of Marketing*, January 2006, 70, pp. 92–106; Matthew B. Myers and David A. Griffith, "Strategies for Combating Gray Market Activity." *Business Horizons*, November-December 1999, 42, pp. 2–8. Counterfeiting: Deborah Kong, "Smart Tech Fights Fakes." *Business*, 2.0, March 2007, p. 30; Eric Shine, "Faking Out the Fakers." *BusinessWeek*, June 4, 2007, pp. 76–80; Geoffrey A. Fowler, "Disney Tries New Antipiracy Tack." *Wall Street Journal*, May 31, 2006, Carol Matlack, "Fed Up with Fakes." *BusinessWeek*, October 9, 2006, pp. 56–57; Justin Mitchell,"China's Blurry Line Between Fake and Real." <www.asiasentinel.com>, May 28, 2007.

General Electric—Rather than striving for larger market share, GE's power systems unit focused on winning a larger percentage of each customer's expenditures. The unit asked its top 100 customers what services were most critical to them and how GE could provide or improve them. The answers prompted GE to cut its response time for replacing old or damaged parts from 12 weeks to six. It began advising customers on the nuances of doing business in the diverse environments of Europe and Asia and providing maintenance staff for occasional equipment upgrades. By adding value and helping customers reduce their costs and become more efficient, GE avoided a move to commodity pricing and generated bigger margins and record revenues.[62]

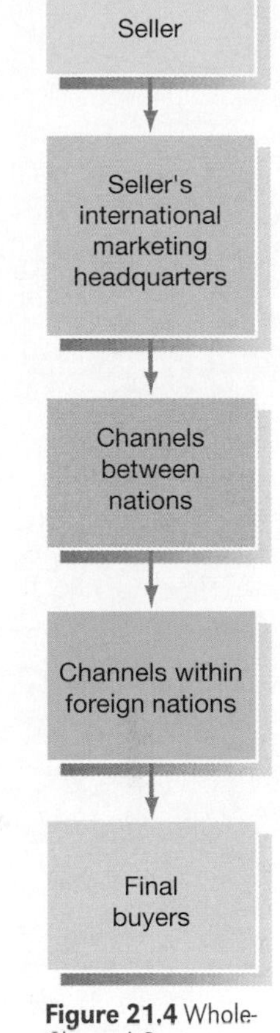

Figure 21.4 Whole-Channel Concept for International Marketing

Nonetheless, Western MNCs are facing relentless price pressure from emerging-market companies with lower product costs and comparable technology. Some have coined the term "China price" to refer to the price pressure U.S. businesses are facing from China's low wages and high technology. Such pressure is not only felt in low-tech sectors, but also in knowledge-intensive industries where the U.S. was assumed to continue domination. For example, in the networking equipment market, a made-in-China datacom switch for 3Com has a list price of $183,000 compared to $245,000 for a comparable switch by Cisco. XCel Mold of Ohio bid $2.07 million to supply a set of plastic molds to a U.S. appliance maker but lost the business when a Chinese supplier bid $1.44 million.[63]

Distribution Channels

Many manufacturers think their job is done once the product leaves the factory. They should pay attention to how the product moves within the foreign country. They should take a whole-channel view of the problem of distributing products to final users. Figure 21.4 shows the three major links between seller and ultimate buyer. In the first link, seller's international marketing headquarters, the export department or international division makes decisions on channels and other marketing-mix elements. The second link, channels between nations, gets the products to the borders of the foreign nation. The decisions made in this link include the types of intermediaries (agents, trading companies) that will be used, the type of transportation (air, sea), and the financing and risk arrangements. The third link, channels within foreign nations, gets the products from their entry point to final buyers and users.

Distribution channels within countries vary considerably. To sell soap in Japan, Procter & Gamble has to work through one of the most complicated distribution systems in the world. It must sell to a general wholesaler, who sells to a product wholesaler, who sells to a product-specialty wholesaler, who sells to a regional wholesaler, who sells to a local wholesaler, who finally sells to retailers. All these distribution levels can mean that the consumer's price ends up double or triple the importer's price. If P&G takes the soap to tropical Africa, the company might sell to an import wholesaler, who sells to several jobbers, who sell to petty traders (mostly women) working in local markets.

Retail outlets vary widely in size and character, forcing marketers to adapt their package sizes, price, and distribution channels to environments such as rural India.

Another difference lies in the size and character of retail units abroad. Large-scale retail chains dominate the developed Asian economies, but much regional retailing is in the hands of small, independent retailers. In India, millions of retailers operate tiny shops or sell in open markets. Their markups are high, but the real price is brought down through haggling. Incomes are low, and people must shop daily for small amounts; they are limited to whatever quantity can be carried home on foot or on a bicycle. Most homes lack storage space and refrigeration. Packaging costs are kept low to keep prices low. In India, cigarettes are often bought singly. Breaking bulk remains an important function of intermediaries and helps perpetuate the long channels of distribution, which are a major obstacle to the expansion of large-scale retailing in developing countries.

One distribution network unique to India is its *dabbawalas*. A *dabbawala* is a person who delivers lunch boxes. In Mumbai, a total of 5,000 *dabbawalas* deliver almost 2,00,000 lunches everyday with precision and punctuality. There is only one error in every 6,00,000 deliveries—a standard that has earned them the Six Sigma Certification for Quality. This has prompted both local and foreign companies to use them as agents for direct marketing. Airtel, India's telecom provider, uses the network of *dabbawalas* to deliver and promote handsets, new connections, and prepaid user cards. Microsoft used the *dabbawalas* to promote its Windows package for a campaign called "Asli PC," meaning "Genuine PC." The use of this channel reinforces the value of authenticity associated with its brand.[64]

When multinationals first enter a country, they prefer to work with local distributors who have good local knowledge, but friction often arises later.[65] The multinational complains that the local distributor does not invest in business growth, does not follow company policy, and does not share enough information. The local distributor complains of insufficient corporate support, impossible goals, and confusing policies. The multinational must choose the right distributors, invest in them, and set up performance goals to which they can agree.[66]

American retail giant Wal-Mart is also expanding overseas, although sometimes to mixed results.[67]

Wal-Mart—Wal-Mart has international operations in 13 countries outside the U.S. including China, Japan, and Korea, serving more than 49 million customers weekly. In 2007, Wal-Mart's international sales increased 17.5 percent over 2006, more than triple the growth rate of its U.S. stores. The company has learned along the way. It does well in China and Mexico but has pulled out of Germany and South Korea. When it first entered Hong Kong in 1994, it was a failure. Hong Kong has a highly dense population. Thus few residents own cars, relying on the city's public transportation system. Wal-Mart's warehouse-style hypermarket, called Value Club, did not do well as Hong Kongers could not easily travel to and from the store on the subway carrying large packages of household items, despite their low price. Nor could they store them in their small apartments. Further, Hong Kongers prefer shopping on a daily basis, stocking up small quantities of household groceries for the family. In Japan, Wal-Mart is struggling to survive. Since it bought over 51 percent stake in Seiyu, a Japanese retail chain, for $1 billion, national-brand food prices come down but high-quality merchandise have also disappeared. While Wal-Mart's "always low prices" may work in developing, under-retailed markets, it does not appear to work in countries like Japan where consumers are willing to pay top prices for exclusive products of the highest quality.[68]

Sometimes, governmental regulations dictate the distribution strategy that is acceptable and firms have to adapt accordingly:

Avon—Avon sought to break China's fragmented distribution barriers through its fabled direct-selling model. But this method was banned in 1998 after the Chinese government lost its patience with a series of failed pyramid schemes. Avon was forced to switch to a retail model overnight. It has since opened 5,500 beauty boutiques and 1,300 beauty counters. With this formidable network, Avon is poised to take on the return of direct selling when the Chinese government lifts the ban.[69]

Attention should also be paid to ensuring good logistical support overseas. When Bojangles, a fast-food chain, opened its first franchise restaurant in Tianjin, it had to find suppliers for 190 components from Cajun-style spices to equipment for the mini-basketball court in the restaurant. This is on top of typical government and real estate issues. Bojangles' due diligence with local suppliers was key because "people are very quick to say that they have the ability to do something by a certain date, and yet you find out very late that they don't." Local attorneys and consultants were hired to find suppliers with good reputation and track records. One Bojangles manager notes, "You always have to be careful who you are dealing with. But in China, you have to be three times as careful."[70]

Supply chain challenges also ensue when Asian companies expand outside the region. For example, Japanese logistics companies face a supply-chain culture clash when they operate in Europe. They struggle to satisfy total quality management and just-in-time procurement. Concepts of service, flexibility, and quality that take precedence in the Japanese approach, sometimes conflict with supply chain efficiency. Non-Japanese employees become frustrated when proposals move slowly through multiple channels before decisions are made and feel that high-ranking Japanese executives spend too much time apologizing for service failures and focus less on planning. Better adaptation to Western business practices seems necessary, including refusing unreasonable requests for services even if this means risking the relationship with the customer, explicitly factoring in the cost of services into the cost of doing business, and selecting Japanese managers for Western subsidiaries based on their communication skills.[71]

Country-of-Origin Effects

In an increasingly connected, highly competitive global marketplace, government officials and marketers are concerned with how attitudes and beliefs about their country affect consumer and business decision making. Country-of-origin perceptions are the mental associations and beliefs triggered by a country. Government officials want to strengthen their country's image to help domestic marketers export, and to attract foreign firms and investors. Marketers want to use country-of-origin perceptions in the most advantageous way possible to sell their products and services.

Building Country Image

Governments now recognize that the image of their cities and countries affects more than tourism and has important value in commerce. Attracting foreign business can improve the local economy, providing jobs and improving infrastructure. City officials in Kobe, Japan, were able to entice multinationals Procter & Gamble, Nestlé, and Eli Lilly to locate their Japanese headquarters in the city through traditional marketing techniques, with careful targeting and positioning.[72] Across the globe, after seeing its name being used to help sell everything from pizza to perfume to blinds, the city of Venice made it a priority to capitalize on its image. City officials developed a trademark that could be licensed to product marketers.[73] Hong Kong officials also developed a symbol—a stylized dragon—to represent their city's core brand values.[74]

Countries worldwide are being marketed like any other brand. New Zealand has developed concerted marketing programs to both sell its products outside the country, via its New Zealand Way program, and to attract tourists by showing the dramatic landscapes featured in *The Lord of the Rings* film trilogy. Both efforts reinforce the image of New Zealand as fresh and pure.

Attitudes toward country-of-origin can change over time. After World War II, Japan had a poor quality image. The success of Sony and its Trinitron TV sets and Japanese automakers Honda and Toyota helped to change people's opinions. Relying partly on the global success of Nokia, Finland launched a campaign to enhance its image as a center of high-tech innovation.[75]

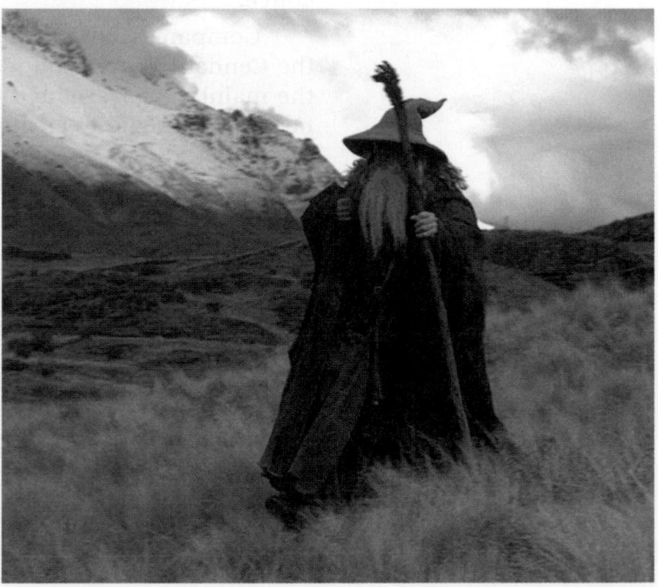

The spectacular landscapes of New Zealand were brought to millions of viewers through the hugely successful *Lord of the Rings* film trilogy, shot there in its entirety. Marketing for a new surge of tourism to New Zealand has carefully played on the films' popularity.

Consumer Perceptions of Country-of-Origin

Global marketers know that buyers hold distinct attitudes and beliefs about brands or products from different countries.[76] These country-of-origin perceptions can affect consumer decision making directly and indirectly. The perceptions may be included as an attribute in decision-making or influence other attributes in the process ("if it is French, it must be stylish"). The mere fact that a brand is perceived as being successful on a global stage may lend credibility and respect.[77] Several studies have found the following:[78]

- **People are often ethnocentric and favorably predisposed to their own country's products,** unless they come from a less developed country.
- **The more favorable a country's image, the more prominently the "Made in..." label should be displayed.**
- **The impact of country-of-origin varies with the type of product.** Consumers want to know where a car was made but not the lubricating oil.
- **Certain countries enjoy a reputation for certain goods:** Japan and Korea for automobiles and consumer electronics; China for toys and textiles; the U.S. for high-tech innovations, soft drinks, toys, cigarettes, and jeans; France for wine, perfume, and luxury goods.
- **Sometimes country-of-origin perception can encompass an entire country's products.** In one study, Chinese consumers in Hong Kong perceived American products as prestigious, Japanese products as innovative, and Chinese products as cheap.

The favorability of country-of-origin perceptions must be considered both from a domestic and foreign perspective. In the domestic market, country-of-origin perceptions may stir consumers' patriotic notions or remind them of their past. As international trade grows, consumers may view certain brands as symbolically important of their own cultural heritage and identity.

A company has several options when its products are competitively priced but their place of origin turns consumers off. The company can consider co-production with a foreign company that has a better name: South Korea could make a fine leather jacket that it sends to Italy for finishing; or the company can adopt a strategy to achieve world-class quality in the local industry, as with Belgian chocolates and Colombian coffee.

Companies can target niches to establish a footing in new markets. For example, the Cendant Hotel Group is launching its Super 8 motel chain in China, in line with the mainland government's call to offer more affordable rooms to tourists and business travelers and to create more jobs in services. Its CEO says, "Overlay the personal income of China's growing middle-class with a country with 21,000 miles of highway and big events coming up like the Beijing Olympics, and we are very bullish on business opportunities."[79]

Companies can also build local roots to increase relevance, as exemplified by Toyota:

Toyota—Toyota has made sales in North America a top priority. As one executive bluntly stated, "We must Americanize." As proof of its conviction, consider the following. Toyota produces one of every six cars sold in the United States, and 60 percent of its cars sold in North America are made in North America. It has the top-selling car (the Camry) and hybrid (the Prius). To publicize its efforts and its convictions, Toyota has run ads touting its $16.6 billion investment in 13 North America factories and its 37,000-plus U.S. employee base. As much as 60 percent of its corporate operating profit comes from the United States, and it sells more cars there than in Japan.[80]

Deciding on the Marketing Organization

Companies manage their international marketing activities in three ways: through export departments, international divisions, or a global organization.

Export Department

A firm normally gets into international marketing by simply shipping out its goods. If its international sales expand, the company organizes an export department consisting of a sales manager and a few assistants. As sales increase, the export department is expanded to include various marketing services so that the company can go after business more aggressively. If the firm moves into joint ventures or direct investment, the export department will no longer be adequate to manage international operations.

International Division

Many companies become involved in several international markets and ventures. Sooner or later they will create international divisions to handle all their international activity. The international division is headed by a division president, who sets goals and budgets and is responsible for the company's international growth.

The international division's corporate staff consists of functional specialists who provide services to various operating units. Operating units can be organized in several ways. First, they can be geographical organizations. Reporting to the international-division president might be regional vice presidents for North America, Latin America, Europe, Africa, the Middle East, and the Far East. Reporting to the regional vice presidents are country managers who are responsible for a sales force, sales branches, distributors, and licensees in the respective countries. The operating units may be world product groups, each with an international vice president responsible for worldwide sales of each product group. The vice presidents may draw on corporate-staff area specialists for expertise on different geographical areas. Finally, operating units may be international subsidiaries, each headed by a president. The various subsidiary presidents report to the president of the international division.

Global Organization

Several firms have become truly global organizations. Their top corporate management and staff plan worldwide manufacturing facilities, marketing policies, financial flows, and logistical systems. The global operating units report directly to the chief executive or executive committee, not to the head of an international division. Executives are trained in worldwide operations. Management is recruited from many countries; components and supplies are purchased where they can be obtained at the least cost; and investments are made where the anticipated returns are greatest.

These companies face several organizational complexities. For example, when pricing a company's mainframe computers to a large banking system in Malaysia, how much influence should the headquarters product manager have? And the company's market manager for the banking sector? And the company's Malaysian country manager?

Different circumstances will dictate different approaches.[81] When forces for "global integration" (capital-intensive production, homogeneous demand) are strong and forces for "national responsiveness" (local standards and barriers, strong local preferences) are weak, a global strategy that treats the world as a single market can make sense (for example, with consumer electronics). When the reverse is true, then a multinational strategy that treats the world as a portfolio of national opportunities can be more appropriate (such as for food or cleaning products).

When both forces prevail to some extent, a "glocal" strategy that standardizes certain elements and localizes other elements can be the way to go (for instance, with telecommunications). As this is often the case, many firms seek a blend of centralized global control from corporate headquarters with input from local and regional marketers. Finding that balance can be tricky, though. Coca-Cola's "think local, act local" philosophy, which decentralized much of the power and responsibility for designing marketing programs and activities, fell apart because many local managers lacked the necessary skills or discipline to do the job. Decidedly un-Coke-like ads appeared—such as skinny-dippers streaking down a beach in Italy—and sales stalled. The pendulum swung back, and Coke executives in Atlanta began to play a stronger strategic role again.[82]

Summary

1. Despite the many challenges in the international arena (shifting borders, unstable governments, foreign-exchange problems, corruption, and technological pirating), companies selling in global industries need to internationalize their operations. Companies cannot stay domestic and expect to maintain their markets.
2. In deciding to go abroad, a company needs to define its international marketing objectives and policies. The company must determine whether to market in a few countries or many countries. It must decide which countries to enter. In general, the candidate countries should be rated on three criteria: market attractiveness, risk, and competitive advantage. Developing countries offer a unique set of opportunities and risks.
3. Once a company decides on a particular country, it must determine the best mode of entry. Its broad choices are indirect exporting, direct exporting, licensing, joint ventures, and direct investment. Each succeeding strategy involves more commitment, risk, control, and profit potential.
4. In developing its marketing program, a company must decide how much to adapt its marketing program—product, communications, distribution, and price—to local conditions. At the product level, firms can pursue a strategy of straight extension, product adaptation, or product invention. At the communication level, firms may choose communication adaptation or dual adaptation. At the price level, firms may encounter price escalation and gray markets. At the distribution level, firms must take a whole-channel view of the challenge of distributing products to the final users. In creating the marketing program, firms must be aware of the cultural, social, political, technological, environmental, and legal limitations they face in other countries.
5. Country-of-origin perceptions can affect consumers and businesses alike. Managing those perceptions in the most advantageous way possible is an important marketing priority.
6. Depending on the level of international involvement, companies manage their international marketing activity in three ways: through export departments, international divisions, or a global organization.

Application

Marketing Debate—Is the World Coming Closer Together?

Many social commentators maintain that youth and teens are becoming more and more alike as time goes on. Others, while not disputing that fact, point out that the differences between cultures at even younger ages by far exceed the similarities.

Take a position: *People are becoming more and more similar* versus *The differences between people of different cultures far outweigh their similarities.*

Marketing Discussion

Think of some of your favorite brands. Do you know where they come from? Where and how are they made or provided? Do you think this would affect your perceptions of quality or satisfaction?

PART 8

A L'Oréal advertisement featuring Gong Li.

22

Managing a Holistic Marketing Organization

Healthy long-term growth for a brand requires that the marketing organization be managed properly. Holistic marketers must engage in a host of carefully planned, interconnected marketing activities and satisfy an increasingly broader set of constituents.[1] They must also consider a wider range of effects of their actions. Corporate social responsibility and sustainability have become a priority as organizations grapple with the short- and long-term effects of their marketing. Some firms have embraced this new vision of corporate enlightenment and made it the very core of what they do. Consider L'Oréal.

L'Oréal, the world's most successful cosmetic company, has experienced almost two decades of double-digit profit growth. The century-old €17 billion company has leveraged its cultural heritage and Parisian origins to sell products that make its customers feel special. Higher-than-average R&D expenditures have led to numerous breakthroughs and a strong technological reputation. Innovative products and glamorous endorsers such as actresses Gong Li, Michelle Reis, Eva Longoria, supermodel Claudia Schiffer, and singer Beyoncé Knowles have sustained L'Oréal's premium pricing strategy and justified its enticing slogan, "Because You're Worth It." Although French actress Catherine Deneuve is one of the official company faces, L'Oréal does not impose one type of beauty in its marketing. The company has acquired local cosmetics brands, such as Maybelline and Soft Sheen, and skillfully given them a facelift before exporting them around the world. CEO Lindsay Owen-Jones notes: "It's a very carefully crafted portfolio ... each brand is positioned in a very precise market segment which overlaps as little as possible with others."[2]

In this chapter, we will address the following questions:

1. What are important trends in marketing practices?
2. What are the keys to effective internal marketing?
3. How can companies be responsible social marketers?
4. How can a company improve its marketing skills?
5. What tools are available to help companies monitor and improve their marketing activities?

Successful holistic marketing requires effective relationship marketing, integrated marketing, internal marketing, and social marketing. Previous chapters addressed the first two topics and the strategy and tactics of marketing.[3] In this chapter, we consider internal and social marketing and how marketing should be administered and conducted responsibly. In our discussion, we look at how firms organize, implement, evaluate, and control marketing activities. We also discuss the increased importance of social responsibility. We begin by examining changes in how companies conduct marketing today.

Trends in Marketing Practices

Chapters 1 and 3 described some important changes in the marketing macroenvironment, such as globalization, deregulation, technological advances, customer empowerment, and market fragmentation. In response to this rapidly changing environment, companies have restructured their business and marketing practices in some of the following ways:

- **Re-engineering.** Appointing teams to manage customer-value-building processes and break down walls between departments.
- **Outsourcing.** Greater willingness to buy more goods and services from external vendors.
- **Benchmarking.** Studying "best practice companies" to improve performance.
- **Supplier partnering.** Increased partnering with fewer but better value-adding suppliers.
- **Customer partnering.** Working more closely with customers to add value to their operations.
- **Merging.** Acquiring or merging with firms in the same or complementary industries to gain economies of scale and scope.
- **Globalizing.** Increased effort to "think global" and "act local."
- **Flattening.** Reducing the number of organizational levels to get closer to the customer.
- **Focusing.** Determining the most profitable businesses and customers and focusing on them.
- **Accelerating.** Designing the organization and setting up processes to respond more quickly to changes in the environment.
- **Empowering.** Encouraging and empowering personnel to produce more ideas and take more initiative.

The role of marketing in the organization is also changing.[4] Traditionally, marketers have played the role of middleman, charged with understanding customer needs and transmitting the voice of the customer to various functional areas in the organization. In a networked enterprise, every functional area can interact directly with customers. Marketing no longer has sole ownership of customer interactions; rather, it needs to integrate all customer-facing processes so that customers see a single face and hear a single voice when they interact with the firm.

Internal Marketing

Internal marketing requires that everyone in the organization buy into the concepts and goals of marketing and engage in choosing, providing, and communicating customer value. Over the years, marketing has evolved as it has grown from work done by the sales department into a complex group of activities spread through the organization.[5]

A company can have an excellent marketing department and yet fail at marketing. Much depends on how *other* company departments view customers. If they point to the marketing department and say, "They do the marketing," the company has not implemented effective marketing. Only when *all* employees realize that their jobs are to create, serve, and satisfy customers does the company become an effective marketer.[6] "Marketing Memo: Characteristics of Customer-Driven Company Departments" presents a measurement tool that

MARKETING MEMO • CHARACTERISTICS OF CUSTOMER-DRIVEN COMPANY DEPARTMENTS

R&D

- They spend time meeting customers and listening to their problems.
- They welcome the involvement of marketing, manufacturing, and other departments on each new project.
- They benchmark competitors' products and seek "best of class" solutions.
- They solicit customer reactions and suggestions as the project progresses.
- They continuously improve and refine the product on the basis of market feedback.

Purchasing

- They proactively search for the best suppliers rather than choose only from those who solicit their business.
- They build long-term relations with fewer but more reliable high-quality suppliers.
- They do not compromise quality for price savings.

Manufacturing

- They invite customers to visit and tour their plants.
- They visit customer factories to see how customers use the company's products.
- They willingly work overtime when it is important to meet promised delivery schedules.
- They continuously search for ways to produce goods faster and/or at lower costs.
- They continuously improve product quality, aiming for zero defects.
- They meet customer requirements for customization where this can be done profitably.

Marketing

- They study customer needs and wants in well-defined market segments.
- They allocate marketing effort in relation to the long-run profit potential of the targeted segments.
- They develop winning offerings for each target segment.
- They measure company image and customer satisfaction on a continuous basis.
- They continuously gather and evaluate ideas for new products, product improvements, and services to meet customers' needs.
- They influence all company departments and employees to be customer-centered in their thinking and practice.

Sales

- They have specialized knowledge of the customer's industry.
- They strive to give the customer the best solution.
- They make only promises that they can keep.
- They feed back customers' needs and ideas to those in charge of product development.
- They serve the same customers for a long period of time.

Logistics

- They set a high standard for service delivery time and they meet this standard consistently.
- They operate a knowledgeable and friendly customer service department that can answer questions, handle complaints, and resolve problems in a satisfactory and timely manner.

Accounting

- They prepare periodic profitability reports by product, market segment, geographic areas (regions, sales territories), order sizes, and individual customers.
- They prepare invoices tailored to customer needs and answer customer queries courteously and quickly.

Finance

- They understand and support marketing expenditures (e.g., image advertising) that represent marketing investments that produce long-term customer preference and loyalty.
- They tailor the financial package to the customers' financial requirements.
- They make quick decisions on customer creditworthiness.

Public Relations

- They disseminate favorable news about the company and they damage control unfavorable news.
- They act as an internal customer and public advocate for better company policies and practices.

Other Customer-Contact Personnel

- They are competent, courteous, cheerful, credible, reliable, and responsive.

can be used to evaluate which company departments have fully embraced the importance of being customer-driven.[7]

Let's look at how marketing departments are being organized, how they can work effectively with other departments, and how firms can foster a creative marketing culture within the entire organization.

Organizing the Marketing Department

Modern marketing departments may be organized in a number of different, sometimes overlapping ways[8]: functionally, geographically, by product or brand, by market, in a matrix, by corporate/division.

FUNCTIONAL ORGANIZATION

The most common form of marketing organization consists of functional specialists reporting to a marketing vice president, who coordinates their activities. Figure 22.1 shows five specialists. Additional specialists might include a customer service manager, a marketing planning manager, a market logistics manager, a direct marketing manager, and an Internet marketing manager.

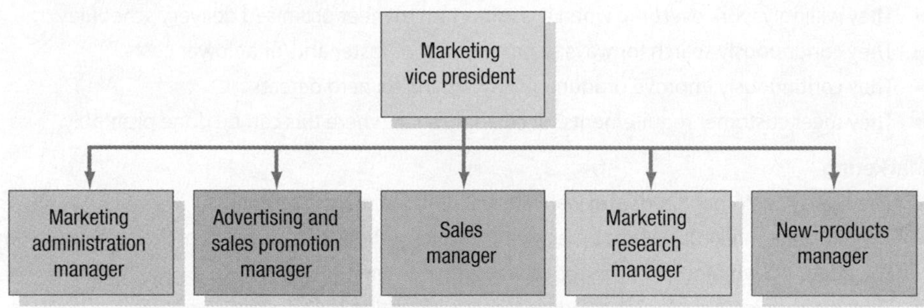

Figure 22.1 Functional Organization

The main advantage of a functional marketing organization is its administrative simplicity. However, it can be quite a challenge to develop smooth working relations within the marketing department.[9] This form can also lose its effectiveness as products and markets increase. A functional organization often leads to inadequate planning for specific products and markets. Products that are not favored by anyone are neglected. Then, each functional group competes with others for budget and status. The marketing vice president constantly has to weigh the claims of competing functional specialists and faces a difficult coordination problem.

GEOGRAPHIC ORGANIZATION

A company selling in a national market often organizes its sales force (and sometimes other functions, including marketing) along geographic lines. The national sales manager may supervise four regional sales managers, who each supervise six zone managers, who in turn supervise eight district sales managers, who supervise ten salespeople.

Several companies are now adding *area market specialists* (regional or local marketing managers) to support the sales efforts in high-volume markets. One such market might be Malaysia. The Malaysia specialist would know Malaysia's customer and trade makeup, help marketing managers at headquarters adjust their marketing mix for Malaysia, and prepare local annual and long-range plans for selling all the company's products in Malaysia.

Improved information and marketing research technologies have spurred regionalization. Some companies have installed retail-store scanners that allow instant tracking of product sales, helping them pinpoint local problems and opportunities. Retailers themselves strongly prefer local programs aimed at consumers in their cities and neighborhoods. To keep retailers happy, manufacturers now create more local marketing plans.

PRODUCT- OR BRAND-MANAGEMENT ORGANIZATION

Companies producing a variety of products and brands often establish a product- (or brand-) management organization. The product-management organization does not replace the functional organization, but serves as another layer of management. A product manager supervises product category managers, who in turn supervise specific product and brand managers.

A product-management organization makes sense if the company's products are quite different, or if the sheer number of products is beyond the ability of a functional organization to handle. Kraft has used a product-management organization, with separate product category managers in charge of cereals, pet food, and beverages. Within the cereal product group, Kraft has separate subcategory managers for nutritional cereals, children's presweetened cereals, family cereals, and miscellaneous cereals.

Product and brand management is sometimes characterized as a **hub-and-spoke** system. The brand or product manager is figuratively at the center with spokes emanating out to various departments (see Figure 22.2). Some of the tasks that product or brand managers may perform include:

- Developing a long-range and competitive strategy for the product.
- Preparing an annual marketing plan and sales forecast.
- Working with advertising and merchandising agencies to develop copy, programs, and campaigns.
- Increasing support of the product among the sales force and distributors.
- Gathering continuous intelligence on the product's performance, customer and dealer attitudes, and new problems and opportunities.
- Initiating product improvements to meet changing market needs.

Figure 22.2 The Product Manager's Interaction

The product-management organization has several advantages. The product manager can concentrate on developing a cost-effective marketing mix for the product. He or she can react more quickly to new products in the marketplace. The company's smaller brands have a product advocate. However, this organization has some disadvantages too:

- Product and brand managers may lack authority to carry out their responsibilities.
- Product and brand managers become experts in their product area but rarely achieve functional expertise.
- The product management system often turns out to be costly.

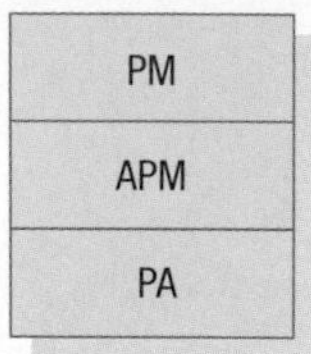

(a) Vertical Product Team

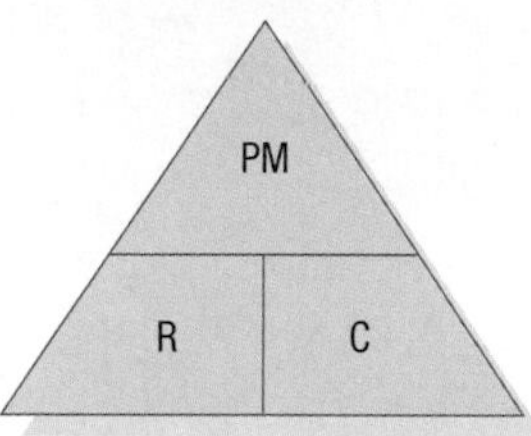

(b) Triangular Product Team

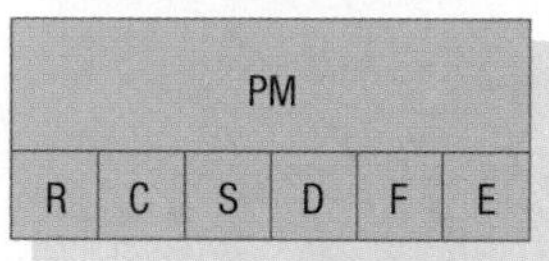

(c) Horizontal Product Team

PM = product manager
AP = associate product manager
PA = product assistant
R = market researcher
C = communication specialist
S = sales manager
D = distribution specialist
F = finance/accounting specialist
E = engineer

Figure 22.3
Three Types of Product Teams

- Brand managers normally manage a brand for only a short time. Short-term involvement leads to short-term planning and fails to build long-term strengths.
- The fragmentation of markets makes it harder to develop a national strategy. Brand managers must please regional and local sales groups, transferring power from marketing to sales.
- Product and brand managers focus the company on building market share rather than customer relationship.

A second alternative in a product-management organization is *product teams.* There are three types of potential product-team structures: vertical product team, triangular product team, and the horizontal product team (see Figure 22.3).

The triangular and horizontal product-team approaches let each major brand be run by a **Brand Asset Management Team (BAMT)** consisting of key representatives from major functions affecting the brand's performance. The company is comprised of several BAMTs which periodically report to a BAMT Directors Committee, which itself reports to a Chief Branding Officer. This is quite different from the way brands have traditionally been handled.

A third alternative for product-management organization is to eliminate product manager positions for minor products and assign two or more products to each remaining manager. This is feasible where two or more products appeal to a similar set of needs. A cosmetics company does not need separate product managers for each product because cosmetics serve one major need—beauty. A toiletries company needs different managers for headache remedies, toothpaste, soap, and shampoo, because these products differ in use and appeal.

A fourth alternative is to introduce *category management,* in which a company focuses on product categories to manage its brands. Procter & Gamble, pioneers of the brand management system, and several other top firms have made a significant shift in recent years to category management.[10]

P&G cites a number of advantages to a category management structure. By fostering internal competition among brand managers, the traditional brand management system created strong incentives to excel, but also much internal competition for resources and a lack of coordination. Whereas a smaller share category might have become relatively neglected before (e.g., in product categories such as "hard surface cleaners"), the new scheme was designed to ensure that all categories would be able to receive adequate resources.[11]

Another rationale for category management is the increasing power of the trade. Because the retail trade has tended to think in terms of product categories and the profitability derived from different departments and sections of their stores, P&G felt it only made sense for them to deal with the trade along similar lines. Retailers such as Wal-Mart have embraced category management themselves as a means to define a particular product category's strategic role within the store and to address such operating issues as logistics, the role of private label products, and the tradeoffs between offering product variety and avoiding inefficient duplication.[12]

Category management is not a panacea. It is still a product-driven system. Colgate has moved from brand management (Colgate toothpaste) to category management (toothpaste category) to a new stage called "customer-need management" (mouth care). This last step finally focuses the organization on a basic customer need.[13]

MARKET-MANAGEMENT ORGANIZATION

Many companies sell their products to different markets. Canon sells its fax machines to consumer, business, and government markets. Nippon Steel sells its steel to the railroad, construction, and public utility industries. When customers fall into different user groups with distinct buying preferences and practices, a ***market-management organization*** is desirable. A market manager supervises several market managers (also called market-development managers, market specialists, or industry specialists). The market managers draw on functional services as needed. Market managers of important markets might even have functional specialists reporting to them.

Market managers are staff (not line) people, with duties similar to those of product managers. Market managers develop long-range and annual plans for their markets. Their performance is judged by their market's growth and profitability. This system carries many of the same advantages and disadvantages of product-management systems. Its strongest advantage is that the marketing activity is organized to meet the needs of distinct customer groups rather than being focused on marketing functions, regions, or products. Many companies are re-organizing along market lines and becoming ***market-centered organizations***. Xerox has converted from geographic selling to selling by industry, as have IBM and Hewlett-Packard.

In a ***customer-management organization***, companies can organize themselves to understand and deal with individual customers rather than with the mass market or even market segments. Technology has facilitated the creation of customer-management organizations, as the following example shows.

Li & Fung—This Hong Kong-based supply chain company has developed extranet sites to serve its largest customers such as Avon, Coca-Cola, Disney, and Kohl's Department Store, who rely on Li & Fung for their promotional items. For example, Coke executives and bottlers can go to a dedicated Web site either to order specific items they designed with Li & Fung or to find out what other bottlers have ordered. If they see a product that would be useful in their market, they can piggyback on an existing order, thereby reducing cost through increased production volume.[14]

MATRIX-MANAGEMENT ORGANIZATION

Companies that produce many products flowing into many markets may adopt a matrix organization. DuPont was a pioneer in developing the matrix structure (see Figure 22.4).

Market Managers

Product Managers	Menswear	Women's wear	Home furnishings	Industrial markets
Rayon				
Acetate				
Nylon				
Orlon				
Dacron				

Figure 22.4 Product- /Market-Management Matrix System

DuPont—Before being spun off, DuPont's textile fibers department consisted of separate product managers for rayon, acetate, nylon, orlon, and dacron; and separate market managers for men's wear, women's wear, home furnishings, and industrial markets. The product managers planned the sales and profits for their respective fibers. They asked market managers to estimate how much of their fiber they could sell in each market at a proposed price. Market managers, however, were generally more interested in meeting their market's needs than pushing a particular fiber. In preparing their market plans, they asked each product manager about the fiber's planned prices and availabilities. The final sales forecast of the market managers and the product managers should have added to the same grand total.

Companies like DuPont can go one step further and view the market managers as the main marketers, and their product managers as suppliers. The menswear market manager, for example, would be empowered to buy textile fibers from DuPont's product managers or, if DuPont's price is too high, from outside suppliers. This system would force Dupont product managers to become more efficient. If a DuPont product manager could not match the "arm's length pricing" levels of competitive suppliers, then perhaps Dupont should not continue to produce that fiber.

A matrix organization seems desirable in a multiproduct, multimarket company. The rub is that this system is costly and often creates conflicts. There is the cost of supporting all the managers. There are also questions about where authority and responsibility should reside.

Relations with Other Departments

Under the marketing concept, all departments need to "think customer" and work together to satisfy customer needs and expectations. The marketing department must drive this point home. The marketing vice president, or CMO, has two tasks: (1) to coordinate the company's internal marketing activities; and (2) to coordinate marketing with finance, operations, and other company functions to serve the customer.

Yet, there is little agreement on how much influence and authority marketing should have over other departments. Departments define company problems and goals from their viewpoint. Conflicts of interest are unavoidable.

To develop a balanced orientation in which marketing and other functions jointly determine what is in the company's best interests, companies can include joint seminars to understand each other's viewpoints, joint committees and liaison personnel, personnel exchange programs, and analytical methods to determine the most profitable course of action.[15]

Perhaps the best solution is for marketing to periodically propose a *function-to-function* meeting with departments where greater understanding and collaboration is warranted. Even if each function indulges in stereotypical charges and complaints about the other, such a meeting can lead to a clearing of the air and a basis for a more constructive collaboration. Each department needs to understand the operating logic of the other departments. When departments work together towards common goals, marketing is more effective.

Procter & Gamble—With 19 of their 20 largest brands gaining share and a stock price that doubled, Procter & Gamble was clearly on a roll during 2002–2004. Organic growth in core businesses provided much of the impetus. P&G's new product hit rate, defined in terms of when returns exceeded the cost of capital, was 70 to 90 percent. Although this extraordinary performance was due to many factors, close interactions between marketing and 7,500 R&D personnel worldwide was critical. To facilitate interaction, problems and solutions are posted on an internal Web site and "communities of practice" dedicated to particular expertise (e.g., "whiteners") meet frequently. Joint collaboration between different units of P&G has produced such diverse products as Crest Whitestrips teeth whiteners, Iams Dental Defense tartar-fighting pet food, and Olay Daily facial cleansing cloths. Mr. Clean AutoDry carwash system was designed with input from R&D experts who worked on the Pur water purification and Cascade automatic dishwasher powder brands.[16]

Building a Creative Marketing Organization

Many companies are beginning to realize that they are not really market- and customer-driven—they are product-and-sales driven. Asian companies such as Samsung, Singapore Airlines, and Toyota are attempting to transform themselves into true market-driven companies. This will require:

1. Developing a company-wide passion for customers.
2. Organizing around customer segments instead of around products.
3. Developing a deep understanding of customers through qualitative and quantitative research.

The payoffs are considerable. It will not happen as a result of the CEO making speeches and urging every employee to "think customer." "Marketing Insight: The Marketing CEO" describes actions a CEO can take to improve marketing capabilities.

Although it is necessary to be customer-oriented, it is not enough. The organization must also be creative. Companies today copy each other's advantages and strategies with increasing speed. Differentiation gets harder to achieve, let alone maintain. Margins fall when firms become more alike. The only answer is for the firm to build a capability in strategic innovation and imagination (see "Marketing Insight: Fueling Strategic Innovation"). This capability comes from assembling tools, processes, skills, and measures that will enable the firm to generate more and better new ideas than its competitors.[17]

Companies must watch trends and be ready to capitalize on them. Motorola was 18 months late in moving from analog to digital cellular phones, giving Nokia and Ericsson a big lead. Sony was late in recognizing the trend toward portable digital music players, giving Apple the lead when it introduced the iPod. Nestlé was late in recognizing the trend toward coffee houses such as Starbucks. Market leaders tend to miss trends when they are risk-averse, obsessed about protecting their existing markets and physical resources, and more interested in efficiency than innovation.

MARKETING INSIGHT • THE MARKETING CEO

What steps can a CEO take to create a market- and customer-focused company?

1. **Convince senior management of the need to become customer-focused.** The CEO personally exemplifies strong customer commitment and rewards those in the organization who do likewise. For example, former CEOs Jack Welch of GE and Lou Gerstner of IBM are said to have spent 100 days a year visiting customers, despite their many strategic, financial, and administrative burdens.
2. **Appoint a senior marketing officer and marketing task force.** The marketing task force should include the CEO; the vice presidents of sales, R&D, purchasing, manufacturing, finance, and human resources; and other key individuals.
3. **Get outside help and guidance.** Consulting firms have considerable experience in helping companies move toward a marketing orientation.
4. **Change the company's reward measurement and system.** As long as purchasing and manufacturing are rewarded for keeping costs low, they will resist accepting some costs required to serve customers better. As long as finance focuses on short-term profit, it will oppose major investments designed to build satisfied, loyal customers.
5. **Hire strong marketing talent.** The company needs a strong marketing vice president who not only manages the marketing department but also gains respect from and influence with the other vice presidents. A multidivisional company would benefit from establishing a strong corporate marketing department.
6. **Develop strong in-house marketing training programs.** The company should design well-crafted marketing training programs for corporate management, divisional general managers, marketing and sales personnel, manufacturing personnel, R&D personnel, and others. Sony and Samsung have such programs.
7. **Install a modern marketing planning system.** The planning format will require managers to think about the marketing environment, opportunities, competitive trends, and other forces. These managers then prepare strategies and sales and profit forecasts for specific products and segments and are accountable for performance.
8. **Establish an annual marketing excellence recognition program.** Business units that believe they have developed exemplary marketing plans should submit a description of their plans and results. The winning teams would be rewarded at a special ceremony. The plans would be disseminated to the other business units as "models of marketing thinking."
9. **Shift from a department focus to a process-outcome focus.** After defining the fundamental business processes that determine its success, the company should appoint process leaders and cross-disciplinary teams to reengineer and implement these processes.
10. **Empower the employees.** Progressive companies encourage and reward their employees for coming up with new ideas. They also empower them to settle customer complaints to save the customer's business.

MARKETING INSIGHT • FUELING STRATEGIC INNOVATION

Stephen Brown has challenged a number of fundamental assumptions underlying the marketing concept. He thinks that marketers make too much of researching and satisfying consumers, and as a result, risk losing marketing imagination and significant consumer impact. Here are his criticisms:

1. If marketers pay too much attention to what consumers say they need or want, marketers will simply make products similar to those that already exist. Consumers normally start from what they know, not from what might be possible. For example, they might say they want a smaller cell phone but would not ask for one that includes a Palm Pilot or voice recognition. It is the marketer's job to go beyond what customers say they want.
2. The marketing concept assumes that consumers have clear goals and pursue them rationally. But consumers are buffeted by all kinds of forces. Many respond to hyped products and stories. Therefore, marketers need skills beyond APIC—analysis, planning, implementation, and control. Marketers need to be able to create dramas, new realities, artificial scarcities, celebrations, and the like.
3. The marketing concept implies that marketers must be submissive to customers, and go all out to please them. Any suggestion that marketers might "play" with the customer, even manipulate the public, is taboo. Yet some of the greatest marketers of the past teased the public, overdramatized offerings, and yet the public loved it. Why should the customer be dominant and the marketer always be submissive?

How can companies build a capability for strategic innovation? Here are some approaches:

- **Hire marketers who are unusually creative to counterbalance the majority who do marketing by the book.** These people may be more unconventional, more rule-breaking, more risk-taking, and even more argumentative, but their ideas will at least present a challenge.
- **Train your employees in the use of creativity techniques,** including group techniques (brainstorming, synectics) and individual techniques (visualization, attribute listing, forced relationships, morphological analysis, mind-mapping).
- **List observable trends** such as longer working hours, single parents, and new lifestyles, and tease out their implications for your firm.
- **List unmet needs and imagine new offerings or solutions:** how to help people lose weight, stop smoking, relieve stress, meet others, and so on.
- **Set up rewards and prizes for new ideas.** Run a "best idea" competition once a month. Give a cash reward, extra vacation time, or travel awards to those who come up with the best ideas.
- **Senior managers should take small sets of employees out for a meal once a week to** discuss ideas they might have on improving the business. Sometimes take them into new settings, such as a wrestling match, a drug rehabilitation center, a poor neighborhood.
- **Set up groups of employees to critique the company's and competitors' products and services.** Also have them critique the company's cherished beliefs and consider turning them upside down.
- **Occasionally hire creative resources from outside the firm.** Many large advertising agencies, such as Leo Burnett, run a creativity service for clients.

Sources: For more on Brown's views, see Stephen Brown, *Marketing–The Retro Revolution*, (Thousand Oaks, CA: Sage Publications, 2001); For more on creativity, see Michael Michalko, *Cracking Creativity: The Secrets of Creative Genius,* (Berkeley, CA: Ten Speed Press, 1998); James M. Higgins, *Creative Problem Solving Techniques*, (New York: New Management Publishing Company, 1994) p. 101; and the books by Edward De Bono.

Socially Responsible Marketing

Effective internal marketing must be matched by a strong sense of social responsibility.[18] Companies need to evaluate whether they are truly practicing ethical and socially responsible marketing. Several forces are driving companies to practice a higher level of corporate social responsibility: rising customer expectations, changing employee expectations, government legislation and pressure, investor interest in social criteria, and changing business procurement practices.[19]

Citigroup—A scandal caused Citigroup's Japanese private banking division to be closed in 2005. An internal audit revealed that Citi officials blamed unclear lines of authority for the problems in Japan as several heads of key divisions reported to different bosses in New York. Japan's Financial Services Agency also faulted a culture where profits were pursued at any cost, and bank officials allegedly misled some clients about their investments and approved loans that were used to manipulate stock prices. To resolve these problems, Citi learned that it was important to appoint a CEO that all Japanese staff report to. A compliance officer post was also created to ensure due corporate governance. Finally, a mid-level team, called Project K (a play on the Japanese word for "respect"), was created to draft a tougher set of internal ethical guidelines.[20]

Business success and continually satisfying the customer and other stakeholders are closely tied to adoption and implementation of high standards of business and marketing conduct. The most admired companies abide by a code of serving people's interests, not only their own.

Business practices are often under attack because business situations routinely pose tough ethical dilemmas. Clearly, certain business practices are unethical or illegal, including stealing trade secrets; false and deceptive advertising; quality or safety defects; false warranties; and inaccurate labeling. However, drawing a clear line between normal marketing practice and unethical behavior is not always easy.

Falsifying records—In China, the phenomenon of record forgery is becoming increasingly prevalent. Factory managers falsify worker time cards and payroll documents to disguise such systemic abuses as underpayment, excessive hours, and inadequate health and safety provision. Double bookkeeping is common because they do not want to lose business from international buyers or incur compliance costs. Auditors estimate that more than half of factories they handle in China are involved in forgery, but evidence is hard to collect. To protect themselves, factory managers are reluctant to explain their methods, while multinationals operating in China do not come clean for fear of bad publicity. Therefore, workers are coached ahead of auditors' visits on how to answer their questions. In some cases, those who give auditors the impression that a facility is compliant are rewarded with bonuses. In a stunning example, one sign posted in a footwear factory in Guangzhou says, "Please educate the workers well to avoid telling the client the truth."[21]

Today companies that do not perform ethically or well are at greater risk of being exposed, thanks to the Internet. In the past, a disgruntled customer might bad-mouth a manufacturer or merchant to 12 other people; today he or she can reach thousands of people on the Internet. "Breakthrough Marketing: Starbucks" showcases the firm's social responsibilities.

Companies are increasingly working with public interest groups to avoid perceptions of "greenwashing"—insincere, phony efforts to appear more environmentally sensitive than they really are. Alliances with environmentalists can achieve more satisfying solutions that both address public concerns and increase the firm's image and profits. DuPont once viewed Greenpeace as an enemy; the firm now uses Greenpeace's former head as a consultant. Greenpeace has also worked with McDonald's and others to stop farmers cutting down the Amazon rainforest to grow soybeans. When Greenpeace called out Coca-Cola on the eve of the 2000 Sydney Olympics for using a potent greenhouse gas in its nearly 10 million coolers and vending machines, Coke, along with PepsiCo, Unilever, and McDonald's, invested $30 million in a less damaging system that now displays a "technology approved by Greenpeace" banner.[22]

Adobe Systems' award-winning headquarters in San Jose is the greenest corporate site on record. Adobe has dramatically reduced electricity and gas consumption in the building over a five-year period.

Firms are fundamentally changing the way they conduct their business, sometimes even where they work. In 2006, $2 billion software maker Adobe Systems became the first company to receive a platinum award from the U.S. Green Building Council, making the firm's San Jose headquarters the greenest corporate site on record. By retrofitting its building with automatic faucets, waterless urinals, timed outages, energy-saver compact fluorescent lights, weather-controlled irrigation systems, and motion sensors, Adobe reduced electricity use by 35 percent and gas consumption by 41 percent over a five-year period while still increasing its head count by 80 percent.[23]

BREAKTHROUGH • MARKETING

STARBUCKS

Starbucks believes that by focusing and aligning the giving priorities of Starbucks Coffee Company with The Starbucks Foundation, a separate 501(c)(3) charitable organization, its contributions will have greater impact and provide more benefit to communities around the world. The Starbucks Foundation celebrated its 10-year anniversary in 2007 with the announcement of Starbucks About Youth, a global philanthropic endeavor focused on supporting educational initiatives and youth leadership in Starbucks retail markets around the world.

Starbucks opened in 1971, at a time when coffee consumption in America had been declining for a decade. The decline stemmed from rivalry among the major coffee brands, which were competing on price. As a result, they used cheaper coffee beans to reduce costs, compromising the quality of their coffee. Starbucks' founders decided to experiment with a new concept: a store that would sell only the finest imported coffee beans and coffee brewing equipment. The original store did not sell coffee by the cup, only beans. You could get a good cup of coffee, but you had to make it yourself at home.

Howard Schultz came to Starbucks in 1982 and saw a new possibility for the company. While in Milan on business, Schultz walked into an Italian coffee bar and had an epiphany with his espresso. "There was nothing like this in America. It was an extension of people's front porch. It was an emotional experience," he said. Schultz set about creating an environment for Starbucks coffeehouses that would reflect Italian elegance melded with American informality. Schultz envisioned that Starbucks would become a "Third Place"—a comfortable, sociable gathering spot bridging the workplace and the home.

Part of the success of Starbucks undoubtedly lies in its products and services, and its relentless commitment to providing customers with the richest possible sensory experiences. But another key is the enlightened sense of responsibility that manifests itself in a number of different ways.

Schultz believes to exceed the expectations of customers it is first necessary to exceed the expectations of employees. As far back as 1990, Starbucks provided comprehensive health care to all employees, including part-timers. Health insurance now costs Starbucks more each year than coffee. The firm also introduced a stock option plan called "Bean Stock," which allows Starbucks' employees to participate in the company's financial success.

The company donates millions of dollars to charities via The Starbucks Foundation, created in 1997 with proceeds from the sale of Schultz's book. The mission of the foundation is to "create hope, discovery, and opportunity in communities where Starbucks partners [employees] live and work." The primary focus of the foundation has been on improving young peoples' lives by supporting literacy programs for children and families. By 2007, the foundation had provided over $12 million to more than 700 youth-focused organizations in the U.S. and Canada. Starbucks also has donated 5 cents of every sale of its Ethos bottled water to improving the quality of water in poor countries as part of a five-year, $10 million pledge.

Starbucks also promotes "fair-trade" export practices with third-world coffee bean producers—no other retailer in North America sells more fair-trade coffee—and pays its producers in those countries an average of 23 percent above market price. It took the company 10 years of development to create the world's first recycled beverage cup made from 10 percent postconsumer fiber, conserving five million pounds of paper or approximately 78,000 trees a year. The company has 87 urban locations co-owned by Earvin "Magic" Johnson.

Starbucks employed a "hub" expansion strategy, in which coffeehouses entered a new market in a clustered group. For each region, a large city served as the hub. Teams of trained professionals supported the new cluster of stores. In the large hub markets, the company rapidly opened 20 or more stores within the first two years. From the established hub, Starbucks stores then spread to new "spoke" markets: smaller satellite cities and nearby suburban locations.

The joke about two Starbucks across the street from each other reflects Starbucks' strategy. The deliberate saturation often cannibalizes 30 percent of one store's sales by introducing a store nearby. But this drop in revenue is offset by efficiencies in marketing and distribution costs, and the enhanced image of convenience. A typical customer stops by Starbucks 18 times a month. No American retailer has a higher frequency of customer visits.

Starbucks also expanded internationally, entering Japan with an outlet in Tokyo in 1996. Although detractors reasoned that the fastidious tea-drinking Japanese would never buy coffee in paper cups, Starbucks proved them wrong. Locations in Japan produced two-and-a-half times the annual sales of those in the U.S. There are now over 500 Starbucks locations in Japan, and the country became the

(Continued ...)

(*Continued ...*)

company's most profitable region. However, in recent years, store sales fell 17 percent. One reason is that Starbucks is cannibalizing its success by building too many stores. There is brand fatigue with its "Starbucks Everywhere" approach. Tough and cheaper competition also presents challenges. Tully's Coffee, a Seattle rival, is becoming popular. Unlike Starbucks, it allows for smoking. Local rivals adopting Starbucks-like practices, such as Doutor, appeal to "old Japan." Their low-cost no-frills coffee houses called Excelsior cafés also allow customers to smoke.

Starbucks later entered China, where it is walking the tightrope between being hip and Western. It is a barely affordable luxury, even for middle-class Chinese. But it has no plans to cut prices. In fact, Starbucks has increased them. In a Shanghai survey, most of its customers said they were happy with the charges. Retailers say a top marketing weapon in urban China is to charge more for public consumption, where price can serve as an indicator of quality and sophistication. That is because Chinese customers have different attitudes from their American yuppie counterparts. They go there not only for the coffee but also to publicly associate themselves with the notion of being modern.

Howard Schultz stepped down as CEO in 2000, but remained chairman and "Chief Global Strategist." He returned as CEO in 2008. Starbucks currently has over 15,000 stores in 43 countries. Schultz wants to see a Starbucks in every country in the world. But there's one country that he especially has his eye on: Italy, where the whole Starbucks concept began.

Sources: Howard Schultz. "Dare to Be a Social Entrepreneur." *Business 2.0*, December 2006, p. 87; Edward Iwata, "Owner of Small Coffee Shop Takes On Java Titan Starbucks." *USA Today*, December 20, 2006. "Staying Pure: Howard Schultz's Formula for Starbucks." *The Economist*, February 25, 2006, p. 72; Diane Anderson, "Evolution of the Eco Cup." *Business 2.0*, June 2006, p. 50; Bruce Horovitz, "Starbucks Nation." *USA Today*, May 19, 2006. Theresa Howard, "Starbucks Takes Up Cause for Safe Drinking Water," *USA Today*, August 2, 2005. Howard Schultz and Dori Jones Yang, *Pour Your Heart into It: How Starbucks Built a Company One Cup at a Time*, (New York: Hyperion, 1999); <www.starbucks.com> (1997); Michael Barbaro and Andrew Martin, "Overhaul, Make it a Venti." <http://www.nytimes.com/2008/01/30/business/30sbux.html?ref=business>, January 30, 2008. Andy Serwer, "Starbucks Fix." *Fortune*, January 18, 2008; <www. starbucks.com>.

Corporate Social Responsibility

Raising the level of socially responsible marketing calls for a three-pronged attack that relies on proper legal, ethical, and social responsibility behavior.

What do Chick-fil-A, Ben & Jerry's ice cream, and Patagonia clothing company have in common? To learn how seriously these companies and others treat the concept of corporate social responsibility, visit wps.prenhall.com/bp_kotler_mm_13/.

LEGAL BEHAVIOR

Society must use the law to define, as clearly as possible, those practices that are illegal, antisocial, or anticompetitive. Organizations must ensure that every employee knows and observes any relevant laws. For example, sales managers can check that sales representatives know and observe the law, such as the fact that it is illegal for salespeople to lie to consumers or mislead them about the advantages of buying a product.

ETHICAL BEHAVIOR

Companies must adopt and disseminate a written code of ethics, build a company tradition of ethical behavior, and hold its people fully responsible for observing ethical and legal guidelines.[24] Nike has long been attacked by labor activists who charge the company with using sweatshop labor, especially from Asia, to produce its sneakers and clothes.

SOCIAL RESPONSIBILITY BEHAVIOR

Individual marketers must practice a "social conscience" in specific dealings with customers and stakeholders.[25] Increasingly, people say that they want information about a company's record on social and environmental responsibility to help decide which companies to buy from, invest in, and work for.[26] Table 22.1 lists the companies who received the highest scores, with HSBC being an example:[27]

HSBC—Ranked fourth among ***Fortune*** companies on social responsibility, HSBC has named a subcommittee of its board to oversee corporate responsibility and make that its number one strategic goal. In 2005, it committed to using the World Bank's Equator Principles in deciding whether to lend to dam and forestry projects and started using an external standard, London CSR think tank AccountAbility's AA1000, to help verify that the new governance structures were a good response to stakeholder needs. "HSBC wants to be seen as a CSR brand," says Francis Sullivan, the bank's advisor on the environment.

Table 22.1 Top 10 Companies for Social Responsibility

Overall
1. BP
2. Barclays
3. EN1
4. HSBC
5. Vodafone
6. Royal Dutch Shell
7. Peugeot
8. HBOS
9. Chevron
10. Daimler Chrysler

Source: Account Ability and CSR network, *The Accountability Report*, <www.accountability21.net>, 2007, accessed on April 21, 2008.

SUSTAINABILITY

Sustainability—the importance of meeting humanity's needs without harming future generations—has risen to the top of many corporate agendas. Major corporations now outline in great detail how they are trying to improve the long-term impact of their actions on communities and the environment. As one sustainability consultant put it, "There is a triple bottom line—people, planet, and profit—and the people part of the equation must come first. Sustainability means more than being eco-friendly, it also means you are in it for the long haul."[28]

Many CEOs believe embracing sustainability can avoid the negative consequences of environmental disasters, political protests, and human rights or workplace abuses. Often a target of environmental criticism in the past, DuPont has moved through two phases of sustainability in the past 15 years: first, drastically reducing the emission of greenhouse gases, release of carcinogens, and discharge of hazardous wastes; and second, embracing sustainability as a strategic goal via the introduction of alternative biofuels and energy-saving materials such as its new bio-PDO fiber.[29]

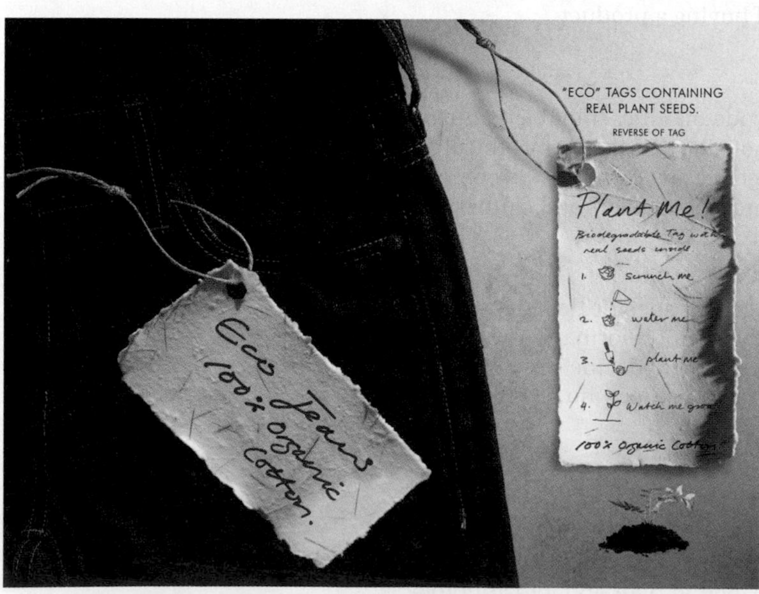

As part of a global launch of products made of 100% organic cotton, Levi's introduced its new Eco jeans for customers who want to "minimize their personal impact on the environment." Even the garment tags and packaging are made of organic fabric or recycled paper and printed with soy-based ink.

Investors are even demanding more concrete information about what firms are doing to achieve sustainability. Sustainability ratings exist, although there is little agreement about what the appropriate metrics might be.[30]

Some feel companies that score well on sustainability factors typically exhibit high levels of management quality in that "they tend to be more strategically nimble and better equipped to compete in the complex, high-velocity, global environment."[31]

Many companies in diverse industries beyond edible food products are embracing organic offerings that avoid the use of chemicals and pesticides to stress ecological preservation. Apparel and other non-food items make up the second-fastest growth category of the organic product industry. Organic cotton grown by farmers who fight boll weevils with ladybugs, weed their crops by hand, and use manure for fertilizer has become a hot product at retail. Sustainability is becoming more mainstream, and consumers are increasingly willing to pay more to support the environment.[32]

Socially Responsible Business Models

The future holds a wealth of opportunities for companies.[33] Technological advances in solar energy, online networks, cable and satellite television, biotechnology, and telecommunications promise to change the world as we know it. At the same time, forces in the socioeconomic, cultural, and natural environments will impose new limits on marketing and business practices. Companies that can innovate new solutions and values in a socially responsible way are the most likely to succeed.[34] Indeed, socially responsible marketing also strikes a resonant chord in Asia as it is consistent with Confucian values (see "Marketing Insight: Confucius and Marketing in East Asia"). Some Asian companies even go overboard in their corporate social responsibility efforts:

MARKETING INSIGHT • CONFUCIUS AND MARKETING IN EAST ASIA

Two Confucian values, *li* (礼) and *ren* (仁), have become the cornerstones of social structure in East Asia. *Li* has been translated as rites, ceremonies, etiquette, and propriety. It provides the appropriate behavior for every social situation. Confucius also maintained that human relations should be based on the moral sentiment of *ren*, leading to positive efforts for the good of others. These concepts created a culture based on the solidarity of the family. Confucius viewed family relationships as a social system of the community rather than of blood families.

The Japanese, in particular, have been deeply influenced by Confucian tradition, extending the values of loyalty and filial piety to commerce. Two exemplars relate to Soichiro Honda and Konosuke Matsushita, who founded leading businesses which bear their names. Viewing their organizations as a family, both leaders had a sense of social responsibility beyond providing meaningful employment, upgrading the level of their employees, and ensuring stable and profitable operations from serving customer needs. Both men established their own foundations to facilitate societal progress. The Honda Foundation promotes new uses for technology, while the PHP Institute propagated Matsushita's ideals to society. Matsushita was also very often the highest taxpayer in Japan.

Confucianism also explains certain marketing mix practices in Asia. The Confucian loyalty of friendship among overseas Chinese businesses provides a channel advantage for local over foreign companies in regional markets. For example, when Kmart tried to enter Asia, it ran into local retailers which could match its prices through the ability to accept even lower margins at the same time that they matched or bettered Kmart's quality. This was due to local retailers receiving the support of most, if not all, of their long-term suppliers who were loyal to them. Successful ad campaigns have been based on Confucian values. In the early 1990s, when state-owned market leader China Life Insurance was still using ads that equated buying its policies with patriotism, Ping An Insurance promoted its products based on personal and family security. Such consumer-based thinking has made Ping An China's second-largest insurer.

However, one negative facet pertains to product management in Asia, which is adversely affected by the widespread lack of respect for Intellectual Property Rights (IPR). In Confucian Asia, to respect the property rights of those with which you have no relationship depends on associating those rights with social harmony. Where there is no historical precedence for the particular property rights in question, as in the case of IPR, this becomes highly problematic. IPR never existed under Confucian custom and tradition. Thus it is very easy, when confronted with IPR piracy, for local legal authorities to look the other way given even a minimal incentive to do so.

Recently, some critics have doubted the role of Asian values in explaining the region's successes and failures. Others have argued that the region's problems look suspiciously like Asian values gone wrong. The attachment to family can be viewed as nepotism. The importance of personal relationships rather than legal formality becomes cronyism. Consensus becomes wheel-greasing and corrupt politics. Conservatism and respect for authority is perceived as rigidity and an inability to innovate. Much vaunted educational achievements become rote learning and a refusal to question those in authority.

Interestingly, Confucius has been cited favorably by those on both sides of the debate about Asian values. As his classical writings are terse and elliptical, they can be interpreted in different ways by different scholars. Nevertheless, socially responsible marketers in the region can take a leaf from his work like Honda and Matsushita have done successfully.

Sources: "What Would Confucius Say Now?" *Economist*, July 25, 1998, pp. 23–25; "The Sage, 2,549 Years On." *Economist*, July 25, 1998, p. 24; Leonardo R. Silos, "What Confucius (Really) Said (About Mismanagement)." *Asian Manager*, April–June 1992, pp. 30–36; David Sanger, "Honda—Rebellious Mechanic, Fiery Maverick, and Trail Blazer." *Straits Times*, (Singapore) August 7, 1991, p. 11; Etsu Inaba, "Matsushita Konosuke's Management Philosophy and Its Relevance to Asian Countries." *Asian Manager*, April–June 1992, pp. 65–68; Daniel P. Reid, "The Legacy of Confucius." *Mercedes*, 1997, 2, pp. 46–56; Konosuke Matsushita, "The Mission of Enterprise." In Dinna Louis C. Dayao, ed., *Asian Business Wisdom: From Deals to Dot.Coms*, (Singapore: John Wiley, 2001) pp. 17–23; George T. Haley, and Chin Tiong Tan, "East vs West: Strategic Marketing Management Meets the Asian Networks." *Journal of Business and Industrial Marketing*, 1999, 14(2), pp. 91–101; Allen T. Cheng, "Insuring China's Future." *Fortune*, 20, January 20, 2003, p. 29.

Tata—The Tata Group not only wants to make money but to "improve the quality of life of the communities" it serves. Tata has a reputation for being an enlightened employer and an honest company. It has lost some deals because it would not pay bribes. Tata Steel exemplifies Tata's culture. The company is based in Jamshedpur, a town named after Tata's founder, where it is the biggest employer. Statues of Tata chairmen (some erected by grateful employees) are testaments to Tata Steel's providing the most comprehensive social services of any Indian city. At an annual cost of $30 million, it pays for water supplies, garbage removal, hospital and school subsidies, and even rogue elephant hunters. When Tata Steel laid off 35,000 workers in 1999, the company agreed to pay the workers' salaries until the age of 60. With 45,000 employees, Tata Steel remains overstaffed. Rival competitor Essar produces about half of Tata Steel's output with only 1,300 employees. Tata wants to "privatize" its urban services to scale back its capital outlay. However, as chairman Ratan Tata notes, "we are also proud that we've never had serious industrial problems." Perhaps being loved may be more highly prized than being profitable.[35]

Corporate philanthropy as a whole is on the rise. More firms are coming to the belief that corporate social responsibility in the form of cash donations, in-kind contributions, cause marketing, and employee volunteerism programs is the not just the "right thing" but also the "smart thing to do."[36] "Marketing Insight: New Views on Corporate Social Responsibility" offers two high-profile perspectives on how to make progress in that area.

Cause-Related Marketing

Many firms are blending their corporate social responsibility initiatives with their marketing activities.[37] **Cause-related marketing** is marketing that links the firm's contributions to a designated cause to customers' engaging directly or indirectly in revenue-producing transactions with the firm.[38] Cause marketing has also been called a part of *Corporate Societal Marketing* (CSM) which Drumwright and Murphy define as marketing efforts "... that have at least one non-economic objective related to social welfare and use the resources of the company and/or of its partners."[39] They also include other activities such as traditional and strategic philanthropy and volunteerism as part of CSM. Cause-related marketing comes in many forms. Consider Canon and *American Idol:*

Canon—Canon engages in a wide spectrum of cause-related marketing. It embraces a philosophy called ***kyosei***, which means living and working together for the common good. It supports the intellectually disabled and underprivileged children by sponsoring the 2005 Special Olympics World Winter Games; donating uniforms and other clothes through Hoa Binh Red Cross in Vietnam; giving out school bags in rural areas through the "Spring Care" project in Malaysia; and donating office equipment to the Sikkha Asia Foundation—a training program for underprivileged children—in Thailand. In New Zealand, Canon raises funds for leukaemia research and patient care, and supports the SPCA. Besides such philanthropic activities, Canon also sponsors entertainment programs. In Malaysia, it was the major sponsor of "Annie the Musical," while Canon Japan supports the Canon Cup Junior Soccer tournament. It is also a corporate member of WWF and supports the "Adopt a Plant" project.[40]

MARKETING INSIGHT • NEW VIEWS ON CORPORATE SOCIAL RESPONSIBILITY

Two of management's most renowned thinkers have turned their attention to corporate social responsibility, offering some unique perspectives that builds on their past management research and thinking.

Michael Porter

Michael Porter and Mark Kramer believe good corporate citizenship can be a source of opportunity, innovation, and competitive advantage, as long as firms evaluate it using the same frameworks and concepts that guide their core business strategies. They feel corporate social responsibility must mesh with a firm's strengths, capabilities, and positioning. They assert that *strategic corporate social responsibility* results when firms (1) transform value chain activities to benefit society while reinforcing strategy; and (2) engage in strategic philanthropy that leverages capabilities to improve salient areas of competitive context.

According to the authors, firms should select causes that intersect their particular businesses to create shared value for the firm and society. For example, Toyota addressed public concerns about auto emissions by creating a competitively strong and environmentally friendly hybrid vehicle, Prius.

Porter and Kramer note that, "By providing jobs, investing capital, purchasing goods, and doing business every day, corporations have a profound and positive influence on society. The most important thing a corporation can do for society, and for any community, is to contribute to a prosperous economy." Although companies can address hundreds of social issues, only a handful offer the opportunity to build focused, proactive, and integrated social initiatives that link with core business strategies to make a real difference to society and create a competitive advantage in the marketplace.

Clayton Christensen

Clayton Christensen, along with his research colleagues, advocates *catalytic innovations* to address social sector problems. Like Christensen's disruptive innovations—which challenge industry incumbents by offering simpler, good enough alternatives to an underserved group of customers—catalytic innovations offer good enough solutions to inadequately addressed social problems. Catalytic innovators share five qualities:

1. They create systemic social change through scaling and replication.
2. They meet a need that is either overserved (because the existing solution is more complex than many people require) or not served at all.
3. They offer simpler, less costly products and services that may have a lower level of performance, but that users consider to be good enough.
4. They generate resources, such as donations, grants, volunteer manpower, or intellectual capital, in ways that are initially unattractive to competitors.
5. They are often ignored, disparaged, or even encouraged by existing players for whom the business model is unprofitable or otherwise unattractive and who therefore avoid or retreat from the market segment.

To find organizations that creating a catalytic innovation for investment or other purposes, Christensen and his colleagues offer some guidelines:

1. **Look for signs of disruption in the process.** Although not necessarily easily observed, preexisting catalytic innovators may already be present in a market.
2. **Identify specific catalytic innovations.** Apply the five criteria listed.
3. **Assess the business model.** Determine whether the organization can effectively introduce the innovation and scale it up and sustain it.

Sources: Michael F. Porter and Mark R. Kramer, "Strategy & Society." *Harvard Business Review*, December 2006, pp. 78–82; Clayton M. Christensen, Heiner Baumann, Rudy Ruggles, and Thomas M. Stadtler, "Disruption Innovation for Social Change." *Harvard Business Review*, December 2006, pp. 94–101. See also Richard Steckel, Elizabeth Ford, Casey Hilliard, and Traci Sanders, *Cold Cash for Warm Hearts: 101 Best Social Marketing Initiatives*, (Homewood, IL: High Tide Press, 2004).

American Idol—In 2007, the "Idol Gives Back Foundation," a not-for-profit organization established by the producers of ***American Idol*** and FOX to raise money and awareness for children and families living in poverty and at risk in the U.S. and abroad. It stages a star-studded event during the series where singers, politicians, sports personalities, and movie stars urge the American audience to donate using a toll-free line or the Internet. The first fund-raising event raised $76 million and won an Emmy award. In 2008, Idol Gives Back returned and raised awareness and funds to benefit the following charities—The Children's Defense Fund, Children's Health Fund, The Global Fund, Make It Right, Malaria No More, Save the Children. By associating with such causes, ***American Idol*** benefits from humanizing itself and endearing to the public, gets the publicity from the stars who, and generate more viewership.[41]

CAUSE MARKETING BENEFITS AND COSTS

A successful cause marketing program can produce a number of benefits: improving social welfare; creating differentiated brand positioning; building strong consumer bonds; enhancing the company's public image with government officials and other decision makers; creating a reservoir of goodwill; boosting internal morale and galvanizing employees; and driving sales.[42]

By humanizing the firm, consumers may develop a strong, unique bond with the firm that transcends normal marketplace transactions.[43] Some of the specific means by which cause marketing programs can build brand equity with consumers include: (1) building brand awareness; (2) enhancing brand image; (3) establishing brand credibility; (4) evoking brand feelings; (5) creating a sense of brand community; and (6) eliciting brand engagement.[44]

LG Electronics—LG carries out its corporate activities with the goal of serving society. In Korea, LG executives donate one percent of their salary and other employees one percent of their performance incentives. The company then matches the monthly contributions and donates the entirety as corporate social contribution funds. LG provides meals and constructs homes for the homeless. It also supports outstanding researchers in the LG Junior Scientists Classroom program. LG has a LG Champion Quiz program that is aired during prime time in Asia, a region with a passion for education and learning. The program thus positions LG as a people-oriented corporation that contributes to the development of local communities.[45]

However, the danger is that the promotional efforts behind a cause-related marketing program could backfire if cynical consumers question the link between the product and the cause, and see the firm as being self-serving and exploitative.[46]

Nike's alliance with the Lance Armstrong Foundation for cancer research has sold over 70 million yellow LIVE**STRONG** bracelets for $1, but deliberately, the famed Nike swoosh logo is nowhere to be seen.[47] One of the more interesting cause programs in recent years is the Project Red campaign.[48]

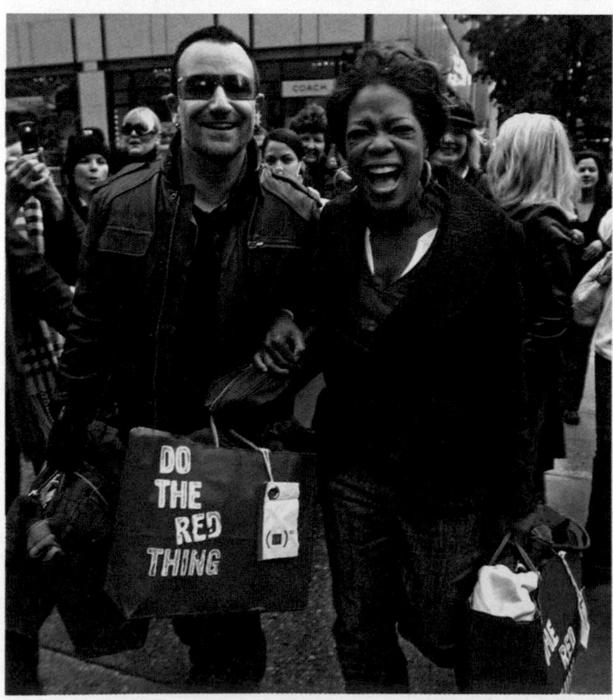

The brainchild of U2's Bono and Bobby Shriver, chairman of DATA, (RED) was a highly publicized effort to raise money for AIDS relief in Africa through partnerships with iconic brands such as Apple, Motorola, American Express, and Gap. Bono and talk show host Oprah Winfrey are shown here shopping at the Red launch in Chicago.

(RED)—2006 saw the highly publicized launch of (RED), championed by U2 singer and activist Bono and Bobby Shriver, Chairman of DATA. (RED) was created to raise awareness and money for The Global Fund by teaming with some of the world's most iconic branded products—American Express cards, Motorola phones, Converse sneakers, Gap T-shirts, Apple iPods, and Emperio Armani sunglasses—to produce (PRODUCT)RED branded products. Up to 50 percent of the profits from the sale of (PRODUCT)RED products are given to The Global Fund to help women and children affected by HIV/AIDS in Africa. The parentheses or brackets in the logo were designed to signify "the embrace"—each company that becomes (RED) places its logo in this embrace and is then "elevated to the power of red." Although some critics felt the project was overmarketed, in the first 18 months of its existence, (RED) contributed more than $36 million to The Global Fund, more than seven times the amount businesses had contributed since it was founded in 2002.

The knowledge, skills, resources, and experiences of a top firm may even be more important to a non-profit or community group than funding. Non-profits must be clear about what their goals are, communicate clearly what they hope to accomplish, and have an organizational structure in place to work with different firms. Developing a long-term relationship with a firm can take a long time. As one consultant noted, "What's often a problem between corporations and non-profits is different expectations and different understanding about the amount of time everything will take."[49]

A number of decisions must be made in designing and implementing a cause marketing program, such as how many and which cause(s) to choose and how to brand the cause program.

CHOOSING A CAUSE

Some experts believe that the positive impact on a brand from cause-related marketing may be lessened by sporadic involvement with numerous causes.

Many companies choose to focus on one or a few main causes to simplify execution and maximize impact. However, constraining support to a single cause may limit the pool of consumers or other stakeholders who could transfer positive feelings from the cause to the firm. In addition, many popular causes already have numerous corporate sponsors. Reportedly, companies such as Avon, Ford, Estée Lauder, Revlon, Lee Jeans, Polo Ralph Lauren, Yoplait, BMW, and American Express associate themselves with breast cancer as a cause in some way.[50] As a consequence, the brand may find itself "lost in the shuffle," overlooked in a sea of symbolic pink ribbons.

Opportunities can potentially be greater with "orphan causes"—causes such as diseases that afflict less than 200,000 people.[51] Another option is overlooked diseases, such as pancreatic cancer, which is the fourth deadliest form of cancer behind skin, lung, and breast cancer and yet has received little or no corporate support. For example, LG Electronics sponsors medical operation services for cleft lip and palate among children in Middle-Eastern and African countries.

Most firms tend to choose causes that fit their corporate or brand image and matter to their employees and shareholders. "Marketing Memo: Making A Difference" provides some tips from a top cause-marketing firm.

Social Marketing

Cause-related marketing supports a cause. **Social marketing** is done by a non-profit or government organization to further a cause, such as "say no to drugs" or "exercise more and eat better."[52]

Social marketing is a global phenomenon that goes back for years. In the 1950s, India started family planning campaigns. Singapore is well-known for its social marketing campaigns, beginning with family planning in the 1960s, and subsequently launching such diverse drives as saving water and electricity, eating more wheat than rice, being more courteous, encouraging Chinese to speak more Mandarin than dialects, promoting marriage among graduates, and promoting larger families for those who can afford to have more children.

Choosing the right goal or objective for a social marketing program is critical. Should a family planning campaign focus on abstinence or birth control? Should a campaign to fight air pollution focus on ride-sharing or mass transit? Social marketing campaigns may have objectives related to changing people's cognitions, values, actions, or behaviors. The following examples illustrate the range of possible objectives.

Cognitive campaigns

- Explain the nutritional value of different foods.
- Explain the importance of conservation.

Action campaigns

- Attract people for mass immunization.
- Motivate people to vote "yes" on a certain issue.
- Motivate people to donate blood.
- Motivate women to take a Pap test.

MARKETING MEMO • MAKING A DIFFERENCE

One of the most accomplished cause marketing consultants is Boston's Cone, Inc. It offers the following perspectives on how cause marketing or Corporate Social Responsibility (CSR) should best be practiced:

- **Define CSR for your company.** Make sure that your senior executives are all talking about the same thing. CSR includes a broad range of complex internal and external business practices. Although they are vital components of the CSR mix, corporate philanthropy and community relations do not define CSR alone.
- **Build a diverse team.** The development and execution of CSR strategies require a collaborative, concerted team effort. Create a decision-making taskforce that integrates and brings together a range of expertise and resources, including marketing, public affairs, community relations, legal, human resources, manufacturing, and others. Install a formal process to approach CSR strategy development, ongoing implementation, and continuous improvement.
- **Analyze your current CSR-related activities and revamp them if necessary.** Do your due diligence at the outset to understand CSR gaps and risks specific to your company. Research industry examples and cull best practices from leading case studies. Make sure to consider global trends.
- **Forge and strengthen NGO relationships.** The more than 300,000 non-governmental organizations (NGOs) around the world are a powerful force on corporate policies and behavior, serving as both advocates and loud critics. Forge sincere partnerships with organizations that can offer you independent, unbiased insight into and evaluation of your CSR activities; provide expertise on social issues and developing global markets; and offer access to key influentials.
- **Develop a cause branding initiative.** Create a public face for your citizenship activities through a signature Cause Branding initiative that integrates philanthropy, community relations, marketing, and human resource assets.
- **Walk your talk.** Critics often assert that companies exploit CSR as a PR smokescreen to conceal or divert attention from corporate misdeeds and blemishes. Before introducing any new CSR initiative or drawing attention to good corporate behavior, make sure that your company is addressing stakeholder expectations of CSR at the most basic level.
- **Don't be silent.** Not only do consumers expect businesses to behave socially, the majority want companies to tell them how they are doing so. Most also say they prefer to find out about CSR activities from a third-party source, particularly the media.
- **Beware.** Greater public awareness for your corporate citizenship record can be double-edged. Claims of socially responsible behavior, even sincere ones, often invite public scrutiny. Be prepared. Even if your company is not ready to proactively communicate about your CSR activities, be ready to respond to public inquiries immediately. Do not let the threat of public scrutiny keep you mute, though. More often than not, silence regarding CSR issues is translated as indifference, or worse, inaction.

Source: *Cone Buzz* (April 2004). See also Carol L. Cone, Mark A. Feldman, and Alison T. DaSilva, "Cause and Effects." *Harvard Business Review,* July 2003. pp. 95–101.

Behavioral campaigns

- Demotivate cigarette smoking.
- Demotivate hard drug usage.
- Demotivate excessive consumption of alcohol.

Value campaigns

- Alter ideas about abortion.
- Change attitudes of getting married and having children.

Social marketing may employ a number of different tactics to achieve its goals.[53] The social marketing planning process follows many of the same steps as for traditional products and services (see Table 22.2). Some key success factors in developing and implementing a social marketing program include:

- Study the literature and previous campaigns.
- Choose target markets that are most ready to respond.
- Promote a single, doable behavior in clear, simple terms.
- Explain the benefits in compelling terms.
- Make it easy to adopt the behavior.
- Develop attention-grabbing messages and media.
- Consider an education-entertainment approach.

Table 22.2 Social Marketing Planning Process

Where Are We?
• Determine program focus. • Identify campaign purpose. • Conduct an analysis of Strengths, Weaknesses, Opportunities, and Threats (SWOT). • Review past and similar efforts.
Where Do We Want To Go?
• Select target audiences. • Set objectives and goals. • Analyze target audiences and the competition.
How Will We Get There?
• Product: Design the market offering. • Price: Manage costs of behavior change. • Distribution: Make the product available. • Communications: Create messages and choose media.
How Will We Stay on Course?
• Develop a plan for evaluation and monitoring. • Establish budgets and find funding sources. • Complete an implementation plan.

Given the complexity and challenges of the issues involved with social marketing, it is important to take a long-run view. Social marketing programs take time and may involve a series of phased programs or actions. For example, take the sequence of actions that have been involved in discouraging smoking: cancer reports, labeling of cigarettes, banning cigarette advertising, education about secondary smoke effects, no smoking in restaurants, no smoking on planes, raising taxes on cigarettes to pay for antismoking campaigns, states suing cigarette companies.

Social marketing program must be evaluated in terms of the program objectives. Criteria might include the following: high incidence of adoption, high speed of adoption, high continuance of adoption, low cost per unit of adoption, and no major counterproductive consequences.

Marketing Implementation

Table 22.3 summarizes the characteristics of a great marketing company. A marketing company is great not by "what it is," but by "what it does."[54] **Marketing implementation** is the process that turns marketing plans into action assignments and ensures that such assignments are executed in a manner that accomplishes the plan's stated objectives.[55]

Strategy addresses the *what* and *why* of marketing activities; implementation addresses the *who, where, when,* and *how*. Strategy and implementation are closely related: one layer of strategy implies certain tactical implementation assignments at a lower level. For example, top management's strategic decision to "harvest" a product must be translated into specific actions and assignments.

Companies today are striving to make their marketing operations more efficient and their return on marketing investment more measurable (see Chapter 4). Marketing costs

Table 22.3 Characteristics of a Great Marketing Company

- The company selects target markets in which it enjoys superior advantages, and exits or avoids markets where it is intrinsically weak.
- Virtually all the company's employees and departments are customer- and market-minded.
- There is a good working relationship between marketing, R&D, and manufacturing.
- There is a good working relationship between marketing, sales, and customer service.
- The company has installed incentives designed to lead to the right behaviors.
- The company continuously builds and tracks customer satisfaction and loyalty.
- The company manages a value-delivery system in partnership with strong suppliers and distributors.
- The company is skilled in building its brand name(s) and image.
- The company is flexible in meeting customers' varying requirements.

can amount to 20 to 40 percent of a company's total operating budget. Companies recognize significant waste in many practices: too many meetings lasting too long, undue time spent in looking for documents, delays in receiving approvals, and difficulties in coordinating vendor partners. An A.C. Nielsen study found that multinational and local retailers in China were concerned that supply chains were inadequate due to the country's massive geography, inefficient information support systems, and shortage of logistics management expertise. Another problem is the high cost relating to staff turnover as the pool of retailing talent at management level and skilled staff at the frontline is over-extended.[56]

Most marketing departments use a limited number of unconnected technology tools such as email, spreadsheets, project management software, and customer databases. Such tools cannot deal with the increasingly complex nature of business, the increased number of collaborators, and the global scope of operations. Companies use information technology to improve the management of their marketing resources. They need better templates for marketing processes, better management of marketing assets, and better allocation of marketing resources. Certain repetitive processes can be automated. This drive is going under such names as *Marketing Resource Management* (MRM), *Enterprise Marketing Management* (EMM), and *Marketing Automation Systems* (MAS).[57]

Several software companies now offer software packages to help companies better manage their marketing processes, assets, and resources. The packages are customized so different marketing managers—vice president of marketing, product and brand managers, field sales managers, marketing communications managers—can do their planning, implementation, and control.

Marketing Resource Management (MRM) software provides a set of Web-based applications that automate and integrate such activities as project management, campaign management, budget management, asset management, brand management, customer-relationship management, and knowledge management. The knowledge management component consists of process templates, how-to wizards, and best practices.

The software packages are Web-hosted and available to users with passwords. They add up to what some have called *desktop marketing* in that marketers can find whatever information and decision structures they need on their computers. The computer will host a dashboard on which marketers can manage their activities. MRM software will soon enable marketers to greatly improve spending and investment decisions, bring new products to market more quickly, and reduce decision time and costs.

Evaluation and Control

Despite the need to monitor and control marketing activities, many companies have inadequate control procedures. Table 22.4 lists four types of marketing control needed by companies: annual-plan control, profitability control, efficiency control, and strategic control. We consider each.

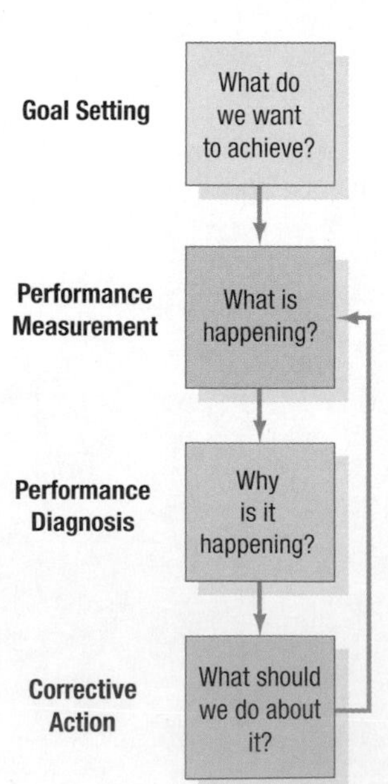
Goal Setting
What do we want to achieve?
Performance Measurement
What is happening?
Performance Diagnosis
Why is it happening?
Corrective Action
What should we do about it?
Figure 22.5 The Control Process

Annual-plan Control

Annual-plan control aims to ensure that the company achieves the sales, profits, and other goals established in its annual plan. The heart of annual-plan control is management by objectives. Four steps are involved (see Figure 22.5). First, management sets monthly or quarterly goals. Second, management monitors its performance in the marketplace. Third, management determines the causes of serious performance deviations. Fourth, management takes corrective action to close the gaps between goals and performance.

This control model applies to all levels of the organization. Top management sets annual sales and profit goals that become specific goals for lower levels of management. Each product manager is committed to attaining specified levels of sales and costs; each regional district and sales manager and each sales representative is also committed to specific goals. Each period, top management reviews and interprets the results.

Marketers today have better marketing metrics for measuring the performance of marketing plans (see Table 22.5 for some sample ones).[58] They can use four tools to check on plan performance: sales analysis, market share analysis, marketing expense-to-sales analysis, and financial analysis.

Table 22.4 Types of Marketing Control

Type of Control	Prime Responsibility	Purpose of Control	Approaches
I. Annual-plan control	Top management Middle management	To examine whether the planned results are being achieved	• Sales analysis • Market share analysis • Sales-to-expense ratios • Financial analysis • Market-based scorecard analysis
II. Profitability control	Marketing controller	To examine where the company is making and losing money	Profitability by: • product • territory • customer • segment • trade channel • order size
III. Efficiency control	Line and staff management Marketing controller	To evaluate and improve the spending efficiency and impact of marketing expenditures	Efficiency of: • sales force • advertising • sales promotion • distribution
IV. Strategic control	Top management Marketing auditor	To examine whether the company is pursuing its best opportunities with respect to markets, products, and channels	• Marketing-effectiveness rating instrument • Marketing audit • Marketing excellence review • Company ethical and social responsibility review

Table 22.5 Marketing Metrics

Sales Metrics
- Sales growth
- Market share
- Sales from new products

Customer Readiness to Buy Metrics
- Awareness
- Preference
- Purchase intention
- Trial rate
- Repurchase rate

Customer Metrics
- Customer complaints
- Customer satisfaction
- Number of promoters to detractors
- Customer acquisition costs
- New-customer gains
- Customer losses
- Customer churn
- Retention rate
- Customer lifetime value
- Customer equity
- Customer profitability
- Return on customer

Distribution Metrics
- Number of outlets
- Share in shops handling
- Weighted distribution
- Distribution gains
- Average stocks volume (value)
- Stocks cover in days
- Out of stock frequency
- Share of shelf
- Average sales per point of sale

Communication Metrics
- Spontaneous (unaided) brand awareness
- Top of mind brand awareness
- Prompted (aided) brand awareness
- Spontaneous (unaided) advertising awareness
- Prompted (aided) advertising awareness
- Effective reach
- Effective frequency
- Gross rating points (GRP)
- Response rate

SALES ANALYSIS

Sales analysis measures and evaluates actual sales in relationship to goals. Two specific tools make it work.

Sales-variance analysis measures the relative contribution of different factors to a gap in sales performance. Suppose the annual plan called for selling 4,000 widgets in the first quarter at $1 per widget, for total revenue of $4,000. At quarter's end, only 3,000 widgets were sold at $.80 per widget, for total revenue of $2,400. How much of the sales performance gap is due to the price decline, and how much to the volume decline? This calculation answers the question:

Variance due to price decline	= ($1.00–$0.80) (3,000) =	$600	37.5%
Variance due to volume decline	= ($1.00) (4,000–3,000) =	$1,000	62.5%
		$1,600	100.0%

Almost two-thirds of the variance is due to failure to achieve the volume target. The company should look closely at why it failed to achieve expected sales volume.

Microsales analysis looks at specific products, territories, and so forth that failed to produce expected sales. Suppose the company sells in three territories, and expected sales were 1,500 units, 500 units, and 2,000 units, respectively. Actual volumes were 1,400 units, 525 units, and 1,075 units, respectively. Thus territory 1 showed a 7 percent shortfall in terms of expected sales; territory 2, a 5 percent improvement over expectations; and territory 3, a 46 percent shortfall! Territory 3 is causing most of the trouble. Maybe territory 3's sales rep is underperforming; a major competitor has entered this territory; or business is in a recession there.

MARKET SHARE ANALYSIS

Company sales do not reveal how well the company is performing relative to competitors. For this purpose, management needs to track its market share in one of three ways.

Overall market share expresses the company's sales as a percentage of total market sales. **Served market share** is sales as a percentage of the total sales to the market. The **served market** is all the buyers able and willing to buy the product, and served market share is always larger than overall market share. A company could capture 100 percent of its served market and yet have a relatively small share of the total market. **Relative market share** is market share in relationship to the largest competitor. A relative market share over 100 percent indicates a market leader. A relative market share of exactly 100 percent means the company is tied for the lead. A rise in relative market share means a company is gaining on its leading competitor.

Conclusions from market share analysis, however, are subject to certain qualifications:

- **The assumption that outside forces affect all companies in the same way is often not true.** A medical report on the harmful consequences of cigarette smoking caused total cigarette sales to falter, but not equally for all companies.
- **The assumption that a company's performance should be judged against the average performance of all companies is not always valid.** A company's performance is best judged against that of its closest competitors.
- **If a new firm enters the industry, every existing firm's market share might fall.** A decline in market share might not mean the company is performing any worse than other companies. Share loss depends on the degree to which the new firm hits the company's specific markets.
- **Sometimes a market share decline is deliberately engineered to improve profits.** For example, management might drop unprofitable customers or products.
- **Market share can fluctuate for many minor reasons.** For example, it can be affected by whether a large sale occurs on the last day of the month or at the beginning of the next month. Not all shifts in market share have marketing significance.[59]

A useful way to analyze market share movements is in terms of four components:

Overall market share = Customer penetration × Customer loyalty × Customer selectivity × Price selectivity

where:

Customer penetration	Percentage of all customers who buy from the company.
Customer loyalty	Purchases from the company by its customers as a percentage of their total purchases from all suppliers of the same products.
Customer selectivity	Size of the average customer purchase from the company as a percentage of the size of the average customer purchase from an average company.
Price selectivity	Average price charged by the company as a percentage of the average price charged by all companies.

Now suppose the company's dollar market share falls during the period. The overall market share equation provides four possible explanations: The company lost some customers (lower customer penetration); existing customers are buying less from the company (lower customer loyalty); the company's remaining customers are smaller in size (lower customer selectivity); or the company's price has slipped relative to competition (lower price selectivity).

MARKETING EXPENSE-TO-SALES ANALYSIS

Annual-plan control requires making sure the company isn't overspending to achieve sales goals. The key ratio to watch is *marketing expense-to-sales.* In one company, this ratio was 30 percent and consisted of five component expense-to-sales ratios: sales force-to-sales (15 percent); advertising-to-sales (5 percent); sales promotion-to-sales (6 percent); marketing research-to-sales (1 percent); and sales administration-to-sales (3 percent).

Fluctuations outside normal range are cause for concern. Management needs to monitor period-to-period fluctuations in each ratio on a *control chart* (see Figure 22.6). This chart shows the advertising expense-to-sales ratio normally fluctuates between 8 percent and 12 percent, say 99 out of 100 times. In the 15th period, however, the ratio exceeded the upper control limit. One of two hypotheses can explain: (1) The company still has good expense control, and this situation represents a rare chance event; (2) The company has lost control over this expense and should find the cause. If there is no investigation, the risk is that some real change might have occurred, and the company will fall behind. An investigation may also uncover nothing and be a waste of time and effort.

Managers should watch the behavior of successive observations even within the upper and lower control limits. Note in Figure 22.6 that the level of the expense-to-sales ratio rose steadily from the 9th period onward. The probability of encountering six successive increases in what should be independent events is only 1 in 64.[60] This unusual pattern should have led to an investigation sometime before the 15th observation.

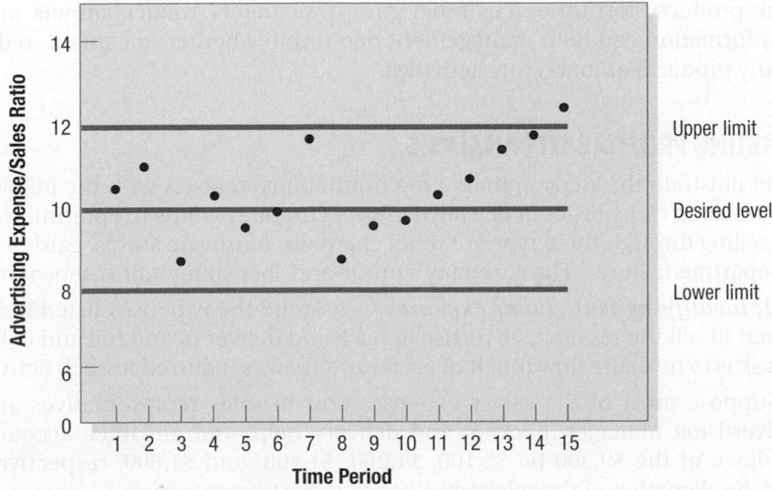

Figure 22.6 The Control-Chart Model

FINANCIAL ANALYSIS

Marketers should analyze the expense-to-sales ratios in an overall financial framework to determine how and where the company is making its money. They can, and are increasingly, using financial analysis to find profitable strategies beyond building sales.

Management uses financial analysis to identify factors that affect the company's *rate of return on net worth*.[61] The main factors are shown in Figure 22.7, along with illustrative numbers for a large chain-store retailer. The retailer is earning a 12.5 percent return on net worth. The return on net worth is the product of two ratios, the company's *return on assets* and its *financial leverage*. To improve its return on net worth, the company must increase its ratio of net profits to assets, or increase the ratio of assets to net worth. The company should analyze the composition of its assets (cash, accounts receivable, inventory, and plant and equipment) and see whether it can improve its asset management.

The return on assets is the product of two ratios, the *profit margin* and the *asset turnover*. The profit margin in Figure 22.7 seems low, whereas the asset turnover is more normal for retailing. The marketing executive can seek to improve performance in two ways: (1) increase the profit margin by increasing sales or cutting costs; and (2) increase the asset turnover by increasing sales or reducing assets (inventory, receivables) held against a given level of sales.[62]

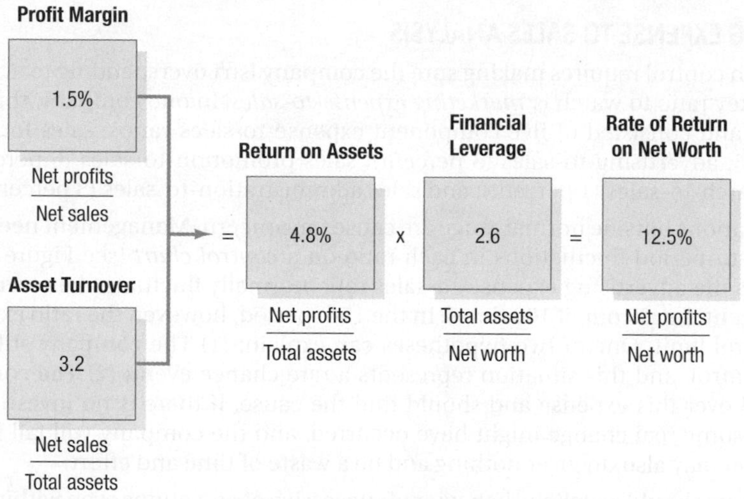

Figure 22.7 Financial Model of Return on Net Worth

Profitability Control

Companies can benefit from deeper financial analysis and should measure the profitability of their products, territories, customer groups, segments, trade channels, and order sizes. This information can help management determine whether to expand, reduce, or eliminate any products or marketing activities.

MARKETING PROFITABILITY ANALYSIS

We will illustrate the steps in marketing profitability analysis with the following example: The marketing vice president of a lawn mower company wants to determine the profitability of selling through three types of retail channels: hardware stores, garden supply shops, and department stores. The company's profit-and-loss statement is shown in Table 22.6.

Step 1: Identifying Functional Expenses — Assume the expenses listed in Table 22.6 are incurred to sell the product, advertise it, pack and deliver it, and bill and collect for it. The first task is to measure how much of each expense was incurred in each activity.

Suppose most of the salary expense went to sales representatives and the rest to an advertising manager, packing and delivery help, and an office accountant. Let the breakdown of the $9,300 be $5,100, $1,200, $1,400, and $1,600, respectively. Table 22.7 shows the allocation of the salary expense to these four activities.

Table 22.6 A Simplified Profit-and-loss Statement

Sales		$60,000
Cost of goods sold		39,000
Gross margin		21,000
Expenses		
Salaries	$9,300	
Rent	3,000	
Supplies	3,500	
		15,800
Net profit		$5,200

Table 22.7 Mapping Natural Expenses into Functional Expenses

Natural Accounts	Total	Selling	Advertising	Packing and Delivery	Billing and Collecting
Salaries	$9,300	$5,100	$1,200	$1,400	$1,600
Rent	3,000	—	400	2,000	600
Supplies	3,500	400	1,500	1,400	200
	$15,800	$5,500	$3,100	$4,800	$2,400

Table 22.7 also shows the rent account of $3,000 allocated to the four activities. Because the sales reps work away from the office, none of the building's rent expense is assigned to selling. Most of the expenses for floor space and rented equipment are for packing and delivery. The supplies account covers promotional materials, packing materials, fuel purchases for delivery, and home office stationery. The $3,500 in this account is reassigned to functional uses of the supplies.

Step 2: Assigning Functional Expenses to Marketing Entities— The next task is to measure how much functional expense was associated with selling through each type of channel. Consider the selling effort, indicated by the number of sales in each channel. This number is in the selling column of Table 22.8. Altogether, 275 sales calls were made during the period. Because the total selling expense amounted to $5,500 (see Table 22.8), the selling expense averaged $20 per call.

We can allocate advertising expense according to the number of ads addressed to different channels. Because there were 100 ads altogether, the average ad cost $31.

The packing and delivery expense is allocated according to the number of orders placed by each type of channel. This same basis was used for allocating billing and collection expense.

Table 22.8 Bases for Allocating Functional Expenses to Channels

Channel Type	Selling	Advertising	Packing and Delivery	Billing and Collecting
Hardware	200	50	50	50
Garden supply	65	20	21	21
Department stores	10	30	9	9
	275	**100**	**80**	**80**
Functional expense	$5,500	$3,100	$4,800	$2,400
÷ No. of Units	275	100	80	80
Equals	**$ 20**	**$ 31**	**$ 60**	**$ 30**

Table 22.9 Profit-and-Loss Statements for Channels

	Hardware	Garden Supply	Dept. Stores	Whole Company
Sales	$30,000	$10,000	$20,000	$60,000
Cost of goods sold	19,500	6,500	13,000	39,000
Gross margin	$10,500	$ 3,500	$ 7,000	$21,000
Expenses				
Selling ($20 per call)	$ 4,000	$ 1,300	$ 200	$ 5,500
Advertising ($31 per advertisement)	1,550	620	930	3,100
Packing and delivery ($60 per order)	3,000	1,260	540	4,800
Billing ($30 per order)	1,500	630	270	2,400
Total expenses	$10,050	$ 3,810	$ 1,940	$ 15,800
Net profit or loss	$ 450	$ (310)	$ 5,060	$ 5,200

Step 3: Preparing a Profit-and-Loss Statement for Each Marketing Entity—We can now prepare a profit-and-loss statement for each type of channel (see Table 22.9). Because hardware stores accounted for half of total sales ($30,000 out of $60,000), charge this channel with half the cost of goods sold ($19,500 out of $39,000). This leaves a gross margin from hardware stores of $10,500. From this we deduct the proportions of functional expenses hardware stores consumed. According to Table 22.8, hardware stores received 200 of 275 total sales calls. At an imputed value of $20 a call, hardware stores must bear a $4,000 selling expense. Table 22.8 also shows hardware stores were the target of 50 ads. At $31 an ad, the hardware stores are charged with $1,550 of advertising. The same reasoning applies in computing the share of the other functional expenses. The result is that hardware stores gave rise to $10,050 of the total expenses. Subtracting this from gross margin, we find the profit of selling through hardware stores is only $450.

Repeat this analysis for the other channels. The company is losing money in selling through garden supply shops and makes virtually all its profits through department stores. Notice that gross sales is not a reliable indicator of the net profits for each channel.

DETERMINING CORRECTIVE ACTION

It would be naive to conclude the company should drop garden supply shops and possibly hardware stores so that it can concentrate on department stores. We need to answer the following questions first:

- To what extent do buyers buy on the basis of type of retail outlet versus brand?
- What are the trends with respect to the importance of these three channels?
- How good are the company marketing strategies directed at the three channels?

On the basis of the answers, marketing management can evaluate five alternatives:

1. Establish a special charge for handling smaller orders.
2. Give more promotional aid to garden supply shops and hardware stores.
3. Reduce the number of sales calls and the amount of advertising going to garden supply shops and hardware stores.
4. Do not abandon any channel entirely, but only the weakest retail units in each channel.
5. Do nothing.

In general, marketing profitability analysis indicates the relative profitability of different channels, products, territories, or other marketing entities. It does not prove that the best course of action is to drop the unprofitable marketing entities, nor does it capture the likely profit improvement if these marginal marketing entities are dropped.

DIRECT VERSUS FULL COSTING

Like all information tools, marketing profitability analysis can lead or mislead marketing executives, depending on how well they understand its methods and limitations. The lawn mower company showed some arbitrariness in its choice of bases for allocating the functional expenses to its marketing entities. It used "number of sales calls" to allocate selling expenses, generating less recordkeeping and computation, when in principle "number of sales working hours" is a more accurate indicator of cost.

Far more serious is another judgmental element affecting profitability analysis—whether to allocate full costs or only direct and traceable costs in evaluating a marketing entity's performance. The lawn mower company sidestepped this problem by assuming only simple costs that fit in with marketing activities, but we cannot avoid the question in real-world analyses of profitability. We distinguish three types of costs:

1. ***Direct costs*** — We can assign direct costs directly to the proper marketing entities. Sales commissions are a direct cost in a profitability analysis of sales territories, sales representatives, or customers. Advertising expenditures are a direct cost in a profitability analysis of products to the extent that each advertisement promotes only one product. Other direct costs for specific purposes are sales-force salaries and traveling expenses.
2. ***Traceable common costs*** — We can assign traceable common costs only indirectly, but on a plausible basis, to the marketing entities. In the example, we analyzed rent this way.
3. ***Non-traceable common costs***— Common costs whose allocation to the marketing entities is highly arbitrary are non-traceable common costs. To allocate "corporate image" expenditures equally to all products would be arbitrary, because all products do not benefit equally. To allocate them proportionately to the sales of the various products would be arbitrary, because relative product sales reflect many factors besides corporate image making. Other examples are top management salaries, taxes, interest, and other overhead.

No one disputes the inclusion of direct costs in marketing cost analysis. There is some controversy about including traceable common costs, which lump together costs that would and would not change with the scale of marketing activity. If the lawn mower company drops garden supply shops, it would probably continue to pay the same rent. In this event, its profits would not rise immediately by the amount of the present loss in selling to garden supply shops ($310).

The major controversy is about whether to allocate the non traceable common costs to the marketing entities. Such allocation is called the *full-cost approach,* and its advocates argue that all costs must ultimately be imputed in order to determine true profitability. However, this argument confuses the use of accounting for financial reporting with its use for managerial decision making. Full costing has three major weaknesses:

1. The relative profitability of different marketing entities can shift radically when we replace one arbitrary way to allocate non-traceable common costs by another.
2. The arbitrariness demoralizes managers, who feel their performance is judged adversely.
3. The inclusion of non traceable common costs could weaken efforts at real cost control.

Operating management is most effective in controlling direct costs and traceable common costs. Arbitrary assignments of non-traceable common costs can lead managers to spend their time fighting cost allocations instead of managing controllable costs well.

Companies show growing interest in using marketing profitability analysis, or its broader version, activity-based cost accounting (ABC), to quantify the true profitability of different activities.[63] Managers can then reduce the resources required to perform various activities, make the resources more productive, acquire them at lower cost, or raise prices on products that consume heavy amounts of support resources. The contribution of ABC is to refocus management's attention away from using only labor or material standard costs to allocate full cost, and toward capturing the actual costs of supporting individual products, customers, and other entities.

Efficiency Control

Suppose a profitability analysis reveals that the company is earning poor profits in certain products, territories, or markets. Are there more efficient ways to manage the sales force, advertising, sales promotion, and distribution in connection with these marketing entities?

Some companies have established a *marketing controller* position to improve marketing efficiency. Marketing controllers work out of the controller's office but specialize in the marketing side of the business. Companies such as General Foods, DuPont, and Johnson & Johnson perform a sophisticated financial analysis of marketing expenditures and results. They examine adherence to profit plans, help prepare brand managers' budgets, measure the efficiency of promotions, analyze media production costs, evaluate customer and geographic profitability, and educate marketing personnel on the financial implications of marketing decisions.[64]

They examine adherence to profit plans, help prepare brand managers' budgets, measure the efficiency of promotions, analyze media production costs, evaluate customer and geographic profitability, and educate marketing personnel on the financial implications of marketing decisions.[65] They can examine the efficiency of the channel, sales force, advertising, or any other form of marketing communication.

For example, in assessing channel efficiency, management needs to search for distribution economies in inventory control, warehouse locations, and transportation modes. It should track such measures as:

- Logistics costs as a percentage of sales
- Percentage of orders filled correctly
- Percentage of on time deliveries
- Number of billing errors

Management should strive to reduce inventory while at the same time speeding up the order-to-delivery cycle. Dell Computer shows how to do both simultaneously.

> **Dell**—A customer-customized computer ordered from Dell's Web site at 9:00 a.m. on Wednesday can be on the delivery truck by 9:00 p.m. Thursday. In that short period, Dell electronically orders the computer components from its suppliers' warehouses. Equally impressive, Dell gets paid electronically within 24 hours, whereas Compaq, supplying its computers to retailers, receives payment days later.

Strategic Control

Each company should periodically reassess its strategic approach to the marketplace with marketing effectiveness reviews and marketing audits. Companies can also perform marketing excellence reviews and ethical/social responsibility reviews.

THE MARKETING AUDIT

The average U.S. corporation loses half of its customers in five years, half of its employees in four years, and half of its investors in less than one year. Clearly, this points to some weaknesses. Companies that discover weaknesses should undertake a thorough study known as a marketing audit.[66] A **marketing audit** is a comprehensive, systematic, independent, and periodic examination of a company's or business unit's marketing environment, objectives, strategies, and activities to determine problem areas and opportunities and recommend a plan of action to improve the company's marketing performance.

Let us examine the marketing audit's four characteristics:

1. ***Comprehensive*** — The marketing audit covers all the major marketing activities of a business, not just a few trouble spots. It would be called a functional audit if it covered only the sales force, pricing, or some other marketing activity. Although functional audits are useful, they sometimes mislead management. For example, excessive sales-force turnover could be a symptom not of poor sales-force training or compensation but of weak company products and promotion. A comprehensive marketing audit usually is more effective in locating the real source of problems.
2. ***Systematic*** — The marketing audit is an orderly examination of the organization's macro- and micromarketing environments, marketing objectives and strategies, marketing systems, and specific activities. The audit indicates the most-needed improvements, which are then incorporated into a corrective action plan involving both short-run and long-run steps to improve overall effectiveness.
3. ***Independent*** — A marketing audit can be conducted in six ways: self-audit, audit from across, audit from above, company auditing office, company taskforce audit, and outsider audit. Self-audits, in which managers use a checklist to rate their own operations, lack objectivity and independence.[67] 3M has made good use of a corporate auditing office, which provides marketing audit services to divisions on request.[68] However, the best audits generally come from outside consultants who have the necessary objectivity, broad experience in multiple industries, some familiarity with the industry being audited, and the undivided time and attention to give to the audit.
4. ***Periodic*** — Typically, marketing audits are initiated only after sales have turned down, sales-force morale has fallen, and other problems have occurred. Companies are thrown into a crisis partly because they failed to review their marketing operations during good times. A periodic marketing audit can benefit companies in good health as well as those in trouble.

A marketing audit starts with a meeting between the company officer(s) and the marketing auditor(s) to work out an agreement on the audit's objectives, coverage, depth, data sources, report format, and time frame. A detailed plan regarding who is to be interviewed, the questions to be asked, the time and place of contact, and so on is prepared so that auditing time and cost are kept to a minimum. The cardinal rule in marketing auditing is: Do not rely solely on company managers for data and opinions. Customers, dealers, and other outside groups must also be interviewed. Many companies do not really know how their customers and dealers see them, nor do they fully understand customer needs.

The marketing audit examines six major components of the company's marketing situation. The major questions are listed in Table 22.10.

THE MARKETING EXCELLENCE REVIEW

Companies can use another instrument to rate their performance in relation to the best practices of high-performing businesses. The three columns in Table 22.10 distinguish among poor, good, and excellent business and marketing practices. Management can place a checkmark to indicate its perception of where the business stands. The resulting profile exposes weaknesses and strengths, highlighting where the company might make changes to become a truly outstanding player in the marketplace.

Table 22.10 Components of a Marketing Audit

Part I. Marketing Environment Audit	
Macroenvironment	
A. Demographic	What major demographic developments and trends pose opportunities or threats to this company? What actions has the company taken in response to these developments and trends?
B. Economic	What major developments in income, prices, savings, and credit will affect the company? What actions has the company been taking in response to these developments and trends?
C. Environmental	What is the outlook for the cost and availability of natural resources and energy needed by the company? What concerns have been expressed about the company's role in pollution and conservation, and what steps has the company taken?
D. Technological	What major changes are occurring in product and process technology? What is the company's position in these technologies? What major generic substitutes might replace this product?
E. Political	What changes in laws and regulations might affect marketing strategy and tactics? What is happening in the areas of pollution control, equal employment opportunity, product safety, advertising, price control, and so forth, that affects marketing strategy?
F. Cultural	What is the public's attitude toward business and toward the company's products? What changes in customer lifestyles and values might affect the company?
Task Environment	
A. Markets	What is happening to market size, growth, geographical distribution, and profits? What are the major market segments?
B. Customers	What are the customers' needs and buying processes? How do customers and prospects rate the company and its competitors on reputation, product quality, service, sales force, and price? How do different customer segments make their buying decisions?
C. Competitors	Who are the major competitors? What are their objectives, strategies, strengths, weaknesses, sizes, and market shares? What trends will affect future competition and substitutes for the company's products?
D. Distribution and Dealers	What are the main trade channels for bringing products to customers? What are the efficiency levels and growth potentials of the different trade channels?
E. Suppliers	What is the outlook for the availability of key resources used in production? What trends are occurring among suppliers?
F. Facilitators and Marketing Firms	What is the cost and availability outlook for transportation services, warehousing facilities, and financial resources? How effective are the company's advertising agencies and marketing research firms?
G. Publics	Which publics represent particular opportunities or problems for the company? What steps has the company taken to deal effectively with each public?
Part II. Marketing Strategy Audit	
A. Business Mission	Is the business mission clearly stated in market-oriented terms? Is it feasible?
B. Marketing Objectives and Goals	Are the company and marketing objectives and goals stated clearly enough to guide marketing planning and performance measurement? Are the marketing objectives appropriate, given the company's competitive position, resources, and opportunities?
C. Strategy	Has the management articulated a clear marketing strategy for achieving its marketing objectives? Is the strategy convincing? Is the strategy appropriate to the stage of the product life cycle, competitors' strategies, and the state of the economy? Is the company using the best basis for market segmentation? Does it have clear criteria for rating the segments and choosing the best ones? Has it developed accurate profiles of each target segment? Has the company developed an effective positioning and marketing mix for each target segment? Are marketing resources allocated optimally to the major elements of the marketing mix? Are enough resources or too many resources budgeted to accomplish the marketing objectives?

Table 22.10 *Continued ...*

Part III. Marketing Organization Audit	
A. Formal Structure	Does the marketing vice president have adequate authority and responsibility for company activities that affect customers' satisfaction? Are the marketing activities optimally structured along functional, product, segment, end-user, and geographical lines?
B. Functional Efficiency	Are there good communication and working relations between marketing and sales? Is the product-management system working effectively? Are product managers able to plan profits or only sales volume? Are there any groups in marketing that need more training, motivation, supervision, or evaluation?
C. Interface Efficiency	Are there any problems between marketing and manufacturing, R&D, purchasing, finance, accounting, and/or legal that need attention?
Part IV. Marketing Systems Audit	
A. Marketing Information System	Is the marketing intelligence system producing accurate, sufficient, and timely information about marketplace developments with respect to customers, prospects, distributors and dealers, competitors, suppliers, and various publics? Are company decision makers asking for enough marketing research, and are they using the results? Is the company employing the best methods for market measurement and sales forecasting?
B. Marketing Planning System	Is the marketing planning system well-conceived and effectively used? Do marketers have decision support systems available? Does the planning system result in acceptable sales targets and quotas?
C. Marketing Control System	Are the control procedures adequate to ensure that the annual-plan objectives are being achieved? Does management periodically analyze the profitability of products, markets, territories, and channels of distribution? Are marketing costs and productivity periodically examined?
D. New-Product Development System	Is the company well-organized to gather, generate, and screen new-product ideas? Does the company do adequate concept research and business analysis before investing in new ideas? Does the company carry out adequate product and market testing before launching new products?
Part V. Marketing Productivity Audit	
A. Profitability Analysis	What is the profitability of the company's different products, markets, territories, and channels of distribution? Should the company enter, expand, contract, or withdraw from any business segments?
B. Cost-Effectiveness Analysis	Do any marketing activities seem to have excessive costs? Can cost-reducing steps be taken?
Part VI. Marketing Function Audits	
A. Products	What are the company's product-line objectives? Are they sound? Is the current product line meeting the objectives? Should the product line be stretched or contracted upward, downward, or both ways? Which products should be phased out? Which products should be added? What are the buyers' knowledge and attitudes toward the company's and competitors' product quality, features, styling, brand names, and so on? What areas of product and brand strategy need improvement?
B. Price	What are the company's pricing objectives, policies, strategies, and procedures? To what extent are prices set on cost, demand, and competitive criteria? Do the customers see the company's prices as being in line with the value of its offer? What does management know about the price elasticity of demand, experience-curve effects, and competitors' prices and pricing policies? To what extent are price policies compatible with the needs of distributors and dealers, suppliers, and government regulation?

Table 22.10 *Continued ...*

C. Distribution	What are the company's distribution objectives and strategies? Is there adequate market coverage and service? How effective are distributors, dealers, manufacturers' representatives, brokers, agents, and others? Should the company consider changing its distribution channels?
D. Marketing Communications	What are the organization's advertising objectives? Are they sound? Is the right amount being spent on advertising? Are the ad themes and copy effective? What do customers and the public think about the advertising? Are the advertising media well chosen? Is the internal advertising staff adequate? Is the sales promotion budget adequate? Is there effective and sufficient use of sales promotion tools such as samples, coupons, displays, and sales contests? Is the public relations staff competent and creative? Is the company making enough use of direct, online, and database marketing?
E. Sales Force	What are the sales force's objectives? Is the sales force large enough to accomplish the company's objectives? Is the sales force organized along the proper principles of specialization (territory, market, product)? Are there enough (or too many) sales managers to guide the field sales representatives? Do the sales compensation level and structure provide adequate incentive and reward? Does the sales force show high morale, ability, and effort? Are the procedures adequate for setting quotas and evaluating performance? How does the company's sales force compare to competitors' sales forces?

The Future of Marketing

Top management has recognized that past marketing has been highly wasteful and is demanding more accountability from marketing departments. "Marketing Memo: Major Marketing Weaknesses" summarizes the major deficiencies that companies have in marketing, how to spot these deficiencies, and what to do about them.

Going forward, there are a number of imperatives to achieve marketing excellence. Marketing must be "holistic" and less departmental. Marketers must achieve larger influence in the company if they are to be the main architect of business strategy. Marketers must continuously create new ideas if the company is to prosper in a hyper-competitive economy. Marketers must strive for customer insight and treat customers differently but appropriately. Marketers must build their brands through performance, more than through promotion. Marketers must go electronic and win through building superior information and communication systems.

In these ways, modern marketing will continue to evolve and confront new challenges and opportunities. As a result, the coming years will see:

- The demise of the marketing department and the rise of holistic marketing.
- The demise of free-spending marketing and the rise of ROI marketing.
- The demise of marketing intuition and the rise of marketing science.
- The demise of manual marketing and the rise of automated marketing.
- The demise of mass marketing and the rise of precision marketing.

To accomplish these changes and become truly holistic in marketing, a new set of skills and competencies is needed. Proficiency will be demanded in areas such as:

- Customer Relationship Management (CRM).
- Partner Relationship Management (PRM).
- Database marketing and data-mining.
- Contact center management and telemarketing.
- Public relations marketing (including event and sponsorship marketing).
- Brand building and brand asset management.
- Experiential marketing.
- Integrated marketing communications.
- Profitability analysis by segment, customer, channel.

It is an exciting time for marketing. In the relentless pursuit of marketing superiority and dominance, new rules and practices are emerging. The benefits of successful 21st century marketing are many, but will only come with hard work, insight, and inspiration. The words of 19th century American author Ralph Waldo Emerson may never have been more true: "This time like all times is a good one, if we but know what to do with it."

MARKETING MEMO • MAJOR MARKETING WEAKNESSES

A number of "deadly sins" signal that the marketing program is in trouble. Here are ten deadly sins, the signs, and some solutions.

DEADLY SIN: The company is not sufficiently market-focused and customer-driven.

Signs: Poor identification of market segments, poor prioritization of market segments, no market segment managers, employees who think it is the job of marketing and sales to serve customers, no training program to create a customer culture, no incentives to treat the customer especially well.

Solutions: Use more advanced segmentation techniques, prioritize segments, specialize the sales force, develop a clear hierarchy of company values, foster more customer consciousness in employees and company agents, make it easy for customers to reach the company and respond quickly to any communication.

DEADLY SIN: The company does not fully understand its target customers.

Signs: Latest study of customers is three years old, customers are not buying your product like they once did, competitor's products are selling better, high level of customer returns and complaints.

Solutions: Do more sophisticated consumer research, use more analytical techniques, establish customer and dealer panels, use customer relationship software, do data mining.

DEADLY SIN: The company needs to better define and monitor its competitors.

Signs: The company focuses on near competitors, misses distant competitors and disruptive technologies, no system for gathering and distributing competitive intelligence.

Solutions: Establish an office for competitive intelligence, hire competitors' people, watch for technology that might affect the company, prepare offerings like competitors'.

DEADLY SIN: The company does not properly manage relationships with stakeholders.

Signs: Employees, dealers, and investors are not happy, good suppliers do not come.

Solutions: Move from zero-sum thinking to positive-sum thinking, do a better job of managing employees, supplier relations, distributors, dealers, and investors.

DEADLY SIN: The company is not good at finding new opportunities.

Signs: The company has not identified any exciting new opportunities for years, the new ideas the company has launched have largely failed.

Solutions: Set up a system for stimulating the flow of new ideas.

DEADLY SIN: The company's marketing planning process is deficient.

Signs: The marketing plan format does not have the right components, there is no way to estimate the financial implications of different strategies, there is no contingency planning.

Solutions: Establish a standard format including situational analysis, SWOT, major issues, objectives, strategy, tactics, budgets, and controls; ask marketers what changes they would make if they were given 20 percent more or less budget; run an annual marketing awards program with prizes for best plans and performance.

DEADLY SIN: Product and service policies need tightening.

Signs: Too many products and many are losing money, the company is giving away too many services, the company is poor at cross-selling products and services.

Solutions: Establish a system to track weak products and fix or drop them, offer and price services at different levels, improve processes for cross-selling and upselling.

DEADLY SIN: The company's brand-building and communication skills are weak.

Signs: The target market does not know much about the company, the brand is not seen as distinctive, the company allocates its budget to the same marketing tools in about the same proportion each year, there is little evaluation of the ROI impact of promotions.

Solutions: Improve brand-building strategies and measurement of results, shift money into effective marketing instruments, require marketers to estimate the ROI impact in advance of funding requests.

DEADLY SIN: The company is not organized for effective and efficient marketing.

Signs: Staff lacks 21st century marketing skills, bad vibes between marketing/sales and other departments.

Solutions: Appoint a strong leader and build new skills in the marketing department, improve marketing's relations with other departments.

DEADLY SIN: The company has not made maximum use of technology.

Signs: Minimal use of the Internet, outdated sales automation system, no market automation, no decision-support models, no marketing dashboards.

Solutions: Use the Internet more, improve the sales automation system, apply market automation to routine decisions, develop formal marketing decision models and marketing dashboards.

Source: Philip Kotler, *Ten Deadly Marketing Sins: Signs and Solutions*, (Hoboken, NJ: John Wiley, 2004).

Summary

1. The modern marketing department has evolved through the years from a simple sales department to an organizational structure where marketing personnel work mainly in cross-disciplinary teams.
2. Modern marketing departments can be organized in a number of ways. Some companies are organized by functional specialization, while others focus on geography and regionalization. Still others emphasize product and brand management or market-segment management. Some companies establish a matrix organization consisting of both product and market managers. Finally, some companies have strong corporate marketing, others have limited corporate marketing, and still others place marketing only in the divisions.
3. Effective modern marketing organizations are marked by a strong cooperation and customer focus among the company's departments: marketing, R&D, engineering, purchasing, manufacturing, operations, finance, accounting, and credit.
4. Companies must practice social responsibility through their legal, ethical, and social words and actions. Cause marketing can used to productively link social responsibility to consumer marketing programs.
5. A brilliant strategic marketing plan counts for little if it is not implemented properly. Implementing marketing plans calls for skills in recognizing and diagnosing a problem, assessing the company level where the problem exists, implementation skills, and skills in evaluating the results.
6. The marketing department has to monitor and control marketing activities continuously. Efficiency control focuses on finding ways to increase the efficiency of the sales force, advertising, sales promotion, and distribution. Strategic control entails a periodic reassessment of the company and its strategic approach to the marketplace, using the tools of marketing effectiveness and excellence reviews, and the marketing audit.

Application

Marketing Debate—Is Marketing Management an Art or a Science?

Some marketing observers maintain that good marketing is something that is more an art and does not lend itself to rigorous analysis and deliberation. Others strongly disagree and contend that marketing management is a highly disciplined enterprise that shares much in common with other business disciplines.

Take a position: *Marketing management is largely an artistic exercise and therefore highly subjective* versus *Marketing management is largely a scientific exercise with well-established guidelines and criteria.*

Marketing Discussion

How does cause or corporate societal marketing affect your personal consumption behavior? Do you ever buy or not buy any products or services from a company because of its environmental policies or programs? Why or why not?

Sonic Marketing Plan and Exercises

The Marketing Plan: An Introduction

As a marketer, you'll need a good marketing plan to provide direction and focus for your brand, product, or company. With a detailed plan, any business will be better prepared to launch an innovative new product or increase sales to current customers. Nonprofit organizations also use marketing plans to guide their fundraising and outreach efforts. Even government agencies put together marketing plans for initiatives such as building public awareness of proper nutrition and stimulating area tourism.

THE PURPOSE AND CONTENT OF A MARKETING PLAN

A marketing plan has a more limited scope than a business plan, which offers a broad overview of the entire organization's mission, objectives, strategy, and resource allocation. The marketing plan documents how the organization's strategic objectives will be achieved through specific marketing strategies and tactics, with the customer as the starting point. It is also linked to the plans of other organizational departments. Suppose a marketing plan calls for selling 200,000 units annually. The production department must gear up to make that many units, finance must arrange funding to cover the expenses, human resources must be ready to hire and train staff, and so on. Without the appropriate level of organizational support and resources, no marketing plan can succeed.

Although the exact length and layout varies from company to company, a marketing plan usually contains the sections described in Chapter 2. Smaller businesses may create shorter or less formal marketing plans, whereas corporations generally require highly structured marketing plans. To guide implementation effectively, every part of the plan must be described in considerable detail. Sometimes a company will post its marketing plan on an internal Web site so managers and employees in different locations can consult specific sections and collaborate on additions or changes.

THE ROLE OF RESEARCH

To develop innovative products, successful strategies, and action programs, marketers need up-to-date information about the environment, the competition, and the selected market segments. Often, analysis of internal data is the starting point for assessing the current marketing situation, supplemented by marketing intelligence and research investigating the overall market, the competition, key issues, threats, and opportunities. As the plan is put into effect, marketers use research to measure progress toward objectives and to identify areas for improvement if results fall short of projections.

Finally, marketing research helps marketers learn more about their customers' requirements, expectations, perceptions, satisfaction, and loyalty. This deeper understanding provides a foundation for building competitive advantage through well-informed segmenting, targeting, and positioning decisions. Thus, the marketing plan should outline what marketing research will be conducted and when, as well as how the findings will be applied.

THE ROLE OF RELATIONSHIPS

Although the marketing plan shows how the company will establish and maintain profitable customer relationships, it also affects both internal and external relationships. First, it influences how marketing personnel work with each other and with other departments to deliver value and satisfy customers. Second, it affects how the company works with suppliers, distributors, and partners to achieve the plan's objectives. Third, it influences the company's dealings with other stakeholders, including government regulators, the media, and the community at large. All these relationships are important to the organization's success and must be considered when developing a marketing plan.

FROM MARKETING PLAN TO MARKETING ACTION

Most companies create yearly marketing plans, although some plans cover a longer period. Marketers start planning well in advance of the implementation date to allow time for marketing research, analysis, management review, and coordination between departments. Then, after each action program begins, marketers monitor ongoing results, investigate any deviation from the projected outcome, and take corrective steps as needed. Some marketers also prepare contingency plans for implementation if certain conditions emerge. Because of inevitable and sometimes unpredictable environmental changes, marketers must be ready to update and adapt marketing plans at any time.

For effective implementation and control, the marketing plan should define how progress toward objectives will be measured. Managers typically use budgets, schedules, and marketing metrics for monitoring and evaluating results. With budgets, they can compare planned expenditures with actual expenditures for a given period. Schedules allow management to see when tasks were supposed to be completed and when they were actually completed. Marketing metrics track the actual outcomes of marketing programs to see whether the company is moving forward toward its objectives.

Sample Marketing Plan for Sonic

This section takes you inside the sample marketing plan for Sonic, a hypothetical start-up company. The company's first product is the Sonic 1000, a multimedia, cellular/Wi-Fi enabled personal digital assistant (PDA), also known as a handheld computer. Sonic will be competing with Palm, Hewlett-Packard, Motorola, Apple, and other well-established rivals in a crowded, fast-changing marketplace where smart phones and many other electronics devices have PDA functionality as well as entertainment capabilities. The annotations explain more about what each section of the plan should contain.

This section summarizes market opportunities, marketing strategy, and marketing and financial objectives for senior managers who will read and approve the marketing plan.

1.0 EXECUTIVE SUMMARY

Sonic is preparing to launch a new multimedia, dual-mode PDA product, the Sonic 1000, in a mature market. We can compete with both PDAs and smart phones because our product offers a unique combination of advanced features and functionality at a value-added price. We are targeting specific segments in the consumer and business markets, taking advantage of the growing interest in a single device with communication, organization, and entertainment benefits.

The primary marketing objective is to achieve first-year national market share of 3 percent with unit sales of 240,000. The primary financial objectives are to achieve first-year sales revenues of $60 million, keep first-year losses to less than $10 million, and break even early in the second year.

The situation analysis describes the market, the company's capability to serve targeted segments, and the competition.

2.0 SITUATION ANALYSIS

Sonic, founded 18 months ago by two entrepreneurs with telecommunications experience, is about to enter the now mature PDA market. Multifunction mobile phones, e-mail devices, and wireless communication devices are increasingly popular for both personal and professional use, with more than five million PDAs and 22 million smart phones sold worldwide each year. Competition is increasingly intense even as technology evolves, industry consolidation continues, and pricing pressures squeeze profitability. Palm, a PDA pioneer, is one of several key players having difficulty adapting to the smart-phone challenge. To gain market share in this dynamic environment, Sonic must carefully target specific segments with valued features and plan for a next-generation product to keep brand momentum going.

2.1 Market Summary

Sonic's market consists of consumers and business users who prefer to use a single device for communication, information storage and exchange, organization, and entertainment on the go. Specific segments being targeted during the first year include professionals, corporations, students, entrepreneurs, and medical users. Exhibit A-1 shows how the Sonic 1000 addresses the needs of targeted consumer and business segments.

PDA purchasers can choose between models based on several different operating systems, including systems from Palm, Microsoft, and Symbian, plus Linux variations. Sonic licenses a Linux-based system because it is somewhat less vulnerable to attack by hackers and viruses. Storage capacity (hard drive or flash drive) is an expected feature for PDAs, so Sonic is equipping its first product with an ultra-fast 20-gigabyte drive that can be supplemented by extra storage. Technology costs are decreasing even as capabilities are increasing, which makes value-priced models more appealing to consumers and to business users with older PDAs who want to trade up to new, high-end multifunction units.

2.2 Strengths, Weaknesses, Opportunities, and Threat Analysis

Sonic has several powerful strengths on which to build, but our major weakness is lack of brand awareness and image. The major opportunity is demand for multifunction communication, organization, and entertainment devices that deliver a number of valued benefits. We also face the threat of ever-higher competition and downward pricing pressure.

Strengths Sonic can build on three important strengths:

Strengths are internal capabilities that can help the company reach its objectives.

1. ***Innovative product***—The Sonic 1000 offers a combination of features that would otherwise require customers to carry multiple devices, such as speedy, hands-free dual-mode mobile/Wi-Fi telecommunications capabilities, and digital video/music/TV program storage/playback.
2. ***Security***—Our PDA uses a Linux-based operating system that is less vulnerable to hackers and other security threats that can result in stolen or corrupted data.

Exhibit A-1: Needs and Corresponding Features/Benefits of Sonic PDA

Targeted Segment	Customer Need	Corresponding Feature/Benefit
Professionals (consumer market)	• Stay in touch while on the go • Record information while on the go	• Wireless e-mail to conveniently send and receive messages from anywhere; cell phone capability for voice communication from anywhere • Voice recognition for no-hands recording
Students (consumer market)	• Perform many functions without carrying multiple gadgets • Express style and individuality	• Compatible with numerous applications and peripherals for convenient, cost-effective functionality • Case wardrobe of different colors and patterns allows users to make a fashion statement
Corporate users (business market)	• Input and access critical data on the go • Use for proprietary tasks	• Compatible with widely available software • Customizable to fit diverse corporate tasks and networks
Entrepreneurs (business market)	• Organize and access contacts, schedule details	• No-hands, wireless access to calendar and address book to easily check appointments and connect with contacts
Medical users (business market)	• Update, access, and exchange medical records	• No-hands, wireless recording and exchange of information to reduce paperwork and increase productivity

3. ***Pricing***—Our product is priced lower than competing multifunction PDAs—none of which offer the same bundle of features—which gives us an edge with price-conscious customers.

Weaknesses are internal elements that may interfere with the company's ability to achieve its objectives.

Weaknesses By waiting to enter the PDA market until considerable consolidation of competitors has occurred, Sonic has learned from the successes and mistakes of others. Nonetheless, we have two main weaknesses:

1. ***Lack of brand awareness***—Sonic has no established brand or image, whereas Palm, Apple, and others have strong brand recognition. We will address this issue with aggressive promotion.
2. ***Heavier and thicker unit***—The Sonic 1000 is slightly heavier and thicker than most competing models because it incorporates many multimedia features and offers far more storage capacity than the average PDA. To counteract this weakness, we will emphasize our product's benefits and value-added pricing, two compelling competitive strengths.

Opportunities are areas of buyer need or potential interest in which the company might perform profitably.

Opportunities Sonic can take advantage of two major market opportunities:

1. ***Increasing demand for multimedia devices with communication functions***—The market for multimedia, multifunction devices is growing much faster than the market for single-use devices. Growth is accelerating as dual-mode capabilities become mainstream, giving customers the flexibility to make phone calls over mobile or Internet connections. PDAs and smart phones are already commonplace in public, work, and educational settings; in fact, users who bought entry-level models are now trading up.
2. ***Lower technology costs***—Better technology is now available at a lower cost than ever before. Thus, Sonic can incorporate advanced features at a value-added price that allows for reasonable profits.

Threats are challenges posed by an unfavorable trend or development that could lead to lower sales and profits.

Threats We face three main threats at the introduction of the Sonic 1000:

1. ***Increased competition***—More companies are offering devices with some but not all of the features and benefits provided by the Sonic PDA. Therefore, Sonic's marketing communications must stress our clear differentiation and value-added pricing.
2. ***Downward pressure on pricing***—Increased competition and market share strategies are pushing PDA prices down. Still, our objective of seeking a 10 percent profit on second-year sales of the original model is realistic, given the lower margins in the PDA market.
3. ***Compressed product life cycle***—PDAs have reached the maturity stage of their life cycle more quickly than earlier technology products. Because of this compressed life cycle, we plan to introduce a media-oriented second product during the year following the Sonic 1000's launch.

This section identifies key competitors, describes their market positions, and provides an overview of their strategies.

2.3 Competition

The emergence of new multifunction smart phones, including the Apple iPhone, has increased competitive pressure. Dell has already left the PDA market; the remaining competitors are continually adding features and sharpening price points. Competition from specialized devices for text and e-mail messaging, such as Blackberry devices, is another major factor. Key competitors:

- ***Palm.*** As the PDA market leader, with a 34 percent share, Palm has excellent distribution in multiple channels and alliances with a number of U.S. and European telecommunications carriers. However, Palm's smart phone share is well below that of Nokia and other handset marketers. Palm products use either the proprietary Palm operating system or Windows.
- ***Hewlett-Packard.*** HP holds 22 percent of the PDA market and targets business segments with its numerous iPAQ Pocket PC devices. Some of its PDAs can send documents

Exhibit A-2 Selected PDA Products and Pricing

Competitor	Model	Features	Price
PalmOne	Tungsten C	PDA functions, wireless capabilities, color screen, tiny keyboard, wireless capabilities	$499
PalmOne	M130	PDA functions, color screen, expandable functionality	$199
Handspring	Treo 270	PDA and mobile phone functions, color screen, tiny keyboard, speakerphone capabilities; no expansion slot	$499
Samsung	i500	PDA functions, mobile phone functions, MP3 player, color screen, video capabilities	$599
Garmin	iQue 3600	PDA functions, global positioning system technology, voice recorder, expansion slot, MP3 player	$589
Dell	Axim X5	PDA functions, color screen, e-mail capable, voice recorder, speaker, expandable	$199
Sony	Clie PEG-NX73V	PDA functions, digital camera, tiny keyboard, games, presentation software, MP3 player, voice recorder	$499

to Bluetooth equipped printers and prevent data loss if batteries run down. For extra security, one model allows access by fingerprint match as well as by password. HP enjoys widespread distribution and offers a full line of PDAs at various price points.

- ***Motorola.*** Motorola sold 100 million of its RAZR clamshell phones worldwide in three years and now offers the RAZR2, smaller and lighter than earlier models and with two operating system options. The Motorola Q targets professionals and business users with PDA and e-mail functions, a tiny keyboard, Bluetooth connections, multimedia capabilities, and more.
- ***Apple.*** The iPhone, a smart phone with a 3.5-inch color screen, has been designed with entertainment enthusiasts in mind. It's well equipped for music, video, and Web access, plus calendar and contact management functions. Apple initially partnered only with the AT&T network and cut the product's price to $399 two months after introduction to speed market penetration. Its iPod Touch media player has iPhone styling without phone functionality.
- ***RIM.*** Research in Motion makes the lightweight BlackBerry wireless phone/PDA products that are popular among corporate users. RIM's continuous innovation and solid customer service support strengthen its competitive standing as it introduces more smart phones and PDAs.
- ***Samsung.*** Value, style, function: Samsung is a powerful competitor, offering a variety of smart phones and Ultra mobile PCs for consumer and business segments. Some of its smart phones are available for specific telecommunications carriers and some are "unlocked," ready for any compatible telecommunications network.

Despite strong competition, Sonic can carve out a definite image and gain recognition among targeted segments. Our voice-recognition system for hands-off operation is a critical point of differentiation for competitive advantage. Our second product will have PDA functions but will be more media-oriented to appeal to segments where we will have strong brand recognition. Exhibit A-2 shows a sample of competitive products and prices.

2.4 Product Offerings

This section summarizes the main features of the company's various products.

The Sonic PDA 1000 offers the following standard features:

- Voice recognition for hands-free operation
- Organization functions, including calendar, address book, synchronization

- Built-in dual mobile phone/Internet phone and push-to-talk instant calling
- Digital music/video/television recording, wireless downloading, and instant playback
- Wireless Web and e-mail, text messaging, instant messaging
- Three-inch color screen for easy viewing
- Ultra-fast 20-gigabyte drive and expansion slots
- Four megapixel camera with flash and photo editing/sharing tools

First-year sales revenues are projected to be $60 million, based on sales of 240,000 of the Sonic 1000 model at a wholesale price of $250 each. Our second-year product will be the Sonic All Media 2000, stressing multimedia communication, networking, and entertainment functions with PDA capabilities as secondary features. The Sonic All Media 2000 will include Sonic 1000 features plus:

- Built-in media beaming to share music, video, television files with other devices
- Web cam for instant video capture and uploading to popular video Web sites
- Voice-command access to popular social networking Web sites
- Integrated eight megapixel camera, flash, and photo editing/sharing tools

Distribution explains each channel for the company's products and mentions new developments and trends.

2.5 Distribution

Sonic-branded products will be distributed through a network of retailers in the top 50 national markets. Among the most important channel partners being contacted are:

- ***Office supply superstores.*** Popular Bookstore and Evergreen Stationery will both carry Sonic products in stores, in catalogs, and online.
- ***Computer stores.*** Challenger and independent computer retailers will carry Sonic products.
- ***Electronics specialty stores.*** Best Denki will feature Sonic PDAs in its stores, online, and in its media advertising.
- ***Online retailers.*** Amazon.com will carry Sonic PDAs and, for a promotional fee, will give Sonic prominent placement on its home page during the introduction.

Distribution will initially be restricted to a national market, with appropriate sales promotion support. Later, we plan to expand into Asia and beyond.

3.0 MARKETING STRATEGY

Objectives should be defined in specific terms so management can measure progress and take corrective action to stay on track.

3.1 Objectives

We have set aggressive but achievable objectives for the first and second years of market entry.

- ***First-year Objectives.*** We are aiming for a 3 percent share of the PDA market through unit sales volume of 240,000.
- ***Second-year Objectives.*** Our second-year objective is to achieve break-even on the Sonic 1000 and launch our second model.

All marketing strategies start with segmentation, targeting, and positioning.

3.2 Target Markets

Sonic's strategy is based on a positioning of product differentiation. Our primary consumer target for the Sonic 1000 is middle- to upper-income professionals who need one device to coordinate their busy schedules, stay in touch with family and colleagues, and be entertained on the go. Our secondary consumer target is high school, college, and graduate students who want a multimedia, dual-mode device. This segment can be described demographically by age (16–30) and education status. Our Sonic All Media 2000 will be aimed at teens and twenty-somethings who want a device with features to support social networking and heavier entertainment media consumption.

The primary business target for the Sonic 1000 is mid- to large-sized corporations that want to help their managers and employees stay in touch and input or access critical data when out of the office. This segment consists of companies with more than $25 million in annual sales and more than 100 employees. A secondary target is entrepreneurs and small business owners. Also we will target medical users who want to update or access patients' medical records.

Each of the marketing-mix strategies conveys Sonic's differentiation to these target market segments.

3.3 Positioning

Positioning identifies the brand, benefits, points of difference, and parity for the product or line.

Using product differentiation, we are positioning the Sonic PDA as the most versatile, convenient, value-added model for personal and professional use. Our marketing will focus on the hands-free operation of multiple communication, entertainment, and information capabilities differentiating the Sonic 1000.

3.4 Strategies

Product strategy includes decisions about product mix and lines, brands, packaging and labeling, and warranties.

Product The Sonic 1000, including all the features described in the earlier Product Review section, will be sold with a one-year warranty. We will introduce the Sonic All Media 2000 during the following year, after we have established our Sonic brand. The brand and logo (Sonic's distinctive yellow thunderbolt) will be displayed on our products and packaging as well as in all marketing campaigns.

Pricing strategy covers decisions about setting initial prices and adapting prices in response to opportunities and competitive challenges.

Pricing The Sonic 1000 will be introduced at $250 wholesale/$350 estimated retail price per unit. We expect to lower the price of this model when we expand the product line by launching the Sonic All Media 2000, to be priced at $350 wholesale per unit. These prices reflect a strategy of (1) attracting desirable channel partners and (2) taking share from established competitors.

Distribution strategy includes selection and management of channel relationships to deliver value to customers.

Distribution Our channel strategy is to use selective distribution, marketing Sonic PDAs through well-known stores and online retailers. During the first year, we will add channel partners until we have coverage in all major national markets and the product is included in the major electronics catalogs and Web sites. We will also investigate distribution through cell-phone outlets maintained by major carriers such as SingTel. In support of channel partners, we will provide demonstration products, detailed specification handouts, and full-color photos and displays featuring the product. Finally, we plan to arrange special payment terms for retailers that place volume orders.

Marketing communications strategy covers all efforts to communicate to target audiences and channel members.

Marketing Communications By integrating all messages in all media, we will reinforce the brand name and the main points of product differentiation. Research about media consumption patterns will help our advertising agency choose appropriate media and timing to reach prospects before and during product introduction. Thereafter, advertising will appear on a pulsing basis to maintain brand awareness and communicate various differentiation messages. The agency will also coordinate public relations efforts to build the Sonic brand and support the differentiation message. To generate buzz, we will host a user-generated video contest on our Web site. To attract, retain, and motivate channel partners for a push strategy, we will use trade sales promotions and personal selling. Until the Sonic brand has been established, our communications will encourage purchases through channel partners rather than from our Web site.

3.5 Marketing Mix

The marketing mix includes tactics and programs that support product, pricing, distribution, and marketing communications strategy.

The Sonic 1000 will be introduced in February. Here are summaries of action programs we will use during the first six months to achieve our stated objectives.

- ***January*** We will launch a $200,000 trade sales promotion campaign and participate in major industry trade shows to educate dealers and generate channel support for the product launch in February. Also, we will create buzz by providing samples to selected product reviewers, opinion leaders, influential bloggers, and celebrities. Our training staff will work with retail sales personnel at major chains to explain the Sonic 1000's features, benefits, and advantages.

- ***February*** We will start an integrated print/radio/Internet campaign targeting professionals and consumers. The campaign will show how many functions the Sonic PDA can perform and emphasize the convenience of a single, powerful handheld device. This multimedia campaign will be supported by point-of-sale signage as well as online-only ads and video tours.

Programs should coordinate with the resources and activities of other departments that contribute to customer value for each product.

- ***March*** As the multimedia advertising campaign continues, we will add consumer sales promotions such as a contest in which consumers post videos to our Web site, showing how they use the Sonic in creative and unusual ways. We will also distribute new point-of-purchase displays to support our retailers.
- ***April*** We will hold a trade sales contest offering prizes for the salesperson and retail organization that sells the most Sonic PDAs during the four-week period.
- ***May*** We plan to roll out a new national advertising campaign this month. The radio ads will feature celebrity voices telling their Sonic PDAs to perform functions such as initiating a phone call, sending an e-mail, playing a song or video, and so on. The stylized print and online ads will feature avatars of these celebrities holding their Sonic PDAs. We plan to reprise this theme for next year's product launch.
- ***June*** Our radio campaign will add a new voice-over tag line promoting the Sonic 1000 as a graduation gift. We will exhibit at the semiannual electronics trade show and provide retailers with new competitive comparison handouts as a sales aid. In addition, we will analyze the results of customer satisfaction research for use in future campaigns and product development efforts.

This section shows how marketing research will support the development, implementation, and evaluation of marketing strategies and programs.

3.6 Marketing Research

Using research, we will identify specific features and benefits our target market segments value. Feedback from market tests, surveys, and focus groups will help us develop and fine-tune the Sonic All Media 2000. We are also measuring and analyzing customers' attitudes toward competing brands and products. Brand awareness research will help us determine the effectiveness and efficiency of our messages and media. Finally, we will use customer satisfaction studies to gauge market reaction.

Financials include budgets and forecasts to plan for marketing expenditures, scheduling, and operations.

4.0 FINANCIALS

Total first-year sales revenue for the Sonic 1000 is projected at $60 million, with an average wholesale price of $250 per unit and variable cost per unit of $150 for unit sales volume of 240,000. We anticipate a first-year loss of up to $10 million. Break-even calculations indicate that the Sonic 1000 will become profitable after the sales volume exceeds 267,500 during the product's second year. Our break-even analysis assumes per-unit wholesale revenue of $250 per unit, variable cost of $150 per unit, and estimated first-year fixed costs of $26,750,000. With these assumptions, the break-even calculation is:

$$\frac{26{,}750{,}000}{\$250 - \$510} = 267{,}500 \text{ units}$$

Controls help management measure results and identify any problems or performance variations that need corrective action.

5.0 CONTROLS

Controls are being established to cover implementation and the organization of our marketing activities.

5.1 Implementation

We are planning tight control measures to closely monitor quality and customer service satisfaction. This will enable us to react very quickly in correcting any problems that may occur. Other early warning signals that will be monitored for signs of deviation from the plan include monthly sales (by segment and channel) and monthly expenses.

5.2 Marketing Organization

Sonic's chief marketing officer, Jane Lim, holds overall responsibility for all of the company's marketing activities. Exhibit A-3 shows the structure of the eight-person marketing organization. Sonic has hired Worldwide Marketing to handle national sales campaigns, trade and consumer sales promotions, and public relations efforts.

The marketing department may be organized by function, as in this sample, or by geography, product, customer, or some combination of these.

Sonic Marketing Plan Chapter Assignments[1]

CHAPTER 2

As an assistant to Jane Lim, Sonic's chief marketing officer, you've been assigned to draft a mission statement for top management's review. This should cover the competitive spheres within which the firm will operate and your recommendation of an appropriate generic competitive strategy. Using your knowledge of marketing, the information you have about Sonic, and library or Internet resources, answer the following questions.

- What should Sonic's mission be?
- In what competitive spheres (industry, products and applications, competence, market segment, vertical, and geographic) should Sonic operate?
- Which of Porter's generic competitive strategies would you recommend Sonic follow in formulating overall strategy?

As your instructor directs, enter your answers and supporting information in a written marketing plan.

CHAPTER 3

Jane Lim asks you to scan Sonic's external environment for early warning signals of new opportunities and emerging threats that could affect the success of the Sonic 1000 PDA. Using Internet or library sources (or both), locate information to answer three questions about key areas of the macroenvironment.

- What demographic changes are likely to affect Sonic's targeted segments?
- What economic trends might influence buyer behavior in Sonic's targeted segments?

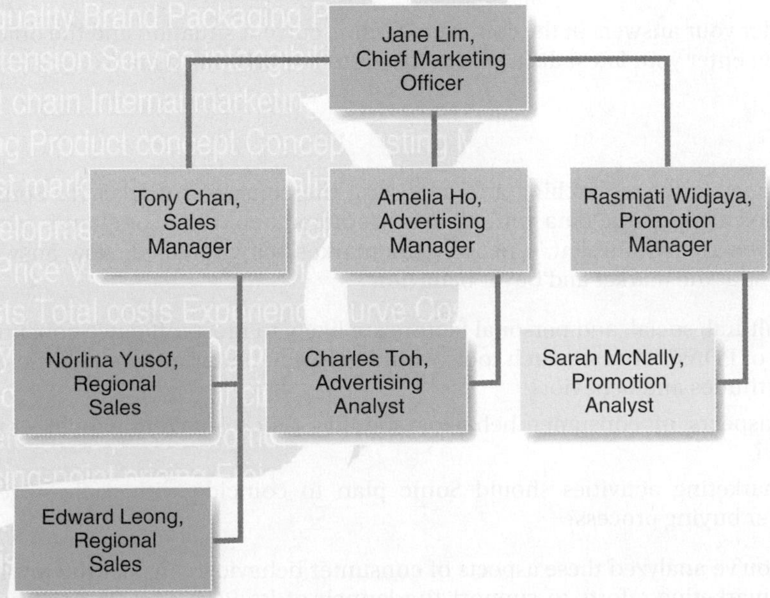

Exhibit A-3 Sonic's Marketing Organization

- How might the rapid pace of technological change/alter Sonic's competitive situation?

Enter your answers about Sonic's environment in the appropriate sections of a written marketing plan.

CHAPTER 4

Your next task is to consider how marketing research can help Sonic support its marketing strategy. Jane Lim also asks you how Sonic can measure results after the marketing plan is implemented. She wants you to answer the following three questions.

- What surveys, focus groups, observation, behavioral data, or experiments will Sonic need to support its marketing strategy? Be specific about the questions or issues that Sonic needs to resolve using marketing research.
- Where can you find suitable secondary data about total demand for PDAs over the next two years? Identify at least two sources (online or off-line), describe what you plan to draw from each source, and indicate how the data would be useful for Sonic's marketing planning.
- Recommend three specific marketing metrics for Sonic to apply in determining marketing effectiveness and efficiency.

Enter this information in the marketing plan you've been writing.

CHAPTER 5

Sonic has decided to focus on total customer satisfaction as a way of encouraging brand loyalty in a highly competitive marketplace. With this in mind, you've been assigned to analyze three specific issues as you continue working on Sonic's marketing plan.

- How (and how often) should Sonic monitor customer satisfaction?
- Would you recommend that Sonic use the Net Promoter method? Explain your reasoning.
- Which customer touch points should Sonic pay particularly close attention to, and why?

Consider your answers in the context of Sonic's current situation and the objectives it has set. Then enter your latest decisions in the written marketing plan.

CHAPTER 6

You're responsible for researching and analyzing the consumer market for Sonic's PDA product. Look again at the data you've already entered about the company's current situation and macroenvironment, especially the market being targeted. Now answer these questions about the market and buyer behavior.

- What cultural, social, and personal factors are likely to most influence consumer purchasing of PDAs? What research tools would help you better understand the effect on buyer attitudes and behavior?
- Which aspects of consumer behavior should Sonic's marketing plan emphasize and why?
- What marketing activities should Sonic plan to coincide with each stage of the consumer buying process?

After you've analyzed these aspects of consumer behavior, consider the implications for Sonic's marketing efforts to support the launch of its PDA. Finally, document your findings and conclusions in a written marketing plan.

CHAPTER 7

You've been learning more about the business market for Sonic's PDA. Jane Lim has defined this market as mid- to large-sized corporations that want their employees to stay in touch and be able to input or access data from any location. Respond to the following three questions based on your knowledge of Sonic's current situation and business-to-business marketing.

- What types of businesses appear to fit Lim's market definition? How can you research the number of employees and find other data about these types of businesses?
- What type of purchase would a Sonic PDA represent for these businesses? Who would participate in and influence this type of purchase?
- Would demand for PDAs among corporate buyers tend to be inelastic? What are the implications for Sonic's marketing plan?

Your answers to these questions will affect how Sonic plans marketing activities for the business segments to be targeted. Take a few minutes to note your ideas in a written marketing plan.

CHAPTER 8

Identifying suitable market segments and selecting targets are critical to the success of any marketing plan. As Jane Lim's assistant, you're responsible for market segmentation and targeting. Look back at the market information, buyer behavior data, and competitive details you previously gathered as you answer the following questions.

- Which variables should Sonic use to segment its consumer and business markets?
- How can Sonic evaluate the attractiveness of each identified segment? Should Sonic market to one consumer segment and one business segment or target more than one in each market? Why?
- Should Sonic pursue full market coverage, market specialization, product specialization, selective specialization, or single-segment concentration? Why?

Next, consider how your decisions about segmentation and targeting will affect Sonic's marketing efforts. Summarize your conclusions in a written marketing plan.

CHAPTER 9

Sonic is a new brand with no prior brand associations, which presents a number of marketing opportunities and challenges. Jane Lim has given you responsibility for making recommendations about three brand equity issues that are important to Sonic's marketing plan.

- What brand elements would be most useful for differentiating the Sonic brand from competing brands?
- How can Sonic sum up its brand promise for the new PDA?
- Should Sonic add a brand for its second product or retain the Sonic name?

Be sure your brand ideas are appropriate in light of what you've learned about your targeted segments and the competition. Then add this information to your written marketing plan.

CHAPTER 10

As before, you're working with Jane Lim on Sonic's marketing plan for launching a new PDA. Now you're focusing on Sonic's positioning and product life-cycle strategies by answering three specific questions.

- In a sentence or two, what is an appropriate positioning statement for the Sonic 1000 PDA?

- Knowing the stage of Sonic's PDA in the product life cycle, what are the implications for pricing, promotion, and distribution?
- In which stage of its evolution does the PDA market appear to be? What does this mean for Sonic's marketing plans?

Document your ideas in a written marketing plan. Note any additional research you may need to determine how to proceed after the Sonic 1000 has been launched.

CHAPTER 11

Sonic is a new entrant in an established industry characterized by competitors with relatively high brand identity and strong market positions. Use research and your knowledge of how to deal with competitors to consider three issues that will affect the company's ability to successfully introduce its first product:

- What factors will you use to determine Sonic's strategic group?
- Should Sonic select a class of competitor to attack on the basis of strength versus weakness, closeness versus distance, or good versus bad? Why is this appropriate in the PDA market?
- As a start-up company, what competitive strategy would be most effective as Sonic introduces its first product?

Take time to analyze how Sonic's competitive strategy will affect its marketing strategy and tactics. Now summarize your ideas in a written marketing plan.

CHAPTER 12

Introducing a new product entails a variety of decisions about product strategy, including differentiation, ingredient branding, packaging, labeling, warranty, and guarantee. Your next task is to answer the following questions about Sonic's product strategy.

- Which aspect of product differentiation would be most valuable in setting Sonic apart from its competitors, and why?
- Should Sonic use ingredient branding to tout the Linux-based operating system that it says makes its PDA more secure than PDAs based on some other operating systems?
- How can Sonic use packaging and labeling to support its brand image and help its channel partners sell the PDA product more effectively?

Once you've answered these questions, incorporate your ideas into the marketing plan you've been writing.

CHAPTER 13

You're planning customer support services for Sonic's new PDA product. Review what you know about your target market and its needs; also think about what Sonic's competitors are offering. Then respond to these three questions about designing and managing services.

- What support services are buyers of PDA products likely to want and need?
- How can Sonic manage gaps between perceived service and expected service to satisfy customers?
- What post-sale service arrangements must Sonic make and how would you expect these to affect customer satisfaction?

Consider how your service strategy will support Sonic's overall marketing efforts. Summarize your recommendations in a written marketing plan.

CHAPTER 14

You're in charge of pricing Sonic's product for its launch early next year. Review the SWOT analysis you previously prepared as well as Sonic's competitive environment, targeting strategy, and product positioning. Now continue working on your marketing plan by responding to the following questions.

- What should Sonic's primary pricing objective be? Explain your reasoning.
- Are PDA customers likely to be price sensitive? What are the implications for your pricing decisions?
- What price adaptations (such as discounts, allowances, and promotional pricing) should Sonic include in its marketing plan?

Make notes about your answers to these questions and then document the information in a written marketing plan.

CHAPTER 15

At Sonic, you have been asked to develop a marketing channel system for the new Sonic 1000 PDA. Based on what you know about designing and managing integrated marketing channels, answer the three questions that follow.

- Do you agree with Jane Lim's decision to use a push strategy for the new product? Explain your reasoning.
- How many channel levels are appropriate for Sonic's targeted consumer and business segments?
- In determining the number of channel members, should you use exclusive, selective, or intensive distribution? Why?

Be sure your marketing channel ideas support the product positioning and are consistent with the goals that have been set. Record your recommendations in a written marketing plan.

CHAPTER 16

At this point, you need to make more specific decisions about managing the marketing intermediaries for Sonic's first product. Formulate your ideas by answering the following questions.

- What types of retailers would be most appropriate for distributing Sonic's PDA? What are the advantages and disadvantages of selling through these types of retailers?
- What role should wholesalers play in Sonic's distribution strategy? Why?
- What market-logistics issues must Sonic consider for the launch of its first PDA?

Summarize your decisions about retailing, wholesaling, and logistics in the marketing plan you've been writing.

CHAPTER 17

Jane Lim has assigned you to plan integrated marketing communications for Sonic's new product introduction. Review the data, decisions, and strategies you previously documented in your marketing plan before you answer the next three questions.

- What communications objectives are appropriate for Sonic's initial campaign?
- How can Sonic use personal communications channels to influence its target audience?
- Which communication tools would you recommend using after Sonic's initial product has been in the market for six months? Why?

Confirm that your marketing communications plans make sense in light of Sonic's overall marketing efforts. Now, as your instructor directs, summarize your thoughts in a written marketing plan.

CHAPTER 18

Mass communications will play a key role in Sonic's product introduction. After reviewing your earlier decisions and thinking about the current situation (especially your competitive circumstances), respond to the following questions to continue planning Sonic's marketing communications strategy.

- Once Sonic begins to use consumer advertising, what goals would be appropriate?
- Should Sonic continue consumer and trade sales promotion after the new product has been in the market for six months? Explain your reasoning.
- Jane Lim wants you to recommend an event sponsorship possibility that would be appropriate for the new product campaign. What type of event would you suggest and what objectives would you set for the sponsorship?

Record your ideas about mass communications in the marketing plan you've been writing.

CHAPTER 19

Sonic needs a strategy for managing personal communications during its new product launch. This is the time to look at interactive marketing, word-of-mouth, and personal selling. Answer these three questions as you consider Sonic's personal communications strategy.

- Which forms of interactive marketing are appropriate for Sonic, given its objectives, mass communications arrangements, and channel decisions?
- How should Sonic use word-of-mouth to generate brand awareness and encourage potential buyers to visit retailers to see the new PDA in person?
- Does Sonic need a direct sales force or can it sell through agents and other outside representatives?

Look back at earlier decisions and ideas before you document your comments about personal communications in your written marketing plan.

CHAPTER 20

Knowing that the PDA market isn't growing as quickly as the market for multimedia, multifunction communication devices, Jane Lim wants you to look ahead at Sonic how can develop new products outside the PDA market. Review the competitive situation and the market situation before you continue working on the Sonic marketing plan.

- List three new-product ideas that build on Sonic's strengths and the needs of its various target segments. What criteria should Sonic use to screen these ideas?
- Develop the most promising idea into a product concept and explain how Sonic can test this concept. What particular dimensions must be tested?
- Assume that the most promising idea tests well. Now develop a marketing strategy for introducing it, including: a description of the target market; the product positioning; the estimated sales, profit, and market share goals for the first year; your channel strategy; and the marketing budget you will recommend for this new product introduction. If possible, estimate Sonic's costs and conduct a break-even analysis.

Document all the details of your new-product development ideas in the written marketing plan.

CHAPTER 21

As Jane Lim's assistant, you're researching how to market the Sonic 1000 PDA product outside your country within a year. You've been asked to answer the following questions about Sonic's use of global marketing.

- As a start-up company, should Sonic use indirect or direct exporting, licensing, joint ventures, or direct investment to enter the Asian market next year? To enter other markets? Explain your answers.
- If Sonic starts marketing its PDA in other countries, which of the international product strategies is most appropriate? Why?
- Although some components are made in Asia, Sonic's PDAs will be assembled in Mexico through a contractual arrangement with a local factory. How are country-of-origin perceptions likely to affect your marketing recommendations?

Think about how these global marketing issues fit into Sonic's overall marketing strategy. Now document your ideas in the marketing plan you've been writing.

CHAPTER 22

With the rest of the marketing plan in place, you're ready to make recommendations about how to manage Sonic's marketing activities. Here are some specific questions Jane Lim wants you to consider.

- How can Sonic drive customer-focused marketing and strategic innovation throughout the organization?
- What role should social responsibility play in Sonic's marketing?
- How can Sonic evaluate its marketing? Suggest several specific steps the company should take.

To complete your marketing plan, enter your answers to these questions in the written marketing plan. Finally, draft the executive summary of the plan's highlights.

Chapter 1

1. Sandra Ward, "Warming Up the Copier." *Barron's*, May 1, 2006, 18:86, pp. 19, 21.
2. Peter D. Bennett, ed., *Dictionary of Marketing Terms*, 2nd ed., (Chicago: American Marketing Association, 1995).
3. Peter Drucker, *Management: Tasks, Responsibilities, Practices*, (New York: Harper and Row, 1973), pp. 64–65.
4. Irving J. Rein, Philip Kotler, and Martin Stoller, *High Visibility*, (Chicago: NTC Publishers, 1998).
5. Philip Kotler, Irving J. Rein, and Donald Haider, *Marketing Places: Attracting Investment, Industry, and Tourism to Cities, States, and Nations*, (New York: Free Press, 1993); Philip Kotler, Christer Asplund, and Irving Rein, *Marketing Places in Europe: Attracting Investment, Industry, and Tourism to Cities, States and Nations*, (London: Financial Times Prentice Hall, 1999).
6. Kerry Capell, "Thinking Simple at Philips." *BusinessWeek*, December 11, 2006, p. 50, <www.philips.com>.
7. Carl Shapiro and Hal R. Varian, "Versioning: The Smart Way to Sell Information." *Harvard Business Review*, November–December 1998, pp. 106–114.
8. John R. Brandt, "Dare to be Different." *Chief Executive*, May 2003, pp. 34–38.
9. Mark Kleinman, "Great Haul of China's Burgers." *The West Australian*, November 25, 2006, p. 91.
10. Jeffrey Rayport and John Sviokla, "Managing in the Marketspace." *Harvard Business Review*, November–December 1994, pp. 141–150. See also their "Exploring the Virtual Value Chain." *Harvard Business Review*, November–December 1995, pp. 75–85.
11. Mohan Sawhney, *Seven Steps to Nirvana* (New York: McGraw-Hill, 2001).
12. Constantine von Hoffman. "Armed With Intelligence." *BrandWeek*, May 29, 2006, pp. 17–20.
13. Ibid, p. 19.
14. Richard Rawlinson, "Beyond Brand Management." *Strategy+Business*, Summer 2006.
15. Gail McGovern and John A. Quelch, "The Fall and Rise of the CMO." *Strategy+Business*, Winter 2004.
16. John Quelch, "Samsung Electronics Company: Global Marketing Operations." *Harvard Business School Case*, 2004, N2, pp. 504–051.
17. Adam Lashinsky, "Shoutout in Gadget Land." *Fortune*, November 10, 2003, pp. 77–86.
18. Anya Kamenetz, "The Network Unbound." *Fast Company*, June 2006, pp. 69–73.
19. Bruce Einhorn, "Mad as Hell in China's Blogosphere." *BusinessWeek*, August 14, 2006, p. 39.
20. Laura Mazur, "Personal Touch is Now Crucial to Growing Profits." *Marketing*, November 27, 2003, p. 18.
21. Kenneth Hein, "Marketers Map out Their GPS Ad Plans." *BrandWeek*, April 24, 2006, p. 4.
22. Suzanne Vranica, "Marketers Aim New Ads at Video iPod Users." *Wall Street Journal*, January 31, 2006.
23. Stanley Holmes, "Into the Wild Blog Yonder." *BusinessWeek*, May 22, 2006, pp. 84–85.
24. Gerry Khermouch, "Breaking into the Name Game." *BusinessWeek*, April 7, 2003, p. 54; Anonymous, "China's Challenge." *Marketing Week*, October 2, 2003, pp. 22–24.
25. Bruce I. Newman, ed. *Handbook of Political Marketing* (Thousand Oaks, CA: Sage Publications, 1999); Bruce I. Newman, *The Mass Marketing of Politics* (Thousand Oaks, CA: Sage Publications, 1999).
26. John B. McKitterick, "What Is the Marketing Management Concept?" In Frank M. Bass, ed., *The Frontiers of Marketing Thought and Action* (Chicago: American Marketing Association, 1957), pp. 71–82; Fred J. Borch, "The Marketing Philosophy as a Way of Business Life." *The Marketing Concept: Its Meaning to Management* (Marketing series, no. 99, New York: American Management Association, 1957), pp. 3–5; Robert J. Keith, "The Marketing Revolution." *Journal of Marketing*, January 1960, pp. 35–38.
27. Theodore Levitt, "Marketing Myopia." *Harvard Business Review*, July–August 1960, p. 50.
28. Ajay K. Kohli and Bernard J. Jaworski, "Market Orientation: The Construct, Research Propositions, and Managerial Implications." *Journal of Marketing*, April 1990, pp. 1–18; John C. Narver and Stanley F. Slater, "The Effect of a Market Orientation on Business Profitability." *Journal of Marketing*, October 1990, pp. 20–35; Stanley F. Slater and John C. Narver, "Market Orientation, Customer Value, and Superior Performance." *Business Horizons*, March–April 1994, pp. 22–28; A. Pelham and D. Wilson, "A Longitudinal Study of the Impact of Market Structure, Firm Structure, Strategy and Market Orientation Culture on Dimensions of Business +Performance." *Journal of the Academy of Marketing Science*, 1996, 24(1), pp. 27–43; Rohit Deshpandé and John U. Farley, "Measuring Market Orientation: Generalization and Synthesis." *Journal of Marketing Management*, 1998, pp. 213–232.

29. John C. Narver, Stanley F. Slater, and Douglas L. MacLachlan, "Total Market Orientation, Business Performance, and Innovation." Working Paper Series, Marketing Science Institute, Report No. 00–116, 2000, pp. 1–34. See also Ken Matsuno and John T. Mentzer. "The Effects of Strategy Type on the Market Orientation–Performance Relationship." *Journal of Marketing*, October 2000, pp. 1–16.
30. Evert Gummesson, *Total Relationship Marketing* (Boston: Butterworth-Heinemann, 1999); Regis McKenna, *Relationship Marketing*, (Reading, MA: Addison-Wesley, 1991); Martin Christopher, Adrian Payne, and David Ballantyne, *Relationship Marketing: Bringing Quality, Customer Service, and Marketing Together*, (Oxford, UK: Butterworth-Heinemann, 1991).
31. James C. Anderson, Hakan Hakansson, and Jan Johanson, "Dyadic Business Relationships within a Business Network Context." *Journal of Marketing*, October 15, 1994, pp. 1–15.
32. Jerome E. McCarthy, *Basic Marketing: A Managerial Approach*, 12th ed., (Homewood, IL: Irwin, 1996). Two alternative classifications are worth noting. Frey proposed that all marketing decision variables could be categorized into two factors: the offering (product, packaging, brand, price, and service) and methods and tools (distribution channels, personal selling, advertising, sales promotion, and publicity). See Albert W. Frey, *Advertising*, 3rd ed., (New York: Ronald Press, 1961), p. 30. Lazer and Kelly proposed a three-factor classification: goods and services mix, distribution mix, and communications mix. See William Lazer and Eugene J. Kelly, *Managerial Marketing: Perspectives and Viewpoints*, rev. ed., (Homewood, IL: Irwin, 1962), p. 413.
33. Robert Shaw and David Merrick. *Marketing Payback: Is Your Marketing Profitable?*, (London, UK: Pearson Education, 2005).
34. Rajendra Sisodia, David Wolfe, and Jagdish Sheth, *Firms of Endearment: How World-Class Companies Profit from Passion* (Upper Saddle River, NJ: Wharton School Publishing, 2007).
35. *Point*, June 2005, p. 4.
36. John Ehernfield, "Feeding the Beast." *Fast Company*, December 2006/January 2007, pp. 41–43.
37. If choosing to develop a strategic corporate social responsibility program, see Michael E. Porter and Mark R. Kramer, "Strategy and Society: The Link between Competitive Advantage and Corporate Social Responsibility." *Harvard Business Review*, December 2006, pp. 78–92.
38. Jeremy Wagstaff and Joseph Pereira, "Good Sports Say No to Sweat." *Far Eastern Economic Review*, May 20, 2004, pp. 32–34.
39. Jonathan Glancey, "The Private World of the Walkman." *Guardian*, October 11, 1999.
40. Joann Muller, "Ford: Why It's Worse Than You Think." *BusinessWeek*, June 25, 2001; Ford *1999 Annual Report*; Greg Keenan, "Six Degrees of Perfection." *Globe and Mail*, December 20, 2000.

Chapter 2

1. Keith H. Hammonds, "Michael Porter's Big Ideas." *Fast Company*, March 2001, pp. 150–154.
2. "Zara, A Spanish Success Story." <CNN.com>, June 15, 2001; <www.zara.com> accessed on July 27, 2004; Lorna Tan, "Singapore Fits Well into Zara's Asian Strategy." *Straits Times* (Singapore), August 22, 2005, p. H18.
3. Ilene R. Prusher, "Japanese Retailers Turn into 'Shetailers'." *Christian Science Monitor*, August 29, 2001; Takashi Hidemine, "SCOCO—A Convenience Store Developed by Women for Women." *Nipponia*, December 15, 2001; Takahashi Hidemnie, "Convenience Stores Take Off in New Directions." *Nipponia*, December 15, 2001.
4. Nirmalya Kumar, *Marketing as Strategy: The CEO's Agenda for Driving Growth and Innovation* (Boston: Harvard Business School Press, 2004).
5. Frederick E. Webster Jr., "The Future Role of Marketing in the Organization." In *Reflections on the Futures of Marketing*, Donald R. Lehmann and Katherine Jocz, eds., (Cambridge, MA: Marketing Science Institute, 1997), pp. 39–66.
6. Michael E. Porter, *Competitive Advantage: Creating and Sustaining Superior Performance* (New York: The Free Press, 1985).
7. Robert Hiebeler, Thomas B. Kelly, and Charles Ketteman. *Best Practices: Building Your Business with Customer-Focused Solutions* (New York: Simon and Schuster, 1998).
8. James Carbone, "At Today's Cisco Systems, the Fewer Suppliers the Better." *Purchasing*, April 20, 2006, pp. 18–21.
9. Michael Hammer and James Champy, *Reengineering the Corporation: A Manifesto for Business Revolution* (New York: Harper Business, 1993).

10. Jon R. Katzenbach and Douglas K. Smith, *The Wisdom of Teams: Creating the High-Performance Organization* (Boston: Harvard Business School Press, 1993); Michael Hammer and James Champy, *Reengineering the Corporation: A Manifesto for Business Revolution*, (New York: Harper Business, 1993).

11. Myron Magnet, "The New Golden Rule of Business." *Fortune*, November 28, 1994, pp. 60–64.

12. C. K. Prahalad and Gary Hamel, "The Core Competence of the Corporation." *Harvard Business Review*, May–June 1990, pp. 79–91.

13. George S. Day, "The Capabilities of Market-Driven Organizations." *Journal of Marketing*, October 1994, p. 38.

14. George S. Day and Paul J.H. Shoemaker, *Peripheral Vision: Detecting the Weak Signals That Will Make or Break Your Company* (Cambridge, MA: Harvard Business School Press, 2006).

15. "Kodak Plans to Cut Up to 5,000 More Jobs." *Bloomberg News*, February 8, 2007; Leon Lazaroff, "Kodak's Big Picture Focusing on Image Change." *Chicago Tribune*, January 29, 2006.

16. Peter Williamson, and Ming Zeng, "Strategies for Competing in a Changed China." *MIT Sloan Management Review*, Summer 2004, 45(4), pp. 85–91.

17. "Winning Asian Strategies." *McKinsey Quarterly*, 1, 2002.

18. *Pew Internet and American Life Project Survey*, November–December 2000.

19. Kasuaki Ushikubo, "A Method of Structure Analysis for Developing Product Concepts and Its Applications." *European Research*, 1986, 14(4), pp. 174–175.

20. "Shanda Pushes Games Overseas." June 11, 2007, <www.chinatechnews.com>.

21. Heather Timmons, "Cosmetics Makers tell Indian Women that They have Power, Even over Skin Tone." *International Herald Tribune*, May 31, 2007.

22. "Coca-Cola Japan to Debut Beer-flavored Soda Next Month." *AsiaPulse News*, February 13, 2004; "Japanese Coke Machines to Accept Cellphone Payment." September 27, 2006, <www.canada.com>.

23. Yoram J. Wind, Vijay Mahajan, and Robert E. Gunther, *Convergence Marketing: Strategies for Reaching the New Hybrid Consumer* (Upper Saddle River, NJ: Prentice Hall PTR, 2002).

24. Peter Drucker, *Management: Tasks, Responsibilities and Practices* (New York: Harper and Row, 1973), chapter 7.

25. Ralph A. Oliva, "Nowhere to Hide." *Marketing Management*, July/August 2001, pp. 44–46.

26. *Pew Internet and American Life Project Survey*, November–December 2000.

27. Chuck Martin, *Net Future* (New York: McGraw-Hill, 1999).

28. Jeffrey F. Rayport and Bernard J. Jaworski, *e-commerce* (New York: McGraw-Hill, 2001), p. 116.

29. Tilman Kemmler, Monika Kubicová, Robert Musslewhite, and Rodney Prezeau. "E-Performance II—The Good, the Bad, and the Merely Average." An exclusive to <www.mckinseyquarterly.com>, (2001).

30. The same matrix can be expanded into nine cells by adding modified products and modified markets. See Johnson, S. J., and Conrad Jones, "How to Organize for New Products." *Harvard Business Review*, May–June 1957, pp. 49–62.

31. <www.starbucks.com>; Howard Schultz, *Pour Your Heart into It* (New York: Hyperion, 1997); Andy Serwer, "Hot Starbucks To Go." *Fortune*, January 26, 2004, pp. 60–74.

32. Tim Goodman, "NBC Everywhere?" *San Francisco Chronicle*, September 4, 2003.

33. "Business: Microsoft's Contradiction." *Economist*, January 31, 1998, pp. 65–67; Andrew J. Glass, "Microsoft Pushes Forward, Playing to Win the Market." *Atlanta Constitution*, June 24, 1998, p. D12.

34. George T. Haley, Chin Tiong Tan, and Usha C.V. Haley, *The New Asian Emperors: The Overseas Chinese, Their Strategies, and Competitive Advantages* (Oxford: Butterworth-Heinemann, 1998); "Asian Capitalism: The End of Tycoons." *Economist*, April 29, 2002, pp. 75–78.

35. Louis Kraar, "Samsung's Tech Wizard." *Fortune*, January 24, 2000, pp. 54–58; William J. Holstein, "Samsung's Golden Touch." *Fortune*, April 1, 2002, pp. 28–34.

36. Daniel Howe, "Note to DaimlerChrysler: It's Not a Small World After All." *Detroit News*, May 19, 1998, p. B4; Bill Vlasic, "The First Global Car Colossus." *BusinessWeek*, May 18, 1998, pp. 40–43; Pamela Harper, "Business 'Cultures' at War." *Electronic News*, August 3, 1998, pp. 50, 55.

37. Bill Vlasic and Bradley Stertz, "Taken for a Ride." *BusinessWeek*, June 5, 2000; Jeffrey Ball and Scott Miller, "DaimlerChrysler Isn't Living Up to Its Promise." *Wall Street Journal*, July 26, 2000; Eric Reguly, "Daimler, Chrysler Still a Culture Clash." *Globe and Mail*, January 30, 2001.

38. Brian Bremner, Gail Edmondson, and Chester Dawson, "Nissan's Boss." *BusinessWeek Asian Edition*, October 4, 2004, pp. 48–56; Gail Edmondson, "Smoothest Combo On the Road." *BusinessWeek Asian Edition*, October 4, 2004, pp. 56–57; Brian Bremner, "The *Gaijin* Who Saved Nissan." *BusinessWeek Asian*

Edition, January 31, 2005, p. 12; Susan Tong, "From Public Enemy No. 1 to Corporate Hero." *Straits Times* (Singapore), November 1, 2002, p. H16; Alex Taylor III, "Nissan's Turnaround Artist." *Fortune*, February 18, 2002, pp. 34–37; Chester Dawson, "Ghosn's Way: Why Japan Inc. Is Following a *Gaijin*." *BusinessWeek Asian Edition*, May 20, 2002, p. 27. See also Ghosn Carlos and Philippe Riès, *Shift: Inside Nissan's Historic Revival* (New York: Currency/Doubleday, 2005).

39. Rohit Deshpandé and John U. Farley, "Tigers and Dragons: Profiling High-Performance Asian Firms." *MSI Report* No. 01–101, 2001; Betsy Read, "Profiling High Performance Asian Firms." *Insights from MSI*, Fall 2001, pp. 7–8.
40. E. Jerome McCarthy, *Basic Marketing: A Managerial Approach*. 12th ed. (Homewood, IL: Irwin, 1996).
41. Ian Wylie, "Calling for a Renewable Future." *Fast Company*, May 2003, pp. 46–48.
42. Dev Patnaik, "Insight." *In*, June 2006, p. 32.
43. Paul J. H. Shoemaker, "Scenario Plannning: A Tool for Strategic Thinking." *Sloan Management Review*, Winter 1995, pp. 25–40.
44. Philip Kotler, *Kotler on Marketing* (New York: Free Press, 1999).
45. Ibid.
46. Ram Charan and Noel M. Tichy, *Every Business Is a Growth Business: How Your Company Can Prosper Year after Year* (New York: Times Business, Random House, 1998).
47. Michael E. Porter, *Competitive Strategy: Techniques for Analyzing Industries and Competitors* (New York: The Free Press, 1980), chapter 2.
48. Michael E. Porter, "What Is Strategy?" *Harvard Business Review*, November–December 1996, pp. 61–78.
49. For some readings on strategic alliances, see Peter Lorange and Johan Roos, *Strategic Alliances: Formation, Implementation and Evolution* (Cambridge, MA: Blackwell, 1992);. Jordan D. Lewis, *Partnerships for Profit: Structuring and Managing Strategic Alliances* (New York: The Free Press, 1990); John R. Harbison and Peter Pekar Jr., *Smart Alliances: A Practical Guide to Repeatable Success* (San Francisco: Jossey-Bass, 1998); *Harvard Business Review on Strategic Alliances*, (Cambridge, MA: Harvard Business School Press, 2002).
50. Robin Cooper and Robert S. Kaplan, "Profit Priorities from Activity-Based Costing." *Harvard Business Review*, May–June 1991, pp. 130–135.
51. Robert S. Kaplan and David P. Norton, *The Balanced Scorecard: Translating Strategy into Action* (Boston: Harvard Business School Press, 1996) as a tool for monitoring stakeholder satisfaction.
52. Thomas J. Peters and Robert H. Waterman Jr., *In Search of Excellence: Lessons from America's Best-Run Companies* (New York: Harper and Row, 1982), pp. 9–12.
53. Terrence E. Deal and Allan A. Kennedy, *Corporate Cultures: The Rites and Rituals of Corporate Life* (Reading, MA: Addison-Wesley, 1982); "Corporate Culture." *BusinessWeek,* October 27, 1980, pp. 148–160; Stanley M. Davis, *Managing Corporate Culture* (Cambridge, MA: Ballinger, 1984); John P. Kotter and James L. Heskett. *Corporate Culture and Performance* (New York: The Free Press, 1992).
54. Nitin Nohria, William Joyce, and Bruce Roberson, "What Really Works." *Harvard Business Review*, 2003, 81(7), pp. 42–53.
55. Dexter Roberts, Michael Arndt, and Andrea Zammert, "Tough Trip from China: The Mainland's Top Appliance Maker Aims to Go Global." *BusinessWeek Asian Edition*, April 1, 2002; <www.haier.com>.
56. Marian Burk Wood, *The Marketing Plan: A Handbook* (Upper Saddle River, NJ: Prentice Hall, 2003).
57. Donald R. Lehmann and Russell S. Winer, *Product Management*, 3rd ed., (Boston, MA: McGraw-Hill/Irwin, 2001).

Chapter 3

1. Frederik Balfour, "Fakes!" *BusinessWeek*, February 7, 2005, pp. 46–53; Stephanie Bodoni, Hugo Miller, and Naween Mangi, "Asian Counterfeiters Shift Focus to Consumer Goods from Luxury Goods." *International Herald Tribune*, June 15, 2007; John Liu and Chinmei Sung, "Fake iPhones Fill Gap Left by Apple." *International Herald Tribune*, September 11, 2007.
2. Dexter Roberts and David Rocks, "Let a Thousand Brands Bloom." *BusinessWeek*, October 17, 2005, pp. 20–22.
3. Julie Scholsser, "Looking for Intelligence in Ice Cream." *Fortune*, March 17, 2003, pp. 114–120.
4. Julie Forster, "You Deserve a Better Break Today." *BusinessWeek*, September 30, 2002, p. 42.

5. Kevin Helliker, "Smile: That Cranky Shopper May Be a Store Spy." *Wall Street Journal*, November 30, 1994, pp. B1, B6; Edward F. McQuarrie, *Customer Visits: Building a Better Market Focus*, 2nd ed., (Newbury Park, CA: Sage Press, 1998).

6. Sacha Pfeiffer, "A Little Market Strategy Can Go a Long Way." *Boston Globe*, July 9, 2006.

7. Andy Serwer, "P&G's Covert Operation." *Fortune*, September 17, 2001, pp. 42–44.

8. Robin T. Peterson and Zhilin Yang, "Web Product Reviews Help Strategy." *Marketing News*, April 7, 2004, p. 18.

9. See <www.badfads.com> for examples of fads and collectibles through the years.

10. John Naisbitt and Patricia Aburdene, *Megatrends 2000*, (New York: Avon Books, 2004).

11. Indata. *IN*. June 2006, p. 27.

12. World POPClock, *U.S. Census Bureau* <www.census.gov>, September 1999.

13. Although over 10 years old, this breakdown provides useful perspective. See Donella H. Meadows, Dennis L. Meadows, and Jorgen Randers, *Beyond the Limits*, (Port Mills, VT: Chelsea Green Publishing Company, 1993) for some commentary.

14. Sally D. Goll, "Marketing: China (Only) Children Get the Royal Treatment." *Wall Street Journal*, February 8, 1995, p. B1.

15. Frederik Balfour and Dexter Roberts, "Turning Playtime into Payday." *BusinessWeek*, November 14, 2005, pp. 60–61.

16. Zhang Shidong, "Around the Markets: Catering to 'Little Emperors.'" *International Herald Tribune*, April 24, 2007.

17. Ian Rowley and Hiroko Tashiro, "For Seniors, Good Care at Good Prices." *BusinessWeek*, November 14, 2005, pp. 62, 64.

18. Manjeet Kripalani, "Trying to Tame the Blackboard Jungle." *BusinessWeek*, August 22/29, 2005, pp. 78–80.

19. Josey Puliyenthuruthel, "The Other MIT." *BusinessWeek*, August 22/29, 2005, pp. 82–84.

20. Manjeet Kripalani and Pete Engardio, "The Rise of India." *BusinessWeek*, December 8, 2003, pp. 66–76; Joanna Slater, "Call of the West." *Wall Street Journal*, January 2, 2004, p. A1.

21. Doung Young, "For Taiwan's Middle Class, A Hidden Struggle." *International Herald Tribune*, January 16, 2008.

22. Dexter Roberts and David Rocks. "China: Let a Thousand Brands Bloom." *BusinessWeek*, October 17, 2005.

23. "Cautious Japanese Changing Buying Habits." *Economist*, as reported in *Straits Times* (Singapore), April 15, 1999, p. 35.

24. Sheridan Passo, "Japan Goes Wild For 100-Yen Prices." *Fortune*, November 28, 2005, p. 21; Hideko Takayama, "Small-Box is Beautiful." *Newsweek*, July 29/August 1, 2005, p. 40.

25. Pete Engardio, "A New World Economy." *BusinessWeek*, August 22/29, 2005, pp. 38–44.

26. Paul Wenske, "You Too Could Lose $19,000!" *Kansas City Star*, October 31, 1999; "Clearing House Suit Chronology," *Associated Press*, January 26, 2001.

27. Vivek Shankar, "Metrosexuals in India Groom New Market." *International Herald Tribune*, November 16, 2006.

28. Clay Chandler, "Full Speed Ahead." *Fortune*, February 7, 2005, pp. 78–84; "What You Can Learn from Toyota." *Business 2.0*, January–February 2005, pp. 67–72; Keith Naughton, "Red, White, and Bold." *Newsweek*, April 25, 2005, pp. 34–36.

29. Brad Stone, "Your Next Computer." *Newsweek*, June 7, 2004, p. 65.

30. Cliff Edwards, "Ready to Buy a Home Robot?" *BusinessWeek*, July 19, 2004, pp. 52–56.

31. Moon Ihlwan, "Wireless Wonders: Samsung Gets Wired On Wireless." *BusinessWeek*, April 26, 2004; Richard Shim and Michael Kannelos, "Networked Homes Move Closer to Reality." <www.CNETNews.com>, May 28, 2004.

32. Manjeet Kripalani, "Pharma Karma." *BusinessWeek*, April 18, 2005, pp. 20–21.

33. Geoffrey A. Fowler, "Butt Out." *Far Eastern Economic Review*, December 4, 2003, p. 35.

34. <www.cisco.com>; Peter Burrows and Manjeet Kripalani, "Cisco: Sold on India." *BusinessWeek*, November 28, 2005, pp. 20–22; Dexter Roberts, "China's Power Brands." *BusinessWeek*, November 8, 2004, pp. 50–56; "The Struggle of the Champions." *Economist*, January 8, 2005, pp. 57–59.

35. Rebecca Gardyn, "Swap Meet." *American Demographics*, July 2001, pp. 51–55.

36. Pamela Paul, "Mixed Signals." *American Demographics*, July 2001, pp. 45–49.

Chapter 4

1. A. G. Lafley, interview, "It Was a No-Brainer." *Fortune,* February 21, 2005, p. 96; Naomi Aoki, "Gillette Hopes to Create a Buzz with Vibrating Women's Razor." *Boston Globe,* December 17, 2004; Chris Reidy, "The Unveiling of a New Venus." *Boston Globe,* November 3, 2000.
2. *1994 Survey of Market Research*, eds. Thomas Kinnear and Ann Root (Los Angeles: American Marketing Association, 1994).
3. Prasad Sangameshwaran and Shweta Jain, "Where is Research Headed?" *Business Standard*, January 28, 2003.
4. For some background information on in-flight Internet service, see "In-Flight Dogfight." *Business2.Com*, January 9, 2001, pp. 84–91; John Blau, "In-Flight Internet Service Ready for Takeoff." *IDG News Service*, June 14, 2002; "Boeing In-Flight Internet Plan Goes Airborne." *Associated Press*, April 18, 2004.
5. For a discussion of the decision-theory approach to the value of research, see Donald R. Lehmann, Sunil Gupta, and Joel Steckel, *Market Research*, (Reading, MA: Addison-Wesley, 1997).
6. Allison Stein Wellner, "Look Who's Watching." *Continental*, April 2003, pp. 39–41; Linda Tischler, "Every Move You Make." *Fast Company*, April 2004, pp. 73–75.
7. For a detailed review of relevant academic work, see Eric J. Arnould and Amber Epp, "Deep Engagement with Consumer Experience." In the *Handbook of Marketing Research*, Rajiv Grover and Marco Vriens, eds., (Thousand Oaks, CA: Sage Publications, 2006). For a range of academic discussion, see the following special issue, "Can Ethnography Uncover Richer Consumer Insights?" *Journal of Advertising Research*, September 2006, 46. For some practical tips, see Richard Durante and Michael Feehan, "Leverage Ethnography to Improve Strategic Decision Making." *Marketing Research*, Winter 2005.
8. Eric J. Arnould and Linda L. Price, "Market-Oriented Ethnography Revisited." *Journal of Advertising Research*, September 2006, 46, pp. 251–62; Eric J. Arnould and Melanie Wallendorf, "Market-Oriented Ethnography: Interpretation Building and Marketing Strategy Formulation." *Journal of Marketing Research*, 31, November 1994, pp. 484–504.
9. Michael Fielding, "Shift the Focus." *Marketing News*, September 1, 2006, pp. 18–20.
10. Bruce Nussbaum, "The Power of Design." *BusinessWeek*, May 17, 2004, pp. 86–94.
11. Louise Witt, "Inside Intent." *American Demographics*, March 2004, pp. 34–39; Andy Raskin, "A Face Any Business Can Trust." *Business 2.0*, December 2003, pp. 58–60; Gerald Zaltman, "Rethinking Market Research: Putting People Back In." *Journal of Marketing Research*, November 1997, 34, pp. 424–37; Wally Wood, "The Race to Replace Memory." *Marketing and Media Decisions*, July 1986, pp. 166–67; Roger D. Blackwell, James S. Hensel, Michael B. Phillips, and Brian Sternthal, *Laboratory Equipment for Marketing Research*, (Dubuque, IA: Kendall/Hunt, 1970).
12. Stephen Baker, "Wiser about the Web." *BusinessWeek*, March 27, 2006, pp. 54–62.
13. Abhik Roy, Peter G.P. Walters, and Sherriff T. K. Luk, "Chinese Puzzles and Paradoxes: Consucting Business Research in China." *Journal of Business Research,* 2001, 52(2), pp. 203–210.
14. Peter Fuller, "A Two-way Conversation." *BrandWeek*, February 25, 2002, pp. 21–27.
15. Catherine Arnold, "Hershey Research Sees Net Gain." *Marketing News*, November 25, 2002, p. 17.
16. "China: Online Marketing Comes of Age." *BusinessWeek*, June 12, 2007, <www.businessweek.com/print/globalbiz/content/jun2007/gb20070612_084967.htm>, accessed on January 30, 2008.
17. Will Wade, "Care and Feeding of Cyberpets Rivets Tag-Along Marketers." *New York Times*, February 26, 2004, p. G5.
18. "Businesses Need to Improve Personal Info Management." *Nikkei Report*, April 1, 2005.
19. Kevin J. Clancy and Peter C. Krieg, *Counterintuitive Marketing: How Great Results Come from Uncommon Sense*, (New York: The Free Press, 2000).
20. John D.C. Little, "Decision Support Systems for Marketing Managers." *Journal of Marketing*, Summer 1979, 11. See "Special Issue on Managerial Decision Making." *Marketing Science,* 1999, 18(3), for some contemporary perspectives.
21. Leonard M. Lodish, "CALLPLAN: An Interactive Salesman's Call Planning System." *Management Science*, December 1971, pp. 25–40.
22. Christine Moorman, Gerald Zaltman, and Rohit Deshpandé, "Relationships Between Providers and Users of Market Research: The Dynamics of Trust Within and Between Organizations." *Journal of Marketing Research,* August 1992, 29, pp. 314–328.
23. Quote excerpted from: Arthur Shapiro, "Let's Redefine Market Research." *BrandWeek*, June 21, 2004, p. 20.

24. See "In Search of Quality Control." *Media*, April 23, 2004; Abhik Roy, Peter G.P. Walters, and Sheriff T.K. Luk, "Chinese Puzzles and Paradoxes: Conducting Business Research in China" *Journal of Business Research*, 2001, 52(2), pp. 203–210; Susan P. Douglas and C. Samuel Craig, *International Marketing Research: Concepts and Methods*, (Chichester, UK: Wiley, 2000); Sabra E. Brock, "Marketing Research in Asia: Problems, Opportunities, and Decisions." *Marketing Research*, September 1989, pp. 44–51; Helen Deal, "Has the Bell Tolled for Asian Profiles." *Asian Advertising & Marketing*, October 4, 1996, p. 10.
25. John McManus, "Stumbling Into Intelligence." *American Demographics*, April 2004, pp. 22–25.
26. John Gaffney, "The Buzz Must Go on." *Business 2.0*, February 2002, pp. 49–50.
27. Tim Ambler, *Marketing and the Bottom Line: The Marketing Metrics to pump up Cash Flow*, 2nd ed., (London: FT Prentice Hall, 2003).
28. Ibid.
29. Jack Neff, "P&G, Clorox Rediscover Modeling." *Advertising Age*, March 29, 2004, p. 10.
30. Laura Q. Hughes, "Econometrics Take Root." *Advertising Age*, August 5, 2002, p. S-4.
31. David J. Reibstein, "Connect the Dots." *CMO Magazine*, May 2005.
32. Jeff Zabin, "Marketing Dashboards: The Visual Display of Marketing Data." *Chief Marketer*.
33. Robert S. Kaplan and David P. Norton, *The Balanced Scorecard*, (Boston: Harvard Business School Press, 1996).
34. Spencer Ante, "Giving the Boss the Big Picture." *BusinessWeek*, February 13, 2006, pp. 48–50.
35. For a good discussion and illustration, see Roger J. Best, *Market-Based Management*, 2nd ed., (Upper Saddle River, NJ: Prentice Hall, 2000), pp. 71–75.
36. For further discussion, see Gary L. Lilien, Philip Kotler, and K. Sridhar Moorthy, *Marketing Models*, (Upper Saddle River, NJ: Prentice Hall, 1992).
37. Brian Sternthal and Alice M. Tybout, "Segmentation and Targeting." In *Kellogg on Marketing*, ed., Dawn Iacobucci (New York: John Wiley, 2001), pp. 3–30.
38. Norman Dalkey and Olaf Helmer, "An Experimental Application of the Delphi Method to the Use of Experts." *Management Science*, April 1963, pp. 458–467. See also Roger J. Best, "An Experiment in Delphi Estimation in Marketing Decision Making." *Journal of Marketing Research*, November 1974, pp. 447–452. For an excellent overview of market forecasting, see Scott Armstrong, ed., *Principles of Forecasting: A Handbook for Researchers and Practitioners* (Norwell, MA: Kluwer Academic Publishers, 2001) and his Web site: <http://fourps.wharton.upenn.edu/forecast/handbook.html>.

Chapter 5

1. <ritzcarlton.com>; <www.brandkeys.com>.
2. Robert Schieffer, *Ten Key Consumer Insights*, (Mason, OH: Thomson, 2005).
3. Don Peppers and Martha Rogers, "Customers Don't Grow on Trees." *Fast Company*, July 2005, pp. 25–26.
4. Tina Arceo-Dumlao, "Customer Relationship Management: Retailers Maintain Competitive Edge with CRM Strategies." *Retail Asia*, February 25, 2005.
5. Glen L. Urban, "The Emerging Era of Customer Advocacy." *MIT Sloan Management Review*, Winter 2004, pp. 77–82.
6. Irwin P. Levin and Richard D. Johnson, "Estimating Price-Quality Tradeoffs Using Comparative Judgments." *Journal of Consumer Research*, June 11, 1984, pp. 593–600. Customer perceived value can be measured as a difference or as a ratio. If total customer value is $20,000 and total customer cost is $16,000, then the customer perceived value is $4,000 (measured as a difference) or 1.25 (measured as a ratio). Ratios that are used to compare offers are often called *value price ratios*.
7. Jenn Abelson, "Gillette Battles for Japanese Hearts and Chins." *International Herald Tribune*, June 25, 2007.
8. For more on customer perceived value, see David C. Swaddling and Charles Miller, *Customer Power* (Dublin, OH: The Wellington Press, 2001).
9. Gary Hamel, "Strategy as Revolution." *Harvard Business Review*, July–August 1996, pp. 69–82.
10. <www.singaporeair.com>.
11. For some provocative analysis, see Susan Fournier and David Glen Mick, "Rediscovering Satisfaction." *Journal of Marketing*, October 1999, pp. 5–23.
12. "$2M for Smiles of Satisfaction," *Today*, May 26, 2005, p. 8.

13. For an interesting analysis of the effects of different types of expectations, see William Boulding, Ajay Kalra, and Richard Staelin, "The Quality Double Whammy." *Marketing Service*, 1999, 18(4), pp. 463–484.

14. Thomas O. Jones and W. Earl Sasser, Jr., "Why Satisfied Customers Defect." *Harvard Business Review*, November–December 1995, pp. 88–99.

15. Companies should also note that managers and salespeople can manipulate customer satisfaction ratings. They can be especially nice to customers just before the survey. They can also try to exclude unhappy customers. Another danger is that if customers know the company will go out of its way to please them, some may express high dissatisfaction to receive more concessions.

16. Frederick K. Reichheld, "The One Number You Need to Grow." *Harvard Business Review*, December 2003, pp. 46–54.

17. Alex Taylor III, "Mercedes Hits a Pothole." *Fortune*, October 27, 2003, pp. 140–146.

18. Technical Assistance Research Programs (Tarp), *U.S. Office of Consumer Affairs Study on Complaint Handling in America*, 1986.

19. Stephen S. Tax and Stephen W. Brown, "Recovering and Learning from Service Failure." *Sloan Management Review*, Fall 1998, 40(1), pp. 75–88; Ruth Bolton and Tina M. Bronkhorst, "The Relationship between Customer Complaints to the Firm and Subsequent Exit Behavior." In *Advances in Consumer Research*, 22 (Provo, UT: Association for Consumer Research, 1995); Roland T. Rust, Bala Subramanian, and Mark Wells, "Making Complaints a Management Tool." *Marketing Management*, March 1992, 1(3), pp. 40–45; Karl Albrecht and Ron Zemke, *Service America!* (Homewood, IL: Dow Jones-Irwin, 1985), pp. 6–7.

20. Christian Homburg and Andreas Fürst, "How Organizational Complaint Handling Drives Customer Loyalty: An Analysis of the Mechanistic and the Organic Approach." *Journal of Marketing*, July 2005, 69, pp. 95–114.

21. Philip Kotler, *Kotler on Marketing*, (New York: The Free Press, 1999), pp. 21–22.

22. "The Gurus of Quality: American Companies Are Heading the Quality Gospel Preached by Deming, Juran, Crosby, and Taguchi." *Traffic Management*, July 1990, pp. 35–39.

23. Cyndee Miller, "U.S. Firms Lag in Meeting Global Quality Standards." *Marketing News*, February 15, 1993.

24. Nona Walia, "He's Tailored to be a Rich Man." *Calcutta Times*, September 13, 2004; James Arnold, "Hong Kong's Travelling Tailor." *BBC News Online*, June 3, 2002.

25. "Quality: The U.S. Drives to Catch Up." *BusinessWeek*, November 1, 1982, pp. 66–80. For a more recent assessment of progress, see Gilbert Fuchsberg's "Quality Programs Show Shoddy Results." *Wall Street Journal*, May 14, 1992, p. B1. See also Roland R. Rust, Anthony J. Zahorik, and Timothy L. Keiningham, "Return on Quality (ROQ): Making Service Quality Financially Accountable." *Journal of Marketing*, April 1995, 59(2), pp. 58–70.

26. Robert D. Buzzell and Bradley T. Gale, *The PIMS Principles: Linking Strategy to Performance*, (New York: The Free Press, 1987), chapter 6 (PIMS stands for Profit Impact of Market Strategy.)

27. Brian Hindo, "Satisfaction Not Guaranteed." *BusinessWeek*, June 19, 2006, pp. 32–36.

28. Lerzan Aksoy, Timothy L. Keiningham, and Terry G. Vavra, "Nearly Everything You Know about Loyalty Is Wrong." *Marketing News*, October 1, 2005, pp. 20–21; Timothy L. Keiningham, Terry G. Vavra, Lerzan Aksoy, and Henri Wallard, *Loyalty Myths* (Hoboken, NJ: John Wiley, 2005).

29. Werner J. Reinartz and V. Kumar, "The Impact of Customer Relationship Characteristics on Profitable Lifetime Duration." *Journal of Marketing*, January 2003, 67, pp. 77–99; Werner J. Reinartz and V. Kumar, "On the Profitability of Long-Life Customers in a Noncontractual Setting: An Empirical Investigation and Implications for Marketing." *Journal of Marketing*, October 2000, 64, pp. 17–35.

30. Rakesh Niraj, Mahendra Gupta, and Chakravarthi Narasimhan, "Customer Profitability in a Supply Chain." *Journal of Marketing*, July 2001, pp. 1–16.

31. Thomas M. Petro, "Profitability: The Fifth 'P' of Marketing." *Bank Marketing*, September 1990, pp. 48–52; "Who Are Your Best Customers?" *Bank Marketing*, October 1990, pp. 48–52.

32. Michael D. Johnson and Fred Selnes, "Diversifying Your Customer Portfolio." *MIT Sloan Management Review*, Spring 2005, 46(3), pp. 11–14.

33. Michael D. Johnson and Fred Selnes, "Customer Portfolio Management." *Journal of Marketing*, April 2004, 68(2), pp. 1–17.

34. Ravi Dhar and Rashi Glazer, "Hedging Customers." *Harvard Business Review*, May 2003, pp. 86–92.

35. Michael E. Porter, *Competitive Strategy: Techniques for Analyzing Industries and Competitors*, (New York: Free Press, 1980).

36. For some recent analysis and discussion, see Michael Heanlein, Andreas M. Kaplan, and Detlef Schoder, "Valuing the Real Option of Abandoning Unprofitable Customers When Calculating Customer Lifetime

Value." *Journal of Marketing*, July 2006, 70, pp. 5–20; Teck-Hua Ho, Young-Hoon Park, and Yong-Pin Zhou, "Incorporating Satisfaction into Customer Value Analysis: Optimal Investment in Lifetime Value." *Marketing Science*, May–June 2006, 25, pp. 260–277; and Peter S. Fader, Bruce G. S. Hardie, and Ka Lok Lee, "RFM and CLV: Using Iso-Value Curves for Customer Base Analysis." *Journal of Marketing Research*, November 2005, 62, pp. 415–430.

37. Nicole E. Coviello, Roderick J. Brodie, Peter J. Danaher, and Wesley J. Johnston, "How Firms Relate to Their Markets: An Empirical Examination of Contemporary Marketing Practices." *Journal of Marketing*, July 2002, 66, pp. 33–46.

38. Nora A. Aufreiter, David Elzinga, and Jonathan W. Gordon, "Better Branding." *The McKinsey Quarterly*, 2003, 4, pp. 29–39.

39. Suzanne Loh, "Customer Relationship Management: CRM Programmes—Empowering Retailers to Meet the Best of Customer Leads." *Retail Asia*, February 28, 2005.

40. Michael J. Lanning, *Delivering Profitable Value* (Oxford, U.K.: Capstone, 1998).

41. Martha Rogers, "Nintendo Plays for Keeps." *Inside 1to1*, Febraury 23, 2004.

42. Don Peppers and Martha Rogers, *The One-to-One Future: Building Relationships One Customer at a Time*, (New York: Currency Doubleday, 1993); Don Peppers and Martha Rogers, *Enterprise One-to-One: Tools for Competing in the Interactive Age*, (New York: Currency, 1997); Don Peppers and Martha Rogers, *The One-to-One Manager: Real-World Lessons in Customer Relationship Management*, (New York: Doubleday, 1999); Don Peppers, Martha Rogers, and Bob Dorf, *The One-to-One Fieldbook: The Complete Toolkit for Implementing a One-to-One Marketing Program*, (New York: Bantam, 1999); Don Peppers and Martha Rogers, *One-to-One B2B: Customer Development Strategies for the Business-To-Business World*, (New York: Doubleday, 2001).

43. Alan W. H. Grant and Leonard A. Schlesinger, "Realize Your Customer's Full Profit Potential." *Harvard Business Review*, September–October 1995, pp. 59–72.

44. Michael Lewis, "Customer Acquisition Promotions and Customer Asset Value." *Journal of Marketing Research*, May 2006, 63, pp. 195–203.

45. Frederick F. Reichheld, "Learning from Customer Defections." *Harvard Business Review*, March–April 1996, pp. 56–69.

46. Kenji Hall, "Fad Marketing's Balancing Act." *BusinessWeek*, August 6, 2007.

47. Frederick F. Reichheld, *Loyalty Rules*, (Boston: Harvard Business School Press, 2001); Frederick F. Reichheld, *The Loyalty Effect*, (Boston: Harvard Business School Press, 1996).

48. Leonard L. Berry and A. Parasuraman, *Marketing Services: Computing through Quality*, (New York: The Free Press, 1991), pp. 136–142. For an academic examination in a business-to-business context, see Robert W. Palmatier, Srinath Gopalakrishna, and Mark B. Houston, "Returns on Business-to-Business Relationship Marketing Investments: Strategies for Leveraging Profits." *Marketing Science*, September–October 2006, 25, pp. 477–93.

49. Utpal M. Dholakia, "How Consumer Self-Determination Influences Relational Marketing Outcomes: Evidence from Longitudinal Field Studies." *Journal of Marketing Research*, February 2006, 43, pp. 109–120.

50. For a review, see Grahame R. Dowling and Mark Uncles, "Do Customer Loyalty Programs Really Work?" *Sloan Management Review*, 1997, 38(4), pp. 71–82.

51. Thomas Lee, "Retailers Look for a Hook." *St. Louis Post-Dispatch*, December 4, 2004, p. A.1.

52. <www.hog.com>.

53. James H. Donnelly, Jr., Leonard L. Berry, and Thomas W. Thompson, *Marketing Financial Services—A Strategic Vision*, (Homewood, IL: Dow Jones-Irwin, 1985), p. 113.

54. Michael Totty, "E-Commerce (A Special Report): Business Solutions." *Wall Street Journal*, October 20, 2003.

55. Jeffrey Pfeffer, "The Face of Your Business." *Business 2.0*, December 2002–January 2003, pp. 58.

56. From a privately circulated paper, Lester Wunderman, "The Most Elusive Word in Marketing." June 2000. See also Lester Wunderman, *Being Direct*, (New York: Random House, 1996).

57. Jacquelyn S. Thomas, Robert C. Blattberg, and Edward J. Fox. "Recapturing Lost Customers." *Journal of Marketing Research*, February 2004, 61, pp. 31–45.

58. Werner Reinartz and V. Kumar, "The Impact of Customer Relationship Characteristics on Profitable Lifetime Duration." *Journal of Marketing*, January 2003, 67(1), pp. 77–99; Werner Reinartz and V. Kumar, "The Mismanagement of Customer Loyalty." *Harvard Business Review*, July 2002, pp. 86–97.

59. Tom Spitale and John Strabley, "Customer Strategy Shift Brightens Tata's Future." *Inside 1to1*, August 23, 2004.

60. Peter R. Peacock, "Data Mining in Marketing: Part 1." *Marketing Management*, Winter 1998, pp. 9–18, and "Data Mining in Marketing: Part 2." *Marketing Management*, Spring 1998, pp. 15–25; Ginger Conlon, "What the !@#!*?!! Is a Data Warehouse?" *Sales & Marketing Management*, April 1997, pp. 41–48; Skip Press, "Fool's Gold? As Companies Rush to Mine Data, They May Dig Up Real Gems—Or False Trends." *Sales & Marketing Management*, April 1997, pp. 58, 60, 62; John Verity, "A Trillion-Byte Weapon." *BusinessWeek*, July 31, 1995, pp. 80–81.

61. James Lattin, Doug Carroll, and Paul Green, *Analyzing Multivariate Data*, (Florence, KY: Thomson Brooks/Cole, 2003); Simon Haykin, *Neural Networks: A Comprehensive Foundation*, 2nd ed., (Upper Saddle River, NJ: Prentice Hall, 1998); Michael J. A. Berry and Gordon Linoff, *Data Mining Techniques: For Marketing, Sales, and Customer Support*, (New York: John Wiley, 1997).

62. Peppers and Rogers Group (Asia), "Customer Relationship Management in Asia." *Inside 1to1*, January 14, 2002.

63. Ibid.

64. Werner Reinartz and V. Kumar, "The Mismanagement of Customer Loyalty." *Harvard Business Review*, July 2002, pp. 86–94; Susan M. Fournier, Susan Dobscha, and David Glen Mick, "Preventing the Premature Death of Relationship Marketing." *Harvard Business Review*, January–February 1998, pp. 42–51.

65. Jon Swartz, "Ebay Faithful Expect Loyalty in Return." *USA Today*, July 1, 2002, pp. B1–B2.

66. Darrell K. Rigby, Frederick F. Reichheld, and Phil Schefter, "Avoid the Four Perils of CRM." *Harvard Business Review*, February 2002, pp. 101–109.

67. George S. Day, "Creating a Superior Customer-Relating Capability." *Sloan Management Review*, Spring 2003, 44(3), pp. 77–82; George S. Day, "Creating a Superior Customer-Relating Capability." *MSI Report*, No. 03-101, (Cambridge, MA: Marketing Science Institute, 2003); "Why Some Companies Succeed at CRM (and Many Fail)." *Knowledge at Wharton*, <knowledge.wharton.upenn.edu>, accessed on January 15, 2003.

Chapter 6

1. Marianne Bray, "Skin Deep: Dying to be White." <http://edition.cnn.com/2002/WORLD/asiapc/east/05/13/asia.whitening>; "White is Still Right? On the Surface Anyway." *The Taipei Times* (Taiwan), March 25, 2004, p. 16; Cris Prystay, "Critics Say Ads for Skin Whiteners Capitalize on Malaysian Prejudice." *Wall Street Journal (Online)*, April 30, 2002; Naresh Puri, "Beyond the Pale?" *BBC News*, September 25, 2007.

2. "Disney Uses *Feng Shui* to Build Mickey's New Kingdom in Hong Kong." <english.sina.com/taiwan_hk/1/2005/0907/45097.html>, September 7, 2005.

3. Richard P. Coleman, "The Continuing Significance of Social Class to Marketing." *Journal of Consumer Research*, December 1983, pp. 265–280.

4. Leon G. Schiffman and Leslie Lazar Kanuk, *Consumer Behavior*, 8th ed., (Upper Saddle River, NJ: Prentice Hall, 2004).

5. Norihiko Shirouzu, "Japan's High School Girls Excel in Art of Setting Trends." *Wall Street Journal*, April 27, 1998, pp. B1–B6.

6. Rosann L. Spiro, "Persuasion in Family Decision Making." *Journal of Consumer Research*, March 1983, pp. 393–402; David J. Burns, "Husband-Wife Innovative Consumer Decision Making: Exploring the Effect of Family Power." *Psychology and Marketing*, May–June 1992, pp. 175–189; Robert Boutilier, "Pulling the Family's Strings." *American Demographics*, August 1993, pp. 44–48; Elizabeth S. Moore, William L. Wilkie, and Richard J. Lutz, "Passing the Torch: Intergenerational Influences as a Source of Brand Equity." *Journal of Marketing*, April 2002, pp. 17–37. For cross-cultural comparisons of husband-wife buying roles, see John B. Ford, Michael S. LaTour, and Tony L. Henthorne, "Perception of Marital Roles in Purchase-Decision Processes: A Cross-Cultural Study." *Journal of the Academy of Marketing Science*, Spring 1995, pp. 120–131.

7. Kay M. Palan and Robert E. Wilkes, "Adolescent-Parent Interaction in Family Decision Making." *Journal of Consumer Research*, 1997, 24(2), pp. 159–169; Sharon E. Beatty and Salil Talpade, "Adolescent Influence in Family Decision Making: A Replication with Extension." *Journal of Consumer Research*, 1994, 21, pp. 332–341.

8. "Korean Carmakers Have Eyes on Women Drivers." *Straits Times* (Singapore), September 25, 2004, pp. A17.

9. Susan Fenton, "Women at Forefront of Consumer Spending in China." *International Herald Tribune*, September 17, 2007.

10. Hillary Chura, "Failing to Connect: Marketing Messages for Women Fall Short." *Advertising Age*, September 23, 2002, pp. 13–14.

11. James U. McNeal, "Tapping the Three Kids' Markets." *American Demographics*, April 1998, pp. 37–41.

12. Jennifer Bayot, "The Teenage Market; Young, Hip, and Looking for a Bargain." *New York Times*, December 1, 2003, p. C8.

13. Julia Boorstin, "Disney's 'Tween Machine." *Fortune*, September 29, 2003, pp. 111–114; Disney Launches Two Channels in Cambodia, *Entertainment Magazine Interactive*, June 20, 2005, "Making of a Legend." *Asia Image*, September 1, 2003.

14. Lawrence Lepisto, "A Life Span Perspective of Consumer Behavior." In Elizabeth Hirshman and Morris Holbrook (eds.), *Advances in Consumer Research 12* (Provo, UT: Association for Consumer Research, 1985), p. 47. See also Gail Sheehy, *New Passages: Mapping Your Life Across Time,* (New York: Random House, 1995).

15. Frederick Herzberg, *Work and the Nature of Man*, (Cleveland: William Collins, 1966); Henk Thierry and Agnes M. Koopman-Iwerna, "Motivation and Satisfaction." In P. J. Drenth, ed., *Handbook of Work and Organizational Psychology*, (New York: John Wiley, 1984), pp. 141–142.

16. Harold H. Kassarjian and Mary Jane Sheffet, "Personality and Consumer Behavior: An Update." In Harold H. Kassarjian and Thomas S. Robertson, eds., *Perspectives in Consumer Behavior*, (Glenview, IL: Scott, Foresman, 1981), pp. 160–180.

17. Jennifer Aaker, "Dimensions of Brand Personality." *Journal of Marketing Research*, August 1997, 34, pp. 347–356; Jennifer Aaker, Veronica Benet-Martinez, and Jodi Garolera, "Consumption Symbols as Carriers of Culture: A Study of Japanese, Spanish, and North American Brand Personality Constructs." *Journal of Personality and Social Psychology*, 2001, 81, pp. 492–508. Some dimensions may be culturally specific: ruggedness (the U.S.), passion (Spain), and peacefulness (Spain and Japan).

18. Jennifer L. Aaker, Veronica Benet-Martinez, and Jordi Garolera, "Consumption Symbols as Carriers of Culture: A Study of Japanese and Spanish Brand Personality Constructs." *Journal of Personality and Social Psychology*, March 2001, 81(3), pp. 492–508.

19. Yongjun Sung and Spencer F. Tinkham, "Brand Personality Structures in the United States and Korea: Common and Culture-Specific Factors." *Journal of Consumer Psychology*, December 2005, 15(4), pp. 334–350.

20. M. Joseph Sirgy, "Self Concept in Consumer Behavior: A Critical Review." *Journal of Consumer Research*, December 9, 1982, pp. 287–300.

21. Timothy R. Graeff, "Consumption Situations and the Effects of Brand Image on Consumers' Brand Evaluations." *Psychology and Marketing*, 1997, 14(1), pp. 49–70; Timothy R. Graeff, "Image Congruence Effects on Product Evaluations: The Role of Self-Monitoring and Public/Private Consumption." *Psychology and Marketing*, 1996, 13(5), pp. 481–499.

22. Jennifer L. Aaker, "The Malleable Self: The Role of Self-Expression in Persuasion." *Journal of Marketing Research*, 1996, 36(2), pp. 45–57.

23. "16m. Young High-Earning Consumers Are Targets of High-End Lifestyle Products 2006." *News India – Times*, August 4, 2006, 37(31), p. 16.

24. "The World's First Individual Electronic Consumer Panel, I-Scan Findings Confirm Hong Kong's Strong Fast Food Culture." <www.acnielsen.com.hk/news.asp?newsID= 124>.

25. "Chinese Men Get Looks Conscious." *Business Times* (Singapore), January 20, 2005.

26. Toby Weber, "All Three? Gee." *Wireless Review*, May 2003, pp. 12–14.

27. Krist Boo, "Fuss-free 'Pets' the Latest Craze in Japan." *Straits Times* (Singapore), September 25, 2004, p. A14; "Pet Ownership is Big Biz in China." *Business Times* (Singapore), February 15, 2005, p. 15.

28. Thomas J. Reynolds and Jonathan Gutman, "Laddering Theory, Method, Analysis, and Interpretation." *Journal of Advertising Research*, February–March 1988, pp. 11–34.

29. Ernest Dichter, *Handbook of Consumer Motivations*, (New York: McGraw-Hill, 1964).

30. Abraham Maslow, *Motivation and Personality*, (New York: Harper and Row), pp. 80–106.

31. Boon Lai Hau, "Japan's Phone Clubs." *Sunday Times* (Singapore), March 12, 2000, p. 18.

32. Hellmut Schütte and Deana Ciarlante, *Consumer Behavior in Asia*, (London: MacMillan Business, 1998).

33. Frederick Herzberg, *Work and the Nature of Man*, (Cleveland: William Collins, 1966); He Thierry and Agnes M. Koopman-Iwerna, "Motivation and Satisfaction." pp. 141–142.

34. Bernard Berelson and Gary A. Steiner, *Human Behavior: An Inventory of Scientific Findings*, (New York: Harcourt, Brace Jovanovich, 1964), p. 88.

35. Gavin Heron, "'Made in China' Not a Negative for Savvy Consumers of Today." *Media* (Hong Kong), 13, February 2004, p. 11; Dexter Roberts, "How to Beat 'Made-in-China' Fear." *BusinessWeek*, October 2007, p. 8.

36. Brian Bremner, "BW's 20 Best Chinese Brands." *BusinessWeek*, August 28, 2006; Dexter Roberts, "How to Beat 'Made-in-China' Fear." *BusinessWeek*, October 2007, p. 8.

37. J. Edward Russo, Margaret G. Meloy, and T.J. Wilks, "The Distortion of Product Information during Brand Choice." *Journal of Marketing Research*, 1998, 35, pp. 438–452.

38. Leslie de Chernatony and Simon Knox, "How an Appreciation of Consumer Behavior can Help in Product Testing." *Journal of Market Research Society*, July 1990, p. 333. See also Chris Janiszewski and Stiju M. J. Osselar, "A Connectionist Model of Brand-Quality Association." *Journal of Marketing Research*, August 2000, pp. 331–351.

39. Florida's Chris Janiszewski has developed a fascinating research program looking at preconscious processing effects. See Chris Janiszewski, "Preattentive Mere Exposure Effects." *Journal of Consumer Research*, December 1993, 20, pp. 376–392, as well as some of his earlier and subsequent research.

40. See Timothy E. Moore, "Subliminal Advertising: What You See Is What You Get." *Journal of Marketing*, 1982, 46, pp. 38–47 for an early classic and Andrew B. Aylesworth, Ronald C. Goodstein, and Ajay Kalra, "Effect of Archetypal Embeds on Feelings: An Indirect Route to Affecting Attitudes?" *Journal of Advertising*, 1999, 28(3), pp. 73–81 for a more current treatment.

41. "Matsushita Improves China Line." *The Nation*, November 2004, p. 24.

42. "China's Yuppies Say 'I Do' to Diamonds." *Business Times* (Singapore) December 27, 2004, p. 12.

43. John R. Anderson, The Architecture of Cognition (Cambridge, MA: Harvard University Press, 1983); Robert S. Wyer, Jr. and Thomas K. Srull, "Person Memory and Judgment." *Psychological Review*, 1989, 96(1), pp. 58–83.

44. Rasul Bailay, "A Haier Price." *Far Eastern Economic Review*, May 27, 2004, p. 44.

45. For additional discussion, see John G. Lynch, Jr. and Thomas K. Srull, "Memory and Attentional Factors in Consumer Choice: Concepts and Research Methods." *Journal of Consumer Research*, June 1982, 9, pp. 18–36; Joseph W. Alba, J. Wesley Hutchinson, and John G. Lynch, Jr, "Memory and Decision Making." In Harold H. Kassarjian and Thomas S. Robertson, eds., *Handbook of Consumer Theory and Research (*Englewood Cliffs, NJ: Prentice Hall, 1992), pp. 1–49.

46. Fergus I.M. Craik and Robert S. Lockhart, "Levels of Processing: A Framework for Memory Research." *Journal of Verbal Learning and Verbal Behavior*, 1972, 11, pp. 671–684; Fergus I.M. Craik and Endel Tulving, "Depth of Processing and the Retention of Words in Episodic Memory." *Journal of Experimental Psychology*, 1975, 104(3), pp. 268–294; Robert S. Lockhart, Fergus I.M. Craik, and Larry Jacoby, "Depth of Processing, Recognition, and Recall." In John Brown, ed., *Recall and Recognition* (New York: John Wiley, 1976).

47. Leonard M. Lodish, Magid Abraham, Stuart Kalmenson, Jeanne Livelsberger, Beth Lubetkin, Bruce Richardson, and Mary Ellen Stevens, "How T.V. Advertising Works: A Meta Analysis of 389 Real World Split Cable T.V. Advertising Experiments." *Journal of Marketing Research*, May 1995, 32, pp. 125–139.

48. Elizabeth F. Loftus and Gregory R. Loftus, "On the Permanence of Stored Information in the Human Brain." *American Psychologist*, May 1980, 35, pp. 409–420.

49. Eric Pfanner, "Pepsi's Counterintuitive Branding Strategy." *International Herald Tribune*, February 2007, p. 18.

50. Benson Shapiro, V. Kasturi Rangan, and John Sviokla, "Staple Yourself to an Order." *Harvard Business Review*, July–August 1992, pp. 113–122. See also Carrie M. Heilman, Douglas Bowman, and Gordon P. Wright, "The Evolution of Brand Preferences and Choice Behaviors of Consumers New to a Market." *Journal of Marketing Research*, May 2000, pp. 139–155.

51. Marketing scholars have developed several models of the consumer buying process. See John A. Howard and Jagdish N. Sheth, *The Theory of Buyer Behavior*, (New York: John Wiley, 1969); James F. Engel, Roger D. Blackwell, and Paul W. Miniard, *Consumer Behavior*, 8th ed., (Fort Worth, TX: Dryden, 1994); Mary Frances Luce, James R. Bettman, and John W. Payne, *Emotional Decisions: Tradeoff Difficulty and Coping in Consumer Choice*, (Chicago, IL: University of Chicago Press, 2001).

52. William P. Putsis, Jr. and Narasimhan Srinivasan, "Buying or Just Browsing? The Duration of Purchase Deliberation." *Journal of Marketing Research*, August 1994, pp. 393–402.

53. Chem L. Narayana and Rom J. Markin, "Consumer Behavior and Product Performance: An Alternative Conceptualization." *Journal of Marketing*, October 1975, pp. 1–6. See also Wayne S. DeSarbo and Kamel Jedidi, "The Spatial Representation of Heterogeneous Consideration Sets." *Marketing Science*, 1995, 14(3), pt. 2, pp. 326–342; Lee G. Cooper and Akihiro Inoue, "Building Market Structures from Consumer Preferences." *Journal of Marketing Research*, August 1996, 33(3), pp. 293–306.

54. This expectancy-value model was originally developed by Martin Fishbein, "Attitudes and Prediction of Behavior." In *Readings in Attitude Theory and Measurement*, Martin Fishbein, ed., (New York: John Wiley, 1967), pp. 477–92. For a critical review, see Paul W. Miniard and Joel B. Cohen, "An Examination of the Fishbein-Ajzen Behavioral-Intentions Model's Concepts and Measures," *Journal of Experimental Social Psychology*, May 1981, pp. 309–39.

55. Virginia Postrel, "The Lessons of the Grocery Shelf Also Have Something to Say About Affirmative Action." *New York Times*, January 30, 2003, p. C2.

56. Leslie Chang, "China's Consumers Put Product Quality Over Price." *Wall Street Journal* (Eastern Edition), August 6, 2004, p. A7.

57. "Healthy Products, Already Big in Japan, Go Global." *Business Times* (Singapore), January 17, 2005, p. 16.

58. David Krech, Richard S. Crutchfield, and Egerton L. Ballachey. *Individual in Society*, (New York: McGraw-Hill, 1962), chapter 2.

59. Jill Venter, "Milk Mustache Campaign Is a Hit with Teens." *St. Louis Post-Dispatch*, April 1, 1998, p. E1; Dave Fusaro, "The Milk Mustache." *Dairy Foods*, April 1997, p. 75; Judann Pollack, "Milk: Kurt Graetzer." *Advertising Age*, June 30, 1997, p. S1; Kevin Lane Keller, "Milk: Branding a Commodity." *Best Practice Cases in Branding* (Upper Saddle River, NJ: Prentice Hall, 2002).

60. Paul E. Green and Yoram Wind, *Multiattribute Decisions in Marketing: A Measurement Approach* (Hinsdale, IL: Dryden, 1973), chapter 2; Leigh McAlister, "Choosing Multiple Items from a Product Class." *Journal of Consumer Research*, December 1979, pp. 213–224; Richard J. Lutz, "The Role of Attitude Theory in Marketing." in Kassarjian and Robertson (eds.), *Perspectives in Consumer Behavior*, (1991), pp. 317–339.

61. This expectancy-value model was originally developed by Martin Fishbein, "Attitudes and Prediction of Behavior." In Martin Fishbein (ed.), *Readings in Attitude Theory and Measurement*, (New York: John Wiley, 1967), pp. 477–492. For a critical review, see Paul W. Miniard and Joel B. Cohen, "An Examination of the Fishbein-Ajzen Behavioral-Intentions Model's Concepts and Measures." *Journal of Experimental Social Psychology*, May 1981, pp. 309–339.

62. Michael R. Solomon, *Consumer Behavior: Buying, Having and Being* (Upper Saddle River, NJ: Prentice Hall, 2001).

63. James R. Bettman, Eric J. Johnson, and John W. Payne, "Consumer Decision Making." In Harold H. Kassarjian and Thomas S. Robertson, eds., *Handbook of Consumer Theory and Research* (Englewood Cliffs, NJ: Prentice Hall, 1992), pp. 50–84.

64. Jagdish N. Sheth, "An Investigation of Relationships among Evaluative Beliefs, Affect, Behavioral Intention, and Behavior." In John U. Farley, John A. Howard, and L. Winston Ring, eds., *Consumer Behavior: Theory and Application*, (Boston: Allyn & Bacon, 1974), pp. 89–114.

65. Martin Fishbein, "Attitudes and Prediction of Behavior." In Martin Fishbein, ed., *Readings in Attitude Theory and Measurement*, (New York: John Wiley, 1967), pp. 477–492.

66. Raymond A. Bauer, "Consumer Behavior as Risk Taking." In Donald F. Cox (ed.), *Risk Taking and Information Handling in Consumer Behavior*, (Boston: Division of Research, Harvard Business School, 1967); James W. Taylor, "The Role of Risk in Consumer Behavior." *Journal of Marketing*, April 1974, pp. 54–60.

67. Priscilla A. La Barbera and David Mazursky, "A Longitudinal Assessment of Consumer Satisfaction/ Dissatisfaction: The Dynamic Aspect of the Cognitive Process." *Journal of Marketing Research*, November 1983, pp. 393–404.

68. Ralph L. Day, "Modeling Choices among Alternative Responses to Dissatisfaction." *Advances in Consumer Research*, 1984, 11, pp. 496–499. See also Philip Kotler and Murali K. Mantrala, "Flawed Products: Consumer Responses and Marketer Strategies." *Journal of Consumer Marketing*, Summer 1985, pp. 27–36.

69. Albert O. Hirschman, *Exit, Voice, and Loyalty* (Cambridge, MA: Harvard University Press, 1970).

70. Mary C. Gilly and Richard W. Hansen, "Consumer Complaint Handling as a Strategic Marketing Tool." *Journal of Consumer Marketing*, Fall 1985, pp. 5–16.

71. James H. Donnelly, Jr. and John M. Ivancevich, "Post-Purchase Reinforcement and Back-Out Behavior." *Journal of Marketing Research*, August 1970, pp. 399–400.

72. Gong, Wen, Zhan G. Li, and Tiger Li, "Marketing to China's Youth: A Cultural Transformation Perspective." *Business Horizons*, 2004, 47(6), pp. 41–50.

73. John D. Cripps, "Heuristics and Biases in Timing the Replacement of Durable Products." *Journal of Consumer Research*, September 1994, 21, pp. 304–318.

74. Richard E. Petty and John T. Cacioppo, *Attitudes and Persuasion: Classic and Contemporary Approaches*, (New York: McGraw-Hill, 1981); Richard E. Petty, *Communication and Persuasion: Central and Peripheral Routes to Attitude Change*, (New York: Springer-Verlag, 1986).

75. Herbert E. Krugman, "The Impact of Television Advertising: Learning without Involvement." *Public Opinion Quarterly*, Fall 1965, pp. 349–356.

76. Frank R. Kardes, *Consumer Behavior and Managerial Decision Making*, 2nd ed., (Upper Saddle River, NJ: Prentice Hall, 2003).

77. See Richard Thaler, "Mental Accounting and Consumer Choice." *Marketing Science*, 1985, 4(3), pp. 199–214 for a seminal piece and Richard Thaler, "Mental Accounting Matters." *Journal of Behavioral Decision Making*, 1999, 12(3), pp. 183–206, for more contemporary perspectives.
78. Gary L. Gastineau and Mark P. Kritzman, *Dictionary of Financial Risk Management*, 3rd ed., (New York: John Wiley, 1999).
79. Example adapted from Daniel Kahneman and Amos Tversky, "Prospect Theory: An Analysis of Decision under Risk." *Econometrica*, March 1979, 47, pp. 263–291.
80. Harper W. Boyd, Jr. and Sidney Levy, "New Dimensions in Consumer Analysis." *Harvard Business Review*, November–December 1963, pp. 129–140.
81. Sandra Vandermerwe, *Customer Capitalism: Increasing Returns in New Market Spaces*, (London: Nicholas Brealey Publishing), chapter 11.
82. Patricia B. Seybold, "Get Inside the Lives of Your Customers." *Harvard Business Review*, May 2001, pp. 81–89.

Chapter 7

1. Kate Maddox, "BMA Conference Showcases Innovation." *B to B*, June 12, 2006, p. 3.
2. James C. Anderson and James A. Narus, *Business Market Management: Understanding, Creating and Delivering Value*, 2nd ed., (Upper Saddle River, NJ: Prentice Hall, 2004).
3. Frederick E. Webster Jr. and Yoram Wind, *Organizational Buying Behavior*, (Upper Saddle River, NJ: Prentice Hall, 1972), p. 2.
4. Jennifer Gilbert, "Small But Mighty." *Sales and Marketing Management*, January 2004, pp. 30–35.
5. Michael Collins, "Breaking into the Big Leagues." *American Demographics*, January 1996, p. 24.
6. Patrick J. Robinson, Charles W. Faris, and Yoram Wind, *Industrial Buying and Creative Marketing*, (Boston: Allyn & Bacon, 1967).
7. Daniel H. McQuiston, "Novelty, Complexity, and Importance as Causal Determinants of Industrial Buyer Behavior." *Journal of Marketing*, April 1989, pp. 66–79; Peter Doyle, Arch G. Woodside, and Paul Mitchell, "Organizational Buying in New Task and Rebuy Situations." *Industrial Marketing Management*, February 1979, pp. 7–11.
8. Urban B. Ozanne and Gilbert A. Churchill Jr., "Five Dimensions of the Industrial Adoption Process." *Journal of Marketing Research*, August 1971, pp. 322–328.
9. Donald W. Jackson Jr., Janet E. Keith, and Richard K. Burdick, "Purchasing Agents' Perceptions of Industrial Buying Center Influence: A Situational Approach." *Journal of Marketing*, Fall 1984, pp. 75–83.
10. Frederick E. Webster Jr. and Yoram Wind. *Organizational Buying Behavior*, (Upper Saddle River, NJ: Prentice Hall, 1972) p. 6.
11. Ibid.
12. Frederick E. Webster Jr. and Yoram Wind, "A General Model for Understanding Organizational Buying Behavior." *Journal of Marketing*, April 1972, 36, pp. 12–19; Frederick E. Webster Jr. and Yoram Wind. *Organizational Buying Behavior,* (Upper Saddle River, NJ: Prentice Hall, 1972).
13. Frederick E. Webster Jr. and Kevin Lane Keller, "A Roadmap For Branding in Industrial Markets." *Journal of Brand Management,* May 2004, 11, pp. 388–402.
14. Scott Ward and Frederick E. Webster Jr., "Organizational Buying Behavior." In Tom Robertson and Hal Kassarjian eds., *Handbook of Consumer Behavior*, (Upper Saddle River, NJ: Prentice Hall, 1991), chapter 12, pp. 419–458.
15. Frederick E. Webster Jr. and Yoram Wind, *Organizational Buying Behavior*, (Upper Saddle River, NJ: Prentice Hall, 1972), p. 6.
16. Nirmalya Kumar, *Marketing As Strategy: Understanding the CEO's Agenda for Driving Growth and Innovation*, (Boston: Harvard Business School Press, 2004).
17. John Seely Brown, "Innovation Blowback: Disruptive Management Practices from Asia." *McKinsey Quarterly*, 2005, 1, p. 34.
18. James C. Anderson and James A. Narus, *Business Market Management: Understanding, Creating and Delivering Value.*
19. Adapted from Peter Kraljic, "Purchasing Must Become Supply Management." *Harvard Business Review*, September–October 1993, pp. 109–117.

20. Tim Minahan, "OEM Buying Survey-Part 2: Buyers Get New Roles but Keep Old Tasks." *Purchasing*, July 16, 1998, pp. 208–209.
21. Patrick J. Robinson, Charles W. Faris, and Yoram Wind. *Industrial Buying and Creative Marketing*.
22. Rick Mullin, "Taking Customer Relations to the Next Level." *The Journal of Business Strategy*, January–February 1997, pp. 22–26.
23. Rajdeep Grewal, James M. Comer, and Raj Mehta, "An Investigation into the Antecedents of Organizational Participation in Business-to-Business Electronic Markets." *Journal of Marketing*, July 2001, 65, pp. 17–33.
24. "Global Sources to Launch Garments & Textiles Magazines and Web Site." *PR Newswire*, February 28, 2005.
25. Kate Maddox, "#1 Hewlett-Packard Co., www.hp.com." *B to B*, August 11, 2003, pp. 1, 23.
26. "Xerox Multinational Supplier Quality Survey." *Purchasing*, January 12, 1995, p. 112.
27. Daniel J. Flint, Robert B. Woodruff, and Sarah Fisher Gardial, "Exploring the Phenomenon of Customers' Desired Value Change in a Business-to-Business Context." *Journal of Marketing*, 66, October 2002, pp. 102–117.
28. Donald R. Lehmann and John O'Shaughnessy, "Differences in Attribute Importance for Different Industrial Products." *Journal of Marketing*, April 1974, pp. 36–42.
29. Arnt Buvik and George John, "When Does Vertical Coordination Improve Industrial Purchasing Relationships?" *Journal of Marketing*, October 2000, 64, pp. 52–64.
30. Inhye Kim, "How Confuciansim Shapes Korean Culture." *Asia Inc*, May 2005, p. 17.
31. Shankar Ganesan, "Determinants of Long-Term Orientation in Buyer-Seller Relationships." *Journal of Marketing*, April 1994, 58, pp. 1–19; Patricia M. Doney and Joseph P. Cannon, "An Examination of the Nature of Trust in Buyer-Seller Relationships." *Journal of Marketing*, April 1997, 61, pp. 35–51.
32. John H. Sheridan, "An Alliance Built on Trust." *Industry Week*, March 17, 1997, pp. 66–70.
33. William W. Keep, Stanley C. Hollander, and Roger Dickinson, "Forces Impinging on Long-Term Business-to-Business Relationships in the United States: An Historical Perspective." *Journal of Marketing*, April 1998, 62, pp. 31–45.
34. Joseph P. Cannon and William D. Perreault Jr., "Buyer-Seller Relationships in Business Markets." *Journal of Marketing Research*, November 1999, 36, pp. 439–460.
35. Ibid.
36. Thomas G. Noordewier, George John, and John R. Nevin, "Performance Outcomes of Purchasing Arrangements in Industrial Buyer-Vendor Arrangements." *Journal of Marketing*, October 1990, 54, pp. 80–93; Arnt Buvik and George John, "When Does Vertical Coordination Improve Industrial Purchasing Relationships?"
37. Akesel I. Rokkan, Jan B. Heide, and Kenneth H. Wathne, "Specific Investment in Marketing Relationships: Expropriation and Bonding Effects." *Journal of Marketing Research*, May 2003, 40, pp. 210–224.
38. Mrinal Ghosh and George John, "Governance Value Analysis and Marketing Strategy." *Journal of Marketing*, 1999, 63, pp. 131–145.
39. Joan Magretta, "Fast, Global, and Entrepreneurial: Supply Chain Management, Hong Kong Style: An Interview with Victor Fung." *Harvard Business Review*, September–October 1998, pp. 103–114.
40. Arnt Buvik and George John, "When Does Vertical Coordination Improve Industrial Purchasing Relationships?"
41. Simon Burns, "Computers: Reinventing Acer." *Far Eastern Economic Review*, May 24, 2001.
42. Kenneth H. Wathne and Jan B. Heide, "Opportunism in Interfirm Relationships: Forms, Outcomes, and Solutions." *Journal of Marketing*, October 2000, 64, pp. 36–51.
43. Mark B. Houston and Shane A. Johnson, "Buyer-Supplier Contracts Versus Joint Ventures: Determinants and Consequences of Transaction Structure." *Journal of Marketing Research*, February 2000, 37, pp. 1–15.
44. Akesel I. Rokkan, Jan B. Heide, and Kenneth H. Wathne, "Specific Investment in Marketing Relationships: Expropriation and Bonding Effects."
45. There are two other types of *keiretsu*: capital-connected and sales-distribution. The *keiretsu* material in this discussion draws from Shigefumi Makino, "A Note on the Japanese *Keiretsu*." in Paul W. Beamish (ed.), *Asia-Pacific Cases in Strategic Management*, (Boston: Irwin McGraw-Hill, 2000), pp. 213–222; Jai-Beom Kim and Paul Mitchell, "Relationship Marketing in Japan: The Buyer-Seller Relationships of Four Automakers." *Journal of Business and Industrial Marketing*, 1999, 14(2), pp. 118–129. For insights regarding the *chaebol*, see Chang-Bum Choi, "Ssangyong Corporation." in Paul W. Beamish (ed.), *Asia-Pacific Cases in Strategic Management*, (Boston: Irwin McGraw-Hill, 2000), pp. 328–340; Yuji Akaba, Florian Budde, and Jungkiu

Choi, "A Cure for Sick *Chaebol*." *The Asian Wall Street Journal*, November 19, 1998; Ihlwan Moon, "The Dangers of Cracking Down in Korea." *BusinessWeek Online*, December 4, 2000.

46. Kimberly Song, "Rules Can Be Negotiable." *Far Eastern Economic Review*, August 5, 2004, pp. 56–57.
47. Matthew Swibel and Janet Novack, "The Scariest Customer." *Forbes*, November 10, 2003, pp. 96–97.
48. Raju Chellam, "Many SMEs Keen on Linux." *Business Times* (Singapore), January 24, 2005, p. B1.
49. Bruce Einhorn, "Legend's Home-Field Advantage." *BusinessWeek Online*, June 18, 2001.
50. "Analysis—Multinationals in China Require New Strategy." *Asia Pulse*, April 5, 2005.

Chapter 8

1. "Over 60 and Overlooked." *Economist*, August 10, 2002, pp. 51–52.
2. "China's Golden Oldies." *Economist*, February 26, 2005, p. 61.
3. Anthony Bianco, "The Vanishing Mass Market." *BusinessWeek Asian Edition*, July 12, 2004, pp. 46–50.
4. Vinay Kamath and Shamni Pande, "Rural Markets: The New Frontier." *Hindu Business Line*, India, April 15, 1999, p. 1; Manjeet Kripalani, "Rural India, Have a Coke." *BusinessWeek Asian Edition*, May 27, 2002, pp. 24–25.
5. James C. Anderson and James A. Narus, "Capturing the Value of Supplementary Services." *Harvard Business Review*, January–February 1995, pp. 75–83.
6. "Don't Call Him Disabled." *BusinessWeek*, June 9, 2003, p. 42.
7. Tevfik Dalgic and Maarten Leeuw, "Niche Marketing Revisited: Concept, Applications, and Some European Cases." *European Journal of Marketing*, 1994, 28(4), pp. 39–55.
8. Robert D. Hof, "There's Not Enough 'Me' in MySpace." *BusinessWeek*, December 4, 2006, p. 40; Abbey Klaassen "Niche-Targeted Social Networks Find Audiences." *Advertising Age*, November 6, 2006, 77(45), p. 15.
9. Craig Wilson, "Hallmark Hits the Mark." *USA Today*, June 14, 2001, pp. 1D–2D.
10. Chad Terhune and Gabriel Kahn, "Shaking Up Coke in Japan." *Far Eastern Economic Review*, September 11, 2003, pp. 36–40.
11. Gunjan Prasad, "Samsung Ties Up with MTV Awards for 'Cool' Catchet." *Media*, January 14, 2005.
12. Robert Blattberg and John Deighton, "Interactive Marketing: Exploiting the Age of Addressi-bility." *Sloan Management Review*, Fall 1991, 33(1), pp. 5–14.
13. Brian Morrissey, "Dan Myrick on the Spot." *Adweek*, May 8, 2006, p. 28.
14. "China's Consumer Market a Tough Nut to Crack." *Straits Times* (Singapore), December 7, 1994, p. 27.
15. "The Legacy that Got Left on the Shelf." *Economist*, January 31, 2008.
16. Don Peppers and Martha Rogers, *The One-to-One Future: Building Relationships One Customer at a Time*, (New York: Currency/Doubleday, 1993).
17. Jerry Wind and A. Rangaswamy, "Customerization: The Second Revolution in Mass Customi-zation." *Wharton School Working Paper*, June 1999.
18. James C. Anderson and James A. Narus, "Capturing the Value of Supplementary Services."
19. Dexter Roberts, "Scrambling to Bring Crest to the Masses in China." *BusinessWeek*, June 25, 2007.
20. Kate Kane, "It's a Small World." *Working Woman*, October 1997, p. 22.
21. Bruce Einhorn, "Know Your IT, Know Your Customer." *BusinessWeek Online Asia*, October 23, 2001.
22. Michael J. Weiss, "To Be About To Be." *American Demographics*, September 2003, pp. 29–36.
23. Brooks Bames and Monica M. Clark, "Tapping into the Wedding Industry to Sell Broadway Seats." *Wall Street Journal*, July 3, 2006.
24. Jim Rendon, "Rear Window." *Business 2.0*, August 2003, p. 72.
25. <www.campaignforrealbeauty.ph>, accessed on February 26, 2008.
26. Ian Rowley, "A Mortgage of Her Own." *BusinessWeek*, July 12, 2004, p. 27.
27. Erica Tay, "Banyan Tree's Oasis Splendor." *Straits Times*, (Singapore), April 29, 2005, p. 3.
28. Gregory L. White and Shirley Leung, "Middle Market Shrinks As Americans Migrate toward the Higher End." *Wall Street Journal*, March 29, 2002, pp. A1, A8.
29. Linda Tischler, "The Price Is Right." *Fast Company*, November 2003, pp. 83–91.

30. Braema Mathi, "Meet Asia's Young and Educated: The Genies." *Straits Times,* (Singapore), May 16, 1997, p. 17.
31. Fara Warner, "Marketers Question Myths About China." *Asian Wall Street Journal*, March 24, 1997, pp. 1, 6.
32. Geoffrey E. Meredith and Charles D. Schewe with Janice Karlovich, *Defining Markets, Defining Moments*, (New York, NY: Hungry Minds, Inc., 2002).
33. Andrew E. Serwer, "42,496 Secrets Bared." *Fortune*, January 24, 1994, pp. 13–14; Kenneth Labich, "Class in America." *Fortune*, February 7, 1994, pp. 114–126.
34. Leah Rickard, "Gerber Trots Out New Ads Backing Toddler Food Line." *Advertising Age*, April 11, 1994, pp. 1, 48.
35. <www.sric-bi.com/VALS/JVALSbackground.shtml>.
36. Pam Danziger, "Getting More for V-Day." *Brandweek*, February 9, 2004, p. 19.
37. Weng Kin Kwan, "Everyday Life—A Cause for Celebration in Japan." *Straits Times* (Singapore) Life! Section, November 10, 1994, p. 6.
38. Gabriel Kahn, "Can Do: How Coke Caters to Quirky Japanese Tastes." *Far Eastern Economic Review*, September 11, 2003, p. 40.
39. Allana Sullivan, "Mobil Bets Drivers Pick Cappuccino over Parties." *Wall Street Journal*, January 30, 1995.
40. Chester Dawson and David Welch, "Honda's First U.S. Bruiser." *BusinessWeek*, December 27, 2004, pp. 28–29.
41. Clay Chandler, "Mickey Mao." *Fortune*, April 18, 2005, pp. 60–66.
42. This classification was adapted from George H. Brown, *"Brand Loyalty: Fact or Fiction?" Advertising Age*, June 1952–January 1953, a series. See also Peter E. Rossi, R. McCulloch, and G. Allenby, *"The Value of Purchase History Data in Target Marketing." Marketing Science*, 1996, 15(4), pp. 321–340.
43. "China Marketing: Cracking the Code." *BusinessWeek*, June 6, 2007.
44. Chip Walker, "How Strong is Your Brand." *Marketing Tools*, January/February 1995, pp. 46–53.
45. <www.conversionmodel.com>.
46. Daniel Yankelovich and David Meer, "Rediscovering Market Segmentation." *Harvard Business Review*, February 2006, pp. 122–131.
47. Shawn W. Crispin, "Tiger Bikes Do a Roaring Trade." *Far Eastern Economic Review*, October 19, 2003, pp. 42.
48. Wendell R. Smith, "Product Differentiation and Market Segmentation as Alternative Marketing Strategies." *Journal of Marketing*, July 1956, p. 4.
49. <www.esteelauder.com>.
50. Russell Flannery, "As Went IBM, So Goes Legend." *Forbes Global*, February 4, 2002, pp. 30–32.
51. "Hyundai Motor: A Better Drive," *Economist*, May 21, 2005, pp. 61–62.
52. Marc Gunther, "Tree Huggers, Soy Lovers, and Profits." *Fortune*, June 23, 2003, pp. 98–104.
53. Bart Macchiette and Roy Abhijit, "Sensitive Groups and Social Issues." *Journal of Consumer Marketing*, 1994, 11(4), pp. 55–64.

Chapter 9

1. "How Good is Google?" *Economist*, November 21, 2003, pp. 57–58; Fred Vogelstein, "Can Google Grow Up?" *Fortune*, December 8, 2003, pp. 102–111; Paul R. La Monica, "MSN-Yahoo: Watch out Google." <www.cnnmoney.com>, May 4, 2007; "Google Troubled by Microsoft Move." <www.news.bbc.co.uk>, February 4, 2008.
2. Interbrand Group, *World's Greatest Brands: An International Review*, (New York: John Wiley, 1992).
3. Jacob Jacoby, Jerry C. Olson, and Rafael Haddock, "Price, Brand Name, and Product Composition Characteristics as Determinants of Perceived Quality." *Journal of Consumer Research*, 1971, 3(4), pp. 209–216; Jacob Jacoby, George Syzbillo, and Jacqueline Busato-Sehach, "Information Acquisition Behavior in Brand Choice Situations." *Journal of Marketing Research*, 1977, pp. 63–69.
4. Leslie de Chernatony and Gil McWilliam, "The Varying Nature of Brands as Assets." *International Journal of Advertising*, 1989, 8(4), pp. 339–349.
5. Constance E. Bagley, *Managers and the Legal Environment: Strategies for the 21st Century*, 2nd ed., (Cincinnati, OH West Publishing, 1995).
6. Tulin Erdem, "Brand Equity as a Signaling Phenomenon." *Journal of Consumer Psychology*, 1998, 7(2), pp. 131–157.

7. Scott Davis, *Brand Asset Management: Driving Profitable Growth Through Your Brands,* (San Francisco: Jossey-Bass, 2000); D. C. Bello and M. B. Holbrook, "Does an Absence of Brand Equity Generalize Across Product Classes?" *Journal of Business Research*, 1996, 34, pp. 125–131; Mary W. Sullivan, "How Brand Names Affect the Demand for Twin Automobiles." *Journal of Marketing Research,* 1998, 35, pp. 154–165; Adrian J. Slywotzky and Benson P. Shapiro, "Leveraging to Beat the Odds: The New Marketing Mindset." *Harvard Business Review*, September–October 1993, pp. 97–107.

8. The power of branding is not without its critics, however, some of whom reject the commercialism associated with branding activities. See Naomi Klein, *No Logo: Taking Aim at the Brand Bullies,* (Picador, New York, 2000).

9. "Chinese Consumers are Brand Conscious When It Comes to Drugs and Health Supplements Purchase." <www.acnielsen.com>, May 12, 2005.

10. Charles Bymer, "Valuing Your Brands: Lessons from Wall Street and the Impact on Marketers." *ARF Third Annual Advertising and Promotion Workshop*, February 5-6, 1991.

11. Francine Brevetti, "Realigning Public Perceptions." *Asian Business*, December 1995, pp. 41–43.

12. "The Five Challenges for Asian Brands." *I.E. Journal*, February 2005, 18, pp. 24–25.

13. Other approaches are based on economic principles of signaling (e.g., Tulin Erdem, "Brand Equity as a Signaling Phenomenon") or more of a sociological, anthropological, or biological perspective (e.g., Grant McCracken, "Culture and Consumption: A Theoretical Account of the Structure and Movement of the Cultural Meaning of Consumer Goods." *Journal of Consumer Research*, 1986, 13, pp. 71–83; or Susan Fournier, "Consumers and Their Brands: Developing Relationship Theory in Consumer Research." *Journal of Consumer Research*, 1998, 24(3), pp. 343–373).

14. David A. Aaker, *Managing Brand Equity,* (New York: Free Press, 1991); David A. Aaker, *Building Strong Brands*, (New York: Free Press, 1996); David A. Aaker and Erich Joachimsthaler, *Brand Leadership*, (New York: Free Press, 2000); Kevin Lane Keller, *Strategic Brand Management*, 3rd ed., (Upper Saddle River, NJ: Prentice Hall, 2008).

15. Jean-Noel Kapferer, *Strategic Brand Management: New Approaches to Creating and Evaluating Brand Equity*, (London: Kogan Page, 1992): p. 38; Jennifer L. Aaker, "Dimensions of Brand Personality." *Journal of Marketing Research,* August 1997, pp. 347–356; Scott Davis, *Brand Asset Management: Driving Profitable Growth Through Your Brands*. For an overview of academic research on branding, see Kevin Lane Keller, "Branding and Brand Equity." In *Handbook of Marketing*, Bart Weitz and Robin Wensley, eds., (Sage Publications, 2002), pp. 151–178.

16. Kevin Lane Keller, *Strategic Brand Management*, 3rd ed., (Upper Saddle River, NJ: Prentice Hall, 2008).

17. Alfred Siew, "It's All about Branding, Creative." *Straits Times* (Singapore), July 28, 2005, pp. 1–2; Alice Z. Cuneo, "Apple Transcends as Lifestyle Brand." *Advertising Age*, June 15, 2003, pp. S2, S6; Andrea Tan, "Creative Technology Posts Net Income Mark." *Bloomberg News*, January 31, 2007.

18. Douglas Holt, *How Brands Become Icons: The Principle of Cultural Branding*, (Cambridge, MA: Harvard Business School Press, 2004); Douglas Holt, "Branding as Cultural Activism." <zibs.com>; Douglas Holt, "What Becomes an Icon Most." *Harvard Business Review*, March 2003, 81, pp. 43–49.

19. Stuart Elliott, "Letting Consumers Control Marketing: Priceless." *New York Times*, October 9, 2006; Elizabeth Holmes, "On MySpace, Millions of Users Make 'Friends' with Ads." *Wall Street Journal*, August 7, 2006.

20. "The 100 Top Brands," *BusinessWeek*, August 6, 2007, pp. 59–64.

21. Ian Batey, *Asian Branding: A Great Way to Fly*, (Singapore: Prentice Hall, 2002). Another regional branding perspective is offered by ad agency Ogilvy & Mather. See also Mark Blair, Richard Armstrong, and Mike Murphy, *The 360 Degree Brand in Asia*, (Singapore: John Wiley, 2003).

22. Alysha Webb, "China's Next Stars?" *Fortune*, September 16, 2002, p. 45.

23. Ibrid. Lawrence Chung, "Taiwan Catches Tsingtao Fever." *Sunday Times* (Singapore), September 1, 2002, p. 14; Dexter Roberts, "China's Power Brands." *BusinessWeek*, Asian Edition, November 8, 2004, pp. 50–56; "Tsingtao Brewery Profit Up." <www.ce.cn>, August 23, 2005.

24. David A. Aaker, *Building Strong Brands*, (New York: Free Press, 1996).

25. Kevin Lane Keller, "Building Customer-Based Brand Equity: A Blueprint for Creating Strong Brands." *Marketing Management*, July/August 2001, 10, pp. 15–19.

26. Rachel Dodes, "From Tracksuits to Fast Track." *Wall Street Journal*, September 13, 2006.

27. Allen T. Cheng, "The Mainland's Sneaker King." *Time*, August 5, 2002; "Li-Ning Signs NBA star Damon Jones." *China Daily*, January 11, 2006; Dexter Roberts, "Don't Know Li-Ning? Ask Shaq." *BusinessWeek*, October 6, 2007.

28. Douglas MacMillan, "What's in a Name?" *BusinessWeek*, July 6, 2007.

29. Ibid.

30. "For Global Hyatt Corp., Success in the Middle Kingdom means Peddling Luxury to a Rapidly Emerging Moneyed Class." *Crain's Chicago Business*, June 26, 2006, 29(26), p. 20, <www.chicagobusiness.com/cgi-bin/article.pl?article_id=26057>.

31. "Omnicom and China's Tsinghua University Join Hands on Naming Project." *PR Newswire*, April 5, 2004.

32. Doris Ho, "Naming: Entering the Chinese Market." <www.brandchannel.com/features_effect.asp?pf_id=274>, August 1, 2005.

33. Fatimah Hashim, "Dutch Baby Changes Name to Dutch Lady." *Business Times* (Malaysia), May 5, 2000.

34. Han Shih Toh, "Starbucks Sues in Shanghai Café Sign Spat." <www.scmp.com>, January 31, 2004.

35. "Johnson & Johnson Loses Trademark Battle." *Xinhua News Agency*, December 24, 2003.

36. Evan Ramstad, "A Legend Passes: Chinese Company Takes New Name." *Wall Street Journal*, April 1, 2004, p. B6.

37. Kim Robertson, "Strategically Desirable Brand Name Characteristics." *Journal of Consumer Marketing*, Fall 1989, pp. 61–70; C. Kohli and D. W. LaBahn, "Creating Effective Brand Names: A Study of the Naming Process." *Journal of Advertising Research*, January/February 1997, pp. 67–75.

38. Robert Salerno, "We Try Harder: An Ad Creates a Brand." *BrandWeek*, September 8, 2003, pp. 32, 33.

39. Don E. Schultz, Stanley I. Tannenbaum, and Robert F. Lauterborn, *Integrated Marketing Communications*, (Lincolnwood IL, NTC Business Books, 1993).

40. Mohanbir Sawhney, "Don't Harmonize, Synchronize." *Harvard Business Review*, July–August 2001, pp. 101–108.

41. Christopher Locke, Rick Levine, Doc Searls, and David Weinberger, *The Cluetrain Manifesto: The End of Business as Usual*, (Cambridge MA: Perseus Press, 2000).

42. Susan Fournier, "Consumers and Their Brands: Developing Relationship Theory in Consumer Research." *Journal of Consumer Research*, March 1998, pp. 343–373.

43. The subsequent discussion draws from Visa International (Asia Pacific) Consulting and Peppers & Rogers Group (Asia), *One to One in Retail Financial Services*, January 2002.

44. Dawn Iacobucci and Bobby Calder, eds., *Kellogg on Integrated Marketing*, (New York: John Wiley, 2003).

45. "China Fashion Lacks Big Names." *Streats* (Singapore), September 22, 2004, p. 17.

46. Pete Engardio, "Taking a Brand Name Higher." *BusinessWeek*, July 31, 2006, p. 48; Rob Walker, "Haier Goals." *New York Times Magazine*, November 20, 2005.

47. Scott Davis and Michael Dunn, *Building the Brand Driven Business*, (New York: John Wiley, 2002); Colin Mitchell, "Selling the Brand Inside." *Harvard Business Review*, January 2002, pp. 99–105.

48. Stan Maklan and Simon Knox, *Competing On Value*, (Upper Saddle River, NJ: Financial Times Prentice Hall, 2000).

49. The principles and examples from this passage are based on Colin Mitchell, "Selling the Brand Inside." *Harvard Business Review*, January 2002, pp. 99–105. For an in-depth discussion of how two organizations, QuikTrip and Wawa, have developed stellar internal branding programs, see Neeli Bendapudi and Venkat Bendapudi, "Creating the Living Brand." *Harvard Business Review*, May 2005, pp. 124–132.

50. Terence H. Witkowski, Yulong Ma, and Dan Zheng, "Cross-Cultural Influences on Brand Identity Impressions: KFC in China and the United States." *Asia Pacific Journal of Marketing and Logistics*, 2003, 15(1/2), pp. 74–88.

51. David A. Aaker, *Building Strong Brands*, (New York: Free Press, 1996). Also see Patrick Barwise et al, *Accounting for Brands*, (London: Institute of Chartered Accountants in England and Wales, 1990); Peter H. Farquhar, Julia Y. Han, and Yuji Ijiri, "Brands on the Balance Sheet." *Marketing Management*, Winter 1992, pp. 16–22.

52. Geoffrey A. Fowler, "From No Name to Brand Name." *Far Eastern Economic Review*, April 8, 2004, pp. 32–34.

53. David Kiley, "To Boost Sales, Volvo Returns to Its Roots: Safety." *USA Today*, August 26, 2002, p. 6B.

54. Natalie Mizik and Robert Jacobson, "Trading Off Between Value Creation and Value Appropriation: The Financial Implications of Shifts in Strategic Emphasis." *Journal of Marketing*, January 2003, 67, pp. 63–76.

55. Mark Speece, "Marketer's Malady: Fear of Change." *BrandWeek*, August 19, 2002.

56. Peter Farquhar, "Managing Brand Equity." *Marketing Research*, September 1989, 1, pp. 24–33.

57. Geoffrey A. Fowler and Ramin Setoodeh, "A Question of Taste." *Far Eastern Economic Review*, August 12, 2004, pp. 32–33.

58. Steven M. Shugan, "Branded Variants." *1989 AMA Educators' Proceedings* (Chicago: American Marketing Association, 1989), pp. 33–38; M. Bergen, S. Dutta, and S.M. Shugan, "Branded Variants: A Retail Perspective." *Journal of Marketing Research*, February 1996, 33, pp. 9–21.

59. Dan Reed, "Low-fare Rivals Keep a Close Eye on Song." *USA Today*, November 25, 2003, p. 6B.

60. Byung-Do Kim and Mary W. Sullivan, "The Effect of Parent Brand Experience on Line Extension Trial and Repeat Purchase." *Marketing Letters*, April 1998, 9, pp. 181–193.

61. Anil Wanvari, "Flour-Maker Beats a Path toward Progress." *Asian Advertising & Marketing*, December 1995, p. 22.

62. Kevin Lane Keller and David A. Aaker, "The Effects of Sequential Introduction of Brand Extensions." *Journal of Marketing Research*, February 1992, 29, pp. 35–50; John Milewicz and Paul Herbig, "Evaluating the Brand Extension Decision Using a Model of Reputation Building." *Journal of Product & Brand Management*, 1994, 3(1), pp. 39–47.

63. Mary W. Sullivan, "Brand Extensions: When to Use Them." *Management Science*, June 1992, 38(6), pp. 793–806; Daniel C. Smith, "Brand Extension and Advertising Efficiency: What Can and Cannot Be Expected." *Journal of Advertising Research*, November/December 1992, pp. 11–20. See also Daniel C. Smith and C. Whan Park, "The Effects of Brand Extensions on Market Share and Advertising Efficiency." *Journal of Marketing Research*, August 1992, 29, pp. 296–313.

64. Bruce Meyer, "Rubber Firms Extend Brands to Gain Customers, Revenue." *B to B*, October 10, 2005, 90(12), p. 6.

65. Subramanian Balachander and Sanjoy Ghose, "Reciprocal Spillover Effects: A Strategic Benefit of Brand Extensions." *Journal of Marketing*, January 2003, 67(1), pp. 4–13.

66. John A. Quelch and David Kenny, "Extend Profits, Not Product Lines." *Harvard Business Review*, September–October 1994, pp. 153–160; Bruce G. S. Hardle, Leonard M. Lodish, James V. Kilmer, and David R. Beatty et al, "The Logic of Product-Line Extensions." *Harvard Business Review*, November–December 1994, pp. 53–62; J. Andrews and G. S. Low, "New But Not Improved: Factors That Affect the Development of Meaningful Line Extensions." Working Paper Report No. 98–124,(Cambridge, MA: Marketing Science Institute, November 1998); Maureen Morrin, "The Impact of Brand Extensions on Parent Brand Memory Structures and Retrieval Processes." *Journal of Marketing Research*, 1999, 36(4), pp. 517–525.

67. Al Ries and Jack Trout, *Positioning: The Battle for Your Mind*, The 20th Anniversary Edition, (New York: McGraw-Hill, 2000).

68. David A. Aaker, *Brand Portfolio Strategy: Creating Relevance, Differentiation, Energy, Leverage, and Clarity*, (New York: Free Press, 2004).

69. Barbara Loken and Deborah Roedder John, "Diluting Brand Beliefs: When Do Brand Extensions Have a Negative Impact?" *Journal of Marketing*, July 1993, pp. 71–84; Deborah Roedder John, Barbara Loken, and Christopher Joiner, "The Negative Impact of Extensions: Can Flagship Products Be Diluted." *Journal of Marketing*, January 1998, pp. 19–32; Susan M. Broniarcyzk and Joseph W. Alba, "The Importance of the Brand in Brand Extension." *Journal of Marketing Research*, May 1994, pp. 214–228 (this entire issue of *JMR* is devoted to brands and brand equity). See also R. Ahluwalia and Z. Gürhan-Canli, "The Effects of Extensions on the Family Brand Name: An Accessibility-Diagnosticity Perspective." *Journal of Consumer Research*, December 2000, 27, pp. 371–381; Z. Gürhan-Canli and M. Durairaj, "The Effects of Extensions on Brand Name Dilution and Enhancement." *Journal of Marketing Research*, 1998, 35, pp. 464–473; S. J. Milberg, C. W. Park, and M. S. McCarthy, "Managing Negative Feedback Effects Associated with Brand Extensions: The Impact of Alternative Branding Strategies." *Journal of Consumer Psychology*, 1997, 6, pp. 119–140.

70. See also, Franziska Völckner and Henrik Sattler, "Drivers of Brand Extension Success." *Journal of Marketing*, April 2006, 70, pp. 1–17.

71. Andrea Rothman, "France's Bic Bets U.S. Consumers Will Go for Perfume on the Cheap." *Wall Street Journal*, January 12, 1989, p. B6.

72. Philip Kotler, *Marketing Management*, 13th ed., (Upper Saddle River, NJ: Prentice Hall, 2008); Patrick Barwise and Thomas Robertson, "Brand Portfolios." *European Management Journal*, September 1992, 10(3), pp. 277–285.

73. Jack Trout, *Differentiate or Die: Survival in Our Era of Killer Competition*, (New York: John Wiley, 2000).

74. Nirmalya Kumar, "Kill a Brand, Keep a Customer." *Harvard Business Review*, December 2003, pp. 87–95.

75. For a methodological approach for assessing the extent and nature of cannibalization, see Charlotte H. Mason and George R. Milne, "An Approach for Identifying Cannibalization within Product Line Extensions and MultiBrand Strategies." *Journal of Business Research*, October–November 1994, 31, pp. 163–170.

76. Roland T. Rust, Valerie A. Zeithaml, and Katherine A. Lemon, "Measuring Customer Equity and Calculating Marketing ROI." In *Handbook of Marketing Research*, Rajiv Grover and Marco Vriens, eds., (Thousand Oaks, CA: Sage Publications, 2006), pp. 588–601; Roland T. Rust, Valerie A. Zeithaml, and Katherine A. Lemon, *Driving Customer Equity*, (New York: Free Press, 2000).
77. Robert C. Blattberg and John Deighton, "Manage Marketing by the Customer Equity Test." *Harvard Business Review* (July–August 1996): pp. 136–144.
78. Robert C. Blattberg and Jacquelyn S. Thomas, "Valuing, Analyzing, and Managing the Marketing Function using Customer Equity Principles." In *Kellogg on Marketing,* Dawn Iacobucci, ed., (New York: John Wiley, 2002); Robert C. Blattberg, Gary Getz, and Jacquelyn S. Thomas, *Customer Equity: Building and Managing Relationships as Valuable Assets*, (Boston: Harvard Business School Press, 2001).
79. Much of this section is based on Robert Leone, Vithala Rao, Kevin Lane Keller, Man Luo, Leigh McAlister, and Rajendra Srivatstava, "Linking Brand Equity to Customer Equity." *Journal of Service Research*, November 2006, 9, pp. 125–138. This special issue is devoted to customer equity and has a number of thought-provoking articles.
80. Niraj Dawar, "What Are Brands Good For?" *MIT Sloan Management Review*, Fall 2004, pp. 31–37.

Chapter 10

1. Michael J. Silverstein and Neil Fiske, *Trading Up: The New American Luxury*, (New York: Portfolio, 2003); Dylan Machan, "Sharing Victoria's Street." *Forbes*, June 5, 1995, p. 132.
2. David Evans, "A Company By Any Other Name ..." *South China Morning Post*, December 5, 2000.
3. Cris Prystay, "Gadget-Driven Lifestyles." *Far Eastern Economic Review*, August 26, 2004, p. 54.
4. Alice M. Tybout and Brian Sternthal, "Brand Positioning." In *Kellogg on Marketing*, Dawn Iacobucci, ed.,(New York: John Wiley, 2001).
5. "Differentiation the Key to Success for Chain Stores Facing Intensified Competition in China: A.C.Nielsen." <www.acnielsen.com.cn>, April 24, 2004.
6. Jim Hopkins, "When the Devil is in the Design." *USA Today*, December 31, 2001, p. 3B.
7. Keith Naughton, "Ford's 'Perfect Storm.'" *Newsweek*, September 17, 2001, pp. 48–50.
8. Gregory S. Carpenter, Rashi Glazer, and Kent Nakamoto, "Meaningful Brands from Meaningless Differentiation: The Dependence on Irrelevant Attributes." *Journal of Marketing Research*, August 1994, pp. 339–350.
9. Cecilie Rohwedder, "Playing Down the Plaid." *Wall Street Journal*, July 7, 2006, <http://online.wsj.com/article_print/SB115222828906800109.html>; David Kiley, "Best Global Brands," *BusinessWeek*, August 6, 2007.
10. For a similar list, see Leonard L. Berry and A. Parasuraman, *Marketing Services: Competing Through Quality,* (New York: The Free Press, 1991), p. 16.
11. Sarah Fister Gale, "The Bookstore Battle." *Workforce Management*, January 2004, pp. 51–53.
12. Willow Duttge, "Counting sleep." *Advertising Age,* June 5, 2006, p. 4, 50.
13. *Fortune*, April 17, 2006; Katrina Brooker, "The Chairman of the Board Looks Back." *Fortune*, May 28, 2001.
14. Neel Chowdhury, "Dell Cracks China." *Fortune*, June 21, 1999, pp. 32–36; see also Bruce Einhorn, "Will Dell Click in Asia?" *BusinessWeek Online*, April 22, 2002.
15. Some authors distinguished additional stages. Wasson suggested a stage of competitive turbulence between growth and maturity. See Chester R. Wasson, *Dynamic Competitive Strategy and Product Life Cycles*, (Austin, TX: Austin Press, 1978). Maturity describes a stage of sales growth slowdown and saturation, a stage of flat sales after sales have peaked.
16. John E. Swan and David R. Rink, "Fitting Market Strategy to Varying Product Life Cycles." *Business Horizons*, January–February 1982, pp. 72–76; Gerard J. Tellis and C. Merle Crawford, "An Evolutionary Approach to Product Growth Theory." *Journal of Marketing*, Fall 1981, pp. 125–134.
17. William E. Cox Jr., "Product Life Cycles as Marketing Models." *Journal of Business*, October 1967, pp. 375–384.
18. Jordan P. Yale, "The Strategy of Nylon's Growth." *Modern Textiles Magazine*, February 1964, p. 32. See also Theodore Levitt, "Exploit the Product Life Cycle." *Harvard Business Review*, November–December 1965, pp. 81–94.
19. Chester R. Wasson, "How Predictable Are Fashion and Other Product Life Cycles?" *Journal of Marketing,* July 1968, pp. 36–43.

20. Ibid.
21. William H. Reynolds, "Cars and Clothing: Understanding Fashion Trends." *Journal of Marketing*, July 1968, pp. 44–49.
22. *TechJapan*, August 13, 2005.
23. Robert D. Buzzell, "Competitive Behavior and Product Life Cycles." In *New Ideas for Successful Marketing*, John S. Wright and Jack Goldstucker, eds., (Chicago: American Marketing Association, 1956), p. 51.
24. Rajesh J. Chandy, Gerard J. Tellis, Deborah J. MacInnis, and Pattana Thaivanich, "What to Say When: Advertising Appeals in Evolving Markets." *Journal of Marketing Research*, November 2001, 38, pp. 399–414.
25. William T. Robinson and Claes Fornell, "Sources of Market Pioneer Advantages in Consumer Goods Industries." *Journal of Marketing Research*, August 1985, pp. 305–317; Glen L. Urban et al, "Market Share Rewards to Pioneering Brands: An Empirical Analysis and Strategic Implications." *Management Science*, June 1986, pp. 645–659.
26. Gregory S. Carpenter and Kent Nakamoto, "Consumer Preference Formation and Pioneering Advantage." *Journal of Marketing Research*, August 1989, pp. 285–298.
27. William T. Robinson and Sungwook Min, "Is the First to Market the First to Fail? Empirical Evidence for Industrial Goods Businesses." *Journal of Marketing Research*, February 2002, 39, pp. 120–128.
28. Frank R. Kardes, Gurumurthy Kalyanaram, Murali Chankdrashekaran, and Ronald J. Dornoff, "Brand Retrieval, Consideration Set Composition, Consumer Choice, and the Pioneering Advantage." *Journal of Consumer Research*, June 1993, pp. 62–75. See also Frank H. Alpert and Michael A. Kamins, "Pioneer Brand Advantage and Consumer Behavior: A Conceptual Framework and Propositional Inventory." *Journal of the Academy of Marketing Science*, Summer 1994, pp. 244–253.
29. Thomas S. Robertson and Hubert Gatignon, "How Innovators Thwart New Entrants into Their Market." *Planning Review*, September–October 1991, pp. 4–11, 48; Douglas Bowman and Hubert Gatignon, "Order of Entry as a Moderator of the Effect of Marketing Mix on Market Share." *Marketing Science*, 1996, 15(3), pp. 222–242.
30. Yadong Kuo, "Pioneering in China: Risks and Benefits." *Long Range Planning*, 1997, 59(5), pp. 768–776.
31. Venkatesh Shankar, Gregory S. Carpenter, Lakshman Krishnamurthi, "Late Mover Advantage: How Innovative Late Entrants Outsell Pioneers." *Journal of Marketing Research*, February 1998, 35, pp. 54–70.
32. Dexter Roberts, Moon Ihlwan, Ian Rowley, and Gail Edmondsen, "GM and VW: How Not to Succeed in China." *BusinessWeek*, May 9, 2005, pp. 18–19; Gordon Fairclough, "GM-China Joint Venture Offers No-interest Loans." *Wall Street Journal*, August 22, 2007; Tian Ying, "Volkswagen Considers China Expansion." *International Herald Tribune*, October 16, 2007.
33. Steven P. Schnaars, *Managing Imitation Strategies*, (New York: The Free Press, 1994). See also Jin K. Han, Namwoon Kim, and Hony-Bom Kin, "Entry Barriers: A Dull-, One-, or Two-Edged Sword for Incumbents? Unraveling the Paradox from a Contingency Perspective." *Journal of Marketing*, January 2001, pp. 1–14.
34. Victor Kegan, "Second Sight: Second Movers Take All." *Guardian*, October 10, 2002.
35. Peter N. Golder and Gerard J. Tellis, "Pioneer Advantage: Marketing Logic or Marketing Legend?" *Journal of Marketing Research*, May 1992, pp. 34–46; Shi Zhang and Arthur B. Markman, "Overcoming the Early Advantage: The Role of Alignable and Nonalignable Differences." *Journal of Marketing Research*, November 1998, pp. 1–15.
36. Gerard Tellis and Peter Golder, *Will & Vision: How Latecomers Can Grow to Dominate Markets*, (New York: McGraw-Hill, 2001); Rajesh K. Chandy and Gerard J. Tellis, "The Incumbent's Curse? Incumbency, Size, and Radical Product Innovation." *Journal of Marketing Research*, July 2000, pp. 1–17.
37. Sungwook Min, Manohar U. Kalwani, and William T. Robinson, "Market Pioneer and Early Follower Survival Risks: A Contingency Analysis of Really New Versus Incrementally New Product-Markets." *Journal of Marketing*, January 2006, 70, pp. 15–35. See also Raji Srinivasan, Gary L. Lilien, and Arvind Rangaswamy, "First In, First Out? The Effects of Network Externalities on Pioneer Survival." *Journal of Marketing*, January 2004, 68, pp. 41–58.
38. Linda Himelstein, "Yahoo! The Company, the Strategy, the Stock." *BusinessWeek*, September 7, 1998, pp. 66–76; Marc Gunther, "The Cheering Fades for Yahoo." *Fortune*, November 12, 2001; Ben Elgin, "Inside Yahoo! The Untold Story of How Arrogance, Infighting, and Management Missteps Derailed One of the Hottest Companies on the Web." *BusinessWeek*, May 21, 2001, p. 114; Ben Elgin, "The Search War Is About to Get Bloody." *BusinessWeek*, July 28, 2003, pp. 72–73.
39. Trond Riiber Knudsen, "Escaping the Middle-Market Trap: An Interview with CEO of Electrolux." *McKinsey Quarterly*, December 2006, pp. 72–79.

40. Malini Rajendran, Simon Reeve, Carol Hui, and Francoise Joaquin, "Tigers—By Any Other Name." *Asia Magazine*, March 21–23, 1997, pp. 10–14; <www.tigerbalm.com>; Lea Wee, "Earning Its Stripes." *Straits Times* (Singapore), December 10, 2002, p. L20.

41. Brain Wansink and Michael L. Ray, "Advertising Strategies to Increase Usage Frequency." *Journal of Marketing,* January 1996, pp. 31–46. See also Brain Wansink, "Expansion Advertising," in *How Advertising Works,* John Philip Jones, ed., (Thousand Oaks, CA: Sage Publications) pp. 95–103.

42. David Rocks, "Making 3G Look As Slow As Smoke Signals." *BusinessWeek*, November 15, 2004, p. 40; Ian Rowley, "$5,000? Put It On My Cell." *BusinessWeek*, June 6, 2005, pp. 18–19; "Steering DoCoMo Out of the Doldrums." *BusinessWeek*, July 25/August 1, 2005, p. 19; Penn Nee Chow, "Shopping Mall on Your Mobile Phone." *Today* (Singapore), October 15–16, 2005, p. 30.

43. Stephen M. Nowlis and Itamar Simonson, "The Effect of New Product Features on Brand Choice." *Journal of Marketing Research*, February 1996, pp. 36–46.

44. David Rocks and Chen Wu, "A Phoenix Named Flying Pigeon." *BusinessWeek*, September 20, 2004, p. 26.

45. Philip Kotler, "Phasing Out Weak Products." *Harvard Business Review*, March–April 1965, pp. 107–118; Richard T. Hise, A. Parasuraman, and R. Viswanathan, "Product Elimination: The Neglected Management Responsibility." *Journal of Business Strategy*, Spring 1984, pp. 56–63; George J. Avlonitis, "Product Elimination Decision Making: Does Formality Matter?" *Journal of Marketing*, Winter 1985, pp. 41–52.

46. Kathryn Rudie Harrigan, "The Effect of Exit Barriers upon Strategic Flexibility." *Strategic Management Journal*, 1, 1980, pp. 165–176.

47. Philip Kotler, "Harvesting Strategies for Weak Products." *Business Horizons*, August 1978, pp. 15–22; Laurence P. Feldman and Albert L. Page, "Harvesting: The Misunderstood Market Exit Strategy." *Journal of Business Strategy*, Spring 1985, pp. 79–85.

48. Peter N. Golder and Gerard J. Tellis, "Growing, Growing, Gone: Cascades, Diffusion, and Turning Points in the Product Life Cycle." *Marketing Science*, Spring 2004, 23, pp. 207–18.

49. Youngme Moon, "Break Free from the Product Life Cycle." *Harvard Business Review*, May 2005, pp. 87–94.

50. Robert D. Buzzell, "Market Functions and Market Evolution." *Journal of Marketing*, 1999, 63, Special Issue, pp. 61–63.

51. For a discussion of the evolution of the minivan market between 1982 and 1998, see Jose Antonio Rosa, Joseph F. Porac, Jelena Runser-Spanjol, and Michael S. Saxon, "Sociocognitive Dynamics in a Product Market." *Journal of Marketing*, 1999, 63, Special Issue, pp. 64–77.

52. Daniel Fisher, "Six Feet Under." *Forbes*, July 7, 2003, pp. 66–68.

Chapter 11

1. "Toshiba Quits HD DVD 'Format War'." <www.cnn.com>, February 21, 2008.

2. Leonard M. Fuld, *The New Competitor Intelligence: The Complete Resource for Finding, Analyzing, and Using Information about Your Competitors*, (New York: John Wiley, 1995); John A. Czepiel, *Competitive Marketing Strategy*, (Upper Saddle River, NJ: Prentice Hall, 1992).

3. Chester Dawson, "An Endurance Test for Japanese Carmakers." *BusinessWeek*, April 26, 2004, p. 19; Ian Rowley, "Toyota Set to Top 50% Market Share in Japan." *BusinessWeek*, <www.businessweek.com/autos/autobeat/archives/2007/11/toyota_tops_50.html>.

4. Michael E. Porter, *Competitive Strategy*, (New York: The Free Press, 1980), pp. 22–23.

5. Sheridan Prasso, "India's Pizza Wars." *Fortune*, October 1, 2007, 156(7), p. 61.

6. Tarun Khanna and Krishna G. Palepu, "Emerging Giants." *Harvard Business Review*, October 2006, 84(10), pp. 60–69.

7. Ibid.

8. Allan D. Shocker, "Determining the Structure of Product-Markets: Practices, Issues, and Suggestions." In Barton A. Weitz and Robin Wensley, eds., *Handbook of Marketing*, (London, UK: Sage Publications, 2002), pp. 106–125. See also Bruce H. Clark and David B. Montgomery, "Managerial Identification of Competitors." *Journal of Marketing*, July 1999, 63, pp. 67–83.

9. For some definitions, see Peter D. Bennett, ed., *Dictionary of Marketing Terms* (Chicago, IL: American Marketing Association, 1995). Also see, Patrick E. Murphy and Ben M. Enis, "Classifying Products Strategically." *Journal of Marketing*, July 1986, pp. 24–42.

10. Some of these bases are discussed in David A. Garvin, "Competing on the Eight Dimensions of Quality." *Harvard Business Review*, November–December 1987, pp. 101–109.

11. Michael Porter, *Competitive Strategy*, (New York: The Free Press,1980), chapter 7.
12. William E. Rothschild, *How to Gain (and Maintain) the Competitive Advantage*, (New York: McGraw-Hill, 1989), chapter 5.
13. Sarah Skidmore, "Nike and Adidas Gear Up for Olympics Shoe Wars." *International Herald Tribune*, October 4, 2007.
14. Michael Porter, *Competitive Strategy,* (New York: The Free Press,1980), chapter 7.
15. Bruce Nussbaum, "The Power of Design." *BusinessWeek*, May 17, 2004, pp. 88–94; "Masters of Design." *Fast Company*, June 2004, pp. 61–75. Also see Philip Kotler, "Design: A Powerful but Neglected Strategic Tool." *Journal of Business Strategy*, Fall 1984, pp. 16–21.
16. Michael Barbaro and Hillary Chura, "The Gap Is in Need of a Niche." *New York Times*, January 27, 2007.
17. <www.starbucks.com/aboutus/overview.asp>.
18. Brian Wansink, "Can Package Size Accelerate Usage Volume?" *Journal of Marketing*, July 1996, 60, pp. 1–14.
19. Elizabeth Jensen, "Wine Gets a Makeover: A Complex Zinfandel Becomes a Power 'Zin'." *Wall Street Journal*, October 14, 1997, pp. A1, A6.
20. John D. Cripps, "Heuristics and Biases in Timing the Replacement of Durable Products." *Journal of Consumer Research*, September 1994, 21, pp. 304–318.
21. "Business Bubbles." *Economist*, October 12, 2002.
22. Carla Rapoport, "You Can Make Money in Japan." *Fortune*, February 12, 1990, pp. 85–92; Keith H. Hammonds, "A Moment Kodak Wants to Capture." *BusinessWeek*, August 27, 1990, pp. 52–53; Alison Fahey, "Polaroid, Kodak, Fuji Get Clicking." *Advertising Age*, May 20, 1991, p. 18; Peter Nulty, "The New Look of Photography." *Fortune*, July 1, 1991, pp. 36–41.
23. Bruce Upbin, "Sharpening the Claws." *Forbes*, July 26, 1999, pp. 102–105.
24. Akio Morita, *Made in Japan*, (New York: Dutton, 1986), chapter 1.
25. Jonathan Glancey, "The Private World of the Walkman." *Guardian*, October 11, 1999.
26. The intensified competition that takes place worldwide has sparked management interest in models of military warfare; see Sun Tzu, *The Art of War*, (London: Oxford University Press, 1963); Miyamoto Mushashi, *A Book of Five Rings*, (Woodstock, NY: Overlook Press, 1974); Carl von Clausewitz, *On War*, (London: Routledge & Kegan Paul, 1908); B. H. Liddell-Hart, *Strategy*, (New York: Praeger, 1967).
27. These six defense strategies, as well as the five attack strategies, are taken from Philip Kotler and Ravi Singh, "Marketing Warfare in the 1980s." *Journal of Business Strategy*, Winter 1981, pp. 30–41. For additional reading, see Gerald A. Michaelson, *Winning the Marketing War: A Field Manual for Business Leaders*, (Lanham, MD: Abt Books, 1987); Al Ries and Jack Trout, *Marketing Warfare*, (New York: New American Library, 1986); Jay Conrad Levinson, *Guerrilla Marketing*, (Boston: Houghton-Mifflin Co., 1984); Barrie G. James, *Business Wargames*, (Harmondsworth, England: Penguin Books, 1984).
28. Ichiko Fuyuno, "Shiseido's Make-Over." *Far Eastern Economic Review*, May 22, 2003, p. 40.
29. Jehoshua Eliashberg and Thomas S. Robertson, "New Product Preannouncing Behavior: A Market Signaling Study." *Journal of Marketing Research*, August 1988, 25, pp. 282–292; Roger J. Calantone and Kim E. Schatzel, "Strategic Foretelling: Communication-Based Antecedents of a Firm's Propensity to Preannounce." *Journal of Marketing*, January 2000, 64, pp. 17–30.
30. Thomas S. Robertson, Jehoshua Eliashberg, and Talia Rymon, "New Product Announcement Signals and Incumbent Reactions." *Journal of Marketing*, July 1995, 59, pp. 1–15.
31. Barry L. Bayus, Sanjay Jain, and Ambar G. Rao, "Truth or Consequences: An Analysis of Vaporware and New Product Announcements." *Journal of Marketing Research*, February 2001, 38, pp. 3–13.
32. Bruce Einhorn, "DoCoMo vs A Mouse That's Roaring." *BusinessWeek*, April 19, 2004, pp. 20–21.
33. Fons Tuinstra, "Shampoo Wars: Why P&G is Way Ahead of Europe's Unilever in China." *Asiaweek*, January 21, 2000, pp. 48–50.
34. David Scheff, "Goodbaby's Growing Pains." *Fortune*, March 18, 2002, pp. 40–46; "Toy Firms Urged to Go More High-Tech." *China Daily,* June 20, 2002.
35. Brian Bremner, "Quenching a Thirst for New Markets." *BusinessWeek*, October 25, 2004, p. 24.
36. Gerry Kermouch, "Spiking the Booze Business." *BusinessWeek*, May 19, 2003, pp. 77–78.
37. Richard Tomlinson, "SABMiller vs Anheuser-Busch in China." *Fortune*, June 14, 2004, p. 30; "The Beers Are On Anheuser." *Economist*, June 5, 2004, p. 56; Ben Dolven, "Big Brewers Try, Try Again." *Far Eastern Economic Review*, July 22, 2004, pp. 32–34.

38. Philip Kotler and Paul N. Bloom, "Strategies for High Market-Share Companies." *Harvard Business Review*, November–December 1975, pp. 63–72. See also Michael Porter, *Competitive Advantage*, (New York: Free Press, 1980), pp. 221–226.
39. Robert J. Dolan, "Models of Competition: A Review of Theory and Empirical Evidence." In Ben M. Enis and Kenneth J. Roering, eds., *Review of Marketing*, (Chicago: American Marketing Association, 1981), pp. 224–234.
40. Robert D. Buzzell and Frederick D. Wiersema, "Successful Share-Building Strategies." *Harvard Business Review*, January–February 1981, pp. 135–144.
41. Linda Hellofs and Robert Jacobson, "Market Share and Customer's Perceptions of Quality: When Can Firms Grow Their Way to Higher Versus Lower Quality?" *Journal of Marketing*, January 1999, 63, pp. 16–25.
42. Ihlwan Moon and Cliff Edwards, "Samsung Inside?" *BusinessWeek*, October 25, 2004, pp. 22–23; Mark LePadus, "Winners, Losers in 2007 Chip Rankings." November 28, 2007, <www.mobilehandsetdesignline.com/news/204300417>.
43. Adam Lashinsky, "Saving Face at Sony." *Fortune*, February 21, 2005, pp. 47–52.
44. Dexter Roberts, "China's Power Brands." *BusinessWeek*, November 8, 2004, pp. 50–56.
45. Abby Klassen, "Search Davids Take Aim at Goliath Google." *Advertising Age*, January 8, 2007, p. 1+. Anonymous, "Cha-Cha – CEO Interview." *CEO Wire*, January 9, 2007.
46. Katrina Booker, "The Pepsi Machine." *Fortune*, February 6, 2006, pp. 68–72.
47. Eryn Brown, "Sony's Big Bazooka." *Fortune*, December 30, 2002, pp. 111–114.
48. Henny Sender, "Back From the Brink: Samsung Electronics Got Into Trouble By Being Like Many Asian Firms; It Survived By Being Different." *Wall Street Journal*, September 22, 2003, p. R.5.
49. Theodore Levitt, "Innovative Imitation." *Harvard Business Review*, September–October 1966, p. 63. See also Steven P. Schnaars, *Managing Imitation Strategies: How Later Entrants Seize Markets from Pioneers*, (New York: The Free Press, 1994).
50. John Liu and Chinmei Sung, "Fake: Phones Fill Gap Left by Apple." *International Herald Tribune*, September 11, 2007.
51. Allen J. McGrath, "Growth Strategies with a 90s Twist." *Across the Board*, March 1995, pp. 43–46; Antonio Ligi, "The Bottom Line: Logitech Plots Its Escape from Mouse Trap." *Dow Jones Newswire*, February 20, 2001.
52. Reported in E. R. Linneman and L. J. Stanton, *Making Niche Marketing Work*, (New York: McGraw-Hill, 1991).
53. Gerry Khermouch, "Richard Branson: Winning Virgin Territory." *BusinessWeek*, December 22, 2003, p. 45.
54. Robert Spector, *Amazon.com: Get Big Fast*, (New York: HarperBusiness, 2000), p. 151.

Chapter 12

1. Bruce Upbin, "Sharpening the Claws." *Forbes*, July 26, 1999, pp. 102–105.
2. This discussion is adapted from Theodore Levitt, "Marketing Success through Differentiation: Of Anything." *Harvard Business Review*, January–February 1980, pp. 83–91. The first level, core benefit, has been added to Levitt's discussion.
3. Martin Fackler, "Fearing Crime, Japanese Wear the Hiding Place." *New York Times*, October 19, 2007.
4. Jim Rohwer, "DoCoMo's Quiet and Powerful Keiji Tachikawa is Asia's Businessman of the Year." *Fortune*, Janaury 22, 2001, pp. 46, 48.
5. Harper W. Boyd Jr. and Sidney Levy, "New Dimensions in Consumer Analysis." *Harvard Business Review*, November–December 1963, pp. 129–140.
6. For some definitions, see *Dictionary of Marketing Terms*, Peter D. Bennett, ed., (Chicago, IL: American Marketing Association, 1995). See also Patrick E. Murphy and Ben M. Enis, "Classifying Products Strategically." *Journal of Marketing*, July 1986, pp. 24–42.
7. Some of these bases are discussed in David A. Garvin, "Competing on the Eight Dimensions of Quality." *Harvard Business Review*, November–December 1987, pp. 101–109.
8. Normandy Madden, "Pantene Shampoo is Reborn: Grey Pumps Up Hair Care Brand for a New Market." *Ad Age Global*, May 1, 2002, 2(9), p. 18.
9. John Murphy, "Japan's Young Won't Rally Round the Car." *Wall Street Journal*, February 29, 2008, p. B1.
10. James H. Gilmore and B. Joseph Pine, *Markets of One: Creating Customer-Unique Value through Mass Customization*, (Boston: Harvard Business School Press, 2000).

11. Stuart Elliot, "Letting Consumers Control Marketing: Priceless." *New York Times*, October 9, 2006.
12. Paul Grimaldi, "Consumers Design Products Their Way." *Knight Ridder Tribune Business News*, November 25, 2006; Michael A. Prospero, *Fast Company*, September 2005, p. 35.
13. Bernd Schmitt and Alex Simonson, *Marketing Aesthetics: The Strategic Management of Brand, Identity, and Image*, (New York: The Free Press, 1997).
14. Bernd Schmitt and Yigang Pan, "Managing Corporate and Brand Identities in the Asia-Pacific Region." *California Management Review*, Summer 1994, p. 43.
15. Bruce Nussbaum, "The Power of Design." *BusinessWeek*, May 17, 2004, pp. 88–94; "Masters of Design." *Fast Company*, June 2004, pp. 61–75. See also Philip Kotler, "Design: A Powerful but Neglected Strategic Tool." *Journal of Business Strategy*, Fall 1984, pp. 16–21.
16. Christopher Palmeri and Nanette Byrnes "Is Japanese Style Taking Over the World?" *BusinessWeek*, July 26, 2004, pp. 92–94.
17. Ibid. Greg Lindsay, "Bold Strokes." *Time*, Spring 2005, pp. 58–62.
18. Neel Chowdhury, "Dell Cracks China." *Fortune*, June 21, 1999, pp. 32–36.
19. Linda Knapp, "A Sick Computer?" *Seattle Times*, January 28, 2001, pp. D–8.
20. Leslie Earnest and Adrian G. Uribarri, "Costco Halts Liberal Electronics Return Policy; Refunds Were Costing the Warehouse Store Chain 'Tens of Millions of Dollars' a Year." *Los Angeles Times*, February 28, 2007.
21. This section is based on a comprehensive treatment of product returns, James Stock and Thomas Speh, "Managing Product Returns for Competitive Advantage." *MIT Sloan Management Review*, Fall 2006, pp. 57–62.
22. Robert Bordley, "Determining the Appropriate Depth and Breadth of a Firm's Product Portfolio." *Journal of Marketing Research*, February 2003, 40, pp. 39–53; Peter Boatwright and Joseph C. Nunes, "Reducing Assortment: An Attribute-Based Approach." *Journal of Marketing*, July 2001, 65, pp. 50–63.
23. Adapted from a Hamilton Consultants White Paper, December 1, 2000.
24. This illustration is found in Benson P. Shapiro, *Industrial Product Policy: Managing the Existing Product Line*, (Cambridge, MA: Marketing Science Institute, September 1977), pp. 3–5, 98–101.
25. "Brand Challenge." *Economist*, April 6, 2002, p. 68.
26. Chris Woodyard, "Hyundai, Kia Shift Gears to Overtake Competition." *USA Today*, March 25, 2005.
27. Stuart Henderson Britt, "How Weber's Law Can Be Applied to Marketing." *Business Horizons*, February 1975, pp. 21–29.
28. "Haier's Purpose." *Economist*, March 20, 2004, p. 67.
29. Patricia O'Connell, "A Chat with Unilever's Niall FitzGerald." *BusinessWeek Online*, August 2, 2001; John Willman, "Leaner, Cleaner, and Healthier Is the Stated Aim." *Financial Times*, February 23, 2000; "Unilever's Goal: 'Power Brands'." *Advertising Age*, January 3, 2000.
30. George Rädler, Jan Kubes, and Bohdan Wojnar, "Skoda Auto: From 'No-Class' to World-Class in One Decade." *Critical EYE 15*, July 2006; Scott D. Upham, "Beneath the Brand." *Automotive Manufacturing & Production*, June 2001.
31. Erica Tay, "P&Q Asia Chief Aims to Grow Market with Low-Cost, Quality Wares." *Straits Times*, September 24, 2007, p. H21.
32. Robert E. Weigand, "Buy In-Follow On Strategies for Profit." *Sloan Management Review*, Spring 1991, pp. 29–37.
33. Gerard J. Tellis, "Beyond the Many Faces of Price: An Integration of Pricing Strategies." *Journal of Marketing*, October 1986, p. 155. This excellent article also analyzes and illustrates other pricing strategies. See also Dilip Soman and John T. Gourville, "Transaction Decoupling: How Price Bundling Affects the Decision to Consume." *Journal of Marketing Research*, February 2001, 38, pp. 30–44.
34. Adapted from George Wuebker, "Bundles Effectiveness Often Undermined." *Marketing News*, March 18, 2002, pp. 9–12. See Stefan Stremersch and Gerard J. Tellis, "Strategic Bundling of Products & Prices." *Journal of Marketing*, January 2002, 66, pp. 55–72.
35. Akshay R. Rao and Robert W. Ruekert, "Brand Alliances as Signals of Product Quality." *Sloan Management Review*, Fall 1994, pp. 87–97; Akshay R. Rao, Lu Qu, and Robert W. Ruekert, "Signaling Unobservable Quality through a Brand Ally." *Journal of Marketing Research*, 1999, 36(2), pp. 258–268.
36. Bernard L. Simonin and Julie A. Ruth, "Is a Company Known by the Company It Keeps? Assessing the Spillover Effects of Brand Alliances on Consumer Brand Attitudes." *Journal of Marketing Research*, February 1998, pp. 30–42. See also C.W. Park, S.Y. Jun, and A.D. Shocker, "Composite Branding Alliances: An Investigation of Extension and Feedback Effects." *Journal of Marketing Research*, 1996, 33, pp. 453–466.

37. Kenneth Hein, "Coke and L'Oréal Partner on New Health Beverage." <www.brandweek.com>, March 12, 2007.
38. C.W. Park, S.Y. Jun, and A.D. Shocker, "Composite Branding Alliances: An Investigation of Extension and Feedback Effects." *Journal of Marketing Research,* 1996, 33, pp. 453–466; Lance Leuthesser, Chiranjier Kohli, and Rajneesh Suri. "2+2 = 5? A Framework for Using Co-branding to Leverage a Brand." *Journal of Brand Management*, September 2003, 2(1), pp. 35–47.
39. Based in part on a talk by Nancy Bailey, "Using Licensing to Build the Brand." Brand Masters conference, December 7, 2000.
40. Kalpesh Kaushik Desai and Kevin Lane Keller, "The Effects of Brand Expansions and Ingredient Branding Strategies on Host Brand Extendibility." *Journal of Marketing*, January 2002, 66, pp. 73–93; D.C. Denison, "Ingredient Branding Puts Big Names in the Mix." *Boston Globe*, May 26, 2002, p. E2.
41. <www.dupont.com>.
42. Susan B. Bassin, "Value-Added Packaging Cuts Through Store Clutter." *Marketing News*, September 26, 1988, p. 21.
43. Trish Hall, "New Packaging May Soon Lead to Food That Tastes Better and is More Convenient." *Wall Street Journal*, April 21, 1986, p. 25.
44. Kate Fitzgerald, "Packaging is the Capper." *Advertising Age*, May 5, 2003, p. 22.
45. "Campbell Soup Co. Changes the Look Of Its Famous Cans." *Wall Street Journal*, August 26, 1999, p. B10; Kate Novack, "Tomato Soup with a Side of Pop Art." *Time*, May 10, 2004.
46. Jason Stein, "10-year Mitsubishi Warranty is Small Part of a Larger Plan." *Automotive News*, January 12, 2004, p. 16.
47. "More Firms Pledge Guaranteed Service." *Wall Street Journal*, July 17, 1991, pp. B1, B6; Barbara Ettore, "Phenomenal Promises Mean Business." *Management Review*, March 1994, pp. 18–23. See also Christopher W. L. Hart, *Extraordinary Guarantees*, (New York: Amacom, 1993); Sridhar Moorthy and Kannan Srinivasan, "Signaling Quality with a Money-Back Guarantee: The Role of Transaction Costs." *Marketing Science*, 1995, 14(4), pp. 442–446.

Chapter 13

1. Leonard L. Berry, *Discovering the Soul of Service: The Nine Drivers of Sustainable Business Success,* (New York: The Free Press, 1999); Fred Wiersema, *Customer Service: Extraordinary Results at Southwest Airlines, Charles Schwab, Lands' End, American Express, Staples, and USA,* (New York: HarperBusiness, 1998); Valarie A. Zeithaml and Mary Jo Bitner, *Services Marketing*, 3rd ed., (McGraw-Hill/Irwin, 2003).
2. Salma Khalik, "Boom Time for Bumrungrad." *Sunday Times* (Singapore), September 22, 2002, p. 39; Graham Lees, "Travelling for Health." *Asia Inc.*, May 2005, pp. 26–27.
3. *Key Indicators Report*, <www.adb.org>.
4. Arthur Kroeber, "Making Money." *Fortune*, May 16, 2005, pp. 58–59.
5. Jena McGregor, "Customer Service Champs." *BusinessWeek*, March 5, 2007, pp. 52–64; "The Customer Service Elite." *BusinessWeek*, <www.bwnt.businessweek.com/interactive_reports/customer_service>.
6. Theodore Levitt, "Production-Line Approach to Service." *Harvard Business Review*, September–October 1972, pp. 41–42.
7. Further classifications of services are described in Christopher H. Lovelock and Jochen Wirtz, *Services Marketing*, 6th ed., (Upper Saddle River, NJ: Prentice Hall, 2006). See also John E. Bateson and Douglas K. Hoffman, *Managing Services Marketing: Text and Readings*, 4th ed., (Hinsdale, IL: Dryden, 1999).
8. Valarie A. Zeithaml, "How Consumer Evaluation Processes Differ Between Goods and Services." In *Marketing of Services*, J. Donnelly and W. R. George, eds., (Chicago, IL: American Marketing Association, 1981), pp. 186–190.
9. Amy Ostrom and Dawn Iacobucci, "Consumer Trade-offs and the Evaluation of Services." *Journal of Marketing*, January 1995, pp. 17–28.
10. Theodore Levitt, "Marketing Intangible Products and Product Intangibles." *Harvard Business Review*, May–June 1981, pp. 94–102; Leonard B. Berry, "Services Marketing Is Different." *Business*, May–June 1980, pp. 24–30.
11. Bernard H. Booms and Mary J. Bitner, "Marketing Strategies and Organizational Structures for Service Firms." In *Marketing of Services*, J. Donnelly and W. R. George, eds., (Chicago, IL: American Marketing Association, 1981), pp. 47–51.
12. "Hostesses 'Too Fat to Fly' Grounded." *Today*, November 6, 2006, p. 14.

13. Mark Carroll, "Switched-on Services." *Far Eastern Economic Review*, September 14, 2000, p. 163.

14. Arthur Kroeber, "Making Money." *Fortune*, May 16, 2005, pp. 58–59.

15. Lewis P. Carbone and Stephan H. Haeckel, "Engineering Customer Experiences." *Marketing Management*, Winter 1994.

16. Bernd H. Schmitt, *Customer Experience Management*, (New York: John Wiley, 2003).

17. Derek Moscato, "Spreading Luxury Farther Afield." *Asia Inc.*, August 2004, pp. 12–13; Eva Y.H. Kwan and Gerard Tocquer, "Shangri-La Hotels and Resorts–Achieving Service Leadership." Center for Asian Business Cases, 400-001-1.

18. G. Lynn Shostack, "Service Positioning Through Structural Change." *Journal of Marketing*, January 1987, pp. 34–43.

19. Debra Zahay and Abbie Griffin, "Are Customer Information Systems Worth It? Results from B2B Services." *Marketing Science Institute Working Paper*, Report No. 02-113, 2002.

20. W. Earl Sasser, "Match Supply and Demand in Service Industries." *Harvard Business Review*, November–December 1976, pp. 133–140.

21. Carol Krol, "Case Study: Club Med Uses Email to Pitch Unsold, Discounted Packages." *Advertising Age*, December 14, 1998, p. 40; <www.clubmed.com>.

22. Seth Godin, "If It's Broke, Fix It." *Fast Company*, October 2003, p. 131.

23. Bruce Horovitz, "Whatever Happened to Customer Service? Automated Answering, Long Waits Irk Consumers." *USA Today*, September 26, 2003, p. A1.

24. Hannah Clark, "Customer Service Hell." *Forbes*, March 30, 2006.

25. Ibid.

26. Michelle Slatella, "Toll-Free Apology Soothes Savage Beast." *New York Times*, February 12, 2004; Jane Spencer, "Cases of Customer Rage Mount as Bad Service Prompts Venting." *Wall Street Journal*, September 17, 2003; Judi Ketteler, "Grumbling Groundswell." *Cincinnati Business Courier*, September 8, 2003; Richard Halicks, "You Can Count on Customer Disservice." *Atlanta Journal Constitution*, June 29, 2003; Bruce Horovitz, "Whatever Happened to Customer Service?" *USA Today*, September 26, 2003.

27. David Lazarus, "JetBlue Response Praised." *San Francisco Chronicle*, February 25, 2007.

28. Stephen S. Tax, Mark Colgate, and David Bowen, "How to Prevent Your Customers from Failing." *MIT Sloan Management Review*, Spring 2006, pp. 30–38; Mei Xue and Patrick T. Harker, "Customer Efficiency: Concept and Its Impact on E-Business Management." *Journal of Service Research*, May 2002, 4(4), pp. 253–267; Matthew L. Meuter, Amy L. Ostrom, Robert I. Roundtree, and Mary Jo Bitner, "Self-Service Technologies: Understanding Customer Satisfaction with Technology-Based Service Encounters." *Journal of Marketing*, July 2000, 64(3), pp. 50–64.

29. Valarie Zeithaml, Mary Jo Bitner, and Dwayne D. Gremler, *Services Marketing: Integrating Customer Focus across the Firm*, 4th ed., (New York: McGraw-Hill, 2006).

30. Stephen S. Tax, Mark Colgate, and David Bowen, "How to Prevent Your Customers from Failing." *MIT Sloan Management Review*, Spring 2006, pp. 30–38.

31. Susan M. Keaveney, "Customer Switching Behavior in Service Industries: An Exploratory Study." *Journal of Marketing*, April 1995, pp. 71–82. See also Michael D. Hartline and O. C. Ferrell, "The Management of Customer-Contact Service Employees: An Empirical Investigation." *Journal of Marketing*, October 1996, pp. 52–70; Lois A. Mohr, Mary Jo Bitner, and Bernard H. Booms, "Critical Service Encounters: The Employee's Viewpoint." *Journal of Marketing*, October 1994, pp. 95–106; Linda L. Price, Eric J. Arnould, and Patrick Tierney, "Going to Extremes: Managing Service Encounters and Assessing Provider Performance." *Journal of Marketing*, April 1995, pp. 83–97; Jaishankar Ganesh, Mark J. Arnold, and Kristy E. Reynolds, "Understanding the Customer Base of Service Providers: An Examination of the Differences Between Switchers and Stayers." *Journal of Marketing*, July 2000, 64, pp. 65–87.

32. Christian Gronroos, "A Service Quality Model and Its Marketing Implications." *European Journal of Marketing*, 1984, 18(4),pp. 36–44.

33. Leonard Berry, "Big Ideas in Services Marketing." *Journal of Consumer Marketing*, Spring 1986, pp. 47–51. See also Walter E. Greene, Gary D. Walls, and Larry J. Schrest, "Internal Marketing: The Key to External Marketing Success." *Journal of Services Marketing*, 1994, 8(4), pp. 5–13; John R. Hauser, Duncan I. Simester, and Birger Wernerfelt, "Internal Customers and Internal Suppliers." *Journal of Marketing Research*, August 1996, pp. 268–280; Jagdip Singh, "Performance Productivity and Quality of Frontline Employees in Service Organizations." *Journal of Marketing*, 64, April 2000, pp. 15–34.

34. "What Makes Singapore a Service Champion?" *Strategic Direction*, April 2003, pp. 26–28; Justin Doebele, "The Engineer." *Forbes*, January 9, 2006, pp. 122–124; Stanley Holmes, "Creature Comforts at 30,000 Feet." *BusinessWeek*, December 18, 2006, p. 138.

35. Christian Gronroos, "A Service Quality Model and Its Marketing Implications;" Michael D. Hartline, James G. Maxham III, and Daryl O. McKee, "Corridors of Influence in the Dissemination of Customer-Oriented Strategy to Customer Contact Service Employees." *Journal of Marketing*, April 2000, pp. 35–50.

36. Nilly Landau, "Are You Being Served?" *International Business*, March 1995, pp. 38–40.

37. Philip Kotler and Paul N. Bloom, *Marketing Professional Services*, (Upper Saddle River, NJ: Prentice Hall, 1984).

38. Dennis Brown, "Creativity in the Marketing of Healthcare Services." *The Singapore Marketer*, November 1993, pp. 5–9, 13.

39. Anna S. Mattila, "The Role of Culture and Purchase Motivation in Service Encounter Evaluations." *Journal of Services Marketing*, 1999, 13(4/5), pp. 376–389.

40. Bernd H. Schmitt and Yigang Pan, "Managing Corporate and Brand Identities in the Asia-Pacific Region." *California Management Review*, Summer 1994, pp. 32–48.

41. Visa International Asia Pacific and Peppers & Rogers Group Asia, *One to One in Retail Financial Services: Replications of U.S. Studies in Five Asian Countries*, January 2002.

42. Bernd H. Schmitt and Yigang Pan, "Managing Corporate and Brand Identities in the Asia-Pacific Region." *California Management Review*, Summer 1994, pp. 32– 48.

43. Heather Cross, "Takashimaya Department Store Shopping Guide." <www.gonyc.about.com/od/shopping/p/takashimaya.htm>.

44. Glenn B. Voss, A. Parasuraman, and Dhruv Grewal, "The Role of Price, Performance, and Expectations in Determining Satisfaction in Service Exchanges." *Journal of Marketing*, October 1998, 62, pp. 46–61.

45. <www.ritzcarlton.com>.

46. "Dip 'N' Sip." *Straits Times* (Singapore), April 7, 2005.

47. A. Parasuraman, Valarie A. Zeithaml, and Leonard L. Berry, "A Conceptual Model of Service Quality and Its Implications for Future Research." *Journal of Marketing*, Fall 1985, pp. 41–50. See also Susan J. Devlin and H. K. Dong, "Service Quality from the Customers' Perspective." *Marketing Research: A Magazine of Management & Applications*, Winter 1994, pp. 4–13; Michael K. Brady and J. Joseph Cronin Jr., "Some New Thoughts on Conceptualizing Perceived Service Quality." *Journal of Marketing*, July 2001, 65, pp. 34–49.

48. Leonard L. Berry and A. Parasuraman, *Marketing Services: Competing Through Quality*, (New York: The Free Press, 1991), p. 16.

49. A. Parasuraman, Valarie A. Zeithaml, and Leonard L. Berry, "A Conceptual Model of Service Quality and Its Implications for Future Research." *Journal of Marketing*, Fall 1985, pp. 41–50.

50. John Helyar, "At E*Trade, Growing Up is Hard to Do." *Fortune*, March 18, 2002, pp. 88–90.

51. James L. Heskett, W. Earl Sasser Jr., and Christopher W. L. Hart, *Service Breakthroughs*, (New York: The Free Press, 1990).

52. <www.worldairportwards.com/Awards_2007>; Ozgur Tore, "ACI Airport Service Quality Awards 2007." <www.ftnnews.com>, February 25, 2008.

53. William C. Copacino, *Supply Chain Management*, (Boca Raton, FL: St. Lucie Press, 1997).

54. Montira Narkvichien, "Bank of Asia's Weapon Against Its Giant Rivals Is a Ubiquitous ATM." *Asian Wall Street Journal*, October 16–17, 1998, p. 7.

55. Leonard L. Berry, Kathleen Seiders, and Dhruv Grewal, "Understanding Service Convenience." *Journal of Marketing*, July 2002, 66, pp. 1–17.

56. Mary Jo Bitner, "Self-Service Technologies: What Do Customers Expect?" *Marketing Management*, Spring 2001, pp. 10–11; Matthew L. Meuter, Amy L. Ostrom, Robert J. Roundtree, and Mary Jo Bitner, "Self-Service Technologies: Understanding Customer Satisfaction with Technology Based Service Encounters." *Journal of Marketing*, July 2000, 64, pp. 50–64.

57. Peter Burrows, "The Era of Efficiency." *BusinessWeek*, June 18, 2001, pp. 94–98.

58. Matthew L. Meuter, Mary Jo Bitner, Amy L. Ostrom, and Stephen W. Brown, "Choosing among Alternative Service Delivery Modes: An Investigation of Customer Trial of Self-Service Technologies." *Journal of Marketing*, April 2005, 69, pp. 61–83.

59. John A. Martilla and John C. James, "Importance-Performance Analysis." *Journal of Marketing*, January 1977, pp. 77–79.

60. Stephen S. Tax and Stephen W. Brown, "Recovering and Learning from Service Failure." *Sloan Management Review,* Fall 1998, pp. 75–88.
61. D. Todd Donovan, Tom J. Brown, and John C. Mowen, "Internal Benefits of Service Worker Customer Orientation: Job Satisfaction, Commitment, and Organizational Citizenship Behaviors." *Journal of Marketing,* January 2004, 68, pp. 128–146.
62. Ben Dolven, "Under New Management." *Far Eastern Economic Review*, April 15, 2004, pp. 30–33.
63. Allen T. Cheng, "Taking Aim at Attitude." <www.asia-inc.com>, August 1999.
64. Dean Tjosvold, Jane Moy, and Shigeru Sasaki, "Co-operative Teamwork for Service Quality in East Asia." *Managing Service Quality*, 1999, 9(3), p. 209.
65. Ian Rowley, "Bank Services With a Smile?" *BusinessWeek*, March 14, 2005, pp. 48–49.
66. "Singapore Hospital Becomes First in Asia to Deploy Cisco Clinical Connection Suite Solution." <www.fujitsu.com/sg/news/pr/archives/month/2006/20060214.html>, February 14, 2006.
67. Susanna Hamner, "Checking In at the Hotel of Tomorrow." *Business 2.0*, November 2006, pp. 38–40.
68. Geoff Keighley, "The Phantasmagoria Factory." *Business 2.0*, February 2004.
69. Milind M. Lele and Uday S. Karmarkar, "Good Product Support Is Smart Marketing." *Harvard Business Review*, November–December, pp. 124–132.
70. For recent research on the effects of delays in service on service evaluations, see Shirley Taylor, "Waiting for Service: The Relationship between Delays and Evaluations of Service." *Journal of Marketing*, April 1994, pp. 56–69; Michael K. Hui and David K. Tse, "What to Tell Consumers in Waits of Different Lengths: An Integrative Model of Service Evaluation." *Journal of Marketing*, April 1996, pp. 81–90.
71. Emily Chia, "IBM Scrubs Down and Refreshes Old PCs." *Asia Computer Weekly,* November 29, 2004, p. 1.

Chapter 14

1. Dan Beucke, "A Blade Too Far." *BusinessWeek*, August 14, 2006; Jenn Abelson, "And Then There Were Five." *Boston Globe*, September 15, 2005; Jack Neff, "Six-Blade Blitz." *Advertising Age*, September 19, 2005, 53, pp. 3; Editorial, "Gillette Spends Smart on Fusion." *Advertising Age*, September 26, 2005, p. 24.
2. Xavier Dreze and Joseph C. Nunes, "Using Combined-Currency Prices to Lower Consumers' Perceived Cost." *Journal of Marketing Research*, February 2004, 41, pp. 59–72.
3. John L. Graham, "Brazilian, Japanese, and American Business Negotiations." *Journal of International Business Studies*, Spring/Summer 1983, pp. 47–61. See also John L. Graham, Dong Ki Kim, Chi-Yuan Lim, and Michael Robinson, "Buyer–Seller Negotiations Around the Pacific Rim: Differences in Fundamental Exchange Processes." *Journal of Consumer Research*, June 1988, pp. 48–54; John L. Graham, Alma T. Mintu, and Waymond Rogers, "Exploration of Negotiation Behaviors in Ten Foreign Cultures Using a Model Developed in the United States." *Management Science*, January 1994, pp. 72–95.
4. Jack Neff, "Moving to Margins in a New Marketing Age." *Advertising Age*, July 24, 2006, pp. 1, 21.
5. Michael Menduno, "Priced to Perfection." *Business 2.0*, March 6, 2001, pp. 40–42.
6. Paul Markillie, "A Perfect Market: A Survey of E-Commerce." *Economist*, May 5, 2004, pp. 3–20; David Kirpatrick, "How the Open-Source World Plans to Smack Down Microsoft, and Oracle, and . . . " *Fortune*, February 23, 2004, pp. 92–100; Faith Keenan, "The Price Is Really Right." *BusinessWeek*, March 31, 2003, pp. 61–67; Michael Menduno, "Priced to Perfection." *Business 2.0*, March 6, 2001, pp. 40–42; Amy E. Cortese, "Good-Bye to Fixed Pricing?" *BusinessWeek*, May 4, 1998, pp. 71–84. For a discussion of some of the academic issues involved, see Florian Zettelmeyer, "Expanding to the Internet: Pricing and Communication Strategies When Firms Compete on Multiple Channels." *Journal of Marketing Research*, August 2000, 37, pp. 292–308; John G. Lynch Jr. and Dan Ariely, "Wine Online: Search Costs Affect Competition on Price, Quality, and Distribution." *Marketing Science*, Winter 2000, pp. 83–103; Rajiv Lal and Miklos Sarvary, "When and How Is the Internet Likely to Decrease Price Competition?" *Marketing Science*, Fall 1999, 18(4), pp. 485–503.
7. Robert J. Dolan and Hermann Simon, "Power Pricers." *Across the Board*, May 1997, pp. 18–19.
8. For a thorough, up-to-date review of pricing research, see Chezy Ofir and Russell S. Winer, "Pricing: Economic and Behavioral Models." In Bart Weitz and Robin Wensley, eds., *Handbook of Marketing*, (in press).
9. Pia Sarkar, "Which Shirt Costs $275?—Brand Loyalty, Bargain Hunting, and Unbridled Luxury All Play a Part in the Price You'll Pay for a T-Shirt." *Final Edition*, March 15, 2007, p. C1. Reprinted by permission.
10. Peter R. Dickson and Alan G. Sawyer, "The Price Knowledge and Search of Supermarket Shoppers." *Journal of Marketing*, July 1990, pp. 42–53. For a methodological qualification, however, see Hooman Estalami,

Alfred Holden, and Donald R. Lehmann, "Macro-Economic Determinants of Consumer Price Knowledge: A Meta-Analysis of Four Decades of Research." *International Journal of Research in Marketing*, December 18, 2001, pp. 341–355.

11. For a different point of view, see Chris Janiszewski and Donald R. Lichtenstein, "A Range Theory Account of Price Perception." *Journal of Consumer Research*, March 1999, pp. 353–368.
12. K.N. Rajendran and Gerard J. Tellis, "Contextual and Temporal Components of Reference Price." *Journal of Marketing*, January 1994, pp. 22–34; Gurumurthy Kalyanaram and Russell S. Winer, "Empirical Generalizations from Reference Price Research." *Marketing Science*, 1995, 14(3), pp. G161–G169.
13. Robert Strauss, "Prices You Just Can't Believe." *New York Times*, January 17, 2002, p. G1.
14. Gurumurthy Kalyanaram and Russell S. Winter, "Empirical Generalizations from Refrence Research." *Marketing Science*, 1995, 14(3), pp. G161–G169.
15. Glenn E. Mayhew and Russell S. Winter, "An Empirical Analysis of Internal and External Reference Price Effects Using Scanner Data." *Journal of Consumer Research*, June 1992, pp. 62–70.
16. Robert Ziethammer, "Forward-Looking Buying in Online Auctions." *Journal of Marketing Research*, August 2006, 43, pp. 462–476.
17. John T. Gourville, "Pennies-a-Day: The Effect of Temporal Reframing on Transaction Evaluation." *Journal of Consumer Research*, March 1998, pp. 395–408.
18. Gary M. Erickson and Johny K. Johansson, "The Role of Price in Multi-Attribute Product-Evaluations." *Journal of Consumer Research*, September 1985, pp. 195–199.
19. Wilfred Amaldoss and Sanjay Jain, "Pricing of Conspicuous Goods: A Competitive Analysis of Social Effects." *Journal of Marketing Research*, February 2005, 42; Angela Chao and Juliet B. Schor, "Empirical Tests of Status Consumption: Evidence from Women's Cosmetics." *Journal of Economic Psychology*, January 19, 1998, 1, pp. 107–131.
20. Ellen Byron, "Fashion Victim: To Refurbish Its Image, Tiffany Risks Profits; After Silver Took Off, Jeweler Raises Prices to Discourage Teens." *Wall Street Journal*, January 2007, p. 10.
21. Mark Stiving and Russell S. Winer, "An Empirical Analysis of Price Endings with Scanner Data." *Journal of Consumer Research*, June 1997, pp. 57–68.
22. Eric Anderson and Duncan Simester, "The Role of Price Endings: Why Stores May Sell More at $49 than at $44." Unpublished conference paper, April 2001.
23. Eric Anderson and Duncan Simester. "Mind Your Pricing Cues." *Harvard Business Review*, September 2003, pp. 96–103.
24. Liu Jie, "High Stakes for High-end Goods." *China Daily*, January 27, 2005, p. 11.
25. Robert M. Schindler and Patrick N. Kirby, "Patterns of Rightmost Digits Used in Advertised Prices: Implications for Nine-Ending Effects." *Journal of Consumer Research*, September 1997, pp. 192–201.
26. Eric Anderson and Duncan Simester. "Mind Your Pricing Cues." *Harvard Business Review*, September 2003, pp. 96–103.
27. Ibid.
28. Daniel J. Howard and Roger A. Kerin, "Broadening the Scope of Reference-Price Advertising Research: A Field Study of Consumer Shopping Involvement." *Journal of Marketing*, October 2006, 70, pp. 185–204.
29. Robert C. Blattberg and Kenneth Wisniewski, "Price-Induced Patterns of Competition." *Marketing Science*, Fall 1989, 8, pp. 291–309.
30. Shantanu Dutta, Mark J. Zbaracki, and Mark Bergen, "Pricing Process as a Capability: A Resource-Based Perspective." *Strategic Management Journal*, July 24, 2003, 7, pp. 615–530.
31. Edward F. Moltzen, "Lenovo Ships Sub-$400 Desktops." <www.crn.com>, accessed on October 18, 2005.
32. David Welch, "Toyota's Risky Ride in the Incentive Lane." *BusinessWeek*, May 23, 2005, p. 42.
33. Mei Fong, "IKEA Hits Home in China: The Swedish Design Giant, Unlike Other Retailers, Slashes Prices for the Chinese." *Wall Street Journal*, March 3, 2006, p. B1. Reprinted by permission of Dow Jones via Copyright Clearance Center.
34. Michael Silverstein and Neil Fiske, *Trading Up: The New American Luxury*, (New York, NY: Portfolio, 2003).
35. Moon Ihlwan and Dexter Roberts, "How Samsung Plugged into China." *BusinessWeek*, March 4, 2002, pp. 22–23.
36. Peter Burrows and Dexter Roberts, "Ringing Off the Hook." *BusinessWeek*, June 9, 2003, p. 20.
37. The discussion on culture and pricing is drawn from David Ackerman and Gerard Tellis. "Can Culture Affect Prices? A Cross-Cultural Study of Shopping and Retail Prices." *Journal of Retailing*, 2001, 77, pp. 57–82.

38. Walter Baker, Mike Marn, and Craig Zawada, "Price Smarter on the Net." *Harvard Business Review*, February 2001, pp. 122–127.

39. "Brand Loyalty Low Amongst Chinese Car Buyers." <www.acnielsen.com>, accessed on May 12, 2004; Frederik Balfour and Chen Wu, "Letting Up on the Gas." *BusinessWeek*, September 20, 2004, pp. 24–25.

40. Thomas T. Nagle and Reed K. Holden, *The Strategy and Tactics of Pricing*, 4th ed., (Upper Saddle River, NJ: Prentice Hall, 2006).

41. For summary of elasticity studies, see Dominique M. Hanssens, Leonard J. Parsons, and Randall L. Schultz, *Market Response Models: Econometric and Time Series Analysis*, (Boston: Kluwer Academic Publishers, 1990), pp. 187–191.

42. Tammo H.A. Bijmolt, Harald J. Van Heerde, and Rik G.M. Pieters, "New Empirical Generalizations on the Determinants of Price Elasticity." *Journal of Marketing Research*, May 2005, 42, pp. 141–156.

43. William W. Alberts, "The Experience Curve Doctrine Reconsidered." *Journal of Marketing*, July 1989, pp. 36–49.

44. Robin Cooper and Robert S. Kaplan. "Profit Priorities from Activity-Based Costing." *Harvard Business Review*, May–June 1991, pp. 130–135. For more on ABC, see chapter 24.

45. "Easier Than ABC." *Economist*, October 25, 2003, p. 56

46. "Japan's Smart Secret Weapon." *Fortune*, August 12, 1991, p. 75.

47. Ben Dolven, "Getting a Grip On the Market." *Far Eastern Economic Review*, August 5, 2004, pp. 42–44.

48. Raissa Espinosa-Robles, "Crisis Survivor." *Asiaweek*, May 21, 1999, pp. 58–59.

49. Adapted from Robert J. Dolan and Hermann Simon, "Power Pricers." *Across the Board*, May 1997, pp. 18–19.

50. Kusum L. Ailawadi, Donald R. Lehmann, and Scott A. Neslin, "Market Response to a Major Policy Change in the Marketing Mix: Learning from Procter & Gamble's Value Pricing Strategy." *Journal of Marketing*, January 2001, 65, pp. 44–61.

51. Tung-Zong Chang and Albert R. Wildt, "Price, Product Information, and Purchase Intention: An Empirical Study." *Journal of the Academy of Marketing Science*, Winter 1994, pp. 16–27. See also G. Dean Kortge and Patrick A. Okonkwo, "Perceived Value Approach to Pricing." *Industrial Marketing Management*, May 1993, pp. 133–140.

52. James C. Anderson, Dipak C. Jain, and Pradeep K. Chintagunta, "Customer Value Assessment in Business Markets: A State-of-Practice Study." *Journal of Business-to-Business Marketing*, 1993, 1(1), pp. 3–29.

53. Chester Dawson and Karen Nickel, "A 'China Price' for Toyota." *BusinessWeek*, February 21, 2005, pp. 18–20.

54. Stephen J. Hoch, Xavier Dreze, and Mary J. Purk, "EDLP, Hi-Lo, and Margin Arithmetic." *Journal of Marketing*, October 1994, pp. 16–27; Rajiv Lal and R. Rao, "Supermarket Competition: The Case of Everyday Low Pricing." *Marketing Science*, 1997, 16(1), pp. 60–80.

55. Joseph W. Alba, Carl F. Mela, Terence A. Shimp, and Joel E. Urbany, "The Effect of Discount Frequency and Depth on Consumer Price Judgments." *Journal of Consumer Research*, September 1999, pp. 99–114.

56. Matsuoka Satoshi, "100-Yen Shops are the Rage All Over Japan." *Nipponia*, 17, June 15, 2001; Chi-dong Lee, "S. Korea Creates Sensation in 100-Yen Shop." *Korea Times*, March 6, 2003.

57. Becky Bull, "No Consensus on Pricing." *Progressive Grocer*, November 1998, pp. 87–90.

58. Sandy D. Jap, "The Impact of Online Reverse Auction Design on Buyer-Supplier Relationships." *Journal of Marketing*, January 2007, 71, pp. 146–159; Sandy D. Jap, "An Exploratory Study of the Introduction of Online Reverse Auctions." *Journal of Marketing*, July 2003, 67, pp. 96–107.

59. Paul W. Farris and David J. Reibstein, "How Prices, Expenditures, and Profits Are Linked." *Harvard Business Review*, November–December 1979, pp. 173–184. See also Makoto Abe, "Price and Advertising Strategy of a National Brand against Its Private-Label Clone: A Signaling Game Approach." *Journal of Business Research*, July 1995, pp. 241–250.

60. J.P. Morgan Report, "eTailing and the Five C's." March 2000.

61. Eugene H. Fram and Michael S. McCarthy, "The True Price of Penalties." *Marketing Management*, October 1999, pp. 49–56.

62. Kissan Joseph, "On the Optimality of Delegating Pricing Authority to the Sales Force." *Journal of Marketing*, January 2001, 65, pp. 62–70.

63. Gary McWilliams, "How Dell Fine-Tunes Its PC Pricing to Gain Edge in a Slow Market." *Wall Street Journal*, June 8, 2001, p. A1.

64. Joel E. Urbany, "Justifying Profitable Pricing." *Journal of Product and Brand Management*, 2001, 10(3), pp. 141–157.

65. Normandy Madden, "P&G Adapts Attitude Toward Local Markets." *Advertising Age*, February 23, 2004, pp. 28–29.

66. Michael Rowe, *Countertrade*, (London: Euromoney Books, 1989); P.N. Agarwala. *Countertrade: A Global Perspective*, (New Delhi: Vikas Publishing House, 1991); Christopher M. Korth, ed., *International Countertrade*, (New York: Quorum Books, 1987).

67. For an interesting discussion of a quantity surcharge, see David E. Sprott, Kenneth C. Manning, and Anthony Miyazaki, "Grocery Price Settings and Quantity Surcharges." *Journal of Marketing*, July 2003, 67, pp. 34–46.

68. Michael V. Marn and Robert L. Rosiello, "Managing Price, Gaining Profit." *Harvard Business Review*, September–October 1992, pp. 84–94. See also Gerard J. Tellis, "Tackling the Retailer Decision Maze: Which Brands to Discount, How Much, When, and Why?" *Marketing Science*, 1995, 14(3), pt. 2: 271–299; Kusom L. Ailawadi, Scott A. Neslin, and Karen Gedeak, "Pursuing the Value-Conscious Consumer: Store Brands Versus National Brand Promotions." *Journal of Marketing*, January 2001, 65, pp. 71–89.

69. Siddharth Srivastava, "Price War Erupts on India-US Routes." *Business Times*, August 18, 2007.

70. Kevin J. Clancy, "At What Profit Price?" *Brandweek*, June 23, 1997.

71. Ramarao Deesiraju and Steven M. Shugan, "Strategic Service Pricing and Yield Management." *Journal of Marketing*, January 1999, 63, pp. 44–56; Robert E. Weigand, "Yield Management: Filling Buckets, Papering the House." *Business Horizons*, September–October 1999, pp. 55–64.

72. Charles Fishman, "Which Price is Right?" *Fast Company*, March 2003, pp. 92–102; John Sviokla, "Value Poaching." *Across the Board*, March/April 2003, pp. 11–12.

73. Mike France, "Does Predatory Pricing Make Microsoft a Predator?" *BusinessWeek*, November 1998, 23, pp. 130–132. See also Joseph P. Guiltinan and Gregory T. Gundlack. "Aggressive and Predatory Pricing: A Framework for Analysis." *Journal of Advertising*, July 1996, pp. 87–102.

74. For more information on specific types of price discrimination that are illegal, see Henry Cheesman, *Contemporary Business Law*, (Upper Saddle River, NJ: Prentice Hall, 1995).

75. Bob Donath, "Dispel Major Myths about Pricing." *Marketing News*, February 3, 2003, p. 10.

76. For a classic review, see Kent B. Monroe, "Buyers' Subjective Perceptions of Price." *Journal of Marketing Research*, February 1973, pp. 70–80. See also Z. John Zhang, Fred Feinberg, and Aradhna Krishna, "Do We Care What Others Get? A Behaviorist Approach to Targeted Promotions." *Journal of Marketing Research*, August 2002, 39, pp. 277–291.

77. Margaret C. Campbell, "Perceptions of Pricing Unfairness: Antecedents and Consequences." *Journal of Marketing Research*, May 1999, 36, pp. 187–199.

78. Eric Mitchell, "How Not to Raise Prices." *Small Business Reports*, November 1990, pp. 64–67.

79. Ian Rowley, "Where the Net Has Telecom on the Run." *BusinessWeek*, June 27, 2005, p. 28.

Chapter 15

1. Adam Luck, "Fish Tales." *Asia Inc.*, July 2003, pp. 60–61.

2. Anne T. Coughlan, Erin Anderson, Louis W. Stern, and Adel I. El-Ansary, *Marketing Channels*, 7th edition (Upper Saddle River, NJ: Prentice Hall, 2005).

3. Louis W. Stern and Barton A. Weitz, "The Revolution in Distribution: Challenges and Opportunities." *Long Range Planning*, 1997, 30(6), pp. 823–829.

4. For an insightful summary of academic research, see Erin Anderson and Anne T. Coughlan, "Channel Management: Structure, Governance, and Relationship Management." In *Handbook of Marketing*, Bart Weitz and Robin Wensley eds., (London: Sage Publications, 2002), pp. 223–247. See also Gary L. Frazier, "Organizing and Managing Channels of Distribution." *Journal of the Academy of Marketing Science*, 1999, 27(2), pp. 226–240.

5. E. Raymond Corey, *Industrial Marketing: Cases and Concepts*, 4th ed., (Upper Saddle River, NJ: Prentice Hall, 1991), chapter 5.

6. For a technical discussion of how service-oriented firms choose to enter international markets, see M. Krishna Erramilli, "Service Firms' International Entry-Mode Approach: A Modified Transaction-Cost Analysis Approach." *Journal of Marketing*, July 1993, pp. 19–38.

7. David Whitford, "Uh ... Maybe Should I Drive." *Fortune*, April 30, 2007, pp. 125–28; Louise Lee, "It's Dell vs. the Dell Way." *BusinessWeek*, March 6, 2006, pp. 61–62; David Kirkpatrick, "Dell in the Penalty Box." *Fortune*, September 18, 2006,

pp. 70–78; Nanette Byrnes, Peter Burrows, and Louise Lee, "Dark Days at Dell." *BusinessWeek*, September 4, 2006, pp. 27–30; Elizabeth Corcoran, "A Bad Spell for Dell." *Forbes*, June 19, 2006, pp. 44–46.

8. Simon Hayes, "Lenovo Drops Plans for Retail Push." *The Australian*, May 3, 2005.
9. Teresa Leung, "HP Adds Direct Delivery to Channels Strategy." *Asia Computer Weekly* (Singapore), October 25, 2004, p. 1.
10. Asim Ansari, Carl F. Mela, and Scott A. Neslin, "Customer Channel Migration." *Journal of marketing Research*, February 2008, 45(1); Jacquelyn S. Thomas and Ursula Y. Sullivan, "Managing Marketing Communications." *Journal of Marketing*, October 2005, 69, pp. 239–251; Sridhar Balasubramanian, Rajagopal Raghunathan, and Vijay Mahajan, "Consumers in a Multichannel Environment: Product Utility, Process Utility, and Channel Choice." *Journal of Interactive Marketing*, Spring 2005, 19(2), pp. 12–30; Edward J. Fox, Alan L. Montgomery, and Leonard M. Lodish, "Consumer Shopping and Spending across Retail Formats." *Journal of Business*, April 2004, 77(2), pp. S25–S60.
11. Paul F. Nunes and Frank V. Cespedes, "The Customer Has Escaped." *Harvard Business Review*, November 2003, pp. 96–105.
12. Mike Troy, "From Supply Chain to Demand Chain, a New View of the Marketplace." *DSN Retailing Today*, October 13, 2003, pp. 8–9.
13. David Murphy, "Up Close and Personal." *Far Eastern Economic Review*, August 5, 2004, pp. 50–51.
14. Anne T. Coughlan, et al., *Marketing Channels*, 7th ed., (Upper Saddle River, NJ: Prentice Hall, 2005).
15. Cui Rong, "Privileged Position." *Far Eastern Economic Review*, August 5, 2004, pp. 45–48.
16. David A. Reid, *Effective Marketing for Japan: The Consumer Gods Experience*, (Hong Kong: Business International Asia/ Pacific Ltd, June 1991).
17. Craig S. Smith, "Doublemint in China: Distribution Isn't Double the Fun." *Wall Street Journal*, December 5, 1995, p. B1.
18. For additional information on backward channels, see Marianne Jahre, "Household Waste Collection as a Reverse Channel: A Theoretical Perspective." *International Journal of Physical Distribution and Logistics*, 25(2), 1995, pp. 39–55; Terrance L. Pohlen and M. Theodore Farris II, "Reverse Logistics in Plastics Recycling." *International Journal of Physical Distribution and Logistics*, 1992, 22(7), pp. 35–37.
19. John Colapinto, "When I'm Sixty-Four." *New Yorker*, June 4, 2007.
20. Irving Rein, Philip Kotler, and Martin Stoller, *High Visibility*, (New York: Dodd, Mead, 1987).
21. Louis P. Bucklin, *Competition and Evolution in the Distributive Trades*, (Upper Saddle River, NJ: Prentice Hall, 1972). See also Anne T. Coughlan et al., *Marketing Channels*, 7th ed., (Upper Saddle River, NJ: Prentice Hall, 2005).
22. Louis P. Bucklin, *A Theory of Distribution Channel Structure*, (Berkeley: Institute of Business and Economic Research, University of California, 1966).
23. Pauline Ng, P. Lovelock, and Ali F. Farhoomand, "Dell: Selling Directly, Globally." *Center for Asian Business Cases*, (University of Hong Kong, 2000).
24. Peter Baldwin, *Consumer Marketing in Indonesia: Harnessing Purchasing Power*, (Hong Kong: Economist Intelligence Unit, March 1994).
25. Thomas Crampton, "Market Research on Asian Nations Is Often Lacking." *International Herald Tribune*, Sponsored Section, November 1994, p. IX.
26. Joanna Slater, "Squeezing the Middlemen." *Far Eastern Economic Review*, January 14, 1999, pp. 20–21.
27. Anne T. Coughlan et al., *Marketing Channels*, 7th ed., (Upper Saddle River, NJ: Prentice Hall, 2005); <www.jinjapan.org/access/dereg/>; Michael Czinkota and Masaaki Kotabe, "Entering the Japanese Market: A Reassessment of Foreign Firm's Entry and Distribution Strategies." *Industrial Marketing Management*, 29, pp. 483–491; Paul Reithmuller and Joseph Chai, "Japan's Large Scale Retail Law: A Cause for Concern for Food Exporters?" *Paper Presented at the International Agribusiness Marketing Association Conference*, Florence, June 1999, pp. 13–16.
28. Anne T. Coughlan et al., *Marketing Channels*, 7th ed., (Upper Saddle River, NJ: Prentice Hall, 2005).
29. Matthew de Paula, "Bank One Buffs Its Image, Care of Avon." *USBanker*, February 2004, p. 26.
30. Carolyn Hong, "Need to Book a Flight? AirAsia Lets You Do It via Cellphone." *Straits Times* (Singapore), August 24, 2005, p. 12.
31. Norihiko Suzuki, "The Trading House and the Challenge from the Far East." In *Advances in International Marketing*, Tamer Cavusgil, Lars Hallen, and Jan Johanson, eds., 3, (Greenwich, CT: JAI Press, 1989), pp. 249–258.
32. "Trouser Suit." *Economist*, November 24, 2001, p. 56.
33. "Exclusives Becoming a Common Practice." *DSN Retailing Today*, February 9, 2004, pp. 38, 44.
34. <www.disney.com>; Edward Helmore, "Media: Why House of Mouse Is Haunted by Failures." *Observer*, February 11, 2001, p. 10.
35. Mongkol Jullayothin, "Thai Telecommunications Firm Set to Expand Retail Outlets." *Knight Ridder Tribune Business News*, November 23, 2002, p. 1.

36. For more on relationship marketing and the governance of marketing channels, see Jan B. Heide, "Interorganizational Governance in Marketing Channels." *Journal of Marketing*, January 1994, pp. 71–85.

37. Lawrence G. Friedman and Timothy R. Furey, *The Channel Advantage: Going to Marketing with Multiple Sales Channels*, (Woburn, MA: Butterworth-Heinemann, 2004). They suggest measuring a channel's profitability by the expense-to-revenue ratio, or E/R. E/R is the average transaction cost divided by the average order size. The average transaction cost is found by dividing the total expense in operating the channel by the total number of transactions. The lower the E/R, the more profitable the channel because less money is spent on selling cost for each dollar of revenue.

38. May Czarina A. Baetiong, "Mitsubishi RP Unit Expects to Sell Mercedes Vehicles Soon." *BusinessWorld* (Manila), January 26, 2001, p. 1.

39. Arthur Bragg, "Undercover Recruiting: Epson America's Sly Distributor Switch." *Sales and Marketing Management*, March 11, 1985, pp. 45–49.

40. Erin Anderson and Anne T. Coughlan, "Channel Management: Structure, Governance, and Relationship Management." In *Handbook of Marketing*, Bart Weitz and Robin Wensley, eds., (London Sage Publications, 2002, pp. 223–247.

41. Bert Rosenbloom, *Marketing Channels: A Management View*, 5th ed., (Hinsdale, IL: Dryden, 1995).

42. Moon Ihlwan and Dexter Roberts, "How Samsung Plugged into China." *BusinessWeek Asian Edition*, March 4, 2002, p. 23.

43. Cui Rong, "Privileged Position." *Far Eastern Economic Review*, August 5, 2004, pp. 45–48.

44. Joanna Slater and Eriko Amaha, "Masters of the Trade." *Far Eastern Economic Review*, July 22, 1999, p. 13.

45. Jerry Useem, "Simply Irresistible." *Fortune*, March 19, 2007, pp. 107–112; Nick Wingfield, "How Apple's Store Strategy Beat the Odds." *Wall Street Journal*, May 17, 2006; Tobi Elkin, "Apple Gambles with Retail Plan." *Advertising Age*, June 24, 2001.

46. For an excellent report on this issue, see Howard Sutton, *Rethinking the Company's Selling and Distribution Channels*, Research Report No. 885, Conference Board: 26, 1986.

47. John Elliott, "How South Korea Conquered India." *Fortune*, April 19, 2004, p. 24.

48. Shigefumi Makino, "A Note on the Japanese *Keiretsu*." In *Asia-Pacific Cases in Strategic Management*, Paul W. Beamish, ed., (Boston: Irwin McGraw-Hill, 2000): chapter 16.

49. Russell Johnston and Paul R. Lawrence, "Beyond Vertical Integration: The Rise of the Value-Adding Partnership." *Harvard Business Review*, July–August 1988, pp. 94–101. See also Judy A. Siguaw, Penny M. Simpson, and Thomas L. Baker, "Effects of Supplier Market Orientation on Distributor Market Orientation and the Channel Relationship: The Distribution Perspective." *Journal of Marketing*, July 1998, pp. 99–111; Narakesari Narayandas and Manohar U. Kalwani, "Long-Term Manufacturer-Supplier Relationships: Do They Pay Off for Supplier Firms?" *Journal of Marketing*, January 1995, pp. 1–16; Arnt Bovik and George John, "When Does Vertical Coordination Improve Industrial Purchasing Relationships." *Journal of Marketing*, October 2000, 64, pp. 52–64.

50. Avery Johnson, "The Next Wave in Private-Jet Travel." *Wall Street Journal*, March 10, 2005, p. D1.

51. "*Yugoka* in Japan—Inter-industry Alliances." *Pins and Needles*, July–August 1992, pp. 9–13.

52. Peking University, Tsinghua University, and the University of South Carolina, *Economic Impact of the Coca-Cola System on China*, August 2000, chapter 4 (see <www.research. moore.sc.edu>).

53. Based on Rowland T. Moriarty and Ursula Moran, "Marketing Hybrid Marketing Systems." *Harvard Business Review*, November–December 1990, pp. 146–155.

54. Anne T. Coughlan and Louis W. Stern, "Marketing Channel Design and Management." In Dawn Iacobucci , ed., *Kellogg on Marketing*, (New York: John Wiley, 2001), pp. 247–269.

55. Rob Wheery, "Pedal Pushers." *Forbes*, October 14, 2002, pp. 205–206.

56. This section draws on Anne T. Coughlan et al., *Marketing Channels*, 7th ed., (Upper Saddle River, NJ: Prentice Hall, 2005), chapter 6. See also Jonathan D. Hibbard, Nirmalya Kumar, and Louis W. Stern, "Examining the Impact of Destructive Acts in Marketing Channel Relationships." *Journal of Marketing Research*, February 2001, 38, pp. 45–61; Kersi D. Antia and Gary L. Frazier, "The Severity of Contract Enforcement in Interfirm Channel Relationships." *Journal of Marketing*, October 2001, 65, pp. 67–81; James R. Brown, Chekitan S. Dev, and Dong-Jin Lee, "Managing Marketing Channel Opportunism: The Efficency of Alternative Governance Mechanisms." *Journal of Marketing*, April 2001, 64, pp. 51–65.

57. Allison Fass, "Trading Up." *Forbes*, January 29, 2007, pp. 48–49; Diane Brady, "Coach's Split Personality." *BusinessWeek*, November 7, 2005, pp. 60–62.

58. Christina Passriello, "Fashionably Late? Designer Brands Are Starting to Embrace E-Commerce." *Wall Street Journal*, May 19, 2006.

59. David A. Soberman and Anne T. Coughlan, "When Is the Best Ship a Leaky One? Segmentation, Competition, and Gray Markets." INSEAD working paper 98/60/MKT summarized in David Champion, "Marketing: The Brighter Side of Gray Markets." *Harvard Business Review*, September–October 1998, 76, pp. 19–22; Robert Weigand, "Parallel

Import Channels—Options for Preserving Territorial Integrity." *Columbia Journal of World Business*, Spring 1991, 26, pp. 53–60; Gert Assmus and Carsten Wiese, "How to Address the Gray Market Threat Using Price Coordination." *Sloan Management Review*, Spring 1995, 36, pp. 31–41.

60. Mark Henricks, "Harmful Diversions." *Apparel Industry Magazine*, 58, September 1997, pp. 72–78.
61. Adapted from Anne T. Coughlan et al., *Marketing Channels*, 7th ed., (Upper Saddle River, NJ: Prentice Hall, 2005).
62. Hellmutt Schütte and Deanna Ciarlante, *Consumer Behavior in Asia*, (London: Macmillan, 1998), p. 179.
63. Mark Bergen, Jan B. Heide, and Shantanu Dutta, "Managing Gray Markets Through Tolerance of Violations: A Transactions Cost Perspective." *Managerial and Decision Economics*, 1998, 19(1), pp. 157–165.
64. Hellmutt Schütte and Deanna Ciarlante, *Consumer Behavior in Asia*, (London: Macmillan, 1998).
65. William G. Zikmund, and William J. Stanton, "Recycling Solid Wastes: A Channels-of-Distribution Problem." *Journal of Marketing*, July 1971, p. 34.
66. Susan Cunningham, "Sparkle of Success." *Asia Inc.*, December 2003, pp. 74–75.
67. Alexis K.J. Barlow, Noreen Q. Siddiqui, and Mike Mannion, "Development in Information and Communication Technologies for Retail Marketing Channels." *International Journal of Retail and Distribution Management*, March 2004, pp. 157–163; G&J Electronic Media Services. *7th Wave of the GfK-Online-Monitor*, (Hamburg: GfK Press, 2001).
68. Kate Maddox, "Online Marketing Summit Probes New Technologies." *BtoB*, March 12, 2007, 92(3), pp. 3, 39. Reprinted by permission.
69. Martin Holzwarth, Chris Janiszewski, and Marcus M. Newmann, "The Influence of Avatars on Online Consumer Shopping Behavior." *Journal of Marketing*, October 2006, 70, pp. 19–36.
70. Ann E. Schlosser, Tiffany Barnett White, and Susan M. Lloyd, "Converting Web Site Visitors into Buyers: How Web Site Investment Increases Consumer Trusting Beliefs and Online Purchase Intentions." *Journal of Marketing*, April 2006, 70, pp. 133–148.
71. "Trends in Online Shopping: A Global Nielsen Consumer Report." *A.C. Nielsen Report*, February 2008.
72. Ronald Abler, John S. Adams, and Peter Gould, *Spatial Organizations: The Geographer's View of the World* (Upper Saddle River, NJ: Prentice Hall, 1971), pp. 531–532.
73. "China's Pied Piper." *Economist*, September 23, 2006, p. 80; <www.alibaba.com>.
74. For an in-depth academic examination, see John G. Lynch Jr. and Dan Ariely, "Wine Online: Search Costs and Competition on Price, Quality, and Distribution." *Marketing Science*, Winter 2000, 19, pp. 83–103.
75. Described in *Inside 1-to-1*, Peppers and Rogers Group newsletter, May 14, 2001.
76. Bob Tedeshi, "How Harley Revved Online Sales." *Business 2.0*, December 2002/January 2003, p. 44.
77. Pallavi Gogoi, "The Hot News in Banking: Bricks and Mortar." *BusinessWeek*, April 21, 2003, pp. 83–84.
78. Marc Weingarten, "The Medium Is the Instant Message." *Business 2.0*, February 2002, pp. 98–99; Douglas Lamont, *Conquering the Wireless World: The Age of M-Commerce*, (New York: John Wiley, 2001).

Chapter 16

1. Kerry Capell, "Fashion Conquistador." *BusinessWeek*, September 4, 2006, pp. 38–39; Rachel Tipaldy, "Zara: Taking the Lead in Fast-Fashion." *BusinessWeek*, April 4, 2006; Kasra Ferdows, Michael A. Lewis, and Jose A.D. Machuca, "Zara's Secret for Fast Fashion." *Harvard Business School Working Knowledge*, February 21, 2005; Vivian Manning-Schaffel, "Zara-Zesty." <brandchannel.com> , August 23, 2004.
2. William R. Davidson, Albert D. Bates, and Stephen J. Bass, "Retail Life Cycle." *Harvard Business Review*, November–December 1976, pp. 89–96.
3. Stanley C. Hollander, "The Wheel of Retailing." *Journal of Marketing*, July 1960, pp. 37–42.
4. A.C. Nielsen, *Asia Pacific Retail and Shopper Trends 2005*.
5. "Franchise Frenzy." "Xinhua News Agency and China Chain Stores and Franchise Association." Statistics found in report in *Straits Times* (Singapore), April 6, 2005, pp. 13.
6. Wendy Liebmann, "Consumers Push Back." *Brandweek*, February 23, 2004, pp. 19–20.
7. Manjeet Kripalani "Here Come the Wal-Mart Wannabes." *BusinessWeek*, April 4, 2005, p. 20.
8. A. C. Nielsen, *Asia Pacific Retail and Shopper Trends 2005*.
9. The Changing Moods of Malaysian Consumers." October 10, 2003; <www.acnielsen.com.my>.
10. Catherine Yang, "Maybe They Should Call Them Scammers." *BusinessWeek*, January 16, 1995, pp. 32–33; Ronald C. Goodstein, "UPC Scanner Pricing Systems: Are They Accurate?" *Journal of Marketing*, April 1994, pp. 20–30.

11. For a listing of the key factors involved in success with an EDI system, see R.P. Vlosky, D.T. Wilson, and P.M. Smith, "Electronic Data Interchange Implementation Strategies: A Case Study." *Journal of Business and Industrial Marketing*, 1994, 9(4), pp. 5–18.
12. "Business Bulletin: Shopper Scanner." *Wall Street Journal*, February 18, 1995, p. A1.
13. For further discussion of retail trends, see Anne T. Coughlan, Erin Anderson, Louis W. Stern, and Adel I. El-Ansary, *Marketing Channels*, 7th ed., (Upper Saddle River, NJ: Prentice Hall, 2005).
14. "Foreign Retailers in China Expanding." *Business Times* (Singapore), May 2, 2005, p. 13.
15. Jane Lanhee Lee, "Spread of Superstores Adds New Choice for China Shoppers." *Dow Jones International News*, October 29, 2002.
16. A.C. Nielsen. *Asia Pacific Retail and Shopper Trends 2005*.
17. <www.giordano.com.hk>; Alexandra A. Seno, "An All-New Dress for Success." *Asiaweek*, October 15, 1999, pp. 64–67; Amy Louise Kasmin, "Giordano Comes in Out of the Cold." *BusinessWeek*, May 31, 1999, p. 26.
18. Irene M. Kunii, "How Do You Say 'Cool' in Japanese? Tsutaya." *BusinessWeek Asian Edition*, May 13, 2002, p. 24.
19. Jonathan Sprague, "The Retailer: Ariga Breaks the Rules—and Wins." *Asiaweek*, August 14, 1998, p. 57.
20. Mary Kwang, "Cashing in on the Maid Market." *Sunday Times* (Singapore), September 1, 2002, p. 38.
21. Sarah Schafer, "A Welcome to Wal-Mart." *Newsweek*, December 20, 2004, pp. 30–34; Clay Chandler, "The Great Wal-Mart of China." *Fortune*, July 25, 2005, pp. 60–68.
22. Uta Werner, John McDermott, and Greg Rotz, "Retailers at the Crossroads: How to Develop Profitable New Growth Strategies." *Journal of Business Strategy*, 2004, 25(2), pp. 10–17.
23. Cecilie Rohwedder, "Viva la Differenza." *Wall Street Journal*, January 29, 2003, pp. B1, B8.
24. Frank Feather, *The Future Consumer*, (Toronto: Warwick Publishing, 1994), p. 171. See also Stephen J. Hoch, Xavier Dreze, and Mary E. Purk "EDLP, Hi-Lo, and Margin Arithmetic." *Journal of Marketing*, October 1994, pp. 1–15; David Bell and James M. Lattin, "Shopping Behavior and Consumer Preference for Retail Price Format: Why 'Large Basket' Shoppers Prefer EDLP." *Marketing Science*, Spring 1998, 17, pp. 66–68.
25. Kenneth T. Rosen and Amanda L. Howard, "E-tail: Gold Rush or Fool's Gold?" *California Management Review*, April 1, 2000, pp. 72–100; Moira Cotler, "Census Releases First E-commerce Report." *Catalog Age*, May 1, 2001; Associated Press, "Online Sales Boomed at End of 2000." *Star-Tribune of Twin Cities*, February 17, 2001; "Reinventing the Store." *Economist*, November 22, 2003, pp. 65–68.
26. "A Busy Bee in the Hamburger Hive." *Economist*, February 28, 2002.
27. R.L. Davies and D.S. Rogers, *Store Location and Store Assessment Research,* (New York: John Wiley, 1984).
28. Sara L. McLafferty, *Location Strategies for Retail and Service Firms*, (Lexington, MA: Lexington Books, 1987).
29. Georges Desvaux, Guangyu Li, and Jacques Penhirin, "Shanghai Shopping." *McKinsey Quarterly*, 2002, 2, pp. 17–20.
30. Sarah Raper Larenaudie, "Luxury for the People!" *Time*, Spring 2005, pp. 48–50.
31. A.C. Nielsen, *Asia Pacific Retail and Shopper Trends 2005*.
32. Kelvin Wong, "House Brands Gaining Favor with Singaporeans." *Straits Times* (Singapore), October 11, 2005, p. H18.
33. Dexter Roberts, Wendy Zellner, and Carol Matlack, "Let the Retail Wars Begin." *BusinessWeek*, January 24, 2005, pp. 18–19.
34. Kenji Hall, "Zen and the Art of Selling Minimalism." *BusinessWeek*, April 9, 2007, p. 45; Rob Walker, "Musuem Quality." *New York Times Magazine*, January 9, 2005, p. 25.
35. James A. Narus and James C. Anderson, "Contributing as a Distributor to Partnerships with Manufacturers." *Business Horizons*, September–October 1987. See also James D. Hlavecek and Tommy J. McCuistion, "Industrial Distributors—When, Who, and How." *Harvard Business Review*, March–April 1983, pp. 96–101.
36. Nirmalya Kumar and Jan-Benedict E.M. Steenkamp, *Private Label Strategy: How to Meet the Store-Brand Challenge* (Boston: Harvard Business School Press, 2007).
37. James A. Narus and James R. Anderson, "Contributing as a Distributor to Partnerships with Manufacturers." *Business Horizons*, September-October 1987. See also James D. Hlavecek and Tommy J. McCuistion, "Industrial Distributors—When, Who, and How." *Harvard Business Review*, March–April 1983, pp. 96–101.
38. Peking University, Tsinghua University, and University of South Carolina, *Economic Impact of the Coca-Cola System in China*, August 2000; <www.research.moore.sc.edu>.
39. "Distribution in China: The End of the Beginning." <www.chinabusinessreview.com>; "China Industry—Networking in Distribution and Logistics Sectors." *EIU Wireswire*, Economist Intelligence Unit Ltd., December 4, 2001.
40. William C. Copacino, *Supply Chain Management,* (Boca Raton, FL: St. Lucie Press, 1997).
41. Joanna Slater and Erika Amaha, "Masters of the Trade." *Far Eastern Economic Review*, July 22, 1999, pp. 10–13; Joanna Slater, "One-Stop Shop." *Far Eastern Economic Review*, July 22, 1999, p. 14.

42. Alfred Siew, "Sir, Your Vegetarian Meal as Requested." *Straits Times* (Singapore), October 2, 2002, p. CT3.
43. Ronald Henkoff, "Delivering the Goods." *Fortune*, November 28, 1994, pp. 64–78.
44. The optimal order quantity is given by the formula $Q^* = 2DS/IC$, where, D = annual demand, S = cost to place one order, and IC = annual carrying cost per unit. Known as the economic-order quantity formula, it assumes a constant ordering cost, a constant cost of carrying an additional unit in inventory, a known demand, and no quantity discounts. For further reading on this subject, see Richard J. Tersine *Principles of Inventory and Materials Management*, 4th ed., (Upper Saddle River, NJ: Prentice Hall, 1994).
45. William C. Copacino, *Supply Chain Management*, (Boca Baton, FL: St. Lucie Press, 1997), pp. 122–123.
46. Jonathan Sprague and Murakami Mutsuko, "The New Japan Inc." *Asiaweek*, August 14, 1998, pp. 58–59.

Chapter 17

1. Noah Brier, "Buzz Giant Poster Boy." *American Demographics*, June 2004, pp. 11–16.
2. Randall Rothenberg, "Dove Effort Gives Packaged-Goods Marketers Lessons for the Future." *Advertising Age*, March 5, 2007; Theresa Howard, "Ad Campaign Tells Women to Celebrate Who They Are." *USA Today*, July 8, 2005; Jack Neff, "In Dove Ads, Normal Is the New Beautiful." *Advertising Age*, September 27, 2004; <www.campaignforrealbeauty.com>.
3. David Kiley, "Hey Advertisers, TiVo Is Your Friend." *BusinessWeek*, October 17, 2005, pp. 97–98; Linda Kaplan Thaler and Robin Koval with Delia Marshall, *Bang! Getting Your Message Heard in a Noisy World*, (New York: Currency, 2003).
4. Anthony Bianco, "The Vanishing Mass Market." *BusinessWeek*, July 12, 2004, pp. 60–68; Susan Thea Posnock, "It Can Control Madison Avenue." *American Demographics*, February 2004, pp. 28–33; Jennifer Pendleton, "Multi TASKERS." *Advertising Age*, March 29, 2004, pp. S1, S8; Christopher Reynolds, "Game Over." *American Demographics*, February 2004, pp. 34–38; Noreen O'Leary, "The 30-Second Spot Is Dead, Long Live the 30-Second Spot." *Adweek*, November 17, 2003, pp. 12–21; Hank Kim, "Madison Ave. Melds Pitches and Content." *Advertising Age*, October 7, 2002, pp. 1, 14.
5. "AirAsia Unveils Red Devil Airbus." *New Straits Times*, May 11, 2006, p. 88.
6. Louise Story, "Anywhere the Eye Can See, It's Likely to See an Ad." *New York Times*, January 15, 2007; Laura Petrecca, "Product Placement – You Can't Escape It." *USA Today*, October 11, 2006.
7. Stuart Elliott, "Nike Reaches Deeper into New Media to Find Young Buyers." *Wall Street Journal*, October 31, 2006.
8. Some of these definitions are adapted from Peter D. Bennett, ed., *Dictionary of Marketing Terms*, (Chicago: American Marketing Association, 1995).
9. "Nike Hones Rebel Reputation with Controversial Asia Ads." 2004, <www.showmenews.com> (accessed on December 8, 2004),
10. Joseph W. Alba and J. Wesley Hutchinson, "Dimensions of Consumer Expertise," *Journal of Consumer Research*, March 1987, 13, 411–453.
11. Wen Gong, Zhan G. Li, and Tiger Li, "Marketing to China's Youth: A Cultural Transformation Perspective." *Business Horizons*, 2004, 47(6), pp. 41–50.
12. For an alternate communications model developed specifically for advertising communications, see Barbara B. Stern, "A Revised Communication Model for Advertising: Multiple Dimensions of the Source, the Message, and the Recipient." *Journal of Advertising*, June 1994, pp. 5–15. For some additional perspectives, see Tom Duncan and Sandra E. Moriarity, "A Communication-Based Marketing Model for Managing Relationships." *Journal of Marketing*, April 1998, pp. 1–13.
13. Demetrios Vakratsas and Tim Ambler "How Advertising Works: What Do We Really Know." *Journal of Marketing*, January 1999, 63(1), pp. 26–43.
14. "Heavyweight Advertising Not Necessarily Lead to Higher Brand Awareness." <www.acnielsen.com.cn>, accessed on September 14, 2004.
15. Sangeeta Mulchand, "Za Shifts Target After Cool Teen Response." *Media*, October 2004, p. 13.
16. James F. Engel, Roger D. Blackwell, and Paul W. Minard, *Consumer Behavior*, 10th ed., (Fort Worth, TX: Dryden, 2005).
17. John R. Rossiter and Larry Percy. *Advertising and Promotion Management*, 2nd ed., (New York: McGraw-Hill, 1997).
18. James E. Engel, Roger D. Blackwell, and Paul W. Minard. *Consumer Behavior*, 10th ed., (Fort Worth, TX: Dryden, 2005).
19. Ayn E. Crowley and Wayne D. Hoyer, "An Integrative Framework for Understanding Two-Sided Persuasion." *Journal of Consumer Research*, March 1994, pp. 561–574.
20. C.I. Hovland, A.A. Lumsdaine, and F.D. Sheffield, *Experiments on Mass Communication*, (Princeton, NJ: Princeton University Press, 1948), p. 3, chapter 8; Ayn E. Crowley and Wayne D. Hoyer, "An Integrative Framework for Understanding Two-Sided Persuasion." For an alternative viewpoint, see George E. Belch, "The Effects of Message Modality on One and Two-Sided Advertising Messages." In Richard P. Bagozzi and Alice M. Tybout, eds., *Advances in Consumer Research*, (Ann Arbor, MI: Association for Consumer Research, 1983) pp. 21–26.

21. Curtis P. Haugtvedt and Duane T. Wegener, "Message Order Effects in Persuasion: An Attitude Strength Perspective." *Journal of Consumer Research*, June 1994, pp. 205–218; H. Rao Unnava, Robert E. Burnkrant, and Sunil Erevelles, "Effects of Presentation Order and Communication Modality on Recall and Attitude." *Journal of Consumer Research*, December 1994, pp. 481–490.

22. Brian Sternthal and C. Samuel Craig, *Consumer Behavior: An Information Processing Perspective*, (Upper Saddle River, NJ: Prentice Hall, 1982), pp. 282–284.

23. Michael R. Solomon, *Consumer Behavior*, 8th ed., (Upper Saddle River, NJ: Prentice Hall, 2008).

24. "The Death of the Jingle." *Economist*, February 8, 2003, p. 61.

25. Kevin Goldman, "Advertising: Knock, Knock. Who's There? The Same Old Funny Ad Again." *Wall Street Journal*, November 2, 1993, p. B10. See also Marc G. Weinberger, Harlan Spotts, Leland Campbell, and Amy L. Parsons, "The Use and Effect of Humor in Different Advertising Media." *Journal of Advertising Research*, May–June 1995, pp. 44–55.

26. Herbert C. Kelman and Carl I. Hovland, "Reinstatement of the Communication in Delayed Measurement of Opinion Change." *Journal of Abnormal and Social Psychology*, 1953, 48, pp. 327–335.

27. David J. Moore, John C. Mowen, and Richard Reardon, "Multiple Sources in Advertising Appeals: When Product Endorsers Are Paid by the Advertising Sponsor." *Journal of the Academy of Marketing Science*, Summer 1994, pp. 234–243.

28. Tom Lowry, "Wow! Yao!" *BusinessWeek*, October 25, 2004, pp. 52–55.

29. C.E. Osgood and P. H. Tannenbaum, "The Principles of Congruity in the Prediction of Attitude Change." *Psychological Review*, 1955, 62, pp. 42–55.

30. Richard C. Morais, "Mobile Mayhem." *Forbes*, July 6, 1998, p. 138; "Working in Harmony." *Soap Perfumery and Cosmetics*, July 1, 1998, p. 27; Rodger Harrabin, "A Commercial Break for Parents." *Independent*, September 8, 1998, p. 19; Naveen Donthu, "A Cross Country Investigation of Recall of and Attitude toward Comparative Advertising." *Journal of Advertising*, June 1998, 27(22), p. 111; "EU to Try Again on Tobacco Advertising Ban." *Associated Press*, May 9, 2001.

31. See also Frederik Balfour and David Kiley, "Ad Agencies Unchanged." *BusinessWeek*, April 25, 2005, pp. 18–19.

32. "Stringham Turns HSBC from Guest to Resident." *Brand Strategy*, October 9, 2002.

33. Magz Osborne, "Asia Multinationals—Structure: The Most Popular Methods Used for Successful Asian Marketing." *Advertising Age International*, April 1, 2000.

34. Susan H.C. Tai, "Factors Affecting Advertising Approach in Asia." *Journal of Current Issues and Research in Advertising*, Spring 1998, pp. 33–45.

35. T.B. Song, and Leo Wong, "Getting the Word Out." *The China Business Review*, September 1, 1998; "Avon Campaign Repositions Company in China." <AdAgeInternational.com>, July 1998; Donthu, "A Cross Country Investigation of Recall of and Attitude toward Comparative Advertising."

36. Betsy McKay, "Coca-Cola Restructuring Effort Has Yet to Prove Effective." *Asian Wall Street Journal*, March 2, 2001, p. N4; James Kynge and Mure Dickie, "Coke Forced to Dump Taiwanese Diva." *Financial Times*, May 2000, p. C12.

37. Susan H.C. Tai, "Factors Affecting Advertising." *Journal of Current Issues and Research in Advertising*, Spring 1998, pp. 33–45.

38. David K. Tse, Russell W. Belk, and Nan Zhou, "Becoming a Consumer Society: A Longitudinal and Cross-Cultural Content Analysis of Print Ads from Hong Kong, the People's Republic of China, and Taiwan." *Journal of Consumer Research*, March 1989, pp. 457–472; Peter Baldwin, *Consumer Marketing in Indonesia: Harnessing Purchasing Power*, (Hong Kong: Business International Asia/Pacific Ltd, March 1994), p. 132.

39. M. Flagg, "Savvy Urban People in China." *Asian Wall Street Journal*, June 9, 2001.

40. Susan H.C. Tai, "Factors Affecting Advertising." *Journal of Current Issues and Research in Advertising*, Spring 1998, pp. 33–45. This author proposes several other factors which impact the management of pan-Asian marketing communications program: product category, country-of-origin of the advertiser, competitive situation, product life-cycle stage, and organization experience and control.

41. Hellmut Schütte and Deanna Ciarlante, *Consumer Behavior in Asia*, (London: MacMillan, 1998), p. 173.

42. J. Clammer, *Difference and Modernity*, (New York: Kegan Paul, 1995), pp. 38–40.

43. Ian Mount, "Marketing." *Business 2.0*, August/September 2001, p. 84.

44. Joy Su, "Mister Donut Eyes Permanent Spot on Taiwan's Culinary Landscape." *Taipei Times*, February 28, 2005, p. 11.

45. "Samsung Backs Olympics to 2008." *Marketing Week*, October 24, 2002; Jon E. Hilsenrath, "Samsung Plays the Brand in Olympics." *Asian Wall Street Journal*, September 28, 2000, pp. 1, 7; "Chelsea Football Club Announces Samsung Electronics as Official Club Sponsor." *Samsung Press Release*, May 2, 2005.

46. Steve Miller, "Mini Making Big Claims about Mileage in New Push." *Brandweek*, June 4, 2007, p. 7; Barnaby Feder, "Billboards That Know You by Name." *New York Times*, January 29, 2007; <www.kellyawardsgallery.org>; Burt Helm, "For Your Eyes Only." *BusinessWeek*, July 31, 2006, pp. 66–67; Warren Berger, "Dare-Devils. 2004." *Business 2.0*,

April, pp. 111–116; Karen Lundegaard, "BMW 'Mini' Campaign: Odd to the Max." *Wall Street Journal* 28, February 2002; John Gaffney, "Most Innovative Campaign." *Business 2.0*, May 2002, pp. 98–99.

47. Adapted from G. Maxwell Ule, "A Media Plan for 'Sputnik' Cigarettes." *How to Plan Media Strategy*, (American Association of Advertising Agencies, Regional Convention, 1957), pp. 41–52.
48. Thomas C. Kinnear and Kenneth L. Bernhardt, *Principles of Marketing*, 2nd ed., (Glenview, IL: Scott Foresman and Co., 1986).
49. Amna Kirmani, "The Effect of Perceived Advertising Costs on Brand Perceptions." *Journal of Consumer Research*, September 17, 1990, pp. 160–171; Amna Kirmani and Peter Wright, "Money Talks: Perceived Advertising Expense and Expected Product Quality." *Journal of Consumer Research*, December 16, 1989, pp. 344–353.
50. Demetrios Vakratsas and Tim Ambler, "How Advertising Works: What Do We Really Know." *Journal of Marketing*, January 1999, pp. 26–43.
51. *How Advertising Works in Today's Marketplace: The Morrill Study*, (New York: McGraw-Hill, 1971), p. 4.
52. Theodore Levitt, *Industrial Purchasing Behavior: A Study in Communication Effects*, (Boston: Division of Research, Harvard Business School, 1965).
53. Leithan Francis, "Thai Paper Firm Steps Up TV Branding Drive." *Media*, October 18, 2002.
54. Ernan Roman, *Integrated Direct Marketing: The Cutting Edge Strategy for Synchronizing Advertising, Direct Mail, Telemarketing, and Field Sales*, (Lincolnwood, IL: NTC Business Books, 1995).
55. William T. Moran, "Insights from Pricing Research." In E.B. Bailey, ed., *Pricing Practices and Strategies* (New York, NY: The Conference Board, 1978), pp. 7–13.
56. Bob Tedeschi, "E-Commerce Report." *New York Times*, June 24, 2002, p. C8.
57. Dale Buss, "On Again, Off Again." *Brand Marketing*, February 2001, p. 51; Kenneth Hein, "Pepsi: This Time It's 'All About the Dew'." *Brandweek*, January 19, 2004, p. 4.
58. Heather Green, "Online Ads Take Off Again." *BusinessWeek*, May 5, 2003, p. 75.
59. Don E. Shultz, Stanley I. Tannenbaum, and Robert F. Lauterborn, *Integrated Marketing Communications: Putting It Together and Making It Work*, (Lincolnwood, IL: NTC Business Books, 1992); Don E. Schultz and Heidi Schultz, *IMC, The Next Generation: Five Steps For Delivering Value and Measuring Financial Returns*, (New York: McGraw-Hill, 2003).
60. Mark Blair, Richard Armstrong, and Mike Murphy, *The 360 Degree Brand in Asia: Creating More Effective Marketing Communications*, (Singapore: John Wiley, 2003), pp. 96–101. See also Don E. Schultz, "The Next Step in IMC?" *Marketing News*, August 15, 1994, pp. 8–9; Birger Wernerfelt, "Efficient Marketing Communications: Helping the Customer Learn." *Journal of Marketing Research*, May 1996, pp. 239–246.

Chapter 18

1. Ellen Neuborne, "Ads That Actually Sell Stuff." *Business 2.0*, June 2004, p. 78.
2. Russell H. Colley, *Defining Advertising Goals for Measured Advertising Results*, (New York: Association of National Advertisers, 1961).
3. Joanna Slater, "How Do I Love Thee?" *Far Eastern Economic Review*, March 18, 1999, pp. 48–49.
4. Frederik Balfour and David Kiley, "Ad Agencies Unchanged." *BusinessWeek*, April 25, 2005, pp. 18–19.
5. For a good discussion, see David A. Aaker and James M. Carman, "Are You Overadvertising?" *Journal of Advertising Research*, August–September 1982, pp. 57–70.
6. Donald E. Schultz, Dennis Martin, and William P. Brown, *Strategic Advertising Campaigns*, (Chicago: Crain Books, 1984), pp. 192–197.
7. Rajesh Chandy, Gerard J. Tellis, Debbie MacInnis, and Pattana Thaivanich, "What to Say When: Advertising Appeals in Evolving Markets." *Journal of Marketing Research*, November 2001, 38(4), pp. 399–414; Gerard J. Tellis, Rajesh Chandy, and Pattana Thaivanich, "Decomposing the Effects of Direct Advertising: Which Brand Works, When, Where, and How Long?" *Journal of Marketing Research*, February 2000, 37, pp. 32–46.
8. See George S. Low and Jakki J. Mohr, "Brand Managers' Perceptions of the Marketing Communications Budget Allocation Process." Cambridge, MA: Marketing Science Institute, Report No. 98-105, March 1998; and their "The Advertising Sales Promotion Trade-Off: Theory and Practice." Cambridge, MA: Marketing Science Institute, Report No. 92-127, October 1992. See also Gabriel J. Beihal and Daniel A. Sheinen, "Managing the Brand in a Corporate Advertising Environment: A Decision-Making Framework for Brand Managers." *Journal of Advertising*, June 22, 1998, 17, p. 99.
9. For an excellent review, see Greg Allenby and Dominique Hanssens, "Advertising Response." Marketing Science Institute, *Special Report*, No. 05-200, 2005.
10. Demetrios Vakratsas, Fred M. Feinberg, Frank M. Bass, and Gurumurthy Kalyanaram, "The Shape of Advertising Response Functions Revisited: A Model of Dynamic Probabilistic Thresholds." *Marketing Science*, Winter 2004, 23(1), pp. 109–19.

11. Leonard M. Lodish, Magid Abraham, Stuart Kalmenson, Jeanne Livelsberger, Beth Lubetkin, Bruce Richardson, and Mary Ellen Stevens, "How T.V. Advertising Works: A Meta-Analysis of 389 Real-World Split Cable T.V. Advertising Experiments." *Journal of Marketing Research*, May 1995, 32, pp. 125–39.
12. Greg Allenby and Dominique Hanssens, "Advertising Response." Marketing Science Institute, *Special Report*, No. 05-200, 2005; Jack Neff, "TV Doesn't Sell Package Goods." *Advertising Age*, May 24, 2004, pp. 1, 30.
13. Jim Aitchinson, *Cutting Edge Advertising*, 2nd ed., (Singapore: Prentice Hall, 2003).
14. Cleve Langton, "Searching for the Holy Global Ad Grail." *Brandweek*, June 5, 2006, p. 16.
15. Jessi Hempel, "Crowdsourcing: Milk the Masses for Inspiration." *BusinessWeek*, September 25, 2006, p. 38.
16. Todd Wasserman, "Intelligence Gathering." *Brandweek*, June 19, 2006, 47(25), pp. S8–S15, S18; Catherine P. Taylor, "Chevy's Crash, Burn." *Adweek*, April 17, 2006, 47(16), p. 14.
17. Craig Simons, "They Don't Kill Dragons, Do They?" *Newsweek*, May 9, 2005, p. 22.
18. Lian H. Wang, "Problems and Solutions." *Zhongguo Guanggao, China Advertising*, 3, pp. 14–15.
19. Gerard Prendergast, Yizheng Shi, and Douglas West, "Organizational Buying and Advertising Agency-Client Relationships in China." *Journal of Advertising*, 30(2), pp. 61–71.
20. Geoffrey A. Fowler, "China's Cultural Fabric Is a Challenge to Marketers." *Wall Street Journal* (Eastern edition), January 21, 2004, p. B7.
21. David Ogilvy, *Ogilvy on Advertising*, (New York, NY: Vintage Books, 1983).
22. Craig Simons, "Marketing to the Masses." *Far Eastern Economic Review*, September 4, 2003, p. 32.
23. For further reading, see Dorothy Cohen, *Legal Issues in Marketing Decision Making*, (Cincinnati, OH: South–Western, 1995).
24. Kim Bartel Sheehan, *Controversies in Contemporary Advertising*, (Thousand Oaks, CA: Sage Publications, 2003).
25. Geoffrey A. Fowler, "China's Cultural Fabric Is a Challenge to Marketers." *Wall Street Journal* (Eastern edition), January 21, 2004, p. B7.
26. Cris Prystay, "Unilever Ads Cause Irritation." *Asian Wall Street Journal*, April 20, 2002, p. A8.
27. The discussion on sex appeals in Asia is based on "Pushing the Sex Envelope." *Media*, September 20, 2002; "Asia Showing Penchant to Shock." *Media*, April 13, 2001.
28. Donald E. Schultz et al., *Strategic Advertising Campaigns*, (Chicago: Crain Books, 1984), p. 340.
29. Herbert E. Krugman, "What Makes Advertising Effective?" *Harvard Business Review*, March–April 1975, p. 98.
30. Thomas H. Davenport and John C. Beck, *The Attention Economy: Understanding the New Currency of Business*, (Boston: Harvard Business School Press, 2000).
31. "China Marketing: Cracking the Code." *BusinessWeek*, June 6, 2007.
32. Susan Thea Posnock, "It Can Control Madison Avenue." *American Demographics*, February 2004, pp. 29–33.
33. Sam Jaffe, "Easy Riders." *American Demographics*, March 2004, pp. 20–23.
34. Theresa Howard, "Ads Seek Greatness." *USA Today*, June 23, 2004, pp. 4B.
35. Geoffrey A. Fowler, "Outdoor Is In." *Far Eastern Economic Review*, February 12, 2002, pp. 34–35.
36. Jeff Pelline, "New Commercial Twist in Corporate Restrooms." *San Francisco Chronicle*, October 6, 1986.
37. "Toilets Offer No Escape." *Bangkok Post*, August 8, 2002.
38. Kong Ho Chua, "Unilever, DBS in ATM Ads Trial." *Streats* (Singapore), September 6, 2004.
39. Brian Steinberg and Suzanne Vranica, "Prime-Time TV's New Guest Stars: Products." *Wall Street Journal*, January 13, 2004, pp. B1, B4.
40. "Heineken Bonds with Casino Royale." May 29, 2006 <www.heinekeninternational.com>; "James Bond: Licensed to Brand." November 18, 2006 <www.namedevelopment.com>.
41. Joanne Lipman, "Product Placement Can Be Free Lunch." *Wall Street Journal*, November 25, 1991; John Lippman and Rick Brooks, "Hot Holiday Flick Pairs FedEx, Hanks." *Wall Street Journal*, December 11, 2000, pp. B1, B6.
42. Warren Berger, "That's Advertainment." *Business 2.0*, March 2003, pp. 91–95.
43. The discussion and examples are from Geoffrey A. Fowler and Helena Yu, "Switched On For a Hard Sell." *Far Eastern Economic Review*, June 3, 2004, pp. 36–38.
44. Kenneth R. Lord and Robert E. Burnkrant, "Attention versus Distraction: The Interactive Effect of Program Involvement and Attentional Devices on Commercial Processing." *Journal of Advertising*, March 1993, pp. 47–60; Kenneth R. Lord, Myung-Soo Lee, and Paul L. Sauer, "Program Context Antecedents of Attitude Toward Radio Commercials." *Journal of the Academy of Marketing Science*, Winter 1994, pp. 3–15.
45. Roland T. Rust, *Advertising Media Models: A Practical Guide*, (Lexington, MA: Lexington Books, 1986).

46. Craig Simons, "Marketing to the Masses." *Far Eastern Economic Review,* September 4, 2003, p. 32.

47. Kineta Hung, Flora Fang Gu, and David K. Tse, "Improving Media Decisions in China: A Targetability and Cost-Benefit Analysis." *Journal of Advertising*, 2005, 34(1), pp. 49–63.

48. Hani I. Mesak, "An Aggregate Advertising Pulsing Model with Wearout Effects." *Marketing Science*, Summer 1992, pp. 310–326; Fred M. Feinberg, "Pulsing Policies for Aggregate Advertising Models." *Marketing Science*, Summer 1992, pp. 221–234.

49. Josephine L.C.M. Woltman Elpers, Michel Wedel, and Rik G.M. Pieters, "Why Do Consumers Stop Viewing Television Commercials? Two Experiments on the Influence of Moment-to-Moment Entertainment and Information Value." *Journal of Marketing Research*, November 2003, 40, pp. 437–453.

50. Cris Prystay, "Sexing Up Asia's Ads." *Far Eastern Economic Review*, May 13, 2004, pp. 34–36.

51. "China Bans Nike Ad for Insulting National Dignity." *Straits Times* (Singapore) December 7, 2004, p. 7.

52. Craig Simons, "They Don't Kill Dragons, Do They?" *Newsweek,* May 9, 2005, p. 22.

53. Kristian S. Palda, *The Measurement of Cumulative Advertising Effect,* (Upper Saddle River, NJ: Prentice Hall, 1964), p. 87; David B. Montgomery and Alvin J. Silk, "Estimating Dynamic Effects of Market Communications Expenditures." *Management Science*, June 1972, pp. 485–501.

54. Gerard J. Tellis, Rajesh K. Chandy, and Pattana Thaivanich, "Which Ad Works, When, Where, and How Often? Modeling the Effects of Direct Television Advertising." *Journal of Marketing Research*, February 2000, 37, pp. 32–46; Ajay Kalra and Ronald C. Goodstein, "The Impact of Advertising Positioning Strategies on Consumer Price Sensitivity." *Journal of Marketing Research*, May 1998, pp. 210–24; Anil Kaul and Dick R. Wittink, "Empirical Generalizations about the Impact of Advertising on Price Sensitivity and Price." *Marketing Science*, Summer 1995, 14(3), pt. 1, pp. G151–60; David Walker and Tony M. Dubitsky, "Why Liking Matters." *Journal of Advertising Research*, May–June 1994, pp. 9–18; Abhilasha Mehta, "How Advertising Response Modeling (ARM) Can Increase Ad Effectiveness." *Journal of Advertising Research*, May–June 1994, pp. 62–74; John Deighton, Caroline Henderson, and Scott Neslin, "The Effects of Advertising on Brand Switching and Repeat Purchasing." *Journal of Marketing Research*, February 1994, pp. 28–43; Karin Holstius, "Sales Response to Advertising." *International Journal of Advertising*, September 1990, 9(1), pp. 38–56.

55. Nigel Hollis, "The Future of Tracking Studies." *Admap*, October 2004, pp. 151–53.

56. Laura Petrecca and Theresa Howard, "Nielsen Wants to Track Who Watches Commercials." *USA Today*, July 11, 2006.

57. From Robert C. Blattberg and Scott A. Neslin, *Sales Promotion: Concepts, Methods, and Strategies* (Upper Saddle River, NJ: Prentice Hall, 1990). This text provides the most comprehensive and analytical treatment of sales promotion to date. An up-to-date and comprehensive review of academic work on sales promotions can be found in Scott Neslin, "Sales Promotion." In *Handbook of Marketing*, Bart Weitz and Robin Wensley, eds., (London: Sage Publications, 2002), pp. 310–338.

58. Kusum Ailawadi, Karen Gedenk, and Scott A. Neslin, "Heterogeneity and Purchase Event Feedback in Choice Models: An Empirical Analysis with Implications for Model Building." *International Journal of Research in Marketing,* 1999, 16, pp. 177–198. See also Eric T. Anderson and Duncan Simester, "The Long-Run Effects of Promotion Depth on New Versus Established Customers: Three Field Studies." *Marketing Science*, Winter 2004, 23(1), pp. 4–20.

59. Carl Mela, Kamel Jedidi, and Douglas Bowman, "The Long-Term Impact of Promotions on Consumer Stockpiling." *Journal of Marketing Research*, May 1998, 35(2), pp. 250–262.

60. Harald J. Van Heerde, Peter S. H. Leeflang, and Dick Wittink, "The Estimation of Pre and Post-promotion Dips with Store-Level Scanner Data." *Journal of Marketing Research*, August 2000, 37(3), pp. 383–395.

61. Paul W. Farris and John A. Quelch, "In Defense of Price Promotion." *Sloan Management Review*, Fall 1987, pp. 63–69.

62. Roger A. Strang, "Sales Promotion: Fast Growth, Faulty Management." *Harvard Business Review*, July–August 1976, pp. 116–119.

63. "In-Store Promotions Grabbed More Attention." <www.acnielsen.com.cn>, July 6, 2005.

64. For a good summary of the research on whether promotion erodes the consumer franchise of leading brands, see Robert C. Blattberg and Scott A. Neslin, *Sales Promotion: Concepts, Methods, and Strategies*, (Upper Saddle River, NJ: Prentice Hall, 1990).

65. Robert George Brown, "Sales Response to Promotions and Advertising." *Journal of Advertising Research*, August 1974, pp. 36–37. See also Carl F. Mela, Sunil Gupta, and Donald R. Lehmann, "The Long-Term Impact of Promotion and Advertising on Consumer Brand Choice." *Journal of Marketing Research*, May 1997, pp. 248–261; Purushottam Papatla and Lakshman Krishnamurti, "Measuring the Dynamic Effects of Promotions on Brand Choice." *Journal of Marketing Research*, February 1996, pp. 20–35; Kamel Jedidi, Carl F. Mela, and Sunil Gupta, "Managing Advertising and Promotion for Long-Run Profitability." *Marketing Science*, 1999, 18(1), pp. 1–22.

66. Ibid.

67. "Bronze Reggie: Winners." *Brandweek*, March 26, 2007, 48(73), pp. R21+; Tammy la Gorce, "For Card-Carrying Members, Lounging at the Mall." *New York Times*, December 24, 2006.

68. Magid M. Abraham and Leonard M. Lodish, "Getting the Most Out of Advertising and Promotion." *Harvard Business Review*, May–June 1990, pp. 50–60. See also Shuba Srinivasan, Koen Pauwels, Dominique Hanssens, and Marnik Dekimpe, "Do Promotions Benefit Manufacturers, Retailers, or Both?" *Management Science*, May 2004, 50(5), pp. 617–629.

69. F. Kent Mitchel, "Advertising/Promotion Budgets: How Did We Get Here, and What Do We Do Now?" *Journal of Consumer Marketing*, Fall 1985, pp. 405–447.

70. For a model for setting sales-promotions objectives, see David B. Jones, "Setting Promotional Goals: A Communications Relationship Model." *Journal of Consumer Marketing*, 1994, 11(1), pp. 38–49.

71. <www.pmalink.org/awards/>; Jane L. Levere, "Body by Milk: More Than Just a White Mustache." *New York Times*, August 30, 2006.

72. See John C. Totten and Martin P. Block, *Analyzing Sales Promotion: Text and Cases*, 2nd ed., (Chicago: Dartnell, 1994), pp. 69–70.

73. Paul W. Farris and Kusum L. Ailawadi, "Retail Power: Monster or Mouse?" *Journal of Retailing*, Winter 1992, pp. 351–369.

74. "Retailers Buy Far in Advance to Exploit Trade Promotions." *Wall Street Journal*, October 9, 1986, p. 35; Rajiv Lal, J. Little, and J. M. Vilas-Boas, "A Theory of Forward Buying, Merchandising, and Trade Deals." *Marketing Science*, 1996, 15(1), pp. 21–37.

75. <www.pmalink.org/awards/>.

76. Arthur Stern, "Measuring the Effectiveness of Package Goods Promotion Strategies" (paper presented to the Association of National Advertisers, Glen Cove, NY, February 1978).

77. Kurt H. Schaffir and H. George Trenten, *Marketing Information Systems* (New York: Amacom, 1973), p. 81.

78. Joe A. Dodson, Alice M. Tybout, and Brian Sternthal, "Impact of Deals and Deal Retraction on Brand Switching." *Journal of Marketing Research*, February 1978, pp. 72–81.

79. Books on sales promotion include John C. Totten and Martin P. Block, *Analyzing Sales Promotion: Text and Cases*, 2nd ed., (Chicago: Dartnell, 1994); Don E. Schultz, William A. Robinson, and Lisa A. Petrison, *Sales Promotion Essentials*, 2nd ed. (Lincolnwood, IL: NTC Business Books, 1994); John Wilmshurst, *Below-the-Line Promotion* (Oxford, England: Butterworth/Heinemann, 1993); Robert C. Blattberg and Scott A. Neslin, *Sales Promotion*. For an expert systems approach to sales promotion, see John W. Keon and Judy Bayer, "An Expert Approach to Sales Promotion Management." *Journal of Advertising Research*, June–July 1986, pp. 19–26.

80. Frederik Balfour, "Free-Range Cash Cow." *BusinessWeek*, October 24, 2005, pp. 26–27.

81. Philip Kotler, "Atmospherics as a Marketing Tool." *Journal of Retailing*, Winter 1973–1974, pp. 48–64.

82. Craig Simon, "They Don't Kill Dragons, Do They?" *NewsWeek*, May 9, 2005, p. 22.

83. Shing Huel Peh, "The Lucrative Business of Sports in China." *Sunday Times* (Singapore), June 19, 2005, pp. L25; <www.theautochannel.com/news/2008/03/25/081849.html> accessed on April 9, 2008.

84. Wen Gong, Zhan G. Li, and Tiger Li, "Marketing to China's Youth: A Cultural Transformation Perspective." *Business Horizons*, 2004, 47(6), pp. 41–50.

85. "The Biggest Thing: Activation Holds Key to Sponsorship Success." *IEG Sponsorship Report*, April 2, 2007, pp. 1–3.

86. "Levi's Gives Away $285,000 for Women and Youth." *CSR Asia*, December 1, 2004.

87. The Association of National Advertisers has a useful source, *Event Marketing: A Management Guide*, which is available at <www.ana.net/bookstore>.

88. David Kiley, "Best Global Brands." *BusinessWeek*, August 6, 2007.

89. Dwight W. Catherwood and Richard L. Van Kirk, *The Complete Guide to Special Event Management* (New York: John Wiley, 1992).

90. William L. Shankin and John Kuzma, "Buying That Sporting Image." *Marketing Management*, Spring 1992, p. 65.

91. "The Sponsorship Factor." *IEG Sponsorship Report*, April 2, 2007, p. 7.

92. Peter Post, "Beyond Brand—The Power of Experience Branding." *ANA/ Advertiser* (October–November 2000).

93. B. Joseph Pine and James H. Gilmore, *The Experience Economy: Work Is Theatre and Every Business a Stage*, (Cambridge, MA: Harvard University Press, 1999).

94 "2006 Experiential Marketing Study," <www.jackmorton.com>.

95. For an excellent account, see Thomas L. Harris, *The Marketer's Guide to Public Relations*, (New York: John Wiley, 1991). See also Harris, *Value-Added Public Relations*, (Chicago: NTC Business Books, 1998).

96. Tom Duncan, *A Study of How Manufacturers and Service Companies Perceive and Use Marketing Public Relations*, (Muncie, IN: Ball State University, December 1985). For more on how to contrast the effectiveness of advertising with the effectiveness of PR, see Kenneth R. Lord and Sanjay Putrevu, "Advertising and Publicity: An Information Processing Perspective." *Journal of Economic Psychology*, March 1993, pp. 57–84.

97. Gary Lim, "Cruel Stunt or Crazy Game?" *Streats* (Singapore), November 20, 2002, p. 6.

98. For further reading on cause-related marketing, see P. Rajan Varadarajan and Anil Menon, "Cause-Related Marketing: A Co-Alignment of Marketing Strategy and Corporate Philanthropy." *Journal of Marketing*, July 1988, pp. 58–74.

99. Sui Noi Goh, "How Everton is Helping to Sell Mobile Phones Across China." *Sunday Times* (Singapore), January 12, 2003, p. 12.

100. Arthur M. Merims, "Marketing's Stepchild: Product Publicity." *Harvard Business Review*, November– December 1972, pp. 111–112. See also Katerine D. Paine, "There Is a Method for Measuring PR." *Marketing News*, November 6, 1987, p. 5.

Chapter 19

1. Assif Shameen, "Land of the Wired." *Asia Inc.*, April, 2004, pp. 22–26; <www.internetworldstats.com> accessed on April 10, 2008; Ian Stewart, Talk given at *New Rules, New ROI Conference*, February 27, 2008; "Trends in Online Shopping: A Global Nielsen Consumer Report." *A.C. Nielsen Report*, February 2008.

2. The terms *direct-order marketing* and *direct-relationship marketing* were suggested as subsets of direct marketing by Stan Rapp and Tom Collins in *The Great Marketing Turnaround (*Upper Saddle River, NJ: Prentice Hall, 1990).

3. Eric Wan, "Chinese Mainland Internet Population Tops 200 Million." January 17, 2008, <http://www.chinatechnews.com/2008/01/17/6302-chinese-mainlands-internet-population-tops-200-million/>.

4. Geoffrey A. Fowler, "Junk Mail Joys." *Far Eastern Economic Review*, March 6, 2003, p. 36.

5. Bill McNutt III, "Opportunity to the East." *Direct*, November 1, 2002.

6. Geoffrey A. Fowler, "Junk Mail Joys." *Far Eastern Economic Review*, March 6, 2003, p. 36.

7. Bob Stone, *Successful Direct Marketing Methods*, 8th ed., (Lincolnwood, IL: NTC Business Books, 2007). See also David Shepard Associates, *The New Direct Marketing*, 3rd ed., (Chicago: Irwin, 1998); Amiya K. Basu, Atasi Basu, and Rajeev Batra, "Modeling the Response Pattern to Direct Marketing Campaigns." *Journal of Marketing Research*, May 1995, pp. 204–212.

8. Edward L. Nash, *Direct Marketing: Strategy, Planning, Execution*, 5th ed., (New York: McGraw-Hill, 2007).

9. Rachel McLaughlin, "Get the Envelope Opened!" *Target Marketing*, September 1998, pp. 37–39.

10. The *average customer longevity (N)* is related to the *customer retention rate (CR)*. Suppose the company retains 80 percent of its customers each year. Then the average customer longevity is given by: $N = 1 / (1 - CR) = 1 / .2 = 5$.

11. "L.L. Bean Achieves a Perfect Fit in Japan." *Investing in Japan*, <www.jetro.go.jp>, October 2003; Mari Yamaguchi, "Japanese Customers Shun Local Catalogs to Buy American." *Marketing News*, December 2, 1996, p. 12.

12. Geoffrey A. Fowler, "Junk Mail Joys." *Far Eastern Economic Review*, March 6, 2003, p. 36.

13. Heinz Bulos, "Filipinos are Getting the Message." *BusinessWeek*, November 22, 2004, p. 28.

14. Siew Hua Seah, "Making M-Commerce a Success." *Today* (Singapore), July 12, 2005, p. 28.

15. Charles Duhigg, "Telemarketing Thieves Sharpen Their Focus on the Elderly." *New York Times*, May 20, 2007.

16. Tony Case, "Growing Up." *Interactive Quarterly*, April 19, 2004, pp. 32–34.

17. David L. Smith and Karen McFee, "Media Mix 101: Online Media for Traditional Marketers." accessed September 2003, at <advantage.msn.com/articles/MediaMix101_2.asp>.

18. Emily Steel, "Advertising's Brave New World." *Wall Street Journal*, May 25, 2007; Johnnie L. Roberts, "How to Count Eyeballs." *Newsweek*, November 27, 2006, p. 42.

19. Online Publisher's Association, "OPA Media Consumption Study." January 2002.

20. "China's Online Ad Boom." *BusinessWeek*, May 15, 2006.

21. Kevin J. Delaney, "Once-Wary Industry Giants Embrace Internet Advertising." *Wall Street Journal*, April 17, 2006; "China: Online Marketing Comes of Age." *BusinessWeek*, June 12, 2007.

22. Ian Stewart (2008) based on a conference presentation at *New Rules, New ROI Conference,* February 27, 2008.

23. Asim Ansari and Carl F. Mela, "E-Customization." *Journal of Marketing Research,* May 2003, 40(2),pp. 131–45.

24. Daniel Michaels and J. Lynn Lunsford, "Ad-Sales Woes Likely to Continue." *Wall Street Journal*, December 4, 2006; Jack Neff, "Axe Cuts Past Competitors, Claims Market Lead." *Advertising Age*, May 14, 2006; Byron Acohido, "Rich Media Enriching PC Ads." *USA Today,* February 25, 2004.

25. "China's Online Ad Boom." *BusinessWeek*, May 15, 2006; "China: Online Marketing Comes of Age." *BusinessWeek*, June 12, 2007.

26. Philip Kotler, *According to Kotler*, (New York: American Management Association, 2005).

27. Peter J. Danaher, Guy W. Mullarkey, and Skander Essegaier, "Factors Affecting Web Site Visit Duration: A Cross-Domain Analysis." *Journal of Marketing Research*, May 2006, 43, pp. 182–194.

28. Jeffrey F. Rayport and Bernard J. Jaworski, *e-commerce*, (New York: McGraw-Hill, 2001), p. 116.

29. Bob Tedeschi, "E-Commerce Report." *New York Times*, June 24, 2002.

30. Jan-Benedict E.M. Steenkamp and Inge Geyskens, "How Country Characteristics Affect the Perceived Value of Web Sites." *Journal of Marketing*, July 2006, 70, pp. 136–50.

31. Nitish Singh and Hisako Matsuo, "Measuring Cultural Adaptation on the Web: A Content Analytic Study of U.S. and Japanese Web Sites." *Journal of Business Research*, 2004, 57, pp. 864–872.

32. Allison Fass, "A Kingdom Seeks Magic." *Forbes*, October 16, 2006, pp. 68–70; David Kiley, "The Craziest Ad Guys in America." *BusinessWeek*, May 22, 2006, pp. 72–80; <www.subservientchicken.com>.

33. "Prime Clicking Time." *Economist*, May 31, 2003, p. 65; Ben Elgin, "Search Engines Are Picking Up Steam." *BusinessWeek*, March 24, 2003, p. 86–87.

34. Ned Desmond, "Google's Next Runaway Success." *Business 2.0*, November 2002, p. 73.

35. Heather Green, "Online Ads Take Off Again." *BusinessWeek*, May 5, 2003, p. 75.

36. Paul Sloan, "The Quest for the Perfect Online Ad." *Business 2.0*, March 2007, pp. 88–93; Catherine Holahan, "The Promise of Online Display Ads." *BusinessWeek*, May 1, 2007.

37. Jessica Mintz, "Microsoft Adds Behavioral Targeting." *Associated Press*, December 28, 2006.

38. Stephen Baker, "Pop-Up Ads Had Better Start Pleasing." *BusinessWeek*, December 8, 2003, p. 40.

39. Youngme Moon, "BMW Films." Harvard Business School Case #9-5-2-046.

40. Heather Green, "Searching for the Pod of Gold." *BusinessWeek*, November 14, 2005, pp. 88–90.

41. Seth Godin, *Permission Marketing: Turning Strangers into Friends and Friends into Customers*, (New York: Simon & Schuster, 1999).

42. Chana R. Schoenberger, "Web? What Web?" *Forbes*, June 10, 2002, p. 132.

43. Suzanne Vranica, "Marketers Give E-Mail Another Look." *Wall Street Journal*, July 17, 2006.

44. "eMarketer: Worldwide Mobile Ad Spending to Hit $19.1 billion by 2012." <www.sfnblog.com>, March 27, 2008.

45. Craig Harvey (2008), paper presented at *New Rules, New ROI Conference*, February 27, 2008.

46. Norimitsu Onishi, "Japan's Best Sellers Go Cellular." *International Herald Tribune*, January 20, 2008.

47. Brooks Barnes, "Toyota Aims Young, Sponsors Fox Spinoff for Cell Phone Screens." *Wall Street Journal*, April 24, 2006; Matt Richtel, "Verizon to Allow Ads on Its Mobile Phones." *New York Times*, December 26, 2006.

48. For a thorough review of relevant academic literature, see Christophe Van Den Bulte and Stefan Wuyts, *Social Networks and Marketing*, (Marketing Science Institute Relevant Knowledge Series, Cambridge, MA, 2007).

49. Louise Story, "What We Talk About When We Talk about Brands." *New York Times*, November 24, 2006.

50. Elizabeth Wellington, "Freebies and Chitchat Are Hot Marketing Tools." *Philadelphia Inquirer*, December 31, 2003; Bob Sperber, "Krispy Kreme Word-of-Mouth Tactics Continue to Go Against the Grain." *Brandweek*, October 21, 2002, p. 9.

51. Renée Dye, "The Buzz on Buzz." *Harvard Business Review*, November–December 2000, pp. 139–46.

52. <http://discussions.apple.com/index.jspa>; <http://socialize.morningstar.com/newsocialize/asp/coverpage.asp?pgid=hetabdi>; <www.fool.com/>; Nanette Byrnes, "Leader of the Packs." *BusinessWeek*, October 31, 2005; <www.quickbooksgroup.com>.

53. Dave Balter and John Butman, "Clutter Cutter." *Marketing Management*, July–August 2006, pp. 49–50.

54. Emanuel Rosen, *The Anatomy of Buzz* (New York: Currency, 2000).

55. Elison A.C. Lim, Swee Hoon Ang, and Soo Jiuan Tan (2008), "Careful Whispers: The Effects of Disclosure, Expertise, and Skepticism in Stealth Marketing Effectiveness." *Working* Paper, University of Melbourne; George Silverman, *The Secrets of Word-of-Mouth Marketing*, (New York: Amacom, 2001); Emanuel Rosen, *The Anatomy of Buzz*, (New York: Currency, 2000), chapter 12; "Viral Marketing." *Sales & Marketing Automation*, November 1999, pp. 12–14.

56. Robert Berner, "I Sold It through the Grapevine." *BusinessWeek*, May 29, 2006, pp. 32–34.

57. Danielle Sacks, "Down the Rabbit Hole." *Fast Company*, November 2006, pp. 86–93; "Fast Talk." *Fast Company*, September 2006, pp. 21–24.

58. Jacqueline Johnson Brown, Peter M. Reingen, and Everett M. Rogers, *Diffusion of Innovations*, 4th ed., (New York: Free Press, 1995); J. Johnson Brown and Peter Reingen, "Social Ties and Word-of-Mouth Referral Behavior." *Journal of Consumer Research*, December 3, 1987, 14, pp. 350–62; Peter H. Riengen and Jerome B. Kernan, "Analysis of Referral Networks in Marketing: Methods and Illustration." *Journal of Marketing Research*, November 1986, pp. 37–78.

59. Malcolm Gladwell, *The Tipping Point: How Little Things Can Make a Big Difference*, (Boston: Little, Brown & Company, 2000).

60. Douglas Atkin, *The Culting of Brands: When Customers Become True Believers*, (New York: Penguin, 2004); Marian Salzman, Ira Matathia, and Ann O'Reilly, *Buzz: Harness the Power of Influence and Create Demand*, (New York: John Wiley, 2003).

61. Dave Balter and John Butman, "Clutter Cutter." "Is There a Reliable Way to Measure Word-of-Mouth Marketing?" *Marketing NPV* 3, 3, 2006, pp. 3–9.

62. Stephen Baker, "Looking for a Blog in a Haystack." *BusinessWeek*, July 25, 2006, p. 38.

63. Pew Internet & American Life Project, July 2006; <www.pewinternet.org>.

64. Todd Wasserman, "Report: Consumers Don't Trust Blogs." *Brandweek*, September 4, 2006, p. 10; For an academic discussion of chat rooms, recommendation sites, and customer review sections online, see Dina Mayzlin, "Promotional Chat on the Internet." *Marketing Science*, March–April 2006, 25, pp. 155–63; and Judith Chevalier and Dina Mayzlin, "The Effect of Word of Mouth on Sales: Online Book Reviews." *Journal of Marketing Research*, August 2006, 43, pp. 345–54.

65. This section is based on an excellent summary, "Is There a Reliable Way to Measure Word-of-Mouth Marketing?" *Marketing NPV* 3, 3, 2006, pp. 3–9, available at <www.marketingnpv.com>.

66. Bamrung Amnatcharoenrit, "Asia Poised to Stay Atop Direct-Sales Growth Table." *Knight Ridder Tribune Business News*, October 1, 2003, p. 1.

67. Carl Quintanilla and Liz Claman, "Nu Skin Asia Pacific—CEO Interview." *CNBC/Dow Jones Business Video*, October 1, 2002.

68. Cris Prystay, "Unilever Raises Its India Game." *Far Eastern Economic Review*, October 30, 2003, p. 50.

69. "One-to-One for Over 1.3 Billion." *Precision Marketing*, November 29, 2002.

70. Carl Quintanilla and Liz Claman, "Nu Skin Asia Pacific—CEO Interview." *CNBC/Dow Jones Business Video*, October 1, 2002.

71. Adapted from Robert N. McMurry, "The Mystique of Super-Salesmanship." *Harvard Business Review*, March–April 1961, p. 114. See also William C. Moncrief III, "Selling Activity and Sales Position Taxonomies for Industrial Salesforces." *Journal of Marketing Research*, August 1986, pp. 261–270.

72. Margot Cohen, "More than a Pretty Face." *Far Eastern Economic Review*, April 1, 2004, pp. 36–37.

73. Lawrence G. Friedman and Timothy R. Furey, *The Channel Advantage: Going to Marketing with Multiple Sales Channels* (Oxford, UK: Butterworth-Heinemann, 1999).

74. Philip Kotler, Neil Rackham, and Suj Krishnaswamy, "Ending the War between Sales & Marketing." *Harvard Business Review*, July–August 2006, pp. 68–78; Timothy M. Smith, Srinath Gopalakrishna, and Rubikar Chaterjee, "A Three-Stage Model of Integrated Marketing Communications at the Marketing–Sales Interface." *Journal of Marketing Research*, November 2006, 43, pp. 546–79.

75. Christopher Hosford, "Rebooting Hewlett-Packard." *Sales and Marketing Management*, July–August 2006, 158(6), p. 32+.

76. "Hitachi Data Systems Announces Expansion of Global Sales Operation." *Business Wire*, April 4, 2005.

77. John S. Hill, Richard R. Still, and Unal O. Boya, "Managing the Multinational Sales Force." *International Marketing Review*, 1991, 8(1), p. 23; Bryan Batson, "Chinese Fortunes." *Sales & Marketing Management*, March 1994, pp. 94–95.

78. Luis R. Gomez-Mejia, David B. Balkin, and Robert L. Cardy, *Managing Human Resources*, (Upper Saddle River, NJ: Prentice Hall, 1995), pp. 416–418.

79. "What Salespeople Are Paid." *Sales & Marketing Management*, February 1995, pp. 30–31; Christopher Power, Lisa Driscoll, and Earl Bohn, "Smart Selling." *BusinessWeek*, August 3, 1992, pp. 46–48; William Keenan Jr., *The Sales & Marketing Management Guide to Sales Compensation Planning: Commissions, Bonuses & Beyond*, (Chicago: Probus Publishing, 1994).

80. Sonke Albers, "Sales-Force Management—Compensation, Motivation, Selection, and Training." In *Handbook of Marketing*, Bart Weitz and Robin Wensley, eds., (London: Sage, 2002), pp. 248–266.

81. Earl D. Honeycutt, Jr. and John B. Ford, "Guidelines for Managing an International Sales Force." *Industrial Marketing Management*, 1995, 24(2), pp. 135–144; Sandra S. Liu, Lucette B. Comer, and Alan J. Dubinsky, "Gender Differences in Attitudes Toward Women as Sales Managers in the People's Republic of China." *Journal of Personal Selling & Sales Management*, Fall 2001, pp. 303–311.

82. John S. Hill and Meg Birdseye, "Salesperson Selection in Multinational Corporations: An Empirical Study." *Journal of Personal Selling and Sales Force Management*, Summer 1989, pp. 39–47; Jeffrey E. Lewin and Wesley J. Johnson, "International Salesforce Management: A Relationship Perspective." *Journal of Business & Industrial Marketing*, 1997, 12(3/4), pp. 232–247.

83. Earl D. Honeycutt, Jr., John B. Ford, Robert A. Lupton, and Theresa B. Flaherty, "Selecting and Training the International Sales Force." *Industrial Marketing Management*, 28, 1999, pp. 627–635.

84. A. Mukund, "Amway's Indian Network Marketing Experience." *ECCH Collection*, Case #501-059-1.

85. Ibid.

86. M. Asri Jantan and Earl D. Honeycutt, Jr., "Sales Training Practices in Malaysia." *Multinational Business Review*, Spring 2002, pp. 72–78.

87. The discussion of Japanese sales training relies on John S. Hill, Richard R. Still, and Unal O. Boya, "Managing the Multi-national Sales Force." *International Marketing Review*, 1991, 8(1), p. 23. Mauricio Lorence, "Assignment USA: The Japanese Solution." *Sales & Marketing Management*, October 1992, p. 63.

88. Margot Cohen, "More than a Pretty Face." *Far Eastern Economic Review*, April 1, 2004, pp. 36–37.

89. Nanette Byrnes, "Avon Calling—Lots of New Reps." *BusinessWeek*, June 2, 2003, pp. 53–54.

90. Margot Cohen, "More than a Pretty Face." *Far Eastern Economic Review*, April 1, 2004, pp. 36–37.

91. Michael R. W. Bommer, Brian F. O'Neil, and Beheruz N. Sethna, "A Methodology for Optimizing Selling Time of Salespersons." *Journal of Marketing Theory and Practice*, Spring 1994, pp. 61–75; See also Joseph Kissen, "On the Optimality of Delegating Pricing Authority to the Sales Force." *Journal of Marketing*, January 2001, 65, pp. 62–70.

92. Thomas Blackshear and Richard E. Plank, "The Impact of Adaptive Selling on Sales Effectiveness Within the Pharmaceutical Industry." *Journal of Marketing Theory and Practice*, Summer 1994, pp. 106–125.

93. Dartnell Corporation, *30th Sales Force Compensation Survey*. Other breakdowns show that 12.7 percent is spent in service calls, 16 percent in administrative tasks, 25.1 percent in telephone selling, and 17.4 percent in waiting/traveling.

94. James A. Narus and James C. Anderson, "Industrial Distributor Selling: The Roles of Outside and Inside Sales." *Industrial Marketing Management*, 15, 1986, pp. 55–62.

95. Willem Verbeke and Richard P. Bagozzi, "Sales Call Anxiety: Exploring What it Means When Fear Rules a Sales Encounter." *Journal of Marketing*, July 2000, 64, pp. 88–101.

96. Gilbert A. Churchill Jr., Neil M. Ford, and Orville C. Walker Jr., *Sales Force Management: Planning, Implementation and Control*, 4th ed., (Homewood, IL: Irwin, 1993). See also Jhinuk Chowdhury, "The Motivational Impact of Sales Quotas on Effort." *Journal of Marketing Research*, February 1993, pp. 28–41; Murali K. Mantrala, Prabhakant Sinha, and Andris A. Zoltners, "Structuring a Multiproduct Sales Quota-Bonus Plan for a Heterogeneous Sales Force: A Practical Model-Based Approach." *Marketing Science*, 1994, 13(2), pp. 121–144; Wujin Chu, Eitan Gerstner, and James D. Hess, "Costs and Benefits of Hard-Sell." *Journal of Marketing Research*, February 1995, pp. 97–102; Manfred Krafft, "In Empirical Investigation of the Antecedents of Sales Force Control Systems." *Journal of Marketing*, July 1999, 63, pp. 120–134.

97. Eilene Zimmerman, "Quota Busters." *Sales & Marketing Management*, January 2001, pp. 59–63.

98. Melanie Warner, "Confessions of a Control Freak." *Fortune*, September 4, 2000, p. 30; Peter Burrows, "The Era of Efficiency." *BusinessWeek*, June 18, 2001, p. 92.

99. Lisa Vaas, "Oracle Teaches Its Sales Force to Play Nice." *eWeek*, July 28, 2004; Lisa Vaas, "Oracle's Sales Force, Reorg Finally Bears Fruit." *eWeek*, December 17, 2003; Ian Mount, "Out of Control." *Business 2.0*, August 2002, pp. 38–44.

100. John S. Hill and Arthur W. Allaway, "How U.S.-based Companies Manage Sales in Foreign Countries." *Industrial Marketing Management*, February 1993, pp. 7–16; John S. Hill, Richard R. Still, and Unal O. Boya, "Managing the Multinational Sales Force." *International Marketing Review*, 1991, 8(1), p. 23.

101. Philip M. Posdakoff and Scott B. MacKenzie, "Organizational Citizenship Behaviors and Sales Unit Effectiveness." *Journal of Marketing Research*, August 1994, pp. 351–363. See also Andrea L. Dixon, Rosann L. Spiro, and Magbul Jamil, "Successful and Unsuccessful Sales Calls: Measuring Salesperson Attributions and Behavioral Intentions." *Journal of Marketing*, July 2001, 65, pp. 64–78; Willem Verbeke and Richard P. Bagozzi, "Sales Call Anxiety: Exploring What It Means When Fear Rules a Sales Encounter"; Siew Meng Leong, Donna M. Randall, and Joseph A. Cote, "Exploring the Organizational Commitment–Performance Linkage of Life Insurance Salespeople." *Journal of Business Research*, January 1994, pp. 57–64.

102. Andrea L. Dixon, Rosann L. Spiro, and Magbul Jamil, "Successful and Unsuccessful Sales Calls: Measuring Salesperson Attributions and Behavioral Intentions." *Journal of Marketing*, July 2001, 65, pp. 64–78.

103. Neil Rackham, *SPIN Selling*, (New York: McGraw-Hill, 1988). Also see his *The SPIN Selling Fieldbook* (New York: McGraw-Hill, 1996); James Lardner, "Selling Salesmanship." *Business 2.0*, December 2002–January 2003, p. 66; Sharon Drew Morgen, *Selling with Integrity: Reinventing Sales through Collaboration, Respect, and Serving* (New York: Berkeley Books, 1999); Neil Rackham and John De Vincentis, *Rethinking the Sales Force* (New York: McGraw-Hill, 1996).

104. Some of the following discussion is based on W. J. E. Crissy, William H. Cunningham, and Isabella C. M. Cunningham, *Selling: The Personal Force in Marketing* (New York: John Wiley, 1977), pp. 119–29.

105. Gerard Prendergast, Yizheng Shi, and Douglas West, "Organizational Buying and Advertising Agency–Client Relationships in China." *Journal of Advertising*, 2001, 30(2), pp. 61–71.

106. Joel E. Urbany, "Justifying Profitable Pricing." Working Paper Series, Marketing Science Institute, Report No. 00-117, 2000, pp. 17–18.

107. For additional reading, see Howard Raiffa, *The Art and Science of Negotiation*, (Cambridge, MA: Harvard University Press, 1982); Max H. Bazerman and Margaret A. Neale, *Negotiating Rationally*, (New York: The Free Press, 1992);

James C. Freund, *Smart Negotiating*, (New York: Simon & Schuster, 1992); Frank L. Acuff, *How to Negotiate Anything with Anyone Anywhere Around the World*, (New York: American Management Association, 1993); Jehoshua Eliashberg, Gary L. Lilien, and Nam Kim, "Searching for Generalizations in Business Marketing Negotiations." *Marketing Science*, 1995, 14(3) (pt. 1), pp. G47–G60.

108. This discussion draws from Gary Bonvillian and William A. Nowlin, "Cultural Awareness: An Essential Element of Doing Business Abroad." *Business Horizons*, November–December 1994, pp. 44–50; Jon P. Alston, "*Wa, Guanxi*, and *Inhwa*: Managerial Principles in Japan, China, and Korea." *Business Horizons*, March–April 1989, pp. 26–31; Dean C. Barnlund, "Public and Private Self in Communicating with Japan." *Business Horizons*, March–April 1989, pp. 32–40; Sergy Frank, "Global Negotiating." *Sales & Marketing Management*, May 1992, pp. 67–70; "Tips for Successful Business in Asia." *Biz-in-Thailand.com*, <www.business-in-asia.com/th_bihours.html>, viewed on November 21, 2002; "Understanding Asia: Principles of Negotiation." <www.qtte.com.au/international/asia/negotiation.htm>, viewed on November 21, 2002.

109. Kwaku Atuahene-Gima and Haiyang Li, "When Does Trust Matter? Antecedents and Contingent Effects of Supervisee Trust on Performance of Selling New Products in China and the United States." *Journal of Marketing*, July 2002, pp. 61–81.

110. Wai-Sum Siu, "Marketing Philosophies and Company Performance of Small Chinese Firms in Hong Kong." *Journal of Marketing Theory & Practice*, Winter 2000, pp. 25–37.

111. Jon P. Alston, "*Wa, Guanxi*, and *Inhwa*: Managerial Principles in Japan, China, and Korea." *Business Horizons*, March–April 1989, pp. 26–31.

112. W. K. Tsang, "Can *Guanxi* Be a Source of Sustained Competitive Advantage for Doing Business in China?" *Academy of Management Executive* 12(2), 1998, pp. 64–74; Lr. Chon-Phung Lim, "MNCs Need to Learn the Art of Doing Business in Asia." *Business Times* (Singapore), February 22, 1999, p. 9.

113. Yadong Luo, "*Guanxi* and Performance of Foreign-Invested Enterprises in China: An Empirical Inquiry." *Management International Review*, January 1997, pp. 51–70.

114. Stephen S. Standifird and Scott Marshall, "The Transaction Cost Advantage of *Guanxi*-Based Business Practices." *Journal of World Business*, Spring 2000, pp. 21–42.

115. Hellmut Schütte and Deanna Ciarlante, *Consumer Behavior in Asia*, (London: MacMillan, 1998), pp. 187–189.

116. Robert W. Armstrong and Siew Min Yee, "Do Chinese Trust Chinese: A Study of Chinese Buyers and Sellers in Malaysia." *Journal of International Marketing*, 2001, 9(3), pp. 63–86.

117. David M. Reid, *Effective Marketing for Japan: The Consumer Goods Experience*, (Hong Kong:Business International Asia/Pacific Ltd, June 1991), pp. 107–110; Sergy Frank, "Global Negotiating." *Sales & Marketing Management*, May 1992, pp. 64–70.

118. Manjeet Kripalani and Steve Hamm, "Leaving a Vacuum at Wipro." *BusinessWeek*, July 11, 2005, p. 22.

119. David M. Reid, *Effective Marketing for Japan: The Consumer Goods Experience*; Sergy Frank, "Global Negotiating." *Sales & Marketing Management*, May 1992, pp. 64–70.

120. Douglas Daft, "Teach the World To Sell." *Newsweek Special Edition: Asia*, July–September 2001, p. 43.

Chapter 20

1. Amy Barrett, "J&J: Reinventing How It Invents." *BusinessWeek*, April 17, 2006, pp. 60–61.

2. For some scholarly reviews, see Ely Dahan and John R. Hauser, "Product Development: Managing a Dispersed Process." In *Handbook of Marketing*, Bart Weitz and Robin Wensley, eds., (London: Sage, 2002), pp. 179–222; Dipak Jain, "Managing New-Product Development for Strategic Competitive Advantage." In *Kellogg on Marketing*, Dawn Iacobucci, ed., (New York: John Wiley, 2001), pp. 130–48; Jerry Wind and Vijay Mahajan, "Issues and Opportunities in New-Product Development: An Introduction to the Special Issue." *Journal of Marketing Research*, February 1997, 34, pp. 1–12.

3. "Beware of China's Rise in R&D, Japan Warns." *Straits Times* (Singapore), July 2, 2005, p. 15.

4. Booz, Allen & Hamilton, *New Products Management for the 1980s*, (New York: Booz, Allen & Hamilton, 1982).

5. "Don't Laugh at Gilded Butterflies." *Economist*, April 24, 2004, pp. 71–73. For some academic discussion of the effects of new-product introductions on markets, see Harald J. Van Heerde, Carl F. Mela, and Puneet Manchanda, "The Dynamic Effect of Innovation on Market Structure." *Journal of Marketing Research*, May 2004, 41, pp. 166–83.

6. Stefan Wuyts, Shantanu Dutta, and Stefan Stremersch, "Portfolios of Interfirm Agreements in Technology-Intensive Markets: Consequences for Innovation and Profitability." *Journal of Marketing*, April 2004, 68, pp. 88–100; Aric Rindfleisch and Christine Moorman, "The Acquisition and Utilization of Information in New-Product Alliance: A Strength-of-Ties Perspective." *Journal of Marketing*, April 2001, 65, pp. 1–18.

7. Steve Hoeffler, "Measuring Preferences for Really New Products." *Journal of Marketing Research*, November 2003, 40, pp. 406–20; Glen Urban, Bruce Weinberg, and John R. Hauser, "Premarket Forecasting of Really New Products." *Journal of Marketing*, January 1996, 60, pp. 47–60.

8. Ashish Sood and Gerard J. Tellis, "Technological Evolution and Radical Innovation." *Journal of Marketing*, July 2005, 69, pp. 152–68.

9. For more discussion, see Jakki Mohr, *Marketing of High-Technology Products and Innovations*, 2nd ed., (Upper Saddle River, NJ: Prentice Hall, 2005).

10. Steve Hamm, "Speed Demons." *BusinessWeek*, March 27, 2006, pp. 69–76.

11. Christina Passariello, "Brand New Bag: Louis Vuitton Tries Modern Methods on Factory Lines." *Wall Street Journal*, October 9, 2006.

12. Rajan Varadarajan, "Business Insight (A Special Report); Think Small: Every Company Wants to Hit It Big with Market-Shattering Innovations; But the Little Changes, Too, Can Make a Huge Difference." *Wall Street Journal*, March 3, 2007.

13. "How Consumer Goods Companies Are Coping with Complexity." McKinsey Quarterly, May 2007; Clayton M. Christensen, *The Innovator's Dilemma: When New Technologies Cause Great Firms to Fail*, (Boston, MA: Harvard University Press, 1997).

14. Ely Dahan and John R. Hauser, "Product Development: Managing a Dispersed Process." In *Handbook of Marketing*, Bart Weitz and Robin Wensley, eds., (London: Sage Publications, 2002), pp. 179–222.

15. David Welch, Kathleen Kerwin, Gail Edmonson, and John Carey, "Gentlemen, Start Your Hybrids." *BusinessWeek*, April 26, 2004, pp. 42–43; David Ibison, "Hybrid Cars 'Terrible Prospect' says Ghosn." *Financial Times*, September 23, 2005, p. 21. See also Alex Taylor III, "Do Hybrid Motors Have Sex Appeal." *Fortune*, October 3, 2005, p. 13; Norihiko Shorouzu and Jathon Sapsford, "Hybrid-Engine Race Gathers Steam." *Wall Street Journal*, October 19, 2005, pp. 16–17; "Toward the Ultimate Eco-car: Toyota." <www.enn.com/business/article/37601>, July 9, 2008.

16. Robert G. Cooper and Elko J. Kleinschmidt, *New Products: The Key Factors in Success*, (Chicago: American Marketing Association, 1990).

17. Ian Rowley, "TV Screens Face a Dazzling New Rival." *BusinessWeek*, July 25/August 1, 2005, p. 18.

18. Bruce Nussbaum, "Get Creative!" *BusinessWeek*, August 8/15, 2005, pp. 40–52.

19. Thomas N. Burton, "By Learning from Failures Lilly Keeps Drug Pipelines Full." *Wall Street Journal*, April 21, 2004.

20. Lauren Swanson, "A Chinese View of Birthing and Growing Ideas." *Marketing News*, March 31, 1997, p. 17.

21. Nanette Byrnes, "Xerox's New Design Team Customers." *BusinessWeek*, May 7, 2007, p. 72.

22. David Welch, "Can Stodgy GM Turn Stylish?" *BusinessWeek*, November 11, 2002, pp. 111–112.

23. David S. Hopkins, *Options In New-Product Organization*, (New York: Conference Board, 1974); Doug Ayers, Robert Dahlstrom, and Steven J. Skinner, "An Exploratory Investigation of Organizational Antecedents to New Product Success." *Journal of Marketing Research*, February 1997, pp. 107–116.

24. Danielle Sacks, Chuck Salter, Alan Deutschman, and Scott Kirsner, "Innovation Scouts." *Fast Company*, May 2007, pp. 90+.

25. Rajesh Sethi, Daniel C. Smith, and C. Whan Park, "Cross Functional Product Development Teams, Creativity, and the Innovativeness of New Consumer Products." *Journal of Marketing Research*, February 2001, 38, pp. 73–85.

26. Michael Song and Mark E. Parry, "The Determinants of Japanese New Product Successes." *Journal of Marketing Research*, February 1997, 34, pp. 64–76. See also Michael Song and Mark E. Parry, "A Cross-National Comparative Study of New Product Development Processes: Japan and the United States." *Journal of Marketing*, April 1997, 61, pp. 1–18.

27. Robert G. Cooper, "Stage-Gate Systems: A New Tool for Managing New Products." *Business Horizons*, May-June 1990, pp. 44–54. See also "The New Prod System: The Industry Experience." *Journal of Product Innovation Management*, 1992, 9, pp. 113–127.

28. Robert Cooper, *Product Leadership: Creating and Launching Superior New Products*, (New York: Perseus Books, 1998).

29. Ely Dahan and John R. Hauser, "Product Development: Managing a Dispersed Process." In *Handbook of Marketing*, Bart Weitz and Robin Wensley, eds., (London: Sage Publications, 2002), pp. 179–222.

30. John Hauser and Gerard J. Tellis, "Research on Innovation: A Review and Agenda for Marketing." 2004, working paper.

31. David Rocks, "China Design." *BusinessWeek*, November 21, 2005, pp. 64–72.

32. Abbie J. Griffin and John Hauser, "The Voice of the Customer." *Marketing Science*, Winter 1993, pp. 1–27.

33. Peter C. Honebein and Roy F. Cammarano, "Customers at Work." *Marketing Management*, January–February 2006, pp. 26–31; Peter C. Honebein and Roy F. Cammarano, *Creating Do-It-Yourself Customers: How Great Customer Experiences Build Great Companies*, (Mason, OH: Texere Southwestern Educational Publishing, 2005).

34. Patricia Seybold, *Outside Innovation: How Your Customers Will Codesign Your Company's Future*, (New York: Collins, 2006).

35. Eric von Hippel, "Lead Users: A Source of Novel Product Concepts." *Management Science*, July 1986, pp. 791–805. See also *The Sources of Innovation*, (New York: Oxford University Press, 1988); "Learning from Lead Users." In *Marketing in an Electronic Age*, Robert D. Buzzell, ed., (Cambridge, MA: Harvard Business School Press, 1985), pp. 308–317.

36. Steven Levy, "Microsoft Gets a Clue From its Kiddie Corps." *Newsweek*, February 24, 2003, pp. 56–57.

37. Khushwant Singh, "Informal Style Works for Samsung Designers." *Streats* (Singapore), June 17, 2004; Peter Lewis, "Samsung's Crisis Machine." *Fortune*, September 5, 2005, pp. 34–41.

38. Jane Ng, "Soya Sauce Maker Sets Up Lab in NUS." *Straits Times* (Singapore), October 7, 2005, p. H13.

39. Michael Michalko, *Cracking Creativity: The Secrets of Creative Genius*, (Berkeley, CA: Ten Speed Press, 1998); James M. Higgins, *101 Creative Problem Solving Techniques*, (New York: New Management Publishing Company, 1994); Darren W. Dahl and Page Moreau, "The Influence and Value of Analogical Thinking During New Product Ideation." *Journal of Marketing Research*, February 2002, 39, pp. 47–60.

40. <www.smokinggun.com>.

41. Bruce Einhorn, Jay Greene, and Irene M. Kunii, "Tablet PCs: Thanks for All the Hype, Bill." *BusinessWeek*, February 23, 2004, p. 25.

42. "Miniature-sized Credit Card Launched by Visa, Citibank." *BusinessWorld* (Manila), February 16, 2004, p. 1.

43. "The Ultimate Widget: 3-D 'Printing' May Revolutionize Product Design and Manufacturing." *U.S. News & World Report*, July 20, 1992, p. 55.

44. For additional information, see also Paul E. Green and V. Srinivasan "Conjoint Analysis in Marketing: New Developments with Implications for Research and Practice." *Journal of Marketing*, October 1990, pp. 3–19; Dick R. Wittnick, Marco Vriens, and Wim Burhenne, "Commercial Uses of Conjoint Analysis in Europe: Results and Critical Reflections." *International Journal of Research in Marketing*, January 1994, pp. 41–52; Jordan J. Louviere, David A. Hensher, and Joffre D. Swait, *Stated Choice Models: Analysis and Applications*, (New York: Cambridge University Press, 2000).

45. The full-profile example was taken from Paul E. Green and Yoram Wind, "New Ways to Measure Consumers' Judgments." *Harvard Business Review*, July–August 1975, pp. 107–117.

46. Robert Blattberg and John Golany, "Tracker: An Early Test Market Forecasting and Diagnostic Model for New Product Planning." *Journal of Marketing Research*, May 1978, pp. 192–202; Glen L. Urban, Bruce D. Weinberg, and John R. Hauser, "Premarket Forecasting of Really New Products." *Journal of Marketing*, January 1996, pp. 47–60; Peter N. Golder and Gerard J. Tellis, "Will It Ever Fly? Modeling the Takeoff of Really New Consumer Durables." *Marketing Science*, 1997, 16(3), pp. 256–270.

47. Roger A. Kerin, Michael G. Harvey, and James T. Rothe, "Cannibalism and New Product Development." *Business Horizons*, October 1978, pp. 25–31.

48. The present value (V) of a future sum (I) to be received t years from today and discounted at the interest rate (r) is given by $V = I_t/(1 + r)^t$. Thus $\$4,761,000/(1.15)^5 = \$2,346,000$.

49. David B. Hertz, "Risk Analysis in Capital Investment." *Harvard Business Review*, January-February 1964, pp. 96–106.

50. John Hauser, "House of Quality." *Harvard Business Review*, May–June 1988, pp. 63–73. Customer-driven engineering is also called "quality function deployment." See Lawrence R. Guinta and Nancy C. Praizler, *The QFD Book: The Team Approach to Solving Problems and Satisfying Customers through Quality Function Deployment* (New York: AMACOM, 1993); V. Srinivasan, William S. Lovejoy, and David Beach, "Integrated Product Design for Marketability and Manufacturing." *Journal of Marketing Research*, February 1997, pp. 154–163.

51. Marco Iansiti and Alan MacCormack, "Developing Products on Internet Time." *Harvard Business Review*, September-October 1997, pp. 108–117; Srikant Datar, C. Clark Jordan, and Kannan Srinivasan, "Advantages of Time-Based New Product Development in a Fast-Cycle Industry." *Journal of Marketing Research*, February 1997, pp. 36–49; Christopher D. Ittner and David F. Larcker, "Product Development Cycle Time and Organizational Performance." *Journal of Marketing Research*, February 1997, pp. 13–23.

52. Tom Peters, *The Circle of Innovation*, (New York: Alfred A. Knopf, 1997), p. 96. For more general discussion, see also Rajesh Sethi, "New Product Quality and Product Development Teams." *Journal of Marketing*, April 2000, pp. 1–14; Christine Moorman and Anne S. Miner, "The Convergence of Planning and Execution Improvisation in New Product Development." *Journal of Marketing*, July 1998, pp. 1–20; Ravinchoanath MacChavan and Rajiv Graver, "From Embedded Knowledge to Embodied Knowledge: New Product Development as Knowledge Management." *Journal of Marketing*, October 1998, pp. 1–12.

53. "Consumers Personalize Coke Bottle Wrappers in Singapore." *Ad Age's Daily World Wire*, October 31, 2002.

54. Grace Ng, "Mickey Mouse Marching in with Disney Gadgets Soon." *Straits Times* (Singapore), August 2, 2005, p. H15.

55. Christopher Power, "Will It Sell in Podunk? Hard to Say." *BusinessWeek*, August 10, 1992, pp. 46–47.

56. Kevin J. Clancy, Robert S. Shulman, and Marianne Wolf, *Simulated Test Marketing: Technology for Launching Successful New Products*, (New York: Lexington Books, 1994); V. Mahajan and Jerry Wind, "New Product Models: Practice, Shortcomings, and Desired Improvements." *Journal of Product Innovation Management*, 1992, 9, pp. 129–139; Glen L. Urban, John R. Hauser, and Roberta A. Chicos, "Information Acceleration: Validation and Lessons from the Field." *Journal of Marketing Research*, February 1997, pp. 143–153.

57. For further discussion, see Robert J. Thomas, "Timing: The Key to Market Entry." *Journal of Consumer Marketing*, Summer 1985, pp. 77–87; Thomas S. Robertson, Jehoshua Eliashberg, and Talia Rymon, "New Product Announcement Signals and Incumbent Reactions." *Journal of Marketing*, July 1995, pp. 1–15; Frank H. Alpert and Michael A. Kamins, "Pioneer Brand Advantages and Consumer Behavior: A Conceptual Framework and Propositional Inventory." *Journal of the Academy of Marketing Science*, Summer 1994, pp. 244–236; Barry L. Bayos, Sanjay Jain, and Ambar Rao, "Consequences: An Analysis of Truth or Vaporware and New Product Announcements." *Journal of Marketing Research*, February 2001, pp. 3–13.

58. Michael Backman and Charlotte Butler, "Tapping the China Potential." *Business Times* (Singapore), November 11, 2002, p. 16.

59. George G. Cooper and Elko J. Kleinschmidt, *New Products: The Key Factors in Success*, (Chicago: American Marketing Association, 1990), pp. 35–38.

60. Steve Hamm, "Tech's Future." *BusinessWeek*, September 27, 2004, pp. 50–57.

61. Philip Kotler and Gerald Zaltman, "Targeting Prospects for a New Product." *Journal of Advertising Research*, February 1976, pp. 7–20.

62. Mark Leslie and Charles A. Holloway, "The Sales Learning Curve." *Harvard Business Review*, July–August 2006, pp. 114–23.

63. For details, see Keith G. Lockyer, *Critical Path Analysis and Other Project Network Techniques*, (London: Pitman, 1984). See also Arvind Rangaswamy and Gary L. Lilien, "Software Tools for New Product Development." *Journal of Marketing Research*, February 1997, pp. 177–184.

64. The following discussion leans heavily on Everett M. Rogers, *Diffusion of Innovation*, 5th ed., (New York: The Free Press, 1995.

65. C. Page Moreau, Donald R. Lehmann, and Arthur B. Markman, "Entrenched Knowledge Structures and Consumer Response to New Products." *Journal of Marketing Research*, February 2001, 38, pp. 14–29.

66. Steve Hoeffler, "Measuring Preferences for Really New Products." *Journal of Marketing Research*, November 2003, 40, pp. 406–420.

67. Everett M. Rogers, *Diffusion of Innovation*, 5th ed., (New York: The Free Press, 1995); Geoffrey A. Moore, *Crossing the Chasm: Marketing and Selling High-Tech Products to Mainstream Customers*, (New York: HarperBusiness, 1999).

68. A. Parasuraman and Charles L. Colby, *Techno-Ready Marketing*, (New York: The Free Press, 2001); Jakki Mohr, *Marketing of High-Technology Products and Innovations*, 2nd ed., (Upper Saddle River, NJ: Prentice Hall, 2005).

69. Bernd Schmitt and Yigang Pan, "Managing Corporate and Brand Identities in the Asia-Pacific Region." *California Management Review*, Summer 1994, 36, pp. 32–48.

70. Chol Lee and Robert T. Green, "Cross-Cultural Examination of the Fishbein Behavioral Intentions Model." *Journal of International Business Studies*, 1991, 22(2), pp. 289–305.

71. C.F. Yang, S.C. Ho, and O.H.M. Yau, "A Conception of Chinese Consumer Behavior." In *Hong Kong Marketing Management: A Case Analysis Approach*, C.F. Yang, S.C. Ho, and O.H.M. Yau, eds., (Hong Kong: Commercial Press, 1989), pp. 317–342.

72. Hellmut Schütte and Deanna Cialante, *Consumer Behavior in Asia*, (London: MacMillan, 1998), pp. 75–79.

73. Hirokazu Takada and Dipak Jain, "Cross-National Analysis of Diffusion of Consumer Durable Goods in Pacific Rim Countries." *Journal of Marketing*, April 1991, 55, pp. 48–54.

74. Siew Meng Leong, "Consumer Decision Making for Common, Repeat-Purchase Products: A Dual Replication." *Journal of Consumer Psychology*, 1993, 2(2), pp. 193–208.

75. Carrie La Ferle, Steven M. Edwards, and Yukata Mizuno, "Internet Diffusion in Japan: Cultural Considerations." *Journal of Advertising Research*, 2002, 42(2), pp. 65–79.

76. The discussion is based on Peter Lewis, "It's Fun and Games Again at Sony." *Fortune*, April 4, 2005, p. 38.

77. Hubert Gatignon, and Thomas S. Robertson, "A Propositional Inventory for New Diffusion Research." *Journal of Consumer Research*, March 1985, pp. 849–867; Vijay Mahajan, Eitan Muller, and Frank M. Bass, "Diffusion of New Products: Empirical Generalizations and Managerial Uses." *Marketing Science*, 1995, 14(3:2), pp. G79–G89; Fareena Sultan, John U. Farley, and Donald R. Lehman, "Reflection on 'A Meta-Analysis of Applications of Diffusion Models'." *Journal of Marketing Research*, May 1996, pp. 247–249; Minhi Hahn, Sehoon Park, and Andris A. Zoltners, "Analysis of New Product Diffusion Using a Four-Segment Trial-Repeat Model." *Marketing Science*, 1994, 13(3), pp. 224–247.

Chapter 21

1. Jack Ewing, "Nokia: Lesson Learned, Reward Reaped." *BusinessWeek*, July 30, 2007, p. 32; "Face Value." *Economist*, May 27, 2006, p. 24; Bruce Upbin, "The Next Billion." <www.forbes.com>, November 12, 2007.
2. Ted C. Fishman, "Will 21st Century Become the Chinese Century?" *Seoul Times* (Korea), October 18, 2005.
3. Michael E. Porter, *Competitive Strategy* (New York: The Free Press, 1980): p. 275.
4. Richard Tomlinson, "L'Oréal's Global Makeover." *Fortune*, September 2, 2002, pp. 54–60; "L'Oréal Builds 4th R&D Center in China." <www.crienglish.com>, September 26, 2005.
5. Joanna Slater, "Spreading the Sauce." *Far Eastern Economic Review*, May 20, 1999, pp. 60–61.
6. Jack Ewing and Dexter Roberts, "The Chinese are Coming . . . to Germany." *BusinessWeek*, February 21, 2005, pp. 24–25.
7. Jan Johanson and Finn Wiedersheim-Paul, "The Internationalization of the Firm." *Journal of Management Studies*, October 1975, pp. 305–322.
8. Stan Reid, "The Decision Maker and Export Entry and Expansion." *Journal of International Business Studies*, Fall 1981, pp. 101–112; Igal Ayal, "Industry Export Performance: Assessment and Prediction." *Journal of Marketing*, Summer 1982, pp. 54–61; Somkid Jatusripitak, *The Exporting Behavior of Manufacturing Firms* (Ann Arbor: University of Michigan Press, 1986).
9. Michael R. Czinkota and Ilkka A. Ronkainen, *International Marketing*, 8th ed., (New York: Harcourt Brace Jovanovich, 2007).
10. Igal Ayal and Jehiel Zif, "Market Expansion Strategies in Multinational Marketing." *Journal of Marketing*, Spring 1979, pp. 84–94.
11. Bill Powell, "The Legend of Legend." *Fortune*, September 16, 2002, pp. 34–38; "Lenovo's IBM Bid Gets U.S. Go-Ahead." <www.news.bbc.co.uk>, March 9, 2005.
12. For a timely and thorough review of academic research on global marketing, see Johny K. Johansson, "Global Marketing: Research on Foreign Entry, Local Marketing, Global Management." In *Handbook of Marketing*, Bart Weitz and Robin Wensley, eds., (London: Sage Publications, 2002), pp. 457–483. See also Johny K. Johansson, *Global Marketing*, 2nd ed., (New York: McGraw-Hill, 2003). For some global marketing research issues, see Susan Douglas and Samuel R. Craig, *International Marketing Research*, 2nd ed., (Upper Saddle River, NJ: Prentice Hall, 2000).
13. Kenichi Ohmae, *Triad Power*, (New York: The Free Press, 1985); Philip Kotler and Nikhilesh Dholakia, "Ending Global Stagnation: Linking the Fortunes of the Industrial and Developing Countries." *Business in the Contemporary World*, Spring 1989, pp. 86–97.
14. Adapted from Vijay Mahajan, Marcos V. Pratini De Moraes, and Jerry Wind, "The Invisible Global Market." *Marketing Management*, Winter 2000, pp. 31–35; C.K. Prahalad, "Myths of the BOP Market." *The Edge* (Singapore), June 20, 2005, pp. 8–9.
15. Niraj Dawar and Amitava Chattopadhyay, "Rethinking Marketing Programs for Emerging Markets." *Long Range Planning*, October 2002, 35(5).
16. Manjeet Kripalani, "Finally, Coke Gets It Right." *BusinessWeek*, February 10, 2003, p. 47; Manjeet Kripalani, "Battling for Pennies in India's Villages." *BusinessWeek*, June 10, 2002, p. 22E7.
17. "Not So Fizzy." *Economist*, February 23, 2002, pp. 66–67; Rajeev Batra, Venkatram Ramaswamy, Dan L. Alden, Jan-Benedict E.M. Steenkamp, and S. Ramachander, "Effects of Brand Local and Nonlocal Origin on Consumer Attitudes in Developing Countries." *Journal of Consumer Psychology*, 2000, 9(2), pp. 83–95.
18. Paul Betts, "Danone's Taste for Microfinance Pays Dividends." *Financial Times*, March 30, 2007, p. 24; "The Bottom of the Pyramid Is Where the Real Gold Is Hidden." *Marketing Week*, February 8, 2007, p. 18; Adam Jones, "Danone and Yunus Extend Partnership." *Financial Times*, December 19, 2006, p. 19.
19. David Welch, "GM: Gunning It In China." *BusinessWeek*, June 21, 2004, pp. 112–115; Muller, "Thanks, Now Move Over;" "GM is China's Top-Selling Automaker." <www.edmunds.com>, Januay 7, 2006; <http://media.gm.com/cn/gm/en/company/china/index.html>, accessed on April 17, 2008.
20. Patrick Williamson, "Toto—Porcelain Gods." <www.brandchannel.com>, February 18, 2008.
21. Gabriel Kahn, "Local Brands Outgun Foreigners in China's Advertising Market." *Wall Street Journal*, October 8, 2003, p. B6A; "The Local Touch." *Economist*, March 8, 2003, p. 58.
22. Dennis Normile, "Branded in China." *Electronic Business*, March 2005, 31(3), pp. 61–64.
23. Michael Vatikiotis, "Outward Bound." *Far Eastern Economic Review*, February 5, 2004, pp. 24–27.
24. Johny K. Johansson, "Global Marketing: Research on Foreign Entry, Local Marketing, Global Management." In *Handbook of Marketing*, Bart Weitz and Robin Wensley, eds., (London: Sage Publications, 2002), pp. 457–483.

25. David Murphy, "Chinese Builders Go Global." *Far Eastern Economic Review*, May 13, 2004, pp. 28–32.

26. Charlene Marmer Solomon, "Don't Get Burned by Hot Markets." *Workforce*, January 1998, pp. 12–22.

27. For an academic review, see Leonidas C. Leonidou, Constantine S. Katsikeas, and Nigel F. Piercy, "Identifying Managerial Influences on Exporting: Past Research and Future Directions." *Journal of International Marketing*, (1998), 6(2), pp. 74–102.

28. Paul Gao, Jonathan R. Woetzel, and Yibing Wu, "Can Chinese Brands Make it Abroad?" *McKinsey Quarterly*, 4, 2003.

29. Brandon Mitchener, "E-Commerce: Border Crossings." *Wall Street Journal*, November 22, 1999, p. R41.

30. Michael Arndt and Dexter Roberts, "A Finger-Lickin' Good Time in China." *BusinessWeek*, October 30, 2006, p. 50; "Cola down Mexico Way." *Economist*, October 11, 2003, pp. 69–70.

31. Russell Flannery, "Franchise Lure Taiwan Entrepreneurs." *Asian Wall Street Journal*, May 11, 1999.

32. Laura Mazur and Annik Hogg, *The Marketing Challenge* (Wokingham, England: Addison-Wesley, 1993): pp. 42–44; Jan Willem Karel, "Brand Strategy Positions Products Worldwide." *Journal of Business Strategy*, May-June 1991, 12(3), pp. 16–19.

33. Paula Dwyer, "Tearing Up Today's Organization Chart." *Business Week*, November 18, 1994, pp. 80–90.

34. Shawn W. Crispin, "Thailand's Rocky Road." *Far Eastern Economic Review*, September 23, 2004, pp. 39–40.

35. George Wehrfritz, "Going Global." *Newsweek*, March 1, 2004, pp. 28–31.

36. Joann Muller, "Global Motors." *Forbes*, January 12, 2004, pp. 62–68.

37. Wilfried Vanhonacker, "Entering China: An Unconventional Approach." *Harvard Business Review*, March-April 1997, pp. 130–141.

38. Shaoming Zou and S. Tamer Cavusgil "The GMS: A Broad Conceptualization of Global Marketing Strategy and Its Effect on Firm Performance." *Journal of Marketing*, October 2002, 66, pp. 40–56.

39. Geert Hofstede, *Culture's Consequences*, (Thousand Oaks, CA: Sage Publications, 2001).

40. For some recent treatments of branding in Asia in particular, see S. Ramesh Kumar, *Marketing & Branding: The Indian Scenario*, (Delhi: Pearson Education, 2007); Martin Roll, *Asian Brand Strategy: How Asia Builds Strong Brands*, (New York: Palgrave MacMillan, 2006); Paul Temporal, *Branding in Asia: The Creation, Development, and Management of Asian Brands for the Global Market*, (Singapore: John Wiley, 2001).

41. Pankaj Ghemawat, "Globalization: The Strategy of Differences." *Harvard Business School Working Knowledge*, November 10, 2003; Pankaj Ghemawat, "The Forgotten Strategy." *Harvard Business Review*, November 2003, 81, 76–84.

42. Paulo Prada and Bruce Orwall, "A Certain *'Je Ne Sais Quoi'* at Disney's New Park." *Wall Street Journal*, March 12, 2003, p. B1; Paul Wiseman, "A Bit of East, A Lot of West in Hong Kong Disneyland." <www.usatoday.com>, October 21, 2005.

43. Arundhati Parmar, "Dependent Variables: Sounds Global Strategies Rely on Certain Factors." *Marketing News*, September 16, 2002, p. 4.

44. Warren J. Keegan, *Global Marketing Management*, 7th ed., (Upper Saddle River, NJ: Prentice Hall, 2001).

45. "What Makes a Company Great?" *Fortune*, October 26, 1998, pp. 218–226.

46. Cris Prystay, "Sizing Up the Asian Market." *Far Eastern Economic Review*, March 18, 2004, p. 62.

47. "All Business is Local." *Straits Times* (Singapore), February 18, 1999, pp. 1–2; "Big Macs Make Way for Congee at McThai." *Straits Times* (Singapore), September 28, 2002, pp. A12; Lawrence Chung, "When Burgers Fail to Excite, McRice Just Might." *Sunday Times* (Singapore), December 15, 2002, p. 15.

48. Richard P. Carpenter and the Globe Staff, "What They Meant to Say Was ... ." *Boston Globe*, August 2, 1998, p. M6.

49. Adam Schwarz and Roland Villinger, "Integrating Southeast Asia's Economies." *McKinsey Quarterly*, 1, 2004, pp.36–37.

50. For an interesting distinction based on the concept of global consumer culture positioning, see Dana L. Alden, Jan-Benedict E.M. Steenkamp, and Rajeev Batra, "Brand Positioning Through Advertising in Asia, North America, and Europe: The Role of Global Consumer Culture." *Journal of Marketing*, January 1999, 63, pp. 75–87.

51. Thomas J. Madden, Kelly Hewett, and Martin S. Roth, "Managing Images in Different Cultures: A Cross-National Study of Color Meanings and Preferences." *Journal of International Marketing*, 2000, 8(4), pp. 90–107; Zeynep Gürhan-Canli, and Durairaj Maheswaran, "Cultural Variations in Country-of-Origin Effects." *Journal of Marketing Research*, August 2000, 37, pp. 309–317.

52. Geoffrey Fowler, Brian Steinberg, and Aaron O. Patrick, "Globalizing Apple's Ads." *Wall Street Journal*, March 1, 2007.

53. Jo Bowman, "Heineken." *Media* (Hong Kong), December 17, 2004, pp. 18–19.

54. Nan Zhou and Russell W. Belk, "Chinese Consumer Readings of Global and Local Advertising Appeals." *Journal of Advertising*, Fall 2004, pp. 63–76.

55. Loretta Chao, "Cell Phone Ads Are Easier Pitch in China Interactive Campaigns." *Wall Street Journal*, January 4, 2007.

56. John L. Graham, Alma T. Mintu, and Raymond Rogers, "Explorations of Negotiations Behaviors in Ten Foreign Cultures Using a Model Developed in the United States." *Management Science*, January 1994, 40, pp. 72–95.
57. David Kirkpatrick, "How Microsoft Conquered China." *Fortune* 156, no. 2, July 23, 2007, pp. 78–84.
58. "The New Language of Emerging Markets." *Financial Times*, August 7, 2002.
59. Bruce Upbin, "The Next Billion." <www.forbes.com>, November 12, 2007.
60. Elliott Masie, "Global Pricing in an Internet World." *Computer Reseller News*, May 11, 1998, pp. 55, 58.
61. Ram Charan, "The Rules Have Changed." *Fortune*, March 16, 1998, pp. 159–162.
62. <www.ge.com>.
63. Pete Engardio and Dexter Roberts, "The China Price." *BusinessWeek*, December 6, 2004, pp. 48–58.
64. Preeti Chaturvedi, "*Dabbawala*—Fast Food." <www.brandchannel.com>, February 11, 2008.
65. David Arnold, "Seven Rules of International Distribution." *Harvard Business Review*, November-December 2000, pp. 131–137.
66. Ibid.
67. Jack Ewing, "The Next Wal-Mart?" *BusinessWeek*, April 26, 2004, pp. 60–62.
68. Katie Benner, "Wal-Mart's Everyday Low Stock Price." <www.money.cnn.com>, August 16, 2005; Bruce Upbin, "Wall-to-Wall Wal-Mart." <www.forbes.com>, April 12, 2004; <walmartstores.com/FactsNews/NewsRoom/8205.aspx>, accessed on April 17, 2008; William J. Holstein, "Why Wal-Mart Can't Find Happiness in Japan." <www.cnnmoney.com>, July 27, 2007.
69. Adam Luck, "Beauty Contest." *Asia Inc*, July 2004, pp. 16–17.
70. Tamara Loomis, "The China Syndrome." <www.law.com>, May 26, 2005.
71. R. de Koster and M. Shinohara, "Supply-Chain Culture Clash." *MIT Sloan Management Review*, Fall 2004, 46(1).
72. "From Head & Shoulders to Kobe." *Economist*, March 27, 2004, pp. 64.
73. Alessandra Galloni, "Venice: Gondoliers, Lagoons, Moonlight—and Meatballs?" *Wall Street Journal*, August 9, 2002, pp. B1, B4.
74. "A Dragon With Core Values." *Economist*, March 30, 2002.
75. Jim Rendon, "When Nations Need a Little Marketing." *New York Times*, November 23, 2003.
76. Zeynep Gurhan-Canli and Durairaj Maheswaran, "Cultural Variations in Country-of-Origin Effects." *Journal of Marketing Research*, August 2000, 37, pp. 309–317.
77. Jan-Benedict E.M. Steenkamp, Rajeev Batra, and Dana L. Alden, "How Perceived Brand Globalness Creates Brand Value." *Journal of International Business Studies*, 2003, 34, pp. 53–65.
78. Johny K. Johansson, "Global Marketing: Research on Foreign Entry, Local Marketing, Global Management." In *Handbook of Marketing*, Bart Weitz and Robin Wensley, eds., (London: Sage Publications, 2002), pp. 457–483. Johny K. Johansson, "Determinants and Effects of the Use of 'Made In' Labels." *International Marketing Review*, (UK) 1989, 6(1), pp. 47–58; Warren J. Bilkey, and Erik Nes, "Country-of-Origin Effects on Product Evaluations." *Journal of International Business Studies*, Spring–Summer 1982, pp. 89–99; "Old Wine in New Bottles." *The Economist*, February 21, 1998, p. 45; Zeynep Gurhan-Canli and Durairaj Maheswaran, "Cultural Variations in Country of Origin Effects." *Journal of Marketing Research*, August 2000, 37, pp. 309–317.
79. Dexter Roberts and Michael Arndt, "It's Getting Hotter in the East." *BusinessWeek*, August 22/29, 2005, pp. 64–67.
80. Charles Fishman, "No Satisfaction at Toyota." *Fast Company*, December 2006–January 2007; Roben Farzad, "The Toyota Enigma." *BusinessWeek*, July 10, 2006, p. 30; Keith Naughton, "Red, White, & Bold." *Newsweek*, April 25, 2005, pp. 34–36; Alex Taylor III, "The Americanization of Toyota." *Fortune*, December 8, 2003, pp. 165–70.
81. Christopher A. Bartlett and Sumantra Ghoshal, *Managing Across Borders*, (Cambridge, MA: Harvard Business School Press, 1989).
82. Betsy McKay, "Coke Hunts for Talent to Re-Establish Its Marketing Might." *Wall Street Journal*, March 6, 2002, p. B4.

Chapter 22

1. Keith Fox, Katherine Jocz, and Bernard Jaworski, "A Common Language." *Marketing Management*, May–June 2003, pp. 14–17.
2. Richard Tomlinson, "L'Orèal's Global Makeover." *Fortune*, September 30, 2002, pp. 141–146; "The Color of Money." *Economist*, March 8, 2003, p. 59; Sarah Ellison and John Carreyrou, "An Unlikely Rival Challenges L'Orèal in Beauty Market." *Wall Street Journal*, January 9, 2003, pp. A1, A6; <investing.businessweek.com/research/stocks/earnings/earnings.asp?symbol=OREP.PA>, accessed on April 22, 2008.

3. For additional updates on the latest academic thinking on marketing strategy and tactics, see *Kellogg on Marketing*, Dawn Iacobucci, ed., (New York: John Wiley, 2001); and *Kellogg on Integrated Marketing*, Dawn Iacobucci and Bobby Calder, eds., (New York: John Wiley, 2003).
4. Frederick E. Webster Jr., Alan J. Malter, and Shankar Ganesan, "Can Marketing Regain Its Seat at the Table?" *Marketing Science Institute Report No. 03–113*. Marketing Science Institute, Cambridge, MA.
5. For a broad historical treatment of marketing thought, see D.G. Brian Jones and Eric H. Shaw, "A History of Marketing Thought." In *Handbook of Marketing*, Barton A. Weitz and Robin Wensley, eds., (London: Sage Publications, 2002), pp. 39–65.
6. Frederick E. Webster Jr., "The Changing Role of Marketing in the Corporation." *Journal of Marketing*, October 1992, pp. 1–17. See also Ravi S. Achrol, "Evolution of the Marketing Organization: New Forms for Turbulent Environment." *Journal of Marketing*, October 1991, pp. 77–93; John P. Workman Jr., Christian Homburg, and Kjell Gruner, "Marketing Organization: An Integrative Framework of Dimensions and Determinants." *Journal of Marketing*, July 1998, pp. 21–41. For some contemporary perspectives, see Special Issue 1999 of *Journal Marketing Fundamental Issues and Directions for Marketing*.
7. For an excellent account of how to convert a company into a market-driven organization, see George Day, *The Market-Driven Organization: Aligning Culture, Capabilities, and Configuation to the Market*, (New York: The Free Press, 1989).
8. Frederick E. Webster Jr, "The Role of Marketing and the Firm." In *Handbook of Marketing*, Barton A. Weitz and Robin Wensley, eds., (London: Sage Publications, 2002), pp. 39–65.
9. Frank V. Cespedes. *Concurrent Marketing: Integrating Product, Sales, and Service*, (Boston, MA: Harvard Business School Press, 1995); Frank V. Cespedes, *Managing Marketing Linkages: Text, Cases, and Readings*, (Upper Saddle River, NJ: Prentice Hall, 1996).
10. Zachary Schiller, "The Marketing Revolution at Procter & Gamble." *BusinessWeek*, July 25, 1998, pp. 72–76; Laurie Freeman, "P&G Widens Power Base: Adds Category Managers." *Advertising Age*.
11. Michael J. Zenor, "The Profit Benefits of Category Management." *Journal of Marketing Research*, May 31, 1994, pp. 202–213.
12. Gerry Khermouch, "Brands Overboard." *Brandweek*, August 22, 1994, pp. 25–39.
13. For further reading, see Robert Dewar and Don Shultz, "The Product Manager, an Idea Whose Time Has Gone." *Marketing Communications*, May 1998, pp. 28–35; "The Marketing Revolution at Proctor & Gamble." *BusinessWeek*, July 25, 1988, pp. 72–76; Kevin T. Higgins, "Category Management: New Tools Changing Life for Manufacturers, Retailers." *Marketing News*, September 25, 1989, pp. 2, 19; George S. Low and Ronald A. Fullerton, "Brands, Brand Management, and the Brand Manager System: A Critical Historical Evaluation." *Journal of Marketing Research*, May 1994, pp. 173–190; Michael J. Zenor, "The Profit Benefits of Category Management."
14. William J. Holstein, "Middleman Becomes Master." *Chief Executive*, October 2002.
15. Benson P. Shapiro, "Can Marketing and Manufacturing Coexist?" *Harvard Business Review*, September–October 1977, pp. 104–114. See also Robert W. Ruekert and Orville C. Walker Jr., "Marketing's Interaction with Other Functional Units: A Conceptual Framework with Other Empirical Evidence." *Journal of Marketing*, January 1987, pp. 1–19.
16. Patricia Sellers, "P&G: Teaching an Old Dog New Tricks." *Fortune*, May 31, 2004, pp. 167–180.
17. Gary Hamel, *Leading the Revolution*, (Boston: Harvard Business School Press, 2000).
18. William L. Wilkie and Elizabeth S. Moore, "Marketing's Relationship to Society." In *Handbook of Marketing*, Barton A. Weitz and Robin Wensley, eds., (London: Sage Publications, 2002), pp. 1–38.
19. "Special Report: Corporate Social Responsibility." *Economist*, December 14, 2002, pp. 62–63.
20. Chester Dawson and Mara Der Hovanesian, "Damage Control in Japan." *BusinessWeek*, February 14, 2005, pp. 48–49.
21. Lauren Foster and Alexandra Harney, "Doctored Records on Working Hours and Pay Are Causing Problems for Consumer Multinationals." *Financial Times*, April 22, 2005, p. 17.
22. John Carey, "Hugging the Tree Huggers." *BusinessWeek*, March 12, 2007, pp. 66–68.
23. Jeff Nachtigal, "It's Easy and Cheap Being Green." *Fortune*, October 16, 2006, p. 53.
24. Shelby D. Hunt and Scott Vitell, "The General Theory of Marketing Ethics: A Retrospective and Revision." In *Ethics in Marketing*, John Quelch and Craig Smith, eds., (Irwin, Chicago, IL, 1992).
25. Marc Gunther, "Tree Huggers, Soy Lovers, and Profits." *Fortune*, June 23, 2003, pp. 98–104.
26. Ronald J. Alsop, "Perils of Corporate Philanthropy." *Wall Street Journal*, January 16, 2002, p. B1; Ronald J. Alsop, *The 18 Immutable Laws of Corporate Reputation: Creating, Protecting, and Repairing Your Most Valuable Asset*, (New York: Free Press, 2004).
27. Telis Demos, "Managing Beyond The Bottom Line." *Fortune*, October 3, 2005, pp. 70–75.

28. Sandra O'Loughlin, "The Wearin' o' the Green." *Brandweek*, April 23, 2007, pp. 26–27. For a critical response, see also, John R. Ehrenfield, "Feeding the Beast." *Fast Company,* December 2006–January 2007, pp. 42–43.
29. Nicholas Varchaver, "Chemical Reaction." *Fortune*, April 2, 2007, pp. 53–58.
30. Pete Engardio, "Beyond the Green Corporation." *BusinessWeek,* January 29, 2007, pp. 50–64.
31. Ibid.
32. Kenneth Hein, "The World on a Platter." *Brandweek*, April 23, 2007, pp. 27–28; Megan Johnston, "Hard Sell for a Soft Fabric." *Forbes*, October 30, 2006, pp. 73–80.
33. See Philip Kotler and Nancy Lee. *Corporate Social Responsibility: Doing the Most Good for Your Company and Your Cause*, (New York: John Wiley, 2005).
34. For a discussion of some public health marketing issues and opportunities, see Michael L. Rothschild, "Carrots, Sticks, and Promises: A Conceptual Framework for the Management of Public Health and Social Issue Behaviors." *Journal of Marketing*, October 1999, 63, pp. 24–37.
35. Eric Ellis, "Tata Steels Itself for Change." *Fortune*, April 29, 2002, pp. 44–50.
36. Robert Berner, "Smarter Corporate Giving." *BusinessWeek*, November 28, 2005, pp. 68–76; Craig N. Smith, "Corporate Social Responsibility: Whether or How?" *California Management Review*, Summer 2003, 45(4), pp. 52–76.
37. Hamish Pringle and Marjorie Thompson. *How Cause Related Marketing Builds Brands*, (New York: John Wiley, 1999); Christine Bittar, "Seeking Cause and Effect." *Brandweek*, November 11, 2002, pp. 19–24; "Marketing, Corporate Social Initiatives, and the Bottom Line." Marketing Science Institute Conference Summary, *MSI Report No. 01–106, 2001).*
38. Rajan Varadarajan and Anil Menon, "Cause-Related Marketing: A Co-Alignment of Marketing Strategy and Corporate Philanthropy." *Journal of Marketing*, 1988, 52, pp. 58–74.
39. Minette Drumwright and Patrick E. Murphy, "Corporate Societal Marketing." In *Handbook of Marketing and Society*, Paul N. Bloom and Gregory T. Gundlach, eds., (Thousand Oaks, CA: Sage Publications, 2001): pp. 162–183. See also Minette Drumwright, "Company Advertising With a Social Dimension: The Role of Noneconomic Criteria." *Journal of Marketing*, October 1996, 60, pp. 71–87.
40. <www.canon.com>.
41. <www.americanidol.com>; <www.hollywoodreporter.com/hr/content_display/television/news/ e3i639db5ad9522 d8c746ec25a1de62b168>. Both accessed on April 22, 2008.
42. Pat Auger, Paul Burke, Timothy Devinney, and Jordan J. Loviere, "What Will Consumers Pay for Social Product Features?" *Journal of Business Ethics*, 2003, 42, pp. 281–304.
43. C.B. Bhattacharya and Sankar Sen, "Consumer-Company Identification: A Framework for Understanding Consumers' Relationships with Companies." *Journal of Marketing*, April 2003, 67, pp. 76–88; Sankar Sen and C.B. Bhattacharya, "Does Doing Good Always Lead to Doing Better? Consumer Reactions to Corporate Social Responsibility." *Journal of Marketing Research*, 2001, 38(2),pp. 225–244; Dennis B. Arnett, Steve D. German, and Shelby D. Hunt, "The Identity Salience Model of Relationship Marketing Success: The Case of Nonprofit Marketing." *Journal of Marketing*, April 2003, 67, pp. 89–105.
44. Stephen Hoeffler and Kevin Lane Keller, "Building Brand Equity through Corporate Societal Marketing." *Journal of Public Policy and Marketing*, Spring, 21(1), pp. 78–89. See also Special Issue: Corporate Responsibility. *Journal of Brand Management*, May 2003, 10 (4–5).
45. <www.lge.com>.
46. Mark R. Forehand and Sonya Grier, "When Is Honesty the Best Policy? The Effect of Stated Company Intent of Consumer Skepticism." *Journal of Consumer Psychology*, 2003, 13(3), pp. 349–356; Dwane Hal Dean, "Associating the Corporation with a Charitable Event Through Sponsorship: Measuring the Effects on Corporate Community Relations." *Journal of Advertising*, 2002, 31(4), pp. 77–87.
47. Lauren Gard, "We're Good Guys, Buy from Us." *BusinessWeek*, November 22, 2004, pp. 72–74.
48. Mya Frazier, "Costly Red Campaign Reaps Meager $18 Million." *Advertising Age*, March 5, 2007; Viewpoint: Bobby Shriver, "CEO: Red's Raised Lots of Green." *Advertising Age*, March 12, 2007; Michelle Conlin, "Shop (in the Name of Love)." *BusinessWeek*, October 2, 2006, p. 9.
49. Todd Cohen, "Corporations Aim for Strategic Engagement." *Philanthropy Journal*, September 20, 2006; John A. Quelch and Nathalie Laidler-Kylander. *The New Global Brands: Managing Non-Governmental Organizations in the 21st Century*, (Cincinnati, OH: South-Western College Publishing, 2005).
50. Susan Orenstein, "The Selling of Breast Cancer." *Business 2.0*, February 2003, pp. 88–94; H. Meyer, "When the Cause is Just." *Journal of Business Strategy*, November/December 1999, pp. 27–31.
51. Christine Bittar, "Seeking Cause & Effect." *Brandweek*, November 11, 2002, pp. 18–24.
52. Philip Kotler, Ned Roberto, and Nancy Lee. *Social Marketing: Improving the Quality of Life*, (Thousand Oaks, CA: Sage Publications, 2002).

53. See Michael L. Rothschild, "Carrots, Sticks, and Promises: A Conceptual Framework for the Management of Public Health and Social Issue Behaviors." *Journal of Marketing*, October 1999, pp. 24–37.

54. For more on developing and implementing marketing plans, see H.W. Goetsch. *Developing, Implementing, and Managing an Effective Marketing Plan*, (Chicago: NTC Business Books, 1993).

55. Ibid.

56. "Vital to Retailer's Success in China: Alignment between Business Strategy and Value Proposition." <www.acnielsen.com.cn>, accessed on October 20, 2004.

57. C. Marcus, "Marketing Resource Management: Key Components." *Gartner Research Note*, August 22, 2001.

58. For other examples, see Paul W. Farris, Neil T. Bendle, Phillip E. Pfeifer, and David J. Reibstein. *Marketing Metrics: 50+ Metrics Every Executive Should Master*, (Upper Saddle River, NJ: Wharton School Publishing, 2006); Marion Debruyne and Katrina Hubbard, "Marketing Metrics." *Working Paper Series, Conference Summary*. Marketing Science Institute, Report No. 00-119 (2000).

59. Alfred R. Oxenfeldt, "How to Use Market-Share Measurement." *Harvard Business Review*, January–February 1969, pp. 59–68.

60. There is a one-half chance that a successive observation will be higher or lower. Therefore, the probability of finding six successively higher values is given by (1/2) to the sixth, or 1/64.

61. Alternatively, companies need to focus on factors affecting shareholder value. The goal of marketing planning is to increase shareholder value, which is the present value of the future income stream created by the company's present actions. Rate-of-return analysis usually focuses on only one year's results. See Alfred Rapport, *Creating Shareholder Value*, (New York: Free Press, 1998).

62. For additional reading on financial analysis, see Peter L. Mullins, *Measuring Customer and Product-Line Profitability*, (Washington, DC: Distribution Research and Education Foundation, 1984).

63. Robin Cooper and Robert S. Kaplan, "Profit Priorities from Activity-Based Costing." *Harvard Business Review*, May–June 1991, pp. 130–35.

64. Sam R. Goodman, *Increasing Corporate Profitability*, (New York: Ronald Press, 1982), chapter 1. See also Bernard J. Jaworski, Vlasis Stathakopoulos, and H. Shanker Krishnan, "Control Combinations in Marketing: Conceptual Framework and Empirical Evidence." *Journal of Marketing*, January 1993, pp. 57–69.

65. Ibid.

66. Philip Kotler, William Gregor, and William Rodgers, "The Marketing Audit Comes of Age." *Sloan Management Review*, Winter 1989, pp. 49–62.

67. Useful checklists for a marketing self-audit can be found in Aubrey Wilson, *Aubrey Wilson's Marketing Audit Checklists*, (London: McGraw-Hill, 1982); Mike Wilson, *The Management of Marketing*, (Westmead, England: Gower Publishing, 1980). A marketing audit software program is described in Ben M. Enis, and Stephen J. Garfein, "The Computer-Driven Marketing Audit." *Journal of Management Inquiry*, December 1992, pp. 306–318.

68. Philip Kotler, William Gregor, and William Rodgers, "The Marketing Audit Comes of Age." *Sloan Management Review*, Winter 1989, pp. 49–62.

Glossary

A

activity-based cost (ABC) accounting procedures that can quantify the true profitability of different activities by identifying their actual costs.

advertising any paid form of nonpersonal presentation and promotion of ideas, goods, or services by an identified sponsor.

advertorials print ads that offer editorial content that reflects favorably on the brand and resemble newspaper or magazine content.

anchoring and adjustment heuristic when consumers arrive at an initial judgment and then make adjustments of their first impressions based on additional information.

arm's-length price the price charged by other competitors for the same or a similar product.

aspirational groups groups a person hopes or would like to join.

associative network memory model a conceptual representation that views memory as consisting of a set of nodes and interconnecting links where nodes represent stored information or concepts and links represent the strength of association between this information or concepts.

attitude a person's enduring favorable or unfavorable evaluation, emotional feeling, and action tendencies toward some object or idea.

augmented product a product that includes features that go beyond consumer expectations and differentiate the product from competitors.

available market the set of consumers who have interest, income, and access to a particular offer.

availability heuristic when consumers base their predictions on the quickness and ease with which a particular example of an outcome comes to mind.

average cost the cost per unit at a given level of production; it is equal to total costs divided by production.

B

backward invention reintroducing earlier product forms that can be well adapted to a foreign country's needs.

banner ads (Internet) small, rectangular boxes containing text and perhaps a picture to support a brand.

basic product what specifically the actual product is.

belief a descriptive thought that a person holds about something.

brand a name, term, sign, symbol, or design, or a combination of them, intended to identify the goods or services of one seller or group of sellers and to differentiate them from those of competitors.

brand associations all brand-related thoughts, feelings, perceptions, images, experiences, beliefs, attitudes, and so on that become linked to the brand node.

brand audit a consumer-focused exercise that involves a series of procedures to assess the health of the brand, uncover its sources of brand equity, and suggest ways to improve and leverage its equity.

brand awareness consumers' ability to identify the brand under different conditions, as reflected by their brand recognition or recall performance.

brand contact any information-bearing experience a customer or prospect has with the brand, the product category, or the market that relates to the marketer's product or service.

brand development index (BDI) the index of brand sales to category sales.

brand dilution when consumers no longer associate a brand with a specific product or highly similar products or start thinking less favorably about the brand.

brand elements those trademarkable devices that serve to identify and differentiate the brand such as a brand name, logo, or character.

brand equity the added value endowed to products and services.

brand extension a company's use of an established brand to introduce a new product.

brand image the perceptions and beliefs held by consumers, as reflected in the associations held in consumer memory.

brand knowledge all the thoughts, feelings, images, experiences, beliefs, and so on that become associated with the brand.

brand line all products, original as well as line and category extensions, sold under a particular brand name.

brand mix the set of all brand lines that a particular seller makes available to buyers.

brand personality the specific mix of human traits that may be attributed to a particular brand.

brand portfolio the set of all brands and brand lines a particular firm offers for sale to buyers in a particular category.

brand promise the marketer's vision of what the brand must be and do for consumers.

brand valuation an estimate of the total financial value of the brand.

brand value chain a structured approach to assessing the sources and outcomes of brand equity and the manner in which marketing activities create brand value.

branded entertainment using sports, music, arts, or other entertainment activities to build brand equity.

branded variants specific brand lines uniquely supplied to different retailers or distribution channels.

branding endowing products and services with the power of a brand.

branding strategy the number and nature of common and distinctive brand elements applied to the different products sold by the firm.

breakeven analysis a means by which management estimates how many units of the product the company would have to sell to break even with the given price and cost structure.

brick-and-click existing companies that have added an online site for information and/or e-commerce.

business database complete information about business customers' past purchases; past volumes, prices, and profits.

business market all the organizations that acquire goods and services used in the production of other products or services that are sold, rented, or supplied to others.

C

capital items long-lasting goods that facilitate developing or managing the finished product.

captive products products that are necessary to the use of other products, such as razor blades or film.

category extension using the parent brand to brand a new product outside the product category currently served by the parent brand.

category membership the products or sets of products with which a brand competes and which function as close substitutes.

cause-related marketing marketing that links a firm's contributions to a designated cause to customers' engaging directly or indirectly in revenue-producing transactions with the firm.

channel advantage when a company successfully switches its customers to lower-cost channels, while assuming no loss of sales or deterioration in service quality.

channel conflict when one channel member's actions prevent the channel from achieving its goal.

channel coordination when channel members are brought together to advance the goals of the channel, as opposed to their own potentially incompatible goals.

channel power the ability to alter channel members' behavior so that they take actions they would not have taken otherwise.

communication adaptation changing marketing communications programs for each local market.

communication-effect research determining whether an ad is communicating effectively.

company demand the company's estimated share of market demand at alternative levels of company marketing effort in a given time period.

company sales forecast the expected level of company sales based on a chosen marketing plan and an assumed marketing environment.

competitive advantage a company's ability to perform in one or more ways that competitors cannot or will not match.

conformance quality the degree to which all the produced units are identical and meet the promised specifications.

conjoint analysis a method for deriving the utility values that consumers attach to varying levels of a product's attributes.

conjunctive heuristic the consumer sets a minimum acceptable cutoff level for each attribute and chooses the first alternative that meets the minimum standard for all attributes.

consumer involvement the level of engagement and active processing undertaken by the consumer in responding to a marketing stimulus.

consumerist movement an organized movement of citizens and government to strengthen the rights and powers of buyers in relation to sellers.

consumption system the way the user performs the tasks of getting and using products and related services.

containerization putting the goods in boxes or trailers that are easy to transfer between two transportation modes.

content-target advertising links ads not to keywords but to the contents of Web pages.

contractual sales force manufacturers' reps, sales agents, and brokers, who are paid a commission based on sales.

convenience goods goods the consumer purchases frequently, immediately, and with a minimum of effort.

conventional marketing channel an independent producer, wholesaler(s), and retailer(s).

core benefit the service or benefit the customer is really buying.

core competency attribute that (1) is a source of competitive advantage in that it makes a significant contribution to perceived customer benefits, (2) has applications in a wide variety of markets, (3) is difficult for competitors to imitate.

core values the belief systems that underlie consumer attitudes and behavior, and that determine people's choices and desires over the long term.

corporate culture the shared experiences, stories, beliefs, and norms that characterize an organization.

corporate retailing corporately owned retailing outlets that achieve economies of scale, greater purchasing power, wider brand recognition, and better-trained employees.

cues stimuli that determine when, where, and how a person responds.

culture the fundamental determinant of a person's wants and behavior.

customer-based brand equity the differential effect that brand knowledge has on a consumer response to the marketing of that brand.

customer churn high customer defection.

customer consulting data, information systems, and advice services that the seller offers to buyers.

customer database an organized collection of comprehensive information about individual customers or prospects that is current, accessible, and actionable for marketing purposes.

customer lifetime value (CLV) the net present value of the stream of future profits expected over the customer's lifetime purchases.

customer mailing list a set of names, addresses, and telephone numbers.

customer perceived value (CPV) the difference between the prospective customer's evaluation of all the benefits and all the costs of an offering and the perceived alternatives.

customer-performance scorecard how well the company is doing year after year on particular customer-based measures.

customer profitability analysis (CPA) a means of assessing and ranking customer profitability through accounting techniques such as Activity-Based Costing (ABC).

customer training training the customer's employees to use the vendor's equipment properly and efficiently.

customer value analysis report of the company's strengths and weaknesses relative to various competitors.

customer value hierarchy five product levels that must be addressed by marketers in planning a market offering.

customerization combination of operationally driven mass customization with customized marketing in a way that empowers consumers to design the product and service offering of their choice.

D

data warehouse a collection of current data captured, organized, and stored in a company's contact center.

database marketing the process of building, maintaining, and using customer databases and other databases for the purpose of contacting, transacting, and building customer relationships.

datamining the extracting of useful information about individuals, trends, and segments from the mass of data.

delivery how well the product or service is delivered to the customer.

demand chain planning the process of designing the supply chain based on adopting a target market perspective and working backward.

direct marketing the use of consumer-direct (CD) channels to reach and deliver goods and services to customers without using marketing middlemen.

direct-order marketing marketing in which direct marketers seek a measurable response, typically a customer order.

direct product profitability (DDP) a way of measuring a product's handling costs from the time it reaches the warehouse until a customer buys it in the retail store.

direct (company) sales force full- or part-time paid employees who work exclusively for the company.

discrimination the process of recognizing differences in sets of similar stimuli and adjusting responses accordingly.

dissociative groups those groups whose values or behavior an individual rejects.

distribution programming building a planned, professionally managed, vertical marketing system that meets the needs of both manufacturer and distributors.

drive a strong internal stimulus impelling action.

dual adaptation adapting both the product and the communications to the local market.

dumping situation in which a company charges either less than its costs or less than it charges in its home market, in order to enter or win a market.

durability a measure of a product's expected operating life under natural or stressful conditions.

E

e-business the use of electronic means and platforms to conduct a company's business.

e-commerce a company or site offers to transact or facilitate the selling of products and services online.

e-marketing company efforts to inform buyers, communicate, promote, and sell its products and services over the Internet.

e-purchasing purchase of goods, services, and information from various online suppliers.

elimination-by-aspects heuristic situation in which the consumer compares brands on an attribute selected probabilistically, and brands are eliminated if they do not meet minimum acceptable cutoff levels.

environmental threat a challenge posed by an unfavorable trend or development that would lead to lower sales or profit.

everyday low pricing (EDLP) in retailing, a constant low price with few or no price promotions and special sales.

exchange the process of obtaining a desired product from someone by offering something in return.

exclusive distribution severely limiting the number of intermediaries, in order to maintain control over the service level and outputs offered by resellers.

expectancy-value model consumers evaluate products and services by combining their brand beliefs—positive and negative—according to their weighted importance.

expected product a set of attributes and conditions buyers normally expect when they purchase this product.

experience curve (learning curve) a decline in the average cost with accumulated production experience.

F

fad a craze that is unpredictable, short-lived, and without social, economic and political significance.

family brand situation in which the parent brand is already associated with multiple products through brand extensions.

family of orientation parents and siblings.

family of procreation spouse and children.

features things that enhance the basic function of a product.

fixed costs (overhead) costs that do not vary with production or sales revenue.

flexible market offering (1) a naked solution containing the product and service elements that all segment members value, and (2) discretionary options that some segment members value.

focus group a gathering of six to ten people who are carefully selected based on certain demographic, psychographic, or other considerations and brought together to discuss various topics of interest.

forecasting the art of anticipating what buyers are likely to do under a given set of conditions.

form the size, shape, or physical structure of a product.

forward invention creating a new product to meet a need in another country.

frequency programs (FPs) designed to provide rewards to customers who buy frequently and in substantial amounts.

G

global firm a firm that operates in more than one country and captures R&D, production, logistical, marketing, and financial advantages in its costs and reputation that are not available to purely domestic competitors.

global industry an industry in which the strategic positions of competitors in major geographic or national markets are fundamentally affected by their overall global positions.

goal formulation the process of developing specific goals for the planning period.

going-rate pricing price based largely on competitors' prices.

gray market branded products diverted from normal or authorized distributions channels in the country of product origin or across international borders.

H

heuristics rules of thumb or mental shortcuts in the decision process.

high-low pricing charging higher prices on an everyday basis but then running frequent promotions and special sales.

holistic marketing a concept based on the development, design, and implementation of marketing programs, processes, and activities that recognizes their breadth and interdependencies.

horizontal marketing system two or more unrelated companies put together resources or programs to exploit an emerging market opportunity.

hybrid channels use of multiple channels of distribution to reach customers in a defined market.

I

image the set of beliefs, ideas, and impressions a person holds regarding an object.

industry a group of firms that offer a product or class of products that are close substitutes for one another.

ingredient branding a special case of co-branding that involves creating brand equity for materials, components, or parts that are necessarily contained within other branded products.

innovation any good, service, or idea that is perceived by someone as new.

innovation diffusion process the spread of a new idea from its source of invention or creation to its ultimate users or adopters.

installation the work done to make a product operational in its planned location.

institutional market schools, hospitals, nursing homes, prisons, and other institutions that must provide goods and services to people in their care.

integrated logistics systems (ILS) materials management, material flow systems, and physical distribution, abetted by information technology (IT).

integrated marketing mixing and matching marketing activities to maximize their individual and collective efforts.

integrated marketing communications (IMC) a concept of marketing communications planning that recognizes the added value of a comprehensive plan.

intensive distribution the manufacturer placing the goods or services in as many outlets as possible.

internal branding activities and processes that help to inform and inspire employees.

interstitials advertisements, often with video or animation, that pop up between changes on a Web site.

J

joint venture a company in which multiple investors share ownership and control.

L

learning changes in an individual's behavior arising from experience.

lexicographic heuristic a consumer choosing the best brand on the basis of its perceived most important attribute.

licensed product one whose brand name has been licensed to other manufacturers who actually make the product.

life-cycle cost the product's purchase cost plus the discounted cost of maintenance and repair less the discounted salvage value.

lifestyle a person's pattern of living in the world as expressed in activities, interests, and opinions.

line extension the parent brand is used to brand a new product that targets a new market segment within a product category currently served by the parent brand.

line stretching a company lengthens its product line beyond its current range.

long-term memory (LTM) a permanent repository of information.

loyalty a commitment to rebuy or re-patronize a preferred product or service.

M

maintenance and repair the service program for helping customers keep purchased products in good working order.

market-buildup method identifying all the potential buyers in each market and estimating their potential purchases.

market demand the total volume of a product that would be bought by a defined customer group in a defined geographical area in a defined time period in a defined marketing environment under a defined marketing program.

market forecast the market demand corresponding to the level of industry marketing expenditure.

market logistics planning the infrastructure to meet demand, then implementing and controlling the physical flows or materials and final goods from points of origin to points of use, to meet customer requirements at a profit.

market opportunity analysis (MOA) system used to determine the attractiveness and probability of success.

market partitioning the process of investigating the hierarchy of attributes consumers examine in choosing a brand if they use phased decision strategies.

market penetration index a comparison of the current level of market demand to the potential demand level.

market-penetration pricing pricing strategy where prices start low to drive higher sales volume from price-sensitive customers and produce productivity gains.

market potential the upper limit to market demand whereby increased marketing expenditures would not be expected to stimulate further demand.

market-skimming pricing pricing strategy where prices start high and are slowly lowered over time to maximize profits from less price-sensitive customers.

marketer someone who seeks a response (attention, a purchase, a vote, a donation) from another party, called the prospect.

marketing process of planning and executing the conception, pricing, promotion, and distribution of ideas, goods, and services to create exchanges that satisfy individual and organizational goals.

marketing audit a comprehensive, systematic, independent, and periodic examination of a company's or business unit's marketing environment, objectives, strategies, and activities.

marketing channel system the particular set of marketing channels employed by a firm.

marketing channels sets of interdependent organizations involved in the process of making a product or service available for use or consumption.

marketing communications the means by which firms attempt to inform, persuade, and remind consumers—directly or indirectly—about products and brands that they sell.

marketing communications mix advertising, sales promotion, events and experiences, public relations and publicity, direct marketing, and personal selling.

marketing decision support system (MDSS) a coordinated collection of data, systems, tools, and techniques with supporting software and hardware by which an organization gathers and interprets relevant information from business and the environment and turns it into a basis for marketing action.

marketing implementation the process that turns marketing plans into action assignments and ensures that such assignments are executed in a manner that accomplishes the plan's stated objectives.

marketing information system (MIS) people, equipment, and procedures to gather, sort, analyze, evaluate, and distribute information to marketing decision makers.

marketing intelligence system a set of procedures and sources managers use to obtain everyday information about developments in the marketing environment.

marketing management the art and science of choosing target markets and getting, keeping, and growing customers through creating, delivering, and communicating superior customer value.

marketing metrics the set of measures that helps firms to quantify, compare, and interpret their marketing performance.

marketing network the company and its supporting stakeholders, with whom it has built mutually profitable business relationships.

marketing opportunity an area of buyer need and interest in which there is a high probability that a company can profitably satisfy that need.

marketing plan written document that summarizes what the marketer has learned about the marketplace, indicates how the firm plans to reach its marketing objectives, and helps direct and coordinate the marketing effort.

marketing public relations (MPR) publicity and other activities that build corporate or product image to facilitate marketing goals.

marketing research the systematic design, collection, analysis, and reporting of data and findings relevant to a specific marketing situation facing the company.

markup pricing an item by adding a standard increase to the product's cost.

materials and parts goods that enter the manufacturer's product completely.

media selection finding the most cost-effective media to deliver the desired number and type of exposures to the target audience.

megamarketing the strategic coordination of economic, psychological, political, and public relations skills, to gain the cooperation of a number of parties in order to enter or operate in a given market.

megatrends large social, economic, political, and technological changes that are slow to form, and once in place, have an influence for seven to ten years or longer.

membership groups groups having a direct influence on a person.

memory encoding how and where information gets into memory.

memory retrieval how and from where information gets out of memory.

mental accounting the manner by which consumers code, categorize, and evaluate financial outcomes of choices.

microsales analysis examination of specific products and territories that fail to produce expected sales.

microsite a limited area on the Web managed and paid for by an external advertiser/company.

mission statements statements that organizations develop to share with managers, employees, and (in many cases) customers.

mixed bundling the seller offers goods both individually and in bundles.

multichannel marketing a single firm uses two or more marketing channels to reach one or more customer segments.

multitasking doing two or more things at the same time.

N

net price analysis analysis that encompasses company list price, average discount, promotional spending, and co-op advertising to arrive at net price.

noncompensatory models in consumer choice, when consumers do not simultaneously consider all positive and negative attribute considerations in making a decision.

O

online alliances and affiliate programs when one Internet company works with another one and they advertise each other.

opinion leader the person in informal, product-related communications who offers advice or information about a specific product or product category.

ordering ease how easy it is for the customer to place an order with the company.

organization a company's structures, policies, and corporate culture.

organizational buying the decision-making process by which formal organizations establish the need for purchased products and services and identify, evaluate, and choose among alternative brands and suppliers.

overall market share the company's sales expressed as a percentage of total market sales.

P

parent brand an existing brand that gives birth to a brand extension.

partner relationship management (PRM) activities the firm undertakes to build mutually satisfying long-term relations with key partners such as suppliers, distributors, ad agencies, and marketing research suppliers.

penetrated market the set of consumers who are buying a company's product.

perceived value the value promised by the company's value proposition and perceived by the customer.

perception the process by which an individual selects, organizes, and interprets information inputs to create a meaningful picture of the world.

performance quality the level at which the product's primary characteristics operate.

personal communications channels two or more persons communicating directly face-to-face, person-to-audience, over the telephone, or through e-mail.

personal influence the effect one person has on another's attitude or purchase probability.

personality a set of distinguishing human psychological traits that lead to relatively consistent responses to environmental stimuli.

place advertising (also out-of-home advertising) ads that appear outside of home and where consumers work and play.

point-of-purchase (P-O-P) the location where a purchase is made, typically thought of in terms of a retail setting.

potential market the set of consumers who profess a sufficient level of interest in a market offer.

potential product all the possible augmentations and transformations the product or offering might undergo in the future.

price discrimination a company sells a product or service at two or more prices that do not reflect a proportional difference in costs.

price escalation an increase in the price of a product due to added costs of selling it in different countries.

primary groups groups with which a person interacts continuously and informally, such as family, friends, neighbors, and coworkers.

principle of congruity psychological mechanism that states that consumers like to see seemingly related objects as being as similar as possible in their favorability.

private label brand brands that retailers and wholesalers develop and market.

product adaptation altering the product to meet local conditions or preferences.

product assortment the set of all products and items a particular seller offers for sale.

product invention creating something new via product development or other means.

product mix see product assortment.

product penetration percentage the percentage of ownership or use of a product or service in a population.

product system a group of diverse but related items that function in a compatible manner.

profitable customer a person, household, or company that over time yields a revenue stream that exceeds by an acceptable amount the company's cost stream of attracting, selling, and servicing that customer.

prospect theory when consumers frame decision alternatives in terms of gains and losses according to a value function.

public any group that has an actual or potential interest in or impact on a company's ability to achieve its objectives.

public relations (PR) a variety of programs designed to promote or protect a company's image or its individual products.

publicity the task of securing editorial space—as opposed to paid space—in print and broadcast media to promote something.

pull strategy when the manufacturer uses advertising and promotion to persuade consumers to ask intermediaries for the product, thus inducing the intermediaries to order it.

purchase probability scale a scale to measure the probability of a buyer making a particular purchase.

pure bundling a firm only offers its products as a bundle.

pure-click companies that have launched a Web site without any previous existence as a firm.

push strategy when the manufacturer uses its sales force and trade promotion money to induce intermediaries to carry, promote, and sell the product to end users.

R

reference groups all the groups that have a direct or indirect influence on a person's attitudes or behavior.

reference prices pricing information a consumer retains in memory which is used to interpret and evaluate a new price.

relational equity the cumulative value of the firm's network of relationships with its customers, partners, suppliers, employees, and investors.

relationship marketing building mutually satisfying long-term relationships with key parties, in order to earn and retain their business.

relative market share market share in relation to a company's largest competitor.

reliability a measure of the probability that a product will not malfunction or fail within a specified time period.

repairability a measure of the ease of fixing a product when it malfunctions or fails.

representativeness heuristic when consumers base their predictions on how representative or similar an outcome is to other examples.

risk analysis a method by which possible rates of returns and their probabilities are calculated by obtaining estimates for uncertain variables affecting profitability.

role the activities a person is expected to perform.

S

sales analysis measuring and evaluating actual sales in relation to goals.

sales budget a conservative estimate of the expected volume of sales, used for making current purchasing, production, and cash flow decisions.

sales promotion a collection of incentive tools, mostly short term, designed to stimulate quicker or greater purchase of particular products or services by consumers or the trade.

sales quota the sales goal set for a product line, company division, or sales representative.

sales-variance analysis a measure of the relative contribution of different factors to a gap in sales performance.

satisfaction a person's feelings of pleasure or disappointment resulting from comparing a product's perceived performance or outcome in relation to his or her expectations.

scenario analysis developing plausible representations of a firm's possible future that make different assumptions about forces driving the market and include different uncertainties.

search-related ads ads in which search terms are used as a proxy for the consumer's consumption interests and relevant links to product or service offerings are listed alongside the search results.

secondary groups groups which tend to be more formal and require less interaction than primary groups, such as religious, professional, and trade-union groups.

selective attention the mental process of screening out certain stimuli while noticing others.

selective distortion the tendency to interpret product information in a way that fits consumer perceptions.

selective distribution the use of more than a few but less than all of the intermediaries who are willing to carry a particular product.

selective retention good points about a product that consumers like are remembered and good points about competing products are forgotten.

served market all the buyers who are able and willing to buy a company's product.

served market share a company's sales expressed as a percentage of the total sales to its served market.

service any act or performance that one party can offer to another that is essentially intangible and does not result in the ownership of anything.

share penetration index a comparison of a company's current market share to its potential market share.

shopping goods goods that the consumer, in the process of selection and purchase, characteristically compares on such bases as suitability, quality, price, and style.

short-term memory (STM) a temporary repository of information.

social classes homogeneous and enduring divisions in a society, which are hierarchically ordered and whose members share similar values, interests, and behavior.

social marketing marketing done by a nonprofit or government organization to further a cause, such as "say no to drugs."

specialty goods goods that have unique characteristics or brand identification for which a sufficient number of buyers are willing to make a special purchasing effort.

sponsorship financial support of an event or activity in return for recognition and acknowledgment as the sponsor.

stakeholder-performance scorecard a measure to track the satisfaction of various constituencies who have a critical interest in and impact on the company's performance.

status one's position within his or her own hierarchy or culture.

straight extension introducing a product in a foreign market without any change in the product.

strategic brand management the design and implementation of marketing activities and programs to build, measure, and manage brands to maximize their value.

strategic business units (SBUs) a single business or collection of related businesses that can be planned separately from the rest of the company, with its own set of competitors and a manager who is responsible for strategic planning and profit performance.

strategic group firms pursuing the same strategy directed to the same target market.

strategic marketing plan laying out the target markets and the value proposition that will be offered, based on analysis of the best market opportunities.

strategy a company's game plan for achieving its goals.

style a product's look and feel to the buyer.

sub-brand a new brand combined with an existing brand.

subculture subdivisions of a culture that provide more specific identification and socialization, such as nationalities, religions, racial groups, and geographical regions.

subliminal perception receiving and processing subconscious messages that affect behavior.

supersegment a set of segments sharing some exploitable similarity.

supplies and business services short-term goods and services that facilitate developing or managing the finished product.

supply chain management (SCM) procuring the right inputs (raw materials, components, and capital equipment); converting them efficiently into finished products; and dispatching them to the final destinations.

T

tactical marketing plan marketing tactics, including product features, promotion, merchandising, pricing, sales channels, and service.

target costing deducting the desired profit margin from the price at which a product will sell, given its appeal and competitors' prices.

target market the part of the qualified available market the company decides to pursue.

target-return pricing determining the price that would yield the firm's target rate of return on investment (ROI).

telemarketing the use of telephone and call centers to attract prospects, sell to existing customers, and provide service by taking orders and answering questions.

total costs the sum of the fixed and variable costs for any given level of production.

total customer cost the bundle of costs customers expect to incur in evaluating, obtaining, using, and disposing of the given market offering, including monetary, time, energy, and psychic costs.

total customer value the perceived monetary value of the bundle of economic, functional, and psychological benefits customers expect from a given market offering.

total quality management (TQM) an organizationwide approach to continuously improving the quality of all the organization's processes, products, and services.

tracking studies collecting information from consumers on a routine basis over time.

transaction a trade of values between two or more parties: A gives X to B and receives Y in return.

transfer in the case of gifts, subsidies, and charitable contributions: A gives X to B but does not receive anything tangible in return.

transfer price the price a company charges another unit in the company for goods it ships to foreign subsidiaries.

trend a direction or sequence of events that has some momentum and durability.

two-part pricing a fixed fee plus a variable usage fee.

tying agreements agreement in which producers of strong brands sell their products to dealers only if dealers purchase related products or services, such as other products in the brand line.

U

unsought goods those the consumer does not know about or does not normally think of buying, like smoke detectors.

V

value-delivery network a company's supply chain and how it partners with specific suppliers and distributors to make products and bring them to markets.

value-delivery system all the expectancies the customer will have on the way to obtaining and using the offering.

value network a system of partnerships and alliances that a firm creates to source, augment, and deliver its offerings.

value pricing winning loyal customers by charging a fairly low price for a high-quality offering.

value proposition the whole cluster of benefits the company promises to deliver.

variable costs costs that vary directly with the level of production.

venture team a cross-functional group charged with developing a specific product or business.

vertical integration situation in which manufacturers try to control or own their suppliers, distributors, or other intermediaries.

vertical marketing system (VMS) producer, wholesaler(s), and retailer(s) acting as a unified system.

viral marketing using the Internet to create word of mouth effects to support marketing efforts and goals.

Y

yield pricing situation in which companies offer (1) discounted but limited early purchases, (2) higher-priced late purchases, and (3) the lowest rates on unsold inventory just before it expires.

Z

zero-level channel (direct-marketing channel) a manufacturer selling directly to the final customer.

Image Credits

Chapter 1
2 Dallas and John Heaton / The Stock Connection; **6** Courtesy of Borneo Motors Singapore / Saatchi & Saatchi Singapore; **7** Courtesy of the Singapore Zoo; **7** Lawrence Ang; **11** Galen Frysinger; **13** Courtesy of Volvo Cars of North America, LLC; **16** Shiseido Co., Ltd. Tokyo, Japan; **22** Bill Aron / PhotoEdit, Inc.; **24** Used with permission of Kinokuniya Singapore, 2008.

Chapter 2
32 Vincent Tan; **40** Used with permission of MMOsite.com; **41** © 2008 Hindustan Unilever; **43** © 2007 Intel Corporation. All rights reserved. Photographer: Trevor Pearson. Used with permission; **48** Courtesy of AP Wide World Photos; **51** Used with permission from Li & Fung Group; **52** Courtesy of the authors; **60** Photo courtesy of Star Alliance™; **63** Courtesy of the authors.

Chapter 3
72 Courtesy of TBWA / Santiago Mangada Puno Philippines, ad agency for Adidas Philippines; **75** Lawrence S. Grodeska; **80** HO/AFP/Getty Images; **81** Courtesy of the authors; **82** HOT WHEELS is a trademark owned by and used with permission from Mattel, Inc. © 2005 Mattel, Inc. All rights reserved; **88** Kent Yu; **89** Courtesy of the authors; **90** Used with permission from Hyundai Motor India Ltd.; **95** Courtesy of Ivan Png.

Chapter 4
98 Courtesy of Gillette; **104** Courtesy of the authors.

Chapter 5
130 Spencer Grant / PhotoEdit, Inc.; **139** Lawrence Ang; **145** Text and artwork copyright © 1998 by Yahoo! Inc. All rights reserved. YAHOO! and the YAHOO! logo are trademarks of YAHOO! Inc.; **149** Reprinted with permission of Cerebos Pacific Limited; **154** Used with permission of Tesco plc.

Chapter 6
158 Image courtesy of Shiseido Co., Ltd; **160** Courtesy of Billabong; **161** Courtesy of the authors; **161** Lawrence Ang; **163** Will Tung; **166** John Yarbrough; **167** Lawrence Ang; **169** Lawrence Ang; **170** A. Kuncoro; **173** Melissa / Flickr; **175** Courtesy of Lenovo; **177** Image used with permission from Japan Sangaria Beverage Co., Ltd.; **179** David Baker; **179** inspector_81 / Flickr.com; **183** Courtesy of the National Fluid Milk Processor Promotion Board.

Chapter 7
194 Photographer: Robert Delahanty. Used with permissions from CISCO Systems, Inc.; **202** Courtesy of Eastman Kodak Company; **206** Courtesy of HP.

Chapter 8
224 Mindy Tom; **227** Lawrence Ang; **230** Chapman Behler; **236** American Honda Motor Co., Inc. Photography by Uwe Breitkpof, illustration by Matt Wood; **237** Used with permission of Unilever Singapore Pte Ltd – Dove; **238** Courtesy of Banyan Tree Hotels and Resorts; **245** Courtesy of ICICI Prudential Life Insurance Company Ltd.; **254** Courtesy of PepsiCo International.

Chapter 9
258 Courtesy of Corbis / Bettman; **262** Amy Etra / PhotoEdit Inc.; **270** © 2006 MasterCard. All rights reserved; **272** Courtesy of the authors; **275** Courtesy of the authors; **279** Lawrence Ang; **286** Courtesy of Eu Yan Sang (Singapore) Private Limited; **286** Harley-Davidson Motor Company; **287** Courtesy of the authors; **290** Courtesy of Essilor Singapore; **293** © Daniela La Monaca / Reuters / Corbis.

Chapter 10
298 AP Wide World Photos; **304** AP Wide World Photos; **306** Serena Chong; **309** Roslan Rahman / Agence France Presses / Getty Images; **309** Perry L. Aragon; **317** Courtesy of Haw Par Healthcare.

Chapter 11
326 Courtesy of Sony Corporation; **335** PhotoEdit, Inc.; **338** Stephan F. Faust / www.photographersdirect.com; **340** Courtesy of AP Wide World Photos; **348** Courtesy of the Quaker Oats Company; **352** Courtesy of the authors.

Chapter 12
358 Douglas C. Pizac / AP Wide World Photos; **366** Courtesy of Essilor Singapore; **367** © John van Hasselt / Corbis. All rights reserved; **376** Michael Newman / PhotoEdit, Inc.; **379** Courtesy of the authors; **382** Courtesy of the authors.

Chapter 13
388 Scott Christian; **393** Courtesy of the authors; **394** Courtesy of the authors; **399** Courtesy of Southwest Airlines; **402** Roslan Rahman / AFP / Getty Images, Inc.; **408** Tom Bodley; **413** Courtesy of Young & Rubicam Singapore; **415** Robert E. Klein / AP Wide World Photos.

Chapter 14
420 Don Ryan / AP Wide World Photos; **422** Courtesy of the authors; **423** Getty Images, Inc.; **424** Alamy Images; **427** Alamy Images; **428** Joey Nigh / Corbis; **429** Courtesy of the authors; **431** Skip Nelson / Image Tree Productions; **442** Courtesy of the authors.

Chapter 15
458 Gert Noroðy; **477** Alamy Images; **488** © Amazon.com. All rights reserved; **489** Lawrence Ang.

Chapter 16
494 Handout / epa / Corbis; **496** Alamay Images; **498** Courtesy of the authors; **502** Courtesy of Joe and Jane Cote; **505** Courtesy of the authors; **506** Courtesy of the authors; **509** Courtesy of the authors; **510** Courtesy of the authors; **510** Courtesy of the authors; **512** Courtesy of the authors.

Chapter 17
526 Used with permission from Unilever; **529** Used with permission from Nike; **536** Courtesy of J. Walter Thompson Singapore, ad agency for Kraft Singapore; **537** Courtesy of Osim International; **540** Image courtesy of HSBC Singapore; **546** Courtesy of Young & Rubicam Singapore; **547** Courtesy of Young & Rubicam Singapore; **553** © 2004 Accenture. All rights reserved. Reprinted with permission.

Chapter 18
558 Courtesy of MasterCard International—Georgette Tan and Venture Liang; **561** Copyright © 2008 by Population Services International (PSI). All rights reserved. Reprinted by permission of PSI; **566** ABSOLUT®VODKA. Absolut Country of Sweden Vodka & Logo, Absolut, Absolut Bottle Design and Absolut Calligraphy are trademarks owned by V&S VIN & SPRIT AB (publ.) © 2004 V&S VIN & SPRIT AB (publ.); **568** Courtesy of the authors; **571** Courtesy of Young & Rubicam Singapore; **572** Courtesy of the authors; **573** Lawrence Ang; **591** Lawrence Ang; **594** © Shawn Thew / epa / Corbis.

Chapter 19
598 Keren Su / Corbis; **607** Tim Lehman; **609** Lawrence Ang; **612** BMW / Ritta and Associates.

Chapter 20
640 Mike Derer / AP Wide World Photos; **643** Courtesy of Lion Corporation Singapore; **648** Courtesy of Xerox Corporation; **652** Zuma Press / NewsCom; **657** Warner Brothers TV / Bright / Kauffman / Crane Pro / The Kobal Collection / Chris Haston; **670** Getty Image.

Chapter 21
676 Panos Pictures; **680** Courtesy of the authors; **688** David Noton Photography / Alamy Images; **692** Zhu Gang / FeatureChina / NewsCom; **698** Courtesy of the authors; **700** Courtesy of the authors; **702** Courtesy of Billabong; **706** Claro Cortes IV CC / Reuters Limited; **707** Robert Harding / Alamy Images; **709** New Line / Saul Zaentz / Wing Nut / The Kobal Collection.

Chapter 22
714 Courtesy of The Image Works; **725** Paul Sakuma / AP Wide World Photos; **726** Used with permission of Starbucks Corporation; **728** © Simon Harshent. Courtesy of Bartle Bogle Hegarty Singapore; **732** M. Spencer Green / AP Wide World Photos.

Index

Name Index

Aaker, David, A., 167, 268, 316
Ahrendt, Angela, 307
Aitchison, Jim, 565
Ambler, Tim, 117
Anderson, Chris, 230
Anderson, James C., 227, 517
Ayal, Igal, 681

Batey, Ian, 265, 267
Beckham, David, 584
Bedbury, Scott, 294
Bell, Genevieve, 113
Berry, Leonard L., 150, 397, 404, 406
Bezos, Jeff, 355, 488
Bond, John, 232
Bonoma, Thomas V., 248
Boulding, William, 406
Branson, Richard, 594
Brin, Sergey, 271
Brown, Stephen, 724
Butterfield, Peter, 377

Carpenter, Gregory S., 312, 353
Cast, Carter, 12
Cespedes, Frank V., 462
Chan, Raymond, 301
Chang, Morris, 39
Charron, Paul R., 335
Chen, Frank, 273
Chen, Tianqiao, 302
Christensen, Clayton, 731
Christensen, Juha, 369
Collins, Jim, 55
Comstock, Beth, 213
Confucius, 729
Cooper, Robert G., 645, 668, 669
Cotsakos, Christos, 407

Daft, Douglas, 637
Daswani, Raja, 1 39
Day, George, 37, 156
Deshpandé, Rohit, 53
Dichter, Ernest, 172
Doctoroff, Tom, 247
Donnelly, James H., 150
Doyle, Peter, 63
Drucker, Peter, 5, 44
Drumwright, Minette, 730
Dunaway, Cammie, 145

Edison, Thomas, 213

Farley, John U., 53
Filo, David, 608
Fiske, Neil, 239
FitzGerald, Niall, 378
Fournier, Susan, 277, 278
Freud, Sigmund, 172
Fung, Victor, 50

Gardner, Susannah, 542
Gates, Bill, 704
Ghosn, Carlos, 53, 219
Gilly, Mary C., 407
Godin, Seth, 277
Goizueta, Roberto, 121
Golder, Peter N., 313
Gong, Li, 537
Gong, Wen, 164
Grove, Andrew, 655
Griffin, Abbie J., 651
Gupta, Sunil, 143

Hampden-Turner, Charles M., 636
Hauser, John, 651
Hawkins, Jeff, 92
Herzberg, Frederick, 173
Ho, Kwon Ping, 261
Honda, Soichiro, 729
Horvath, David, 369
Hovland, Carl, 536
Hu, Judy, 213
Huba, Jackie, 149
Hurd, Mark, 621

James, Damon, 270
James, LeBron, 22, 529, 579
Jaworski, Bernard J., 410, 609
Johnston, Russell, 480
Jones, Scott A., 348
Jordan, Michael, 22
Joseph, Robert, 133

Kalra, Ajay, 406
Kamprad, Ingvar, 170
Karlovich, Janice, 241
Kelly, Francis J., 322
Khan, Shah Rukh, 90
Kim, W. Chan, 331
Kimoto, Tetsu, 176
Kinney, Rik, 112
Klein, Russ, 265
Kleinschmidt, Elko J., 645, 668, 669
Kraljic, Peter, 203
Kramer, Mark, 731
Kumar, Kishore, 669
Kumar, Nirmalya, 35, 454, 455, 516
Kumar, V., 143

Lafley, A. G., 145, 265, 652
LaPointe, Pat, 119
Lau, Peter, 409
Lawrence, Paul R., 480
Lee, Jae H., 444
Lehmann, Donald R., 143
Letz, Jim, 367
Levitt, Theodore, 19, 46, 270, 350, 391
Li, Ning, 270
Li, Richard, 693
Li, Tiger, 164
Li, Zhan G., 164
Liak, Teng Lit, 413
Lim, Chon-Phung, 635
Liu, Richie, 177
Liu, Xiang, 22, 332
Low, George S., 562
Lu, Hong Liang, 433

Ma, Jack, 489
MacMillan, Ian C., 308
Malhotra, Arvind, 407
Maloney, John, 535
Manomaiphibul, Piti, 251
Martin, Nan, 113
Maslow, Abraham, 172
Matsushita, Konosuke, 729
Mauborgne, Renée, 331
McCausland, Tom, 8
McConnell, Ben, 149
McGovern, Gail, 12
McGrath, Rita Gunther, 308
Meredith, Geoffrey E., 84, 241
Min, Sungwook, 312
Mohr, Jakki J., 562
Morgan, Adam, 349
Morita, Akio, 44, 340, 655
Morrison, Alasdair, 343
Murdoch, Rupert, 663
Murphy, Patrick E., 730
Myrick, Dan, 229

Nagle, Thomas T., 435
Nakamoto, Kent, 312, 353
Nakata, Cheryl, 647
Narus, James A., 227, 517
Neeleman, David 400
Nunes, Paul F., 462

Okuda, Hiroshi, 343
O'Leary, Michael, 424
Omidayar, Pierre, 443
O'Neal, Shaquille, 270
Osgood, C. E., 538
Osher, John, 652
Owen-Jones, Lindsay, 715

Packard, David, 12
Page, Larry, 271
Palmisano, Samuel, 55
Parasuraman, A., 397, 404, 406, 407
Parker, Mark, 145
Paul, Vivek, 637
Peppers, Don, 145
Peters, Tom, 6
Pfeffer, Jeffrey, 151
Phelps, Sherry, 399
Porter, Michael, 35, 59, 731
Prahalad, C. K., 55

Quelch, John, 12

Rangan, V. Kasturi, 479
Rangaswamy, Arvind, 233
Rayport, Jeffrey F., 410, 609
Reichheld, Frederick K., 138
Ries, Al, 290
Robinson, William T., 312
Rogers, Everett, 671
Rogers, Martha, 145
Russo, J. Edward, 191

Sawhney, Mohan, 11, 55
Schewe, Charles D., 84, 241
Schmitt, Bernd, 590
Schnaars, Steven P., 313
Schoemaker, Paul J. H., 191
Schultz, Don, 462
Schultz, Howard, 26, 726
Shapiro, Benson P., 248
Silverstein, Barry, 322
Silverstein, Michael, 239
Sivakumar, K., 647
Smith, Adam, 134
Staelin, Richard, 406
Stafford, Dale, 396
Stanat, Michael, 240
Steenkamp, Jan-Benedict E. M., 516
Stern, Louis W., 464
Stråberg, Hans, 316
Stuart, John, 283
Sun Tzu, 340

Tannenbaum, P. H., 538
Tatelman, Michael, 74
Tellis, Gerard J., 313
Thaler, Richard, 191
Thompson, Thomas W., 150
Trompenaars, Fons, 636
Trout, Jack, 290

Underhill, Paco, 509
Underwood, Carrie, 584

Vandebroek, Sophie V., 648
Vanhonacker, Wilfried, 61

Wales, Jim, 348
Webster Jr., Frederick E., 35, 200, 201
Welch Jr., John F., 139
West, Dan, 448
Wexner, Leslie, 299
Williamson, Peter, 38
Wind, Yoram, 200, 233
Wolfinbarger, Mary, 407
Wong, Hansel, 477
Woods, Tiger, 22, 336, 538, 588
Wunderman, Lester, 152

Yan, Vincent, 285
Yang, Jerry, 608
Yano, Hirotake, 442
Yao, Ming, 538
Yeh, Ying, 220
Yoshida, Tatsuo, 367
Yun, Jong-Yong, 51, 370

Zeithaml, Valarie A., 397, 404, 407
Zeng, Ming, 38

Zhang, Ziyi, 183
Zhu, Rongji, 344
Zif, Jehiel, 681
Zyman, Sergio, 19

Company, Brand, and Organization Index

(RED), 732
1Up.com, 229
2001 Outlet, 144
3721, 608
3Com, 707
3M, 138, 649, 650, 691
7dream.com, 491
7-Eleven, 75
999 Ointment, 533

A.C. Nielsen, 168, 261, 434, 489, 497, 499, 506, 512, 533, 548, 581, 736
A.C. Nielsen Media Research, 126
A.T. Cross, 386
Absolut, 566
Accenture, 117, 336, 553, 588
Acer, 91, 217, 651
Acushnet, 706
Adec, 375
Adidas, 332, 571, 587
Adobe Systems Inc., 649, 725
Aetna Malaysia, 153
Agro Asia (Double A), 552
Air China, 481
Air Deccan, 449
AirAsia, 471, 528
Airtel, 708
Ajinomoto, 345, 702
Akzo Nobel, 210
Alba, 375
Alcatel, 642, 684
Alexandra Hospital, 413
Alibaba, 207, 208, 315, 444, 489, 608
Altria, 678
Amazon.com, 355, 488
American Express, 197, 304, 582
American Idol, 731
Amul, 685
Amway, 625
Andersen Consulting, 336
Anheuser Busch, 691, 266, 345
AOL-Time Warner, 221
Apple, 264, 347, 350, 477, 572, 653, 670, 677, 701, A-5
Armani, 293, 426
Arthur Andersen, 336
Asahi Breweries, 316, 524
Asimco, 385
ATG, 668
Auprés, 342
Aveda, 252
Avis, 276
Avon, 60, 470, 520, 541, 708

B&Q, 503, 574
BabyCare, 82
Baidu, 608
Bak Foong Yun, 286
Bandai, 312
Bank of Asia, 409
Bank of China, 514, 689
Bank One, 470
Banyan Tree, 238, 261
Baosteel Group, 692
Barbie, 273, 697
Bata Indonesia, 28
Bates Asia, 703
BayanTrade, 207
Bechtel Corporation, 688
Beijing Economic Technology Investment Development Corporation, 693
Beijing Hualian Group, 694
Beijing Wan Yuan Industry Corporation, 693
Ben & Jerry's, 76
Berjaya Times Square, 509
Bert Claeys, 331
BeXcom, 208
BIC, 291
Bienestar, 28
Big Bazaar, 502
Billabong, 160, 681, 702
Biotherm, 273
Blu-ray, 327
BMW, 18, 55, 233, 293, 305, 469, 612, 653
BMW Films, 612
Body by Milk, 584
Boeing, 18, 664
Bojangles, 708
Boon Rawd Brewery, 108, 568
Booz Allen Hamilton, 25
Borders, 410, 505
Bosch, 274
Boston Consulting Group, 491, 643
Boston's Cone, Inc., 734
BP, 280
Brand's, 149, 188, 555
Britannia, 227
British Airways, 594
BSkyB, 663
Build-a-Bear Workshop, 149
Bumrungrad International, 389
Burberry Ltd, 307
Burger King, 145, 265, 593, 610
Burson-Marsteller, 542
Business Software Alliance, 351

Café de Coral, 168, 169
Café de Make-up, 237
California Milk Processor Board, 183
Callaway Golf, 331
CALLPLAN model, 115
Calvin Klein, 272
Caltex, 23
Campbell Soup, 386
Campfire, 614
Canon, 207, 265, 351, 585, 645, 677, 730
Carefree, 275
Careful, 275
Carrefour, 513
Casio, 351
Caterpillar, 339, 359
Cathay Pacific, 45, 272, 377, 403
Cendant Hotel Group, 710
Cerebos, 555
ChaCha, 348
Changi International Airport Services, 522
Charoen Pokphand, 687
ChemConnect, 207
Chem-Cross, 207
Chery, 313
Chevrolet, 145
China Airlines, 261
China Bicycle, 276
China Fisheries, 459
China International Water & Electric, 687
China Life Insurance, 729
China National Bluestar Group, 694
China Resources Enterprise (CRE), 512
Chinatrust Commercial Bank, 393
Chrysler, 52. *See also* DaimlerChrysler
Chuo Mitsui Trust, 237
CIC, 111
Circle K, 235
Cirque du Soleil, 331, 415
Cisco Systems Inc, 36, 95, 195, 487, 653, 707
Citibank, 395, 553, 659, 703
Citicorp, 688
Citigroup, 724
Citizen, 375
CJ Home Shopping, 599
CKin2u, 272
Clear Blue, 533
Clear Media, 571
Clinique, 252, 567
Coach, 485
Coca-Cola, 14, 41, 76, 115, 121, 207, 229, 244, 316, 318, 348, 382, 423, 451, 481, 498, 507, 518, 541, 585, 592, 637, 665, 682, 691, 692, 696, 701, 703, 711, 725
Coke Blak, 423
Coles Group, 144
Colgate Junior, 255
Colgate-Palmolive, 255, 287, 667
Columbia Records, 400
Comite Colberg, 351
Compaq, 209, 541
Converse, 17, 149
Coopers & Lybrand, 52
Costco, 371
Cover Girl Outlast, 664
CR Asia, 235
Creative Technology, 264
Crest, 233, 252, 262, 287, 607, 652, 701, 722
Cummins, 202

Daewoo, 163
Dahongying, 94
Daimler, 52
DaimlerChrysler, 136, 469, 474, 645
Dairy Farm, 500
Dairy Queen, 352
Daiso, 442
Danone, 682, 705
Daum Corporation, 599
DBS Bank, 578
DCW Home Products, 289
De Beers, 176, 561
Del Monte, 476, 600
Dell, 249, 309, 446, 461, 468
Delta, 449
Denso, 218
Derwent Valley Foods, 274
Diamond Back, 276
Diet Coke, 175
Diet Pepsi, 175
Dindings Poultry Processing, 272
Disney, 49, 161, 246, 344, 396, 471, 472, 665, 698, 706
Disney Channel, 165
Disneyland, 13, 161, 698
DoCoMo, 318, 343, 498
Dodge, 240
Dogster, 229
Dolce & Gabbana, 491
Dome Coffee, 217
Domino's Pizza, 329, 500, 523
Dongfeng, 689
Doosan Group, 691
Dove, 237, 526
Dow, 649
DuPont, 383, 721, 725, 728
Dutch Baby, 274
Dutch Lady, 274

E*Trade, 407
EachNet, 302
eBay, 156, 207, 302, 608
Electrolux AB, 316
Electrolux, 564
Eli Lilly, 646
Emami, 90
E-Mart, 685
EMI, 467
Epson, 474
ER, 657
Ericsson, 272, 683
Escalator Handrail Company (EHC), 438
Escotel, 227

Eslite Bookstore, 277
Essilor, 290, 366
Estée Lauder, 252
Eu Yan Sang, 286
EVA Airways, 261
Evista, 646
ExxonMobil, 23

FaceBook, 229, 614
Fair & Lovely Foundation, 163
Fanta, 316, 579
Febreze, 262
FedEx, 275, 386
Feichang, 306
Five Star, 385
Flying Pigeon, 319
Foo Fighters, 240
Ford, 273, 305, 316, 542, 588, 608, 616, 645
Forever Living, 626
Formula1, 572
France Telecom, 694
French Connection, 574
Friends, 657
Frito-Lay, 145, 287
Fuji, 500, 655
Fuji/Xerox, 274
Fujitsu, 655
Fuld & Co., 77
Future Cola, 306

Gai Zhong Gai, 568
Galaxy, 316
Gallup & Robinson, Inc., 578
Gap, 335, 426, 477
Gateway, The, 514
Gather.com, 229
Gatorade, 538
Geely, 87, 306
General Electric (GE), 103, 139, 213, 273, 588, 653, 707
General Mills, 649
General Motors (GM), 87, 238, 313, 434, 491, 564, 607, 645, 683, 689, 693, 694
Gerber, 592
Gillette, 90, 99, 135, 207, 236, 262, 293, 339, 421, 507, 624, 652
Gillette Venus, 236
Giordano, 370, 409, 412, 499, 504
Glico Pocky, 350
Global Sources Garments & Textiles Online, 206
Golden Hope Plantations, 381
GoodBaby, 344
Goodyear, 290
Google, 46, 259, 272, 315, 348, 608, 653
Grameen Bank, 682
Grameen-Phone, 682
Greenpeace, 725
Grey Global's, 87
Grey Worldwide, 548

Groupe Michelin, 290
Gucci, 471, 511
Guibiewan, 225

H&M, 426
H.P. France NY, 517
Haier, 63, 174, 177, 279, 306, 378, 404, 547
Hallmark, 229
Handi Network International, 228
Hanjaya Mandala Sampoerna, 353
Hanmi Whole Soymilk Company, 270
Happy Jacks, 593
Harbin Brewery, 345
Harley-Davidson, 146, 150, 286, 490, 653
Hasbro, 379, 691
Hazema, 219
Head & Shoulders, 288
Health Food Enterprises, 384
Heineken, 703
Heinz, 287, 600
Hello Kitty, 60
Helmut Lang, 491
Hero-Honda, 227
Hershey's Food Corp., 111
Hertz, 276
Heublein, 342
Hewlett-Packard (HP), 27, 197, 206, 207, 209, 254, 288, 371, 398, 461, 621, 635, 650, A-4
Hidesign, 270
Hindustan Unilever, 41, 77, 101, 163, 227, 618, 682, 692
Hitachi, 288, 655
Holo Holo, 171
Home Depot, 140
Home Show, 574
Honda, 218, 235, 244, 265, 287, 288, 313, 351, 398, 574, 645, 729
Honda Element, 235
Honda Fit, 235
Hong Kong International Airport, 408
Hong Kong Tourism Board, 116
HSBC, 60, 232, 514, 539, 572, 727
Hualu Electronics, 61
Huapeng Trading, 680
Huawei Technologies, 95
Hyatt, 273, 691
Hyatt Regency, 309
Hyundai, 163, 253, 265, 313, 377, 434

Iams, 722
IBM, 55, 137, 197, 207, 280, 336, 371, 416, 575, 613, 623, 625, 681
ICI Dulux, 243
ICICI Prudential, 245
IDT International, 301
IKEA, 170, 370, 431, 519
iMac, 669
i-mode, 16, 343
Indian Airlines, 392

Infosys Technologies, 330, 683
ING Group, 548
ING Insurance, 534
Intel, 43, 113, 185, 383, 547
Interbrand, 284
International Flavors & Fragrances, 653
Inventec, 330
iPhone, 92, 350, 670, A-5
iPod, 264, 347, 656, 670
iTunes, 347, 467, 670

J. Walter Thompson, 514
J.D. Power & Associates, 136, 140
Jaguar, 542
Jansenn Pharmaceutical, 605
Jardine Matheson, 343
Jet Airways, 449
JetBlue, 400
Jianlibao, 682
Jin Bei, 693
Johnson & Johnson, 252, 275, 611, 641, 649
Johnson Electric, 39
Jollibee, 438, 510, 685
Juicy Couture, 270, 335
Jump Associates, 54
JVC, 427
JWT, 247

Kajima, 219
Kanebo, 273
Kansai International Airport, 408
Kasikornbank, 45, 382
KDDI, 343
Kejian, 595
Kelkoo, 315
Key Clinic, 567
KFC, 17, 94, 95, 187, 281, 393, 691
Kia Motors, 137, 163, 377
Kikkoman, 656
Kinepolis, 331
Kingfisher, 392, 449
Kinokuniya, 24
Kirin, 316, 672
KitKat, 376, 570
Kmart, 337
Knorr, 368, 378
Kodak, 38, 202, 220, 376, 524, 691
Komatsu heavy equipment, 653
Kong-Doo Soy Milk, 270
Konica, 304
Konka, 177
Kraft, 207, 465, 476, 536, 719
Krohne, 61
Kuala Lumpur International Airport, 219, 408
Kyobo Books, 491

L.L. Bean, 605
L'Oréal, 169, 382, 541, 564, 679, 715
Lakme Lever, 692
Lawson, 499

Lee Kum Kee, 680
Legend, 275, 681
LEGO, 323, 365, 650, 653
Lenovo, 87, 174, 221, 252, 275, 430, 642, 681
Leo Beer, 568
Leo Burnett, 239, 541, 548
Levi's, 88, 588, 653, 700, 701, 728
Lexus, 6, 265, 637, 377, 390
LG, 91, 177, 478, 499, 619, 626
LG Electronics, 63, 227, 732
LG Electronics MobileComm, 588
LG Home Shopping, 599
Li & Fung, 39, 50, 60, 208, 217, 477, 520, 721
Li Ning Sports Goods, 270
Lifebuoy, 704
Limited Brands, 299
Liz Claiborne, 270
Logitech International, 352
Loppi, 499
Louis Vuitton, 167, 511, 643
LSI Logic, 653
Lucky Brand, 335
Lululemon, 338
Lumaé, 382
Luvs, 262
LVMH Moët Hennessy Louis Vuitton, 706
Lycra My Show, 573

M.A.C., 252
Macromedia, 369
Malaysian Airline System, 514
Manchester United, 528
Mandom, 237
Marlboro, 309
Marriott International, 131, 430
Marushin Foods, 275
MasterCard, 269, 270, 561
Matsushita Electric Industrial, 61, 176, 288, 479, 645, 646, 647, 729
Mattel, 111
Max New York Life, 227
Maxim, 168
Maybelline, 679
McCann-Erickson, 600
McDonald's, 11, 27, 77, 91, 168, 241, 275, 287, 438, 500, 587, 685, 696, 700, 725
McDonnell Douglas, 448
McGraw-Hill, 197
McKinsey & Company, 42, 61, 62, 336, 435, 511, 643
Medtronic, 653
Meiya Power, 219
Mengniu Dairy, 587
Mercedes, 375, 376
Mercedes A-Class, 375
Message Co., 83
Microsoft, 50, 61, 197, 259, 315, 475, 541, 611, 613, 654, 704, 708

Miller Brewing, 280
Millward Brown International, 268, 580
Mini, 544
Mininurse, 679
Minolta, 653
Mirinda, 540
Mister Donut, 542
Mitsubishi Corporation, 471
Mitsubishi Motors, 218, 328, 386, 474, 699
Mitsubishi Tokyo Financial Group, 413
Mittal, 683
Mizuho Financial Group, 413
M-Link Asia, 472
Mobil, 244
Moto Photo, 500
Motoman Inc., 216
Motorola, 74, 103, 531, 609, 677, 683
Mount Elizabeth Hospital (MEH), 403
Mountain Dew, 307
Mr. Clean, 262, 652, 722
Mujirushi Ryohin, 505, 515
MySpace, 229, 265, 614

Narayana Hrudayalaya Hospital, 55
National University of Singapore, 656
National, 288
NBC Universal, 49
NEC, 655
NECX, 208
Neopets.com, 112
Nestlé, 152, 225, 376, 588, 602, 691, 692
Netease, 221, 302
Network Walkman, 347
New Coke, 318
Nice Group, 38, 300
Nike, 145, 272, 332, 344, 529, 531, 573, 588, 727, 732
Nikon, 290
Nintendo, 144, 265, 348, 589
Nippon Lever, 465
Nissan, 218, 219, 365, 398, 53, 645
Nivea, 283
Nokia, 111, 370, 54, 677, 683, 705
Northwest Airlines, 140
NTT DoCoMo, 41, 318, 361, 490, 613
Nu Skin, 618

Oak Industries, 691
OCBC, 552
Ogilvy & Mather, 237, 238, 103
OgilvyOne, 600
Olay, 233, 722
Olympus, 427
Omnicom, 273
Omron, 655
Open Source, 423
Oracle, 628
Oral-B, 262
Oregon Scientific, 301
Oriflame, 626
Oshkosh, 344
Osim, 537
Otis Elevator, 38

Pacific Andes, 459
Pacific Century CyberWorks, 300
Paetec, 149
Palm Pilot, 92
PalmOne, 92
Pampers, 233, 262
Panasonic, 265, 288, 699
Pantene, 262, 288, 364
Paramount, 327
PCH International, 463
Pearl River Piano, 276, 686
Pepsi, 147, 179, 272, 538, 540, 553, 592, 607
Pepsico, 253, 254
Petronas, 571
Philip Morris, 227, 353, 614, 678
Philips, 8
Phineas Fogg, 274
Ping An Insurance, 729
Pizza Hut, 329, 500
Plastics.com, 207
PlayStation, 150, 348
Polaroid, 524
PowerBar, 316
Prada, 511
Prado SUV, 567
President chain stores, 342
Pret A Manger, 590
PricewaterhouseCoopers, 334
Pringles, 652
Procter & Gamble, 55, 87, 100, 145, 207, 233, 251–252, 262, 287, 287, 288, 306, 380, 421, 447, 476, 555, 607, 614, 652, 653, 664, 720, 722
Project Shakti, 682
Promet, 514
Publicis New York, 703
Pulsar, 375
Pure Mild, 342

Qatar Airways, 481
Quaker Chemical, 210
Quaker Oats, 283
Quality Brands Protection Committee, 351

Raja Fashions, 139
Ralph's, 133
RCA, 285, 684
Red Bull, 240
Reeb, 533, 540
Rejoice, 233, 287, 288
Reliance, 683
Renault, 372
Resona Bank, 237
Retin-A, 605
Reynolds, 313, 345
Ritz-Carlton, 131, 404
Rockwell Automation, 210
Roper Starch Worldwide, 542,
Royal Philips Electronics, 8, 376
Ryanair, 424
Ryukakusan, 694

SAB Miller, 345
Sainsbury's, 154
Saint Gobain, 62
SAM's Clubs, 513
Samsung, 14, 177, 207, 227, 229, 265, 346, 349, 369, 370, 432
Samsung Aerospace, 448
Samsung Electronics, 51
Sangaria Oxygen Water, 177, 235
Sankyo, 647
Sanrio, 60
Sanyo, 61
Sara Lee, 207, 468
SAS, 151, 452
Satyam Computer Services, 330
Schiess, 680
SCOCO, 35
Seagrams, 691
Searle, 647
Sears, 344
Sega/Genesis, 348, 614
Seibu, 542
Seiko, 375
Seinfeld, 657
Seiyu, 513, 708
Seoul Incheon Airport, 408
Shagaku, 274
Shanda Interactive Entertainement, 40, 302
Shanghai Automotive, 642, 689
Shanghai Bell, 61
Shangri-La Hotel, 394
Sharp, 182
Shell, 23, 199
Shenyang Machine Tool Group, 680
Shimano, 588
Shimizu, 219, 655
Shinsegae, 685
Shiseido, 16, 236, 316, 342, 655
Shijingshan Amusement Park, 706
Shoktidoi, 682
Showa Kirin Brewery, 691
Shu Uemera, 679
Siebel, 316, 628
Siemens, 61
Siemens Medical Systems, 8
SilkAir, 288
Sina.com, 274, 302, 608
Singapore Airlines (SIA), 60, 136, 150, 265, 288, 293, 309, 343, 377, 395, 402, 462, 565
Singapore Changi Airport, 104, 408
Singapore Ministry of Health, 565
Singapore Telecoms, 565
Singapore Zoo, 7
Singer Company, 81
Sinohydro, 687
Skyjet International, 481
SmarTone Vodafone, 429
Smirnoff, 342
SmithKline Beecham, 252
Softbank Yahoo! BB, 453
Sohu.com, 221
Sony, 101, 265, 288, 327, 340, 347, 348, 369, 370
Sony Connect, 347
Sony Ericsson, 616
Southwest Airlines, 309, 331, 399, 643
SPC, 23
Spice Jet, 392
Sprite, 547, 703
SRI Consulting Business Intelligence's, 241
Ssangyong Motor, 642, 694
Stanford University, 259
Star Alliance, 60
Star TV, 693
Star Wars, 115
Starbucks, 26, 275, 338, 382, 467, 48, 726
Starbucks Foundation, The, 726
Stattera, 646
Stella Artois, 606
Sterling Airlines, 452
Stillwater Technologies, 216
Stockstar.com, 491
Subaru, 593
Sumstar, 692
Suntory, 540
Suruga Bank, 237
SVA Group, 690
Swedish Match, 624
Swiffer, 262
Swipe, 571
Synovate, 113, 159

Taisei, 219
Taiwan Semiconductor Manufacturing Company, 39
Takashimaya, 404
Tamagotchi, 274, 312
Taobao.com, 208, 444
Tata, 730
Tata Consultancy Services, 330
Tata Telecom, 153, 683, 692, 730
TCL Corp., 285, 177, 642, 684
Tele Vital, 669
Telecom Asia, 694
Telstra, 335
Tesco Clubcard, 18, 154
Tesco plc, 154, 503
Thaigem.com, 487
The9, 302
Thomson 800, 446
Thomson Electronics, 285, 684
Tide, 233, 447
Tiffany & Co. 428, 607
Tiger Airways, 293

Tiger Balm, 317, 694
Tiger Motorcycles, 251
Titleist, 706
TiVo, 316
Tokyo DisneySea, 393
Tokyo Hands, 171
Tokyo Star Bank, 237
Toshiba, 327, 38, 645, 91
Toto, 684
Tourism Thailand, 7
Toyota Camry, 377
Toyota Corolla, 377
Toyota Prius, 90, 367, 710, 731
Toyota Scion, 367
Transora, 207
Tremor, 614
Trust-Mart, 513
Tsingtao, 266, 350
Tsutaya, 504

UCLA, 109
Ugly Dolls, 369
U-Like Coffee, 275
Unilever, 231, 287, 344, 378, 472, 527, 547, 567, 572, 682, 692, 704, 725
Uni-President, 512
United Airlines, 403
United Microelectronics, 211
Universal Music, 230, 573
UTStarcom, 433

Value Club, 469, 513, 708
Vaseline, 571
Victoria's Secret, 299
Vios, 377
Virgin Atlantic, 403
Virgin Group, 594, 663
Virgin Media, 663
Virgin Mobile, 354
Visa, 304, 659
Vitro, 61
Vocalpoint, 614
Volkswagen, 272, 313, 379, 434, 533
Volvo, 13, 272, 285, 588

Wahaha, 306, 347
Wal-Mart, 20, 207, 337, 344, 469, 471, 506, 507, 513, 678, 685, 708
Walt Disney Company. *See* Disney
Weiden + Kennedy Amsterdam, 703
Welz, 680
Westin Stamford, 306
Wii, 348
Wikipedia, 348, 653
Wipro Technologies, 637, 330, 683
Wolfschmidt, 342
World Trade Organization, 688
WPP, 268
Wrigley's, 17, 463, 466

XCel Mold, 707
Xerox, 209, 275
Xilinx, 211

Yahoo! Music, 145, 145, 259, 315, 315, 348, 444, 553, 608
Yamaha, 320
Yangshengtang, 703
Yisou.com, 608
Yoox, 491
Young and Rubicam (Y&R), 267
YouTube, 265, 527, 653
YTL Corporation, 199
Yue Sai, 679
Yujin Robotics, 92
Yum Brands, 393

Za, 342, 535
Zaitun, 274
Zara, 33, 495
Zing, 286
Zoom Technologies, 205

Subject Index

Aaker model, 268
Absolute product failure, 657
Accelerating, 716
Acceleration effect, 198
Access, 24
Accessibility, 250
Account management, 622
Accounting departments, 26
Accumulated production, 436–437
Achievers, 242
Acquisition, 642
Action campaigns, 733
Active information search, 180
Activity plans, 628
Activity-based cost (ABC) accounting, 62, 142, 437
Actual self-concept, 168
Adaptation, 696
Adapted marketing mix, 698
Adapters, 350
Adaptive conjoint analysis (ACA), 661
Add-on spending, 294
Administered VMS, 479
Administrative costs, 586
Admiration, 173
Adoption, 665, 671–674, 725, 735
Ad placement policies, 576
Advantages, 631
Advertising,
  global markets, 701–704
  marketing communications mix, 529, 549
  marketing plan example, 69
  marketing program and, 319
  online, 609–613
  program development and management, 560–568
  specialty, 585
  versus sales promotion, 581–582
Advertising budget, 562–563
Advertising campaign, 563–568
  message generation and evaluation, 563–564
  creative development and execution, 565–567
Advertising effectiveness, 577–580
Advertising elasticity, 562–563
Advertising expenditure share, 580
Advertising frequency, 562
Advertising goal, 560
Advertising research techniques, 578
Advertorials, 574
Advocate channels, 542
Advocates, 147
Affiliate programs, 612
Affluence, 384
Affordable budgeting method, 544
Age, 165–166, 235
Agents, 460
AIDA Model, 533
Airtruck, 523
Alliances, 61, 612
Allocating, 619
Allowance, 449, 584
Alpha testing, 664, 667
Alternatives, evaluation of, 182–184
Ambivalent brand nonusers, 248
Anchoring and adjustment heuristic, 189
Ancillary products. *See* Captive products
Annual-plan control, 736–740
Anticipatory pricing, 452
Antitrust actions, 345
Applications, 45
Apprentice, The (television show), 564
Approach, 631
Approvers, 200
Arbitration, 484
Area market potential, 125–126
Area marketing specialists, 718
Area sample, 110
Areas of dominant influence (ADI), 577
Arm's-length price, 705
Arranged interviews, 110
Ascending bids, 445
Ascribed status, 636
Aspirational groups, 162
Asset turnover, 740
Associative network memory model, 177, 178
Assortment building, 516
Atmosphere, 587
  event marketing, 587–588
  retail stores, 508
Attack strategy, 347–349
Attitudes, 183, 247
Attitudes of others, 185
Attribute listing, 656
Auction-type pricing, 443
Audience, 574
Audience quality, 576
Audience-attention probability, 576
Augmented product, 360
Automated warehouses, 522
Automatic vending, 498
Availability heuristic, 189
Available brand nonusers, 248
Available market, 121
Avatars, 489
Average brand users, 248
Average cost, 436
Awareness, 532, 595, 671
Awareness set, 181, 182

Baby boomers, 84, 235, 239
Backward flow, 464
Backward invention, 699
Bad competitors, 334
Balance, 316
Banded pack, 583
Banking, in-store, 481
Banner ads, 611
Bargaining power, 329
Barriers, 115, 330
  entry, 260, 328, 477, 699
  exit, 320, 328
Barter markets, 207
Bartering, 447–448
Bases for segmenting
  business markets, 248–250
  consumer markets, 233–248
Basic product, 360
BAV power grid, 268
BCG's Growth-Share Matrix, 47
Behavior mapping, 107
Behavioral campaigns, 734
Behavioral data, 104
Behavioral decision theory (BDT), 190
Behavioral factors, in marketing plan example, 67
Behavioral segmentation, 243–248
Behavioral variables, 243–248
Beliefs, 89, 183
Believability, 306, 659
Believers, 242
Benchmarks, 36, 210, 334, 716
Benefits, 244, 623, 631
Beta testing, 664, 667
Biases, decision, 189
Billboards, 571
Biogenic needs, 171
Blair Witch Project, The (movie), 229
Blanket contract, 211
Blanket family names, 288
Blogs, 18, 78, 542, 616
Blue-ocean strategy, 331
"Body by Milk" promotional campaign, 584
Borrowed interest techniques, 536
Bottleneck products, 204

Brain science, 109
Brand asset management team (BAMT), 720
Brand asset valuator (BAV), 267
Brand associations, 177, 280
Brand attributes, 305
Brand audit, 281
Brand awareness, 278, 295, 530, 533, 732
Brand benefits, 305
Brand bonding, 279
Brand concept, 658
Brand contact, 277, 529
Brand development index (BDI), 125–126
Brand development stages, 269
Brand dilution, 291
Brand earnings, 284
Brand elements, 271, 698
  choosing, 271–275, 414
  developing, 276
Brand equity, 260, 263–264
  as bridge, 265
  branding strategy, 287–294
  building, 271–275
  customer-based, 263
  customer equity and, 294–295
  defining, 263
  global markets, 698
  managing, 283–287
  marketing communications and, 528
  measuring, 281
Brand equity models, 267–270
Brand essence, 268
Brand expansion, 294
Brand extension, 287, 289–291
  advantages of, 289–290
  disadvantages of, 290–291
  success characteristics, 291
Brand feelings, 270
Brand funnel, 246
Brand identity, 268, 279
Brand image, 270, 278, 384, 588
Brand judgments, 270
Brand knowledge, 263–264, 265
  secondary sources of, 280
Brand line, 287
Brand loyalty, 246, 260, 581
Brand metrics pathway, 119
Brand mix, 287
Brand overlap, 293
Brand partnerships, 698
Brand performance, 270
Brand personality, 167–168
Brand personification, 108
Brand portfolios, 292–294
  market evolution, 322
  product life-cycle marketing strategies, 310
Brand positioning, 300–301
  differentiation strategies, 308
  product life-cycle marketing strategies, 310
Brand promise, 265
Brand purchase intention, 556
Brand reinforcement, 283–285
Brand relationship spectrum position, 278, 288
Brand report card, 267
Brand resonance model, 269–270
Brand resonance pyramid, 245
Brand resonance, 269–270
Brand revitalization, 285–287
Brands/branding, 14, 381–383
  advantages, 275
  breakaway, 322
  building, 271
  co-branding and ingredient branding, 381–383
  crisis management for, 592
  customer loyalty and, 136
  definition of, 260
  exclusive, 505
  global marketing, 698
  innovation and, 55
  private labels, 512, 516
  role of, 260-262, 284
  scope of, 263
  self-branding, 6
  service, 412–415
Brand salience, 270
Brand signatures, 43, 547
Brand stature, 267, 268
Brand strategies, for services, 414–415
Brand strength, 268, 284
Brand valuation, 283, 284
Brand value calculation, 284
Brand value, 260
Brand value chain, 282
Brand-as-organization, 268
Brand-as-person, 268
Brand-as-product, 268
Brand-as-symbol, 268
Brand-dominant hierarchy, 181
Brand-management organization, 718–720
Brand-product relationships, 372
Brand-tracking studies, 283
Branded entertainment, 302
Branded variants, 287
Branding. *See* Brands/branding
Branding decision, 288
  internal, 279
  scope of, 263
Branding strategy, 287–294, 415
Branding decisions, 288–294
Brandstorming, 336
BRANDZ, 268
Breadth, 504
Breakaway brands, 322
Breakeven analysis, 69, 663
Breakeven cost chart, 474
Brick-and-click companies, 490
Bridges, 615
Broad environment, 15
Broadcast advertising research techniques, 578
Brochures, 570
Brokers, 15, 620
Budgets/budgeting
  advertising, 562–563
  marketing communications, 544–546
  marketing plan example, 70
  new-product development, 648–649
  research and development, 93
  sales, 124
Bulk breaking, 516
Business advisory services, 364
Business analysis, 662–663
Business buying process, 200–202
Business database, 152
Business customers, types of, 202
Business legislation, 94–95
Business markets, 10, 248–250
  business buying process, 200–202
  business-to-business customer relationship, 212
  buying process stages, 204–212
  consumer markets versus, 196–198
  institutional and government, 219–221
  organizational buying, 196
  purchasing/procurement process, 203–204
Business mission, 56
Business models, socially responsible, 729
Business partnership management, 41
Business promotion, 580, 585
Business realignment, 37–38
Business relationships, 217–218
Business sector, retail sector, 390
Business services, 363–364
Business unit strategic planning, 55–64
  feedback and control, 63–64
  goal formulation, 58–59
  program formulation and implementation, 62
  strategic formulation, 59–61
  SWOT analysis, 56–58
Business unit strategic planning, 55
Business-goods market testing, 667
Business-need services, 391
Business-to-business customer relationships, 212, 215
Business-to-business ecommerce, 207
Buyback agreement, 448
Buyer turnover, 576
Buyer-readiness stage, 246, 551
Buyer's intentions survey, 127
Buyer-supplier relationships
  categories of, 216
Buyers,
  buying center and, 200
  competitive forces and, 330
  geographically concentrated, 198
Buygrid framework, 204
Buying, wholesalers, 516. *See also* Purchasing
Buying alliances, 207
Buying center, 200
Buying center influences, 201
Buying center targeting, 201–202
Buying decision process, 179–188
Buying influences, 196
Buying power, 17
Buying process stages, 204–212
Buying service, 498
Buying sites, 207
Buying situations, 198–199
Buyphases, 204
Buzz marketing, 614
Bypass attack, 348
By-product pricing, 380

Call centers, 412
Call reports, 529
CALLPLAN model, 115
Camera journals, 107
Cannibalization, 291, 484
Cannibalized income, 663
Capital items, 363
Capital shortages, 646
Captive-product pricing, 380
Carpet bombing, 76
Carrying costs, 522–523
Cash, 447–448
Cash cows, 293
Cash discounts, 472
Cash rebates, 450
Cash refund offers, 583
Cash-flow metrics pathway, 119
Catalog marketing, 604–605
Catalog sites, 207
Catalytic innovations, 731
Category benefits, 305
Category extension, 287
Category killers, 497
Category management, 505, 720
Category membership, 301, 304–305
Category points-of-parity, 303
Causal research, 102
Cause marketing, 27
Cause-related marketing, 27, 588, 730–733
Customer-driven engineering, 647
Celebrity marketing, 6
Census tracts, 126
Central business districts, 510
Central route, 188
Cents-off deals, 583
Chaebol, 678
Chain-ratio method, 124

Channel alternatives, 470–472
Channel bonding, 37
Channel captain, 478
Channel conflict, 483–484
Channel coordination, 483
Channel design, 467–470
Channel differentiation, 309
Channel integration, 462
Channel levels, 465–467
Channel members
 evaluating, 476
 selection of, 474–475
 terms and responsibilities of, 472
 training and motivating, 475–476
Channel objectives, 468
Channel power, 475
Channel pricing, 451
Channel specialists, 353
Channel stewards, 479
Characteristics of the innovation, 673
Chief executive officer (CEO), 12, 42
Chief marketing officer (CMO), 12, 722
China/Chinese, 16, 109, 144, 163, 169, 170, 174, 176, 254, 434, 511, 541, 688–689, 725,
 advertising in, 540, 541, 567
 business etiquette, 214, 634
 business landscape characteristics, 38, 221, 412, 498, 503
 consumers, 164, 225, 231, 239, 240, 548
 corruption in, 96
 counterfeit goods in, 73, 706
 culture, 434, 703
 families, 82
 fashion, 279
 farm brands, 363
 feng shui in, 161, 514
 folklore, 11
 guanxi, 21, 635, 693
 languages in, 84, 273
 Law Against Unfair Competition, 540
 market, 61–62, 600, 683
 media market, 576
 MNCs in, 625
 promotions in, 581
 occupational classes in, 161
 religions in, 85
 Sun Tzu Bing Fa, 340–341
 symbols, 22, 368
 tea houses, 404
 wholly-owned foreign enterprises in, 695
Choice heuristics, 185
Choice set, 181–182
Choices and implications, 135
Circulation, 574
City product adaptation, 699
Civic positioning, 254
Clients, 147
Cliques, 615
Cloners, 350
Closed-end questions, 105, 106
Closing, 632
Club membership programs, 150
Cluster sample, 110
Clustered preferences, 228
Clutter, 562
Co-branding, 381–383
Coercive power, 475
Cognitive campaigns, 733
Cognitive space, 39, 40
Cohorts, 83, 84, 238
Collectivism, 539, 697
Commercial information sources, 181
Commercialization, 668–669
Commodity business, 591
Commonality, 554
Common carrier, 523
Communicability, 306, 659, 673
Communication adaptation, 701
Communication channels, 14, 542
 integration of, 544
 non-personal, 543
 personal, 542
Communication metrics, 737
Communication platforms, 530
Communication-effect research, 578–579
Communications, 15, 18
 brand-positioning strategy, 300–309
 category membership, 305
 in retailing, 510
 value, 30. *See also* Marketing communications; Mass communications; Personal communications
Communications companies, 555–556
Communications model, 533
Communications process models, 532–534
 response hierarchy model, 532
 hierarchy-of-effects model, 532
Communications results measurement, 551–552
Communitarianism, 636
Community influentials, 616
Community involvement, corporate, 27
Community shopping centers, 511
Companies, pricing methods of, 423–425
Company buying sites, 207
Company capabilities, affecting marketing, 17–18
Company demand, 123
Company departments, 717
Company image, 384
Company marketing orientation, 18–27
Company name awareness, 587
Company performance, 411
Company pricing policies, 445–446
Company sales force, 620
Company sales forecast, 123–124
Company sales potential, 124
Comparative advertising, 540
Compatibility, 673
Compatibility, 673
Compensation, for sales-force, 623
Compensation deal, 448
Competence, 395
Competency space, 40
Competition, 15, 327
 advertising budget and, 562
 balancing customer and, 354
 global markets, 678–679
 intertype, 501
 marketing channels and, 483–486
 private labels, 516
 retailing, 480
 societal forces affecting, 15–17
Competitive advantage, 37–38, 142, 308
Competitive category dynamics, 316
Competitive forces, 328–329
Competitive frame of reference, for brand positioning, 301
Competitor orientations, 354–355
Competitive performance, 334
Competitive points-of-parity, 301
Competitive repositioning, 184
Competitive strategies, 335
 market-challenger, 346–349
 market-follower, 350
 market leaders and, 335–346
 market-nicher, 352
Competitive-parity budgeting method, 545
Competitor-centered companies, 354
Competitors
 analyzing, 330–335
 definition of, 330
 identifying, 329–330
 low-cost, 454–455
 marketing research and, 101
 pricing and, 438,
 selection of, 453–454
Complaints. *See* Customer complaints
Complementarity, 554
Complementary services, 395
Complexity, 673
Component materials, 363
Component parts, 363
Compositional approach, 210
Comprehensive marketing audit, 745
Computer games, 240
Concentrated marketing, 228
Concentration, 577
Concept development, 649, 658–659
Concept testing, 659
 rapid prototyping, 659
 virtual reality, 659
Conditions of sale, 472
Conflict, in marketing channels. *See* Channel conflict
Conformance quality, 139, 366
Confucian dynamic, 647
Confucianism, 672, 729
 li, 729
 ren, 729
Congruity, 538
Conjoint analysis, 210, 660–661
Conjunctive heuristic, 185
Connectors, 615
Consideration set, 181–182
Consultative selling, 202
Consumer affluence, 384
Consumer and market knowledge (CMK), 100
Consumer base, 562
Consumer behavior, 160–171
Consumer behavior model, 171
Consumer cooperative, 501
Consumer decision making, 188–192
Consumer electronics, 427
Consumer feedback method, 578
Consumer franchise building, 583
Consumer involvement level, 188–189
Consumer journey, 107
Consumer knowledge, 264
Consumer lifestyle, 469
Consumer marketing channel, 466
Consumer markets, 10, 160
 buying decision process in, 179–188
 consumer behavior and, 160
 consumer decision making, 188–192
 psychological processes and, 171–179
 segmenting, 233–248
Consumer participation, 396
Consumer perceptions, of country of origin, 710
Consumer power, 164
Consumer promotion, 580, 582–584
Consumer psychology, pricing and, 425–429
Consumer surveys, 586
Consumer tests, 385
Consumer-adoption process, 671–674
Consumer-goods classification, 362
Consumer-goods market testing, 665–667
 trial, 665
 first repeat, 665

adoption, 665
purchase frequency, 665
Consumerist movement, 95–96
Consumers, 17, 18
Consumption chain method, 56
Consumption system, 192, 361
Contact methods, 110–111
Containerization, 523
ontender, 685
Contests, 583
Context, 656
Contextual placement, 607
Contingency planning, in marketing plan example, 70
Continuity, 577
Continuous innovation, 339
Continuous replenishment programs, 212
Contract carrier, 523
Contract manufacturing, 691
Contraction defense, 345
Contractual VMS, 480
Contribution, 554
Control, 63
global markets, 698
holistic marketing, 736–748
marketing channels and, 474
marketing plan example, 70
Control chart, 739
Controllable returns, 372
Controlled test marketing, 666
Convenience goods, 362
Convenience items, 374
Convenience sample, 110
Convenience stores, 497, 499
Conventional marketing channel, 478
Conventions, 585
Conversion Model, 248
Convertible brand users, 248
Conviction, 534
Cooperation, in marketing channels, 483–486
Cooperative organizations, 689
Co-optation, 484
Co-production, 400–401
Core beliefs, 89
Core benefit, 360
Core brand identity elements, 268
Core business processes, 36
Core competencies, 37–39
Core products, 374
Corporate chain store, 501
Corporate communications, 592
Corporate community involvement, 27
Corporate credibility, 215
Corporate culture, 50
Corporate expertise, 215
Corporate identity, 7
Corporate image, 588, 593
Corporate likability, 215
Corporate mission, 44–46
Corporate philanthropy, 27
Corporate retail organizations, 501
Corporate retailing, 498
Corporate social initiatives, 27
Corporate social marketing, 27
Corporate social responsibility, 727–728, 731
Corporate societal marketing, 730
Corporate strategic planning, 44–50
Corporate trust and credibility, 215
Corporate VMS, 479
Corporate-product brand names, 288
Corrective action, 742–743
Corruption, 96
Cost behavior, 436
Cost estimation, 435–437, 662–663
Cost inflation, 452
Cost leadership, 59
Cost structure, 282
Cost-based price, 704
Costing, direct versus full, 743–744. *See also*, Activity-based costing
Costs
competitors, 438–439
estimating, 435–437, 662–663
integrated marketing communications, 554
inventory, 522–523
media types and, 569
out-of-pocket, 416
target, 437
types of, 435–436
Counseling, 592
Counterfeiting, 351, 706
Counteroffensive defense, 343–344
Countertrade, 447
Country images, 709
Country product adaptations, 699
Country-of-origin effects, 709–710
Coupons, 583
Courtesy, 394
Coverage, in integrated marketing, 554
Creative briefs, 563
Creative development and execution, 565–567
Creative marketers, 339
Creative marketing organization, 722–723
Creative strategy, marketing communications, 535–537, 604
Creativity techniques, 656
Credence qualities, 391
Credibility, 215, 394, 537, 539, 549, 595
Credit, 87
Critical life events or transitions, 166
Critical path scheduling (CPS), 669
Cross-promotions, 583
Cross-selling, 146
Cues, 176
Cultivation, 550
Cultural environment. *See* Socio-cultural environment
Cultural factors, affecting consumer behavior, 160–162
Cultural values, 89
Culture
definition of, 160
effects of, on new product-development, 647
Currency, 447
Current demand estimation, 124–126
Custom marketing research firms, 100
Customer acquisition, 36, 147, 294
Customer activity cycle, 192
Customer advantage, 308
Customer advisory panel, 77
Customer attributes (CAs), 664
Customer base, 146, 148
Customer bonds, 148
Customer churn, 146
Customer citizenship, 401
Customer cloning, 234
Customer communities, 489
Customer complaints, 138
Customer consulting, 371
Customer databases, 152
Customer defection, 146, 148
Customer empowerment, 144, 145, 398, 400
Customer equity, 294–295
Customer evangelists, creating, 149
Customer expectations, 404–406
Customer experience management (CEM), 590
Customer failure, root causes of, 400
Customer feedback systems, online, 77
Customer importance, 411
Customer interface systems, 410
Customer lifetime value (CLV), 142, 143
Customer linking, 37
Customer loss rate, 137
Customer loyalty, 136
building, 132–143, 148–152
datamining and, 155–156
loyalty status, 246–247
market share and, 739
Customer mailing list, 152
Customer markets, 10–11
Customer metrics, 119, 737
Customer multiplier, 282
Customer needs, 416, 462
Customer orientations, 412
Customer partnering, 716
Customer penetration, 739
Customer perceived value (CPV), 133
Customer portfolios, 142
Customer profitability analysis (CPA), 141–142
Customer readiness to buy metrics, 737
Customer relationship capital, 148
Customer relationship management (CRM), 41, 144–146, 151, 294
customer equity and, 294
downside of, 155–156
process, 36
value delivery, 41
Customer relationships, business-to-business, 212
service firms and, 396
Customer responses, micromodel of, 532–534
Customer retention, 137, 146–148, 294
Customer risk, 202
Customer satisfaction, 136–137
measuring, 137–138
Customer scenario, 192
Customer selectivity, 739
Customer service, 67, 403, 407
Customer switching behavior, 402
Customer tests, 664
Customer touch point, 144
Customer training, 371
Customer value
building, 132–140
delivering, 136
holistic marketing and, 39–40
marketing and, 34–44
Customer value analysis, 134
Customer value assessment (CVA), 210
Customer value hierarchy, 360–361
Customer value propositions, 210
Customer value triad, 14
Customer-based brand equity, 263
Customer-centered companies, 354–355
Customer-delivered value, determinants of, 133
Customer-development process, 147
Customer-driven engineering, 647
Customer-focused value proposition, 300
Customerization, 233
Customer-oriented organization chart, 132
Customer-performance scorecard, 118, 119
Customers,
connecting with, 29
innovation and, 55, 653
selection of, 334–335
service output levels and, 467
total market expansion and, 338–339
Customization, 365, 409, 506, 550, 698
Cycle-recycle pattern, 310, 311

Data
behavioral, 104
interdependence of, 104. *See also* Marketing research
Data analysis, 75
Database marketing, 152–153
Databases, 76–77
Data collection, 111
Data mining, 76, 153–155
Data sources, for marketing research, 102
Data warehouses, 76, 153
Dealer tests, 385
Debt, 87
Deception, 606
Deciders, 200
Decision alternatives, 102
Decision heuristics and biases, 189
Decision-making advertising budgets, 499–500
branding, 288–289
buying decision process, 179–188
consumer, 188–192
customer-perceived value, 135
global market entry, 681–689
global marketing organization, 697
globall marketing program, 546
logistics, 521–524
marketing channel design, 467
marketing channel management, 474–478
marketing public relations, 593–596
market research and, 115
market offerings, 29
mass communications, 559
retailing, 496
sales promotions, 543
sponsorships, 595, 612
Decision roles, 243
Decision traps, 191
Decision-making style, 665
Decline stage, 319, 324
Declining demand, 9
Decoding, 532
Defection rate, of customers, 148
Defects, 26, 34
Defender, 685
defending, 339
expanding, 345
Defenses, of market share, 339, 345
Delayed quotation pricing, 452
Delight needs, 13
Delivery, 370
Deliverability, 306
Deliverer, 618
Delivery channel, 464
Delivery time, 418
Delivery, of services, 369–370
Delphi method, 128
Demand, 9
elastic, 435
estimating current, 124–126
estimating future, 126–128
fluctuating, 198
hyperconsumption and, inelastic, 198, 432
marketing sensitivity of, 122
nonpeak, 395
pricing and, 445
price elasticity of, 435
Demand chain planning, 462
Demand creator, 619
Demand curve estimation, 434–435
Demand measurement, 122
Demand states, 9
Demands, 13
Demand-side measurement method, 589
Demographic, 249
educational groups, 85
ethnic and other markets, 83, 84
geographical shifts in population, 86
household patterns, 85
population age mix, 83
worldwide population growth, 81–82
Demographic environment, 79–86
Demographic segmentation, 235–241
Demographic trends, 79
Demonstrations, sales, 583, 631
Department stores, 496
Dependence asymmetry, 216
Depression cohort, 84
Depth, 373
Deregulation, 16
Derived demand, 196
Descending bids, 445
Descriptive research, 102
Design, marketing channels, 467–473, 477–478
marketing communications, 435–442
product, 369
services, 406
Web sites, 410
Designated marketing areas (DMAs), 577
Desirability, 306
Desktop marketing, 736
Developed markets, 682–684
Development costs, 646
Differential pricing, 395
Differentiated marketing costs, 262, 263, 247
channel, 309
image, 309
personnel, 309
Differentiation, 59, 308
brand asset valuator, 267
brand positioning, 307
competitors and, 337
distribution, 466
marketing, 230
market segmentation, 228
pricing, 400–402
product strategy, 367, 383
services, 412–414
strategic formulation, 59
Diffuseness, 636
Diffused preference, 228
Diffused-preference market, 323
Dilution, 484
Diplomacy, 484
Direct and interactive marketing, 550
Direct approach, 281
Direct brand equity, 263
Direct costing, vs. full costing, 130–131
Direct costs, 751
Direct export, 689–690
Direct investment, 694
Direct mail, 602
Direct marketing, 498, 529, 600
Direct marketing channel, 466
Direct-order marketing, 600
Direct product profitability (DPP), 507
Direct purchasing, 198
Direct-response marketing, 595
Direct sales force, 469
Direct selling, 498
Direct survey questions, 210
Discount pricing, 449
Discount stores, 467
Discretionary options, 228
Discrimination, 176
Disintermediation, 16
Display ads, 611
Disruptive technologies, 569–670
Dissatisfiers, 173
Dissociative groups, 162
Distinctive capabilities, 37–39
international marketing and, 701
Distinctiveness, 306
Distribution
differentiated, 252
global markets, 10
marketing plan example, 66
marketing program and, 64
Distribution channels, 14
Distribution efficiency, 503
Distribution innovation, 349
Distribution method, 604
Distribution metrics, 737
Distribution programming, 479
Distribution warehouses, 522
Distribution systems, 478
Distributor feedback sites, 78
Distributor-relations planning, 480
Distributors, 15
Diversification growth, 49–50
Diversification strategy, 48
Diversity, 84–86
Diverting, 585
Divesting, 50
Divisibility, 673
Division strategic planning, 44
Dodger, 685
Dollar stores, 442
Domestic-based export agents, 689
Domestic-based export department, 690
Domestic-based export merchants, 689
Dot-com, 16
Down-market stretch, 375
Downsizing, 50
Downtime, 416
Dragalong income, 663
Drive, 172
Drop shippers, 459
DROP-error, 656
Dual adaptation, 709
Dumping, 712
Durability, 366
Durable goods, 362
Dutch auctions, 445
Dynamic process model, 406
Early adopters, 671
Early majority, 672
E-business, 486
Echo Boomers. *See* Generation Y
E-commerce marketing practices, 486
Econometric analysis, 128
Economic circumstances, 166
Economic costs, of market share expansion, 345
Economic criteria, for marketing channels, 473
Economic environment, 86
Economies of scale, 216
Editing, 479
Eco-tourism, 6
Editorial quality, 576
Educational groups, 85
Effective ad-exposed audience, 575
Effective communication, steps in, 575
Effective audience, 575
Efficient customer response (ECR) practices, 480
Effective segmentation criteria, 250
ethical choice of, 254
segments, 224
segment-by-segment invasion, 253
Efficiency control, 744
marketing audit, 745
Elaboration likelihood model, 188
Elastic demand, 435
Elasticity, advertising, 562
Electronics shopping, 498
Electronic data interchange, 520
Electronic funds transfer, 520
order-cycle time, 520

Electronic media, 543
Elimination-by-aspects heuristic, 185
Email, 613
Emergence, 323
Emotional appeals, 536
Empathy, 405
Employees, 401
branding and, 363
event marketing and, 590
part-time, 395
Employee research, 397
Employee satisfaction, 407
Empowering, 716
Encirclement attack, 348
Encoding, 532
Endorsements, 538
End-user specialists, 353
Energy, 279
Engineering customer-driven, 647
Engineering attributes (EAs), 664
Engineering tests, 385
English auctions, 445
Enterprise marketing management (EMM), 736
Enterprise resource planning (ERP), 463
Enterprise selling, 202
Entertainment, through event marketing, 467
Enthusiasm building, 490, 527
Enthusiast segment, 226
Entrants, new, 295
Entrenched brand users, 226
Environment, 236
Environmental threat, 57
Environmental trends, 73
E-procurement, 206
E-purchasing, 486
Equipment-based services, 391
Enthusiast, 247
Entrants, 328
Entry barriers, 328
Escalator clauses, 452
E-service quality, 407
Esteem, 267
Esteem needs, 172
Ethical behavior, 727
Ethical issues, 485,
direct marketing, 600
marketing channel relations, 485
market targets, 254
See also Social responsibility marketing
Event creation, 589
Ethical marketing, 114
Ethnic markets, 83
Ethnographic research, 103
Euro, 698
European consumer, 379
European Union, 82
Evaluating sales representatives, 628
Evaluation and control, 736–740
Evaluation, 671
Event creation, 589
Event marketing, 277
Generation Y, 240
marketing communications, 528
marketing PR and, 595
Events and experiences, 529, 543, 549, 587
Everyday low pricing (EDLP), 441
Exchange, 423
Exchange markets, 207
Exclusive brands, 505
Exchange process, 5
Exclusive dealing, 471
Exclusive distribution, 471, 485
Executive summary, 65,
Exemplars, 305
Exit barriers, 328
Exit option, 186
Expansible market, 122
Expectancy-value model, 183
Expectations, 406
Expected product, 360
Expected service, 404
Expense allowances, 623
Expense forecast, in marketing plan example, 70
Experience business, 591
Experience curve, 436
Experience-curve pricing, 437
Experience qualities, 391–392
Experiencers, 242
Experiential information sources, 181
Experiential marketing, 6
marketing communications, 528
Experimental design, 580
Experimental research, 104
Experiments, 105
Expert opinions, 129
Expert power, 475
Expertise, 215
Exploratory research, 105
Exponential smoothing, 128
Export department, 711
Export-management companies, 690
Export, 689
Export sales reps, 690
Extended brand identity elements, 268
Extended warranties, 416
External environment analysis, 56
Extender, 685
External marketing, 280
Extranet links, 207
Extranet, 15, 212, 423
Extra-role behaviors, 412
Extreme user interviews, 107
Extrinsic rewards, 626

Face (mianzi), 165
guanxi, 21, 221
Facilitating services, 416
Facilities, 405
Fad life cycles, 311–312
Fads, 78
Failure frequency, 416
Fairness, 397
Family, 162–165
Family, as consumer buying organization, 162–164
Family brand, 372
Family life cycle, 234, 235
Family of orientation, 162
Family of procreation, 162
Farm products, 363
Feasibility, 306
Feature improvement, 318
Features, 364
Feedback, 64, 627
brand extensions and, 291
decision traps, 191
marketing communications and, 532
online, 77, 78
sales reps, 628
Feed-forward, 628
Feng shui, 512, 514
Fiberglass, 281
Field value-in-use assessment, 211
Final price, 445–447
Financial accountability, 25
Financial analysis, 284, 740
Financial leverage, 740
Financial objectives, in marketing plan example, 64
Financial projections, 65
Financial risk, 186
Financing
low-interest, 450
wholesalers, 516
Finite renewable resources, 92
First entry, 668
First repeat, 665
First-time customers, 147
Fishyback, 523
Five Ms of advertising, 560
Fixed compensation, 623
Fixed costs, 435
Flagship brands, 293
Flank attack, 347
Flank defense, 342
Flankers, 293
Flattening, 716
Flexible market offering, 227, 228
Flighting, 577
Fluctuating demand, 198
Fluid contracts, 633
Focus, 59
Focus groups, 103
Focus-group research, 104
Focus-group value assessment, 210
Focusing, 716
Follow-up, 632
Forced relationships, 656
Forecast measurement, 117
Forecasting, 127–128
Foreign-based distributors or agents, 607
Forgetting rate, 577
Form, 363, 364
Formal evaluations, of sales force, 629–630
Forward buying, 585
Forward flow, 464
Forward invention, 699
Four Cs of customer relationships, 24
Four Ps, 23–24, 462
Fragile-market-share trap, 452
Fragmented markets, 646
Frame blindness, 191
Frame control, 191
Franchise, 500
Franchise organizations, 480
Franchisees, 500
Franchising, 691
Fraud, 606
Free goods, 584
Free trade, 87
Free trade zones, 684
Free trials, 583
Frequency programs (FPs), 148, 583
Frequency, 568
Frontal attack, 344, 347
Fulfillment management process, 36
Fulfillment, 407
Full costing, 743–744
Full demand, 9
Full market coverage, 252
Full service, 497
Full-cost approach, 743
Full-line forcing, 485
Functional discounts, 449
Functional expenses, 741
Functional hubs, 206
Functional organization, 718
Functional quality, 403
Functional risk, 186

Gain-and-risk-sharing pricing, 446
Gatekeepers, 200
Gen Next (India), 168
Gender segmentation, 237
General need description, 204
Generation X, 84, 240
Generation Y, 240
Generics, 515, 238
Geographic organization, 718
Geographic segmentation, 233
Geographic strategy, 668
Geographical-expansion strategy, 338
Geographically concentrated buyers, 198
Global Asian brands, developing, 266, 267
Global branding, 698
Global business units (GBU), 213
Global markets, 10
Global organization, 711

Global service brands, 699
Global standardization, 696
Global web strategy, 690
Globalization, 16, 330
Glocal strategy, 711
Goal formulation, 58–59
GO-error, 657
Going-rate pricing, 443
Gold customers, 142
Good competitors, 334
Goods, 6, 10,
Got Milk campaign, 183
Government data resources, 77
Government sector, 390
Grassroots marketing, 231
Gray market, 705–706
Green marketing myopia, 91
Green marketing, 91
Group failure, 191
Group-discussion method, 128
Growth, 47–50
  accessing, 47–50
  diversification, 49–50
  downsizing and divesting, 50
  integrative, 49
  intensive, 48–49
  worldwide population, 81–83
Growth Champions, 25
Growth stage, 314, 321, 323
Growth-slump-maturity pattern, 310, 311
Guanxi (personal connections), 21, 221, 693
Guarantees, 383, 386
Guided searches, 348

Habitual shoppers, 462
Halo effect, 670
Hard-core loyals, 246
Harvesting, 320
Headline, 566
Heart share, 7, 272, 333
Hedonic bias, 176
Heightened attention, 180
Heightened competition, 16
Herds, 548
Heterogeneous shopping goods, 362
Heuristics, 189
Hierarchy of needs, 172
Hierarchy-of-Effects model, 532, 533
High context, 610
High value deal seekers, 462
High-context cultures, 542
High-end prestige brands, 294
High-involvement shoppers, 462
High-level management committee, 649
High-low pricing, 441
High-markup, lower-volume, 508
Hiring procedures, of service firms, 394–395
Hispanic market segment, 162
Historical approach, 580
Hold, 650
Holistic marketing concept, 20, 39–40, 715–716
  brand equity and, 732
  customer value and, 41
  evaluation and control, 737–748
  future of marketing, 748–749
  integrated marketing, 23–24
  internal marketing, 24–25, 716–724
  marketing implementation, 735–736
  overview of, 20
  relationship marketing, 20–22
  social responsibility marketing, 28
  services and, 401–404
Homogeneous preferences, 228
Homogeneous shopping goods, 362
Horizontal channel conflict, 483
Horizontal marketing systems, 481
House brands, 453
Household patterns, 85
Hub-and-spoke system, 399, 719
Hybrid cars, 645
Hybrid grid, 483
Hybrid marketing channels, 461
Hypersegmentation, 237

Idea generation, 651
Idea screening, 656–658
Ideal method, 56
Ideal self-concept, 168
Ideas, 55
Identity media, 530, 596
Identity, 279
Illiteracy, 85
Image, 279, 309
Image analysis, 534
Image differentiation, 309
Image dimensions, for services, 414
Image pricing, 450–451
Imitators, 313
I-mode, 16
Impact, 568
Implementation controls, 65
Implementation skills, 750
Implementation, 62
Implication questions, 630
Implicitness, 550
Importance ratings, 210
Impulse goods, 362
Inbound telemarketing, 605
Incentives, sales promotion and, 549
Income distribution, 86–87
Income segmentation, 238
Income, 234
Income-distribution patterns, 87
Incremental innovation, 643
Independent marketing audit, 747
India, 85, 86, 94, 392, 449, 683
Indirect approach, 281
Indirect export, 689, 690
Individual brand names, 288
Individual marketing, 233
Individualism, 647, 697
Individualism-collectivism, 539, 697
Individualization, 606
Individuals, marketing through, 7
Indonesia, 207
Industrial economies, 86
Industrial marketing channel, 466
Industrial-goods classification, 241
Industrializing economies, 86
Industry competitors, 328
Industry convergence, 16
Industry sales, 126
Industry trends, 56
Industry, definition of, 330
Inelastic demand, 198
Influencers, 200
Influencing, 479, 593, 671
Infomediaries, 489
Informal communications, 634
Information access, 17, 78
Information age, 15
Information asymmetry, 216
Information collection, 146
Information flow, 465
Information gathering, 619
Information needs probes, 75
Information search, 171, 180
Information sources, 17, 181
Information systems, 520, 74
Information technology (IT), 463, 519
Information, 8
  SIVA, 24
  value and cost of, 114
Informational appeals, 535–536
Informative advertising, 561
Ingredient branding, 383
In-home tests, 584
Inhwa, 635
Initiators, 200
Innovation
  characteristics of, 673
  continuous, 339, 590, 643
  marketing, 55
  new-product, 590, 643, 652
  organizations and, 674
  packaging and, 384
  strategic, 724
  value, 331
Innovation diffusion process, 384, 671
Innovation, 91, 93
Innovation-adoption model, 533
Innovativeness, 408
Innovators, 241, 671
Inseparability, 394
Installation, 363, 371
Institutional markets, 219–221
Institutional ties, 151
In-store banking, 481
Intangibility, 392–393
Integrated logistic systems, 519, 520
Integrated marketing channels, 426–430
Integrated marketing communications, 552–554, 612
Integrated marketing, 21, 23–24, 279–280
Integrative growth, 47
Integrators, 242
Intelligence. *See* Marketing intelligence system
Intensive distribution, 472
Intensive growth, 48
Interactive marketing, 403, 529, 530, 550, 606–612
Interactive marketing, 403, 550, 606
Intercept interviews, 110
Interest, 671
Intermediaries
  channel conflict and, 484
  number of, 484
  types of, 484
Intermediary markets, 9
Internal branding, 279
Internal engineering assessment, 210
Internal environment analysis, 57, 58, 67
Internal marketing metrics, 118
Internal marketing, 21, 24–25, 280, 401, 593–596, 716–724
Internal records, 75–78
Internal resource management, 39, 41
Internalization, 279–280
International division, 711
International marketing. *See* Global markets
International subsidiaries, 711
Internationalization process, 680
Internet
  global Web strategy, 690–691
  marketers and, 17
  marketing research, 101
  online advertising and promotions, 609–613
  online auctions and exchanges, 423, 445
  profile of, 570
Internet marketing, 718. *See* Online marketing
Internet niching, 229
Internet searches, 57, 347
Interstitials, 611
Intertype competition, 501
Intervening factors, in consumer purchasing, 185
Intranet, 15
Intrinsic, 626
Introduction stage, 312
Introductory market strategy, 669
Introspective method, 191, 522
Inventor, 656
Inventory, 395

Inventory-carrying, 522, 523
Investment, 63
Investment companies, 7
Invitation, 549
Involvement, 188
Iron customers, 142
Irregular demand, 9
Item, 372

Japan, 200
Japan VALS, 242
Job-shop specialist, 353
Joint venture co-branding, 381
Joint ventures, 692, 695
Judgment sample, 110

Keiretsu, 218
Key buying influencers, 201
Kill, 650
Kiosks, 572
Knowledge, 267, 533, 630
Koreans, 96

Labeling, 385–386
Labels, 512
  private, 385–386
Laboratory tests, 578
Laddering, 108, 172
Laggards, 672
Language, 632
Late entry, 668
Late majority, 672
Latent demand, 9
Lateral marketing, 656
Lead customers, 142
Lead generation, 152, 483
Lead time, 586
Learning curve, 436
Learning tests, 276
Learning, 176–177
Legal behavior, 727
Legal environment, 93. *See* Political-legal environment
Legal issues
  advertising, 504–505
  marketing channel relations, 485–486
Legitimate power, 475
Leisure activities, 162
Leverage products, 203
Leverageable advantage, 142, 308
Leveraged sales force, 619
Lexicographic heuristic, 185
Li, 729
Licensed product, 288
Licensing, 691
Life stage, 236
Life-cycle cost, 416
Life-cycle stage, of demographic segmentation, 165–166, 235
Lifestyle, 168–171
Lighting, 46, 56
Likability, 537
Liking, 533
Limited service, 497
Line extension, 287
Line filling, 377–378
Line modernization, 378–379
Line pruning, 378–379
Line stretching, 375–377
Line-extension trap, 290
Links, 177
Listening, 397
Lobbying, 530, 592
Lobbyists, 94
Local firms, 347
Local marketing, 231
Location pricing, 451
Location, of retail stores, 504
Logical resistance, 631
Logistics, 26
Logistics alliances, 60
Long tail, 230
Long-run average cost curve (LRAC), 436
Long-term memory (LTM), 177
Loss of face, 626, 634, 672
Loss-leader pricing, 450
Lot size, 467
Low pragmatics, 243
Low-involvement marketing strategies, 188–189
Low-markup, higher-volume, 508
Low-quality trap, 452
Low-trust cultures, 635
Loyal buyers, 441
Loyalty programs, 148–150
Loyalty status, 246–247
Loyalty, 118, 136. *See* Customer loyalty
Luxury automobile, 390

Macroenvironment, 582
Macroenvironment analysis, 78–79, 86–96
Macroenvironment forces, 56
Macromodels of communications process, 600
Macroscheduling problem, 576
Magazines, 8
Mail questionnaire, 110
Maintenance, 417, 722
Maintenance and repair items, 363
Maintenance and repair services, 364
Maintenance, 371, 632
Major accounts, 622
Major account management (MAM), 711
Major service, 391
Makers, 242
Management, 17
Management by objectives (MBO), 67
Management contracts, 691
Manufactured materials and parts, 363
Manufacturer markets, 9
Manufacturer promotions, 582
Manufacturer-sponsored retailer franchise, 480
Manufacturer-sponsored wholesaler franchise, 480
Manufacturing departments, 26
Manufacturing sector, 390
Mapping, 479
Markets, 9, 10, 11, 361
Margins, 352
Market-based price, 704
Market broadening, 344
Market-buildup method, 125
Market-centered organizations, 721
Market challenger, 335
Market-challenger strategies, 346
Market consolidation, 324
Market coverage, 293
Market definitions, 46
Market demand, 121
  functions, 122
  measures of, 120
Market demassification, 600
Market demographics, in marketing plan example, 67
Market development organizations (MDOs), 100
Market-development strategy, 48
Market diversification, 334
Market-driving firms, 340
Market entry, global markets, 689–696
Marketers, 8–9
Market evolution, 322–324
Market follower strategies, 350
Market forecast, 123
Market fragmentation, 324
Market growth, in marketing plan example, 67
Market information, 517
Market minimum, 122
Market needs, in marketing plan example, 66
  innovation and, 55
Market pioneer, 313
Market places, 14
  brand value, 284
Market potential, 123
Market profile, 374–375
Market reform, 96
  customization, 233
  demographic, 233
  geographic, 233
  levels of, 226
  local marketing, 231
  niche marketing, 228
  psychographic, 241
  segment marketing, 226
  sequential, 249
  small businesses, 249
Market sensing, 36, 37
  competitors and, 346
  defending, 321
  expansion of, 332
  maximum, 430
Market share analysis, 123, 126, 562, 738
Market shares, industry sales and, 126
Market skimming, 431
Market spaces, 11
Market specialization, 252
Market targeting, 250–255
Market-test method, 128
Market testing, 665
Market trends, in marketing plan example, 66
Market-buildup method, 125
Market-challenger strategies, 48, 346–349
Market-driving firm, 340
Marketer, 7, 8–9
Market-follower strategies, 350
Market-growth stage, 323
Marketing
  company capabilities and, 17–18
  company orientation toward, 18–28
  consumer capabilities and, 17–18
  core concepts, 13–15
  customer value and, 34–43
  defining, 5–6
  future of, 748, 749–750
  importance of, 4
  scope of, 5–12
  shareholder value and, 63
  societal forces affecting, 15–17
  ten commandments of, 20
  ten deadly sins of, 20, 749
Marketing activities, pricing and, 445
Marketing alliances, 60
Marketing channels, 14
  conflict, cooperation, and competition, 483–486
  design and arrangements, 478–479
  design decisions, 467–474
  e-commerce marketing practices, 486–492
  integration and systems, 478–482
  management decisions, 474–478
  role of, 463–467
Marketing channel stewards, 479
Marketing communications, 528
  development of, 534–546
  expenditures, 570
  global markets, 701–704
  integrated, 552–555
  role of, 528–534
  See also Communications; Mass communications; Personal communications
Marketing communications budget, 544

Marketing communications
channels, 542–544
Marketing communications mix, 529
Marketing concept, 19
Marketing controller, 744
Marketing dashboards, 117, 118–122
Marketing decision support system
(MDSS), 115
Marketing departments, 26, 716–718
Marketing environment, 15
Marketing excellence review, 745
Marketing expense-to-sales analysis,
126
Marketing information systems
(MIS), 74
components of, 74–75
demographic environment, 79–86
economic environment, 86–87
internal records and marketing
intelligence, 75–78
marcroenvironment analysis,
78–79
natural environment, 90–91
political-legal environment, 93–96
social-cultural environment,
87–96
technological environment, 92–93
Marketing infrastructure, 698
Marketing innovation, 54
Marketing insights, 29
forecast and demand
measurement, 122
marketing productivity
measurement, 117
marketing research process, 101
marketing research system, 100
Marketing intelligence system, 75
Marketing investment management
(MIM), 648
Marketing management tasks, 28
definition of, 5
Marketing metrics, 117–118
Marketing mix, 23, 69, 278
Marketing-mix modeling, 118
Marketing network, 21
Marketing objectives, in marketing
plan example, 68
Marketing organizations
creative, 722–724
global markets, 682–683
marketing plan example, 70
types of, 25
Marketing plans, 41
business unit, 55–64
developing, 29
nature and contents of, 63–64
See also Strategic planning
Marketing organization charts, 132
Marketing productivity audit, 747
Marketing productivity
measurement, 117–128
Marketing profitability analysis, 740
Marketing program, 319
Marketing public relations (MPR),
593–596
Marketing plan example, 64
process, 101
system, 101
Marketing research, 69
developing, 29
low-involvement, 188
Marketing resistance, 15
Marketing resource management
(MRM), 735
Marketing sensitivity of demand, 122
Marketing strategy, 9
developing, 28
low-involvement, 188
marketing plan example, 69
market offerings, 650
product life cycle, 310–318
product planning, 64
service firms, 396–399
See also Strategic planning
Marketing strategy audit, 746
Marketing systems audit, 746
Marketing weaknesses, 749
Market leaders, 380–381
Market logistics, 584
Market makers, 489
Market-management organization,
720
Market minimum, 123
Market modification, 318
Market multiplier, 283
Market needs, in marketing plan
example, 67
Market-nicher strategies, 396–398
components of, 79
Market offerings, 13, 28, 614–634
business analysis, 650–652
commercialization, 668–669
components of, 360
concept development and
testing, 658–661
consumer-adoption process,
671–674
idea generation, 651–658
idea screening, 656–659
market testing, 664–666
marketing strategy development,
650
new-product development,
643–671
new-product options, 642
organizational arrangements,
647–650
product development, 663–670
Market opportunity analysis (MOA),
56
Market partitioning, 181
Market penetration index, 123
Market-penetration pricing, 431
Market-penetration strategy, 338, 48
Market pioneer, 313
Marketplaces, 11, 12
company orientations toward, 18
vs. one-to-one marketing, 159
Market potential, 123,124
Market profile, 374–375
Markets, 9–10, 361
brand value, 282–283
business markets, 248–249
consumer markets, 233–248
evaluation and selection, 251–252
global marketing
communications, 539
level of, 226–233
market targeting, 250–255
mission statements and, 44
tech users, 542
Market sensing, 36, 37
Market share, 123, 126
advertising budget and, 562
advertising research and, 579–580
competitors and, 332, 334
defending, 339–345
expansion of, 345–346
maximum, 430–431
optimal, 346
Market share analysis, 123, 126,
562, 738
Market skimming, 431
Market spaces, 11
Market specialization, 252
Market targeting, 250–255. *See also*
Target marketing
Market testing, 665
Market-test method, 129
Market trends, in marketing plan
example, 438–439
Markup pricing, 439
Marriage, 236
Marriott, 408
Masculine, 697
Mass affluent segment, 160
Mass communications, 559–561
advertising program
development and
management, 560–568
events and experiences, 587–591
media decisions, 581–582
public relations, 591–596
sales promotion, 580–586
See also Marketing
communications
Mass customization, 365
Mass marketing, 226
Mass-market, 38
Mass-market strategy, 323
Masstige goods, 239
Materials and parts, 362, 363
Matrix-management organization,
721–722
Maturity stage, 315–319, 323
Mavens, 615
Maximum current profit, 430
Maximum market share, 383–384
M-Commerce, 490
Measuring performance of, 137
Measuring satisfaction, 150–151
Mechanical devices, 113
Media, 543
direct marketing and, 603
timing and allocation, 576–577
types of, 574–575
Media coordination, 553–555
Media decisions, 568–580
Media graphics, 272
Media habits, 164
Media selection, 568
Mediation, 634
Megamarketing, 254
Megatrends, 78
Members, 147
Membership groups, 162
Memory, 177–179
Memory encoding, 178
Memory processes, 178
Memory retrieval, 178–179
Memory tests, 276
Mental accounting, 189–191
Mental maps, 177
Mentoring, 626
Merchandise customization, 506
Merchandising, 588
Merchandising conglomerate, 501
Merchants, 460
Merchant wholesalers, 525
Merging, 716
Message, 532, 595
Message generation and evalution,
563–564
Message source, 537
Message strategy, 535
Metamarkets, 11, 361
Metamediaries, 11, 361
Microenvironment actors, 56
Micromarketing, 226
Micromodel of customer responses,
532–534
Microsales analysis, 738
Microscheduling problem, 576
Microsites, 610
Mind-mapping, 656
Mind share, 332, 333
Minor goods and services, 391
Mission, 44–45, 56, 68
Missionary sales force, 199
Missionary selling, 551
Mission statements, 44–45
Mixed bundling, 381
Mobile defense, 344
Mobile marketing, 613
Mobility barriers, 332
Modified rebuy, 198–199
Modernization, 378
Monadic-rating method, 665
Monetary amount, 602
Money-constrained consumers, 169
Monitoring systems, 410–411
Morphological analysis, 656

Motive, 171
Motivation, 171–173
channel members, 474–478
sales reps, 627–628
transformational appeals, 536
MRO, 199
Multichannel conflict, 483
Multichannel marketing systems, 481
Multicultural marketing, 160
Multilevel selling, 201, 626
Multiple segments, 303
Multiple-factor index method, 125–126
Multiple-niche strategy, 323
Multiple-sponsor co-branding, 381
Multiple-vehicle, multiple-stage campaign, 553
Multitasking, 169
Mutual services and responsibilities, 472
Mystery shoppers, 137

N generation cohort, 84
Naked solution, 228
National brands, 505
Nation-dominant hierarchy, 181
Natural environment, 90
Natural expenses, 741
Natural market segments, 228
Natural products, 363
Natural resources, 127
Near-zero inventory, 523
Need descriptions, 205–206
Need family, 372
Need level, 659
Need-gap score, 659
Need-payoff questions, 630
Needs, 13
customer, 416, 462
information, 74–75
macroenvironment, 78–79
marketing, 67
Needs hierarchy, 172
Needs-based segmentation, 250
Negative demand, 9
Negotiation, 632
Negotiated exchange, 632
Nepotism, 693
Net price analysis, 450
Network information technology, 15
Network marketing. *See* Direct selling
Networking, 145
Neuromarketing, 109
New contexts, 656
New entrants, threat of, 328
New Luxury goods, 239
New task, 198
Newlyweds, 603
New-market segment strategy, 338
New-product department, 649
New-product development, 647
New-product failure, 645
New-product introductions, 643
New-product mangers, 649
New-product options, 642
New-product success, 289
News, 595
Newsletters, 570
Newspapers, 570
New-task buying, 198
Niche marketing, 228
Niche specialist roles, 313
Niching, 229
Nodes, 177
Noise, 532
Non-compensatory models of consumer choice, 200
Non-controllables, 79
Non-durable goods, 362
Non-existent demand, 9
Non-expansible market, 122
Non-peak demand, 395
Non-personal communication channels, 543
Non-probability sample, 109
Non-profit markets, 11
Non-profit sector, 390
Non-store retailing, 498
Non-traceable common costs, 743

Objective-and-task method, 545
Objectives, of competitors, 332
Observational research, 103
Occasions, 243
Occupation, 166
Offer elements, of direct marketing, 604
Offerings, 14
Offers, 439–439, 604
Office staff, 620
Off-invoice, 584
Off-lists, 584
Off-price retailers, 510
Offset, 448
Oil, 199
Old Luxury brand extensions, 239
Oligopoly mass marketing, 144
Olympics, 6
On-air tests, 578
On-the-job training, 625
One-level channel, 466
One-to-one marketing, 145
Online advertising and promotions, 609
Online auctions and exchanges, 423
Online buzz, 240
Online communities, 612
Online customer feedback systems, 77
Online information sources, 78
Online interviews, 110
Online research, 112
Online shopping, 230
OPEC, 329
Open innovation, 651
Open-dating, 411
Open-end questions, 105
Operating supplies, 363
Operating variables, 248
Opinion leaders, 162
Opportunism, in business relationships, 217–218
Opportunity analysis, 56
Opportunity matrix, 57
Optimal market share, 346
Optional-feature pricing, 380
Order point, 522
Order processing, 521
Order processing costs, 522
Order taker, 618
Ordering ease, 370
Order-routine specification, 211
Orders, placing and receiving, 17
Order-cycle time, 520
Order-to-payment cycle, 75, 521
Organization, 402
innovation and, 55
logistics and, 524
market offerings and, 647–650
Organization charts, 132
Organizational buying, 196
Organizational culture, 50
Organizations, 7, 88. *See also* Marketing organizations
Organizations, marketing of, 8
Original equipment manufacturer (OEM), 281
Origins, 49
Others, perceptions of, 88
Others' self-concept, 168
Outbound telemarketing, 605
Outdoor media, 570
Outer direction, 636
Out-of-pocket costs, 416
Outsourcing, 716
Overall cost leadership, 59
Overall market share, 738
Overcoming objections, 631
Overdemand, 452
Overfull demand, 9
Overhead costs, 437
Overhead, 437
Overseas Chinese, 50
Ownership, services, 391

Packaging, 384–385
Paid-search ads, 611
Paired-comparison method, 664
Paper towels, 360
Parallel entry, 668
Parent brand, 287
Partial cost recovery, 434
Partial product failure, 657
Participation marketing, 67
Particularism, 636
Partner relationship management (PRM), 23, 61
Partners, 147
Parts, 362
Part-time employees, 396
Past-sales analysis, 128
Patronage awards, 583
Payment equity, 406
Payment flow, 406
Payment terms, 406
Pay-per-click ads, 611
Peak-time efficiency, 396
Peer influences, 17
Penetrated market, 122
People-based services, 391
Perceived risk, 186
Perceived service, 404
Perceived value, 659
perceived-value pricing, 439–441
Percentage labeling, 386
Percentage-of-sales method, 545
Perception, 174, 484, 710
Performance marketing, 25
Performance quality, 139, 365–366
Performance review, 212
Periodic surveys, 137
Peripheral cues, 176
Peripheral route, 176
Perishability, 395–396
Permission marketing, 277
Personal characteristics, market segmentation and, 248–250
Personal communications, 599
direct marketing, 600
interactive marketing, 606
personal selling, 630
sales force design, 618
sales force management, 623
word-of-mouth marketing, 550
See also marketing communications
Personal communications channels, 542
Personal factors, affecting consumer behavior, 165–171
age, 165
economic circumstances, 166
occupation circumstances, 166
Personal influence, 653
Personal information sources, 157
Personal interactions, 550
Personal interview, 110
Personal selling, 319, 529, 550
Personality, 115, 167–168, 630
Personalization, 277–278
Personalized marketing, 150
Personal-need services, 391
Personnel differentiation, 309
Persons, marketing of, 6
Persuasive advertising, 561
Pervasiveness, 549
Philanthropy, corporate, 28
Physical evidence, 392
Physical flow, 436
Physical prototypes, 664

Physical risk, 186
Physiological needs, 172
Piggyback, 523
Pioneer advantage, 312–314
Piracy, 704
Place, 23
Place advertising, 571
Place marketing, 7
Planned contraction, 345
Plant capacity, excess, 377
Platform, 303
Platinum customers, 23
Podcasts, 612
Point-of purchase, 574
 Point-of-Purchase (POP) Displays and Demonstrations, 583
Points-of-difference (PODs), 324, 325
Points-of-parity, 301–303
Political-legal environment, 93–96
Pooling of individual estimates, 128
Population
 educational groups, 85
 ethnic and other markets, 85
 geographical shifts in, 86
 household patterns, 85
 worldwide growth of, 81–83
Population, aging of, 83
Population age mix of, 83
Porter's generic strategies, 59–60
Portfolio tests, 578
Position defense, 342
Positioning, 310
 marketing plan example, 67
 marketing segmentation, 251
 product and brand, 658
 See also Brand positioning
Positioning statement, 306
Positioning strategy
 choosing POPs and PODs, 306–308
 competitive frame of reference, 301
 creating POPs and PODs, 306–308
 membership, 304–30
 points-of-difference, 301–304
 points-of-parity, 301–304
Positive feedback effects, 209
Post-purchase actions, 186
Post-purchase behavior, 186–188
Post-purchase satisfaction, 186
Post-purchase use and disposal, 186
Post-sales analysis, 74
Post-sale service strategy, 417
Postwar cohort, 84
Potential entrants, 296
Potential market, evaluation of, 686
Potential product, 361
Potentials, 147
Power distance, 697
Power grid, 267
Preannouncements, 343
Preapproach, 631
Predatory pricing, 451
Preemptive cannibalization, 291
Pre-emptive defense, 343
Preference, 533
Preference segments, 228
Premiums, 583
Prescriptive method, 192
Presentation sales, 631
 service companies and, 279
Presentational problems, in marketing research, 107
Press relations, 592
Prestige brands, 294
Prices. *See* Pricing/price, 513
Price changes, 451–454
Price cuts, 451–452
Price discrimination, 450
Price elasticity of demand, 435
Price endings, 426
Price experiments, 434
Price increases, 452–453
Price indifference band, 435
Price-off, 584
Price packs, 583
Price policy, 472
Price pressures, 211
Price-quality inferences, 427
Price premium, 261
Price selectivity, 426
Price wars, 472
Price-oriented customers, 202
Price-quality inferences, 427–428
Price-war trap, 452
Pricing/price, 421
 adapting, 447
 competitors and, 437
 consumer psychology and, 425
 differential, 395
 differentiated, 450
 four Ps, 23
 marketing plan example, 70
 marketing program and, 319
 product-mix, 379
 promotional, 450
 retailing and, 740
 setting, 430
 understanding, 422
Pricing collaborations, 60
Pricing environment, 422
Pricing method, 439
Pricing objectives, 432
Product-bundling, 381
Product-line, 380
Primary activities, 35
Primary data, 102
Primary demand, 122
Primary groups, 162
Primary package, 384
Primary service package, 413
Prime contractors, 199
Principle of congruity, 539
Print advertising, 566
 print advertising research techniques, 577–578
Privacy issues, 96, 492
Private carrier, 523
Private exchanges, 207
Private labels, 515, 516
Private nonprofit sector, 390
Privatization, 16
Prizes, 583
Proactive market orientation, 19
Probability sample, 110
Problem definition, 102
Problem detection method, 56
Problem recognition, 180, 205
Processes, core business, 44
Procurement, 203, 506
 procurement orientation, 203
 procurement process, 203
Product adaption, 699
Product alliances, 60
Product assortment,in retailing, 504
Product-brand relationships, 372
Product-bundling pricing, 381
Product categories, 593
Product class, 372
Product concept, 18, 19
Product descriptor, 305
Product development, 48, 664
 See also Market offerings
Product differentiation, 364–368
Product family, 372
Product-feature specialists, 353
Product-form pricing, 450
Product hierarchy, 372
Product idea, 658
Product imitation, 350
Product innovation, 262, 350
Product invention, 699–700
Production, accumulated, 431
Production concept, 18–19
Production levels, 360
Productivity, of sales reps, 626
Product launches, 562
Product levels, 360
Product life cycle, 310
 advertising budget and, 562
 marketing communications mix, 529
 marketing strategies, 310
Product line, 372
Product line analysis, 373
Product-management organization, 718–720
Product managers, 648
Product map, 374
Product-market expansion grid, 48
Product markets, 550
Product mix, 372–373
 product-mix pricing, 379
 product-mix width, 373
Product modification, 318
Product offering, in marketing plan example, 68
Product penetration percentage, 123
Product pioneer, 312, 313
Product placement, 573
Product planning, 44, 64
Product-positioning map, 658
Product publicity, 592
Product quality, 53, 463
Prouct-quality leadership, 432
Product review forums, 78
Product, 8
 classifications, 360–364
 co-branding, 381–383
 differentiation, 369–372
 four Ps, 23
 evaluation continuum, 288
 hierarchy, 372
 ingredient branding, 381–383
 labeling, 385–386
 levels, 360–361
 licensed, 286–287
 marketing channel objectives and, 467
 mission statements and, 45
 new luxury, 239
 variety of, 24
Product sample, 616
Product specialists, 205–206, 252, 314
Product specialization, 252
Product specifications, 205
Product strategy, 387
 differentiation, 309
 packaging, labeling, warranties, and guarantees, 358
 product characteristics and classifications, 433
Product substitutability, 562
Product support services, 416–417
Product systems, 372–373
Product type, 372
Product value analysis (PVA), 206
Product variant, 372, 229
Product variety, 467
Product warranties, 583
Professional purchasing, 195
Profiling, 190
Profitability analysis, 141–142
Profitable customers, 140. *See also* Customer profitability analysis
Profitability control, 740
Profit-and-loss statement, 740
Profit life cycle, 310
Profit margin, 352
Profit tiers, 398
Program formulation and implementation, 62
Program multiplier, 282
Projective techniques, 108, 172
Promotion event marketing, 587–588
 four Ps, 23–24, 462
 marketing plan example, 64
 online, 609–613
 wholesalers, 516
 See Sales promotion

Promotional alliances, 60
Promotional allowances, 449
Promotional pricing, 450
Promotion flow, 465
Propective method, 192
Properties, 7
Proposal solicitation, 203
Prospect calls, 626
Prospecting, 619
Prospects, 8–9, 145, 147
Prospect theory, 191
Prototypes, 664
Psychogenic needs, 171
Psychographic segmentation, 241–243
Psychological discounting, 450
Psychological life cycle, 166
Psychological processes, 171–179
Psychological repositioning, 184
Psychological resistance, 631
Psychological risk, 186
Public, 549
Public information sources, 181–82
Public issues. *See* Social issues
Public opinion, 17
Public relations, 26, 591, 593
Public relations department, 592
Public service activities, 361
Public space advertising, 572
Publications, 595
Publicity. *See* Public relations
Pull strategy, 460
Pulsing, 577
Purchase, 534
Purchase decision, 171, 184–185
Purchase frequency, 576, 665, 659
Purchase intention, 659
Purchasing consumer responses, 26
  decision-making process, 191
  direct, 198
  market segmentation and, 226
  organizational, 196
Purchasing approached, 249
Purchasing departments, 196
Purchasing organization and administration, 204
Purchasing process, 203
Purchasing orientations, 203
Purchasing power parity, 704
Purchasing time, 35
Purchasing/procurement, 203–204
Pure bundling, 381
Pure-click companies, 487
Pure play auction sites, 207
Pure service, 391
Pure tangible goods, 362

Q factor, 538
Qualified available market, 121
Qualifying, 631
Qualitative research, 107, 108
Quality, 139–140
  conformance, 366
  definition of, 139
  impact of, 140
  market share expansion and, 346
  pricing, 427
  services, 396
Quality function deployment (QFD), 664
Quality improvcment, 318
Quality-price specialists, 353
Quantitative analysis, 590
Quantity discounts, 449
Questionnaires, 105, 110
Questions, types of, 106
Quick response systems (QRS), 370
Quota sample, 110

Racial markets, 83
Radio, 570
Radio advertising, 541
Radio Frequency Identification (RFID), 506
Rank-order method, 664
Rapid prototyping, 659
Rate of return on net worth, 740
Raw-material-exporting economies, 86
Raw materials, 363
Reach, 568
Reactive market orientation, 19
Real estate marketing, 7
Real needs, 13
Real repositioning, 184
Receiver, 532
Recency, Frequency, Monetary amount (RFM), 602
Records, internal, 74
Recovery, 397
Recruiting and selecting Representatives, 474
Recruiting, 18
Reduced-price pack, 583
Reengineering, 410
Reference groups, 162
Reference prices, 426–427
Referent power, 475
Regional firms, 347
Regional shopping centers, 510
Regulation of technological change, 93
Reinforcement advertising, 562
Reintermediation, 16
Relationship marketing, 634
Relationship. *See* customer relationship management
Reminder advertising, 562
Relative advantage, 673
Relative market share, 738
Relative product failure, 657
Relevance, 267, 306
Reminder advertising, 562
Reorder point, 522
Repair, 371
Repairability, 366
Repeat customers, 147
Repositioning, 184, 642
Representativeness heuristic, 189
Requests for proposals (RFPs), 196
Research, 17. *See also* marketing research
Research and development budgets, 68
Research approaches, 103
Research creativity, 114
Research finding presenting, 114
Research instruments, 105–108
Research objectives, 102
Research plans, 102
Reservation systems, 395
Resiliency, 408
Resonance, 269
Resource markets, 9
Resource space, 40
Response, 533
Response hierarchy models, 532–533
Responsibilities, mutual, 472
Responsive marketing, 339
Responsiveness, 404
Retail category management, 505
Retail co-branding, 381
Retail environment, 501
Retail transformation, 16
Retailer cooperatives, 480
Retailer product adaptions, 699
Retailer promotions, 582
Retailer branches and offices, 516–517
Retailing, 496
  competition in, 480
  marketing decisions in, 503
Retail life cycle, 497
Retrospective method, 59, 63
Return on assets, 740
Return on investment (ROI), 59
Returns, 371–372
Reverse assumption analysis, 656
Reverse auction, 17
Reverse-flow channels, 466
Review forums, 78
Reward power, 475
Ring-seido, 663
Risk, 186
  business relationships, 217
  customer, 227
  wholesalers and, 516
Risk analysis, 663
Rivals. *See* competitors, 663
Risk and gain sharing, 202
Roles, 165
Routine products, 203
Running costs, 522

Safety needs, 172
Salary, 623
Sales
  conditions of, 479
  estimating, 662
  industry, 126
  marketing communications and, 471–474
  product-line analysis and, 373
  tied-in, 381
Sales agent feedback sites, 78
Sales analysis, 738
Sales assistants, 626
Sales branch, overseas, 690
Sales budget, 124
Sales calls, 197
Sales channel, 464
Sales contests, 585
Sales departments, 75, 628
Sales-effect research, 579
  sales force objectives and strategy, 619
Sales force, 618
  design, 618–623
  management, 623–630
  marketing intelligence and, 76
Sales-force compensation, 623
Sales-force opinions, 127
Sales-force promotion, 580
Sales-force promotion tools, 585
Sales-force size, 622
  workload approach, 622
Sales-force structure, 620
Sales forecast, 69, 124
Sales information systems, 75
Sales life cycle, 310
Salesmen, 615
Sales metrics, 737
Sales potential company, 124
Sales process, steps in, 631
Sales promotion, 529, 549, 580
  marketing communications channels, 544
  marketing program and, 589
  mass communications, 559
  consumer promotion, 580
  trade promotion, 580
  business and sales-force, 549
  promotion, 580
Sales quota, 134
Sales rep productivity, 626
  time-and-duty analysis, 626
Sales representatives, 624–626
Sales time, 626
Sales-variance analysis, 738
Sales volume, 317
Sales-wave research, 666
Same-company co-branding, 381
Samples, 583
Sample size, 108
Sampling plan, 108
Sampling procedures, 109
Sampling units, 108
Smart tags, 506
Satisfaction, 14
Satisfied shoppers, 245
Satisfiers, 173, 410
Savings, 87

Scalloped PLC, 311
Scarcity, 14
Scenario analysis, 54
Scientific credibility, 673
Scientific method, 129
Sealed-bid auctions, 445
Search ads, 611
Search dynamics, 181–82
Search engines, 348
Search qualities, 391
Seasonal discount, 14
Secondary beliefs, 89
Secondary brand associations, 280–281
Secondary data, 102
Secondary groups, 162
Secondary package, 384
Secondary service features, 413, 418
Second-tier contractors, 199
Secret needs, 13
Security, 407
Segment "acid test," 250
Segment attractiveness, 250
Segment-by-segment invasion plans, 253–255
Segment identification, 250
Segment marketing, 226
Segmentation, 13
  effective criteria for, 250
  steps in process of, 250
  targeting, positioning (STP), 34
Segmenting consumer markets, 233–248
Selecting market segments, 251–255
Selective attention, 174
Selective distortion, 175, 471
Selective distribution, 471
Selective retention, 176
Selective specialization, 251
Self adopters, 242
Self-innovators, 242
Self-actualization needs, 172
Self-branding, 6, 383
Self-concept, 168
Self-liquidating premiums, 583
Self-selection, 497
Self-service, 384, 497
Self-service technologies (SSTs), 409
Sell-in time, 586
Selling, 619
  missionary, 551
  retailing and, 454
  wholesalers, 458
Selling concept, 19
Senders, 532
Sentiment, 616
Sequential segmentation, 266
Servant leadership, 435
Served market share, 125
Service alliances, 60
Service backup, 495
Service blueprint, 424
Service brands, 441
Service business, 419
Service channel, 14
Service contracts, 416
Service dependability, 443
Service design,435
Service firms, 393–396
Service firms, marketing strategies for, 425
Service firm-sponsored retailer franchise, 508
Service industries, 390
Service mix categories, 420
Service output levels, 495
Service quality, 151
Service/quality customers, 413
Service/quality management, 433
Service quality perceptions, 406
Service review forums, 81
Service(s), 413
  categories of, 391–392
  characteristics of, 392–396
  definition of, 390
  holistic marketing, 401–403
  intangibility of, 414
  managing product support, 416–417
  mutual, 472
  nature of, 390–96
  product-support, 398–400
  quality, 396, 397
  retailing, 508–09
  variety of, 162
Services differentiation, 369–372
Service-performance-process map, 395
Service-quality model, 404
Service sector channels, 467
Services mix, 508
Service specialists, 353
Servicing, 619
SERVQUAL, 405
Setup costs, 522
Sets, in consumer decision making, 181
Seven deadly sins, service management, 409
Sex appeals, 568
Shadowing, 107
Shallow brand users, 248
Shallow-pockets trap, 452
Shared services, 396
Shared values, 62
Share of heart, 383
Share of market, 123, 333
Share of mind, 333
Shareholder value analysis (SVA), 63
Share-penetration index, 123
Shifting loyals, 246
Shipping package, 384
Shopping goods, 362
Shopping strips, 511
Short-term memory (STM), 177
Simple random sample, 110
Simulated test marketing, 666
Single-niche strategy, 323, 352
Single-segment concentration, 251
Single-vehicle, single-stage campaign, 553
Situation analysis, 65, 66
Situational factors, 185, 249
Situation questions, 630
SIVA, 24, 462
Skepticism, 114
Skills, 61
Slotting fee, 515
Slogans, 276
Small businesses, 443
  guidelines for selling to, 197
  marketing to, 199
Small Business Administration, 197, 228
Small business, sales to, 197
Smart tags, 506
SMS marketing, 606
Social approval, 672
  personal influence, 673
  collectivistic, 673
  power distance, 673
  uncertainty, 673
Social benefits, 148
Social channels, 542
Social class, 161
Social class segmentation, 241
Social constraints, 646
Social-cultural environment, 87–90
Social factors, affecting consumer behavior, 162–165
Social factors, of consumer family, 162
  reference groups, 162
  roles and statuses, 165
Social issues
  advertising, 567–68
  direct marketing, 707
Social marketing, 733
Social needs, 172
Social networks, 16–17
Social networking, 635
Social responsibility marketing, 26, 27
Social risk, 186
Social stratification, 161
Social trends, 78
Societal forces, affecting marketing, 15–16
Societal marketing concept, 27
Society, perceptions of, 88
Solutions, 24, 55
Solution selling, 202
Solution vendor, 619
Solution-oriented customers, 202
Sourcing strategy, 59
Spatial convenience, 467
Special-interest groups, 94, 95, 97
Specialized wholesalers, 545
Specialties, 374
Specialty advertising, 585
Specialty goods, 362
Specialty-line marketing research firms, 100
Specific customer specialists, 353
Specific investments, 217
Speeches, 595
SPIN method, 630
Spiral development process, 650
Split loyals, 246
Sponsorship, 589, 612
Sports marketing, for Generation Y, 240
Spot markets, 207
Sprinkler approach, 681
SSWD group, 85
Stability, 284
Staffing, 62
Stage-gate system, 650
Stakeholder-performance scorecard, 119
Stakeholders, 62
Standardization, 696
Standards, of service quality, 405
Staples, 362
Star Wars (movie), 115
Stated needs, 13
Statistical analysis, 434
Statistical demand analysis, 128
Status, 165
Status and title, 633
Stealth price increases, 446
Stickiness, 615
Stealth marketing, 615
Stockkeeping unit, 372
Stock position, 551
Stockless purchase plans, 211
Storage warehouses, 522
Store atmosphere, 508
  feng shui, 512
Store-based retailing, 501
Store brands. *See* Private labels
Stores-within-stores, 511
Storytelling, 107
Straddle positioning, 305
Straight extension, 699
Straight rebuy, 198
Strategy, definition of, 59
  role of, 41
  products, 64
  corporate and division, 44
Strategy/ies, 300
  concentric, 50
  conglomerate, 50
  diversification, 49
  market challenger, 335, 346–349
  market-development, 48
  market follower, 335, 350–352
  market nicher, 335, 352–354
  market-penetration, 48
  new-market segment, 338
  Porter's generic, 59–60

price cutting, 453
product-development, 48
sourcing, 34, 59
technology, 59
Strategic alliances, 60–61
Strategic brand management, 260
Strategic business units (SBUs), 46–47
Strategic concept, 407
Strategic control, 737, 744–48
Strategic formulation, 59
Strategic group, 60
Strategic innovation, 723
Strategic market definition, 46
Strategic marketing plans, 41–44
Strategic planning, 63
corporate and division, 44–55
products, 64–71
role of, 41–44
Strategic-planning gap, 47
Strategic products, 203
Strategic withdrawal, 345
Strategic-value customers, 202
Stratification, 161
Stratified random sample, 115
Street teams, 240
Strength, of competitors, 333
Strengths and weaknesses analysis, 57, 58, 67
Strivers, 242
Strongly unavailable brand nonusers, 248
Structural ties, 148
Strugglers, 242
Student ambassadors, 240
Style, 311, 368
Style improvement, 318
Style life cycle, 311
Sub-brand, 287
Subcultures, 89, 160
Subliminal perception, 176
Subsistence economies, 86
Substance of style, 370
Substitutability, 562
Substitutes, 330
Super Bowl, 145
Supercenters, 502
Supermarkets, 524
Superpremium products, 239
Supersegment, 251
Superstores, 524
Supervision, of sales reps, 624
Supplier search, 206
Supplier selection, 209–211
Supplier partnering, 716
Supplier-customer relationship, 196
Suppliers, 363
competitive forces and, 330
extranet links to, 207
information from, 77
number of, 211
Supplies, 363
Supply chain, 15, 37
Supply-side measurement method, 589
Support, 282
Support activities, 35
Survey research, 104
number of, 211
information from, 77
extranet links to, 207
competitive forces and, 328
Surveys, 103, 434
Survival, 430
Survival-age distribution, 662
Survivors, 242
Suspects, 147
Sustainability, 306
Sustainers, 243
Sweepstakes, 621
Switchers, 246
SWOT analysis, 56, 58, 67
Synchronous Time, 636
Syndicated-service research firms, 100
Systems buying and selling, 199
Systems contracting, 199
Systems, as element of successful business, 62

Table of contents, 65
Tactical marketing plan, 44
Tangibility, 362
Tangible goods, 362
Tangibles, 405, 406
Target, 41
Target audience, 533, 569
Target costing, 437
Target market, 13, 231
Target market definition, 46
Target marketing, 208, 250. *See also* Market targeting
buying center, 201–202
definition, 46
direct mail, 602–604
in marketing plan example, 66, 68
market demand and, 122
marketing PR, 593
market offerings, 590–591
market segmentation, 251
retailing, 503
Targeting, 619
Target-market prospects, 669
Target-return pricing, 440
Teamwork, 397
market segmentation, 250
marketing plan example, 66
market demand and, 122
definition, 46
buying center, 201
Technical people, 620
Technical quality, 403
Technical support people, 626
Technician, 619
Technological devices, for marketing research, 107
Technological environment, 92–96
Technological investments, in retailing, 540–41
Technological leapfrogging, 374
Technological trends, 78
Technology strategy, 59
Telemarketers, 626
Telemarketing, 605
Telematics, 490
Telephone, profile of, 608
Telephone interview, 110
Television, 608
Television advertising, 565–66
Television direct-response marketing, 498
Territorial rights, of distributors, 472
Terekura, 172
Testing elements, of direct marketing, 604
Test markets, 666
Theater tests, 616
Thinkers, 241
Threat analysis, 56
Threat matrix, 57
Threats, 328–329, 515–517
Threats, to market segments, 328–329
Three-level channel, 466
Tied-in sales, 381
Tie-in promotions, 583
Time, 633
Time pricing, 451
Time risk, 186
Time-and-duty analysis, 626
Timing strategy, of market offerings, 669
Time-constrained consumers, 169
Time-series analysis, 127
Title flow, 465
Top management, 408
Total costs, 436
Total cost of ownership, 433
Total customer benefit, 133
Total customer cost, 133
Total customer satisfaction, 136–137
Total customer value, 133
Total market expansion, 339
Total market orientation, 19
Total market potential, 124
Total quality, 140
Total quality management (TQM), 140
Total sales estimation, 662
Total set, in consumer decision making, 181
Traceable common costs, 743
Tracking studies, 282
Trade discount, 449
Trade promotion tools, 584
Trade shows, 585
Trade-in allowances, 449
Trade-offs, 59
Trading up, 138
Tradition, 243
adapters, 243
innovators, 241
Traditional organization chart, 132
Traditional segment, 243
Trailer tests, 578
Training
channel members, 475–76
customer, 371
sales reps, 624
service firms and, 394–95
Trainship, 523
Trailing-edge baby boomer cohort, 84
Training and supervising sales representatives, 624
sales training, 625
collectivism, 625
power distance, 625
sensitivity training, 625
on-the-job training, 625
formal training, 625
Transactions, 56
Transactional selling, 202, 266
Transfer, 6
Transfer price, 704
Transformational appeals, 536
emotional appeals, 536
borrowed interest, 536
Transportation, 543
Trends, 67, 78
holistic marketing, 716
macroenvironment, 78–79
wholesaling, 517–18
Trends in wholesaling, 517
Trial, 671
Truck wholesalers, 545
Trust, corporate, 215
Trustworthiness, 537
Two-level channel, 494
Two-part pricing, 380
Two-way stretch, 377
Type of costs, 435–436
in marketing practices, 715
in retailing, 480
in wholesaling, 518
Types of intermediaries, 470

Unanticipated situational factors, 185
Unbundling, 452
Uncertainty avoidance, 647, 697
Uncontrollable returns, 372
Undifferentiated marketing, 252
Unfairness,
Uniform pricing, 622
Unit metrics pathway, 119
Universe, perceptions of, 89
Unsought goods, 362
Unstated needs, 13
Unwholesome demand, 9
Up-market stretch, 377
Up-selling, 146

Urban Chinese consumer, 546
Usage rate, 245
Usage, total market expansion, 338
Users, 200
User status, 234, 245
User targets, 659

Value, 168–170
communicating, 30
perceived, 659
SIVA, 24
See also Customer value
Value-added reseller (VAR), 353
Value-adding partnerships (VAPs), 480
Value-augmenting services, 416
Value-based marketing, 63
Value buyers, 441
Value campaigns, 374
Value chain, 35
Value creation, 40
Value delivery, 42, 43
Value delivery network, 35
Value delivery process, 34
Value delivery system, 136
Value-developing processes, 35
Value exploration, 40
Value innovation, 331
Value network, 35, 462–463
Value pricing, 441–442
Value proposition, 14, 35, 136, 300
Values, 168–170
Value segment, 35
Variability, 394–395
Variable costs, 436
Variable compensation, 623
Variety-loving shoppers, 189, 462
Variety-seeking buying behavior, 189
Velocity, 616
Vending machines, 498
Vendor analysis, 210
Vendor-managed inventory, 221
Venture teams, 649
Versatility, 554
Vertical channel conflict, 483
Vertical coordination, 212–214
Vertical hubs, 206
Vertical-level specialists,
Vertical marketing systems, 478–480
Vertical markets, 207
Vertical competitive sphere, 45
Vertical-level, 353
Video games, 575
Videos, 240, 611
Vigilant organizations, 37
Viral marketing, 614
Virtual reality, 659
Visualization, 108
Voice of the customer (VOC) measurements, 410
Voice option, 186
Voice quality, 616
Voice share, 580
Volume, 352
Voluntary chain, 480

Wa, 635
Waiting time, 413
Wants, 13
Warehousing, 522
Warranties, 383, 386–387
Waterfall approach, 681
Weakly unavailable brand nonusers, 248
Web site design, 407
Website(s), 206
Web strategy, global, 690–691
Wholesaler-sponsored voluntary chains, 480
Wholesaling, 516
Win-backs, 152
With-pack premiums, 583
Word association, 108
Word of mouth, 614–618, 672, 673
Word-of-mouth marketing, 550
Workload approach, 622
World product groups, 711
World War II cohort, 84
Write-ups of activity results, 628

Yield pricing, 451
Yugoka, 481

Zero-defects, 35
Zero level channel, 466
Zone of tolerance, 405